The Norton Reader

SEVENTH EDITION

The Norton Reader

An Anthology of Expository Prose

SEVENTH EDITION

Arthur M. Eastman, *General Editor*
VIRGINIA POLYTECHNIC INSTITUTE AND STATE UNIVERSITY

Caesar R. Blake
UNIVERSITY OF TORONTO

Hubert M. English, Jr.
UNIVERSITY OF MICHIGAN

Joan E. Hartman
COLLEGE OF STATEN ISLAND,
CITY UNIVERSITY OF NEW YORK

Alan B. Howes
UNIVERSITY OF MICHIGAN

Robert T. Lenaghan
UNIVERSITY OF MICHIGAN

Leo F. McNamara
UNIVERSITY OF MICHIGAN

James Rosier
UNIVERSITY OF PENNSYLVANIA

W · W · NORTON & COMPANY · *New York* · *London*

The text of this book is composed in Electra.
Composition by Vance Weaver Composition.
Manufacturing by R. R. Donnelley.
Book design by Antonina Krass.

Library of Congress Cataloging-in-Publication Data

The Norton reader.

    Includes bibliographies and index.
    1. College readers. I. Eastman, Arthur M.,
1918-   . II. Blake, Caesar R. (Caesar Robert),
1925-   .
PE1122.N68   1988   808.88'8   87-24046

          ISBN 0-393-95645-8

W. W. Norton & Company, Inc., 500 Fifth Avenue, New York, N.Y. 10110

W. W. Norton & Company, Ltd., 37 Great Russell Street, London WC1B 3NU

          1 2 3 4 5 6 7 8 9 0

Contents

[Entries marked with • are followed by questions.]

INDEX OF RHETORICAL MODES AND STRATEGIES   xiii

PREFACE   xix

NOTES ON READING AND WRITING   xxiii

PERSONAL REPORT

Dylan Thomas *Memories of Christmas*	1
Margaret Laurence *Where the World Began*	6
Wallace Stegner *The Town Dump* •	10
Al Young *"Java Jive," by the Ink Spots* •	16
Zora Neale Hurston *How It Feels to Be Colored Me*	19
Maya Angelou *Graduation*	22
Richard Hugo *How I Never Met Eudora Welty* •	32
Hans A. Schmitt *January 30, 1933: A Memoir*	36
Bruno Bettelheim *A Victim*	41
Paul Fussell *My War* •	44
Alice Walker *Beauty: When the Other Dancer Is the Self* •	52
Scott Sanders *Listening to Owls*	59
Joan Didion *On Going Home* •	69
Loren Eiseley *The Brown Wasps* •	72
E. B. White *Once More to the Lake* •	79

PROSE FORMS: JOURNALS   85

Ralph Waldo Emerson from *Journal*	88
Henry David Thoreau from *Journal*	91
Walt Whitman *Abraham Lincoln*	92
May Sarton from *Journal of a Solitude*	95

Woody Allen *Selections from the Allen
     Notebooks*   101

PEOPLE, PLACES

Thomas Jefferson *George Washington* •   105
Nathaniel Hawthorne *Abraham Lincoln* •   108
June Callwood *Portrait of Canada*   112
N. Scott Momaday *The Way to Rainy Mountain*   129
Jane Howard *Pomp and Circumstance in Groundhog Hollow*   134
Virginia Woolf *Great Men's Houses* •   142
Virginia Woolf *My Father: Leslie Stephen* •   146
Doris Lessing *My Father* •   151
Daniel Mark Epstein *The Case of Harry Houdini* •   159

MIND

Benjamin Franklin *The Convenience of Being "Reasonable"* 172
William Golding *Thinking as a Hobby* •   173
Carl Sagan *The Abstractions of Beasts*   180
Neil Postman *Confusing Levels of Abstraction* •   187
Henry David Thoreau *Observation*   193
Jacob Bronowski *The Reach of Imagination* •   194
Isaac Asimov *The Eureka Phenomenon* •   201

EDUCATION

Eudora Welty *Clamorous to Learn*   212
Caroline Bird *College Is a Waste of Time and Money*   217
Barbara Ehrenreich *College Today: Tune In, Drop Out, and
     Take the Cash*   226
James Thurber *University Days* •   229
William Zinsser *College Pressures* •   234
William G. Perry, Jr. *Examsmanship and the Liberal Arts: A
     Study in Educational Epistemology* •   242
Lewis Thomas *Humanities and Science* •   253
Lord Ashby *The University Ideal: A View from Britain*   261
Wayne C. Booth *Is There Any Knowledge That a Man Must
     Have?*   268
Francis E. Sparshott *Nothing to Say* •   283

LANGUAGE AND COMMUNICATION

Robert M. Adams *Soft Soap and the Nitty-Gritty* •   288
John Leo *Journalese for the Lay Reader* •   298

H. L. Mencken   *Gamalielese* •   301
Gloria Naylor   *"Mommy, What Does 'Nigger' Mean?"*   305
Robert Burchfield   *Dictionaries and Ethnic Sensibilities* •   308
Richard Rodriguez   *Aria* •   315
Lewis Thomas   *Notes on Punctuation* •   322
Erich Fromm   *The Nature of Symbolic Language*   325
Wayne C. Booth   *Boring from Within: The Art of the Freshman
   Essay* •   332
Nancy Sommers   *Revision Strategies of Student Writers and
   Experienced Adult Writers*   344
George Orwell   *Politics and the English Language* •   353

AN ALBUM OF STYLES   365

Francis Bacon   *Of Revenge*   365
John Donne   *Men Are Sleeping Prisoners*   366
Samuel Johnson   *The Pyramids*   367
Laurence Sterne   *Of Door Hinges and Life in
   General*   368
John Henry Newman   *Knowledge and Virtue*   368
Abraham Lincoln   *The Gettysburg Address*   369
Matthew Arnold   *Culture*   370
Walter Pater   *The Mona Lisa*   371
Anonymous   *No Dawn to the East*   372
Ernest Hemingway   from *A Farewell to
   Arms*   373
Virginia Woolf   *What the Novelist Gives Us*   373
E. B. White   *Progress and Change*   375
Joyce Cary   *Art and Education*   376
William Faulkner   *Nobel Prize Award
   Speech*   376
James Thurber   *A Dog's Eye View of Man*   378
John Updike   *Beer Can*   379
Tom Wolfe   *The Legend of Junior Johnson*   379
Robert Pirsig   *Concrete, Brick, and Neon*   380
John McPhee   *The Grizzly*   381

SIGNS OF THE TIMES

Anthony Burgess   *Is America Falling Apart?* •   384
Wendell Berry   *Home of the Free*   391
Phyllis Rose   *Shopping and Other Spiritual Adventures* •   394
Ian Frazier   *Just a Country Boy*   397

John McMurtry *Kill 'Em! Crush 'Em! Eat 'Em Raw!* • 399
S. J. Perelman *The Machismo Mystique* • 406
Adrienne Rich *When We Dead Awaken: Writing as Re-Vision* • 411
Gloria Steinem *The Good News Is: These Are Not the Best Years of Your Life* 424
Betty Rollin *Motherhood: Who Needs It?* 430
Brent Staples *Black Men and Public Space* • 440
Jessica Mitford *Behind the Formaldehyde Curtain* 443
Lewis Thomas *On Magic in Medicine* • 450
Dan Lacy *Reading in an Audiovisual and Electronic Era* 455
Joan Didion *Salvador* • 464
Jonathan Schell *The Destructive Power of a One-Megaton Bomb on New York City* 472
Garrison Keillor *The Tower Project* • 478

HUMAN NATURE

Jerome S. Bruner *Freud and the Image of Man* 481
Carol Gilligan *Images of Relationship* 488
Judith Viorst *Good as Guilt* • 501
Desmond Morris *Territorial Behavior* • 510
Barbara Garson *Whistle While You Work* 518
Robert Finch *Very Like a Whale* • 521
Paul West *A Passion to Learn* 527
Oliver Sacks *The Disembodied Lady* • 538
James Baldwin *Stranger in the Village* • 547
Norman Podhoretz *My Negro Problem—and Ours* 558
Malcolm Cowley *The View from 80* 569
Lewis Thomas *The Long Habit* • 575
Elisabeth Kübler-Ross *On the Fear of Death* • 579

ETHICS

James Thurber *The Bear Who Let It Alone* 587
Samuel Johnson *On Self-Love and Indolence* 588
Francis Bacon *Of Simulation and Dissimulation* • 592
Samuel Johnson *Letter to Lord Chesterfield* 595
Lord Chesterfield *Letter to His Son* • 596
Samuel L. Clemens *Advice to Youth* • 599
Judith Martin *Some Thoughts on the Mannerly Way of Life* 602
Stanley Milgram *The Perils of Obedience* • 606
Michael Levin *The Case for Torture* • 619
Tom Regan *The Case for Animal Rights* 621
Carl Cohen *The Case for the Use of Animals in Biomedical Research* 633
Stephen Jay Gould *The Terrifying Normalcy of AIDS* 643

Michael Stone   *Should Testing for the AIDS Virus Be
    Mandatory?*   646
Thomas Murray   *The Growing Danger* •   650
Gilbert Ryle   *On Forgetting the Difference between Right and
    Wrong*   655
Willard Gaylin   *What You See Is the Real You* •   664

PROSE FORMS: APOTHEGMS   667

W. H. Auden   *Apothegms*   670
Ambrose Bierce   from *The Devil's
    Dictionary*   671
William Blake   *Proverbs of Hell*   674
Benjamin Franklin   from *Poor Richard's
    Almanack*   676
La Rochefoucauld   from *Maxims*   678
George Bernard Shaw   from *The
    Revolutionist's Handbook*   681

HISTORY

Herbert Butterfield   *The Originality of the Old Testament* •   685
Henry David Thoreau   *The Battle of the Ants* •   690
Chief Seattle   *Address*   693
Walt Whitman   *Death of Abraham Lincoln* •   696
John Houseman   *The War of the Worlds*   704
Hannah Arendt   *Denmark and the Jews*   714
Michael Arlen   *Griefspeak* •   719
Michael Herr   *"How Bad Do You Want to Get to Danang?"*   722
Kildare Dobbs   *The Shatterer of Worlds*   725
Joan Didion   *On Keeping a Notebook* •   731
Virginia Woolf   *The New Biography* •   738
Frances FitzGerald   *Rewriting American History* •   744
Edward Hallett Carr   *The Historian and His Facts* •   751

POLITICS AND GOVERNMENT

George Orwell   *Shooting an Elephant* •   768
Ngũgĩ wa Thiong'o   *Decolonizing the Mind* •   775
Charles R. Morris   *Civil Disobedience* •   785
Ralph W. Conant   *The Justification of Civil Protest, Nonviolent
    and Violent* •   788
Martin Luther King, Jr.   *Letter from Birmingham Jail*   792
James Thurber   *The Rabbits Who Caused All the Trouble*   806

Jonathan Swift   A Modest Proposal •   807
Niccolò Machiavelli   The Morals of the Prince •   815
Abraham Lincoln   Second Inaugural Address   822
Thomas Jefferson   Original Draft of the Declaration of
    Independence   824
Thomas Jefferson and Others   The Declaration of
    Independence •   828
Carl Becker   Democracy   832
E. B. White   Democracy •   833
E. B. White   Four Letters on Freedom of Expression   834
Walter Lippmann   The Indispensable Opposition •   841
Jonathan Schell   The Roots of Nuclear Peril   848

SCIENCE

Edward O. Wilson   The Superorganism   856
Michael J. Katz   On the Wings of an Angel: An Exploration of
    the Limits of Biological Enterprise   866
Konrad Z. Lorenz   The Taming of the Shrew •   879
Niko Tinbergen   The Bee-Hunters of Hulshorst •   892
Alexander Petrunkevitch   The Spider and the Wasp •   905
Stephen Jay Gould   Our Allotted Lifetimes   910
Nigel Calder   Heads and Tails   914
Arthur Koestler   Gravity and the Holy Ghost •   920
Jacob Bronowski   The Nature of Scientific Reasoning •   927
Richard S. Westfall   The Career of Isaac Newton: A Scientific
    Life in the Seventeenth Century •   931
Stephen Jay Gould   Darwin's Middle Road   945
Tom Bethell   Agnostic Evolutionists •   952
Thomas S. Kuhn   The Route to Normal Science •   966

LITERATURE AND THE ARTS

Eudora Welty   One Writer's Beginnings •   976
John Gardner   What Writers Do   982
Vladimir Nabokov   Good Readers and Good Writers   992
Northrop Frye   The Motive for Metaphor •   997
Annie Dillard   About Symbol •   1006
Susanne K. Langer   Expressiveness   1013
Carl Gustav Jung   The Poet •   1021
Robert Frost   Education by Poetry: A Meditative Monologue •   1026
Robertson Davies   Ham and Tongue   1035
Margaret Atwood   Writing the Male Character •   1042
Virginia Woolf   In Search of a Room of One's Own   1053
S. I. Hayakawa   Sex Is Not a Spectator Sport •   1064
Vicki Hearne   Horses in Partnership with Time   1066
Christopher Fry   Laughter   1074

E. B. White   *Some Remarks on Humor* •   1076
Aaron Copland   *How We Listen*   1078
Lord Clark   *The Blot and the Diagram* •   1083
Joan Didion   *Georgia O'Keeffe* •   1098

PROSE FORMS: PARABLES   1102

Aesop   *The Frogs Desiring a King*   1105
Plato   *The Allegory of the Cave*   1105
Jesus   *Parables of the Kingdom*   1109
Zen Parables   *Muddy Road, A Parable,*
   Learning to Be Silent   1111
Jonathan Swift   *The Spider and the Bee*   1112
Samuel L. Clemens   *The War Prayer*   1115
Franz Kafka   *Parable of the Law*   1117

PHILOSOPHY AND RELIGION

James Thurber   *The Owl Who Was God*   1123
Robert Graves   *Mythology*   1124
E. F. Schumacher   *Levels of Being*   1129
John Donne   *Let Me Wither* •   1137
Langston Hughes   *Salvation* •   1139
C. S. Lewis   *Three Screwtape Letters* •   1141
Paul Tillich   *The Riddle of Inequality*   1147
Stephen Jay Gould   *Nonmoral Nature* •   1153
E. M. Forster   *What I Believe*   1162
Gilbert Highet   *The Mystery of Zen* •   1170
Virginia Woolf   *The Death of the Moth* •   1179
Annie Dillard   *Sight into Insight* •   1182
Jean-Paul Sartre   *Existentialism* •   1193

AUTHORS   1203

INDEX   1231

ACKNOWLEDGMENTS   1235

Index of
Rhetorical Modes
and Strategies

RHETORICAL MODES

Narrative

Dylan Thomas: Memories of Christmas   (p. 1)
Wallace Stegner: The Town Dump   (p. 10)
Maya Angelou: Graduation   (p. 22)
Richard Hugo: How I Never Met Eudora Welty   (p. 32)
Hans A. Schmitt: January 30, 1933: A Memoir   (p. 36)
Paul Fussell: My War   (p. 44)
Loren Eiseley: The Brown Wasps   (p. 72)
E. B. White: Once More to the Lake   (p. 79)
James Thurber: University Days   (p. 229)
Eudora Welty: One Writer's Beginnings   (p. 976)
Ian Frazier: Just A Country Boy   (p. 397)
Barbara Garson: Whistle While You Work   (p. 518)
Walt Whitman: Death of Abraham Lincoln   (p. 696)
Langston Hughes: Salvation   (p. 1139)
N. Scott Momaday: The Way to Rainy Mountain   (p. 129)
Tom Wolfe: The Legend of Junior Johnson   (p. 379)
John McPhee: The Grizzly   (p. 381)
Malcolm Cowley: The View from 80   (p. 569)
John Houseman: The War of the Worlds   (p. 704)
Richard S. Westfall: The Career of Isaac Newton: A Scientific Life
    in the Seventeenth Century   (p. 931)
Robertson Davies: Ham and Tongue   (p. 1035)
Samuel Johnson: Letter to Lord Chesterfield   (p. 595)

DESCRIPTION

Margaret Laurence: Where the World Began (p. 6)
Al Young: "Java Jive," by the Ink Spots (p. 16)
Scott Sanders: Listening to Owls (p. 59)
Jane Howard: Pomp and Circumstance in Groundhog Hollow
  (p. 134)
Thomas Jefferson: George Washington (p. 105)
Nathaniel Hawthorne: Abraham Lincoln (p. 108)
Virginia Woolf: Great Men's Houses (p. 142)
Virginia Woolf: My Father: Leslie Stephen (p. 146)
Doris Lessing: My Father (p. 151)
Daniel Mark Epstein: The Case of Harry Houdini (p. 159)
Eudora Welty: Clamorous to Learn (p. 212)
George Orwell: Shooting an Elephant (p. 768)
Joan Didion: Georgia O'Keeffe (p. 1098)
Michael Herr: "How Bad Do You Want to Get to Danang?"
  (p. 722)
Joan Didion: Salvador (p. 464)
Walter Pater: The Mona Lisa (p. 371)

EXPOSITION

Essays That Compare and Contrast
June Callwood: Portrait of Canada (p. 112)
William G. Perry, Jr: Examsmanship and the Liberal Arts: A Study
  in Educational Epistemology (p. 242)
Dan Lacy: Reading in an Audiovisual and Electronic Era (p. 455)
Chief Seattle: Address (p. 693)
Frances FitzGerald: Rewriting American History (p. 744)
John McMurtry: Kill 'Em! Crush 'Em! Eat 'Em Raw! (p. 399)
E. B. White: Once More to the Lake (p. 79)
John Updike: Beer Can (p. 79)
Michael Stone: Should Testing for the AIDS Virus Be
  Mandatory? (p. 646)
Virginia Woolf: The New Biography (p. 738)
Virginia Woolf: In Search of a Room of One's Own (p. 1053)
James Thurber: A Dog's Eye View of Man (p. 378)
Alexander Petrunkevitch: The Spider and the Wasp (p. 905)
Lord Clark: The Blot and the Diagram (p. 1083)

Essays That Classify and Divide
William Golding: Thinking as a Hobby (p. 173)
William Zinsser: College Pressures (p. 234)
Francis E. Sparshott: Nothing to Say (p. 283)
Aaron Copland: How We Listen (p. 1078)
Judith Viorst: Good as Guilt (p. 501)
Charles R. Morris: Civil Disobedience (p. 785)

Michael J. Katz: On the Wings of an Angel: An Exploration of the Limits of Biological Enterprise (p. 866)
Northrop Frye: The Motive for Metaphor (p. 997)
Robert Frost: Education by Poetry: A Meditative Monologue (p. 1026)
E. F. Schumacher: Levels of Being (p. 1129)

Essays That Define

Benjamin Franklin: The Convenience of Being "Reasonable" (p. 172)
Henry David Thoreau: Observation (p. 193)
Jacob Bronowski: The Reach of Imagination (p. 194)
Neil Postman: Confusing Levels of Abstraction (p. 187)
S. J. Perelman: The Machismo Mystique (p. 406)
E. B. White: Some Remarks on Humor (p. 1076)
Christopher Fry: Laughter (p. 1074)
E. B. White: Democracy (p. 833)
Carl Becker: Democracy (p. 832)
Michael Arlen: Griefspeak (p. 719)
Joan Didion: On Going Home (p. 69)
Jean-Paul Sartre: Existentialism (p. 1193)
Lewis Thomas: Notes on Punctuation (p. 322)
Virginia Woolf: The Death of the Moth (p. 1179)
Nigel Calder: Heads and Tails (p. 914)
Jacob Bronowski: The Nature of Scientific Reasoning (p. 927)
John Gardner: What Writers Do (p. 982)
Carl Gustav Jung: The Poet (p. 1021)
Gilbert Highet: The Mystery of Zen (p. 1170)
E. M. Forster: What I Believe (p. 1162)
Ernest Hemingway: from A Farewell to Arms (p. 373)
John Donne: Men Are Sleeping Prisoners (p. 366)
Robert M. Adams: Soft Soap and the Nitty-Gritty (p. 288)
H. L. Mencken: Gamalielese (p. 301)
Gloria Naylor: "Mommy, What Does 'Nigger' Mean?" (p. 305)
Erich Fromm: The Nature of Symbolic Language (p. 325)
John Henry Newman: Knowledge and Virtue (p. 368)
Matthew Arnold: Culture (p. 370)
Robert Pirsig: Concrete, Brick, and Neon (p. 380)
Wendell Berry: Home of the Free (p. 391)
Francis Bacon: Of Simulation and Dissimulation (p. 592)
Herbert Butterfield: The Originality of the Old Testament (p. 685)
Walter Lippmann: The Indispensable Opposition (p. 841)
Thomas S. Kuhn: The Route to Normal Science (p. 966)
Vladimir Nabokov: Good Readers and Good Writers (p. 992)
Annie Dillard: About Symbol (p. 1006)
Robert Graves: Mythology (p. 1124)
John Donne: Let Me Wither (p. 1137)
Annie Dillard: Sight into Insight (p. 1182)

Essays That Analyze a Process
   Alice Walker: Beauty: When the Other Dancer Is the Self   (p. 52)
   Isaac Asimov: The Eureka Phenomenon   (p. 201)
   Wayne C. Booth: Boring from Within: The Art of the Freshman
      Essay   (p. 332)
   Robert Burchfield: Dictionaries and Ethnic Sensibilities   (p. 308)
   Jonathan Schell: The Destructive Power of One-Megaton Bomb on
      New York City   (p. 472)
   Elisabeth Kübler-Ross: On the Fear of Death   (p. 579)
   Nancy Sommers: Revision Strategies of Student Writers and
      Experienced Adult Writers   (p. 344)
   E. B. White: Progress and Change   (p. 375)
   Ngũgĩ wa Thiong'o: Decolonizing the Mind   (p. 775)
   Edward O. Wilson: The Superorganism   (p. 856)
   Konrad Z. Lorenz: The Taming of the Shrew   (p. 879)
   Virginia Woolf: What the Novelist Gives Us   (p. 373)
   Jessica Mitford: Behind the Formaldehyde Curtain   (p. 443)
   Paul West: A Passion to Learn   (p. 527)
   Stanley Milgram: The Perils of Obedience   (p. 606)
   Niko Tinbergen: The Bee-Hunters of Hulshorst   (p. 892)

Essays That Analyze Cause/Effect
   Bruno Bettelheim: A Victim   (p. 41)
   Arthur Koestler: Gravity and the Holy Ghost   (p. 920)
   Richard Rodriguez: Aria   (p. 315)
   Samuel Johnson: The Pyramids   (p. 367)
   George Orwell: Politics and the English Language   (p. 353)
   Robert Finch: Very Like a Whale   (p. 521)
   Gloria Steinem: The Good News Is: These Are Not the Best Years
      of Your Life   (p. 424)
   Kildare Dobbs: The Shatterer of Worlds   (p. 725)
   Oliver Sacks: The Disembodied Lady   (p. 538)
   James Thurber: The Bear Who Let It Alone   (p. 587)
   Joan Didion: On Keeping a Notebook   (p. 731)
   Henry David Thoreau: The Battle of the Ants   (p. 690)
   E. B. White: Four Letters on Freedom of Expression   (p. 834)
   James Thurber: The Owl Who Was God   (p. 1123)

PERSUASION/ARGUMENT

   Caroline Bird: College Is a Waste of Time and Money   (p. 217)
   Lord Ashby: The University Ideal: A View from Britain   (p. 261)
   Laurence Sterne: Of Door Hinges and Life in General   (p. 368)
   Joyce Cary: Art and Education   (p. 376)
   Adrienne Rich: When We Dead Awaken: Writing as Re-
      Vision   (p. 411)
   Jerome S. Bruner: Freud and the Image of Man   (p. 481)
   Carol Gilligan: Images of Relationship   (p. 488)
   Norman Podhoretz: My Negro Problem—and Ours   (p. 558)

Lord Chesterfield: Letter to His Son   (p. 596)
Tom Regan: The Case for Animal Rights   (p. 621)
Carl Cohen: The Case for the Use of Animals in Biomedical
  Research   (p. 633)
Vicki Hearne: Horses in Partnership with Time   (p. 1066)
C. S. Lewis: Three Screwtape Letters   (p. 1141)
Stephen Jay Gould: Nonmoral Nature   (p. 1153)
Wayne C. Booth: Is There Any Knowledge That a Man Must
  Have?   (p. 268)
Anthony Burgess: Is America Falling Apart?   (p. 384)
Betty Rollin: Motherhood: Who Needs It?   (p. 430)
Garrison Keillor: The Tower Project   (p. 478)
Jonathan Swift: A Modest Proposal   (p. 807)
Willard Gaylin: What You See Is the Real You   (p. 664)
Michael Levin: The Case for Torture   (p. 619)
James Thurber: The Rabbits Who Caused All the Trouble
  (p. 806)
Hannah Arendt: Denmark and the Jews   (p. 714)
Carl Sagan: The Abstractions of Beasts   (p. 180)
Martin Luther King, Jr.: Letter from Birmingham Jail   (p. 792)
Margaret Atwood: Writing the Male Character   (p. 1042)
Brent Staples: Black Men and Public Space   (p. 440)
Barbara Ehrenreich: College Today: Tune In, Drop Out, and Take
  the Cash   (p. 226)
John Leo: Journalese for the Lay Reader   (p. 298)
Edward Hallett Carr: The Historian and His Facts   (p. 751)
Thomas Murray: The Growing Danger   (p. 650)
Stephen Jay Gould: The Terrifying Normalcy of AIDS   (p. 643)
Charles R. Morris: Civil Disobedience   (p. 785)
Ralph W. Conant: The Justification of Civil Protest, Nonviolent
  and Violent   (p. 788)
Abraham Lincoln: Second Inaugural Address   (p. 822)
Thomas Jefferson: Original Draft of the Declaration of
  Independence   (p. 824)
Thomas Jefferson and Others: The Declaration of
  Independence   (p. 828)
Lewis Thomas: Humanities and Science   (p. 253)
Lewis Thomas: On Magic in Medicine   (p. 450)
Lewis Thomas: The Long Habit   (p. 575)
Tom Bethell: Agnostic Evolutionists   (p. 952)
Stephen Jay Gould: Our Allotted Lifetimes   (p. 910)
Stephen Jay Gould: Darwin's Middle Road   (p. 945)
Plato: The Allegory of the Cave   (p. 1105)
Paul Tillich: The Riddle of Inequality   (p. 1147)
S. I. Hayakawa: Sex Is Not a Spectator Sport   (p. 1064)
Abraham Lincoln: The Gettysburg Address   (p. 369)
William Faulkner: Nobel Prize Award Speech   (p. 376)
Francis Bacon: Of Revenge   (p. 365)

RHETORICAL STRATEGIES

TITLE, AND OPENING AND CLOSING PARAGRAPHS

Stephen Jay Gould: Our Allotted Lifetimes   (p. 910)
Jacob Bronowski: The Nature of Scientific Reasoning   (p. 927)
Nathaniel Hawthorne: Abraham Lincoln   (p. 108)
Thomas Jefferson: George Washington   (p. 105)
Doris Lessing: My Father   (p. 151)
Alice Walker: Beauty: When the Other Dancer Is the Self   (p. 52)
Gloria Naylor: "Mommy, What Does 'Nigger' Mean?"   (p. 305)
Michael J. Katz: On the Wings of an Angel: An Exploration of the
    Limits of Biological Enterprise   (p. 866)

THESIS, DEVELOPMENT, AND SUPPORT

E. F. Schumacher: Levels of Being   (p. 1129)
Judith Viorst: Good as Guilt   (p. 501)
Langston Hughes: Salvation   (p. 1139)
Phyllis Rose: Shopping and Other Spiritual Adventures   (p. 394)
Walter Lippmann: The Indispensable Opposition   (p. 841)
Herbert Butterfield: The Originality of the Old Testament   (p. 685)
Jerome S. Bruner: Freud and the Image of Man   (p. 481)

ORGANIZATION

Caroline Bird: College Is a Waste of Time and Money   (p. 217)
Ngũgĩ wa Thiong'o: Decolonizing the Mind   (p. 775)
Tom Regan: The Case for Animal Rights   (p. 621)
Desmond Morris: Territorial Behavior   (p. 510)
Stephen Jay Gould: Nonmoral Nature   (p. 1153)
Martin Luther King, Jr. : Letter from Birmingham Jail   (p. 792)
Aaron Copland: How We Listen   (p. 1078)
George Orwell: Politics and the English Language   (p. 353)

PERSONA

Chief Seattle: Address   (p. 693)
Richard Rodriguez: Aria   (p. 315)
Eudora Welty: One Writer's Beginnings   (p. 976)
Adrienne Rich: When We Dead Awaken: Writing as Re-
    Vision   (p. 411)
Robert Frost: Education by Poetry: A Meditative Monologue
    (p. 1026)
Woody Allen: Selections from the Allen Notebooks   (p. 101)
James Baldwin: Stranger in the Village   (p. 547)
Annie Dillard: Sight into Insight   (p. 1182)
Niccolò Machiavelli: The Morals of the Prince   (p. 815)

Preface

Editors of texts that undergo repeated revision inevitably regard their latest effort as especially fine. Certainly the editors of this seventh edition of *The Norton Reader* consider it the equal of its progenitors and possibly the best since the first edition of 1965. Its generous contents are varied in many ways—in length, style, tone, immediacy, difficulty, and subject; and period, nationality, age, and sex of the author. Eight essays, for example, are by Canadian authors, forty-one by women. New and familiar essays by Native American, black, Asian American, and Chicano writers reflect the range of the *Reader*. All entries have been approved by at least three of the editors: quality has continued to be essential for inclusion.

Having satisfied the demands of most readers, two-thirds of the selections remain from earlier editions. It is a pleasure—simply to name selections from "Personal Report"—to print again old favorites by Dylan Thomas, Maya Angelou, Loren Eiseley, and E. B. White. It is no less a pleasure to introduce new selections that account for one-third of this edition. They come from such authors as June Callwood, Jane Howard, Neil Postman, Richard Rodriguez, Nancy Sommers, Gloria Steinem, and Michael J. Katz. Further, inclusion of these new essayists points up a sharpened focus on modern and contemporary writing. Thirty essays were published between 1900 and 1950, eighty-five between 1950 and 1980, and fifty-one since 1980.

As heretofore, the essays are gathered into sections according to major fields of human concern, some of them familiar ground to students— "Personal Report," "Mind," "Education," "Language and Communication"—and others inviting ventures toward more specialized kinds of knowledge, such as "History," "Science," "Philosophy and Religion." Teachers familiar with earlier editions will, however, note important changes in the manner of presenting essays. The editors have sought a middle ground between anthologies that offer essays with little or no editorial help and others in which editorial advice overwhelms the readings. The editors, realizing that writing and reading can engage in dialogues to the benefit of both, have sought to stimulate such dialogues in several ways:

1. By increasing the number of essays for which study questions are provided.
2. By dividing these study questions into two complementary categories: "The Reader" and "The Writer." The first focuses on content and interpretation—in short, on meaning. The second focuses on means and ends, on the strategies of style, tone, and arrangement by which an author seeks to effect changes in the readers' mind.
3. By multiplying to four the offerings of certain gifted essayists—E. B. White, Virginia Woolf, Lewis Thomas, and Joan Didion—so that students may discover how authors, like baseball pitchers, vary their delivery to suit the occasion. There are, too, other less frequent manifestations of the same voice employing in different essays different means for different ends: Henry David Thoreau, for example, or Thomas Jefferson, Benjamin Franklin, Eudora Welty, Wayne C. Booth, George Orwell, Samuel Johnson, and Stephen Jay Gould.
4. By providing more cross-referencing questions that invite discrimination among the ways different authors treat related subjects—Loren Eiseley, E. B. White, Lewis Thomas, and Elisabeth Kübler-Ross on mortality, for example, or the paired essays, one by Virginia Woolf and one by Doris Lessing, entitled "My Father."
5. By providing a totally new introductory (rather than final) essay on reading and writing. The work of Robert E. Hosmer, Jr. of Mount Holyoke, it explicitly yet informally coaches young readers in analyzing the processes of writing and reasoned response.
6. By expanding the authors' biographies to help students determine the contexts from which writings emerge.
7. And by securing from Professor Hosmer a new teachers' *Guide*, one that treats the rhetoric and content of *all* essays in the *Reader*, focusing especially on the aforementioned quartets of essays by E. B. White, Virginia Woolf, Lewis Thomas, and Joan Didion.

Many of these improvements derive from suggestions from the field, and much of what remains does so because of support from teachers across the country. Among those whose aid it is a pleasure to acknowledge are the following: Christine Barkley, San Diego Mesa College; Ruth M. Bradley, Diablo Valley College; Roger D. Carlstrom, Yakima Valley Community College; Joseph J. Comprone, University of Louisville; Virginia Cooke, Simon Fraser University; Richard Hauer Costa, Texas A&M University; Carrol Daniels, Stephen F. Austin State University; Charles H. Daughaday, Murray State University; Wilfred O. Dietrich, Blinn College; J. L. Dillard, Northwestern State University of Louisiana; M. Elaine Dolan, Tulane University of Louisiana; Anita Gandolfo, West Virginia University; Marshall Gillaland, University of Saskatchewan; Frederick Goldberg, Clayton Junior College; Katherine K. Gottschalk,

Cornell University; Theodore Haddin, University of Alabama in Birmingham; James Harrison, University of Guelph; Michael Hennessy, Southwest Texas State University; Charles Hofmiller, University of Bridgeport; Elsie B. Holmes, Trinity University; M. Hoskinson, Los Angeles Pierce College; Patricia J. Howard, Baylor University; Susan Hunter, Harvey Mudd College; Joseph Johnson, Northwestern State University of Louisiana; Nancy Johnson, University of British Columbia; Paul Klemp, Oklahoma State University; John Lammers, University of Central Arkansas; Frank E. LaRosa, San Diego City College; Jane LeMoine, Florida Institute of Technology; Jonathan Loesberg, American University; Steve Lynn, University of South Carolina; Karen Lyons, University of Nebraska at Lincoln; Mary McBride, Texas Tech University; Paul J. McGinnis, California State University, Sacramento; Jay Macpherson, Victoria College, University of Toronto; Irene Makaryk, Université d'Ottawa; Sara Murray, University of Texas at San Antonio; J. Walter Nelson, Eastern Kentucky University; Karen C. Ogden, University of Manitoba; Walter O'Grady, University of Toronto; Herbert Perluck, Brooklyn College, City University of New York; Catherine Reyner, University of Missouri at Kansas City; Mary Beth Richards, University of Nebraska at Lincoln; Eleanor M. Robinson, Niagara County Community College; Robert Ross, Southern Methodist University; Dennis Rygiel, Auburn University; Gary D. Schmidt, Calvin College; H. W. Sheridan, Brown University; Sam Solecki, University of Toronto; H. M. Solomon, Auburn University; David E. Stacey, University of Louisville; Neal Steiger, University of Massachusetts—Amherst; Judith Stein, University of Maryland at College Park; Philip J. Tama, Marywood College; David Tangeman, Washburn University of Topeka; Eva Taube, Southwestern College; Mary Kay Temple, University of North Florida; Robert Wiltenburg, Washington University; L. Westervelt, University of Houston.

—Arthur M. Eastman

Notes on Reading and Writing

> Despair is no good—for the writer, for anyone. Only hope can carry us aloft, can keep us afloat. Only hope, and a certain faith that the incredible structure that has been fashioned by this most strange and ingenious of all mammals cannot end in ruin and disaster. This faith is a writer's faith, for writing itself is an act of faith, nothing else.
>
> —E. B. White, "The Faith of a Writer"

E. B. White's eloquent remarks, delivered on his receiving the National Medal for Literature in 1971, encourage all of us engaged in writing. His words provide a point of departure as we consider the whole project of reading and writing, and the role that *The Norton Reader* can play in enabling you to become a better writer. A *better* writer, for you can already write. That is not just to say that you know the language and some of the "mechanics," like exclamation points, periods, and paragraph indentions, needed to put your thoughts on paper. It also means that you know how to communicate your thoughts in writing, at least some of the time. Sometimes you know what you want to say, other times you do not; sometimes you can find the words to say exactly what you want to, other times you cannot; sometimes you are satisfied with what you have written, other times you are not. If you feel that these last remarks apply to you, do not despair—you are in the company of almost every writer, amateur and professional.

One of the first things to remember about writing derives from an awareness of what human beings are: limited, capable of mistakes, and constantly seeking to understand and express themselves. To recognize this is not to give way to despair; rather, it is to recognize two positive implications for you as a writer. First, your writing cannot be "perfect," and no one is asking you to write the perfect essay. Work toward producing the best piece of writing you can deliver today, but do not be crippled by unrealistic expectations, your own or your instructor's. Second, because you are unique and your experiences and objectives are solely your own, you always have something to add to a text you have read, whether in thought, discussion, or writing.

Recognizing this should give you confidence. Writing, like many other human activities, goes hand in hand with self-confidence: if you think you can do it, you are halfway there. "Writing itself is an act of faith," primarily in yourself and your abilities, secondarily in language. If you remember how you learned to do certain things—prepare a meal, play a sport, pass an exam—you recall just how important self-confidence is. Of course, preparation and practice are equally important elements in any process. In the process of learning to write better, your preparation—reading, thinking, discussing—and your practice—writing, revising, editing—are essential. In addition, the work of your instructor and your classmates will be invaluable for you. They, too, are writers confronting the same problems that you confront.

The Norton Reader has been designed to play a significant part in that process. It offers a selection of well-written, thought-provoking essays for you to read, reflect on, discuss, and write about. These essays are here for you. The meaning of each essay does not reside "there" on the page, in the essay; nor does it reside solely in you. Furthermore, the essay does not mean whatever you want it to mean. Rather, meaning will emerge from the text and your response to it in that intervening distance between you and the printed page. The meaning that you derive will be tested, modified, rejected, or enhanced when you discuss your ideas in class and when you write. The remarks that follow may offer some helpful strategies as you work with the essays in this reader.

The Essay

It is far easier to say what the essay is *not* than to say what it is; it is not a poem or drama or catalogue or lab report or any one of a long list of other forms of writing we might cite. But definition by negation does not help much, nor does a definition such as Aldous Huxley's flippant "The essay is a literary device for saying almost everything about anything." One way to define the essay is to describe it as a "brief prose composition that attempts to make and develop an assertion in an engaging manner." It is worth pausing to consider the different elements of this definition. First, the essay is brief, perhaps only a few typed pages. Second, the essay is prose. Alexander Pope referred to his verse compositions, the "Essay on Criticism" and the "Essay on Man," as essays, but few writers since the eighteenth century have followed his example. Essays today are works of nonfiction in prose. Third, the essay writer attempts to develop an assertion, to make one point clearly and effectively. Finally, the word "essay," from the French noun *essai*, a "trial," reflects the view of Michel de Montaigne, a sixteenth-century French philosopher and creator of the "essai." Montaigne considered his essays attempts to respond to a wide variety of issues and events in a thoughtful, personal way.

One way to classify essays in general is to distinguish the formal essay from the informal essay. The formal essay most often presents a serious subject for a specialized audience; its author writes as an acknowledged authority whose purpose is to inform the reader; the tone of the formal essay tends to be impersonal. Nancy Sommers's "Revision Strategies of Student Writers and Experienced Adult Writers," Niccolò Machiavelli's "The Morals of the Prince," and Jean-Paul Sartre's "Existentialism" illustrate the formal essay. The informal essay, on the other hand, deals with events from everyday life and presents its subject matter for a general reader; its author is often a keen observer or participant who writes in a personal way. Examples of informal essays in *The Norton Reader* include Dylan Thomas's "Memories of Christmas," Daniel Mark Epstein's "The Case of Harry Houdini," and Phyllis Rose's "Shopping and Other Spiritual Adventures."

Every essay, whether formal or informal, focuses attention on a particular subject and seeks to make a definite point for a specific audience. It is a combination of objective elements and subjective responses. In writing essays in college, keep in mind the importance of balancing personal response with objective material. You limit the effectiveness of your writing when the reader is left with the impression that all you have written is opinion.

Rhetoric and the Modes of Essay Writing

When you hear someone's remarks dismissed as "mere rhetoric," you know that the term is less than glowing: the speaker or writer may have mastered the means of expression—style and delivery—but is found lacking in substance. Politicians often face this charge. Yet *rhetoric* also has positive meaning, for it refers to both knowledge and skill of strategies for effective communication. Aristotle's *Rhetoric* is the central document in the study of rhetoric. For Aristotle, rhetoric has mostly to do with persuasion, with inventing arguments, arranging evidence, and expressing ideas in aptly chosen language. For our purpose, rhetoric is the knowledge of the skills and strategies needed to communicate ideas, with grace and fluency, to a designated audience.

Rhetorical tradition provides a convenient way of distinguishing one type of essay from another. We can speak of four basic "modes" or types of essay writing: narrative, descriptive, expository, and argumentative.

Narrative essays, which relate an event or a series of events, demonstrate a particular dimension of the storyteller's art: creating a story from factual material. Unlike a short story or novel or fable, narrative essays deal exclusively with "real world" events. Descriptive essays create impressions that appeal to our senses. Expository essays offer explanations, most often by supplying substantial information presented in a logical manner. Among the most common forms of exposition, which can also be called analysis, are essays of comparison/contrast, classification, definition, process analysis, and causal analysis. Finally, argumentative essays seek to convince the reader of the correctness of a particular point of view. Strictly speaking, argument and persuasion are two different activities (argument appeals to reason and seeks assent; persuasion appeals to emotion and seeks action), but they are often combined in effective writing. Likewise, while it is possible to write an essay that is pure narrative or pure description or pure exposition, it is much more likely that you will mix modes in your own writing.

Writing as Process

The composing process involves all stages of your work, from the first ideas you have or notes you jot down through the presentation of the final copy. It extends well beyond the physical acts of putting pen to paper or hands to keyboard, for, in the process of composing—in reading, reflecting, discussing, and writing—you are actively involved in creating a text.

Consider the kinds of writing activities you might use in working on an essay: preliminary writing (notes, journal entries, freewriting); inventing a thesis and designing an essay (trial thesis statements and outlines); working up a draft; revising; editing the best draft for final copy. Seen in this way, writing is a process by and through which you can progress from tentative responses and jottings to a final draft worthy of submission.

Writing is also a cognitive process, a means by which you learn more about a particular subject, about other people, and about yourself. At no point will you or any writer know everything about a specific topic, but in most cases you will know more by the time you submit the final copy than you did when you invented your thesis or wrote your first draft. The status of writing as a cognitive process means two things for you. First, you can expect to learn from your writing. And second, you can be confident that your writing will improve with effort, for you and the essay are proceeding toward a goal.

Reading and Writing

Reading and writing might seem to be opposing activities. Careful reading calls for analysis, splitting a text apart in order to understand how it is constructed. Effective writing, on the other hand, demands synthesis, binding elements together so that they function as a whole. Yet reading and writing are complementary activities, for the better you understand how a given essay "works," the more you learn about how to make your own writing "work."

In considering anything you have read, you need to ask yourself two important questions, both of them posed by a distinguished teacher, Robert Scholes: What does this text mean? How does it mean? When you have finished reading, you will have some tentative responses; when you have discussed the reading in class, you will have clearer answers; and when you have written your essay, you will have significantly deepened your understanding of the text. Put another way, writing will complete the experience of reading.

How to Read: Some Practical Suggestions

A good understanding of any serious essay requires more than just one reading. You might adopt a three-part method for reading your assigned essays: first, an uninterrupted narrative reading to acquire a basic sense of the text (What does it mean?); then, a close, analytical, annotated reading to appreciate the structure and logic of the text (How does it mean?); finally, a "review reading" to synthesize your earlier readings. Because careful reading is analysis, you will want to be precise as you examine all the elements—even the title—of the essays you read.

As you read, annotate your text with a free but directed hand. Underline important ideas and essential terms; underline passages you do not understand; put question marks and comments in the margins. Imagine that you are in conversation with the writer and respond accordingly. If a particular idea strikes you as insightful, make a note. If the writer's thought seems unclear, note that you want to focus on it in your next reading or in discussion. Refer to your annotated text in class to remind you what ideas provoked you and where you had questions. Use your annotation to bring your personal perspective and experience to bear on what you read. This is an essential part of the composing process.

What to Look for When You Read

To get at the structure and substance of an essay, spend some time considering the following elements:

1. TITLE, AND OPENING AND CLOSING PARAGRAPHS
   Notice the title—it can be an important aspect of the essay, serving to catch the reader's interest and sometimes giving a clear indication of what the essay is about. Study the opening paragraph, a vital part of an

essay, one which establishes some common ground with the reader. The opening paragraph often articulates the thesis of the essay. Take a look at how Brent Staples in "Black Men and Public Space" and Betty Rollin in "Motherhood: Who Needs It?" startle the reader in their opening paragraphs. Consider the closing paragraph. It should reinforce the thesis and offer an assessment, an observation, or a prediction; it should leave the reader with something to think about. Look at the provocative closing paragraphs of "Decolonizing the Mind" by Ngũgĩ wa Thiong'o and "Shopping and Other Spiritual Adventures" by Phyllis Rose.

2. THESIS, DEVELOPMENT, AND SUPPORT

Examine the essay for a thesis statement, a sentence in which the writer takes a stand and indicates his or her central purpose. Sometimes, as in Judith Viorst's "Good as Guilt," the writer's thesis is explicitly stated. Other times, as in E. B. White's "Once More to the Lake," where there is probably no single sentence that will satisfactorily represent the entire essay, the writer implies it. In such cases the careful reader should be able to construct a thesis statement.

How does the writer develop the main idea of the essay? Sometimes a thesis will rest on assumptions, related ideas that the writer does not mention directly but expects the reader to understand or to agree to or, if the real purpose is deception, to overlook. Machiavelli, in "The Morals of the Prince," appears to assume that it is more important for a prince to stay in power than to be a "good" man. In considering what you read, always ask yourself: What assumptions has the writer made? Apply that question to Elisabeth Kübler-Ross's "On the Fear of Death" or Stephen Jay Gould's "The Terrifying Normalcy of AIDS."

How does the writer support the main idea of the essay? Determine what kinds of support have been enlisted. Factual evidence (material easily verifiable or attested to by reliable witnesses) or opinion? If opinion, whose? That of a recognized authority? Furthermore, consider whether or not the support is sufficient for the subject, purpose, and audience. Is the evidence appropriate and convincing? Evaluate the evidence Anthony Burgess draws on in his essay "Is America Falling Apart?"

3. ORGANIZATION

A well-written essay is clearly, logically, and carefully organized. Its skeletal structure can be discerned, removed, and examined. Think of this process as something like boning a fish: if the essay has been organized well, you should be able to delineate its structure as easily as you can separate the skeletal system from a freshly caught trout. As an exercise in discerning structure, see if you can "bone" George Orwell's "Shooting an Elephant" or Desmond Morris's "Territorial Behavior."

4. PERSONA

When you read an essay, you should be able to form an impression of the writer from the text. In response to choices of subject, purpose, and, most importantly, audience, the writer creates a particular image. Elements like tone, word choice, figures of speech, sentence complexity, and paragraph length—that is, the writer's "style"—create a persona. Your response to the writer's persona is of crucial importance, particularly in argument, where, if the writer fails to create a persona that is fair, knowledgeable, and trustworthy, the argument is lost. You should be able to characterize the writer's persona. One way to do this is to draw up a short list of adjectives that describe the voice you heard in the essay you read. Try this exercise on Margaret Atwood's "Writing the Male Character" or Eudora Welty's "One Writer's Beginnings."

Upon completion of your close reading, you should be able to summarize the essay as a whole, describe the strategies that the writer has used, and offer your view of the success or failure of the essay by pointing to specific elements in the text.

How to Write: Some Suggestions Based upon Reading

Through reading, you sharpen your sense of what a good essay is. You develop an awareness of the elements that determine its success or failure, taking into consideration title, opening and closing paragraphs, thesis, development and support, and persona. Now your work as a writer begins. The nine brief points that follow are suggestions for developing your understanding of writing.

1. Have something to say. You can know all the fine points of form and style, but unless you have discovered something to say, there is no sense in writing.
2. Know your subject. Review your annotated text and class notes.
3. Articulate your purpose. If it has not been assigned in class, determine it for yourself.
4. Develop a clear sense of your audience. Ask yourself two questions: For whom am I writing this? What must I do to communicate successfully with my reader? Develop a clear sense of your own voice—know your persona.
5. Once you have these four aspects defined, formulate a thesis statement that expresses the central idea of your essay. Use whatever method works for you—freewriting, brainstorming, cataloguing responses to what you have read—but put your thesis, however tentative, in writing.

6. Design your essay by drawing up an outline to guide its development.
7. Write a rough draft. Go ahead and write, no matter what you think of the quality. A first draft, however rough, gives you something to work with.
8 Revise the draft. "Re-see" your essay in light of its subject, purpose, and audience. Examine its design. Judge how effectively it supports its central thesis.
9. Edit your revised draft. Proofread your final essay.

—Robert E. Hosmer, Jr.,
Mount Holyoke College

The Norton Reader

SEVENTH EDITION

Personal Report

Dylan Thomas

MEMORIES OF CHRISTMAS

One Christmas was so much like another, in those years, around the sea-town corner now and out of all sound except the distant speaking of the voices I sometimes hear a moment before sleep, that I can never remember whether it snowed for six days and six nights when I was twelve or whether it snowed for twelve days and twelve nights when I was six; or whether the ice broke and the skating grocer vanished like a snowman through a white trap-door on that same Christmas Day that the mince-pies finished Uncle Arnold and we tobogganed down the seaward hill, all the afternoon, on the best tea-tray, and Mrs. Griffiths complained, and we threw a snowball at her niece, and my hands burned so, with the heat and the cold, when I held them in front of the fire, that I cried for twenty minutes and then had some jelly.

All the Christmases roll down the hill towards the Welsh-speaking sea, like a snowball growing whiter and bigger and rounder, like a cold and headlong moon bundling down the sky that was our street; and they stop at the rim of the ice-edged, fish-freezing waves, and I plunge my hands in the snow and bring out whatever I can find; holly or robins or pudding, squabbles and carols and oranges and tin whistles, and the fire in the front room, and bang go the crackers, and holy, holy, holy, ring the bells, and the glass bells shaking on the tree, and Mother Goose, and Struwelpeter[1] —oh! the baby-burning flames and the clacking scissorman!—Billy Bunter[2] and Black Beauty, Little Women and boys who have three helpings, Alice and Mrs. Potter's badgers,[3] penknives, teddy-bears—

1. The title character of *Struwelpeter (Slovenly Peter),* or *Merry Tales and Funny Pictures,* a children's book originally in German, by Dr. Heinrich Hoffmann, containing gaily grim admonitory narratives in verse about little Pauline, for example, who played with matches and got burned up; or the little boy who sucked his thumbs until the tall scissorman cut them off.
2. The humorous fat boy in Frank Richards' tales of English school life.
3. Beatrix Potter, creator of *Peter Rabbit* and other animal tales for children, among them *The Tale of Mr. Tod,* a badger.

named after a Mr. Theodore Bear, their inventor, or father, who died recently in the United States—mouth-organs, tin-soldiers, and blancmange, and Auntie Bessie playing "Pop Goes the Weasel" and "Nuts in May" and "Oranges and Lemons" on the untuned piano in the parlor all through the thimble-hiding musical-chairing blind-man's-buffing party at the end of the never-to-be-forgotten day at the end of the unremembered year.

In goes my hand into that wool-white bell-tongued ball of holidays resting at the margin of the carol-singing sea, and out come Mrs. Prothero and the firemen.

It was on the afternoon of the day of Christmas Eve, and I was in Mrs. Prothero's garden, waiting for cats, with her son Jim. It was snowing. It was always snowing at Christmas; December, in my memory, is white as Lapland, though there were no reindeers. But there were cats. Patient, cold, and callous, our hands wrapped in socks, we waited to snowball the cats. Sleek and long as jaguars and terrible-whiskered, spitting and snarling they would slink and sidle over the white back-garden walls, and the lynx-eyed hunters, Jim and I, fur-capped and moccasined trappers from Hudson's Bay off Eversley Road, would hurl our deadly snowballs at the green of their eyes. The wise cats never appeared. We were so still, Eskimo-footed arctic marksmen in the muffling silence of the eternal snows—eternal, ever since Wednesday—that we never heard Mrs. Prothero's first cry from her igloo at the bottom of the garden. Or, if we heard it at all, it was, to us, like the far-off challenge of our enemy and prey, the neighbor's Polar Cat. But soon the voice grew louder. "Fire!" cried Mrs. Prothero, and she beat the dinner-gong. And we ran down the garden, with the snowballs in our arms, towards the house, and smoke, indeed, was pouring out of the dining-room, and the gong was bombilating, and Mrs. Prothero was announcing ruin like a town-crier in Pompeii. This was better than all the cats in Wales standing on the wall in a row. We bounded into the house, laden with snowballs, and stopped at the open door of the smoke-filled room. Something was burning all right; perhaps it was Mr. Prothero, who always slept there after midday dinner with a newspaper over his face; but he was standing in the middle of the room, saying "A fine Christmas!" and smacking at the smoke with a slipper.

"Call the fire-brigade," cried Mrs. Prothero as she beat the gong.

"They won't be there," said Mr. Prothero, "it's Christmas."

There was no fire to be seen, only clouds of smoke and Mr. Prothero standing in the middle of them, waving his slipper as though he were conducting.

"Do something," he said.

And we threw all our snowballs into the smoke—I think we missed Mr. Prothero—and ran out of the house to the telephone-box.

"Let's call the police as well," Jim said.

"And the ambulance."

"And Ernie Jenkins, he likes fires."

But we only called the fire-brigade, and soon the fire-engine came and three tall men in helmets brought a hose into the house and Mr. Prothero got out just in time before they turned it on. Nobody could have had a noisier Christmas Eve. And when the firemen turned off the hose and were standing in the wet and smoky room, Jim's aunt, Miss Prothero, came downstairs and peered in at them. Jim and I waited, very quietly, to hear what she would say to them. She said the right thing, always. She looked at the three tall firemen in their shining helmets, standing among the smoke and cinders and dissolving snowballs, and she said: "Would you like something to read?"

Now out of that bright white snowball of Christmas gone comes the stocking, the stocking of stockings, that hung at the foot of the bed with the arm of a golliwog dangling over the top and small bells ringing in the toes. There was a company, gallant and scarlet but never nice to taste though I always tried when very young, of belted and busbied and musketed lead soldiers so soon to lose their heads and legs in the wars on the kitchen table after the tea-things, the mince-pies, and the cakes that I helped to make by stoning the raisins and eating them, had been cleared away; and a bag of moist and many-colored jelly-babies and a folded flag and a false nose and a tram-conductor's cap and a machine that punched tickets and rang a bell; never a catapult; once, by a mistake that no one could explain, a little hatchet; and a rubber buffalo, or it may have been a horse, with a yellow head and haphazard legs; and a celluloid duck that made, when you pressed it, a most unducklike noise, a mewing moo that an ambitious cat might make who wishes to be a cow; and a painting-book in which I could make the grass, the trees, the sea, and the animals any color I pleased: and still the dazzling sky-blue sheep are grazing in the red field under a flight of rainbow-beaked and pea-green birds.

Christmas morning was always over before you could say Jack Frost. And look! suddenly the pudding was burning! Bang the gong and call the fire-brigade and the book-loving firemen! Someone found the silver three-penny-bit with a currant on it; and the someone was always Uncle Arnold. The motto in my cracker read:

> Let's all have fun this Christmas Day,
> Let's play and sing and shout hooray!

and the grown-ups turned their eyes towards the ceiling, and Auntie Bessie, who had already been frightened, twice, by a clockwork mouse, whimpered at the sideboard and had some elderberry wine. And some-one put a glass bowl full of nuts on the littered table, and my uncle said, as he said once every year: "I've got a shoe-nut here. Fetch me a shoehorn to open it, boy."

And dinner was ended.

And I remember that on the afternoon of Christmas Day, when the others sat around the fire and told each other that this was nothing, no, nothing, to the great snowbound and turkey-proud yule-log-crackling holly-berry-bedizined and kissing-under-the mistletoe Christmas when *they* were children, I would go out, school-capped and gloved and muffered, with my bright new boots squeaking, into the white world on to the seaward hill, to call on Jim and Dan and Jack and to walk with them through the silent snowscape of our town.

We went padding through the streets, leaving huge deep footprints in the snow, on the hidden pavements.

"I bet people'll think there's been hippoes."

"What would you do if you saw a hippo coming down Terrace Road?"

"I'd go like this, bang! I'd throw him over the railings and roll him down the hill and then I'd tickle him under the ear and he'd wag his tail . . ."

"What would you do if you saw *two* hippoes . . . ?"

Iron-flanked and bellowing he-hippoes clanked and blundered and battered through the scudding snow towards us as we passed by Mr. Daniel's house.

"Let's post Mr. Daniel a snowball through his letter box."

"Let's write things in the snow."

"Let's write 'Mr. Daniel looks like a spaniel' all over his lawn."

"Look," Jack said, "I'm eating snow-pie."

"What's it taste like?"

"Like snow-pie," Jack said.

Or we walked on the white shore.

"Can the fishes see it's snowing?"

"They think it's the sky falling down."

The silent one-clouded heavens drifted on to the sea.

"All the old dogs have gone."

Dogs of a hundred mingled makes yapped in the summer at the sea-rim and yelped at the trespassing mountains of the waves.

"I bet St. Bernards would like it now."

And we were snowblind travelers lost on the north hills, and the great dewlapped dogs, with brandy-flasks round their necks, ambled and shambled up to us, baying "Excelsior."[4]

We returned home through the desolate poor sea-facing streets where only a few children fumbled with bare red fingers in the thick wheel-rutted snow and catcalled after us, their voices fading away, as we

---

4. "Higher"—recalling Henry Wadsworth Longfellow's poem "Excelsior," in which a traveler who has adopted that word as his motto perishes while climbing a dangerous, snowy mountain trail, and is found by monks of Saint Bernard and their "faithful hound."

trudged uphill, into the cries of the dock-birds and the hooters of ships out in the white and whirling bay.

Bring out the tall tales now that we told by the fire as we roasted chestnuts and the gaslight bubbled low. Ghosts with their heads under their arms trailed their chains and said "whooo" like owls in the long nights when I dared not look over my shoulder; wild beasts lurked in the cubby-hole under the stairs where the gas-meter ticked. "Once upon a time," Jim said, "there were three boys, just like us, who got lost in the dark in the snow, near Bethesda Chapel, and this is what happened to them . . ." It was the most dreadful happening I had ever heard.

And I remember that we went singing carols once, a night or two before Christmas Eve, when there wasn't the shaving of a moon to light the secret, white-flying streets. At the end of a long road was a drive that led to a large house, and we stumbled up the darkness of the drive that night, each one of us afraid, each one holding a stone in his hand in case, and all of us too brave to say a word. The wind made through the drive-trees noises as of old and unpleasant and maybe web-footed men wheezing in caves. We reached the black bulk of the house.

"What shall we give them?" Dan whispered.

"'Hark the Herald'? 'Christmas comes but Once a Year'?"

"No," Jack said: "We'll sing 'Good King Wenceslas.' I'll count three."

One, two, three, and we began to sing, our voices high and seemingly distant in the snow-felted darkness round the house that was occupied by nobody we knew. We stood close together, near the dark door.

> Good King Wenceslas looked out
> On the Feast of Stephen.

And then a small, dry voice, like the voice of someone who has not spoken for a long time, suddenly joined our singing: a small, dry voice from the other side of the door: a small, dry voice through the keyhole. And when we stopped running we were outside our house; the front room was lovely and bright; the gramophone was playing; we saw the red and white balloons hanging from the gas-bracket; uncles and aunts sat by the fire; I thought I smelt our supper being fried in the kitchen. Everything was good again, and Christmas shone through all the familiar town.

"Perhaps it was a ghost," Jim said.

"Perhaps it was trolls," Dan said, who was always reading.

"Let's go in and see if there's any jelly left," Jack said. And we did that.

1945

Margaret Laurence

WHERE THE WORLD BEGAN

A strange place it was, that place where the world began. A place of incredible happenings, splendors and revelations, despairs like multitudinous pits of isolated hells. A place of shadow-spookiness, inhabited by the unknowable dead. A place of jubilation and of mourning, horrible and beautiful.

It was, in fact, a small prairie town.

Because that settlement and that land were my first and for many years my only real knowledge of this planet, in some profound way they remain my world, my way of viewing. My eyes were formed there. Towns like ours, set in a sea of land, have been described thousands of times as dull, bleak, flat, uninteresting. I have had it said to me that the railway trip across Canada is spectacular, except for the prairies, when it would be desirable to go to sleep for several days, until the ordeal is over. I am always unable to argue this point effectively. All I can say is—well, you really have to live there to know that country. The town of my childhood could be called bizarre, agonizingly repressive or cruel at times, and the land in which it grew could be called harsh in the violence of its seasonal changes. But never merely flat or uninteresting. Never dull.

In winter, we used to hitch rides on the back of the milk sleigh, our moccasins squeaking and slithering on the hard rutted snow of the roads, our hands in ice-bubbled mitts hanging onto the box edge of the sleigh for dear life, while Bert grinned at us through his great frosted mustache and shouted the horse into speed, daring us to stay put. Those mornings, rising, there would be the perpetual fascination of the frost feathers on windows, the ferns and flowers and eerie faces traced there during the night by unseen artists of the wind. Evenings, coming back from skating, the sky would be black but not dark, for you could see a cold glitter of stars from one side of the earth's rim to the other. And then the sometime astonishment when you saw the Northern Lights flaring across the sky, like the scrawled signature of God. After a blizzard, when the snowplow hadn't yet got through, school would be closed for the day, the assumption being that the town's young could not possibly flounder through five feet of snow in the pursuit of education. We would then gaily don snowshoes and flounder for miles out into the white dazzling deserts, in pursuit of a different kind of knowing. If you came back too close to night, through the woods at the foot of the town hill, the thin black branches of poplar and chokecherry now meringued with frost, sometimes you heard coyotes. Or maybe the banshee wolf-voices were really only inside your head.

Summers were scorching, and when no rain came and the wheat became bleached and dried before it headed, the faces of farmers and townsfolk would not smile much, and you took for granted, because it never seemed to have been any different, the frequent knocking at the back door and the young men standing there, mumbling or thrusting defiantly their requests for a drink of water and a sandwich if you could spare it. They were riding the freights, and you never knew where they had come from, or where they might end up, if anywhere. The Drought and Depression were like evil deities which had been there always. You understood and did not understand.

Yet the outside world had its continuing marvels. The poplar bluffs and the small river were filled and surrounded with a zillion different grasses, stones, and weed flowers. The meadowlarks sang undaunted from the twanging telephone wires along the gravel highway. Once we found an old flat-bottomed scow, and launched her, poling along the shallow brown waters, mending her with wodges of hastily chewed Spearmint, grounding her among the tangles of yellow marsh marigolds that grew succulently along the banks of the shrunken river, while the sun made our skins smell dusty-warm.

My best friend lived in an apartment above some stores on Main Street (its real name was Mountain Avenue, goodness knows why), an elegant apartment with royal-blue velvet curtains. The back roof, scarcely sloping at all, was corrugated tin, of a furnace-like warmth on a July afternoon, and we would sit there drinking lemonade and looking across the back lane at the Fire Hall. Sometimes our vigil would be rewarded. Oh joy! Somebody's house burning down! We had an almost-perfect callousness in some ways. Then the wooden tower's bronze bell would clonk and toll like a thousand speeded funerals in a time of plague, and in a few minutes the team of giant black horses would cannon forth, pulling the fire wagon like some scarlet chariot of the Goths, while the firemen clung with one hand, adjusting their helmets as they went.

The oddities of the place were endless. An elderly lady used to serve, as her afternoon tea offering to other ladies, soda biscuits spread with peanut butter and topped with a whole marshmallow. Some considered this slightly eccentric, when compared with chopped egg sandwiches, and admittedly talked about her behind her back, but no one ever refused these delicacies or indicated to her that they thought she had slipped a cog. Another lady dyed her hair a bright and cheery orange, by strangers often mistaken at twenty paces for a feather hat. My own beloved stepmother wore a silver fox neckpiece, a whole pelt, *with the embalmed head still on.* My Ontario Irish grandfather said, "sparrow grass," a more interesting term than asparagus. The town dump was known as "the nuisance grounds," a phrase fraught with weird connotations, as though the effluvia of our lives was beneath contempt but at the same time was subtly threatening to the determined and sometimes hysterical propriety of our ways.

Some oddities were, as idiom had it, "funny ha ha"; others were "funny peculiar." Some were not so very funny at all. An old man lived, deranged, in a shack in the valley. Perhaps he wasn't even all that old, but to us he seemed a wild Methuselah figure, shambling among the underbrush and the tall couchgrass, muttering indecipherable curses or blessings, a prophet who had forgotten his prophecies. Everyone in town knew him, but no one knew him. He lived among us as though only occasionally and momentarily visible. The kids called him Andy Gump,[1] and feared him. Some sought to prove their bravery by tormenting him. They were the medieval bear baiters, and he the lumbering bewildered bear, half blind, only rarely turning to snarl. Everything is to be found in a town like mine. Belsen,[2] writ small but with the same ink.

All of us cast stones in one shape or another. In grade school, among the vulnerable and violet girls we were, the feared and despised were those few older girls from what was charmingly termed "the wrong side of the tracks." Tough in talk and tougher in muscle, they were said to be whores already. And may have been, that being about the only profession readily available to them.

The dead lived in that place, too. Not only the grandparents who had, in local parlance, "passed on" and who gloomed, bearded or bonneted, from the sepia photographs in old albums, but also the uncles, forever eighteen or nineteen, whose names were carved on the granite family stones in the cemetery, but whose bones lay in France.[3] My own young mother lay in that graveyard, beside other dead of our kin, and when I was ten, my father, too, only forty, left the living town for the dead dwelling on the hill.

When I was eighteen, I couldn't wait to get out of that town, away from the prairies. I did not know then that I would carry the land and town all my life within my skull, that they would form the mainspring and source of the writing I was to do, wherever and however far away I might live.

This was my territory in the time of my youth, and in a sense my life since then has been an attempt to look at it, to come to terms with it. Stultifying to the mind it certainly could be, and sometimes was, but not to the imagination. It was many things, but it was never dull.

The same, I now see, could be said for Canada in general. Why on earth did generations of Canadians pretend to believe this country dull?

1. Chinless character in a comic strip popular in the 1920s and 1930s.
2. The Nazi concentration camp Bergen-Belsen.
3. That is, who had been killed in World War I. The Canadian war dead were buried in Canadian cemeteries in northeastern France and Belgium.

We knew perfectly well it wasn't. Yet for so long we did not proclaim what we knew. If our upsurge of so-called nationalism seems odd or irrelevant to outsiders, and even to some of our own people (*what's all the fuss about?*), they might try to understand that for many years we valued ourselves insufficiently, living as we did under the huge shadows of those two dominating figures, Uncle Sam and Britannia. We have only just begun to value ourselves, our land, our abilities. We have only just begun to recognize our legends and to give shape to our myths.

There are, God knows, enough aspects to deplore about this country. When I see the killing of our lakes and rivers with industrial wastes, I feel rage and despair. When I see our industries and natural resources increasingly taken over by America, I feel an overwhelming discouragement, especially as I cannot simply say "damn Yankees." It should never be forgotten that it is we ourselves who have sold such a large amount of our birthright for a mess of plastic Progress. When I saw the War Measures Act being invoked in 1970,[4] I lost forever the vestigial remains of the naïve wish-belief that repression could not happen here, or would not. And yet, of course, I had known all along in the deepest and often hidden caves of the heart that anything can happen anywhere, for the seeds of both man's freedom and his captivity are found everywhere, even in the microcosm of a prairie town. But in raging against our injustices, our stupidities, I do so *as family*, as I did, and still do in writing, about those aspects of my town which I hated and which are always in some ways aspects of myself.

The land still draws me more than other lands. I have lived in Africa and in England, but splendid as both can be, they do not have the power to move me in the same way as, for example, that part of southern Ontario where I spent four months last summer in a cedar cabin beside a river. "Scratch a Canadian, and you find a phony pioneer," I used to say to myself in warning. But all the same it is true, I think, that we are not yet totally alienated from physical earth, and let us only pray we do not become so. I once thought that my lifelong fear and mistrust of cities made me a kind of old-fashioned freak; now I see it differently.

The cabin has a long window across its front western wall, and sitting at the oak table there in the mornings, I used to look out at the river and at the tall trees beyond, green-gold in the early light. The river was bronze; the sun caught it strangely, reflecting upon its surface the near-shore sand ripples underneath. Suddenly, the crescenting of a fish, gone before the eye could clearly give image to it. The old man next door said these

4. By Prime Minister Pierre Elliott Trudeau, citing an "apprehended insurrection" in the wake of terrorist kidnapings by the separatist FLQ (Front de Libération du Québec). Under the provisions of this act, the armed forces took over many police functions, and certain civil liberties—notably habeas corpus—were suspended so that suspected terrorists could be held in jail without being charged.

leaping fish were carp. Himself, he preferred muskie, for he was a real fisherman and the muskie gave him a fight. The wind most often blew from the south, and the river flowed toward the south, so when the water was wind-riffled, and the current was strong, the river seemed to be flowing both ways. I liked this, and interpreted it as an omen, a natural symbol.

A few years ago, when I was back in Winnipeg, I gave a talk at my old college. It was open to the public, and afterward a very old man came up to me and asked me if my maiden name had been Wemyss. I said yes, thinking he might have known my father or my grandfather. But no. "When I was a young lad," he said, "I once worked for your great-grandfather, Robert Wemyss, when he had the sheep ranch at Raeburn." I think that was a moment when I realized all over again something of great importance to me. My long-ago families came from Scotland and Ireland, but in a sense that no longer mattered so much. My true roots were here.

I am not very patriotic, in the usual meaning of that word. I cannot say "My country right or wrong" in any political, social or literary context. But one thing is inalterable, for better or worse, for life.

This is where my world began. A world which includes the ancestors —both my own and other people's ancestors who become mine. A world which formed me, and continues to do so, even while I found it in some of its aspects, and continue to do so. A world which gave me my own lifework to do, because it was here that I learned the sight of my own particular eyes.

1970

Wallace Stegner

THE TOWN DUMP

The town dump of Whitemud, Saskatchewan, could only have been a few years old when I knew it, for the village was born in 1913 and I left there in 1919. But I remember the dump better than I remember most things in that town, better than I remember most of the people. I spent more time with it, for one thing; it has more poetry and excitement in it than people did.

It lay in the southeast corner of town, in a section that was always full of adventure for me. Just there the Whitemud River left the hills, bent a little south, and started its long traverse across the prairie and international boundary to join the Milk. For all I knew, it might have been on its way to join the Alph:[1] simply, before my eyes, it disappeared into strangeness and wonder.

Also, where it passed below the dumpground, it ran through willowed bottoms that were a favorite campsite for passing teamsters, gypsies, sometimes Indians. The very straw scattered around those camps, the ashes of those strangers' campfires, the manure of their teams and saddle horses, were hot with adventurous possibilities.

It was as an extension, a living suburb, as it were, of the dumpground that we most valued those camps. We scoured them for artifacts of their migrant tenants as if they had been archaeological sites full of the secrets of ancient civilizations. I remember toting around for weeks the broken cheek strap of a bridle. Somehow or other its buckle looked as if it had been fashioned in a far place, a place where they were accustomed to flatten the tongues of buckles for reasons that could only be exciting, and where they made a habit of plating the silver with some valuable alloy, probably silver. In places where the silver was worn away the buckle underneath shone dull yellow: probably gold.

It seemed that excitement liked that end of town better than our end. Once old Mrs. Gustafson, deeply religious and a little raddled in the head, went over there with a buckboard full of trash, and as she was driving home along the river she looked and saw a spent catfish, washed in from Cypress Lake or some other part of the watershed, floating on the yellow water. He was two feet long, his whiskers hung down, his fins and tail were limp. He was a kind of fish that no one had seen in the Whitemud in the three or four years of the town's life, and a kind that none of us children had ever seen anywhere. Mrs. Gustafson had never seen one like him either; she perceived at once that he was the devil, and she whipped up the team and reported him at Hoffman's elevator.

We could hear her screeching as we legged it for the river to see for ourselves. Sure enough, there he was. He looked very tired, and he made no great effort to get away as we pushed out a half-sunken rowboat from below the flume, submerged it under him, and brought him ashore. When he died three days later we experimentally fed him to two half-wild cats, but they seemed to suffer no ill effects.

At that same end of town the irrigation flume crossed the river. It always seemed to me giddily high when I hung my chin over its plank edge and looked down, but it probably walked no more than twenty feet above the water on its spidery legs. Ordinarily in summer it carried about six or eight inches of smooth water, and under the glassy hurrying of the little boxed stream the planks were coated with deep sun-warmed moss as slick as frogs' eggs. A boy could sit in the flume with the water walling up against his back, and grab a cross brace above him, and pull, shooting

1. The imaginary, mysterious river of Samuel Taylor Coleridge's poem "Kubla Khan."

himself sledlike ahead until he could reach the next brace for another pull and another slide, and so on across the river in four scoots.

After ten minutes in the flume he would come out wearing a dozen or more limber black leeches, and could sit in the green shade where darning needles flashed blue, and dragonflies hummed and darted and stopped, and skaters dimpled slack and eddy with their delicate transitory footprints, and there stretch the leeches out one by one while their sucking ends clung and clung, until at last, stretched far out, they let go with a tiny wet *puk* and snapped together like rubber bands. The smell of the river and the flume and the clay cutbanks and the bars of that part of the river was the smell of wolf willow.

But nothing in that end of town was as good as the dumpground that scattered along a little runoff coulee dipping down toward the river from the south bench. Through a historical process that went back, probably, to the roots of community sanitation and distaste for eyesores, but that in law dated from the Unincorporated Towns Ordinance of the territorial government, passed in 1888, the dump was one of the very first community enterprises, almost our town's first institution.

More than that, it contained relics of every individual who had ever lived there, and of every phase of the town's history.

The bedsprings on which the town's first child was begotten might be there; the skeleton of a boy's pet colt; two or three volumes of Shakespeare bought in haste and error from a peddler, later loaned in carelessness, soaked with water and chemicals in a house fire, and finally thrown out to flap their stained eloquence in the prairie wind.

Broken dishes, rusty tinware, spoons that had been used to mix paint; once a box of percussion caps, sign and symbol of the carelessness that most of those people felt about all matters of personal or public safety. We put them on the railroad tracks and were anonymously denounced in the *Enterprise*. There were also old iron, old brass, for which we hunted assiduously, by night conning junkmen's catalogues and the pages of the *Enterprise* to find how much wartime value there might be in the geared insides of clocks or in a pound of tea lead[2] carefully wrapped in a ball whose weight astonished and delighted us. Sometimes the unimaginable outside world reached in and laid a finger on us. I recall that, aged no more than seven, I wrote a St. Louis junk house asking if they preferred their tea lead and tinfoil wrapped in balls, or whether they would rather have it pressed flat in sheets, and I got back a typewritten letter in a window envelope instructing me that they would be happy to have it in any way that was convenient for me. They added that they valued my business and were mine very truly. Dazed, I carried that windowed grandeur around in my pocket until I wore it out, and for months I saved

2. An alloy used for lining the chests in which tea was stored and transported.

the letter as a souvenir of the wondering time when something strange and distinguished had singled me out.

We hunted old bottles in the dump, bottles caked with dirt and filth, half buried, full of cobwebs, and we washed them out at the horse trough by the elevator, putting in a handful of shot along with the water to knock the dirt loose; and when we had shaken them until our arms were tired, we hauled them off in somebody's coaster wagon and turned them in at Bill Anderson's pool hall, where the smell of lemon pop was so sweet on the dark pool-hall air that I am sometimes awakened by it in the night, even yet.

Smashed wheels of wagons and buggies, tangles of rusty barbed wire, the collapsed perambulator that the French wife of one of the town's doctors had once pushed proudly up the planked sidewalks and along the ditchbank paths. A welter of foul-smelling feathers and coyote-scattered carrion which was all that remained of somebody's dream of a chicken ranch. The chickens had all got some mysterious pip at the same time, and died as one, and the dream lay out there with the rest of the town's history to rustle to the empty sky on the border of the hills.

There was melted glass in curious forms, and the half-melted office safe left from the burning of Bill Day's Hotel. On very lucky days we might find a piece of the lead casing that had enclosed the wires of the town's first telephone system. The casing was just the right size for rings, and so soft that it could be whittled with a jackknife. It was a material that might have made artists of us. If we had been Indians of fifty years before, that bright soft metal would have enlisted our maximum patience and craft and come out as ring and metal and amulet inscribed with the symbols of our observed world. Perhaps there were too many ready-made alternatives in the local drug, hardware, and general stores; perhaps our feeble artistic response was a measure of the insufficiency of the challenge we felt. In any case I do not remember that we did any more with the metal than to shape it into crude seal rings with our initials or pierced hearts carved in them; and these, though they served a purpose in juvenile courtship, stopped something short of art.

The dump held very little wood, for in that country anything burnable got burned. But it had plenty of old iron, furniture, papers, mattresses that were the delight of field mice, and jugs and demijohns that were sometimes their bane, for they crawled into the necks and drowned in the rain water or redeye that was inside.

If the history of our town was not exactly written, it was at least hinted, in the dump. I think I had a pretty sound notion even at eight or nine of how significant was that first institution of our forming Canadian civilization. For rummaging through its foul purlieus I had several times been surprised and shocked to find relics of my own life tossed out there to rot or blow away.

The volumes of Shakespeare belonged to a set that my father had bought before I was born. It had been carried through successive moves from town to town in the Dakotas, and from Dakota to Seattle, and from Seattle to Bellingham, and Bellingham to Redmond, and from Redmond back to Iowa, and from there to Saskatchewan. Then, stained in a stranger's house fire, these volumes had suffered from a house-cleaning impulse and been thrown away for me to stumble upon in the dump. One of the Cratchet girls had borrowed them, a hatchet-faced, thin, eager, transplanted Cockney girl with a frenzy, almost a hysteria, for reading. And yet somehow, through her hands, they found the dump, to become a symbol of how much was lost, how much thrown aside, how much carelessly or of necessity given up, in the making of a new country. We had so few books that I was familiar with them all, had handled them, looked at their pictures, perhaps even read them. They were the lares and penates, part of the skimpy impedimenta of household gods we had brought with us into Latium.[3] Finding those three thrown away was a little like finding my own name on a gravestone.

And yet not the blow that something else was, something that impressed me even more with the dump's close reflection of the town's intimate life. The colt whose picked skeleton lay out there was mine. He had been incurably crippled when dogs chased our mare, Daisy, the morning after she foaled. I had labored for months to make him well; had fed him by hand, curried him, exercised him, adjusted the iron braces that I had talked my father into having made. And I had not known that he would have to be destroyed. One weekend I turned him over to the foreman of one of the ranches, presumably so that he could be cared for. A few days later I found his skinned body, with the braces still on his crippled front legs, lying on the dump.

Not even that, I think, cured me of going there, though our parents all forbade us on pain of cholera or worse to do so. The place fascinated us, as it should have. For this was the kitchen midden of all the civilization we knew; it gave us the most tantalizing glimpses into our lives as well as into those of the neighbors. It gave us an aesthetic distance from which to know ourselves.

The dump was our poetry and our history. We took it home with us by the wagonload, bringing back into town the things the town had used and thrown away. Some little part of what we gathered, mainly bottles, we managed to bring back to usefulness, but most of our gleanings we left lying around barn or attic or cellar until in some renewed fury of spring cleanup our families carted them off to the dump again, to be rescued and briefly treasured by some other boy with schemes for making them

3. The region of Italy settled by the Trojans after their defeat by the Greeks in the Trojan War. Later, in Roman families, the lares and penates were the ancestral household gods; they came to embody the continuity of the family.

useful. Occasionally something we really valued with a passion was snatched from us in horror and returned at once. That happened to the mounted head of a white mountain goat, somebody's trophy from old times and the far Rocky Mountains, that I brought home one day in transports of delight. My mother took one look and discovered that his beard was full of moths.

I remember that goat; I regret him yet. Poetry is seldom useful, but always memorable. I think I learned more from the town dump than I learned from school: more about people, more about how life is lived, not elsewhere but here, not in other times but now. If I were a sociologist anxious to study in detail the life of any community, I would go very early to its refuse piles. For a community may be as well judged by what it throws away—what it has to throw away and what it chooses to—as by any other evidence. For whole civilizations we have sometimes no more of the poetry and little more of the history than this.

1959

THE READER

1. Is Stegner's description of the dump and its surroundings vivid? Where does his writing directly appeal to the senses, and which senses are called into play?
2. Why does Stegner say (p. 14) that finding the three volumes of Shakespeare in the dump was "a little like finding my own name on a gravestone"? What is the purpose and effect of his allusion to Virgil's Aeneid in the sentence just before that?
3. Through what particular details does Stegner portray the dump as a record of his childhood? How is it shown to be also a record of the brief history of the town? In what respects does it more widely reflect and suggest European and American history and culture and, ultimately, the ancient past, the foundations of civilization?

THE WRITER

1. Stegner begins his reminiscence of the town dump by saying that it had "poetry and excitement" in it. In what ways does he seek to convey those qualities to the reader?
2. In his second paragraph, Stegner speaks of the Alph, the "sacred river" of Coleridge's poem "Kubla Khan." Why? How does allusion to that poem help him convey the strangeness and wonder he then felt? (For "Kubla Khan," see p. 1010.)
3. In paragraphs 5-8, Stegner departs, as he had departed to a lesser degree in the two preceding paragraphs, from his description of the dump. Explain how that departure is justified and whether the writing there is appropriate to the essay as a whole.
4. Write an essay in which you deduce things about a person or a family from a room. You might use your room or an attic or a basement.

Al Young

"JAVA JIVE," BY THE INK SPOTS

For several mornings at the age of three I stood quietly by the living-room window in our little one-story house in Ocean Springs, Mississippi, and studied the way a spider trapped a fly in his web and carefully devoured her. Why I thought the fly was a she and the spider a he would be tough to explain, but that was the way it played in my literal head of dream pictures, whose images, now that I think about it, were clearly made up of tiny quivering dots the way magazine or newspaper photos look when you subject them to intensive magnification.

Words didn't come easily for what I was seeing, yet somehow I knew deep beneath or beyond what little mind I must've had by then that I was glimpsing a mystery of some kind; some important, worldly essence was being vividly played out before my unblinking eyes.

Then, finally, it all fell into place. The sun—like a hot, luminous magnet—happened to be shining powerfully that antique afternoon. My father was busy being his auto mechanic self, and I could see him through the dusty window screen out there in the grass and dirt and clay of the side-yard driveway, fixing on our dark blue Chevy coupe, grease all over his face and forearms; black on black. Pious as a minister or metaphysician, he was bent on fixing that car.

My mother was in the next room, the kitchen, fixing red beans and rice. My very intestines were tingling with gladness, for red beans and rice, as far as I was concerned, had no parallel; there simply wasn't anything like it anywhere in the world, whatever the world was. To dine every day on red beans and rice—or to breakfast, lunch, or snack on them—would've suited me just fine. Lifetimes from my spider-and-fly moment, just before nightfall, I knew we children would be gobbling our portions of dinner—complete with chopped onions and oleomargarined slices of white Bond bread—on the linoleum down under the kitchen table with newspaper for placemats. And I'd be spoiling to tell everybody about the spider and how he'd stuck it to the fly with his web, even though it was going to be years—and I seem to have glimpsed this too—before I'd be able to make heads or tails of any of it, in words anyway.

From the big Zenith radio console, the wood case shining with furniture oil, probably lemon, the Ink Spots were singing "Java Jive." Except for "I like coffee/I like tea," the words made no sense to me, but I liked the way the tune kept winding around and around to make its point, and I loved the way they came out of it all with: "A cup/a cup/a cup/a cup/a cup, ahhhhhhh!" That sigh at the tag meant everything, said it all: it

signaled my Aunt Ethel, the big coffee addict in the family, who, even
then, always came to mind with her lips cradling the edge of some hot
cup, breathing and exhaling steam and steaminess; big fogs of warmth in
which sugar and sweetmilk or Pet Milk played some part. Watching her I
could not fail to get the idea that something glad was going on between
Aunt Ethel and that coffee of hers. If you or anyone else had taken time
out to explain that the coffee bean and its narcotizing effect on people
everywhere was an industry that involved colored poeples doing the
picking all over the world, I wouldn't have connected with what you were
saying any more than I would've understood the meaning of the Man in
the Moon, but I might've had a notion. Around the same time, you see,
the Andrews Sisters were drawing checks off something called "They've
Got an Awful Lot of Coffee in Brazil."

Being three, you see, isn't that much different from being a hundred
and three, particularly when you begin to understand it's all a matter of
putting two and two together.

July seeped into the room, quiescent with harmony and heat, the beat;
the beating of the fly's wings as the spider ingested her from head to toe,
boodie and sole. I stood there. I stood still. Time stood still and the whole
of Mississippi, maybe the whole world, stood there soaking up this three-
year-old's vision of how the world really works whether you realize it or
not. It was as if, for me at least at that moment, my father had pried open
the engine of life itself and motioned me over to have a look at how it
worked and then, without so much as a seventh-grade shop class explanation, snapped the lid back on, leaving me the idea that there was something, some mechanism or cause, that lay behind any and everything I
would ever experience in this ever-shifting, not-to-be-believed existence
that mystics—when you boil what they say down to a simmering, low
gravy—say is only a movie, the acting out of something vaster than
ourselves; the cosmic drama, if you will.

I wanted to taste this java, sample this coffee, this tea they were
rhythmizing so invitingly. Feeling my insides beginning to gladden, I
rushed out into the yard to hear my father say, "Hey, Skippy! C'mere,
boy, and gimme some sugar!"—meaning: Let me kiss you smack on the
jaw. I liked that. I liked it so much, I got confused. I wanted to race over
and blurt out to him everything I'd just figured out about the spider and
the world and the mystery and the tingling I felt inside, even though I
didn't feel ready yet to pull the words together. There were no words,
really; there was only this soundless understanding puffing up with
feeling like a rainbow-colored balloon filling up all too fast with smooth
summer air.

Just then, just as I was about to make my move toward Daddy, I saw a
bright aquaplane zoom in close overhead, low enough for me to see the
pilot, a white man, making me think at once of a crisp, airborne Nabisco

saltine. He was wearing one of those old-time aviator helmets with earflaps and goggles. He waved at me. He waved and smiled and now, millions of mind-hours later, I can draw a wayward cloud of a comic strip balloon over his head that shows him thinking: "Long as I'm up here foolin around, lemme just wave at that lil ole colored boy on the ground down there and give him a thrill!"

This bubbling moment and all that led up to it—like the family's first tentative move to Detroit and the unbelievable coldness of ice and snow and the tight light of what my folks kept calling "movin upnorth to the city"—are etched into me like the lines of some play; a kind of play that's had to settle for being sliced up over the years into what I eventually learned to call poetry or prose.

We lived close enough to the Gulf of Mexico for low-flying aquaplanes to be a commonplace, but that was the very first time I'd ever seen a pilot up close. It was entirely different from those blackout nights when coastal air raid alerts were up, when Ella Mae Morse would be on the Zenith singing "The House of Blue Lights," and there we'd be, me and my brothers, sprawled on the floor or blanketed down in bed, listening and remembering, with those blue emergency lightbulbs screwed into the lamp and ceiling sockets, their cooling glow softening the edge that was forever cutting a line between the seeable and the hearable worlds.

I rushed into my father's arms, gave him that sugar, wondering why we called those people crackers and why kids weren't supposed to fool with coffee.

As for the spider and the fly and my insights into the mystery of that spectacle, all I can say is that the craziness of my excitement has thickened over the years. Now I'm given to believing that the web is only the world, the spider desire, and the fly the fickle, innocent, and positively neutral nature of existence. Beyond that stands some youthful presence, more consciousness than thing, taking it all in with astonishment and, as a matter of fact, aiding and abetting and allowing it all to happen as if— like the web—it were either staged or created by design.

1984

THE READER

1. What became evident to Young as he watched the spider and the fly? What do you understand him to mean by "a mystery" and "some important, worldly essence"?

2. Does Young's writing seem especially vivid to you? Where does his writing show how the world impinged on the senses of a child? Which senses?

3. How large a part in the experience Young describes is played by what might be called just "fooling around"?

THE WRITER

1. *With what devices of writing does Young, as an adult, convey the feelings and thoughts of the child that afternoon?*
2. *Are there any details in this piece that are irrelevant to or distract from its main subject? What is that subject?*
3. *Write an essay exploring your earliest memory of some sense of how the world works. Was it a puzzling experience then? Was it exciting? Hopeful? Daunting? What details are impressed on your memory? What do you make of it all now?*

Zora Neale Hurston

HOW IT FEELS TO BE COLORED ME

I am colored but I offer nothing in the way of extenuating circumstances except the fact that I am the only Negro in the United States whose grandfather on the mother's side was *not* an Indian chief.

I remember the very day that I became colored. Up to my thirteenth year I lived in the little Negro town of Eatonville, Florida. It is exclusively a colored town. The only white people I knew passed through the town going to or coming from Orlando. The native whites rode dusty horses, the Northern tourists chugged down the sandy village road in automobiles. The town knew the Southerners and never stopped cane chewing[1] when they passed. But the Northerners were something else again. They were peered at cautiously from behind curtains by the timid. The more venturesome would come out on the porch to watch them go past and got just as much pleasure out of the tourists as the tourists got out of the village.

The front porch might seem a daring place for the rest of the town, but it was a gallery seat for me. My favorite place was atop the gate-post. Proscenium box for a born first-nighter. Not only did I enjoy the show, but I didn't mind the actors knowing that I liked it. I usually spoke to them in passing. I'd wave at them and when they returned my salute, I would say something like this: "Howdy-do-well-I-thank-you-where-you-goin'?" Usually automobile or the horse paused at this, and after a queer exchange of compliments, I would probably "go a piece of the way" with them, as we say in farthest Florida. If one of my family happened to come to the front in time to see me, of course negotiations would be rudely broken off. But even so, it is clear that I was the first "welcome-to-our-state" Floridian, and I hope the Miami Chamber of Commerce will

1. Chewing sugar cane.

please take notice.

During this period, white people differed from colored to me only in that they rode through town and never lived there. They liked to hear me "speak pieces" and sing and wanted to see me dance the parse-me-la, and gave me generously of their small silver for doing these things, which seemed strange to me for I wanted to do them so much that I needed bribing to stop. Only they didn't know it. The colored people gave no dimes. They deplored any joyful tendencies in me, but I was their Zora nevertheless. I belonged to them, to the nearby hotels, to the county— everybody's Zora.

But changes came in the family when I was thirteen, and I was sent to school in Jacksonville. I left Eatonville, the town of the oleanders,[2] as Zora. When I disembarked from the river-boat at Jacksonville, she was no more. It seemed that I had suffered a sea change. I was not Zora of Orange County any more, I was now a little colored girl. I found it out in certain ways. In my heart as well as in the mirror, I became a fast brown— warranted not to rub nor run.

But I am not tragically colored. There is no great sorrow dammed up in my soul, nor lurking behind my eyes. I do not mind at all. I do not belong to the sobbing school of Negrohood who hold that nature somehow has given them a lowdown dirty deal and whose feelings are all hurt about it. Even in the helter-skelter skirmish that is my life, I have seen that the world is to the strong regardless of a little pigmentation more or less. No, I do not weep at the world—I am too busy sharpening my oyster knife.[3]

Someone is always at my elbow reminding me that I am the grand-daughter of slaves. It fails to register depression with me. Slavery is sixty years in the past. The operation was successful and the patient is doing well, thank you. The terrible struggle[4] that made me an American out of a potential slave said "On the line!" The Reconstruction said "Get set!"; and the generation before said "Go!" I am off to a flying start and I must not halt in the stretch to look behind and weep. Slavery is the price I paid for civilization, and the choice was not with me. It is a bully adventure and worth all that I have paid through my ancestors for it. No one on earth ever had a greater chance for glory. The world to be won and nothing to be lost. It is thrilling to think—to know that for any act of mine, I shall get twice as much praise or twice as much blame. It is quite exciting to hold the center of the national stage, with the spectators not knowing whether to laugh or to weep.

The position of my white neighbor is much more difficult. No brown

2. Fragrant tropical flowers.
3. Cf. the popular expression "The world is my oyster."
4. I.e., the Civil War. The Reconstruction was the period immediately following the war; one of its better effects was that northern educators came south to teach newly freed slaves.

specter pulls up a chair beside me when I sit down to eat. No dark ghost thrusts its leg against mine in bed. The game of keeping what one has is never so exciting as the game of getting.

I do not always feel colored. Even now I often achieve the unconscious Zora of Eatonville before the Hegira.[5] I feel most colored when I am thrown against a sharp white background.

For instance at Barnard.[6] "Beside the waters of the Hudson" I feel my race. Among the thousand white persons, I am a dark rock surged upon, and overswept, but through it all, I remain myself. When covered by the waters, I am; and the ebb but reveals me again.

Sometimes it is the other way around. A white person is set down in our midst, but the contrast is just as sharp for me. For instance, when I sit in the drafty basement that is The New World Cabaret with a white person, my color comes. We enter chatting about any little nothing that we have in common and are seated by the jazz waiters. In the abrupt way that jazz orchestras have, this one plunges into a number. It loses no time in circumlocutions, but gets right down to business. It constricts the thorax and splits the heart with its tempo and narcotic harmonies. This orchestra grows rambunctious, rears on its hind legs and attacks the tonal veil with primitive fury, rending it, clawing it until it breaks through to the jungle beyond. I follow those heathen—follow them exultingly. I dance wildly inside myself; I yell within, I whoop; I shake my assegai[7] above my head, I hurl it true to the mark yeeeeooww! I am in the jungle and living in the jungle way. My face is painted red and yellow and my body is painted blue. My pulse is throbbing like a war drum. I want to slaughter something—give paid, give death to what, I do not know. But the piece ends. The men of the orchestra wipe their lips and rest their fingers. I creep back slowly to the veneer we call civilization with the last tone and find the white friend sitting motionless in his seat, smoking calmly.

"Good music they have here," he remarks, drumming the table with his fingertips.

Music. The great blobs of purple and red emotion have not touched him. He has only heard what I felt. He is far away and I see him but dimly across the ocean and the continent that have fallen between us. He is so pale with his whiteness then and I am *so* colored.

At certain times I have no race, I am *me*. When I set my hat at a certain angle and saunter down Seventh Avenue, Harlem City, feeling as snooty

5. I.e., a journey undertaken away from a dangerous situation into a more highly desirable one (literally, the flight of Mohammed from Mecca in A.D. 622).

6. American women's college in New York City, near the Hudson River (cf. the psalmist's "by the waters of Babylon").
7. South African hunting spear.

as the lions in front of the Forty-Second Street Library, for instance. So far as my feelings are concerned, Peggy Hopkins Joyce[8] on the Boule Mich with her gorgeous raiment, stately carriage, knees knocking together in a most aristocratic manner, has nothing on me. The cosmic Zora emerges. I belong to no race nor time. I am the eternal feminine with its string of beads.

I have no separate feeling about being an American citizen and colored. I am merely a fragment of the Great Soul that surges within the boundaries. My country, right or wrong.

Sometimes, I feel discriminated against, but it does not make me angry. It merely astonishes me. How can any deny themselves the pleasure of my company? It's beyond me.

But in the main, I feel like a brown bag of miscellany propped against a wall. Against a wall in company with other bags, white, red and yellow. Pour out the contents, and there is discovered a jumble of small things priceless and worthless. A first-water diamond, an empty spool, bits of broken glass, lengths of string, a key to a door long since crumbled away, a rusty knife-blade, old shoes saved for a road that never was and never will be, a nail bent under the weight of things too heavy for any nail, a dried flower or two still a little fragrant. In your hand is the brown bag. On the ground before you is the jumble it held—so much like the jumble in the bags, could they be emptied, that all might be dumped in a single heap and the bags refilled without altering the content of any greatly. A bit of colored glass more or less would not matter. Perhaps that is how the Great Stuffer of Bags filled them in the first place—who knows?

1928

8. Peggy Hopkins Joyce: American beauty and fashion-setter of the twenties; the Boule Mich is the Boulevard Saint-Michel, a fashionable Parisian street.

Maya Angelou

GRADUATION

The children in Stamps[1] trembled visibly with anticipation. Some adults were excited too, but to be certain the whole young population had come down with graduation epidemic. Large classes were graduating from both the grammar school and the high school. Even those who were years removed from their own day of glorious release were anxious to help with preparations as a kind of dry run. The junior students who were moving into the vacating classes' chairs were tradition-bound to show

1. A town in Arkansas.

their talents for leadership and management. They strutted through the school and around the campus exerting pressure on the lower grades. Their authority was so new that occasionally if they pressed a little too hard it had to be overlooked. After all, next term was coming, and it never hurt a sixth grader to have a play sister in the eighth grade, or a tenth-year student to be able to call a twelfth grader Bubba. So all was endured in a spirit of shared understanding. But the graduating classes themselves were the nobility. Like travelers with exotic destinations on their minds, the graduates were remarkably forgetful. They came to school without their books, or tablets or even pencils. Volunteers fell over themselves to secure replacements for the missing equipment. When accepted, the willing workers might or might not be thanked, and it was of no importance to the pregraduation rites. Even teachers were respectful of the now quiet and aging seniors, and tended to speak to them, if not as equals, as beings only slightly lower than themselves. After tests were returned and grades given, the student body, which acted like an extended family, knew who did well, who excelled, and what piteous ones had failed.

Unlike the white high school, Lafayette County Training School distinguished itself by having neither lawn, nor hedges, nor tennis court, nor climbing ivy. Its two buildings (main classrooms, the grade school and home economics) were set on a dirt hill with no fence to limit either its boundaries or those of bordering farms. There was a large expanse to the left of the school which was used alternately as a baseball diamond or basketball court. Rusty hoops on swaying poles represented the permanent recreational equipment, although bats and balls could be borrowed from the P.E. teacher if the borrower was qualified and if the diamond wasn't occupied.

Over this rocky area relieved by a few shady tall persimmon trees the graduating class walked. The girls often held hands and no longer bothered to speak to the lower students. There was a sadness about them, as if this old world was not their home and they were bound for higher ground. The boys, on the other hand, had become more friendly, more outgoing. A decided change from the closed attitude they projected while studying for finals. Now they seemed not ready to give up the old school, the familiar paths and classrooms. Only a small percentage would be continuing on to college—one of the South's A & M (agricultural and mechanical) schools, which trained Negro youths to be carpenters, farmers, handymen, masons, maids, cooks and baby nurses. Their future rode heavily on their shoulders, and blinded them to the collective joy that had pervaded the lives of the boys and girls in the grammar school graduating class.

Parents who could afford it had ordered new shoes and readymade clothes for themselves from Sears and Roebuck or Montgomery Ward.

They also engaged the best seamstresses to make the floating graduating dresses and to cut down secondhand pants which would be pressed to a military slickness for the important event.

Oh, it was important, all right. Whitefolks would attend the ceremony, and two or three would speak of God and home, and the Southern way of life, and Mrs. Parsons, the principal's wife, would play the graduation march while the lower-grade graduates paraded down the aisles and took their seats below the platform. The high school seniors would wait in empty classrooms to make their dramatic entrance.

In the Store I was the person of the moment. The birthday girl. The center. Bailey[2] had graduated the year before, although to do so he had had to forfeit all pleasures to make up for his time lost in Baton Rouge.

My class was wearing butter-yellow piqué dresses, and Momma launched out on mine. She smocked the yoke into tiny crisscrossing puckers, then shirred the rest of the bodice. Her dark fingers ducked in and out of the lemony cloth as she embroidered raised daisies around the hem. Before she considered herself finished she had added a crocheted cuff on the puff sleeves, and a pointy crocheted collar.

I was going to be lovely. A walking model of all the various styles of fine hand sewing and it didn't worry me that I was only twelve years old and merely graduating from the eighth grade. Besides, many teachers in Arkansas Negro schools had only that diploma and were licensed to impart wisdom.

The days had become longer and more noticeable. The faded beige of former times had been replaced with strong and sure colors. I began to see my classmates' clothes, their skin tones, and the dust that waved off pussy willows. Clouds that lazed across the sky were objects of great concern to me. Their shiftier shapes might have held a message that in my new happiness and with a little bit of time I'd soon decipher. During that period I looked at the arch of heaven so religiously my neck kept a steady ache. I had taken to smiling more often, and my jaws hurt from the unaccustomed activity. Between the two physical sore spots, I suppose I could have been uncomfortable, but that was not the case. As a member of the winning team (the graduating class of 1940) I had outdistanced unpleasant sensations by miles. I was headed for the freedom of open fields.

Youth and social approval allied themselves with me and we trammeled memories of slights and insults. The wind of our swift passage remodeled my features. Lost tears were pounded to mud and then to dust. Years of withdrawal were brushed aside and left behind, as hanging ropes of parasitic moss.

2. The author's brother.

My work alone had awarded me a top place and I was going to be one of the first called in the graduating ceremonies. On the classroom blackboard, as well as on the bulletin board in the auditorium, there were blue stars and white stars and red stars. No absences, no tardinesses, and my academic work was among the best of the year. I could say the preamble to the Constitution even faster than Bailey. We timed ourselves often: "WethepeopleoftheUnitedStatesinordertoformamoreperfectunion . . ." I had memorized the Presidents of the United States from Washington to Roosevelt in chronological as well as alphabetical order.

My hair pleased me too. Gradually the black mass had lengthened and thickened, so that it kept at last to its braided pattern, and I didn't have to yank my scalp off when I tried to comb it.

Louise and I had rehearsed the exercises until we tired out ourselves. Henry Reed was class valedictorian. He was a small, very black boy with hooded eyes, a long, broad nose and an oddly shaped head. I had admired him for years because each term he and I vied for the best grades in our class. Most often he bested me, but instead of being disappointed I was pleased that we shared top places between us. Like many Southern Black children, he lived with his grandmother, who was as strict as Momma and as kind as she knew how to be. He was courteous, respectful and soft-spoken to elders, but on the playground he chose to play the roughest games. I admired him. Anyone, I reckoned, sufficiently afraid or sufficiently dull could be polite. But to be able to operate at a top level with both adults and children was admirable.

His valedictory speech was entitled "To Be or Not to Be." The rigid tenth-grade teacher had helped him write it. He'd been working on the dramatic stresses for months.

The weeks until graduation were filled with heady activities. A group of small children were to be presented in a play about buttercups and daisies and bunny rabbits. They could be heard throughout the building practicing their hops and their little songs that sounded like silver bells. The older girls (nongraduates, of course) were assigned the task of making refreshments for the night's festivities. A tangy scent of ginger, cinnamon, nutmeg and chocolate wafted around the home economics building as the budding cooks made samples for themselves and their teachers.

In every corner of the workshop, axes and saws split fresh timber as the woodshop boys made sets and stage scenery. Only the graduates were left out of the general bustle. We were free to sit in the library at the back of the building or look in quite detachedly, naturally, on the measures being taken for our event.

Even the minister preached on graduation the Sunday before. His subject was, "Let your light so shine that men will see your good works and praise your Father, Who is in Heaven." Although the sermon was purported to be addressed to us, he used the occasion to speak to back-sliders, gamblers and general ne'er-do-wells. But since he had called our names at the beginning of the service we were mollified.

Among Negroes the tradition was to give presents to children going only from one grade to another. How much more important this was when the person was graduating at the top of the class. Uncle Willie and Momma had sent away for a Mickey Mouse watch like Bailey's. Louise gave me four embroidered handkerchiefs. (I gave her crocheted doilies.) Mrs. Sneed, the minister's wife, made me an undershirt to wear for graduation, and nearly every customer gave me a nickel or maybe even a dime with the instruction "Keep on moving to higher ground," or some such encouragement.

Amazingly the great day finally dawned and I was out of bed before I knew it. I threw open the back door to see it more clearly, but Momma said, "Sister, come away from that door and put your robe on."

I hoped the memory of that morning would never leave me. Sunlight was itself young, and the day had none of the insistence maturity would bring it in a few hours. In my robe and barefoot in the backyard, under cover of going to see about my new beans, I gave myself up to the gentle warmth and thanked God that no matter what evil I had done in my life He had allowed me to live to see this day. Somewhere in my fatalism I had expected to die, accidentally, and never have the chance to walk up the stairs in the auditorium and gracefully receive my hard-earned diploma. Out of God's merciful bosom I had won reprieve.

Bailey came out in his robe and gave me a box wrapped in Christmas paper. He said he had saved his money for months to pay for it. It felt like a box of chocolates, but I knew Bailey wouldn't save money to buy candy when we had all we could want under our noses.

He was as proud of the gift as I. It was a soft-leather-bound copy of a collection of poems by Edgar Allan Poe, or, as Bailey and I called him, "Eap." I turned to "Annabel Lee" and we walked up and down the garden rows, the cool dirt between our toes, reciting the beautifully sad lines.

Momma made a Sunday breakfast although it was only Friday. After we finished the blessing, I opened my eyes to find the watch on my plate. It was a dream of a day. Everything went smoothly and to my credit. I didn't have to be reminded or scolded for anything. Near evening I was too jittery to attend to chores, so Bailey volunteered to do all before his bath.

Days before, we had made a sign for the Store, and as we turned out the lights Momma hung the cardboard over the doorknob. It read clearly: CLOSED. GRADUATION.

My dress fitted perfectly and everyone said that I looked like a sunbeam in it. On the hill, going toward the school, Bailey walked behind with Uncle Willie, who muttered, "Go on, Ju." He wanted him to walk ahead with us because it embarrassed him to have to walk so slowly. Bailey said he'd let the ladies walk together, and the men would bring up the rear. We all laughed, nicely.

Little children dashed by out of the dark like fireflies. Their crepe-paper dresses and butterfly wings were not made for running and we heard more than one rip, dryly, and the regretful "uh uh" that followed.

The school blazed without gaiety. The windows seemed cold and unfriendly from the lower hill. A sense of ill-fated timing crept over me, and if Momma hadn't reached for my hand I would have drifted back to Bailey and Uncle Willie, and possibly beyond. She made a few slow jokes about my feet getting cold, and tugged me along to the now-strange building.

Around the front steps, assurance came back. There were my fellow "greats," the graduating class. Hair brushed back, legs oiled, new dresses and pressed pleats, fresh pocket handkerchiefs and little handbags, all homesewn. Oh, we were up to snuff, all right. I joined my comrades and didn't even see my family go in to find seats in the crowded auditorium.

The school band struck up a march and all classes filed in as had been rehearsed. We stood in front of our seats, as assigned, and on a signal from the choir director, we sat. No sooner had this been accomplished than the band started to play the national anthem. We rose again and sang the song, after which we recited the pledge of allegiance. We remained standing for a brief minute before the choir director and the principal signaled to us, rather desperately I thought, to take our seats. The command was so unusual that our carefully rehearsed and smooth-running machine was thrown off. For a full minute we fumbled for our chairs and bumped into each other awkwardly. Habits change or solidify under pressure, so in our state of nervous tension we had been ready to follow our usual assembly pattern: the American national anthem, then the pledge of allegiance, then the song every Black person I knew called the Negro National Anthem. All done in the same key, with the same passion and most often standing on the same foot.

Finding my seat at last, I was overcome with a presentiment of worse things to come. Something unrehearsed, unplanned, was going to happen, and we were going to be made to look bad. I distinctly remember being explicit in the choice of pronoun. It was "we," the graduating class, the unit, that concerned me then.

The principal welcomed "parents and friends" and asked the Baptist minister to lead us in prayer. His invocation was brief and punchy, and for a second I thought we were getting on the high road to right action. When the principal came back to the dais, however, his voice had changed. Sounds always affected me profoundly and the principal's voice was one of my favorites. During assembly it melted and lowed weakly into the audience. It had not been in my plan to listen to him, but my curiosity was piqued and I straightened up to give him my attention.

He was talking about Booker T. Washington, our "late great leader," who said we can be as close as the fingers on the hand, etc. . . . Then he said a few vague things about friendship and the friendship of kindly people to those less fortunate than themselves. With that his voice nearly faded, thin, away. Like a river diminishing to a stream and then to a trickle. But he cleared his throat and said, "Our speaker tonight, who is also our friend, came from Texarkana to deliver the commencement address, but due to the irregularity of the train schedule, he's going to, as they say, 'speak and run.'" He said that we understood and wanted the man to know that we were most grateful for the time he was able to give us and then something about how we were willing always to adjust to another's program, and without more ado—"I give you Mr. Edward Donleavy."

Not one but two white men came through the door off-stage. The shorter one walked to the speaker's platform, and the tall one moved to the center seat and sat down. But that was our principal's seat, and already occupied. The dislodged gentleman bounced around for a long breath or two before the Baptist minister gave him his chair, then with more dignity than the situation deserved, the minister walked off the stage.

Donleavy looked at the audience once (on reflection, I'm sure that he wanted only to reassure himself that we were really there), adjusted his glasses and began to read from a sheaf of papers.

He was glad "to be here and to see the work going on just as it was in the other schools."

At the first "Amen" from the audience I willed the offender to immediate death by choking on the word. But Amens and Yes, sir's began to fall around the room like rain through a ragged umbrella.

He told us of the wonderful changes we children in Stamps had in store. The Central School (naturally, the white school was Central) had already been granted improvements that would be in use in the fall. A well-known artist was coming from Little Rock to teach art to them. They were going to have the newest microscopes and chemistry equipment for their laboratory. Mr. Donleavy didn't leave us long in the dark over who made these improvements available to Central High. Nor were we to be ignored in the general betterment scheme he had in mind.

He said that he had pointed out to people at a very high level that one of the first-line football tacklers at Arkansas Agricultural and Mechanical College had graduated from good old Lafayette County Training School. Here fewer Amen's were heard. Those few that did break through lay dully in the air with the heaviness of habit.

He went on to praise us. He went on to say how he had bragged that "one of the best basketball players at Fisk sank his first ball right here at Lafayette County Training School."

The white kids were going to have a chance to become Galileos and Madame Curies and Edisons and Gauguins, and our boys (the girls weren't even in on it) would try to be Jesse Owenses and Joe Louises.

Owens and the Brown Bomber were great heroes in our world, but what school official in the white-goddom of Little Rock had the right to decide that those two men must be our only heroes? Who decided that for Henry Reed to become a scientist he had to work like George Washington Carver, as a bootblack, to buy a lousy microscope? Bailey was obviously always going to be too small to be an athlete, so which concrete angel glued to what country seat had decided that if my brother wanted to become a lawyer he had to first pay penance for his skin by picking cotton and hoeing corn and studying correspondence books at night for twenty years?

The man's dead words fell like bricks around the auditorium and too many settled in my belly. Constrained by hard-learned manners I couldn't look behind me, but to my left and right the proud graduating class of 1940 had dropped their heads. Every girl in my row had found something new to do with her handkerchief. Some folded the tiny squares into love knots, some into triangles, but most were wadding them, then pressing them flat on their yellow laps.

On the dais, the ancient tragedy was being replayed. Professor Parsons sat, a sculptor's reject, rigid. His large, heavy body seemed devoid of will or willingness, and his eyes said he was no longer with us. The other teachers examined the flag (which was draped stage right) or their notes, or the windows which opened on our now-famous playing diamond.

Graduation, the hush-hush magic time of frills and gifts and congratulations and diplomas, was finished for me before my name was called. The accomplishment was nothing. The meticulous maps, drawn in three colors of ink, learning and spelling decasyllabic words, memorizing the whole of *The Rape of Lucrece*[3]—it was for nothing. Donleavy had exposed us.

We were maids and farmers, handymen and washerwomen, and anything higher that we aspired to was farcical and presumptuous.

Then I wished that Gabriel Prosser and Nat Turner[4] had killed all whitefolks in their beds and that Abraham Lincoln had been assassinated before the signing of the Emancipation Proclamation, and that Harriet Tubman[5] had been killed by that blow on her head and Christopher Columbus had drowned in the *Santa Maria*.

It was awful to be a Negro and have no control over my life. It was

3. A narrative poem of 1,855 lines, by Shakespeare.
4. Leaders of Virginia slave rebellions in 1800 and 1831 respectively.
5. Nineteenth-century black abolitionist, a "conductor" on the Underground Railroad.

brutal to be young and already trained to sit quietly and listen to charges brought against my color with no chance of defense. We should all be dead. I thought I should like to see us all dead, one on top of the other. A pyramid of flesh with the whitefolks on the bottom, as the broad base, then the Indians with their silly tomahawks and teepees and wigwams and treaties, the Negroes with their mops and recipes and cotton sacks and spirituals sticking out of their mouths. The Dutch children should all stumble in their wooden shoes and break their necks. The French should choke to death on the Louisiana Purchase (1803) while silkworms ate all the Chinese with their stupid pigtails. As a species, we were an abomination. All of us.

Donleavy was running for election, and assured our parents that if he won we could count on having the only colored paved playing field in that part of Arkansas. Also—he never looked up to acknowledge the grunts of acceptance—also, we were bound to get some new equipment for the home economics building and the workshop.

He finished, and since there was no need to give any more than the most perfunctory thank-you's, he nodded to the men on the stage, and the tall white man who was never introduced joined him at the door. They left with the attitude that now they were off to something really important. (The graduation ceremonies at Lafayette County Training School had been a mere preliminary.)

The ugliness they left was palpable. An uninvited guest who wouldn't leave. The choir was summoned and sang a modern arrangement of "Onward, Christian Soldiers," with new words pertaining to graduates seeking their place in the world. But it didn't work. Elouise, the daughter of the Baptist minister, recited "Invictus,"[6] and I could have cried at the impertinence of "I am the master of my fate, I am the captain of my soul."

My name had lost its ring of familiarity and I had to be nudged to go and receive my diploma. All my preparations had fled. I neither marched up to the stage like a conquering Amazon, nor did I look in the audience for Bailey's nod of approval. Marguerite Johnson, I heard the name again, my honors were read, there were noises in the audience of appreciation, and I took my place on the stage as rehearsed.

I thought about colors I hated: ecru, puce, lavender, beige and black.

There was shuffling and rustling around me, then Henry Reed was giving his valedictory address, "To Be or Not to Be." Hadn't he heard the whitefolks? We couldn't *be*, so the question was a waste of time. Henry's voice came out clear and strong. I feared to look at him. Hadn't he got the message? There was no "nobler in the mind" for Negroes because the world didn't think we had minds, and they let us know it. "Outrageous fortune"? Now, that was a joke. When the ceremony was over I had to

6. An inspirational poem by the nineteenth-century poet William Ernest Henley, once very popular for occasions such as this one.

tell Henry Reed some things. That is, if I still cared. Not "rub," Henry, "erase." "Ah, there's the erase." Us.

Henry had been a good student in elocution. His voice rose on tides of promise and fell on waves of warnings. The English teacher had helped him to create a sermon winging through Hamlet's soliloquy. To be a man, a doer, a builder, a leader, or to be a tool, an unfunny joke, a crusher of funky toadstools. I marveled that Henry could go through with the speech as if we had a choice.

I had been listening and silently rebutting each sentence with my eyes closed; then there was a hush, which in an audience warns that something unplanned is happening. I looked up and saw Henry Reed, the conservative, the proper, the A student, turn his back to the audience and turn to us (the proud graduating class of 1940) and sing, nearly speaking,

> "Lift ev'ry voice and sing
> Till earth and heaven ring
> Ring with the harmonies of Liberty . . ."

It was the poem written by James Weldon Johnson. It was the music composed by J. Rosamond Johnson. It was the Negro national anthem. Out of habit we were singing it.

Our mothers and fathers stood in the dark hall and joined the hymn of encouragement. A kindergarten teacher led the small children onto the stage and the buttercups and daisies and bunny rabbits marked time and tried to follow:

> "Stony the road we trod
> Bitter the chastening rod
> Felt in the days when hope, unborn, had died.
> Yet with a steady beat
> Have not our weary feet
> Come to the place for which our fathers sighed?"

Each child I knew had learned that song with his ABC's and along with "Jesus Loves Me This I Know." But I personally had never heard it before. Never heard the words, despite the thousands of times I had sung them. Never thought they had anything to do with me.

On the other hand, the words of Patrick Henry had made such an impression on me that I had been able to stretch myself tall and trembling and say, "I know not what course others may take, but as for me, give me liberty or give me death."

And now I heard, really for the first time:

> "We have come over a way that with tears
> has been watered,
> We have come, treading our path through
> the blood of the slaughtered."

While echoes of the song shivered in the air, Henry Reed bowed his head, said "Thank you," and returned to his place in the line. The tears that slipped down many faces were not wiped away in shame.

We were on top again. As always, again. We survived. The depths had been icy and dark, but now a bright sun spoke to our souls. I was no longer simply a member of the proud graduating class of 1940; I was a proud member of the wonderful, beautiful Negro race.

Oh, Black known and unknown poets, how often have your auctioned pains sustained us? Who will compute the lonely nights made less lonely by your songs, or the empty pots made less tragic by your tales?

If we were a people much given to revealing secrets, we might raise monuments and sacrifice to the memories of our poets, but slavery cured us of that weakness. It may be enough, however, to have it said that we survive in exact relationship to the dedication of our poets (include preachers, musicians and blues singers).

1969

Richard Hugo

HOW I NEVER MET EUDORA WELTY[1]

Logan The Finger and H. Reed Fulton are dead, and if anyone reading this happens to have attended West Seattle High School in the 30s and 40s, his sighs of regret should not appreciably compound the noise pollution problem.

Logan The Finger was the study hall monitor and Logan The Finger was called Logan The Finger because Logan The Finger had the thumb and index finger missing from his right hand. When he signaled you to his desk to give you demerits for talking to the girl in the next seat, he was not only inviting you to his desk, he was giving you the finger. A humorless man, his job was anything but easy. Boys would swing open the back doors and roll handfuls of steel bearings across the floor of the huge auditorium room where we held study hall, and they would rattle off the steel legs of our desks making a hell of a racket. Sometimes, the students released pigeons in the study hall. The room had a very high ceiling and there was no way to get the pigeons out during the day. They would sit high on the ornamental arch over the stage, and we would stare at them with some sort of envy for their freedom and their obliviousness to boredom. Then, someone would tie an alarm clock onto the curtain

---

1. Well-known Southern writer of fiction (b. 1909).

cord and snap the blind high up out of reach where the clock would hang like a bomb until it went off at the set hour.

Logan The Finger oversaw all this from his chair and desk, raised on a platform about a foot above the floor. He was available for help with study problems and I suppose must have had a broad though no doubt shallow understanding of a lot of different subjects. I never went to him with a math problem, math being easy for me then, but students who did told me he often illustrated his explanations with an example of how you could cheat the Bon Marche department store. My hero of the day was Amos Laudet who crawled commando style on his stomach yards and yards under desks and between student legs, gave Logan The Finger a hot foot and returned to his seat completely undetected by Logan or by the woman in charge of seating assignments, sitting across the room from Logan. I also considered it a tribute to the many students who saw it that they played it cool and Logan never knew what was happening until his foot started to burn.

H. Reed Fulton was the principal. He was also a successful author of boys' books. *Laddie The Great, The Powder Dock Mystery*, and *Moccasin Trail* were his best known works, and West Seattle was probably the only high school in the nation that included H. Reed Fulton on the Recommended Reading List along with Thomas Wolfe, Ernest Hemingway, John dos Passos and John Steinbeck, in the American Literature courses.

H. Reed Fulton had two favorite words, "guts" and "democracy." When he mounted the stage in the auditorium, which was also the study hall, to address the assembly kicking off the new school year, his speech would go something like this: "It was but a scant two weeks ago that I stood on the banks of the Dosewallips river, my creel brimming with trout, and reflected on how it takes guts to live in a democracy. And if you don't have the guts to live in a democracy, then I suggest you find an undemocratic nation where the guts required by a democracy are no longer necessary." And on and on.

The worst thing Logan The Finger could do was send you to see H. Reed Fulton. You might get kicked out of school. Certainly you were in for it one way or another. "Watch out for the lamp," some students warned, those who had been to see Fulton. Logan usually sent you there if you did something he considered wrong but didn't know what punishment it called for. In those days I played the ocarina or sweet potato.[2] Not very well either. I could play "The Organ Grinder's Swing" and that was it. On the first day of the second semester in my freshman year, I was sitting in study hall with nothing to do. No lesson assignments had been given and even if they had, studying was impossible because students were in a long line waiting for seat assignments. People were chatting.

2. Simple wind instrument; it has an oval body, finger holes, and a projecting mouthpiece.

The hall was noisy and unorganized, though rest assured Logan The Finger was on the job. With nothing to do, I sat in my assigned seat in the back row and played the ocarina. When I saw Logan approaching, I could tell by his expression he'd heard me and I hid the ocarina under the desk. He looked about, obviously perplexed by the eerie sound he'd heard, then walked over to me and asked if I had been whistling.

"No," I said, exuberantly, naive enough to believe honesty the best policy, "I was playing my ocarina," and I held it up so he could see it. It was too much. Never had he found a student playing an ocarina in study hall and he wrote a note for me to take to Fulton. He was trembling when he wrote it, and I realize now that it must have been the unique nature of the offense that upset him so. Ocarinas in themselves are not that important.

I waited on the bench outside Fulton's office, and I was nervous and frightened. I hated the woman at the desk who asked me to wait there and who smiled at me, sadistically I thought, while I played with my hands.

The first thing H. Reed Fulton did in his office after I sat down across from him was turn the shade on his lamp so that the light poured into my eyes. He took his time while I squinted trying to see him through the glare. And he started very low key. In a quiet calm voice he said, after he'd read the note, "How old are you, Richard?"

"Fourteen, Mr. Fulton."

"Fourteen." Very soft and quiet. He mused on fourteen for a moment, Again soft and quiet, "And do you like this school, Richard?"

"Yes sir, I do."

He jumped up so suddenly I flinched and he screamed at me over the glaring lamp, "Then why don't you have the guts to live up to its democratic ideals?"

He might as well have fired a cannon. I withered on the spot. It was so startling that I don't remember what happened after that, what was said, how long I was there or when I left.

I graduated in 1941 and of course got caught in the war. In 1945 I was out, twenty-one years old, veteran of thirty-five bombing missions and at the University of Washington taking creative writing courses, something I'd looked forward to all through the Army Air Corps, now called the Air Force. I'd started writing when I was nine and writing seemed to be the only thing I'd ever be able or want to do. My teacher was a new man named Grant Redford, a very good short story writing teacher and a sad man who was to commit suicide twenty years later. He was from Montana and had been connected with the old *Rocky Mountain Review*. I think it became the *Western Review* but I'm not sure and I'm not going to look it up. I'm afraid I was never much of a student for Redford. My stories were hopelessly self indulgent, on and on about my personal problems, without form, wihout development, and without even any good writing. However, I did write humor in those days and had no trouble getting it published in the campus magazine, though I'd hate to see it now. Mostly my writing was used to get myself attention, to satisfy a terrible streak of narcissism, and it wasn't until I concentrated all my efforts on poems that I was to realize the only real reward of writing, that special way you feel just when you've done something you like. That's far more satisfying than seeing your name in print, good reviews, flattery or applause after a reading. And more enduring.

The Northwest Writers Conference was scheduled for the summer of 1946 and Grant Redford was one of the organizers. I felt then that artists, writers, jazz musicians were touched with a strange kind of magic and that if you could make contact with one some of the magic would rub off on you. I remember climbing some sawhorses in 1942 in the old Trianon Ballroom in Seattle, just to stand against the tiered bandstand next to an old Chicago jazz trombone player named Floyd O'Brien who was playing with Bob Crosby's Bobcats. I was balanced on a sawhorse within two or three feet of this magic man when he turned to me and said, "Shit, it's hot in here." I thought then how wonderful it was that this great musician, touched as he was by some gift from heaven, would make such a down-to-earth statement. So when I heard Eudora Welty was coming to the Northwest Writers Conference, nothing would do but that I get to talk to her.

I approached Redford and explained my problem. I wouldn't pay the ten dollar conference fee unless I got to talk alone with Eudora Welty. Redford promised to look into it for me. What a chance this seemed. Miss Welty might give some magic advice that would open my soul. Maybe she would say in a burst of insight (didn't all great writers have equally great bursts of insight?), "I can tell, Mr. Hugo, that you'll be a fine writer some day." Or maybe she'd advise me to go to Australia to broaden my base of experience. I would not have gone, but I would have considered it.

Had I ever met her I'm sure she would have said, though no doubt more graciously, what Roethke said two or three years later, "Get your fat ass to work." But I never did meet her. It turned out that she was in much demand and Redford couldn't guarantee a private audience with her though he could insure an audience with a very successful author, H. Reed Fulton. Ten dollars seemed high.

1986

THE READER

1. Does Hugo consider H. Reed Fulton a good writer? How do you know?
2. What does Hugo consider to be the only real reward of writing? Why might it be that this discovery came only after he concentrated all his efforts on poems instead of on stories?

3. *What piece of advice do you suppose Hugo might give to aspiring writers?*

THE WRITER

1. *Do you see in the way his essay is written any indication that Hugo usually writes poems rather than stories?*
2. *Rewrite Hugo's essay in the style of H. Reed Fulton.*
3. *Write an essay comparing and contrasting Hugo's recollection of school with that given by Hans A. Schmitt in "January 30, 1933: A Memoir" (below). Are German and American schools fundamentally different?*

Hans A. Schmitt

JANUARY 30, 1933: A MEMOIR

I remember January 30, 1933. In Germany the next-to-last day of the first month is invariably unpleasant. If the sun should shine, in defiance of all metereological odds, it would illuminate a world lashed by crackling cold. If the clouds which rule the central European heavens from September to May claim this day as their own, as they generally do, then sleet or slushy brown snow covers the pavement. Children amble to school, and their elders walk purposefully to work, through a world suffused in a spectrum ranging from black to gray.

The best holidays of the year are over, and before every German schoolchild there stretches an expanse of dreary, homework-laden days before the academic term ends at Easter. It is the time when youngsters pray for an attack of influenza, or measles, in fact any affliction that promises to lighten life with an unscheduled holiday.

When I woke that morning, I felt the deep depression engendered by the approach of another day of educational misery: my geometry homework was only half done, the assigned passage in Ernest Lavisse's *Histoire de France* (simplified and expurgated beyond recognition) imperfectly understood. I was to face a scene with the German master for defiantly writing, once again, a composition in Latin rather than in German script. French irregular verbs were the only burden which the dismal morning found me ready to carry with a degree of authoritative ease. The day promised to be like any other day in school life, a day hardly worth living.

But wait! I swallowed and my head jerked upward, jolted by a sudden pain. Could it be? Eagerly I swallowed again. No doubt about it, my throat hurt. I repeated the process several times. I wanted to be sure that this was no dream. Evidence mounted: I had a sore throat. Lying back, I closed my eyes and prayed that the symptoms would not go away.

I remembered at once that the morning of a school day never found me well. I always had to wrestle with a powerful urge to go back to sleep. I always suffered from a matutinal heaviness of limb, coupled with slight dizziness. These were symptoms of chronic disaffection, the protests of a disconsolate soul. But the sore throat signaled a distempered body, and while the world of authority around me, my parents and my teachers, cared not about my psychic sufferings, it kept a 24-hour watch on my physical health. Every sport I enjoyed was proscribed as a source of potential injury. As soon as the daily rounds of school and chores had been completed and I seemed ready to claim a life of my own, other rules and curfews intervened. When I began the initiation into the mysteries of the English language in my fourth year of *Gymnasium*, "early to bed and early to rise makes a man healthy, wealthy and wise" was the first Anglo-Saxon maxim my classmates and I were forced to recite in unison. Duty without end promised a long, useful life, a gram of pleasure portended decay.

Now the time had come to turn the obstructive wisdom of my elders to my own advantage. Indifferent to suffering of my spirit, they would rise to the challenge of bodily disease.

I bolted out of bed to carry the day's first medical bulletin to my mother. By now it must have become clear that I was not looking for sympathy. The world in which I grew up gave none. It was divided by a two-party system which pitted the eternal majority of school and home against the child. Both harnessed me into a six-day curriculum of joyless obligations from which Sunday, punctuated by familial excursions on foot and indiscreet parental inquiries into scholastic progress, offered little relief. There was no escape, except vacation and illness, the latter afforded only after thorough tests by thermometer, careful examination of relevant sectors of the anatomy, and, in case of doubt, an earnest consultation with a third, part-time member of this grand coalition of adults, the family physician. These tests made up a daunting obstacle course, separating the claim of illness from its official recognition, but the defeats of life had not extinguished my will to tackle it once more.

"Open your mouth," my mother commanded. She peered intently down my throat. "Your throat is red," she announced. "I shall take your temperature." Under the covers I squeezed my thumbs between the second and third fingers of each hand, the German equivalent of keeping my fingers crossed. The first test had been passed.

German home medicine in those days decreed that body temperature be measured not by the easy introduction of the thermometer under the tongue, but by a far more degrading maneuver. Instead of sitting or lying on his back, the victim, in my case a pubescent boy of twelve, lay on his stomach waiting to learn whether submission to this indignity would turn out to be justified by the results.

Having thus impaled me, my mother hurried off to get my father's breakfast and supervise my younger brother's daily mobilization. She returned after half an hour and disclosed the thermometer reading: "You have a temperature. Cover up well and stay in bed. I shall call Dr. Wetzler." I pulled up my pajama trousers and slipped under the covers. Life had its moments, after all. January 30 would pass without geometry, without joining Caesar on his forays into Gaul. (Lavisse's summary was at least a kindlier guide than his Latin source, whose reading the modern language curriculum of my school spared me.) It would be a day of peace, spent alone, interrupted only by surreptitious reading of my latest favorite, a German translation of that congenial classic *Tom Sawyer*, the recent gift of an understanding friend of the family.

The morning passed gently in dozing, daydreaming, and reading. Whenever steps echoed outside my room, I deftly slipped *Tom Sawyer* under the mattress. The doctor appeared in time to confirm my mother's diagnosis and to prescribe that I stay in bed until the temperature was gone. On the other hand, he agreed that she should call the home of my friend Fritz, asking that he bring me the day's assignments, confirming that I was certainly not too ill to keep up with schoolwork.

At one-thirty Fritz duly appeared with a depressing list of new tasks. After my mother had left the room, not before warning him to keep his distance from my bed to avoid contamination, he leaned over with understandable unconcern and whispered excitedly:

"Do you know what I heard?"

"What?"

"Hitler has just become chancellor."

We always whispered. It was a convention of our age group, inured to live in constant opposition. Secretiveness was our way. We whispered to each other in class, when talking was naturally prohibited. We whispered in the schoolyard when exchanging a limited, unchanging repertory of anal and sexual jokes, or swapping derogatory remarks about teachers, parents, or other members of the adult world. Our existence was a furtive, resistant, sneaky microcosm of trivial secrets, our own only as long as it remained hidden from our elders.

"Is it true?" I asked.

"It went around school, and I saw storm troopers everywhere on my way home. Reif, the milkman, was in uniform today. You know, he wouldn't wear that get-up on his route unless it was safe."

Fritz was excited. Throughout the past year he had not passed a brownshirt on the street without sidling up to him, raising his hand, and whispering, "Heil Hitler." Sometimes his low voiced greeting had been noticed and returned, sometimes merely acknowledged with a condescending smile (the Nazis proclaimed their commitment to youth, but treated children no better than did other adults), sometimes disregarded. His father, with whom I seldom heard him exchange a friendly word and whom we avoided even more doggedly than we were wont to avoid fathers in general, was a Jewish lawyer whose sister had married a colonel in Germany's purportedly 100,000-man army. Fritz envied his cousins for having a father in uniform. He bragged about his uncle, and in our class he was the resident authority on Germany's glorious future in arms. We accepted his claim to being privy to all kinds of exciting martial secrets which his uncle, "who knew what was going on," supposedly passed on to him.

By the time my exultant friend left, the personal triumph with which the day had begun had soured. I, too, had an uncle who in my own mind stood apart from the hostile adult phalanx. He was no colonel, but a Jewish businessman who lived in an elegant house in a western suburb of Berlin. His establishment included a cook and two maids: family dinners were sumptuous and far tastier than ordinary German middle-class fare, and he never asked me how I was doing in school. I wondered whether he had heard the news and what he thought of it.

For the rest of the afternoon I left *Tom Sawyer* under the mattress and brooded. About what had happened, about Fritz, about myself, about my family. There was nothing unnatural or precocious about this. In my house, politics was a commonplace subject of conversation. Like many proverbially "nonpolitical" Germans, my parents subscribed to several newspapers and talked about what they read. In a typical middle-class home adults and children possessed a working knowledge of the shifting panorama of current affairs, including the major questions before parliament and the frequent rise and fall of ministerial coalitions, without recognizing any obligation to join the process.

I therefore understood enough of what had happened to reflect uneasily on what it might mean. I tried to translate apprehension into personal terms. What effect would the new government have on me and on my friend? Here was Fritz with his harsh and querulous Jewish father with the martial connections. Here was I with a Jewish mother and a gentile father who barely kept us afloat on the shallow waters of petty bourgeois gentility. The members of Fritz' family would be pulling even harder in opposite directions. What would happen to us? Would my mother's ancestry put her, and us, outside the pale? It was a reasonable question, for no one knew at this point what action to expect from Hitler, the strident, anti-Semitic head of government. My father was a Social-Democrat, not very active recently but of an intractable, intolerant, and choleric nature, an outsider by inclination. How was he taking the latest news? How would he face it?

I found out that evening when he came home from the office. As soon as he heard that I was ill, he came to my room, followed by my mother and brother. He opened his mouth as if to speak, hesitated, looked about, and then abruptly barked at my brother: "Close the door." I shrank back in my pillow. Ordinarily that phrase served as prelude to a tongue-lashing or a whipping for something I had or had not done that day. Doors were closed to muffle stormy passages. Surely he was not going to give me hell for missing a day of school?

After my brother had carried out his order my father burst out: "So that old asshole the Field Marshal has gone and done it!"

Never in my life had I heard my father use such language. Never in the lives of any of my friends had any father used such language, at least not in the hearing of his children. My world was transformed! I sat up, barely restraining myself from jumping out of bed. What excitement to hear my father describe a person of authority in terms with which we expressed our alienation from the adult world around us.

Only he was not whispering. He had flung the word loudly into the room, to characterize the 86-year-old president of the republic, Paul von Hindenburg, respectfully designated by the press of all political shades (except the Communists) as "aged," which was correct and "venerable," which in some quarters was secretly qualified as a matter of opinion. So far as I was concerned my father was the first to call him an asshole. Astonishingly, my mother who, according to my view of the world, did not even know the word my father had used, uttered neither protest nor reproof.

"You voted for that senile bastard last year," my father turned on her. "I told you this would happen. I told you. My God!" He sat down on the chair by my writing desk and pounded it with his right fist. The long discussions at the dinner table during the previous year's presidential elections came back to me. Faced by two serious choices, Hindenburg or Hitler, my mother like most citizens supporting the fragile republic, had cast ballots for the old soldier of the vanished empire. My father, veteran though he was, voted for the Communist candidate, as much, I am inclined to think today, in defiance of my mother's imperturbably rational arguments against such a step as out of conviction. Now he thought that he had been vindicated, for it seemed that a vote for the winner had also turned into a mandate for his closest rival.

While my father raged and my mother remained inscrutably silent, I looked at my brother. He winked. His round cheeks were even redder than usual. He shared my excitement of discovery. At that moment we both loved our father as never before. What a man! Asshole indeed. That's what they all were, principals, teachers, school janitors, and neighbors who confiscated our soccer balls after they had landed in their flower beds.

Assholes ruled the world, but my father had drawn the line now. He was no longer part of the coalition of oppressors.

I looked at him in speechless admiration. He glanced at me and then at the floor, suddenly embarrassed. "Well, how are you feeling?"

"Better," I said firmly and to my own surprise. It was a diagnosis one ordinarily left to adults.

"Good. Then let us go down to dinner."

"Don't you think he should have his meal in bed," my mother interposed, speaking for the first time now that the conversation had shifted to her jurisdiction.

Before I could protest, my father declared firmly: "No, tonight we all eat together." He rose and led the procession out of my room. This time he left the door open.

From that evening on, closing doors and windows before speaking became an undeclared general order in our household. What we had to say to each other at the end of a day was henceforth shielded from alien ears. Maids, repairmen, and passers-by represented the ubiquitous enemy, not merely oppressive, but threatening and brutal, bent not on controling but on destroying. The struggle against the tyranny of authority and custom had been turned into a struggle for survival. Inside the family bastion, however, the barrier between generations had been lowered. After January 30, 1933, we children and our parents moved closer together as the distance between ourselves and the outside world increased rapidly.

We could not know this as we ate our dinner that glum, historic evening, just as we could not know what a divide the day would forever constitute in our lives. Nor had my father's reaction brought us to such a prophetic understanding. But when he asked my brother to close the door he had responded to an inner voice, to a sensible warning. He had begun to prepare for our survival before he knew that it was threatened.

1983

Bruno Bettelheim

A VICTIM

Many students of discrimination are aware that the victim often reacts in ways as undesirable as the action of the aggressor. Less attention is paid to this because it is easier to excuse a defendant than an offender, and because they assume that once the aggression stops the victim's reactions will stop too. But I doubt if this is of real service to the persecuted. His main interest is that the persecution cease. But that is less apt to happen if he lacks a real understanding of the phenomenon of persecution, in which victim and persecutor are inseparably interlocked.

Let me illustrate with the following example: in the winter of 1938 a Polish Jew murdered the German attaché in Paris, vom Rath. The Gestapo used the event to step up anti-Semitic actions, and in the camp new hardships were inflicted on Jewish prisoners. One of these was an order barring them from the medical clinic unless the need for treatment had originated in work accident.

Nearly all prisoners suffered from frostbite which often led to gangrene and then amputation. Whether or not a Jewish prisoner was admitted to the clinic to prevent such a fate depended on the whim of an SS private. On reaching the clinic entrance, the prisoner explained the nature of his ailment to the SS man, who then decided if he should get treatment or not.

I too suffered from frostbite. At first I was discouraged from trying to get medical care by the fate of Jewish prisoners whose attempts had ended up in no treatment, only abuse. Finally things got worse and I was afraid that waiting longer would mean amputation. So I decided to make the effort.

When I got to the clinic, there were many prisoners lined up as usual, a score of them Jews suffering from severe frostbite. The main topic of discussion was one's chances of being admitted to the clinic. Most Jews had planned their procedure in detail. Some thought it best to stress their service in the German army during World War I: wounds received or decorations won. Others planned to stress the severity of their frostbite. A few decided it was best to tell some "tall story," such as that an SS officer had ordered them to report at the clinic.

Most of them seemed convinced that the SS man on duty would not see through their schemes. Eventually they asked me about my plans. Having no definite ones, I said I would go by the way the SS man dealt with other Jewish prisoners who had frostbite like me, and proceed accordingly. I doubted how wise it was to follow a preconceived plan, because it was hard to anticipate the reactions of a person you didn't know.

The prisoners reacted as they had at other times when I had voiced similar ideas on how to deal with the SS. They insisted that one SS man was like another, all equally vicious and stupid. As usual, any frustration was immediately discharged against the person who caused it, or was nearest at hand. So in abusive terms they accused me of not wanting to share my plan with them, or of intending to use one of theirs; it angered them that I was ready to meet the enemy unprepared.

No Jewish prisoner ahead of me in the line was admitted to the clinic. The more a prisoner pleaded, the more annoyed and violent the SS became. Expressions of pain amused him; stories of previous services rendered to Germany outraged him. He proudly remarked that *he* could not be taken in by Jews, that fortunately the time had passed when Jews could reach their goal by lamentations.

When my turn came he asked me in a screeching voice if I knew that work accidents were the only reason for admitting Jews to the clinic, and if I came because of such an accident. I replied that I knew the rules, but that I couldn't work unless my hands were freed of the dead flesh. Since prisoners were not allowed to have knives, I asked to have the dead flesh cut away. I tried to be matter-of-fact, avoiding pleading, deference, or arrogance. He replied: "If that's all you want, I'll tear the flesh off myself." And he started to pull at the festering skin. Because it did not come off as easily as he may have expected, or for some other reason, he waved me into the clinic.

Inside, he gave me a malevolent look and pushed me into the treatment room. There he told the prisoner orderly to attend to the wound. While this was being done, the guard watched me closely for signs of pain but I was able to suppress them. As soon as the cutting was over, I started to leave. He showed surprise and asked why I didn't wait for further treatment. I said I had gotten the service I asked for, at which he told the orderly to make an exception and treat my hand. After I had left the room, he called me back and gave me a card entitling me to further treatment, and admittance to the clinic without inspection at the entrance.

* * *

Because my behavior did not correspond to what he expected of Jewish prisoners on the basis of his projection, he could not use his prepared defenses against being touched by the prisoner's plight. Since I did not act as the dangerous Jew was expected to, I did not activate the anxieties that went with his stereotype. Still he did not altogether trust me, so he continued to watch while I received treatment.

Throughout these dealings, the SS felt uneasy with me, though he did not unload on me the annoyance his uneasiness aroused. Perhaps he watched me closely because he expected that sooner or later I would slip up and behave the way his projected image of the Jew was expected to act. This would have meant that his delusional creation had become real.

1960

Paul Fussell

MY WAR[1]

* * *

My war is virtually synonymous with my life. I entered the war when I was nineteen, and I have been in it ever since. Melville's Ishmael[2] says that a whale-ship was his Yale College and his Harvard. An infantry division was mine, the 103rd, whose dispirited personnel wore a colorful green and yellow cactus on their left shoulders. These hillbillies and Okies, drop-outs and used-car salesmen and petty criminals were my teachers and friends.

How did an upper-middle-class young gentleman find himself in so unseemly a place? Why wasn't he in the Navy, at least, or in the OSS or Air Corps administration or editing the *Stars and Stripes* or being a general's aide?[3] The answer is comic: at the age of twenty I found myself leading forty riflemen over the Vosges Mountains[4] and watching them torn apart by German artillery and machine-guns because when I was sixteen, in junior college, I was fat and flabby, with feminine tits and a big behind. For years the thing I'd hated most about school was gym, for there I was obliged to strip and shower communally. Thus I chose to join the R.O.T.C. (infantry, as it happened) because that was a way to get out of gym, which meant you never had to take off your clothes and invite—indeed, compel—ridicule. You rationalized by noting that this was 1939 and that a little "military training" might not, in the long run, be wasted. Besides, if you worked up to be a cadet officer, you got to wear a Sam Browne belt, from which depended a nifty saber.

When I went on to college, it was natural to continue my technique for not exposing my naked person, and luckily my college had an infantry R.O.T.C. unit, where I was welcomed as something of an experienced hand. This was in 1941. When the war began for the United States, college students were solicited by various "programs" of the navy and marine corps and coast guard with plans for transforming them into officers. But people enrolled in the R.O.T.C. unit were felt to have committed themselves already. They had opted for the infantry, most of them all unaware, and that's where they were going to stay. Thus while

---

1. Excerpted from a longer essay, also entitled "My War," in which Fussell explores and explains what he calls his "dark, ironical, flip view" of World War II and its effect, afterward, on his life and thinking.
2. Narrator of Herman Melville's novel *Moby-Dick* (1851).
3. I.e., all comparably safe and "intellectual" wartime assignments; specifically, the OSS, or Office of Strategic Services, was the American military-civilian intelligence organization, while The *Stars and Stripes* was a popular illustrated magazine put out for the information and enjoyment of the armed forces.
4. Mountains in the north of France, where Fussell's troops underwent their hardest fighting.

shrewder friends were enrolling in Navy V-1[5] or signing up for the pacific exercises of the Naval Japanese Language Program or the Air Corps Meteorological Program, I signed up for the Infantry Enlisted Reserve Corps, an act guaranteeing me one extra semester in college before I was called. After basic training, advancement to officer training was promised, and that seemed a desirable thing, even if the crossed rifles on the collar did seem to betoken some hard physical exertion and discomfort— marching, sleeping outdoors, that sort of thing. But it would help "build you up," and besides officers, even in the Infantry, got to wear those wonderful pink trousers and receive constant salutes.

It was such imagery of future grandeur that in spring, 1943, sustained me through eighteen weeks of basic training in 100-degree heat at dreary Camp Roberts, California, where to toughen us, it was said, water was forbidden from 8:00 a.m. to 5:00 p.m. ("water discipline," this was called). Within a few weeks I'd lost all my flab and with it the whole ironic "reason" I found myself there at all. It was abundantly clear already that "infantry" had been a big mistake: it was not just stupid and boring and bloody, it was athletic, and thus not at all for me. But supported by vanity and pride I somehow managed to march thirty-five miles and tumble through the obstacle course, and a few months later I found myself at the Infantry School, Fort Benning, Georgia, where, training to become an officer, I went through virtually the same thing over again. As a Second Lieutenant of Infantry I "graduated" in the spring of 1944 and was assigned to the 103rd Division at Camp Howze, Texas, the local equivalent of Camp Roberts, only worse: Roberts had white-painted two-storey clapboard barracks, Howze one-storey tar-paper shacks. But the heat was the same, and the boredom, and the local whore-culture, and the hillbilly songs:

> Who's that gal with the red dress on?
> Some folks call her Dinah.
> She stole my heart away,
> Down in Carolina.

The 103rd Division had never been overseas, and all the time I was putting my rifle platoon through its futile exercises we were being prepared for the invasion of southern France, which followed the landings in Normandy.[6] Of course we didn't know this, and assumed from the training ("water discipline" again) that we were destined for the South Pacific. There were some exercises involving towed gliders that seemed to portend nothing at all but self-immolation, we were so inept with these devices. In October, 1944, we were all conveyed by troop transports to

5. An intensive college-training program for naval officers.
6. On June 6, 1944, British and American forces began their invasion of Nazi-occupied Europe by crossing the English Channel and landing on the beaches at Normandy.

Marseilles.[7]

It was my first experience of abroad, and my life-long affair with France dates from the moment I first experienced such un-American phenomena as: formal manners and a respect for the language; a well-founded skepticism; the pollarded plane trees on the Av. R. Schuman; the red wine and real bread; the *pissoirs*[8] in the streets; the international traffic signs and the visual public language hinting a special French understanding of things: *Hôtel de Ville, Defense d'afficher;*[9] the smell of Turkish tobacco when one has been brought up on Virginia and Burley. An intimation of what we might be opposing was supplied by the aluminum Vichy coinage. On one side, a fasces and *Etat Français*. No more Republic. On the other, *Liberté, Egalité, Fraternité replaced by Travail* (as in *Arbeit Macht Frei*), *Famille,* and *Patrie* (as in *Vaterland*).[1] But before we had time to contemplate all this, we were moving rapidly northeast. After a truck ride up the Rhone Valley, still pleasant with girls and flowers and wine, our civilized period came to an abrupt end. On the night of November 11 (nice irony there) we were introduced into the line at St. Dié, in Alsace.[2]

We were in "combat." I find the word embarrassing, carrying as it does false chivalric overtones (as in "single combat"). But synonyms are worse: *fighting* is not accurate, because much of the time you are being shelled, which is not fighting but suffering; *battle* is too high and remote; *in action* is a euphemism suited more to dire telegrams than description. "Combat" will have to do, and my first hours of it I recall daily, even now. They fueled, and they still fuel, my view of things.

Everyone knows that a night relief is among the most difficult of infantry maneuvers. But we didn't know it, and in our innocence we expected it to go according to plan. We and the company we were replacing were cleverly and severely shelled: it was as if the Germans a few hundred feet away could see us in the dark and through the thick pine growth. When the shelling finally stopped, at about midnight, we realized that, although near the place we were supposed to be, until daylight we would remain hopelessly lost. The order came down to stop where we were, lie down among the trees, and get some sleep. We would finish the relief at first light. Scattered over several hundred yards, the two hundred and fifty of us in F Company lay down in a darkness so thick we could see nothing at all. Despite the terror of our first shelling (and several people

---

7. Large seaport city in southern France.
8. Public urinals—a feature of French cities.
9. "Town Hall; Post No Bills."
1. The "Vichy government" of France during World War II was essentially the Nazis' means of controlling that country; its coinage was aluminum because other materials were pressed into war service. As Fussell describes the coins, one side bore the ancient Roman symbol of authority (the "fasces"), which the Italian dictator Mussolini had made his symbol, and the words "French State"; on the other side, the French motto "Liberty, Equality, Brotherhood" was replaced by "Work" (as in the Nazi slogan "Work Makes Freedom"), "Family," and "Country" (as in the German "Fatherland").
2. In northern France.

had been hit), we slept as soundly as babes. At dawn I awoke, and what I saw all around were numerous objects I'd miraculously not tripped over in the dark. These objects were dozens of dead German boys in greenish-gray uniforms, killed a day or two before by the company we were relieving. If darkness had hidden them from us, dawn disclosed them with open eyes and greenish-white faces like marble, still clutching their rifles and machine-pistols in their seventeen-year-old hands, fixed where they had fallen. (For the first time I understood the German phrase for the war-dead: *die Gefallenen*.[3]) Michelangelo could have made something beautiful out of these forms, in the *Dying Gaul* tradition,[4] and I was startled to find that in a way I couldn't understand, at first they struck me as beautiful. But after a moment, no feeling but shock and horror. My adolescent illusions, largely intact to that moment, fell away all at once, and I suddenly knew I was not and never would be in a world that was reasonable or just. The scene was less apocalyptic than shabbily ironic: it sorted so ill with modern popular assumptions about the idea of progress and attendant improvements in public health, social welfare, and social justice. To transform guiltless boys into cold marble after passing them through unbearable fear and humiliation and pain and contempt seemed to do them an interesting injustice. I decided to ponder these things. In 1917, shocked by the Battle of the Somme and recovering from neurasthenia, Wilfred Owen[5] was reading a life of Tennyson. He wrote his mother: "Tennyson, it seems, was always a great child. So should I have been but for Beaumont Hamel." So should I have been but for St. Dié.

After that, one day was much like another: attack at dawn, run and fall and crawl and sweat and worry and shoot and be shot at and cower from mortar shells, always keeping up a jaunty carriage in front of one's platoon; and at night, "consolidate" the objective, usually another hill, sometimes a small town, and plan the attack for the next morning. Before we knew it we'd lost half the company, and we all realized then that for us there would be no way out until the war ended but sickness, wounds, or oblivion. And the war would end only as we pressed our painful daily advance. Getting it over was our sole motive. Yes, we knew about the Jews. But our skins seemed to us more valuable at the time.

The word for the German defense all along was clever, a word that never could have been applied to our procedures. It was my first experience, to be repeated many times in later years, of the cunning ways of Europe versus the blunter ways of the New World. Although manned largely by tired thirty-year-old veterans (but sharp enough to have got out of Normandy alive), old men, and crazy youths, the German infantry

---

3. "The Fallen."
4. A reference to a starkly idealized statue by the great Renaissance artist.
5. British poet (1893–1918), killed in World War I; the Battle of the Somme was one of that war's worst battles; Tennyson, the great Victorian poet (1809–92).

was officered superbly, and their defense, which we experienced for many months, was disciplined and orderly. My people would have run, or at least "snaked off." But the Germans didn't, until the very end. Their uniforms were a scandal—rags and beat-up boots and unauthorized articles—but somehow they held together. Nazis or not, they did themselves credit. Lacking our lavish means, they compensated by patience and shrewdness. Not until well after the war did I discover that many times when they unaccountably located us hidden in deep woods and shelled us accurately, they had done so by inferring electronically the precise positions of the radios over which we innocently conversed.

As the war went on, the destruction of people became its sole means. I felt sorry for the Germans I saw killed in quantity everywhere—along the roads, in cellars, on roof-tops—for many reasons. They were losing, for one thing, and their deaths meant nothing, though they had been persuaded that resistance might "win the war." And they were so pitifully dressed and accoutered: that was touching. Boys with raggedy ad hoc uniforms and *Panzerfausts*[6] and too few comrades. What were they doing? They were killing themselves; and for me, who couldn't imagine being killed, for people my age voluntarily to get themselves killed caused my mouth to drop open.

Irony describes the emotion, whatever it is, occasioned by perceiving some great gulf, half-comic, half-tragic, between what one expects and what one finds. It's not quite "disillusion," but it's adjacent to it. My experience in the war was ironic because my innocence before had prepared me to encounter in it something like the same reasonableness that governed prewar life. This, after all, was the tone dominating the American relation to the war: talk of "the future," allotments and bond purchases carefully sent home,[7] hopeful fantasies of "the postwar world." I assumed, in short, that everyone would behave according to the clear advantages offered by reason. I had assumed that in war, like chess, when you were beaten you "resigned"; that when outnumbered and outgunned you retreated; that when you were surrounded you surrendered. I found out differently, and with a vengeance. What I found was people obeying fatuous and murderous "orders" for no reason I could understand, killing themselves because someone "told them to," prolonging the war when it was hopelessly lost because—because it was unreasonable to do so. It was my introduction to the shakiness of civilization. It was my first experience of the profoundly irrational element, and it made ridiculous all talk of plans and preparations for the future and goodwill and intelligent arrangements. Why did the red-haired young German machine-gunner firing at us in the woods not go on living—marrying, going to university,

---

6. Literally, "tank-fists," i.e., hand-carried antitank rockets.
7. "Allotments": portions of a soldier's pay

sent home to his family; "bond" refers to "War Bonds" (now "U. S. Savings Bonds").

going to the beach, laughing, smiling—but keep firing long after he had made his point, and require us to kill him with a grenade?

Before we knew it it was winter, and the winter in 1944–1945 was the coldest in Europe for twenty-five years. For the ground troops conditions were unspeakable, and even the official history admits the disaster, imputing the failure to provide adequate winter clothing—analogous to the similar German oversight when the Russian winter of 1941–1942 surprised the planners[8]—to optimism, innocence, and "confidence":

> Confidence born of the rapid sweep across Europe in the summer of 1944 and the conviction on the part of many that the successes of Allied arms would be rewarded by victory before the onset of winter contributed to the unpreparedness for winter combat.

The result of thus ignoring the injunction "Be Prepared" was 64,008 casualties from "cold injury"—not wounds but pneumonia and trench-foot. The official history sums up: "This constitutes more than four 15,000-man divisions. Approximately 90 percent of cold casualties involved riflemen and there were about 4,000 riflemen per infantry division. Thus closer to 13 divisions were critically disabled for combat." We can appreciate those figures by recalling that the invasion of Normany was initially accomplished by only six divisions (nine if we add the airborne). Thus crucial were little things like decent mittens and gloves, fur-lined parkas, thermal underwear—all of which any normal peacetime hiker or skier would demand as protection against prolonged exposure. But "the winter campaign in Europe was fought by most combat personnel in a uniform that did not give proper protection": we wore silly long overcoats, right out of the nineteenth century; thin field jackets, designed to convey an image of manliness at Fort Bragg; and dress wool trousers. We wore the same shirts and huddled under the same blankets as Pershing's troops in the expedition against Pancho Villa in 1916.[9] Of the 64,008 who suffered "cold injury" I was one. During February, 1945, I was back in various hospitals for a month with pneumonia. I told my parents it was flu.

That month away from the line helped me survive for four weeks more but it broke the rhythm and, never badly scared before, when I returned to the line early in March I found for the first time that I was terrified, unwilling to take the chances which before had seemed rather sporting. My month of safety had renewed my interest in survival, and I was psychologically and morally ill-prepared to lead my platoon in the great Seventh Army attack of March 15, 1945. But lead it I did, or rather push it, staying as far in the rear as was barely decent. And before the day was

8. A drastically heavy winter was one cause of the Germans' failure to conquer Russia.
9. Referring to General John Pershing's un-
successful punitive expedition against the Mexican revolutionary Francisco ("Pancho") Villa.

over I had been severely rebuked by a sharp-eyed lieutenant-colonel who threatened court martial if I didn't pull myself together. Before that day was over I was sprayed with the contents of a soldier's torso when I was lying behind him and he knelt to fire at a machine-gun holding us up: he was struck in the heart, and out of the holes in the back of his field jacket flew little clouds of tissue, blood, and powdered cloth. Near him another man raised himself to fire, but the machine-gun caught him in the mouth, and as he fell he looked back at me with surprise, blood and teeth dribbling out onto the leaves. He was one to whom early on I had given the Silver Star for heroism, and he didn't want to let me down.

As if in retribution for my cowardice, in the late afternoon, near Engwiller, Alsace, clearing a woods full of Germans cleverly dug in, my platoon was raked by shells from an 88, and I was hit in the back and leg by shell fragments. They felt like red-hot knives going in, but I was as interested in the few quiet moans, like those of a hurt child drifting off to sleep, of my thirty-seven-year-old platoon sergeant—we'd been together since Camp Howze—killed instantly by the same shell. We were lying together, and his immediate neighbor on the other side, a lieutenant in charge of a section of heavy machine-guns, was killed instantly too. And my platoon was virtually wiped away. I was in disgrace, I was hurt, I was clearly expendable—while I lay there the supply sergeant removed my issue wristwatch to pass on to my replacement—and I was twenty years old.

I bore up all right while being removed from "the field" and passed back through the first-aid stations where I was known. I was deeply on morphine, and managed brave smiles as called for. But when I got to the evacuation hospital thirty miles behind the lines and was coming out from the anesthetic of my first operation, all my affectations of control collapsed, and I did what I'd wanted to do for months. I cried, noisily and publicly, and for hours. I was the scandal of the ward. There were lots of tears back there: in the operating room I saw a nurse dissolve in shoulder-shaking sobs when a boy died with great stertorous gasps on the operating table she was attending. That was the first time I'd seen anyone cry in the whole European Theater of Operations, and I must have cried because I felt that there, out of "combat," tears were licensed. I was crying because I was ashamed and because I'd let my men be killed and because my sergeant had been killed and because I recognized as never before that he might have been me and that statistically if in no other way he was me, and that I had been killed too. But ironically I had saved my life by almost losing it, for my leg wound providentially became infected, and by the time it was healed and I was ready for duty again, the European war was over, and I journeyed back up through a silent Germany to re-join my reconstituted platoon "occupying" a lovely Tyrolean valley near Innsbruck.[1] For the infantry there was still the Japanese war to sweat out, and I was destined for it, despite the dramatic gash in my leg. But thank God the Bomb[2] was dropped while I was on my way there, with the result that I can write this.

* * *

1982

1. In Austria.
2. The atomic bombs dropped on Japanese cities in 1945, which effectively ended the war in the Pacific.

THE READER

1. Fussell says that he first realized the shakiness of civilization when he saw that the Germans were resisting in obedience to fatuous and murderous orders. He then implies that the civilized thing to do would have been to stop fighting, and this implication would seem to be supported by his description of his own behavior in the attack of March 15. Yet the reasons he gives for crying at the evacuation hospital are more complicated. Explain whether these reasons modify his idea of civilization or whether he has shifted to a larger, perhaps more basic topic.
2. Check your dictionary for a definition of irony; compare it with Fussell's (p. 48). What does he accomplish by classifying it, as he does, as an emotion?

THE WRITER

1. This is a basically chronological narrative, but on p. 48 Fussell begins an interruption that takes up half of the discussion. Is the interruption justified? What is the point or points?
2. Elsewhere Fussell describes the speaker in this account of his war as a "pissed-off infantryman." What do you find in his account that supports that self-identification Presuming that not all of what you find will be equally important, what seems essential?
3. Write a brief essay in which you compare Fussell's view of war with Hemingway's in A Farewell to Arms (p. 373).

Alice Walker

BEAUTY: WHEN THE OTHER DANCER IS THE SELF

It is a bright summer day in 1947. My father, a fat, funny man with beautiful eyes and a subversive wit, is trying to decide which of his eight children he will take with him to the county fair. My mother, of course, will not go. She is knocked out from getting most of us ready: I hold my neck stiff against the pressure of her knuckles as she hastily completes the braiding and then beribboning of my hair.

My father is the driver for the rich old white lady up the road. Her name is Miss Mey. She owns all the land for miles around, as well as the house in which we live. All I remember about her is that she once offered to pay my mother thirty-five cents for cleaning her house, raking up piles of her magnolia leaves, and washing her family's clothes, and that my mother—she of no money, eight children, and a chronic earache—refused it. But I do not think of this in 1947. I am two and a half years old. I want to go everywhere my daddy goes. I am excited at the prospect of riding in a car. Someone has told me fairs are fun. That there is room in the car for only three of us doesn't faze me at all. Whirling happily in my starchy frock, showing off my biscuit-polished patent-leather shoes and lavender socks, tossing my head in a way that makes my ribbons bounce, I stand, hands on hips, before my father. "Take me, Daddy," I say with assurance; "I'm the prettiest!"

Later, it does not surprise me to find myself in Miss Mey's shiny black car, sharing the back seat with the other lucky ones. Does not surprise me that I thoroughly enjoy the fair. At home that night I tell the unlucky ones all I can remember about the merry-go-round, the man who eats live chickens, and the teddy bears, until they say: that's enough, baby Alice. Shut up now, and go to sleep.

It is Easter Sunday, 1950. I am dressed in a green, flocked, scalloped-hem dress (handmade by my adoring sister, Ruth) that has its own smooth satin petticoat and tiny hot-pink roses tucked into each scallop. My shoes, new T-strap patent leather, again highly biscuit-polished. I am six years old and have learned one of the longest Easter speeches to be heard that day, totally unlike the speech I said when I was two: "Easter lilies/pure and white/blossom in/the morning light." When I rise to give my speech I do so on a great wave of love and pride and expectation. People in the church stop rustling their new crinolines. They seem to hold their breath. I can tell they admire my dress, but it is my spirit, bordering on sassiness (womanishness), they secretly applaud.

"That girl's a little *mess*," they whisper to each other, pleased.

Naturally I say my speech without stammer or pause, unlike those who stutter, stammer, or, worst of all, forget. This is before the word "beautiful" exists in people's vocabulary, but "Oh, isn't she the *cutest* thing!" frequently floats my way. "And got so much sense!" they gratefully add . . . for which thoughtful addition I thank them to this day.

It was great fun being cute. But then, one day, it ended.

I am eight years old and a tomboy. I have a cowboy hat, cowboy boots, checkered shirt and pants, all red. My playmates are my brothers, two and four years older than I. Their colors are black and green, the only difference in the way we are dressed. On Saturday nights we all go to the picture show, even my mother; Westerns are her favorite kind of movie. Back home, "on the ranch," we pretend we are Tom Mix, Hopalong Cassidy, Lash LaRue (we've even named one of our dogs Lash LaRue); we chase each other for hours rustling cattle, being outlaws, delivering damsels from distress. Then my parents decide to buy my brothers guns. These are not "real" guns. They shoot "BBs," copper pellets my brothers say will kill birds. Because I am a girl, I do not get a gun. Instantly I am relegated to the position of Indian. Now there appears a great distance between us. They shoot and shoot at everything with their new guns. I try to keep up with my bow and arrows.

One day while I am standing on top of our makeshift "garage"—pieces of tin nailed across some poles—holding my bow and arrow and looking out toward the fields, I feel an incredible blow in my right eye. I look down just in time to see my brother lower his gun.

Both brothers rush to my side. My eye stings, and I cover it with my hand. "If you tell," they say, "we will get a whipping. You don't want that to happen, do you?" I do not. "Here is a piece of wire," says the older brother, picking it up from the roof; "say you stepped on one end of it and the other flew up and hit you." The pain is beginning to start. "Yes," I say, "Yes, I will say that is what happened." If I do not say this is what happened, I know my brothers will find ways to make me wish I had. But now I will say anything that gets me to my mother.

Confronted by our parents we stick to the lie agreed upon. They place me on a bench on the porch and I close my left eye while they examine the right. There is a tree growing from underneath the porch that climbs past the railing to the roof. It is the last thing my right eye sees. I watch as its trunk, its branches, and then its leaves are blotted out by the rising blood.

I am in shock. First there is intense fever, which my father tries to break using lily leaves bound around my head. Then there are chills: my mother tries to get me to eat soup. Eventually, I do not know how, my parents learn what has happened. A week after the "accident" they take me to see a doctor. "Why did you wait so long to come?" he asks, looking into my eye and shaking his head. "Eyes are sympathetic," he says. "If one is blind, the other will likely become blind too."

This comment of the doctor's terrifies me. But it is really how I look that bothers me most. Where the BB pellet struck there is a glob of whitish scar tissue, a hideous cataract, on my eye. Now when I stare at people—a favorite pastime, up to now—they will stare back. Not at the "cute" little girl, but at her scar. For six years I do not stare at anyone, because I do not raise my head.

Years later, in the throes of a mid-life crisis, I ask my mother and sister whether I changed after the "accident." "No," they say, puzzled. "What do you mean?"

What do I mean?

I am eight, and, for the first time, doing poorly in school, where I have been something of a whiz since I was four. We have just moved to the place where the "accident" occurred. We do not know any of the people around us because this is a different county. The only time I see the friends I knew is when we go back to our old church. The new school is the former state penitentiary. It is a large stone building, cold and drafty, crammed to overflowing with boisterous, ill-disciplined children. On the third floor there is a huge circular imprint of some partition that has been torn out.

"What used to be here?" I ask a sullen girl next to me on our way past it to lunch.

"The electric chair," says she.

At night I have nightmares about the electric chair, and about all the people reputedly "fried" in it. I am afraid of the school, where all the students seem to be budding criminals.

"What's the matter with your eye?" they ask, critically.

When I don't answer (I cannot decide whether it was an "accident" or not), they shove me, insist on a fight.

My brother, the one who created the story about the wire, comes to my rescue. But then brags so much about "protecting" me, I become sick.

After months of torture at the school, my parents decide to send me back to our old community, to my old school. I live with my grandparents and the teacher they board. But there is no room for Phoebe, my cat. By the time my grandparents decide there is room, and I ask for my cat, she cannot be found. Miss Yarborough, the boarding teacher, takes me under her wing, and begins to teach me to play the piano. But soon she marries an African—a "prince," she says—and is whisked away to his continent.

At my old school there is at least one teacher who loves me. She is the teacher who "knew me before I was born" and bought my first baby clothes. It is she who makes life bearable. It is her presence that finally helps me turn on the one child at the school who continually calls me "one-eyed bitch." One day I simply grab him by his coat and beat him until I am satisfied. It is my teacher who tells me my mother is ill.

My mother is lying in bed in the middle of the day, something I have never seen. She is in too much pain to speak. She has an abscess in her ear. I stand looking down on her, knowing that if she dies, I cannot live. She is being treated with warm oils and hot bricks held against her cheek. Finally a doctor comes. But I must go back to my grandparents' house. The weeks pass but I am hardly aware of it. All I know is that my mother might die, my father is not so jolly, my brothers still have their guns, and I am the one sent away from home.

"You did not change," they say.

Did I imagine the anguish of never looking up?

I am twelve. When relatives come to visit I hide in my room. My cousin Brenda, just my age, whose father works in the post office and whose mother is a nurse, comes to find me. "Hello," she says. And then she asks, looking at my recent school picture, which I did not want taken, and on which the "glob," as I think of it, is clearly visible, "You still can't see out of that eye?"

"No," I say, and flop back on the bed over my book.

That night, as I do almost every night, I abuse my eye. I rant and rave at it, in front of the mirror. I plead with it to clear up before morning. I tell it I hate and despise it. I do not pray for sight. I pray for beauty.

"You did not change," they say.

I am fourteen and baby-sitting for my brother Bill, who lives in Boston. He is my favorite brother and there is a strong bond between us. Understanding my feelings of shame and ugliness he and his wife take me to a local hospital, where the "glob" is removed by a doctor named O. Henry. There is still a small bluish crater where the scar tissue was, but the ugly white stuff is gone. Almost immediately I become a different person from the girl who does not raise her head. Or so I think. Now that I've raised my head I win the boyfriend of my dreams. Now that I've raised my head I have plenty of friends. Now that I've raised my head classwork comes from my lips as faultlessly as Easter speeches did, and I leave high school as valedictorian, most popular student, and queen, hardly believing my luck. Ironically, the girl who was voted most beautiful in our class (and was) was later shot twice through the chest by a male companion, using a "real" gun, while she was pregnant. But that's another story in itself. Or is it?

"You did not change," they say.

It is now thirty years since the "accident." A beautiful journalist comes to visit and to interview me. She is going to write a cover story for her magazine that focuses on my latest book. "Decide how you want to look on the cover," she says. "Glamorous, or whatever."

Never mind "glamorous," it is the "whatever" that I hear. Suddenly all I can think of is whether I will get enough sleep the night before the photography session: if I don't, my eye will be tired and wander, as blind eyes will.

At night in bed with my lover I think up reasons why I should not appear on the cover of a magazine. "My meanest critics will say I've sold out," I say. "My family will now realize I write scandalous books."

"But what's the real reason you don't want to do this?" he asks.

"Because in all probability," I say in a rush, "my eye won't be straight."

"It will be straight enough," he says. Then, "Besides, I thought you'd made your peace with that."

And I suddenly remember that I have.

I remember:

I am talking to my brother Jimmy, asking if he remembers anything unusual about the day I was shot. He does not know I consider that day the last time my father, with his sweet home remedy of cool lily leaves, chose me, and that I suffered and raged inside because of this. "Well," he says, "all I remember is standing by the side of the highway with Daddy, trying to flag down a car. A white man stopped, but when Daddy said he needed somebody to take his little girl to the doctor, he drove off."

I remember:

I am in the desert for the first time. I fall totally in love with it. I am so overwhelmed by its beauty, I confront for the first time, consciously, the meaning of the doctor's words years ago: "Eyes are sympathetic. If one is blind, the other will likely become blind too." I realize I have dashed about the world madly, looking at this, looking at that, storing up images against the fading of the light. *But I might have missed seeing the desert!* The shock of that possibility—and gratitude for over twenty-five years of sight—sends me literally to my knees. Poem after poem comes—which is perhaps how poets pray.

On Sight

I am so thankful I have seen
The Desert

And the creatures in the desert
And the desert Itself.

The desert has its own moon
Which I have seen
With my own eye.
There is no flag on it.

Trees of the desert have arms
All of which are always up
That is because the moon is up
The sun is up
Also the sky
The stars
Clouds
None with flags.

If there were flags, I doubt
the trees would point.
Would you?

But mostly, I remember this:

I am twenty-seven, and my baby daughter is almost three. Since her birth I have worried about her discovery that her mother's eyes are different from other people's. Will she be embarrassed? I think. What will she say? Every day she watches a television program called "Big Blue Marble." It begins with a picture of the earth as it appears from the moon. It is bluish, a little battered-looking, but full of light, with whitish clouds swirling around it. Every time I see it I weep with love, as if it is a picture of Grandma's house. One day when I am putting Rebecca down for her nap, she suddenly focues on my eye. Something inside me cringes, gets ready to try to protect myself. All children are cruel about physical differences, I know from experience, and that they don't always mean to be is another matter. I assume Rebecca will be the same.

But no-o-o-o. She studies my face intently as we stand, her inside and me outside her crib. She even holds my face maternally between her dimpled little hands. Then, looking every bit as serious and lawyerlike as her father, she says, as if it may just possibly have slipped my attention: "Mommy, there's a *world* in your eye." (As in, "Don't be alarmed, or do anything crazy.") And then, gently, but with great interest: "Mommy, where did you *get* that world in your eye?"

For the most part, the pain left then. (So what, if my brothers grew up to buy even more powerful pellet guns for their sons and to carry real guns themselves. So what, if a young "Morehouse man"[1] once nearly fell off the steps of Trevor Arnett Library because he thought my eyes were blue.) Crying and laughing I ran to the bathroom, while Rebecca mumbled and sang herself off to sleep. Yes indeed, I realized, looking into the mirror. There was a world in my eye. And I saw that it was possible to love it: that in fact, for all it had taught me of shame and anger and inner vision, I *did* love it. Even to see it drifting out of orbit in boredom, or rolling up out of fatigue, not to mention floating back at attention in excitement (bearing witness, a friend has called it), deeply suitable to my personality, and even characteristic of me.

That night I dream I am dancing to Stevie Wonder's song "Always" (the name of the song is really "As," but I hear it as "Always"). As I dance, whirling and joyous, happier than I've ever been in my life, another bright-faced dancer joins me. We dance and kiss each other and hold each other through the night. The other dancer has obviously come through all right, as I have done. She is beautiful, whole and free. And she is also me.

1983

1. A student at Morehouse College in Atlanta, Georgia.

THE READER

1. *Walker's essay frequently uses the word "beautiful." Does this word always have the same meaning, or is it used in more than one sense?*
2. *Throughout her essay, Walker refers to the "accident." Why does she put the word in quotation marks?*
3. *Had the "accident" changed Walker? In what ways? What might account for others assuring her that it had not changed her?*
4. *Writing of the girl who was voted most beautiful in her high-school class and who was later shot—with a "real" gun—by a male companion, Walker says, "That's another story in itself. Or is it?" Why does she question whether that's another story in itself?*
5. *Has Walker made her peace with the "accident" and its consequences?*

THE WRITER

1. *Walker writes her essay by selecting particular moments in her life. What does each moment show? How does her writing bring out the immediacy of each moment? How do these moments relate to Walker's theme?*
2. *Does Walker's essay gain by having a poem included in it?*
3. *What is the effect of ending the essay by recounting a dream? What is the relation of the dream to the essay's title?*
4. *Write an essay comparing and contrasting Walker's essay and Hurston's "How It Feels to Be Colored Me" (p. 19). Consider especially their subjects and their attitudes toward those subjects.*

Scott Sanders

LISTENING TO OWLS

On the morning after the winter solstice, two hours before sunrise, moon full, I stood on frozen feet beside a pine grove in southern Indiana and listened for owls. The pine boughs were dark featherings on darkness. Every winter weed and bush in the meadow cast a pale moon-shadow. Burst milkweed pods hung upon last year's stems like giant commas. Breath haloed about my face in the five-degree air. In such stillness an owl could hear the footpads of mice, the rustling of rabbits, but I with my clumsy ears could hear nothing.

The friend who had brought me to this owl country—Don White-head, a husky man with sun-creases around his eyes, who indulges his passion for the outdoors by teaching ecology—cupped gloved hands to his mouth and uttered a long cry, rather like the noise a strangled rooster might make. This was the barred owl's call, which bird books will tell you sounds like a guttural rendering of "Who cooks for you, who cooks for you all?" But don't let the cozy sentences fool you. The cry of the barred owl, even the counterfeit cry my friend Don was making, resembles no human speech. It is night-speech. So there we stood, on the longest night of the year, two grown men hooting into the darkness and listening.

Presently a cow answered, lowing mournfully. Next a dog yapped, then two more, then a fourth, all at a great distance from us and seemingly from all four points of the compass. We were surrounded by domestication. When a rooster chimed in, I began to despair of owls. Gingerly, afraid my iced toes might shatter, I rocked from foot to foot.

Don motioned for me to keep still. Dogs, cow, and rooster also obligingly hushed. A moonlit smile stole across his face. He pointed, away from the pine woods and across the meadow, toward a cedar-topped ridge. I faced where he pointed, shut my eyes, and listened, listened so hard my shivering body grew calm. What I heard sounded at first like a distant creek splashing over rocks. I disappeared into my listening. The water-sound grew sharper, divided into syllables, spoke to me at last in the sixty-million-year-old voice of an owl.

Sixty million years is only an estimate, of course, and might be off by an eon or two. The bones of owls, like those of all other birds, are hollow and flimsy, and consequently make poor fossils. Reading the rocks, scientists find dinosaurs by the truckload, seashells and gigantic ferns by the long ton, but scant trace of birds. Some dinosaurs had wings, but they must have been clumsy fliers. Maybe they could not truly fly, but had to climb trees or cliffs and then leap in one hungry swoop onto their prey.

Some one hundred eighty million years ago, one of these winged dinosaurs lay down in the mud and left its fossilized imprint, including a toothed jaw, a long bony tail, and the ghostly trace of feathers. Feathers! Here was a new invention, and a durable one, to judge by the chickadee on my windowsill. Life shoving through the sluggish bodies of dinosaurs —so the scientists theorize—chopped off the heavy tail, feathered the wings, hollowed the bones, and eventually produced birds. This takes some getting used to, holding dinosaur and bird together in the mind, a lumbering swamp monster on one side and an ounce of fluff on the other, with a dotted line connecting them. But next time you get close to a pigeon, or any other patient bird, notice the reptilian scales on its legs, and see if you don't catch a whiff of ancient mud.

While the barred owl called, I shook, as if I were a plucked string. Of course the five-degree weather probably had something to do with my shaking. But mainly it was that night-voice plucking at the strings of wonder and dread in me. Listening in that moonshadowed meadow, the grasses and weeds curling from the soil like delicate brush-stokes, I understood why so many ancient peoples regarded the owl's cry as an omen of death.

In the old days, when the Chinese heard that cry they called it "digging a grave," and knew an owl was on its way to snatch some dying soul. Australian Aborigines believed that owls trafficked only in the souls of women, the souls of men being reserved for bats. Sicilians used to say that an owl cry meant an ailing person would die within three days. If nobody in the neighborhood was sick, well then, somebody would come down with tonsil trouble; no point in wasting an evil omen. The Old Testament warned the Israelites not to eat owls, lumping them with vultures as pariahs of the waste lands. Sumerians and Hebrews associated owls with Lilith, the goddess of death, who struck in the night. This death-dealing hag became, in the Middle Ages, a witch, and the owl became one of her familiars, a worker of wickedness.

"Death's dreadful messenger," that's what Edmund Spenser called the bird. And Shakespeare found it difficult to murder anyone on stage without the help of a preliminary announcement from owls. The king's murder in *Macbeth*, for example, is accompanied by the shriek of an owl, "the fatal bellman which gives the stern'st goodnight."

Even the word *owl* is funereal, coming as it does from a Latin root meaning "to howl," the same root that gives us *ululation*—the sound of wailing and lamentation. The birds have not helped their reputation any by showing a fondness for nesting in ruins and graveyards. Their flight is silent, thanks to the downy edge of their primary feathers and oversized wings. Like death, they arrive unannounced and gobble their victims whole.

These are not comforting details to recollect at two hours before sunrise, with your extremities frozen and ice forming in your arteries and the whole universe seized by a winter that might last forever, not comforting at all, especially if you are given, as I am, to brooding about death even in daylight and without the aid of owls.

Don yelped his strangled-rooster cry again. I flinched. He grinned— not at me, it turned out, but at the voice of a second barred owl which joined the first in a courting duet. The twin songs spiraled about one another, twisting the birds together in a rope of desire. At the far end of that rope, if things worked out, would be a nest, eggs, four weeks of incubation, and two or three owlets looking like handfuls of dandelion fluff. So here were voices crying at the other gate, the gate of birth rather than death. Night and Eros also go together. A century ago, in the streets of London, if you had inquired about "owls" you would have been led to a brothel. Night hags bring the big death, nightwalkers bring the small one.

Once they tuned up, our pair of lovers kept hooting yearnfully, like Romeo and Juliet in their balcony scene. What business did I have eavesdropping on this erotic serenade? How would I like finding them perched one midnight on my bedroom windowsill, their radar-dish ears catching every rustle of my sheets? But I had no intention of budging from that icy meadow so long as they kept singing. Now that love had been introduced, I could hear enough gaiety in their call to understand why Audubon, trailing barred owls in the swamps of Louisiana, compared their cry "to the affected bursts of laughter which you may have heard from some of the fashionable members of our own species."

If you listen to recordings of owls you will hear an eerie babel of moans and cackling, snores and screeches. There are about one hundred thirty species worldwide in sizes ranging from sparrow to eagle, and they speak in as many dialects as people do. Some of the voices are liquid trills. Others resemble the harsh buzz of locusts. Some make you think of murder victims, sirens, the sickening squeal cars make before a crash. Defending their nests, many owls snap their bills, clicking like geigercounters. Burrowing owls, which like to set up house in abandoned prairie dog tunnels, scare away predators by hissing like a rattlesnake. With wings spread and tail ruffled, a hissing owl might remind other predators rather uncomfortably of a wildcat. Saw-whet owls derive their name from the saw-sharpening whine they make. More than one early traveler in the American wilderness reports having been fooled by this bird-whistle into thinking a sawmill was just ahead.

Owls do all this muttering for purposes of courtship, as our yearnful pair of barreds were doing, and also for establishing territory. Wolves mark out the boundaries of their turf by urinating and defecating. Humans build fences and guard-posts. Owls, more fastidious than either, embroider the edges of their territory with song. They also fly their boundaries, regular as mailmen. When threatened, they will cry out like sirens to announce alarms. Nestlings clamor for food in the universally raucous manner of the young. Nocturnal owls often sing for a spell at dusk before the evening's hunt, like children at hide-and-seek counting to a hundred before going in search of victims.

They probably conduct other business with their hoots and gurgles—commenting on the weather, say, or estimating the population of field mice—including business we will never understand. Taken all together, the vocabulary of owls is about as complex as that of the average telephone conversation. Once you've spoken about hunger and fear, weather and territory, sex and death, what more is there to say?

Listening to screech owls beside Walden Pond, Thoreau was reminded of wailing women and mournful lovers, as if their call "were the dark and tearful side of music." Others have heard melancholy in these voices. The Kootenay Indians used to warn that children crying in the night would be mistaken by owls for their own young and be carried away. (I tried this warning on my three-year-old, but he seemed to like the idea of being snatched out of bed and flown high above the night-country). A brooding and sometimes melancholy bird himself, Thoreau welcomed the screech owls, saying, "They give me a sense of the variety and capacity of that nature which is our common dwelling."

Screech owls do not actually screech, but gently whinny, or give a voiceless, quavering whistle, like the syncopated whooshing sound of a revolving door. Fans of science fiction movies might be reminded of the sounds flying saucers are supposed to make. My friend Don had perfected that call as well. He had spent his teen years in the Adirondacks imitating birds, the way ordinary teenagers imitate television comedians or rock singers. When the barred owls tired of their love-duet and fell silent, Don gave a tremulous whistle. Within moments a screech owl whistled back, as if to say, "I thought you'd never call." This time the voice rose from the pine woods, so we shifted around to face the shaggy boughs. It would probably be a solitary male, staking out his territory. The whistling came only once more. Here I am, he was announcing. This is my realm of bugs and frogs and field-mice. Don spoke back to him, but the owl apparently had said his say. The pines bristled silently in the moonlight.

Audubon once carried a live screech owl in his coat pocket from Philadelphia to New York, over land and water, feeding it by hand. Audubon did things like that. On one occasion he was presented with a live duck. Lacking any other place to store it, he carried the bird half a day under his tophat. (I specify that both duck and owl were alive, since

Audubon's ordinary method of studying birds, like that of all early ornithologists, was to shoot first and ask scientific questions later. "I have not shot but have seen a Hawk of great size entirely *new*—" he wrote to his wife from Florida, and then added hopefully, "—may perhaps kill him tomorrow." He sometimes shot upwards of three hundred birds to secure one fine specimen for illustration). He once fell into quicksand while chasing a great horned owl. The slime was up to his armpits before someone heard his cries and pulled him out. Audubon held no grudge against the bird, to judge from his portrait of a male and female pair. They stare at you regally from the page, "ear" tufts erect, yellow-rimmed eyes somewhat crossed, feathers subtle as fine-threaded tapestry.

Studying those eyes, you can see where owls get their reputation for wisdom. We guess at the intelligence of strangers by watching their eyes. Here are two strangers, these Audubon owls, who bore holes through you with their stare. You could use either face for a mantra, lose yourself among the concentric rings of feathers. Their eyes proclaim that they know exactly who they are and what they are about. They have seen to the heart of things, while we grope around on the surface. Since the eyes of owls are fixed in their sockets, the bird must swivel its entire head in order to look to the side or rear. You receive no sly glances from an owl, but always a full stare. Its neck is so flexible that it can even gaze directly behind itself, thus keeping watch on the past. When a cartoon owl gazes at me and poses its cartoon question—"Whooo?"—I wish I had as clear an answer as the owl appears to have. Like all wild creatures, owls are serenely and unambiguously themselves. They do not suffer from existential angst. They do not wake themselves up four hours early and fly into town in hopes of hearing the overtones of truth in human chatter.

But are owls wise? The Greeks thought so, identifying them with Athena, goddess of wisdom. In medieval illustrations, owls accompany Merlin and share in his sorcery. In fairytales they rival the fox for cunning. Children's picture books show them wearing spectacles, mortarboard, and scholar's gown. Soups and other confections made from owls have been credited with curing whooping cough, drunkenness, epilepsy, famine, and insomnia. The Cherokee Indians used to bathe their children's eyes with a broth of owl feathers to keep the kids awake at night. Recipes using owl eggs are reputed to bestow keen eyesight and wisdom. Yet these birds are no smarter, ornithologists assure us, than most others. A museum guide in Boston once displayed a drowsy-looking barn owl on his gloved wrist, explaining to those of us assembled there how small the bird's brain actually was. "You'll notice the head of this live specimen appears to be about the size of a grapefruit," he said, "but it's mostly feathers." Lifting his other hand, he added, "The skull, you see, is the size of a lemon. There's only room enough inside for a bird-brain, not enough for Einstein!" We all laughed politely. But I was not convinced. Sure, the skull was small. The lower half was devoted to jaw and most of the upper half to beak and eye-holes. Yet enough neurons could be fitted into the remaining space to enable the barn owl to catch mice in total darness. They can even snatch bats on the wing, these princes of night-time stealth. We have to invent sonar for locating submarines, radar for locating airplanes; neither is much use with mice or bats. Barn owls can also see dead—and therefore silent—prey in light one-hundredth as bright as we would need. Like the ability to saw a board square or judge the consistency of bread dough, that might not amount to scholarship, but it is certainly a wisdom of the body. It has worked for some sixty million years. Farmers in Scandinavia, not caring about I.Q., often build roosts and special doors near the peaks of their barns for these efficient rodent-killers.

Most likely the reason we give owls credit for wisdom is because they look like us. Behold the rounded head, the prominent eyes set in front, a disk of feathers radiating outward from each eye like cheeks, dark slashes across the forehead like eyebrows, the lethal beak protruding only far enough to resemble a nose. Aha, we think, here are feathered, midget versions of ourselves; they must be smart. I suppose the owls, noting the same resemblance, would assume we are expert killers, and they would be right.

You can't judge owls by appearance. Their daytime faces—glimpsed in zoos and museums and books, occasionally on birds I discover at their perches—don't match the night-time voices Don and I were hearing. The face of a screech owl could belong to Cotton Mather or some other Puritan divine, full of wrath and fiery judgment, yet its quavering whistle falls as forgivingly as rain. Round facial markings make the barred owl look like a pilot in goggles, jet black eyes fresh from outer-space, rotund head filled with unearthly lore. Yet when I hear the "Who cooks for you, who cooks for you all?" cry, I can only think of lovers yodeling beneath balconies or strangling from disappointment. Barn owls, with faces pale and heart-shaped as old valentines, look like sad elves. But their repertoire of cries includes a screech that will set your teeth on edge and stiffen your neck hairs.

One of these elfin-looking barn owls once scared me nearly witless. I was camping with some other boys on a ridge overlooking the Mahoning River in northern Ohio. The sun was down. We'd made a fire, the light splashing on the undersides of sycamore leaves, and while we sat with our backs towards the dark woods, my father was telling us a ghost story. I can't remember the gory details, but the story climaxed with a squadron of ghouls pouncing on some unsuspecting boys as they sat around a campfire. "And the blood-drinking ghosts hooked their claws in the sycamore bark," my father was whispering, "and they spied down on those poor boys, kind of sizing them up. And then the ghosts tilted forward just a little bit on the sycamore limbs, and they"—my father's voice suddenly rose to a shout—"JUMPED!" We jumped. Then *he* jumped, as a scream burst over our heads, so loud it seemed to crack the night open. My heart quit, lungs quit, brain played turtle in my skull. I was doing my best to imitate a rock, so the blood-sucking ghouls would nab the guy next to me. Only when the scream sounded again, farther away, down along the river did I open my eyes. The other boys looked like prisoners of war, like pale stowaways who had just come blinking onto deck. My father's voice still shook as he explained, "It was just a barn owl. I expect we scared it off its roost."

Don and I heard no barn owls on the night of the winter solstice. Never common in the Middle West, this prowler has become even scarcer in recent years due to pesticide-poisoning. Like all predators, owls are near the top of the food-chain, and so they gobble toxins in concentrated doses. We're predators, too, feeding on the whole of nature. Although we don't eat owls, we poison them, with chemicals designed to protect our corn from worms, our apples from blemishes. One price of the perfection we expect on our dinner table is the death of night-hunters, the death of singers, the death of birds that impersonate ghosts.

We did hope to rouse a great-horned owl before daylight. Don knew a likely place, a hillside planted to sweetgum and pine, about a mile from the ridge where we had listened to the barred and screech owls. So we hiked the mile on ice-cake feet, scaring up a rabbit and a meadowlark along the way. Although the sun was rising, the temperature wasn't. The messages coming from my hands and feet were as shrill as the static on a shortwave radio during electrical storms.

By the time we reached the hillside, both eastern and western horizons were glowing, with rising sun and setting moon. The tips of pines and cedars fretted the skyline like saw-teeth. It was a dangerous hour, this lull between night and day, for any beast small enough to become owl food. Rabbits, squirrels, porcupines, skunks, mice and rats, snakes and all manner of birds, any of these might provide breakfast for the great horned owl. Here is a formidable bird, growing to a height of two feet and a wingspan of nearly five, capable of killing (but not carrying) animals that outweigh it. Pound-for-pound—as announcers say about bantam-weight boxers—this character is fiercer than a mountain lion. Any sort of owl is likely to get mobbed in daytime if smaller birds find it roosting. But great horneds drive crows into a particular frenzy. I once saw fifteen of those braggart birds pestering a great horned owl, diving and jabbering at him until he suddenly lashed out with a taloned foot and sent a ragged clump of feathers tumbling. Unenlightened, the fourteen survivors resumed their pestering, and the owl dispatched two more before they left.

If you have the bad luck or bad judgment to climb into its nesting tree while the youngsters are about, the great horned will greet you with a wallop and give your head and arms a good raking.

A friend of mine, a gangling man who assembles color televisions for a living and who has lost two wives because of his passion for birding, told me about meeting a great horned owl in a tulip tree. He had climbed the tree before dawn to wait to photograph the sunrise over Lake Monroe. There he waited, on a morning warmer than the one Don and I had picked for owling, his legs straddling a limb and his back against the trunk. Presently, the branch just above his head shook, as if someone had given it a single karate chop. Looking up, he saw the solemn bird. It was scanning the territory, head tilted forward and slowly pivoting, ear-tufts raised like twin antennae, saucer eyes making a murderous survey of the lakeside. When it spied my friend, the owl glanced casually away, and then did a comical double-take. For a moment the two perchers stared eye-to-eye, the man calculating whether there was light enough for a photo, the bird probably calculating whether this gawky beast would do for breakfast. Evidently deciding no, the owl gave a noncommittal hoot and flew away. My friend was lucky this was a hunting rather than a nesting tree, for had he approached the nest, the bird would probably have mauled him.

The great horned owl typically gives a gurgling call of one, two, and then three notes, as if it were learning to count. Don, as you might have guessed, can gurgle convincingly, and did so, on that brightening hillside. No answer. He tried again and again, pausing between calls, but the great horned owls had apparently clocked out for the night. I was so ecstatic with sunrise and moonset, so intoxicated with the night-voices we had already heard, that I would have turned entirely to ice before giving up on this last of our neighborhood owls. Don patiently crowed, I rocked on numb legs, the sun opened in the east like the mouth of a furnace. At last a gurgling voice answered from the woods. When I finally distinguished the sound, I realized I had been hearing it for several minutes, but had not recognized it amidst the wind noises and the chatter of awakening songbirds. Guessing the direction, I peered intently, hoping to catch a glimpse of the bird. The song unraveled for five minutes or more, and then came to an abrupt end. In the first moment of quiet I saw a huge shadow rise above the treetops, wings large enough for an angel. It flapped once, twice, and then swerved and was gone. I blinked, wondering if I had really seen it, or only conjured it out of the dawn sky. But Don had seen it, too. Beside me he was murmuring, "Wonderful, wonderful!"

When I try to explain to friends why I rise so early of a December day to go shiver in the owl-haunted woods, I find that those who have to ask my reasons cannot be made to understand them. When you sit near a waterfall, with the mist playing over your skin and the roar shaking your spine, you either realize that this is one of the authentic experiences, one of the touchstones for all living, or you don't. If you don't feel that thrill in the presence of a waterfall, or a stand of virgin timber, or a mountain peak, or a calling owl, then no explanation on earth will make you feel it.

Think of it, carrying on half of a love-duet with a bird. There you stand in your human shape, flightless and nightblind, conversing with a killer that navigates through darkness. Our literature and film are crowded with aliens from outer space, tentacled and bug-eyed, possessed of mysterious powers. But is any of these extraterrestrials stranger than an owl? Until visitors actually arrive from some remote planet, let me talk with owls or whales or even Sufis,[1] and I will find my conversation alien enough. Such talk makes us the visitors, the invaders from Ultima Thule.[2] The owl cannot speak in our tongue, but we can speak in his. The creation lures us out of ourselves, while the owl remains tucked snugly in the pouch of his instincts. He only speaks to us because we have entered his precinct, gone out to meet him, put off for a while our human garments and assumed his.

Chilled and triumphant, Don and I hiked back toward the car, neither of us speaking, as if we had tacitly agreed to keep the owls in our ears as long as possible. Our path took us along the shore of the lake, where cattails and reeds stood rigid in a frozen border of ice. In the deeper parts, waves lapped against the hem of ice with the sound of polite applause. In the shallow bays, where ice glinted like gun-metal from shore to shore, steam rising from the surface turned rose and violet in the early sunlight. It was like the smoke from incense, an offering fit for owl-gods or any other deities. Here and there a whirlwind lifted columns of steam twenty or thirty feet into the air. The spouts trailed across the ice, sinuous as snakes, and then collapsed back into the lower mists.

As the light grew stronger, we noticed that near the lake's edge the black ice was covered with a rough white fur. Bending closer, we could see that the fur was really a miniature forest of ice crystals, each crystal fern-shaped, a tiny glistening lattice. The boughs of this frozen forest were so delicate that they swayed when I breathed on them. The tallest thicket of crystals was no higher than the knuckle on a flattened hand, yet within those pygmy thickets there was more intricacy than the eye could follow.

Every weed and twig on the shore was covered with the same fragile wafers of ice. I plucked a stem of foxtail grass and held it between me and the sun. The light shattered on the crystals as I gently twirled the stem; a sliver of ice, thinner than an eyelash, broke the glow from a hydrogen

1. Islamic mystics, particularly inaccessible to Westerners.   2. A faraway place, the farthest land, a region of the North.

explosion into rainbows. Soon the frost on my foxtail melted. Before my very eyes the ice forest was evaporating from the margins of the lake, a disappearing-trick more astonishing than any Saturday-afternoon magic. The mists and spouts over the brozen bays were thinning away. I wanted to seize this moment of ice-beauty, hold it still for my perpetual delight. But it would not linger, any more than the owls would.

All the way up the hillside, whenever I turned to face the sun, I saw ice crystals needling through the air. Blown or shaken loose from trees, they drifted slantwise like silver seeds, like migrating sparks.

We heard, arising from somewhere near the car, the raucous scolding of blue jays. "They're pestering something," said Don. "A hawk?" I guessed. "Or an owl maybe," he said.

Putting off our weariness, we jogged on numb legs toward the noise. There were six or eight jays swooping and squawking about the hollow crown of a dead beech. "That's got to be an owl tree," Don whispered.

At our approach, the jays spiraled away, screeching indignantly. Don and I circled the beech in opposite directions, eyes alert for any movement in the tree's rot-blackened top. But we met on the far side of the circle without having spied anything. "You go beat on the trunk with a stick," Don suggested, "and I'll keep watch." "How would a great horned owl, say, feel about somebody come knocking on his tree?" I asked. "He wouldn't like it one bit," Don allowed. "What's he likely to do about it?" The creases about Don's eyes deepened. "He's likely to come out fast," he said, "too fast for messing with you or me, and then he's going to disappear in about half a blink."

Unreassured, I picked up a stout branch from the ground, approached the hollow beech, and gave the trunk a polite thwack, "Hit it hard," Don urged. So I grasped the stick with both hands and slammed the tree a few homerun blows. Between strokes I glanced up, to catch a glimpse of anything that might fly from the rotten peak. Or anything that might come plummeting down on me, talons lowered for the kill. Nothing flew, nothing plummeted. After a few more thumps, Don called "It's no use. If the jays had an owl in there, it was gone before we got here."

I dropped the stick, feeling a little ashamed, as if, in the daylight, I had tried to summon up by brute force what only patience and stillness had been able to summon up in the darkness. The hollow beech was a reminder, if I needed a reminder, that owls will not be bullied. You can hoot at them until you're blue in the face, but they will only answer when they please, if they please. Talking with them is like soliciting a word from the gods. There are rituals to be observed, such as choosing the right season of year and time of day. Certain owl-callers, like certain priests, enjoy better luck than others. But after you have made all your preparations, you can only wait. If the owls choose to remain invisible and silent, then, like the gods, silent and invisible they will remain. There are no switches you can throw to make them perform. They fly their own missions, speak their own messages, with no more regard for us than the moon has.

From the car, I turned to look back down at the lake. The mists had now almost all dissolved away into daylight. The whirlwinds of steam had ceased their revels. In the ragged patches of open water near the middle of the lake, a few ducks and geese congregated. The two bald eagles spotted here this season would find the hunting poor. Another week of freezing weather would close the lake entirely, driving water birds south, and the eagles after them. But the owls would stay on. Adaptable, stealthy, expert at killing and not overly particular about what they eat, they would endure. They *will* endure. By keeping to the night-side, owls avoid their one dangerous enemy—us, lords of the day-side. So long as there are woods, and not too much poison, there will be owls. So long as there are owls, we can hear night-voices and remain humble.

"I rejoice that there are owls," says Thoreau. "Let them do the idiotic and maniacal hooting for men. It is a sound admirably suited to swamps and woods which no day illustrates, suggesting a vast and undeveloped nature which men have not recognized." Most of us still don't recognize that "undeveloped nature," that nature which dances and unfurls its life without regard to human purposes. We can't hear the earth sing above all the racket our species makes. Listening to owls is a cure for such deafness.

1982

Joan Didion

ON GOING HOME

I am home for my daughter's first birthday. By "home" I do not mean the house in Los Angeles where my husband and I and the baby live, but the place where my family is, in the Central Valley of California. It is a vital although troublesome distinction. My husband likes my family but is uneasy in their house, because once there I fall into their ways, which are difficult, oblique, deliberately inarticulate, not my husband's ways. We live in dusty houses ("D-U-S-T," he once wrote with his finger on surfaces all over the house, but no one noticed it) filled with mementos quite without value to him (what could the Canton dessert plates mean to him? how could he have known about the assay scales, why should he care if he did know?), and we appear to talk exclusively about people we know who have been committed to mental hospitals, about people we know who have been booked on drunk-driving charges, and about property, particularly about property, land, price per acre and C-2 zoning and assessments and freeway access. My brother does not understand my husband's inability to perceive the advantage in the rather common real-estate transaction known as "sale-leaseback," and my husband in turn does not understand why so many of the people he hears about in my father's house have recently been committed to mental hospitals or booked on drunk-driving charges. Nor does he understand that when we talk about sale-leasebacks and right-of-way condemnations we are talking in code about the things we like best, the yellow fields and the cotton-woods and the rivers rising and falling and the mountain roads closing when the heavy snow comes in. We miss each other's points, have another drink and regard the fire. My brother refers to my husband, in his presence, as "Joan's husband." Marriage is the classic betrayal.

Or perhaps it is not any more. Sometimes I think that those of us who are now in our thirties were born into the last generation to carry the burden of "home," to find in family life the source of all tension and drama. I had by all objective accounts a "normal" and a "happy" family situation, and yet I was almost thirty years old before I could talk to my family on the telephone without crying after I had hung up. We did not fight. Nothing was wrong. And yet some nameless anxiety colored the emotional charges between me and the place that I came from. The question of whether or not you could go home again was a very real part of the sentimental and largely literary baggage with which we left home in the fifties; I suspect that it is irrelevant to the children born of the fragmentation after World War II. A few weeks ago in a San Francisco bar I saw a pretty young girl on crystal take off her clothes and dance for the cash prize in an "amateur-topless" contest. There was no particular sense of moment about this, none of the effect of romantic degradation, of "dark journey," for which my generation strived so assiduously. What sense could that girl possibly make of, say, Long Day's Journey into Night?[1] Who is beside the point?

That I am trapped in this particular irrelevancy is never more apparent to me than when I am home. Paralyzed by the neurotic lassitude engendered by meeting one's past at every turn, around every corner, inside every cupboard, I go aimlessly from room to room. I decide to meet it head-on and clean out a drawer, and I spread the contents on the bed. A bathing suit I wore the summer I was seventeen. A letter of rejection from The Nation, an aerial photograph of the site for a shopping center

1. A powerful domestic tragedy by the modern American playwright Eugene O'Neill, based on his early life.

my father did not build in 1954. Three teacups hand-painted with cabbage roses and signed "E.M.," my grandmother's initials. There is no final solution for letters of rejection from The Nation and teacups hand-painted in 1900. Nor is there any answer to snapshots of one's grandfather as a young man on skis, surveying around Donner Pass in the year 1910. I smooth out the snapshot and look into his face, and do and do not see my own. I close the drawer, and have another cup of coffee with my mother. We get along very well, veterans of a guerrilla war we never understood.

Days pass. I see no one. I come to dread my husband's evening call, not only because he is full of news of what by now seems to me our remote life in Los Angeles, people he has seen, letters which require attention, but because he asks what I have been doing, suggests uneasily that I get out, drive to San Francisco or Berkeley. Instead I drive across the river to a family graveyard. It has been vandalized since my last visit and the monuments are broken, overturned in the dry grass. Because I once saw a rattlesnake in the grass I stay in the car and listen to a country-and-Western station. Later I drive with my father to a ranch he has in the foothills. The man who runs his cattle on it asks us to the roundup, a week from Sunday, and although I know that I will be in Los Angeles I say, in the oblique way my family talks, that I will come. Once home I mention the broken monuments in the graveyard. My mother shrugs.

I go to visit my great-aunts. A few of them think now that I am my cousin, or their daughter who died young. We recall an anecdote about a relative last seen in 1948, and they ask if I still like living in New York City. I have lived in Los Angeles for three years, but I say that I do. The baby is offered a horehound drop, and I am slipped a dollar bill "to buy a treat." Questions trail off, answers are abandoned, the baby plays with the dust motes in a shaft of afternoon sun.

It is time for the baby's birthday party: a white cake, strawberry-marshmallow ice cream, a bottle of champagne saved from another party. In the evening, after she has gone to sleep, I kneel beside the crib and touch her face, where it is pressed against the slats, with mine. She is an open and trusting child, unprepared for and unaccustomed to the ambushes of family life, and perhaps it is just as well that I can offer her little of that life. I would like to give her more. I would like to promise her that she will grow up with a sense of her cousins and of rivers and of her great-grandmother's teacups, would like to pledge her a picnic on a river with fried chicken and her hair uncombed, would like to give her home for her birthday, but we live differently now and I can promise her nothing like that. I give her a xylophone and a sundress from Madeira, and promise to tell her a funny story.

1966

THE READER

1. Does the author take a single attitude or several toward "home"? Try to specify the attitude or attitudes.
2. What does the author mean by "the ambushes of family life" (p. 71)?
3. Explain whether the essay gives you any clues as to why so much of the talk at home is "about people we know who have been committed to mental hospitals, about people we know who have been booked on drunk-driving charges, and about property" (p. 70)?
4. In her concluding sentence, the author tells us she gives as birthday gifts to her daughter "a xylophone and a sundress from Madeira." Are these appropriate? Why or why not? Explain why she would like to give other gifts.
5. In "On Keeping a Notebook," Didion says that it is good to keep in touch with the people we used to be (p. 733). Is her account of this visit an effort to do that? Are there recalled phrases and observations in "On Going Home" like those she quotes from her notebooks, or does the different argument change the character of the phrases and observations she recalls?

THE WRITER

1. The author speaks of herself at home as "paralyzed by the neurotic lassitude engendered by meeting one's past at every turn" (p. 70). What details in the essay help explain that feeling?
2. If you have read or seen the play, explain the appropriateness of the author's reference (p. 70) to O'Neill's Long Day's Journey into Night.
3. Didion speaks of family life as "the source of all tension and drama." Point to details in the essay that illustrate that view. What kinds of details about her family might she have considered but rejected because they didn't advance that view or, indeed, contradicted it?
4. Write an essay about a trip you have made back to your home or back to a place you were once familiar with.

Loren Eiseley

THE BROWN WASPS

There is a corner in the waiting room of one of the great Eastern stations where women never sit. It is always in the shadow and overhung by rows of lockers. It is, however, always frequented—not so much by genuine travelers as by the dying. It is here that a certain element of the abandoned poor seeks a refuge out of the weather, clinging for a few hours longer to the city that has fathered them. In a precisely similar manner I have seen, on a sunny day in midwinter, a few old brown wasps creep slowly over an abandoned wasp nest in a thicket. Numbed and forgetful and frost-blackened, the hum of the spring hive still resounded faintly in their sodden tissues. Then the temperature would fall and they would drop away into the white oblivion of the snow. Here in the station it is in no way different save that the city is busy in its snows. But the old ones cling to their seats as though these were symbolic and could not be given up. Now and then they sleep, their gray old heads resting with painful awkwardness on the backs of the benches.

Also they are not at rest. For an hour they may sleep in the gasping exhaustion of the ill-nourished and aged who have to walk in the night. Then a policeman comes by on his round and nudges them upright.

"You can't sleep here," he growls.

A strange ritual then begins. An old man is difficult to waken. After a muttered conversation the policeman presses a coin into his hand and passes fiercely along the benches prodding and gesturing toward the door. In his wake, like birds rising and settling behind the passage of a farmer through a cornfield, the men totter up, move a few paces and subside once more upon the benches.

One man, after a slight, apologetic lurch, does not move at all. Tubercularly thin, he sleeps on steadily. The policeman does not look back. To him, too, this has become a ritual. He will not have to notice it again officially for another hour.

Once in a while one of the sleepers will not awake. Like the brown wasps, he will have had his wish to die in the great droning center of the hive rather than in some lonely room. It is not so bad here with the shuffle of footsteps and the knowledge that there are others who share the bad luck of the world. There are also the whistles and the sounds of everyone, everyone in the world, starting on journeys. Amidst so many journeys somebody is bound to come out all right. Somebody.

Maybe it was on a like thought that the brown wasps fell away from the old paper nest in the thicket. You hold till the last, even if it is only to a public seat in a railroad station. You want your place in the hive more than you want a room or a place where the aged can be eased gently out of the way. It is the place that matters, the place at the heart of things. It is life that you want, that bruises your gray old head with the hard chairs; a man has a right to his place.

But sometimes the place is lost in the years behind us. Or sometimes it is a thing of air, a kind of vaporous distortion above a heap of rubble. We cling to a time and place because without them man is lost, not only man but life. This is why the voices, real or unreal, which speak from the floating trumpets at spiritualist seances are so unnerving. They are voices out of nowhere whose only reality lies in their ability to stir the memory of a living person with some fragment of the past. Before the medium's cabinet both the dead and the living revolve endlessly about an episode, a place, an event that has already been engulfed by time.

This feeling runs deep in life; it brings stray cats running over endless miles, and birds homing from the ends of the earth. It is as though all living creatures, and particularly the more intelligent, can survive only by fixing or transforming a bit of time into space or by securing a bit of space with its objects immortalized and made permanent in time. For example, I once saw, on a flower pot in my own living room, the efforts of a field mouse to build a remembered field. I have lived to see this episode repeated in a thousand guises, and since I have spent a large portion of my life in the shade of a nonexistent tree, I think I am entitled to speak for the field mouse.

One day as I cut across the field which at that time extended on one side of our suburban shopping center, I found a giant slug feeding from a runnel of pink ice cream in an abandoned Dixie cup. I could see his eyes telescope and protrude in a kind of dim, uncertain ecstasy as his dark body bunched and elongated in the curve of the cup. Then, as I stood there at the edge of the concrete, contemplating the slug, I began to realize it was like standing on a shore where a different type of life creeps up and fumbles tentatively among the rocks and sea wrack. It knows its place and will only creep so far until something changes. Little by little as I stood there I began to see more of this shore that surrounds the place of man. I looked with sudden care and attention at things I had been running over thoughtlessly for years. I even waded out a short way into the grass and the wild-rose thickets to see more. A huge black-belted bee went droning by and there were some indistinct scurryings in the underbrush.

Then I came to a sign which informed me that this field was to be the site of a new Wanamaker suburban store. Thousands of obscure lives were about to perish, the spores of puffballs would go smoking off to new fields, and the bodies of little white-footed mice would be crunched under the inexorable wheels of the bulldozers. Life disappears or modifies its appearances so fast that everything takes on an aspect of illusion— a momentary fizzing and boiling with smoke rings, like pouring dissident chemicals into a retort. Here man was advancing, but in a few years his plaster and bricks would be disappearing once more into the insatiable maw of the clover. Being of an archaeological cast of mind, I thought of this fact with an obscure sense of satisfaction and waded back through the rose thickets to the concrete parking lot. As I did so, a mouse scurried ahead of me, frightened of my steps if not of that ominous Wanamaker sign. I saw him vanish in the general direction of my apartment house, his little body quivering with fear in the great open sun on the blazing concrete. Blinded and confused, he was running straight away from his field. In another week scores would follow him.

I forgot the episode then and went home to the quiet of my living room. It was not until a week later, letting myself into the apartment, that I realized I had a visitor. I am fond of plants and had several ferns standing on the floor in pots to avoid the noon glare by the south window.

As I snapped on the light and glanced carelessly around the room, I saw a little heap of earth on the carpet and a scrabble of pebbles that had been kicked merrily over the edge of one of the flower pots. To my astonishment I discovered a full-fledged burrow delving downward among the fern roots. I waited silently. The creature who had made the burrow did not appear. I remembered the wild field then, and the flight of the mice. No house mouse, no *Mus domesticus*, had kicked up this little heap of earth or sought refuge under a fern root in a flower pot. I thought of the desperate little creature I had seen fleeing from the wild-rose thicket. Through intricacies of pipes and attics, he, or one of his fellows, had climbed to this high green solitary room. I could visualize what had occurred. He had an image in his head, a world of seed pods and quiet, of green sheltering leaves in the dim light among the weed stems. It was the only world he knew and it was gone.

Somehow in his flight he had found his way to this room with drawn shades where no one would come till nightfall. And here he had smelled green leaves and run quickly up the flower pot to dabble his paws in common earth. He had even struggled half the afternoon to carry his burrow deeper and had failed. I examined the hole, but no whiskered twitching face appeared. He was gone. I gathered up the earth and refilled the burrow. I did not expect to find traces of him again.

Yet for three nights thereafter I came home to the darkened room and my ferns to find the dirt kicked gaily about the rug and the burrow reopened, though I was never able to catch the field mouse within it. I dropped a little food about the mouth of the burrow, but it was never touched. I looked under beds or sat reading with one ear cocked for rustlings in the ferns. It was all in vain; I never saw him. Probably he ended in a trap in some other tenant's room.

But before he disappeared I had come to look hopefully for his evening burrow. About my ferns there had begun to linger the insubstantial vapor of an autumn field, the distilled essence, as it were, of a mouse brain in exile from its home. It was a small dream, like our dreams, carried a long and weary journey along pipes and through spider webs, past holes over which loomed the shadows of waiting cats, and finally, desperately, into this room where he had played in the shuttered daylight for an hour among the green ferns on the floor. Every day these invisible dreams pass us on the street, or rise from beneath our feet, or look out upon us from beneath a bush.

Some years ago the old elevated railway in Philadelphia was torn down and replaced by a subway system. This ancient El with its barnlike stations containing nut-vending machines and scattered food scraps had, for generations, been the favorite feeding ground of flocks of pigeons, generally one flock to a station along the route of the El. Hundreds of pigeons were dependent upon the system. They flapped in and out of its stanchions and steel work or gathered in watchful little audiences about the feet of anyone who rattled the peanut-vending machines. They even watched people who jingled change in their hands, and prospected for food under the feet of the crowds who gathered between trains. Probably very few among the waiting people who tossed a crumb to an eager pigeon realized that this El was like a food-bearing river, and that the life which haunted its banks was dependent upon the running of the trains with their human freight.

I saw the river stop.

The time came when the underground tubes were ready; the traffic was transferred to a realm unreachable by pigeons. It was like a great river subsiding suddenly into desert sands. For a day, for two days, pigeons continued to circle over the El or stand close to the red vending machines. They were patient birds, and surely this great river which had flowed through the lives of unnumbered generations was merely suffering from some momentary drought.

They listened for the familiar vibrations that had always heralded an approaching train; they flapped hopefully about the head of an occasional workman walking along the steel runways. They passed from one empty station to another, all the while growing hungrier. Finally they flew away.

I thought I had seen the last of them about the El, but there was a revival and it provided a curious instance of the memory of living things for a way of life or a locality that has long been cherished. Some weeks after the El was abandoned workmen began to tear it down. I went to work every morning by one particular station, and the time came when the demolition crews reached this spot. Acetylene torches showered passersby with sparks, pneumatic drills hammered at the base of the structure, and a blind man who, like the pigeons, had clung with his cup to a stairway leading to the change booth, was forced to give up his place.

It was then, strangely, momentarily, one morning that I witnessed the return of a little band of the familiar pigeons. I even recognized one or two members of the flock that had lived around this particular station before they were dispersed into the streets. They flew bravely in and out among the sparks and the hammers and the shouting workmen. They had returned—and they had returned because the hubbub of the wreckers had convinced them that the river was about to flow once more. For several hours they flapped in and out through the empty windows, nodding their heads and watching the fall of girders with attentive little eyes. By the following morning the station was reduced to some burned-off stanchions in the street. My bird friends had gone. It was plain, however, that they retained a memory for an insubstantial structure now compounded of air and time. Even the blind man clung to it. Someone had provided him with a chair, and he sat at the same corner staring sightlessly at an invisible stairway where, so far as he was concerned, the crowds were still ascending to the trains.

I have said my life has been passed in the shade of a nonexistent tree, so that such sights do not offend me. Prematurely I am one of the brown wasps and I often sit with them in the great droning hive of the station, dreaming sometimes of a certain tree. It was planted sixty years ago by a boy with a bucket and a toy spade in a little Nebraska town. That boy was myself. It was a cottonwood sapling and the boy remembered it because of some words spoken by his father and because everyone died or moved away who was supposed to wait and grow old under its shade. The boy was passed from hand to hand, but the tree for some intangible reason had taken root in his mind. It was under its branches that he sheltered; it was from this tree that his memories, which are my memories, led away into the world.

After sixty years the mood of the brown wasps grows heavier upon one. During a long inward struggle I thought it would do me good to go and look upon that actual tree. I found a rational excuse in which to clothe this madness. I purchased a ticket and at the end of two thousand miles I walked another mile to an address that was still the same. The house had not been altered.

I came close to the white picket fence and reluctantly, with great effort, looked down the long vista of the yard. There was nothing there to see. For sixty years that cottonwood had been growing in my mind. Season by season its seeds had been floating farther on the hot prairie winds. We had planted it lovingly there, my father and I, because he had a great hunger for soil and live things growing, and because none of these things had long been ours to protect. We had planted the little sapling and watered it faithfully, and I remembered that I had run out with my small bucket to drench its roots the day we moved away. And all the years since it had been growing in my mind, a huge tree that somehow stood for my father and the love I bore him. I took a grasp on the picket fence and forced myself to look again.

A boy with the hard bird eye of youth pedaled a tricycle slowly up beside me.

"What'cha lookin' at?" he asked curiously.

"A tree," I said.

"What for?" he said.

"It isn't there," I said, to myself mostly, and began to walk away at a pace just slow enough not to seem to be running.

"What isn't there?" the boy asked. I didn't answer. It was obvious I was attached by a thread to a thing that had never been there, or certainly not for long. Something that had to be held in the air, or sustained in the mind, because it was part of my orientation in the universe and I could not survive without it. There was more than an animal's attachment to a place. There was something else, the attachment of the spirit to a grouping of events in time; it was part of our morality.

So I had come home at last, driven by a memory in the brain as surely as the field mouse who had delved long ago into my flower pot or the pigeons flying forever amidst the rattle of nut-vending machines. These, the burrow under the greenery in my living room and the red-bellied bowls of peanuts now hovering in midair in the minds of pigeons, were all part of an elusive world that existed nowhere and yet everywhere. I looked once at the real world about me while the persistent boy pedaled at my heels.

It was without meaning, though my feet took a remembered path. In sixty years the house and street had rotted out of my mind. But the tree, the tree that no longer was, that had perished in its first season, bloomed on in my individual mind, unblemished as my father's words. "We'll plant a tree here, son, and we're not going to move any more. And when you're an old, old man you can sit under it and think how we planted it here, you and me, together."

I began to outpace the boy on the tricycle.

"Do you live here, Mister?" he shouted after me suspiciously. I took a firm grasp on airy nothing—to be precise, on the bole of a great tree. "I do," I said. I spoke for myself, one field mouse, and several pigeons. We were all out of touch but somehow permanent. It was the world that had changed.

1971

THE READER

1. Eiseley writes of old men in train stations, brown wasps, a field mouse, pigeons near the El, and his own return to his boyhood home in Nebraska. What do these matters have in common? Can you state the essay's theme?

2. In "Once More to the Lake" (p. 79), White describes his return to a lake he had known years earlier. What reflections arise in his mind on this occasion? Are they similar to, or different from, Eiseley's thoughts upon returning to his Nebraska home and the nonexistent tree?

3. Would Eiseley agree with Thoreau's remarks in "Observation" (p. 193)? If so, in what particular ways would he agree?

THE WRITER

1. Some psychologists study animal behavior in order to learn about human behavior, but many of them write about animals in a very different fashion. Do you think that Eiseley's way of relating the behavior of animals to human behavior makes sense? If you are studying psychology, it might be interesting to compare a selection from

your textbook with this essay.

2. *Eiseley's essay contains sentences like "We cling to a time and place because without them man is lost, not only man but life" (p. 73) and "A boy with the hard bird eye of youth pedaled a tricycle slowly up beside me" (p. 77). What is the difference between these two kinds of sentences? Can you show how Eiseley manages to connect one kind with the other?*

3. *Write an essay comparing the theme or purpose of "The Brown Wasps" with that of Lorenz's "The Taming of the Shrew" (p. 879). Does Lorenz take a similar approach to his subject? Consider also the manner of the writing: how would you characterize it in each instance?*

E. B. White

ONCE MORE TO THE LAKE

One summer, along about 1904, my father rented a camp on a lake in Maine and took us all there for the month of August. We all got ringworm from some kittens and had to rub Pond's Extract on our arms and legs night and morning, and my father rolled over in a canoe with all his clothes on; but outside of that the vacation was a success and from then on none of us ever thought there was any place in the world like that lake in Maine. We returned summer after summer—always on August 1st for one month. I have since become a salt-water man, but sometimes in summer there are days when the restlessness of the tides and the fearful cold of the sea water and the incessant wind which blows across the afternoon and into the evening make me wish for the placidity of a lake in the woods. A few weeks ago this feeling got so strong I bought myself a couple of bass hooks and a spinner and returned to the lake where we used to go, for a week's fishing and to revisit old haunts.

I took along my son, who had never had any fresh water up his nose and who had seen lily pads only from train windows. On the journey over to the lake I began to wonder what it would be like. I wondered how time would have marred this unique, this holy spot—the coves and streams, the hills that the sun set behind, the camps and the paths behind the camps. I was sure the tarred road would have found it out and I wondered in what other ways it would be desolated. It is strange how much you can remember about places like that once you allow your mind to return into the grooves which lead back. You remember one thing, and that suddenly reminds you of another thing. I guess I remembered clearest of all the early mornings, when the lake was cool and motionless, remembered how the bedroom smelled of the lumber it was made of and of the wet woods whose scent entered through the screen. The partitions in the camp were thin and did not extend clear to the top of the rooms, and as I was always the first up I would dress softly so as not to wake the others, and sneak out into the sweet outdoors and start out in the canoe, keeping close along the shore in the long shadows of the pines. I remembered being very careful never to rub my paddle against the gunwale for fear of disturbing the stillness of the cathedral.

The lake had never been what you would call a wild lake. There were cottages sprinkled around the shores, and it was in farming country although the shores of the lake were quite heavily wooded. Some of the cottages were owned by nearby farmers, and you would live at the shore and eat your meals at the farmhouse. That's what our family did. But although it wasn't wild, it was a fairly large and undisturbed lake and there were places in it which, to a child at least, seemed infinitely remote and primeval.

I was right about the tar: it led to within half a mile of the shore. But when I got back there, with my boy, and we settled into a camp near a farmhouse and into the kind of summertime I had known, I could tell that it was going to be pretty much the same as it had been before—I knew it, lying in bed the first morning, smelling the bedroom, and hearing the boy sneak quietly out and go off along the shore in a boat. I began to sustain the illusion that he was I, and therefore, by simple transposition, that I was my father. This sensation persisted, kept cropping up all the time we were there. It was not an entirely new feeling, but in this setting it grew much stronger. I seemed to be living a dual existence. I would be in the middle of some simple act, I would be picking up a bait box or laying down a table fork, or I would be saying something, and suddenly it would be not I but my father who was saying the words or making the gesture. It gave me a creepy sensation.

We went fishing the first morning. I felt the same damp moss covering the worms in the bait can, and saw the dragonfly alight on the tip of my rod as it hovered a few inches from the surface of the water. It was the arrival of this fly that convinced me beyond any doubt that everything was as it always had been, that the years were a mirage and there had been no years. The small waves were the same, chucking the rowboat under the chin as we fished at anchor, and the boat was the same boat, the same color green and the ribs broken in the same places, and under the floor-boards the same fresh-water leavings and débris—the dead helgramite,[1] the wisps of moss, the rusty discarded fishhook, the dried blood from yesterday's catch. We stared silently at the tips of our rods, at the dragonflies that came and went. I lowered the tip of mine into the water, tentatively, pensively dislodging the fly, which darted two feet away,

1. The nymph of the May-fly, used as bait.

poised, darted two feet back, and came to rest again a little farther up the rod. There had been no years between the ducking of this dragonfly and the other one—the one that was part of memory. I looked at the boy, who was silently watching his fly, and it was my hands that held his rod, my eyes watching. I felt dizzy and didn't know which rod I was at the end of.

We caught two bass, hauling them in briskly as though they were mackerel, pulling them over the side of the boat in a businesslike manner without any landing net, and stunning them with a blow on the back of the head. When we got back for a swim before lunch, the lake was exactly where we had left it, the same number of inches from the dock, and there was only the merest suggestion of a breeze. This seemed an utterly enchanted sea, this lake you could leave to its own devices for a few hours and come back to, and find that it had not stirred, this constant and trustworthy body of water. In the shallows, the dark, water-soaked sticks and twigs, smooth and old, were undulating in clusters on the bottom against the clean ribbed sand, and the track of the mussel was plain. A school of minnows swam by, each minnow with its small individual shadow, doubling the attendance, so clear and sharp in the sunlight. Some of the other campers were in swimming, along the shore, one of them with a cake of soap, and the water felt thin and clear and unsubstantial. Over the years there had been this person with the cake of soap, this cultist, and here he was. There had been no years.

Up to the farmhouse to dinner through the teeming, dusty field, the road under our sneakers was only a two-track road. The middle track was missing, the one with the marks of the hooves and the splotches of dried, flaky manure. There had always been three tracks to choose from in choosing which track to walk in; now the choice was narrowed down to two. For a moment I missed terribly the middle alternative. But the way led past the tennis court, and something about the way it lay there in the sun reassured me; the tape had loosened along the backline, the alleys were green with plantains and other weeds, and the net (installed in June and removed in September) sagged in the dry noon, and the whole place steamed with midday heat and hunger and emptiness. There was a choice of pie for dessert, and one was blueberry and one was apple, and the waitresses were the same country girls, there having been no passage of time, only the illusion of it as in a dropped curtain—the waitresses were still fifteen; their hair had been washed, that was the only difference —they had been to the movies and seen the pretty girls with the clean hair.

Summertime, oh summertime, pattern of life indelible, the fade-proof lake, the woods unshatterable, the pasture with the sweetfern and the juniper forever and ever, summer without end; this was the background, and the life along the shore was the design, the cottagers with their innocent and tranquil design, their tiny docks with the flagpole and the

American flag floating against the white clouds in the blue sky, the little paths over the roots of the trees leading from camp to camp and the paths leading back to the outhouses and the can of lime for sprinkling, and at the souvenir counters at the store the miniature birch-bark canoes and the post cards that showed things looking a little better than they looked. This was the American family at play, escaping the city heat, wondering whether the newcomers in the camp at the head of the cove were "common" or "nice," wondering whether it was true that the people who drove up for Sunday dinner at the farmhouse were turned away because there wasn't enough chicken.

It seemed to me, as I kept remembering all this, that those times and those summers had been infinitely precious and worth saving. There had been jollity and peace and goodness. The arriving (at the beginning of August) had been so big a business in itself, at the railway station the farm wagon drawn up, the first smell of the pine-laden air, the first glimpse of the smiling farmer, and the great importance of the trunks and your father's enormous authority in such matters, and the feel of the wagon under you for the long ten-mile haul, and at the top of the last long hill catching the first view of the lake after eleven months of not seeing this cherished body of water. The shouts and cries of the other campers when they saw you, and the trunks to be unpacked, to give up their rich burden. (Arriving was less exciting nowadays, when you sneaked up in your car and parked it under a tree near the camp and took out the bags and in five minutes it was all over, no fuss, no loud wonderful fuss about trunks.)

Peace and goodness and jollity. The only thing that was wrong now, really, was the sound of the place, an unfamiliar nervous sound of the outboard motors. This was the note that jarred, the one thing that would sometimes break the illusion and set the years moving. In those other summertimes all motors were inboard; and when they were at a little distance, the noise they made was a sedative, an ingredient of summer sleep. They were one-cylinder and two-cylinder engines, and some were make-and-break and some were jump-spark,[2] but they all made a sleepy sound across the lake. The one-lungers throbbed and fluttered, and the twin-cylinder ones purred and purred, and that was a quiet sound too. But now the campers all had outboards. In the daytime, in the hot mornings, these motors made a petulant, irritable sound; at night, in the still evening when the afterglow lit the water, they whined about one's ears like mosquitoes. My boy loved our rented outboard, and his great desire was to achieve singlehanded mastery over it, and authority, and he soon learned the trick of choking it a little (but not too much), and the adjustment of the needle valve. Watching him I would remember the

2. Methods of ignition timing.

things you could do with the old one-cylinder engine with the heavy flywheel, how you could have it eating out of your hand if you got really close to it spiritually. Motor boats in those days didn't have clutches, and you would make a landing by shutting off the motor at the proper time and coasting in with a dead rudder. But there was a way of reversing them, if you learned the trick, by cutting the switch and putting it on again exactly on the final dying revolution of the flywheel, so that it would kick back against compression and begin reversing. Approaching a dock in a strong following breeze, it was difficult to slow up sufficiently by the ordinary coasting method, and if a boy felt he had complete mastery over his motor, he was tempted to keep it running beyond its time and then reverse it a few feet from the dock. It took a cool nerve, because if you threw the switch a twentieth of a second too soon you would catch the flywheel when it still had speed enough to go up past center, and the boat would leap ahead, charging bull-fashion at the dock.

We had a good week at the camp. The bass were biting well and the sun shone endlessly, day after day. We would be tired at night and lie down in the accumulated heat of the little bedrooms after the long hot day and the breeze would stir almost imperceptibly outside and the smell of the swamp drift in through the rusty screens. Sleep would come easily and in the morning the red squirrel would be on the roof, tapping out his gay routine. I kept remembering everything, lying in bed in the mornings —the small steamboat that had a long rounded stern like the lip of a Ubangi, and how quietly she ran on the moonlight sails, when the older boys played their mandolins and the girls sang and we ate doughnuts dipped in sugar, and how sweet the music was on the water in the shining night, and what it had felt like to think about girls then. After breakfast we would go up to the store and the things were in the same place—the minnows in a bottle, the plugs and spinners disarranged and pawed over by the youngsters from the boys' camp, the fig newtons and the Beeman's gum. Outside, the road was tarred and cars stood in front of the store. Inside, all was just as it had always been, except there was more Coca-Cola and not so much Moxie and root beer and birch beer and sarsaparilla. We would walk out with a bottle of pop apiece and sometimes the pop would backfire up our noses and hurt. We explored the streams, quietly, where the turtles slid off the sunny logs and dug their way into the soft bottom; and we lay on the town wharf and fed worms to the tame bass. Everywhere we went I had trouble making out which was I, the one walking at my side, the one walking in my pants.

One afternoon while we were there at that lake a thunderstorm came up. It was like the revival of an old melodrama that I had seen long ago with childish awe. The second-act climax of the drama of the electrical disturbance over a lake in America had not changed in any important respect. This was the big scene, still the big scene. The whole thing was so familiar, the first feeling of oppression and heat and a general air around camp of not wanting to go very far away. In midafternoon (it was all the same) a curious darkening of the sky, and a lull in everything that had made life tick; and then the way the boats suddenly swung the other way at their moorings with the coming of a breeze out of the new quarter, and the premonitory rumble. Then the kettle drum, then the snare, then the bass drum and cymbals, then crackling light against the dark, and the gods grinning and licking their chops in the hills. Afterward the calm, the rain steadily rustling in the calm lake, the return of light and hope and spirits, and the campers running out in joy and relief to go swimming in the rain, their bright cries perpetuating the deathless joke about how they were getting simply drenched, and the children screaming with delight at the new sensation of bathing in the rain, and the joke about getting drenched linking the generations in a strong indestructible chain. And the comedian who waded in carrying an umbrella.

When the others went swimming my son said he was going in too. He pulled his dripping trunks from the line where they had hung all through the shower, and wrung them out. Languidly, and with no thought of going in, I watched him, his hard little body, skinny and bare, saw him wince slightly as he pulled up around his vitals the small, soggy, icy garment. As he buckled the swollen belt suddenly my groin felt the chill of death.

1941

THE READER

1. *White had not been back to the lake for many years. What bearing has this fact on the experience the essay describes?*
2. *How do the differences between boats of the past and boats of today relate to or support the point of the essay?*
3. *What is the meaning of White's last sentence? What relation has it to the sentence just preceding? How has White prepared us for this ending?*
4. *Read White's "Some Remarks on Humor" (p. 1076). Is he writing humor in "Once More to the Lake"?*

THE WRITER

1. *What has guided White in his selection of the details he gives about the trip? Why, for example, does he talk about the road, the dragonfly, the bather with the cake of soap?*
2. *In "On Keeping a Notebook," Didion says that it is good to keep in touch with the people we used to be (p. 733). Is that what White is doing here?*
3. *Write an account of an experience, real or imagined, in which you return to a place you haven't seen for a while. Think about what point you wish to make through your narrative.*

Prose Forms: Journals

Occasionally one catches oneself having said something aloud, obviously with no concern to be heard, even by oneself. And all of us have overheard, perhaps while walking, a solitary person muttering or laughing softly or exclaiming abruptly. Something floats up from the world within, forces itself to be expressed, takes no real account of the time or the place, and certainly intends no conscious communication.

With more self-consciousness, and yet without a specific audience, one sometimes speaks out at something that has momentarily filled attention from the world without. A sharp play at the ball game, the twist of a political speech, an old photograph—something from the outer world impresses the mind, stimulates it, focuses certain of its memories and values, interests and needs. Thus stimulated, one may wish to share an experience with another, to inform or amuse that person, to rouse him or her to action or persuade someone to a certain belief. Often, though, the person experiencing may want most to talk to himself or herself, to give a public shape in words to thoughts and feelings but for the sake of a kind of private dialogue. Communication to another may be an ultimate desire, but the immediate motive is to articulate the experience for oneself.

To articulate, to shape the experience in language for one's own sake, one may keep a journal. Literally a day-book, the journal enables one to write down something about the experiences of a day which for a great variety of reasons may have been especially memorable or impressive. The journal entry may be merely a few words to call to mind a thing done, a person seen, a menu enjoyed at a dinner party. It may be concerned at length with a political crisis in the community, or a personal crisis in the home. It may even as noble as it was with some pious people in the past who used the journal to keep a record of their consciences, a periodic reckoning of their moral and spiritual accounts. In its most public aspect, the idea of a journal calls to mind the newspaper or the record of proceedings like the U.S. Congressional Record *and the Canadian* Hansard. *In its most closely private form, the journal becomes the* diary.

To keep a journal is to hold onto experiences through writing. But to get it down on paper begins another adventure. For the journalist has to focus on what he or she has experienced, and to be able to say what, in fact, the experience is. What of it is new? What of it is remarkable because of associations in the memory it stirs up? Is this like anything I— or others—have experienced before? Is it a good or a bad thing to have happened? And why, specifically? The questions multiply themselves quickly, and as the journalist seeks to answer the appropriate ones, he or she begins to know what is being contemplated. As one tries to find the words that best represent this discovery, the experience becomes even more clear in its shape and meaning. We can imagine Emerson going to the ballet, being absorbed in the spectacle, thinking casually of this or that association the dancer and the movements suggest. When he writes about the experience in his journal, a good many questions, judgments, and speculations get tied up with the spectacle, and it is this complex of event and this total relation to it that becomes the experience he records. The simple facts of time, place, people, and actions drop down into one's consciousness and set in motion ideas and feelings which give those facts their real meaning to oneself.

Once this consciousness of events is formulated in words, the journalist has it, not only in the sense of understanding what has been seen or felt or thought, but also in the sense of having it there to contemplate long after the event itself. When we read a carefully kept journal covering a long period and varied experiences, we have the pleasure of a small world re-created for us in the consciousness of one who experienced it. Even more, we feel the continuity, the wholeness, of the writer. Something of the same feeling is there for the person who kept the journal: a whole world of events preserved in the form of their experienced reality, and with it the persistent self in the midst of that world. That world and that self are always accessible on the page and ultimately, therefore, usably real.

Beyond the value of the journal as record, there is the instructive value of the habit of mind and hand journal keeping can assure. One begins to attend more carefully to what happens to and around oneself. One learns the resources of language as a means of representing what one sees, and gains skill and certainty in doing justice to experience and to one's own consciousness. And the journal represents a discipline. It brings together an individual and a complex environment in a relation that teaches the individual something of himself or herself, something of the world, and something of the meaning of their relation. There is scarcely a moment in life when one is not poised for the lesson. When it comes with the promise of special force, there is the almost irresistible temptation to catch the impulse, give it form, make it permanent, assert its meaning. And so one commits oneself to language. To have given up one's experience to words is to have begun marking out the limits and potential of its meaning. In the journal that meaning is developed and clarified to oneself primarily. When the whole intention of the development and the clarification is the consideration of another reader, the method of the journal redirects itself to become that of the essay.

Ralph Waldo Emerson: FROM JOURNAL

I like to have a man's knowledge comprehend more than one class of topics, one row of shelves. I like a man who likes to see a fine barn as well as a good tragedy. [1828]

The Religion that is afraid of science dishonors God and commits suicide. [1831]

The things taught in colleges and schools are not an education, but the means of education. [1831]

Don't tell me to get ready to die. I know not what shall be. The only preparation I can make is by fulfilling my present duties. This is the everlasting life. [1832]

My aunt [Mary Moody Emerson] had an eye that went through and through you like a needle. "She was endowed," she said, "with the fatal gift of penetration." She disgusted everybody because she knew them too well. [1832]

I am sure of this, that by going much alone a man will get more of a noble courage in thought and word than from all the wisdom that is in books. [1833]

I fretted the other night at the hotel at the stranger who broke into my chamber after midnight, claiming to share it. But after his lamp had smoked the chamber full and I had turned round to the wall in despair, the man blew out his lamp, knelt down at his bedside, and made in low whisper a long earnest prayer. Then was the relation entirely changed between us. I fretted no more, but respected and liked him. [1835]

I believe I shall some time cease to be an individual, that the eternal tendency of the soul is to become Universal, to animate the last extremities of organization. [1837]

It is very hard to be simple enough to be good. [1837]

A man must have aunts and cousins, must buy carrots and turnips, must have barn and woodshed, must go to market and to the blacksmith's shop, must saunter and sleep and be inferior and silly. [1838]

How sad a spectacle, so frequent nowadays, to see a young man after ten years of college education come out, ready for his voyage of life—and to see that the entire ship is made of rotten timber, of rotten, honeycombed, traditional timber without so much as an inch of new plank in the hull. [1839]

A sleeping child gives me the impression of a traveler in a very far country. [1840]

In reading these letters of M.M.E. I acknowledge (with surprise that I could ever forget it) the debt of myself and my brothers to that old religion which, in those years, still dwelt like a Sabbath peace in the country population of New England, which taught privation, self-denial, and sorrow. A man was born, not for prosperity, but to suffer for the benefit of others, like the noble rock-maple tree which all around the villages bleeds for the service of man.[1] Not praise, not men's acceptance of our doing, but the Spirit's holy errand through us, absorbed the thought. How dignified is this! how all that is called talents and worth in Paris and in Washington dwindles before it! [1841]

All writing is by the grace of God. People do not deserve to have good writing, they are so pleased with bad. In these sentences that you show me, I can find no beauty, for I see death in every clause and every word. There is a fossil or a mummy character which pervades this book. The best sepulchers, the vastest catacombs, Thebes and Cairo, Pyramids, are sepulchers to me. I like gardens and nurseries. Give me initiative, spermatic, prophesying, man-making words. [1841]

When summer opens, I see how fast it matures, and fear it will be short; but after the heats of July and August, I am reconciled, like one who has had his swing, to the cool of autumn. So will it be with the coming of death. [1846]

In England every man you meet is some man's son; in America, he may be some man's father. [1848]

Every poem must be made up of lines that are poems. [1848]

Love is necessary to the righting the estate of woman in this world. Otherwise nature itself seems to be in conspiracy against her dignity and welfare; for the cultivated, high-thoughted, beauty-loving, saintly woman finds herself unconsciously desired for her sex, and even enhancing the appetite of her savage pursuers by these fine ornaments she has piously laid on herself. She finds with indignation that she is herself a snare, and was made such. I do not wonder at her occasional protest, violent protest against nature, in fleeing to nunneries, and taking black veils. Love rights all this deep wrong. [1848]

Natural Aristocracy. It is a vulgar error to suppose that a gentleman must be ready to fight. The utmost that can be demanded of the gentleman is that he be incapable of a lie. There is a man who has good sense, is well informed, well-read, obliging, cultivated, capable, and has an

1. The sap of the rock or sugar maple is collected and made into maple syrup.

absolute devotion to truth. He always means what he says, and says what he means, however courteously. You may spit upon him—nothing could induce him to spit upon you—no praises, and no possessions, no compulsion of public opinion. You may kick him—he will think it the kick of a brute—but he is not a brute, and will not kick you in return. But neither your knife and pistol, nor your gifts and courting will ever make the smallest impression on his vote or word; for he is the truth's man, and will speak and act the truth until he dies. [1849]

Love is temporary and ends with marriage. Marriage is the perfection which love aimed at, ignorant of what it sought. Marriage is a good known only to the parties—a relation of perfect understanding, aid, contentment, possession of themselves and of the world—which dwarfs love to green fruit. [1850]

I found when I had finished my new lecture that it was a very good house, only the architect had unfortunately omitted the stairs. [1851]

This filthy enactment [The Fugitive Slave Law[2]] was made in the nineteenth century, by people who could read and write. I will not obey it, by God. [1851]

Henry [Thoreau] is military. He seemed stubborn and implacable; always manly and wise, but rarely sweet. One would say that, as Webster could never speak without an antagonist, so Henry does not feel himself except in opposition. He wants a fallacy to expose, a blunder to pillory, requires a little sense of victory, a roll of the drums, to call his powers into full exercise. [1853]

Shall we judge the country by the majority or by the minority? Certainly, by the minority. The mass are animal, in state of pupilage, and nearer the chimpanzee. [1854]

All the thoughts of a turtle are turtle. [1854]

Resources or feats. I like people who can do things. When Edward and I struggled in vain to drag our big calf into the barn, the Irish girl put her finger into the calf's mouth, and led her in directly. [1862]

George Francis Train said in a public speech in New York, "Slavery is a divine institution." "So is hell," exclaimed an old man in the crowd. [1862]

You complain that the Negroes are a base class. Who makes and keeps the Jew or the Negro base, who but you, who exclude them from the rights which others enjoy? [1867]

---

2. A law enacted in 1850 to compel the arrest of runaway slaves and their return to their owners.

Henry David Thoreau: FROM JOURNAL

As the least drop of wine tinges the whole goblet, so the least particle of truth colors our whole life. It is never isolated, or simply added as treasure to our stock. When any real progress is made, we unlearn and learn anew what we thought we knew before. [1837]

Not by constraint or severity shall you have access to true wisdom, but by abandonment, and childlike mirthfulness. If you would know aught, be gay before it. [1840]

It is the man determines what is said, not the words. If a mean person uses a wise maxim, I bethink me how it can be interpreted so as to commend itself to his meanness; but if a wise man makes a commonplace remark, I consider what wider construction it will admit. [1840]

Nothing goes by luck in composition. It allows of no tricks. The best you can write will be the best you are. Every sentence is the result of a long probation. The author's character is read from title-page to end. Of this he never corrects the proofs. We read it as the essential character of a handwriting without regard to the flourishes. And so of the rest of our actions; it runs as straight as a ruled line through them all, no matter how many curvets about it. Our whole life is taxed for the least thing well done: it is its net result. How we eat, drink, sleep, and use our desultory hours, now in these indifferent days, with no eye to observe and no occasion [to] excite us, determines our authority and capacity for the time to come. [1841]

What does education often do? It makes a straight-cut ditch of a free, meandering brook. [1850]

All perception of truth is the detection of an analogy; we reason from our hands to our head. [1851]

To set down such choice experiences that my own writings may inspire me and at last I may make wholes of parts. Certainly it is a distinct profession to rescue from oblivion and to fix the sentiments and thoughts which visit all men more or less generally, that the contemplation of the unfinished picture may suggest its harmonious completion. Associate reverently and as much as you can with your loftiest thoughts. Each thought that is welcomed and recorded is a nest egg, by the side of which more will be laid. Thoughts accidentally thrown together become a frame in which more may be developed and exhibited. Perhaps this is the main value of a habit of writing, of keeping a journal—that so we remember our best hours and stimulate ourselves. My thoughts are my company. They have a certain individuality and separate existence, aye, personality. Having by chance recorded a few disconnected thoughts and then brought them into juxtaposition, they suggest a whole new field in which it was possible to labor and to think. Thought begat thought. [1852]

It is pardonable when we spurn the proprieties, even the sanctities, making them stepping-stones to something higher. [1858]

There is always some accident in the best things, whether thoughts or expressions or deeds. The memorable thought, the happy expression, the admirable deed are only partly ours. The thought came to us because we were in a fit mood; also we were unconscious and did not know that we had said or done a good thing. We must walk consciously only part way toward our goal, and then leap in the dark to our success. What we do best or most perfectly is what we have most thoroughly learned by the longest practice, and at length it falls from us without our notice, as a leaf from a tree. It is the *last* time we shall do it—our unconscious leavings. [1859]

The expression "a *liberal* education" originally meant one worthy of freemen. Such is education simply in a true and broad sense. But education ordinarily so called—the learning of trades and professions which is designed to enable men to earn their living, or to fit them for a particular station in life—is *servile*. [1859]

Walt Whitman

ABRAHAM LINCOLN

August 12th.—I see the President almost every day, as I happen to live where he passes to or from his lodgings out of town. He never sleeps at the White House during the hot season, but has quarters at a healthy location some three miles north of the city, the Soldiers' home, a United States military establishment. I saw him this morning about 8½ coming in to business, riding on Vermont avenue, near L street. He always has a company of twenty-five or thirty cavalry, with sabres drawn and held upright over their shoulders. They say this guard was against his personal wish, but he let his counselors have their way. The party makes no great show in uniform or horses. Mr. Lincoln on the saddle generally rides a good-sized, easy-going gray horse, is dress'd in plain black, somewhat rusty and dusty, wears a black stiff hat, and looks about as ordinary in attire, &c., as the commonest man. A lieutenant, with yellow straps, rides at his left, and following behind, two by two, come the cavalry men, in their yellow-striped jackets. They are generally going at a slow trot, as that is the pace set them by the one they wait upon. The sabres and accoutrements clank, and the entirely unornamental *cortège* as it trots towards Lafayette square arouses no sensation, only some curious stranger stops and gazes. I see very plainly ABRAHAM LINCOLN's dark brown face, with the deep-cut lines, the eyes, always to me with a deep latent sadness in the expression. We have got so that we exchange bows, and very cordial ones. Sometimes the President goes and comes in an open barouche. The cavalry always accompany him, with drawn sabres. Often I notice as he goes out evenings—and sometimes in the morning, when he returns early—he turns off and halts at the large and handsome residence of the Secretary of War, on K street, and holds conference there. If in his barouche, I can see from my window he does not alight, but sits in his vehicle, and Mr. Stanton comes out to attend him. Sometimes one of his sons, a boy of ten or twelve, accompanies him, riding at his right on a pony. Earlier in the summer I occasionally saw the President and his wife, toward the latter part of the afternoon, out in a barouche, on a pleasure ride through the city. Mrs. Lincoln was dress'd in complete black, with a long crape veil. The equipage is of the plainest kind, only two horses, and they nothing extra. They pass'd me once very close, and I saw the President in the face fully, as they were moving slowly, and his look, though abstracted, happen'd to be directed steadily in my eye. He bow'd and smiled, but far beneath his smile I noticed well the expression I have alluded to. None of the artists or pictures has caught the deep, though subtle and indirect expression of this man's face. There is something else there. One of the great portrait painters of two or three centuries ago is needed.

The Inauguration

March 4.—The President very quietly rode down to the capitol in his own carriage, by himself, on a sharp trot, about noon, either because he wish'd to be on hand to sign bills, or to get rid of marching in line with the absurd procession, the muslin temple of liberty, and pasteboard monitor. I saw him on his return, at three o'clock, after the performance was over. He was in his plain two-horse barouche, and look'd very much worn and tired; the lines, indeed, of vast responsibilities, intricate questions, and demands of life and death, cut deeper than ever upon his dark brown face; yet all the old goodness, tenderness, sadness, and canny shrewdness, underneath the furrows. (I never see that man without feeling that he is one to become personally attach'd to, for his combination of purest, heartiest tenderness, and native western form of manliness.) By his side sat his little boy, of ten years. There were no soldiers, only a lot of civilians on horseback, with huge yellow scarfs over their shoulders, riding around the carriage. (At the inauguration four years ago, he rode down and back again surrounded by a dense mass of arm'd cavalrymen eight deep, with drawn sabres; and there were sharpshooters station'd at every corner on the route.) I ought to make mention of the closing levee[1] of Saturday night last. Never before was such a compact jam in front of the White House—all the grounds fill'd, and away out to the spacious sidewalks. I was there, as I took a notion to go—was in the rush inside with the crowd—surged along the passage-ways, the blue and other rooms, and through the great east room. Crowds of country people, some very funny. Fine music from the Marine band, off in a side place. I saw Mr. Lincoln, drest all in black, with white kid gloves and a claw-hammer coat, receiving, as in duty bound, shaking hands, looking very disconsolate, and as if he would give anything to be somewhere else.

Death of President Lincoln

April 16, '65.—I find in my notes of the time, this passage on the death of Abraham Lincoln: He leaves for America's history and biography, so far, not only its most dramatic reminiscence—he leaves, in my opinion, the greatest, best, most characteristic, artistic, moral personality. Not but that he had faults, and show'd them in the Presidency; but honesty, goodness, shrewdness, conscience, and (a new virtue, unknown to other lands, and hardly yet really known here, but the foundation and tie of all, as the future will grandly develop,) UNIONISM, in its truest and amplest sense, form'd the hard-pan of his character. These he seal'd with his life. The tragic splendor of his death, purging, illuminating all, throws round his form, his head, an aureole that will remain and will grow brighter through time, while history lives, and love of country lasts. By many has this Union been help'd; but if one name, one man, must be pick'd out, he, most of all, is the conservator of it, to the future. He was assassinated— but the Union is not assassinated—ça ira![2] One falls, and another falls. The soldier drops, sinks like a wave—but the ranks of the ocean eternally press on. Death does its work, obliterates a hundred, a thousand— President, general, captain, private—but the Nation is immortal.

No Good Portrait of Lincoln

Probably the reader has seen physiognomies (often old farmers, sea-captains, and such) that, behind their homeliness, or even ugliness, held superior points so subtle, yet so palpable, making the real life of their

1. An occasion of state for the receiving of visits, ceremonial greetings, and interviews.   2. It goes on; it succeeds.

faces almost as impossible to depict as a wild perfume or fruit-taste, or a passionate tone of the living voice—and such was Lincoln's face, the peculiar color, the lines of it, the eyes, mouth, expression. Of technical beauty it had nothing—but to the eye of a great artist it furnished a rare study, a feast and fascination. The current portraits are all failures—most of them caricatures.

1882

May Sarton: FROM JOURNAL OF A SOLITUDE

September 17th. Cracking open the inner world again, writing even a couple of pages, threw me back into depression, not made easier by the weather, two gloomy days of darkness and rain. I was attacked by a storm of tears, those tears that appear to be related to frustration, to buried anger, and come upon me without warning. I woke yesterday so depressed that I did not get up till after eight.

I drove to Brattleboro[1] to read poems at the new Unitarian church there in a state of dread and exhaustion. How to summon the vitality needed? I had made an arrangement of religious poems, going back to early books and forward into the new book not yet published. I suppose it went all right—at least it was not a disaster—but I felt (perhaps I am wrong) that the kind, intelligent people gathered in a big room looking out on pine trees did not really want to think about God. His absence (many of the poems speak of that) or His presence. Both are too frightening.

On the way back I stopped to see Perley Cole, my dear old friend, who is dying, separated from his wife, and has just been moved from a Dickensian nursing home into what seems like a far better one. He grows more transparent every day, a skeleton or nearly. Clasping his hand, I fear to break a bone. Yet the only real communication between us now (he is very deaf) is a handclasp. I want to lift him in my arms and hold him like a baby. He is dying a terribly lonely death. Each time I see him he says, "It is rough" or "I did not think it would end like this."

Everywhere I look about this place I see his handiwork: the three small trees by a granite boulder that he pruned and trimmed so they pivot the whole meadow; the new shady border he dug out for me one of the last days he worked here; the pruned-out stone wall between my field and the church. The second field where he cut brush twice a year and cleared out to the stone wall is growing back to wilderness now. What is done here

1. Brattleboro, Vermont.

has to be done over and over and needs the dogged strength of a man like Perley. I could have never managed it alone. We cherished this piece of land together, and fought together to bring it to some semblance of order and beauty.

I like to think that this last effort of Perley's had a certain ease about it, a game compared to the hard work of his farming years, and a game where his expert knowledge and skill could be well used. How he enjoyed teasing me about my ignorance!

While he scythed and trimmed, I struggled in somewhat the same way at my desk here, and we were each aware of the companionship. We each looked forward to noon, when I could stop for the day and he sat on a high stool in the kitchen, drank a glass or two of sherry with me, said, "Court's in session!" and then told me some tall tale he had been cogitating all morning.

It was a strange relationship, for he knew next to nothing about my life, really; yet below all the talk we recognized each other as the same kind. He enjoyed my anger as much as I enjoyed his. Perhaps that was part of it. Deep down there was understanding, not of the facts of our lives so much as of our essential natures. Even now in his hard, lonely end he has immense dignity. But I wish there were some way to make it easier. I leave him with bitter resentment against the circumstances of this death. "I know. But I did not approve. And I am not resigned."

In the mail a letter from a twelve-year-old child, enclosing poems, her mother having pushed her to ask my opinion. The child does really look at things, and I can write something helpful, I think. But it is troubling how many people expect applause, recognition, when they have not even begun to learn an art or a craft. Instant success is the order of the day; "I want it *now!*" I wonder whether this is not part of our corruption by machines. Machines do things very quickly and outside the natural rhythm of life, and we are indignant if a car doesn't start at the first try. So the few things that we still do, such as cooking (though there are TV dinners!), knitting, gardening, anything at all that cannot be hurried, have a very particular value.

September 18th. The value of solitude—one of its values—is, of course, that there is nothing to *cushion* against attacks from within, just as there is nothing to help balance at times of particular stress or depression. A few moments of desultory conversation with dear Arnold Miner, when he comes to take the trash, may calm an inner storm. But the storm, painful as it is, might have had some truth in it. So sometimes one has simply to endure a period of depression for what it may hold of illumination if one can live through it, attentive to what it exposes or demands.

The reasons for depression are not so interesting as the way one handles it, simply to stay alive. This morning I woke at four and lay awake for an hour or so in a bad state. It is raining again. I got up finally and went about the daily chores, waiting for the sense of doom to lift—and what did it was watering the house plants. Suddenly joy came back because I was fulfilling a simple need, a living one. Dusting never has this effect (and that may be why I am such a poor housekeeper!), but feeding the cats when they are hungry, giving Punch clean water, makes me suddenly feel calm and happy.

Whatever peace I know rests in the natural world, in feeling myself a part of it, even in a small way. Maybe the gaiety of the Warner family, their wisdom, comes from this, that they work close to nature all the time. As simple as that? But it is not simple. Their life requires patient understanding, imagination, the power to endure constant adversity—the weather, for example! To go with, not against the elements, an inexhaustible vitality summoned back each day to do the same tasks, to feed the animals, clean out barns and pens, keep that complex world alive.

October 6th. A day when I am expecting someone for lunch is quite unlike ordinary days. There is a reason to make the flowers look beautiful all over the house, and I know that Anne Woodson, who is coming today, will notice them, for she sees this house in a way that few of my friends do, perhaps because she has lived here without me, has lived her way into the place by pruning and weeding, and once even tidying the linen cupboard!

It is a mellow day, very gentle. The ash has lost its leaves and when I went out to get the mail and stopped to look up at it, I rejoiced to think that soon everything here will be honed down to structure. It is all a rich farewell now to leaves, to color. I think of the trees and how simply they let go, let fall the riches of a season, how without grief (it seems) they can let go and go deep into their roots for renewal and sleep. Eliot's statement comes back to me these days:

> Teach us to care and not to care
> Teach us to sit still.[2]

It is there in Mahler's *Der Abschied*, which I play again every autumn (Bruno Walter with Kathleen Ferrier).[3] But in Mahler it is a cry of loss, a long lyrical cry just *before* letting go, at least until those last long phrases that suggest peace, renunciation. But I think of it as the golden leaves and the brilliant small red maple that shone transparent against the shimmer of the lake yesterday when I went over to have a picnic with Helen

2. From T. S. Eliot's *Ash Wednesday* (1930), lines 38-39.
3. A famous record of Mahler's song "The Farewell," evocative of the coming of winter and death. Mahler died before it could be performed, and the premiere was conducted by his disciple Bruno Walter. Kathleen Ferrier was to die within a few years of recording the song.

Milbank.

Does anything in nature despair except man? An animal with a foot caught in a trap does not seem to despair. It is too busy trying to survive. It is all closed in, to a kind of still, intense waiting. Is this a key? Keep busy with survival. Imitate the trees. Learn to lose in order to recover, and remember that nothing stays the same for long, not even pain, psychic pain. Sit it out. Let it all pass. Let it go.

Yesterday I weeded out violets from the iris bed. The iris was being choked by thick bunches of roots, so much like fruit under the earth. I found one single very fragrant violet and some small autumn crocuses. Now, after an hour's work as the light failed and I drank in the damp smell of earth, it looks orderly again.

October 9th. Has it really happened at last? I feel released from the rack, set free, in touch with the deep source that is only *good,* where poetry lives. We have waited long this year for the glory, but suddenly the big maple is all gold and the beeches yellow with a touch of green that makes the yellow even more intense. There are still nasturtiums to be picked, and now I must get seriously to work to get the remaining bulbs in.

It has been stupidly difficult to let go, but that is what has been needed. I had allowed myself to get overanxious, clutching at what seemed sure to pass, and clutching is the surest way to murder love, as if it were a kitten, not to be squeezed so hard, or a flower to fade in a tight hand. Letting go, I have come back yesterday and today to a sense of my life here in all its riches, depth, freedom for soulmaking.

It's a real break-through. I have not written in sonnet form for a long time, but at every major crisis in my life when I reach a point of clarification, where pain is transcended by the quality of the experience itself, sonnets come. Whole lines run through my head and I cannot *stop* writing until whatever it is gets said.

Found three huge mushrooms when I went out before breakfast to fill the bird feeder. So far only jays come, but the word will get around.

October 11th. The joke is on me. I filled this weekend with friends so that I would not go down into depression, not knowing that I should have turned the corner and be writing poems. It is the climactic moment of autumn, but already I feel like Sleeping Beauty as the carpet of leaves on the front lawn gets thicker and thicker. The avenue of beeches as I drive up the winding road along the brook is glorious beyond words, wall on wall of transparent gold. Laurie Armstrong came for roast beef Sunday dinner. Then I went out for two hours late in the afternoon and put in a hundred tulips. In itself that would not be a big job, but everywhere I have to clear space for them, weed, divide perennials, rescue iris that is being choked by violets. I really get to weeding only in spring and autumn, so I am working through a jungle now. Doing it I feel strenuously happy and at peace. At the end of the afternoon on a gray day, the light is sad and one feels the chill, but the bitter smell of earth is a tonic.

I can hardly believe that relief from the anguish of these past months is here to stay, but so far it does feel like a true change of mood—or rather, a change of being where I can stand alone. So much of my life here is precarious. I cannot always believe even in my work. But I have come in these last days to feel again the validity of my struggle here, that it is meaningful whether I ever "succeed" as a writer or not, and that even its failures, failures of nerve, failures due to a difficult temperament, can be meaningful. It is an age where more and more human beings are caught up in lives where fewer and fewer inward decisions can be made, where fewer and fewer real choices exist. The fact that a middle-aged, single woman, without any vestige of family left, lives in this house in a silent village and is responsible only to her own soul means something. The fact that she is a writer and can tell where she is and what it is like on the pilgrimage inward can be of comfort. It is comforting to know there are lighthouse keepers on rocky islands along the coast. Sometimes, when I have been for a walk after dark and see my house lighted up, looking so alive, I feel that my presence here is worth all the Hell.

I have time to think. That is the great, the greatest luxury. I have time to be. Therefore my responsibility is huge. To use time well and to be all that I can in whatever years are left to me. This does not dismay. The dismay comes when I lose the sense of my life as connected (as if by an aerial) to many, many other lives whom I do not even know and cannot ever know. The signals go out and come in all the time.

Why is it that poetry always seems to me so much more a true work of the soul than prose? I never feel elated after writing a page of prose, though I have written good things on concentrated will, and at least in a novel the imagination is fully engaged. Perhaps it is that prose is earned and poetry given. Both can be revised almost indefinitely. I do not mean to say that I do not work at poetry. When I am really inspired I can put a poem through a hundred drafts and keep my excitement. But this sustained battle is possible only when I am in a state of grace, when the deep channels are open, and when they are, when I am both profoundly stirred and balanced, then poetry comes as a gift from powers beyond my will.

I have often imagined that if I were in solitary confinement for an indefinite time and knew that no one would ever read what I wrote, I would still write poetry, but I would not write novels. Why? Perhaps because the poem is primarily a dialogue with the self and the novel a dialogue with others. They come from entirely different modes of being. I suppose I have written novels to find out what I thought about something and poems to find out what I felt about something.

January 7th. I have worked all morning—and it is now afternoon—to try to make by sheer art and craft an ending to the first stanza of a lyric that shot through my head intact. I should not feel so pressed for time, but I do, and I suppose I always shall. Yeats[4] speaks of spending a week on one stanza. The danger, of course, is overmanipulation, when one finds oneself manipulating *words*, not images or concepts. My problem was to make a transition viable between lovers in a snowstorm and the whiteness of a huge amaryllis I look at across the hall in the cosy room—seven huge flowers that make constant silent hosannas as I sit here.

In a period of happy and fruitful isolation such as this, any interruption, any intrusion of the social, any obligation breaks the thread on my loom, breaks the pattern. Two nights ago I was called at the last minute to attend the caucus of Town Meeting . . . and it threw me. But at least the companionship gave me one insight: a neighbor told me she had been in a small car accident and had managed to persuade the local paper to ignore her true age (as it appears on her license) and to print her age as thirty-nine! I was really astonished by this confidence. I am proud of being fifty-eight, and still alive and kicking, in love, more creative, balanced, and potent than I have ever been. I mind certain physical deteriorations, but not *really*. And not at all when I look at the marvelous photograph that Bill sent me of Isak Dinesen[5] just before she died. For after all we make our faces as we go along, and who when young could ever look as she does? The ineffable sweetness of the smile, the total acceptance and joy one receives from it, life, death, everything taken in and, as it were, savored—and let go.

Wrinkles here and there seem unimportant compared to *Gestalt* of the whole person I have become in this past year. Somewhere in *The Poet and the Donkey* Andy speaks for me when he says, "Do not deprive me of my age. I have earned it."

My neighbor's wish to be known forever as thirty-nine years old made me think again of what K said in her letter about the people in their thirties mourning their lost youth because we have given them no ethos that makes maturity appear an asset. Yet we have many examples before us. It looks as if T. S. Eliot came into a fully consummated happy marriage only when he was seventy. Yeats married when he was fifty or over. I am coming into the most fulfilled love of my life now. But for some reason Americans are terrified of the very idea of passionate love going on past middle age. Are they afraid of being alive? Do they want to be dead, i.e., *safe*? For of course one is never safe when in love. Growth is demanding and may seem dangerous, for there is loss as well as gain in growth. But why go on living if one has ceased to grow? And what more

4. William Butler Yeats, 1865–1939. Irish poet and dramatist.
5. Modern Danish short-story writer who de-   spite painful illness in her later years continued writing until her death at seventy-seven.

demanding atmosphere for growth than love in any form, than any relationship which can call out and requires of us our most secret and deepest selves?

My neighbor who wishes to remain thirty-nine indefinitely does so out of anxiety—she is afraid she will no longer be "attractive" if people know her age. But if one wants mature relationships, one will look for them among one's peers. I cannot imagine being in love with someone much younger than I because I have looked on love as an *éducation sentimentale*. About love I have little to learn from the young.

January 8th. Yesterday was a strange, hurried, uncentered day; yet I did not have to go out, the sun shone. Today I feel centered and time is a friend instead of the old enemy. It was zero this morning. I have a fire burning in my study, yellow roses and mimosa on my desk. There is an atmosphere of festival, of release, in the house. We are one, the house and I, and I am happy to be alone—time to think, time to be. This kind of open-ended time is the only luxury that really counts and I feel stupendously rich to have it. And for the moment I have a sense of fulfillment both about my life and about my work that I have rarely experienced until this year, or perhaps until these last weeks. I look to my left and the transparent blue sky behind a flame-colored cyclamen, lifting about thirty winged flowers to the light, makes an impression of stained glass, light-flooded. I have put the vast heap of unanswered letters into a box at my feet, so I don't see them. And now I am going to make one more try to get that poem right. The last line is still the problem.

1970, 1971   1973

Woody Allen: SELECTIONS FROM THE ALLEN NOTEBOOKS

Following are excerpts from the hitherto secret private journal of Woody Allen, which will be published posthumously or after his death, whichever comes first.

Getting through the night is becoming harder and harder. Last evening, I had the uneasy feeling that some men were trying to break into my room to shampoo me. But why? I kept imagining I saw shadowy forms, and at 3 A.M. the underwear I had draped over a chair resembled the Kaiser on roller skates. When I finally did fall asleep, I had that same hideous nightmare in which a woodchuck is trying to claim my prize at a raffle. Despair.

I believe my consumption has grown worse. Also my asthma. The wheezing comes and goes, and I get dizzy more and more frequently. I have taken to violent choking and fainting. My room is damp and I have perpetual chills and palpitations of the heart. I noticed, too, that I am out of napkins. Will it never stop?

Idea for a story: A man awakens to find his parrot has been made Secretary of Agriculture. He is consumed with jealousy and shoots himself, but unfortunately the gun is the type with a little flag that pops out, with the word "Bang" on it. The flag pokes his eye out, and he lives—a chastened human being who, for the first time, enjoys the simple pleasures of life, like farming or sitting on an air hose.

Thought: Why does man kill? He kills for food. And not only food: frequently there must be a beverage.

Should I marry W.? Not if she won't tell me the other letters in her name. And what about her career? How can I ask a woman of her beauty to give up the Roller Derby? Decisions . . .

Once again I tried committing suicide—this time by wetting my nose and inserting it into the light socket. Unfortunately, there was a short in the wiring, and I merely caromed off the icebox. Still obsessed by thoughts of death, I brood constantly. I keep wondering if there is an afterlife, and if there is will they be able to break a twenty?

I ran into my brother today at a funeral. We had not seen one another for fifteen years, but as usual he produced a pig bladder from his pocket and began hitting me on the head with it. Time has helped me understand him better. I finally realize his remark that I am "some loathsome vermin fit only for extermination" was said more out of compassion than anger. Let's face it: he was always much brighter than me—wittier, more cultured, better educated. Why he is still working at McDonald's is a mystery.

Idea for story: Some beavers take over Carnegie Hall and perform Wozzeck.[1] (Strong theme. What will be the structure?)

Good Lord, why am I so guilty? Is it because I hated my father? Probably it was the veal-parmigian' incident. Well, what *was* it doing in his wallet? If I had listened to him, I would be blocking hats for a living. I can hear him now: "To block hats—that is everything." I remember his reaction when I told him I wanted to write. "The only writing you'll do is

1. A lurid and dissonant opera by the modern composer Alban Berg. Carnegie Hall is a famous concert hall in New York City.

in collaboration with an owl." I still have no idea what he meant. What a sad man! When my first play, *A Cyst for Gus*, was produced at the Lyceum, he attended opening night in tails and a gas mask.

Today I saw a red-and-yellow sunset and thought, How insignificant I am! Of course, I thought that yesterday, too, and it rained. I was overcome with self-loathing and contemplated suicide again—this time by inhaling next to an insurance salesman.

Short story: A man awakens in the morning and finds himself transformed into his own arch supports (This idea can work on many levels. Psychologically, it is the quintessence of Kruger, Freud's disciple who discovered sexuality in bacon.)

How wrong Emily Dickinson was! Hope is not "the thing with feathers." The thing with feathers has turned out to be my nephew. I must take him to a specialist in Zurich.

I have decided to break off my engagement with W. She doesn't understand my writing, and said last night that my *Critique of Metaphysical Reality* reminded her of *Airport*. We quarreled, and she brought up the subject of children again, but I convinced her they would be too young.

Do I believe in God? I did until Mother's accident. She fell on some meat loaf, and it penetrated her spleen. She lay in a coma for months, unable to do anything but sing "Granada" to an imaginary herring. Why was this woman in the prime of life so afflicted—because in her youth she dared to defy convention and got married with a brown paper bag on her head? And how can I believe in God when just last week I got my tongue caught in the roller of an electric typewriter? I am plagued by doubts. What if everything is an illusion and nothing exists? In that case, I definitely overpaid for my carpet. If only God would give me some clear sign! Like making a large deposit in my name at a Swiss bank.

Had coffee with Melnick today. He talked to me about his idea of having all government officials dress like hens.

Play idea: A character based on my father, but without quite so prominent a big toe. He is sent to the Sorbonne[2] to study the harmonica. In the end, he dies, never realizing his one dream—to sit up to his waist in

2. The University of Paris.

gravy. (I see a brilliant second-act curtain, where two midgets come upon a severed head in a shipment of volleyballs.)

While taking my noon walk today, I had more morbid thoughts. What *is* it about death that bothers me so much? Probably the hours. Melnick says the soul is immortal and lives on after the body drops away, but if my soul exists without my body I am convinced all my clothes will be too loose-fitting. Oh, well . . .

Did not have to break off with W. after all, for as luck would have it, she ran off to Finland with a professional circus geek. All for the best, I suppose, although I had another of those attacks where I start coughing out of my ears.

Last night, I burned all my plays and poetry. Ironically as I was burning my masterpiece, *Dark Penguin*, the room caught fire, and I am now the object of a lawsuit by some men named Pinchunk and Schlosser. Kierkegaard was right.

                                                                    1972

People, Places

Thomas Jefferson

GEORGE WASHINGTON[1]

I think I knew General Washington intimately and thoroughly; and were I called on to delineate his character, it should be in terms like these.

His mind was great and powerful, without being of the very first order; his penetration strong, though not so acute as that of a Newton, Bacon, or Locke; and as far as he saw, no judgment was ever sounder. It was slow in operation, being little aided by invention or imagination, but sure in conclusion. Hence the common remark of his officers, of the advantage he derived from councils of war, where hearing all suggestions, he selected whatever was best; and certainly no general ever planned his battles more judiciously. But if deranged during the course of the action, if any member of his plan was dislocated by sudden circumstances, he was slow in re-adjustment. The consequence was, that he often failed in the field, and rarely against an enemy in station, as at Boston and York. He was incapable of fear, meeting personal dangers with the calmest unconcern. Perhaps the strongest feature in his character was prudence, never acting until every circumstance, every consideration, was maturely weighed; refraining if he saw a doubt, but, when once decided, going through with his purpose, whatever obstacles opposed. His integrity was most pure, his justice the most inflexible I have ever known, no motives of interest or consanguinity, of friendship or hatred, being able to bias his decision. He was, indeed, in every sense of the words, a wise, a good, and a great man. His temper was naturally irritable and high toned; but reflection and resolution had obtained a firm and habitual ascendency over it. If ever, however, it broke its bonds, he was most tremendous in his wrath. In his expenses he was honorable, but exact; liberal in contri-

1. From a letter written in 1814 to a Doctor Jones, who was writing a history and wanted to know about Washington's role in the Federalist-Republican controversy.

butions to whatever promised utility; but frowning and unyielding on all visionary projects, and all unworthy calls on his charity. His heart was not warm in its affections; but he exactly calculated every man's value, and gave him a solid esteem proportioned to it. His person, you know, was fine, his stature exactly what one would wish, his deportment easy, erect and noble; the best horseman of his age, and the most graceful figure that could be seen on horseback. Although in the circle of his friends, where he might be unreserved with safety, he took a free share in conversation, his colloquial talents were not above mediocrity, possessing neither copiousness of ideas, nor fluency of words. In public, when called on for a sudden opinion, he was unready, short and embarrassed. Yet he wrote readily, rather diffusely, in an easy and correct style. This he had acquired by conversation with the world, for his education was merely reading, writing and common arithmetic, to which he added surveying at a later day. His time was employed in action chiefly, reading little, and that only in agriculture and English history. His correspondence became necessarily extensive, and, with journalizing his agricultural proceedings, occupied most of his leisure hours within doors. On the whole, his character was, in its mass, perfect, in nothing bad, in few points indifferent; and it may truly be said, that never did nature and fortune combine more perfectly to make a man great, and to place him in the same constellation with whatever worthies have merited from man an everlasting remembrance. For his was the singular destiny and merit, of leading the armies of his country successfully through an arduous war, for the establishment of its independence; of conducting its councils through the birth of a government, new in its forms and principles, until it had settled down into a quiet and orderly train; and of scrupulously obeying the laws through the whole of his career, civil and military, of which the history of the world furnishes no other example.

    * * * I am satisfied, the great body of republicans think of him as I do. We were, indeed, dissatisfied with him on his ratification of the British treaty. But this was short lived. We knew his honesty, the wiles with which he was encompassed, and that age had already begun to relax the firmness of his purposes; and I am convinced he is more deeply seated in the love and gratitude of the republicans, than in the Pharisaical homage of the federal monarchists.[2] For he was no monarchist from preference of his judgment. The soundness of that gave him correct views of the rights of man, and his severe justice devoted him to them. He has often declared to me that he considered our new Constitution as an experiment on the practicability of republican government, and with what dose of liberty man could be trusted for his own good; that he was determined the experiment should have a fair trial, and would lose the last drop of his

2. Jefferson here compares those who sought to make the new United States a kingdom, with Washington as king, to the biblical Pharisees, the haughty sect of ancient Israel.

blood in support of it. And these declarations he repeated to me the oftener and more pointedly, because he knew my suspicions of Colonel Hamilton's views,[3] and probably had heard from him the same declarations which I had, to wit, "that the British constitution, with its unequal representation, corruption and other existing abuses, was the most perfect government which had ever been established on earth, and that a reformation of those abuses would make it an impracticable government." I do believe that General Washington had not a firm confidence in the durability of our government. He was naturally distrustful of men, and inclined to gloomy apprehensions; and I was ever persuaded that a belief that we must at length end in something like a British constitution, had some weight in his adoption of the ceremonies of levees,[4] birthdays, pompous meetings with Congress, and other forms of the same character, calculated to prepare us gradually for a change which he believed possible, and to let it come on with as little shock as might be to the public mind.

These are my opinions of General Washington which I would vouch at the judgment seat of God, having been formed on an acquaintance of thirty years. I served with him in the Virginia legislature from 1769 to the Revolutionary war, and again, a short time in Congress, until he left us to take command of the army. During the war and after it we corresponded occasionally, and in the four years of my continuance in the office of Secretary of State, our intercourse was daily, confidential and cordial. After I retired from that office, great and malignant pains were taken by our federal monarchists, and not entirely without effect, to make him view me as a theorist, holding French principles of government,[5] which would lead infallibly to licentiousness and anarchy. And to this he listened the more easily, from my known disapprobation of the British treaty. I never saw him afterwards, or these malignant insinuations should have been dissipated before his just judgment, as mists before the sun. I felt on his death, with my countrymen, that "verily a great man hath fallen this day in Israel."

1814

3. Alexander Hamilton (1755–1804) advocated a strong central federal government, led by the "wealthy, good, and wise." His views were opposed by the relatively more democratic views of Jefferson.
4. Morning receptions held by a head of state

to enable him to attend to public affairs while rising and dressing. The form was characteristic of European monarchs.
5. Radical political views advanced by extreme democrats in the course of the French Revolution.

THE READER

1. What, in Jefferson's view, are Washington's outstanding virtues? What are Washington's greatest defects? What is Jefferson's overall judgment of the character of Washington? Does this portrait of Washington agree with what you have been taught and have learned about

the man?

2. From what he writes about Washington, can you infer those qualities of character that Jefferson most admires? If so, do you agree?

3. Do we learn anything from Jefferson's portrait about what Washington looked like? About his family life? About his hobbies? About his religion? If not, are these important omissions in the characterization of a person in public life?

THE WRITER

1. What does Jefferson produce by including in his portrait certain defects or shortcomings of Washington?

2. Is Jefferson's characterization of Washington persuasive? What kinds of authority (explicit and implicit) does this piece set forth for the correctness of its view?

3. Write in the manner of Jefferson a characterization of an important figure in public life today. Consider whether this manner enables you to bring out what you think is essential truth, and whether the attempt brings to light any special problems concerning either the task itself or public life today.

Nathaniel Hawthorne

ABRAHAM LINCOLN

Of course, there was one other personage, in the class of statesmen, whom I should have been truly mortified to leave Washington without seeing; since (temporarily, at least, and by force of circumstances) he was the man of men. But a private grief had built up a barrier about him, impeding the customary free intercourse of Americans with their chief magistrate; so that I might have come away without a glimpse of his very remarkable physiognomy, save for a semi-official opportunity of which I was glad to take advantage. The fact is, we were invited to annex ourselves, as supernumeraries, to a deputation that was about to wait upon the President, from a Massachusetts whip factory, with a present of a splendid whip.

Our immediate party consisted only of four or five (including Major Ben Perley Poore,[1] with his note-book and pencil), but we were joined by several other persons, who seemed to have been lounging about the precincts of the White House, under the spacious porch, or within the hall, and who swarmed in with us to take the chances of a presentation. Nine o'clock had been appointed as the time for receiving the deputa-

1. American journalist and biographer.

tion, and we were punctual to the moment; but not so the President, who sent us word that he was eating his breakfast, and would come as soon as he could. His appetite, we were glad to think, must have been a pretty fair one; for we waited about half an hour in one of the antechambers, and then were ushered into a reception-room, in one corner of which sat the Secretaries of War and of the Treasury, expecting, like ourselves, the termination of the Presidential breakfast. During this interval there were several new additions to our group, one or two of whom were in a working-garb, so that we formed a very miscellaneous collection of people, mostly unknown to each other, and without any common sponsor, but all with an equal right to look our head servant in the face.

By and by there was a little stir on the staircase and in the passageway, and in lounged a tall, loose-jointed figure, of an exaggerated Yankee port and demeanor, whom (as being about the homeliest man I ever saw, yet by no means repulsive or disagreeable) it was impossible not to recognize as Uncle Abe.

Unquestionably, Western man though he be, and Kentuckian by birth, President Lincoln is the essential representative of all Yankees, and the veritable specimen, physically, of what the world seems determined to regard as our characteristic qualities. It is the strangest and yet the fittest thing in the jumble of human vicissitudes, that he, out of so many millions, unlooked for, unselected by any intelligible process that could be based upon his genuine qualities, unknown to those who chose him, and unsuspected of what endowments may adapt him for his tremendous responsibility, should have found the way open for him to fling his lank personality into the chair of state—where, I presume, it was his first impulse to throw his legs on the council-table, and tell the Cabinet Ministers a story. There is no describing his lengthy awkwardness, nor the uncouthness of his movement; and yet it seemed as if I had been in the habit of seeing him daily, and had shaken hands with him a thousand times in some village street; so true was he to the aspect of the pattern American, though with a certain extravagance which, possibly, I exaggerated still further by the delighted eagerness with which I took it in. If put to guess his calling and livelihood, I should have taken him for a country school-master as soon as anything else. He was dressed in a rusty black frock coat and pantaloons, unbrushed, and worn so faithfully that the suit had adapted itself to the curves and angularities of his figure, and had grown to be an outer skin of the man. His hair was black, still unmixed with gray, stiff, somewhat bushy, and had apparently been acquainted with neither brush nor comb that morning, after the disarrangement of the pillow; and as to a nightcap, Uncle Abe probably knows nothing of such effeminacies. His complexion is dark and sallow, betokening, I fear, a insalubrious atmosphere around the White House; he has thick black eyebrows and an impending brow; his nose is large, and the lines about his mouth are very strongly defined.

The whole physiognomy is as coarse a one as you would meet anywhere in the length and breadth of the States; but, withal, it is redeemed, illuminated, softened, and brightened by a kindly though serious look out of his eyes, and an expression of homely sagacity, that seems weighted with rich results of village experience. A great deal of native sense; no bookish cultivation, no refinement; honest at heart, and thoroughly so, and yet, in some sort, sly—at least, endowed with a sort of tact and wisdom that are akin to craft, and would impel him, I think, to take an antagonist in flank, rather than to make a bull-run at him right in front. But, on the whole, I like this sallow, queer, sagacious visage, with the homely human sympathies that warmed it; and, for my small share in the matter, would as lief have Uncle Abe for a ruler as any man whom it would have been practicable to put in his place.

Immediately on his entrance the President accosted our member of Congress, who had us in charge, and, with a comical twist of his face, made some jocular remark about the length of his breakfast. He then greeted us all round, not waiting for an introduction, but shaking and squeezing everybody's hand with the utmost cordiality, whether the individual's name was announced to him or not. His manner towards us was wholly without pretence, but yet had a kind of natural dignity, quite sufficient to keep the forwardest of us from clapping him on the shoulder and asking him for a story. A mutual acquaintance being established, our leader took the whip out of its case, and began to read the address of presentation. The whip was an exceedingly long one, its handle wrought in ivory (by some artist in the Massachusetts State Prison, I believe), and ornamented with a medallion of the President, and other equally beautiful devices; and along its whole length there was a succession of golden bands and ferrules. The address was shorter than the whip, but equally well made, consisting chiefly of an explanatory description of these artistic designs, and closing with a hint that the gift was a suggestive and emblematic one, and that the President would recognize the use to which such an instrument should be put.

This suggestion gave Uncle Abe rather a delicate task in his reply, because, slight as the matter seemed, it apparently called for some declaration, or intimation, or faint foreshadowing of policy in reference to the conduct of the war, and the final treatment of the Rebels. But the President's Yankee aptness and not-to-be-caughtness stood him in good stead, and he jerked or wiggled himself out of the dilemma with an uncouth dexterity that was entirely in character; although, without his gesticulation of eye and mouth—and especially the flourish of the whip, with which he imagined himself touching up a pair of fat horses—I doubt whether his words would be worth recording, even if I could remember them. The gist of the reply was, that he accepted the whip as an emblem of peace, not punishment; and, this great affair over, we retired out of the presence in high good humor, only regretting that we could not have seen the President sit down and fold up his legs (which is said to be a most extraordinary spectacle), or have heard him tell one of those delectable stories for which he is so celebrated. A good many of them are afloat upon the common talk of Washington, and are certainly the aptest, pithiest, and funniest little things imaginable; though, to be sure, they smack of the frontier freedom, and would not always bear repetition in a drawing-room, or on the immaculate page of the *Atlantic*.[2]

Good Heavens! what liberties have I been taking with one of the potentates of the earth, and the man on whose conduct more important consequences depend than on that of any other historical personage of the century! But with whom is an American citizen entitled to take a liberty, if not with his own chief magistrate? However, lest the above allusions to President Lincoln's little peculiarities (already well known to the country and to the world) should be misinterpreted, I deem it proper to say a word or two in regard to him, of unfeigned respect and measurable confidence. He is evidently a man of keen faculties, and, what is still more to the purpose, of powerful character. As to his integrity, the people have that intuition of it which is never deceived. Before he actually entered upon his great office, and for a considerable time afterwards, there is no reason to suppose that he adequately estimated the gigantic task about to be imposed on him, or, at least, had any distinct idea how it was to be managed; and I presume there may have been more than one veteran politician who proposed to himself to take the power out of President Lincoln's hands into his own, leaving our honest friend only the public responsibility for the good or ill success of the career. The extremely imperfect development of his statesmanly qualities, at that period, may have justified such designs. But the President is teachable by events, and has now spent a year in a very arduous course of education; he has a flexible mind, capable of much expansion, and convertible towards far loftier studies and activities than those of his early life; and if he came to Washington a backwoods humorist, he has already transformed himself into as good a statesman (to speak moderately) as his prime minister.[3]

                                                                                    1862

2. This passage was one of those omitted from the article as originally published, and the following note was appended to explain the omission, which had been indicated by a line of points:
"We are compelled to omit two or three pages, in which the author describes the interview, and gives his idea of the personal appearance and deportment of the President. The sketch appears to have been written in a benign spirit, and perhaps conveys a not inaccurate impression of its august subject; but it lacks *reverence*, and it pains us to see a gentleman of ripe age, and who has spent years under the corrective influence of foreign institutions, falling into the characteristic and most ominous fault of Young America."

3. Presumably the Secretary of State, William H. Seward.

THE READER

1. In one sentence, summarize Hawthorne's attitude toward Lincoln in the first seven paragraphs.
2. In his final paragraph, Hawthorne seeks to prevent misunderstanding by stressing his respect for and confidence in Lincoln. Is there anything in the paragraph that runs counter to that expression? To what effect?

THE WRITER

1. What is the basic pattern of the opening sentence of the fifth paragraph? Find other examples of this pattern. What is their total impact on Hawthorne's description?
2. Write a paragraph of description of someone you know, using the same pattern for the entire paragraph that you discovered for Hawthorne's sentence in the previous question.
3. In the footnote to the seventh paragraph, the editor of the Atlantic Monthly explains his omission of the first seven paragraphs. On the evidence of this statement, what sort of person does the editor seem to be? Is there anything in the omitted paragraphs that would tend to justify his decision as editor? Is the full description superior to the last paragraph printed alone? Explain.
4. Describe someone you know who has a strong personality that has contrasting characteristics.

June Callwood

PORTRAIT OF CANADA

When the province of Québec elected a government, on November 15, 1976, that promised to take Québec out of Canada, Canadians were too stunned to believe it, though the country has never been without a strong secessionist movement since its beginning. Nova Scotia's first reaction to the birth of Canada in 1867 was to vote to leave it. In the wake of the re-election in February 1980 of Pierre Trudeau, the country's stylish, haughty prime minister, a prominent western Progressive Conservative, Richard Collver, leader of the party in Saskatchewan, resigned and said he would work to take western Canada out of federation and join the United States.

It isn't true that Canadians don't care about Canada. Canadians dislike (a) other Canadians, and (b) their governments, but will fight to the death if either is threatened. They reserve their most intense loyalty for the landscape of their own neighborhoods, for the certain lovely light of a winter dawn, for a skyline that lifts the eye, for waves ruffled white in a bay. Canadians, excepting only those descended from the French and living in Québec, have never created a myth that would unify them into nationhood.

The country was not designed that way. The base for its existence was a strong aversion to being absorbed into the United States following the Civil War, together with the anxiety of the founding fathers, many of whom were railway speculators, to make money from building a transcontinental railway. To that end they patched together four wary, doubtful, newly self-governing British colonies and called them Canada.

To add to the difficulty of poor carpentry, the country is illogical. It runs east and west on a continent where rivers and mountains, commerce and people flow north and south. Canada is uneconomic and absurd in its demographic outline: its 23 million people live along the United States border in a band about 100 miles wide and 3,987 miles long. The peculiar population distribution makes Canadians world-class masters of communication. Since there are too few customers to attract private industry, the government has been obliged to subsidize or own outright an airline, a railway, television networks (French and English), radio networks (French and English), oil and gas pipelines; enthusiasm for public enterprise overflowed into a government-owned oil company, government ownership of all beer and liquor sales, government-owned hydroelectric power, nuclear power, and a third of all Canadian-controlled corporations.

Canada has centralist churches, banks, insurance companies, and businesses, a theme dating to the country's beginnings when it was a fur farm owned by European monopolies. French and English investors controlled all commerce and had feudal authority over every living creature. Settlers had no civil rights but received protection from invading Americans, start-up supplies and copious amounts of law and order provided first by agents of the monopolies, then by armies, and then, today, by paramilitary police.

At a hint of trouble, the Canadian custom is to call out the Army, jail all suspects, all relatives of suspects, all associates of suspects, all whose names or addresses resemble those of suspects, and, human nature being what it is, all to whom none of the above applies but who have offended the authorities.

No nonsense about habeas corpus;[1] suspects go to jail and stay there. In Canada, 85 percent of those charged with indictable offenses are convicted. Small wonder: in Canada courts allow illegally obtained evidence. Canadian police have been opening private mail illegally for years. When Canadians heard of it in 1979, they were indignant: they demanded that the law be changed so that police could open mail freely,

1. Habeas corpus: a written document requiring an individual to appear before a court.

without breaking the law. When Canadians also learned that police bugged the conversations of cabinet ministers, they approved.

The Supreme Court of Canada recently rejected the tradition in English law that an accused person has the right to remain silent. In Canada, if you don't reply to the police, you go to jail. Juries in the 1970s twice found a man innocent of the crime with which he was charged. Each time higher courts ruled he should go to jail anyway—and he did.

Those arrested for offending the government customarily are held without bail, without being allowed to notify relatives or lawyers, without visits from anyone but teams of interrogators, without appearing before judges, and without being informed what the charge might eventually be. Canadians who *looked* as though they might disagree with the government have been deported to the country of their birth, or their parents' birth; also without trial.

In 1970 in Canada, those who protested such draconian methods were described by Prime Minister Pierre Elliott Trudeau as "bleeding hearts." The occasion was his invocation of the War Measures Act[2] after terrorists in Montréal had kidnapped two people. As a result of the act, 465 people were put in jail, almost none even remotely connected with the kidnapping.

Canada teemed with Vietnam War draft resisters then, most of whom had imagined themselves in a liberal Utopia. When Trudeau invoked the War Measures Act, they were among the few residents of Canada dismayed by it. A Gallup opinion poll showed 87 percent of Canadians in favor of the War Measures Act, making it the single most popular piece of legislation in the country's history. Canadian university students, fresh from picket lines protesting the Vietnam War, or for boycotting California grapes, or demonstrating solidarity with the Selma, Alabama, march for black rights—all causes romantically distant—turned out by the thousands after the War Measures Act *to support it.*

Employees in the Canadian Embassy in Washington tried to explain to astonished Americans how a modern democracy could impose behavior appropriate to Vlad the Impaler without provoking riots. The United States, which had just survived a presidential assassination without violating the rights of its citizens, began to feel it hadn't understood Canada at all.

Unlike Americans, whose natural response to an invasion of rights by the state is to fill Washington with demonstrators, Canadians tolerate even brutal use of authority with approval. Unless it is directed at them personally, they don't mind. They trust the government and police to act in the best interests of society even when they do not seem to be doing so. They trust that authority knows best.

2. The War Measures Act permits the government to assume emergency powers in the event of war or insurrection.

When a train spill in Mississauga released chlorine gas over that Toronto suburb in 1979, 250,000 people left their homes wihout fuss at the request of the police. The largest peacetime evacuation in world history, the refugees slept for a week on the floors of shopping plazas, uncomplaining. Meanwhile, though their homes and businesses were deserted, the crime rate went *down*.

The Royal Canadian Mounted Politce celebrated its hundredth birthday in 1973 and was honored across the country. An Ottawa columnist, Charles Lynch, was impressed. He could not imagine, he wrote, a similar outpouring of good wishes on the anniversary of Scotland Yard or the FBI. Later it was revealed that the RCMP at that time was stealing dynamite to create an illusion of an active underground, forging seditious documents, burning down a barn, copying membership lists of legitimate political parties, and burglarizing a newspaper. Canadians defended the police. If Mounties were breaking the law, Canadians reasoned, the law was wrong.

Alan Borovoy, general counsel for the Canadian Civil Liberties Association, an organization with an almost unblemished record of failure in such a climate, describes the Canadian style as "autocracy with decency," a tribute to the government's restraint. The government limits retaliation to a target group, wipes it out, and withdraws well short of tyranny.

Canadians are not Americans who live in a colder climate: they are different people. While they resemble Americans—wear the same jeans, use the same expletives, drink the same booze, bet the same point spread, pop the same pills for the same reasons, watch Johnny Carson, and goggle at the same center folds—they are not the same. In a clutch, an American goes for a gun; a Canadian calls the police, who arrive promptly and in great numbers.

A Canadian who doesn't care for that kind of passive reliance on authority, one who has uppity feelings about private enterprise and individual freedom, can always move south of the border to an environment as familiar-looking as his own where his quirks will be appreciated. A radio pioneer in Canada, Graham Spry, once observed, "The state or the United States."

The U.S. economist-statesman John Kenneth Galbraith, Canadian-born, expressed a similar sentiment. "In southwestern Ontario," he wrote, "we were taught that patriotism should not withstand anything more than a $5-a-month wage difference. Anything more than that and you went to Detroit."

Canadians drift back and forth over the border. Always have. Only in recent years have they been obliged to confide their intentions to customs or immigration officers. In 1885 a harried official in Washington declared, "No futher reference will be made to the subject (of Canadian immigration) till a more effective system can be devised for enumeration."

Officially, "Canadian foreign stock" in the United States is calculated at 3 million, an unlikely figure. Estimates are that there are close to 2 million of French-Canadian heritage in New England alone. There are more Québécois in the Los Angeles area (200,000) than there are in Québec City (186,000).

The United States often forgets to identify Canadians as a racial entity. When the American Museum of Immigration in New York City was opened in 1972, Canada was not represented. The explanation was that Canadians aren't really foreigners. The U.S. Bureau of Statistics does recognize them as such: it reports Canadians are the third-largest ethnic group in America.

In the late 1890s, the governor-general's lady, wandering among her countrymen on the Québec City docks to welcome newcomers to Canada, was disconcerted that the question she was asked most frequently was the direction to the United States border. In the 1950s, when Canada was developing a middle class, the expression "the brain drain," referred to the scholars, scientists, actors, inventors, manufacturers, doctors, writers, and engineers flowing south.

Canada has received two mass migrations moving the other way, one after the War of Indepedence in 1776, and one during the Vietnam War of the late 1960s. Both times, Canada got American conservatives in search of stability and structure.

Culture, however, travels in but one direction: north. Canada is afloat in American films, American television, American music, American books, American magazines, American sport, American fads—all of which stimulate defensive government support of artists, publishers, dance companies, theaters, magazines, galleries, orchestras, and radio and television networks in order to nourish the frail flower of indigenous culture. To offset the fact of the deluge of Americana, Canadian schools in the 1970s began to stress Canadian history and offer Canadian literature in English courses. The country now is festooned with ceremonies in which Canadians receive awards for singing Canadian songs, or writing Canadian books, or for some aspect of the Canadian identity, the pursuit of which is a national obsession.

All this applies to English-speaking Canada. Québec, a French island in English North America, is steeped in its own culture. Writers, singers, and artists have been dowsing for the wellspring of the Québécois sense of patrie[3] for more than a century. Before that, the Roman Catholic Church held people together in defiance of a Protestant anti-Catholic British Empire. For a very long time, French-speaking Canadians have

3. *Patrie:* nation.

known, and admired, themselves; English-speaking Canadians have no similar imploded racial commonality and pride.

Communication problems are a result of treaty makers in the eighteenth century who constructed the border to give maximum advantage to the United States. In all such negotiations, Canada was never represented. Instead, the British team speaking for Canada usually was made up of men with close financial ties to the United States, men who had no interest in Canada but were determined to help America prosper.

Accordingly, Canadians got two million square miles of lunar rock, some treeless tundra, and a thin strip of arable land so eccentrically arranged that transportation between the parts was almost impossible. The British had given the United States the Mississippi-Ohio valley, Maine, upper New York State, and the Oregon country, all once legitimately part of Canada.

For most of history, the fastest and most comfortable way to travel from central Canada to another part of Canada or to Britain was through the United States. This meant that Canadian politicians from Toronto went down the Hudson in order to get to London, and British governors-general bound for Ottawa got off the boat at Portland, Maine. Such accommodations had to be suspended during those periods when the United States was actively invading Canada, or planning to, at which time British redcoats had to march the longer all-Canada route over terrain that killed many of them.

Pressed by the weight of ice and rocks at their backs, most Canadians live as close to the American border as they can without changing citizenship. Their communities form a chain of beads; if one, say Québec, drops off, the necklace comes apart.

Some Canadians are resigned to the inevitability of dissolution, even after a referendum in Québec in May 1980 rejected separation by a margin of 60-40. The Atlantic provinces resent that Ontario has prospered in Canada at their expense. Alberta, rich in oil and gas pegged by the Ottawa government well below world prices, seethes with resentment. British Columbia, remote beyond the mountains, has never felt itself very Canadian. And Newfoundland in 1980 observed the thirty-first anniversary of its joining Canada with a suggestion in its largest newspaper that the island separate.

Only Ontario, which profited most in 1867 from confederation which provided markets for its factories and a high tariff wall to enrich manufacturers, shows any real passion for keeping the country together. Everywhere else, Canadians talk mutinously of leaving. Vancouver Island has a group ready to leave British Columbia. The *Parti Acadien*[4] has its own flag and talks of leaving New Brunswick. Newfoundlanders have a new

---

4. *Parti Acadien*: a separatist party within the maritime province of New Brunswick.

flag (June 1980) and an anthem they sing with tears in their eyes; when they became Canada's tenth province, they donned black armbands in grief. Labrador has a secessionist movement; northern Ontario has an element hopeful of separating from southern Ontario.

"I can report to you that national unity is far from being a dead issue," wrote Dalton Camp, former head of the Progressive Conservative party of Canada, after a coast-to-coast tour in November 1979. "Instead, there may be as many as 23 million people out there ready and eager to march against it."

Efforts to control the runaway pieces of the country are hampered by damage to the constitution committed by members of the Judicial Committee of the British Privy Council. For most of Canada's history they functioned as a supreme court on constitutional matters. Almost without exception, they dismantled the authority of the central government.

The founding fathers, almost all of them immigrants except for the French-Canadians, drew up a constitution that is a business agreement, a dispersal of powers. They were lawyers and railway speculators, not philosophers. When the Canadian constitution was drafted in 1864, the American Civil War was raging. Fearful that they would be invaded by the victorious Union Army, Canadians wrote clauses to invest most authority in the central government. To sell federation to the locals, particularly French-Canadians nervous of assimilation, provinces got authority over minor matters like culture. Thanks to the Privy Council, culture turned out to be the whole ball game.

The constitution could not be enacted in Canada because the provinces then were colonies of the British Empire. So it was addressed to the House of Commons in London, England, which passed what it called the British North America Act[5] only moments before considering the big business of the day—a tax on dogs. Disputes over interpretation had to be referred back to the British Government, which effectively eroded federal authority.

Thus, modern Canada is almost ungovernable. Every matter touching the personal lives of Canadians is in limbo between federal and provincial jurisdiction. Thousands of federal and provincial civil servants ponder the pieces. Hundreds of federal-provincial conferences are held annually—a good many ending without agreement.

Deplorable evidence of this awkwardness came to world attention in the fall of 1948, when Canada abstained from signing the first draft of the United Nations Declaration on Human Rights. Six other dissenting countries were from beyond the Iron Curtain: Byelorussia, Czechoslovakia, Poland, the Ukraine, the Soviet Union, and Yugoslavia. Canada eventually endorsed it but the signature is technically unconstitutional.

5. British North America Act: a British parliamentary act passed in 1867, creating the Confederation of the Dominion of Canada.

In Canada civil rights fall within provincial jurisdiction, not federal. A federally enacted Canadian Bill of Rights makes a handsome wall hanging but rarely intrudes upon the solemn deliberations of Canadian judges.

Still, the peculiarities of sailing a ship of state with eleven captains pacing the bridge have developed in Canadians a genius for compromise. During the Suez Crisis of 1956, when it seemed that a third world war was inevitable, Canadian diplomat and later Prime Minister Lester B. ("Mike") Pearson produced in the United Nations a resolution that received unanimous support, ended the crisis, and won him the only Nobel Peace Prize ever awarded a Canadian. Another Canadian who became prime minister, William Lyon Mackenzie King, earned a generous cash payment for teaching John D. Rockefeller a better way to get along with labor unions than by shooting strikers.

That was the same prime minister who, when confronted during World War II with a country violently divided on the issue of sending draftees overseas, pronounced that his government's quintessentially Canadian policy was "conscription if necessary, but not necessarily conscription."

As a legacy to hand down the generations, in the way that Americans believe in their gift for enterprise and the English in their grit, the Canadian ability to straddle issues lacks snap. So does the suggestion that English-speaking Canada derives from discards of the American Revolution. The Revolutionary War of 1776 created not one but two nations. The United States of America grew from the Revolution, Anglo-Canada from the counterrevolution.

The central fact of North American history is that there were fifteen British colonies before 1776. Thirteen rebelled and two did not. "The great refusal," Canadian historian Frank Underhill called it. In truth, neither northern colony had much choice. The Royal Navy was based in one, Nova Scotia, and the British Army in the other, Québec.

The characters of both new nations were molded in the crucible of that revolution and in the migrations that followed. The thirteen colonies that became a republic rid themselves of conservatives, change resisters, traditionalists: American Tories moved north and reestablished under a monarchy in a military state, blissful to have order and security. The two British colonies gradually emptied of dissenters, authority shakers, individualists, free enterprisers, liberty mongers. Nova Scotian Congregationalists with a taste for egalitarianism went back to New England, passing New Englanders who couldn't abide disorder and were moving to Halifax.

Canada developed from people who consciously, and with some considerable sacrifice, chose structure rather than individualism and wanted a powerful state rather than citizen rights. While the American constitution speaks of liberty, the Canadian one says "peace, order and good government."

Northrop Frye, an esteemed academic at the University of Toronto, has written extensively on what he describes as "the garrison mentality" of Canadians. Frye's theory is that because Canadians have lived for more than two centuries in fear of an American invasion, they are scarred. Generations of Canadians depended on first the British Army and now on a faintly militaristic government. The concept of citizen justice, of vigilantes and posses, is as foreign to Canada as to Switzerland.

Even the word *liberty* was alien to early Canadians. It was as reviled as *communist* is in North America today, since it represented a sloganeering and dangerous enemy. In the Canadian context, democracy was an outside agitator.

The United States put its faith in the individual American and got dazzling achievement at the cost of independent Americans choosing to become muggers. Canada put its faith in a paternalistic state and police power, at the cost of flair and private enterprise.

"Anemia was their heritage," grumbled Canadian novelist Mordecai Richler, who frequently despairs upon contemplaing his countrymen's amiable lassitude. Kaspar Naegele, a Canadian sociologist, put it more gently: "There is less emphasis in Canada on equality than there is in the United States. In Canada there seems to be a greater acceptance of limitation, of hierarchial patterns. There seems to be less optimism, less faith in the future, less willingness to risk capital or reputation. In contrast to America, Canada is a country of greater caution, reserve, restraint."

One side of the border has a policeman for a hero, the red-coated Mountie. The other celebrates mavericks. One country believes father is always right; the other may put a bullet in father's head. In the United States the entrepreneur, the person who stands out from the crowd, becomes immortal; the Canadian ideal is the one who emerges from a snowdrift with the toes intact—a survivor.

Differences in style were sharper in the last century. American miners who stampeded north from California in 1860 were met by soldiers and a British judge who hospitably cautioned them to "remember on which side of the line the camp is—for boys, if there is shooting in Kootenay, there will be hanging in Kootenay."

When the great cattle drives of the American Midwest flowed north to railheads in Canada, cowboys adjusted to the shock of being asked to surrender their guns to the single policeman who met them at the border. One Mountie rode into Sitting Bull's camp a few days after the Battle at Little Big Horn, noted fresh American scalps and horses with U.S. cavalry brands, and advised Sitting Bull to obey Canadian laws or he, the Mountie, would deport the whole tribe. And Sitting Bull nodded.

During the Klondike gold rush of the nineties, the American town of Skagway in the Alaskan panhandle was run by a ruthless American gangster and gunfights in the streets were common. Across the border in Canada, Yukon mining towns were so law-abiding that a miner safely could leave his poke of gold in an unlocked cabin.

Canadians don't even litter. Office workers eating picnic lunches in city squares pick up every scrap. The Canadian crime rate is startlingly lower than that in the United States. Detroit policemen visiting their Toronto counterparts noted a chart listing eighteen murders in July. "Pretty heavy weekend," one observed. Toronto police were shocked. Eighteen was the score for the year.

Good behavior, while laudatory, makes people yawn. The world appears to be little impressed with Canada as an important power. The impression is widespread that Canadians, despite some differences with the United States over matters such as scallop fishing in the Atlantic, are in America's hip pocket. There was little surprise during the Vietnam War that Canadians on the United Nations International Control Commission used the opportunity to spy for the American Army. Third World nations, which twenty-five years ago looked to Canada for moral leadership against the Big Powers, no longer count Canada as a neutral.

Also, there is a tendency abroad to dismiss Canada as a small country which isn't too bright. Canadians protest that what seems a pathological willingness to be conned is instead only anxiety to be liked. And, assuredly, the world is wrong about the size. Canada is big, the largest country in the world except for the Soviet Union. It is larger by 300,000 square miles than all of the United States, including Alaska. It stretches from sea to sea to sea—Atlantic, Arctic, and Pacific—giving it the longest coastline of any nation on earth.

"The immense searching distance," Northrop Frye once called it. Few Canadians live more than an afternoon's drive from wilderness. Beyond the towns are woods and lakes, and then rock, tundra, and ice that stretches to the top of the world. The country's small population of 23 million is lost in the big land. There are fewer Canadians than there are people in the Philippine Islands or South Korea; Canada's population is approximately the same as that of Yugoslavia or New York State. But South Korea could be floated on one of Canada's anonymous lakes without disturbing the fish, Yugoslavia is about half the size of Baffin Island, and if New York State were transported north a little, it would find itself lost in the Otish Mountains without a road map, since the Otish Mountains have almost no roads.

The crushing problem the economy has faced since the first commerce, fur trading, is that distances are too enormous for cheap distribution, making private enterprise an endeavor highly likely to lead to bankruptcy. Canadians therefore are employees. What the government doesn't own, multinationals do; no one else can afford costs of transportation. Canadians welcome multinationals: the government gives bonuses and tax breaks; the combines legislation is as weak as that of an African dictatorship; natural resources can be taken from the ground with negligible interference from royalty collectors. For instance, 90 percent of gold taken from the Canadian Klondike at the turn of the century wound up in Fort Knox, the Canadian Government pocketing pennies in return.

The Canadian civil service has been described as the country's only growth industry. It administers extensive welfare services paid, in good part, by foreign investment in Canada. Canada has been providing monthly allowances for mothers for more than thirty years, hospital insurance since 1947, medical insurance since 1962. It supplies unemployment insurance, disability benefits, rape-crisis centers, day-care centers, pensions for the elderly, and, in one province, compensation for victims of crime, and, in two provinces, state-run car insurance.

Canadians expect no less. A semi-feudal system with paternalistic *seigneurs*[6] existed in Canada for a century after it had been abolished in France. Also, Canada through most of its development had no middle class. There was the top of the ladder and there was the bottom of the ladder; in between, there was no ladder. States with a rigid ruling class not uncommonly bestow broad social services to the masses.

By contrast, America's backwardness in such fundamental considerations as Medicare owes much to the Horatio Alger myth of individual invincibility and the American dream of upward mobility for all.

The high cost of Canada's welfare services resulted in the 1980s in a government picturesquely sinking into unmanageable debt, borrowing extravagantly on natural resources fast being leeched from the ground, mostly by the United States. America controls 99.4 percent of Canada's oil and gas deposits, and almost all the coal, iron, asbestos, nickel, pulp and paper mills. Most of Canada's manufacturing sector is U.S.-owned. The country's largest industry, automobiles and automotive parts, is wholly owned by Americans; Americans own 89 percent of all chemical producers, 88 percent of all electrical products, 87 percent of all machinery, 87 percent of all rubber products; only 5 percent of all patents registered in Canada are held by Canadians. Canada is the only country where the domimant labor unions have headquarters in the United States.

Since most Canadian industry is a branch plant of an American conglomerate, Canadians find it almost impossible to compete. There is no Canadian-designed car, few Canadian-designed appliances, and a Canadian clothing industry that would collapse like a three-dollar suit without a tariff wall to protect it. In recent years, as multinational corporations

---

6. *Seigneurs*: members of the landed gentry.

have relocated in Third World countries with right-wing, union-bashing governments, Canada has seen a sharp decline in industry. Whole communities in Canada are thrown out of work when the U.S. parent makes a better business deal in Guatemala or the Philippines.

Canada and the United States are each other's major trading partners, but the exchange is ominous for Canadians. While 70 percent of Canadian exports go to the United States, most are non-renewable natural resources, shipped raw and providing few jobs. But 70 percent of American exports to Canada are manufactured labor-intensive goods.

Canadians appear to have little confidence in their country. Small businesses and factories find it easier to borrow money in New York than in Toronto, while Canadian investors have plunged $20 billion into American enterprise, a sum exceeded in the United States only by the Netherlands and Britain.

Canadians see themselves as hewers of wood and drawers of water, first for France, then for Great Britain, and now for the United States. When the country's natural resources give out, as they will begin to do in the 1980s, the country will be destitute.

Frank Underhill, Canadian historian, once wrote that Canadians are the world's oldest continuing anti-Americans. There are still Canadian nationalists who talk of buying back the country's industries and resources from Yankee carpetbaggers, but most people accept that Canada hasn't enough money for such a grand design. Irritation with the United States in the 1980s was focused instead on border problems. Canadians drink water full of asbestos dumped by Silver Bay, Minnesota, the American switch to coal meant acid rain in Ontario, the U.S.-Canada fish treaty was being held up in the U.S. Senate for years while New England fishing fleets depleted the scallops in contested waters, and the Garrison Dam in North Dakota threatened to back pollution into Manitoba. An American judge, pondering a project in Washington State that would flood British Columbia, raised hackles when he mused aloud, "We have a third dimension here and it's called Canada, and every time I look at it I wonder what I'm going to do about it."

Canadians like to say that when the United States catches a cold, Canada sneezes; also, that being on the same continent as the United States is like being a guppy in a tank of piranhas—it's okay so long as the piranhas aren't hungry. Prime Minister Pierre Elliott Trudeau once observed that Canada is a mouse in bed with an elephant.

Canadians, in truth, admire and envy Americans and imitate them wistfully. Success within Canada is often suspect: most Canadians reason, if the person is really good, why isn't he or she in the United States?

Still, the Parti Québécois victory in 1976 created an invisible shift along the old fault lines.[7] English-speaking Canadians were amazed by their depth of feelings as the country neared the precipice in the weeks leading to the 1980 May referendum. A *Péquiste*[8] cabinet minister, Lise Payette, emerged shaken from a federal-provincial conference. A man wept on her shoulder and said, "Lise, don't go." She reflected, "We had expected English Canadians to react to separatism with cool arguments. We were not prepared for the sheer emotion."

English-Canadians were equally surprised. Their patriotism has been a slow process. Canada was ninety-eight years old before it had its own flag. It was sixty years old before it started to handle its own negotiations with the United States. It was eighty-two years old before it stopped allowing Britain to rearrange its constitution. It was eighty years old before there were Canadian passports and Canadian citizenship. It was eighty-five years old before the governor-general was a Canadian. As recently as 1959, Queen Elizabeth II signed a United Nations document on behalf of Canada; she is the Canadian head of state. Only in 1977 did Canada take power from the Queen of England to accredit and recall diplomats, declare war, and sign peace treaties for Canada. In June 1980 the Canadian Parliament decided to make *O Canada* the national anthem.

"What do you think of a country that has no flag?" an irate nationalist asked American comedian Mort Sahl during a show on Canadian television in the 1950s.

Sahl considered carefully, "Well," he offered, "it's a start."

A national disinterest in Canadian history has created a vacuum in which a variety of desultory emblems and anthems have found accommodation. The beaver, which has come to represent Canada as the eagle does the United States and the lion Britain, is a flat-tailed, slow-witted, toothy rodent known to bite off its own testicles or to stand under its own falling trees.

The maple leaf, another Canadian symbol and the natural choice for the design-a-flag contest in 1965, does not take well to city life in Canada. When Canadians wish to foliate downtown parks with the national tree, they import hardier species from Norway.

As a tourist attraction, Ottawa stages in summer a changing-of-the-guard ceremony in front of the Parliament buildings. The uniforms worn in this operetta are patterned on those last seen on a British expedition on the Nile in 1884. The country's internationally recognized red-coated Mountie is encased in a montage of European cavalry castoffs topped with a hat adapted from the Texas Rangers of the last century.

7. *Parti Québécois*: separatist party within the French-speaking province of Québec. The PQ, under Premier Réné Lévesque, came to power in 1976; in the May 1980 referendum, the electorate voted against political independence for Québec.
8. *Péquiste*: member of the PQ.

There are nearly twenty English versions of the national anthem, *O Canada*. In 1972 the government considered 615 suggestions for lyrics, and finally, in 1980, chose one. No Canadian adult is yet certain which one is official; on formal occasions the last three lines are an incomprehensible babble as loyal Canadians sing whichever version they know best. The French lyrics of *O Canada* bear no similarity to the English. In any event, separatists won't sing it; they prefer *Gens du Pays*.[9]

In the spring of 1973 the *Canadian Magazine* sponsored a contest asking Canadians to submit a better set of lyrics for the national anthem. The editors abandoned the project when two thirds of the suggestions were derisive or obscene, and the word *bland* was overused. The music for *O Canada* was written by a French-Canadian who subsequently moved to the United States and spent his money on pamphlets urging his countrymen to do likewise.

His defection is not unique. Louis Riel, a rebel hanged in Regina, Saskatchewan, in 1885 and commemorated as a hero in 1973 on a Canadian stamp, died an American citizen. Alexander Graham Bell, of Brantford, Ontario, inventor of the telephone, couldn't interest Canadians in backing his device. He's buried under a tombstone inscribed, as he wished, "Died a Citizen of the U.S.A." The first man to sail alone around the world, Joshua Slocum, was born in Nova Scotia in 1844 and was raised there; his thirty-seven-foot yawl flew the Stars and Stripes.

Yet Canada is populated by people who will live nowhere else. They are held in good part by the land. All Canadians share a rapture about the beauty of their country. Canadian calendars usually feature scenery. Until the 1930s, Canadian artists painted little else. During the American bicentennial of 1976, Canada's official gift to the United States was a book of superb photographs of—what else?—scenery.

Canadians are attached to their country by private ecstasies: small, religious experiences that dissolve the senses, as when a loon cries across a still northern lake, or the ocean thunders against the rocks of Cape Breton, or the Rockies leap up out of the prairies at Calgary, or wheat fields under the aching blue arch of the great sky, or the eerie flickering of the aurora borealis above the ice, or even the monotonous tundra that author Farley Mowat described as "a terrestrial ocean whose waves are the rolling ridges."

Canadians tend to be fanatical about the particular part of the country they inhabit: it's the best. In 1973 residents of a desolate Labrador village named Black Tickle refused to relocate on a better site only twelve miles away.

Some of the bliss that Canadians feel contemplating a view is charged with pure pride. The geography everywhere is unforgiving; to survive is

9. *Gens du Pays*: "People of the Country."

an achievement. Half of Canada is covered by the Canadian Shield, the oldest exposed rock on earth. It sprawls in boomerang shape from Labrador to the Great Lakes, covering four fifths of Québec and nine tenths of Ontario. It is rock, the age of which in places is measured at 2.5 billion years, ideal for U.S. astronauts to practice sample-gathering before setting off for the moon.

Only 4 percent of Canada is under cultivation. Another 3 percent is marginally arable but isn't farmed because the yield would be uneconomic. A semi-desert covers the north, a treeless waste carpeted in summer by moss and exquisite miniature flowers. Prairie wheat must grow in a latitude frost-free a mere ninety days a year. The heart of the western plains is a potential dust bowl. A glacier covers 75,000 square miles of Canada, and in Saskatchewan there is a patch of shifting sand stretching for 115 square miles.

People who choose to remain in such a land are magnificently perverse. What the cruel land doesn't clobber the climate will. Though parts of Canada lie as far south as Madrid and Istanbul, and parts are farther south than northern California, it is not apparent in winter. Between the Rockies and the Maritimes, Canada is a scoop that catches the polar cold and hurls it at school children.

Only Siberia and northern Scandinavia are as cold as most of Canada in winter. Montréal spends more money on snow removal than the entire budgets of some emerging nations. Canadians are not surprised that a man ice-fishing in Canada, Clarence Birdseye of Massachusetts, was inspired there to discover the principle of fast-freezing food. Inuit[1] on Baffin Island find it *really* cold only when the temperature drops to −80° F. When it's a mere −40° F and breath frosts eyebrows, Canadians at bus stops exchange looks of pure pleasure: they are feisty; they are invincible; they can take it.

No one on earth appreciates the first warm day of spring as intensely as a Canadian does. The west coast, where golf courses never close, takes spring for granted, but elsewhere it is an armistice. The war is over for a while.

Summers can be torrid with heat waves in the nineties. Even the Yukon has days when the temperature reaches the seventies (or 21° Celsius: to their disgust, Canadians were compelled to begin converting to metric measure in the mid-1970s). Resolute, a weather station five hundred miles north of the Arctic Circle, has two weeks under the midnight sun in July when there is no frost.

Climate shapes character. Climate extremes shape character profoundly. Remorseless winters have forged in Canadians fortitude, endurance, and an ingenuity for survival. The special qualities of Canadians

---

1. Inuit: Eskimos of the Arctic and Labrador coastal areas.

are nowhere more dramatically evinced than in wartime. The only soldiers who didn't run from humankind's first poison gas attack in World War I were Canadians; later, the person who designed a gas mask to withstand the deadly fumes was a Canadian. The army selected by the British to be slaughtered on the Dieppe[2] beaches in World War II was Canadian. The air crews who took the heaviest casualities in that war were Canadians. The men in the dirtiest convoy duty, sailing the North Atlantic in little minesweepers and corvettes, were Canadians.

A character in a Bernard Malamud[3] novel asks, in essence, "Why are you doing this insane thing?"

The answer is, "Because I can."

Military historians agree that Canadians are among the best fighters in the world, not as predictable as the British, not as erratic as the Americans. Instead, they think hard and they don't bolt. That's what Canadians at a bus stop are doing when glittering ice sheathes the city and a wind shrieks mercilessly all the way from the arctic, thinking hard about Florida, but staying.

Canadian novelist and poet Margaret Atwood explored Canadian literature in search of the theme. In a book Survival she demonstrated that the essence of Canadianism is endurance. Canadians, she maintained, are an endangered species, which is why they empathize readily with the plight of baby seals, whooping cranes, and miners trapped in cave-ins. Survival is a Canadian's ideal of epic achievement. She concluded that, if a Canadian had written Moby Dick, the book would have been done from the perspective of the whale.

Canadian bush pilots flew in the arctic in open-cockpit planes in winter. Canadians fish on the Atlantic from open dories so exposed their hands freeze to the nets. It was a Canadian who put on a wet suit and went first under the ice at the North Pole. Canadians walked all over North America a century before Americans dared to leave the safety of the Atlantic coast.

That's heroism on a grand scale. But somehow it hasn't permeated the country's psyche in a way that emerges as national self-esteem and identity. Canadian unity founders on particularism. Poeple who come to Canada do not surrender the past and don a new nationality as immigrants to the United States do. They come to Canada because it's available, because it's all right, because it's preferable to whatever they left. In Canada they keep their roots; there is little repotting even to the third generation. They remain Scots, Ukrainians, Haitians; no altered loyalty seizes their imaginations.

The Melting Pot is American. Immigrants there dissolve in bubbling

2. Dieppe: French coastal town on the English Channel where, in 1942, Allied forces, mostly Canadians, suffered a loss against the Germans.

3. Bernard Malamud (1914–1986): American novelist.

assimilation; they become Americans. Canada has the *Mosaic*. The country doesn't assimilate and never aspired to. The pieces of the Canadian Mosaic are beautiful, as in Cape Breton towns where people converse in Gaelic still, or the spanking clean Hutterite[4] villages of Alberta, or the Portuguese neighborhoods of Toronto where black-eyed babies wear tiny gold rings in their ears. But the parts don't merge as a conherent whole.

Canadians suspect that an invasion by the United States would unite them overnight. The country's fingers closed into a fist in the 1970s when an American ship, *Manhattan*, took liberties in Canadian territorial water in the arctic. Such an event, however gratifying to nationalists, is hardly likely. American presidents since Franklin Delano Roosevelt have been unable to restrain their speech writers from admiring the world's longest undefended border. In truth, the United States doesn't arm the border because it doesn't need to, and Canada doesn't arm the border because people would fall down laughing at the presumption.

The border indeed is undefended. It is porous. The Haskell Free Library in Vermont, for instance, has black tape across the floor to designate the border. The librarian is Canadian, but her office is on the American side of the tape. A fire in the bathroom in 1976 brought a surveyor to determine whether a Canadian or an American firm would pay.

Pinecreek, Minnesota, has a binational airport. Planes landing on the Canadian end of the runway finish their taxiing in the United States. In Washington State, Metcalfe's Cafe in Point Roberts straddles the border. When patrons imbibe too much in the Canadian end of the room, the proprietor calls the Canadian police. Patrons then pick up their glasses and move to the other end of the bar. There's a woman in Edmundston, New Brunswick, whose parlor is in Canada and kitchen in the United States.

A Canadian general in the 1920s drafted a contingency plan for the invasion of the United States by Canada. He based it on military intelligence obtained by asking for the free road maps available at American gasoline stations. Eventually he was led away with a butterfly net over his head. The Pentagon, on the other hand, has detailed campaigns designed for the invasion of Canada which were adjusted in 1976 when the separatists won the election.

If Québec ever leaves Canada the new nation will call its people *Québécois*; Canadians will be foreigners. That's ironic. Canada is the name French settlers insisted upon in the seventeenth century. They rejected the king's efforts to call their country La Nouvelle France. They were not French, they said. They were a new breed of people, *Canadiens*.

4. Hutterite: a member of a Christian sect, closely related to the Mennonites, who believes in common ownership of property.

The word *Canada* comes from a journal of the sixteenth-century explorer Jacques Cartier, who spelled it *Kanata*. The most accepted translation of the lost Iroquois word is that it meant "a collection of huts." When Cartier indicated by sign language that he wanted to know what natives called their land, the Iroquois told him "Kanata." Etymologists now believe the Iroquois thought Cartier referred to the nearby village, a collection of huts.

The other plausible explanation is that the Iroquois used a phrase picked up from Portuguese fishermen who made annual voyages to catch cod and whales long before Cartier's time. According to this theory, the visitors impressed the natives with the fervent comment, "*Aca nada, aca nada!*" which means, "There is nothing here *nothing!*"

"No one knows my country," historian Bruce Hutchison wrote sadly. "My country has not found itself."

Québec has. Alberta has. Newfoundland has. The Yukon is in the process. Vancouver Island has. Cape Breton has. Northern Ontario is in the process. . . .

A collection of huts.

1981

N. Scott Momaday

THE WAY TO RAINY MOUNTAIN

A single knoll rises out of the plain in Oklahoma, north and west of the Wichita Range. For my people, the Kiowas, it is an old landmark, and they gave it the name Rainy Mountain. The hardest weather in the world is there. Winter brings blizzards, hot tornadic winds arise in the spring, and in summer the prairie is an anvil's edge. The grass turns brittle and brown, and it cracks beneath your feet. There are green belts along the rivers and creeks, linear groves of hickory and pecan, willow and witch hazel. At a distance in July or August the steaming foliage seems almost to writhe in fire. Great green and yellow grasshoppers are everywhere in the tall grass, popping up like corn to sting the flesh, and tortoises crawl about on the red earth, going nowhere in the plenty of time. Loneliness is an aspect of the land. All things in the plain are isolate; there is no confusion of objects in the eye, but *one* hill or *one* tree or *one* man. To look upon that landscape in the early morning, with the sun at your back, is to lose the sense of proportion. Your imagination comes to life, and this, you think, is where Creation was begun.

I returned to Rainy Mountain in July. My grandmother had died in the spring, and I wanted to be at her grave. She had lived to be very old and at last infirm. Her only living daughter was with her when she died, and I was told that in death her face was that of a child.

I like to think of her as a child. When she was born, the Kiowas were living the last great moment of their history. For more than a hundred years they had controlled the open range from the Smoky Hill River to the Red, from the headwaters of the Canadian to the fork of the Arkansas and Cimarron. In alliance with the Comanches, they had ruled the whole of the southern Plains. War was their sacred business, and they were among the finest horsemen the world has ever known. But warfare for the Kiowas was preeminently a matter of disposition rather than of survival, and they never understood the grim, unrelenting advance of the U.S. Cavalry. When at last, divided and ill-provisioned, they were driven onto the Staked Plains in the cold rains of autumn, they fell into panic. In Palo Duro Canyon they abandoned their crucial stores to pillage and had nothing then but their lives. In order to save themselves, they surrendered to the soldiers at Fort Sill and were imprisoned in the old stone corral that now stands as a military museum. My grandmother was spared the humiliation of those high gray walls by eight or ten years, but she must have known from birth the affliction of defeat, the dark brooding of old warriors.

Her name was Aho, and she belonged to the last culture to evolve in North America. Her forebears came down from the high country in western Montana nearly three centuries ago. They were a mountain people, a mysterious tribe of hunters whose language has never been positively classified in any major group. In the late seventeenth century they began a long migration to the south and east. It was a journey toward the dawn, and it led to a golden age. Along the way the Kiowas were befriended by the Crows, who gave them the culture and religion of the Plains. They acquired horses, and their ancient nomadic spirit was suddenly free of the ground. They acquired Tai-me, the sacred Sun Dance doll, from that moment the object and symbol of their worship, and so shared in the divinity of the sun. Not least, they acquired the sense of destiny, therefore courage and pride. When they entered upon the southern Plains they had been transformed. No longer were they slaves to the simple necessity of survival; they were a lordly and dangerous society of fighters and thieves, hunters and priests of the sun. According to their origin myth, they entered the world through a hollow log. From one point of view, their migration was the fruit of an old prophecy, for indeed they emerged from a sunless world.

Although my grandmother lived out her long life in the shadow of Rainy Mountain, the immense landscape of the continental interior lay like memory in her blood. She could tell of the Crows, whom she had never seen, and of the Black Hills, where she had never been. I wanted to see in reality what she had seen more perfectly in the mind's eye, and traveled fifteen hundred miles to begin my pilgrimage.

Yellowstone, it seemed to me, was the top of the world, a region of deep lakes and dark timber, canyons and waterfalls. But, beautiful as it is, one might have the sense of confinement there. The skyline in all directions is close at hand, the high wall of the woods and deep cleavages of shade. There is a perfect freedom in the mountains, but it belongs to the eagle and the elk, the badger and the bear. The Kiowas reckoned their stature by the distance they could see, and they were bent and blind in the wilderness.

Descending eastward, the highland meadows are a stairway to the plain. In July the inland slope of the Rockies is luxuriant with flax and buckwheat, stonecrop and larkspur. The earth unfolds and the limit of the land recedes. Clusters of trees, and animals grazing far in the distance, cause the vision to reach away and wonder to build upon the mind. The sun follows a longer course in the day, and the sky is immense beyond all comparison. The great billowing clouds that sail upon it are the shadows that move upon the grain like water, dividing light. Farther down, in the land of the Crows and Blackfeet, the plain is yellow. Sweet clover takes hold of the hills and bends upon itself to cover and seal the soil. There the Kiowas paused on their way; they had come to the place where they must change their lives. The sun is at home on the plains. Precisely there does it have the certain character of a god. When the Kiowas came to the land of the Crows, they could see the dark lees of the hills at dawn across the Bighorn River, the profusion of light on the grain shelves, the oldest deity ranging after the solstices. Not yet would they veer southward to the caldron of the land that lay below; they must wean their blood from the northern winter and hold the mountains a while longer in their view. They bore Tai-me in procession to the east.

A dark mist lay over the Black Hills, and the land was like iron. At the top of a ridge I caught sight of Devil's Tower upthrust against the gray sky as if in the birth of time the core of the earth had broken through its crust and the motion of the world was begun. There are things in nature that engender an awful quiet in the heart of man; Devil's Tower is one of them. Two centuries ago, because they could not do otherwise, the Kiowas made a legend at the base of the rock. My grandmother said:
Eight children were there at play, seven sisters and their brother. Suddenly the boy was struck dumb; he trembled and began to run upon his hands and feet. His fingers became claws, and his body was covered with fur. Directly there was a bear where the boy had been. The sisters were terrified; they ran, and the bear after them. They came to the stump of a great tree, and the tree spoke to them. It bade them climb upon it, and as they did so it began to rise into the air. The bear came to kill them, but they were just beyond its reach. It reared against the tree and scored the bark all around with its claws.

The seven sisters were borne into the sky, and they became the stars of the Big Dipper.

From that moment, and so long as the legend lives, the Kiowas have kinsmen in the night sky. Whatever they were in the mountains, they could be no more. However tenuous their well-being, however much they had suffered and would suffer again, they had found a way out of the wilderness.

My grandmother had a reverence for the sun, a holy regard that now is all but gone out of mankind. There was a wariness in her, and an ancient awe. She was a Christian in her later years, but she had come a long way about, and she never forgot her birthright. As a child she had been to the Sun Dances; she had taken part in those annual rites, and by them she had learned the restoration of her people in the presence of Tai-me. She was about seven when the last Kiowa Sun Dance was held in 1887 on the Washita River above Rainy Mountain Creek. The buffalo were gone. In order to consummate the ancient sacrifice—to impale the head of a buffalo bull upon the medicine tree—a delegation of old men journeyed into Texas, there to beg and barter for an animal from the Goodnight herd. She was ten when the Kiowas came together for the last time as a living Sun Dance culture. They could find no buffalo; they had to hang an old hide from the sacred tree. Before the dance could begin, a company of soldiers rode out from Fort Sill under orders to disperse the tribe. Forbidden without cause the essential act of their faith, having seen the wild herds slaughtered and left to rot upon the ground, the Kiowas backed away forever from the medicine tree. That was July 20, 1890, at the great bend of the Washita. My grandmother was there. Without bitterness, and for as long as she lived, she bore a vision of deicide.

Now that I can have her only in memory, I see my grandmother in the several postures that were peculiar to her: standing at the wood stove on a winter morning and turning meat in a great iron skillet; sitting at the south window, bent above her beadwork, and afterwards, when her vision failed, looking down for a long time into the fold of her hands; going out upon a cane, very slowly as she did when the weight of age came upon her; praying. I remember her most often at prayer. She made long, rambling prayers out of suffering and hope, having seen many things. I was never sure that I had the right to hear, so exclusive where they of all mere custom and company. The last time I saw her she prayed standing by the side of her bed at night, naked to the waist, the light of a kerosene lamp moving upon her dark skin. Her long, black hair, always drawn and braided in the day, lay upon her shoulders and against her breasts like a shawl. I do not speak Kiowa, and I never understood her prayers, but there was something inherently sad in the sound, some merest hesitation upon the syllables of sorrow. She began in a high and descending pitch, exhausting her breath to silence; then again and again

—and always the same intensity of effort, of something that is, and is not, like urgency in the human voice. Transported so in the dancing light among the shadows of her room, she seemed beyond the reach of time. But that was illusion; I think I knew then that I should not see her again.

Houses are like sentinels in the plain, old keepers of the weather watch. There, in a very little while, wood takes on the appearance of great age. All colors wear soon away in the wind and rain, and then the wood is burned gray and the grain appears and the nails turn red with rust. The windowpanes are black and opaque; you imagine there is nothing within, and indeed there are many ghosts, bones given up to the land. They stand here and there against the sky, and you approach them for a longer time than you expect. They belong in the distance; it is their domain.

Once there was a lot of sound in my grandmother's house, a lot of coming and going, feasting and talk. The summers there were full of excitement and reunion. The Kiowas are a summer people; they abide the cold and keep to themselves, but when the season turns and the land becomes warm and vital they cannot hold still; an old love of going returns upon them. The aged visitors who came to my grandmother's house when I was a child were made of lean and leather, and they bore themselves upright. They wore great black hats and bright ample shirts that shook in the wind. They rubbed fat upon their hair and wound their braids with strips of colored cloth. Some of them painted their faces and carried the scars of old and cherished enmities. They were an old council of warlords, come to remind and be reminded of who they were. Their wives and daughters served them well. The women might indulge themselves; gossip was at once the mark and compensation of their servitude. They made loud and elaborate talk among themselves, full of jest and gesture, fright and false alarm. They went abroad in fringed and flowered shawls, bright beadwork and German silver. They were at home in the kitchen, and they prepared meals that were banquets.

There were frequent prayer meetings, and great nocturnal feasts. When I was a child I played with my cousins outside, where the lamplight fell upon the ground and the singing of the old people rose up around us and carried away into the darkness. There were a lot of good things to eat, a lot of laughter and surprise. And afterwards, when the quiet returned, I lay down with my grandmother and could hear the frogs away by the river and feel the motion of the air.

Now there is a funeral silence in the rooms, the endless wake of some final word. The walls have closed in upon my grandmother's house. When I returned to it in mourning, I saw for the first time in my life how small it was. It was late at night, and there was a white moon, nearly full. I sat for a long time on the stone steps by the kitchen door. From there I could see out across the land; I could see the long row of trees by the creek, the low light upon the rolling plains, and the stars of the Big Dipper. Once I looked at the moon and caught sight of a strange thing. A cricket had perched upon the handrail, only a few inches away from me. My line of vision was such that the creature filled the moon like a fossil. It had gone there, I thought, to live and die, for there, of all places, was its small definition made whole and eternal. A warm wind rose up and purled like the longing within me.

The next morning I awoke at dawn and went out on the dirt road to Rainy Mountain. It was already hot, and the grasshoppers began to fill the air. Still, it was early in the morning, and the birds sang out of the shadows. The long yellow grass on the mountain shone in the bright light, and a scissortail hied above the land. There, where it ought to be, at the end of a long and legendary way, was my grandmother's grave. Here and there on the dark stones were ancestral names. Looking back once, I saw the mountain and came away.

1969

Jane Howard

POMP AND CIRCUMSTANCE IN GROUNDHOG HOLLOW

Every morning Matilda Titus Hastings fixes her husband, Wayne, a panful of biscuits and gravy to go with his specially fried eggs. Perhaps as a subtle consequence of this repeated alchemy, in the same way that dogs come to resemble their masters, Matilda looks something like a biscuit herself, wholesomely puffy. "Only one woman in Atkins, West Virginia," she likes to say, "is bigger than I am—the lady who runs the tavern."

But Tildy, as she is usually known except to the twelve who call her Mama and the three dozen or so to whom she is Granny, is not really all that fat. What she is is comfortable looking. Her hair, which never in her life has been cut, is pinned up in braids. "Before it got so thin," she says, "the braids were about as wide as my wrist."

She wears glasses for sewing, the only work for which she has ever been paid, and for reading, which is her furtive pleasure. (She reads on the sly, the way some people gamble.) Outside, on bright days, she puts on a homemade sunbonnet. Most of her dresses she makes herself, for about a dollar each, but once she spent sixteen dollars on a three-piece lace outfit. She owns two costume-jewelry pins. One, crown-shaped, is composed of the birthstones of her ten daughters and two sons. The other, made of coal, is shaped like West Virginia.

* * *

The Hastingses' two-story house is modest by many standards, but in West Virginia it is thought to be imposing. To get to that house you have to take a rough ride up Groundhog Hollow Road. The car bounces and jounces and rattles and shakes and so, if you are a passenger, do you. "I tell people that's how come I had so many girl babies," Tildy jokes during one such ride. "Going up and down this road all the time, I shook the balls off them."

Groundhog Hollow Road leads down a steep hill to Atkins, where the Hastingses shop. Turn right there and drive four miles and you will come to Rollo, where they get their mail. All around that region you will see cars with Kentucky and Virginia license plates, because both state borders are nearby. Medical facilities, however, are not. If something is wrong with the Hastingses' teeth, for example, they have to drive thirty-five miles to Welch. "There's supposed to be a dentist in War, sixteen miles over," says Tildy, "but seems like you never can find him in."

McDowell County, in which the Hastingses live, has been called the Coal Bin of America. Slag heaps in the wake of strip mines desecrate the lyrically lovely hillsides. Abandoned car hulks rot, with all deliberate speed, in stream beds. The best of the roads are poor. All change comes slowly. Incest is not unheard of—"They try to hush it up, but word gets around."—nor is illiteracy. "A lot of people," says Tildy, "have to have the postmistress read them their Black Lung checks." Ninety percent of the men in McDowell County who work or have worked in mines, including Wayne Hastings, suffer from silicosis.

Movie theaters and libraries are scarce, but churches abound. Just down the road from Groundhog Hollow, in Atkins, is a church whose members believe that the command given in Mark 16:18, "They shall take up serpents," must be followed literally. On Saturday evenings they really do handle real snakes. I wanted to visit this church the weekend I spent with the Hastingses; to me it sounded as exotic as a mosque. Wayne said we could, but first we would go to the Church of Christ, where he sometimes preaches. The service there lasted so long that by the time we got out the snake-handlers had gone home.

Tildy does not share her husband's enthusiasm for the Church of Christ, by which he is in fact ordained and to which he converted dramatically in 1953. Nothing can lure her away from the Jacob's Ladder Branch Church of the Old Hosanna Regular Primitive Baptist Association. She and Wayne can argue for hours about theology.

"It like to kill her daddy when Grace Ellen joined the Primitive Baptists," Tildy said of one of her daughters. "He said he'd rather see them dead than join my church. Several of the others joined his. On the surface you might think they cared more for their daddy than for me, because they make over him more. But they feared him, while I was more their friend. I'd stop them if they ever said anything disrespectful. I'd say 'That's your father, so don't you say that.'

"Wayne is interested in death and the hereafter," she says. "He believes in hell and damnation, everlasting fires. I'm interested in Christ and salvation. I believe we get our punishments and our blessings right here on earth. I can't believe I need to be water-baptized in total immersion to avoid eternal damnation. You should come here sometime the first Sunday in August, when we have, in my church, our old-time foot-washing.

"We wash each other's feet with two towels sewed together. Ladies wait on female members, men on men, and it doesn't matter whose feet we wash, because we all just love each other so much we want to be at each other's feet in humility. As we wash each other's feet, we keep on singing."

If you were setting Tildy's life to a musical score, you would draw from three sources: "Earnestly, Tenderly, Jesus Is Calling," "Turkey in the Straw," and "Pomp and Circumstance." Nothing in all the Hastings house is more arresting than the array in the living room of twelve high-school graduation pictures. Six graduates on top, six below, born between 1928 and 1947, each one dressed in cap and gown, some with diplomas clutched close to their cheeks.

The youngest of these children did not technically get a diploma but a certificate of attendance. "She had to fight to finish high school; she wanted so bad to have that picture up there with the others. Her I.Q. is 85, and she doesn't retain information. Wayne thought it was the teachers' fault; he thought they didn't try hard enough to pound the learning into her. In his own childhood, you see, people weren't retarded. They were crazy.

"But Wayne is as proud of those pictures as I am. He drives around even now, with all our children grown and gone, to visit the schoolrooms, or he tries to, anyway." In one schoolroom, a couple of years ago, a teacher told Wayne he could not pay an impromptu visit without special permission from the Board of Education. This hurt him. "If that ain't communism," he asked rhetorically, "could you tell me what is?"

Tildy herself, the second of nine children, only went as far as the eighth grade, because her father didn't believe in sending girls to high school. Sometimes, even when ice covered the ground, she would walk to school barefoot and contemplate stealing something from the country store so that she might be sent to reform school, "because at least it was a school.

"I was born in nineteen and eleven and raised up at the top of this same mountain," she says, "and I like to say my father moved just about every time the moon changed. We had a lot of superstitions in those days. If your nose itched, it meant somebody coming. If a rooster crowed on your porch before breakfast, you'd have company. If you stepped on a rusty nail, the thing to do was pull it out, rub it with bacon rind, and hang it on a hook. If you got a snake bite, you'd wrap the bite in black tape and try to kill the snake before it got to water—then the bite would heal."

From the moment she first saw Wayne Hastings, "I thought he was about the handsomest guy in the world. I was at a spring, dipping water, and he passed by and said, 'How do you do?' There was never another man in my life before and there hasn't been one since. Once I said I knew of two women around here who were decent, and someone said, 'Oh? Which two?' I said, 'Well, I know I am, and I'm pretty sure Mama is.' Mama was there, and she said, ''Pon my word, daughter, I am.'

"One night Wayne walked me home from a tent meeting and we started keeping company. He never proposed and I didn't, either. One day he said, 'I'm not going to walk this ridge so much.' I said, 'Oh? Why not?' He said, 'I'm going to make them come to see us.' He was twenty-two and I was seventeen when we got married on September nineteenth, nineteen and twenty-eight. It was a Wednesday, a popular day to be married in those times, and we never knew what a honeymoon was, except that somebody caught us a catfish so long it wouldn't lay flat in a three-dollar washtub.

"My mama warned me that Wayne was from a family that drank right much, and for a long time he did. He could be mean: he'd fuss at the children and once when he was cleaning onions with a butcher knife he looked at me and said, 'I ought to cut your throat.' I said, 'Go ahead, if you can,' and took off my glasses and stood right there, but he didn't. I left him once, over drinking, but I couldn't abandon the babies, so I came back. He never missed a day's work over it, and he was always a good provider. In October of nineteen and fifty-three he joined the church and never had a drop since, not even after the accident."

A rock "as big as a mattress on a bed" fell onto Wayne's spine inside the Island Creek Coal Company mine in 1959. "He was hunkered on his heels—they were blasting to get the coal out and he was shot fireman. Compared to what could have happened he was lucky. The hole he was caught in, they said, didn't look big enough for an eight-year-old child to survive in. And they weren't sure he would be able to walk at all, or have any use whatsoever of his sexual organs." A two-year period of rehabilitation at a United Mine Workers hospital in New Jersey restored partial use of the lower half of Wayne's body, but life has been difficult ever since then both for him and his wife.

"His morale was right bad after the accident. Once he said he felt so worthless we'd be better off without him, and he told me to get a divorce. I said, 'You can't drive me away—I don't want a divorce and you can't get one. When we were married I said it would be for life, and I've always held to that.' My one prayer is that I'll outlive him, so I can care for him as long as he lives. I don't think the children could cope with him. When I'm gone he subsists, but he never eats the right food, and he won't go visit his sisters. They offer to do for him, but he won't have it."

Tildy still likes to read visitors a letter she once received from her eighth child, Louella: "I think about when I was younger," Louella wrote, "maybe twenty or twenty-five years ago. I think about good things. I see the beauty of the mountains we lived in. All the fields cleared, with all the dandelions growing everywhere and the milkweeds and polk berries, the log house and the spring in the holler. Beautiful, beautiful sunshine everywhere. The cows, chickens, cats, and dogs. I don't believe the sun could shine any brighter than in the spring and fall as it did then. In spring everything seemed greener than green and in fall, everything red, yellow, and colors that can't be named. Hickory nuts and walnuts and squirrels. Watching the house being built was one long, beautiful movie."

Before they moved into their present house, in 1949, the Hastingses lived in a four-room log cabin half a mile or so down Groundhog Hollow. Before Wayne's illness there was no telephone; only since 1962 have they had indoor plumbing. Tildy can remember the first car she ever saw: "In nineteen and eighteen it sounded like a helicopter sounds now. When I heard it coming up the hill, I ran and hid." Not so long ago she herself washed on a board, cooked on a wood stove, and hand-ground entire 250-pound hogs, storing the meat in Mason jars.

Her babies were delivered in the old log cabin, with the help of a midwife. "When it was time, we'd send a neighbor boy over the mountain on a mule to fetch her, and she'd walk down with a bag that had in it a scale, a scissors, and a cord. Her fee was five dollars, and if she had to she'd stay around for a week at a time. She wasn't in any hurry to go. She was a wonderful woman, and I was blessed to sit by her bed and hold her hand when she left this world.

"If I had it to do over I'd have fewer children, because there isn't room enough in the world for everyone to have as many as I did, but I sure can't tell you which of them I'd give up. Without anesthetics it wasn't easy having them, but you just grit you teeth and bear it. Once I had six under the age of five, and when my youngest daughter was three months old my system wasn't too strong, and I almost had a nervous breakdown. If the company doctor hadn't got my tubes tied, I might have had more still. Wayne would divorce me if he heard me say so, but I feel more strongly about sterilization than abortions, though I think there are times when abortions should be permitted too."

Tildy tells of a doctor's visit to an equally fecund friend of hers. The doctor, calling on the woman in another old log cabin, suggested that properly timed cold baths might help to reduce chances of pregnancy. "Doctor," the woman asked him, "do you see that creek down there?" He saw it, a good 150 yards away. "Doctor, do you think I'm going to go down there four or five times a night to take a cold bath? Because, Doctor, if you do, you'd better think again."

Wayne and Tildy, like many American couples, have their failures in communication. "A lot of times I find out from other people what's going on with him," says Tildy. They have chronic disagreements, too. Wayne, for example, is still not persuaded that reading anything other than the Holy Scripture is a worthwhile activity. "Wayne says that reading costs money and that time spent reading could be better spent doing something different. But I've always read, all my life, and I'm not about to stop. I used to read to the kids, one on either knee, whether they wanted me to or not. Once, when I was missing my copies of *Life* magazine, I went to ask the postmistress how come they hadn't been coming, and she hinted that Wayne had them sent back. I said to him that if my magazine didn't come that next week, I'd go to the drugstore and buy a copy, so that was the end of that.

"But when the children were in school and he was working on the night shift, I'd read all the school books I missed as a child, and a novel a night. I've read *Franklin and Eleanor* and *My Life with Jackie* (I liked it but thought that author lady was very disloyal) and several of Taylor Caldwell's books and *Jane Eyre* and *I Know Why the Caged Bird Sings* and *Tap Roots*, a Civil War story that dealt with the Negro race, and a lot of Reader's Digest Condensed Books and *A Lion in the Streets* and *For Whom the Bell Tolls* and *Forever Amber* and another one I can't remember.

"I watch television some, but not as much as a lot of people do. Television's changed things a lot. Before television people used to be more friendlier, pay more attention, be more relaxed and settle-minded. Used to be whole families would come for a visit and stay overnight. Now sometimes weeks pass and nobody stops by here."

Not one of the Hastings children has settled in West Virginia: "They all went other places to find work, and they all found it too." It saddens the parents that none of the children wants to inherit the house they struggled so hard to build. "It's a dream," says Tildy, "but we'd like to make the house, after we pass on, into a home for wayward girls or old people or maybe disabled miners."

Most of the children live close enough, in neighboring states, to make occasional visits. Once in a while, in a masterful triumph of choreogra-

phy, the whole family is reunited. On one such occasion somebody had
made a sign which still hangs: OCCUPANCY BY MORE THAN 25
PERSONS IN THIS BATHROOM IS BOTH ILLEGAL AND UN-
LAWFUL. And one July, when many of the dozen came home, they
chipped in to buy their parents a new dinette set. "A couple of them took
us down to the store in their car," Tildy remembers, "and when we drove
back, they'd keep saying, 'Wonder if Santy Claus has been here?' When
we got home, we saw the old chairs we'd been using out on the porch and
the new set inside. Both our reclining chairs were gifts from the children
too. Oh, we couldn't be more proud of them all."

Had she not had so many children, Tildy thinks she might have been a
nurse or a writer. "I love to take care of people and I love to tell about
people. You don't raise twelve children and help with a lot of grandchildren without doing a lot of nursing. I've helped in hospitals and had
patients to ask me how long I've been in nursing. I delivered a baby one
time in an emergency and helped with a lot of other deliveries. I put the
first diaper on Clifford's wife's baby and the first diaper on Clifford's wife
herself too.

"Once, out on Atkins mountain, a favorite uncle of mine had a stroke. I
was out there caring for him when another daughter in Indiana was about
to have surgery, and another one's babies were ill, and Wayne's mother
had taken a turn for the worse. I debated which to go to: Grace Ellen or
Velma Jean, and decided Velma Jean needed me worse. I stayed at the
hospital a couple of nights and helped in the house, too. Wayne called
and said Grace Ellen had to have brain surgery.

"Wilma, the one whose husband was in jail for being an alcoholic, she
was about to go to the hospital for a baby. So I called her the next morning
in Dayton, and the nurse said she was coming along fine. Wayne and I
went to see Grace Ellen and found her mother-in-law already there. She
said Grace Ellen was getting along all right, but Lord, how she looked. I
got home Saturday evening, went to church Sunday morning, and on
Monday morning went to Tennessee to get Wilma's boys. Tuesday
morning I went to the hospital myself, from what I guess you might call
an overdose of motherhood. I've had a heart condition, and spells off and
on, ever since. I have to take it pretty easy these days.

"But there's lots of things I want to do. For one, I'd like right much to
look into genealogy. They tell me my people go back to 1066, and that
we're descended from a queen of England. I'd like to travel too, right
much more than Wayne ever wanted to. It's hard for the kids to entertain
their daddy when he and I come to visit. One thing he did like, when we
went to Washington to see Louella, he liked the Wax Museum."

* * *

"I don't think I can stay on the Mountain Artisans[1] board," Tildy said, "because of my health. But being *paid* to do the kind of work I've always done anyway since I was seven has given me a self-confidence I never had before. Somebody said the quilts we make aren't art, because we make them to a design and art's something there's only one of, but I said, 'What could be more artistic than something our grandmothers taught us how to do?'

"Besides, one year I earned $841, and some have made plenty more than that. For some, including me, it's the first money we ever made in our lives, and for others it's the only source of income at all. Not that I expect to be paid for all I do. I like working in the community too, trying to get school buses to go up into the hollers to get to the children, organizing a buyers' club, helping with Head Start, and helping with the old people too. Seems to me whatever more pleasure they can get, they sure do deserve it.

"Old women seem to me more lonely than old men, because old men can get together more, on street corners and in barber shops. Women are more sure of themselves than men, in this area anyway, but to me women'll always be women, and they shouldn't try not to." Tildy put on a checkered sunbonnet and walked out her back door to look up over the hill. "But I don't think any person, male or female, should be a doormat," she went on. "I've heard married couples to say they've never had an argument in their lives. All I can say to that is they must be mighty meek and mild. I'm sure glad *I'm* not married to a man like that, and I'll bet the men wouldn't like it much either. I guess it works out about equal most of the time, but you could put it this way, if you understand what I mean: we make men *think* they run the show."

1973, 1982

.

---

1. A cooperative that marketed patchwork quilts and other products of West Virginia seamstresses.

Virginia Woolf

GREAT MEN'S HOUSES

London, happily, is becoming full of great men's houses, bought for the nation and preserved entire with the chairs they sat on and the cups they drank from, their umbrellas and their chests of drawers. And it is no frivolous curiosity that sends us to Dickens's house and Johnson's house and Carlyle's house and Keats's house. We know them from their houses —it would seem to be a fact that writers stamp themselves upon their possessions more indelibly than other people. Of artistic taste they may have none; but they seem always to possess a much rarer and more interesting gift—a faculty for housing themselves appropriately, for making the table, the chair, the curtain, the carpet into their own image.

Take the Carlyles, for instance. One hour spent in 5 Cheyne Row will tell us more about them and their lives than we can learn from all the biographies. Go down into the kitchen. There, in two seconds, one is made acquainted with a fact that escaped the attention of Froude,[1] and yet was of incalculable importance—they had no water laid on. Every drop that the Carlyles used—and they were Scots, fanatical in their cleanliness—had to be pumped by hand from a well in the kitchen. There is the well at this moment and the pump and the stone trough into which the cold water trickled. And here, too, is the wide and wasteful old grate upon which all kettles had to be boiled if they wanted a hot bath; and here is the cracked yellow tin bath, so deep and so narrow, which had to be filled with the cans of hot water that the maid first pumped and then boiled and then carried up three flights of stairs from the basement.

The high old house without water, without electric light, without gas fires, full of books and coal smoke and four-poster beds and mahogany cupboards, where two of the most nervous and exacting people of their time lived, year in year out, was served by one unfortunate maid. All through the mid-Victorian age the house was necessarily a battlefield where daily, summer and winter, mistress and maid fought against dirt and cold for cleanliness and warmth. The stairs, carved as they are and wide and dignified, seem worn by the feet of harassed women carrying tin cans. The high panelled rooms seem to echo with the sound of pumping and the swish of scrubbing. The voice of the house—and all houses have voices—is the voice of pumping and scrubbing, of coughing and groaning. Up in the attic under a skylight Carlyle groaned, as he wrestled with his history,[2] on a horsehair chair, while a yellow shaft of London light fell

---

1. James Anthony Froude (1818–1894): Car-   2. *History of the French Revolution* (1837).
lyle's biographer.

upon his papers and the rattle of a barrel organ and the raucous shouts of street hawkers came through walls whose double thickness distorted but by no means excluded the sound. And the season of the house—for every house has its season—seems to be always the month of February, when cold and fog are in the street and torches flare and the rattle of wheels grows suddenly loud and dies away. February after February Mrs. Carlyle lay coughing[3] in the large four-poster hung with maroon curtains in which she was born, and as she coughed the many problems of the incessant battle, against dirt, against cold, came before her. The horsehair couch needed recovering; the drawing-room paper with its small, dark pattern needed cleaning; the yellow varnish on the panels was cracked and peeling—all must be stitched, cleansed, scoured with her own hands; and had she, or had she not, demolished the bugs that bred and bred in the ancient wood panelling? So the long watches of the sleepless night passed, and then she heard Mr. Carlyle stir above her, and held her breath and wondered if Helen were up and had lit the fire and heated the water for his shaving. Another day had dawned and the pumping and the scrubbing must begin again.

Thus number 5 Cheyne Row is not so much a dwelling-place as a battlefield—the scene of labor, effort and perpetual struggle. Few of the spoils of life—its graces and its luxuries—survive to tell us that the battle was worth the effort. The relics of drawing-room and study are like the relics picked up on other battlefields. Here is a packet of old steel nibs; a broken clay pipe; a pen-holder such as schoolboys use; a few cups of white and gold china, much chipped; a horsehair sofa and a yellow tin bath. Here, too, is a cast of the thin worn hands that worked here, and of the excruciated and ravished face of Carlyle when his life was done and he lay dead here. Even the garden at the back of the house seems to be not a place of rest and recreation, but another smaller battlefield marked with a tombstone beneath which a dog lies buried. By pumping and by scrubbing, days of victory, evenings of peace and splendor were won, of course. Mrs. Carlyle sat, as we see from the picture, in a fine silk dress, in a chair pulled up to a blazing fire and had everything seemly and solid about her; but at what cost had she won it! Her cheeks are hollow; bitterness and suffering mingle in the half-tender, half-tortured expression of the eyes. Such is the effect of a pump in the basement and a yellow tin bath up three pairs of stairs. Both husband and wife had genius; they loved each other; but what can genius and love avail against bugs and tin baths and pumps in the basement?

It is impossible not to believe that half their quarrels might have been spared and their lives immeasurably sweetened if only number 5 Cheyne Row had possessed, as the house agents put it, bath, h. and c., gas fires in

3. Jane Carlyle suffered frequent bouts of influenza—eight times a year, according to a contemporary.

the bedrooms, all modern conveniences and indoor sanitation. But then, we reflect, as we cross the worn threshold, Carlyle with hot water laid on would not have been Carlyle; and Mrs. Carlyle without bugs to kill would have been a different woman from the one we know.

An age seems to separate the house in Chelsea where the Carlyles lived from the house in Hampstead which was shared by Keats and Brown and the Brawnes. If houses have their voices and places their seasons, it is always spring in Hampstead as it is always February in Cheyne Row. By some miracle, too, Hampstead has always remained not a suburb or a piece of antiquity engulfed in the modern world, but a place with a character peculiar to itself. It is not a place where one makes money, or goes when one has money to spend. The signs of discreet retirement are stamped on it. Its houses are neat boxes such as front the sea at Brighton with bow windows and balconies and deck chairs on verandahs. It has style and intention as if designed for people of modest income and some leisure who seek rest and recreation. Its prevailing colors are the pale pinks and blues that seem to harmonize with the blue sea and the white sand; and yet there is an urbanity in the style which proclaims the neighborhood of a great city. Even in the twentieth century this serenity still pervades the suburb of Hampstead. Its bow windows still look out upon vales and trees and ponds and barking dogs and couples sauntering arm in arm and pausing, here on the hill-top, to look at the distant domes and pinnacles of London, as they sauntered and paused and looked when Keats lived here. For Keats lived up the lane in a little white house behind wooden palings. Nothing has been much changed since his day. But as we enter the house in which Keats lived some mournful shadow seems to fall across the garden. A tree has fallen and lies propped. Waving branches cast their shadows up and down over the flat white walls of the house. Here, for all the gaiety and serenity of the neighborhood, the nightingale sang; here, if anywhere, fever and anguish had their dwelling and paced this little green plot oppressed with the sense of quick-coming death and the shortness of life[4] and the passion of love and its misery.

Yet if Keats left any impress upon his house it is the impression not of fever, but of that clarity and dignity which come from order and self-control. The rooms are small but shapely; downstairs the long windows are so large that half the wall seems made of light. Two chairs turned together are close to the window as if someone had sat there reading and had just got up and left the room. The figure of the reader must have been splashed with shade and sun as the hanging leaves stirred in the breeze. Birds must have hopped close to his foot. The room is empty save for the two chairs, for Keats had few possessions, little furniture and not more,

4. John Keats (1795–1821) died of tuberculosis.

he said, than one hundred and fifty books. And perhaps it is because the rooms are so empty and furnished rather with light and shadow than with chairs and tables that one does not think of people, here where so many people have lived. The imagination does not evoke scenes. It does not strike one that there must have been eating and drinking here; people must have come in and out; they must have put down bags, left parcels; they must have scrubbed and cleaned and done battle with dirt and disorder and carried cans of water from the basement to the bedrooms. All the traffic of life is silenced. The voice of the house is the voice of leaves brushing in the wind; of branches stirring in the garden. Only one presence—that of Keats himself—dwells here. And even he, though his picture is on every wall, seems to come silently, on the broad shafts of light, without body or footfall. Here he sat on the chair in the window and listened without moving, and saw without starting, and turned the page without haste though his time was so short.

There is an air of heroic equanimity about the house in spite of the death masks and the brittle yellow wreaths and the other grisly memorials which remind us that Keats died young and unknown and in exile.[5] Life goes on outside the window. Behind this calm, this rustling of leaves, one hears the far-off rattle of wheels, the bark of dogs fetching and carrying sticks from the pond. Life goes on outside the wooden paling. When we shut the gate upon the grass and the tree where the nightingale sang we find, quite rightly, the butcher delivering his meat from a small red motor van at the house next door. If we cross the road, taking care not to be cut down by some rash driver—for they drive at a great pace down these wide streets—we shall find ourselves on top of the hill and beneath shall see the whole of London lying below us. It is a view of perpetual fascination at all hours and in all seasons. One sees London as a whole— London crowded and ribbed and compact, with its dominant domes, its guardian cathedrals; its chimneys and spires; its cranes and gasometers; and the perpetual smoke which no spring or autumn ever blows away. London has lain there time out of mind scarring that stretch of earth deeper and deeper, making it more uneasy, lumped and tumultuous, branding it for ever with an indelible scar. There it lies in layers, in strata, bristling and billowing with rolls of smoke always caught on its pinnacles. Ant yet from Parliament Hill one can see, too, the country beyond. There are hills on the further side in whose woods birds are singing, and some stoat or rabbit pauses, in dead silence, with paw lifted to listen intently to rustlings among the leaves. To look over London from this hill Keats came and Coleridge and Shakespeare, perhaps. And here at this

5. In Rome.

very moment the usual young man sits on an iron bench clasping to his arms the usual young woman.

1932

THE READER

1. Why is Woolf glad that great men's houses are being "preserved entire with the chairs they sat on and the cups they drank from"?
2. Woolf says that "all houses have voices" and that "every house has its season." What does she mean by these statements? Are they true of the houses you know?
3. Why does Woolf end her essay the way she does?
4. Does Woolf's biographical sketch of the Carlyles conform to her theory of what constitutes good biography, as she describes it in "The New Biography" (p. 738)?

THE WRITER

1. Woolf makes a major assertion in her first paragraph. How is that assertion illustrated and supported in the rest of the essay? How convincing a case does she make for the assertion?
2. How many of Woolf's conclusions about the Carlyles come from her observation of the house itself? How many from other sources? What might those other sources include?
3. Write a brief comparison of Woolf's biographical sketch of her father (p. 146) with her sketch of the Carlyles. Does she use any of the same techniques?
4. Write a short essay describing a house or a room in such a way as to reveal something about the character of its occupant(s).

Virginia Woolf

MY FATHER: LESLIE STEPHEN

By the time that his children were growing up, the great days of my father's life were over. His feats on the river and on the mountains had been won before they were born. Relics of them were to be found lying about the house—the silver cup on the study mantelpiece; the rusty alpenstocks that leaned against the bookcase in the corner; and to the end of his days he would speak of great climbers and explorers with a peculiar mixture of admiration and envy. But his own years of activity were over, and my father had to content himself with pottering about the Swiss valleys or taking a stroll across the Cornish moors.

That to potter and to stroll meant more on his lips than on other people's is becoming obvious now that some of his friends have given their own version of those expeditions. He would start off after breakfast alone, or with one companion. Shortly after dinner he would return. If the walk had been successful, he would have out his great map and commemorate a new short cut in red ink. And he was quite capable, it appears, of striding all day across the moors without speaking more than a word or two to his companion. By that time, too, he had written the *History of English Thought in the Eighteenth Century*, which is said by some to be his masterpiece; and the *Science of Ethics*—the book which interested him most; and *The Playground of Europe,* in which is to be found "The Sunset on Mont Blanc"—in his opinion the best thing he ever wrote. He still wrote daily and methodically, though never for long at a time.

In London he wrote in the large room with three long windows at the top of the house. He wrote lying almost recumbent in a low rocking chair which he tipped to and fro as he wrote, like a cradle, and as he wrote he smoked a short clay pipe, and he scattered books round him in a circle. The thud of a book dropped on the floor could be heard in the room beneath. And often as he mounted the stairs to his study with his firm, regular tread he would burst, not into song, for he was entirely unmusical, but into a strange rhythmical chant, for verse of all kinds, both "utter trash," as he called it, and the most sublime words of Milton and Wordsworth, stuck in his memory, and the act of walking or climbing seemed to inspire him to recite whichever it was that came uppermost or suited his mood.

But it was his dexterity with his fingers that delighted his children before they could potter along the lanes at his heels or read his books. He would twist a sheet of paper beneath a pair of scissors and out would drop an elephant, a stag, or a monkey, with trunks, horns, and tails delicately and exactly formed. Or, taking a pencil, he would draw beast after beast —an art that he practiced almost unconsciously as he read, so that the flyleaves of his books swarm with owls and donkeys as if to illustrate the "Oh, you ass!" or "Conceited dunce" that he was wont to scribble impatiently in the margin. Such brief comments, in which one may find the germ of the more temperate statements of his essays, recall some of the characteristics of his talk. He could be very silent, as his friends have testified. But his remarks, made suddenly in a low voice between the puffs of his pipe, were extremely effective. Sometimes with one word— but his one word was accompanied by a gesture of the hand—he would dispose of the tissue of exaggerations which his own sobriety seemed to provoke. "There are 40,000,000 unmarried women in London alone!" Lady Ritchie once informed him. "Oh, Annie, Annie!" my father exclaimed in tones of horrified but affectionate rebuke. But Lady Ritchie, as if she enjoyed being rebuked, would pile it up even higher next time she came.

The stories he told to amuse his children of adventures in the Alps—

but accidents only happened, he would explain, if you were so foolish as to disobey your guides—or of those long walks, after one of which, from Cambridge to London on a hot day, "I drank, I am sorry to say, rather more than was good for me," were told very briefly, but with a curious power to impress the scene. The things that he did not say were always there in the background. So, too, though he seldom told anecdotes, and his memory for facts was bad, when he described a person—and he had known many people, both famous and obscure—he would convey exactly what he thought of him in two or three words. And what he thought might be the opposite of what other people thought. He had a way of upsetting established reputations and disregarding conventional values that could be disconcerting, and sometimes perhaps wounding, though no one was more respectful of any feeling that seemed to him genuine. But when, suddenly opening his bright blue eyes and rousing himself from what had seemed complete abstraction, he gave his opinion, it was difficult to disregard it. It was a habit, especially when deafness made him unaware that this opinion could be heard, that had its inconveniences.

"I am the most easily bored of men," he wrote, truthfully as usual; and when, as was inevitable in a large family, some visitor threatened to stay not merely for tea but also for dinner, my father would express his anguish at first by twisting and untwisting a certain lock of hair. Then he would burst out, half to himself, half to the powers above, but quite audibly, "Why can't he go? Why can't he go?" Yet such is the charm of simplicity—and did he not say, also truthfully, that "bores are the salt of the earth"?—that the bores seldom went, or, if they did, forgave him and came again.

Too much, perhaps, has been said of his silence; too much stress has been laid upon his reserve. He loved clear thinking; he hated sentimentality and gush; but this by no means meant that he was cold and unemotional, perpetually critical and condemnatory in daily life. On the contrary, it was his power of feeling strongly and of expressing his feeling with vigor that made him sometimes so alarming as a companion. A lady, for instance, complained of the wet summer that was spoiling her tour in Cornwall. But to my father, though he never called himself a democrat, the rain meant that the corn was being laid; some poor man was being ruined; and the energy with which he expressed his sympathy—not with the lady—left her discomfited. He had something of the same respect for farmers and fishermen that he had for climbers and explorers. So, too, he talked little of patriotism, but during the South African War—and all wars were hateful to him—he lay awake thinking that he heard the guns on the battlefield. Again, neither his reason nor his cold common sense helped to convince him that a child could be late for dinner without having been maimed or killed in an accident. And not all his mathematics together with a bank balance which he insisted must be ample in the extreme could persuade him, when it came to signing a check, that the whole family was not "shooting Niagara to ruin,"[1] as he put it. The pictures that he would draw of old age and the bankruptcy court, of ruined men of letters who have to support large families in small houses at Wimbledon (he owned a very small house at Wimbledon), might have convinced those who complain of his understatements that hyperbole was well within his reach had he chosen.

Yet the unreasonable mood was superficial, as the rapidity with which it vanished would prove. The checkbook was shut; Wimbledon and the workhouse were forgotten. Some thought of a humorous kind made him chuckle. Taking his hat and his stick, calling for his dog and his daughter, he would stride off into Kensington Gardens, where he had walked as a little boy, where his brother Fitzjames and he had made beautiful bows to young Queen Victoria and she had swept them a curtsy; and so, round the Serpentine, to Hyde Park Corner, where he had once saluted the great Duke himself; and so home. He was not then in the least "alarming"; he was very simple, very confiding; and his silence, though one might last unbroken from the Round Pond to the Marble Arch, was curiously full of meaning, as if he were thinking half aloud, about poetry and philosophy and people he had known.

He himself was the most abstemious of men. He smoked a pipe perpetually, but never a cigar. He wore his clothes until they were too shabby to be tolerable; and he held old-fashioned and rather puritanical views as to the vice of luxury and the sin of idleness. The relations between parents and children today have a freedom that would have been impossible with my father. He expected a certain standard of behavior, even of ceremony, in family life. Yet if freedom means the right to think one's own thoughts and to follow one's own pursuits, then no one respected and indeed insisted upon freedom more completely than he did. His sons, with the exception of the Army and Navy, should follow whatever professions they chose; his daughters, though he cared little enough for the higher education of women, should have the same liberty. If at one moment he rebuked a daughter sharply for smoking a cigarette —smoking was not in his opinion a nice habit in the other sex—she had only to ask him if she might become a painter, and he assured her that so long as she took her work seriously he would give her all the help he could. He had no special love for painting; but he kept his word. Freedom of that sort was worth thousands of cigarettes.

It was the same with the perhaps more difficult problem of literature. Even today there may be parents who would doubt the wisdom of allowing a girl of fifteen the free run of a large and quite unexpurgated library. But my father allowed it. There were certain facts—very briefly,

1. The reference is to going over Niagara Falls in a boat.

very shyly he referred to them. Yet "Read what you like," he said, and all his books, "mangy and worthless," as he called them, but certainly they were many and various, were to be had without asking. To read what one liked because one liked it, never to pretend to admire what one did not—that was his only lesson in the art of reading. To write in the fewest possible words, as clearly as possible, exactly what one meant—that was his only lesson in the art of writing. All the rest must be learned for oneself. Yet a child must have been childish in the extreme not to feel that such was the teaching of a man of great learning and wide experience, though he would never impose his own views or parade his own knowledge. For, as his tailor remarked when he saw my father walk past his shop up Bond Street, "There goes a gentleman that wears good clothes without knowing it."

In those last years, grown solitary and very deaf, he would sometimes call himself a failure as a writer; he had been "jack of all trades, and master of none." But whether he failed or succeeded as a writer, it is permissible to believe that he left a distinct impression of himself on the minds of his friends. Meredith[2] saw him as "Phoebus Apollo turned fasting friar" in his earlier days; Thomas Hardy, years later, looked at the "spare and desolate figure" of the Schreckhorn[3] and thought of

> him,
> Who scaled its horn with ventured life and limb,
> Drawn on by vague imaginings, maybe,
> Of semblance to his personality
> In its quaint glooms, keen lights, and rugged trim.

But the praise he would have valued most, for though he was an agnostic nobody believed more profoundly in the worth of human relationships, was Meredith's tribute after his death: "He was the one man to my knowledge worthy to have married your mother." And Lowell,[4] when he called him "L.S., the most lovable of men," has best described the quality that makes him, after all these years, unforgettable.

1950[5]

2. George Meredith (1828–1909), English novelist and poet.
3. One of the peaks in the Swiss Alps.
4. James Russell Lowell, nineteenth-century American poet, essayist, and editor.
5. Published posthumously.

THE READER

1. *What are the basic qualities Woolf admires, as revealed in this selection?*

2. *Would you like to have been Leslie Stephen's son or daughter? Why, or why not?*

3. *In some of her other work, Woolf shows a deep and sensitive concern for women's experience and awareness. Do you find a feminist awareness here? In what way?*

4. *In her novel* To the Lighthouse, *Woolf creates the fictional character of Mr. Ramsay from recollections of her father. Compare the characterization in her essay with this passage from the novel: "What he said was true. It was always true. He was incapable of untruth; never tampered with a fact; never altered a disagreeable word to suit the pleasure or convenience of any mortal being, least of all of his own children, who, sprung from his loins, should be aware from childhood that life is difficult; facts uncompromising; and the passage to that fabled land where our brightest hopes are extinguished, our frail barks founder in darkness (here Mr. Ramsay would straighten his back and narrow his little blue eyes upon the horizon), one that needs, above all, courage, truth, and the power to endure." (*To the Lighthouse, Harcourt, Brace & World, 1927; © 1955 Leonard Woolf, pp. 10–11.*)

THE WRITER

1. *Giving praise can be a difficult rhetorical and social undertaking. How does Woolf avoid the pitfalls or try to? Compare Lessing's "My Father" (p. 151) to this selection. Does Lessing take similar risks?*
2. *Does Woolf's portrait of her father conform to her criteria for such writing as she defines them in "The New Biography" (p. 738)?*
3. *What are the main currents of the Stephens' family life as revealed here? Since any such description must be selective, what does Woolf leave out? Do the omissions detract from her essay? If you think so, say why.*
4. *If you didn't know that Leslie Stephen was Woolf's father, could you deduce that fact from the way she writes about him? Why, or why not?*
5. *Write a sketch about a father, real or fictional, adopting a tone similar to Woolf's in this sketch.*

Doris Lessing

MY FATHER

We use our parents like recurring dreams, to be entered into when needed; they are always there for love or for hate; but it occurs to me that I was not always there for my father. I've written about him before, but novels, stories, don't have to be "true." Writing this article is difficult because it has to be "true." I knew him when his best years were over.

There are photographs of him. The largest is of an officer in the 1914–18 war. A new uniform—buttoned, badged, strapped, tabbed—confines a handsome, dark young man who holds himself stiffly to confront what he certainly thought of as his duty. His eyes are steady, serious, and responsible, and show no signs of what he became later. A photograph at sixteen is of a dark, introspective youth with the same intent eyes. But it is his mouth you notice—a heavily-jutting upper lip contradicts the rest of a regular face. His moustache was to hide it: "Had to do something—a damned fleshy mouth. Always made me uncomfortable, that mouth of mine."

Earlier a baby (eyes already alert) appears in a lace waterfall that cascades from the pillowy bosom of a fat, plain woman to her feet. It is the face of a head cook. "Lord, but my mother was a practical female—almost as bad as you!" as he used to say, or throw at my mother in moments of exasperation. Beside her stands, or droops, arms dangling, his father, the source of the dark, arresting eyes, but otherwise masked by a long beard.

The birth certificate says: Born 3rd August, 1886, Walton Villa, Crefield Road, S. Mary at the Wall, R.S.D. Name, Alfred Cook. Name and surname of Father: Alfred Cook Tayler. Name and maiden name of Mother: Caroline May Batley. Rank or Profession: Bank Clerk. Colchester, Essex.

They were very poor. Clothes and boots were a problem. They "made their own amusements." Books were mostly the Bible and *The Pilgrim's Progress*.[1] Every Saturday night they bathed in a hipbath in front of the kitchen fire. No servants. Church three times on Sundays. "Lord, when I think of those Sundays! I dreaded them all week, like a nightmare coming at you full tilt and no escape." But he rabbited with ferrets along the lanes and fields, bird-nested, stole fruit, picked nuts and mushrooms, paid visits to the blacksmith and the mill and rode a farmer's carthorse.

They ate economically, but when he got diabetes in his forties and subsisted on lean meat and lettuce leaves, he remembered suet puddings, treacle puddings, raisin and currant puddings, steak and kidney puddings, bread and butter pudding, "batter cooked in the gravy with the meat," potato cake, plum cake, butter cake, porridge with treacle, fruit tarts and pies, brawn, pig's trotters and pig's cheek and home-smoked ham and sausages. And "lashings of fresh butter and cream and eggs." He wondered if this diet had produced the diabetes, but said it was worth it.

There was an elder brother described by my father as: "Too damned clever by half. One of those quick, clever brains. Now I've always had a slow brain, but I get there in the end, damn it!"

The brothers went to a local school and the elder did well, but my father was beaten for being slow. They both became bank clerks in, I think, the Westminster Bank, and one must have found it congenial, for he became a manager, the "rich brother," who had cars and even a yacht. But my father did not like it, though he was conscientious. For instance, he changed his writing, letter by letter, because a senior criticised it. I never saw his unregenerate hand, but the one he created was elegant,

1. An allegory of Christian's progress toward heaven through a world filled with tempters, by the seventeenth-century writer John Bunyan.

spiky, careful. Did this mean he created a new personality for himself, hiding one he did not like, as he hid his "damned fleshy mouth"? I don't know.

Nor do I know when he left home to live in Luton, or why. He found family life too narrow? A safe guess—he found everything too narrow. His mother was too down-to-earth? He had to get away from his clever elder brother?

Being a young man in Luton was the best part of his life. It ended in 1914, so he had a decade of happiness. His reminiscences of it were all of pleasure, the delight of physical movement, of dancing in particular. All his girls were "a beautiful dancer, light as a feather." He played billiards and ping-pong (both for his country); he swam, boated, played cricket and football,[2] went to picnics and horse races, sang at musical evenings. One family of a mother and two daughters treated him "like a son only better. I didn't know whether I was in love with the mother or the daughters, but oh I did love going there; we had such good times." He was engaged to one daughter, then, for a time, to the other. An engagement was broken off because she was rude to a waiter. "I could not marry a woman who allowed herself to insult someone who was defenceless." He used to say to my wryly smiling mother: "Just as well I didn't marry either of them; they would never have stuck it out the way you have, old girl."

Just before he died he told me he had dreamed he was standing in a kitchen on a very high mountain holding X in his arms. "Ah, yes, that's what I've missed in my life. Now don't you let yourself be cheated out of life by the old dears. They take all the colour out of everything if you let them."

But in that decade—"I'd walk 10, 15 miles to a dance two or three times a week and think nothing of it. Then I'd dance every dance and walk home again over the fields. Sometimes it was moonlight, but I liked the snow best, all crisp and fresh. I loved walking back and getting into my digs[3] just as the sun was rising. My little dog was so happy to see me, and I'd feed her, and make myself porridge and tea, then I'd wash and shave and go off to work."

The boy who was beaten at school, who went too much to church, who carried the fear of poverty all his life, but who nevertheless was filled with the memories of country pleasures; the young bank clerk who worked such long hours for so little money, but who danced, sang, played, flirted —this naturally vigorous, sensuous being was killed in 1914, 1915, 1916. I think the best of my father died in that war, that his spirit was crippled by it. The people I've met, particularly the women, who knew him young, speak of his high spirits, his energy, his enjoyment of life. Also of his

2. Soccer.   3. Lodgings.

kindness, his compassion and—a word that keeps recurring—his wisdom. "Even when he was just a boy he understood things that you'd think even an old man would find it easy to condemn." I do not think these people would have easily recognised the ill, irritable, abstracted, hypochondriac man I knew.

He "joined up" as an ordinary soldier out of a characteristically quirky scruple: it wasn't right to enjoy officers' privileges when the Tommies[4] had such a bad time. But he could not stick the communal latrines, the obligatory drinking, the collective visits to brothels, the jokes about girls. So next time he was offered a commission he took it.

His childhood and young man's memories, kept fluid, were added to, grew, as living memories do. But his war memories were congealed in stories that he told again and again, with the same words and gestures, in stereotyped phrases. They were anonymous, general, as if they had come out of a communal war memoir. He met a German in no-man's-land, but both slowly lowered their rifles and smiled and walked away. The Tommies were the salt of the earth, the British fighting men the best in the world. He had never known such comradeship. A certain brutal officer was shot in a sortie by his men, but the other officers, recognising rough justice, said nothing. He had known men intimately who saw the Angels at Mons.[5] He wished he could force all the generals on both sides into the trenches for just one day, to see what the common soldiers endured—*that* would have ended the war at once.

There was an undercurrent of memories, dreams, and emotions much deeper, more personal. This dark region in him, fate-ruled, where nothing was true but horror, was expressed inarticulately, in brief, bitter exclamations or phrases of rage, incredulity, betrayal. The men who went to fight in that war believed it when they said it was to end war. My father believed it. And he was never able to reconcile his belief in his country with his anger at the cynicism of its leaders. And the anger, the sense of betrayal, strengthened as he grew old and ill.

But in 1914 he was naïve, the German atrocities in Belgium inflamed him, and he enlisted out of idealism, although he knew he would have a hard time. He knew because a fortuneteller told him. (He could be described as uncritically superstitious or as psychically gifted.) He would be in great danger twice, yet not die—he was being protected by a famous soldier who was his ancestor. "And sure enough, later I heard from the Little Aunties that the church records showed we were descended the backstairs way from the Duke of Wellington, or was it Marlborough? Damn it, I forget. But one of them would be beside me all through the war, she said." (He was romantic, not only about this solicitous ghost, but also about being a descendant of the Huguenots, on the

4. Foot soldiers.   World War I battle.
5. An apparition that appeared during a

strength of the "e" in Tayler; and about "the wild blood" in his veins from a great uncle who, sent unjustly to prison for smuggling, came out of a ten-year sentence and earned it, very efficiently, along the coasts of Cornwall until he died.)

The luckiest thing that ever happened to my father, he said, was getting his leg shattered by shrapnel ten days before Passchendaele.[6] His whole company was killed. He knew he was going to be wounded because of the fortuneteller, who had said he would know. "I did not understand what she meant, but both times in the trenches, first when my appendix burst and I nearly died, and then just before Passchendaele, I felt for some days as if a thick, black velvet pall was settled over me. I can't tell you what it was like. Oh, it was awful, awful, and the second time it was so bad I wrote to the old people and told them I was going to be killed."

His leg was cut off at mid-thigh, he was shell-shocked, he was very ill for many months, with a prolonged depression afterwards. "You should always remember that sometimes people are all seething underneath. You don't know what terrible things people have to fight against. You should look at a person's eyes, that's how you tell. . . . When I was like that, after I lost my leg, I went to a nice doctor man and said I was going mad, but he said, don't worry, everyone locks up things like that. You don't know—horrible, horrible, awful things. I was afraid of myself, of what I used to dream. I wasn't myself at all."

In the Royal Free Hospital was my mother, Sister McVeagh. He married his nurse which, as they both said often enough (though in different tones of voice), was just as well. That was 1919. He could not face being a bank clerk in England, he said, not after the trenches. Besides, England was too narrow and conventional. Besides, the civilians did not know what the soldiers had suffered, they didn't want to know, and now it wasn't done even to remember "The Great Unmentionable." He went off to the Imperial Bank of Persia, in which country I was born.

The house was beautiful, with great stone-floored high-ceilinged rooms whose windows showed ranges of snow-streaked mountains. The gardens were full of roses, jasmine, pomegranates, walnuts. Kermanshah he spoke of with liking, but soon they went to Teheran, populous with "Embassy people," and my gregarious mother created a lively social life about which he was irritable even in recollection.

Irritableness—that note was first struck here, about Persia. He did not like, he said, "the graft and the corruption." But here it is time to try and describe something difficult—how a man's good qualities can also be his bad ones, or if not bad, a danger to him.

My father was honourable—he always knew exactly what that word

6. A prolonged and futile battle of World War I, in which British and Commonwealth forces sustained massive casualties.

meant. He had integrity. His "one does not do that sort of thing," his "no, it is *not* right," sounded throughout my childhood and were final for all of us. I am sure it was true he wanted to leave Persia because of "the corruption." But it was also because he was already unconsciously longing for something freer, because as a bank official he could not let go into the dream-logged personality that was waiting for him. And later in Rhodesia, too, what was best in him was also what prevented him from shaking away the shadows: it was always in the name of honesty or decency that he refused to take this step or that out of the slow decay of the family's fortunes.

In 1925 there was leave from Persia. That year in London there was an Empire Exhibition, and on the Southern Rhodesian stand some very fine maize cobs and a poster saying that fortunes could be made on maize at 25/-[7] a bag. So on an impulse, turning his back forever on England, washing his hands of the corruption of the East, my father collected all his capital, £800, I think, while my mother packed curtains from Liberty's, clothes from Harrods, visiting cards, a piano, Persian rugs, a governess and two small children.

Soon, there was my father in a cigar-shaped house of thatch and mud on the top of a kopje[8] that overlooked in all directions a great system of mountains, rivers, valleys, while overhead the sky arched from horizon to empty horizon. This was a couple of hundred miles south from the Zambesi, a hundred or so west from Mozambique, in the district of Banket, so called because certain of its reefs were of the same formation as those called *banket* on the Rand. Lomagundi—gold country, tobacco country, maize country—wild, almost empty. (The Africans had been turned off it into reserves.) Our neighbours were four, five, seven miles off. In front of the house . . . no neighbours, nothing; no farms, just wild bush with two rivers but no fences to the mountains seven miles away. And beyond these mountains and bush again to the Portuguese border,[9] over which "our boys" used to escape when wanted by the police for pass or other offences.

And then? There was bad luck. For instance, the price of maize dropped from 25/- to 9/- a bag. The seasons were bad, prices bad, crops failed. This was the sort of thing that made it impossible for him ever to "get off the farm," which, he agreed with my mother, was what he most wanted to do.

It was an absurd country, he said. A man could "own" a farm for years that was totally mortgaged to the Government and run from the Land Bank, meanwhile employing half-a-hundred Africans at 12/- a month and none of them knew how to do a day's work. Why, two farm labourers

---

7. Twenty-five shillings. A shilling was then worth about twenty-five cents.
8. Small hill. The term is South African Dutch.
9. That is, the border of Mozambique, then a Portuguese possession.

from Europe could do in a day what twenty of these ignorant black savages would take a week to do. (Yet he was proud that he had a name as a just employer, that he gave "a square deal.") Things got worse. A fortuneteller had told him that her heart ached when she saw the misery ahead for my father: this was the misery.

But it was my mother who suffered. After a period of neurotic illness, which was a protest against her situation, she became brave and resourceful. But she never saw that her husband was not living in a real world, that he had made a captive of her common sense. We were always about to "get off the farm." A miracle would do it—a sweepstake, a goldmine, a legacy. And then? What a question! We would go to England where life would be normal with people coming in for musical evenings and nice supper parties at the Trocadero after a show. Poor woman, for the twenty years we were on the farm, she waited for when life would begin for her and for her children, for she never understood that what was a calamity for her was for them a blessing.

Meanwhile my father sank towards his death (at 61). Everything changed in him. He had been a dandy and fastidious, now he hated to change out of shabby khaki. He had been sociable, now he was misanthropic. His body's disorders—soon diabetes and all kinds of stomach ailments—dominated him. He was brave about his wooden leg, and even went down mine shafts and climbed trees with it, but he walked clumsily and it irked him badly. He greyed fast, and slept more in the day, but would be awake half the night pondering about. . . .

It could be gold divining. For ten years he experimented on private theories to do with the attractions and repulsions of metals. His whole soul went into it but his theories were wrong or he was *unlucky*—after all, if he had found a mine he would have had to leave the farm. It could be the relation between the minerals of the earth and of the moon; his decision to make infusions of all the plants on the farm and drink them himself in the interests of science; the criminal folly of the British Government in not realising that the Germans and the Russians were conspiring as Anti-Christ to . . . the inevitability of war because no one would listen to Churchill, but it would be all right because God (by then he was a British Israelite[1]) had destined Britain to rule the world; a prophecy said 10 million dead would surround Jerusalem—how would the corpses be cleared away?; people who wished to abolish flogging should be flogged; the natives understood nothing but a good beating; hanging must not be abolished because the Old Testament said "an eye for an eye and a tooth for a tooth. . . ."

Yet, as this side of him darkened, so that it seemed all his thoughts

1. A reference to the contention that the English-speaking peoples are the descendants of the "ten tribes" of Israel, deported by Sargon of Assyria on the fall of Samaria in 721 B.C.

were of violence, illness, war, still no one dared to make an unkind comment in his presence or to gossip. Criticism of people, particularly of women, made him more and more uncomfortable till at last he burst out with: "It's all very well, but no one has the right to say that about another person."

In Africa, when the sun goes down, the stars spring up, all of them in their expected places, glittering and moving. In the rainy season, the sky flashed and thundered. In the dry season, the great dark hollow of night was lit by veld fires: the mountains burned through September and October in chains of red fire. Every night my father took out his chair to watch the sky and the mountains, smoking, silent, a thin shabby fly-away figure under the stars. "Makes you think—there are so many worlds up there, wouldn't really matter if we did blow ourselves up—plenty more where we came from."

The Second World War, so long foreseen by him, was a bad time. His son was in the Navy and in danger, and his daughter a sorrow to him. He became very ill. More and more often it was necessary to drive him into Salisbury with him in a coma, or in danger of one, on the back seat. My mother moved him into a pretty little suburban house in town near the hospitals, where he took to his bed and a couple of years later died. For the most part he was unconscious under drugs. When awake he talked obsessively (a tongue licking a nagging sore place) about "the old war." Or he remembered his youth. "I've been dreaming—Lord, to see those horses come lickety-split down the course with their necks stretched out and the sun on their coats and everyone shouting. . . . I've been dreaming how I walked along the river in the mist as the sun was rising. . . . Lord, lord, lord, what a time that was, what good times we all had then, before the old war."

1974

THE READER

1. Find facts about Lessing's father that are repeated or referred to more than once. Why does she repeat them?
2. Lessing says that it was difficult for her to write about her father because she "knew him when his best years were over." What other things about those "best years" might she have wanted to know that she apparently didn't?

THE WRITER

1. Lessing says that "writing this article is difficult because it has to be 'true.'" Why does she put quotation marks around "true"? Why would it be more difficult to write something that has to be "true" than, as she says, stories that "don't have to be 'true'"? How has she tried to make this sketch "true"? How well do you think she has succeeded?

2. *If a stranger were writing about Lessing's father but had the same facts available, might the account differ in any ways? Explain.*
3. *If you wrote a sketch of a father after reading Woolf's "My Father: Leslie Stephen" (p. 146), write another sketch about the same or a different father, adopting a tone similar to Lessing's.*

Daniel Mark Epstein

THE CASE OF HARRY HOUDINI

When my grandfather was a boy he saw the wild-haired magician escape from a riveted boiler. He would remember that image as long as he lived, and how Harry Houdini, the rabbi's son, defeated the German Imperial Police at the beginning of the twentieth century. Hearing those tales and others even more incredible, sixty years after the magician's death we cannot help but wonder: What did the historical Houdini *really* do? And how on earth did he do it?

The newspaper accounts are voluminous, and consistent. The mere cataloguing of Houdini's escapes soon grows tedious, which they were not, to be sure, in the flesh. But quickly: the police stripped him naked and searched him thoroughly before binding his wrists and ankles with five pairs of irons. Then they would slam him into a cell and turn the key of a three-bond burglar-proof lock. He escaped, hundreds of times, from the most secure prisons in the world. He hung upside down in a strait-jacket from the tallest buildings in America, and escaped in full view of the populace. He was chained hand and foot and nailed into a packing case weighted with lead; the packing case was dropped from a tugboat into New York's East River and ninety seconds later Houdini surfaced. The packing case was hauled up intact, with the manacles inside, still fastened. He was sealed into a paper bag and got out without disturbing the seal. He was sewn into a huge football, into the belly of a whale, and escaped. In California he was buried six feet underground, and clawed his way out. He did this, he did that. These are facts that cannot be exaggerated, for they were conceived as exaggerations. We know he did these things beccause his actions were more public than the proceedings of Congress, and most of them he performed over and over, so no one would miss the point.

How did he do such things? For all rational people who are curious, sixty years after the magician's death, there is good news and bad news. The good news is that we know how the vast majority of Houdini's tricks were done, and the explanations are as fascinating as the mystery was.

Much of our knowledge comes from the magician's writings, for Houdini kept ahead of his imitators by exposing his cast-off tricks. We have additional information from technicians and theater historians. No magician will reveal Houdini's secrets—their code forbids it. But so much controversy has arisen concerning his powers—so much conjecture they may have been supernatural—that extraordinary measures have been taken to assure us Houdini was a *mortal* genius. Many secrets have leaked out, and others have been discovered from examining the props. So at last we know more about Houdini's technique than any other magician's.

The disturbing news is that, sixty years after his last performance, some of his more spectacular escapes remain unexplained. And while magicians such as Doug Henning are bound not to expose their colleagues, they are free to admit what mystifies them. They know how Houdini walked through the brick wall at Hammerstein's Roof Garden, in 1914, but they do not know how he made the elephant disappear in 1918. This trick he performed only for a few months in New York. And when people asked him why he did not continue he told them that Teddy Roosevelt, a great hunter, had begged him to stop before he exhausted the world's supply of pachyderms.

But before we grapple with the mysteries, let us begin with what we can understand. Let us begin with my grandfather's favorite story, the case of Harry Houdini versus the German Police. Houdini's first tour of Europe depended upon the good will and cooperation of the law. When he arrived in London in 1900 the twenty-six-year-old magician did not have a single booking. His news clippings eventually inspired an English agent, who had Houdini manacled to a pillar in Scotland Yard. Seeing that Houdini was securely fastened, Superintendent Melville of the Criminal Investigation Department said he would return in a couple of hours, when the escapist had worn himself out. By the time Melville got to the door the magician was free to open it for him.

The publicity surrounding his escape from the most prestigious police force in the world opened up many another door for the young magician. Booked at the Alhambra Theater in London, he performed his "Challenge" handcuff act, which had made him famous on the vaudeville circuit. After some card tricks and standard illusions, Houdini would stand before the proscenium and challenge the world to restrain him with ropes, straitjackets, handcuffs, whatever they could bring on, from lockshops, prisons, and museums. A single failure might have ruined him. There is no evidence that he ever failed, though in several cases he nearly died from the effort required to escape from sadistic shackles. The "Challenge" act filled the Alhambra Theater for two months. Houdini might have stayed there if Germany had not already booked him; the Germans could hardly wait to get a look at Houdini.

As he had done in America and England, Houdini began his tour of

Germany with a visit to police headquarters. The Dresden officers were not enthusiastic, yet they could hardly refuse the magician's invitation to lock him up. That might suggest a crisis of confidence. And like their colleagues the world over, the Dresden police viewed Houdini's news clippings as so much paper in the balance with their locks and chains. Of course the Dresden police had no more success than those of Kansas City, or San Francisco, or Scotland Yard. Their manacles were paper to him. The police chief reluctantly signed the certificate Houdini demanded, but the newspapers gave him little coverage.

So on his opening night at Dresden's Central Theatre, Houdini arranged to be fettered in the leg irons and manacles of the Mathildegasse Prison. Some of the locks weighed forty pounds. The audience, packed to the walls, went wild over his escape, and the fact that he spoke their language further endeared him. If anything could have held him captive it would have been the adoring burghers of Dresden, who mobbed the theater for weeks. The manager wanted to buy out Houdini's contract with the Wintergarten of Berlin, so as to hold him over in Dresden, but the people of Berlin could not wait to see the magician.

Houdini arrived in Berlin in October of 1900. The first thing he did was march into the police station, strip stark naked, and challenge the jailors. They could not hold him. This time Count von Windheim, the highest ranking policeman in Germany, signed the certificate of Houdini's escape. The Wintergarten was overrun. The management appealed to the theater of Houdini's next engagement, in Vienna, so they might hold him over an extra month in Berlin. The Viennese finally yielded, demanding an indemnity equal to Houdini's salary for one month. When the magician, at long last, opened at the Olympic Theater in Paris, in December of 1901, he was the highest paid foreign entertainer in French history.

But meanwhile there was big trouble brewing in Germany. It seems the police there had little sense of humor about Houdini's peculiar gifts, and the Jew had quickly exhausted what little there was. In Dortmund he escaped from the irons that had bound Glowisky, a notorious murderer, beheaded three days before. At Hanover the police chief, Count von Schwerin, plotted to disgrace Houdini, challenging him to escape from a special straitjacket reinforced with thick leather. Houdini agonized for one and a half hours while von Schwerin looked on, his jubilant smile melting in wonder, then rage, as the magician worked himself free.

The cumulative anger of the German police went public in July of 1901. Inspector Werner Graff witnessed Houdini's escape from all the manacles at the Cologne police station and vowed to end the humiliation. It was not a simple matter of pride. Graff, along with von Schwerin and other officials, feared Houdini was weakening their authority and inviting jailbreaks, if not other kinds of antisocial behavior. So Graff wrote a letter to Cologne's newspaper, the *Rheinische Zeitung*. The letter stated that Houdini had escaped from simple restraints at the police headquarters, by trickery; but his publicity boasted he could escape from restraints *of any kind*. Such a claim, Graff wrote, was a lie, and Houdini ought to be prosecuted for fraud.

Though he knew the letter was nonsense the magician could not ignore it, for it was dangerous nonsense. If the police began calling him a fraud in every town he visited, Houdini would lose his audience. So he demanded that Graff apologize and the newspaper publish a retraction. Graff refused, and other German dailies reprinted his letter. Should Harry Houdini sue the German policeman for libel? Consider the circumstances. Germany, even in 1901, was one of the most authoritarian states in the world. Houdini was an American, a Jew who embarrassed the police. A libel case against Graff would turn upon the magician's claim that he could escape from *any* restraint, and the courtroom would become an international theater. There a German judge and jury would try his skill, and, should they find it wanting, Houdini would be washed up, exiled to play beer halls and dime museums. Only an artist with colossal pride and total confidence in his methods would act as Houdini did. He hired the most prominent trial lawyer in Cologne, and ordered him to sue Werner Graff and the Imperial Police of Germany for criminal libel.

There was standing room only in the Cologne *Schöffengericht*. The judge allowed Werner Graff to seek out the most stubborn locks and chains he could find, and tangle Houdini in them, in full view of everyone. Here was a hitch, for Houdini did not wish to show the crowd his technique. He asked the judge to clear the courtroom, and in the ensuing turmoil the magician released himself so quickly no one knew how he had done it. The *Schöffengericht* fined the astonished policeman and ordered a public apology. So Graff's lawyer appealed the case.

Two months later Graff was better prepared. In the *Strafkammer*, or court of appeals, he presented thirty letters from legal authorities declaring that the escape artist could not justify his advertisements. And Graff had a shiny new pair of handcuffs. The premier locksmith of Germany had engineered the cuffs especially for the occasion. Werner Graff explained to the judge that the lock, once closed, could never be opened, even with its own key. Let Houdini try to get out of these.

This time the court permitted Houdini to work in privacy, and a guard led the magician to an adjacent chamber. Everyone else settled down for a long wait, in a chatter of anticipation. They were interrupted four minutes later by the entrance of Houdini, who tossed the manacles on the judge's bench. So the *Strafkammer* upheld the lower court's decision, as did the *Oberlandesgericht* in a "paper" appeal. The court fined Werner Graff thirty marks and ordered him to pay for the trials as well as a published apology. Houdini's next poster showed him in evening dress, his hands manacled, standing before the judge, jurors, and a battery of mustachioed policemen. Looking down on the scene is a bust of the Kaiser against a crimson background, and a scroll that reads: "The Imperial Police of Cologne slandered Harry Houdini . . . were compelled to advertise 'An Honorary Apology' and pay costs of the trials. By command of Kaiser Wilhelm II, Emperor of Germany."

Now this is surely a wondrous tale, like something out of the Arabian Nights, and it will seem no less wonderful when we understand the technique that made it come true. In 1901, when Houdini took on the Imperial Police, he was not whistling in the dark. By the time he left America at the end of the nineteenth century he had dissected every kind of lock he could find in the New World, and whatever he could import from the old one. Arriving in London Houdini could write that there were only a few kinds of British handcuffs, "seven or eight at the utmost," and these were some of the simplest he had ever seen. He searched the markets, antique shops, and locksmiths, buying up all the European locks he could find so he could dismantle and study them.

Then during his Berlin engagement he worked up to ten hours a day at Mueller's locksmith on the Mittelstrasse, studying restraints. He was the Bobby Fischer of locks. With a chessmaster's foresight Houdini devised a set of picks to release every lock in existence, as well as *any he could imagine*. Such tireless ingenuity produced the incandescent light bulb and the atom bomb. Houdini's creation of a theatrical metaphor made a comparable impact on the human spirit. He had a message which he delivered so forcefully it goes without mentioning in theater courses: humankind cannot be held in chains. The European middle class had reached an impressionable age, and the meaning of Houdini's theater was not lost upon them. Nor was he mistaken by the aristocracy, who stayed away in droves. The spectacle of this American Jew bursting from chains by dint of ingenuity did not amuse the rich. They wanted desperately to demythologize him.

It was not about to happen in the German courtroom. When Werner Graff snapped the "new" handcuffs on Houdini, they were not strange to the magician. He had already invented them, so to speak, as well as the pick to open them, and the pick was in his pocket. Only a locksmith whose knowledge surpassed Houdini's could stop him; diligent study assured him that, as of 1901, there could be no such locksmith on the face of the earth.

What else can we understand about the methods of Harry Houdini, born Ehrich Weiss? We know he was a superbly conditioned athlete who did not smoke or take a drop of alcohol. His straitjacket escapes he performed in full view of the world so they could see it was by main force and flexibility that he freed himself. He may or may not have been able to dislocate his shoulders at will—he said he could, and it seems no more marvelous than certain other skills he demonstrated. Friends reported that his toes could untie knots most of us could not manage with our fingers. And routinely the magician would hold his breath for as long as four minutes to work underwater escapes. To cheapen the supernatural claims of the fakir Rahman Bey, Houdini remained underwater in an iron box for ninety minutes, as against the Egyptian's sixty. Examining Houdini, a physician testified that the fifty-year-old wizard had halved his blood pressure while doubling his pulse. Of course, more wonderful than any of these skills was the courage allowing him to employ them, in predicaments where any normal person would panic.

These things are known about Houdini. The same tireless ingenuity, when applied to locks and jails, packing cases and riveted boilers; the same athletic prowess, when applied at the bottom of the East River, or while dangling from a rope attached to the cornice of the Sun Building in Baltimore—these talents account for the vast majority of Houdini's exploits. As we have mentioned, theater historians, notably Raymund Fitzsimons in his *Death and the Magician*, have carefully exposed Houdini's ingenuity, knowing that nothing can tarnish the miracle of the man's existence. Their accounts are technical and we need not dwell on them, except to say they *mostly* support Houdini's oath that his effects were achieved by natural, or mechanical means. The Houdini problem arises from certain outrageous effects no one has ever been able to explain, though capable technicians have been trying for more than sixty years.

Let us briefly recall those effects. We have mentioned the Disappearing Elephant. On January 7, 1918, Houdini had a ten-thousand-pound elephant led onto the bright stage of the Hippodrome in New York City. A trainer marched the elephant around a cabinet large enough for an elephant, proving there was space behind. There was no trapdoor in the floor of the Hippodrome, and the elephant could not fly. Houdini ushered the pachyderm into the cabinet and closed the curtains. Then he opened them, and where the elephant had stood there was nothing but empty space. Houdini went on with his program, which might have been making the Hippodrome disappear, for all the audience knew. A reporter for the *Brooklyn Eagle* noted: "The program says that the elephant vanished into thin air. The trick is performed fifteen feet from the backdrop and the cabinet is slightly elevated. That explanation is as good as any." After Houdini stopped making elephants disappear, nineteen weeks later, the trick would never be precisely duplicated.

That is the single "conventional" illusion of Houdini's repertoire that remains unexplained. He was not the greatest illusionist of his time, though he was among them. His expertise was the "escape" act, that specialty of magic furthest removed from theater, for its challenges are quite real and sometimes beyond the magician's control. It was the escapes, as his wife later wrote, that were truly dangerous, and Houdini privately admitted some anxieties about them. Give a wizard twenty years to build a cabinet which snuffs an elephant, and you will applaud his cleverness if he succeeds, in the controlled environment of his theater. But surrender the same man, stark naked, to the Russian police, who stake their honor upon detaining him in a convict van, and you may well suspect the intercession of angels should he get out.

And that is exactly what Houdini did, in one of the strangest and most celebrated escapes of his career. Strange, because it was Houdini's habit to escape only from barred jail cells where the locks were within easy reach, and then only after inspection, so he might hide picks in crannies, or excuse himself if he foresaw failure. But the Siberian Transport Cell made his blood boil. On May 11, 1903, the chief of the Russian secret police searched the naked Houdini inside and out. The revolt of 1905 was in its planning stages and the Imperial Police were understandably touchy. The magician's wrists were padlocked and his ankles fettered before the police locked him into the carette. Mounted on a wagon, the zinc-lined steel cell stood in the prison courtyard in view of chief Lebedoeff, his staff, and a number of civilians. Twenty-eight minutes later Houdini was walking around the courtyard, stretching. Nobody saw him get out, but he was out. The police ran to the door of the carette. The door was still locked and the shackles lay on the floor of the undamaged van. The police were so furious they would not sign the certificate of escape, but so many people had witnessed the event that the news was soon being shouted all over Moscow. Doug Henning has written: "It remains one of his escapes about which the real method is pure conjecture."

In the Houdini Museum at Niagara Falls, Canada, you may view the famous Mirror Handcuffs. If you are a scholar you can inspect them. In March of 1904 the London *Daily Mirror* discovered a blacksmith who had been working for five years to build a set of handcuffs no mortal man could pick. Examining the cuffs, the best locksmiths in London agreed they had never seen such an ingenious mechanism. The newspaper challenged Houdini to escape from them. On March 17, before a house of four thousand in the London Hippodrome, a journalist fastened the cuffs on Houdini's wrists and turned the key six times. The magician retired to his cabinet onstage, and the band struck up a march. He did not emerge for twenty minutes. When he did, it was to hold the lock up to the light. Remember that most "Challenge" handcuffs were regulation, and familiar to Houdini. He studied the lock in the light, and then went back into the cabinet, as the band played a waltz.

Ten minutes later Houdini stuck his head out, asking if he could have a cushion to kneel on. He was denied. After almost an hour Houdini came out of the cabinet again, obviously worn out, and his audience groaned. He wanted the handcuffs to be unlocked for a moment so he could take off his coat, as he was sweating profusely. The journalist denied the request, since Houdini had never before seen the handcuffs unlocked, and that might give him an advantage. Whereupon Houdini, in full view of the four thousand, extracted a penknife from his pocket and opened it with his teeth. Turning the coat inside out over his head, he shredded it loose with the penknife, and returned to the cabinet. Someone called out that Houdini had been handcuffed for more than an hour. As the band played on, the journalists of the London *Daily Mirror* could taste the greatest scoop of the twentieth century. But ten minutes later there was a cry from the cabinet and Houdini leapt out of it, free, waving the handcuffs high in the air. While the crowd roared, several men from the audience carried Houdini on their shoulders around the theater. He was crying as if his heart would break.

For all his other talents Houdini was a notoriously wooden actor, and we may assume the rare tears were altogether real, the product of an uncounterfeitable emotion. It is as if the man himself had been over-whelmed by his escape. Eighty years of technological progress have shed no light upon it. We know how Houdini got out of other handcuffs, but not these. As far as anyone can tell, the Mirror Handcuffs remain as the blacksmith described them—a set of handcuffs no mortal man could pick. One is tempted to dismiss the whole affair as mass hypnosis.

In the same Canadian museum you may view the Chinese Water Torture Cell, in which the magician was hung upside down, in water, his ankles padlocked to the riveted roof. His escape from this cell was the crowning achievement of his stage career, and though he performed it on tour during the last ten years of his life, no one has the slightest notion how he did it. The gifted Doug Henning revived the act in 1975, on television. But he would be the first to tell you his was *not* Houdini's version, but his own, and he would not do it onstage before a live audience seven nights a week, with matinees on Wednesday and Saturday, because the trick would be unspeakably dangerous even if he could perform it there. When Houdini died he willed the contraption to his brother Hardeen, a fine magician in his own right. But Hardeen would not get in it either, and the instructions were to be burned upon his death. Again, as with the Vanishing Elephant, we are reviewing a stage illusion under controlled conditions, and may bow to a master's technical superiority, without fretting that he has used supernatural powers.

But the Mirror Handcuffs and the Siberian Van Escape are trouble-some, as are certain of Houdini's escapes from reinforced straitjackets, and packing cases underwater. So is the fact that he was buried six feet underground, and clawed his way out. He only tried it once, and nearly died in the struggle, but the feat was attested, and you do not need a degree in physics to know it is as preposterous as rising from the dead. The weight of the earth is so crushing you could not lift it in the open air. Try doing this with no oxygen. The maestro himself misjudged the weight, and, realizing his folly, tried to signal his crew when the grave was not yet full. They could not hear him and kept right on shoveling as fast as they could, so as not to keep him waiting. Then they stood back, to watch. A while later they saw his bleeding hands appear above the ground.

If we find Houdini's record unsettling, imagine what our grandparents must have thought of him. They knew almost nothing of his technique. Where we remain troubled by a few of his illusions and escapes, our ancestors were horrified by most of them. The European journalists thought he was some kind of hobgoblin, a shapeshifter who could crawl through keyholes, or dematerialize and reappear at will. One can hardly blame them. Despite his constant reassurances that his effects were technical, and natural, the practical-minded layman could not believe it, and even fellow magicians were disturbed by his behavior.

So we come to the central issue in the case of Harry Houdini. It is an issue he carefully avoided in public, while studying it diligently in private. To wit: Can a magician, by the ultimate perfection of a technique, generate a force which, at critical moments, will achieve a supernatural result? Houdini's writings show this was the abiding concern of his intellectual life. It is, of course, the essential mystery of classical magic since before the Babylonians. Yet it remained a private and professional concern until Houdini's career forced it upon the public.

With the same determination that opened the world's locks, Houdini searched for an answer. His own technique was so highly evolved that its practice might have satisfied him, but his curiosity was unquenchable. He amassed the world's largest collection of books pertaining to magic and the occult, and no less a scholar than Edmund Wilson honored Houdini's authority. The son of a rabbi, Houdini pursued his studies with rabbinic thoroughness. And, from the beginning of his career, he sought out the living legends of magic and badgered them in retirement, sometimes with tragicomic results.

As far back as 1895 it seemed to Houdini something peculiar was going on when he performed the Metamorphosis with his wife Bess. You have probably seen this classic illusion. Two friends of mine once acted it in my living room, as a birthday present. When the Houdinis performed the Metamorphosis, Bess whould handcuff Harry, tie him in a sack, and lock him in a trunk. She would draw a curtain hiding the trunk and then it would open, showing Houdini free upon the stage. Where was Bess? Inside the trunk, inside the sack, handcuffed—there was Bess. The method of this trick is only mysterious if you cannot pay for it. But the Houdinis' *timing* of the Metamorphosis got very mysterious indeed. They polished the act until it happened in less than three seconds—three rather blurred seconds in their own minds, to be sure. Believe me, you cannot get *into* the trunk in less than three seconds. So when the Houdinis had done the trick they were often as stunned as their audience. It seemed a sure case of technique unleashing a supernatural force. Perplexed, Houdini planned to interview Hermann the Great, the pre-eminent conjuror in America in 1895, and ask Hermann what was up. But Hermann died as Houdini was about to ask him the question.

And Houdini shadowed the marvelous Harry Kellar, cross-examining him, and Alexander Heimburger, and the decrepit Ira Davenport, who had been a medium as well as a magician. But the great magicians flatly denied the psychic possibility, and Davenport would not answer to Houdini's satisfaction. In 1903 he discovered that Wiljalba Frikell, a seemingly mythic wizard of the nineteenth century, was still alive, in retirement near Dresden. When the ancient mage would not acknowl-edge his letters, Houdini grew convinced Wiljalba Frikell was the man to answer his question. He took the train to Dresden and knocked on Frikell's door. His wife sent Houdini away. On the road in Germany and Russia, Houdini continued to send letters and gifts to Frikell. And at last, six months after he had been turned away from Frikell's door, the reclusive magician agreed to see him.

Houdini rang the doorbell at 2:00 P.M. on October 8, 1903, the exact hour of his appointment. The door swung open. An hour earlier Wiljalba Frikell had dressed in his best suit, and laid out his scrapbooks, programs, and medals for Houdini to view. Houdini excitedly followed Frikell's wife into the room where the master sat surrounded by the mementos of his glorious career. But he would not be answering any of the questions that buzzed in Houdini's brain. The old man was stone dead.

Throughout his life Houdini categorically denied that any of his effects were achieved by supernatural means. He crusaded against mediums, clairvoyants, and all who claimed psychic power, advertising that he would reproduce any of their manifestations by mechanical means. In the face of spiritualists who accused *him* of being a physical medium, he protested that all his escapes and illusions were tricks. He was probably telling the truth, as he understood it. But Rabbi Drachman, who spoke at Houdini's funeral, and had been in a position to receive confidences, said: "Houdini possessed a wondrous power that he never understood, and which he never revealed to anyone in life."

Houdini was not Solomon; he was a vaudeville specialist. If he ever experienced a psychic power it surely humbled his understanding. And to admit such a power, in his position, would have been a monumental stupidity. Why? If for no other reason, Talmudic law forbids the performance of miracles, and Houdini was the obedient son of Rabbi Weiss. Also, in case he should forget the Jewish law, it is strictly against the magician's code to claim a supernatural power, for reasons impossible to ignore. Mediums made such claims, at their own risk. Two of the more famous mediums of the nineteenth century, Ira and William Davenport, achieved manifestations similar to Houdini's. Audiences in Liverpool, Leeds, and Paris rioted, stormed the stage, and ran the mediums out of town, crying their performances were an outrage against God and a danger to man. Whether or not the acts were supernatural is beside the point—billing them as such was bad business, and hazardous to life and limb. Yet the Davenports were no more than a sideshow, compared to Houdini. The man was blinding. There had not been such a public display of apparent miracles in nearly two thousand years. Had the Jew so much as hinted his powers were spiritual he might have expected no better treatment than the renegade Hebrew of Nazareth.

Houdini was the self-proclaimed avatar of nothing but good old American know-how, and that is how he wished to be remembered. His wife of thirty years, Beatrice Houdini (known as "Bess"), was loyal to him in this, as in all other things. Pestered for revelations about Houdini's magic long after his death, the widow swore by her husband's account. But against her best intentions, Bess clouded the issue by saying just a little more than was necessary. It was in a letter to Sir Arthur Conan Doyle, who had been a close friend of hers and Houdini's.

The friendship was an odd one. The author of Sherlock Holmes believed in Spiritualism, and championed the séance with all the fervor with which Houdini opposed it. There were two great mysteries in Doyle's life: the powers of Sherlock Holmes and Harry Houdini. Doyle knew the Houdinis intimately, and nothing the magician said could shake Sir Arthur's conviction that certain of Houdini's escapes were supernatural. Doyle never stopped trying to get Houdini to confess. In 1922 it was more than a personal issue. The séance had become big business in America, with millions of bereaved relatives paying to communicate with their dear departed. Spiritualism was a home-grown, persuasive religious movement, a bizarre reaction to American science and pragmatism. The great critic Edmund Wilson, who admired Houdini and understood his gifts, recognized that the magician had appeared at a critical moment in the history of Spiritualism. Houdini was the only man living who had the authority, and the competence, to expose the predatory mediums, and his success was decisive.

Yet Houdini's lecture-demonstrations, and exposures of false mediums, only fueled Doyle's suspicions that his friend was the real thing, a physical medium. In all fairness, Sir Arthur Conan Doyle was a credulous old gentleman, who knew nothing of Houdini's techniques. But his instinct was sound. Two months after Houdini died, Sir Arthur wrote to Bess in despair of ever learning the truth from the magician's lips, and she wrote Doyle a long letter. What concerns us here are a few sentences which, coming from the woman who shared his life and work, and maintained her loyalty to Houdini alive and dead, we must regard as altogether startling.

> I will never be offended by anything you say for him or about him, but that he possessed psychic powers—he never knew it. As I told Lady Doyle often he would get a difficult lock, I stood by the cabinet and I would hear him say, "This is beyond me," and after many minutes when the audience became restless I nervously would say "Harry, if there is anything in this belief in Spiritism,—why don't you call on them to assist you," and before many minutes had passed Houdini had mastered the lock.
>
> We never attributed this to psychic help. We just knew that that particular instrument was the one to open that lock, and so did all his tricks.

The tone of this letter penned so soon after her husband's death is somber throughout, painfully sincere. This was not a subject for levity, this being the central issue in the life of Harry Houdini. So what on earth is Bess trying to tell Sir Arthur when she testifies to the invocation of spirits in one sentence, and repudiates psychic help in the next? What kind of double-talk is this, when the widow refers to the summoning of spiritual aid as "that particular instrument," as if a spirit were no different from any other skeleton key? It sounds like sheer euphemism; it sounds like the Houdinis' lifetime of work had uncovered a power so terrifying they would not admit it to each other, let alone the world. Would that Albert Einstein had been so discreet in 1905.

So what if Harry Houdini, once in a while, "spirited" himself out of a Siberian Van, or a pair of Mirror Handcuffs, or a packing case at the bottom of the East River? It is perhaps no more remarkable than that an American Jew won a verdict against the German Police for criminal libel in 1901, or reversed a religious movement in America in 1922. Houdini died in Detroit on Halloween in 1926, of acute appendicitis. He was born in Budapest on March 24, 1874, but told the world he was born in Appleton, Wisconsin on April 6. Not until after World War II did Americans discover that their greatest magician was an alien. Houdini's work was no more miraculous than his life. His life was no more miraculous than the opening and closing of a flower.

1986

THE READER

1. Do you find the figure of Houdini appealing, attractive, as Epstein presents him? What do you take to be the outstanding qualities of his character?
2. How important to this account of Houdini is the fact that he was a Jew?

What are some of the implications here of that fact? What might Epstein be saying (even if unexpressed) in his account of the confrontations between Houdini and the German police?

3. *What, according to Epstein, was the message to mankind of Houdini's career? What details in the essay exemplify that message?*

THE WRITER

1. *At several points in his account of Houdini, Epstein creates an effect of suspense. How does he manage that effect? What purposes does it serve?*

2. *Epstein's account of Houdini leaves some unanswered questions. What are they? Why are they unanswered? Would it be a better account if there were no questions left unanswered? Do you see any connection between the fact of unanswered questions and the theme of the essay?*

Mind

Benjamin Franklin

THE CONVENIENCE OF BEING "REASONABLE"

I believe I have omitted mentioning that, in my first voyage from Boston, being becalmed off Block Island, our people set about catching cod, and hauled up a great many. Hitherto I had stuck to my resolution of not eating animal food, and on this occasion I considered, with my master Tryon,[1] the taking every fish as a kind of unprovoked murder, since none of them had, or ever could do us any injury that might justify the slaughter. All this seemed very reasonable. But I had formerly been a great lover of fish, and, when this came hot out of the frying-pan, it smelled admirably well. I balanced some time between principle and inclination, till I recollected that, when the fish were opened, I saw smaller fish taken out of their stomachs; then thought I, "if you eat one another, I don't see why we mayn't eat you." So I dined upon cod very heartily, and continued to eat with other people, returning only now and then occasionally to a vegetable diet. So convenient a thing it is to be a *reasonable creature*, since it enables one to find or make a reason for everything one has a mind to do.

1791

---

1. "When about 16 years of age, I happened to meet with a book written by one [Thomas] Tryon [*The Way to Health, Wealth, and Happiness*, 1682] recommending a vegetable diet. I determined to go into it. * * * My refusing to eat flesh occasioned an inconveniency, and I was frequently chid for my singularity" [Franklin, *Autobiography*].

William Golding

THINKING AS A HOBBY

While I was still a boy, I came to the conclusion that there were three grades of thinking; and since I was later to claim thinking as my hobby, I came to an even stranger conclusion—namely, that I myself could not think at all.

I must have been an unsatisfactory child for grownups to deal with. I remember how incomprehensible they appeared to me at first, but not, of course, how I appeared to them. It was the headmaster of my grammar school who first brought the subject of thinking before me—though neither in the way, nor with the result he intended. He had some statuettes in his study. They stood on a high cupboard behind his desk. One was a lady wearing nothing but a bath towel. She seemed frozen in an eternal panic lest the bath towel slip down any farther; and since she had no arms, she was in an unfortunate position to pull the towel up again. Next to her, crouched the statuette of a leopard, ready to spring down at the top drawer of a filing cabinet labeled A-AH. My innocence interpreted this as the victim's last, despairing cry. Beyond the leopard was a naked, muscular gentleman, who sat, looking down, with his chin on his fist and his elbow on his knee. He seemed utterly miserable.

Some time later, I learned about these statuettes. The headmaster had placed them where they would face delinquent children, because they symbolized to him the whole of life. The naked lady was the Venus of Milo. She was Love. She was not worried about the towel. She was just busy being beautiful. The leopard was Nature, and he was being natural. The naked, muscular gentleman was not miserable. He was Rodin's Thinker, an image of pure thought. It is easy to buy small plaster models of what you think life is like.

I had better explain that I was a frequent visitor to the headmaster's study, because of the latest thing I had done or left undone. As we now say, I was not integrated. I was, if anything, disintegrated; and I was puzzled. Grownups never made sense. Whenever I found myself in a penal position before the headmaster's desk, with the statuettes glimmering whitely above him, I would sink my head, clasp my hands behind my back and writhe one shoe over the other.

The headmaster would look opaquely at me through flashing spectacles.

"What are we going to do with you?"

Well, what were they going to do with me? I would writhe my shoe some more and stare down at the worn rug.

"Look up, boy! Can't you look up?"

Then I would look up at the cupboard, where the naked lady was frozen in her panic and the muscular gentleman contemplated the hindquarters of the leopard in endless gloom. I had nothing to say to the headmaster. His spectacles caught the light so that you could see nothing human behind them. There was no possibility of communication.

"Don't you ever think at all?"

No, I didn't think, wasn't thinking, couldn't think—I was simply waiting in anguish for the interview to stop.

"Then you'd better learn—hadn't you?"

On one occasion the headmaster leaped to his feet, reached up and plonked Rodin's masterpiece on the desk before me.

"That's what a man looks like when he's really thinking."

I surveyed the gentleman without interest or comprehension.

"Go back to your class."

Clearly there was something missing in me. Nature had endowed the rest of the human race with a sixth sense and left me out. This must be so, I mused, on my way back to the class, since whether I had broken a window, or failed to remember Boyle's Law, or been late for school, my teachers produced me one, adult answer: "Why can't you think?"

As I saw the case, I had broken the window because I had tried to hit Jack Arney with a cricket ball and missed him; I could not remember Boyle's Law because I had never bothered to learn it; and I was late for school because I preferred looking over the bridge into the river. In fact, I was wicked. Were my teachers, perhaps, so good that they could not understand the depths of my depravity? Were they clear, untormented people who could direct their every action by this mysterious business of thinking? The whole thing was incomprehensible. In my earlier years, I found even the statuette of the Thinker confusing. I did not believe any of my teachers were naked, ever. Like someone born deaf, but bitterly determined to find out about sound, I watched my teachers to find out about thought.

There was Mr. Houghton. He was always telling me to think. With a modest satisfaction, he would tell me that he had thought a bit himself. Then why did he spend so much time drinking? Or was there more sense in drinking than there appeared to be? But if not, and if drinking were in fact ruinous to health—and Mr. Houghton was ruined, there was no doubt about that—why was he always talking about the clean life and the virtues of fresh air? He would spread his arms wide with the action of a man who habitually spent his time striding along mountain ridges.

"Open air does me good, boys—I know it!"

Sometimes, exalted by his own oratory, he would leap from his desk and hustle us outside into a hideous wind.

"Now, boys! Deep breaths! Feel it right down inside you—huge draughts of God's good air!"

He would stand before us, rejoicing in his perfect health, an open-air man. He would put his hands on his waist and take a tremendous breath. You could hear the wind, trapped in the cavern of his chest and struggling with all the unnatural impediments. His body would reel with shock and his ruined face go white at the unaccustomed visitation. He would stagger back to his desk and collapse there, useless for the rest of the morning.

Mr. Houghton was given to high-minded monologues about the good life, sexless and full of duty. Yet in the middle of one of these monologues, if a girl passed the window, tapping along on her neat little feet, he would interrupt his discourse, his neck would turn of itself and he would watch her out of sight. In this instance, he seemed to me ruled not by thought but by an invisible and irresistible spring in his nape.

His neck was an object of great interest to me. Normally it bulged a bit over his collar. But Mr. Houghton had fought in the First World War alongside both Americans and French, and had come—by who knows what illogic?—to a settled detestation of both countries. If either country happened to be prominent in current affairs, no argument could make Mr. Houghton think well of it. He would bang the desk, his neck would bulge still further and go red. "You can say what you like," he would cry, "but I've thought about this—and I know what I think!"

Mr. Houghton thought with his neck.

There was Miss Parsons. She assured us that her dearest wish was our welfare, but I knew even then, with the mysterious clairvoyance of childhood, that what she wanted most was the husband she never got. There was Mr. Hands—and so on.

I have dealt at length with my teachers because this was my introduction to the nature of what is commonly called thought. Through them I discovered that thought is often full of unconscious prejudice, ignorance and hypocrisy. It will lecture on disinterested purity while its neck is being remorselessly twisted toward a skirt. Technically, it is about as proficient as most businessmen's golf, as honest as most politicians' intentions, or—to come near my own preoccupation—as coherent as most books that get written. It is what I came to call grade-three thinking, though more properly, it is feeling, rather than thought.

True, often there is a kind of innocence in prejudices, but in those days I viewed grade-three thinking with an intolerant contempt and an incautious mockery. I delighted to confront a pious lady who hated the Germans with the proposition that we should love our enemies. She taught me a great truth in dealing with grade-three thinkers; because of her, I no longer dismiss lightly a mental process which for nine-tenths of the population is the nearest they will ever get to thought. They have immense solidarity. We had better respect them, for we are outnumbered and surrounded. A crowd of grade-three thinkers, all shouting the same thing, all warming their hands at the fire of their own prejudices, will not thank you for pointing out the contradictions in their beliefs. Man is a gregarious animal, and enjoys agreement as cows will graze all the same way on the side of a hill.

Grade-two thinking is the detection of contradictions. I reached grade two when I trapped the poor, pious lady. Grade-two thinkers do not stampede easily, though often they fall into the other fault and lap behind. Grade-two thinking is a withdrawal, with eyes and ears open. It became my hobby and brought satisfaction and loneliness in either hand. For grade-two thinking destroys without having the power to create. It set me watching the crowds cheering His Majesty and King and asking myself what all the fuss was about, without giving me anything positive to put in the place of that heady patriotism. But there were compensations. To hear people justify their habit of hunting foxes and tearing them to pieces by claiming that the foxes liked it. To hear our Prime Minister talk about the great benefit we conferred on India by jailing people like Pandit Nehru and Gandhi. To hear American politicians talk about peace in one sentence and refuse to join the League of Nations in the next. Yes, there were moments of delight.

But I was growing toward adolescence and had to admit that Mr. Houghton was not the only one with an irresistible spring in his neck. I, too, felt the compulsive hand of nature and began to find that pointing out contradiction could be costly as well as fun. There was Ruth, for example, a serious and attractive girl. I was an atheist at the time. Grade-two thinking is a menace to religion and knocks down sects like skittles. I put myself in a position to be converted by her with an hypocrisy worthy of grade three. She was a Methodist—or at least, her parents were, and Ruth had to follow suit. But, alas, instead of relying on the Holy Spirit to convert me, Ruth was foolish enough to open her pretty mouth in argument. She claimed that the Bible (King James Version) was literally inspired. I countered by saying that the Catholics believed in the literal inspiration of Saint Jerome's *Vulgate*,[1] and the two books were different. Argument flagged.

At last she remarked that there were an awful lot of Methodists, and they couldn't be wrong, could they—not all those millions? That was too easy, said I restively (for the nearer you were to Ruth, the nicer she was to be near to) since there were more Roman Catholics than Methodists anyway; and they couldn't be wrong, could they—not all those hundreds of millions? An awful flicker of doubt appeared in her eyes. I slid my arm around her waist and murmured breathlessly that if we were counting heads, the Buddhists were the boys for my money. But Ruth had *really*

1. The Latin Bible as revised in the fourth century A.D. by Jerome and used thereafter as the authoritative text for Roman Catholic ritual.

wanted to do me good, because I was so nice. She fled. The combination of my arm and those countless Buddhists was too much for her.

That night her father visited my father and left, red-cheeked and indignant. I was given the third degree to find out what had happened. It was lucky we were both of us only fourteen. I lost Ruth and gained an undeserved reputation as a potential libertine.

So grade-two thinking could be dangerous. It was in this knowledge, at the age of fifteen, that I remember making a comment from the heights of grade two, on the limitations of grade three. One evening I found myself alone in the school hall, preparing it for a party. The door of the headmaster's study was open. I went in. The headmaster had ceased to thump Rodin's Thinker down on the desk as an example to the young. Perhaps he had not found any more candidates, but the statuettes were still there, glimmering and gathering dust on top of the cupboard. I stood on a chair and rearranged them. I stood Venus in her bath towel on the filing cabinet, so that now the top drawer caught its breath in a gasp of sexy excitement. "A-ah!" The portentous Thinker I placed on the edge of the cupboard so that he looked down at the bath towel and waited for it to slip.

Grade-two thinking, though it filled life with fun and excitement, did not make for content. To find out the deficiencies of our elders bolsters the young ego but does not make for personal security. I found that grade two was not only the power to point out contradictions. It took the swimmer some distance from the shore and left him there, out of his depth. I decided that Pontius Pilate was a typical grade-two thinker. "What is truth?" he said, a very common grade-two thought, but one that is used always as the end of an argument instead of the beginning. There is still a higher grade of thought which says, "What is truth?" and sets out to find it.

But these grade-one thinkers were few and far between. They did not visit my grammar school in the flesh though they were there in books. I aspired to them, partly because I was ambitious and partly because I now saw my hobby as an unsatisfactory thing if it went no further. If you set out to climb a mountain, however high you climb, you have failed if you cannot reach the top.

I *did* meet an undeniably grade-one thinker in my first year at Oxford. I was looking over a small bridge in Magdalen Deer Park, and a tiny mustached and hatted figure came and stood by my side. He was a German who had just fled from the Nazis to Oxford as a temporary refuge. His name was Einstein.

But Professor Einstein knew no English at that time and I knew only two words of German. I beamed at him, trying wordlessly to convey by my bearing all the affection and respect that the English felt for him. It is possible—and I have to make the admission—that I felt here were two grade-one thinkers standing side by side; yet I doubt if my face conveyed more than a formless awe. I would have given my Greek and Latin and French and a good slice of my English for enough German to communicate. But we were divided; he was as inscrutable as my headmaster. For perhaps five minutes we stood together on the bridge, undeniable grade-one thinker and breathless aspirant. With true greatness, Professor Einstein realized that my contact was better than none. He pointed to a trout wavering in midstream.

He spoke: *"Fisch."*

My brain reeled. Here I was, mingling with the great, and yet helpless as the veriest grade-three thinker. Desperately I sought for some sign by which I might convey that I, too, revered pure reason. I nodded vehemently. In a brilliant flash I used up half of my German vocabulary.

"Fisch. Ja Ja."

For perhaps another five minutes we stood side by side. Then Professor Einstein, his whole figure still conveying good will and amiability, drifted away out of sight.

I, too, would be a grade-one thinker. I was irreverent at the best of times. Political and religious systems, social customs, loyalties and traditions, they all came tumbling down like so many rotten apples off a tree. This was a fine hobby and a sensible substitute for cricket, since you could play it all the year round. I came up in the end with what must always remain the justification for grade-one thinking, its sign, seal and charter. I devised a coherent system for living. It was a moral system, which was wholly logical. Of course, as I readily admitted, conversion of the world to my way of thinking might be difficult, since my system did away with a number of trifles, such as big business, centralized government, armies, marriage. . . .

It was Ruth all over again. I had some very good friends who stood by me, and still do. But my acquaintances vanished, taking the girls with them. Young women seemed oddly contented with the world as it was. They valued the meaningless ceremony with a ring. Young men, while willing to concede the chaining sordidness of marriage, were hesitant about abandoning the organizations which they hoped would give them a career. A young man on the first rung of the Royal Navy, while perfectly agreeable to doing away with big business and marriage, got as rednecked as Mr. Houghton when I proposed a world without any battleships in it.

Had the game gone too far? Was it a game any longer? In those prewar days, I stood to lose a great deal, for the sake of a hobby.

Now you are expecting me to describe how I saw the folly of my ways and came back to the warm nest, where prejudices are so often called loyalties, where pointless actions are hallowed into custom by repetition, where we are content to say we think when all we do is feel.

But you would be wrong. I dropped my hobby and turned professional.

If I were to go back to the headmaster's study and find the dusty statuettes still there, I would arrange them differently. I would dust Venus and put her aside, for I have come to love her and know her for the fair thing she is. But I would put the Thinker, sunk in his desperate thought, where there were shadows before him—and at his back, I would put the leopard, crouched and ready to spring.

1961

THE READER

1. It has been said: "Third-rate thinkers think like everybody else because everybody else thinks the same way. Second-rate thinkers think differently from everybody else because everybody else thinks the same way. First-rate thinkers think." Does this saying correspond to Golding's message? Would you modify it in any way in light of what he writes?

2. What are the special attractions and what are the penalties of grade-three thinking? Grade-two? Grade-one?

3. Are Golding's three categories all-encompassing? If so, how? If not, what additional ones would you add?

4. Are Golding's categories useful for assessing the value of a person's statements? Choose several selections in this book, and examine them by Golding's implied criteria.

THE WRITER

1. Why does Golding, at the end of his essay, return to the three statuettes? Have the statuettes anything to do with the three kinds of thinking described in the essay? Why would Golding rearrange the statuettes as he does in the final paragraph?

2. Why does Golding include the anecdote about Einstein? Does it have any bearing upon his account of the three categories of thinking?

3. One would not usually consider thinking a "hobby." Why does Golding do so? Write an essay on something else not usually considered a hobby, using the title "_____ as a Hobby."

4. Golding is the author of Lord of the Flies. If you have read that novel, write an essay attempting to relate his depiction of characters and events to the three categories of thinking.

Carl Sagan

THE ABSTRACTIONS OF BEASTS

"Beasts abstract not," announced John Locke, expressing mankind's prevailing opinion throughout recorded history: Bishop Berkeley[1] had, however, a sardonic rejoinder: "If the fact that brutes abstract not be made the distinguishing property of that sort of animal, I fear a great many of those that pass for men must be reckoned into their numbers." Abstract thought, at least in its more subtle varieties, is not an invariable accompaniment of everyday life for the average man. Could abstract thought be a matter not of kind but of degree? Could other animals be capable of abstract thought but more rarely or less deeply than humans?

We have the impression that other animals are not very intelligent. But have we examined the possibility of animal intelligence carefully enough, or, as in François Truffaut's poignant film *The Wild Child*, do we simply equate the absence of our style of expression of intelligence with the absence of intelligence? In discussing communication with the animals, the French philosopher Montaigne remarked, "The defect that hinders communication betwixt them and us, why may it not be on our part as well as theirs?"

There is, of course, a considerable body of anecdotal information suggesting chimpanzee intelligence. The first serious study of the behavior of simians—including their behavior in the wild—was made in Indonesia by Alfred Russel Wallace, the co-discoverer of evolution by natural selection. Wallace concluded that a baby orangutan he studied behaved "exactly like a human child in similar circumstances." In fact, "orangutan" is a Malay phrase meaning not ape but "man of the woods." Teuber recounted many stories told by his parents, pioneer German ethologists who founded and operated the first research station devoted to chimpanzee behavior on Tenerife in the Canary Islands early in the second decade of this century. It was here that Wolfgang Kohler performed his famous studies of Sultan, a chimpanzee "genius" who was able to connect two rods in order to reach an otherwise inaccessible banana. On Tenerife, also, two chimpanzees were observed maltreating a chicken: One would extend some food to the fowl, encouraging it to approach; whereupon the other would thrust at it with a piece of wire it had concealed behind its back. The chicken would retreat but soon allow itself to approach once again—and be beaten once again. Here is a fine

---

1. John Locke, English philosopher, author of *An Essay Concerning Human Understanding* (1690); Bishop George Berkeley, Irish philosopher, author of *A Treatise Concerning the Principles of Human Knowledge* (1710).

combination of behavior sometimes thought to be uniquely human: cooperation, planning a future course of action, deception and cruelty. It also reveals that chickens have a very low capacity for avoidance learning.

Until a few years ago, the most extensive attempt to communicate with chimpanzees went something like this: A newborn chimp was taken into a household with a newborn baby, and both would be raised together —twin cribs, twin bassinets, twin high chairs, twin potties, twin diaper pails, twin babypowder cans. At the end of three years, the young chimp had, of course, far outstripped the young human in manual dexterity, running, leaping, climbing and other motor skills. But while the child was happily babbling away, the chimp could say only, and with enormous difficulty, "Mama," "Papa," and "cup." From this it was widely concluded that in language, reasoning and other higher mental functions, chimpanzees were only minimally competent: "Beasts abstract not."

But in thinking over these experiments, two psychologists, Beatrice and Robert Gardner, at the University of Nevada, realized that the pharynx and larynx of the chimp are not suited for human speech. Human beings exhibit a curious multiple use of the mouth for eating, breathing and communicating. In insects such as crickets, which call to one another by rubbing their legs, these three functions are performed by completely separate organ systems. Human spoken language seems to be adventitious. The exploitation of organ systems with other functions for communication in humans is also indicative of the comparatively recent evolution of our linguistic abilities. It might be, the Gardners reasoned, that chimpanzees have substantial language abilities which could not be expressed because of the limitations of their anatomy. Was there any symbolic language, they asked, that could employ the strengths rather than the weaknesses of chimpanzee anatomy?

The Gardners hit upon a brilliant idea: Teach a chimpanzee American sign language, known by its acronym Ameslan, and sometimes as "American deaf and dumb language" (the "dumb" refers, of course, to the inability to speak and not to any failure of intelligence). It is ideally suited to the immense manual dexterity of the chimpanzee. It also may have all the crucial design features of verbal languages.

There is by now a vast library of described and filmed conversations, employing Ameslan and other gestural languages, with Washoe, Lucy, Lana and other chimpanzees studied by the Gardners and others. Not only are there chimpanzees with working vocabularies of 100 to 200 words; they are also able to distinguish among nontrivially different grammatical patterns and syntaxes. What is more, they have been remarkably inventive in the construction of new words and phrases.

On seeing for the first time a duck land quacking in a pond, Washoe gestured "waterbird," which is the same phrase used in English and other languages, but which Washoe invented for the occasion. Having never seen a spherical fruit other than an apple, but knowing the signs for the principal colors, Lana, upon spying a technician eating an orange, signed "orange apple." After tasting a watermelon, Lucy described it as "candy drink" or "drink fruit," which is essentially the same word form as the English "water melon." But after she had burned her mouth on her first radish, Lucy forever after described them as "cry hurt food." A small doll placed unexpectedly in Washoe's cup elicited the response "Baby in my drink." When Washoe soiled, particularly clothing or furniture, she was taught the sign "dirty," which she then extrapolated as a general term of abuse. A rhesus monkey that evoked her displeasure was repeatedly signed at: "Dirty monkey, dirty monkey, dirty monkey." Occasionally Washoe would say things like "Dirty Jack, gimme drink." Lana, in a moment of creative annoyance, called her trainer "You green shit." Chimpanzees have invented swear words. Washoe also seems to have a sort of sense of humor; once, when riding on her trainer's shoulders and, perhaps inadvertently, wetting him, she signed: "Funny, funny."

Lucy was eventually able to distinguish clearly the meanings of the phrases "Roger tickle Lucy" and "Lucy tickle Roger," both of which activities she enjoyed with gusto. Likewise, Lana extrapolated from "Tim groom Lana" to "Lana groom Tim." Washoe was observed "reading" a magazine—i.e., slowly turning the pages, peering intently at the pictures and making, to no one in particular, an appropriate sign, such as "cat" when viewing a photograph of a tiger, and "drink" when examining a Vermouth advertisement. Having learned the sign "open" with a door, Washoe extended the concept to a briefcase. She also attempted to converse in Ameslan with the laboratory cat, who turned out to be the only illiterate in the facility. Having acquired this marvelous method of communication, Washoe may have been surprised that the cat was not also competent in Ameslan. And when one day Jane, Lucy's foster mother, left the laboratory, Lucy gazed after her and signed: "Cry me. Me cry."

Boyce Rensberger is a sensitive and gifted reporter for the New York Times whose parents could neither speak nor hear, although he is in both respects normal. His first language, however, was Ameslan. He had been abroad on a European assignment for the Times for some years. On his return to the United States, one of his first domestic duties was to look into the Gardners' experiments with Washoe. After some little time with the chimpanzee, Rensberger reported, "Suddenly I realized I was conversing with a member of another species in my native tongue." The use of the word tongue is, of course, figurative: it is built deeply into the structure of the language (a word that also means "tongue"). In fact, Rensberger was conversing with a member of another species in his native "hand." And it is just this transition from tongue to hand that has permitted humans to regain the ability—lost, according to Josephus,[2] since Eden—to communicate with the animals.

In addition to Ameslan, chimpanzees and other nonhuman primates are being taught a variety of other gestural languages. At the Yerkes Regional Primate Research Center in Atlanta, Georgia, they are learning a specific computer language called (by the humans, not the chimps) "Yerkish." The computer records all of its subjects' conversations, even during the night when no humans are in attendance; and from its ministrations we have learned that chimpanzees prefer jazz to rock and movies about chimpanzees to movies about human beings. Lana had, by January 1976, viewed *The Developmental Anatomy of the Chimpanzee* 245 times. She would undoubtedly appreciate a larger film library.

* * * The machine provides for many of Lana's needs, but not all. Sometimes, in the middle of the night, she forlornly types out: "Please, machine, tickle Lana." More elaborate requests and commentaries, each requiring a creative use of a set grammatical form, have been developed subsequently.

Lana monitors her sentences on a computer display, and erases those with grammatical errors. Once, in the midst of Lana's construction of an elaborate sentence, her trainer mischievously and repeatedly interposed, from his separate computer console, a word that made nonsense of Lana's sentence. She gazed at her computer display, spied her trainer at his console, and composed a new sentence: "Please, Tim, leave room." Just as Washoe and Lucy can be said to speak, Lana can be said to write.

At an early stage in the development of Washoe's verbal abilities, Jacob Bronowski and a colleague wrote a scientific paper denying the significance of Washoe's use of gestural language because, in the limited data available to Bronowski, Washoe neither inquired nor negated. But later observations showed that Washoe and other chimpanzees were perfectly able both to ask questions and to deny assertions put to them. And it is difficult to see any significant difference in quality between chimpanzee use of gestural language and the use of ordinary speech by children in a manner that we unhesitatingly attribute to intelligence. In reading Bronowski's paper I cannot help but feel that a little pinch of human chauvinsim has crept in, an echo of Locke's "Beasts abstract not." In 1949, the American anthropologist Leslie White stated unequivocally: "Human behavior is symbolic behavior; symbolic behavior is human behavior." What would White have made of Washoe, Lucy and Lana?

These findings on chimpanzee language and intelligence have an intriguing bearing on "Rubicon" arguments[3]—the contention that the

2. First-century Jewish general and historian.
3. Those assuming a definitive boundary between different kinds of intelligence. The allusion is to the river Rubicon, in ancient

total brain mass, or at least the ratio of brain to body mass, is a useful index of intelligence. Against this point of view it was once argued that the lower range of the brain masses of microcephalic humans overlaps the upper range of brain masses of adult chimpanzees and gorillas; and yet, it was said, microcephalics have some, although severely impaired, use of language—while the apes have none. But in only relatively few cases are microcephalics capable of human speech. One of the best behavioral descriptions of microcephalics was written by a Russian physician, S. Korsakov, who in 1893 observed a female microcephalic named "Masha." She could understand a very few questions and commands and could occasionally reminisce on her childhood. She sometimes chattered away, but there was little coherence to what she uttered. Korsakov characterized her speech as having "an extreme poverty of logical associations." As an example of her poorly adapted and automaton-like intelligence, Korsakov described her eating habits. When food was present on the table, Masha would eat. But if the food was abruptly removed in the midst of a meal, she would behave as if the meal had ended, thanking those in charge and piously blessing herself. If the food were returned, she would eat again. The pattern apparently was subject to indefinite repetition. My own impression is that Lucy or Washoe would be a far more interesting dinner companion than Masha, and that the comparison of microcephalic humans with normal apes is not inconsistent with some sort of "Rubicon" of intelligence. Of course, both the quality and the quantity of neural connections are probably vital for the sorts of intelligence that we can easily recognize.

Recent experiments performed by James Dewson of the Stanford University School of Medicine and his colleagues give some physiological support to the idea of language centers in the simian neocortex—in particular, like humans, in the left hemisphere. Monkeys were trained to press a green light when they heard a hiss and a red light when they heard a tone. Some seconds after a sound was heard, the red or the green light would appear at some unpredictable position—different each time—on the control panel. The monkey pressed the appropriate light and, in the case of a correct guess, was rewarded with a pellet of food. Then the time interval between hearing the sound and seeing the light was increased up to twenty seconds. In order to be rewarded, the monkeys now had to remember for twenty seconds which noise they had heard. Dewson's team then surgically excised part of the so-called auditory association cortex from the left hemisphere of the neocortex in the temporal lobe. When retested, the monkeys had very poor recall of which sound they were then hearing. After less than a second they could not recall whether it was a hiss or a tone. The removal of a comparable part of the temporal

---

times the boundary between Rome and its "barbaric" Germanic provinces.

lobe from the right hemisphere produced no effect whatever on this task. "It looks," Dewson was reported to say, "as if we removed the structure in the monkeys' brains that may be analogous to human language centers." Similar studies on rhesus monkeys, but using visual rather than auditory stimuli, seem to show no evidence of a difference between the hemispheres of the neocortex.

Because adult chimpanzees are generally thought (at least by zookeepers) to be too dangerous to retain in a home or home environment, Washoe and other verbally accomplished chimpanzees have been involuntarily "retired" soon after reaching puberty. Thus we do not yet have experience with the adult language abilities of monkeys and apes. One of the most intriguing questions is whether a verbally accomplished chimpanzee mother will be able to communicate language to her offspring. It seems very likely that this should be possible and that a community of chimps initially competent in gestural language could pass down the language to subsequent generations.

Where such communication is essential for survival, there is already some evidence that apes transmit extragenetic or cultural information. Jane Goodall observed baby chimps in the wild emulating the behavior of their mothers and learning the reasonably complex task of finding an appropriate twig and using it to prod into a termite's nest so as to acquire some of these tasty delicacies.

Differences in group behavior—something that it is very tempting to call cultural differences—have been reported among chimpanzees, baboons, macaques and many other primates. For example, one group of monkeys may know how to eat bird's eggs, while an adjacent band of precisely the same species may not. Such primates have a few dozen sounds or cries, which are used for intra-group communication, with such meanings as "Flee; here is a predator." But the sound of the cries differs somewhat from group to group: there are regional accents.

An even more striking experiment was performed accidentally by Japanese primatologists attempting to relieve an overpopulation and hunger problem in a community of macaques on an island in south Japan. The anthropologists threw grains of wheat on a sandy beach. Now it is very difficult to separate wheat grains one by one from sand grains; such an effort might even expend more energy than eating the collected wheat would provide. But one brilliant macaque, Imo, perhaps by accident or out of pique, threw handfuls of the mixture into the water. Wheat floats; sand sinks, a fact that Imo clearly noted. Through the sifting process she was able to eat well (on a diet of soggy wheat, to be sure). While older macaques, set in their ways, ignored her, the younger monkeys appeared to grasp the importance of her discovery, and imitate it. In the next generation, the practice was more widespread; today all macaques on the island are competent at water sifting, an example of a cultural tradition among the monkeys.

Earlier studies on Takasakiyama, a mountain in northeast Kyushu inhabited by macaques, show a similar pattern in cultural evolution. Visitors to Takasakiyama threw caramels wrapped in paper to the monkeys—a common practice in Japanese zoos, but one the Takasakiyama macaques had never before encountered. In the course of play, some young monkeys discovered how to unwrap the caramels and eat them. The habit was passed on successively to their playmates, their mothers, the dominant males (who among the macaques act as babysitters for the very young) and finally to the subadult males, who were at the furthest social remove from the monkey children. The process of acculturation took more than three years. In natural primate communities, the existing nonverbal communications are so rich that there is little pressure for the development of a more elaborate gestural language. But if gestural language were necessary for chimpanzee survival, there can be little doubt that it would be transmitted culturally down through the generations.

I would expect a significant development and elaboration of language in only a few generations if all the chimps unable to communicate were to die or fail to reproduce. Basic English corresponds to about 1,000 words. Chimpanzees are already accomplished in vocabularies exceeding 10 percent of that number. Although a few years ago it would have seemed the most implausible science fiction, it does not appear to me out of the question that, after a few generations in such a verbal chimpanzee community, there might emerge the memoirs of the natural history and mental life of a chimpanzee, published in English or Japanese (with perhaps an "as told to" after the by-line).

If chimpanzees have consciousness, if they are capable of abstractions, do they not have what until now has been described as "human rights"? How smart does a chimpanzee have to be before killing him constitutes murder? What further properties must he show before religious missionaries must consider him worthy of attempts at conversion?

I recently was escorted through a large primate research laboratory by its director. We approached a long corridor lined, to the vanishing point as in a perspective drawing, with caged chimpanzees. They were one, two or three to a cage, and I am sure the accommodations were exemplary as far as such institutions (or for that matter traditional zoos) go. As we approached the nearest cage, its two inmates bared their teeth and with incredible accuracy let fly great sweeping arcs of spittle, fairly drenching the lightweight suit of the facility's director. They then uttered a staccato of short shrieks, which echoed down the corridor to be repeated and amplified by other caged chimps, who had certainly not seen us, until the corridor fairly shook with the screeching and banging and rattling of bars. The director informed me that not only spit is apt to fly in such a situation; and at his urging we retreated.

I was powerfully reminded of those American motion pictures of the 1930s and '40s, set in some vast and dehumanized state or federal penitentiary, in which the prisoners banged their eating utensils against the bars at the appearance of the tyrannical warden. These chimps are healthy and well-fed. If they are "only" animals, if they are beasts which abstract not, then my comparison is a piece of sentimental foolishness. But chimpanzees *can* abstract. Like other mammals, they are capable of strong emotions. They have certainly committed no crimes. I do not claim to have the answer, but I think it is certainly worthwhile to raise the question: Why, exactly, all over the civilized world, in virtually every major city, are apes in prison?

For all we know, occasional viable crosses between humans and chimpanzees are possible. The natural experiment must have been tried very infrequently, at least recently. If such off-spring are ever produced, what will their legal status be? The cognitive abilities of chimpanzees force us, I think, to raise searching questions about the boundaries of the community of beings to which special ethical considerations are due, and can, I hope, help to extend our ethical perspectives downward through the taxa on Earth and upwards to extraterrestial organisms, if they exist.

* * *

1977

Neil Postman

CONFUSING LEVELS OF ABSTRACTION

Many years ago, mathematicians and logicians were confounded by a certain paradox for which their intellectual habits could produce no solutions. The paradox, which had been known about for centuries, is easily stated in the following way: A Cretan says, "All Cretans are liars." If the statement is true, then it is also false (because at least one Cretan, the speaker, has told the truth). We have a proposition, in other words, that is both true and false at the same time, which is terrifying to mathematicians and logicians. Bertrand Russell and Alfred North Whitehead solved this paradox in their great work, published in 1913, *Principia Mathematica*. They called their solution The Theory of Logical Types, and it, also, may be easily stated: A class of things must not be considered a member of that class. Or, to quote Russell and Whitehead, "Whatever involves *all* of a collection must not be one of that collection." And so, a particular statement by one Cretan about all of the statements made by Cretans is not itself to be considered part of what he is talking about. It is of a different logical type, a different order of things. To confuse them would be like confusing the word *finger* with a finger itself, so that if I asked you to count the number of fingers on your hand, you would (if you were confused) say six—five fingers plus the name of the class of things.

To take another example: There is no paradox in the statement "Never say never" because the first *never* is not at the same level of abstraction as the second, the first *never* referring to all statements, the second to particular ones.

Now, all of this has made mathematicians and logicians reasonably happy, but what about the rest of us? If does not happen very often, not even on the isle of Crete, that a Cretan will approach anybody and announce, "All Cretans are liars." And as for fingers, not even a deranged logician will say he has six fingers on each hand—five plus the class of things. And yet, for all that, The Theory of Logical Types has some practical implications for reducing our stupid and crazy talk. For one thing, it provides us with a certain awareness of the different types of statements we customarily make. For example, we make statements about things and processes in the world, such as, "The temperature is now ninety degrees." And we make statements about our *reactions* to things and processes in the world, such as, "It is hot." If you think that those two statements are virtually the same, you are on a path that is bound to lead to some interesting stupid talk. Whether or not a thermometer registers ninety degrees is an issue that can be settled by anyone who knows how to read a thermometer. But whether or not something is "hot" depends on who is being heated. To a Laplander, a temperature of fifty-eight degrees may be "hot," to a South African it may be "cold." The statement "It is hot (or cold)" is a statement about what is going on inside one's body. The statement "The temperature is now ninety degress (or fifty-eight degrees)" is a statement about what is going on outside one's body. Alfred Korzybski[1] provided us with two terms which are useful in talking about these different types of statements: *Extensional* statements are those which try to point to observable processes that are occurring outside our skins. *Intensional* statements are those which point to processes occurring inside our skins.

This distinction is by no means trivial. As I mentioned earlier, more than a few arguments and misunderstandings are generated by people who have confused the two types of statements and who, therefore, look in the wrong direction for verification of what they are saying. I can never prove to a Laplander that fifty-eight degrees is "cool," but I can prove to him that it is fifty-eight degrees. In other words, there is no paradox in

1. American scientist and writer (1879–1950), born in Poland, founder of the science of general semantics, the study of how language conveys meaning.

two different people's concluding that the weather is both "hot" and "cold" at the same time. As long as they know that each of them is talking about a different reality, their conversation can proceed in a fairly orderly way.

In addition to the differing "horizontal" directions of our statements (inside and outside), there are differing "vertical" directions of our statements. For example, assuming you and I are talking about some event that has occurred, and that we are trying to describe it "objectively," we may still differ in the degree of specificity of our sentences. I may say, "Two vehicles collided." And you may say, "Two Chevy Impalas collided." We are both being extensional in our remarks, but you have included more details than I and, to that extent, come closer to depicting "reality." We may say that my level of abstraction is higher than yours. And as a general rule, the higher the level of abstraction, the less able it is to denote the color and texture and uniqueness of specific realities. I do not say—please note—the less "true" it is. The statement "$E = mc^2$," I am told, is about as "true" as a statement can be, but it is at such a high level of abstraction—it leaves out so many details—as to be virtually useless to all but a select few who use it for specialized purposes. Einstein himself remarked that the more "true" mathematics is, the less it has to do with reality. Nowhere can this be seen more clearly than in our attempts to apply statistical statements to "real" situations. There is, for example, an apocryphal story about a pregnant woman (let us call her Mrs. Green) who went to see her obstetrician in a state of agitation bordering on hysteria. She had read in a magazine that one out of every five babies born in the world is Chinese. She already had given birth to four children and feared that her next would be a victim of the inexorable laws of statistics. The point is that the statement "one out of every five babies in the world is Chinese" is "true," but it is at such a high level of abstraction that it bears no relation to the realities of any *particular* person. It is of a different logical type from any statement made about Mrs. Green's situation and what she, in particular, might expect.

Mrs. Green's problem is apocryphal, but her confusion is not. There are plenty of people who worry themselves to death because they have discovered that they are "below average" in some respect. And there is no shortage of people who falsely assess their own expectations and, indeed, merit, because they have determined they are "above average." For example, a person whose IQ score is "above average" ought not to assume that he or she will have a better chance of understanding a certain situation than a person whose IQ score is "below average." For one thing, a score on a test is a highly abstract statement in itself. For another, a statement about one's score in relation to a thousand other scores is a further abstraction—so far removed from one's performance in a particular situation as to be meaningless. The point is that statistical language of even the most rudimentary sort leaves out so many details that it is, almost literally, not about anything. There is nothing "personal" about it, and therefore it is best to regard it as being of a different logical type from statements about what is actually happening to people.

Generalizations about groups of people present a similar problem. It may be "true," for example, that Jews, as a class of people, have a higher income than Italians, but it does not follow that Al Schwartz, in particular, earns more than Dominick Alfieri, in particular. One of the roots of what may be called prejudice lies somewhere in our confusion over what may be "true" in a general sense and what may be "true" in a particular sense.

The Theory of Logical Types, then, is useful in helping us to sort out our different modalities of talk. There are statements about what we observe and statements about how we feel and statements about our statements (of which self-reflexiveness is an example) and statements about how we classify things—in a phrase, statements about different orders of "reality."

It does not always matter, of course, that we be aware of these distinctions. No one is more obnoxious than the fanatical semanticist who insists upon straightening everyone out even though they have no wish to be straightened. But, obviously, there are many situations in which people descend into argument, confusion, or despair because they are not aware of the differing types of statements being made. In these cases, knowledge of logical types, levels of abstraction, and extensionality-intensionality can be very useful.

But there is still another application to all of this that is even more useful. I am referring to our efforts at solving problems. The basic distinction that is required here is between "first-order" thinking and "second-order" thinking. (I am lifting these terms from a remarkable book, Change, by Paul Watzlawick, John Weakland, and Richard Fisch, in which the authors explain, in great detail, how to apply The Theory of Logical Types to the resolution of practical human problems.) The difference between first- and second-order thinking is a difference in the level of abstraction at which we perceive a problem. When we try to solve a problem through first-order thinking, we work within the framework of the system, accepting the assumptions on which the system is based. For instance, suppose you were given this problem to solve: Here is a number, VI. By the addition of one line, can you make it into a seven? The answer is simple enough—VII. First-order perceptions are entirely adequate for such a problem. But now suppose you are given the following problem: Here is a number, IX. By the addition of one line, can you make it into a six? This problem does not yield to first-order thinking. If you try to solve it by rearranging the elements of the system, you will not come up with a solution. But if you go to another level of abstraction, if you step outside the system, so to speak, an answer suggests itself: SIX. People who cannot solve this problem have usually failed for the following reasons: They assume that IX is a Roman number, and only a Roman number. They assume that the answer must, therefore, be expressed in a Roman number. And they assume that "a line" must be a straight line. In other words, they have "framed" the problem in a certain way and have tried to solve it by staying within that frame. Second-order thinking means going outside the "frame" of a problem and drawing on resources not contained in the original "frame."

There are several different names for second-order thinking. Some have referred to it simply as "creative thinking." The authors of *Change* call it "reframing." Edward de Bono calls it *lateral thinking*, of which he gives the following example:

> There is made in Switzerland a pear brandy in which a whole pear is to be seen within the bottle. How did the pear get into the bottle? The usual guess is that the bottle neck has been closed after the pear has been put into the bottle. Others guess that the bottom of the bottle was added after the pear was inside. It is always assumed that since the pear is a fully grown pear that it must have been placed in the bottle as a fully grown pear. In fact if a branch bearing a tiny bud was inserted through the neck of the bottle then the pear would actually grow within the bottle and there would be no question of how it got inside.   (*Lateral Thinking*, pp. 93 and 94)

One must grant that problems about Roman numbers and pears in bottles are not of the type which ordinarily worry poeple. But the process by which they are solved—going to another level of perception—can be of substantial practical value. For example, in some New York City public schools, the teachers have a great deal of trouble keeping their students inside the classrooms. Students wander through the hallways during class time, sometimes running, fighting, and screaming, which is not only dangerous but also distracting to those inside the classrooms. Now, if you assume that a classroom is the only place where learning can occur and that those who are not in their classrooms are a "problem," you will spend all your energy trying to get the problems to go where the solution is. You will threaten, plead, and even call the police, none of which works very well. But suppose you "reframe" the problem. Suppose, for example, you say that the issue is not how to get the students into a room but how to get them to learn something. All sorts of possibilities will now become available. In one New York City school, the assistant principal came up with this solution: She announced that the school was instituting a radical educational plan, known as "the open hall policy." The plan made *staying in the halls* a legitimate educational activity. A few teachers were made available to talk with students about a variety of subjects, and thus the halls *became* the classroom. The screaming, running, and fighting stopped, and I have been told on good authority that other principals now visit this school to observe this startling educational innovation.

To take another example, in *Change*, Watzlawick and his associates suggest that people suffering from insomnia will often choose the worst possible path to sleep. They will tell themselves that their problem is "to get to sleep." But since sleep must come spontaneously or it does not come, to work at getting to sleep will defeat its purpose. They recommend a little reverse English: Tell yourself that your problem is to stay awake, and try to do so.

Another example: The New York State Thruway Authority faced the problem of an excessive number of speed-limit violations. They could have, at great expense, hired more troopers to track down the violators. Instead, they raised the speed limit, and thus eliminated much of the problem, with no increase in the accident rate.

The point of all this is that a great deal of stupid talk can be eliminated if we can get beyond and outside of our own assumptions. We too often become tyrannized by the way we have framed a certain situation; that is, we allow a set of words and sentences to define for us the level of perception at which we will view a matter. But if we change our words, we may change the matter. And, therefore, the solution.

1976

THE READER

1. Postman shows several implications of The Theory of Logical Types. What are these? Do you find them of value for practical thinking? Can you think of further implications and uses?
2. What point is exemplified by Postman's discussion of the difference between saying "The temperature is now ninety degrees" and "It is hot" (pp. 188–189)?
3. At the close of his essay, Postman offers several instances of creative solutions to practical problems arrived at by the application of second-order thinking (pp. 190–192). Do the solutions seem satisfactory to you? What assumptions underlie his judgment that these are good solutions to the problems posed?
4. What similarities do you find between Postman's discussion of different orders of abstraction and the discussion in Golding's "Thinking as a Hobby" (p. 173)? Are there important differences between them?

THE WRITER

1. Postman says (p. 190) that in many situations "people descend into argument, confusion, or despair because they are not aware of the differing types of statements being made." Has this ever happened to you? Have you ever known anyone who seemed to delight in using "logic" to confuse and confound you? Write an account of your per-

sonal experience in one such situation or with one such logic-monger-
ing acquaintance.
2. Why does Postman include in his essay a discussion of the use and
misuse of statistics? Consider the following (actual) newspaper headline: "Study shows half of U.S. population below average intelligence."
Survey one issue of a newspaper for all instances of stories or analyses
based on statistical material, and write a report of your findings.
3. In grappling with a vexing problem, have you ever experienced the
sudden finding of a solution that seemed to result from a shift from
first- to second-order thinking? Write an account of it, tracing as
carefully as you can the precise sequence of details in the process.
4. Write an essay comparing and contrasting Postman's discussion of
first- and second-order thinking with Bronowski's discussion of imagination (p. 194) or Asimov's discussion of the "eureka" phenomenon
(p. 201).

Henry David Thoreau

OBSERVATION

There is no such thing as pure *objective* observation. Your observation, to be interesting, *i.e.* to be significant, must be *subjective*. The sum
of what the writer of whatever class has to report is simply some human
experience, whether he be poet or philosopher or man of science. The
man of most science is the man most alive, whose life is the greatest
event. Senses that take cognizance of outward things merely are of no
avail. It matters not where or how far you travel—the farther commonly
the worse—but how much alive you are. If it is possible to conceive of an
event outside to humanity, it is not of the slightest significance, though it
were the explosion of a planet. Every important worker will report what
life there is in him. It makes no odds into what seeming deserts the poet is
born. Though all his neighbors pronounce it a Sahara, it will be a paradise
to him; for the desert which we see is the result of the barrenness of our
experience. No mere willful activity whatever, whether in writing verses
or collecting statistics, will produce true poetry or science. If you are
really a sick man, it is indeed to be regretted, for you cannot accomplish
so much as if you were well. All that a man has to say or do that can
possibly concern mankind, is in some shape or other to tell the story of his
love—to sing, and, if he is fortunate and keeps alive, he will be forever in
love. This alone is to be alive to the extremities. It is a pity that this
divine creature should ever suffer from cold feet; a still greater pity that
the coldness so often reaches to his heart. I look over the report of the

doings of a scientific association and am surprised that there is so little life to be reported; I am put off with a parcel of dry technical terms. Anything living is easily and naturally expressed in popular language. I cannot help suspecting that the life of these learned professors has been almost as inhuman and wooden as a rain-gauge or self-registering magnetic machine. They communicate no fact which rises to the temperature of bloodheat. It doesn't all amount to one rhyme.

May 6, 1854

Jacob Bronowski

THE REACH OF IMAGINATION

For three thousand years, poets have been enchanted and moved and perplexed by the power of their own imagination. In a short and summary essay I can hope at most to lift one small corner of that mystery; and yet it is a critical corner. I shall ask, What goes on in the mind when we imagine? You will hear from me that one answer to this question is fairly specific: which is to say, that we can describe the working of the imagination. And when we describe it as I shall do, it becomes plain that imagination is a specifically *human* gift. To imagine is the characteristic act, not of the poet's mind, or the painter's, or the scientist's, but of the mind of man.

My stress here on the word *human* implies that there is a clear difference in this between the actions of men and those of other animals. Let me then start with a classical experiment with animals and children which Walter Hunter thought out in Chicago about 1910. That was the time when scientists were agog with the success of Ivan Pavlov in forming and changing the reflex actions of dogs, which Pavlov had first announced in 1903. Pavlov had been given a Nobel prize the next year, in 1904; although in fairness I should say that the award did not cite his work on the conditioned reflex, but on the digestive gland.

Hunter duly trained some dogs and other animals on Pavlov's lines. They were taught that when a light came on over one of three tunnels out of their cage, that tunnel would be open; they could escape down it, and were rewarded with food if they did. But once he had fixed that conditioned reflex, Hunter added to it a deeper idea: he gave the mechanical experiment a new dimension, literally—the dimension of time. Now he no longer let the dog go to the lighted tunnel at once; instead, he put out the light, and then kept the dog waiting a little while before he let him go. In this way Hunter timed how long an animal can remember where he has last seen the signal light to his escape route.

The results were and are staggering. A dog or a rat forgets which one of three tunnels has been lit up within a matter of seconds—in Hunter's experiment, ten seconds at most. If you want such an animal to do much better than this, you must make the task much simpler: you must face him with only two tunnels to choose from. Even so, the best that Hunter could do was to have a dog remember for five minutes which one of two tunnels had been lit up.

I am not quoting these times as if they were exact and universal: they surely are not. Hunter's experiment, more than fifty years old now, had many faults of detail. For example, there were too few animals, they were oddly picked, and they did not all behave consistently. It may be unfair to test a dog for what he *saw*, when he commonly follows his nose rather than his eyes. It may be unfair to test any animal in the unnatural setting of a laboratory cage. And there are higher animals, such as chimpanzees and other primates, which certainly have longer memories than the animals that Hunter tried.

Yet when all these provisos have been made (and met, by more modern experiments) the facts are still startling and characteristic. An animal cannot recall a signal from the past for even a short fraction of the time that a man can—for even a short fraction of the time that a child can. Hunter made comparable tests with six-year-old children, and found, of course, that they were incomparably better than the best of his animals. There is a striking and basic difference between a man's ability to imagine something that he saw or experienced, and an animal's failure.

Animals make up for this by other and extraordinary gifts. The salmon and the carrier pigeon can find their way home as we cannot: they have, as it were, a practical memory that man cannot match. But their actions always depend on some form of habit: on instinct or on learning, which reproduce by rote a train of known responses. They do not depend, as human memory does, on calling to mind the recollection of absent things.

Where is it that the animal falls short? We get a clue to the answer, I think, when Hunter tells us how the animals in his experiment tried to fix their recollection. They most often pointed themselves at the light before it went out, as some gun dogs point rigidly at the game they scent —and get the name *pointer* from the posture. The animal makes ready to act by building the signal into its action. There is a primitive imagery in its stance, it seems to me; it is as if the animal were trying to fix the light on its mind by fixing it in its body. And indeed, how else can a dog mark and (as it were) name one of three tunnels, when he has no such words as *left* and *right*, and no such numbers as *one, two, three*? The directed gesture of attention and readiness is perhaps the only symbolic device that the dog commands to hold on to the past, and thereby to guide himself into the future.

I used the verb *to imagine* a moment ago, and now I have some ground for giving it a meaning. *To imagine* means to make images and to move them about inside one's head in new arrangements. When you and I recall the past, we imagine it in this direct and homely sense. The tool that puts the human mind ahead of the animal is imagery. For us, memory does not demand the preoccupation that it demands in animals, and it lasts immensely longer, because we fix it in images or other substitute symbols. With the same symbolic vocabulary we spell out the future—not one but many futures, which we weigh one against another.

I am using the word *image* in a wide meaning, which does not restrict it to the mind's eye as a visual organ. An image in my usage is what Charles Peirce called a *sign*, without regard for its sensory quality. Peirce distinguished between different forms of signs, but there is no reason to make his distinction here, for the imagination works equally with them all, and that is why I call them all images.

Indeed, the most important images for human beings are simply words, which are abstract symbols. Animals do not have words, in our sense: there is no specific center for language in the brain of any animal, as there is in the human being. In this respect at least we know that the human imagination depends on a configuration in the brain that has only evolved in the last one or two million years. In the same period, evolution has greatly enlarged the front lobes in the human brain, which govern the sense of the past and the future; and it is a fair guess that they are probably the seat of our other images. (Part of the evidence for this guess is that damage to the front lobes in primates reduces them to the state of Hunter's animals.) If the guess turns out to be right, we shall know why man has come to look like a highbrow or an egghead: because otherwise there would not be room in his head for his imagination.

The images play out for us events which are not present to our senses, and thereby guard the past and create the future—a future that does not yet exist, and may never come to exist in that form. By contrast, the lack of symbolic ideas, or their rudimentary poverty, cuts off an animal from the past and the future alike, and imprisons him in the present. Of all the distinctions between man and animal, the characteristic gift which makes us human is the power to work with symbolic images: the gift of imagination.

This is really a remarkable finding. When Philip Sidney in 1580 defended poets (and all unconventional thinkers) from the Puritan charge that they were liars, he said that a maker must imagine things that are not. Halfway between Sidney and us, William Blake said, "What is now proved was once only imagined." About the same time, in 1796, Samuel Taylor Coleridge for the first time distinguished between the passive fancy and the active imagination, "the living Power and prime Agent of all human Perception." Now we see that they were right, and precisely right: the human gift is the gift of imagination—and that is not just a literary phrase.

Nor is it just a literary gift; it is, I repeat, characteristically human. Almost everything that we do that is worth doing is done in the first place in the mind's eye. The richness of human life is that we have many lives; we live the events that do not happen (and some that cannot) as vividly as those that do; and if thereby we die a thousand deaths, that is the price we pay for living a thousand lives. (A cat, of course, has only nine.) Literature is alive to us because we live its images, but so is any play of the mind—so is chess: the lines of play that we foresee and try in our heads and dismiss are as much a part of the game as the moves that we make. John Keats said that the unheard melodies are sweeter, and all chess players sadly recall that the combinations that they planned and which never came to be played were the best.

I make this point to remind you, insistently, that imagination is the manipulation of images in one's head; and that the rational manipulation belongs to that, as well as the literary and artistic manipulation. When a child begins to play games with things that stand for other things, with chairs or chessmen, he enters the gateway to reason and imagination together. For the human reason discovers new relations between things not by deduction, but by that unpredictable blend of speculation and insight that scientists call induction, which—like other forms of imagination—cannot be formalized. We see it at work when Walter Hunter inquires into a child's memory, as much as when Blake and Coleridge do. Only a restless and original mind would have asked Hunter's questions and could have conceived his experiments, in a science that was dominated by Pavlov's reflex arcs and was heading toward the behaviorism of John Watson.[1]

Let me find a spectacular example for you from history. What is the most famous experiment that you had described to you as a child? I will hazard that it is the experiment that Galileo is said to have made in Sidney's age, in Pisa about 1590, by dropping two unequal balls from the Leaning Tower. There, we say, is a man in the modern mold, a man after our own hearts: he insisted on questioning the authority of Aristotle and St. Thomas Aquinas, and seeing with his own eyes whether (as they said) the heavy ball would reach the ground before the light one. Seeing is believing.

Yet seeing is also imagining. Galileo did challenge the authority of Aristotle, and he did look at his mechanics. But the eye that Galileo used was the mind's eye. He did not drop balls from the Leaning Tower of Pisa —and if he had, he would have got a very doubtful answer. Instead, Galileo made an imaginary experiment in his head, which I will describe as he did years later in the book he wrote after the Holy Office silenced

---

1. Watson, a forerunner of B. F. Skinner, argued that all human behavior consists of conditioned reflexes in response to environmental stimuli.

him: the *Discorsi . . . intorno a due nuove scienze*,[2] which was smuggled out to be printed in the Netherlands in 1638.

Suppose, said Galileo, that you drop two unequal balls from the tower at the same time. And suppose that Aristotle is right—suppose that the heavy ball falls faster, so that it steadily gains on the light ball, and hits the ground first. Very well. Now imagine the same experiment done again, with only one difference: this time the two unequal balls are joined by a string between them. The heavy ball will again move ahead, but now the light ball holds it back and acts as a drag or brake. So the light ball will be speeded up and the heavy ball will be slowed down; they must reach the ground together because they are tied together, but they cannot reach the ground as quickly as the heavy ball alone. Yet the string between them has turned the two balls into a single mass which is heavier than either ball—and surely (according to Aristotle) this mass should therefore move faster than either ball? Galileo's imaginary experiment has uncovered a contradiction; he says trenchantly, "You see how, from your assumption that a heavier body falls more rapidly than a lighter one, I infer that a (still) heavier body falls more slowly." There is only one way out of the contradiction: the heavy ball and the light ball must fall at the same rate, so that they go on falling at the same rate when they are tied together.

This argument is not conclusive, for nature might be more subtle (when the two balls are joined) than Galileo has allowed. And yet it is something more important: it is suggestive, it is stimulating, it opens a new view—in a word, it is imaginative. It cannot be settled without an actual experiment, because nothing that we imagine can become knowledge until we have translated it into, and backed it by, real experience. The test of imagination is experience. But then, that is as true of literature and the arts as it is of science. In science, the imaginary experiment is tested by confronting it with physical experience; and in literature, the imaginative conception is tested by confronting it with human experience. The superficial speculation in science is dismissed because it is found to falsify nature; and the shallow work of art is discarded because it is found to be untrue to our own nature. So when Ella Wheeler Wilcox died in 1919, more people were reading her verses than Shakespeare's; yet in a few years her work was dead. It had been buried by its poverty of emotion and its trivialness of thought: which is to say that it had been proved to be as false to the nature of man as, say, Jean Baptiste Lamarck and Trofim Lysenko[3] were false to the nature of inheritance. The

2. *Treatise . . . on Two New Sciences.* In 1630, after publishing his heretical theory that the earth moves around the sun, Galileo was forced by the Inquisition to recant it under threat of torture.

3. Lamarck was a French biologist (1744–1829) who held that characteristics acquired by experience were biologically transmittable. Lysenko is a Russian biologist (1898–) who has held that hereditary properties of organisms could be changed by manipulating the environment.

strength of the imagination, its enriching power and excitement, lies in its interplay with reality—physical and emotional.

I doubt if there is much to choose here between science and the arts: the imagination is not much more free, and not much less free, in one than in the other. All great scientists have used their imagination freely, and let it ride them to outrageous conclusions without crying "Halt!" Albert Einstein fiddled with imaginary experiments from boyhood, and was wonderfully ignorant of the facts that they were supposed to bear on. When he wrote the first of his beautiful papers on the random movement of atoms, he did not know that the Brownian motion which it predicted could be seen in any laboratory. He was sixteen when he invented the paradox that he resolved ten years later, in 1905, in the theory of relativity, and it bulked much larger in his mind than the experiment of Albert Michelson and Edward Morley[4] which had upset every other physicist since 1881. All his life Einstein loved to make up teasing puzzles like Galileo's, about falling lifts and the detection of gravity; and they carry the nub of the problems of general relativity on which he was working.

Indeed, it could not be otherwise. The power that man has over nature and himself, and that a dog lacks, lies in his command of imaginary experience. He alone has the symbols which fix the past and play with the future, possible and impossible. In the Renaissance, the symbolism of memory was thought to be mystical, and devices that were invented as mnemonics (by Giordano Bruno, for example, and by Robert Fludd) were interpreted as magic signs. The symbol is the tool which gives man his power, and it is the same tool whether the symbols are images or words, mathematical signs or mesons. And the symbols have a reach and a roundness that goes beyond their literal and practical meaning. They are the rich concepts under which the mind gathers many particulars into one name, and many instances into one general induction. When a man says *left* and *right*, he is outdistancing the dog not only in looking for a light; he is setting in train all the shifts of meaning, the overtones and the ambiguities, between *gauche* and *adroit* and *dexterous*, between *sinister* and the sense of right. When a man counts *one, two, three*, he is not only doing mathematics; he is on the path to the mysticism of numbers in Pythagoras and Vitruvius and Kepler, to the Trinity and the signs of the Zodiac.

I have described imagination as the ability to make images and to move them about inside one's head in new arrangements. This is the faculty that is specifically human, and it is the common root from which science

4. Physicists had believed space to be filled with an ether which made possible the propagation of light and magnetism; the Michelson-Morley experiment proved this untrue. Einstein, an outsider, always claimed not to have heard of the experiment until after he published his special theory of relativity, which not only accounted for the Michelson-Morley findings but resolved such paradoxes as the impossibility of distinguishing qualitatively between gravity and the pull caused by the acceleration of an elevator, or lift.

and literature both spring and grow and flourish together. For they do flourish (and languish) together; the great ages of science are the great ages of all the arts, because in them powerful minds have taken fire from one another, breathless and higgledy-piggledy, without asking too nicely whether they ought to tie their imagination to falling balls or a haunted island. Galileo and Shakespeare, who were born in the same year, grew into greatness in the same age; when Galileo was looking through his telescope at the moon, Shakespeare was writing *The Tempest* and all Europe was in ferment, from Johannes Kepler to Peter Paul Rubens, and from the first table of logarithms by John Napier to the Authorized Version of the Bible.

Let me end with a last and spirited example of the common inspiration of literature and science, because it is as much alive today as it was three hundred years ago. What I have in mind is man's ageless fantasy, to fly to the moon. I do not display this to you as a high scientific enterprise; on the contrary, I think we have more important discoveries to make here on earth than wait for us, beckoning, at the horned surface of the moon. Yet I cannot belittle the fascination which that ice-blue journey has had for the imagination of men, long before it drew us to our television screens to watch the tumbling astronauts. Plutarch and Lucian, Ariosto and Ben Jonson wrote about it, before the days of Jules Verne and H. G. Wells and science fiction. The seventeenth century was heady with new dreams and fables about voyages to the moon. Kepler wrote one full of deep scientific ideas, which (alas) simply got his mother accused of witchcraft. In England, Francis Godwin wrote a wild and splendid work, *The Man in the Moone,* and the astronomer John Wilkins wrote a wild and learned one, *The Discovery of a New World.* They did not draw a line between science and fancy; for example, they all tried to guess just where in the journey the earth's gravity would stop. Only Kepler understood that gravity has no boundary, and put a law to it—which happened to be the wrong law.

All this was a few years before Isaac Newton was born, and it was all in his head that day in 1666 when he sat in his mother's garden, a young man of twenty-three, and thought about the reach of gravity. This was how he came to conceive his brilliant image, that the moon is like a ball which has been thrown so hard that it falls exactly as fast as the horizon, all the way round the earth. The image will do for any satellite, and Newton modestly calculated how long therefore an astronaut would take to fall round the earth once. He made it ninety minutes, and we have all seen now that he was right; but Newton had no way to check that. Instead he went on to calculate how long in that case the distant moon would take to round the earth, if indeed it behaves like a thrown ball that falls in the earth's gravity, and if gravity obeyed a law of inverse squares. He found that the answer would be twenty-eight days.

In that telling figure, the imagination that day chimed with nature, and made a harmony. We shall hear an echo of that harmony on the day when we land on the moon, because it will be not a technical but an imaginative triumph, that reaches back to the beginning of modern science and literature both. All great acts of imagination are like this, in the arts and in science, and convince us because they fill out reality with a deeper sense of rightness. We start with the simplest vocabulary of images, with *left* and *right* and *one, two, three,* and before we know how it happened the words and the numbers have conspired to make a match with nature: we catch in them the pattern of mind and matter as one.

1967

THE READER

1. How does the Hunter experiment provide Bronowski with the ground for defining the imagination?
2. On p. 196, Bronowski attributes the imagination to a "configuration" in the brain. Configuration *seems vague here. What else shows uncertainty about exactly what happens in the brain? Does this uncertainty compromise the argument of this essay?*

THE WRITER

1. Bronowski discusses the work of Galileo and Newton in the middle and at the end of his essay. What use does he make of their work? Does it justify placing them in the central and final positions?
2. What function is given to the mind by the title metaphor of reaching (later extended to symbols on p. 199)? What words does Bronowski use to indicate the objects reached for? What is the significance of his selecting these words?
3. Bronowski says that "seeing is also imagining." Write a brief essay exploring that assertion.

Isaac Asimov

THE EUREKA PHENOMENON

In the old days, when I was writing a great deal of fiction, there would come, once in a while, moments when I was stymied. Suddenly, I would find I had written myself into a hole and could see no way out. To take care of that, I developed a technique which invariably worked.

It was simply this—I went to the movies. Not just any movie. I had to pick a movie which was loaded with action but which made no demands on the intellect. As I watched, I did my best to avoid any conscious thinking concerning my problem, and when I came out of the movie I knew exactly what I would have to do to put the story back on the track.

It never failed.

In fact, when I was working on my doctoral dissertation, too many years ago, I suddenly came across a flaw in my logic that I had not noticed before and that knocked out everything I had done. In utter panic, I made my way to a Bob Hope movie—and came out with the necessary change in point of view.

It is my belief, you see, that thinking is a double phenomenon like breathing.

You can control breathing by deliberate voluntary action: you can breathe deeply and quickly, or you can hold your breath altogether, regardless of the body's needs at the time. This, however, doesn't work well for very long. Your chest muscles grow tired, your body clamors for more oxygen, or less, and you relax. The automatic involuntary control of breathing takes over, adjusts it to the body's needs and unless you have some respiratory disorder, you can forget about the whole thing.

Well, you can think by deliberate voluntary action, too, and I don't think it is much more efficient on the whole than voluntary breath control is. You can deliberately force your mind through channels of deductions and associations in search of a solution to some problem and before long you have dug mental furrows for yourself and find yourself circling round and round the same limited pathways. If those pathways yield no solution, no amount of further conscious thought will help.

On the other hand, if you let go, then the thinking process comes under automatic involuntary control and is more apt to take new pathways and make erratic associations you would not think of consciously. The solution will then come while you *think* you are *not* thinking.

The trouble is, though, that conscious thought involves no muscular action and so there is no sensation of physical weariness that would force you to quit. What's more, the panic of necessity tends to force you to go on uselessly, with each added bit of useless effort adding to the panic in a vicious cycle.

It is my feeling that it helps to relax, deliberately, by subjecting your mind to material complicated enough to occupy the voluntary faculty of thought, but superficial enough not to engage the deeper involuntary one. In my case, it is an action movie; in your case, it might be something else.

I suspect it is the involuntary faculty of thought that gives rise to what we call "a flash of intuition," something that I imagine must be merely the result of unnoticed thinking.

Perhaps the most famous flash of intuition in the history of science took place in the city of Syracuse in third-century B.C. Sicily. Bear with me and I will tell you the story—

About 250 B.C., the city of Syracuse was experiencing a kind of Golden Age. It was under the protection of the rising power of Rome, but it retained a king of its own and considerable self-government; it was prosperous; and it had a flourishing intellectual life.

The king was Hieron II, and he had commissioned a new golden crown from a goldsmith, to whom he had given an ingot of gold as raw material. Hieron, being a practical man, had carefully weighed the ingot and then weighed the crown he received back. The two weights were precisely equal. Good deal!

But then he sat and thought for a while. Suppose the goldsmith had subtracted a little bit of the gold, not too much, and had substituted an equal weight of the considerably less valuable copper. The resulting alloy would still have the appearance of pure gold, but the goldsmith would be plus a quantity of gold over and above his fee. He would be buying gold with copper, so to speak, and Hieron would be neatly cheated.

Hieron didn't like the thought of being cheated any more than you or I would, but he didn't know how to find out for sure if he had been. He could scarcely punish the goldsmith on mere suspicion. What to do?

Fortunately, Hieron had an advantage few rulers in the history of the world could boast. He had a relative of considerable talent. The relative was named Archimedes and he probably had the greatest intellect the world was to see prior to the birth of Newton.

Archimedes was called in and was posed the problem. He had to determine whether the crown Hieron showed him was pure gold, or was gold to which a small but significant quantity of copper had been added.

If we were to reconstruct Archimedes' reasoning, it might go as follows. Gold was the densest known substance (at that time). Its density in modern terms is 19.3 grams per cubic centimeter. This means that a given weight of gold takes up less volume than the same weight of anything else! In fact, a given weight of pure gold takes up less volume than the same weight of any kind of impure gold.

The density of copper is 8.92 grams per cubic centimeter, just about half that of gold. If we consider 100 grams of pure gold, for instance, it is easy to calculate it to have a volume of 5.18 cubic centimeters. But suppose that 100 grams of what looked like pure gold was really only 90 grams of gold and 10 grams of copper. The 90 grams of gold would have a volume of 4.66 cubic centimeters, while the 10 grams of copper would have a volume of 1.12 cubic centimeters; for a total value of 5.78 cubic centimeters.

The difference between 5.18 cubic centimeters and 5.78 cubic centimeters is quite a noticeable one, and would instantly tell if the crown were of pure gold, or if it contained 10 per cent copper (with the missing 10 per cent of gold tucked neatly in the goldsmith's strongbox).

All one had to do, then, was measure the volume of the crown and compare it with the volume of the same weight of pure gold.

The mathematics of the time made it easy to measure the volume of many simple shapes: a cube, a sphere, a cone, a cylinder, any flattened object of simple regular shape and known thickness, and so on.

We can imagine Archimedes saying, "All that is necessary, sire, is to pound that crown flat, shape it into a square of uniform thickness, and then I can have the answer for you in a moment."

Whereupon Hieron must certainly have snatched the crown away and said, "No such thing. I can do that much without you; I've studied the principles of mathematics, too. This crown is a highly satisfactory work of art and I won't have it damaged. Just calculate its volume without in any way altering it."

But Greek mathematics had no way of determining the volume of anything with a shape as irregular as the crown, since integral calculus had not yet been invented (and wouldn't be for two thousand years, almost). Archimedes would have had to say, "There is no known way, sire, to carry through a non-destructive determination of volume."

"Then think of one," said Hieron testily.

And Archimedes must have set about thinking of one, and gotten nowhere. Nobody knows how long he thought, or how hard, or what hypotheses he considered and discarded, or any of the details.

What we do know is that, worn out with thinking, Archimedes decided to visit the public baths and relax. I think we are quite safe in saying that Archimedes had no intention of taking his problem to the baths with him. It would be ridiculous to imagine he would, for the public baths of a Greek metropolis weren't intended for that sort of thing.

The Greek baths were a place for relaxation. Half the social aristocracy of the town would be there and there was a great deal more to do than wash. One steamed one's self, got a massage, exercised, and engaged in general socializing. We can be sure that Archimedes intended to forget the stupid crown for a while.

One can envisage him engaging in light talk, discussing the latest news from Alexandria and Carthage, the latest scandals in town, the latest funny jokes at the expense of the country-squire Romans—and then he lowered himself into a nice hot bath which some bumbling attendant had filled too full.

The water in the bath slopped over as Archimedes got in. Did Archimedes notice that at once, or did he sigh, sink back, and paddle his feet awhile before noting the water-slop. I guess the latter. But, whether soon or late, he noticed, and that one fact, added to all the chains of reasoning his brain had been working on during the period of relaxation when it was unhampered by the comparative stupidities (even in Archimedes) of voluntary thought, gave Archimedes his answer in one blinding flash of insight.

Jumping out of the bath, he proceeded to run home at top speed through the streets of Syracuse. He did *not* bother to put on his clothes. The thought of Archimedes running naked through Syracuse has titillated dozens of generations of youngsters who have heard this story, but I must explain that the ancient Greeks were quite lighthearted in their attitude toward nudity. They thought no more of seeing a naked man on the streets of Syracuse, than we would on the Broadway stage.

And as he ran, Archimedes shouted over and over, "I've got it! I've got it!" Of course, knowing no English, he was compelled to shout it in Greek, so it came out, *"Eureka! Eureka!"*

Archimedes' solution was so simple that anyone could understand it— once Archimedes explained it.

If an object that is not affected by water in any way, is immersed in water, it is bound to displace an amount of water equal to its own volume, since two objects cannot occupy the same space at the same time.

Suppose, then, you had a vessel large enough to hold the crown and suppose it had a small overflow spout set into the middle of its side. And suppose further that the vessel was filled with water exactly to the spout, so that if the water level were raised a bit higher, however slightly, some would overflow.

Next, suppose that you carefully lower the crown into the water. The water level would rise by an amount equal to the volume of the crown, and that volume of water would pour out the overflow and be caught in a small vessel. Next, a lump of gold, known to be pure and exactly equal in weight to the crown, is also immersed in the water and again the level rises and the overflow is caught in a second vessel.

If the crown were pure gold, the overflow would be exactly the same in each case, and the volume of water caught in the two small vessels would be equal. If, however, the crown were of alloy, it would produce a larger overflow than the pure gold would and this would be easily noticeable.

What's more, the crown would in no way be harmed, defaced, or even as much as scratched. More important, Archimedes had discovered the "principle of buoyancy."

And was the crown pure gold? I've heard that it turned out to be alloy and that the goldsmith was executed, but I wouldn't swear to it.

How often does this "Eureka phenomenon" happen? How often is there this flash of deep insight during a moment of relaxation, this triumphant cry of "I've got it! I've got it!" which must surely be a moment of the purest ecstasy this sorry world can afford?

I wish there were some way we could tell. I suspect that in the history of science it happens *often*; I suspect that very few significant discoveries are made by the pure technique of voluntary thought; I suspect that voluntary thought may possibly prepare the ground (if even that), but that the final touch, the real inspiration, comes when thinking is under involuntary control.

But the world is in a conspiracy to hide the fact. Scientists are wedded to reason, to the meticulous working out of consequences from assumptions to the careful organization of experiments designed to check those consequences. If a certain line of experiments ends nowhere, it is omitted from the final report. If an inspired guess turns out to be correct, it is *not* reported as an inspired guess. Instead, a solid line of voluntary thought is invented after the fact to lead up to the thought, and that is what is inserted in the final report.

The result is that anyone reading scientific papers would swear that *nothing* took place but voluntary thought maintaining a steady clumping stride from origin to destination, and that just can't be true.

It's such a shame. Not only does it deprive science of much of its glamour (how much of the dramatic story in Watson's *Double Helix* do you suppose got into the final reports announcing the great discovery of the structure of DNA?[1]), but it hands over the important process of "insight," "inspiration," "revelation" to the mystic.

The scientist actually becomes ashamed of having what we might call a revelation, as though to have one is to betray reason—when actually what we call revelation in a man who has devoted his life to reasoned thought, is after all merely reasoned thought that is not under voluntary control.

Only once in a while in modern times do we ever get a glimpse into the workings of involuntary reasoning, and when we do, it is always fascinating. Consider, for instance, the case of Friedrich August Kekule von Stradonitz.

In Kekule's time, a century and a quarter ago, a subject of great interest to chemists was the structure of organic molecules (those associated with living tissue). Inorganic molecules were generally simple in the sense that they were made up of few atoms. Water molecules, for instance, are made up of two atoms of hydrogen and one of oxygen (H_2O). Molecules of ordinary salt are made up of one atom of sodium and one of chlorine ($NaCl$), and so on.

Organic molecules, on the other hand, often contained a large number of atoms. Ethyl alcohol molecules have two carbon atoms, six hydrogen atoms, and an oxygen atom (C_2H_6O); the molecule of ordinary cane sugar is $C_{12}H_{22}O_{11}$, and other molecules are even more complex.

Then, too, it is sufficient, in the case of inorganic molecules generally, merely to know the kinds and numbers of atoms in the molecule; in

1. I'll tell you, in case you're curious. None! [Asimov's note]. How Francis Crick and James Watson discovered the molecular structure of this vital substance is told in Watson's autobiographical book, *The Double Helix*.

organic molecules, more is necessary. Thus, dimethyl ether has the formula C_2H_6O, just as ethyl alcohol does, and yet the two are quite different in properties. Apparently, the atoms are arranged differently within the molecules—but how to determine the arrangements?

In 1852, an English chemist, Edward Frankland, had noticed that the atoms of a particular element tended to combine with a fixed number of other atoms. This combining number was called "valence." Kekule in 1858 reduced this notion to a system. The carbon atom, he decided (on the basis of plenty of chemical evidence) had a valence of four; the hydrogen atom, a valence of one; and the oxygen atom, a valence of two (and so on).

Why not represent the atoms as their symbols plus a number of attached dashes, that number being equal to the valence. Such atoms could then be put together as though they were so many Tinker Toy units and "structural formulas" could be built up.

It was possible to reason out that the structural formula of ethyl alcohol was

$$\begin{array}{ccc} H & H & \\ | & | & \\ H-C-C-O-H, \\ | & | & \\ H & H & \end{array}$$

while that of dimethyl ether was

$$\begin{array}{ccc} H & & H \\ | & & | \\ H-C-O-C-H. \\ | & & | \\ H & & H \end{array}$$

In each case, there were two carbon atoms, each with four dashes attached; six hydrogen atoms, each with one dash attached; and an oxygen atom with two dashes attached. The molecules were built up of the same components, but in different arrangements.

Kekule's theory worked beautifully. It has been immensely deepened and elaborated since his day, but you can still find structures very much like Kekule's Tinker Toy formulas in any modern chemical textbook. They represent oversimplifications of the true situation, but they remain extremely useful in practice even so.

The Kekule structures were applied to many organic molecules in the years after 1858 and the similarities and contrasts in the structures neatly matched similarities and contrasts in properties. The key to the rationalization of organic chemistry had, it seemed, been found.

Yet there was one disturbing fact. The well-known chemical benzene wouldn't fit. It was known to have a molecule made up of equal numbers of carbon and hydrogen atoms. Its molecular weight was known to be 78 and a single carbon-hydrogen combination had a weight of 13. Therefore, the benzene molecule had to contain six carbon-hydrogen combinations and its formula had to be C_6H_6.

But that meant trouble. By the Kekule formulas, the hydrocarbons (molecules made up of carbon and hydrogen atoms only) could easily be envisioned as chains of carbon atoms with hydrogen atoms attached. If all the valences of the carbon atoms were filled with hydrogen atoms, as in "hexane," whose molecule looks like this—

$$
\begin{array}{ccccccc}
H & H & H & H & H & H \\
| & | & | & | & | & | \\
H-C-C-C-C-C-C-H \\
| & | & | & | & | & | \\
H & H & H & H & H & H
\end{array}
$$

the compound is said to be saturated. Such saturated hydrocarbons were found to have very little tendency to react with other substances.

If some of the valences were not filled, unused bonds were added to those connecting the carbon atoms. Double bonds were formed as in "hexene"—

$$
\begin{array}{ccccccc}
H & H & H & H & H & H \\
| & | & | & | & | & | \\
H-C-C-C=C-C-C-H \\
| & | & & & | & | \\
H & H & & & H & H
\end{array}
$$

Hexene is unsaturated, for that double bond has a tendency to open up and add other atoms. Hexene is chemically active.

When six carbons are present in a molecule, it takes fourteen hydrogen atoms to occupy all the valence bonds and make it inert—as in hexane. In hexene, on the other hand, there are only twelve hydrogens. If there were still fewer hydrogen atoms, there would be more than one double bond; there might even be triple bonds, and the compound would be still more active than hexene.

Yet benzene, which is C_6H_6 and has eight fewer hydrogen atoms than hexane, is *less* active than hexene, which has only two fewer hydrogen atoms than hexane. In fact, benzene is even less active than hexane itself. The six hydrogen atoms in the benzene molecule seem to satisfy the six carbon atoms to a greater extent than do the fourteen hydrogen atoms in hexane.

For heaven's sake, why?

This might seem unimportant. The Kekule formulas were so beauti-fully suitable in the case of so many compounds that one might simply dismiss benzene as an exception to the general rule.

Science, however, is not English grammar. You can't just categorize something as an exception. If the exception doesn't fit into the general system, then the general system must be wrong.

Or, take the more positive approach. An exception can often be made to fit into a general system, provided the general system is broadened. Such broadening generally represents a great advance and for this reason, exceptions ought to be paid great attention.

For some seven years, Kekule faced the problem of benzene and tried to puzzle out how a chain of six carbon atoms could be completely satisfied with as few as six hydrogen atoms in benzene and yet be left unsatisfied with twelve hydrogen atoms in hexene.

Nothing came to him!

And then one day in 1865 (he tells the story himself) he was in Ghent, Belgium, and in order to get to some destination, he boarded a public bus. He was tired and, undoubtedly, the droning beat of the horses' hooves on the cobblestones, lulled him. He fell into a comatose half-sleep.

In that sleep, he seemed to see a vision of atoms attaching themselves to each other in chains that moved about. (Why not? It was the sort of thing that constantly occupied his waking thoughts.) But then one chain twisted in such a way that head and tail joined, forming a ring—and Kekule woke with a start.

To himself, he must surely have shouted "Eureka," for indeed he had it. The six carbon atoms of benzene formed a ring and not a chain, so that the structural formula looked like this:

To be sure, there were still three double bonds, so you might think the molecule had to be very active—but now there was a difference. Atoms in a ring might be expected to have different properties from those in a chain and double bonds in one case might not have the properties of those in the other. At least, chemists could work on that assumption and see if it involved them in contradictions.

It didn't. The assumption worked excellently well. It turned out that organic molecules could be divided into two groups: aromatic and aliphatic. The former had the benzene ring (or certain other similar rings) as part of the structure and the latter did not. Allowing for different properties within each group, the Kekule structures worked very well.

For nearly seventy years, Kekule's vision held good in the hard field of actual chemical techniques, guiding the chemist through the jungle of reactions that led to the synthesis of more and more molecules. Then, in 1932, Linus Pauling applied quantum mechanics to chemical structure with sufficient subtlety to explain just why the benzene ring was so special and what had proven correct in practice proved correct in theory as well.

Other cases? Certainly.

In 1764, the Scottish engineer James Watt was working as an instrument maker for the University of Glasgow. The university gave him a model of a Newcomen steam engine, which didn't work well, and asked him to fix it. Watt fixed it without trouble, but even when it worked perfectly, it didn't work well. It was far too inefficient and consumed incredible quantities of fuel. Was there a way to improve that?

Thought didn't help; but a peaceful, relaxed walk on a Sunday afternoon did. Watt returned with the key notion in mind of using two separate chambers, one for steam only and one for cold water only, so that the same chamber did not have to be constantly cooled and reheated to the infinite waste of fuel.

The Irish mathematician William Rowan Hamilton worked up a theory of "quaternions" in 1843 but couldn't complete that theory until he grasped the fact that there were conditions under which $p \times q$ was *not* equal to $q \times p$. The necessary thought came to him in a flash one time when he was walking to town with his wife.

The German physiologist Otto Loewi was working on the mechanism of nerve action, in particular, on the chemicals produced by nerve endings. He awoke at 3 A.M. one night in 1921 with a perfectly clear notion of the type of experiment he would have to run to settle a key point that was puzzling him. He wrote it down and went back to sleep. When he woke in the morning, he found he couldn't remember what his inspiration had been. He remembered he had written it down, but he couldn't read his writing.

The next night, he woke again at 3 A.M. with the clear thought once more in mind. This time, he didn't fool around. He got up, dressed himself, went straight to the laboratory and began work. By 5 A.M. he had proved his point and the consequences of his findings became important enough in later years so that in 1936 he received a share in the Nobel prize in medicine and physiology.

How very often this sort of thing must happen, and what a shame that scientists are so devoted to their belief in conscious thought that they so consistently obscure the actual methods by which they obtain their results.

1971

THE READER

1. Does Asimov argue that science ought to abandon reasoned thought in favor of intuition?
2. Is cultivation of "the Eureka phenomenon" encouraged in any of the science courses you may have taken or are now taking? Why, or why not?
3. In the preceding essay, Bronowski discusses imagination and science. Are there points on which Asimov and Bronowski would seem to be in agreement concerning science?

THE WRITER

1. What does Asimov find wrong about scientific reports as they are customarily written? Do you agree? If scientific writing were not strictly reasonable, wouldn't there be a danger of misrepresenting science?
2. Have you ever experienced anything like "the Eureka phenomenon" Asimov describes? If so, write an account of what happened. Tell what your feelings were when the phenomenon occurred. Did you ever report the discovery in just that way to any one else (to a teacher, for example)? If so, what was the other person's response?

Education

Eudora Welty

CLAMOROUS TO LEARN

From the first I was clamorous to learn—I wanted to know and begged to be told not so much what, or how, or why, or where, as when. How soon?

> Pear tree by the garden gate,
> How much longer must I wait?

This rhyme from one of my nursery books was the one that spoke for me. But I lived not at all unhappily in this craving, for my wild curiosity was in large part suspense, which carries its own secret pleasure. And so one of the godmothers of fiction was already bending over me.

When I was five years old, I knew the alphabet, I'd been vaccinated (for smallpox), and I could read. So my mother walked across the street to Jefferson Davis Grammar School[1] and asked the principal if she would allow me to enter the first grade after Christmas.

"Oh, all right," Said Miss Duling. "Probably the best thing you could do with her."

Miss Duling, a lifelong subscriber to perfection, was a figure of authority, the most whole-souled I have ever come to know. She was a dedicated schoolteacher who denied herself all she might have done or whatever other way she might have lived (this possibility was the last that could have occurred to us, her subjects in school). I believe she came of well-off people, well-educated, in Kentucky, and certainly old photographs show she was a beautiful, high-spirited-looking young lady—and came down to Jackson to its new grammar school that was going begging for a principal. She must have earned next to nothing; Mississippi then as now was the

---

1. Named after the president of the Confederate States of America (1861–65) and located in Jackson, Mississippi.

nation's lowest-ranking state economically, and our legislature has always shown a painfully loud reluctance to give money to public education. That challenge *brought* her.

In the long run she came into touch, as teacher or principal. with three generations of Jacksonians. My parents had not, but everybody else's parents had gone to school to her. She'd taught most of our leaders somewhere along the line. When she wanted something done—some civic oversight corrected, some injustice made right overnight, or even a tree spared that the fool telephone people were about to cut down—she telephoned the mayor, or the chief of police, or the president of the power company, or the head doctor at the hospital, or the judge in charge of a case, or whoever, and calling them by their first names, *told* them. It is impossible to imagine her meeting with anything less than compliance. The ringing of her brass bell from their days at Davis School would still be in their ears. She also proposed a spelling match between the fourth grade at Davis School and the Mississippi Legislature, who went through with it; and that told the Legislature.

Her standards were very high and of course inflexible, her authority was total; why *wouldn't* this carry with it a brass bell that could be heard ringing for a block in all directions? That bell belonged to the figure of Miss Duling as though it grew directly out of her right arm, as wings grew out of an angel or a tail out of the devil. When we entered, marching, into her school, by strictest teaching, surveillance, and order we learned grammar, arithmetic, spelling, reading, writing, and geography; and she, not the teachers, I believe, wrote out the examinations: need I tell you, they were "hard."

She's not the only teacher who has influenced me, but Miss Duling, in some fictional shape or form, has stridden into a larger part of my work than I'd realized until now. She emerges in my perhaps inordinate number of schoolteacher characters. I loved those characters in the writing. But I did not, in life, love Miss Duling. I was afraid of her high-arched bony nose, her eyebrows lifted in half-circles above her hooded, brilliant eyes, and of the Kentucky R's in her speech, and the long steps she took in her hightop shoes. I did nothing but fear her bearing-down authority, and did not connect this (as of course we were meant to) with our own need or desire to learn, perhaps because I already had this wish, and did not need to be driven.

She was impervious to lies or foolish excuses or the insufferable plea of not knowing any better. She wasn't going to have any frills, either, at Davis School. When a new governor moved into the mansion, he sent his daughter to Davis School; her name was Lady Rachel Conner. Miss Duling at once called the governor to the telephone and told him, "She'll be plain Rachel here."

Miss Duling dressed as plainly as a Pilgrim on a Thanksgiving poster

we made in the schoolroom, in a longish black-and-white checked ging-
ham dress, a bright thick wool sweater the red of a railroad lantern—
she'd knitted it herself—black stockings and her narrow elegant feet in
black hightop shoes with heels you could hear coming, rhythmical as a
parade drum down the hall. Her silky black curly hair was drawn back out
of curl, fastened by high combs, and knotted behind. She carried her
spectacles on a gold chain hung around her neck. Her gaze was in general
sweeping, then suddenly at the point of concentration upon you. With a
swing of her bell that took her whole right arm and shoulder, she rang it,
militant and impartial, from the head of the front steps of Davis School
when it was time for us all to line up, girls on one side, boys on the other.
We were to march past her into the school building, while the fourth-
grader she nabbed played time on the piano, mostly to a tune we could
have skipped to, but we didn't skip into Davis School.

Little recess (open-air exercises) and big recess (lunch-boxes from
home opened and eaten on the grass, on the girls' side and the boys' side
of the yard) and dismissal were also regulated by Miss Duling's bell. The
bell was also used to catch us off guard with fire drill.

It was examinations that drove my wits away, as all emergencies do.
Being expected to measure up was paralyzing. I failed to make 100 on my
spelling exam because I missed one word and that word was "uncle."
Mother, as I knew she would, took it personally. "You couldn't spell
uncle? When you've got those five perfectly splendid uncles in West
Virginia? What would *they* say to that?"

It was never that Mother wanted me to beat my classmates in grades;
what she wanted was for me to have my answers right. It was unclouded
perfection I was up against.

My father was much more tolerant of possible error. He only said, as he
steeply and impeccably sharpened my pencils on examination morning,
"Now just keep remembering: the examinations were made out for the
average student to pass. That's the majority. And if the majority can pass,
think how much better you can do."

I looked to my mother, who had her own opinions about the majority.
My father wished to treat it with respect, she didn't. I'd been born left-
handed, but the habit was broken when I entered the first grade in Davis
School. My father had insisted. He pointed out that everything in life had
been made for the convenience of right-handed people, because they
were the majority, and he often used "what the majority wants" as a
criterion for what was for the best. My mother said she could not promise
him, could not promise him at all, that I wouldn't stutter as a consequence. Mother had been born left-handed too; her family consisted of
five left-handed brothers, a left-handed mother, and a father who could
write with both hands at the same time, also backwards and forwards and
upside down, different words with each hand. She had been broken of it

when she was young, and she said she used to stutter.

"But you still stutter," I'd remind her, only to hear her say loftily, "You should have heard me when I was your age."

In my childhood days, a great deal of stock was put, in general, in the value of doing well in school. Both daily newspapers in Jackson saw the honor roll as news and published the lists, and the grades, of all the honor students. The city fathers gave the children who made the honor roll free season tickets to the baseball games down at the grandstand. We all attended and all worshiped some player on the Jackson Senators: I offered up my 100's in arithmetic and spelling, reading and writing, attendance and, yes, deportment—I must have been a prig!—to Red McDermott, the third baseman. And our happiness matched that of knowing Miss Duling was on her summer vacation, far, far away in Kentucky.

Every school week, visiting teachers came on their days for special lessons. On Mondays, the singing teacher blew into the room fresh from the early outdoors, singing in her high soprano "How do you do?" to do-mi-sol-do,[2] and we responded in chorus from our desks, "I'm ve-ry well" to do-sol-mi-do. Miss Johnson taught us rounds—"Row row row your boat gently down the stream"—and "Little Sir Echo," with half the room singing the words and the other half being the echo, a competition. She was from the North, and she was the one who wanted us all to stop the Christmas carols and see snow. The snow falling that morning outside the window was the first most of us had ever seen, and Miss Johnson threw up the window and held out wide her own black cape and caught flakes on it and ran, as fast as she could go, up and down the aisles to show us the real thing before it melted.

Thursday was Miss Eyrich and Miss Eyrich was Thursday. She came to give us physical training. She wasted no time on nonsense. Without greeting, we were marched straight outside and summarily divided into teams (no choosing sides), put on the mark, and ordered to get set for a relay race. Miss Eyrich cracked out "Go!" Dread rose in my throat. My head swam. Here was my turn, nearly upon me. (Wait, have I been touched—was that slap the touch? Go on! Do I go on without our passing a word? What word? Now am I racing too fast to turn around? Now I'm nearly home, but where is the hand waiting for mine to touch? Am I too late? Have I lost the whole race for our side?) I lost the relay race for our side before I started, through living ahead of myself, dreading to make my start, feeling too late prematurely, and standing transfixed by emergency, trying to think of a password. Thursdays still can make me hear Miss Eyrich's voice. "On your mark—get set—GO!"

Very composedly and very slowly, the art teacher, who visited each

2. Syllables indicating the first, third, fifth, and eighth tones of the scale.

room on Fridays, paced the aisle and looked down over your shoulder at what you were drawing for her. This was Miss Ascher. Coming from behind you, her deep, resonant voice reached you without being a word at all, but a sort of purr. It was much the sound given out by our family doctor when he read the thermometer and found you were running a slight fever: "Um-hm. Um-hm." Both alike, they let you go right ahead with it.

The school toilets were in the boys' and girls' respective basements. After Miss Duling had rung to dismiss school, a friend and I were making our plans for Saturday from adjoining cubicles. "Can you come spend the day with me?" I called out, and she called back, "I might could."

"Who—said—MIGHT—COULD?" It sounded like "Fe Fi Fo Fum!"

We both were petrified, for we knew whose deep measured words those were that came from just outside our doors. That was the voice of Mrs. McWillie, who taught the other fourth grade across the hall from ours. She was not even our teacher, but a very heavy, stern lady who dressed entirely in widow's weeds with a pleated black shirtwaist with a high net collar and velvet ribbon, and a black skirt to her ankles, with black circles under her eyes and a mournful, Presbyterian expression. We children took her to be a hundred years old. We held still.

"You might as well tell me," continued Mrs. McWillie. "I'm going to plant myself right here and wait till you come out. Then I'll see who it was I heard saying 'MIGHT-COULD.'"

If Elizabeth wouldn't go out, of course I wouldn't either. We knew her to be a teacher who would not flinch from standing there in the basement all afternoon, perhaps even all day Saturday. So we surrendered and came out. I priggishly hoped Elizabeth would clear it up which child it was—it wasn't me.

"So it's you." She regarded us as a brace, made no distinction: whoever didn't say it was guilty by association. "If I ever catch you down here one more time saying 'MIGHT-COULD,' I'm going to carry it to Miss Duling. You'll be kept in every day for a week! I hope you're both sufficiently ashamed of yourselves?" Saying "might-could" was bad, but saying it in the basement made bad grammar a sin. I knew Presbyterians believed that you could go to Hell.

Mrs. McWillie never scared us into grammar, of course. It was my first-year Latin teacher in high school who made me discover I'd fallen in love with it. It took Latin to thrust me into bona fide alliance with words in their true meaning. Learning Latin (once I was free of Caesar) fed my love for words upon words, words in continuation and modification, and the beautiful, sober, accretion of a sentence. I could see the achieved sentence finally standing there, as real, intact, and built to stay as the Mississippi State Capitol at the top of my street, where I could walk through it on my way to school and hear underfoot the echo of its marble floor, and over me the bell of its rotunda.

On winter's rainy days, the schoolrooms would grow so dark that sometimes you couldn't see the figures on the blackboard. At that point, Mrs. McWillie, that stern fourth-grade teacher, would let her children close their books, and she would move, broad in widow's weeds like darkness itself, to the window and by what light there was she would stand and read aloud "The King of the Golden River."[3] But I was excluded—in the other fourth grade, across the hall. Miss Louella Varnado, my teacher, didn't copy Mrs. McWillie; we had a spelling match: you could spell in the dark. I did not then suspect that there was any other way I could learn the story of "The King of the Golden River" than to have been assigned in the beginning to Mrs. McWillie's cowering fourth grade, then wait for her to treat you to it on the rainy day of her choice. I only now realize how much the treat depended, too, on there not having been money enough to put electric lights in Davis School. John Ruskin had to come in through courtesy of darkness. When in time I found the story in a book and read it to myself, it didn't seem to live up to my longings for a story with that name; as indeed, how could it?

1985

3. A fantasy for children by the English author John Ruskin (1819–1900).

Caroline Bird

COLLEGE IS A WASTE OF TIME AND MONEY

A great majority of our nine million college students are not in school because they want to be or because they want to learn. They are there because it has become the thing to do or because college is a pleasant place to be; because it's the only way they can get parents or taxpayers to support them without working at a job they don't like; because Mother wanted them to go, or some other reason entirely irrelevant to the course of studies for which college is supposedly organized.

As I crisscross the United States lecturing on college campuses, I am dismayed to find that professors and administrators, when pressed for a candid opinion, estimate that no more than 25 percent of their students are turned on by classwork. For the rest, college is at best a social center or aging vat, and at worst a young folks' home or even a prison that keeps them out of the mainstream of economic life for a few more years.

The premise—which I no longer accept—that college is the best place for all high-school graduates grew out of a noble American ideal. Just as the United States was the first nation to aspire to teach every small child to read and write, so, during the 1950s, we became the first and only great nation to aspire to higher education for all. During the '60s we damned the expense and built great state university systems as fast as we could. And adults—parents, employers, high-school counselors—began to push, shove and cajole youngsters to "get an education."

It became a mammoth industry, with taxpayers footing more than half the bill. By 1970, colleges and universities were spending more than 30 billion dollars annually. But still only half our highschool graduates were going on. According to estimates made by the economist Fritz Machlup, if we had been educating every young person until age 22 in that year of 1970, the bill for higher education would have reached 47.5 billion dollars, 12.5 billion more than the total corporate profits for the year.

Figures such as these have begun to make higher education for all look financially prohibitive, particularly now when colleges are squeezed by the pressures of inflation and a drop-off in the growth of their traditional market.

Predictable demography has caught up with the university empire builders. Now that the record crop of postwar babies has graduated from college, the rate of growth of the student population has begun to decline. To keep their mammoth plants financially solvent, many institutions have begun to use hard-sell, Madison-Avenue techniques to attract students. They sell college like soap, promoting features they think students want: innovative programs, an environment conducive to meaningful personal relationships, and a curriculum so free that it doesn't sound like college at all.

Pleasing the customers is something new for college administrators. Colleges have always known that most students don't like to study, and that at least part of the time they are ambivalent about college, but before the student riots of the 1960s educators never thought it either right or necessary to pay any attention to student feelings. But when students rebelling against the Vietnam war and the draft discovered they could disrupt a campus completely, administrators had to act on some student complaints. Few understood that the protests had tapped the basic discontent with college itself, a discontent that did not go away when the riots subsided.

Today students protest individually rather than in concert. They turn inward and withdraw from active participation. They drop out to travel to India or to feed themselves on subsistence farms. Some refuse to go to college at all. Most, of course, have neither the funds nor the self-confidence for constructive articulation of their discontent. They simply hang around college unhappily and reluctantly.

All across the country, I have been overwhelmed by the prevailing sadness on American campuses. Too many young people speak little, and then only in drowned voices. Sometimes the mood surfaces as diffidence, wariness, or coolness, but whatever its form, it looks like a defense mechanism, and that rings a bell. This is the way it used to be with women, and just as society had systematically damaged women by insisting that their proper place was in the home, so we may be systematically damaging 18-year-olds by insisting that their proper place is in college.

Campus watchers everywhere know what I mean when I say students are sad, but they don't agree on the reason for it. During the Vietnam war some ascribed the sadness to the draft; now others blame affluence, or say it has something to do with permissive upbringing.

Not satisfied with any of these explanations, I looked for some answers with the journalistic tools of my trade—scholarly studies, economic analyses, the historical record, the opinions of the especially knowledgeable, conversations with parents, professors, college administrators, and employers, all of whom spoke as alumni too. Mostly I learned from my interviews with hundreds of young people on and off campuses all over the country.

My unnerving conclusion is that students are sad because they are not needed. Somewhere between the nursery and the employment office, they become unwanted adults. No one has anything in particular against them. But no one knows what to do with them either. We already have too many people in the world of the 1970s, and there is no room for so many newly minted 18-year-olds. So we temporarily get them out of the way by sending them to college where in fact only a few belong.

To make it more palatable, we fool ourselves into believing that we are sending them there for their own best interests, and that it's good for them, like spinach. Some, of course, learn to like it, but most wind up preferring green peas.

Educators admit as much. Nevitt Sanford, distinguished student of higher education, says students feel they are "capitulating to a kind of voluntary servitude." Some of them talk about their time in college as if it were a sentence to be served. I listened to a 1970 Mount Holyoke graduate: "For two years I was really interested in science, but in my junior and senior years I just kept saying, 'I've done two years; I'm going to finish'. When I got out I made up my mind that I wasn't going to school anymore because so many of my courses had been bullshit."

But bad as it is, college is often preferable to a far worse fate. It is better than the drudgery of an uninspiring nine-to-five job, and better than doing nothing when no jobs are available. For some young people, it is a graceful way to get away from home and become independent without losing the financial support of their parents. And sometimes it is the only alternative to an intolerable home situation.

It is difficult to assess how many students are in college reluctantly.

The conservative Carnegie Commission estimates from 5 to 30 percent. Sol Linowitz, who was once chairman of a special committee on campus tension of the American Council on Education, found that "a significant number were not happy with their college experience because they felt they were there only in order to get the 'ticket to the big show' rather than to spend the years as productively as they otherwise could."

Older alumni will identify with Richard Baloga, a policeman's son, who stayed in school even though he "hated it" because he thought it would do him some good. But fewer students each year feel this way. Daniel Yankelovich has surveyed undergraduate attitudes for a number of years, and reported in 1971 that 74 percent thought education was "very important." But just two years earlier, 80 percent thought so.

The doubters don't mind speaking up. Leon Lefkowitz, chairman of the department of social studies at Central High School in Valley Stream, New York, interviewed 300 college students at random, and reports that 200 of them didn't think that the education they were getting was worth the effort. "In two years I'll pick up a diploma," said one student, "and I can honestly say it was a waste of my father's bread."

Nowadays, says one sociologist, you don't have to have a reason for going to college; it's an institution. His definition of an institution is an arrangement everyone accepts without question; the burden of proof is not on why you go, but why anyone thinks there might be a reason for not going. The implication is that an 18-year-old is too young and confused to know what he wants to do, and that he should listen to those who know best and go to college.

I don't agree. I believe that college has to be judged not on what other people think is good for students, but on how good it feels to the students themselves.

I believe that people have an inside view of what's good for them. If a child doesn't want to go to school some morning, better let him stay at home, at least until you find out why. Maybe he knows something you don't. It's the same with college. If high-school graduates don't want to go, or if they don't want to go right away, they may perceive more clearly than their elders that college is not for them. It is no longer obvious that adolescents are best off studying a core curriculum that was constructed when all educated men could agree on what made them educated, or that professors, advisors, or parents can be of any particular help to young people in choosing a major or a career. High-school graduates see college graduates driving cabs, and decide it's not worth going. College students find no intellectual stimulation in their studies and drop out.

If students believe that college isn't necessarily good for them, you can't expect them to stay on for the general good of mankind. They don't go to school to beat the Russians to Jupiter, improve the national defense, increase the GNP, or create a new market for the arts—to mention some of the benefits taxpayers are supposed to get for supporting higher education.

Nor should we expect to bring about social equality by putting all young people through four years of academic rigor. At best, it's a roundabout and expensive way to narrow the gap between the highest and lowest in our society anyway. At worst, it is unconsciously elitist. Equalizing opportunity through universal higher education subjects the whole population to the intellectual mode natural only to a few. It violates the fundamental egalitarian principle of respect for the differences between people.

Of course, most parents aren't thinking of the "higher" good at all. They send their children to college because they are convinced young people benefit financially from those four years of higher education. But if money is the only goal, college is the dumbest investment you can make. I say this because a young banker in Poughkeepsie, New York, Stephen G. Necel, used a computer to compare college as an investment with other investments available in 1974 and college did not come out on top.

For the sake of argument, the two of us invented a young man whose rich uncle gave him, in cold cash, the cost of a four-year education at any college he chose, but the young man didn't have to spend the money on college. After bales of computer paper, we had our mythical student write to his uncle: "Since you said I could spend the money foolishly if I wished, I am going to blow it all on Princeton."

The much respected financial columnnist Sylvia Porter echoed the common assumption when she said last year, "A college education is among the very best investments you can make in your entire life." But the truth is not quite so rosy, even if we assume that the Census Bureau is correct when it says that as of 1972, a man who completed four years of college would expect to earn $199,000 more between the ages of 22 and 64 than a man who had only a high-school diploma.

If a 1972 Princeton-bound high-school graduate had put the $34,181 that his four years of college would have cost him into a savings bank at 7.5 percent interest compounded daily, he would have had at age 64 a total of $1,129,200, or $528,200 more than the earnings of a male college graduate, and more than five times as much as the $199,000 extra the more educated man could expect to earn between 22 and 64.

The big advantage of getting your college money in cash now is that you can invest it in something that has a higher return than a diploma. For instance, a Princeton-bound high-school graduate of 1972 who liked fooling around with cars could have banked his $34,181, and gone to work at the local garage at close to $1,000 more per year than the average high-school graduate. Meanwhile, as he was learning to be an expert auto mechanic, his money would be ticking away in the bank. When he became 28, he would have earned $7,199 less on his job from age 22 to 28 than his college-educated friend, but he would have had $73,113 in his passbook—enough to buy out his boss, go into the used-car business, or acquire his own new-car dealership. If successful in business, he could expect to make more than the average college graduate. And if he had the brains to get into Princeton, he would be just as likely to make money without the four years spent on campus. Unfortunately, few college-bound high-school graduates get the opportunity to bank such a large sum of money, and then wait for it to make them rich. And few parents are sophisticated enough to understand that in financial returns alone, their children would be better off with the money than with the education.

Rates of return and dollar signs on education are fascinating brain teasers, but obviously there is a certain unreality to the game. Quite aside from the noneconomic benefits of college, and these should loom larger once the dollars are cleared away, there are grave difficulties in assigning a dollar value to college at all.

In fact there is no real evidence that the higher income of college graduates is due to college. College may simply attract people who are slated to earn more money anyway; those with higher IQs, better family backgrounds, a more enterprising temperament. No one who has wrestled with the problem is prepared to attribute all of the higher income to the impact of college itself.

Christopher Jencks, author of *Inequality,* a book that assesses the effect of family and schooling in America, believes that education in general accounts for less than half of the difference in income in the American population. "The biggest single source of income differences," writes Jencks, "seems to be the fact that men from high-status families have higher incomes than men from low-status families even when they enter the same occupations, have the same amount of education, and have the same test scores."

Jacob Mincer of the National Bureau of Economic Research and Columbia University states flatly that of "20 to 30 percent of students at any level, the additional schooling has been a waste, at least in terms of earnings." College fails to work its income-raising magic for almost a third of those who go. More than half of those people in 1972 who earned $15,000 or more reached that comfortable bracket without the benefit of a college diploma. Jencks says that financial success in the U.S. depends a good deal on luck, and the most sophisticated regression analyses have yet to demonstrate otherwise.

But most of today's students don't go to college to earn more money anyway. In 1968, when jobs were easy to get, Daniel Yankelovich made his first nationwide survey of students. Sixty-five percent of them said they "would welcome less emphasis on money." By 1973, when jobs were scarce, that figure jumped to 80 percent.

The young are not alone. Americans today are all looking less to the pay of a job than to the work itself. They want "interesting" work that permits them "to make a contribution," express themselves" and "use their special abilities," and they think college will help them find it.

Jerry Darring of Indianapolis knows what it is to make a dollar. He worked with his father in the family plumbing business, on the line at Chevrolet, and in the Chrysler foundry. He quit these jobs to enter Wright State University in Dayton, Ohio, because "in a job like that a person only has time to work, and after that he's so tired that he can't do anything else but come home and go to sleep."

Jerry came to college to find work "helping people." And he is perfectly willing to spend the dollars he earns at dull, well-paid work to prepare for lower-paid work that offers the reward of service to others.

Jerry's case is not unusual. No one works for money alone. In order to deal with the nonmonetary rewards of work, economists have coined the concept of "psychic income" which according to one economic dictionary means "income that is reckoned in terms of pleasure, satisfaction, or general feelings of euphoria."

Psychic income is primarily what college students mean when they talk about getting a good job. During the most affluent years of the late 1960s and early 1970s college students told their placement officers that they wanted to be researchers, college professors, artists, city planners, social workers, poets, book publishers, archeologists, ballet dancers, or authors.

The psychic income of these and other occupations popular with students is so high that these jobs can be filled without offering high salaries. According to one study, 93 percent of urban university professors would choose the same vocation again if they had the chance, compared with only 16 percent of unskilled auto workers. Even though the monetary gap between college professor and auto worker is now surprisingly small, the difference in psychic income is enormous.

But colleges fail to warn students that jobs of these kinds are hard to come by, even for qualified applicants, and they rarely accept the responsibility of helping students choose a career that will lead to a job. When a young person says he is interested in helping people, his counselor tells him to become a psychologist. But jobs in psychology are scarce. The Department of Labor, for instance, estimates there will be 4,300 new jobs for psychologists in 1975 while colleges are expected to turn out 58,430 B.A.s in psychology that year.

Of 30 psych majors who reported back to Vassar what they were doing a year after graduation in 1972, only five had jobs in which they could possibly use their courses in psychology, and two of these were working for Vassar.

The outlook isn't much better for students majoring in other psychic-pay disciplines: sociology, English, journalism, anthropology, forestry, education. Whatever college graduates want to do, most of them are going to wind up doing what there is to do.

John Shingleton, director of placement at Michigan State University, accuses the academic community of outright hypocrisy. "Educators have never said, 'Go to college and get a good job,' but this has been implied, and now students expect it. . . . If we care what happens to students after college, then let's get involved with what should be one of the basic purposes of education: career preparation."

In the 1970s, some of the more practical professors began to see that jobs for graduates meant jobs for professors too. Meanwhile, students themselves reacted to the shrinking job market, and a "new vocational-ism" exploded on campus. The press welcomed the change as a return to the ethic of achievement and service. Students were still idealistic, the reporters wrote, but they now saw that they could best make the world better by healing the sick as physicians or righting individual wrongs as lawyers.

But there are no guarantees in these professions either. The American Enterprise Institute estimated in 1971 that there would be more than the target ratio of 100 doctors for every 100,000 people in the population by 1980. And the odds are little better for would-be lawyers. Law schools are already graduating twice as many new lawyers every year as the Department of Labor thinks will be needed, and the oversupply is growing every year.

And it's not at all apparent that what is actually learned in a "professional" education is necessary for success. Teachers, engineers and others I talked to said they find that on the job they rarely use what they learned in school. In order to see how well college prepared engineers and scientists for actual paid work in their fields, The Carnegie Commission queried all the employees with degrees in these fields in two large firms. Only one in five said the work they were doing bore a "very close relationship" to their college studies, while almost a third saw "very little relationship at all." An overwhelming majority could think of many people who were doing their same work, but had majored in different fields.

Majors in nontechnical fields report even less relationship between their studies and their jobs. Charles Lawrence, a communications major in college and now the producer of "Kennedy & Co.," the Chicago morning television show, says, "You have to learn all that stuff and you never use it again. I learned my job doing it." Others employed as architects, nurses, teachers and other members of the so-called learned professions report the same thing.

Most college administrators admit that they don't prepare their graduates for the job market. "I just wish I had the guts to tell parents that when you get out of this place you aren't prepared to do anything," the academic head of a famous liberal-arts college told us. Fortunately, for him, most people believe that you don't have to defend a liberal-arts education on those grounds. A liberal-arts education is supposed to provide you with a value system, a standard, a set of ideas, not a job. "Like Christianity, the liberal arts are seldom practiced and would probably be hated by the majority of the populace if they were," said one defender.

The analogy is apt. The fact is, of course, that the liberal arts are a religion in every sense of that term. When people talk about them, their language becomes elevated, metaphorical, extravagant, theoretical and reverent. And faith in personal salvation by the liberal arts is professed in a creed intoned on ceremonial occasions such as commencements.

If the liberal arts are a religious faith, the professors are its priests. But disseminating ideas in a four-year college curriculum is slow and most expensive. If you want to learn about Milton, Camus, or even Margaret Mead you can find them in paperback books, the public library, and even on television.

And when most people talk about the value of a college education, they are not talking about great books. When at Harvard commencement, the president welcomes the new graduates into "the fellowship of educated men and women," what he could be saying is, "Here is a piece of paper that is a passport to jobs, power and instant prestige." As Glenn Bassett, a personnel specialist at G.E. says, "In some parts of G.E., a college degree appears completely irrelevant to selection to, say, a manager's job. In most, however, it is a ticket of admission."

But now that we have doubled the number of young people attending college, a diploma cannot guarantee even that. The most charitable conclusion we can reach is that college probably has very little, if any, effect on people and things at all. Today, the false premises are easy to see:

First, college doesn't make people intelligent, ambitious, happy, or liberal. It's the other way around. Intelligent, ambitious, happy, liberal people are attracted to higher education in the first place.

Second, college can't claim much credit for the learning experiences that really change students while they are there. Jobs, friends, history, and most of all the sheer passage of time, have as big an impact as anything even indirectly related to the campus.

Third, colleges have changed so radically that a freshman entering in the fall of 1974 can't be sure to gain even the limited value research studies assigned to colleges in the '60s. The sheer size of undergraduate campuses of the 1970s makes college even less stimulating now than it was 10 years ago. Today even motivated students are disappointed with their college courses and professors.

Finally, a college diploma no longer opens as many vocational doors. Employers are beginning to realize that when they pay extra for someone with a diploma, they are paying only for an empty credential. The fact is that most of the work for which employers now expect college training is now or has been capably done in the past by people without higher educations.

College, then, may be a good place for those few young people who are really drawn to academic work, who would rather read than eat, but it has become too expensive, in money, time, and intellectual effort to serve as a holding pen for large numbers of our young. We ought to make it possible for those reluctant, unhappy students to find alternative ways of growing up, and more realistic preparation for the years ahead.

1975

Barbara Ehrenreich

COLLEGE TODAY: TUNE IN, DROP OUT, AND TAKE THE CASH

I would do anything to keep my kids from going to college. It's not just that the cost of tuition is now about the same as a good-size endowment; I am afraid of what will happen to them there. A recent news story described an apparently brilliant college senior who was abandoning her plans for medical school because a medical career couldn't give her "a sufficient return on her investment." Now I would have thought that the practice of medicine—supplemented, perhaps, with a little unnecessary surgery—could support even the most gluttonous standard of living. But no, this young woman will soon be forgetting her organic chemistry, her calculus, her Western Civ, to make a quick killing in finance.

I've heard worse stories, too, like the case of one local boy—a decent, likable kid who went off to college with his hair up in orange spikes, an earring in one ear and a longstanding commitment to the legalization of marijuana and came back for Thanskgiving wearing a Le Tigre shirt and talking about stock options. So it is with deep foreboding that I look at my own children, so unspoiled, so dashing in their little New Wave outfits, so ignorant of the rudiments of capital accumulation. Anything could happen in college. I tell them: "You could fall in with the wrong crowd. You could meet some boy who'd want to take you up to his room and show you his portfolio. Some cynical upper classman could come along and offer you a debenture or a soybean future or whatever, and I hope I don't have to tell you what that could lead to."

Even if college were free I would be opposed to it these days, but the fact that we are expected to pay to have our children transformed into preppies or worse only heightens my antagonism. Between the coming cutbacks in financial aid and the continuing increases in tuition, I will have passed the point of total destitution well before my youngest one's graduation. And I have no reason to believe I will be invited to that event either, because no up-and-coming young man will want his frat brothers to know that his mother is a bag lady. When I think of myself rooting through public trash cans while my children are off on some bucolic campus learning to hold their liquor along with future stockbrokers and purveyors of military hardware, then I too must wonder what constitutes a sufficient return on an investment.

I began to discourage them from college at a very early age. While other children were spending their pre-K years practicing taking the S.A.T.'s in crayon, I encouraged mine to hang out in the kitchen and express themselves in Play-Doh. There were no computer summer camps for my children, no interviews at academically renowned nursery schools. As soon as they could read—an achievement I delayed as long as possible by promising I would still be reading aloud to them until they were 35 or so—I left brochures around the house describing the local college of cosmetology and various correspondence schools advertised on matchbooks. At P.T.A. meetings, while the other mothers clamored for more homework and basics, I ran a lonely campaign for a two-hour recess and an afternoon cookie break. Now that we're in the teen and preteen years, they do sometimes sneak off to their rooms to study, but I can usually distract them with offers of a lift, one way, to the shopping mall.

As they've gotten older and smarter, I've also had to come up with ever more ingenious arguments against college. I tell them that the first thing they will learn from studying the liberal arts is that hardly any of the Great Persons of history were college graduates. It wasn't Marcus Aurelius, Ph.D., or Catherine de' Medici, M.B.A.[1] In fact many of the truly stellar figures, like Joan of Arc and Thomas Edison, were, if I remember right, grade school dropouts; and much of Western philosophy consists of the offhand remarks of carpenters, stonemasons and unemployable misfits. I tell them also about the many members of our own extended family who have never been to college and are perfectly content to be bartenders, telephone operators, factory operatives and the like. And of course I tell them about the many other family members who *have* been to college and are therefore somewhat less content to be bartenders,

---

1. Marcus Aurelius: Roman philosopher (A.D. 121–180); Catherine de' Medici: Italian who became queen of France (1519–89).

telephone operators, etc.

It is not that I'm opposed to learning or even to the learned professions. On the contrary, I am proud that my children are dedicated readers and will be prouder still if they eventually take up some honorable intellectual endeavor, such as philosophy, history, poetry or pure science. But I also know that the job market for, say, historians is very similar to what it is for blacksmiths, so that if you intend to devote your life to the study of 17th-century social movements or the Peloponnesian War,[2] it is a good idea to start by learning to drive a cab. Hence, I tell my son, who shows some promise as a classicist, to avoid Dartmouth where (as I know from a recent book on the subject) he might be drawn into an unsavory right-wing student group, and to keep away from Princeton, where he would have to be interviewed extensively before he could even eat dinner, and to apply himself instead to a study of a Manhattan street map. Anything he wishes to know about Virgil or Hesiod[3] he can find out from a tape deck installed just under the meter.

I suspect that other parents will soon see the wisdom of having their children skip college and go straight on to their careers. If, for example, a son is interested in something that has no market value, such as the liberal arts, the social sciences and many of the natural ones, he should be encouraged to become a busboy at once, without squandering his parents' life savings.

If, on the other hand, a child is drawn to a more highly regarded occupation, like currency speculation, she should be sent into it straight from high school and before her mind is beclouded with the existential dilemmas, habits of critical inquiry and other possible byproducts of higher education. For example, the parents of that young woman who switched from premed to finance should have taken her aside right after her high school prom and handed her the $60,000 or so they were planning to spend on college tuition. "Here, sweetie," they might have said. "It's yours to invest in something that pays better than calculus or chemistry. Just try to get 15 percent on the dollar."

The colleges will soon have to close, of course, and the professors—many of whom are already reduced to wearing second-hand denims and accepting tips from students—will join the best of their former students as janitors or key-punch operators. It will probably not be any harder than it is now to get an education, however. If you want to know about cosmology or French literature or some other recondite field, you'll always be able to ask a cabdriver.

1985

---

2. A war involving Athens and other Greek states, 431–404 B.C.

3. Virgil: Roman poet (70–19 B.C.); Hesiod: Greek poet (eighth century B.C.).

James Thurber

UNIVERSITY DAYS

I passed all the other courses that I took at my university, but I could never pass botany. This was because all botany students had to spend several hours a week in a laboratory looking through a microscope at plant cells, and I could never see through a microscope. I never once saw a cell through a microscope. This used to enrage my instructor. He would wander around the laboratory pleased with the progress all the students were making in drawing the involved and, so I am told, interesting structure of flower cells, until he came to me. I would just be standing there. "I can't see anything," I would say. He would begin patiently enough, explaining how anybody can see through a microscope, but he would always end up in a fury, claiming that I could *too* see through a microscope but just pretended that I couldn't. "It takes away from the beauty of flowers anyway," I used to tell him. "We are not concerned with beauty in this course," he would say. "We are concerned solely with what I may call the *mechanics* of flars." "Well," I'd say, "I can't see anything." "Try it just once again," he'd say, and I would put my eye to the microscope and see nothing at all, except now and again a nebulous milky substance—a phenomenon of maladjustment. You were supposed to see a vivid, restless clockwork of sharply defined plant cells. "I see what looks like a lot of milk," I would tell him. This, he claimed, was the result of my not having adjusted the microscope properly, so he would readjust it for me, or rather, for himself. And I would look again and see milk.

I finally took a deferred pass, as they called it, and waited a year and tried again. (You had to pass one of the biological sciences or you couldn't graduate.) The professor had come back from vacation brown as a berry, bright-eyed, and eager to explain cell-structure again to his classes. "Well," he said to me, cheerily, when we met in the first laboratory hour of the semester, "we're going to see cells this time, aren't we?" "Yes, sir," I said. Students to right of me and to left of me and in front of me were seeing cells; what's more, they were quietly drawing pictures of them in their notebooks. Of course, I didn't see anything.

"We'll try it," the professor said to me, grimly, "with every adjustment of the microscope known to man. As God is my witness, I'll arrange this glass so that you see cells through it or I'll give up teaching. In twenty-two years of botany, I—" He cut off abruptly for he was beginning to quiver all over, like Lionel Barrymore,[1] and he genuinely wished to hold onto his temper; his scenes with me had taken a great deal out of him.

1. Famed American actor (1878–1954), especially noted for elderly roles.

So we tried it with every adjustment of the microscope known to man. With only one of them did I see anything but blackness or the familiar lacteal opacity, and that time I saw, to my pleasure and amazement, a variegated constellation of flecks, specks, and dots. These I hastily drew. The instructor, noting my activity, came back from an adjoining desk, a smile on his lips and his eyebrows high in hope. He looked at my cell drawing. "What's that?" he demanded, with a hint of a squeal in his voice. "That's what I saw," I said. "You didn't, you didn't, you *didn't!*" he screamed, losing control of his temper instantly, and he bent over and squinted into the microscope. His head snapped up. "That's your eye!" he shouted. "You've fixed the lens so that it reflects! You've drawn your eye!"

Another course that I didn't like, but somehow managed to pass, was economics. I went to that class straight from the botany class, which didn't help me any in understanding either subject. I used to get them mixed up. But not as mixed up as another student in my economics class who came there direct from a physics laboratory. He was a tackle on the football team, named Bolenciecwcz. At that time Ohio State University had one of the best football teams in the country, and Bolenciecwcz was one of its outstanding stars. In order to be eligible to play it was necessary for him to keep up in his studies, a very difficult matter, for while he was not dumber than an ox he was not any smarter. Most of his professors were lenient and helped him along. None gave him more hints in answering questions or asked him simpler ones than the economics professor, a thin, timid man named Bassum. One day when we were on the subject of transportation and distribution, it came Bolenciecwcz's turn to answer a question. "Name one means of transportation," the professor said to him. No light came into the big tackle's eyes. "Just any means of transportation," said the professor. Bolenciecwcz sat staring at him. "That is," pursued the professor, "any medium, agency, or method of going from one place to another." Bolenciecwcz had the look of a man who is being led into a trap. "You may choose among steam, horsedrawn, or electrically propelled vehicles," said the instructor. "I might suggest the one which we commonly take in making long journeys across land." There was a profound silence in which everybody stirred uneasily, including Bolenciecwcz and Mr. Bassum, Mr. Bassum abruptly broke this silence in an amazing manner. "Choo-choo-choo," he said, in a low voice, and turned instantly scarlet. He glanced appealingly around the room. All of us, of course, shared Mr. Bassum's desire that Bolenciecwcz should stay abreast of the class in economics, for the Illinois game, one of the hardest and most important of the season, was only a week off. "Toot, toot, too-toooooooot!" some student with a deep voice moaned, and we all looked encouragingly at Bolenciecwcz. Somebody else gave a fine imitation of a locomotive letting off steam. Mr. Bassum himself rounded off the little show. "Ding, dong, ding, dong," he said, hopefully. Bolenciecwcz was staring at the floor now, trying to think, his great brow furrowed, his huge hands rubbing together, his face red.

"How did you come to college this year, Mr. Bolenciecwcz?" asked the professor. "*Chuffa* chuffa, *chuffa* chuffa."

"M'father sent me," said the football player.

"What on?" asked Bassum.

"I git an 'lowance," said the tackle, in a low, husky voice, obviously embarrassed.

"No, no," said Bassum. "Name a means of transportation. What did you *ride* here on?"

"Train," said Bolenciecwcz.

"Quite right," said the professor. "Now, Mr. Nugent, will you tell us—"

If I went through anguish in botany and economics—for different reasons—gymnasium work was even worse. I don't even like to think about it. They wouldn't let you play games or join in the exercises with your glasses on and I couldn't see with mine off. I bumped into professors, horizontal bars, agricultural students, and swinging iron rings. Not being able to see, I could take it but I couldn't dish it out. Also, in order to pass gymnasium (and you had to pass it to graduate) you had to learn to swim if you didn't know how. I didn't like the swimming pool, I didn't like swimming, and I didn't like the swimming instructor, and after all these years I still don't. I never swam but I passed my gym work anyway, by having another student give my gymnasium number (978) and swim across the pool in my place. He was a quiet, amiable blond youth, number 473, and he would have seen through a microscope for me if we could have got away with it, but we couldn't get away with it. Another thing I didn't like about gymnasium work was that they made you strip the day you registered. It is impossible for me to be happy when I am stripped and being asked a lot of questions. Still, I did better than a lanky agricultural student who was cross-examined just before I was. They asked each student what college he was in—that is, whether Arts, Engineering, Commerce, or Agriculture. "What college are you in?" the instructor snapped at the youth in front of me. "Ohio State University," he said promptly.

It wasn't that agricultural student but it was another a whole lot like him who decided to take up journalism, possibly on the ground that when farming went to hell he could fall back on newspaper work. He didn't realize, of course, that that would be very much like falling back full-length on a kit of carpenter's tools. Haskins didn't seem cut out for journalism, being too embarrassed to talk to anybody and unable to use a typewriter, but the editor of the college paper assigned him to the cow barns, the sheep house, the horse pavilion, and the animal husbandry department generally. This was a genuinely big "beat," for it took up five times as much ground and got ten times as great a legislative appropriation as the College of Liberal Arts. The agricultural student knew animals, but nevertheless his stories were dull and colorlessly written. He took all afternoon on each of them, on account of having to hunt for each letter on the typewriter. Once in a while he had to ask somebody to help him hunt. "C" and "L," in particular, were hard letters for him to find. His editor finally got pretty much annoyed at the farmer-journalist because his pieces were so uninteresting. "See here, Haskins," he snapped at him one day, "why is it we never have anything hot from you on the horse pavilion? Here we have two hundred head of horses on this campus —more than any other university in the Western Conference[2] except Purdue—and yet you never get any real lowdown on them. Now shoot over to the horse barns and dig up something lively." Haskins shambled out and came back in about an hour; he said he had something. "Well, start it off snappily," said the editor. "Something people will read." Haskins set to work and in a couple of hours brought a sheet of typewritten paper to the desk; it was a two-hundred-word story about some disease that had broken out among the horses. Its opening sentence was simple but arresting. It read: "Who has noticed the sores on the tops of the horses in the animal husbandry building?"

Ohio State was a land grant university and therefore two years of military drill was compulsory. We drilled with old Springfield rifles and studied the tactics of the Civil War even though the World War was going on at the time. At 11 o'clock each morning thousands of freshmen and sophomores used to deploy over the campus, moodily creeping up on the old chemistry building. It was good training for the kind of warfare that was waged at Shiloh[3] but it had no connection with what was going on in Europe. Some people used to think there was German money behind it, but they didn't dare say so or they would have been thrown in jail as German spies. It was a period of muddy thought and marked, I believe, the decline of higher education in the Middle West.

As a soldier I was never any good at all. Most of the cadets were glumly indifferent soldiers, but I was no good at all. Once General Littlefield, who was commandant of the cadet corps, popped up in front of me during regimental drill and snapped, "You are the main trouble with this university!" I think he meant that my type was the main trouble with the university but he may have meant me individually. I was mediocre at drill, certainly—that is, until my senior year. By that time I had drilled longer than anybody else in the Western Conference, having failed at military at the end of each preceding year so that I had to do it all over again. I was the only senior still in uniform. The uniform which, when

2. The Big Ten.
3. In southwestern Tennessee, site of 1862 Union victory.

new, had made me look like an interurban railway conductor, now that it had become faded and too tight made me look like Bert Williams in his bellboy act.[4] This had a definitely bad effect on my morale. Even so, I had become by sheer practice little short of wonderful at squad maneuvers.

One day General Littlefield picked our company out of the whole regiment and tried to get it mixed up by putting it through one movement after another as fast as we could execute them: squads right, squads left, squads on right into line, squads right about, squads left front into line, etc. In about three minutes one hundred and nine men were marching in one direction and I was marching away from them at an angle of forty degrees, all alone. "Company, halt!" shouted General Littlefield. "That man is the only man who has it right!" I was made a corporal for my achievement.

The next day General Littlefield summoned me to his office. He was swatting flies when I went in. I was silent and he was silent too, for a long time, I don't think he remembered me or why he had sent for me, but he didn't want to admit it. He swatted some more flies, keeping his eyes on them narrowly before he let go with the swatter. "Button up your coat!" he snapped. Looking back on it now I can see that he meant me although he was looking at a fly, but I just stood there. Another fly came to rest on a paper in front of the general and began rubbing its hind legs together. The general lifted the swatter cautiously. I moved restlessly and the fly flew away. "You startled him!" barked General Littlefield, looking at me severely. I said I was sorry. "That won't help the situation!" snapped the General, with cold military logic. I didn't see what I could do except offer to chase some more flies toward his desk, but I didn't say anything. He stared out the window at the faraway figures of co-eds crossing the campus toward the library. Finally, he told me I could go. So I went. He either didn't know which cadet I was or else he forgot what he wanted to see me about. It may have been that he wished to apologize for having called me the main trouble with the university; or maybe he had decided to compliment me on my brilliant drilling of the day before and then at the last minute decided not to. I don't know. I don't think about it much any more.

1933

4. Popular vaudeville comedian.

THE READER

1. *On the basis of this essay, what do you think Thurber's definition or description of an ideal college education would be?*
2. *In "Examsmanship and the Liberal Arts" (p. 242), Perry distinguishes between two kinds of knowledge: "cow" and "bull." Read or review the Perry essay, and then determine, judging by Thurber's essay, which kind of knowledge seems to have been in greater demand at*

Thurber's university.

3. In *"Some Remarks on Humor"* (p. 1076), White says about humorists: *"Humorists fatten on trouble.... You find them wrestling with foreign languages, fighting folding ironing boards and swollen drainpipes, suffering the terrible discomfort of tight boots.... They pour out their sorrows profitably, in a form that is not quite fiction nor quite fact either. Beneath the sparkling surface of these dilemmas flows the strong tide of human woe."* Discuss the validity of White's assertion, and test it by applying it to Thurber's essay.

THE WRITER

1. Why did Thurber pick these particular incidents of his college career to write about? What do they have in common?
2. Take one of the incidents in the essay, and analyze how Thurber describes it. What do you think he may have added to or subtracted from what actually happened? Take a similar incident (real or imagined), and, in a brief essay, try to treat it the way Thurber treats his incidents.

William Zinsser

COLLEGE PRESSURES

Dear Carlos: I desperately need a dean's excuse for my chem midterm which will begin in about 1 hour. All I can say is that I totally blew it this week. I've fallen incredibly, inconceivably behind.

Carlos: Help! I'm anxious to hear from you. I'll be in my room and won't leave it until I hear from you. Tomorrow is the last day for . . .

Carlos: I left town because I started bugging out again. I stayed up all night to finish a take-home make-up exam & am typing it to hand in on the 10th. It was due on the 5th. P.S. I'm going to the dentist. Pain is pretty bad.

Carlos: Probably by Friday I'll be able to get back to my studies. Right now I'm going to take a long walk. This whole thing has taken a lot out of me.

Carlos: I'm really up the proverbial creek. The problem is I really *bombed* the history final. Since I need that course for my major I . . .

Carlos: Here follows a tale of woe. I went home this weekend, had to help my Mom, & caught a fever so didn't have much time to study. My professor . . .

Carlos: Aargh! Trouble. Nothing original but everything's piling up at once. To be brief, my job interview . . .

Hey Carlos, good news! I've got mononucleosis.

Who are these wretched supplicants, scribbling notes so laden with anxiety, seeking such miracles of postponement and balm? They are men and women who belong to Branford College, one of the twelve residential colleges at Yale University, and the messages are just a few of the hundreds that they left for their dean, Carlos Hortas—often slipped under his door at 4 A.M.—last year.

But students like the ones who wrote those notes can also be found on campuses from coast to coast—especially in New England and at many other private colleges across the country that have high academic standards and highly motivated students. Nobody could doubt that the notes are real. In their urgency and their gallows humor they are authentic voices of a generation that is panicky to succeed.

My own connection with the message writers is that I am master of Branford College. I live in its Gothic quadrangle and know the students well. (We have 485 of them.) I am privy to their hopes and fears—and also to their stereo music and their piercing cries in the dead of night ("Does anybody ca-a-are?"). If they went to Carlos to ask how to get through tomorrow, they come to me to ask how to get through the rest of their lives.

Mainly I try to remind them that the road ahead is a long one and that it will have more unexpected turns than they think. There will be plenty of time to change jobs, change careers, change whole attitudes and approaches. They don't want to hear such liberating news. They want a map—right now—that they can follow unswervingly to career security, financial security. Social Security and, presumably, a prepaid grave.

What I wish for all students is some release from the clammy grip of the future. I wish them a chance to savor each segment of their education as an experience in itself and not as a grim preparation for the next step. I wish them the right to experiment, to trip and fall, to learn that defeat is as instructive as victory and is not the end of the world.

My wish, of course, is naïve. One of the few rights that America does not proclaim is the right to fail. Achievement is the national god, venerated in our media—the million-dollar athlete, the wealthy executive—and glorified in our praise of possessions. In the presence of such a potent state religion, the young are growing up old.

I see four kinds of pressure working on college students today: economic pressure, parental pressure, peer pressure, and self-induced pressure. It is easy to look around for villains—to blame the colleges for charging too much money, the professors for assigning too much work, the parents for pushing their children too far, the students for driving themselves too hard. But there are no villains; only victims.

"In the late 1960s," one dean told me, "the typical question that I got from students was 'Why is there so much suffering in the world?' or 'How can I make a contribution?' Today it's 'Do you think it would look better for getting into law school if I did a double major in history and political science, or just majored in one of them?'" Many other deans confirmed this pattern. One said: "They're trying to find an edge—the intangible something that will look better on paper if two students are about equal."

Note the emphasis on looking better. The transcript has become a sacred document, the passport to security. How one appears on paper is more important than how one appears in person. *A* is for Admirable and *B* is for Borderline, even though, in Yale's official system of grading, *A* means "excellent" and *B* means "very good." Today, looking very good is no longer good enough, especially for students who hope to go on to law school or medical school. They know that entrance into the better schools will be an entrance into the better law firms and better medical practices where they will make a lot of money. They also know that the odds are harsh, Yale Law School, for instance, matriculates 170 students from an applicant pool of 3,700; Harvard enrolls 550 from a pool of 7,000.

It's all very well for those of us who write letters of recommendation for our students to stress the qualities of humanity that will make them good lawyers or doctors. And it's nice to think that admission officers are really reading our letters and looking for the extra dimension of commitment or concern. Still, it would be hard for a student not to visualize these officers shuffling so many transcripts studded with *A*s that they regard a *B* as positively shameful.

The pressure is almost as heavy on students who just want to graduate and get a job. Long gone are the days of the "gentleman's C," when students journeyed through college with a certain relaxation, sampling a wide variety of courses—music, art, philosophy, classics, anthropology, poetry, religion—that would send them out as liberally educated men and women. If I were an employer I would rather employ graduates who have this range and curiosity than those who narrowly pursued safe subjects and high grades. I know countless students whose inquiring minds exhilarate me. I like to hear the play of their ideas. I don't know if they are getting *A*s or *C*s, and I don't care. I also like them as people. The country needs them, and they will find satisfying jobs. I tell them to relax. They can't.

Nor can I blame them. They live in a brutal economy. Tuition, room, and board at most private colleges now comes to at least $7,000, not counting books and fees. This might seem to suggest that the colleges are getting rich. But they are equally battered by inflation. Tuition covers only 60 percent of what it costs to educate a student, and ordinarily the remainder comes from what colleges receive in endowments, grants, and gifts. Now the remainder keeps being swallowed by the cruel costs—

higher every year—of just opening the doors. Heating oil is up. Insurance is up. Postage is up. Health-premium costs are up. Everything is up. Deficits are up. We are witnessing in America the creation of a brotherhood of paupers—colleges, parents, and students, joined by the common bond of debt.

Today it is not unusual for a student, even if he works part time at college and full time during the summer, to accrue $5,000 in loans after four years—loans that he must start to repay within one year after graduation. Exhorted at commencement to go forth into the world, he is already behind as he goes forth. How could he not feel under pressure throughout college to prepare for this day of reckoning? I have used "he," incidentally, only for brevity. Women at Yale are under no less pressure to justify their expensive education to themselves, their parents, and society. In fact, they are probably under more pressure. For although they leave college superbly equipped to bring fresh leadership to traditionally male jobs, society hasn't yet caught up with this fact.

Along with economic pressure goes parental pressure. Inevitably, the two are deeply intertwined.

I see many students taking pre-medical courses with joyless tenacity. They go off to their labs as if they were going to the dentist. It saddens me because I know them in other corners of their life as cheerful people.

"Do you want to go to medical school?" I ask them.

"I guess so," they say, without conviction, or "Not really."

"Then why are you going?"

"Well, my parents want me to be a doctor. They're paying all this money and . . ."

Poor students, poor parents. They are caught in one of the oldest webs of love and duty and guilt. The parents mean well; they are trying to steer their sons and daughters toward a secure future. But the sons and daughters want to major in history or classics or philosophy—subjects with no "practical" value. Where's the payoff on the humanities? It's not easy to persuade such loving parents that the humanities do indeed pay off. The intellectual faculties developed by studying subjects like history and classics—an ability to synthesize and relate, to weigh cause and effect, to see events in perspective—are just the faculties that make creative leaders in business or almost any general field. Still, many fathers would rather put their money on courses that point toward a specific profession —courses that are pre-law, pre-medical, pre-business, or, as I sometimes heard it put, "pre-rich."

But the pressure on students is severe. They are truly torn. One part of them feels obligated to fulfill their parents' expectations; after all, their parents are older and presumably wiser. Another part tells them that the expectations that are right for their parents are not right for them.

I know a student who wants to be an artist. She is very obviously an artist and will be a good one—she has already had several modest local exhibits. Meanwhile she is growing as a well-rounded person and taking humanistic subjects that will enrich the inner resources out of which her art will grow. But her father is strongly opposed. He thinks that an artist is a "dumb" thing to be. The student vacillates and tries to please everybody. She keeps up with her art somewhat furtively and takes some of the "dumb" courses her father wants her to take—at least they are dumb courses for her. She is a free spirit on a campus of tense students— no small achievement in itself—and she deserves to follow her muse.

Peer pressure and self-induced pressure are also intertwined, and they begin almost at the beginning of freshman year.

"I had a freshman student I'll call Linda," one dean told me, "who came in and said she was under terrible pressure because her roommate, Barbara, was much brighter and studied all the time. I couldn't tell her that Barbara had come in two hours earlier to say the same thing about Linda."

The story is almost funny—except that it's not. It's symptomatic of all the pressures put together. When every student thinks every other student is working harder and doing better, the only solution is to study harder still. I see students going off to the library every night after dinner and coming back when it closes at midnight. I wish they would some-times forget about their peers and go to a movie. I hear the clacking of typewriters in the hours before dawn. I see the tension in their eyes when exams are approaching and papers are due: "*Will I get everything done?*"

Probably they won't. They will get sick. They will get "blocked." They will sleep. They will oversleep. They will bug out. *Hey Carlos, help!*

Part of the problem is that they do more than they are expected to do. A professor will assign five-page papers. Several students will start writ-ing ten-page papers to impress him. Then more students will write ten-page papers, and a few will raise the ante to fifteen. Pity the poor student who is still just doing the assignment.

Once you have twenty or thirty percent of the student population deliberately overexerting," one dean points out, "it's bad for everybody. When a teacher gets more and more effort from his class, the student who is doing normal work can be perceived as not doing well. The tactic works, psychologically."

Why can't the professor just cut back and not accept longer papers? He can, and he probably will. But by then the term will be half over and the damage done. Grade fever is highly contagious and not easily reversed. Besides, the professor's main concern is with his course. He knows his students only in relation to the course and doesn't know that they are also overexerting in their other courses. Nor is it really his business. He didn't sign up for dealing with the student as a whole person and with all the emotional baggage the student brought along from home. That's what deans, masters, chaplains, and psychiatrists are for.

To some extent this is nothing new: a certain number of professors have always been self-contained islands of scholarship and shyness, more comfortable with books than with people. But the new pauperism has widened the gap still further, for professors who actually like to spend time with students don't have as much time to spend. They also are overexerting. If they are young, they are busy trying to publish in order not to perish, hanging by their finger nails onto a shrinking profession. If they are old and tenured, they are buried under the duties of administering departments—as departmental chairmen or members of committees —that have been thinned out by the budgetary axe.

Ultimately it will be the students' own business to break the circles in which they are trapped. They are too young to be prisoners of their parents' dreams and their classmates' fears. They must be jolted into believing in themselves as unique men and women who have the power to shape their own future.

"Violence is being done to the undergraduate experience," says Carlos Hortas. "College should be open-ended: at the end it should open many, many roads. Instead, students are choosing their goal in advance, and their choices narrow as they go along. It's almost as if they think that the country has been codified in the type of jobs that exist—that they've got to fit into certain slots. Therefore, fit into the best-paying slot.

"They ought to take chances. Not taking chances will lead to a life of colorless mediocrity. They'll be comfortable. But something in the spirit will be missing."

I have painted too drab a portrait of today's students, making them seem a solemn lot. That is only half of their story; if they were so dreary I wouldn't so thoroughly enjoy their company. The other half is that they are easy to like. They are quick to laugh and to offer friendship. They are not introverts. They are unusually kind and are more considerate of one another than any student generation I have known.

Nor are they so obsessed with their studies that they avoid sports and extracurricular activities. On the contrary, they juggle their crowded hours to play on a variety of teams, perform with musical and dramatic groups, and write for campus publications. But this in turn is one more cause of anxiety. There are too many choices. Academically, they have 1,300 courses to select from; outside class they have to decide how much spare time they can spare and how to spend it.

This means that they engage in fewer extracurricular pursuits than their predecessors did. If they want to row on the crew and play in the symphony they will eliminate one; in the '60s they would have done both. They also tend to choose activities that are self-limiting. Drama, for instance, is flourishing in all twelve of Yale's residential colleges as it never has before. Students hurl themselves into these productions—as actors, directors, carpenters, and technicians—with a dedication to create the best possible play, knowing that the day will come when the run will end and they can get back to their studies.

They also can't afford to be the willing slave of organizations like the *Yale Daily News.* Last spring at the one-hundredth anniversary banquet of that paper—whose past chairmen include such once and future kings as Potter Stewart, Kingman Brewster, and William F. Buckley, Jr.— much was made of the fact that the editorial staff used to be small and totally committed and that "newsies" routinely worked fifty hours a week. In effect they belonged to a club; Newsies is how they defined themselves at Yale. Today's student will write one or two articles a week, when he can, and he defines himself as a student. I've never heard the word Newsie except at the banquet.

If I have described the modern undergraduate primarily as a driven creature who is largely ignoring the blithe spirit inside who keeps trying to come out and play, it's because that's where the crunch is, not only at Yale but throughout American education. It's why I think we should all be worried about the values that are nurturing a generation so fearful of risk and so goal-obsessed at such an early age.

I tell students that there is no one "right" way to get ahead—that each of them is a different person, starting from a different point and bound for a different destination. I tell them that change is a tonic and that all the slots are not codified nor the frontiers closed. One of my ways of telling them is to invite men and women who have achieved success outside the academic world to come and talk informally with my students during the year. They are heads of companies or ad agencies, editors of magazines, politicians, public officials, television magnates, labor leaders, business executives, Broadway producers, artists, writers, economists, photographers, scientists, historians—a mixed bag of achievers.

I ask them to say a few words about how they got started. The students assume that they started in their present profession and knew all along that it was what they wanted to do. Luckily for me, most of them got into their field by a circuitous route, to their surprise, after many detours. The students are startled. They can hardly conceive of a career that was not pre-planned. They can hardly imagine allowing the hand of God or chance to nudge them down some unforeseen trail.

1979

THE READER

1. On p. 235, Zinsser names four kinds of pressure on college students. Are there others? Are they equally strong? What counterpressures exist? What would be necessary for a state of equilibrium? Would those changes or that state be desirable?

2. *In his fifth paragraph, Zinsser says he wishes "for all students . . . some release from the clammy grip of the future" so that they could both "savor each segment of their education" and "learn that defeat is as instructive as victory." Are these two compatible? Which is more important, savoring each segment of one's education or learning from defeat? How would a college program designed to fulfill either or both of these two functions differ from that of the average college or from the one you are pursuing?*

THE WRITER

1. *By beginning with quotations from student notes to the counseling dean, Zinsser seeks to establish the problem of college pressures as a concrete personal reality; then he seeks to generalize, using those personal statements to represent also the situation of other students at other colleges. Does this plan work? What makes the statements sound authentic or inauthentic?*

2. *In describing the four kinds of pressure, Zinsser has to make transitions. One of these ("Along with economic pressure . . . " [p. 237] is loose. Could it be tightened? Should it be? What about the others? What are the logical relations among the four kinds of pressure?*

3. *On p. 240, Zinsser refers to "the blithe spirit" inside the "driven" college student. Gaylin, in "What You See Is the Real You" (p. 664), rejects such analyses. Which view do you find more persuasive? Why?*

4. *In the* New York Times *for May 14, 1970, Fred Hechinger reported an apparent increase in cheating by college students and pointed out that, historically, cheating occurs when grades are used to determine success in competition for economic and social rewards. He then concluded that some people are wondering if this process is not damaging the colleges, if "the economic and political system is improperly exploiting the educational system." By making "system" the subject of the clause, he avoided having to say who in particular is responsible for the problem. Write an essay in which you show who is responsible, or show that the problem doesn't exist at present or isn't important, or redefine the problem to lead to different conclusions.*

5. *Write an essay on one of these topics:*
   a) The Value of Failure
   b) The Necessity for Pressures
   c) Ways to Eliminate Pressures
   d) An Alternative to Grading
   Then write a paragraph rebutting the point of view in your essay. Which seems more effective to you? Why?

William G. Perry, Jr.

EXAMSMANSHIP AND THE LIBERAL ARTS: A STUDY IN EDUCATIONAL EPISTEMOLOGY

"But sir, I don't think I really deserve it, it was mostly bull, really." This disclaimer from a student whose examination we have awarded a straight "A" is wondrously depressing. Alfred North Whitehead invented its only possible rejoinder: "Yes sir, what you wrote is nonsense, utter nonsense. But ah! Sir! It's the right *kind* of nonsense!"

Bull, in this university,[1] is customarily a source of laughter, or a problem in ethics. I shall step a little out of fashion to use the subject as a take-off point for a study in comparative epistemology. The phenomenon of bull, in all the honor and opprobrium with which it is regarded by students and faculty, says something, I think, about our theories of knowledge. So too, the grades which we assign on examinations communicate to students what these theories may be.

We do not have to be out-and-out logical-positivists[2] to suppose that we have something to learn about "what we think knowledge is" by having a good look at "what we do when we go about measuring it." We know the straight "A" examination when we see it, of course, and we have reason to hope that the student will understand why his work receives our recognition. He doesn't always. And those who receive lesser honor? Perhaps an understanding of certain anomalies in our customs of grading good bull will explain the students' confusion.

I must beg patience, then, both of the reader's humor and of his morals. Not that I ask him to suspend his sense of humor but that I shall ask him to go beyond it. In a great university the picture of a bright student attempting to outwit his professor while his professor takes pride in not being outwitted is certainly ridiculous. I shall report just such a scene, for its implications bear upon my point. Its comedy need not present a serious obstacle to thought.

As for the ethics of bull, I must ask for a suspension of judgment. I wish that students could suspend theirs. Unlike humor, moral commitment is hard to think beyond. Too early a moral judgment is precisely what stands between many able students and a liberal education. The stunning realization that the Harvard Faculty will often accept, as evidence of knowledge, the cerebrations of a student who has little data at his

---

1. Harvard.
2. Members of a contemporary school of philosophy which sees philosophy as an activity rather than a body of knowledge, and con-

cerns itself not with abstract notions of what a thing is but with empirical observation of what it does.

disposal, confronts every student with an ethical dilemma. For some it forms an academic focus for what used to be thought of as "adolescent disillusion." It is irrelevant that rumor inflates the phenomenon to mythical proportions. The students know that beneath the myth there remains a solid and haunting reality. The moral "bind" consequent on this awareness appears most poignantly in serious students who are reluctant to concede the competitive advantage to the bullster and who yet feel a deep personal shame when, having succumbed to "temptation," they themselves receive a high grade for work they consider "dishonest."

I have spent many hours with students caught in this unwelcome bitterness. These hours lend an urgency to my theme. I have found that students have been able to come to terms with the ethical problem, to the extent that it is real, only after a refined study of the true nature of bull and its relation to "knowledge." I shall submit grounds for my suspicion that we can be found guilty of sharing the students' confusion of moral and epistemological issues.

I

I present as my "premise," then, an amoral *fabliau*. Its hero-villain is the Abominable Mr. Metzger '47. Since I celebrate his virtuosity, I regret giving him a pseudonym, but the peculiar style of his bravado requires me to honor also his modesty. Bull in pure form is rare; there is usually some contamination by data. The community has reason to be grateful to Mr. Metzger for having created an instance of laboratory purity, free from any adulteration by matter. The more credit is due him, I think, because his act was free from premeditation, deliberation, or hope of personal gain.

Mr. Metzger stood one rainy November day in the lobby of Memorial Hall. A junior, concentrating in mathematics, he was fond of diverting himself by taking part in the drama, a penchant which may have had some influence on the events of the next hour. He was waiting to take part in a rehearsal in Sanders Theatre, but, as sometimes happens, no other players appeared. Perhaps the rehearsal had been canceled without his knowledge? He decided to wait another five minutes.

Students, meanwhile, were filing into the Great Hall opposite, and taking seats at the testing tables. Spying a friend crossing the lobby toward the Great Hall's door, Metzger greeted him and extended appropriate condolences. He inquired, too, what course his friend was being tested in. "Oh, Soc. Sci. something-or-other." "What's it all about?" asked Metzger, and this, as Homer remarked of Patroclus, was the beginning of evil for him.

"It's about Modern Perspectives on Man and Society and All That," said his friend. "Pretty interesting, really."

"Always wanted to take a course like that," said Metzger. "Any good reading?"

"Yeah, great. There's this book"—his friend did not have time to finish.

"Take your seats please" said a stern voice beside them. The idle conversation had somehow taken the two friends to one of the tables in the Great Hall. Both students automatically obeyed; the proctor put blue-books before them; another proctor presented them with copies of the printed hour-test.

Mr. Metzger remembered afterwards a brief misgiving that was suddenly overwhelmed by a surge of curiosity and puckish glee. He wrote "George Smith" on the blue book, opened it, and addressed the first question.

I must pause to exonerate the Management. The Faculty has a rule that no student may attend an examination in a course in which he is not enrolled. To the wisdom of this rule the outcome of this deplorable story stands witness. The Registrar, charged with the enforcement of the rule, has developed an organization with procedures which are certainly the finest to be devised. In November, however, class rosters are still shaky, and on this particular day another student, named Smith, was absent. As for the culprit, we can reduce his guilt no further than to suppose that he was ignorant of the rule, or, in the face of the momentous challenge before him, forgetful.

We need not be distracted by Metzger's performance on the "objective" or "spot" questions on the test. His D on these sections can be explained by those versed in the theory of probability. Our interest focuses on the quality of his essay. It appears that when Metzger's friend picked up his own blue book a few days later, he found himself in company with a large proportion of his section in having received on the essay a C. When he quietly picked up "George Smith's" blue book to return it to Metzger, he observed that the grade for the essay was A. In the margin was a note in the section man's hand. It read "Excellent work. Could you have pinned these observations down a bit more closely? Compare . . . in . . . pp. . . . ."

Such news could hardly be kept quiet. There was a leak, and the whole scandal broke on the front page of Tuesday's *Crimson*. With the press Metzger was modest, as becomes a hero. He said that there had been nothing to it at all, really. The essay question had offered a choice of two books, Margaret Mead's *And Keep Your Powder Dry* or Geoffrey Gorer's *The American People*. Metzger reported that having read neither of them, he had chosen the second "because the title gave me some notion as to what the book might be about." On the test, two critical comments were offered on each book, one favorable, one unfavorable. The students were asked to "discuss." Metzger conceded that he had played safe in throwing his lot with the more laudatory of the two comments, "but I did not forget to be balanced."

I do not have Mr. Metzger's essay before me except in vivid memory. As I recall, he took his first cue from the name Geoffrey, and committed his strategy to the premise that Gorer was born into an "Anglo-Saxon" culture, probably English, but certainly "English speaking." Having heard that Margaret Mead was a social anthropologist, he inferred that Gorer was the same. He then entered upon his essay, centering his inquiry upon what he supposed might be the problems inherent in an anthropologist's observation of a culture which was his own, or nearly his own. Drawing in part from memories of table-talk on cultural relativity[3] and in part from creative logic, he rang changes on the relation of observer to observed, and assessed the kind and degree of objectivity which might accrue to an observer through training as an anthropologist. He concluded that the book in question did in fact contribute a considerable range of "'objective', and even 'fresh'," insights into the nature of our culture. "At the same time," he warned, "these observations must be understood within the context of their generation by a person only partly freed from his embeddedness in the culture he is observing, and limited in his capacity to transcend those particular tendencies and biases which he has himself developed as a personality in his interraction with this culture since his birth. In this sense the book portrays as much the character of Geoffrey Gorer as it analyzes that of the American people." It is my regretable duty to report that at this moment of triumph Mr. Metzger was carried away by the temptations of parody and added, "We are thus much the richer."

In any case, this was the essay for which Metzger received his honor grade and his public acclaim. He was now, of course, in serious trouble with the authorities.

I shall leave him for the moment to the mercy of the Administrative Board of Harvard College and turn the reader's attention to the section man who ascribed the grade. He was in much worse trouble. All the consternation in his immediate area of the Faculty and all the glee in other areas fell upon his unprotected head. I shall now undertake his defense.

I do so not simply because I was acquainted with him and feel a respect for his intelligence; I believe in the justice of his grade! Well, perhaps "justice" is the wrong word in a situation so manifestly absurd. This is more a case in "equity." That is, the grade is equitable if we accept other aspects of the situation which are equally absurd. My proposition is this: if we accept as valid those C grades which were accorded students who, like Metzger's friend, demonstrated a thorough familiarity with the details of the book without relating their critique to the methodological

3. "An important part of Harvard's educa-   An Official Publication [Perry's note]. The
tion takes place during meals in the Houses."   Houses are residences for upperclassmen.

problems of social anthropology, then "George Smith" deserved not only the same, but better.

The reader may protest that the C's given to students who showed evidence only of diligence were indeed not valid and that both these students and "George Smith" should have received E's. To give the diligent E is of course not in accord with custom. I shall take up this matter later. For now, were I to allow the protest, I could only restate my thesis: that "George Smith's" E would, in a college of liberal arts, be properly a "better" E.

At this point I need a short-hand. It is a curious fact that there is no academic slang for the presentation of evidence of diligence alone. "Parroting" won't do; it is possible to "parrot" bull. I must beg the reader's pardon, and, for reasons almost too obvious to bear, suggest "cow."

Stated as nouns, the concepts look simple enough:

> cow (pure): data, however relevant, without relevancies.
> bull (pure): relevancies, however relevant, without data.

The reader can see all too clearly where this simplicity would lead. I can assure him that I would not have imposed on him this way were I aiming to say that knowledge in this university is definable as some neuter compromise between cow and bull, some infertile hermaphrodite. This is precisely what many diligent students seem to believe: that what they must learn to do is to "find the right mean" between "amounts" of detail and "amounts" of generalities. Of course this is not the point at all. The problem is not quantitative, nor does its solution lie on a continuum between the particular and the general. Cow and bull are not poles of a single dimension. A clear notion of what they really are is essential to my inquiry, and for heuristic purposes I wish to observe them further in the celibate state.

When the pure concepts are translated into verbs, their complexities become apparent in the assumptions and purposes of the students as they write:

To cow (v. *intrans.*) or the act of cowing:
> To list data (or perform operations) without awareness of, or comment upon, the contexts, frames of reference, or points of observation which determine the origin, nature, and meaning of the data (or procedures). To write on the assumption that "a fact is a fact." To present evidence of hard work as a substitute for understanding, without any intent to deceive.

To bull (v. *intrans.*) or the act of bulling:
> To discourse upon the contexts, frames of reference and points of observation which would determine the origin, nature, and meaning of data if one had any. To present evidence of an understanding of form in the hope that the reader may be deceived into supposing a familiarity with content.

At the level of conscious intent, it is evident that cowing is more moral, or less immoral, than bulling. To speculate about unconscious intent would be either an injustice or a needless elaboration of my theme. It is enough that the impression left by cow is one of earnestness, diligence, and painful naiveté. The grader may feel disappointment or even irritation, but these feelings are usually balanced by pity, compassion, and a reluctance to hit a man when he's both down and moral. He may feel some challenge to his teaching, but none whatever to his one-ups-man-ship. He writes in the margin: "See me."

We are now in a position to understand the anomaly of custom: As instructors, we always assign bull an E, *when we detect it*; whereas we usually give cow a C, *even though it is always obvious*.

After all, we did not ask to be confronted with a choice between morals and understanding (or did we?). We evince a charming humanity, I think, in our decision to grade in favor of morals and pathos. "I simply *can't* give this student an E after he has *worked* so hard." At the same time we tacitly express our respect for the bullster's strength. We recognize a colleague. If he knows so well how to dish it out, we can be sure that he can also take it.

Of course it is just possible that we carry with us, perhaps from our own school-days, an assumption that if a student is willing to work hard and collect "good hard facts" he can always be taught to understand their relevance, whereas a student who has caught onto the forms of relevance without working at all is a lost scholar.

But this is not in accord with our experience.

It is not in accord either, as far as I can see, with the stated values of a liberal education. If a liberal education should teach students "how to think," not only in their own fields but in fields outside their own—that is, to understand "how the other fellow orders knowledge," then bulling, even in its purest form, expresses an important part of what a pluralist university holds dear, surely a more important part than the collecting of "facts that are facts" which schoolboys learn to do. Here then, good bull appears not as ignorance at all but as an aspect of knowledge. It is both relevant and "true." In a university setting good bull is therefore of more value than "facts," which, without a frame of reference, are not even "true" at all.

Perhaps this value accounts for the final anomaly: as instructors, we are inclined to reward bull highly, *where we do not detect its intent*, to the consternation of the bullster's acquaintances. And often we do not examine the matter too closely. After a long evening of reading blue books full of cow, the sudden meeting with a student who at least understands the problems of one's field provides a lift like a draught of refreshing wine, and a strong disposition toward trust.

This was, then, the sense of confidence that came to our unfortunate section man as he read "George Smith's" sympathetic considerations.

II

In my own years of watching over students' shoulders as they work, I have come to believe that this feeling of trust has a firmer basis than the confidence generated by evidence of diligence alone. I believe that the theory of a liberal education holds. Students who have dared to understand man's real relation to his knowledge have shown themselves to be in a strong position to learn content rapidly and meaningfully, and to retain it. I have learned to be less concerned about the education of a student who has come to understand the nature of man's knowledge, even though he has not yet committed himself to hard work, than I am about the education of the student who, after one or two terms at Harvard, is working desperately hard and still believes that collected "facts" constitute knowledge. The latter, when I try to explain to him, too often understands me to be saying that he "doesn't *put in enough generalities.*" Surely he has "put in *enough* facts."

I have come to see such quantitative statements as expressions of an entire, coherent epistemology. In grammar school the student is taught that Columbus discovered America in 1492. The more such items he gets "right" on a given test the more he is credited with "knowing." From years of this sort of thing it is not unnatural to develop the conviction that knowledge consists of the accretion of hard facts by hard work.

The student learns that the more facts and procedures he can get "right" in a given course, the better will be his grade. The more courses he takes, the more subjects he has "had," the more credits he accumulates, the more diplomas he will get, until, after graduate school, he will emerge with his doctorate, a member of the community of scholars.

The foundation of this entire life is the proposition that a fact is a fact. The necessary correlate of this proposition is that a fact is either right or wrong. This implies that the standard against which the rightness or wrongness of a fact may be judged exists *someplace*—perhaps graven upon a tablet in a Platonic world[4] outside and above *this* cave of tears. In grammar school it is evident that the tablets which enshrine the spelling of a word or the answer to an arithmetic problem are visible to my teacher who need only compare my offerings to it. In high school I observe that my English teachers disagree. This can only mean that the tablets in such matters as the goodness of a poem are distant and obscured by clouds. They surely exist. The pleasing of befuddled English teachers degenerates into assessing their prejudices, a game in which I have no protection against my competitors more glib of tongue. I respect only my science teachers, authorities who *really know.* Later I learn from

4. That is, a world of ideal forms, of which this world is but the image. See Plato's "Allegory of the Cave," p. 1107.

them that "this is only what we think *now.*" But eventually, surely. . . .
Into this epistemology of education, apparently shared by teachers in
such terms as "credits," "semester hours" and "years of French" the
student may invest his ideals, his drive, his competitiveness, his safety,
his self-esteem, and even his love.

College raises other questions: by whose calendar is it proper to say
that Columbus discovered America in 1492? How, when and by whom
was the year 1 established in this calendar? What of other calendars? In
view of the evidence for Leif Ericson's previous visit (and the American
Indians), what historical ethnocentrism is suggested by the use of the
word "discover" in this sentence? As for Leif Ericson, in accord with
what assumptions do you order the evidence?

These questions and their answers are not "more" knowledge. They
are devastation. I do not need to elaborate upon the epistemology, or
rather epistemologies, they imply. A fact has become at last "an observation or an operation performed in a frame of reference." A liberal education is founded in an awareness of frame of reference even in the most
immediate and empirical examination of data. Its acquirement involves
relinquishing hope of absolutes and of the protection they afford against
doubt and the glib-tongued competitor. It demands an ever widening
sophistication about systems of thought and observation. It leads, not
away from, but *through* the arts of gamesmanship to a new trust.

This trust is in the value and integrity of systems, their varied character, and the way their apparently incompatible metaphors enlighten,
from complementary facets, the particulars of human experience. As one
student said to me: "I used to be cynical about intellectual games. Now I
want to know them thoroughly. You see I came to realize that it was only
when I knew the rules of the game cold that I could tell whether what I
was saying was tripe."

We too often think of the bullster as cynical. He can be, and not always
in a light-hearted way. We have failed to observe that there can lie
behind cow the potential of a deeper and more dangerous despair. The
moralism of sheer work and obedience can be an ethic that, unwilling to
face a despair of its ends, glorifies its means. The implicit refusal to
consider the relativity of both ends and means leaves the operator in an
unconsidered proprietary absolutism. History bears witness that in the
pinches this moral superiority has no recourse to negotiation, only to
force.

A liberal education proposes that man's hope lies elsewhere: in the
negotiability that can arise from an understanding of the integrity of
systems and of their origins in man's address to his universe. The prerequisite is the courage to accept such a definition of knowledge. From then
on, of course, there is nothing incompatible between such an epistemology and hard work. Rather the contrary.

I can now at last let bull and cow get together. The reader knows best how a productive wedding is arranged in his own field. This is the nuptial he celebrates with a straight A on examinations. The masculine context must embrace the feminine particular, though itself "born of woman." Such a union is knowledge itself, and it alone can generate new contexts and new data which can unite in their turn to form new knowledge.

In this happy setting we can congratulate in particular the Natural Sciences, long thought to be barren ground to the bullster. I have indeed drawn my examples of bull from the Social Sciences, and by analogy from the Humanities. Essay-writing in these fields has long been thought to nurture the art of bull to its prime. I feel, however, that the Natural Sciences have no reason to feel slighted. It is perhaps no accident that Metzger was a mathematician. As part of my researches for this paper, furthermore, a student of considerable talent has recently honored me with an impressive analysis of the art of amassing "partial credits" on examinations in advanced physics. Though beyond me in some respects, his presentation confirmed my impression that instructors of Physics frequently honor on examinations operations structurally similar to those requisite in a good essay.

The very qualities that make the Natural Sciences fields of delight for the eager gamesman have been essential to their marvelous fertility.

III

As priests of these mysteries, how can we make our rites more precisely expressive? The student who merely cows robs himself, without knowing it, of his education and his soul. The student who only bulls robs himself, as he knows full well, of the joys of inductive discovery—that is, of engagement. The introduction of frames of reference in the new curricula of Mathematics and Physics in the schools is a hopeful experiment. We do not know yet how much of these potent revelations the very young can stand, but I suspect they may rejoice in them more than we have supposed. I can't believe they have never wondered about Leif Ericson and that word "discovered," or even about 1492. They have simply been too wise to inquire.

Increasingly in recent years better students in the better high schools and preparatory schools are being allowed to inquire. In fact they appear to be receiving both encouragement and training in their inquiry. I have the evidence before me.

Each year for the past five years all freshmen entering Harvard and Radcliffe have been asked in freshman week to "grade" two essays answering an examination question in History. They are then asked to give their reasons for their grades. One essay, filled with dates, is 99% cow. The other, with hardly a date in it, is a good essay, easily mistaken for bull. The "official" grades of these essays are, for the first (alas!) C "because he has worked so hard," and for the second (soundly, I think) B. Each year a larger majority of freshmen evaluate these essays as would the majority of the faculty, and for the faculty's reasons, and each year a smaller minority give the higher honor to the essay offering data alone. Most interesting, a larger number of students each year, while not over-rating the second essay, award the first the straight E appropriate to it in a college of liberal arts.

For us who must grade such students in a university, these develop-ments imply a new urgency, did we not feel it already. Through our grades we describe for the students, in the showdown, what we believe about the nature of knowledge. The subtleties of bull are not peripheral to our academic concerns. That they penetrate to the center of our care is evident in our feelings when a student whose good work we have awarded a high grade reveals to us that he does not feel he deserves it. Whether he disqualifies himself because "there's too much bull in it," or worse because "I really don't think I've worked that hard," he presents a serious educational problem. Many students feel this sleaziness; only a few reveal it to us.

We can hardly allow a mistaken sense of fraudulence to undermine our students' achievements. We must lead students beyond their concept of bull so that they may honor relevancies that are really relevant. We can willingly acknowledge that, in lieu of the date 1492, a consideration of calendars and of the word "discovered," may well be offered with intent to deceive. We must insist that this does not make such considerations intrinsically immoral, and that, contrariwise, the date 1492 may be no substitute for them. Most of all, we must convey the impression that we grade understanding qua understanding. To be convincing, I suppose we must concede to ourselves in advance that a bright student's understand-ing is understanding even if he achieved it by osmosis rather than by hard work in our course.

These are delicate matters. As for cow, its complexities are not what need concern us. Unlike good bull, it does not represent partial knowl-edge at all. It belongs to a different theory of knowledge entirely. In our theories of knowledge it represents total ignorance, or worse yet, a knowledge downright inimical to understanding. I even go so far as to propose that we award no more C's for cow. To do so is rarely, I feel, the act of mercy it seems. Mercy lies in clarity.

The reader may be afflicted by a lingering curiosity about the fate of Mr. Metzger. I hasten to reassure him. The Administrative Board of Harvard College, whatever its satanic reputations, is a benign body. Its members, to be sure, were on the spot. They delighted in Metzger's exploit, but they were responsible to the Faculty's rule. The hero stood in danger of probation. The debate was painful. Suddenly one member, of a refined legalistic sensibility, observed that the rule applied specifically to "examinations" and that the occasion had been simply an hour-test. Mr. Metzger was merely "admonished."

1963

THE READER

1. Perry speaks several times of "good bull." Explain what "bad bull" would be in Perry's view, and give an example of it.
2. Perry points out the essential inaccuracy of such a supposedly simple statement of fact as "Columbus discovered America in 1492." Analyze one or two other such commonly accepted statements of fact in the same way Perry does.
3. Perry says that the ideal is "a productive wedding" between bull and cow. Find another essay in this book that you think represents such a "productive wedding," and explain how the author has brought that wedding about.

THE WRITER

1. Near the beginning of his essay, Perry says that he must "beg patience . . . both of the reader's humor and of his morals" (p. 242). Why does he find this necessary, and what assumptions does he make about his readers?
2. What tone does Perry adopt in his essay? Explain how the indicated words in these phrases contribute to Perry's creation of a tone appropriate to his thesis: (1) "the stunning realization that the Harvard Faculty will often accept, as evidence of knowledge, the cerebrations of a student who has little data at his disposal"; (2) "the peculiar style of his bravado requires me to honor also his modesty"; (3) "Bull in pure form is rare; there is usually some contamination by data"; (4) "some neuter compromise between cow and bull, some infertile hermaphrodite." Find and comment on other examples that help to define the tone of the essay.
3. In "Education by Poetry" (p. 1026), Frost talks about the importance of metaphor in a liberal education. Write an essay relating Frost's remarks about metaphor to Perry's remarks about the place of bull and cow in a liberal education.

Lewis Thomas

HUMANITIES AND SCIENCE

Lord Kelvin was one of the great British physicists of the late nineteenth century, an extraordinarily influential figure in his time, and in some ways a paradigm of conventional, established scientific leadership. He did a lot of good and useful things, but once or twice he, like Homer, nodded. The instances are worth recalling today, for we have nodders among our scientific eminences still, from time to time, needing to have their elbows shaken.

On one occasion, Kelvin made a speech on the overarching importance of numbers. He maintained that no observation of nature was worth paying serious attention to unless it could be stated in precisely quantitative terms. The numbers were the final and only test, not only of truth but about meaning as well. He said, "When you can measure what you are speaking about, and express it in numbers, you know something about it. But when you cannot—your knowledge is of a meagre and unsatisfactory kind."

But, as at least one subsequent event showed, Kelvin may have had things exactly the wrong way round. The task of converting observations into numbers is the hardest of all, the last task rather than the first thing to be done, and it can be done only when you have learned, beforehand, a great deal about the observations themselves. You can, to be sure, achieve a very deep understanding of nature by quantitative measurement, but you must know what you are talking about before you can begin applying the numbers for making predictions. In Kelvin's case, the problem at hand was the age of the earth and solar sytem. Using what was then known about the sources of energy and the loss of energy from the physics of that day, he calculated that neither the earth nor the sun were [sic] older than several hundred million years. This caused a considerable stir in biological and geological circles, especially among the evolutionists. Darwin himself was distressed by the numbers; the time was much too short for the theory of evolution. Kelvin's figures were described by Darwin as one of his "sorest troubles."

T. H. Huxley had long been aware of the risks involved in premature extrapolations from mathematical treatment of biological problems. He said, in an 1869 speech to the Geological Society concerning numbers, "This seems to be one of the many cases in which the admitted accuracy of mathematical processes is allowed to throw a wholly inadmissible appearance of authority over the results obtained by them. . . . As the grandest mill in the world will not extract wheat flour from peascods, so pages of formulas will not get a definite result out of loose data."

The trouble was that the world of physics had not moved fast enough to allow for Kelvin's assumptions. Nuclear fusion and fission had not yet been dreamed of, and the true age of the earth could not even be guessed from the data in hand. It was not yet the time for mathematics in this subject.

There have been other examples, since those days, of the folly of using numbers and calculations uncritically. Kelvin's own strong conviction that science could not be genuine science without measuring things was catching. People in other fields of endeavor, hankering to turn their disciplines into exact sciences, beset by what has since been called "physics envy," set about converting whatever they knew into numbers and thence into equations with predictive pretensions. We have it with us still, in economics, sociology, psychology, history, even, I fear, in English-literature criticism and linguistics, and it frequently works, when it works at all, with indifferent success. The risks of untoward social consequences in work of this kind are considerable. It is as important— and as hard—to learn *when* to use mathematics as *how* to use it, and this matter should remain high on the agenda of consideration for education in the social and behavioral sciences.

Of course, Kelvin's difficulty with the age of the earth was an exceptional, almost isolated instance of failure in quantitative measurement in nineteenth-century physics. The instruments devised for approaching nature by way of physics became increasingly precise and powerful, carrying the field through electromagnetic theory, triumph after triumph, and setting the stage for the great revolution of twentieth-century physics. There is no doubt about it: measurement works when the instruments work, and when you have a fairly clear idea of what it is that is being measured, and when you know what to do with the numbers when they tumble out. The system for gaining information and comprehension about nature works so well, indeed, that it carries another hazard: the risk of convincing yourself that you know everything.

Kelvin himself fell into this trap toward the end of the century. (I don't mean to keep picking on Kelvin, who was a very great scientist; it is just that he happened to say a couple of things I find useful for this discussion.) He stated, in a summary of the achievements of nineteenth-century physics, that it was an almost completed science; virtually everything that needed knowing about the material universe had been learned; there were still a few anomalies and inconsistencies in electromagnetic theory, a few loose ends to be tidied up, but this would be done within the next several years. Physics, in these terms, was not a field any longer likely to attract, as it previously had, the brightest and most imaginative young brains. The most interesting part of the work had already been done. Then, within the next decade, came radiation, Planck, the quantum,

Einstein, Rutherford, Bohr, and all the rest—quantum mechanics—and the whole field turned over and became a brand-new sort of human endeavor, still now, in the view of many physicists, almost a full century later, a field only at its beginnings.

But even today, despite the amazements that are turning up in physics each year, despite the jumps taken from the smallest parts of nature—particle physics—to the largest of all—the cosmos itself—the impression of science that the public gains is rather like the impression left in the nineteenth-century public mind by Kelvin. Science, in this view, is first of all a matter of simply getting all the numbers together. The numbers are sitting out there in nature, waiting to be found, sorted and totted up. If only they had enough robots and enough computers, the scientists could go off to the beach and wait for their papers to be written for them. Second of all, what we know about nature today is pretty much the whole story: we are very nearly home and dry. From here on, it is largely a problem of tying up loose ends, tidying nature up, getting the files in order. The only real surprises for the future—and it is about those that the public is becoming more concerned and apprehensive—are the technological applications that the scientists may be cooking up from today's knowledge.

I suggest that the scientific community is to blame. If there are disagreements between the world of the humanities and the scientific enterprise as to the place and importance of science in a liberal-arts education, and the role of science in twentieth-century culture, I believe that the scientists are themselves responsible for a general misunderstanding of what they are really up to.

Over the past half century, we have been teaching the sciences as though they were the same academic collection of cut-and-dried subjects as always, and—here is what has really gone wrong—as though they would always be the same. The teaching of today's biology, for example, is pretty much the same kind of exercise as the teaching of Latin was when I was in high school long ago. First of all, the fundamentals, the underlying laws, the essential grammar, and then the reading of texts. Once mastered, that is that: Latin is Latin and forever after will be Latin. And biology is precisely biology, a vast array of hard facts to be learned as fundamentals, followed by a reading of the texts.

Moreover, we have been teaching science as though its facts were somehow superior to the facts in all other scholarly disciplines, more fundamental, more solid, less subject to subjectivism, immutable. English literature is not just one way of thinking, it is all sorts of ways. Poetry is a moving target. The facts that underlie art, architecture, and music are not really hard facts, and you can change them any way you like by arguing about them, but science is treated as an altogether different kind of learning: an unambiguous, unalterable, and endlessly useful display of data needing only to be packaged and installed somewhere in one's temporal lobe in order to achieve a full understanding of the natural world.

And it is, of course, not like this at all. In real life, every field of science that I can think of is incomplete, and most of them—whatever the record of accomplishment over the past two hundred years—are still in the earliest stage of their starting point. In the fields I know best, among the life sciences, it is required that the most expert and sophisticated minds be capable of changing those minds, often with a great lurch, every few years. In some branches of biology the mind-changing is occurring with accelerating velocities. The next week's issue of any scientific journal can turn a whole field upside down, shaking out any number of immutable ideas and installing new bodies of dogma, and this is happening all the time. It is an almost everyday event in physics, in chemistry, in materials research, in neurobiology, in genetics, in immunology. The hard facts tend to soften overnight, melt away, and vanish under the pressure of new hard facts, and the interpretations of what appear to be the most solid aspects of nature are subject to change, now more than at any other time in history. The conclusions reached in science are always, when looked at closely, far more provisional and tentative than are most of the assumptions arrived at by our colleagues in the humanities.

The running battle now in progress between the sociobiologists and the antisociobiologists is a marvel for students to behold, close up. To observe, in open-mouthed astonishment, the polarized extremes, one group of highly intelligent, beautifully trained, knowledgeable, and imaginative scientists maintaining that all sorts of behavior, animal and human, are governed exclusively by genes, and another group of equally talented scientists saying precisely the opposite and asserting that all behavior is set and determined by the environment, or by culture, and both sides brawling in the pages of periodicals such as *The New York Review of Books*, is an educational experience that no college student should be allowed to miss. The essential lesson to be learned has nothing to do with the relative validity of the facts underlying the argument, it is the argument itself that is the education: we do not yet know enough to settle such questions.

It is true that any given moment there is the appearance of satisfaction, even self-satisfaction, within every scientific discipline. On any Tuesday morning, if asked, a good working scientist will gladly tell you that the affairs of the field are nicely in order, that things are finally looking clear and making sense, and all is well. But come back again, on another Tuesday, and he may let you know that the roof has just fallen in on his life's work, that all the old ideas—last week's ideas in some cases—are no longer good ideas, that something strange has happened.

It is the very strangeness of nature that makes science engrossing. That ought to be at the center of science teaching. There are more than seven-times-seven types of ambiguity in science, awaiting analysis. The poetry of Wallace Stevens is crystal-clear alongside the genetic code.

I prefer to turn things around in order to make precisely the opposite case. Science, especially twentieth-century science, has provided us with a glimpse of something we never really knew before, the revelation of human ignorance. We have been used to the belief, down one century after another, that we more or less comprehend everything bar one or two mysteries like the mental processes of our gods. Every age, not just the eighteenth century, regarded itself as the Age of Reason, and we have never lacked for explanations of the world and its ways. Now, we are being brought up short, and this has been the work of science. We have a wilderness of mystery to make our way through in the centuries ahead, and we will need science for this but not science alone. Science will, in its own time, produce the data and some of the meaning in the data, but never the full meaning. For getting a full grasp, for perceiving real significance when significance is at hand, we shall need minds at work from all sorts of brains outside the fields of science, most of all the brains of poets, of course, but also those of artists, musicians, philosophers, historians, writers in general.

It is primarily because of this need that I would press for changes in the way science is taught. There is a need to teach the young people who will be doing the science themselves, but this will always be a small minority among us. There is a deeper need to teach science to those who will be needed for thinking about it, and this means pretty nearly everyone else, in hopes that a few of these people—a much smaller minority than the scientific community and probably a lot harder to find—will, in the thinking, be able to imagine new levels of meaning that are likely to be lost on the rest of us.

In addition, it is time to develop a new group of professional thinkers, perhaps a somewhat larger group than the working scientists, who can create a discipline of scientific criticism. We have had good luck so far in the emergence of a few people ranking as philosophers of science and historians and journalists of science, and I hope more of these will be coming along, but we have not yet seen a Ruskin or a Leavis or an Edmund Wilson. Science needs critics of this sort, but the public at large needs them more urgently.

I suggest that the introductory courses in science, at all levels from grade school through college, be radically revised. Leave the fundamentals, the so-called basics, aside for a while, and concentrate the attention of all students on the things that are not known. You cannot possibly teach quantum mechanics without mathematics, to be sure, but you can describe the strangeness of the world opened up by quantum theory. Let it be known, early on, that there are deep mysteries, and profound paradoxes, revealed in their distant outlines, by the quantum. Let it be known that these can be approached more closely, and puzzled over, once the language of mathematics has been sufficiently mastered.

Teach at the outset, before any of the fundamentals, the still imponderable puzzles of cosmology. Let it be known, as clearly as possible, by the youngest minds, that there are some things going on in the universe that lie beyond comprehension, and make it plain how little is known.

Do not teach that biology is a useful and perhaps profitable science; that can come later. Teach instead that there are structures squirming inside all our cells, providing all the energy for living, that are essentially foreign creatures, brought in for symbiotic living a billion or so years ago, the lineal descendants of bacteria. Teach that we do not have the ghost of an idea how they got there, where they came from, or how they evolved to their present structure and function. The details of oxidative phosphorylation[1] and photosynthesis can come later.

Teach ecology early on. Let it be understood that the earth's life is a system of interliving, interdependent creatures, and that we do not understand at all how it works. The earth's environment, from the range of atmospheric gases to the chemical constituents of the sea, has been held in an almost unbelievably improbable state of regulated balance since life began, and the regulation of stability and balance is accomplished solely by the life itself, like the internal environment of an immense organism, and we do not know how *that* one works, even less what it means. Teach that.

Go easy, I suggest, on the promises sometimes freely offered by science. Technology relies and depends on science these days, more than ever before, but technology is nothing like the first justification for doing research, nor is it necessarily an essential product to be expected from science. Public decisions about what to have in the way of technology are totally different problems from decisions about science, and the two enterprises should not be tangled together. The central task of science is to arrive, stage by stage, at a clearer comprehension of nature, but this does not mean, as it is sometimes claimed to mean, a search for mastery over nature. Science may provide us, one day, with a better understanding of ourselves, but never, I hope, with a set of technologies for doing something or other to improve ourselves. I am made nervous by assertions that human consciousness will someday be unraveled by research, laid out for close scrutiny like the workings of a computer, and then, *and then*! I hope with some fervor that we can learn a lot more than we now know about the human mind, and I see no reason why this strange puzzle should remain forever and entirely beyond us. But I would be deeply disturbed by any prospect that we might use the new knowledge in order

1. "A vital process of intracellular respiration" (*American Heritage Dictionary*).

to begin doing something about it, to improve it, say. This is a different matter from searching for information to use against schizophrenia or dementia, where we are badly in need of technologies, indeed likely one day to be sunk without them. But the ordinary, everyday, more or less normal human mind is too marvelous an instrument ever to be tampered with by anyone, science or no science.

The education of humanists cannot be regarded as complete, or even adequate, without exposure in some depth to where things stand in the various branches of science, and particularly, as I have said, in the areas of our ignorance. This does not mean that I know how to go about doing it, nor am I unaware of the difficulties involved. Physics professors, most of them, look with revulsion on assignments to teach their subject to poets. Biologists, caught up by the enchantment of their new power, armed with flawless instruments to tell the nucleotide sequences of the entire human genome, nearly matching the physicists in the precision of their measurements of living processes, will resist the prospect of broad survey courses; each biology professor will demand that any student in his path must master every fine detail within that professor's research program. The liberal-arts faculties, for their part, will continue to view the scientists with suspicion and apprehension. "What do the scientists want?" asked a Cambridge professor in Francis Cornford's wonderful *Microcosmographia Academica*. "Everything that's going," was the quick answer. That was back in 1912, and universities haven't much changed.

The worst thing that has happened to science education is that the great fun has gone out of it. A very large number of good students look at it as slogging work to be got through on the way to medical school. Others look closely at the premedical students themselves, embattled and bleeding for grades and class standing, and are turned off. Very few see science as the high adventure it really is, the wildest of all explorations ever undertaken by human beings, the chance to catch close views of things never seen before, the shrewdest maneuver for discovering how the world works. Instead, they become baffled early on, and they are misled into thinking that bafflement is simply the result of not having learned all the facts. They are not told, as they should be told, that everyone else—from the professor in his endowed chair down to the platoons of postdoctoral students in the laboratory all night—is baffled as well. Every important scientific advance that has come in looking like an answer has turned, sooner or later—usually sooner—into a question. And the game is just beginning.

An appreciation of what is happening in science today, and of how great a distance lies ahead for exploring, ought to be one of the rewards of a liberal-arts education. It ought to be a good in itself, not something to be acquired on the way to a professional career but part of the cast of thought needed for getting into the kind of century that is now just down the road. Part of the intellectual equipment of an educated person, however his or her time is to be spent, ought to be a feel for the queernesses of nature, the inexplicable things.

And maybe, just maybe, a new set of courses dealing systematically with ignorance in science might take hold. The scientists might discover in it a new and subversive technique for catching the attention of students driven by curiosity, delighted and surprised to learn that science is exactly as Bush described it: an "endless frontier." The humanists, for their part, might take considerable satisfaction watching their scientific colleagues confess openly to not knowing everything about everything. And the poets, on whose shoulders the future rests, might, late nights, thinking things over, begin to see some meanings that elude the rest of us. It is worth a try.

1983

THE READER

1. What does Thomas believe that scientists "are really up to"?
2. What, in Thomas's view, is the relationship between science and technology? The differences? Why is it important that science and technology be distinguished?
3. Thomas describes the battle between the sociobiologists and the antisociobiologists, and says, "it is the argument itself that is the education" (p. 256). Take Wilson's "The Superorganism" (p. 856) as an example of sociobiology. How do you think Wilson would react to Thomas's assertion?
4. Does Thomas imply that there are often things wrong about the way the humanities are usually taught? Have you been taught that English literature is "one way of thinking," or have you been taught to regard poetry as a "moving target" (p. 255)?

THE WRITER

1. Thomas's essay implies that science and the humanities have more in common than is customarily supposed. What details in the discussion lead to that implication?
2. Write a brief essay supporting or denying Thomas's assertion that "the conclusions reached in science are always . . . far more provisional and tentative than are most of the assumptions arrived at . . . in the humanities."
3. Thomas suggests that "a new set of courses dealing systematically with ignorance in science might take hold." Write a brief description of one such course. Then compare it with some courses it might replace, coming to some conclusion as to which might be more valuable for you.
4. Write a definition of "the scientific method," as you take that term to be commonly understood. Then write a critique of that definition as Thomas's view might suggest.
5. Here Thomas is dealing with a subject that is sweeping and important

and in "Notes on Punctuation" (p. 322) with one that is restricted and minor. Describe the personality Thomas presents to you here and then the one he presents in "Notes on Puctuation." Are they similar? Different? Do they overlap? Is his analysis in "On Magic in Medicine" (p. 450) consistent with this personality or these personalities?

6. *In "About Symbol," Dillard says: "All our knowledge is partial and approximate; if we are to know electrons and chimpanzees less than perfectly, and call it good enough, we may as well understand phenomena like love and death, or art and freedom, imperfectly also" (p. 1008). Write a brief essay comparing Dillard's idea with Thomas's assertion that conclusions in science are "far more provisional and tentative than are most of the assumptions . . . in the humanities."*

Lord Ashby

THE UNIVERSITY IDEAL: A VIEW FROM BRITAIN

The story is told that in the medieval University of Paris the professors were disputing about the number of teeth in a horse's mouth. They agreed that the number could not be a multiple of three, for that would be an offense to the Trinity; nor could it be a multiple of seven, for God created the world in six days and rested on the seventh. Neither the records of Aristotle nor the arguments of St. Thomas enabled them to solve the problem. Then a shocking thing happened. A student who had been listening to the discussion went out, opened a horse's mouth, and counted the teeth.

I want to draw two conclusions from this parable. The first is that our present perplexities about universities derive from the act of this medieval student. He symbolizes the beginning of objective inquiry, the revolt against authority, the empirical attitude, the linking of academic study with the facts of life. His act introduced research into the university. After the horse's mouth was opened knowledge became an open system. The second conclusion is that we must think twice before we become nostalgic about the traditional university ideal. Not everything about the traditional university is worth preserving. The medieval university was hostile to what we now call academic freedom. To stray outside the corpus academicum of set books, even to interpret them in novel ways, was to court heresy. The traditional university was not much interested in discovery: it was preoccupied with transmission of a crystallized culture. It was at certain periods not even interested in knowledge for its own sake; many scholars pursued knowledge if not for preferment, then as a means of spiritual and intellectual health, just as a man plays golf not for the sake of golf but to keep down his weight.

I want to follow these two lines of thought by raising three questions. The first is this. What do we want to perpetuate from the university's long tradition? What, in other words, is the content of our loyalty to the university ideal? Secondly, what obligations does the university have— what loyalties ought it to foster—toward contemporary society? And thirdly, what are the prospects that these two loyalties—one to a traditional university ideal, the other to the society in which we live—can be reconciled?

On the very spot where I sat to prepare these remarks Clare College had existed since 1326. Six centuries ago it was a row of cottages, with an iron box in which some books were stored. In the cottages, under the Lady Clare's foundation, lived the Master and a dozen Fellows and about the same number of students, sharing the Fellows' rooms. There was a hall where lectures were held and where Fellows and scholars ate together, but much of the teaching was a private contract between Fellow and pupil; we still have records of the fees they paid. Fellows and scholars lived austerely. Their food was plain. They clustered in winter round a common fire. The little community was virtually independent of the University. It governed itself as it still does, sealing contracts in the name of the Master, Fellows, and Scholars of Clare; we still have the seal Lady Clare gave us.

In this simple society was to be found the secret of excellence in universities, the one element of tradition which we do want to preserve. It was an environment for the continuous polishing of one mind by another. Its basic formula was very simple. The essential ingredients were on the one hand a reflective, disciplined, learned man willing to teach; on the other hand an intelligent, motivated student willing to learn; and, thirdly, a balance of numbers between teacher and student so that the relation between them was intimate and personal. Given these ingredients, the university ideal can be realized whatever other shortcomings there may be. Without these ingredients, no institution can realize fully the university ideal.

The characteristic of university teaching is quality in communication, which must be distinguished from standards of achievement. Standards vary enormously in time and place. For example, the standards of achievement necessary for admission to Cambridge, Harvard, and Göttingen are very different. The standard of achievement necessary to get a degree in physics in Cambridge in 1900 was about the same as the standard now necessary to get entry to Cambridge as a freshman. But quality of teaching in Cambridge, Harvard, and Göttingen is—I believe —about the same; and the quality of teaching in Cambridge two generations ago was certainly not lower than it is today. So when we talk of preserving traditional academic values, we mean quality. This we must preserve.

Now let me turn again to the student who opened the horse's mouth. He was the pioneer of academic freedom, the *Lern-* and *Lehrfreiheit*[1] of the Germans. He gave the university a new mission; not to preserve the *status quo* but to question it. From this all sorts of consequences flow: the university as a disruptive rather than a consolidating influence in society; the proliferation, and hence the fragmentation, of knowledge; the consequent inevitable increase in size and cost of universities, which threaten to deprive the university of its identity because it has become—I suppose for the first time since the middle ages—too dependent upon outside influence, an influence which in those days was the orthodoxy of the Church and in these days is the orthodoxy of alumni or legislature.

This brings me to the university's obligation to the present. Being modern is not necessarily a virtue; indeed it is one sign of a small mind to want to be contemporary in one's generation, just as it is to want to be parochial in one's geography. We face a problem in what a biologist would call selective permeability. Which outside pressures should we allow to act upon the university, and which should we resist?

It has been said of medieval universities "that they placed the administration of human affairs . . . in the hands of educated men." There could be no better summary than this of the obligations of universities to our present society; nor is it likely to be disputed. Our disputes center round the definition of an educated man. For some people still this is synonymous with a knowledge of the languages and civilizations of Greece and Rome, and consistent with an ignorance of science, technology, and modern society. It is still possible to rise to the highest ranks of public life in Britain having done no science since the age of 15, no social science at all, and at the university nothing but the classics for three years. Diversification of the curriculum has always met with fierce opposition. When history was introduced into Oxford one of the faculty wrote, "I can but fear the worst, a majority of fourteen in convocation voted in favor of . . . modern history. We did indeed by a large majority reject the details of this novelty, but the principle has been admitted . . . we have fallen into the weakness of yielding to the spirit of the age." A century later Flexner[2] was issuing similar Jeremiads about the introduction of journalism and business studies into American universities.

I believe Flexner was wrong. I believe that to admit into the college curriculum new professional schools on our terms—the terms of the faculty not of the legislature or the alumni—is an essential obligation of universities. But, let it be emphasized, on our terms, for we are the experts. And our terms are uncompromising and unambiguous. They are that any and every university subject must be mastered in the medium of

1. Freedom to learn and freedom to teach.   educator and educational reformer.
2. Abraham Flexner (1866–1959), American

one or other (or both) of two systems of symbols: language and mathematics. Indeed, the quintessence of higher education is the mastery of these systems of symbols and their application to real, and relevant, situations. To me, the touchstone of university studies is not to teach great truths but rather to teach truth in a great way; not simply to inherit orthodoxy but to master the dialectic between orthodoxy and dissent. It is a style of thought, which at its best transcends subject-matter; a style which cannot be acquired except from someone who is constantly exploring at the limits of understanding (hence the necessity for academics to do what is commonly, and erroneously, called "research").

One of the great contributions which the United States has made to the university tradition is to overcome the resistance to desirable adaptation of the curriculum. In permitting the proliferation of professional schools following a bachelor's degree in liberal arts, the United States has done no more than reinstate in modern dress the traditional medieval pattern of the university, which had been lost in nineteenth century Oxford and Cambridge. I believe this is a great achievement, but it has brought in its wake two problems. One is the enormous increase in size of universities, inevitable if they are to encompass this novel diversity of studies. The other is that you cannot have professional schools without professionals, and a professional's first loyalty is to his guild of other professionals, to chemists, historians, lawyers, outside the university. And so the university finds itself with a faculty which, if not exactly alienated, certainly does not give its total allegiance to the institution it serves.

Size and divided loyalty: these are not new problems. Estimates of student numbers in medieval universities have been greatly exaggerated, but it is very likely that at times there were about 7,000 students in some of the bigger ones. And a student population of 7,000 on one campus under medieval conditions must have been as formidable as a population ten times the size under modern conditions. As for divided loyalties, we only have to remember that the faculty in a medieval university were clerics, under church discipline, to realize where their first loyalty lay.

Let me say that in British universities we have, by and large, preserved the ark of the covenant,[3] which is dedication to quality in the transmission of learning and a sustained and rigorous training in the symbolism of language and mathematics. But, it is essential to point out at what cost we have done this. For the price has been high.

First, we have denied an opportunity for higher education to tens of thousands of British children who deserved to have one. At the time of the Robbins Committee (1963) it was estimated that about 1 in 3 Ameri-

---

3. A sacred symbol of the biblical Hebrews, the ark was the wooden chest overlaid with gold in which Moses placed the stone tablets containing the ten commandments. See Exodus xxv. 10–21.

can children of university age were receiving full-time education. The corresponding figures for British children were about 1 in 14; and, if you count only degree-granting institutions, more like 1 in 25. Even when all allowances are made for our very different patterns of high school education, there is still no escape from the conclusion that we in Britain have avoided one of your problems simply by shutting college doors to thousands of our children. We are changing all that now (and hence running into troubles similar to yours), but even when our educational revolution is over, in 1980, we plan to have only 1 child in 6 attending college.

Secondly, we have virtually eliminated general education from our system, though some of our newer institutions are beginning in a modest way to reinstate it.

This is the price we are paying. Now let me tell you what we have bought for the price.

First, we have avoided some of the dangers of size. Rightly or wrongly (it is too early to say yet), we have met the demand for higher education not by enlarging our universities to 20,000 or 30,000 as you have but by creating new universities. And even our larger universities, such as my own, are divided into small units. Clare College has 360 undergraduates. We give personal tuition to every one of these undergraduates about twice a week and we draw on nearly 100 people, part time, to do this college teaching for us. And even in universities where there is no college system, students (since they are reading one-subject honors degrees) spend nearly all their time in one department, so it becomes their intellectual and largely their social home, and the faculty knows them as individuals.

One consequence of this restriction on student numbers and preservation of small units of size is that the ratio of teachers to students is high. We try to aim at a faculty-student ratio of 1 in 8. In small universities and in Cambridge colleges the "mix" is even richer; in these, every week the student receives two or three supervisions (called tutorials in Oxford) either alone with his teacher, or in pairs or at most threes, when he reads an essay and has it criticized. Faculty members become as enthusiastic about the performance of their pupils as though the pupils were horses entered in a race. It is the determined and deliberate policy of the British University Grants Committee that this "hand-made" method of teaching shall be adopted by all British universities, and some of them are well on the way to adopting it.

One may wonder where the faculty comes from. I can say for Cambridge. Of course we use Ph.D. teaching assistants as American universities do, but not to the same extent. We use also—and they are absolutely essential to our system—members of research teams and faculty wives, a device which could, I believe, be adopted effectively in American universities. But above all we expect our faculty members, however distinguished, to teach. No British university would offer even a Nobel Price-winner a job with the understanding that he need teach only one quarter a year. In my own College there are Fellows of Royal Society who are teaching up to ten hours a week. The "flight from teaching" is, of course, a problem for us as well as you, but apart from the "flight across the Atlantic," it is less severe for us for two reasons: because we give tenure to academics earlier in their careers than America does, which means that the drive to publish is less pressing; and because we have uniform salary scales for all British universities; hence our faculty composition is more stable and one university cannot easily buy up scholars from another.

Of course it is an expensive method of education, this "hand-made" teaching. And Britain is not a wealthy country. But I wonder whether some of the troubles in America might be due to the fact (I hesitate to say such a surprising thing) that despite the astronomical bill for colleges, higher education is being done "on the cheap," insofar as it is not employing enough senior faculty to match the student numbers. For the sacred thread of transmission between teacher and pupil, does America perhaps rely more than we do on inexperienced teachers?

Secondly, our very neglect of general education does enable us to insist on mastery of a narrow field. If a student studies nothing but history (or chemistry) for three years, under the personal tutelage of an expert, he is likely to acquire a sense of values, standards of self-criticism, a mastery in handling data and concepts, which is one hallmark of higher education. Particularly is this so if the student is highly motivated. Since there is such competition for places, and selection nowadays is strictly on academic merit, we in Britain are able to select intelligent and often earnest students. Not exclusively, of course; but the frivolous student, the playboy, and the dullard do not easily slip into British universities. So our drop-out rate is low: in Cambridge less than 3 percent of those who enter fail to graduate; and the national average of drop-outs in Britain is around 12 percent.

Finally—and this is a controversial virtue—we meet the challenge of maintaining quality in higher education by our system of examination. Every university in every subject has an external examiner, usually from another university. It is the external examiner's business to see that the standards for the award of degrees are about the same as those in his own university. So (for example) the level of achievement which we call "a first" in history or chemistry is locked into a common standard for all British universities. In this way we have, I am sure, consolidated throughout the whole of our system of higher education our loyalty to the ideal of what a university should be. But, by putting on the market, as it were, only Cadillacs and no Fords, we have not fulfilled adequately our loyalty to contemporary society.

If one accepts my description of the university ideal as quality in the transmission of knowledge, possible ways to preserve this ideal are: (1) to insist on a rich faculty-student ratio and to require the faculty to teach at least eight hours a week; (2) to maintain comparatively small units of size: this is not inconsistent with the large university—one can build clusters of colleges around massive central amenities (the Residential College at the University of Michigan is one experimental prototype) and (3) at some stage of university education to require intense concentration in scope of studies.

It is time to sum up. Let us try to cast a balance for the modern university. In standards of achievement demanded of students and faculty, in a willingness to incorporate new areas of knowledge, in giving faculty and students freedom to teach and to learn, modern universities are incomparably better than were those in the middle ages, or indeed those in the nineteenth century.

It is the very success of universities which endangers their cohesion internally and their integrity from outside. It does not matter much if the external structure of universities changes, or if new subjects appear in the curriculum, or if universities open their doors to a greater proportion of the age group: provided always that the thin stream of excellence on which the intellectual health of the nation ultimately depends is not contaminated. In our present social climate I do not believe excellence can be safeguarded (as we have tried to safeguard it in Britain) by keeping mediocrity out of higher education. This is simply unrealistic. I believe it must be safeguarded as America is trying to do it, by the peaceful coexistence of mediocrity and excellence. They have, after all, got to coexist elsewhere in society, and it is an educational commonplace that Gresham's law[4] does not hold for college degrees; indeed mediocrity is improved by association with excellence. Fords do not drive Cadillacs off the market.

What we have to devise, on both sides of the Atlantic, are ways to foster motivation among students and quality in communication among teachers. That is why I venture to come back to the paradigm of Clare College six hundred years ago. I have faith in the American university because I believe that even with its immense numbers of students it can (and indeed is) solving the problem of cultivating quality as well as accommodating quantity. It is reconciling loyalty to the university ideal and loyalty to contemporary society.

c. 1965

---

4. The economic principle that "bad money drives out good"—that is, that the introduction of a debased coinage will result in the disappearance of coins made of precious metals.

Wayne C. Booth

IS THERE ANY KNOWLEDGE THAT A MAN *MUST* HAVE?

Everyone lives on the assumption that a great deal of knowledge is not worth bothering about; though we all know that what looks trivial in one man's hands may turn out to be earth-shaking in another's, we simply cannot know very much, compared with what might be known, and we must therefore choose. What is shocking is not the act of choice which we all commit openly but the claim that some choices are wrong. Especially shocking is the claim implied by my title: There is some knowledge that a man *must* have.

There clearly is no such thing, if by knowledge we mean mere acquaintance with this or that thing, fact, concept, literary work, or scientific law. When C. P. Snow and F. R. Leavis exchanged blows on whether knowledge of Shakespeare is more important than knowledge of the second law of thermodynamics, they were both, it seemed to me, much too ready to assume as indispensable what a great many wise and good men have quite obviously got along without. And it is not only nonprofessionals who can survive in happy ignorance of this or that bit of lore. I suspect that many successful scientists (in biology, say) have lost whatever hold they might once have had on the second law; I know that a great many literary scholars survive and even flourish without knowing certain "indispensable" classics. We all get along without vast loads of learning that other men take as necessary marks of an educated man. If we once begin to "reason the need" we will find, like Lear, that "our basest beggars/Are in the poorest thing superfluous." Indeed, we can survive, in a manner of speaking, even in the modern world, with little more than the bare literacy necessary to tell the "off" buttons from the "on."

Herbert Spencer would remind us at this point that we are interpreting *need* as if it were entirely a question of private survival. Though he talks about what a man must know to stay alive, he is more interested, in his defense of science, in what a *society* must know to survive: "Is there any knowledge that *man* must have?"—not a man; but *man*. This question is put to us much more acutely in our time than it was in Spencer's, and it is by no means as easy to argue now as it was then that the knowledge needed for man's survival is scientific knowledge. The threats of atomic annihilation, of engulfing population growth, of depleted air, water, and food must obviously be met, if man is to survive, and in meeting them man will, it is true, need more and more scientific knowledge; but it is not at all clear that more and more scientific knowledge will by itself suffice. Even so, a modern Herbert Spencer might well argue that a conference like this one, with its emphasis on the individual and his cognitive needs, is simply repeating the mistakes of the classical tradition. The knowledge most worth having would be, from his point of view, that of how to pull mankind through the next century or so without absolute self-destruction. The precise proportions of different kinds of knowledge—physical, biological, political, ethical, psychological, historical, or whatever— would be different from those prescribed in Spencer's essay, but the nature of the search would be precisely the same.

We can admit the relevance of this emphasis on social utility and at the same time argue that our business here is with other matters entirely. If the only knowledge a man *must* have is how to cross the street without getting knocked down—or, in other words, how to navigate the centuries without blowing himself up—then we may as well close the conference and go home. We may as well also roll up the college and mail it to a research institute, because almost any place that is not cluttered up with notions of liberal education will be able to discover and transmit practical bits of survival-lore better than we can. Our problem of survival is a rather different one, thrust at us as soon as we change our title slightly once again to "Is there any knowledge (other than the knowledge for survival) that a man must have?" That slight shift opens a new perspective on the problem, because the question of what it is to be a man, of what it is to be fully human, is the question at the heart of liberal education.

To be human, to be human, to be fully human. What does it mean? What is required? Immediately, we start feeling nervous again. Is the speaker suggesting that some of us are not fully human yet? Here come those hierarchies again. Surely in our pluralistic society we can admit an unlimited number of legitimate ways to be a man, without prescribing some outmoded aristocratic code!

Who—or what—is the creature we would educate? Our answer will determine our answers to educational questions, and it is therefore, I think, worth far more vigorous effort than it usually receives. I find it convenient, and only slightly unfair, to classify the educational talk I encounter these days under four notions of man, three of them metaphorical, only one literal. Though nobody's position, I suppose, fits my types neatly, some educators talk as if they were programming machines, some talk as if they were conditioning rats, some talk as if they were training ants to take a position in the anthill, and some—precious few—talk as if they thought of themselves as men dealing with men.

One traditional division of the human soul, you will remember, was into three parts: the vegetable, the animal, and the rational. Nobody, so far as I know, has devised an educational program treating students as vegetables, though one runs into the analogy used negatively in academic sermons from time to time. Similarly, no one ever really says that men are ants, though there is a marvelous passage in Kwame Nkrumah's autobiography in which he meditates longingly on the order and pure functionality of an anthill.[1] Educators do talk of men as machines or as animals, but of course they always point out that men are much more complicated than any other known animals or machines. My point here is not so much to attack any one of these metaphors—dangerous as I think they are—but to describe briefly what answers to our question each of them might suggest.

Ever since Descartes, La Mettrie,[2] and others explicitly called a man a machine, the metaphor has been a dominant one in educational thinking. Some have thought of man as a very complex machine, needing very elaborate programming; others have thought of him as a very simple machine, requiring little more than a systematic pattern of stimuli to produce foretellable responses. I heard a psychologist recently repeat the old behaviorist claim (first made by John B. Watson, I believe) that if you would give him complete control over any normal child's life from birth, he could turn that child into a great musician or a great mathematician or a great poet—you name it and he could produce it. On being pressed, the professor admitted that this claim was only "in theory," because we don't yet have the necessary knowledge. When I pushed further by asking why he was so confident in advance of experimental proof, it became clear that his faith in the fundamental metaphor of man as a programmable machine was unshakable.

When the notion of man as machine was first advanced, the machine was a very simple collection of pulleys and billiard balls and levers. Such original simplicities have been badly battered by our growing awareness both of how complex real machines can be and of how much more complex man is than any known machine. Modern notions of stimulus-response patterns are immeasurably more complicated than anything Descartes imagined, because we are now aware of the fantastic variety of stimuli that the man-machine is subject to and of the even more fantastic complexity of the responding circuits.

But whether the machine is simple or complex, the educational task for those who think of man under this metaphor is to program the mechanism so that it will produce the results that we have foreordained. We do not simply fill the little pitchers, like Mr. Gradgrind in Dickens' *Hard*

---

1. Nkrumah was the first premier of the African republic of Ghana; he was ultimately deposed in a coup and went to live in China.
2. René Descartes (1596–1650), French phi-losopher and mathematician; Julian Offray de La Mettrie (1709–1751), French physician and philosopher.

Times;[3] we are much too sophisticated to want only undigested "pour-back," as he might have called his product. But we still program the information channels so that the proper if-loops and do-loops will be followed and the right feedback produced. The "programming" can be done by human teachers, of course, and not only by machines; but it is not surprising that those whose thinking is dominated by this metaphor tend to discover that machines are better teachers than men. The more ambitious programmers do not hesitate to claim that they can teach both thought and creativity in this way. But I have yet to see a program that can deal effectively with any subject that cannot be reduced to simple yes and no answers, that is, to answers that are known in advance by the programmer and can thus be fixed for all time.

We can assume that subtler machines will be invented that can engage in simulated dialogue with the pupil, and perhaps even recognize when a particularly bright pupil has discovered something new that refutes the program. But even the subtlest teaching machine imaginable will still be subject, one must assume, to a final limitation: it can teach only what a machine can "learn." For those who believe that man is literally nothing but a very complicated machine, this is not in fact a limitation; machines will ultimately be able to duplicate all mental processes, thus "learning" everything learnable, and they will be able in consequence to teach everything.

I doubt this claim for many reasons, and I am glad to find the testimony of Norbert Wiener, the first and best known cyberneticist, to the effect that there will always remain a radical gap between computers and the human mind. But "ultimately" is a long way off, and I am not so much concerned with whether ultimately man's mind will closely resemble some ultimately inventable machine as I am with the effects, here and now, of thinking about men under the analogy with machines of today. Let me simply close this section with an illustration of how the mechanistic model can permeate our thought in destructive ways. Ask yourselves what picture of creature-to-be-educated emerges from this professor of teacher education:

> To implement the TEAM Project new curriculum proposal . . . our first concerns are with instructional systems, materials to feed the system, and personnel to operate the system. We have defined an instructional system as the optimal blending of the demands of content, communication, and learning. While numerous models have been developed, our simplified model of an instructional system would look like Figure 2. . . . We look at the process of communication—communicating content to produce learning—as something involving the senses: . . . [aural, oral, tactile, visual]. And I think in

3. Thomas Gradgrind thought of his students as "little pitchers . . . who were to be filled so full of facts."

teacher education we had better think of the communications aspect of the instructional system as a package that includes the teacher, textbook, new media, classroom, and environment. To integrate these elements to more effectively transmit content into permanent learning, new and better instructional materials are needed and a new focus on the teacher of teachers is required. The teacher of teachers must: (1) examine critically the content of traditional courses in relation to desired behavioral outcomes; (2) become more sophisticated in the techniques of communicating course content; and (3) learn to work in concert with media specialists to develop the materials and procedures requisite to the efficient instructional system. And if the media specialist were to be charged with the efficient operation of the system, his upgrading would demand a broad-based "media generalist" orientation.

I submit that the author of this passage was thinking of human beings as stimulus-response systems on the simplest possible model, and that he was thinking of the purpose of education as the transfer of information from one machine to another. Though he would certainly deny it if we asked him, he has come to think about the human mind so habitually in the mechanistic mode that he doesn't even know he's doing it.[4]

But it is time to move from the machine metaphor to animal metaphors. They are closely related, of course, because everybody who believes that man is a machine also believes that animals are machines, only simpler ones. But many people who would resist the word "machine" do tend to analogize man to one or another characteristic of animals. Since man is obviously an animal in one sense, he can be studied as an animal, and he can be taught as an animal is taught. Most of the fundamental research in learning theory underlying the use of teaching machines has been done, in fact, on animals like rats and pigeons. You can teach pigeons to play Ping-Pong rather quickly by rewarding every gesture they make that moves them toward success in the game and refusing to reward those gestures that you want to efface. Though everybody admits that human beings are more complicated than rats and pigeons, just as everyone admits that human beings are more complicated than computers, the basic picture of the animal as a collection of drives or instincts, "conditioned" to learn according to rewards or punishments, has underlain much modern educational theory.

The notion of the human being as a collection of drives different from animal drives only in being more complex carries with it implications for education planners. If you and I are motivated only by sex or hunger or more complex drives like desire for power or for ego-satisfaction, then of course all education depends on the provision of satisfactions along our route to knowledge. If our teachers can just program carrots along the

4. I am not of course suggesting that any use of teaching machines implies a mechanistic reduction of persons to machines; programmers rightly point out that machines can free teachers from the mechanical and save time for the personal [Booth's note].

path at the proper distance, we donkey-headed students will plod along the path from carrot to carrot and end up as educated men.

I cannot take time here to deal with this view adequately, but it seems to me that it is highly questionable even about animals themselves. What kind of thing, really, is a rat or a monkey? The question of whether animals have souls has been debated actively for at least nine centuries; now psychologists find themselves dealing with the same question under another guise: What are these little creatures that we kill so blithely for the sake of knowledge? What are these strangely resistant little bundles of energy that will prefer—as experiments with rats have shown—a complicated interesting maze without food to a dull one with food?

There are, in fact, many experiments by now showing that at the very least we must postulate, for animals, a strong independent drive for mastery of the environment or satisfaction of curiosity about it. All the more advanced animals will learn to push levers that produce interesting results—clicks or bells or flashing lights or sliding panels—when no other reward is offered. It seems clear that even to be a fulfilled animal, as it were, something more than "animal satisfaction" is needed!

I am reminded here of the experiments on mother-love in monkeys reported by Harry F. Harlow in the *Scientific American* some years ago. Harlow called his article "Love in Infant Monkeys," and the subtitle of his article read, "Affection in infants was long thought to be generated by the satisfactions of feeding. Studies of young rhesus monkeys now indicate that love derives mainly from close bodily contact." The experiment consisted of giving infant monkeys a choice between a plain wire figure that offered the infant milk and a terry-cloth covered figure without milk. There was a pathetic picture of an infant clinging to the terry-cloth figure, and a caption that read "The infants spent most of their time clinging to the soft cloth 'mother' even when nursing bottles were attached to the wire mother." The article concluded—rather prematurely, I thought—that "contact comfort" had been shown to be a "prime requisite in the formation of an infant's love for its mother," that the act of nursing had been shown to be unimportant if not totally irrelevant in forming such love (though it was evident to any reader, even at the time, that no genuine "act of nursing" had figured in the experiment at all), and that "our investigations have established a secure experimental approach to this realm of dramatic and subtle emotional relationships." The only real problem, Harlow said, was the availability of enough infant monkeys for experiment.

Now I would not want to underrate the importance of Harlow's demonstration to the scientific community that monkeys do not live by bread alone. But I think that most scientists and humanists reading the article would have been struck by two things. The first is the automatic assumption that the way to study a subject like love is to break it down into its component parts; nobody looking at that little monkey clinging to the terry-cloth could possibly have said, "This is love," unless he had been blinded by a hidden conviction that love in animals is—must be—a mere cumulative result of a collection of drive satisfactions. This assumption is given quite plainly in Harlow's concluding sentence: "Finally with such techniques established, there appears to be no reason why we cannot at some future time investigate the fundamental neurophysiological and biochemical variables underlying affection and love." For Harlow monkeys (and people) seem to be mere collections of neurophysiological and biochemical variables, and love will be best explained when we can explain the genesis of each of its parts. The second striking point is that for Harlow animals do not matter, except as they are useful for experiment. If he had felt that they mattered, he might have noticed the look on his infant's face—a look that predicted for me, and for other readers of the *Scientific American* I've talked with, that these monkeys were doomed.

And indeed they were. A year or so later another article appeared, reporting Harlow's astonished discovery that all of the little monkeys on which he had earlier experimented had turned out to be incurably psychotic. Not a single monkey could mate, not a single monkey could play, not a single monkey could in fact become anything more than the twisted half-creatures that Harlow's deprivations had made of them. Harlow's new discovery was that monkeys needed close association with their peers during infancy and that such association was even more important to their development than genuine mothering. There was no sign that Harlow had learned any fundamental lessons from his earlier gross mistakes; he had landed nicely on his feet, still convinced that the way to study love is to break it down into its component parts and that the way to study animals is to maim them or reduce them to something less than themselves. As Robert White says, summarizing his reasons for rejecting similar methods in studying human infancy, it is too often assumed that the scientific way is to analyze behavior until one can find a small enough unit to allow for detailed research, but in the process "very vital common properties" are lost from view.

I cite Harlow's two reports not, of course, to attack animal experimentation—though I must confess that I am horrified by much that goes on in its name—nor to claim that animals are more like human beings than they are. Rather, I want simply to suggest that the danger of thinking of men as animals is heightened if the animals we think of are reduced to machines on a simple model.

The effects of reducing education to conditioning can be seen throughout America today. Usually they appear in subtle forms, disguised with the language of personalism; you will look a long time before you find anyone (except a very few Skinnerians) saying that he thinks of education as exactly like conditioning pigeons. But there are plenty of honest, blunt folk around to let the cat out of the bag—like the author of an article this year in *College Composition and Communications*: "The Use of a Multiple Response Device in the Teaching of Remedial English." The author claimed to have evidence that if you give each student four buttons to be pushed on multiple-choice questions, with all the buttons wired into a lighted grid at the front of the room, the resulting "instantaneous feedback"—every child learning immediately whether he agrees with the rest of the class—speeds up the learning of grammatical rules considerably over the usual workbook procedures. I daresay it does—but meanwhile what has happened to education? Or take the author of an article on "Procedures and Techniques of Teaching," who wrote as follows: "If we expect students to learn skills, they have to practice, but practice doesn't make perfect. Practice works if the learner *learns the results* of his practice, i.e., if he receives feedback. Feedback is most effective when it is contiguous to the response being learned. One of the chief advantages of teaching machines is that the learner finds out quickly whether his response is right or wrong ... [Pressey] has published the results of an extensive program of research with tests that students score for themselves by punching alternatives until they hit the correct one. ... [Thus] teaching machines or workbooks have many theoretical advantages over lecturing or other conventional methods of instruction." But according to what theory, one must ask, *do* systematic feedback mechanisms, perfected to whatever degree, have "theoretical advantages" over human contact? Whatever else can be said for such a theory, it will be based on the simplest of comparisons with animal learning. Unfortunately, the author goes on, experimental evidence is on the whole rather discouraging: "Experiments at the Systems Development Corporation ... suggest that teaching incorporating ... human characteristics is more effective than the typical fixed-sequence machines. (In this experiment instead of using teaching machines to simulate human teachers, the experimenters used humans to simulate teaching machines!)"

So far I have dealt with analogies for man that apply only to individuals. My third analogy turns to the picture of men in groups, and it is given to me partly by discussions of education, like those of Admiral Rickover, that see it simply as filling society's needs. I know of only one prominent educator who has publicly praised the anthill as a model for the kind of society a university should serve—a society of specialists each trained to do his part. But the notion pervades many of the defenses of the emerging multiversities.[5]

5. A 1960s term for the gargantuan universities which often set government and corporate research, and the training of graduate students to do that research, above under-

If knowledge is needed to enable men to function as units in society, and if the health of society is taken as the purpose of their existence, then there is nothing wrong in training the ants to fill their niches; it would be wrong not to. "Education is our first line of defense—make it strong," so reads the title of the first chapter of Admiral Rickover's book, *Education and Freedom* (New York: Dutton, 1959). "We must upgrade our schools" in order to "guarantee the future prosperity and freedom of the Republic." You can tell whether the ant-analogy is dominating a man's thinking by a simple test of how he orders his ends and means. In Admiral Rickover's statement, the schools must be upgraded in order to guarantee future prosperity, that is, we improve education for the sake of some presumed social good.

I seldom find anyone putting it the other way round: we must guarantee prosperity so that we can improve the schools, and the reason we want to improve the schools is that we want to insure the development of certain kinds of persons, both as teachers and as students. You cannot even say what I just said so long as you are really thinking of ants and anthills. Ants are not ends in themselves, ultimately more valuable than the hills they live in (I *think* they are not; maybe to themselves, or in the eyes of God, even ants are ultimate, self-justifying ends). At least from our point of view, ants are expendable, or to put it another way, their society is more beautiful, more interesting, more admirable than they are. And I would want to argue that too many people think of human beings in the same way when they think of educating them. The Communists make this quite explicit: the ends of Communist society justify whatever distortion or destruction of individual purposes is necessary to achieve them; men are educated for the state, not for their own well-being. They are basically political animals, not in the Aristotelian sense that they require society if they are to achieve their full natures and thus their own special, human kind of happiness, but in the sense that they exist, like ants, for the sake of the body politic.

If the social order is the final justification of what we do in education, then a certain attitude toward teaching and research will result: all of us little workmen, down inside the anthill, will go on happily contributing our tiny bit to the total scheme without worrying much about larger questions of the why and wherefore. I know a graduate student who says that she sometimes sees her graduate professors as an army of tiny industrious miners at the bottom of a vast mine, chipping away at the edges and shipping their bits of knowledge up to the surface, blindly hoping that someone up there will know what to do with it all. An order is received for such-and-such new organic compounds; society needs them. Another order is received for an atomic bomb; it is needed, and it is

---

graduate education.

therefore produced. Often no orders come down, but the chipping goes on anyway, and the shipments are made, because everyone knows that the health of the mine depends on a certain tonnage of specialized knowledge each working day.

We have learned lately that "they" are going to establish a great new atom-smasher, perhaps near Chicago. The atom-smasher will employ two thousand scientists and technicians. I look out at you here, knowing that some of you are physics majors, and I wonder whether any of you will ultimately be employed in that new installation, and if you are, whether it will be as an ant or as a human being. Which it will be must depend not on your ultimate employers but on yourself and on what happens to your education between now and then: if you have been given nothing but training to be that ultimate unit in that ultimate system, only a miracle can save you from formic dissolution of your human lineaments.

But it is long past time for me to turn from these negative, truncated portraits of what man really is not and attempt to say what he is. And here we encounter a difficulty that I find very curious. You will note that each of these metaphors has reduced man to something less than man, or at least to a partial aspect of man. It is easy to say that man is not a machine, though he is in some limited respects organized like a machine and even to some degree "programmable." It is also easy to say that man is not simply a complicated rat or monkey, though he is in some ways like rats and monkeys. Nor is man an ant, though he lives and must function in a complicated social milieu. All these metaphors break down not because they are flatly false but because they are metaphors, and any metaphorical definition is inevitably misleading. The ones I have been dealing with are especially misleading, because in every case they have reduced something more complex to something much less complex. But even if we were to analogize man to something more complex, say, the universe, we would be dissatisfied. What we want is some notion of what man really is, so that we will know what or whom we are trying to educate.

And here it is that we discover something very important about man, something that even the least religious person must find himself mystified by: man is the one "thing" we know that is completely resistant to our efforts at metaphor or analogy or image-making. What seems to be the most important literal characteristic of man is his resistance to definitions in terms of anything else. If you call me a machine, even a very complicated machine, I know that you deny what I care most about, my selfhood, my sense of being a person, my consciousness, my conviction of freedom and dignity, my awareness of love, my laughter. Machines have none of these things, and even if we were generous to their prospects, and imagined machines immeasurably superior to the most complicated ones now in existence, we would still feel an infinite gap between them and what we know to be a basic truth about ourselves: machines are expendable, ultimately expendable, and men are mysteriously ends in themselves.

I hear people deny this, but when they do they always argue for their position by claiming marvelous feats of super-machine calculation that machines can now do or will someday be able to do. But that is not the point; of course machines can outcalculate us. The question to ask is entirely a different one: Will they ever outlove us, outlive us, outvalue us? Do we build machines because machines are good things in themselves? Do we nurture them for their own good, as we nurture our children? An obvious way to test our sense of worth in men and machines is to ask ourselves whether we would ever campaign to liberate the poor downtrodden machines who have been enslaved. Shall we form a National Association for the Advancement of Machinery? Will anyone ever feel a smidgeon of moral indignation because this or that piece of machinery is not given equal rights before the law? Or put it another way: Does anyone value Gemini[6] more than the twins? There may be men now alive who would rather "destruct," as we say, the pilot than the experimental rocket, but most of us still believe that the human being in the space ship is more important than the space ship.

When college students protest the so-called depersonalization of education, what they mean, finally, is not simply that they want to meet their professors socially or that they want small classes or that they do not want to be dealt with by IBM machines. All these things are but symptoms of a deeper sense of a violation of their literal reality as persons, ends in themselves rather than mere expendable things. Similarly, the current deep-spirited revolt against racial and economic injustice seems to me best explained as a sudden assertion that people, of whatever color or class, are not reducible to social conveniences. When you organize your labor force or your educational system as if men were mere social conveniences, "human resources," as we say, contributors to the gross national product, you violate something that we all know, in a form of knowledge much deeper than our knowledge of the times tables or the second law of thermodynamics: those field hands, those children crowded into the deadening classroom, those men laboring without dignity in the city anthills are men, creatures whose worth is mysteriously more than any description of it we might make in justifying what we do to them.

Ants, rats, and machines can all learn a great deal. Taken together, they "know" a very great part of what our schools and colleges are now designed to teach. But is there any kind of knowledge that a creature

6. Here referring not to the astrological sign but to the space rockets.

must have to qualify as a man? Is there any part of the educational task that is demanded of us by virtue of our claim to educate this curious entity, this *person* that cannot be reduced to mechanism or animality alone?

You will not be surprised, by now, to have me sound, in my answer, terribly traditional, not to say square: the education that a *man* must have is what has traditionally been called liberal education. The knowledge it yields is the knowledge or capacity or power of how to act freely as a man. That's why we call liberal education liberal: it is intended to liberate from whatever it is that makes animals act like animals and machines act like machines.

I'll return in a moment to what it means to act freely as a man. But we are already in a position to say something about what knowledge a man must have—he must first of all be able to learn for himself. If he cannot learn for himself, he is enslaved by his teachers' ideas, or by the ideas of his more persuasive contemporaries, or by machines programmed by other men. He may have what we call a good formal education, yet still be totally bound by whatever opinions happen to have come his way in attractive garb. One wonders how many of our graduates have learned how to take hold of a subject and "work it up," so that they can make themselves experts on what other men have concluded. In some ways this is not a very demanding goal, and it is certainly not very exciting. It says nothing about that popular concept, creativity, or about imagination or originality. All it says is that anyone who is dependent on his teachers *is* dependent, not free, and that anyone who knows how to learn for himself is less like animals and machines than anyone who does not know how to learn for himself.

We see already that a college is not being merely capricious or arbitrary when it insists that some kinds of learning are more important than some others. The world is overflowing with interesting subjects and valuable skills, but surely any college worth the name will put first things first: it will try to insure, as one inescapable goal, that every graduate can dig out from the printed page what he needs to know. And it will not let the desire to tamp in additional tidbits of knowledge, however delicious, interfere with training minds for whom a formal teacher is no longer required.

To put our first goal in this way raises some real problems that we cannot solve. Obviously no college can produce self-learners in very many subjects. Are we not lucky if a graduate can learn for himself even in one field, now that knowledge in all areas has advanced as far as it has? Surely we cannot expect our graduates to reach a stage of independence in mathematics and physics, in political science and psychology, in philosophy and English, *and* in all the other nice subjects that one would like to master.

Rather than answer this objection right away, let me make things even more difficult by saying that it is not enough to learn how to learn. The man who cannot *think* for himself, going beyond what other men have learned or thought, is still enslaved to other men's ideas. Obviously the goal of learning to think is even more difficult than the goal of learning to learn. But difficult as it is we must add it to our list. It is simply not enough to be able to get up a subject on one's own, like a good encyclopedia employee, even though any college would take pride if all its graduates could do so. To be fully human means in part to think one's own thoughts, to reach a point at which, whether one's ideas are different from or similar to other men's, they are truly one's own.

The art of asking oneself critical questions that lead either to new answers or to genuine revitalizing of old answers, the art of making thought live anew in each new generation, may not be entirely amenable to instruction. But it is a necessary art nonetheless, for any man who wants to be free. It is an art that all philosophers have tried to pursue, and many of them have given direct guidance in how to pursue it. Needless to say, it is an art the pursuit of which is never fully completed. No one thinks for himself very much of the time or in very many subjects. Yet the habitual effort to ask the right critical questions and to apply rigorous tests to our hunches is a clearer mark than any other of an educated man.

But again we stumble upon the question, "Learn to think about *what?*" The modern world presents us with innumerable subjects to think about. Does it matter whether anyone achieves this rare and difficult point in more than one subject? And if not, won't the best education simply be the one that brings a man into mastery of a narrow specialty as soon as possible, so that he can learn to think for himself as soon as possible? Even at best most of us are enslaved to opinions provided for us by experts in *most* fields. So far, it might be argued, I still have not shown that there is any kind of knowledge that a man must have, only that there are certain skills that he must be able to exercise in at least one field.

To provide a proper grounding for my answer to that objection would require far more time than I have left, and I'm not at all sure that I could do so even with all the time in the world. The question of whether it is possible to maintain a human stance toward any more than a tiny fraction of modern knowledge is not clearly answerable at this stage in our history. It will be answered, if at all, only when men have learned how to store and retrieve all "machinable" knowledge, freeing themselves for distinctively human tasks. But in the meantime, I find myself unable to surrender, as it were, three distinct kinds of knowledge that seem to me indispensable to being human.

To be a man, a man must first know something about his own nature and his place in Nature, with a capital N—something about the truth of things, as men used to say in the old-fashioned days before the word "truth" was banned from academia. Machines are not curious, so far as I can judge; animals are, but presumably they never go, in their philosophies, even at the furthest, beyond a kind of solipsistic existentialism. But in science, in philosophy (ancient and modern), in theology, in psychology and anthropology, and in literature (of some kinds), we are presented with accounts of our universe and of our place in it that as men we can respond to in only one manly way: by thinking about them, by speculating and testing our speculations.

We know before we start that our thought is doomed to incompleteness and error and downright chanciness. Even the most rigorously scientific view will be changed, we know, within a decade, or perhaps even by tomorrow. But to refuse the effort to understand is to resign from the human race; the unexamined life can no doubt be worth living in other respects—after all, it is no mean thing to be a vegetable, an oak tree, an elephant, or a lion.[7] But a man, a man will want to see, in this speculative domain, beyond his next dinner.

By putting it in this way, I think we can avoid the claim that to be a man I must have studied any one field—philosophy, science, theology. But to be a man, *I must speculate*, and I must learn how to test my speculations so that they are not simply capricious, unchecked by other men's speculations. A college education, surely, should throw every student into a regular torrent of speculation, and it should school him to recognize the different standards of validation proper to different kinds of claims to truth. You cannot distinguish a man who in this respect is educated from other men by whether or not he believes in God, or in UFO's. But you can tell an educated man by the way he takes hold of the question of whether God exists, or whether UFO's are from Mars. Do you know your own reasons for your beliefs, or do you absorb your beliefs from whatever happens to be in your environment, like plankton taking in nourishment?

Second, the man who has not learned how to make the great human achievements in the arts his own, who does not know what it means to earn a great novel or symphony or painting for himself, is enslaved either to caprice or to other men's testimony or to a life of ugliness. You will notice that as I turn thus to "beauty"—another old-fashioned term—I do not say that a man must know how to prove what is beautiful or how to discourse on aesthetics. Such speculative activities are pleasant and worthwhile in themselves, but they belong in my first domain. Here we are asking that a man be educated to the experience of beauty; speculation about it can then follow. My point is simply that a man is less than a

7. Here Booth echoes the assertion of Socrates, defending his practice of probing students' conventional beliefs, that the unexamined life is not worth living.

man if he cannot respond to the art made by his fellow man.

Again I have tried to put the standard in a way that allows for the impossibility of any one man's achieving independent responses in very many arts. Some would argue that education should insure some minimal human competence in all of the arts, or at least in music, painting, and literature. I suppose I would be satisfied if all of our graduates had been "hooked" by at least one art, hooked so deeply that they could never get free. As in the domain of speculation, we could say that the more types of distinctively human activity a man can master, the better, but we are today talking about floors, not ceilings, and I shall simply rest content with saying that to be a man, a man must know artistic beauty, in some form, and know it in the way that beauty can be known. (The distinction between natural and man-made beauty might give me trouble if you pushed me on it here, but let me just say, dogmatically, that I would not be satisfied simply to know natural beauty—women and sunsets, say—as a substitute for art.)

Finally, the man who has not learned anything about how to understand his own intentions and to make them effective in the world, who has not, through experience and books, learned something about what is possible and what impossible, what desirable and what undesirable, will be enslaved by the political and social intentions of other men, benign or malign. The domain of practical wisdom is at least as complex and troublesome as the other two, and at the same time it is even more self-evidently indispensable. How should a man live? How should a society be run? What direction should a university take in 1966? For that matter what should be the proportion, in a good university, of inquiry into truth, beauty, and "goodness"? What kind of knowledge of self or of society is pertinent to living the life proper to a man? In short, the very question of this conference falls within this final domain: What knowledge, if any, is most worthy of pursuit? You cannot distinguish the men from the boys according to any one set of conclusions, but you *can* recognize a man, in this domain, simply by discovering whether he can think for himself about practical questions, with some degree of freedom from blind psychological or political or economic compulsions. Ernest Hemingway tells somewhere of a man who had "moved one dollar's width to the [political] right for every dollar that he'd ever earned." Perhaps no man ever achieves the opposite extreme, complete freedom in his choices from irrelevant compulsions. But all of us who believe in education believe that it is possible for any man, through study and conscientious thought, to school his choices—that is, to free them through coming to understand the forces working on them.

Even from this brief discussion of the three domains, I think we are put in a position to see how it can be said that there is some knowledge that a man must have. The line I have been pursuing will not lead to a list of great books, or even to a list of indispensable departments in a university. Nor will it lead, in any clear-cut fashion, to a pattern of requirements in each of the divisions. Truth, beauty, and goodness (or "right choice") are relevant to study in every division within the university; the humanities, for example, have no corner on beauty or imagination or art, and the sciences have no corner on speculative truth. What is more, a man can be ignorant even of Shakespeare, Aristotle, Beethoven, and Einstein, and be a man for a' that—if he has learned how to think his own thoughts, experience beauty for himself, and choose his own actions.

It is not the business of a college to determine or limit what a man will know; if it tries to, he will properly resent its impositions, perhaps immediately, perhaps ten years later when the imposed information is outmoded. But I think that it is the business of a college to help teach a man how to use his mind for himself, in at least the three directions I have suggested * * * To think for oneself is, as we all know, hard enough. To design a program and assemble faculty to assist rather than hinder students in their efforts to think for themselves is even harder. But in an age that is oppressed by huge accumulations of unassimilated knowledge, the task of discovering what it means to educate a man is perhaps more important than ever before.

1967

Francis E. Sparshott

NOTHING TO SAY

The following is the text of the convocation address delivered by Professor Sparshott to Victoria College and bachelor of commerce graduates.

There are many jokes about convocation addresses. Most of the jokes are bad. Almost all of them are true. Few are truer than what Sir Peter Medawar said in this very hall last winter. The purpose of a convocation address, he said, is to say nothing; and that is why they are always entrusted to people with nothing to say.

Certainly there is nothing that I could say to you, the graduating class, on this occasion. I can give you no advice, offer you no opinion. How could I advise you? Your presence here suggests that you have discovered for yourselves the important thing that I never learned: how to get out of the University. If I offered you advice, I would be like a hen, who had been set to rear a brood of duck eggs, telling her former charges how to swim. Besides, if you had wanted my advice, you would have asked me for it. You never did. It would be grave impertinence in me to offer it to you now, when you could only avoid it by leaving the hall en masse and thus missing the bit of the ceremony you came here for.

If I can't advise you, I am in no better position to offer my opinions. Again, if you had wanted my opinions, you would have asked for them. And there is nothing special about them. I have no opinion, on anything, that is not contradicted by people who, so far as the public record shows, are at least as well-informed, well-intentioned, and intelligent as I am.

Besides, I remember that when I was a younger man everyone used to prefer my father's opinions to mine, to the point where my mother would often request me to be silent and let my father continue speaking. And yet I remember distinctly that I thought much more highly of the opinions I held then than I do of the opinions I hold now. So, if you wanted opinions, you should have asked my father. In short, what with one thing and another, I have nothing to say.

Perhaps it would help if I repeated for you the messages of the last two convocation speakers I heard. One of these, a poet and a Victoria graduate, seemed to suggest that the world is a warm, snug, and cozy place, whether your own position be on the right or on the left. Her exact words were: "I'm here to tell you, it's an armpit out there." But the other speaker, and eminent scientist, seemed to suggest rather that the world is a dangerous place. He pointed out, with facts and figures to support him, that nuclear weapons are dangerous and far too numerous. A measure of disarmament, he felt, would be in order. I am sure he is right, for the responsible leaders of the world's great powers all agree that nuclear disarmament would be a good thing. However, my father told me when I was young that how much a person valued a thing was shown by how much that person was prepared to give up for it. Next time you hear a political leader speaking in favor of nuclear disarmament, or anything else for that matter, ask yourself this question: what price is this politician ready to pay for what he says he wants? If the answer is nothing, that is how much the politician's statement is worth. Or so my father would say. And you remember how good his opinions were. Meanwhile, one of those two convocation speakers seems to think the world is rather a safe place, the other that is rather a dangerous place, so that kind of cancels out.

I am to say nothing, then. Fortunately, I am a philosopher by trade, and philosophers know better than anyone how to say nothing. It is a matter of logic, you see. The surest way to say nothing is to contradict oneself. If I say the world is a safe place, and this is the best of times, I have said something, though not much. If I say the world is a dangerous place and thus not safe at all, so that this is the worst of times, I have said something, though very little. But if I say that the world is a safe place and also is not a safe place, I contradict myself, and I have said nothing. After a contradiction, one of my colleagues was saying the other day, one does not know how to go on. After one has said "It was the best of times, it was the worst of times,"[1] how could one possibly continue? If one were a novelist, perhaps one could go on to write a novel about the French Revolution; but that only shows that novelists are unreliable people and not to be believed.

I suppose the nearest I can decently come to actually contradicting myself is to utter, separately, two equal and opposite truths. If we keep them separate, we are all right. It is only if we put them together that we get a contradiction. My truths will be: "Whatever is, is wrong" and "Whatever is, is right."[2]

First, whatever is, is wrong. That must be true. The present, God's unique gift to us, is all we have; but no sooner is it offered to us than it is withdrawn and replaced by another, somewhat different and therefore, presumably, meant to be an improvement. Of course, the changes between successive moments are not very big. The world is like a Volkswagen Beetle with innumerable very small modifications leaving the basic design intact. Some of us live in hopes that one day the world will be withdrawn altogether and replaced by a rabbit. But what is certain is that the world is constantly being changed; so, presumably, whatever is, is wrong.

But it is no less certain that what is, is right. Whatever happens is simply the resultant of all the forces actually effective at the time, including all the operative interests. How could it be otherwise? But if whatever happens is the most perfect expression of the sum of the prevailing interests, given the totality of the objective conditions, how could that be improved on? Whatever is, then, is right. This does not imply that you should not complain or fight, if you find it useful or comforting to do so, or that you should not try to bring it about that your own interests are better satisfied at some future time. What is now is right for now; that does not make it right for the future. But, if it is true that whatever is, is right, that does mean that it is foolish to act on the supposition that the present state of affairs, whatever it may be, is anything other than the best expression of the prevailing interests. It is foolish for two reasons: first, because it substitutes your own wishes for the recognition of reality; and, second, because it makes you ineffective. If you want to change a situation you must know what it is; and, in any social or economic situation, knowing what it is is the same as knowing why it is right. If one wishes to promote nuclear disarmament, it is little use to tell oneself, or to tell the world, that the conduct of the major powers is lunatic and wicked. What one has to do is master the viewpoint

---

1. The opening sentence of Charles Dickens's *A Tale of Two Cities* (1859), a novel of the French Revolution.

2. Line 294 from Alexander Pope's "An Essay on Man" (1733).

from which what they are doing is the best possible policy, becuase the factors that go to make up that viewpoint, and nothing else, are what one has to change. Or again, if one wishes to change the policy, current here and in many other places, of continually reducing expenditures on university education, it is pointless to say over and over again that the policy is wrong, unless one has a clear idea of just why it is right. Personally, I have never seen a public plea for the reversal of this trend that made any realistic attempt to understand the justification for the trend that was to be reversed. Consequently, since the underfunders are never shown what is wrong with their reasons for underfunding, they see no reason to change their policies.

We must not, however, jump to conclusions. Since whatever is is right, this widespread habit of calling for change without understanding what it is that has to be changed must be right too. Karl Marx once said that philosophers had sought to understand the world in this way or that, but the point is, he said, to change it. Many people quote this remark with approval, so there are obviously a lot of people around who think it is a good idea to change things without understanding them. The history of revolutions and their aftermaths in this century provides bitter food for thought here.

Of course, it is really not worth saying that whatever is, is right, except to console or hearten oneself at times when things are, to all appearances, going very badly wrong. In his oratorio *Jephtha*, the composer George Frideric Handel sets the words "Whatever is, is right," to music. The music for the words "whatever is," as one might expect, is dreary and despondent. And one would have expected that the following words, "is right," would express triumphant jubilation, or serene confidence in the ultimate goodness of the world. But they don't. What we hear from the chorus is something between a defiant shout and a despairing yell. As every condemned criminal knows, the fact that something is right does not mean that you have to like it. After all, as I said before, it appears that Providence does not like it either. Every state of affairs in the world is immediately replaced by a new, improved state of affairs in a new package. So whatever is, is wrong.

Well, there you have it. Whatever is, is right; whatever is, is wrong. It is the best of times, it is the worst of times. Do I contradict myself? Very well, then, I contradict myself.[3] But mind you, as they say in Ireland— mind you, I've said nothing . . .

I wish you good fortune in the world, such as you find it, such as you make it.

1984

---

3. From Walt Whitman's "Song of Myself."

THE READER

1. What do you make of all this? Does Sparshott have anything to say?
2. Sparshott quotes a previous commencement speaker as saying: "I'm here to tell you, it's an armpit out there." He seems to think this means "that the world is a warm, snug, and cozy place, whether your own position be on the right or on the left." But surely this is to misunderstand her meaning. How do you account for such a mistake? Is it because she is a poet and he a philosopher?
3. Having compared the world to a Volkswagen Beetle, Sparshott says that some hope "that one day the world will be withdrawn altogether and replaced by a rabbit." Is there a misprint there—should this word be "Rabbit," with a capital R?
4. Sparshott says he has no advice to give nor opinions to offer. Is this true?

THE WRITER

1. In what ways is Sparshott's address adapted to the occasion and to his audience?
2. What is the function in Sparshott's address of his reference to Marx? To Handel? To his own mother and father?
3. Would you call Sparshott's address humorous or witty?
4. Two of the things philosophers and teachers of philosophy like to talk about are the law of contradiction in logic and the nature of philosophical inquiry (including the examination of assumptions). Does Sparshott do any teaching of this sort in his address?

Language and Communication

Robert M. Adams

SOFT SOAP AND THE NITTY-GRITTY

Because euphemism, which is an effort to make something sound specially nice, implies that unless prettified it will be specially unacceptable, a euphemistic formation can easily turn into its opposite. That would be a "dysphemism," a coinage almost as ugly as what it describes.[1] Easy and obvious examples are found in the troubled area of racial names. For many years, "Afro-Americans," "the colored," and "Negroes" were prevalent as efforts, more or less high-falutin, to say what it is now accepted procedure to express by the word "black." The latest word is notably inexact, since most of the people it designates are different shades of brown, sometimes very light. (It is, to be sure, no more inexact that the word "white" applied to a spectrum of faces from pinko-grey to swarthy.) But it is a "genuine" word, implying in its very overstatement rejection of all efforts to mitigate or evade the basic fact; it is, in addition, "our" word, not the word of outsiders. Recognizing the old euphemisms as really dysphemisms, it confronts and gets rid of them—as in certain social situations it is felt as an insult to use the vaguely honorific word "lady," where the straightforward "woman" is called for. (Try programming this into a computer!) There are youthful circles, I learn, which consider it normal to describe a parent as "my toad"—an interesting euphemism-dysphemism which substitutes frank disgust for the ancient hypocritical professions. It may be ugly, is the implication, but it's

---

1. The coinage owes something to Bentham's "dyslogism," found throughout the *Table of the Springs of Action*. Direct contra- ries of Bentham's word would be "eulogy" and "eulogistic," which have acquired meanings of their own [author's note].

honest; in fact, the proof of its honesty is its ugliness.

A leaven of falsity or avoidance is what causes the euphemism to exist in the first place; but, given the richness of modern vocabulary, using one word almost always involves avoiding another which might be thought uglier and in some judgments more appropriate. For instance, a particular girl could be called slim, slender, willowy, lithe, svelte, graceful—or skinny or bony. Depending on one's taste in girls, or one's feeling about an individual girl, the first six adjectives might be felt as euphemisms for either of the last.

Occasionally there just is no convenient middle term between a vulgarity such as "shit" and an artificial learned word such as "feces." (Who ever stubbed his toe in the dark and cried out, "Oh, feces!"—or, alternatively, "Oh, night-soil"?) Depending on social context, one may have to choose the least unsatisfactory of two evils, or circumlocute, to an inevitably clumsy effect, circumlocution being nothing but euphemism long drawn out. Where there is an unwelcome truth to be hidden from others or oneself, euphemism flourishes, hence its special fondness for situations where codes or ideologies are under pressure. President Reagan, trying to obscure the fact that the MX missile is an awesomely destructive weapon, tries to title it "The Peacekeeper." Just so, "liquidation" used to be a favorite Soviet term for the process of resolving political differences, until the world caught on to what it meant; and Hitler had a "final solution" for the Jewish problem. "They make a solitude and call it peace," said Tacitus[2] of his fellow Romans, noting an uncharacteristic Roman euphemism; it is still available for use in Cambodia. But since politics, above all international politics, is almost exclusively the art of muffling reality in fine words, it would be otiose to multiply examples of this order.

Most of the modern discredit attached to the notion of euphemism stems from use of the formula in service to the proprieties, "Purity's aged grannams," as Meredith[3] called them. Within the last twenty years a book was published which referred to Fanny Cornforth as Rossetti's[4] "housekeeper"; that was going half a dozen better than Fowler, who in Modern English Usage tells us that "mistress" itself is a euphemism for "concubine." We have euphemisms for our euphemisms; the fact will surprise nobody who reflects on the panoply of euphemisms for referring to homosexuals (gays, fairies, pansies, homophiles, saturnians, uranians, queers, queens, faggots, flits, and so forth), most of which contain elements of derision and contempt, but which can also be though of as terms for avoiding heavy expressions like "catamite," "sodomist," "pederast," and all the variations to be played on "buggery." "Toilet" is another

2. Tacitus (A.D. 55?–117?): Roman historian.
3. George Meredith (1828–1909): British novelist; grannams: grandmothers.
4. Dante Gabriel Rossetti (1828–82): British poet and Pre-Raphaelite painter.

concept for which there are so many euphemisms, including a French cousin the Vay-say,[5] that one hardly knows which is not a euphemism for the many others.

If the root act of euphemism is suppression or evasion, and therefore untruth, a frequent precondition is some kind of elevation or pretension (whether moral, social, or stylistic) which the euphemism tries to sustain. Classical rhetorical theory, as formulated by Cicero, Quintilian, Longinus, and other legislators, distinguished three levels of discourse, the sublime, the humble, and the intermediate, and insisted that within each mode the style must be appropriate to the subject, the subject accommodated to the style. Thus it would have shocked a classical historian beyond measure to find Gregory of Tours,[6] in a serious history, describing a posse pausing during a manhunt to take counsel: "dixitque unus, dum equi urinam profecerunt. . . ." Horses just don't *do* that in a dignified literary work. The same sort of shock, but actual not hypothetical, exploded a Paris audience in 1829 when the fatal word "mouchoir"[7] was first pronounced during an elevated drama, and a Dublin audience in 1907 when the word "shift" first sullied, within the fane of a public theater, the purity of Irish ears. In all these instances, the elevated style would be expected either to suppress the offensive act or word, or else to circumlocute. "Poetic diction" is the systematic application of euphemism to maintaining elevation of style, and since nobody to speak of tries to maintain an elevated style any more, this sort of euphemism would seem to be on the verge of obsolescence.

As far as imaginative writing goes, where the exalted style used to be not only accepted but required, this seems to be in good part accomplished fact. For novelists and playwrights, as for movie-makers and constructors of soap operas who follow suit, it seems to have become a formula that every congenial, decorous, "civilized" situation exists only as a whited sepulcher to be torn open amid shrieks of agony and screams of fury; thus one discovers the authentic, i.e. destructive emotions at the core of it. Wherever exposure is the aim and shock the technique, euphemism (which is placatory and concealing by nature) is bound to be inappropriate. And while this is not necessarily or universally the pattern in poetry, revulsion from an elevated or emphatic style is established there too, and euphemism, as a corruption of "natural" language, is repudiated.

It is possible, I think, to write a major composition so consistently framed in euphemisms and other avoidance-terms that they will not be recognized individually as such, because they merge into the smear of

---

5. The French pronunciation of W.C., the English abbreviation for *water closet*.
6. Gregory of Tours (c. 538–594): bishop and the author of *History of the Franks*; "dixitque

unus, dum equi urinam profecerunt": "and one spoke, while the horses urinated."
7. Handkerchief.

the style as a whole. That extraordinary lingua franca[8] of cheap nine-teenth-century novels, in which most lending-library fiction and even some more pretentious works (as by Edward Bulwer-Lytton[9]) were composed, amounts to an unbroken string of artificial and pompous phrases, amid which mere euphemisms pass almost unnoticed. Even contemporary paperback romances, while drenched in smarmy eroticism, generally slither so moistly through the language of innuendo that they have no use for euphemisms as such, or else submerge them in other forms of evasion and suggestion. For the lightly salacious pornographer, avoidance of the explicit and the crude goes readily with a high level of suggestive titillation.

Certain categories of fictional omission occur so often and go so generally unremarked that they hardly qualify as euphemism. Hardly any characters in fiction have occasion to excrete; in the world they inhabit, such acts would be grossly out of place. Neither do women ever menstruate; the process is no more mentioned in the usual fiction than at the usual dinner-party. In real life, all peole secrete various disagreeable effluvia, which most of the time everybody quietly ignores; fiction, having almost total control of its environment, ignores them too, except for special, deliberately chosen effects. Euphemism would enter in only if language, admitting or suggesting the cacodylic hero or heroine, tried to prettify or cosmeticize the effect. You could call euphemism the deodorant of language; if so, a code of silent omissions would correspond to the private preliminary shower-bath that renders anti-perspirants unnecessary.

The reality behind both anti-perspirants and shower-baths is that we naturally stink, and in insisting on that fact much modern literature, which aims at counterstating the accepted conventions and mores, banishes euphemisms from the printed page. Yet in managing its everyday affairs, a complicated cosmopolitan commercial society, which discusses, legislates, and litigates publicly many matters that used to be determined by quiet tradition and domestic consent, needs more euphemisms than ever before. The social sciences, which for years have been trying to develop a sanitized, neutral, and preferably artificial vocabulary, serve as a major source of supply. "Senior citizens," for example, is a standard euphemism for the old. There is nothing wrong with the word "old," or for that matter with the lesser euphemism "elderly," except that both imply the proximate end of life. "Citizen" is supposed to suggest active involvement in the affairs of society, and "senior" the kind of respect given to senators and such. How pitifully far the terms commonly are from reality needs, alas, no demonstration. "Upwardly mobile" is a similarly sanitized form of "ambitious," as "anti-social behavior" illus-

8. Italian term for a hybrid language used by speakers of different languages.

9. Edward Robert Bulwer-Lytton (1831–91): British diplomat and poet.

trates the power of an indefinite abstraction to subsume numerous ugly particulars by packaging them in a phrase with minor varieties of mischief. The phrase "different life-styles" practically enforces a non-judgmental attitude, whatever the alternatives one is comparing; "life-style" itself assumes the individual isn't making any personal decisions, just following a pre-established pattern. The term "exceptional children" is a particularly brilliant educationist's euphemism, because it lumps together those who are too dull, those suffering from physical handicaps, and those who are too brilliant to follow the regular curriculum. The democratic objective is to conceal such elitist categories of achievement as better and worse, so as to prevent damage to the self-esteem of the less competent pupil. Perhaps this makes a bit of sense at the early stages of the educational process, though in fact young children are too quick and too cruel in deciding for themselves which of their classmates are smart and which dumb, to be long deceived. Besides, in society at large the democratic mystique creates many purely artificial and heavily discounted terms of avoidance and glorification to prevent invidious distinctions. Thus garbage men become "environmental engineers," and the sewage disposal plant is the "waste water treatment facility." It is the same principle on which, in Britain, garbage collectors are called "dustmen," though dust is the least of the commodities in which they deal. From the depths of the Victorian era, Henry Mayhew[1] recalls is to us a discreet and elegant euphemism among the street paupers of his day: "pure" collectors were collectors of pure dog-shit, used for various tannery operations. One understands their need for a phrase, however oblique, that would partially disguise their trade.

In despising the dishonesty of euphemisms, as we can and must, we run the risk of overlooking the many destructive and explosive potentialities of language. Though gossip in an infinitely pluralistic society is less deadly than it used to be a hundred years ago, it can still hang a tin can on a dog's tail and rattle him to death. In addition, high-pressure living has added new terrors to the psychopathology of everyday life. The hijacker holding a plane full of terrified passengers under the muzzle of a machine gun, the theater full of people who must be told there is a fire behind the stage, the potential suicide teetering on a ledge far above the street—in these charged and volatile situations, the pressure on language becomes extreme. One wrong word spoken when a convoy of scabs is confronting a picket line, one foolish expression when racial feelings are inflamed, and men are fighting mad—and half a city may go up in smoke. Euphemisms must be among the expressions used on such occasions: there is no formula for them, and if they make themselves too readily felt as what they are, that's bad. So a natural tendency is to say as little as possible.

1. Henry Mayhew (1812–87): British journalist, author of *London Labour and the London Poor.*

When calming a restive horse or soothing a fretful cow about to kick over the milk pail, one is free to use a mere tone of voice, murmuring nonsense or something like. With people one must at least seem to make sense. So General de Gaulle, facing an enraged crowd of *pieds noirs*[2] demonstrating against Algerian independence, told them majestically, "Je vous ai compris," extricated himself from the situation amid cheers, and once in Paris did exactly what they did *not* want, and which he'd intended to do all along.

Euphemisms thus serve as verbal placebos; they are particularly frequent when the ill-timed provocation could expose one to instant retaliation. Sports figures are always careful to speak with respect, even admiration, of their upcoming opponents, however inept. Precautionary and placatory euphemisms include variations on the theme, "They're a much better team than their record shows," and that minimal, threadbare uncompliment, "They never give up." Everywhere except in politics (where it's accepted practice to toot one's own horn as loudly as possible), false modesty is useful protection against overconfidence on one's own part and provocation of the opponent.

Though they commonly involve just language, euphemisms may be expressed in other sorts of signs, as when a hotel numbers its floors "11, 12, 12A, 14," etc., or omits room number 13 entirely. It is a euphemism of sorts when the price of a product is pegged at $9.99—"*under* ten dollars," as the commercials will say. The language of gesture may frequently, though it doesn't necessarily, involve euphemism, as in gestures warding off the evil eye or averting bad luck, which comfort the enactor without requiring him to face or profess a belief of which he is probably ashamed or afraid. Marble fig-leaves on statues and overpainted loincloths on pictures are visual euphemisms; Yahveh or Jhvh, the Tetragrammaton,[3] was such a sacred and terrible name that it must not be pronounced, and eternal penalties were reserved for those who did so: Adonai was substituted as a euphemism, but most commonly mumbled in the public services to prevent anyone from hearing, still less understanding it.

Polite applause at a musical concert one didn't really enjoy, but which showed good will on the part of the performers, is a generally accepted form of social evasion—anywhere but in the opera house at Parma; so is the adjective "interesting," or one of its many devious equivalents, when one is buttonholed in a gallery by the artist demanding to know what one thinks of his work. Placebo answers to awkward questions are legitimate escape-hatches; but the non-statement may have aggressive aspects too.

Pornographic film advertisements ostentatiously decline to list the title
of the skin-flick presently showing, on the score that it's too raunchy, too
offensive for the public prints. That being just what the owners know
their customers want, avoiding real words enables them to have it both
ways. And from this moral highland, we look out on the tumultuous
ocean of commercial sharp practice, with its "pre-owned" automobiles
(in the last stages of disintegration), its "cozy" houses (the size of a
postage stamp), its "natural" or "organic" foods (distinguished from
others only by the exorbitant price) and its "40 per cent off" (off what?)
sales. Folk wisdom enshrines warnings against many of these euphemistic formulas, as in the excellent advice never to eat in a restaurant that
advertises "home cooking," never to play poker with a man known as
"Doc," and never to buy a used car from a man calling himself "Honest
John" or the equivalent thereof.

Special interest groups require special vocabularies, sometimes active
formulas, sometimes avoidance devices, to urge their point of view
without presenting it. Stores in America seem to vie with one another in
seeking euphemistic variations on the blunt old "No Smoking" sign.
"Please try not to smoke" is one plaintive formula; "Thank you for not
smoking" assumes you have already obeyed instructions you have not yet
received; and "Our customers thank you for not smoking" puts the whole
responsibility on some hypothetical customers who (for all anybody
knows) may themselves be sheepish, brow-beaten would-be smokers.
The new puritanism implicit in the women's movement shows itself,
among other places, in a demand for fresh euphemisms, new restrictions
on the traditional English vocabulary. You cannot refer to any female
over the age of three as a "girl"; indeed, even under the age of three, it's
better described as a "child." You cannot refer to the "chairman" or even
the "chairperson" of an organization; male, female, or *tertium quid*,[4] it
must be the "chair"—which is not so bad, considering that some of them
might just as well be pieces of furniture. You cannot mention "bluestockings" for literary ladies, even of an age when the term was commonly
accepted; you cannot intimate that Henry VIII found Anne of Cleves
physically unattractive, since this is treating her as a "sex-object."[5]
Marxist or would-be Marxist historians have their taboos and fetishes as
well, in equal quantity and of equal grossness. One cannot use the
standard eighteenth-century word for a violent crowd, "mob"—rather,
one must circumlocute, periphrase, or euphemize to "the people," or
"the working class," expressions which don't mean the same thing at all.
The same ideologues object to any expression implying disapproval of

4. *Tertium quid*: a middle course, a compromise term.
5. Bluestockings: originally referring to women members of literary clubs; Anne of
Cleves (1515–57): the fourth queen consort
of Henry VIII of England, not known for
beauty.

the Paris massacres of September 1792; large numbers of royalist or accused royalist prisoners were dragged from their cells and murdered out of hand by vigilante gangs. Apparently the proper name for this process is "people's justice," or something like that.

In the euphemistic expression "that's a lot of bull" (to make an easy transition), we recognize the operation of that synecdoche where the whole is asked to stand for the part; in a whole range of softened expletives, from "darn" and "drat" to "Jiminy Christmas" and "by Jove," we recognize deformation. In the "bl" combination which gives us "blasted," "blooming," "blighter," and "bloody" we must have something like onomatopoeia at work. (The sound of the word does duty for any sense it might have, as in the "bleep" which designates an obscenity erased from a tape. Even "blessed," directly opposite in overt meaning, is sometimes co-opted, because of its sound, to the services of profanity— the ultimate euphemism.) Foreign languages used to, and occasionally still do, provide evasion devices. Latin was retained in translations of ancient texts when one wanted the reader to work so hard deciphering it that all obscene pleasures would be obliterated by the labor of translation. French can also be used to circumlocute English tongue-tiedness in expressions like *ménage à trois*[6] or *double entendre*, and Dickens uses the foreign idiom to bury a fecal joke in the name of Mr. Murdstone. Foreign languages reciprocate sometimes by using English expressions where the explicit term in their own tongue would be either unrespectable or illegal. There are cities in Mexico where the expression "Ladies Bar" is euphemistic for "whorehouse."[7]

Emerging social customs create situations for which there really are no words other than euphemisms. In modern America, it is a stock dilemma what to call the young man who shares an apartment with one's daughter, or the young woman with whom one's son happens to be cohabiting. "Lover" and "mistress" imply high passion where often enough a dominant concern is economy; "room-mate," "companion," and "friend" ignore the sexual component entirely, they are euphemisms simon-pure. Some semi-humorous acronyms have been proposed, but none really satisfactory; the term which finally meets the need may be a euphemism to start, but it will not long be felt as one. If shacking-up persists as a custom, the normal word will have to be created, no doubt with satellite euphemisms and dysphemisms around it.[8] The malady syphilis went

6. *Ménage à trois*: three persons living together, two of whom are often married, all of whom share sexual relationships; *double entendre*: literally "double meaning" or "double intent," an ambiguous expression, one meaning of which is often indecent.

7. "Whorehouse" has a tease-fascination for Americans. There is a not-inexpensive restaurant in my town called the "Ore House," and a record shop known as the "Warehouse." Flirting with the taboo word apparently makes the name of an establishment particularly memorable; the accepted euphemism in places like Nevada is, I believe, "Guest Ranch" [author's note].

8. *Dys-* is a prefix meaning "hard" or "bad,"

through a long search for a proper name, various nations and cities all attributing it to one another, analogies with the smallpox asserting their claim, lues and buboes being suggested (no doubt) by the plague. Only the accident of Fracastoro's[9] erudite pastoral contributed the "normal" English name of the disease, more than 200 years after this affliction first appeared in the West. (The poem itself was written in 1530; OED dates the first appearance of the word in English as 1718.) In fact, "syphilis" is a rather remote and allusive euphemism, without even the poor excuse that "St. Vitus's dance" has to be the popular name of chorea[1] (prayer to the saint was said to cure it) or that St. Cecilia has to be the patroness of music (she was notably incompetent at it).

"Chrétien"—Christian—was a kindly euphemism at first for the goiterous idiots who during the Middle Ages inhabited the high Alpine meadows; they too, the word implied, were members of the Christian community, God's sacred simpletons. Corrupted, adapted to English, and tuned to dysphemistic ends, it became "cretin," a term of genera-lized abuse for the stupid. When she was thought to possess occult powers, the name of "witch" may have been a kind of placatory euphe-mism, meaning "the person who knows." As time and competition diminished the witch's prestige, her former euphemism dwindled to a term of contempt. Some violations of the taboos cut so deeply against the grain that there is no way to euphemize them. Though we have many alternative ways to take the edge off words like "murder," "robbery," and "fraud," there are no current euphemisms for "parricide," "rape," and "incest"; perhaps in the happier non-judgmental society to come, the gentler formulas will be invented and domesticated.

Evidently, it's better to think of euphemisms as a variety of processes rather than a collection of expressions; and, given the variety of human judgments, it's more than likely that one man's euphemism will be another man's dysphemism. Once in Japan, I attended a concert of gagaku music with a Japanese couple; at intermission, they asked what I thought of it, and with some hesitation over the implied dispraise, I said gently that I thought it was very melancholy and a bit monotonous. They were enraptured. "Indeed, indeed it is," they cried. "Melancholy and monotonous, just so!" And it was clear I could not have paid a higher tribute. Proust's Albertine[2] was an animated euphemism, and it's not hard to think of novels, from *Tom Jones* to *Felix Krull*, where a love affair serves as a euphemistic cover for social ambition. Petrarch used Laura in good part as a euphemism for poetic fame, and poor Charlotte Haze was a

---

the opposite of *eu-*.
9. Girolamo Fracastoro (1483–1553): an Ital-ian poet, author of the poem (in Latin) *Syphilis; or, the French Disease.*
1. Chorea: a disease causing muscular spasms.

2. Albertine: lesbian protagonist in Marcel Proust's novel *Remembrance of Things Past;* Laura: idealized heroine of Petrarch's son-nets; Charlotte Haze: mother of Lolita in the novel of that name by Vladimir Nabokov.

social euphemism used by Humbert Humbert to mask his pursuit of her fatal daughter. A living euphemism is sometimes known by the alternative name of a "stuffed shirt."

So prevalent and protean is it, that one could argue that euphemism is an essential element of a pluralist society. My particular bent (line of interest, moral slant, or intellectual commitment) is repugnant or ridiculous to others, as theirs are to me. Probably I can learn to tolerate their idiocies; what is much harder to appreciate is that they, in their folly, are politely tolerating me. Euphemisms not only soften disagreeable qualities of the outside world, they may be used to smooth asperities of our own egotistical judgments—thereby keeping us out of jail and on bearable terms with our like-them-or-not associates. The abuse of the process is weaseling, waffling, and something very close to straight lying; its proper use lies in fostering that mutual consideration which underlies civilized conduct and conversation.

Yet a pluralistic society deeply aware of the fragility of its own conventions—challenged as they have been by wars, holocausts, ideologies, social breakdowns, class conflicts, and the abiding mistrust the society has earned by its endless capacity for deception and self-deception—cannot help being uneasy in the presence of euphemisms. That, I suppose, is one rationale for the present volume. The subject cries out for analysis, and the question it poses is basic. How do we distinguish the fraudulent from the authentic euphemism, the specious moral pickpocket from the considerate and soft-spoken idealist? Since in their pure form both types are relatively infrequent, the permutations and combinations are what we must deal with; and here I confess to feeling the study of language does not help much. The mind and the intentions behind it are far subtler than the verbal makeshifts and stuttering formulas with which we try to define its devious workings. Milton said it once and for all:

> For neither man nor angel can discern
> Hypocrisy, the only evil that walks
> Invisible . . .

1985

THE READER

1. What does Adams regard as the basic nature or "root act" of euphemism? What several and different uses for euphemism does he suggest? Are any of these surprising, ones you had not previously thought of? Are there any uses of euphemism that he does not include in his account?

2. Are euphemisms preferable to dysphemisms or vice versa? Why, or why not? Adams suggests that certain situations seem to demand

dysphemism, as a sort of thoughtless or conventional abasement, as much as other situations seem to call for euphemism. What are some of these situations? Can you think of others?

3. *Does Adams treat euphemism primarily as a matter of language or as a matter of modes of thought and behavior? What does he suggest is the relationship among these matters?*

4. *What is the relationship between euphemism and hypocrisy? How much hypocrisy, in your opinion, does daily life require?*

THE WRITER

1. *Throughout his essay, Adams gives many examples of euphemism drawn from many fields (such as social science) and contexts (life in a democratic or pluralistic society). Do these examples contribute to the definition of his subject? Do they confuse the subject?*

2. *Go through one day, noting down instances of euphemism you hear in speech or read in the newspapers for that day. Write an account of these. Are they all of one kind, or do they seem to have various uses? Are they ludicrous? Harmless? Vapid? Boring? Sinister? Necessary?*

3. *Adams suggests that sometimes what was once euphemism becomes dysphemism. Write a brief essay tracing that transformation in one particular expression that he notes or in another that you are familiar with. Explore what you take to be the reasons for that transformation.*

4. *One might infer from Adams that some euphemisms are institutional —that is, as essential feature of a given field or activity (e.g., sports, discussion of public issues, academic discourse). Choose a field or an activity with which you are familiar, and write an essay on the uses and abuses of euphemism in that particular sphere.*

John Leo

JOURNALESE FOR THE LAY READER

Journalese, the native tongue of newsgatherers and pundits, retains a faint similarity to English but is actually closer to Latin. Like Latin, it is primarily a written language, prized for its incantatory powers, and is best learned early, while the mind is still supple. Every cub reporter, for instance, knows that fires rage out of control, minor mischief is perpetrated by Vandals (never Visigoths, Franks, or a single Vandal working alone) and key labor accords are hammered out by weary negotiators in marathon, round-the-clock bargaining sessions, thus narrowly averting threatened walkouts. The discipline required for a winter storm report is awesome. The first reference to seasonal precipitation is "snow," followed by "the white stuff," then either "it" or "the flakes," but not both.

The word snow may be used once again toward the end of the report, directly after discussion of ice-slicked roads and the grim highway toll.

Every so often, an inexperienced reporter attempts to describe a dwelling as "attractive" or "impressive." This is incorrect. In journalese, all homes are either modest or stately. When confronted with a truly ramshackle fixer-upper, knowing scribes will deflect attention to the surrounding area, describing the residence as "off the beaten track" or "in a developing area," that is, a slum. Distaste for the suburbs is conveyed by mentioning "trimmed lawns and neat flower beds," thus artfully suggesting both compulsiveness and a high level of intolerance for life in its hearty, untrimmed state.

Journalese is rich in mystic nouns: gentrification, quichification, greenmail, dealignment, watershed elections and apron strings (the political coattails of a female candidate). But students of the language agree that adjectives do most of the work, smuggling in actual information under the guise of normal journalism. Thus the use of soft-spoken (mousy), loyal (dumb), high-minded (inept), hardworking (plodding), self-made (crooked) and pragmatic (totally immoral). A person who is dangerous as well as immoral can be described as a fierce competitor or gut fighter, and a meddler who cannot leave his subordinates alone is a hands-on executive. When strung together properly, apparently innocent modifiers can acquire megaton force. For instance, a journalist may write, "A private, deliberate man, Frobisher dislikes small talk, but can be charming when he wants to." In translation this means, "An antisocial, sullen plodder, Frobisher is obnoxious and about as articulate as a canteloupe." The familiar phrase "can be charming" is as central to good journalese as "affordable" is to automobile ads and "excellence" is to education reports. It indicates that Frobisher's charm production is a rare result of mighty exertion, yet it manages to end the revelation about his dismal character on an upbeat note.

"Spry" refers to any senior citizen who is not in a wheelchair or a coma, and "stereotype" introduces the discussion of something entirely obvious that the writer wishes to disparage, as in "the stereotype that boys like to play with trucks and girls like to play with dolls." "Life-style" has made the transition from psychobabble to journalese. Though often misused to indicate gays, joggers, wheat-germ consumers and other defiant minorities, it actually refers to any practice that makes the normal citizen's hair stand on end. The fellow who tortures iguanas in his basement has a life-style. The rest of us merely have lives.

Many terms in journalese come from sportswriting. "A complex, sensitive man" (lunatic) and "ebullient" (space cadet) were developed by baseball writers. When baseball players of the 1940s and 1950s were fined for the usual excesses with women and booze, the writers faithfully reported that the penalties were for "nightclubbing." Nowadays the vast consumption of controlled and uncontrolled substances would be covered by circumlocutions like "he works hard and he plays hard." Sportswriters also taught journalese users how to recast a boring story with exciting verbiage. Hence all the crucial issues, dramatic confrontations and stunning breakthroughs. "Arguably" is the most useful adverb on the excitement frontier, because it introduces a sweeping factoid that no one will be able to check: "Frobisher is arguably the richest Rotarian living west of the Susquehanna."

Often English words mean exactly the opposite in journalese. "Multitalented" means "untalented" and is used to identify entertainers who have great pep and perspire a lot but do nothing particularly well. "Community" means non-community, as in the intelligence community, the gay community or the journalese-speaking community. Under this usage, everyone shooting everyone else in and around Beirut, say, could be fairly referred to as the Lebanese community.

"Middle America" has disappeared from political journalese, for the simple reason that in the Age of Reagan, America is all middle, with no edges. Similarly, yesterday's "radical right-winger" is today's "mainstream Republican," while "unabashed" now modifies "liberal" instead of "conservative." Yet most political journalese is timeless. A "savvy political pro" is anyone who has lived through two or more Administrations and can still get a table in a decent restaurant. An elder stateman is an out-of-office politician who is senile, and a neoliberal is any Democrat under 45 with blow-dried hair. All seasoned reporters (old-timers) know that when two or more political appointees are fired on the same day, they need only check their calendars before tapping out "Bloody Wednesday" or "the Thursday Early-Afternoon Massacre." Political journalese has a number of famed option plays. One man's squealer is another's whistle blower, and Frobisher's magnificent five-point agenda can also be described as a shopping list, or worse, a wish list.

One inflexible rule of journalese is that American assassins must have three names: John Wilkes Booth, Lee Harvey Oswald, James Earl Ray, Mark David Chapman. This courtesy of a resonant three-part moniker is also applied to other dangerous folk. This is why the "subway vigilante" is "Bernhard Hugo Goetz" to many journalists who consider him a monster, and just plain "Bernhard Goetz" to almost everyone else. Another rule of the language is that euphemisms for "fat" are understood too quickly by the public and are therefore in constant need of replacement. "Jolly," "Rubenesque" and the like have long been abandoned. A Washington writer scored by praising a woman's "Wagnerian good looks," which is far more polite than saying she is not bad looking for a massive Brünnhilde. The disinfecting compliment is particularly deft. As all practitioners know, a corrective lurch toward balance is the hallmark of good journalese. After all, journalism is a crucially important field that attracts high-minded, multitalented professionals, arguably the finest in the land.

1985

THE READER

1. What are the major characteristics of journalese? What purposes does it serve?
2. Read Orwell's "Politics and the English Language" (p. 353). How does Orwell's tone differ from Leo's? What might Orwell say about Leo's essay?
3. What is Leo doing in his last sentence?

THE WRITER

1. What techniques does Leo use in giving his definition of journalese?
2. How does Leo's use of humor contribute to the effectiveness of his essay?
3. Write a brief sketch of a person or an account of an event. Then rewrite it in journalese as Leo defines and describes it. What are the differences?
4. Write a brief comparison of Leo's journalese with Mencken's Gamalielese (below). What characteristics do they share? How are they different?

H. L. Mencken

GAMALIELESE[1]

On the question of the logical content of Dr. Harding's harangue of last Friday I do not presume to have views. The matter has been debated at great length by the editorial writers of the Republic, all of them experts in logic; moreover, I confess to being prejudiced. When a man arises publicly to argue that the United States entered the late war because of a "concern for preserved civilization," I can only snicker in a superior way and wonder why he isn't holding down the chair of history in some American university. When he says that the U.S. has "never sought territorial aggrandizement through force," the snicker rises to the virulence of a chuckle, and I turn to the first volume of General Grant's memoirs.[2] And when, gaining momentum, he gravely informs the boobery that "ours is a constitutional freedom where the popular will is supreme, and minorities are sacredly protected," then I abandon myself

1. Gamaliel was President Warren Harding's middle name, here nominalized to identify his oratorical style.

2. Dealing with the Mexican-American War (1846–48), in some respects a land-grabbing venture.

to a mirth that transcends, perhaps, the seemly, and send picture post-cards of A. Mitchell Palmer,[3] and the Atlanta Penitentiary to all of my enemies who happen to be Socialists.

But when it comes to the style of a great man's discourse, I can speak with a great deal less prejudice, and maybe with somewhat more compe-tence, for I have earned most of my livelihood for twenty years past by translating the bad English of a multitude of authors into measurably better English. Thus qualified professionally, I rise to pay my small tribute to Dr. Harding. Setting aside a college professor or two and half a dozen dipsomaniacal newspaper reporters, he takes the first place in my Valhall of literati. That is to say, he writes the worst English that I have ever encountered. It reminds me of a string of wet sponges; it reminds me of tattered washing on the line; it reminds me of a stale bean-soup, of college yells, of dogs barking idiotically through endless nights. It is so bad that a sort of grandeur creeps into it. It drags itself out of the dark abysm (I was about to write abscess!) of pish, and crawls insanely up the topmost pinnacle of posh. It is rumble and bumble. It is flap and doodle. It is balder and dash.

But I grow lyrical. More scientifically, what is the matter with it? Why does it seem so flabby, so banal, so confused and childish, so stupidly at war with sense? If you first read the inaugural address and then heard it intoned, as I did (at least in part), then you will perhaps arrive at an answer. That answer is very simple. When Dr. Harding prepares a speech he does not think it out in terms of an educated reader locked up in jail, but in terms of a great horde of stoneheads gathered around a stand. That is to say, the thing is always a stump speech; it is conceived as a stump speech and written as a stump speech. More, it is a stump speech addressed primarily to the sort of audience that the speaker has been used to all his life, to wit, an audience of small town yokels, of low political serfs, or morons scarcely able to understand a word of more than two syllables, and wholly unable to pursue a logical idea for more than two centimeters.

Such imbeciles do not want ideas—that is, new ideas, ideas that are unfamiliar, ideas that challenge their attention. What they want is sim-ply a gaudy series of platitudes, of threadbare phrases terrifically re-peated, of sonorous nonsense driven home with gestures. As I say, they can't understand many words of more than two syllables, but that is not saying that they do not esteem such words. On the contrary, they like them and demand them. The roll of incomprehensible polysyllables enchants them. They like phrases which thunder like salvos of artillery. Let that thunder sound, and they take all the rest on trust. If a sentence begins furiously and then peters out into fatuity, they are still satisfied. If

3. A. Mitchell Palmer: U.S. attorney general (1919–21), initiator of the "Palmer Raids" in which thousands of alleged subversives were arrested for deportation.

a phrase has a punch in it, they do not ask that it also have a meaning. If a word slides off the tongue like a ship going down the ways, they are content and applaud it and wait for the next.

Brought up amid such hinds, trained by long practice to engage and delight them, Dr. Harding carries over his stump manner into everything he writes. He is, perhaps, too old to learn a better way. He is, more likely, too discreet to experiment. The stump speech, put into cold type, maketh the judicious to grieve. But roared from an actual stump, with arms flying and eyes flashing and the old flag overhead, it is certainly and brilliantly effective. Read the inaugural address, and it will gag you. But hear it recited through a sound-magnifier, with grand gestures to ram home its periods, and you will begin to understand it.

Let us turn to a specific example. I exhume a sentence from the latter half of the eminent orator's discourse:

"I would like government to do all it can to mitigate; then, in understanding, in mutuality of interest, in concern for the common good, our tasks will be solved."

I assume that you have read it. I also assume that you set it down as idiotic—a series of words without sense. You are quite right; it is. But now imagine it intoned as it was designed to be intoned. Imagine the slow tempo of a public speech. Imagine the stately unrolling of the first clause, the delicate pause upon the word "then"—and then the loud discharge of the phrases "in understanding," "in mutuality of interest," "in concern for the common good," each with its attendant glare and roll of the eyes, each with its sublime heave, each with its gesture of a blacksmith bringing down his sledge upon an egg—imagine all this, and then ask yourself where you have got. You have got, in brief, to a point where you don't know what it is all about. You hear and applaud the phrases, but their connection has already escaped you. And so, when in violation of all sequence and logic, the final phrase, "our tasks will be solved," assaults you, you do not notice its disharmony—all you notice is that, if this or that, already forgotten, is done, "our tasks will be solved." Whereupon, glad of the assurance and thrilled by the vast gestures that drive it home, you give a cheer.

That is, if you are the sort of man who goes to political meetings, which is to say, if you are the sort of man that Dr. Harding is used to talking to, which is to say, if you are a jackass.

The whole inaugural address reeked with just such nonsense. The thing started off with an error in English in its very first sentence—the confusion of pronouns in the one-he combination, so beloved of bad newspaper reporters. It bristled with words misused; civic for civil, luring for alluring, womanhood for women, referendum for reference, even task for problem. "The task is to be solved"—what could be worse? Yet I find it twice. "The expressed views of world opinion"—what irritating tautology! "The expressed conscience of progress"—what on earth does it mean? "This is not selfishness, it is sanctity"—what intelligible idea do you get out of that? "I know that Congress and the administration will favor every wise government policy to aid the resumption and encourage continued progress"—the resumption of what? "Service is the supreme commitment of life"—*ach, du heiliger!*[4]

But is such bosh out of place in a stump speech? Obviously not. It is precisely and thoroughly in place in a stump speech. A tight fabric of ideas would weary and exasperate the audience; what it wants is simply a loud burble of words, a procession of phrases that roar, a series of whoops. This is what it got in the inaugural address of the Hon. Warren Gamaliel Harding. And this is what it will get for four long years—unless God sends a miracle and the corruptible puts on incorruption . . . Almost I long for the sweeter song, the rubber-stamps of more familiar design, the gentler and more seemly bosh of the late Woodrow.

1921

4. "Good Lord!"

THE READER

1. What are the particular qualities of "Gamalielese," as Mencken uses the term? What are Mencken's specific objections to Gamalielese? Why, if it works so well as a political speech, should we care if the English isn't too good? Mencken says he is talking about the style rather than the content, but what does style matter except to people like Mencken and English teachers and language cops?
2. Mencken writes, "When a man arises publicly to argue that the United States entered the late war because of a 'concern for preserved civilization,' I can only snicker in a superior way and wonder why he isn't holding down the chair of history in some American university" (p. 301). In this sentence, Mencken is fighting on two fronts at once. What are the two objects of his attack? Why in his essay does he use "Dr. Harding" for "President Harding"?
3. Mencken characterizes President Harding's usual audience as "stoneheads," "yokels," "serfs," "morons," "imbeciles," and "hinds." Is this a fair characterization of the American public? Should Mencken have used euphemisms?

THE WRITER

1. What is the purpose of Mencken's essay? What is its tone? How would you describe its intended audience?
2. Write a brief essay comparing "Gamalielese" and "journalese" (Leo, p. 298).
3. Write a brief essay explaining the following poem by E. E. Cummings. Is the characterization of President Harding and his style similar to that in Mencken's characterization?

XXVII

the first president to be loved by his
bitterest enemies" is dead

the only man woman or child who wrote
a simple declarative sentence with seven grammatical
errors "is dead"
beautiful Warren Gamaliel Harding
"is" dead
he's
"dead"
if he wouldn't have eaten them Yapanese Craps

somebody might hardly never have not been unsorry,perhaps

—E. E. Cummings, from ViVa, 1931

Gloria Naylor

"MOMMY, WHAT DOES 'NIGGER' MEAN?"

Language is the subject. It is the written form with which I've managed to keep the wolf away from the door and, in diaries, to keep my sanity. In spite of this, I consider the written word inferior to the spoken, and much of the frustration experienced by novelists is the awareness that whatever we manage to capture in even the most transcendent passages falls far short of the richness of life. Dialogue achieves its power in the dynamics of a fleeting moment of sight, sound, smell and touch.

I'm not going to enter the debate here about whether it is language that shapes reality or vice versa. That battle is doomed to be waged whenever we seek intermittent reprieve from the chicken and egg dispute. I will simply take the position that the spoken word, like the written word, amounts to a nonsensical arrangement of sounds or letters without a consensus that assigns "meaning." And building from the meanings of what we hear, we order reality. Words themselves are innocuous; it is the consensus that gives them true power.

I remember the first time I heard the word nigger. In my third-grade class, our math tests were being passed down the rows, and as I handed the papers to a little boy in back of me, I remarked that once again he had received a much lower mark than I did. He snatched his test from me and spit out that word. Had he called me a nymphomaniac or a necrophiliac, I couldn't have been more puzzled. I didn't know what a nigger was, but I knew that whatever it meant, it was something he shouldn't have called me. This was verified when I raised my hand, and in a loud voice repeated what he had said and watched the teacher scold him for using a "bad" word. I was later to go home and ask the inevitable question that every black parent must face—"Mommy, what does 'nigger' mean?"

And what exactly did it mean? Thinking back, I realize that this could not have been the first time the word was used in my presence. I was part of a large extended family that had migrated from the rural South after World War II and formed a close-knit network that gravitated around my maternal grandparents. Their ground-floor apartment in one of the buildings they owned in Harlem was a weekend mecca for my immediate family, along with countless aunts, uncles and cousins who brought along assorted friends. It was a bustling and open house with assorted neighbors and tenants popping in and out to exchange bits of gossip, pick up an old quarrel or referee the ongoing checkers game in which my grandmother cheated shamelessly. They were all there to let down their hair and put up their feet after a week of labor in the factories, laundries and shipyards of New York.

Amid the clamor, which could reach deafening proportions—two or three conversations going on simultaneously, punctuated by the sound of a baby's crying somewhere in the back rooms or out on the street—there was still a rigid set of rules about what was said and how. Older children were sent out of the living room when it was time to get into the juicy details about "you-know-who" up on the third floor who had gone and gotten herself "p-r-e-g-n-a-n-t!" But my parents, knowing that I could spell well beyond my years, always demanded that I follow the others out to play. Beyond sexual misconduct and death, everything else was considered harmless for our young ears. And so among the anecdotes of the triumphs and disappointments in the various workings of their lives, the word nigger was used in my presence, but it was set within contexts and inflections that caused it to register in my mind as something else.

In the singular, the word was always applied to a man who had distinguished himself in some situation that brought their approval for his strength, intelligence or drive:

"Did Johnny really do that?"

"I'm telling you, that nigger pulled in $6,000 of overtime last year. Said he got enough for a down payment on a house."

When used with a possessive adjective by a woman—"my nigger"—it became a term of endearment for husband or boyfriend. But it could be more than just a term applied to a man. In their mouths it became the pure essence of manhood—a disembodied force that channeled their past history of struggle and present survival against the odds into a victorious statement of being: "Yeah, that old foreman found out quick enough—you don't mess with a nigger."

In the plural, it became a description of some group within the community that had overstepped the bounds of decency as my family defined it: Parents who neglected their children, a drunken couple who fought in public, people who simply refused to look for work, those with excessively dirty mouths or unkempt households were all "trifling niggers." This particular circle could forgive hard times, unemployment, the occasional bout of depression—they had gone through all of that themselves—but the unforgivable sin was lack of self-respect.

A woman could never be a "nigger" in the singular, with its connotation of confirming worth. The noun girl was its closest equivalent in that sense, but only when used in direct address and regardless of the gender doing the addressing. "Girl" was a token of respect for a woman. The one-syllable word was drawn out to sound like three in recognition of the extra ounce of wit, nerve or daring that the woman had shown in the situation under discussion.

"G-i-r-l, stop. You mean you said that to his face?"

But if the word was used in a third-person reference or shortened so that it almost snapped out of the mouth, it always involved some element of communal disapproval. And age became an important factor in these exchanges. It was only between individuals of the same generation, or from an older person to a younger (but never the other way around), that "girl" would be considered a compliment.

I don't agree with the argument that use of the word nigger at this social stratum of the black community was an internalization of racism. The dynamics were the exact opposite: the people in my grandmother's living room took a word that whites used to signify worthlessness or degradation and rendered it impotent. Gathering there together, they transformed "nigger" to signify the varied and complex human beings they knew themselves to be. If the word was to disappear totally from the mouths of even the most liberal of white society, no one in that room was naïve enough to believe it would disappear from white minds. Meeting the word head-on, they proved it had absolutely nothing to do with the way they were determined to live their lives.

So there must have been dozens of times that the word "nigger" was spoken in front of me before I reached the third grade. But I didn't "hear" it until it was said by a small pair of lips that had already learned it could be a way to humiliate me. That was the word I went home and asked my mother about. And since she knew that I had to grow up in America, she took me in her lap and explained.

1986

Robert Burchfield

DICTIONARIES AND ETHNIC SENSIBILITIES

At the beginning of *Macbeth*, a bleeding sergeant describes how brave Macbeth killed the "merciless" rebel, Macdonwald: "he unseamed him from the nave to th' chaps," that is, from the navel to the jaws, "and fixed his head upon our battlements." It may seem a far cry from the rebellious "kerns and gallow-glasses"[1] of Macdonwald to the persevering scholarship involved in dictionary editing, but the connection will be made clear as I proceed.

The head some want to display on the battlements is that of a dictionary, or of its publishers, and, especially, any dictionary that records a meaning that is unacceptable or at best unwelcome to the person or group on the warpath. The ferocity of such assaults is almost unbelievable except as a by-product of what Professor Trevor-Roper calls the twentieth-century "epidemic fury of ideological belief." Key words are *Jew, Palestinian, Arab, Pakistan, Turk, Asiatic, Muhammadan,* and *Negro,* and there are others.

It is impossible to discover exactly when the battle cry was first heard, but certainly by the 1920s a pattern of protest existed. In the *Jewish Chronicle* of 24 October 1924, a leading article expressed "no small gratification" that, in deference to complaints that had been published in the *Jewish Chronicle*, the delegates of the Clarendon Press had decided that the "sinister meaning" attached to the word *Jew* (that is, the meaning "unscrupulous usurer or bargainer," and the corresponding verb meaning "to cheat, overreach") should be labeled to make it clear that it was a derogatory use. The *Jewish Chronicle* had maintained that users of the *Pocket Oxford Dictionary* would conclude that "every Jew is essentially the sort of person thus described." Mr. R. W. Chapman, who at that time was the head of the section of OUP which publishes dictionaries, replied that "it is no part of the duty of a lexicographer to pass judgment on the justice or propriety of current usage." The editor of the *Pocket Oxford Dictionary*, the legendary H. W. Fowler, in a letter to Chapman declared:

> The dictionary-maker has to record what people say, not what he thinks they can politely say: how will you draw the line between this insult to a nation and such others as 'Dutch courage', 'French leave', 'Punic faith', the 'Huns', 'a nation of shopkeepers', and hundreds more? The real question is not whether a phrase is rude, but whether it is current.

1. *Macbeth* I.ii.13: light and heavy infantry.

The *Pocket Oxford* and other Oxford dictionaries, and dictionaries elsewhere, labeled the "sinister meaning" of the word *Jew* "derogatory," "opprobrious," or the like, and an uneasy peace was established. But not for long. Some other "sinister" meanings in the *Pocket Oxford* were pointed out. "*Turk*: Member of the Ottoman race; unmanageable child." "*Tartar*: native of Tartary (etc.); intractable person or awkward customer." "*Jesuit*: member of Society of Jesus (etc.); deceitful person."

Fowler felt that he was being incited, as he said, "to assume an autocratic control of the language and put to death all the words and phrases that do not enjoy our approval." He maintained that the *POD* was not keeping the incriminated senses alive but that, unfortunately, they were not in danger of dying. In a letter to Kenneth Sisam in September 1924, he insisted: "I should like to repeat that I have neither religious, political, nor social antipathy to Jews"—nor, by implication, to Turks, Tartars, or Jesuits. The episode passed, but was not forgotten. The *Jewish Chronicle* at that time appeared to be satisfied by an assurance that the unfavorable senses would be labeled as such. They did not ask for, far less demand, the exclusion of the disapproved meanings.

In the United States in the 1920s, a parallel protest movement aimed at the compulsory capitalization of the initial letter of the word *Negro* and the abandonment, except among black inhabitants of the States, of the word *nigger*. Again, dictionaries were among the main targets, and here, too the lexicographers replied that if writers, including the editors of newspapers, used a capital initial for *Negro*, they would themselves be happy to include this form in their dictionaries, and to give it priority if it became the dominant form in print.

A half-century later, it is easy to see that the lexicographers had "scotch'd the snake, not killed it."[2] Resentment smoldered away in certain quarters, and the issues were brought out into the open again after the 1939–1945 war. But this time there was a difference. Dictionaries remained a prime target, but the protesters brought new assault techniques to bear, especially the threat of sanctions if the lexicographers did not come to heel. Now, dictionary editors, judged by the standards of the broad world, are a soft target. With little personal experience of the broil that forms the daily experience of, for example, politicians, newspaper editors, and psychiatrists, editors of dictionaries tend to be too unworldly and too disdainfully scholarly to recognize the severity of an assault made on them. What is this assault and what form does it take? Quite simply, it is a concerted attempt by various pressure groups to force dictionary editors to give up recording the factual unpleasantnesses of our times and to abandon the tradition of setting down the language as it is actually used, however disagreeable, regrettable, or uncongenial the

2. *Macbeth* III.ii.13.

use.

Two definitions in the *Concise Oxford Dictionary*, one in the early fifties and the other in 1976, exacerbated things. One concerned the word *Pakistan*, and the other, the word *Palestinian*. The editor of the *Concise Oxford Dictionary* unwisely entered the word *Pakistan* in his dictionary in 1951—unwisely, because names of countries as such do not qualify for an entry in Oxford dictionaries—and defined it as "a separate Moslem State in India, Moslem autonomy; (from 1947) the independent Moslem Dominion in India."

It lay apparently unnoticed until 1959, when somebody must have pointed it out. The Pakistanis, understandably, were outraged, and called for a ban on the *COD* in Pakistan and for all unsold copies in Pakistan to be confiscated. The OUP admitted that the definition was "tactless" and "locally irritating," but pointed out that the intention had been to show that Pakistan was in the familiar, triangular section of territory which had always been called India on maps and in geography books. No political motive was in question. The Karachi police raided bookstalls in the city and seized 215 copies of the fourth edition of the *COD*. They also raided the Karachi office of the OUP, and seized the only copy of the dictionary on the premises, which was, in fact, the typist's copy. Copies in government offices were commandeered by the police, and apparently hundreds of copies were collected from public offices, schools, and colleges.

After high-level discussion, the Pakistan government decided to lift its ban on the *COD* in November 1959, after receiving an undertaking by the OUP to issue a correction slip for insertion in all copies of *COD* sold in Pakistan, and to enter a new definition in the next impression of the dictionary. Later, a more permanent solution was found when the word *Pakistan* was dropped from the main-line Oxford dictionaries altogether, as a proper name with no other meanings. It remains in the semi-encyclopedic *Oxford Illustrated Dictionary*, where it is defined as "Muslim State in SE Asia, formed in 1947 from regions where Muslims predominated."

This was a striking example of the serious consequences arising from a simple error of judgment by a lexicographer. There were other minor skirmishes, for example, when it was noticed that the definition of the word *American* in some of the Oxford dictionaries failed to allow for the existence of black Americans and of Latin Americans. The dictionary editors gladly revised the definitions and brought them up to date with a minimum of fuss and with no heat generated on either side.

However, the problem of the word *Jew* kept returning in an increasingly dramatic way. Some correspondents contrasted the derogatory definitions of *Jew* with the colloquial senses of the word *Christian*. *Christian* is defined as "a human being, as distinguished from a brute," for example, in Shaftesbury (1714): "The very word Christian is, in common language, us'd for Man, in opposition to Brute-beast." It is also recorded with the colloquial sense, "a decent, respectable, or presentable person," as in Dickens (1844): "You must take your passage like a Christian; at least as like a Christian as a fore-cabin passenger can."

One correspondent, in 1956, said that she was concerned with the way in which stereotypes about groups of people became formulated, and she argued that the preservation of derogatory definitions in dictionaries did nothing to prevent the persistence of such stereotypes. Others drew attention to the cultural and scholarly achievements of Jews, for example, that thirty-eight Nobel prizes had been awarded to Jews by 1960. A representative of the American Conference of Businessmen came to the OED Department in Oxford in March 1966, and he and I discussed the problem amicably. "Men of good will," he said, "should unite to do everything possible not to give any appearance of acceptance to unfavorable applications of the word *Jew* if they exist." If they exist? But we knew from our quotation files that unfavorable applications of the word *Jew* did and do exist, both in speech and in print, deplorable though they are. All I could do was to repeat the familiar lexicographical arguments. It is the duty of lexicographers to record actual usage, as shown by collected examples, not to express moral approval or disapproval of usage; dictionaries cannot be regulative in matters of social, political, and religious attitudes; there is no question of any animus on the part of the lexicographers against the Jews, or the Arabs, or anyone else.

In 1969, a Jewish businessman from Salford came on the scene and claimed that the definitions of *Jew* were "abusive and insulting and reflected a deplorable attitude toward Jewry." He turned the screw more forcibly by releasing the text of his letters to the national newspapers, who by now realized that the matter was an issue of public controversy. He also wrote to politicians, church leaders, including the chief rabbi and the archbishop of Canterbury, to the commissioner of police, and to other instruments of the church and state.

In 1972, this Salford businessman brought an action against the Clarendon Press, claiming that the secondary definitions of the word *Jew* were "derogatory, defamatory, and deplorable." He lost the case in the High Court in July 1973. Mr. Justice Goff held that, in law, the plaintiff had no maintainable cause of action because he could not, as required by English law, show that the offending words in the dictionary entries "referred to him personally or were capable of being understood by others as referring to him."

The next episode occurred on the other side of the world. Toward the end of 1976, Mr. Al Grassby, Australia's commissioner for community relations, called for the withdrawal of the *Australian Pocket Oxford Dictionary* from circulation because it contained a number of words applied in a derogatory way to ethnic or religious groups: words like *wog*, *wop*, and *dago*.

Knowing very little, if anything, about lexicographical policy, he thought it deplorable that there was no entry for *Italy* but one for *dago*, none for Brazil as a country but one for *Brazil nut*, and so on. This wholly simplistic notion was rejected with humor and scorn by the Australian press. A cartoon in the *Australian* showed two European migrants looking very unhappy, and the caption read: "Did you hear what those ignorant Aussie dingoes called us?" And a headline in the *Melbourne Sunday Press* makes its point quite simply: "You are on a loser, pal Grassby."

The most recent example of hostility toward dictionary definitions occurred a short time ago. On this occasion, as with *Pakistan*, the criticized definition was inadequate, and, curiously, the concession of its inadequacy merely transferred the attack from one quarter to another. In the sixth edition of the *Concise Oxford Dictionary*, published in July 1976, the word *Palestinian* was defined as "(native or inhabitant) of Palestine; (person) seeking to displace Israelis from Palestine." Early in 1977, the definition provoked angry editorial comment in newspapers in the Middle East, and threats were made that if the Oxford University Press did not agree to amend it at once, the matter would be brought to the atttention of the Arab League, with a proposal to place the OUP on the Arab boycott list.

Each day's post brought fresh evidence of what appeared to be a severe reaction throughout Arabic-speaking countries, if the newspapers were anything to go by. The sales records for the *Concise Oxford Dictionary* in Egypt showed that all of eleven copies had been sold there in the financial year 1976–1977! But, sales apart, what was clear was that the Arabs considered the definition to be partisan, and that, in my opinion, would have been the attitude of the man on the Clapham[3] omnibus too.

In two lines of the *COD*—because that was all the space available in such a small dictionary—we concluded that it was not possible to arrive at other than a formulaic definition of *Palestinian*. Any form of words ascribing motives to "Palestinians" simply failed by one test or another when the space available was so limited. We therefore decided to adopt another type of definition, one of the type that is used in every desk dictionary in the world, and the new definition reads as follows: "*n*. Native or inhabitant of Palestine, *a*. Of, pertaining to, or connected with Palestine."

The Arabs were satisfied ("it represents a victory for truth and objectivity," declared the *Egyptian Gazette* of 3 May 1977) and, had the matter rested there, without further publicity, that would probably have been the end of it. Not content with severing the head, however, the Arabs wished to fix it upon the battlements. A press statement was issued to

3. Suburb of London.

British national newspapers by a London-based Arab organization, and even though this statement was factually and unemotionally expressed, it brought an instant reaction from the other side.

Letters of protest began to arrive from various Jewish organizations, and the scholarly lexicographers of the OUP had to endure the kind of concerted campaign with which politicians have always been familiar. The letters expressed "profound distress" and declared that the lexicographers "had departed from their usual standards of scholarly objectivity in yielding to pro-Arab pressure groups." The "selfsame tune and words" came from several directions. "We consider this an encroachment on traditional British integrity and on British values," "Political appeasement for commercial considerations," "I wish to register the strongest protest against such abject and cowardly behaviour on the part of your organization," and so on. It dawned on us, as the letters arrived, that we were dealing with an organized petition. The individuals and groups writing to us had been urged to write to us by some central body. The same phrases occurred in several of the letters; for example: "In describing a Palestinian as a native or inhabitant of Palestine, you impliedly deny the existence of the State of Israel." That "impliedly" rather gave the game away.

This Palestinian affair is for all practical purposes over, though not without bruises on all sides. Dictionary editors are now at last aware that they must give maximum attention to sensitive words, like *Palestinian*, *Jap*, and so on. Politically sensitive words like *Palestine* and *Kashmir* can be entered only as geographical, and not as political entities unless there is adequate space to describe the claims and counterclaims and there are facilities for the frequent updating of the entries.

For the most part lexicographers are agreed about the necessity of recording derogatory applications of words even if some sections of the general public are not. Since the 1960s or so most dictionaries (other than the smallest ones and those prepared for the use of children) have also included most of the more commonly heard expressions used in contexts describing sexual or excretory matters. A different practice, which I believe to be mistaken, is defended in classical manner by David B. Guralnik in the foreword to his *Webster's New World Dictionary of the American Language* (Second College Edition, 1972), p. viii:

> The absence from this dictionary of a handful of old, well-known vulgate terms for sexual and excretory organs and functions is not due to a lack of citations for these words from current literature. On the contrary, the profusion of such citations in recent years would suggest that the terms in question are so well known as to require no explanation. The decision to eliminate them as part of the extensive culling process that is the inevitable task of the lexicographer was made on the practical grounds that there is still objection in many quarters to the appearance of these terms in print and that to risk

keeping this dictionary out of the hands of some students by introducing several terms that require little if any elucidation would be unwise. In a similar vein, it was decided in the selection process that this dictionary could easily dispense with those true obscenities, the terms of racial or ethnic opprobrium, that are, in any case, encountered with diminishing frequency these days.

In respect of such vocabulary, inclusion or exclusion should be governed by the size of the dictionary or by the educational market envisaged for it. In large dictionaries like the *OED*, the *Shorter Oxford English Dictionary* and *Webster's Third New International Dictionary*, such vocabulary should be automatically included, with suitable indications of the status of each item. In desk dictionaries like the *Concise Oxford Dictionary* and *Webster's New Collegiate Dictionary* the editors normally have sufficient space to include such words: a wide range of suitable status labels is available to indicate the degree of vulgarity of words like *crap, cunt, fart, fuck, turd,* and so on; and for terms of racial abuse a special symbol meaning "regarded as offensive in varying degrees by a person to whom the word is applied" is long overdue. Such dictionaries should aim to be regulative or normative in such matters only by the use of cautionary labels and/or symbols and not by censorship. In smaller dictionaries, and in school dictionaries, the absence of such vocabulary needs no defense.

In the end, in their function as "marshallers of words," lexicographers responsible for the compilation of the larger dictionaries must aim to include vocabulary from the disputed areas of vocabulary as well as from safe or uncontroversial subject areas, words that are gracefully formed as well as those that are not, words from sets of religious, political, or social beliefs with which one has no sympathy beside those that one finds acceptable. And to the list of words that must not be excluded I should add those that are explosive and dangerous, like words of ethnic abuse, as well.

1978

THE READER

1. What does Burchfield's title suggest he is going to talk about? Explain why he finds it necessary to talk about other things.
2. Does Burchfield believe that dictionary makers have the responsibility to bring about social change? Do you agree?
3. What is the difference between the use of "cautionary labels" and "censorship"?
4. Why does Burchfield include "expressions used in contexts describing sexual or excretory matters" at the end of his discussion? What do they have in common with terms that might offend ethnic sensibilities?

THE WRITER

1. *Why does Burchfield start with the quotation from* Macbeth?
2. *Burchfield uses the extended metaphor of a war between dictionary makers and some groups among their readers. Write a brief essay comparing this with McMurtry's use of the war metaphor in connection with football (p. 399). Does the metaphor serve different purposes in the two cases?*
3. *Look up in your desk dictionary several words that might offend certain groups. Has your dictionary handled them as Burchfield recommends? Write a brief essay either supporting or attacking the practice followed by your dictionary.*
4. *Write out your answer to question 2 under "The Reader," above.*

Richard Rodriguez

ARIA

Supporters of bilingual education today imply that students like me miss a great deal by not being taught in their family's language. What they seem not to recognize is that, as a socially disadvantaged child, I considered Spanish to be a private language. What I needed to learn in school was that I had the right—and the obligation—to speak the public language of *los gringos*.[1] The odd truth is that my first-grade classmates could have become bilingual, in the conventional sense of that word, more easily than I. Had they been taught (as upper-middle-class children are often taught early) a second language like Spanish or French, they could have regarded it simply as that: another public language. In my case such bilingualism could not have been so quickly achieved. What I did not believe was that I could speak a single public language.

Without question, it would have pleased me to hear my teachers address me in Spanish when I entered the classroom. I would have felt much less afraid. I would have trusted them and responded with ease. But I would have delayed—for how long postponed?—having to learn the language of public society. I would have evaded—and for how long could I have afforded to delay?—learning the great lesson of school, that I had a public identity.

Fortunately, my teachers were unsentimental about their responsibility. What understood was that I needed to speak a public language. So their voices would search me out, asking me questions. Each time I'd hear them, I'd look up in surprise to see a nun's face frowning at me. I'd

1. Foreigners.

mumble, not really meaning to answer. The nun would persist, "Richard, stand up. Don't look at the floor. Speak up. Speak to the entire class, not just to me!" But I couldn't believe that the English language was mine to use. (In part, I did not want to believe it.) I continued to mumble. I resisted the teacher's demands. (Did I somehow suspect that once I learned public language my pleasing family life would be changed?) Silent, waiting for the bell to sound, I remained dazed, diffident, afraid.

Because I wrongly imagined that English was intrinsically a public language and Spanish an intrinsically private one, I easily noted the difference between classroom language and the language of home. At school, words were directed to a general audience of listeners. ("Boys and girls.") Words were meaningfully ordered. And the point was not self-expression alone but to make oneself understood by many others. The teacher quizzed: "Boys and girls, why do we use that word in this sentence? Could we think of a better word to use there? Would the sentence change its meaning if the words were differently arranged? And wasn't there a better way of saying much the same thing?" (I couldn't say. I wouldn't try to say.)

Three months. Five. Half a year passed. Unsmiling, ever watchful, my teachers noted my silence. They began to connect my behavior with the difficult progress my older sister and brother were making. Until one Saturday morning three nuns arrived at the house to talk to our parents. Stiffly, they sat on the blue living room sofa. From the doorway of another room, spying the visitors, I noted the incongruity—the clash of two worlds, the faces and voices of school intruding upon the familiar setting of home. I overheard one voice gently wondering, "Do your children speak only Spanish at home, Mrs. Rodriguez?" While another voice added, "That Richard especially seems so timid and shy."

That Rich-heard!

With great tact the visitors continued, "Is it possible for you and your husband to encourage your children to practice their English when they are home?" Of course, my parents complied. What would they not do for their children's well-being? And how could they have questioned the Church's authority which those women represented? In an instant, they agreed to give up the language (the sounds) that had revealed and accentuated our family's closeness. The moment after the visitors left, the change was observed. "*Ahora,* speak to us *en inglés,*"[2] my father and mother united to tell us.

At first, it seemed a kind of game. After dinner each night, the family gathered to practice "our" English. (It was still then *inglés,* a language foreign to us, so we felt drawn as strangers to it.) Laughing, we would try to define words we could not pronounce. We played with strange English

2. "*Now, speak to us in English.*"

sounds, often overanglicizing our pronunciations. And we filled the smiling gaps of our sentences with familiar Spanish sounds. But that was cheating, somebody shouted. Everyone laughed. In school, meanwhile, like my brother and sister, I was required to attend a daily tutoring session. I needed a full year of special attention. I also needed my teachers to keep my attention from straying in class by calling out, *Rich-heard*— their English voices slowly prying loose my ties to my other name, its three notes, *Ri-car-do*. Most of all I needed to hear my mother and father speak to me in a moment of seriousness in broken—suddenly heartbreaking—English. The scene was inevitable: One Saturday morning I entered the kitchen where my parents were talking in Spanish. I did not realize that they were talking in Spanish however until, at the moment they saw me, I heard their voices change to speak English. Those *gringo* sounds they uttered startled me. Pushed me away. In that moment of trivial misunderstanding and profound insight, I felt my throat twisted by unsounded grief. I turned quickly and left the room. But I had no place to escape to with Spanish. (The spell was broken.) My brother and sisters were speaking English in another part of the house.

Again and again in the days following, increasingly angry, I was obliged to hear my mother and father: "Speak to us *en inglés*." (Speak.) Only then did I determine to learn classroom English. Weeks after, it happened: One day in school I raised my hand to volunteer an answer. I spoke out in a loud voice. And I did not think it remarkable when the entire class understood. That day, I moved very far from the disadvantaged child I had been only days earlier. The belief, that calming assurance that I belonged in public, had at last taken hold.

Shortly after, I stopped hearing the high and loud sounds of *los gringos*. A more and more confident speaker of English, I didn't trouble to listen to *how* strangers sounded, speaking to me. And there simply were too many English-speaking people in my day for me to hear American accents anymore. Conversations quickened. Listening to persons who sounded eccentrically pitched voices, I usually noted their sounds for an initial few seconds before I concentrated on *what* they were saying. Conversations became content-full. Transparent. Hearing someone's *tone* of voice—angry or questioning or sarcastic or happy or sad—I didn't distinguish it from the words it expressed. Sound and word were thus tightly wedded. At the end of a day, I was often bemused, always relieved, to realize how "silent," though crowded with words, my day in public had been. (This public silence measured and quickened the change in my life.)

At last, seven years old, I came to believe what had been technically true since my birth: I was an American citizen.

But the special feeling of closeness at home was diminished by then. Gone was the desperate, urgent, intense feeling of being at home; rare was the experience of feeling myself individualized by family intimates. We remained a loving family, but one greatly changed. No longer so close; no longer bound tight by the pleasing and troubling knowledge of our public separateness. Neither my older brother nor sister rushed home after school anymore. Nor did I. When I arrived home there would often be neighborhood kids in the house. Or the house would be empty of sounds.

Following the dramatic Americanization of their children, even my parents grew more publicly confident. Especially my mother. She learned the names of all the people on our block. And she decided we needed to have a telephone installed in the house. My father continued to use the word *gringo*. But it was no longer charged with the old bitterness or distrust. (Stripped of any emotional content, the word simply became a name for those Americans not of Hispanic descent.) Hearing him, sometimes, I wasn't sure if he was pronouncing the Spanish word *gringo* or saying gringo in English.

Matching the silence I started hearing in public was a new quiet at home. The family's quiet was partly due to the fact that, as we children learned more and more English, we shared fewer and fewer words with our parents. Sentences needed to be spoken slowly when a child addressed his mother or father. (Often the parent wouldn't understand.) The child would need to repeat himself. (Still the parent misunderstood.) The young voice, frustrated, would end up saying, "Never mind"—the subject was closed. Dinners would be noisy with the clinking of knives and forks against dishes. My mother would smile softly between her remarks; my father at the other end of the table would chew and chew at his food, while he stared over the heads of his children.

My mother! My father! After English became my primary language, I no longer knew what words to use in addressing my parents. The old Spanish words (those tender accents of sound) I had used earlier—*mamá* and *papá*—I couldn't use anymore. They would have been too painful reminders of how much had changed in my life. On the other hand, the words I heard neighborhood kids call *their* parents seemed equally unsatisfactory. *Mother* and *Father*; *Ma, Papa, Pa, Dad, Pop* (how I hated the all American sound of that last word especially)—all these terms I felt were unsuitable, not really terms of address for my parents. As a result, I never used them at home. Whenever I'd speak to my parents, I would try to get their attention with eye contact alone, In public conversations, I'd refer to "my parents" or "my mother and father."

My mother and father, for their part, responded differently, as their children spoke to them less. She grew restless, seemed troubled and anxious at the scarcity of words exchanged in the house. It was she who would question me about my day when I came home from school. She smiled at small talk. She pried at the edges of my sentences to get me to say something more. (What?) She'd join conversations she overheard, but her intrusions often stopped her children's talking. By contrast, my father seemed reconciled to the new quiet. Though his English improved somewhat, he retired into silence. At dinner he spoke very little. One night his children and even his wife helplessly giggled at his garbled English pronunciation of the Catholic Grace before Meals. Thereafter he made his wife recite the prayer at the start of each meal, even on formal occasions, when there were guests in the house. Hers became the public voice of the family. On official business, it was she, not my father, one would usually hear on the phone or in stores, talking to strangers. His children grew so accustomed to his silence that, years later, they would speak routinely of his shyness. (My mother would often try to explain: Both his parents died when he was eight. He was raised by an uncle who treated him like little more than a menial servant. He was never encouraged to speak. He grew up alone. A man of few words.) But my father was not shy, I realized, when I'd watch him speaking Spanish with relatives. Using Spanish, he was quickly effusive. Especially when talking with other men, his voice would spark, flicker, flare alive with sounds. In Spanish, he expressed ideas and feelings he rarely revealed in English. With firm Spanish sounds, he conveyed confidence and authority English would never allow him.

The silence at home, however, was finally more than a literal silence. Fewer words passed between parent and child, but more profound was the silence that resulted from my inattention to sounds. At about the time I no longer bothered to listen with care to the sounds of English in public, I grew careless about listening to the sounds family members made when they spoke. Most of the time I heard someone speaking at home and didn't distinguish his sounds from the words people uttered in public. I didn't even pay much attention to my parents' accented and ungrammatical speech. At least not at home. Only when I was with them in public would I grow alert to their accents. Though, even then, their sounds caused me less and less concern. For I was increasingly confident of my own public identity.

I would have been happier about my public success had I not sometimes recalled what it had been like earlier, when my family had conveyed its intimacy through a set of conveniently private sounds. Sometimes in public, hearing a stranger, I'd hark back to my past. A Mexican farmworker approached me downtown to ask directions to somewhere, "*¿Hijito . . . ?*"[3] he said. And his voice summoned deep longing. Another time, standing beside my mother in the visiting room of a Carmelite convent,[4] before the dense screen which rendered the nuns shadowy figures, I heard several Spanish-speaking nuns—their busy,

3. "Little boy . . . ?"   Mount Carmel.
4. Of the Catholic Order of Our Lady of

singsong overlapping voices—assure us that yes, yes, we were remembered, all our family was remembered in their prayers. (Their voices echoed faraway family sounds.) Another day, a dark-faced old woman—her hand light on my shoulder—steadied herself against me as she boarded a bus. She murmured something I couldn't quite comprehend. Her Spanish voice came near, like the face of a never-before-seen relative in the instant before I was kissed. Her voice, like so many of the Spanish voices I'd hear in public, recalled the golden age of my youth. Hearing Spanish then, I continued to be a careful, if sad, listener to sounds. Hearing a Spanish-speaking family walking behind me, I turned to look. I smiled for an instant, before my glance found the Hispanic-looking faces of strangers in the crowd going by.

Today I hear bilingual educators say that children lose a degree of "individuality" by becoming assimilated into public society. (Bilingual schooling was popularized in the seventies, that decade when middle-class ethnics began to resist the process of assimilation—the American melting pot.) But the bilingualists simplistically scorn the value and necessity of assimilation. They do not seem to realize that there are two ways a person is individualized. So they do not realize that while one suffers a diminished sense of *private* individuality by becoming assimilated into public society, such assimilation makes possible the achievement of *public* individuality.

The bilingualists insist that a student should be reminded of his difference from others in mass society, his heritage. But they equate mere separateness with individuality. The fact is that only in private—with intimates—is separateness from the crowd a prerequisite for individuality. (An intimate draws me apart, tells me that I am unique, unlike all others.) In public, by contrast, full individuality is achieved, paradoxically, by those who are able to consider themselves members of the crowd. Thus it happened for me: Only when I was able to think of myself as an American, no longer an alien in *gringo* society, could I seek the rights and opportunities necessary for full public individuality. The social and political advantages I enjoy as a man result from the day that I came to believe that my name, indeed, is *Rich-heard Road-ree-guess*. It is true that my public society today is often impersonal. (My public society is usually mass society). Yet despite the anonymity of the crowd and despite the fact that the individuality I achieve in public is often tenuous —because it depends on my being one in a crowd—I celebrate the day I acquired my new name. Those middle-class ethnics who scorn assimilation seem to me filled with decadent self-pity, obsessed by the burden of public life. Dangerously, they romanticize public separateness and they trivialize the dilemma of the socially disadvantaged.

My awkward childhood does not prove the necessity of bilingual education. My story discloses instead an essential myth of childhood—inevitable pain. If I rehearse here the changes in my private life after my Americanization, it is finally to emphasize the public gain. The loss implies the gain: The house I returned to each afternoon was quiet. Intimate sounds no longer rushed to the door to greet me. There were other noises inside. The telephone rang. Neighborhood kids ran past the door of the bedroom where I was reading my schoolbooks—covered with shopping-bag paper. Once I learned public language, it would never again be easy for me to hear intimate family voices. More and more of my day was spent hearing words. But that may only be a way of saying that the day I raised my hand in class and spoke loudly to an entire roomful of faces, my childhood started to end.

1982

THE READER

1. What did Rodriguez lose because his schooling was in English instead of in Spanish? What did he gain? Was there any pain connected with the loss and gain? Was it worth it?
2. Rodriguez writes of those "middle-class ethnics who scorn assimilation" that they seem to him "filled with decadent self-pity, obsessed by the burden of public life. Dangerously, they romanticize public separateness and they trivialize the dilemma of the socially disadvantaged." Explain what the terms and implications of this judgment are. Is it a fair judgment?
3. Could one argue from Rodriguez's view of the matter that encouragement or advocacy of bilingual education amounts to trying to ensure perpetual childhood for those schooled? If so, is Rodriguez's view a fair one? Is his position elitist? Is it bad to be elitist?

THE WRITER

1. What qualities does Rodriguez ascribe to private language? What is his tone in writing of these? What attitude has he toward them?
2. How does Rodriguez characterize the difference between private and public language? Does he show persuasively the need for public language? By what means does he seek to do this?
3. For Rodriguez, the private language is Spanish, the public English. Could similar considerations apply if both were different kinds of English? Does the English you have learned at school differ from the English of your home and childhood? Do your parents, your friends, your teachers have different languages (all called "English")? Write an essay exploring your personal experience with private and public language.

Lewis Thomas

NOTES ON PUNCTUATION

There are no precise rules about punctuation (Fowler[1] lays out some general advice (as best he can under the complex circumstances of English prose (he points out, for example, that we possess only four stops (the comma, the semicolon, the colon and the period (the question mark and exclamation point are not, strictly speaking, stops; they are indicators of tone (oddly enough, the Greeks employed the semicolon for their question mark (it produces a strange sensation to read a Greek sentence which is a straightforward question: Why weepest thou; (instead of Why weepest thou? (and, of course, there are parentheses (which are surely a kind of punctuation making this whole much more complicated by having to count up the left-handed parentheses in order to be sure of closing with the right number (but if the parentheses were left out, with nothing to work with but the stops, we would have considerably more flexibility in the deploying of layers of meaning than if we tried to separate all the clauses by physical barriers (and in the latter case, while we might have more precision and exactitude for our meaning, we would lose the essential flavor of language, which is its wonderful ambiguity)))))))))))).

The commas are the most useful and usable of all the stops. It is highly important to put them in place as you go along. If you try to come back after doing a paragraph and stick them in the various spots that tempt you you will discover that they tend to swarm like minnows into all sorts of crevices whose existence you hadn't realized and before you know it the whole long sentence becomes immobilized and lashed up squirming in commas. Better to use them sparingly, and with affection, precisely when the need for each one arises, nicely, by itself.

I have grown fond of semicolons in recent years. The semicolon tells you that there is still some question about the preceding full sentence; something needs to be added; it reminds you sometimes of the Greek usage. It is almost always a greater pleasure to come across a semicolon than a period. The period tells you that that is that; if you didn't get all the meaning you wanted or expected, anyway you got all the writer intended to parcel out and now you have to move along. But with a semicolon there you get a pleasant little feeling of expectancy; there is more to come; read on; it will get clearer.

Colons are a lot less attractive, for several reasons: firstly, they give you

1. H. W. Fowler, author of *Modern English Usage* (1926, revised 1965 by Sir Ernest Gowers), a standard reference work.

the feeling of being rather ordered around, or at least having your nose pointed in a direction you might not be inclined to take if left to yourself, and, secondly, you suspect you're in for one of those sentences that will be labeling the points to be made: firstly, secondly and so forth, with the implication that you haven't sense enough to keep track of a sequence of notions without having them numbered. Also, many writers use this system loosely and incompletely, starting out with number one and number two as though counting off on their fingers but then going on and on without the succession of labels you've been led to expect, leaving you floundering about searching for the ninthly or seventeenthly that ought to be there but isn't.

Exclamation points are the most irritating of all. Look! they say, look at what I just said! How amazing is my thought! It is like being forced to watch someone else's small child jumping up and down crazily in the center of the living room shouting to attract attention. If a sentence really has something of importance to say, something quite remarkable, it doesn't need a mark to point it out. And if it is really, after all, a banal sentence needing more zing, the exclamation point simply emphasizes its banality!

Quotation marks should be used honestly and sparingly, when there is a genuine quotation at hand, and it is necessary to be very rigorous about the words enclosed by the marks. If something is to be quoted, the exact words must be used. If part of it must be left out because of space limitations, it is good manners to insert three dots to indicate the omission, but it is unethical to do this if it means connecting two thoughts which the original author did not intend to have tied together. Above all, quotation marks should not be used for ideas that you'd like to disown, things in the air so to speak. Nor should they be put in place around clichés; if you want to use a cliché you must take full responsibility for it yourself and not try to job it off on anon., or on society. The most objectionable misuse of quotation marks, but one which illustrates the dangers of misuse in ordinary prose, is seen in advertising, especially in advertisements for small restaurants, for example "just around the corner," or "a good place to eat." No single, identifiable, citable person ever really said, for the record, "just around the corner," much less "a good place to eat," least likely of all for restaurants of the type that use this type of prose.

The dash is a handy device, informal and essentially playful, telling you that you're about to take off on a different tack but still in some way connected with the present course—only you have to remember that the dash is there, and either put a second dash at the end of the notion to let the reader know that he's back on course, or else end the sentence, as here, with a period.

The greatest danger in punctuation is for poetry. Here it is necessary to be as economical and parsimonious with commas and periods as with the words themselves, and any marks that seem to carry their own subtle meanings, like dashes and little rows of periods, even semicolons and question marks, should be left out altogether rather than inserted to clog up the thing with ambiguity. A single exclamation point in a poem, no matter what else the poem has to say, is enough to destroy the whole work.

The things I like best in T. S. Eliot's poetry, especially in the *Four Quartets*, are the semicolons. You cannot hear them, but they are there, laying out the connections between the images and the ideas. Sometimes you get a glimpse of a semicolon coming, a few lines farther on, and it is like climbing a steep path through woods and seeing a wooden bench just at a bend in the road ahead, a place where you can expect to sit for a moment, catching your breath.

Commas can't do this sort of thing; they can only tell you how the different parts of a complicated thought are to be fitted together, but you can't sit, not even take a breath, just because of a comma,

1979

THE READER

1. Compare Thomas's statements about the various punctuation marks with a handbook's rules on the subject. How do they differ? Do they make any of the same points?
2. Compare the punctuation in two or more of the pieces in "An Album of Styles" (p. 365). You might look particularly at the selections by Bacon, Thurber, and White before making your choices.
3. Gertrude Stein once said: "There are two different ways of thinking about colons and semi-colons you can think of them as commas and as such they are purely servile or you can think of them as periods and then using them can make you feel adventurous." What might Thomas's comment on Stein's statement be?

THE WRITER

1. How soon in this essay do you realize that Thomas is playing a kind of game with the reader? Why doesn't he tell you at the beginning what he is going to do?
2. Here Thomas deals with a restricted, minor subject and, in "Humanities and Science" (p. 253), with one that is sweeping and important. Describe the personality he presents to you here and then the one he presents in "Humanities and Science." Are they similar? Different? Do they overlap? Is his analysis in "On Magic in Medicine" (p. 450) consistent with this personality or these personalities?
3. The first paragraph in Thomas's essay is a single sentence. Rewrite the paragraph so that it is several sentences. What changes in punctuation did you make?

4. Write a short essay on "My Encounters with Punctuation" or "The Semicolon and I."

Erich Fromm

THE NATURE OF SYMBOLIC LANGUAGE

Let us assume you want to tell someone the difference between the taste of white wine and red wine. This may seem quite simple to you. You know the difference very well; why should it not be easy to explain it to someone else? Yet you find the greatest difficulty putting this taste difference into words. And probably you will end up by saying, "Now look here, I can't explain it to you. Just drink red wine and then white wine, and you will know what the difference is." You have no difficulty in finding words to explain the most complicated machine, and yet words seem to be futile to describe a simple taste experience.

Are we not confronted with the same difficulty when we try to explain a feeling experience? Let us take a mood in which you feel lost, deserted, where the world looks gray, a little frightening though not really dangerous. You want to describe this mood to a friend, but again you find yourself groping for words and eventually feel that nothing you have said is an adequate explanation of the many nuances of the mood. The following night you have a dream. You see yourself in the outskirts of a city just before dawn, the streets are empty except for a milk wagon, the houses look poor, the surroundings are unfamiliar, you have no means of accustomed transportation to places familiar to you and where you feel you belong. When you wake up and remember the dream, it occurs to you that the feeling you had in that dream was exactly the feeling of lostness and grayness you tried to describe to your friend the day before. It is just one picture, whose visualization took less than a second. And yet this picture is a more vivid and precise description than you could have given by talking *about* it at length. The picture you see in the dream is a *symbol* of something you felt.

What is a symbol? A symbol is often defined as "something that stands for something else." This definition seems rather disappointing. It becomes more interesting, however, if we concern ourselves with those symbols which are sensory expressions of seeing, hearing, smelling, touching, standing for a "something else" which is an inner experience, a feeling or thought. A symbol of this kind is something outside ourselves; that which it symbolizes is something inside ourselves. Symbolic language is language in which we express inner experience as if it were a sensory experience, as if it were something we were doing or something that was done to us in the world of things. Symbolic language is language in which the world outside is a symbol of the world inside, a symbol for our souls and our minds.

If we define a symbol as "something which stands for something else," the crucial question is: *What is the specific connection between the symbol and that which it symbolizes?*

In answer to this question we can differentiate between three kinds of symbols: the *conventional*, the *accidental* and the *universal* symbol. As will become apparent presently, only the latter two kinds of symbols express inner experiences as if they were sensory experiences, and only they have the elements of symbolic language.

The *conventional* symbol is the best known of the three, since we employ it in everyday language. If we see the word "table" or hear the sound "table," the letters T-A-B-L-E stand for something else. They stand for the thing table that we see, touch and use. What is the connection between the word "table" and the thing "table"? Is there any inherent relationship between them? Obviously not. The thing table has nothing to do with the sound table, and the only reason the word symbolizes the thing is the convention of calling this particular thing by a particular name. We learn this connection as children by the repeated experience of hearing the word in reference to the thing until a lasting association is formed so that we don't have to think to find the right word.

There are some words, however, where the association is not only conventional. When we say "phooey," for instance, we make with our lips a movement of dispelling the air quickly. It is an expression of disgust in which our mouths participate. By this quick expulsion of air we imitate and thus express our intention to expel something, to get it out of our system. In this case, as in some others, the symbol has an inherent connection with the feeling it symbolizes. But even if we assume that originally many or even all words had their origins in some such inherent connection between symbol and the symbolized, most words no longer have this meaning for us when we learn a language.

Words are not the only illustration for conventional symbols, although they are the most frequent and best-known ones. Pictures also can be conventional symbols. A flag, for instance, may stand for a specific country, and yet there is no connection between the specific colors and the country for which they stand. They have been accepted as denoting that particular country, and we translate the visual impression of the flag into the concept of that country, again on conventional grounds. Some pictorial symbols are not entirely conventional; for example, the cross. The cross can be merely a conventional symbol of the Christian church and in that respect no different from a flag. But the specific content of the cross referring to Jesus' death or, beyond that, to the interpenetration of the material and spiritual planes, puts the connection between the symbol and what it symbolizes beyond the level of mere conventional symbols.

The very opposite to the conventional symbol is the *accidental* symbol, although they have one thing in common: there is no intrinsic relationship between the symbol and that which it symbolizes. Let us assume that someone has had a saddening experience in a certain city; when he hears the name of that city, he will easily connect the name with a mood of sadness, just as he would connect it with a mood of joy had his experience been a happy one. Quite obviously there is nothing in the nature of the city that is either sad or joyful. It is the individual experience connected with the city that makes it a symbol of a mood.

The same reaction could occur in connection with a house, a street, a certain dress, certain scenery, or anything once connected with a specific mood. We might find ourselves dreaming that we are in a certain city. In fact, there may be no particular mood connected with it in the dream; all we see is a street or even simply the name of the city. We ask ourselves why we happened to think of that city in our sleep and may discover that we had fallen asleep in a mood similar to the one symbolized by the city. The picture in the dream represents this mood, the city "stands for" the mood once experienced in it. Here the connection between the symbol and the experience symbolized is entirely accidental.

In contrast to the conventional symbol, the accidental symbol cannot be shared by anyone else except as we relate the events connected with the symbol. For this reason accidental symbols are rarely used in myths, fairy tales, or works of art written in symbolic language because they are not communicable unless the writer adds a lengthy comment to each symbol he uses. In dreams, however, accidental symbols are frequent. * * *

The *universal* symbol is one in which there is an intrinsic relationship between the symbol and that which it represents. We have already given one example, that of the outskirts of the city. The sensory experience of a deserted, strange, poor environment has indeed a significant relationship to a mood of lostness and anxiety. True enough, if we have never been in the outskirts of a city we could not use that symbol, just as the word "table" would be meaningless had we never seen a table. This symbol is meaningful only to city dwellers and would be meaningless to people living in cultures that have no big cities. Many other universal symbols, however, are rooted in the experience of every human being. Take, for instance, the symbol of fire. We are fascinated by certain qualities of fire in a fireplace. First of all, by its aliveness. It changes continuously, it moves all the time, and yet there is constancy in it. It remains the same without being the same. It gives the impression of power, of energy, of grace and lightness. It is as if it were dancing and had an inexhaustible source of energy. When we use fire as a symbol, we describe the inner experience characterized by the same elements which we notice in the sensory experience of fire; the mood of energy, lightness, movement, grace, gaiety—sometimes one, sometimes another of these elements being predominant in the feeling.

Similar in some ways and different in others is the symbol of water—of the ocean or of the stream. Here, too, we find the blending of change and permanence, of constant movement and yet of permanence. We also feel the quality of aliveness, continuity and energy. But there is a difference; where fire is adventurous, quick, exciting, water is quiet, slow and steady. Fire has an element of surprise; water an element of predictability. Water symbolizes the mood of aliveness, too, but one which is "heavier," "slower," and more comforting than exciting.

That a phenomenon of the physical world can be the adequate expression of an inner experience, that the world of things can be a symbol of the world of the mind, is not surprising. We all know that our bodies express our minds. Blood rushes to our heads when we are furious, it rushes away from them when we are afraid; our hearts beat more quickly when we are angry, and the whole body has a different tonus if we are happy from the one it has when we are sad. We express our moods by our facial expressions and our attitudes and feelings by movements and gestures so precise that others recognize them more accurately from our gestures than from our words. Indeed, the body is a symbol—and not an allegory—of the mind. Deeply and genuinely felt emotion, and even any genuinely felt thought, is expressed in our whole organism. In the case of the universal symbol, we find the same connection between mental and physical experience. Certain physical phenomena suggest by their very nature certain emotional and mental experiences, and we express emotional experiences in the language of physical experiences, that is to say, symbolically.

The universal symbol is the only one in which the relationship between the symbol and that which is symbolized is not coincidental but intrinsic. It is rooted in the experience of the affinity between an emotion or thought, on the one hand, and a sensory experience, on the other. It can be called universal because it is shared by all men, in contrast not only to the accidental symbol, which is by its very nature entirely personal, but also to the conventional symbol, which is restricted to a group of people sharing the same convention. The universal symbol is rooted in the properties of our body, our senses, and our mind, which are common to all men and, therefore, not restricted to individuals or to specific groups. Indeed, the language of the universal symbol is the one common tongue developed by the human race, a language which it forgot before it succeeded in developing a universal conventional language.

There is no need to speak of a racial inheritance in order to explain the universal character of symbols. Every human being who shares the essential features of bodily and mental equipment with the rest of mankind is capable of speaking and understanding the symbolic language that is based upon these common properties. Just as we do not need to learn to cry when we are sad or to get red in the face when we are angry, and just as these reactions are not restricted to any particular race or group of people, symbolic language does not have to be learned and is not restricted to any segment of the human race. Evidence for this is to be found in the fact that symbolic language as it is employed in myths and dreams is found in all cultures—in so-called primitive as well as such highly developed cultures as Egypt and Greece. Furthermore, the symbols used in these various cultures are strikingly similar since they all go back to the basic sensory as well as emotional experiences shared by men of all cultures. Added evidence is to be found in recent experiments in which people who had no knowledge of the theory of dream interpretation were able, under hypnosis, to interpret the symbolism of their dreams without any difficulty. After emerging from the hypnotic state and being asked to interpret the same dreams, they were puzzled and said, "Well, there is no meaning to them—it is just nonsense."

The foregoing statement needs qualification, however. Some symbols differ in meaning according to the difference in their realistic significance in various cultures. For instance, the function and consequently the meaning of the sun is different in northern countries and in tropical countries. In northern countries, where water is plentiful, all growth depends on sufficient sunshine. The sun is the warm, life-giving, protecting, loving power. In the Near East, where the heat of the sun is much more powerful, the sun is a dangerous and even threatening power from which man must protect himself, while water is felt to be the source of all life and the main condition for growth. We may speak of dialects of universal symbolic language, which are determined by those differences in natural conditions which cause certain symbols to have a different meaning in different regions of the earth.

Quite different from these "symbolic dialects" is the fact that many symbols have more than one meaning in accordance with different kinds of experiences which can be connected with one and the same natural phenomenon. Let us take up the symbol of fire again. If we watch fire in the fireplace, which is a source of pleasure and comfort, it is expressive of a mood of aliveness, warmth, and pleasure. But if we see a building or forest on fire, it conveys to us an experience of threat or terror, of the powerlessness of man against the elements of nature. Fire, then, can be the symbolic representation of inner aliveness and happiness as well as of fear, powerlessness, or of one's own destructive tendencies. The same holds true of the symbol water. Water can be a most destructive force when it is whipped up by a storm or when a swollen river floods its banks. Therefore, it can be the symbolic expression of horror and chaos as well as of comfort and peace.

Another illustration of the same principle is a symbol of a valley. The valley enclosed between mountains can arouse in us the feeling of security and comfort, of protection against all dangers from the outside. But the protecting mountains can also mean isolating walls which do not permit us to get out of the valley and thus the valley can become a symbol of imprisonment. The particular meaning of the symbol in any given place can only be determined from the whole context in which the symbol appears, and in terms of the predominant experiences of the person using the symbol. * * *

A good illustration of the function of the universal symbol is a story, written in symbolic language, which is known to almost everyone in Western culture: the Book of Jonah. Jonah has heard God's voice telling him to go to Nineveh and preach to its inhabitants to give up their evil ways lest they be destroyed. Jonah cannot help hearing God's voice and that is why he is a prophet. But he is an unwilling prophet, who, though knowing what he should do, tries to run away from the command of God (or, as we may say, the voice of his conscience). He is a man who does not care for other human beings. He is a man with a strong sense of law and order, but without love.

How does the story express the inner processes in Jonah?

We are told that Jonah went down to Joppa and found a ship which should bring him to Tarshish. In mid-ocean a storm rises and, while everyone else is excited and afraid, Jonah goes into the ship's belly and falls into a deep sleep. The sailors, believing that God must have sent the storm because someone on the ship is to be punished, wake Jonah, who had told them he was trying to flee from God's command. He tells them to take him and cast him forth into the sea and that the sea would then become calm. The sailors (betraying a remarkable sense of humanity by first trying everything else before following his advice) eventually take Jonah and cast him into the sea, which immediately stops raging. Jonah is swallowed by a big fish and stays in the fish's belly three days and three nights. He prays to God to free him from this prison. God makes the fish vomit out Jonah unto the dry land and Jonah goes to Nineveh, fulfills God's command, and thus saves the inhabitants of the city.

The story is told as if these events had actually happened. However, it is written in symbolic language and all the realistic events described are symbols for the inner experiences of the hero. We find a sequence of symbols which follow one another: going into the ship, going into the ship's belly, falling asleep, being in the ocean, and being in the fish's belly. All these symbols stand for the same inner experience: for a condition of being protected and isolated, of safe withdrawal from communication with other human beings. They represent what could be represented in another symbol, the fetus in the mother's womb. Different as the ship's belly, deep sleep, the ocean, and a fish's belly are realistically, they are expressive of the same inner experience, of the blending between protection and isolation.

In the manifest story events happen in space and time: first, going into the ship's belly; then, falling asleep; then, being thrown into the ocean; then, being swallowed by the fish. One thing happens after the other and, although some events are obviously unrealistic, the story has its own logical consistency in terms of time and space. But if we understand that the writer did not intend to tell us the story of external events, but of the inner experience of a man torn between his conscience and his wish to escape from his inner voice, it becomes clear that his various actions following one after the other express the same mood in him; and that *sequence in time* is expressive of a *growing intensity* of the same feeling. In his attempt to escape from his obligation to his fellow men Jonah isolates himself more and more until, in the belly of the fish, the protective element has so given way to the imprisoning element that he can stand it no longer and is forced to pray to God to be released from where he had put himself. (This is a mechanism which we find so characteristic of neurosis. An attitude is assumed as a defense against a danger, but then it grows far beyond its original defense function and becomes a neurotic symptom from which the person tries to be relieved.) Thus Jonah's escape into protective isolation ends in the terror of being imprisoned, and he takes up his life at the point where he had tried to escape.

There is another difference between the logic of the manifest and of the latent story. In the manifest story the logical connection is one of causality of external events. Jonah wants to go overseas because he wants to flee from God, he falls asleep because he is tired, he is thrown overboard because he is supposed to be the reason for the storm, and he is swallowed by the fish because there are man-eating fish in the ocean. One event occurs because of a previous event. (The last part of the story is unrealistic but not illogical.) But in the latent story the logic is different. The various events are related to each other by their association with the same inner experience. What appears to be a causal sequence of external events stands for a connection of experiences linked with each other by their association in terms of inner events. This is as logical as the manifest story—but it is a logic of a different kind. * * *

1951

Wayne C. Booth

BORING FROM WITHIN: THE ART OF THE FRESHMAN ESSAY[1]

Last week I had for about the hundredth time an experience that always disturbs me. Riding on a train, I found myself talking with my seat-mate, who asked me what I did for a living. "I teach English." Do you have any trouble predicting his response? His face fell, and he groaned, "Oh, dear, I'll have to watch my language." In my experience there are only two other possible reactions. The first is even less inspiriting: "I hated English in school; it was my worst subject." The second, so rare as to make an honest English teacher almost burst into tears of gratitude when it occurs, is an animated conversation about literature, or ideas, or the American language—the kind of conversation that shows a continuing respect for "English" as something more than being sure about *who* and *whom, lie* and *lay.*

Unless the people you meet are a good deal more tactful or better liars than the ones I meet, you've had the two less favorable experiences many times. And it takes no master analyst to figure out why so many of our fellow citizens think of us as unfriendly policemen: it is because too many of us have seen ourselves as unfriendly policemen. I know of a high school English class in Indiana in which the students are explicitly told that their paper grades will not be affected by anything they say; required to write a paper a week, they are graded simply on the number of spelling and grammatical errors. What is more, they are given a standard form for their papers: each paper is to have three paragraphs, a beginning, a middle, and an end—or is it an introduction, a body, and a conclusion? The theory seems to be that if the student is not troubled about having to say anything, or about discovering a good way of saying it, he can then concentrate on the truly important matter of avoiding mistakes.

What's wrong with such assignments? What's wrong with getting the problem of correctness focused sharply enough so that we can really work on it? After all, we do have the job of teaching correct English, don't we? We can't possibly teach our hordes of students to be colorful writers, but by golly, we can beat the bad grammar out of them. Leaving aside the obvious fact that we *can't* beat the bad grammar out of them, not by direct assault, let's think a bit about what that kind of assignment does to the poor teacher who gives it. Those papers must be read, by someone,

1. Adapted by Mr. Booth from a speech delivered in May 1963 to the Illinois Council of College Teachers of English.

and unless the teacher has more trained assistance than you and I have, she's the victim. She can't help being bored silly by her own paper-reading, and we all know what an evening of being bored by a class's papers does to our attitude toward that class the next day. The old formula of John Dewey was that any teaching that bores the student is likely to fail. The formula was subject to abuse, quite obviously, since interest in itself is only one of many tests of adequate teaching. A safer formula, though perhaps also subject to abuse, might be: Any teaching that bores the teacher is sure to fail. And I am haunted by the picture of that poor woman in Indiana, week after week reading batches of papers written by students who have been told that nothing they say can possibly affect her opinion of those papers. Could any hell imagined by Dante or Jean-Paul Sartre[2] match this self-inflicted futility?

I call it self-inflicted, as if it were a simple matter to avoid receiving papers that bore us. But unfortunately it is not. It may be a simple matter to avoid the *total* meaninglessness that the students must give that Indiana teacher, but we all know that it is no easy matter to produce interesting papers; our pet cures for boredom never work as well as they ought to. Every beginning teacher learns quickly and painfully that nothing works with all students, and that on bad days even the most promising ideas work with nobody.

As I try to sort out the various possible cures for those batches of boredom—in ink, double-spaced, on one side of the sheet, only, please—I find them falling into three groups: efforts to give the students a sharper sense of writing to an audience, efforts to give them some substance to express, and efforts to improve their habits of observation and of approach to their task—what might be called improving their mental personalities.

This classification, both obvious and unoriginal, is a useful one not only because it covers—at least I hope it does—all of our efforts to improve what our students can do but also because it reminds us that no one of the three is likely to work unless it is related to each of the others. In fact each of the three types of cure—"develop an awareness of audience," "give them something to say," and "enliven their writing personalities"—threatens us with characteristic dangers and distortions; all three together are indispensable to any lasting cure.

Perhaps the most obvious omission in that Indiana teacher's assignments is all sense of an audience to be persuaded, of a serious rhetorical purpose to be achieved. One tempting cure for this omission is to teach them to put a controversial edge on what they say. So we ask them to write a three-page paper arguing that China should be allowed into the

2. Booth refers to the elaborately described hell of the *Inferno*, by the fourteenth-century Italian poet Dante Alighieri, and to the banal locked room in which the characters of Sartre's *No Exit* discover that hell is "other people."

UN or that women are superior to men or that American colleges are failing in their historic task. Then we are surprised when the papers turn out to be as boring as ever. The papers on Red China are full of abstract pomposities that the students themselves obviously do not understand or care about, since they have gleaned them in a desperate dash through the most readily available sources listed in the *Readers' Guide*. Except for the rare student who has some political background and awareness, and who thus might have written on the subject anyway, they manage to convey little more than their resentment at the assignment and their boredom in carrying it out. One of the worst batches of papers I ever read came out of a good idea we had at Earlham College for getting the whole student body involved in controversial discussion about world affairs. We required them to read Barbara Ward's *Five Ideas that Change the World;* we even had Lady Jackson[3] come to the campus and talk to everyone about her concern for the backward nations. The papers, to our surprise, were a discouraging business. We found ourselves in desperation collecting the boners that are always a sure sign, when present in great numbers, that students are thoroughly disengaged. "I think altruism is all right, so long as we practice it in our own interest." "I would be willing to die for anything fatal." "It sure is a doggie dog world."

It is obvious what had gone wrong: though we had ostensibly given the student a writing purpose, it had not become *his* purpose, and he was really no better off, perhaps worse, than if we had him writing about, say, piccolos or pizza. We might be tempted in revulsion from such overly ambitious failures to search for controversy in the students' own mundane lives. This may be a good move, but we should not be surprised when the papers on "Let's clean up the campus" or "Why must we have traffic fatalities?" turn out to be just as empty as the papers on the UN or the Congo. They may have more exclamation points and underlined adjectives, but they will not interest any teacher who would like to read papers for his own pleasure or edification. "People often fail to realize that nearly 40,000 people are killed on our highways each year. Must this carnage continue?" Well, I suppose it must, until people who write about it learn to see it with their own eyes, and hearts, instead of through a haze of cliché. The truth is that to make students assume a controversial pose before they have any genuine substance to be controversial about is to encourage dishonesty and slovenliness, and to ensure our own boredom. It may very well lead them into the kind of commercial concern for the audience which makes almost every *Reader's Digest* article intelligible to everyone over the chronological age of ten and boring to everyone over the mental age of fifteen. *Newsweek* magazine recently had a readability survey conducted on itself. It was found to be readable by the average

3. Barbara Ward.

twelfth grader, unlike *Time*, which is readable by the average eleventh grader. The editors were advised, and I understand are taking the advice, that by improving their "readability" by one year they could improve their circulation by several hundred thousand. Whether they will thereby lop off a few thousand adult readers in the process was not reported.

The only protection from this destructive type of concern for the audience is the control of substance, of having something solid to say. Our students bore us, even when they take a seemingly lively controversial tone, because they have nothing to say, to us or to anybody else. If and when they discover something to say, they will no longer bore us, and our comments will no longer bore them. Having something to say, they will be interested in learning how to say it better. Having something to say, they can be taught how to give a properly controversial edge to what will by its nature be controversial—nothing, after all, is worth saying that everybody agrees on already.

When we think of providing substance, we are perhaps tempted first to find some way of filling students' minds with a goodly store of general ideas, available on demand. This temptation is not necessarily a bad one. After all, if we think of the adult writers who interest us, most of them have such a store; they have read and thought about man's major problems, and they have opinions and arguments ready to hand about how men ought to live, how society ought to be run, how literature ought to be written. Edmund Wilson, for example, one of the most consistently interesting men alive, seems to have an inexhaustible flow of reasoned opinions on any subject that comes before him. Obviously our students are not going to interest us until they too have some ideas.

But it is not easy to impart ideas. It is not even easy to impart opinions, though a popular teacher can usually manage to get students to parrot his views. But ideas—that is, opinions backed with genuine reasoning—are extremely difficult to develop. If they were not, we wouldn't have a problem in the first place; we could simply send our students off with an assignment to prove their conviction that God does or does not exist or that the American high school system is the best on God's earth, and the interesting arguments would flow.

There is, in fact, no short cut to the development of reasoned ideas. Years and years of daily contact with the world of ideas are required before the child can be expected to begin formulating his own ideas and his own reasons. And for the most part the capacity to handle abstract ideas comes fairly late. I recently saw a paper of a bright high school sophomore, from a good private school, relating the economic growth of China and India to their political development and relative supply of natural resources. It was a terrible paper; the student's hatred of the subject, his sense of frustration in trying to invent generalizations about processes that were still too big for him, showed in every line. The child's parent told me that when the paper was returned by the geography teacher, he had pencilled on the top of one page, "Why do you mix so many bad ideas with your good ones?" The son was almost in tears, his father told me, with anger and helplessness. "He talks as if I'd put bad ideas in on purpose. *I* don't know a bad idea from a good one on this subject."

Yet with all this said, I am still convinced that general ideas are not only a resource but also a duty that cannot be dodged just because it is a dangerous one. There is nothing we touch, as English teachers, that is immune to being tainted by our touch; all the difference lies in how we go about it.

Ideas are a resource because adolescents are surprisingly responsive to any real encouragement to think for themselves, *if* methods of forced feeding are avoided. The seventeen-year-old who has been given nothing but commonplaces and clichés all his life and who finally discovers a teacher with ideas of his own may have his life changed, and, as I shall say in my final point, when his life is changed his writing is changed. Perhaps some of you can remember, as I can, a first experience with a teacher who could think for himself. I can remember going home from a conversation with my high school chemistry teacher and audibly vowing to myself: "Someday I'm going to be able to think for myself like that." There was nothing especially unconventional about Luther Gidding's ideas—at least I can remember few of them now. But what I cannot forget is the way he had with an idea, the genuine curiosity with which he approached it, the pause while he gave his little thoughtful cough, and then the bulldog tenacity with which he would argue it through. And I am convinced that though he never required me to write a line, he did more to improve my writing during the high school years than all of my English teachers put together. The diary I kept to record my sessions with him, never read by anyone, was the best possible writing practice.

If ideas, in this sense of speculation backed up with an attempt to think about things rigorously and constructively, are a great and often neglected resource, they are also our civic responsibility—a far more serious responsibility than our duty to teach spelling and grammar. It is a commonplace to say that democracy depends for its survival on an informed citizenry, but we all know that mere information is not what we are talking about when we say such things. What we mean is that democracy depends on a citizenry that can reason for themselves, on men who know whether a case has been proved, or at least made probable. Democracy depends, if you will forgive some truisms for a moment, on free choices, and choices cannot be in any sense free if they are made blind: free choice is, in fact, choice that is based on knowledge—not just opinions, but knowledge in the sense of reasoned opinion. And if that half of our population who do not go beyond high school do not learn from us how to put two and two together and how to test the efforts of others to do so, and if the colleges continue to fail with most of the other half, we are doomed to become even more sheeplike, as a nation, than we are already.

Papers about ideas written by sheep are boring; papers written by thinking boys and girls are interesting. The problem is always to find ideas at a level that will allow the student to *reason*, that is, to provide support for his ideas, rather than merely assert them in half-baked form. And this means something that is all too often forgotten by the most ambitious teachers—namely, that whatever ideas the student writes about must somehow be connected with his own experience. Teaching machines will never be able to teach the kind of writing we all want, precisely because no machine can ever know which general ideas relate, for a given student, to some meaningful experience. In the same class we'll have one student for whom philosophical and religious ideas are meaningful, another who can talk with confidence about entropy and the second law of thermodynamics, a third who can write about social justice, and a fourth who can discuss the phony world of Holden Caulfield.[4] Each of them can do a good job on his own subject, because he has as part of his equipment a growing awareness of how conclusions in that subject are related to the steps of argument that support conclusions. Ideally, each of these students ought to have the personal attention of a tutor for an hour or so each week, someone who can help him sharpen those connections, and not force him to write on topics not yet appropriate to his interests or experience. But when these four are in a class of thirty or forty others, taught by a teacher who has three or four other similar sections, we all know what happens: the teacher is forced by his circumstances to provide some sort of mold into which all of the students can be poured. Although he is still better able to adapt to individual differences than a machine, he is unfortunately subject to boredom and fatigue, as a machine would not be. Instead of being the philosopher, scientist, political analyst, and literary critic that these four students require him to be, teaching them and learning from them at the same time, the teacher is almost inevitably tempted to force them all to write about the ideas he himself knows best. The result is that at least three of the four must write out of ignorance.

Now clearly the best way out of this impasse would be for legislatures and school boards and college presidents to recognize the teaching of English for what it is: the most demanding of all teaching jobs, justifying the smallest sections and the lightest course loads. No composition teacher can possibly concentrate on finding special interests, making imaginative assignments, and testing the effectiveness and cogency of

4. The hero of *The Catcher in the Rye*, by J. D. Salinger.

papers if he has more than seventy-five students at a time; the really desirable limit would be about forty-five—three sections of fifteen students each. Nobody would ever expect a piano teacher, who has no themes to read, to handle the great masses of pupils that we handle. Everyone recognizes that for all other technical skills individual attention is required. Yet for this, the most delicate of all skills, the one requiring the most subtle interrelationships of training, character, and experience, we fling students and teachers into hopelessly impersonal patterns.

But if I'm not careful I'll find myself saying that our pupils bore us because the superintendents and college presidents hire us to be bored. Administrative neglect and misallocation of educational funds are basic to our problem, and we should let the citizenry know of the scandal on every occasion. But meanwhile, back at the ranch, we are faced with the situation as it now is: we must find some way to train a people to write responsibly even though the people, as represented, don't want this service sufficiently to pay for it.

The tone of political exhortation into which I have now fallen leads me to one natural large source of ideas as we try to encourage writing that is not just lively and controversial but informed and genuinely persuasive. For many students there is obviously more potential interest in social problems and forces, political controversy, and the processes of everyday living around them than in more general ideas. The four students I described a moment ago, students who can say something about philosophy, science, general political theory, or literary criticism, are rare. But most students, including these four, can in theory at least be interested in meaningful argument about social problems in which they are personally involved.

As a profession we have tried, over the past several decades, a variety of approaches attempting to capitalize on such interests. Papers on corruption in TV, arguments about race relations, analyses of distortions in advertising, descriptions of mass communication—these have been combined in various quantities with traditional subjects like grammar, rhetoric, and literature. The "communications" movement, which looked so powerful only a few years ago and which now seems almost dead, had at its heart a perfectly respectable notion, a notion not much different from the one I'm working with today: get them to write about something they know about, and make sure that they see their writing as an act of communication, not as a meaningless exercise. And what better material than other acts of communication.

The dangers of such an approach are by now sufficiently understood. As subject matter for the English course, current "communications media" can at best provide only a supplement to literature and analysis of ideas. But they can be a valuable supplement. Analysis in class of the appeals buried in a New Yorker or Life advertisement followed by a writing assignment requiring similar analyses can be a far more interesting introduction to the intricacies of style than assignments out of a language text on levels of usage or emotion-charged adjectives. Analysis of a Time magazine account, purporting to be objective news but in actual fact a highly emotional editorial, can be not only a valuable experience in itself, but it can lead to papers in which the students do say something to us. Stylistic analysis of the treatment of the same news events by two newspapers or weeklies of different editorial policy can lead to an intellectual awakening of great importance, and thus to papers that will not, cannot, bore the teacher. But this will happen only if the students' critical powers are genuinely developed. It will not do simply to teach the instructor's own prejudices.

There was a time in decades not long past when many of the most lively English teachers thought of their job as primarily to serve as handmaids to liberalism. I had one teacher in college who confessed to me that his overriding purpose was to get students to read and believe The Nation rather than the editorials of their daily paper. I suppose that his approach was not entirely valueless. It seems preferable to the effort to be noncontroversial that marks too many English teachers in the '60's, and at least it stirred some of us out of our dogmatic slumbers. But unfortunately it did nothing whatever about teaching us to think critically. Though we graduated from his course at least aware—as many college graduates do not seem to be today—that you can't believe anything you read in the daily press until you have analyzed it and related it to your past experience and to other accounts, it failed to teach us that you can't believe what you read in The Nation either. It left the job undone of training our ability to think, because it concentrated too heavily on our opinions. The result was, as I remember, that my own papers in that course were generally regurgitated liberalism. I was excited by them, and that was something. But I can't believe that the instructor found reading them anything other than a chore. There was nothing in them that came from my own experience, my own notions of what would constitute evidence for my conclusions. There I was, in Utah in the depths of the depression, writing about the Okies when I could have been writing about the impoverished farmers all around me. I wrote about race relations in the south without ever having talked with a Negro in my life and without recognizing that the bootblack I occasionally saw in Salt Lake City in the Hotel Utah was in any way related to the problem of race relations.

The third element that accounts for our boring papers is the lack of character and personality in the writer. My life, my observations, my insights were not included in those papers on the Okies and race relations and the New Deal. Every opinion was derivative, every observation second-hand. I had no real opinions of my own, and my eyes were not open wide enough for me to make first-hand observations on the world around me. What I wrote was therefore characterless, without true personality, though often full of personal pronouns. My opinions had been changed, my *self* had not. The style was the boy, the opinionated, immature, uninformed boy; whether my teacher knew it or not—and apparently he did not—his real job was to make a man of me if he wanted me to write like a man.

Putting the difficulty in this way naturally leads me to what perhaps many of you have been impatient about from the beginning. Are not the narrative arts, both as encountered in great literature and as practiced by the students themselves, the best road to the infusion of individuality that no good writing can lack? Would not a real look at the life of that bootblack, and an attempt to deal with him in narrative, have led to a more interesting paper than all of my generalized attacks on the prejudiced southerners?

I think it would, but once again I am almost more conscious of the dangers of the cure than of the advantages. As soon as we make our general rule something like, "Have the students write a personal narrative on what they know about, what they can see and feel at first hand," we have opened the floodgates for those dreadful assignments that we all find ourselves using, even though we know better: "My Summer Vacation," "Catching My First Fish," and "Our Trip to the Seattle World's Fair." Here are personal experiences that call for personal observation and narration. What's wrong with them?

Quite simply, they invite triviality, superficiality, puerility. Our students have been writing essays on such non-subjects all their lives, and until they have developed some sort of critical vision, some way of looking at the world they passed through on their vacations or fishing trips, they are going to feed us the same old bromides that have always won their passing grades. "My Summer Vacation" is an invitation to a grocery list of items, because it implies no audience, no point to be made, no point of view, no character in the speaker. A bright student will make something of such an invitation, by dramatizing the comic family quarrel that developed two days out, or by comparing his view of the American motel system with Nabokov's in *Lolita*, or by remembering the types of people seen in the campgrounds. If he had his own eyes and ears open he might have seen, in a men's room in Grand Canyon last summer, a camper with a very thick French accent trying to convert a Brooklyn Jew into believing the story of the Mormon gold plates.[5] Or he could have heard, at Mesa Verde, a young park ranger, left behind toward the end of the season by all of the experienced rangers, struggling ungrammatically

5. Bearing, according to Mormon tradition, the Book of Mormon, divinely revealed to the prophet Joseph Smith in upstate New York in 1827.

through a set speech on the geology of the area and finally breaking down in embarrassment over his lack of education. Such an episode, really *seen*, could be used narratively to say something to other high school students about what education really is.

But mere narration can be in itself just as dull as the most abstract theorizing about the nature of the universe or the most derivative opinion-mongering about politics. Even relatively skilful narration, used too obviously as a gimmick to catch interest, with no real relation to the subject, can be as dull as the most abstract pomposities. We all know the student papers that begin like *Reader's Digest* articles, with stereotyped narration that makes one doubt the event itself: "On a dark night last January, two teen agers were seen etc., etc." One can open any issue of *Time* and find this so-called narrative interest plastered throughout. From the March 29 issue I find, among many others, the following bits of fantasy: #1: "A Bolivian father sadly surveyed his nation's seven universities, then made up his mind. 'I don't want my son mixed up in politics.' . . . So saying, he sent his son off to West Germany to college." So writing, the author sends me into hysterical laughter: the quote is phony, made up for the occasion to disguise the generality of the news item. #2: "Around 12:30 P.M. every Monday and Friday, an aging Cubana Airlines turbo-prop Britannia whistles to a halt at Mexico City's International Airport. Squads of police stand by. All passengers . . . without diplomatic or Mexican passports are photographed and questioned. . . . They always dodge questions. 'Why are you here? Where are you going?' ask the Mexicans. 'None of your business,' answer the secretive travelers." "Why should I go on reading?" ask I. #3: "At 6:30 one morning early this month, a phone shrilled in the small office off the bedroom of Egypt's President. . . Nasser. [All early morning phones "shrill" for *Time*.] Already awake, he lifted the receiver to hear exciting news: a military coup had just been launched against the anti-Nasser government of Syria. The phone rang again. It was the Minister of Culture. . . . How should Radio Cairo handle the Syrian crisis? 'Support the rebels,' snapped Nasser." Oh lucky reporter, I sigh, to have such an efficient wiretapping service. #4: "In South Korea last week, a farmer named Song Kyu Il traveled all the way from the southern provinces to parade before Seoul's Duk Soo Palace with a placard scrawled in his own blood. . . . Farmer Song was thrown in jail, along with some 200 other demonstrators." That's the last we hear of Song, who is invented as an individual for this opening and then dropped. #5: "Defense Secretary Robert McNamara last spring stood beside President Kennedy on the tenth-deck bridge of the nuclear-powered carrier *Enterprise*. For as the eye could see, other U.S. ships deployed over the Atlantic seascape." Well, maybe. But for as far as the eye can see, the narrative clichés are piled, rank on rank. At 12:00 midnight last Thursday a gaunt, harried English professor could be seen hunched over his typewriter, a pile of *Time* magazines beside him on the floor. "What," he murmured to himself, sadly, "Whatever can we do about this trashy imitation of narration?"

Fortunately there is something we can do, and it is directly within our province. We can subject our students to models of genuine narration, with the sharp observation and penetrating critical judgment that underlies all good story telling, whether reportorial or fictional.

> It is a truth universally acknowledged, that a single man in possession of a good fortune must be in want of a wife.
>
> However little known the feelings or views of such a man may be on his first entering a neighborhood, this truth is so well fixed in the minds of the surrounding families, that he is considered as the rightful property of some-one or other of their daughters.
>
> "My dear Mr. Bennet," said his lady to him one day, "have you heard that Netherfield Park is let at last?"

And already we have a strong personal tone established, a tone of mocking irony which leaves Jane Austen's Mrs. Bennet revealed before us as the grasping, silly gossip she is. Or try this one:

> I am an American, Chicago-born—Chicago, that somber city—and go at things as I have taught myself, free-style, and will make the record in my own way: first to knock, first admitted; sometimes an innocent knock, sometimes a not so innocent. But a man's character is his fate, says Heraclitus, and in the end there isn't any way to disguise the nature of the knocks by acoustical work on the door or gloving the knuckles.
>
> Everybody knows there is no fineness or accuracy of suppression; if you hold down one thing you hold down the adjoining.
>
> My own parents were not much to me, though I cared for my mother. She was simple-minded, and what I learned from her was not what she taught. . . .

Do you catch the accent of Saul Bellow here, beneath the accent of his Augie March? You do, of course, but the students, many of them, do not. How do you know, they will ask, that Jane Austen is being ironic? How do you know, they ask again, that Augie is being characterized by his author through what he says? In teaching them how we know, in exposing them to the great narrative voices, ancient and modern, and in teaching them to hear these voices accurately, we are, of course, trying to change their lives, to make them new, to raise their perceptions to a new level altogether. Nobody can really catch these accents who has not grown up sufficiently to see through cheap substitutes. Or, to put it another way, a steady exposure to such voices is the very thing that will produce the maturity that alone can make our students ashamed of beclouded, com-mercial, borrowed spectacles for viewing the world.

It is true that exposure to good fiction will not in itself transform our students into good writers. Even the best-read student still needs endless hours and years of practice, with rigorous criticism. Fiction will not do the job of discipline in reasoned argument and of practice in developing habits of addressing a living audience. But in the great fiction they will learn what it means to look at something with full attention, what it means to see beneath the surface of society's platitudes. If we then give them practice in writing about things close to the home base of their own honest observations, constantly stretching their powers of generalization and argument but never allowing them to drift into pompous inanities or empty controversiality, we may have that rare but wonderful pleasure of witnessing the miracle: a man and a style where before there was only a bag of wind or a bundle of received opinions. Even when, as with most of our students, no miracles occur, we can hope for papers that we can enjoy reading. And as a final bonus, we might hope that when our students encounter someone on a train who says that he teaches English, their automatic response may be something other than looks of pity or, cries of mock alarm.

                                                        1963

THE READER

1. What steps are necessary before an "opinion" can become a "reasoned opnion"? Select some subject on which you have a strong opinion, and decide whether it is a reasoned opinion.
2. Booth characterizes the writing in the Reader's Digest and Time (p. 334). What does he feel the two magazines have in common? Analyze an article from either one of these magazines to see how accurate Booth's characterization is.

THE WRITER

1. Booth is writing for an audience of English teachers. In what ways might the essay differ if he were writing for an audience of students?
2. On p. 338, Booth says he has "now fallen" into a "tone of political exhortation." (Tone may be defined as the reflection in language of the attitude a writer takes toward his or her subject or audience or both.) What other "tones" are there in the essay? Why does Booth find it necessary to vary the tone?
3. Write an account of the process you went through in writing some paper recently or the process you typically go through in writing a paper. Then, in a paragraph or two, tell what you think Booth's comments on your process of writing might be.

Nancy Sommers

REVISION STRATEGIES OF STUDENT WRITERS AND EXPERIENCED ADULT WRITERS

Although various aspects of the writing process have been studied extensively of late, research on revision has been notably absent. * * * Dissatisfied with * * * the lack of attention to the process of revision, I conducted a series of studies over the past three years which examined the revision processes of student writers and experienced writers to see what role revision played in their writing processes. In the course of my work the revision process was redefined as *a sequence of changes in a composition—changes which are initiated by cues and occur continually throughout the writing of a work.*

Methodology

I used a case study approach. The student writers were twenty freshmen at Boston University and the University of Oklahoma with SAT verbal scores ranging from 450–600 in their first semester of composition. The twenty experienced adult writers from Boston and Oklahoma City included journalists, editors, and academics. To refer to the two groups, I use the terms *student writers* and *experienced writers* because the principal difference between these two groups is the amount of experience they have had in writing.

Each writer wrote three essays, expressive, explanatory, and persuasive, and rewrote each essay twice, producing nine written products in draft and final form. Each writer was interviewed three times after the final revision of each essay. And each writer suggested revisions for a composition written by an anonymous author. Thus extensive written and spoken documents were obtained from each writer.

The essays were analyzed by counting and categorizing the changes made. Four revision operations were identified: deletion, substitution, addition, and reordering. And four levels of changes were identified: word, phrase, sentence, theme (the extended statement of one idea). A coding system was developed for identifying the frequency of revision by level and operation. In addition, transcripts of the interviews in which the writers interpreted their revisions were used to develop what was called a *scale of concerns* for each writer. This scale enabled me to codify what were the writer's primary concerns, secondary concerns, tertiary concerns, and whether the writers used the same scale of concerns when revising the second or third drafts as they used in revising the first draft.

Revision Strategies of Student Writers

Most of the students I studied did not use the terms *revision* or *rewriting*. In fact, they did not seem comfortable using the word *revision* and explained that revision was not a word they used, but the word their teachers used. Instead, most of the students had developed various functional terms to describe the type of changes they made. The following are samples of these definitions:

Scratch Out and Do Over Again: "I say scratch out and do over, and that means what it says. Scratching out and cutting out. I read what I have written and I cross out a word and put another word in; a more decent word or a better word. Then if there is somewhere to use a sentence that I have crossed out, I will put it there."

Reviewing: "Reviewing means just using better words and eliminating words that are not needed. I go over and change words around."

Reviewing: "I just review every word and make sure that everything is worded right. I see if I am rambling; I see if I can put a better word in or leave one out. Usually when I read what I have written, I say to myself, 'that word is so bland or so trite,' and then I go and get my thesaurus."

Redoing: "Redoing means cleaning up the paper and crossing out. It is looking at something and saying, no that has to go, or no, that is not right."

Marking Out: "I don't use the word rewriting because I only write one draft and the changes that I make are made on top of the draft. The changes that I make are usually just marking out words and putting different ones in."

Slashing and Throwing Out: "I throw things out and say they are not good. I like to write like Fitzgerald did by inspiration, and if I feel inspired then I don't need to slash and throw much out."

The predominant concern in these definitions is vocabulary. The students understand the revision process as a rewording activity. They do so because they perceive words as the unit of written discourse. That is, they concentrate on particular words apart from their role in the text. Thus one student quoted above thinks in terms of dictionaries, and, following the eighteenth century theory of words parodied in *Gulliver's Travels*,[1] he imagines a load of things carried about to be exchanged. Lexical changes are the major revision activities of the students because economy is their goal. They are governed, like the linear model itself, by the Law of Occam's razor[2] that prohibits logically needless repetition:

1. In Part 3 of Jonathan Swift's work.
2. A principle of parsimony formulated by   the English philosopher William of Occam or Ockham (?1300–?49) that entities should

redundancy and superfluity. Nothing governs speech more than such superfluities; speech constantly repeats itself precisely because spoken words, as Barthes writes, are expendable in the cause of communication.[3] The aim of revision according to the students' own description is therefore to clean up speech; the redundancy of speech is unnecessary in writing, their logic suggests, because writing, unlike speech, can be reread. Thus one student said, "Redoing means cleaning up the paper and crossing out." The remarkable contradiction of cleaning by marking might, indeed, stand for student revision as I have encountered it.

The students place a symbolic importance on their selection and rejection of words as the determiners of success or failure for their compositions. When revising, they primarily ask themselves: can I find a better word or phrase? A more impressive, not so cliched, or less humdrum word? Am I repeating the same word or phrase too often? They approach the revision process with what could be labeled as a "thesaurus philosophy of writing"; the students consider the thesaurus a harvest of lexical substitutions and believe that most problems in their essays can be solved by rewording. What is revealed in the students' use of the thesaurus is a governing attitude toward their writing: that the meaning to be communicated is already there, already finished, already produced, ready to be communicated, and all that is necessary is a better word "rightly worded." One student defined revision as "redoing": "redoing" meant "just using better words and eliminating words that are not needed." For the students, writing is translating: the thought to the page, the language of speech to the more formal language of prose, the word to its synonym. Whatever is translated, an original text already exists for students, one which need not be discovered or acted upon, but simply communicated.[4]

The students list repetition as one of the elements they most worry about. This cue signals to them that they need to eliminate the repetition either by substituting or deleting words or phrases. Repetition occurs, in lage part, because student writing imitates—transcribes—speech: attention to repetitious words is a manner of cleaning speech. Without a sense of the developmental possibilities of revision (and writing in general) students seek, on the authority of many textbooks, simply to clean up their language and prepare to type. What is curious, however, is that students are aware of lexical repetition, but not conceptual repetition. They only notice the repetition if they can "hear" it; they do not diag-

---

not be multiplied unnecessarily—i.e., the simplest of competing theories should be preferred to more complex ones, and explanations of unknown phenomena should be sought in the known.
3. Sommers, in a portion of the essay omitted, cites Roland Barthes's "Writers, Intellectuals, Teachers," in *Image-Music-Text*, trans. Stephen Heath (New York: Hill and Wang, 1977).
4. Nancy Sommers and Ronald Schleifer, "Means and Ends: Some Assumptions of Student Writers," *Composition and Teaching*, [II (1981)] [author's note].

nose lexical repetition as symptomatic of problems on a deeper level. By rewording their sentences to avoid the lexical repetition, the students solve the immediate problem, but blind themselves to problems on a textual level; although they are using different words, they are sometimes merely restating the same idea with different words. Such blindness, as I discovered with student writers, is the inability to "see" revision as a process: the inability to "re-view" their work again, as it were, with different eyes, and to start over.

The revision strategies described above are consistent with the students' understanding of the revision process as requiring lexical changes but not semantic changes. For the students, the extent to which they revise is a function of their level of inspiration. In fact, they use the word *inspiration* to describe the ease or difficulty with which their essay is written, and the extent to which the essay needs to be revised. If students feel inspired, if the writing comes easily, and if they don't get stuck on individual words or phrases, then they say that they cannot see any reason to revise. Because students do not see revision as an acitivity in which they modify and develop perspectives and ideas, they feel that if they know what they want to say, then there is little reason for making revisions.

The only modification of ideas in the students' essays occurred when they tried out two or three introductory paragraphs. This results, in part, because the students have been taught in another version of the linear model of composing to use a thesis statement as a controlling device in their introductory paragraphs. Since they write their introductions and their thesis statements even before they have really discovered what they want to say, their early close attention to the thesis statement, and more generally the linear model, function to restrict and circumscribe not only the development of their ideas, but also their ability to change the direction of these ideas.

Too often as composition teachers we conclude that students do not willingly revise. The evidence from my research suggests that it is not that students are unwilling to revise, but rather that they do what they have been taught to do in a consistently narrow and predictable way. On every occasion when I asked students why they hadn't made any more changes, they essentially replied, "I knew something larger was wrong, but I didn't think it would help to move words around." The students have strategies for handling words and phrases and their strategies helped them on a word or sentence level. What they lack, however, is a set of strategies to help them identify the "something larger" that they sensed was wrong and work from there. The students do not have strategies for handling the whole essay. They lack procedures or heuristics to help them reorder lines of reasoning or ask questions about their purposes and readers. The students view their compositions in a linear way as a series of parts. Even such potentially useful concepts as "unity" or "form" are reduced to the rule that a composition, if it is to have form, must have an introduction, a body, and a conclusion, or the sum total of the necessary parts.

The students decide to stop revising when they decide that they have not violated any of the rules for revising. These rules, such as "Never begin a sentence with a conjunction" or "Never end a sentence with a preposition," are lexically cued and rigidly applied. In general, students will subordinate the demands of the specific problems of their text to the demands of the rules. Changes are made in compliance with abstract rules about the product, rules that quite often do not apply to the specific problems in the text. These revision strategies are teacher-based, directed towards a teacher-reader who expects compliance with rules— with pre-existing "conceptions"—and who will only examine parts of the composition (writing comments about those parts in the margins of their essays) and will cite any violations of rules in those parts. At best the students see their writing altogether passively through the eyes of former teachers or their surrogates, the textbooks, and are bound to the rules which they have been taught.

Revision Strategies of Experienced Writers

One aim of my research has been to contrast how student writers define revision with how a group of experienced writers define their revision processes. Here is a sampling of the definitions from the experienced writers:

Rewriting: "It is a matter of looking at the kernel of what I have written, the content, and then thinking about it, responding to it, making decisions, and actually restructuring it."

Rewriting: "I rewrite as I write. It is hard to tell what is a first draft because it is not determined by time. In one draft, I might cross out three pages, write two, cross out a fourth, rewrite it, and call it a draft. I am constantly writing and rewriting. I can only conceptualize so much in my first draft—only so much information can be held in my head at one time; my rewriting efforts are a reflection of how much information I can encompass at one time. There are levels and agenda which I have to attend to in each draft."

Rewriting: "Rewriting means on one level, finding the argument, and on another level, language changes to make the argument more effective. Most of the time I feel as if I can go on rewriting forever. There is always one part of a piece that I could keep working on. It is always difficult to know at what point to abandon a piece of writing. I like this idea that a piece of writing is never finished, just abandoned.

Rewriting: My first draft is usually very scattered. In rewriting, I find the line of argument. After the argument is resolved, I am much more interested in word choice and phrasing."

Revising: "My cardinal rule in revising is never to fall in love with what I have written in a first or second draft. An idea, sentence, or even a phrase that looks catchy, I don't trust. Part of this idea is to wait a while. I am much more in love with something after I have written it than I am a day or two later. It is much easier to change anything with time."

Revising: "It means taking apart what I have written and putting it back together again. I ask major theoretical questions of my ideas, respond to those questions, and think of proportion and structure, and try to find a controlling metaphor. I find out which ideas can be developed and which should be dropped. I am constantly chiseling and changing as I revise."

The experienced writers describe their primary objective when revising as finding the form or shape of their argument. Although the metaphors vary, the experienced writers often use structural expressions such as "finding a framework," "a pattern," or "a design" for their argument. When questioned about this emphasis, the experienced writers responded that since their first drafts are usually scattered attempts to define their territory, their objective in the second draft is to begin observing general patterns of development and deciding what should be included and what excluded. One writer explained, "I have learned from experience that I need to keep writing a first draft until I figure out what I want to say. Then in a second draft, I begin to see the structure of an argument and how all the various sub-arguments which are buried beneath the sruface of all those sentences are related." What is described here is a process in which the writer is both agent and vehicle. "Writing," says Barthes, unlike speech, "develops like a seed, not a line,"[5] and like a seed it confuses beginning and end, conception and production. Thus, the experienced writers say their drafts are "not determined by time," that rewriting is a "constant process," that they feel as if (they) "can go on forever." Revising confuses the beginning and end, the agent and vehicle; it confuses, *in order to find,* the line of argument.

After a concern for form, the experienced writers have a second objective: a concern for their readership. In this way, "production" precedes "conception." The experienced writers imagine a reader (reading their product) whose existence and whose expectations influence their revision process. They have abstracted the standards of a reader and this reader seems to be partially a reflection of themselves and functions as a critical and productive collaborator—a collaborator who has yet to love their work. The anticipation of a reader's judgment causes a feeling of dissonance when the writer recognizes incongruities between

5. "Writing Degree Zero," in *Writing Degree Zero and Elements of Semiology,* trans. Annette Lavers and Colin Smith (New York: Hill and Wang, 1968), p. 20 [author's note].

intention and execution, and requires these writers to make revisions on all levels. Such a reader gives them just what the students lacked: new eyes to "re-view" their work. The experienced writers believe that they have learned the causes and conditions, the product, which will influence their reader, and their revision strategies are geared towards creating these causes and conditions. They demonstrate a complex understanding of which examples, sentences, or phrases should be included or excluded. For example, one experienced writer decided to delete public examples and add private examples when writing about the energy crisis because "private examples would be less controversial and thus more persuasive." Another writer revised his transitional sentences because "some kinds of transitions are more easily recognized as transitions than others." These examples represent the type of strategic attempts these experienced writers use to manipulate the conventions of discourse in order to communicate to their reader.

But these revision strategies are a process of more than communication; they are part of the process of *discovering meaning* altogether. Here we can see the importance of dissonance; at the heart of revision is the process by which writers recognize and resolve the dissonance they sense in their writing. Ferdinand de Saussure has argued that meaning is differential or "diacritical," based on differences between terms rather than "essential" or inherent qualities of terms. "Phonemes," he said, "are characterized, not, as one might think, by their own positive quality but simply by the fact that they are distinct."[6] In fact, Saussure bases his entire *Course in General Linguistics* on these differences, and such differences are dissonant; like musical dissonances which gain their significance from their relationship to the "key" of the composition which itself is determined by the whole langue, specific language (parole) gains its meaning from the system of language (langue) of which it is a manifestation and part. The musical composition—a "composition" of parts—creates its "key" as in an over-all structure which determines the value (meaning) of its parts. The analogy with music is readily seen in the compositions of experienced writers: both sorts of composition are based precisely on those structures experienced writers seek in their writing. It is this complicated relationship between the parts and the whole in the work of experienced writers which destroys the linear model; writing cannot develop "like a line" because each addition or deletion is a reordering of the whole. Explicating Saussure, Jonathan Culler asserts that "meaning depends on difference of meaning."[7] But student writers constantly struggle to bring their essays into congruence with a predefined meaning. The experienced writers do the opposite: they seek

6. *Course in General Linguistics*, trans. Wade Baskin (New York: [McGraw-Hill,] 1966), p. 119 [author's note].

7. Jonathan Culler, *Saussure* (Penguin Modern Masters Series; London: Penguin Books, 1976), p. 70 [author's note].

to discover (to create) meaning in the engagement with their writing, in revision. They seek to emphasize and exploit the lack of clarity, the differences of meaning, the dissonance, that writing as opposed to speech allows in the possibility of revision. Writing has spatial and temporal features not apparent in speech—words are recorded in space and fixed in time—which is why writing is susceptible to reordering and later addition. Such features make possible the dissonance that both provokes revision and promises, from itself, new meaning.

For the experienced writers the heaviest concentration of changes is on the sentence level, and the changes are predominantly by addition and deletion. But, unlike the students, experienced writers make changes on all levels and use all revision operations. Moreover, the operations the students fail to use—reordering and addition—seem to require a theory of the revision process as a totality—a theory which, in fact, encompasses the whole of the composition. Unlike the students, the experienced writers possess a nonlinear theory in which a sense of the whole writing both precedes and grows out of an examination of the parts. As we saw, one writer said he needed "a first draft to figure out what to say," and "a second draft to see the structure of an argument buried beneath the surface." Such a "theory" is both theoretical and strategical; once again, strategy and theory are conflated in ways that are literally impossible for the linear model. Writing appears to be more like a seed than a line.

Two elements of the experienced writers' theory of the revision process are the adoption of a holistic perspective and the perception that revision is a recursive process. The writers ask: what does my essay as a whole need for form, balance, rhythm, or communication. Details are added, dropped, substituted, or reordered according to their sense of what the essay needs for emphasis and proportion. This sense, however, is constantly in flux as ideas are developed and modified; it is constantly "re-viewed" in relation to the parts. As their ideas change, revision becomes an attempt to make their writing consonant with that changing vision.

The experienced writers see their revision process as a recursive process—a process with significant recurring activities—with different levels of attention and different agenda for each cycle. During the first revision cycle their attention is primarily directed towards narrowing the topic and delimiting their ideas. At this point, they are not as concerned as they are later about vocabulary and style. The experienced writers explained that they get closer to their meaning by not limiting themselves too early to lexical concerns. As one writer commented to explain her revision process, a comment inspired by the summer 1977 New York power failure: "I feel like Con Edison cutting off certain states to keep the generators going. In first and second drafts, I try to cut off as much as I can of my editing generator, and in a third draft, I try to cut off some of my idea generators, so I can make sure that I will actually finish the essay." Although the experienced writers describe their revision process as a series of different levels or cycles, it is inaccurate to assume that they have only one objective for each cycle and that each cycle can be defined by a different objective. The same objectives and sub-processes are present in each cycle, but in different proportions. Even though these experienced writers place the predominant weight upon finding the form of their argument during the first cycle, other concerns exist as well. Conversely, during the later cycles, when the experienced writers' primary attention is focused upon stylistic concerns, they are still attuned, although in a reduced way, to the form of the argument. Since writers are limited in what they can attend to during each cycle (understandings are temporal), revision strategies help balance competing demands on attention. Thus, writers can concentrate on more than one objective at a time by developing strategies to sort out and organize their different concerns in successive cycles of revision.

It is a sense of writing as discovery—a repeated process of beginning over again, starting out new—that the students failed to have. I have used the notion of dissonance because such dissonance, the incongruities between intention and execution, governs both writing and meaning. Students do not see the incongruities. They need to rely on their own internalized sense of good writing and to see their writing with their "own" eyes. Seeing in revision—seeing beyond hearing—is at the root of the word *revision* and the process itself; current dicta on revising blind our students to what is actually involved in revision. In fact, they blind them to what constitutes good writing altogether. Good writing disturbs: it creates dissonance. Students need to seek the dissonance of discovery, utilizing in their writing, as the experienced writers do, the very difference between writing and speech—the possibility of revision.[8]

1980

8. *Acknowledgement*: The author wishes to express her gratitude to Professor William Smith, University of Pittsburgh, for his vital assistance with the research reported in this article and to Patrick Hays, her husband, for extensive discussions and critical help [author's note].

George Orwell

POLITICS AND THE ENGLISH LANGUAGE

Most people who bother with the matter at all would admit that the English language is in a bad way, but it is generally assumed that we cannot by conscious action do anything about it. Our civilization is decadent and our language—so the argument runs—must inevitably share in the general collapse. It follows that any struggle against the abuse of language is a sentimental archaism, like preferring candles to electric light or hansom cabs to aeroplanes. Underneath this lies the half-conscious belief that language is a natural growth and not an instrument which we shape for our own purposes.

Now, it is clear that the decline of a language must ultimately have political and economic causes: it is not due simply to the bad influence of this or that individual writer. But an effect can become a cause, reinforcing the original cause and producing the same effect in an intensified form, and so on indefinitely. A man may take to drink because he feels himself to be a failure, and then fail all the more completely because he drinks. It is rather the same thing that is happening to the English language. It becomes ugly and inaccurate because our thoughts are foolish, but the slovenliness of our language makes it easier for us to have foolish thoughts. The point is that the process is reversible. Modern English, especially written English, is full of bad habits which spread by imitation and which can be avoided if one is willing to take the necessary trouble. If one gets rid of these habits one can think more clearly, and to think clearly is a necessary first step towards political regeneration: so that the fight against bad English is not frivolous and is not the exclusive concern of professional writers. I will come back to this presently, and I hope that by that time the meaning of what I have said here will have become clearer. Meanwhile, here are five specimens of the English language as it is now habitually written.

These five passages have not been picked out because they are especially bad—I could have quoted far worse if I had chosen—but because they illustrate various of the mental vices from which we now suffer. They are a little below the average, but are fairly representative samples. I number them so that I can refer back to them when necessary:

> "(1) I am not, indeed, sure whether it is not true to say that the Milton who once seemed not unlike a seventeenth-century Shelley had not become, out of an experience ever more bitter in each year, more alien [sic] to the founder of that Jesuit sect which nothing could induce him to tolerate."
> Professor Harold Laski (Essay in *Freedom of Expression*).

"(2) Above all, we cannot play ducks and drakes with a native battery of idioms which prescribes such egregious collocations of vocables as the Basic *put up with* for *tolerate* or *put at a loss* for *bewilder*."

Professor Lancelot Hogben (*Interglossa*).

"(3) On the one side we have the free personality: by definition it is not neurotic, for it has neither conflict nor dream. Its desires, such as they are, are transparent, for they are just what institutional approval keeps in the fore-front of consciousness; another institutional pattern would alter their number and intensity; there is little in them that is natural, irreducible, or culturally dangerous. But *on the other side*, the social bond itself is nothing but the mutual reflection of these self-secure integrities. Recall the definition of love. Is not this the very picture of a small academic? Where is there a place in this hall of mirrors for either personality or fraternity?"

Essay on psychology in *Politics* (New York).

"(4) All the 'best people' from the gentlemen's clubs, and all the frantic fascist captains, united in common hatred of Socialism and bestial horror of the rising tide of the mass revolutionary movement, have turned to acts of provocation, to foul incendiarism, to medieval legends of poisoned wells, to legalize their own destruction of proletarian organizations, and rouse the agitated petty-bourgeoisie to chauvinistic fervour on behalf of the fight against the revolutionary way out of the crisis."

Communist pamphlet.

"(5) If a new spirit *is* to be infused into this old country, there is one thorny and contentious reform which must be tackled, and that is the humanization and galvanization of the B.B.C. Timidity here will bespeak cancer and atrophy of the soul. The heart of Britain may be sound and of strong beat, for instance, but the British lion's roar at present is like that of Bottom in Shakespeare's *Midsummer Night's Dream*—as gentle as any sucking dove. A virile new Britain cannot continue indefinitely to be traduced in the eyes or rather ears, of the world by the effete languors of Langham Place, brazenly masquerading as 'standard English'. When the Voice of Britain is heard at nine o'clock, better far and infinitely less ludicrous to hear aitches honestly dropped than the present priggish, inflated, inhibited, school-ma'amish arch braying of blameless bashful mewing maidens!"

Letter in *Tribune*.

Each of these passages has faults of its own, but, quite apart from avoidable ugliness, two qualities are common to all of them. The first is staleness of imagery: the other is lack of precision. The writer either has a meaning and cannot express it, or he inadvertently says something else, or he is almost indifferent as to whether his words mean anything or not. This mixture of vagueness and sheer incompetence is the most marked characteristic of modern English prose, and especially of any kind of political writing. As soon as certain topics are raised, the concrete melts into the abstract and no one seems able to think of turns of speech that are not hackneyed: prose consists less and less of *words* chosen for the sake of their meaning, and more and more of phrases tacked together like the sections of a prefabricated hen-house. I list below, with notes and examples, various of the tricks by means of which the work of prose-construction is habitually dodged:

Dying Metaphors

A newly invented metaphor assists thought by evoking a visual image, while on the other hand a metaphor which is technically "dead" (e.g. iron resolution) has in effect reverted to being an ordinary word and can generally be used without loss of vividness. But in between these two classes there is a huge dump of worn-out metaphors which have lost all evocative power and are merely used because they save people the trouble of inventing phrases for themselves. Examples are: Ring the changes on, take up the cudgels for, toe the line, ride roughshod over, stand shoulder to shoulder with, play into the hands of, no axe to grind, grist to the mill, fishing in troubled waters, on the order of the day, Achilles' heel, swan song, hotbed. Many of these are used without knowledge of their meaning (what is a "rift," for instance?), and incompatible metaphors are frequently mixed, a sure sign that the writer is not interested in what he is saying. Some metaphors now current have been twisted out of their original meaning without those who use them even being aware of the fact. For example, toe the line is sometimes written tow the line. Another example is the hammer and the anvil, now always used with the implication that the anvil gets the worst of it. In real life it is always the anvil that breaks the hammer, never the other way about: a writer who stopped to think what he was saying would be aware of this, and would avoid perverting the original phrase.

Operators or Verbal False Limbs

These save the trouble of picking out appropriate verbs and nouns, and at the same time pad each sentence with extra syllables which give it an appearance of symmetry. Characteristic phrases are: render inoperative, militate against, make contact with, be subjected to, give rise to, give grounds for, have the effect of, play a leading part (role) in, make itself felt, take effect, exhibit a tendency to, serve the purpose of, etc., etc. The keynote is the elimination of simple verbs. Instead of being a single word, such as break, stop, spoil, mend, kill, a verb becomes a phrase, made up of a noun or adjective tacked on to some general-purposes verb such as prove, serve, form, play, render. In addition, the passive voice is wherever possible used in preference to the active, and noun constructions are used instead of gerunds (by examination of instead of by examining). The range of verbs is further cut down by means of the -ize and de- formation, and the banal statements are given an appearance of profundity by means of the *not un-* formation. Simple conjunctions and prepositions are replaced by such phrases as *with respect to, having regard to, the fact that, by dint of, in view of, in the interests of, on the hypothesis that;* and the ends of sentences are saved from anticlimax by such resounding commonplaces as *greatly to be desired, cannot be left out of account, a development to be expected in the near future, deserving of serious consideration, brought to a satisfactory conclusion,* and so on and so forth.

Pretentious Diction

Words like *phenomenon, element, individual* (as noun), *objective, categorical, effective, virtual, basic, primary, promote, constitute, exhibit, exploit, utilize, eliminate, liquidate,* are used to dress up simple statements and give an air of scientific impartiality to biased judgments. Adjectives like *epoch-making, epic, historic, unforgettable, triumphant, age-old, inevitable, inexorable, veritable,* are used to dignify the sordid processes of international politics, while writing that aims at glorifying war usually takes on an archaic colour, its characteristic words being: *realm, throne, chariot, mailed fist, trident, sword, shield, buckler, banner, jackboot, clarion.* Foreign words and expressions such as *cul de sac, ancien régime, deus ex machina, mutatis mutandis, status quo, gleichschaltung, weltanschauung,* are used to give an air of culture and elegance. Except for the useful abbreviations *i.e., e.g.,* and *etc.,* there is no real need for any of the hundreds of foreign phrases now current in English. Bad writers, and especially scientific, political and sociological writers, are nearly always haunted by the notion that Latin or Greek words are grander than Saxon ones, and unnecessary words like *expedite, ameliorate, predict, extraneous, deracinated, clandestine, subaqueous* and hundreds of others constantly gain ground from their Anglo-Saxon opposite numbers.[1] The jargon peculiar to Marxist writing (*hyena, hangman, cannibal, petty bourgeois, these gentry, lacquey, flunkey, mad dog, White Guard,* etc.) consists largely of words and phrases translated from Russian, German or French; but the normal way of coining a new word is to use a Latin or Greek root with the appropriate affix and, where necessary, the *-ize* formation. It is often easier to make up words of this kind (*deregionalize, impermissible, extramarital, nonfragmentatory* and so forth) than to think up the English words that will cover one's meaning. The result, in general, is an increase in slovenliness and vagueness.

1. An interesting illustration of this is the way in which the English flower names which were in use till very recently are being ousted by Greek ones, *snapdragon* becoming *antirrhinum, forget-me-not* becoming *myoso-* *tis,* etc. It is hard to see any practical reason for this change of fashion: it is probably due to an instinctive turning-away from the more homely word and a vague feeling that the Greek word is scientific [Orwell's note].

Meaningless Words

In certain kinds of writing, particularly in art criticism and literary criticism, it is normal to come across long passages which are almost completely lacking in meaning.[2] Words like *romantic, plastic, values, human, dead, sentimental, natural, vitality,* as used in art criticism, are strictly meaningless in the sense that they not only do not point to any discoverable object, but are hardly ever expected to do so by the reader. When one critic writes, "The outstanding feature of Mr. X's work is its living quality", while another writes, "The immediately striking thing about Mr. X's work is its peculiar deadness", the reader accepts this as a simple difference of opinion. If words like *black* and *white* were involved, instead of the jargon words *dead* and *living,* he would see at once that language was being used in an improper way. Many political words are similarly abused. The word *Fascism* has now no meaning except in so far as it signifies "something not desirable." The words *democracy, socialism, freedom, patriotic, realistic, justice,* have each of them several different meanings which cannot be reconciled with one another. In the case of a word like *democracy,* not only is there no agreed definition, but the attempt to make one is resisted from all sides. It is almost universally felt that when we call a country democratic we are praising it: consequently the defenders of every kind of régime claim that it is a democracy, and fear that they might have to stop using the word if it were tied down to any one meaning. Words of this kind are often used in a consciously dishonest way. That is, the person who uses them has his own private definition, but allows his hearer to think he means something quite different. Statements like *Marshal Pétain was a true patriot, The Soviet Press is the freest in the world, The Catholic Church is opposed to persecution,* are almost always made with intent to deceive. Other words used in variable meanings, in most cases more or less dishonestly, are: *class, totalitarian, science, progressive, reactionary, bourgeois, equality.*

Now that I have made this catalogue of swindles and perversions, let me give another example of the kind of writing that they lead to. This time it must of its nature be an imaginary one. I am going to translate a passage of good English into modern English of the worst sort. Here is a well-known verse from *Ecclesiastes:*

"I returned and saw under the sun, that the race is not to the swift, nor the battle to the strong, neither yet bread to the wise, nor yet riches to men of

2. Example: "Comfort's catholicity of perception and image, strangely Whitmanesque in range, almost the exact opposite in aesthetic compulsion, continues to evoke that trembling atmospheric accumulative hinting at a cruel, an inexorably serene timelessness ... Wrey Gardiner scores by aiming at simple bull's-eyes with precision. Only they are not so simple, and through this contented sadness- runs more than the surface bittersweet of resignation" (*Poetry Quarterly*) [Orwell's note].

understanding, nor yet favour to men of skill; but time and chance happeneth to them all."

Here it is in modern English:

"Objective consideration of contemporary phenomena compels the conclusion that success or failure in competitive activities exhibits no tendency to be commensurate with innate capacity, but that a considerable element of the unpredictable must invariably be taken into account."

This is a parody, but not a very gross one. Exhibit (3), above, for instance, contains several patches of the same kind of English. It will be seen that I have not made a full translation. The beginning and ending of the sentence follow the original meaning fairly closely, but in the middle the concrete illustrations—race, battle, bread—dissolve into the vague phrase "success or failure in competitive activities." This had to be so, because no modern writer of the kind I am discussing—no one capable of using phrases like "objective consideration of contemporary phenomena"—would ever tabulate his thoughts in that precise and detailed way. The whole tendency of modern prose is away from concreteness. Now analyse these two sentences a little more closely. The first contains forty-nine words but only sixty syllables, and all its words are those of everyday life. The second contains thirty-eight words of ninety syllables: eighteen of its words are from Latin roots, and one from Greek. The first sentence contains six vivid images, and only one phrase ("time and chance") that could be called vague. The second contains not a single fresh, arresting phrase, and in spite of its ninety syllables it gives only a shortened version of the meaning contained in the first. Yet without a doubt it is the second kind of sentence that is gaining ground in modern English. I do not want to exaggerate. This kind of writing is not yet universal, and outcrops of simplicity will occur here and there in the worst-written page. Still, if you or I were told to write a few lines on the uncertainty of human fortunes, we should probably come much nearer to my imaginary sentence than to the one from *Ecclesiastes*.

As I have tried to show, modern writing at its worst does not consist in picking out words for the sake of their meaning and inventing images in order to make the meaning clearer. It consists in gumming together long strips of words which have already been set in order by someone else, and making the results presentable by sheer humbug. The attraction of this way of writing is that it is easy. It is easier—even quicker, once you have the habit—to say *In my opinion it is a not unjustifiable assumption that* than to say *I think*. If you use ready-made phrases, you not only don't have to hunt about for words; you also don't have to bother with the rhythms of your sentences, since these phrases are generally so arranged as to be more or less euphonious. When you are composing in a hurry—when you are dictating to a stenographer, for instance, or making a public speech—it is natural to fall into a pretentious, Latinized style. Tags like a *consideration which we should do well to bear in mind* or a *conclusion to which all of us would readily assent* will save many a sentence from coming down with a bump. By using stale metaphors, similes and idioms, you save much mental effort, at the cost of leaving your meaning vague, not only for your reader but for yourself. This is the significance of mixed metaphors. The sole aim of a metaphor is to call up a visual image. When these images clash—as in *The Fascist octopus has sung its swan song, the jackboot is thrown into the melting pot*—it can be taken as certain that the writer is not seeing a mental image of the objects he is naming; in other words he is not really thinking. Look again at the examples I gave at the beginning of this essay. Professor Laski (1) uses five negatives in fifty-three words. One of these is superfluous, making nonsense of the whole passage, and in addition there is the slip *alien* for akin, making further nonsense, and several avoidable pieces of clumsiness which increase the general vagueness. Professor Hogben (2) plays ducks and drakes with a battery which is able to write prescriptions, and, while disapproving of the everyday phrase *put up with*, is unwilling to look *egregious* up in the dictionary and see what it means. (3), if one takes an uncharitable attitude towards it, is simply meaningless: probably one could work out its intended meaning by reading the whole of the article in which it occurs. In (4), the writer knows more or less what he wants to say, but an accumulation of stale phrases chokes him like tea leaves blocking a sink. In (5), words and meaning have almost parted company. People who write in this manner usually have a general emotional meaning—they dislike one thing and want to express solidarity with another—but they are not interested in the detail of what they are saying. A scrupulous writer, in every sentence that he writes, will ask himself at least four questions, thus: What am I trying to say? What words will express it? What image or idiom will make it clearer? Is this image fresh enough to have an effect? And he will probably ask himself two more: Could I put it more shortly? Have I said anything that is avoidably ugly? But you are not obliged to go to all this trouble. You can shirk it by simply throwing your mind open and letting the ready-made phrases come crowding in. They will construct your sentences for you—even think your thoughts for you, to a certain extent—and at need they will perform the important service of partially concealing your meaning even from yourself. It is at this point that the special connection between politics and the debasement of language becomes clear.

In our time it is broadly true that political writing is bad writing. Where it is not true, it will generally be found that the writer is some kind of rebel, expressing his private opinions and not a "party line." Orthodoxy, of whatever colour, seems to demand a lifeless, imitative style. The political dialects to be found in pamphlets, leading articles, manifestos, White Papers and the speeches of under-secretaries do, of course, vary from party to party, but they are all alike in that one almost never finds in them a fresh, vivid, home-made turn of speech. When one watches some tired hack on the platform mechanically repeating the familiar phrases—*bestial atrocities, iron heel, bloodstained tyranny, free peoples of the world, stand shoulder to shoulder*—one often has a curious feeling that one is not watching a live human being but some kind of dummy: a feeling which suddenly becomes stronger at moments when the light catches the speaker's spectacles and turns them into blank discs which seem to have no eyes behind them. And this is not altogether fanciful. A speaker who uses that kind of phraseology has gone some distance towards turning himself into a machine. The appropriate noises are coming out of his larynx, but his brain is not involved as it would be if he were choosing his words for himself. If the speech he is making is one that he is accustomed to make over and over again, he may be almost unconscious of what he is saying, as one is when one utters the responses in church. And this reduced state of consciousness, if not indispensable, is at any rate favourable to political conformity.

In our time, political speech and writing are largely the defence of the indefensible. Things like the continuance of British rule in India, the Russian purges and deportations, the dropping of the atom bombs on Japan, can indeed be defended, but only by arguments which are too brutal for most people to face, and which do not square with the professed aims of political parties. Thus political language has to consist largely of euphemism, question-begging and sheer cloudy vagueness. Defenceless villages are bombarded from the air, the inhabitants driven out into the countryside, the cattle machine-gunned, the huts set on fire with incendiary bullets: this is called *pacification*. Millions of peasants are robbed of their farms and sent trudging along the roads with no more than they can carry: this is called *transfer of population* or *rectification of frontiers*. People are imprisoned for years without trial, or shot in the back of the neck or sent to die of scurvy in Arctic lumber camps: this is called *elimination of unreliable elements*. Such phraseology is needed if one wants to name things without calling up mental pictures of them. Consider for instance some comfortable English professor defending Russian totalitarianism. He cannot say outright, "I believe in killing off your opponents when you can get good results by doing so." Probably, therefore, he will say something like this:

"While freely conceding that the Soviet régime exhibits certain features which the humanitarian may be inclined to deplore, we must, I think, agree that a certain curtailment of the right to political opposition is an unavoidable concomitant of transitional periods, and that the rigors which the Russian people have been called upon to undergo have been amply justified in the sphere of concrete achievement."

The inflated style is itself a kind of euphemism. A mass of Latin words falls upon the facts like soft snow, blurring the outlines and covering up all the details. The great enemy of clear language is insincerity. When there is a gap between one's real and one's declared aims, one turns as it were instinctively to long words and exhausted idioms, like a cuttlefish squirting out ink. In our age there is no such thing as "keeping out of politics." All issues are political issues, and politics itself is a mass of lies, evasions, folly, hatred and schizophrenia. When the general atmosphere is bad, language must suffer. I should expect to find—this is a guess which I have not sufficient knowledge to verify—that the German, Russian and Italian languages have all deteriorated in the last ten or fifteen years, as a result of dictatorship.

But if thought corrupts language, language can also corrupt thought. A bad usage can spread by tradition and imitation, even among people who should and do know better. The debased language that I have been discussing is in some ways very convenient. Phrases like a *not unjustifiable assumption, leaves much to be desired, would serve no good purpose, a consideration which we should do well to bear in mind,* are a continuous temptation, a packet of aspirins always at one's elbow. Look back through this essay, and for certain you will find that I have again and again committed the very faults I am protesting against. By this morning's post I have received a pamphlet dealing with conditions in Germany. The author tells me that he "felt impelled" to write it. I open it at random, and here is almost the first sentence that I see: "(The Allies) have an opportunity not only of achieving a radical transformation of Germany's social and political structure in such a way as to avoid a nationalistic reaction in Germany itself, but at the same time of laying the foundations of a co-operative and unified Europe." You see, he "feels impelled" to write—feels, presumably, that he has something new to say—and yet his words, like cavalry horses answering the bugle, group themselves automatically into the familiar dreary pattern. This invasion of one's mind by ready-made phrases (*lay the foundations, achieve a radical transformation*) can only be prevented if one is constantly on guard against them, and every such phrase anaesthetizes a portion of one's brain.

I said earlier that the decadence of our language is probably curable. Those who deny this would argue, if they produced an argument at all, that language merely reflects existing social conditions, and that we cannot influence its development by any direct tinkering with words and constructions. So far as the general tone or spirit of a language goes, this may be true, but it is not true in detail. Silly words and expressions have often disappeared, not through any evolutionary process but owing to the conscious action of a minority. Two recent examples were *explore every avenue* and *leave no stone unturned,* which were killed by the jeers of a few journalists. There is a long list of flyblown metaphors which could similarly be got rid of if enough people would interest themselves in the job; and it should also be possible to laugh the *not un-* formation out of existence,[3] to reduce the amount of Latin and Greek in the average sentence, to drive out foreign phrases and strayed scientific words, and, in general, to make pretentiousness unfashionable. But all these are minor points. The defence of the English language implies more than this, and perhaps it is best to start by saying what it does *not* imply.

To begin with it has nothing to do with archaism, with the salvaging of obsolete words and turns of speech, or with the setting up of a "standard English" which must never be departed from. On the contrary, it is especially concerned with the scrapping of every word or idiom which has outworn its usefulness. It has nothing to do with correct grammar and syntax, which are of no importance so long as one makes one's meaning clear, or with the avoidance of Americanisms, or with having what is called a "good prose style." On the other hand it is not concerned with fake simplicity and the attempt to make written English colloquial. Nor does it even imply in every case preferring the Saxon word to the Latin one, though it does imply using the fewest and shortest words that will cover one's meaning. What is above all needed is to let the meaning choose the word, and not the other way about. In prose, the worst thing one can do with words is to surrender to them. When you think of a concrete object, you think wordlessly, and then, if you want to describe the thing you have been visualizing you probably hunt about till you find the exact words that seem to fit. When you think of something abstract you are more inclined to use words from the start, and unless you make a conscious effort to prevent it, the existing dialect will come rushing in and do the job for you, at the expense of blurring or even changing your meaning. Probably it is better to put off using words as long as possible and get one's meaning as clear as one can through pictures or sensations. Afterwards one can choose—not simply *accept*—the phrases that will best cover the meaning, and then switch round and decide what impression one's words are likely to make on another person. This last effort of the mind cuts out all stale or mixed images, all prefabricated phrases, needless repetitions, and humbug and vagueness generally. But one can often be in doubt about the effect of a word or a phrase, and one needs rules that one can rely on when instinct fails. I think the following rules will cover most cases:

    (i) Never use a metaphor, simile or other figure of speech which you are used to seeing in print.

    (ii) Never use a long word where a short one will do.

    (iii) If it is possible to cut a word out, always cut it out.

3. One can cure oneself of the *not un-*formation by memorizing this sentence: *A not un-black dog was chasing a not unsmall rabbit across a not ungreen field* [Orwell's note].

(iv) Never use the passive where you can use the active.

(v) Never use a foreign phrase, a scientific word or a jargon word if you can think of an everyday English equivalent.

(vi) Break any of these rules sooner than say anything outright barbarous.

These rules sound elementary, and so they are, but they demand a deep change of attitude in anyone who has grown used to writing in the style now fashionable. One could keep all of them and still write bad English, but one could not write the kind of stuff that I quoted in those five specimens at the beginning of this article.

I have not here been considering the literary use of language, but merely language as an instrument for expressing and not for concealing or preventing thought. Stuart Chase and others have come near to claiming that all abstract words are meaningless, and have used this as a pretext for advocating a kind of political quietism. Since you don't know what Fascism is, how can you struggle against Fascism? One need not swallow such absurdities as this, but one ought to recognize that the present political chaos is connected with the decay of language, and that one can probably bring about some improvement by starting at the verbal end. If you simplify your English, you are freed from the worst follies of orthodoxy. You cannot speak any of the necessary dialects, and when you make a stupid remark its stupidity will be obvious, even to yourself. Political language—and with variations this is true of all political parties, from Conservatives to Anarchists—is designed to make lies sound truthful and murder respectable, and to give an appearance of solidity to pure wind. One cannot change this all in a moment, but one can at least change one's own habits, and from time to time one can even, if one jeers loudly enough, send some worn-out and useless phrase—some jackboot, Achilles' heel, hotbed, melting pot, acid test, veritable inferno or other lump of verbal refuse—into the dustbin where it belongs.

1946

THE READER

1. What is Orwell's pivotal point? Where is it best stated?
2. Discuss Orwell's assertion that "the decline of a language must ultimately have political and economic causes." Is this "clear," as he claims?
3. Orwell suggests that if you look back through his essay, you will find that he has "again and again committed the very faults" he is protesting against. Is this true? If it is, does it affect the validity of his major points?

THE WRITER

1. How can you be sure that a metaphor is dying, rather than alive or dead? Is Orwell's test of seeing it often in print a sufficient one? Can you defend any of his examples of dying metaphors as necessary or

useful additions to our vocabularies?

2. Orwell gives a list of questions for the writer to ask himself (p. 359) and a list of rules for the writer to follow (p. 362). Why does he consider it necessary to give both kinds of advice? How much do the two overlap? Are both consistent with Orwell's major ideas expressed elsewhere in the essay? Does his injunction to "break any of these rules sooner than say anything outright barbarous" beg the question?

3. Words create a personality or confer a character. Write a brief essay describing the personality that would be created by following Orwell's six rules. Show that character in action.

grammar → structure that relates part of sentence

statement (problem)

- order for ... - not ... grammar - flow

conclusion (solution)

eg: warranty on a car - overuse warranty in language ex. 18 yr warranty But in reality product was good why is warranty needed.

- think about the similarity between Orwell's example of English language and your own experiences

analysis, account for language is used to manipulate, cheat etc. interpersonal accounts - saying what you mean!!

An Album of Styles

Francis Bacon: OF REVENGE

Revenge is a kind of wild justice; which the more man's nature runs to, the more ought law to weed it out. For as for the first wrong, it doth but offend the law; but the revenge of that wrong putteth the law out of office. Certainly, in taking revenge, a man is but even with his enemy; but in passing it over, he is superior; for it is a prince's part to pardon. And Salomon, I am sure, saith, *It is the glory of a man to pass by an offence.* That which is past is gone, and irrevocable; and wise men have enough to do with things present and to come: therefore they do but trifle with themselves, that labour in past matters. There is no man doth a wrong for the wrong's sake; but thereby to purchase himself profit, or pleasure, or honour, or the like. Therefore why should I be angry with a man for loving himself better than me? And if any man should do wrong merely out of ill nature, why, yet it is but like the thorn or briar, which prick and scratch, because they can do no other. The most tolerable sort of revenge is for those wrongs which there is no law to remedy; but then let a man take heed the revenge be such as there is no law to punish; else a man's enemy is still beforehand, and it is two for one. Some, when they take revenge, are desirous the party should know whence it cometh: this is the more generous. For the delight seemeth to be not so much in doing the hurt as in making the party repent: but base and crafty cowards are like the arrow that flieth in the dark. Cosmus, duke of Florence, had a desperate saying against perfidious or neglecting friends, as if those wrongs were unpardonable: *You shall read* (saith he) *that we are commanded to forgive our enemies; but you never read that we are commanded to forgive our friends.* But yet the spirit of Job was in a better tune: *Shall we* (saith he) *take good at God's hands, and not be content to take evil also?* And so of friends in a proportion. This is certain, that a man that studieth revenge keeps his own wounds green, which otherwise would heal and do well. Public revenges are for the most part fortunate; as that for the death of Caesar; for the death of Pertinax;[1] for the death of Henry the third of France;[2] and many more. But in private revenges it is not so. Nay rather, vindictive persons live the life of witches; who as they are mischievous, so end they infortunate.

1625

1. Publius Helvius Pertinax became Emperor of Rome in 193 and was assassinated three months after his accession to the throne by a soldier in his praetorian Guard.
2. King of France 1574–1589; assassinated during the Siege of Paris.

John Donne: MEN ARE SLEEPING PRISONERS

We are all conceived in close prison; in our Mothers wombs, we are close prisoners all; when we are born, we are born but to the liberty of the house;[1] prisoners still, though within larger walls; and then all our life is but a going out to the place of execution, to death. Now was there ever any man seen to sleep in the cart, between Newgate, and Tyburn?[2] Between the prison and the place of execution, does any man sleep? And we sleep all the way; from the womb to the grave we are never thoroughly awake; but pass on with such dreams, and imaginations as these, I may live as well, as another, and why should I die, rather than another? But awake, and tell me, says this text *Quis homo?*[3] Who is that other that thou talkest of? *What man is he that liveth, and shall not see death?*

1640

1. Donne distinguishes between a prisoner confined to a cell and one given somewhat more liberty.
2. London prisoners were taken in carts from Newgate prison to nearby Tyburn for execution.
3. "Who [is] the man?"

Samuel Johnson: THE PYRAMIDS

Of the wall [of China] it is very easy to assign the motives. It secured a wealthy and timorous nation from the incursions of Barbarians, whose unskillfulness in arts made it easier for them to supply their wants by rapine than by industry, and who from time to time poured in upon the habitations of peaceful commerce, as vultures descend upon domestic fowl. Their celerity and fierceness made the wall necessary, and their ignorance made it efficacious.

But for the pyramids no reason has ever been given adequate to the cost and labor of the work. The narrowness of the chambers proves that it could afford no retreat from enemies, and treasures might have been reposited at far less expense with equal security. It seems to have been erected only in compliance with that hunger of imagination which preys incessantly upon life, and must be always appeased by some employment. Those who have already all that they can enjoy, must enlarge their desires. He that has built for use, till use is supplied must begin to build for vanity, and extend his plan to the utmost power of human performance, that he may not be soon reduced to form another wish.

I consider this mighty structure as a monument of the insufficiency of human enjoyments. A king, whose power is unlimited, and whose treasures surmount all real and imaginary wants, is compelled to solace, by the erection of a pyramid, the satiety of dominion and tastelessness of pleasures, and to amuse the tediousness of declining life, by seeing thousands laboring without end, and one stone, for no purpose, laid upon another. Whoever thou art, that, not content with a moderate condition, imaginest happiness in royal magnificence, and dreamest that command or riches can feed the appetite of novelty with perpetual gratifications, survey the pyramids, and confess thy folly!

1759

Laurence Sterne: Of Door Hinges and Life in General

Every day for at least ten years together did my father resolve to have it mended—'tis not mended yet: no family but ours would have borne with it an hour—and what is most astonishing, there was not a subject in the world upon which my father was so eloquent, as upon that of door-hinges. And yet at the same time, he was certainly one of the greatest bubbles to them, I think, that history can produce: his rhetoric and conduct were at perpetual handycuffs. Never did the parlor-door open—but his philosophy or his principles fell a victim to it; three drops of oyl with a feather, and a smart stroke of a hammer, had saved his honor for ever. Inconsistent soul that man is—languishing under wounds, which he has the power to heal—his whole life a contradiction to his knowledge—his reason, that precious gift of God to him—(instead of pouring in oyl) serving but to sharpen his sensibilities, to multiply his pains and render him more melancholy and uneasy under them—poor unhappy creature, that he should do so! Are not the necessary causes of misery in this life enow, but he must add voluntary ones to his stock of sorrow, struggle against evils which cannot be avoided, and submit to others, which a tenth part of the trouble they create him, would remove from his heart forever?

By all that is good and virtuous! if there are three drops of oyl to be got, and a hammer to be found within ten miles of Shandy-Hall, the parlordoor hinge shall be mended this reign.

1767

John Henry Newman: Knowledge and Virtue

Knowledge is one thing, virtue is another; good sense is not conscience, refinement is not humility, nor is largeness and justness of view faith. Philosophy, however enlightened, however profound, gives no command over the passions, no influential motives, no vivifying principles. Liberal Education makes not the Christian, not the Catholic, but the gentleman. It is well to be a gentleman, it is well to have a cultivated intellect, a delicate taste, a candid, equitable, dispassionate mind, a noble and courteous bearing in the conduct of life—these are the connatural qualities of a large knowledge; they are the objects of a University; I am advocating, I shall illustrate and insist upon them; but still, I repeat, they are no guarantee for sanctity or even for conscientiousness, they may attach to the man of the world, to the profligate, to the heartless, pleasant, alas, and attractive as he shows when decked out in them. Taken by themselves, they do but seem to be what they are not; they look like virtue at a distance, but they are detected by close observers, and on the long run; and hence it is that they are popularly accused of pretense and hypocrisy, not, I repeat, from their own fault, but because their professors and their admirers persist in taking them for what they are not, and are officious in arrogating for them a praise to which they have no claim. Quarry the granite rock with razors, or moor the vessel with a thread of silk; then may you hope with such keen and delicate instruments as human knowledge and human reason to contend against those giants, the passion and the pride of man.

1852

Abraham Lincoln: THE GETTYSBURG ADDRESS

Four score and seven years ago our fathers brought forth on this continent, a new nation, conceived in Liberty, and dedicated to the proposition that all men are created equal.

Now we are engaged in a great civil war, testing whether that nation, or any nation so conceived and so dedicated, can long endure. We are met on a great battle-field of that war. We have come to dedicate a portion of that field, as a final resting place for those who here gave their lives that that nation might live. It is altogether fitting and proper that we should do this.

But, in a larger sense, we can not dedicate—we can not consecrate—we can not hallow—this ground. The brave men, living and dead, who struggled here, have consecrated it, far above our poor power to add or detract. The world will little note, nor long remember what we say here, but it can never forget what they did here. It is for us the living, rather, to be dedicated here to the unfinished work which they who fought here have thus far so nobly advanced. It is rather for us to be here dedicated to the great task remaining before us—that from these honored dead we take increased devotion to that cause for which they gave the last full measure of devotion—that we here highly resolve that these dead shall not have died in vain—that this nation, under God, shall have a new birth of freedom—and that government of the people, by the people, for the people, shall not perish from the earth.

1863

Matthew Arnold: CULTURE

But there is of culture another view, in which not solely the scientific passion, the sheer desire to see things as they are, natural and proper in an intelligent being, appears as the ground of it. There is a view in which all the love of our neighbor, the impulses towards action, help, and benefi-cence, the desire for removing human error, clearing human confusion, and diminishing human misery, the noble aspiration to leave the world better and happier than we found it—motives eminently such as are called social—come in as part of the grounds of culture, and the main and pre-eminent part. Culture is then properly described not as having its origin in curiosity, but as having its origin in the love of perfection; it is a *study of perfection.* It moves by the force, not merely or primarily of the scientific passion for pure knowledge, but also of the moral and social passion for doing good. As, in the first view of it, we took for its worthy motto Montesquieu's words: "To render an intelligent being yet more intelligent!" so, in the second view of it, there is no better motto which it can have than these words of Bishop Wilson: "To make reason and the will of God prevail!"

Only, whereas the passion for doing good is apt to be overhasty in determining what reason and the will of God say, because its turn is for acting rather than thinking, and it wants to be beginning to act; and whereas it is apt to take its own conceptions, which proceed from its own state of development and share in all the imperfections and immaturities of this, for a basis of action; what distinguishes culture is, that it is possessed by the scientific passion as well as by the passion of doing good; that it demands worthy notions of reason and the will of God, and does not readily suffer its own crude conceptions to substitute themselves for them. And knowing that no action or institution can be salutary and stable which is not based on reason and the will of God, it is not so bent on acting and instituting, even with the great aim of diminishing human error and misery ever before its thoughts, but that it can remember that acting and instituting are of little use, unless we know how and what we ought to act and to institute.

1869

Walter Pater: THE MONA LISA

The presence that rose thus so strangely beside the waters, is expressive of what in the ways of a thousand years men had come to desire. Hers is the head upon which all "the ends of the world are come," and the eyelids are a little weary. It is a beauty wrought out from within upon the flesh, the deposit, little cell by cell, of strange thoughts and fantastic reveries and exquisite passions. Set it for a moment beside one of those white Greek goddesses or beautiful women of antiquity, and how would they be troubled by this beauty, into which the soul with all its maladies has passed! All the thoughts and experience of the world have etched and molded there, in that which they have of power to refine and make expressive the outward form, the animalism of Greece, the lust of Rome, the mysticism of the middle ages with its spiritual ambition and imaginative loves, the return of the Pagan world, the sins of the Borgias. She is older than the rocks among which she sits; like the vampire, she has been dead many times, and learned the secrets of the grave; and has been a diver in deep seas, and keeps their fallen day about her; and trafficked for strange webs with Eastern merchants: and, as Leda, was the mother of Helen of Troy, and, as Saint Anne, the mother of Mary; and all this has been to her but as the sound of lyres and flutes, and lives only in the delicacy with which it has molded the changing lineaments, and tinged the eyelids and the hands. The fancy of a perpetual life, sweeping together ten-thousand experiences, is an old one; and modern philosophy has conceived the idea of humanity as wrought upon by, and summing up in itself, all modes of thought and life. Certainly Lady Lisa might stand as the embodiment of the old fancy, the symbol of the modern idea.

1868   1873

371

Anonymous: NO DAWN TO THE EAST

My sun is set. My day is done. Darkness is stealing over me. Before I lie down to rise no more I will speak to my people. Hear me, for this is not the time to tell a lie. The Great Spirit made us, and gave us this land we live in. He gave us the buffalo, antelope, and deer for food and clothing. Our hunting grounds stretched from the Mississippi to the great mountains. We were free as the winds and heard no man's commands. We fought our enemies, and feasted our friends. Our braves drove away all who would take our game. They captured women and horses from our foes. Our children were many and our herds were large. Our old men talked with spirits and made good medicine. Our young men hunted and made love to the girls. Where the tipi was, there we stayed, and no house imprisoned us. No one said, "To this line is my land, to that is yours." Then the white man came to our hunting grounds, a stranger. We gave him meat and presents, and told him go in peace. He looked on our women and stayed to live in our tipis. His fellows came to build their roads across our hunting grounds. He brought among us the mysterious iron that shoots. He brought with him the magic water that makes men foolish. With his trinkets and beads he even bought the girl I loved. I said, "The white man is not a friend, let us kill him." But their numbers were greater than blades of grass. They took away the buffalo and shot down our best warriors. They took away our lands and surrounded us by fences. Their soldiers camped outside with cannon to shoot us down. They wiped the trails of our people from the face of the prairies. They forced our children to forsake the ways of their fathers. When I turn to the east I see no dawn. When I turn to the west the approaching night hides all.

c. 1870

Ernest Hemingway: FROM A FAREWELL TO ARMS

* * * I was always embarrassed by the words sacred, glorious, and sacrifice and the expression in vain. We had heard them, sometimes standing in the rain almost out of earshot, so that only the shouted words came through, and had read them, on proclamations that were slapped up by billposters over other proclamations, now for a long time, and I had seen nothing sacred, and the things that were glorious had no glory and the sacrifices were like the stockyards at Chicago if nothing was done with the meat except to bury it. There were many words that you could not stand to hear and finally only the names of places had dignity. Certain numbers were the same way and certain dates and these with the names of places were all you could say and have them mean anything. Abstract words such as glory, honor, courage, or hallow were obscene beside the concrete names of villages, the numbers of roads, the names of rivers, the numbers of regiments and the dates.

1929

Virginia Woolf: WHAT THE NOVELIST GIVES US

It is simple enough to say that since books have classes—fiction, biography, poetry—we should separate them and take from each what it is right that each should give us. Yet few people ask from books what books can give us. Most commonly we come to books with blurred and divided minds, asking of fiction that it shall be true, of poetry that it shall be false, of biography that it shall be flattering, of history that it shall enforce our own prejudices. If we could banish all such preconceptions when we read, that would be an admirable beginning. Do not dictate to your author; try to become him. Be his fellow-worker and accomplice. If you hang back, and reserve and criticize at first, you are preventing yourself from getting the fullest possible value from what you read. But if you open your mind as widely as possible, then signs and hints of almost imperceptible fineness, from the twist and turn of the first sentences, will bring you into the presence of a human being unlike any other. Steep yourself in this, acquaint yourself with this, and soon you will find that your author is giving you, or attempting to give you, something far more definite. The thirty-two chapters of a novel—if we consider how to read a novel first—are an attempt to make something as formed and controlled as a building: but words are more impalpable than bricks; reading is a longer and more complicated process than seeing. Perhaps the quickest way to understand the elements of what a novelist is doing is not to read, but to write; to make your own experiment with the dangers and difficulties of words. Recall, then, some event that has left a distinct impression on you—how at the corner of the street, perhaps, you passed two people talking. A tree shook; an electric light danced; the tone of the talk was comic, but also tragic; a whole vision, an entire conception, seemed contained in that moment.

But when you attempt to reconstruct it in words, you will find that it breaks into a thousand conflicting impressions. Some must be subdued; others emphasized; in the process you will lose, probably, all grasp upon the emotion itself. Then turn from your blurred and littered pages to the opening pages of some great novelist—Defoe, Jane Austen, Hardy. Now you will be better able to appreciate their mastery. It is not merely that we are in the presence of a different person—Defoe, Jane Austen, or Thomas Hardy—but that we are living in a different world. Here, in *Robinson Crusoe*, we are trudging a plain high road; one thing happens after another; the fact and the order of the fact is enough. But if the open air and adventure mean everything to Defoe they mean nothing to Jane Austen. Hers is the drawing-room, and people talking, and by the many mirrors of their talk revealing their characters. And if, when we have accustomed ourselves to the drawing-room and its reflections, we turn to Hardy, we are once more spun around. The moors are round us and the stars are above our heads. The other side of the mind is now exposed— the dark side that comes uppermost in solitude, not the light side that shows in company. Our relations are not towards people, but towards Nature and destiny. Yet different as these worlds are, each is consistent with itself. The maker of each is careful to observe the laws of his own perspective, and however great a strain they may put upon us they will never confuse us, as lesser writers so frequently do, by introducing two different kinds of reality into the same book. Thus to go from one great novelist to another—from Jane Austen to Hardy, from Peacock to Trollope, from Scott to Meredith—is to be wrenched and uprooted; to be thrown this way and then that. To read a novel is a difficult and complex art. You must be capable not only of great finesse of perception, but of great boldness of imagination if you are going to make use of all that the novelist—the great artist—gives you.

1932

E. B. White: Progress and Change

In resenting progress and change, a man lays himself open to censure. I suppose the explanation of anyone's defending anything as rudimentary and cramped as a Pullman berth is that such things are associated with an earlier period in one's life and that this period in retrospect seems a happy one. People who favor progress and improvements are apt to be people who have had a tough enough time without any extra inconvenience. Reactionaries who pout at innovations are apt to be well-heeled sentimentalists who had the breaks. Yet for all that, there is always a subtle danger in life's refinements, a dim degeneracy in progress. I have just been refining the room in which I sit, yet I sometimes doubt that a writer should refine or improve his workroom by so much as a dictionary: one thing leads to another and the first thing you know he has a stuffed chair and is fast asleep in it. Half a man's life is devoted to what he calls improvements, yet the original had some quality which is lost in the process. There was a fine natural spring of water on this place when I bought it. Our drinking water had to be lugged in a pail, from a wet glade of alder and tamarack. I visited the spring often in those first years, and had friends there—a frog, a woodcock, and an eel which had churned its way all the way up through the pasture creek to enjoy the luxury of pure water. In the normal course of development, the spring was rocked up, fitted with a concrete curb, a copper pipe, and an electric pump. I have visited it only once or twice since. This year my only gesture was the purely perfunctory one of sending a sample to the state bureau of health for analysis. I felt cheap, as though I were smelling an old friend's breath.

1938

Joyce Cary: ART AND EDUCATION

A very large number of people cease when quite young to add anything to a limited stock of judgments. After a certain age, say 25, they consider that their education is finished.

It is perhaps natural that having passed through that painful and boring process, called expressly education, they should suppose it over, and that they are equipped for life to label every event as it occurs and drop it into its given pigeonhole. But one who has a label ready for everything does not bother to observe any more, even such ordinary happenings as he has observed for himself, with attention, before he went to school. He merely acts and reacts.

For people who have stopped noticing, the only possible new or renewed experience, and, therefore, new knowledge, is from a work of art. Because that is the only kind of experience which they are prepared to receive on its own terms, they will come out from their shells and expose themselves to music, to a play, to a book, because it is the accepted method of enjoying such things. True, even to plays and books they may bring artistic prejudices which prevent them from seeing *that* play or comprehending *that* book. Their artistic sensibilities may be as crusted over as their minds.

But it is part of an artist's job to break crusts, or let us say rather that artists who work for the public and not merely for themselves are interested in breaking crusts because they want to communicate their intuitions.

1949

William Faulkner: NOBEL PRIZE AWARD SPEECH

I feel that this award was not made to me as a man but to my work—a life's work in the agony and sweat of the human spirit, not for glory and least of all for profit, but to create out of the materials of the human spirit something which did not exist before. So this award is only mine in trust. It will not be difficult to find a dedication for the money part of it commensurate with the purpose and significance of its origin. But I would like to do the same with the acclaim too, by using this moment as a pinnacle from which I might be listened to by the young men and women already dedicated to the same anguish and travail, among whom is already that one who will some day stand here where I am standing.

Our tragedy today is a general and universal physical fear so long sustained by now that we can even bear it. There are no longer problems of the spirit. There is only the question: When will I be blown up? Because of this, the young man or woman writing today has forgotten the problems of the human heart in conflict with itself which alone can make good writing because only that is worth writing about, worth the agony and the sweat.

He must learn them again. He must teach himself that the basest of all things is to be afraid; and, teaching himself that, forget it forever, leaving no room in his workshop for anything but the old verities and truths of the heart, the old universal truths lacking which any story is ephemeral and doomed—love and honor and pity and pride and compassion and sacrifice. Until he does so, he labors under a curse. He writes not of love but of lust, of defeats in which nobody loses anything of value, of victories without hope and, worst of all, without pity or compassion. His griefs grieve on no universal bones leaving no scars. He writes not of the heart but of the glands.

Until he relearns these things, he will write as though he stood alone and watched the end of man. I decline to accept the end of man. It is easy enough to say that man is immortal simply because he will endure; that when the last ding-dong of doom has clanged and faded from the last worthless rock hanging tideless in the last red and dying evening, that even then there will still be one more sound: that of his puny inexhaustible voice, still talking. I refuse to accept this. I believe that man will not merely endure: he will prevail. He is immortal, not because he alone among creatures has an inexhaustible voice but because he has a soul, a spirit capable of compassion and sacrifice and endurance. The poet's, the writer's, duty is to write about these things. It is his privilege to help man endure by lifting his heart, by reminding him of the courage and honor and hope and pride and compassion and pity and sacrifice which have been the glory of his past. The poet's voice need not merely be the record of man, it can be one of the props, the pillars to help him endure and prevail.

1949

James Thurber: A Dog's Eye View of Man

If Man has benefited immeasurably by his association with the dog, what, you may ask, has the dog got out of it? His scroll has, of course, been heavily charged with punishments: he has known the muzzle, the leash, and the tether; he has suffered the indignities of the show bench, the tin can on the tail, the ribbon in the hair; his love life with the other sex of his species has been regulated by the frigid hand of authority, his digestion ruined by the macaroons and marshmallows of doting women. The list of his woes could be continued indefinitely. But he has also had his fun, for he has been privileged to live with and study at close range the only creature with reason, the most unreasonable of creatures.

The dog has got more fun out of Man than Man has got out of the dog, for the clearly demonstrable reason that Man is the more laughable of the two animals. The dog has long been bemused by the singular activities and the curious practices of men, cocking his head inquiringly to one side, intently watching and listening to the strangest goings-on in the world. He has seen men sing together and fight one another in the same evening. He has watched them go to bed when it is time to get up, and get up when it is time to go to bed. He has observed them destroying the soil in vast areas, and nurturing it in small patches. He has stood by while men built strong and solid houses for rest and quiet, and then filled them with lights and bells and machinery. His sensitive nose, which can detect what's cooking in the next township, has caught at one and the same time the bewildering smells of the hospital and the munitions factory. He has seen men raise up great cities to heaven and then blow them to hell.

1955

John Updike: BEER CAN

This seems to be an era of gratuitous inventions and negative improvements. Consider the beer can. It was beautiful—as beautiful as the clothespin, as inevitable as the wine bottle, as dignified and reassuring as the fire hydrant. A tranquil cylinder of delightfully resonant metal, it could be opened in an instant, requiring only the application of a handy gadget freely dispensed by every grocer. Who can forget the small, symmetrical thrill of those two triangular punctures, the dainty *pffff*, the little crest of suds that foamed eagerly in the exultation of release? Now we are given, instead, a top beetling with an ugly, shmoo-shaped "tab," which, after fiercely resisting the tugging, bleeding fingers of the thirsty man, threatens his lips with a dangerous and hideous hole. However, we have discovered a way to thwart Progress, usually so unthwartable. *Turn the beer can upside down and open the bottom.* The bottom is still the way the top used to be. True, this operation gives the beer an unsettling jolt, and the sight of a consistently inverted beer can might make people edgy, not to say queasy. But the latter difficulty could be eliminated if manufacturers would design cans that looked the same whichever end was up, like playing cards. What we need is Progress with an escape hatch.

1964

Tom Wolfe: THE LEGEND OF JUNIOR JOHNSON

The legend of Junior Johnson! In this legend, here is a country boy, Junior Johnson, who learns to drive by running whiskey for his father, Johnson, Senior, one of the biggest copper-still operators of all time, up in Ingle Hollow, near North Wilkesboro, in northwestern North Carolina, and grows up to be a famous stock car racing driver, rich, grossing $100,000 in 1963, for example, respected, solid, idolized in his hometown and throughout the rural South. There is all this about how good old boys would wake up in the middle of the night in the apple shacks and hear a supercharged Oldsmobile engine roaring over Brushy Mountain and say, "Listen at him—there he goes!" although that part is doubtful, since some nights there were so many good old boys taking off down the road in supercharged automobiles out of Wilkes County, and running loads to Charlotte, Salisbury, Greensboro, Winston-Salem, High Point, or wherever, it would be pretty hard to pick out one. It was Junior Johnson, specifically, however, who was famous for the "bootleg turn" or "about-face," in which, if the Alcohol Tax agents had a roadblock up for you or were too close behind, you threw the car up into second gear, cocked the wheel, stepped on the accelerator and made the car's rear end skid around in a complete 180-degree arc, a complete about-face, and tore on back up the road exactly the way you came from. God! The Alcohol Tax agents used to burn over Junior Johnson. Practically every good old boy in town in Wilkesboro, the county seat, got to know the agents by sight in a very short time. They would rag them practically to their faces on the subject of Junior Johnson, so that it got to be an obsession. Finally, one night they had Junior trapped on the road up toward the bridge around Millersville, there's no way out of there, they had the barricades up and they could hear this souped-up car roaring around the bend, and here it comes—but suddenly they can hear a siren and see a red light flashing in the grille, so they think it's another agent, and boy, they run out like ants and pull those barrels and boards and sawhorses out of the way, and then —Ggghhzzzzzzzzhhhhhhggggggzzzzzzzeeeeeong!—gawdam! there he goes again, it was him, Junior Johnson! with a gawdam agent's sireen and a red light in his grille!

1965

Robert Pirsig: CONCRETE, BRICK, AND NEON

The city closes in on him now, and in his strange perspective it becomes the antithesis of what he believes. The citadel not of Quality, the citadel of form and substance. Substance in the form of steel sheets and girders, substance in the form of concrete piers and roads, in the form of brick, of asphalt, of auto parts, old radios, and rails, dead carcasses of animals that once grazed the prairies. Form and substance without Quality. That is the soul of this place. Blind, huge, sinister and inhuman: seen by the light of fire flaring upward in the night from the blast furnaces in the south, through heavy coal smoke deeper and denser into the neon of BEER and PIZZA and LAUNDROMAT signs and unknown and meaningless signs along meaningless straight streets going off into other straight streets forever.

If it was all bricks and concrete, pure forms of substance, clearly and openly, he might survive. It is the little, pathetic attempts at Quality that kill. The plaster false fireplace in the apartment, shaped and waiting to contain a flame that can never exist. Or the hedge in front of the apartment building with a few square feet of grass behind it. A few square feet of grass, after Montana. If they just left out the hedge and grass it would be all right. Now it serves only to draw attention to what has been lost.

Along the streets that lead away from the apartment he can never see anything through the concrete and brick and neon but he knows that buried within it are grotesque, twisted souls forever trying the manners that will convince themselves they possess Quality, learning strange poses of style and glamour vended by dream magazines and other mass media, and paid for by the vendors of substance. He thinks of them at night alone with their advertised glamorous shoes and stockings and underclothes off, staring through the sooty windows at the grotesque shells revealed beyond them, when the poses weaken and the truth creeps in, the only truth that exists here, crying to heaven, God, there is nothing here but dead neon and cement and brick.

1975

John McPhee: THE GRIZZLY

* * *

We passed first through stands of fireweed, and then over ground that was wine-red with the leaves of bearberries. There were curlewberries, too, which put a deep-purple stain on the hand. We kicked at some wolf scat, old as winter. It was woolly and white and filled with the hair of a snowshoe hare. Nearby was a rich inventory of caribou pellets and, in increasing quantity as we moved downhill, blueberries—an outspreading acreage of blueberries. Fedeler stopped walking. He touched my arm. He had in an instant become even more alert than he usually was, and obviously apprehensive. His gaze followed straight on down our intended course. What he saw there I saw now. It appeared to me to be a hill of fur. "Big boar grizzly," Fedeler said in a near-whisper. The bear was about a hundred steps away, in the blueberries, grazing. The head was down, the hump high. The immensity of muscle seemed to vibrate slowly—to expand and contract, with the grazing. Not berries alone but whole bushes were going into the bear. He was big for a barren-ground grizzly. The brown bears of Arctic Alaska (or grizzlies; they are no longer thought to be different) do not grow to the size they will reach on more ample diets elsewhere. The barren-ground grizzly will rarely grow larger than six hundred pounds.

"What if he got too close?" I said.

Fedeler said, "We'd be in real trouble."

"You can't outrun them," Hession said.

A grizzly, no slower than a racing horse, is about half again as fast as the fastest human being. Watching the great mound of weight in the blueberries, with a fifty-five-inch waist and a neck more than thirty inches around, I had difficulty imagining that he could move with such speed, but I believed it, and was without impulse to test the proposition. Fortunately, a light southerly wind was coming up the Salmon valley. On its way to us, it passed the bear. The wind was relieving, coming into our faces, for had it been moving the other way the bear would not have been placidly grazing. There is an old adage that when a pine needle drops in the forest the eagle will see it fall; the deer will hear it when it hits the ground; the bear will smell it. If the boar grizzly were to catch our scent, he might stand on his hind legs, the better to try to see. Although he could hear well and had an extraordinary sense of smell, his eyesight was not much better than what was required to see a blueberry inches away. For this reason, a grizzly stands and squints, attempting to bring the middle distance into focus, and the gesture is often misunderstood as a sign of anger and forthcoming attack. If the bear were getting ready to attack, he would be on four feet, head low, ears cocked, the hair above his hump muscle standing on end. As if that message were not clear enough, he would also chop his jaws. His teeth would make a sound that would carry like the ringing of an axe.

One could predict, but not with certainty, what a grizzly would do. Odds were very great that one touch of man scent would cause him to stop his activity, pause in a moment of absorbed and alert curiosity, and then move, at a not undignified pace, in a direction other than the one from which the scent was coming. That is what would happen almost every time, but there was, to be sure, no guarantee. The forest Eskimos fear and revere the grizzly. They know that certain individual bears not only will fail to avoid a person who comes into their country but will approach and even stalk the trespasser. It is potentially inaccurate to extrapolate the behavior of any one bear from the behavior of most, since they are both intelligent and independent and will do what they choose to do according to mood, experience, whim. A grizzly that has ever been wounded by a bullet will not forget it, and will probably know that it was a human being who sent the bullet. At sight of a human, such a bear will be likely to charge. Grizzlies hide food sometimes—a caribou calf, say, under a pile of scraped-up moss—and a person the bear might otherwise ignore might suddenly not be ignored if the person were inadvertently to step into the line between the food cache and the bear. A sow grizzly with cubs, of course, will charge anything that suggests danger to the cubs, even if the cubs are nearly as big as she is. They stay with their mother two and a half years.

None of us had a gun. (None of the six of us had brought a gun on the trip.) Among nonhunters who go into the terrain of the grizzly, there are several schools of thought about guns. The preferred one is: Never go without a sufficient weapon—a high-powered rifle or a shotgun and plenty of slug-loaded shells. The option is not without its own inherent peril. A professional hunter, some years ago, spotted a grizzly from the air and—with a client, who happened to be an Anchorage barber— landed on a lake about a mile from the bear. The stalking that followed was evidently conducted not only by the hunters but by the animal as well. The professional hunter was found dead from a broken neck, and had apparently died instantly, unaware of danger, for the cause of death was a single bite, delivered from behind. The barber, noted as clumsy with a rifle, had emptied his magazine, missing the bear with every shot but one, which struck the grizzly in the foot. The damage the bear did to the barber was enough to kill him several times. After the corpses were found, the bear was tracked and killed. To shoot and merely wound is worse than not to shoot at all. A bear that might have turned and gone away will possibly attack if wounded.

* * *

1977

Signs of the Times

Anthony Burgess

IS AMERICA FALLING APART?

I am back in Bracciano, a castellated town about 13 miles north of Rome, after a year in New Jersey. I find the Italian Government still unstable, gasoline more expensive than anywhere in the world, butchers and bank clerks and tobacconists (which also means saltsellers) ready to go on strike at the drop of a *cappello*,[1] neo-Fascists at their dirty work, the hammer and sickle painted on the rumps of public statues, a thousand-lire note (officially worth about $1.63) shrunk to the slightness of a dollar bill.

Nevertheless, it's delightful to be back. People are underpaid but they go through an act of liking their work, the open markets are luscious with esculent color, the community is more important than the state, the human condition is humorously accepted. The *tramontana*[2] blows viciously today, and there's no central heating to turn on, but it will be pleasant when the wind drops. The two television channels are inadequate, but next Wednesday's rerun of an old Western, with Gary Cooper coming into a saloon saying *"Ciao, ragazzi,"*[3] is something to look forward to. Manifold consumption isn't important here. The quality of life has nothing to do with the quantity of brand names. What matters is talk, family, cheap wine in the open air, the wresting of minimal sweetness out of the long-known bitterness of living. I was spoiled in New Jersey. The Italian for *spoiled* is *viziato*, cognate with *vitiated*, which has to do with vice.

Spoiled? Well, yes. I never had to shiver by a fire that wouldn't draw, or go without canned kraut juice or wild rice. America made me develop new appetites in order to make proper use of the supermarket. A charac-

---

ter in Evelyn Waugh's *Put Out More Flags* said that the difference between prewar and postwar life was that, prewar, if one thing went wrong the day was ruined; postwar, if one thing went right the day would be made. America is a prewar country, psychologically unprepared for one thing to go wrong. Now everything seems to be going wrong. Hence the neurosis, despair, the Kafka feeling that the whole marvelous fabric of American life is coming apart at the seams. Italy is used to everything going wrong. This is what the human condition is about.

Let me stay for a while on this subject of consumption. American individualism, on the face of it an admirable philosophy, wishes to manifest itself in independence of the community. You don't share things in common; you have your own things. A family's strength is signalized by its possessions. Herein lies a paradox. For the desire for possessions must eventually mean dependence on possessions. Freedom is slavery. Once let the acquisitive instinct burgeon (enough flour for the winter, not just for the week), and there are ruggedly individual forces only too ready to make it come to full and monstrous blossom. New appetites are invented; what to the European are bizarre luxuries become, to the American, plain necessities.

During my year's stay in New Jersey I let my appetites flower into full Americanism except for one thing. I did not possess an automobile. This self-elected deprivation was a way into the nastier side of the consumer society. Where private ownership prevails, public amenities decay or are prevented from coming into being. The wretched run-down rail services of America are something I try, vainly, to forget. The nightmare of filth, outside and in, that enfolds the trip from Springfield, Mass., to Grand Central Station would not be accepted in backward Europe. But far worse is the nightmare of travel in and around Los Angeles, where public transport does not exist and people are literally choking to death in their exhaust fumes. This is part of the price of the metaphysic of individual ownership.

But if the car owner can ignore the lack of public transport, he can hardly ignore the decay of services in general. His car needs mechanics, and mechanics grow more expensive and less efficient. The gadgets in the home are cheaper to replace than repair. The more efficiently self-contained the home, primary fortress of independence, seems to be, the more dependent it is on the great impersonal corporations, as well as a diminishing army of servitors. Skills at the lowest level have to be wooed slavishly and exorbitantly rewarded. Plumbers will not come. Nor, at the higher level, will doctors. And doctors and dentists, in a nation committed to maiming itself with sugar and cholesterol, know their scarcity value and behave accordingly.

Americans are at last realizing that the acquisition of goods is not the whole of life. Consumption, on one level, is turning insipid, especially as the quality of the artifacts themselves seems to be deteriorating. Planned obsolescence is not conducive to pride in workmanship. On another level, consumption is turning sour. There is a growing guilt about the masses of discarded junk—rusting automobiles and refrigerators and washing machines and dehumidifiers—that it is uneconomical to recycle. Indestructible plastic hasn't even the grace to undergo chemical change. America, the world's biggest consumer, is the world's biggest polluter. Awareness of this is a kind of redemptive grace, but it doesn't appreciably lead to repentance and a revolution in consumer habits. Citizens of Los Angeles are horrified by that daily pall of golden smog, but they don't noticeably clamor for a decrease in the number of owner-vehicles. There is no worse neurosis than that which derives from a consciousness of guilt and an inability to reform.

America is anachronistic in so many ways, and not least in its clinging to a belief—now known to be unviable—in the capacity of the individual citizen to do everything for himself. Americans are admirable in their distrust of the corporate state—they have fought both Fascism and Communism—but they forget that there is a use for everything, even the loathesome bureaucratic machine. America needs a measure of socialization, as Britain needed it. Things—especially those we need most—don't always pay their way, and it is here that the state must enter, dismissing the profit element. Part of the present American neurosis, again, springs from awareness of this but inability to do anything about practical implementation. Perhaps only a country full of bombed cities feels capable of this kind of social revolution.

It would be supererogatory for me to list those areas in which thoughtful Americans feel that collapse is coming. It is enough for me to concentrate on what, during my New Jersey stay, impinged on my own life. Education, for instance, since I have a 6-year-old son to be brought up. America has always despised its teachers and, as a consequence, it has been granted the teachers it deserves. The quality of first-grade education that my son received, in a New Jersey town noted for the excellence of its public schools, could not, I suppose, be faulted on the level of dogged conscientiousness. The principal had read all the right pedagogic books, and was ready to quote these in the footnotes to his circular exhortations to parents. The teachers worked rigidly from the approved rigidly programed primers, ensuring that school textbook publication remains the big business it is.

But there seemed to be no spark; no daring, no madness, no readiness to engage the individual child's mind as anything other than raw material for statistical reductions. The fear of being unorthodox is rooted in the American teacher's soul: you can be fired for treading the path of experimental enterprise. In England, teachers cannot be fired, except for raping girl students and getting boy students drunk. In consequence, there is the kind of security that breeds eccentric genius, the capacity for firing mad enthusiasms.

I know that American technical genius, and most of all the moon landings, seems to give the lie to too summary a condemnation of the educational system, but there is more to education than the segmental equipping of the mind. There is that transmission of the value of the past as a force still miraculously fertile and moving—mostly absent from American education at all levels.

Of course, America was built on a rejection of the past. Even the basic Christianity which was brought to the continent in 1620 was of a novel and bizarre kind that would have nothing to do with the great rank river of belief that produced Dante and Michelangelo. America as a nation has never been able to settle to a common belief more sophisticated than the dangerous naiveté of the Declaration of Independence. "Life, liberty and the pursuit of happiness," indeed. And now America, filling in the vacuum left by the liquefied British Empire, has the task of telling the rest of the world that there's something better than Communism. The something better can only be money-making and consumption for its own sake. In the name of this ghastly creed the jungles must be defoliated.[3]

No wonder the guilt of the thoughtful Americans I met in Princeton and New York and, indeed, all over the Union tended to express itself as an extravagant masochism, a desire for flagellation. Americans want to take on all the blame they can find, gluttons for punishment. "What do Europeans really think of us?" is a common question at parties. The expected answer is: "They think you're a load of decadent, gross-lipped, potbellied, callous, overbearing neoimperialists." Then the head can be bowed and the chest smitten: "*Nostra culpa, nostra maxima culpa....*"[4] But the fact is that such an answer, however much desired, would not be an honest one. Europeans think more highly of Americans now than they ever did. Let me try to explain why.

When Europe, after millennia of war, rapine, slavery, famine, intolerance, had sunk to the level of a sewer, America became the golden dream, the Eden where innocence could be recovered. Original sin was the monopoly of that dirty continent over there; in America man could glow in an aura of natural goodness, driven along his shining path by divine reason. The Declaration of Independence itself is a monument to reason.

3. That is, in order to deny the enemy protective cover—a part of American strategy during the Vietnam war.
4. "Through our fault, through our most grievous fault," a modification of *Mea culpa, mea maxima culpa* ("Through my fault . . ."), part of the act of confession in the Roman Catholic church.

Progress was possible, and the wrongs committed against the Indians, the wildlife, the land itself, could be explained away in terms of the rational control of environment necessary for the building of a New Jerusalem.[5] Right and wrong made up the moral dichotomy; evil—that great eternal inextirpable entity—had no place in America.

At last, with the Vietnam war and especially the Mylai horror,[6] Americans are beginning to realize that they are subject to original sin as much as Europeans are. Some things—the massive crime figures, for instance—can now be explained only in terms of absolute evil. Europe, which has long known about evil and learned to live with it (*live* is *evil* spelled backwards), is now grimly pleased to find that America is becoming like Europe. America is no longer Europe's daughter nor her rich stepmother: she is Europe's sister. The agony that America is undergoing is not to be associated with breakdown so much as with the parturition of self-knowledge.

It has been assumed by many that the youth of America has been in the vanguard of the discovery of both the disease and the cure. The various copping-out movements, however, from the Beats on, have committed the gross error of assuming that original sin rested with their elders, their rulers, and that they themselves could manifest their essential innocence by building little neo-Edens. The drug culture could confirm that the paradisal vision was available to all who sought it. But instant ecstasy has to be purchased, like any other commodity, and, in economic terms, that passive life of pure being involves parasitism. Practically all of the crime I encountered in New York—directly or through report—was a preying of the opium-eaters on the working community. There has to be a snake in paradise. You can't escape the heritage of human evil by building communes, usually on an agronomic ignorance that, intended to be a rejection of inherited knowledge, that suspect property of the elders, does violence to life. The American young are well-meaning but misguided, and must not themselves be taken as guides.

The guides, as always, lie among the writers and artists. And Americans ought to note that, however things may seem to be falling apart, arts and the humane scholarship are flourishing here, as they are not, for instance, in England. I'm not suggesting that Bellow, Mailer, Roth and the rest have the task of finding a solution to the American mess, but they can at least clarify its nature and show how it relates to the human condition in general. Literature, that most directly human of the arts, often reacts magnificently to an ambience of unease or apparent breakdown. The Elizabethans,[7] to whose era we look back as to an irrecovera-

---

5. The holy city described by John in Revelation xxi, here a figurative expression for a perfected society.
6. A massacre by American troops of over a hundred Vietnamese civilians in the village of Mylai.
7. The British during the reign of Elizabeth I, 1558–1603.

ble Golden Age, were far more conscious than modern Americans of the chaos and corruption and incompetence of the state. Shakespeare's period was one of poverty, unemployment, ghastly inflation, violence in the streets. Twenty-six years after his death there was a bloody civil war, followed by a dictatorship of religious fanatics, followed by a calm respite in which the seeds of a revolution were sown. England survived. America will survive.

I'm not suggesting that Americans sit back and wait for a transient period of mistrust and despair to resolve itself, like a disease, through the unconscious healing forces which lie deep in organic nature. Man, as Thornton Wilder showed in The Skin of Our Teeth,[8] always comes through—though sometimes only just. Americans living here and now have a right to an improvement in the quality of their lives, and they themselves, not the remote governors, must do something about it. It is not right that men and women should fear to go on the streets at night, and that they should sometimes fear the police as much as the criminals, both of whom sometimes look like mirror images of each other. I have had too much evidence, in my year in New Jersey, of the police behaving like the "Fascist pigs" of the revolutionary press. There are too many guns about, and the disarming of the police should be a natural aspect of the disarming of the entire citizenry.

American politics, at both the state and the Federal levels, is too much concerned with the protection of large fortunes, America being the only example in history of a genuine timocracy. The wealth qualification for the aspiring politician is taken for granted; a governmental system dedicated to the promotion of personal wealth in a few selected areas will never act for the public good. The time has come, nevertheless, for citizens to demand, from their government, a measure of socialization—the provision of amenities for the many, of which adequate state pensions and sickness benefits, as well as nationalized transport, should be priorities.

As for those remoter solutions to the American nightmare—only an aspect, after all, of the human nightmare—an Englishman must be diffident about suggesting that America made her biggest mistake in becoming America—meaning a revolutionary republic based on a romantic view of human nature. To reject a limited monarchy in favor of an absolute one (which is, after all, what the American Presidency is) argues a trust in the disinterestedness of an elected ruler which is, of course, no more than a reflection of belief in the innate goodness of man—so long as he happens to be American man. The American Constitution is out of date. Republics tend to corruption. Canada and Australia have their own

8. American play depicting man's tragicomic struggle for survival from prehistoric times to the present.

problems, but they are happier countries than America.

This *Angst*[9] about America coming apart at the seams, which apparently is shared by nearly 50 per cent of the entire American population, is something to rejoice about. A sense of sin is always admirable, though it must not be allowed to become neurotic. If electric systems break down and gadgets disintegrate, it doesn't matter much. There is always wine to be drunk by candlelight, uniced. If America's position as a world power collapses, and the Union dissolves into independent states, there is still the life of the family or the individual to be lived. England has survived her own dissolution as an imperial power, and Englishmen seem to be happy enough. But I ask the reader to note that I, an Englishman, no longer live in England, and I can't spend more than six months at a stretch in Italy—or any other European country, for that matter. I come to America as to a country more stimulating than depressing. The future of mankind is being worked out there on a scale typically American—vast, dramatic, almost apocalyptical. I brave the brutality and the guilt in order to be in on the scene. I shall be back.

                                                                          1971

9. Anxiety.

THE READER

1. Burgess wrote this piece in 1971. If he were writing it today, what might he want to leave out, add, or modify?
2. Burgess says that in the school his son attended, there was "no readiness to engage the individual child's mind as anything other than raw material for statistical reductions." Can you recall incidents from your early schooldays that would either support or counter Burgess's criticism of American education?
3. Would any of the ideals for education that Lord Ashby suggests ("The University Ideal: A View from Britain," p. 261) be translatable into improvements in education at the level that Burgess is talking about?

THE WRITER

1. Burgess writes as a visitor to America but a native of Great Britain. How might his account have differed if he had been an American?
2. Burgess's observation about the Italian word for spoiled implies a concern for etymology and precision of language. Is there evidence of that concern in his choice of English words?
3. Write your own brief characterization of one area of American life that Burgess talks about. How does your view differ from Burgess's?
4. Burgess refers to "the dangerous naiveté of the Declaration of Independence." Study the Declaration (p. 828), and write a brief argument either for considering it as a "naive" piece of writing or not.

Wendell Berry

HOME OF THE FREE

I was writing not long ago about a team of Purdue engineers who foresaw that by 2001 practically everything would be done by remote control. The question I asked—because such a "projection" forces one to ask it—was, Where does satisfaction come from? I concluded that there probably wouldn't be much satisfaction in such a world. There would be a lot of what passes for "efficiency," a lot of "production" and "consumption," but little satisfaction.

What I failed to acknowledge was that this "world of the future" is already established among us, and is growing. Two advertisements that I have lately received from correspondents make this clear, and raise the question about the sources of satisfaction more immediately and urgently than any abstract "projection" can do.

The first is the legend from a John Deere display at Waterloo Municipal Airport:

INTRODUCING SOUND-GARD BODY . . .
A DOWN TO EARTH SPACE CAPSULE.

New Sound-Gard body from John Deere, an "earth space capsule" to protect and encourage the American farmer at his job of being "Breadwinner to a world of families."

Outside: dust, noise, heat, storm, fumes.
Inside: all's quiet, comfortable, safe.
Features include a 4 post Roll Gard, space-age metals, plastics, and fibers to isolate driver from noise, vibration, and jolts. He dials 'inside weather', to his liking . . . he push buttons radio or stereo tape entertainment. He breathes filtered, conditioned air in his pressurized compartment. He has remote control over multi-ton and multi-hookups, with control tower visibility . . . from his scientifically padded seat.

The second is an ad for a condominium housing development:

HOME OF THE FREE.

We do the things you hate. You do the things you like. We mow the lawn, shovel the walks, paint and repair and do all exterior maintenance.
You cross-country ski, play tennis, hike, swim, work out, read or nap. Or advise our permanent maintenance staff as they do the things you hate.

Different as they may seem at first, these two ads make the same appeal, and they represent two aspects of the same problem: the widespread, and still spreading, assumption that we somehow have the right to be set free from anything whatsoever that we "hate" or don't want to do. According to this view, what we want to be set free from are the natural conditions of the world and the necessary work of human life; we do not want to experience temperatures that are the least bit too hot or too cold, or to work in the sun, or be exposed to wind or rain, or come in personal contact with anything describable as dirt, or provide for any of our own needs, or clean up after ourselves. Implicit in all this is the desire to be free of the "hassles" of mortality, to be "safe" from the life cycle. Such freedom and safety are always for sale. It is proposed that if we put all earthly obligations and the rites of passage into the charge of experts and machines, then life will become a permanent holiday.

What these people are really selling is insulation—cushions of technology, "space age" materials, and the menial work of other people—to keep fantasy in and reality out. The condominium ad says flat out that it is addressed to people who "hate" the handwork of household maintenance, and who will enjoy "advising" the people who do it for them; it is addressed, in other words, to those who think themselves too good to do work that other people are not too good to do. But it is a little surprising to realize that the John Deere ad is addressed to farmers who not only hate farming (that is, any physical contact with the ground or the weather or the crops), but also hate tractors, from the "dust," "fumes," "noise, vibration, and jolts" of which they wish to be protected by an "earth space capsule" and a "scientifically padded seat."

Of course, the only real way to get this sort of freedom and safety—to escape the hassles of earthly life—is to die. And what I think we see in these advertisements is an appeal to a desire to be dead that is evidently felt by many people. These ads are addressed to the perfect consumers— the self-consumers, who have found nothing of interest here on earth, nothing to do, and are impatient to be shed of earthly concerns. And so I am at a loss to explain the delay. Why hasn't some super salesman sold every one of these people a coffin—an "earth space capsule" in which they would experience no discomfort or inconvenience whatsoever, would have to do no work that they hate, would be spared all extremes of weather and all noises, fumes, vibrations, and jolts?

I wish it were possible for us to let these living dead bury themselves in the earth space capsules of their choice and think no more about them. The problem is that with their insatiable desire for comfort, convenience, remote control, and the rest of it, they cause an unconscionable amount of trouble for the rest of us, who would like a fair crack at living the rest of our lives within the terms and conditions of the real world. Speaking for myself, I acknowledge that the world, the weather, and the life cycle have caused me no end of trouble, and yet I look forward to putting in another forty or so years with them because they have also given me no end of pleasure and instruction. They interest me. I want to see them thrive on their own terms. I hate to see them abused and interfered with for the comfort and convenience of a lot of spoiled people who presume to "hate" the more necessary kinds of work and all the natural consequences of working outdoors.

When people begin to "hate" the life cycle and to try to live outside it and to escape its responsibilities, then the corpses begin to pile up and to get into the wrong places. One of the laws that the world imposes on us is that everything must be returned to its source to be used again. But one of the first principles of the haters is to violate this law in the name of convenience or efficiency. Because it is "inconvenient" to return bottles to the beverage manufacturers, "dead soldiers" pile up in the road ditches and in the waterways. Because it is "inconvenient" to be responsible for wastes, the rivers are polluted with everything from human excrement to various carcinogens and poisons. Because it is "efficient" (by what standard?) to mass-produce meat and milk in food "factories," the animal manures that once would have fertilized the fields have instead become wastes and pollutants. And so to be "free" of "inconvenience" and "inefficiency" we are paying a high price—which the haters among us are happy to charge to posterity.

And what a putrid (and profitable) use they have made of the idea of freedom! What a tragic evolution has taken place when the inheritors of the Bill of Rights are told, and when some of them believe, that "the home of the free" is where somebody else will do your work!

Let me set beside those advertisements a sentence that I consider a responsible statement about freedom: "To be free is precisely the same thing as to be pious, wise, just and temperate, careful of one's own, abstinent from what is another's, and thence, in fine, magnanimous and brave." That is John Milton. He is speaking out of the mainstream of our culture. Reading his sentence after those advertisements is coming home. His words have an atmosphere around them that a living human can breathe in.

How do you get free in Milton's sense of the word? I don't think you can do it in an earth space capsule or a space space capsule or a capsule of any kind. What Milton is saying is that you can do it only by living in this world as you find it, and by taking responsibility for the consequences of your life in it. And that means doing some chores that, highly objectionable in anybody's capsule, may not be at all unpleasant in the world.

Just a few days ago I finished up one of the heaviest of my spring jobs: hauling manure. On a feed lot I think this must be real drudgery even with modern labor-saving equipment—all that "waste" and no fields to put it on! But instead of a feed lot I have a small farm—what would probably be called a subsistence farm. My labor-saving equipment consists of a team of horses and a forty-year-old manure spreader. We forked the manure on by hand—forty-five loads. I made my back tired and my hands sore, but I got a considerable amount of pleasure out of it. Everywhere I spread that manure I knew it was needed. What would have been a nuisance in a feed lot was an opportunity and a benefit here. I enjoyed seeing it go out onto the ground. I was working some two-year-olds in the spreader for the first time, and I enjoyed that—mostly. And, since there were no noises, fumes, or vibrations the loading times were socially pleasant. I had some help from neighbors, from my son, and, toward the end, from my daughter who arrived home well rested from college. She helped me load, and then read *The Portrait of a Lady*[1] while I drove up the hill to empty the spreader. I don't think many young women have read Henry James while forking manure. I enjoyed working with my daughter, and I enjoyed wondering what Henry James would have thought of her.

1978

1. Novel by Henry James.

Phyllis Rose

SHOPPING AND OTHER SPIRITUAL ADVENTURES

Last year a new Waldbaum's Food Mart opened in the shopping mall on Route 66. It belongs to the new generation of superdupermarkets open 24 hours that have computerized checkout. I went to see the place as soon as it opened and I was impressed. There was trail mix in Lucite bins. There was freshly made pasta. There were coffee beans, 4 kinds of tahini, 10 kinds of herb teas, raw shrimp in shells and cooked shelled shrimp, fresh-squeezed orange juice. Every sophistication known to the big city, even goat's cheese covered with ash, was now available in Middletown, Conn. People raced from the warehouse aisle to the bagel bin to the coffee beans to the fresh fish market, exclaiming at all the new things. Many of us felt elevated, graced, complimented by the presence of this food palace in our town.

This is the wonderful egalitarianism of American business. Was it Andy Warhol[1] who said that the nice thing about Coke is, no can is any better or worse than any other? Some people may find it dull to cross the country and find the same chain stores with the same merchandise from coast to coast, but it means that my town is as good as yours, my shopping mall as important as yours, equally filled with wonders.

1. Andy Warhol: American pop artist (?1930–87) who often used repeated images.

Imagine what people ate during the winter as little as 75 years ago. They ate food that was local, long-lasting and dull, like acorn squash, turnips and cabbage. Walk into an American supermarket in February and the world lies before you: grapes, melons, artichokes, fennel, lettuce, peppers, pistachios, dates, even strawberries, to say nothing of ice cream. Have you ever considered what a triumph of civilization it is to be able to buy a pound of chicken livers? If you lived on a farm and had to kill a chicken when you wanted to eat one, you wouldn't ever accumulate a pound of chicken livers.

Another wonder of Middletown is Caldor, the discount department store. Here is man's plenty: tennis racquets, pantyhose, luggage, glassware, records, toothpaste, Timex watches, Cadbury's chocolate, corn poppers, hair dryers, warm-up suits, car wax, light bulbs, television sets. All good quality at low prices with exchanges cheerfully made on defective goods. There are worse rules to live by. I feel good about America whenever I walk into this store, which is almost every midwinter Sunday afternoon, when life elsewhere has closed down. I go to Caldor the way English people go to pubs: out of sociability. To get away from my house. To widen my horizons. For culture's sake. Caldor provides me too with a welcome sense of seasonal change. When the first outdoor grills and lawn furniture appear there, it's as exciting a sign of spring as the first crocus or robin.

Someone told me about a Soviet émigré who practices English by declaiming, at random, sentences that catch his fancy. One of his favorites is, "Fifty percent off all items today only." Refugees from Communist countries appreciate our supermarkets and discount department stores for the wonders they are. An Eastern European scientist visiting Middletown wept when she first saw the meat counter at Waldbaum's. On the other hand, before her year in America was up, her pleasure turned sour. She wanted everything she saw. Her approach to consumer goods was insufficiently abstract, too materialistic. We Americans are beyond a simple, possessive materialism. We're used to abundance and the possibility of possessing things. The things, and the possibility of possessing them, will still be there next week, next year. So today we can walk the aisles calmly.

It is a misunderstanding of the American retail store to think we go there necessarily to buy. Some of us shop. There's a difference. Shopping has many purposes, the least interesting of which is to acquire new articles. We shop to cheer ourselves up. We shop to practice decision-making. We shop to be useful and productive members of our class and society. We shop to remind ourselves how much is available to us. We shop to remind ourselves how much is to be striven for. We shop to assert our superiority to the material objects that spread themselves before us.

Shopping's function as a form of therapy is widely appreciated. You don't really need, let's say, another sweater. You need the feeling of power that comes with buying or not buying it. You need the feeling that someone wants something you have—even if it's just your money. To get the benefit of shopping, you needn't actually purchase the sweater, any more than you have to marry every man you flirt with. In fact, window-shopping, like flirting, can be more rewarding, the same high without the distressing commitment, the material encumbrance. The purest form of shopping is provided by garage sales. A connoisseur goes out with no goal in mind, open to whatever may come his or her way, secure that it will cost very little. Minimum expense, maximum experience. Perfect shopping.

I try to think of the opposite, a kind of shopping in which the object is all-important, the pleasure of shopping at a minimum. For example, the purchase of blue jeans. I buy new blue jeans as seldom as possible because the experience is so humiliating. For every pair that looks good on me, 15 look grotesque. But even shopping for blue jeans at Bob's Surplus on Main Street—no frills, bare-bones shopping—is an event in the life of the spirit. Once again I have to come to terms with the fact that I will never look good in Levi's. Much as I want to be mainstream, I never will be.

In fact, I'm doubly an oddball, neither Misses nor Junior, but Misses Petite. I look in the mirror, I acknowledge the disparity between myself and the ideal, I resign myself to making the best of it: I will buy the Lee's Misses Petite. Shopping is a time of reflection, assessment, spiritual self-discipline.

It is appropriate, I think, that Bob's Surplus has a communal dressing room. I used to shop only in places where I could count on a private dressing room with a mirror inside. My impulse then was to hide my weaknesses. Now I believe in sharing them. There are other women in the dressing room at Bob's Surplus trying on blue jeans who look as bad as I do. We take comfort from one another. Sometimes a woman will ask me which of two items looks better. I always give a definite answer. It's the least I can do. I figure we are all in this together, and I emerge from the dressing room not only with a new pair of jeans but with a renewed sense of belonging to a human community.

When a Solzhenitsyn[2] rants about American materialism, I have to look at my digital Timex and check what year this is. Materialism? Like conformism, a hot moral issue of the 50's, but not now. How to spread the goods, maybe. Whether the goods are the Good, no. Solzhenitsyn, like the visiting scientist who wept at the beauty of Waldbaum's meat counter but came to covet everything she saw, takes American material-

2. Alexandr I. Solzhenitsyn: Russian novelist and émigré (1918–   ).

ism too materialistically. He doesn't see its spiritual side. Caldor, Waldbaum's, Bob's Surplus—these, perhaps, are our cathedrals.

1984

THE READER

1. What, according to Rose, is the spiritual significance of shopping (as opposed to buying things)? How does shopping nourish and enhance the spirit?
2. What is Solzhenitsyn's error and the mistake made by the visiting scientist who wept at the meat counter?
3. It is often said that Americans are "too materialistic." Would Rose agree? Why, or why not? Do you think Americans might be too spiritual?

THE WRITER

1. What is the tone of Rose's article? Does it have a single dominant tone, or are there several tones? What particular elements in the article provide evidence for your answer?
2. Describe Rose's intended audience, specifying details in the article from which you infer that audience.
3. "Caldor, Waldbaum's, Bob's Surplus—these, perhaps, are our cathedrals." Write an essay testing this suggestion. Choose a particular store and a particular cathedral with which you are familiar. Do you find more resemblances or contrasts?

Ian Frazier

JUST A COUNTRY BOY

If you think that when you look at me you're looking at rock, rhythm and blues, jazz, classical, or pop, then you are wrong, because I am country from my head down to my boots. If you're looking at me, then by definition you are looking at country. When I was in my early teens, the great Hank Williams[1] told me, "Son, you ain't country unless you've looked at a lot of miles over the back end of a mule." Unfortunately, because of conflicts in my schedule at the time, I did not have a chance to look at as many miles over the back end of a mule as I would have liked to. Hank, however, made some excellent videotapes of miles with the back end of a mule in the foreground, and I spent countless hours screening those tapes.

Excuse me. That's my phone.

Sorry. That was the lonesome highway calling me. It calls me just

1. Hank Williams: leading country-music singer, musician, and composer (1923–1953).

about every day at this time. Just about every day, I get calls from the lonesome highway, the gentle Southern summer breezes, my Smoky Mountain memories, and that lonesome freight-train whistle's whine. If I'm not in, they leave messages. I don't mind all these calls, because they remind me that I'm just a country boy and that's all I'll ever be. (Although sometimes that lonesome freight-train whistle's whine can be a little irritating. I pick up the phone and all I hear is this whine.)

I like it when the lonesome highway calls, because for a long time it has been my only friend. I don't know exactly why I always keep moving on down the road. One reason might be that I've got a different girl in every town you can name. There's a Cajun[2] Queen down in Baton Rouge who usually tries to avoid me. And in North Dallas there's a rich man's daughter who says she doesn't like me that much. In old San Antone there's a dark-eyed señorita who didn't have a very good time with me, while up in Memphis there are several Tennessee belles whose feelings toward me are lukewarm at best. I tell them all the same thing: "I am not the kind of man to hang around with any one woman for too long, because I am always chasing rainbows. So please bear that in mind." That is not an easy thing to tell someone (particularly if you have to yell it through her locked door), but I know myself well enough to say that it is nothing more or less than the simple truth.

I am country today, and I was country this time last year—I have photographs to prove it. I was country back before Hollywood brought Texas to New York and imitation cowboys turned up all over the Sunset Strip. I was country in '80, '79, '78, '77, '76—it doesn't matter how far back you want to go. I was country when country wasn't cool. In fact, I was country back when it was forbidden by law in most states and the federal government turned a blind eye to this blatant violation of the rights of its people. I was country back when if you were intelligent enough to buy beer and you tried to be country you could be fined, or even imprisoned. Now it is hard to believe that such times ever existed.

My daddy was just a simple backwoods art director (B.F.A., Rhode Island School of Design) out of Checotah, Oklahoma. He raised me right. He insisted that I spend at least three hours out of every day honky-tonking, and he was very strict. I had to bring him bar tabs from as many places as I could, to prove I had really bar-hopped. He also made me practice cheating and slipping around behind my wife's back. Of course, I was much too young to be married, so we pretended I was married to Yeller, my dog. Then I would go over to our neighbor's yard and sweet-talk their dog, Blue. "What part of heaven did you fall from, angel?" I'd say. "No, no, no!" Daddy would holler. "Say it like you mean it! Put some ol' country sorghum in your voice!"[3] And he'd make me try it again and

2. Louisianian descended from Acadian French-speaking ancestors.

3. I.e., be sweetly sentimental ("sorghum": a sweet syrup made from sorgo).

again, until I finally had Yeller howling with jealousy. At that time, I have to admit, I hated my daddy for being so hard on me, but now I understand what he was doing, and I thank him for it.

Many of the experiences of my life were like that; I did not understand at the time that they were molding me into pure country, which is what I am today. Like when I went to tennis camp with Bob Wills and several of the Texas Playboys. Or the time I made a snow sculpture with Ernest Tubb. Or the time I went on a two-month tour of the canals of Europe with Jimmie Rodgers, the Singing Brakeman.[4] Each of these experiences taught me a little bit more about what country really means.

So when people who don't have the benefit of similar experiences ask me "What is country?" I don't know what to tell them. Country is so many things. It's knowing how to find the country station on your radio dial. It's watching the TV pages to see when the next country-music awards show is on. It's knowing the location of the aisle labeled "Country" at your record store . . . It's all these things, and yet, somehow, it's more. It's ineffable, really. And when my friends, all of them country "kickers" like myself, and I watch people who just plain *ain't* country trying to pretend they are—when we watch them fumble with their radios searching for a country station—well, then we just smile. Because if you're not country, then there's nothing you can do about it. Because real, down-home country is something that comes from the heart. Because there is no way if you aren't country that you can ever possibly become country—certainly not without working at it for, at the very least, seven to ten years.

1986

John McMurtry

KILL 'EM! CRUSH 'EM! EAT 'EM RAW!

A few months ago my neck got a hard crick in it. I couldn't turn my head; to look left or right I'd have to turn my whole body. But I'd had cricks in my neck since I started playing grade-school football and hockey, so I just ignored it. Then I began to notice that when I reached for any sort of large book (which I do pretty often as a philosophy teacher at the University of Guelph) I had trouble lifting it with one hand. I was

---

4. Bob Wills and the Texas Playboys: Western swing band popular in the 1930s; Ernest Tubb (b. 1914): Texas balladeer who introduced the electric guitar to country-Western mainstream; Jimmie (James Charles) Rodgers (1897–1933): early and influential star of "hillbilly" music known for his "blue yodels" and sentimental songs.

losing the strength in my left arm, and I had such a steady pain in my back I often had to stretch out on the floor of the room I was in to relieve the pressure.

A few weeks later I mentioned to my brother, an orthopedic surgeon, that I'd lost the power in my arm since my neck began to hurt. Twenty-four hours later I was in a Toronto hospital not sure whether I might end up with a wasted upper limb. Apparently the steady pounding I had received playing college and professional football in the late Fifties and early Sixties had driven my head into my backbone so that the discs had crumpled together at the neck—"acute herniation"—and had cut the nerves to my left arm like a pinched telephone wire (without nerve stimulation, of course, the muscles atrophy, leaving the arm crippled). So I spent my Christmas holidays in the hospital in heavy traction and much of the next three months with my neck in a brace. Today most of the pain has gone, and I've recovered most of the strength in my arm. But from time to time I still have to don the brace, and surgery remains a possibility.

Not much of this will surprise anyone who knows football. It is a sport in which body wreckage is one of the leading conventions. A few days after I went into hospital for that crick in my neck, another brother, an outstanding football player in college, was undergoing spinal surgery in the same hospital two floors above me. In his case it was a lower, more massive herniation, which every now and again buckled him so that he was unable to lift himself off his back for days at a time. By the time he entered the hospital for surgery he had already spent several months in bed. The operation was successful, but, as in all such cases, it will take him a year to recover fully.

These aren't isolated experiences. Just about anybody who has ever played football for any length of time, in high school, college or one of the professional leagues, has suffered for it later physically.

Indeed, it is arguable that body shattering is the very *point* of football, as killing and maiming are of war. (In the United States, for example, the game results in 15 to 20 deaths a year and about 50,000 major operations on knees alone.) To grasp some of the more conspicuous similarities between football and war, it is instructive to listen to the imperatives most frequently issued to the players by their coaches, teammates and fans. "Hurt 'em!" "Level 'em!" "Kill 'em!" "Take 'em apart!" Or watch for the plays that are most enthusiastically applauded by the fans. Where someone is "smeared," "knocked silly," "creamed," "nailed," "broken in two," or even "crucified." (One of my coaches when I played corner linebacker with the Calgary Stampeders in 1961 elaborated, often very inventively, on this language of destruction: admonishing us to "unjoin" the opponent, "make 'im remember you" and "stomp 'im like a bug.") Just as in hockey, where a fight will bring fans to their feet more often than a skillful play, so in football the mouth waters most of all for the really crippling block or tackle. For the kill. Thus the good teams are "hungry," the best players are "mean," and "casualties" are as much a part of the game as they are of a war.

The family resemblance between football and war is, indeed, striking. Their languages are similar: "field general," "long bomb," "blitz," "take a shot," "front line," "pursuit," "good hit," "the draft" and so on. Their principles and practices are alike: mass hysteria, the art of intimidation, absolute command and total obedience, territorial aggression, censorship, inflated insignia and propaganda, blackboard maneuvers and strategies, drills, uniforms, formations, marching bands and training camps. And the virtues they celebrate are almost identical: hyper-aggressiveness, coolness under fire and suicidal bravery. All this has been implicitly recognized by such jock-loving Americans as media stars General Patton and President Nixon, who have talked about war as a football game. Patton wanted to make his Second World War tank men look like football players. And Nixon, as we know, was fond of comparing attacks on Vietnam to football plays and drawing coachly diagrams on a blackboard for TV war fans.

One difference between war and football, though, is that there is little or no protest against football. Perhaps the most extraordinary thing about the game is that the systematic infliction of injuries excites in people not concern, as would be the case if they were sustained at, say, a rock festival, but a collective rejoicing and euphoria. Players and fans alike revel in the spectacle of a combatant felled into semiconsciousness, "blindsided," "clotheslined" or "decapitated." I can remember, in fact, being chided by a coach in pro ball for not "getting my hat" injuriously into a player who was already lying helpless on the ground. (On another occasion, after the Stampeders had traded the celebrated Joe Kapp to BC, we were playing the Lions in Vancouver and Kapp was forced on one play to run with the ball. He was coming "down the chute," his bad knee wobbling uncertainly, so I simply dropped on him like a blanket. After I returned to the bench I was reproved for not exploiting the opportunity to unhinge his bad knee.)

After every game, of course, the papers are full of reports on the day's injuries, a sort of post-battle "body count," and the respective teams go to work with doctors and trainers, tape, whirlpool baths, cortisone and morphine to patch and deaden the wounds before the next game. Then the whole drama is reenacted—injured athletes held together by adhesive, braces and drugs—and the days following it are filled with even more feverish activity to put on the show yet again at the end of the next week. (I remember being so taped up in college that I earned the nickname "mummy.") The team that survives this merry-go-round spectacle of skilled masochism with the fewest incapacitating injuries usually wins.

It is a sort of victory by ordeal: "We hurt them more than they hurt us."

My own initiation into this brutal circus was typical. I loved the game from the moment I could run with a ball. Played shoeless on a green open field with no one keeping score and in a spirit of reckless abandon and laughter, it's a very different sport. Almost no one gets hurt and it's rugged, open and exciting (it still is for me). But then, like everything else, it starts to be regulated and institutionalized by adult authorities. And the fun is over.

So it was as I began the long march through organized football. Now there was a coach and elders to make it clear by their behavior that beating other people was the only thing to celebrate and that trying to shake someone up every play was the only thing to be really proud of. Now there were severe rule enforcers, audiences, formally recorded victors and losers, and heavy equipment to permit crippling bodily moves and collisions (according to one American survey, more than 80% of all football injuries occur to fully equipped players). And now there was the official "given" that the only way to keep playing was to wear suffocating armor, to play to defeat, to follow orders silently and to renounce spontaneity for joyless drill. The game had been, in short, ruined. But because I loved to play and play skillfully, I stayed. And progressively and inexorably, as I moved through high school, college and pro leagues, my body was dismantled. Piece by piece.

I started off with torn ligaments in my knee at 13. Then, as the organization and the competition increased, the injuries came faster and harder. Broken nose (three times), broken jaw (fractured in the first half and dismissed as a "bad wisdom tooth," so I played with it for the rest of the game), ripped knee ligaments again. Torn ligaments in one ankle and a fracture in the other (which I remember feeling relieved about because it meant I could honorably stop drill-blocking a 270-pound defensive end). Repeated rib fractures and cartilage tears (usually carried, again, through the remainder of the game). More dislocations of the left shoulder than I can remember (the last one I played with because, as the Calgary Stampeder doctor said, it "couldn't be damaged any more"). Occasional broken or dislocated fingers and toes. Chronically hurt lower back (I still can't lift with it or change a tire without worrying about folding). Separated right shoulder (as with many other injuries, like badly bruised hips and legs, needled with morphine for the games). And so on. The last pro grame I played—against Winnipeg Blue Bombers in the Western finals in 1961—I had a recently dislocated left shoulder, a more recently wrenched right shoulder and a chronic pain center in one leg. I was so tied up with soreness I couldn't drive my car to the airport. But it never occurred to me or anyone else that I miss a play as a corner linebacker.

By the end of my football career, I had learned that physical injury—

giving it and taking it—is the real currency of the sport. And that in the final analysis the "winner" is the man who can hit to kill even if only half his limbs are working. In brief, a warrior game with a warrior ethos into which (like almost everyone else I played with) my original boyish enthusiasm had been relentlessly taunted and conditioned.

In thinking back on how all this happened, though, I can pick out no villains. As with the social system as a whole, the game has a life of its own. Everyone grows up inside it, accepts it and fulfills its dictates as obediently as helots. Far from ever questioning the principles of the activity, people simply concentrate on executing these principles more aggressively than anybody around them. The result is a group of people who, as the leagues become of a higher and higher class, are progressively insensitive to the possibility that things could be otherwise. Thus, in football, anyone who might question the wisdom or enjoyment of putting on heavy equipment on a hot day and running full speed at someone else with the intention of knocking him senseless would be regarded simply as not really a devoted athlete and probably "chicken." The choice is made straightforward. Either you, too, do your very utmost to efficiently smash and be smashed, or you admit incompetence or cowardice and quit. Since neither of these admissions is very pleasant, people generally keep any doubts they have to themselves and carry on.

Of course, it would be a mistake to suppose that there is more blind acceptance of brutal practices in organized football than elsewhere. On the contrary, a recent Harvard study has approvingly argued that football's characteristics of "impersonal acceptance of inflicted injury," an overriding "organization goal," the "ability to turn oneself on and off" and being, above all, "out to win" are of "inestimable value" to big corporations. Clearly, our sort of football is no sicker than the rest of our society. Even its organized destruction of physical well-being is not anomalous. A very large part of our wealth, work and time is, after all, spent in systematically destroying and harming human life. Manufacturing, selling and using weapons that tear opponents to pieces. Making ever bigger and faster predator-named cars with which to kill and injure one another by the million every year. And devoting our very lives to outgunning one another for power in an ever more destructive rat race. Yet all these practices are accepted without question by most people, even zealously defended and honored. Competitive, organized injuring is integral to our way of life, and football is simply one of the more intelligible mirrors of the whole process: a sort of colorful morality play showing us how exciting and rewarding it is to Smash Thy Neighbor.

Now it is fashionable to rationalize our collaboration in all this by arguing that, well, man *likes* to fight and injure his fellows and such games as football should be encouraged to discharge this original-sin urge into less harmful channels than, say, war. Public-show football, this line goes, plays the same sort of cathartic role as Aristotle said stage tragedy does: without real blood (or not much), it releases players and audience from unhealthy feelings stored up inside them.

As an ex-player in the seasonal coast-to-coast drama, I see little to recommend such a view. What organized football did to me was make me suppress my natural urges and re-express them in an alienating, vicious form. Spontaneous desires for free bodily exuberance and fraternization with competitors were shamed and forced under ("If it ain't hurtin' it ain't helpin'") and in their place were demanded armored mechanical moves and cool hatred of all opposition. Endless authoritarian drill and dressing-room harangues (ever wonder why competing teams can't prepare for a game in the same dressing room?) were the kinds of mechanisms employed to reconstruct joyful energies into mean and alien shapes. I am quite certain that everyone else around me was being similarly forced into this heavily equipped military precision and angry antagonism, because there was always a mutinous attitude about full-dress practices, and everybody (the pros included) had to concentrate incredibly hard for days to whip themselves into just one hour's hostility a week against another club. The players never speak of these things, of course, because everyone is so anxious to appear tough.

The claim that men like seriously to battle one another to some sort of finish is a myth. It only endures because it wears one of the oldest and most propagandized of masks—the romantic combatant. I sometimes wonder whether the violence all around us doesn't depend for its survival on the existence and preservation of this tough-guy disguise.

As for the effect of organized football on the spectator, the fan is not released from supposed feelings of violent aggression by watching his athletic heroes perform it so much as encouraged in the view that people-smashing is an admirable mode of self-expression. The most savage attackers, after all, are, by general agreement, the most efficient and worthy players of all (the biggest applause I ever received as a football player occurred when I ran over people or slammed them so hard they couldn't get up). Such circumstances can hardly be said to lessen the spectators' martial tendencies. Indeed it seems likely that the whole show just further develops and titillates the North American addiction for violent self-assertion. . . . Perhaps, as well, it helps explain why the greater the zeal of U.S. political leaders as football fans (Johnson, Nixon, Agnew), the more enthusiastic the commitment to hard-line politics. At any rate there seems to be a strong correlation between people who relish tough football and people who relish intimidating and beating the hell out of commies, hippies, protest marchers and other opposition groups.

Watching well-advertised strong men knock other people round, make them hurt, is in the end like other tastes. It does not weaken with feeding and variation in form. It grows.

I got out of football in 1962. I had asked to be traded after Calgary had offered me a $25-a-week-plus-commissions off-season job as a clothing-store salesman. ("Dear Mr. Finks:" I wrote. [Jim Finks was then the Stampeders' general manager.] "Somehow I do not think the dialectical subtleties of Hegel, Marx and Plato would be suitably oriented amidst the environmental stimuli of jockey shorts and herringbone suits. I hope you make a profitable sale or trade of my contract to the East.") So the Stampeders traded me to Montreal. In a preseason intersquad game with the Alouettes I ripped the cartilages in my ribs on the hardest block I'd ever thrown. I had trouble breathing and I had to shuffle-walk with my torso on a tilt. The doctor in the local hospital said three weeks rest, the coach said scrimmage in two days. Three days later I was back home reading philosophy.

1971

THE READER

1. What relationship does McMurtry see between football and war? Do you find his suggestion persuasive?
2. Does football, in McMurtry's view, provide for participants and spectators a harmless release of potentially harmful tensions and impulses, like "letting off steam"? Do you agree with McMurtry's view?
3. McMurtry says he can "pick out no villains" for the damage football does to its players. Do you agree? Explain.
4. To what extent is what McMurtry says of football true of any other sport?
5. What relationships does McMurtry see between football and society at large? Do his comparisons make sense to you?

THE WRITER

1. Is McMurtry's essay mainly about his personal experiences in football? What effect is produced by his recounting his experiences in detail?
2. What evidence in the essay, if any, do you find to show that McMurtry is not a "team player"? If he is not a "team player," would that account for the fact that he finds so much to criticize about football and about society?
3. McMurtry says that "our sort of football is no sicker than the rest of our society." Write a brief argument supporting or denying that view.
4. Write an essay drawing connections between "real life" and some kind of game or play familiar to you. Does this illuminate any social arrangements, help you to see them in a new light? How far can you truthfully generalize?

S. J. Perelman

THE MACHISMO MYSTIQUE

It was 3 P.M., that climactic midafternoon moment toward which every gallant worthy of the name bends his energies, and I'd done all the preparatory work time and an unencumbered credit card could accomplish. I had stoked my Chilean vis-à-vis with three vodka martinis, half a gallon of Sancerre, and two balloons of Armagnac until her eyes were veritable liquid pools. Under my bold, not to say outrageous, compliments her damask skin and the alabaster column of her throat glowed like a lovely pink pearl; her hair, black as the raven's wing, shimmered in the reflection of the boudoir lamp shading our discreet banquette; and every now and again as my knee nudged hers under the table, my affinity's magnificent bosom heaved uncontrollably. I had glissed through all those earnest confidences that begin, "You know, I've never said this to anyone before," to, "Look, I'm not very articulate, but I feel that in these parlous times, it behooves us all to reach out, to cling to another lonely person—do you know what I mean?" Suddenly I had the feeling that she knew what I meant, all right. In a swift glance, I encompassed the small chic restaurant whence all but we had fled—its idle barman and the maître d'hôtel stifling a yawn—and I struck.

"Listen," I said as if inspired. "This friend of mine, the Marquis de Cad, who has a wonderful collection of African sculpture, was called away to Cleveland, and I promised to stop by his flat and dust it. Why don't we pick up a bottle of lemon oil . . ."

Inamorata threw back her sleek head and shouted with laughter. "Stop, querido,"[1] she implored. "You're ruining my mascara. Such machismo—who would have expected it from a shrimp like you?"

Quicker than any hidalgo of Old Spain to erase an insult, I sprang up prepared to plunge my poniard into her bosom (a striking demonstration of the maxim that man kills that which he most loves). Unfortunately, I had left my poniard at home on the bureau and was wearing only a tie-tack that could never penetrate anyone so thick-skinned. Nonetheless, I made the hussy smart for her insolence. "Let me tell you something, Chubby," I rasped. "Never underestimate the American male. I may not dance the mambo or reek of garlic, but I'm just as feisty as those caballeros of yours below the Rio Grande. Remember that our first colonial flag in Kentucky, the Dark and Bloody Ground, portrayed a coiled rattlesnake over the legend, 'Don't Tread on Me.'"

"Big deal," she scoffed. "Do you want an example of real machismo—

1. Beloved.

the kind of masculinity Latin-American men are capable of? Tell them to bring me another Armagnac."

Downcast at the realization that our matinee had blown out the back, I sullenly acceded. The story as she related it dealt with a bar in Guatemala City called *Mi apuesta* (The Wager) after a bet once made there. Two young bloods or *machos*, it appeared, had swaggered in one evening, stiff with conceit and supremely self-confident, arrogant as a pair of fighting cocks. Lounging at the bar over a glass of manzanilla, one of them remarked to the other, "*Te apuesto que no eres bastante macho para matar al primero que entre*" (I wager you're not man enough to kill the first hombre who comes in).

The other sneered thinly. "No?" he said. "I bet you fifty *centavos* I will."

The bet was covered, whereupon the challenged party extracted a Beretta from his waistband, and a moment later, as a totally inoffensive stranger stepped through the saloon door, a bullet drilled him through the heart.

"*Madre de Dios*," I exclaimed, shocked. "What happened to the assassin?"

"*Niente*," said Inamorata calmly. "The judge gave him a three months' suspended sentence on the ground that the crime was in no way premeditated."

Needless to say, whenever Inamorata rang up after our abortive meeting and besought me to lunch her again, I showed her a clean pair of heels. (They were two fellows who dispensed towels at the Luxor Baths; they pursued her madly, and I hope with more success than I had.) At any rate, in pondering the whole business of *machismo*, of male bravado and excessive manliness, it occurred to me that I had met quite a few *machos* in my time, both in the entertainment world and belles-lettres. The one I remember most vividly in the former was a Hollywood screenwriter—a big redheaded blowhard I'll call Rick Ferret. A Montanan who claimed to have grown up on the range, Ferret was forever beating his gums about his amatory exploits; by his own blushing admission, he was Casanova reborn, the swordsman supreme, the reincarnation of Don Juan. According to him, women in every walk of life—society leaders and shopgirls, leading ladies and vendeuses—fell in windrows in his path, and though it was obvious to his auditors at the Brown Derby that he dealt in quantity rather than quality, the references he dropped to his nuclear power and durability left us pale with jealousy.

One evening, I attended a party at his house in Laurel Canyon. Living with him at the time was a lady named Susie, quite well-endowed and with a rather sharp tongue. So late was the hour when the bash ended that the two insisted I stay over, and the next morning, while I was adjusting my false lashes, Ferret entered the bathroom and proceeded to take a shower. Just as he was snorting and puffing like a grampus, I chanced to observe a quite formidable scar on his *Sitzfleisch*. With an apology for the personal nature of the question, I asked if it was a war wound of some kind.

"Yes, in a way," he said carelessly, turning off the taps. "There's quite a story attached to it." He opened the door of the bathroom to disperse the steam, and I glimpsed his Susie breakfasting in bed a few feet distant. "The fact is," he went on, "it happened some years ago down on the south fork of the Brazos while I was rounding up some mavericks. This gang of rustlers from Durango way cut into the herd, and I took after them hell for leather. Well, the greasers were spoiling for action, and they got it." He chuckled. "Before I could yank out my six-guns, they creased me here, but I managed to rub out the whole dad-blamed lot."

"Oh, for God's sake, Ferret," I heard Susie's voice croak from the bedroom. "You know perfectly well you had a boil lanced on your tail only last Tuesday."

The two most celebrated *machos* I ever knew, I suppose, were Ernest Hemingway—unquestionably the holder of the black belt in the Anglo-Saxon world—and Mike Todd, who, to pilfer a phrase from Marcel Proust, might aptly be termed the Sweet Cheat Gone. My go-around with Hemingway took place in the winter of 1954, directly after his two widely publicized plane crashes in East Africa. He was borne into the New Stanley Hotel in Nairobi in a somewhat disoriented state, suffering a double concussion, a smashed kidney, and alarming symptoms of *folie de grandeur*.[2] I turned up there two days later from Uganda with fourteen women comprising the first American all-girl safari (quite another story), and since my room was adjacent to his, saw a good bit of him thereafter. What with his tribulations and frequent infusions of hooch, Papa was inclined to ramble somewhat, and it was not always easy to follow the thread of his discourse. Once in a while, though, the clouds dissipated, and we were able to chat about mutual friends in the Montparnasse of the 'twenties. It was on such an occasion, one night, that he told me an anecdote that stunningly dramatized his *machismo*.

It concerned a period when he used to box at Stillman's Gymnasium in New York, a favorite haunt of enthusiasts of what is termed the manly art. His adversaries, Hemingway blushingly admitted, never matched his own speed and strength, but one of them improved so under his tutelage that occasionally the pair had a tolerable scrimmage. Thinking to intensify it, Hemingway suggested they discard their gloves and fight bareknuckle. This, too, while diverting, soon palled, but at last he had an inspiration.

"The room we boxed in," Hemingway explained, "had these rows of

2. Delusions of grandeur.

pipes running along the walls—you know, like backstage in a theater? Well, we flooded the place with steam, so thickly that it looked like a pea-soup fog in London. Then we started charging each other like a couple of rhinos. Butting our heads together and roaring like crazy. God, it was terrific—you could hear the impact of bone on bone, and we bled like stuck pigs. Of course, that made the footwork a bit more difficult, slipping and sliding all over, but it sure heightened the fun. Man, those were the days. You had to have real *cojones*[3] to stand up to it."

The same hormonal doodads were imperative in order to cope with Mike Todd and his vagaries. Todd's *machismo* was that common form that afflicts all undersized men—megalomania. He freely identified himself with Napoleon, P. T. Barnum, and Carl Laemmle, Junior, not to mention the Roman emperors of the decline. Whereas the latter, however, believed in giving the populace bread and circuses, Todd gave them circuses and kept the bread. Rarely if ever has there been anyone more unwilling to fork over what he owed to those actors, writers, and technicians who aided him in his grandiloquent projects of stage and screen. The little corpuscle, in short, believed in flaunting money where it made the most impression—at Deauville, Monaco, and the gaming tables of Las Vegas. In this respect, he was a true *macho*. My sole souvenir of our frenetic association is a replica of the carpetbag Phileas Fogg carried on his celebrated journey, a thousand of which Todd distributed in lordly fashion to Broadway companions, investors, accountants, dentists, and other sycophants. But surely, his admirers have since queried me, I must have been awed by his tremendous vitality; Only in part I respond: *Moi-même*, I prefer the anthropoid apes. The gibbon swings farther, the chimpanzee's reflexes are quicker, the orangutan can scratch faster, and the gorilla—my particular love object—has been known to crunch a Stillson wrench in his teeth.

Of such literary *machos* was the late Robert Ruark, who of course patterned himself on Hemingway. Their careers afford ample demonstration of my two favorite maxims: a) that the gaudier the patter, the cheaper the scribe, and b) that easy writing makes hard reading. The legend of Ruark's fatal charisma with women still gives one a pain in the posterior when recounted, and his press interviews, studded with reference to the millions of words he merchandised, act as a tourniquet on bleeders like myself who labor over a postcard. Even John O'Hara, somewhat more talented, was not above buttonholing acquaintances and boasting that he had written this or that deathless vignette in three quarters of an hour. It is interesting, by the way, that Scott Fitzgerald, with whom O'Hara was given to comparing himself, never made any

3. Testicles.

claims to his own facility when I knew him in Hollywood. On the contrary, both he and Nathanael West were continually obsessed by delusions of their inadequacy with sex and their small literary output.

Looking back over a long and mottled career, I think the best illustration of real *machismo* I ever beheld took place on the terrace of the Café du Dôme in Paris in 1927. I was seated there at dusk one day with a fellow journalist when an enormous yellow Hispano-Suiza landaulet driven by a chauffeur drew up at the curb. From it emerged a tall and beautiful, exquisitely clad lady, followed by another even more photogenic—both clearly high-fashion mannequins. Reaching into the tonneau, they brought forth a wizened homunculus with a yellow face resembling Earl Sande, the celebrated jockey. Hooking their arms through his, they assisted him to a table farther down the terrace. I turned to my *copain* with my eyebrows raised, searching for some explanation of the phenomenon. A slow smile overspread his countenance, and he held his hands apart as does one when asked to steady a skein of wool.

That's *machismo*, sweetheart.

1975

THE READER

1. Perelman says his next-to-last paragraph contains his "best illustration of real machismo." Explain why you agree or disagree.
2. Perelman implies that machismo attitudes are reflected in language. Find examples from contemporary newspapers or magazines.

THE WRITER

1. Write your own definition of machismo, basing it on Perelman's examples.
2. Toward the end of his essay, Perelman talks about writers who boast about how fast and how much they write. Why do you think Perelman includes these examples? Explain whether they are a part of his definition of machismo or merely analogous to it.
3. Perelman has a very distinctive style. Try to determine what its characteristics are by rewriting one of his paragraphs in a more neutral style.
4. Describe an incident (either actual or invented) that illustrates machismo. Then change the incident so that it no longer illustrates machismo. Explain whether the changes involve (a) changes in people, (b) changes in circumstances or social customs, or (c) changes in both. What conclusions can you draw about whether machismo is a part of human nature or is culturally conditioned?

Adrienne Rich

WHEN WE DEAD AWAKEN: WRITING AS RE-VISION

Ibsen's *When We Dead Awaken* is a play about the use that the male artist and thinker—in the process of creating culture as we know it—has made of women, in his life and in his work; and about a woman's slow struggling awakening to the use to which her life has been put. Bernard Shaw wrote in 1900 of this play: "[Ibsen] shows us that no degradation ever devized or permitted is as disastrous as this degradation; that through it women can die into luxuries for men and yet can kill them; that men and women are becoming conscious of this: and that what remains to be seen as perhaps the most interesting of all imminent social developments is what will happen 'when we dead awaken.'"

It's exhilarating to be alive in a time of awakening consciousness; it can also be confusing, disorienting, and painful. This awakening of dead or sleeping consciousness has already affected the lives of millions of women, even those who don't know it yet. It is also affecting the lives of men, even those who deny its claims upon them. The argument will go on whether an oppressive economic class system is responsible for the oppressive nature of male/female relations, or whether, in fact, the sexual class system is the original model on which all the others are based. But in the last few years connections have been drawn between our sexual lives and our political institutions which are inescapable and illuminating. The sleepwalkers are coming awake, and for the first time this awakening has a collective reality; it is no longer such a lonely thing to open one's eyes.

Re-vision—the act of looking back, of seeing with fresh eyes, of entering an old text from a new critical direction—is for us more than a chapter in cultural history: it is an act of survival. Until we can understand the assumptions in which we are drenched we cannot know ourselves. And this drive to self-knowledge, for woman, is more than a search for identity: it is part of her refusal of the destructiveness of male-dominated society. A radical critique of literature, feminist in its impulse, would take the work first of all as a clue to how we live, how we have been living, how we have been led to imagine ourselves, how our language has trapped as well as liberated us; and how we can begin to see —and therefore live—afresh. A change in the concept of sexual identity is essential if we are not going to see the old political order reassert itself in every new revolution. We need to know the writing of the past, and know it differently than we have ever known it; not to pass on a tradition but to break its hold over us.

For writers, and at this moment for women writers in particular, there is the challenge and promise of a whole new psychic geography to be explored. But there is also a difficult and dangerous walking on the ice, as we try to find language and images for a consciousness we are just coming into, and with little in the past to support us. I want to talk about some aspects of this difficulty and this danger.

Jane Harrison, the great classical anthropologist, wrote in 1914 in a letter to her friend Gilbert Murray: "By the by, about 'Women,' it has bothered me often—why do women never want to write poetry about Man as a sex—why is Woman a dream and a terror to man and not the other way around? . . . Is it mere convention and propriety, or something deeper?" I think Jane's question cuts deep into the myth-making tradition, the romantic tradition; deep into what women and men have been to each other; and deep into the psyche of the woman writer. Thinking about that question, I began thinking of the work of two twentieth-century women poets, Sylvia Plath and Diane Wakoski. It strikes me that in the work of both Man appears as, if not a dream, a fascination, and a terror; and that the source of the fascination and the terror is, simply, Man's power—to dominate, tyrannize, choose or reject the woman. The charisma of Man seems to come purely from his power over her, and his control of the world by force; not from anything fertile or life-giving in him. And, in the work of both these poets, it is finally the woman's sense of *herself*—embattled, possessed—that gives the poetry its dynamic charge, its rhythms of struggle, need, will and female energy. Convention and propriety are perhaps not the right words, but until recently this female anger, this furious awareness of the Man's power over her, were not available materials to the female poet, who tended to write of Love as the source of her suffering, and to view that victimization by Love as an almost inevitable fate. Or, like Marianne Moore and Elizabeth Bishop, she kept human sexual relationships at a measured and chiselled distance in her poems.

One answer to Jane Harrison's question has to be that historically men and women have played very different parts in each others' lives. Where woman has been a luxury for man, and has served as the painter's model and the poet's muse, but also as comforter, nurse, cook, bearer of his seed, secretarial assistant, and copyist of manuscripts, man has played a quite different role for the female artist. Henry James repeats an incident which the writer Prosper Mérimée described, of how, while he was living with George Sand,

he once opened his eyes, in the raw winter dawn, to see his companion, in a dressing-gown, on her knees before the domestic hearth, a candle-stick beside her and a red *madras* round her head, making bravely, with her own hands, the fire that was to enable her to sit down betimes to urgent pen and paper. The story represents him as having felt that the spectacle chilled his ardor and tried his taste; her appearance was unfortunate, her occupation an inconsequence, and her industry a reproof—the result of all of which was a lively irritation and an early rupture.

I am suggesting that the specter of this kind of male judgment, along with the active discouragement and thwarting of her needs by a culture controlled by males, has created problems for the woman writer: problems of contact with herself, problems of language and style, problems of energy and survival.

In rereading Virginia Woolf's *A Room of One's Own* for the first time in some years, I was astonished at the sense of effort, of pains taken, of dogged tentativeness, in the tone of that essay. And I recognized that tone. I had heard it often enough, in myself and in other women. It is the tone of a woman almost in touch with her anger, who is determined not to appear angry, who is *willing* herself to be calm, detached, and even charming in a roomful of men where things have been said which are attacks on her very integrity. Virginia Woolf is addressing an audience of women, but she is acutely conscious—as she always was—of being overheard by men: by Morgan and Lytton and Maynard Keynes[1] and for that matter by her father, Leslie Stephen. She drew the language out into an exacerbated thread in her determination to have her own sensibility yet protect it from those masculine presences. Only at rare moments in that essay do you hear the passion in her voice; she was trying to sound as cool as Jane Austen, as Olympian as Shakespeare, because that is the way the men of the culture thought a writer should sound.

No male writer has written primarily or even largely for women, or with the sense of women's criticism as a consideration when he chooses his materials, his theme, his language. But to a lesser or greater extent, every woman writer has written for men even when, like Virginia Woolf, she was supposed to be addressing women. If we have come to the point when this balance might begin to change, when women can stop being haunted, not only by "convention and propriety" but by internalized fears of being and saying themselves, then it is an extraordinary moment for the woman writer—and reader.

I have hesitated to do what I am going to do now, which is to use myself as an illustration. For one thing, it's a lot easier and less dangerous to talk about other women writers. But there is something else. Like Virginia Woolf, I am aware of the women who are not with us here because they

1. E. M. Forster, novelist, and Lytton Strachey, biographer, and John Maynard Keynes, economist—all members of the Bloomsbury group in London during the twenties and thirties.

are washing the dishes and looking after the children. Nearly fifty years after she spoke, that fact remains largely unchanged. And I am thinking also of women whom she left out of the picture altogether—women who are washing other people's dishes and caring for other people's children, not to mention women who went on the streets last night in order to feed their children. We seem to be special women here, we have liked to think of ourselves as special, and we have known that men would tolerate, even romanticize us as special, as long as our words and actions didn't threaten their privilege of tolerating or rejecting us according to *their* ideas of what a special woman ought to be. An important insight of the radical women's movement, for me, has been how divisive and how ultimately destructive is this myth of the special woman, who is also the token woman. Every one of us here in this room has had great luck; our own gifts could not have been enough, for we all know women whose gifts are buried or aborted. Our struggles can have meaning only if they can help to change the lives of women whose gifts—and whose very being— continues to be thwarted.

My own luck was being born white and middle-class into a house full of books, with a father who encouraged me to read and write. So for about twenty years I wrote for a particular man, who criticized and praised me and made me feel I was indeed "special." The obverse side of this, of course, was that I tried for a long time to please him, or rather, not to displease him. And then of course there were other men—writers, teach- ers—the Man, who was not a terror or a dream but a literary master and a master in other ways less easy to acknowledge. And there were all those poems about women, written by men: it seemed to be a given that men wrote poems and women frequently inhabited them. These women were almost always beautiful, but threatened with the loss of beauty, the loss of youth—the fate worse than death. Or, they were beautiful and died young, like Lucy and Lenore.[2] Or, the woman was like Maud Gonne,[3] cruel and disastrously mistaken, and the poem reproached her because she had refused to become a luxury for the poet.

A lot is being said today about the influence that the myths and images of women have on all of us who are products of culture. I think it has been a peculiar confusion to the girl or woman who tries to write, because she is peculiarly susceptible to language. She goes to poetry or fiction looking for *her* way of being in the world, since she too has been putting words and images together; she is looking eagerly for guides, maps, possibilities; and over and over in the "words' masculine persuasive force" of litera- ture she comes up against something that negates everthing she is about: she meets the image of Woman in books written by men. She finds a terror and a dream, she finds a beautiful pale face, she finds La Belle

2. In poems by William Wordsworth and   3. Irish revolutionary activist, subject of
Edgar Allan Poe.   many love poems by William Butler Yeats.

Dame Sans Merci, she finds Juliet or Tess or Salomé,[4] but precisely what she does not find is that absorbed, drudging, puzzled, sometimes inspired creature, herself, who sits at a desk trying to put words together.

So what does she do? What did I do? I read the older women poets with their peculiar keenness and ambivalence: Sappho, Christina Rossetti, Emily Dickinson, Elinor Wylie, Edna Millay, H.D. I discovered that the woman poet most admired at the time (by men) was Marianne Moore, who was maidenly, elegant, intellectual, discreet. But even in reading these women I was looking in them for the same things I had found in the poetry of men, because I wanted women poets to be the equals of men, and to be equal was still confused with sounding the same.

I know that my style was formed first by male poets: by the men I was reading as an undergraduate—Frost, Dylan Thomas, Donne, Auden, MacNiece, Stevens, Yeats. What I chiefly learned from them was craft. But poems are like dreams: in them you put what you don't know you know. Looking back at poems I wrote before I was twenty-one, I'm startled because beneath the conscious craft are glimpses of the split I even then experienced between the girl who wrote poems, who defined herself in writing poems, and the girl who was to define herself by her relationships with men. "Aunt Jennifer's Tigers," written while I was a student, looks with deliberate detachment at this split.

> Aunt Jennifer's tigers stride across a screen,
> Bright topaz denizens of a world of green.
> They do not fear the men beneath the tree,
> They pace in sleek chivalric certainty.
>
> Aunt Jennifer's fingers, fluttering through her wool,
> Find even the ivory needle hard to pull.
> The massive weight of Uncle's wedding-band
> Sits heavily upon Aunt Jennifer's hand.
>
> When Aunt is dead, her terrified hands will lie
> Still ringed with ordeals she was mastered by.
> The tigers in the panel that she made
> Will go on striding, proud and unafraid.

In writing this poem, composed and apparently cool as it is, I thought I was creating a portrait of an imaginary woman. But this woman suffers from the opposition of her imagination, worked out in tapestry, and her life-style, "ringed with ordeals she was mastered by." It was important to me that Aunt Jennifer was a person as distinct from myself as possible—

4. These female figures appear respectively in the poem "La Belle Dame sans Merci" by John Keats, Shakespeare's play *Romeo and Juliet*, Thomas Hardy's novel *Tess of the D'Urbervilles*, and Oscar Wilde's play *Salomé*. The men whom they love, or who love them, all sicken or die.

distanced by the formalism of the poem; by its objective, observant tone; even by putting the woman in a different generation.

In those years formalism was part of the strategy—like asbestos gloves, it allowed me to handle materials I couldn't pick up barehanded. (A later strategy was to use the persona of a man, as I did in "The Loser.")

A man thinks of the woman he once loved: first, after her wedding, and then nearly a decade later.

I

I kissed you, bride and lost, and went
home from that bourgeois sacrament,
your cheek still tasting cold upon
my lips that gave you benison
with all the swagger that they knew—
as losers somehow learn to do.

Your wedding made my eyes ache; soon
the world would be worse off for one
more golden apple dropped to ground
without the least protesting sound,
and you would windfall lie, and we
forget your shimmer on the tree.

Beauty is always wasted: if
not Mignon's song sung to the deaf,
at all events to the unmoved.
A face like yours cannot be loved
long or seriously enough.
Almost, we seem to hold it off.

II

Well, you are tougher than I thought.
Now when the wash with ice hangs taut
this morning of St. Valentine,
I see you strip the squeaking line,
your body weighed against the load,
and all my groans can do no good.

Because you still are beautiful,
though squared and stiffened by the pull
of what nine windy years have done.
You have three daughters, lost a son.
I see all your intelligence
flung into that unwearied stance.

My envy is of no avail.
I turn my head and wish him well
who chafed your beauty into use
and lives forever in a house
lit by the friction of your mind.
You stagger in against the wind.

1958

I finished college, published my first book by a fluke, as it seemed to me, and broke off a love-affair. I took a job, lived alone, went on writing, fell in love. I was young, full of energy, and the book seemed to mean that others agreed I was a poet. Because I was also determined to have a "full" woman's life, I plunged in my early twenties into marriage and had three children before I was thirty. There was nothing overt in the environment to warn me: these were the fifties, and in reaction to the earlier wave of feminism, middle-class women were making careers of domestic perfection, working to send their husbands through professional schools, then retiring to raise large families. People were moving out to the suburbs, technology was going to be the answer to everything, even sex; the family was in its glory. Life was extremely private; women were isolated from each other by the loyalties of marriage. I have a sense that women didn't talk to each other much in the fifties—not about their secret emptinesses, their frustrations. I went on trying to write, my second book and first child appeared in the same month. But by the time that book came out I was already dissatisfied with those poems, which seemed to me mere exercises for poems I hadn't written. The book was praised, however, for its "gracefulness"; I had a marriage and a child. If there were doubts, if there were periods of null depression or active despairing, these could only mean that I was ungrateful, insatiable, perhaps a monster.

About the time my third child was born, I felt that I had either to consider myself a failed woman and a failed poet, or try to find some synthesis by which to understand what was happening to me. What frightened me most was the sense of drift, of being pulled along on a current which called itself my destiny, but in which I seemed to be losing touch with whoever I had been, with the girl who had experienced her own will and energy almost ecstatically at times, walking around a city or riding a train at night or typing in a student room. In a poem about my grandmother, I wrote (of myself): "A young girl, thought sleeping, is certified dead." I was writing very little, partly from fatigue, that female fatigue of suppressed anger and the loss of contact with her own being; partly from the discontinuity of female life with its attention to small chores, errands, work that others constantly undo, small children's constant needs. What I did write was unconvincing to me; my anger and frustration were hard to acknowledge in or out of poem, because in fact I cared a great deal about my husband and my children. Trying to look back and understand that time I have tried to analyze the real nature of the conflict. Most, if not all, human lives are full of fantasy—passive daydreaming which need not be acted on. But to write poetry or fiction, or even to think well, is not to fantasize, or to put fantasies on paper. For a poem to coalesce, for a character or an action to take shape, there has to be an imaginative transformation of reality which is in no way passive. And a certain freedom of the mind is needed—freedom to press on, to enter the currents of your thought like a glider pilot, knowing that your motion can be sustained, that the buoyancy of your attention will not be suddenly snatched away. Moreover, if the imagination is to transcend and transform experience it has to question, to challenge, to conceive of alternatives, perhaps to the very life you are living at that moment. You have to be free to play around with the notion that day might be night, love might be hate; nothing can be too sacred for the imagination to turn into its opposite or to call experimentally by another name. For writing is re-naming. Now, to be maternally with small children all day in the old way, to be with a man in the old way of marriage, requires a holding-back, a putting-aside of that imaginative activity, and seems to demand instead a kind of conservatism. I want to make it clear that I am *not* saying that in order to write well, or think well, it is necessary to become unavailable to others, or to become a devouring ego. This has been the myth of the masculine artist and thinker; and I repeat, I do not accept it. But to be a female human being trying to fulfill traditional female functions in a traditional way *is* in direct conflict with the subversive function of the imagination. The word *traditional* is important here. There must be ways, and we will be finding out more and more about them, in which the energy of creation and the energy of relation can be united. But in those earlier years I always felt the conflict as a failure of love in myself. I had thought I was choosing a full life: the life available to most men, in which sexuality, work and parenthood could coexist. But I felt, at twenty-nine, guilt toward the people closest to me, and guilty toward my own being.

I wanted, then, more than anything, the one thing of which there was never enough: time to think, time to write. The fifties and early sixties were years of rapid revelations: the sit-ins and marches in the South, the Bay of Pigs,[5] the early anti-war movement raised large questions— questions for which the masculine world of the academy around me seemed to have expert and fluent answers. But I needed desperately to think for myself—about pacifism and dissent and violence, about poetry and society and about my own relationship to all these things. For about

5. Site of a failed American invasion of Cuba, intended to overthrow the Castro regime.

ten years I was reading in fierce snatches, scribbling in notebooks, writing poetry in fragments; I was looking desperately for clues, because if there were no clues then I thought I might be insane. I wrote in a notebook about this time: "Paralyzed by the sense that there exists a mesh of relationships—e.g. between my anger at the children, my sensual life, pacifism, sex, (I mean sex in its broadest significance, not merely sexual desire)—an interconnectedness which, if I could see it, make it valid, would give me back myself, make it possible to function lucidly and passionately. Yet I grope in and out among these dark webs." I think I began at this point to feel that politics was not something "out there" but something "in here" and of the essence of my condition.

In the late fifties I was able to write, for the first time, directly about experiencing myself as a woman. The poem was jotted in fragments during children's naps, brief hours in a library, or at 3 A.M. after rising with a wakeful child. I despaired of doing any continuous work at this time. Yet I began to feel that my fragments and scraps had a common consciousness and a common theme, one which I would have been very unwilling to put on paper at an earlier time because I had been taught that poetry should be "universal," which meant, of course, non-female. Until then I had tried very much *not* to identify myself as a female poet. Over two years I wrote a ten-part poem called "Snapshots of A Daughter-in-Law," in a longer, looser mode than I've ever trusted myself with before. It was an extraordinary relief to write that poem. It strikes me now as too literary, too dependent on allusion; I hadn't found the courage yet to do without authorities, or even to use the pronoun *I*—the woman in the poem is *always she*. One section of it, 2, concerns a woman who thinks she is going mad; she is haunted by voices telling her to resist and rebel, voices which she can hear but not obey.

2.

Banging the coffee-pot into the sink
she hears the angels chiding, and looks out
past the raked gardens to the sloppy sky.
Only a week since They said: *Have no patience.*

The next time it was: *Be insatiable.*
Then: *Save yourself; others you cannot save.*
Sometimes she's let the tapstream scald her arm,
a match burn to her thumbnail,

or held her hand above the kettle's spout
right in the woolly steam. They are probably angels,
since nothing hurts her any more, except
each morning's grit blowing into her eyes.

The poem "Orion," written five years later, is a poem of reconnection with a part of myself I had felt I was losing—the active principle, the energetic imagination, the "half-brother" whom I projected, as I had for many years, into the constellation Orion.

> Far back when I went zig-zagging
> through tamarack pastures
> you were my genius, you
> my cast-iron Viking, my helmed
> lion-heart king in prison.
> Years later now you're young
>
> my fierce half-brother, staring
> down from that simplified west
> your breast open, your belt dragged down
> by an oldfashioned thing, a sword
> the last bravado you won't give over
> though it weighs you down as you stride
>
> and the stars in it are dim
> and maybe have stopped burning.
> But you burn, and I know it;
> as I throw back my head to take you in
> an old transfusion happens again:
> divine astronomy is nothing to it.
>
> Indoors I bruise and blunder,
> break faith, leave ill enough
> alone, a dead child born in the dark.
> Night cracks up over the chimney,
> pieces of time, frozen geodes
> come showering down in the grate.
>
> A man reaches behind my eyes
> and finds them empty
> a woman's head turns away
> from my head in the mirror
> children are dying my death
> and eating crumbs of my life.
>
> Pity is not your forte.
> Calmly you ache up there
> pinned aloft in your crow's nest,
> my speechless pirate!
> You take it all for granted
> and when I look you back
>
> it's with a starlike eye

> shooting its cold and egotistical spear
> where it can do least damage.
> Breathe deep! No hurt, no pardon
> out here in the cold with you
> you with your back to the wall.

It's no accident that the words *cold and egotistical* appear in this poem, and are applied to myself. The choice still seemed to be between "love" —womanly, maternal love, altruistic love—a love defined and ruled by the weight of an entire culture—and egotism—a force directed by men into creation, achievement, ambition, often at the expense of others, but justifiably so. For weren't they men, and wasn't that their destiny as womanly love was ours? I know now that the alternatives are false ones— that the word *love* is itself in need of re-vision.

There is a companion poem to "Orion," written three years later, in which at last the woman in the poem and the woman writing the poem become the same person. It is called "Planetarium," and it was written after a visit to a real planetarium, where I read an account of the work of Caroline Herschel, the astronomer, who worked with her brother William, but whose name remained obscure, as his did not.

> *(Thinking of Caroline Herschel, 1750–1848, astronomer, sister of William; and others)*

> A woman in the shape of a monster
> a monster in the shape of a woman
> the skies are full of them
>
> a woman   'in the snow
> among the Clocks and instruments
> or measuring the ground with poles'
>
> in her 98 years to discover
> 8 comets
>
> she whom the moon ruled
> like us
> levitating into the night sky
> riding the polished lenses
>
> Galaxies of women, there
> doing penance for impetuousness
> ribs chilled
> in those spaces   of the mind

An eye,
              'virile, precise and absolutely certain'
              from the mad webs of Uranisborg
                                        encountering the NOVA

every impulse of light exploding
from the core
as life flies out of us

              Tycho whispering at last
              'Let me not seem to have lived in vain'

What we see, we see
and seeing is changing

the light that shrivels a mountain
and leaves a man alive

Heartbeat of the pulsar
heart sweating through my body

The radio impulse
pouring in from Taurus

              I am bombarded yet   I stand

I have been standing all my life in the
direct path of a battery of signals
the most accurately transmitted most
untranslatable language in the universe
I am a galactic cloud so deep   so invo-
luted that a light wave could take 15
years to travel through me   And has
taken   I am an instrument in the shape
of a woman trying to translate pulsations
into images   for the relief of the body
and the reconstruction of the mind.

In closing I want to tell you about a dream I had last summer. I dreamed
I was asked to read my poetry at a mass women's meeting; but when I
began to read, what came out were the lyrics of a blues song. I share this
dream with you because it seemed to me to say a lot about the problems
and the future of the woman writer, and probably of women in general.
The awakening of consciousness is not like the crossing of a frontier—
one step, and you are in another country. Much of women's poetry has
been of the nature of the blues song: a cry of pain, of victimization, or a
lyric of seduction. And today, much poetry by women—and prose for

that matter—is charged with anger. I think we need to go through that anger, and we will betray our own reality if we try, as Virginia Woolf was trying, for an objectivity, a detachment; that would make us sound more like Jane Austen or Shakespeare. We know more than Jane Austen or Shakespeare knew: more than Jane Austen because our lives are more complex, more than Shakespeare because we know more about the lives of women, Jane Austen and Virginia Woolf included.

Both the victimization and the anger experienced by women are real, and have real sources, everywhere in the environment, built into society. They must go on being tapped and explored by poets, among others. We can neither deny them, nor can we rest there. They are our birth-pains, and we are bearing ourselves. We would be failing each other as writers and as women, if we neglected or denied what is negative, regressive or Sisyphean[5] in our inwardness.

We all know that there is another story to be told. I am curious and expectant about the future of the masculine consciousness. I feel in the work of the men whose poetry I read today a deep pessimism and fatalistic grief; and I wonder if it isn't the masculine side of what women have experienced, the price of masculine dominance. One thing I am sure of: just as woman is becoming her own midwife, creating herself anew, so man will have to learn to gestate and give birth to his own subjectivity—something he has frequently wanted woman to do for him. We can go on trying to talk to each other, we can sometimes help each other, poetry and fiction can show us what the other is going through; but women can no longer be primarily mothers and muses for men: we have our own work cut out for us.

                                                                    1972

5. The reference is to the Greek myth of Sisyphus. He was condemned to roll a huge rock to the top of a hill, but the rock always rolled back down before the top was reached.

THE READER

1. A typical male-chauvinist cliché is that women take everything too personally, that they lack the larger (i.e., male) perspective. Does this essay tend to confirm or deny that belief?
2. In the eighth paragraph, Rich asserts that "no male writer has written primarily or even largely for women, or with the sense of women's criticism as a consideration when he chooses his materials, his theme, his languge." How can she know this? Do you think she is right? How do you know?
3. In saying that the need is to break tradition's hold over us (p. 418), Rich clearly implies her assessment of tradition. Looking to the future she says, "Woman is becoming her own midwife, creating herself anew." What view of history is implicit here? What role does the speaker create for herself?

THE WRITER

1. *Why does Rich include some of her own poetry? Explain whether you think she is able to make points through it that she couldn't make otherwise.*
2. *On p. 413, Rich describes Virginia Woolf as being conscious of male listeners even as she addressed women. Can you detect signs of this in Woolf's "In Search of a Room of One's Own" (p. 1053)? Rich will try to avoid this way of speaking and writing. Does she succeed? Find passages to support your answer.*
3. *Why does Rich use the hyphen in re-vision? What does she wish to imply about writing? Compare her view with that of Sommers (p. 344).*
4. *On p. 414, Rich refers to "the influence that the myths and images of women have on all of us." Presumably there are also myths and images of men. Write a brief account of either a male or a female myth and its influence upon attitudes and actions of the other sex.*

Gloria Steinem

THE GOOD NEWS IS: THESE ARE NOT THE BEST YEARS OF YOUR LIFE

If you had asked me a decade or more ago, I certainly would have said the campus was the first place to look for the feminist or any other revolution. I also would have assumed that student-age women, like student-age men, were much more likely to be activist and open to change than their parents. After all, campus revolts have a long and well-publicized tradition, from the students of medieval France, whose "heresy" was suggesting that the university be separate from the church, through the anticolonial student riots of British India; from students who led the cultural revolution of the People's Republic of China, to campus demonstrations against the Shah of Iran. Even in this country, with far less tradition of student activism, the populist movement to end the war in Vietnam was symbolized by campus protests and mistrust of anyone over thirty.

It has taken me many years of traveling as a feminist speaker and organizer to understand that I was wrong about women; at least, about women acting on their own behalf. In activism, as in so many other things, I had been educated to assume that men's cultural pattern was the natural or the only one. If student years were the peak time of rebellion and openness to change for men, then the same must be true for women.

In fact, a decade of listening to every kind of women's group—from brown-bag lunchtime lectures organized by office workers to all-night rap sessions at campus women's centers; from housewives' self-help groups to campus rallies—has convinced me that the reverse is more often true. Women may be the one group that grows more radical with age. Though some students are big exceptions to this rule, women in general don't begin to challenge the politics of our own lives until later.

Looking back, I realize that this pattern has been true for my life, too. My college years were full of uncertainties and the personal conservatism that comes from trying to win approval and fit into the proper grown-up and womanly role whether that means finding a well-to-do man to be supported by or a male radical to support. Nonetheless, I went right on assuming that brave exploring youth and cowardly conservative old age were the norms for everybody, and that I must be just an isolated and guilty accident. Though every generalization based on female culture has many exceptions, and should never be used as a crutch or excuse, I think we might be less hard on ourselves and each other as students, feel better about our potential for change as we grow older—and educate reporters who announce feminism's demise because its red-hot center is not on campus—if we figured out that for most of us as women, the traditional college period is an unrealistic and cautious time. Consider a few of the reasons.

As students, women are probably treated with more equality than we ever will be again. For one thing, we're consumers. The school is only too glad to get the tuitions we pay, or that our families or government grants pay on our behalf. With population rates declining because of women's increased power over childbearing, that money is even more vital to a school's existence. Yet more than most consumers, we're too transient to have much power as a group. If our families are paying our tuition, we may have even less power.

As young women, whether students or not, we're still in the stage most valued by male-dominant cultures: We have our full potential as workers, wives, sex partners, and childbearers.

That means we haven't yet experienced the life events that are most radicalizing for women: entering the paid-labor force and discovering how women are treated there; marrying and finding out that it is not yet an equal partnership; having children and discovering who is responsible for them and who is not; and aging, still a greater penalty for women than for men.

Furthermore, new ambitions nourished by the rebirth of feminism may make young women feel and behave a little like a classical immigrant group. We are determined to prove ourselves, to achieve academic excellence, and to prepare for interesting and successful careers. More noses are kept to more grindstones in an effort to demonstrate newfound abilities, and perhaps to allay suspicions that women still have to have more and better credentials than men. This doesn't leave much time for activism. Indeed, we may not yet know that it is necessary.

In addition, the very progress into previously all-male careers that may be revolutionary for women is seen as conservative and conformist by outside critics. Assuming male radicalism to be the measure of change, they interpret any concern with careers as evidence of "campus conservatism." In fact, "dropping out" may be a departure for men, but "dropping in" is a new thing for women. Progress lies in the direction we have not been.

Like most groups of the newly arrived or awakened, our faith in education and paper degrees also has yet to be shaken. For instance, the percentage of women enrolled in colleges and universities has been increasing at the same time that the percentage of men has been decreasing. Among students entering college in 1978, women *outnumbered* men for the first time. This hope of excelling at the existing game is probably reinforced by the greater cultural pressure on females to be "good girls" and observe somebody else's rules.

Though we may know intellectually that we need to have new games with new rules, we probably haven't quite absorbed such facts as the high unemployment rate among female Ph.D.s; the lower average salary among women college graduates of all races than among counterpart males who graduated from high school or less; the middle-management ceiling against which even those eagerly hired new business-school graduates seem to bump their heads after five or ten years; and the barrier-breaking women in nontraditional fields who become the first fired when recession hits. Sadly enough, we may have to personally experience some of these reality checks before we accept the idea that lawsuits, activism, and group pressure will have to accompany our individual excellence and crisp new degrees.

Then there is the female guilt trip, student edition. If we're not sailing along as planned, it must be *our* fault. If our mothers didn't "do anything" with their educations, it must have been *their* fault. If we can't study as hard as we think we must (because women still have to be better prepared than men), and have a substantial personal and sexual life at the same time (because women are supposed to care more about relationships than men do), then we feel inadequate, as if each of us were individually at fault for a problem that is actually culture-wide.

I've yet to be on a campus where most women weren't worrying about some aspect of combining marriage, children, and a career. I've yet to find one where many men were worrying about the same thing. Yet women will go right on suffering from the double-role problem and terminal guilt until men are encouraged, pressured, or otherwise forced, individually and collectively, to integrate themselves into the "women's work" of raising children and homemaking. Until then, and until there are changed job patterns to allow equal parenthood, children will go right on growing up with the belief that only women can be loving and nurturing, and only men can be intellectual or active outside the home. Each half of the world will go on limiting the full range of its human talent.

Finally, there is the intimate political training that hits women in the teens and early twenties: the countless ways we are still brainwashed into assuming that women are dependent on men for our basic identities, both in our work and our personal lives, much more than vice versa. After all, if we're going to enter a marriage system that's still legally designed for a person and a half, submit to an economy in which women still average about fifty-nine cents on the dollar earned by men, and work mainly as support staff and assistants, or co-directors and vice-presidents at best, then we have to be convinced that we are not whole people on our own.

In order to make sure that we will see ourselves as half-people, and thus be addicted to getting our identity from serving others, society tries hard to convert us as young women into "man junkies"; that is, into people who are addicted to regular shots of male-approval and presence, both professionally and personally. We need a man standing next to us, actually and figuratively, whether it's at work, on Saturday night, or throughout life. (If only men realized how little it matters which man is standing there, they would understand that this addiction depersonalizes them, too.) Given the danger to a male-dominant system if young women stop internalizing this political message of derived identity, it's no wonder that those who try to kick the addiction—and, worse yet, to help other women do the same—are likely to be regarded as odd or dangerous by everyone from parents to peers.

With all that pressure combined with little experience, it's no wonder that younger women are often less able to support each other. Even young women who espouse feminist goals as individuals may refrain from identifying themselves as "feminist": it's okay to want equal pay for yourself (just one small reform) but it's not okay to want equal pay for women as a group (an economic revolution). Some retreat into individualized career obsessions as a way of avoiding this dangerous discovery of shared experience with women as a group. Others retreat into the safe middle ground of "I'm not a feminist but. . . ." Still others become politically active, but only on issues that are taken seriously by their male counterparts.

The same lesson about the personal conservatism of younger women is taught by the history of feminism. If I hadn't been conned into believing the masculine stereotype of youth as the "natural" time for freedom and rebellion, a time of "sowing wild oats" that actually is made possible by the assurance of power and security later on, I could have figured out the female pattern of activism by looking at women's movements of the past.

In this country, for instance, the nineteenth-century wave of feminism was started by older women who had been through the radicalizing experience of getting married and becoming the legal chattel of their husbands (or the equally radicalizing experience of *not* getting married and being treated as spinsters). Most of them had also worked in the antislavery movement and learned from the political parallels between race and sex. In other countries, that wave was also led by women who were past the point of maximum pressure toward marriageability and conservatism.

Looking at the first decade of this second wave, it's clear that the early feminist activist and consciousness-raising groups of the 1960s were organized by women who had experienced the civil rights movement, or homemakers who had discovered that raising kids and cooking didn't occupy all their talents. While most campuses of the late sixties were still circulating the names of illegal abortionists privately (after all, abortion could damage our marriage value), slightly older women were holding press conferences and speak-outs about the reality of abortions (including their own, even though that often meant confessing to an illegal act) and demanding reform or repeal of antichoice laws. Though rape had been a quiet epidemic on campus for generations, younger women victims were still understandably fearful of speaking up, and campuses encouraged silence in order to retain their reputation for safety with tuition-paying parents. It took many off-campus speak-outs, demonstrations against laws of evidence and police procedures, and testimonies in state legislatures before most student groups began to make demands on campus and local cops for greater rape protection. In fact, "date rape"—the common campus phenomenon of a young woman being raped by someone she knows, perhaps even by several students in a fraternity house—is just now being exposed. Marital rape, a more difficult legal issue, was taken up several years ago. As for battered women and the attendant exposé of husbands and lovers as more statistically dangerous than unknown muggers in the street, that issue still seems to be thought of as a largely noncampus concern, yet at many of the colleges and universities where I've spoken, there has been at least one case within current student memory of a young woman beaten or murdered by a jealous lover.

This cultural pattern of youthful conservatism makes the growing number of older women going back to school very important. They are life examples and pragmatic activists who radicalize women young enough to be their daughters. Now that the median female undergraduate age in this country is twenty-seven because so many older women have returned, the campus is becoming a major place for cross-generational connections.

None of this should denigrate the courageous efforts of young women, especially women on campus, and the many changes they've pioneered. On the contrary, they should be seen as even more remarkable for surviving the conservative pressures, recognizing societal problems they haven't yet fully experienced, and organizing successfully in the midst of a transient student population. Every women's history course, rape hot line, or campus newspaper that is finally covering *all* the news; every feminist professor whose job has been created or tenure saved by student pressure, or male administrator whose consciousness has been permanently changed; every counselor who's stopped guiding women one way and men another; every lawsuit that's been fueled by student energies against unequal athletic funds or graduate school requirements: all those accomplishments are even more impressive when seen against the backdrop of the female pattern of activism.

Finally, it would help to remember that a feminist revolution rarely resembles a masculine-style one—just as a young woman's most radical act toward her mother (that is, connecting as women in order to help each other get some power) doesn't look much like a young man's most radical act toward his father (that is, breaking the father-son connection in order to separate identities or take over existing power).

It's those father-son conflicts at a generational, national level that have often provided the conventional definition of revolution; yet they've gone on for centuries without basically changing the role of the female half of the world. They have also failed to reduce the level of violence in society, since both fathers and sons have included some degree of aggressiveness and superiority to women in their definition of masculinity, thus preserving the anthropological model of dominance.

Furthermore, what current leaders and theoreticians define as revolution is usually little more than taking over the army and the radio stations. Women have much more in mind than that. We have to uproot the sexual caste system that is the most pervasive power structure in society, and that means transforming the patriarchal values of those who run the institutions, whether they are politically the "right" or the "left," the fathers or the sons. This cultural part of the change goes very deep, and is often seen as too intimate, and perhaps too threatening, to be considered as either serious or possible. Only conflicts among men are "serious." Only a takeover of existing institutions is "possible."

That's why the definition of "political," on campus as elsewhere, tends to be limited to who's running for president, who's demonstrating against corporate investments in South Africa, or which is the "moral" side of some conventional revolution, preferably one that is thousands of miles away.

As important as such activities are, they are also the most comfortable ones when we're young. They provide a sense of virtue without much disruption in the power structure of our daily lives. Even when the most consistent energies on campus are actually concentrated around feminist issues, they may be treated as apolitical and invisible. Asked "What's happening on campus?" a student may reply, "The antinuke movement," even though that resulted in one demonstration of two hours, while student antirape squads have been patrolling the campus every night for two years and women's studies have begun to transform the very textbooks we read.

No wonder reporters and sociologists looking for revolution on campus often miss the depth of feminist change and activity that is really there. Women students themselves may dismiss it as not political and not serious. Certainly, it rarely comes in the masculine sixties style of bombing buildings or burning draft cards. In fact, it goes much deeper than protesting a temporary sympton—say, the draft—and challenges the right of one group to dominate another, which is the disease itself.

Young women have a big task of resisting pressures and challenging definitions. Their increasing success is a miracle of foresight and courage that should make us all proud. But they should know that they, too, may grow more radical with age.

One day, an army of gray-haired women may quietly take over the earth.

1979

Betty Rollin

MOTHERHOOD: WHO NEEDS IT?

Motherhood is in trouble, and it ought to be. A rude question is long overdue: Who needs it? The answer used to be (1) society and (2) women. But now, with the impending horrors of overpopulation, society desperately *doesn't* need it. And women don't need it either. Thanks to the Motherhood Myth—the idea that having babies is something that all normal women instinctively want and need and will enjoy doing—they just *think* they do.

The notion that the maternal wish and the activity of mothering are instinctive or biologically predestined is baloney. Try asking most sociologists, psychologists, psychoanalysts, biologists—many of whom are mothers—about motherhood being instinctive; it's like asking department store presidents if their Santa Clauses are real. "Motherhood—instinctive?" shouts distinguished sociologist/author Dr. Jessie Bernard. "Biological destiny? Forget biology! If it were biology, people would die from not doing it."

"Women don't need to be mothers any more than they need spaghetti," says Dr. Richard Rabkin, a New York psychiatrist. "But if you're in a world where everyone is eating spaghetti, thinking they need it and want it, you will think so too. Romance has really contaminated science. So-called instincts have to do with stimulation. They are not things that well up inside of you."

"When a woman says with feeling that she craved her baby from within, she is putting into biological language what is psychological," says University of Michigan psychoanalyst and motherhood-researcher Dr. Frederick Wyatt. "There are no instincts," says Dr. William Goode, president-elect of the American Sociological Association. "There are reflexes, like eye-blinking, and drives, like sex. There is no innate drive for children. Otherwise, the enormous cultural pressures that there are to reproduce wouldn't exist. There are no cultural pressures to sell you on getting your hand out of the fire."

There are, to be sure, biologists and others who go on about biological destiny, that is, the innate or instinctive goal of motherhood. (At the turn of the century, even good old capitalism was explained by a theorist as "the *instinct* of acquisitiveness.") And many psychoanalysts will hold the Freudian view that women feel so rotten about not having a penis that they are necessarily propelled into the child-wish to replace the missing organ. Psychoanalysts also make much of the psychological need to repeat what one's parent of the same sex has done. Since every woman has a mother, it is considered normal to wish to imitate one's mother by being a mother.

There is, surely, a wish to pass on love if one has received it, but to insist women must pass it on in the same way is like insisting that every man whose father is a gardener has to be a gardener. One dissenting psychoanalyst says, simply, "There is a wish to comply with one's biology, yes, but we needn't and sometimes we shouldn't." (Interestingly, the woman who has been the greatest contributor to child therapy and who has probably given more to children than anyone alive is Dr. Anna Freud, Freud's magnificent daughter, who is not a mother.)

Anyway, what an expert cast of hundreds is telling us is, simply, that biological *possibility* and desire are not the same as biological *need*. Women have childbearing equipment. To choose not to use the equipment is no more blocking what is instinctive than it is for a man who, muscles or no, chooses not to be a weight lifter.

So much for the wish. What about the "instinctive" *activity* of mothering? One animal study shows that when a young member of a species is put in a cage, say, with an older member of the same species, the latter will act in a protective, "maternal" way. But that goes for both males and females who have been "mothered" themselves. And studies indicate that a human baby will also respond to whoever is around playing mother

—even if it's father. Margaret Mead and many others frequently point out that mothering can be a fine occupation, if you want it, for either sex. Another experiment with monkeys who were brought up without mothers found them lacking in maternal behavior toward their own offspring. A similar study showed that monkeys brought up without other monkeys of the opposite sex had no interest in mating—all of which suggests that both mothering and mating behavior are learned, not instinctual. And, to turn the cart (or the baby carriage) around, baby ducks who lovingly follow their mothers seemed, in the mother's absence, to just as lovingly follow wooden ducks or even vacuum cleaners.

If motherhood isn't instinctive, when and why, then, was the Motherhood Myth born? Until recently, the entire question of maternal motivation was academic. Sex, like it or not, meant babies. Not that there haven't always been a lot of interesting contraceptive tries. But until the creation of the diaphragm in the 1880's, the birth of babies was largely unavoidable. And, generally speaking, nobody really seemed to mind. For one thing, people tend to be sort of good sports about what seems to be inevitable. For another, in the past, the population needed beefing up. Mortality rates were high, and agricultural cultures, particularly, have always needed children to help out. So because it "just happened" and because it was needed, motherhood was assumed to be innate.

Originally, it was the word of God that got the ball rolling with "Be fruitful and multiply," a practical suggestion, since the only people around then were Adam and Eve. But in no time, supermoralists like St. Augustine changed the tone of the message: "Intercourse, even with one's legitimate wife, is unlawful and wicked where the conception of the offspring is prevented," he, we assume, thundered. And the Roman Catholic position was thus cemented. So then and now, procreation took on a curious value among people who viewed (and view) the pleasures of sex as sinful. One could partake in the sinful pleasure, but feel vindicated by the ensuing birth. Motherhood cleaned up sex. Also, it cleaned up women, who have always been considered somewhat evil, because of Eve's transgression ("... but the woman was deceived and became a transgressor. Yet woman will be saved through bearing children ... ," I Timothy, 2:14–15), and somewhat dirty because of menstruation.

And so, based on need, inevitability, and pragmatic fantasy—the Myth *worked*, from society's point of view—the Myth grew like corn in Kansas. And society reinforced it with both laws and propaganda—laws that made woman a chattel, denied her education and personal mobility, and madonna propaganda that she was beautiful and wonderful doing it and it was all beautiful and wonderful to do. (One rarely sees a madonna washing dishes.)

In fact, the Myth persisted—breaking some kind of record for longlasting fallacies—until something like yesterday. For as the truth about the Myth trickled in—as women's rights increased, as women gradually got the message that it was certainly possible for them to do most things that men did, that they live longer, that their brains were not tinier—then, finally, when the really big news rolled in, that they could *choose* whether or not to be mothers—what happened? The Motherhood Myth soared higher than ever. As Betty Friedan made oh-so-clear in *The Feminine Mystique*, the '40's and '50's produced a group of ladies who not only had babies as if they were going out of style (maybe they were) but, as never before, they turned motherhood into a cult. First, they wallowed in the aesthetics of it all—natural childbirth and nursing became maternal musts. Like heavy-bellied ostriches, they grounded their heads in the sands of motherhood, only coming up for air to say how utterly happy and fulfilled they were. But, as Mrs. Friedan says only too plainly, they weren't. The Myth galloped on, moreover, long after making babies had turned from practical asset to liability for both individual parents *and* society. With the average cost of a middle-class child figured conservatively at $30,000 (not including college), any parent knows that the only people who benefit economically from children are manufacturers of consumer goods. Hence all those gooey motherhood commercials. And the Myth gathered momentum long after sheer numbers, while not yet extinguishing us, have made us intensely uncomfortable. Almost all of our societal problems, from minor discomforts like traffic to major ones like hunger, the population people keep reminding us, have to do with there being too many people. And who suffers most? The kids who have been so mindlessly brought into the world, that's who. They are the ones who have to cope with all of the difficult and dehumanizing conditions brought on by overpopulation. They are the ones who have to cope with the psychological nausea of feeling unneeded by society. That's not the only reason for drugs, but, surely, it's a leading contender.

Unfortunately, the population curbers are tripped up by a romantic, stubborn, ideological hurdle. How can birth-control programs really be effective as long as the concept of glorious motherhood remains unchanged? (Even poor old Planned Parenthood has to euphemize—why not Planned Unparenthood?) Particularly among the poor, motherhood is one of the few inherently positive institutions that are accessible. As Berkeley demographer Judith Blake points out, "Poverty-oriented birth control programs do not make sense as a welfare measure . . . as long as existing pronatalist policies . . . encourage mating, pregnancy, and the care, support, and rearing of children." Or, she might have added, as long as the less-than-idyllic child-rearing part of motherhood remains "in small print."

Sure, motherhood gets dumped on sometimes: Philip Wylie's Momism[1] got going in the '40's and Philip Roth's *Portnoy's Complaint* did its best to turn rancid the chicken-soup concept of Jewish motherhood. But these are viewed as the sour cries of a black humorist here, a malcontent there. Everyone shudders, laughs, but it's like the mouse and the elephant joke. Still, the Myth persists. Last April, a Brooklyn woman was indicted on charges of manslaughter and negligent homicide—eleven children died in a fire in a building she owned and criminally neglected—"But," sputtered her lawyer, "my client, Mrs. Breslow, is a mother, a grandmother, and a great-grandmother!"

Most remarkably, the Motherhood Myth persists in the face of the most overwhelming maternal unhappiness and incompetence. If reproduction were merely superfluous and expensive, if the experience were as rich and rewarding as the cliché would have us believe, if it were a predominantly joyous trip for everyone riding—mother, father, child—then the going everybody-should-have-two-children plan would suffice. Certainly, there are a lot of joyous mothers, and their children and (sometimes, not necessarily) their husbands reflect their joy. But a lot of evidence suggests that for more women than anyone wants to admit, motherhood can be miserable. ("If it weren't," says one psychiatrist wryly, "the world wouldn't be in the mess it's in.")

There is a remarkable statistical finding from a recent study of Dr. Bernard's, comparing the mental illness and unhappiness of married mothers and single women. The latter group, it turned out, was both markedly less sick and overtly more happy. Of course, it's not easy to measure slippery attitudes like happiness. "Many women have achieved a kind of reconciliation—a conformity," says Dr. Bernard,

> that they interpret as happiness. Since feminine happiness is supposed to lie in devoting one's life to one's husband and children, they do that; so *ipso facto*, they assume they are happy. And for many women, untrained for independence and "processed" for motherhood, they find their state far preferable to the alternatives, which don't really exist.

Also, unhappy mothers are often loath to admit it. For one thing, if in society's view not to be a mother is to be a freak, not to be a *blissful* mother is to be a witch. Besides, unlike a disappointing marriage, disappointing motherhood cannot be terminated by divorce. Of course, none of that stops such a woman from expressing her dissatisfaction in a variety of ways. Again, it is not only she who suffers but her husband and children as well. Enter the harridan housewife, the carping shrew. The realities of motherhood can turn women into terrible people. And, judging from the 50,000 cases of child abuse in the U.S. each year, some are worse than terrible.

1. Philip Wylie's *A Generation of Vipers* (1942) blamed many of the ills of American society on dominating mothers.

In some cases, the unpleasing realities of motherhood begin even before the beginning. In *Her Infinite Variety*, Morton Hunt describes young married women pregnant for the first time as "very likely to be frightened and depressed, masking these feelings in order not to be considered contemptible. The arrival of pregnancy interrupts a pleasant dream of motherhood and awakens them to the realization that they have too little money, or not enough space, or unresolved marital problems. . . ."

The following are random quotes from interviews with some mothers in Ann Arbor, Mich., who described themselves as reasonably happy. They all had positive things to say about their children, although when asked about the best moment of their day, they *all* confessed it was when the children were in bed. Here is the rest:

Suddenly I had to devote myself to the child totally. I was under the illusion that the baby was going to fit into my life, and I found that I had to switch my life and my schedule to fit *him*. You think, "I'm in love, I'll get married, and we'll have a baby." First there's two, then three, it's simple and romantic. You don't even think about the work. . . .

You never get away from the responsibility. Even when you leave the children with a sitter, you are not out from under the pressure of the responsibility. . . .

I hate ironing their pants and doing their underwear, and they never put their clothes in the laundry basket. . . . As they get older, they make less demands on our time because they're in school, but the demands are greater in forming their values. . . . Best moment of the day is when all the children are in bed. . . . The worst time of the day is 4 P.M., when you have to get dinner started, the kids are tired, hungry and crabby—everybody wants to talk to you about *their* day . . . your day is only half over.

Once a mother, the responsibility and concern for my children became so encompassing. . . . It took a great deal of will to keep up other parts of my personality. . . . To me, motherhood gets harder as they get older because you have less control. . . . In an abstract sense, I'd have several. . . . In the non-abstract, I would not have any . . . .

I had anticipated that the baby would sleep and eat, sleep and eat. Instead, the experience was overwhelming. I really had not thought particularly about what motherhood would mean in a realistic sense. I want to do *other* things, like to become involved in things that are worthwhile—I don't mean women's clubs—but I don't have the physical energy to go out in the evenings. I feel like I'm missing something . . . the experience of being somewhere with people and having them talking about something—something that's going on in the world.

Every grownup person expects to pay a price for his pleasures, but seldom is the price as vast as the one endured "however happily" by most mothers. We have mentioned the literal cost factor. But what does that mean? For middle-class American women, it means a life style with severe and usually unimagined limitations; i.e., life in the suburbs, because who can afford three bedrooms in the city? And what do suburbs mean? For women, suburbs mean other women and children and leftover peanut-butter sandwiches and car pools and seldom-seen husbands. Even the Feminine Mystiqueniks—the housewives who finally admitted that their lives behind brooms (OK, electric brooms) were driving them crazy —were loath to trace their predicament to their children. But it is simply a fact that a childless married woman has no child-work and little housework. She can live in a city, or, if she still chooses the suburbs or the country, she can leave on the commuter train with her husband if she wants to. Even the most ardent job-seeking mother will find little in the way of great opportunities in Scarsdale.[2] Besides, by the time she wakes up, she usually lacks both the preparation for the outside world and the self-confidence to get it. You will say there are plenty of city-dwelling working mothers. But most of those women do additional-funds-for-the-family kind of work, not the interesting career kind that takes plugging during childbearing years.

Nor is it a bed of petunias for the mother who does make it professionally. Says writer critic Marya Mannes:

> If the creative woman has children, she must pay for this indulgence with a long burden of guilt, for her life will be split three ways between them and her husband and her work. . . . No woman with any heart can compose a paragraph when her child is in trouble. . . . The creative woman has no wife to protect her from intrusion. A man at his desk in a room with closed door is a man at work. A woman at a desk in any room is available.

Speaking of jobs, do remember that mothering, salary or not, is a job. Even those who can afford nurses to handle the nitty-gritty still need to put out emotionally. "Well-cared-for" neurotic rich kids are not exactly unknown in our society. One of the more absurd aspects of the Myth is the underlying assumption that, since most women are biologically equipped to bear children, they are psychologically, mentally, emotionally, and technically equipped (or interested) to rear them. Never mind happiness. To assume that such an exacting, consuming, and important task is something almost all women are equipped to do is far more dangerous and ridiculous than assuming that everyone with vocal chords should seek a career in the opera.

A major expectation of the Myth is that children make a not-so-hot marriage hotter, or a hot marriage, hotter still. Yet almost every available

2. A wealthy suburb of New York City.

study indicates that childless marriages are far happier. One of the biggest, of 850 couples, was conducted by Dr. Harold Feldman of Cornell University, who states his finding in no uncertain terms: "Those couples with children had a significantly lower level of marital satisfaction than did those without children." Some of the reasons are obvious. Even the most adorable children make for additional demands, complications, and hardships in the lives of even the most loving parents. If a woman feels disappointed and trapped in her mother role, it is bound to affect her marriage in any number of ways: she may take out her frustrations directly on her husband, or she may count on him too heavily for what she feels she is missing in her daily life.

"... You begin to grow away from your husband," says one of the Michigan ladies. "He's working on his career and you're working on your family. But you both must gear your lives to the children. You do things the children enjoy, more than things you might enjoy." More subtle and possibly more serious is what motherhood may do to a woman's sexuality. Often when the stork flies in, sexuality flies out. Both in the emotional minds of some women *and* in the minds of their husbands, when a woman becomes a mother, she stops being a woman. It's not only that motherhood may destroy her physical attractiveness, but its madonna concept may destroy her *feelings* of sexuality.

And what of the payoff? Usually, even the most self-sacrificing of maternal self-sacrificers expects a little something back. Gratified parents are not unknown to the Western world, but there are probably at least just as many who feel, to put it crudely, shortchanged. The experiment mentioned earlier—where the baby ducks followed vacuum cleaners instead of their mothers—indicates that what passes for love from baby to mother is merely a rudimentary kind of object attachment. Without necessarily feeling like a Hoover, a lot of women become disheartened because babies and children are not only not interesting to talk to (not everyone thrills at the wonders of da-da-ma-ma talk) but they are generally not empathetic, considerate people. Even the nicest children are not capable of empathy, surely a major ingredient of love, until they are much older. Sometimes they're never capable of it. Dr. Wyatt says that often, in later years particularly, when most of the "returns" are in, it is the "good mother" who suffers most of all. It is then she must face a reality: The child—the appendage with her genes—is not an appendage, but a separate person. What's more, he or she may be a separate person who doesn't even like her—or whom she doesn't really like.

So if the music is lousy, how come everyone's dancing? Because the motherhood minuet is taught freely from birth, and whether or not she has rhythm or likes the music, every woman is expected to do it. Indeed, she *wants* to do it. Little girls start learning what to want—and what to be—when they are still in their cribs. Dr. Miriam Keiffer, a young social psychologist at Bensalem, the Experimental College of Fordham University, points to studies showing that

> at six months of age, mothers are already treating their baby girls and boys quite differently. For instance, mothers have been found to touch, comfort, and talk to their females more. If these differences can be found at such an early stage, it's not surprising that the end product is as different as it is. What is surprising is that men and women are, in so many ways, similar.

Some people point to the way little girls play with dolls as proof of their innate motherliness. But remember, little girls are *given* dolls. When Margaret Mead presented some dolls to New Guinea children, it was the boys, not the girls, who wanted to play with them, which they did by crooning lullabies and rocking them in the most maternal fashion.

By the time they reach adolescence, most girls, unconsciously or not, have learned enough about role definition to qualify for a master's degree. In general, the lesson has been that no matter what kind of career thoughts one may entertain, one must, first and foremost, be a wife and mother. A girl's mother is usually her first teacher. As Dr. Goode says, "A woman is not only taught by society to have a child; she is taught to have a child who will have a child." A woman who has hung her life on the Motherhood Myth will almost always reinforce her young married daughter's early training by pushing for grandchildren. Prospective grandmothers are not the only ones. Husbands, too, can be effective sellers. After all, they have the Fatherhood Myth to cope with. A married man is *supposed* to have children. Often, particularly among Latins, children are a sign of potency. They help him assure the world—and himself—that he is the big man he is supposed to be. Plus, children give him both immortality (whatever that means) and possibly the chance to become more in his lifetime through the accomplishments of his children, particularly his son. (Sometimes it's important, however, for the son to do better, but not *too* much better.)

Friends, too, can be counted on as myth-pushers. Naturally one wants to do what one's friends do. One study, by the way, found a correlation between a woman's fertility and that of her three closest friends. The negative sell comes into play here, too. We have seen what the concept of non-mother means (cold, selfish, unwomanly, abnormal). In practice, particularly in the suburbs, it can mean, simply, exclusion—both from child-centered activities (that is, most activities) and child-centered conversations (that is, most conversations). It can also mean being the butt of a lot of unfunny jokes. ("Whaddya waiting for? An immaculate conception? Ha ha.") Worst of all, it can mean being an object of pity.

In case she's escaped all those pressures (that is, if she was brought up in a cave), a young married woman often wants a baby just so that she'll (1) have something to do (motherhood is better than clerk/typist, which is often the only kind of job she can get, since little more has been expected of her and, besides, her boss also expects her to leave and be a mother); (2) have something to hug and possess, to be needed by and have power over; and (3) have something to be—e.g., a baby's mother. Motherhood affords an instant identity. First, through wifehood, you are somebody's wife; then you are somebody's mother. Both give not only identity and activity, but status and stardom of a kind. During pregnancy, a woman can look forward to the kind of attention and pampering she may not ever have gotten or may never otherwise get. Some women consider birth the biggest accomplishment of their lives, which may be interpreted as saying not much for the rest of their lives. As Dr. Goode says, "It's like the gambler who may know the roulette wheel is crooked, but it's the only game in town." Also, with motherhood, the feeling of accomplishment is immediate. It is really much faster and easier to make a baby than paint a painting, or write a book, or get to the point of accomplishment in a job. It is also easier in a way to shift focus from self-development to child development—particularly since, for women, self-development is considered selfish. Even unwed mothers may achieve a feeling of this kind. (As we have seen, little thought is given to the aftermath.) And, again, since so many women are underdeveloped as people, they feel that, besides children, they have little else to give—to themselves, their husbands, to their world.

You may ask why then, when the realities do start pouring in, does a woman want to have a second, third, even fourth child? OK, (1) just because reality is pouring in doesn't mean she wants to face it. A new baby can help bring back some of the old illusions. Says psychoanalyst Dr. Natalie Shainess, "She may view each successive child as a knight in armor that will rescue her from being a 'bad unhappy mother.'" (2) Next on the horror list of having no children, is having one. It suffices to say that only children are not only OK, they even have a high rate of exceptionality. (3) Both parents usually want at least one child of each sex. The husband, for reasons discussed earlier, probably wants a son. (4) The more children one has, the more of an excuse one has not to develop in any other way.

What's the point? A world without children? Of course not. Nothing could be worse or more unlikely. No matter what anyone says in *Look* or anywhere else, motherhood isn't about to go out like a blown bulb, and who says it should? Only the Myth must go out, and now it seems to be dimming.

The younger-generation females who have been reared on the Myth have not rejected it totally, but at least they recognize it can be more loving to children not to have them. And at least they speak of adopting children instead of bearing them. Moreover, since the new nonbreeders are "less hung-up" on ownership, they seem to recognize that if you dig loving children, you don't necessarily have to own one. The end of the Motherhood Myth might make available more loving women (and men!) for those children who already exist.

When motherhood is no longer culturally compulsory, there will, certainly, be less of it. Women are now beginning to think and do more about development of self, of their individual resources. Far from being selfish, such development is probably our only hope. That means more alternatives for women. And more alternatives mean more selective, better, happier, motherhood—and childhood and husbandhood (or manhood) and peoplehood. It is not a question of whether or not children are sweet and marvelous to have and rear; the question is, even if that's so, whether or not one wants to pay the price for it. It doesn't make sense any more to pretend that women need babies, when what they really need is themselves. If God were still speaking to us in a voice we could hear, even He would probably say, "Be fruitful. Don't multiply."

1970

Brent Staples

BLACK MEN AND PUBLIC SPACE

My first victim was a woman—white, well dressed, probably in her early twenties. I came upon her late one evening on a deserted street in Hyde Park, a relatively affluent neighborhood in an otherwise mean, impoverished section of Chicago. As I swung onto the avenue behind her, there seemed to be a discreet, uninflammatory distance between us. Not so. She cast back a worried glance. To her, the youngish black man— a broad six feet two inches with a beard and billowing hair, both hands shoved into the pockets of a bulky military jacket—seemed menacingly close. After a few more quick glimpses, she picked up her pace and was soon running in earnest. Within seconds she disappeared into a cross street.

That was more than a decade ago, I was twenty-two years old, a graduate student newly arrived at the University of Chicago. It was in the echo of that terrified woman's footfalls that I first began to know the unwieldy inheritance I'd come into—the ability to alter public space in ugly ways. It was clear that she thought herself the quarry of a mugger, a rapist, or worse. Suffering a bout of insomnia, however, I was stalking sleep, not defenseless wayfarers. As a softy who is scarcely able to take a knife to a raw chicken—let alone hold one to a person's throat—I was surprised, embarrassed, and dismayed all at once. Her flight made me feel like an accomplice in tyranny. It also made it clear that I was indistinguishable from the muggers who occasionally seeped into the area from the surrounding ghetto. That first encounter, and those that followed, signified that a vast, unnerving gulf lay between nighttime pedestrians—particularly women—and me. And I soon gathered that being perceived as dangerous is a hazard in itself. I only needed to turn a corner into a dicey situation, or crowd some frightened, armed person in a foyer somewhere, or make an errant move after being pulled over by a policeman. Where fear and weapons meet—and they often do in urban America—there is always the possibility of death.

In that first year, my first away from my hometown, I was to become thoroughly familiar with the language of fear. At dark, shadowy intersections, I could cross in front of a car stopped at a traffic light and elicit the *thunk, thunk, thunk, thunk* of the driver—black, white, male, or female—hammering down the door locks. On less traveled streets after dark, I grew accustomed to but never comfortable with people crossing to the other side of the street rather than pass me. Then there were the standard unpleasantries with policemen, doormen, bouncers, cabdrivers, and others whose business it is to screen out troublesome individuals *before* there is any nastiness.

I moved to New York nearly two years ago and I have remained an avid night walker. In central Manhattan, the near-constant crowd cover minimizes tense one-on-one street encounters. Elsewhere—in SoHo, for example, where sidewalks are narrow and tightly spaced buildings shut out the sky—things can get very taut indeed.

After dark, on the warrenlike streets of Brooklyn where I live, I often see women who fear the worst from me. They seem to have set their faces on neutral, and with their purse straps strung across their chests bandolier-style, they forge ahead as though bracing themselves against being tackled. I understand, of course, that the danger they perceive is not a hallucination. Women are particularly vulnerable to street violence, and young black males are drastically overrepresented among the perpetrators of that violence. Yet these truths are no solace against the kind of alienation that comes of being ever the suspect, a fearsome entity with whom pedestrians avoid making eye contact.

It is not altogether clear to me how I reached the ripe old age of twenty-two without being conscious of the lethality nighttime pedestrians attributed to me. Perhaps it was because in Chester, Pennsylvania, the small, angry industrial town where I came of age in the 1960s, I was scarcely noticeable against a backdrop of gang warfare, street knifings, and murders. I grew up one of the good boys, had perhaps a half-dozen fistfights. In retrospect, my shyness of combat has clear sources.

As a boy, I saw countless tough guys locked away; I have since buried several, too. They were babies, really—a teenage cousin, a brother of twenty-two, a childhood friend in his mid-twenties—all gone down in episodes of bravado played out in the streets. I came to doubt the virtues of intimidation early on. I chose, perhaps unconsciously, to remain a shadow—timid, but a survivor.

The fearsomeness mistakenly attributed to me in public places often has a perilous flavor. The most frightening of these confusions occurred in the late 1970s and early 1980s, when I worked as a journalist in Chicago. One day, rushing into the office of a magazine I was writing for with a deadline story in hand, I was mistaken for a burglar. The office manager called security and, with an ad hoc[1] posse, pursued me through the labyrinthine halls, nearly to my editor's door. I had no way of proving who I was. I could only move briskly toward the company of someone who knew me.

Another time I was on assignment for a local paper and killing time before an interview. I entered a jewelry store on the city's affluent Near North Side. The proprietor excused herself and returned with an enormous red Doberman pinscher straining at the end of a leash. She stood, the dog extended toward me, silent to my questions, her eyes bulging nearly out of her head. I took a cursory look around, nodded, and bade her good night.

Relatively speaking, however, I never fared as badly as another black male journalist. He went to nearby Waukegan, Illinois, a couple of summers ago to work on a story about a murderer who was born there. Mistaking the reporter for the killer, police officers hauled him from his car at gunpoint and but for his press credentials would probably have tried to book him. Such episodes are not uncommon. Black men trade tales like this all the time.

Over the years, I learned to smother the rage I felt at so often being taken for a criminal. Not to do so would surely have led to madness. I now take precautions to make myself less threatening. I move about with care, particularly late in the evening. I give a wide berth to nervous people on subway platforms during the wee hours, particularly when I have exchanged business clothes for jeans. If I happen to be entering a building behind some people who appear skittish, I may walk by, letting them clear the lobby before I return, so as not to seem to be following them. I have been calm and extremely congenial on those rare occasions when I've been pulled over by the police.

And on late-evening constitutionals I employ what has proved to be an excellent tension-reducing measure: I whistle melodies from Beethoven and Vivaldi and the more popular classical composers. Even steely New Yorkers hunching toward nighttime destinations seem to relax, and occasionally they even join in the tune. Virtually everybody seems to

1. "Ad hoc": for a particular purpose.

sense that a mugger wouldn't be warbling bright, sunny selections from Vivaldi's *Four Seasons*.[2] It is my equivalent of the cowbell that hikers wear when they know they are in bear country.

1986

2. Work by eighteenth-century composer Antonio Vivaldi celebrating the seasons.

THE READER

1. In his essay, Staples writes of situations correctly perceived as danger-ous and situations misperceived as dangerous. Give specific instances of each. How are they related?
2. Staples shows that his personal background and experiences led him to see things in a particular way. To what degree is that particular way idiosyncratic—specific to him? To what degree is that particular way expressive of general truth—experience common to all or most per-sons?

THE WRITER

1. Does Staples take a humorous approach to his subject at certain points in the essay? If so, does this distract from or contribute to the serious-ness of the matter? Explain.
2. Is the concluding sentence an effective close? Draw out its implica-tions, showing how these relate to the details of his discussion.
3. Do you have perceptions and apprehensions similar to or largely different from those described by Staples? Write an essay on this topic, placing yourself in familiar or in unusual surroundings.

Jessica Mitford

BEHIND THE FORMALDEHYDE CURTAIN

The drama begins to unfold with the arrival of the corpse at the mortuary.

Alas, poor Yorick![1] How surprised he would be to see how his counter-part of today is whisked off to a funeral parlor and is in short order sprayed, sliced, pierced, pickled, trussed, trimmed, creamed, waxed, painted, rouged and neatly dressed—transformed from a common corpse into a Beautiful Memory Picture. This process is known in the trade as embalming and restorative art, and is so universally employed in the United States and Canada that the funeral director does it routinely, without consulting corpse or kin. He regards as eccentric those few who are hardy enough to suggest that it might be dispensed with. Yet no law

1. The phrase is Hamlet's (V.i.184) on the disinterment, identification, and perusal of the skull of the court clown he had known as a child.

requires embalming, no religious doctrine commends it, nor is it dictated by considerations of health, sanitation, or even of personal daintiness. In no part of the world but in Northern America is it widely used. The purpose of embalming is to make the corpse presentable for viewing in a suitably costly container; and here too the funeral director routinely, without first consulting the family, prepares the body for public display.

Is all this legal? The processes to which a dead body may be subjected are after all to some extent circumscribed by law. In most states, for instance, the signature of next of kin must be obtained before an autopsy may be performed, before the deceased may be cremated, before the body may be turned over to a medical school for research purposes; or such provision must be made in the decedent's will. In the case of embalming, no such permission is required nor is it ever sought. A textbook, *The Principles and Practices of Embalming*, comments on this: "There is some question regarding the legality of much that is done within the preparation room." The author points out that it would be most unusual for a responsible member of a bereaved family to instruct the mortician, in so many words, to "embalm" the body of a deceased relative. The very term "embalming" is so seldom used that the mortician must rely upon custom in the matter. The author concludes that unless the family specifies otherwise, the act of entrusting the body to the care of a funeral establishment carries with it an implied permission to go ahead and embalm.

Embalming is indeed a most extraordinary procedure, and one must wonder at the docility of Americans who each year pay hundreds of millions of dollars for its perpetuation, blissfully ignorant of what it is all about, what is done, how it is done. Not one in ten thousand has any idea of what actually takes place. Books on the subject are extremely hard to come by. They are not to be found in most libraries or bookshops.

In an era when huge television audiences watch surgical operations in the comfort of their living rooms, when, thanks to the animated cartoon, the geography of the digestive system has become familiar territory even to the nursery school set, in a land where the satisfaction of curiosity about almost all matters is a national pastime, the secrecy surrounding embalming can, surely, hardly be attributed to the inherent gruesomeness of the subject. Custom in this regard has within this century suffered a complete reversal. In the early days of American embalming, when it was performed in the home of the deceased, it was almost mandatory for some relative to stay by the embalmer's side and witness the procedure. Today, family members who might wish to be in attendance would certainly be dissuaded by the funeral director. All others, except apprentices, are excluded by law from the preparation room.

A close look at what does actually take place may explain in large measure the undertaker's intractable reticence concerning a procedure that has become his major *raison d'être*.[2] Is it possible he fears that public information about embalming might lead patrons to wonder if they really want this service? If the funeral men are loath to discuss the subject outside the trade, the reader may, understandably, be equally loath to go on reading at this point. For those who have the stomach for it, let us part the formaldehyde curtain. . . .

The body is first laid out in the undertaker's morgue—or rather, Mr. Jones is reposing in the preparation room—to be readied to bid the world farewell.

The preparation room in any of the better funeral establishments has the tiled and sterile look of a surgery, and indeed the embalmer-restorative artist who does his chores there is beginning to adopt the term "dermasurgeon" (appropriately corrupted by some mortician-writers as "demi-surgeon") to describe his calling. His equipment, consisting of scalpels, scissors, augers, forceps, clamps, needles, pumps, tubes, bowls and basins, is crudely imitative of the surgeon's, as is his technique, acquired in a nine- or twelve-month post-high-school course in an embalming school. He is supplied by an advanced chemical industry with a bewildering array of fluids, sprays, pastes, oils, powders, creams, to fix or soften tissue, shrink or distend it as needed, dry it here, restore the moisture there. There are cosmetics, waxes and paints to fill and cover features, even plaster of Paris to replace entire limbs. There are ingenious aids to prop and stabilize the cadaver: a Vari-Pose Head Rest, the Edwards Arm and Hand Positioner, the Repose Block (to support the shoulders during the embalming), and the Throop Foot Positioner, which resembles an old-fashioned stocks.

Mr. John H. Eckels, president of the Eckels College of Mortuary Science, thus describes the first part of the embalming procedure: "In the hands of a skilled practitioner, this work may be done in a comparatively short time and without mutilating the body other than by slight incision —so slight that it scarcely would cause serious inconvenience if made upon a living person. It is necessary to remove the blood, and doing this not only helps in the disinfecting, but removes the principal cause of disfigurements due to discoloration."

Another textbook discusses the all-important time element: "The earlier this is done, the better, for every hour that elapses between death and embalming will add to the problems and complications encountered. . . ." Just how soon should one get going on the embalming? The author tells us, "On the basis of such scanty information made available to this profession through its rudimentary and haphazard system of technical research, we must conclude that the best results are to be obtained if the subject is embalmed before life is completely extinct—

2. Reason for being.

that is, before cellular death has occurred. In the average case, this would mean within an hour after somatic death." For those who feel that there is something a little rudimentary, not to say haphazard, about this advice, a comforting thought is offered by another writer. Speaking of fears entertained in early days of premature burial, he points out, "One of the effects of embalming by chemical injection, however, has been to dispel fears of live burial." How true; once the blood is removed, chances of live burial are indeed remote.

To return to Mr. Jones, the blood is drained out through the veins and replaced by embalming fluid pumped in through the arteries. As noted in *The Principles and Practices of Embalming*, "every operator has a favorite injection and drainage point—a fact which becomes a handicap only if he fails or refuses to forsake his favorites when conditions demand it." Typical favorites are the carotid artery, femoral artery, jugular vein, subclavian vein. There are various choices of embalming fluid. If Flextone is used, it will produce a "mild, flexible rigidity. The skin retains a velvety softness, the tissues are rubbery and pliable. Ideal for women and children." It may be blended with B. and G. Products Company's Lyf-Lyk tint, which is guaranteed to reproduce "nature's own skin texture . . . the velvety appearance of living tissue." Suntone comes in three separate tints: Suntan; Special Cosmetic Tint, a pink shade "especially indicated for young female subjects"; and Regular Cosmetic Tint, moderately pink.

About three to six gallons of a dyed and perfumed solution of formaldehyde, glycerin, borax, phenol, alcohol and water is soon circulating through Mr. Jones, whose mouth has been sewn together with a "needle directed upward between the upper lip and gum and brought out through the left nostril," with the corners raised slightly "for a more pleasant expression." If he should be bucktoothed, his teeth are cleaned with Bon Ami and coated with colorless nail polish. His eyes, meanwhile, are closed with flesh-tinted eye caps and eye cement.

The next step is to have at Mr. Jones with a thing called a trocar. This is a long, hollow needle attached to a tube. It is jabbed into the abdomen, poked around the entrails and chest cavity, the contents of which are pumped out and replaced with "cavity fluid." This done, and the hole in the abdomen sewn up, Mr. Jones's face is heavily creamed (to protect the skin from burns which may be caused by leakage of the chemicals), and he is covered with a sheet and left unmolested for a while. But not for long—there is more, much more, in store for him. He has been embalmed, but not yet restored, and the best time to start the restorative work is eight to ten hours after embalming, when the tissues have become firm and dry.

The object of all this attention to the corpse, it must be remembered, is to make it presentable for viewing in an attitude of healthy repose. "Our

customs require the presentation of our dead in the semblance of normality . . . unmarred by the ravages of illness, disease or mutilation," says Mr.
J. Sheridan Mayer in his *Restorative Art*. This is rather a large order since
few people die in the full bloom of health, unravaged by illness and
unmarked by some disfigurement. The funeral industry is equal to the
challenge: "In some cases the gruesome appearance of a mutilated or
disease-ridden subject may be quite discouraging. The task of restoration
may seem impossible and shake the confidence of the embalmer. This is
the time for intestinal fortitude and determination. Once the formative
work is begun and affected tissues are cleaned or removed, all doubts of
success vanish. It is surprising and gratifying to discover the results
which may be obtained."

The embalmer, having allowed an appropriate interval to elapse,
returns to the attack, but now he brings into play the skill and equipment
of sculptor and cosmetician. Is a hand missing? Casting one in plaster of
Paris is a simple matter. "For replacement purposes, only a cast of the
back of the hand is necessary; this is within the ability of the average
operator and is quite adequate." If a lip or two, a nose or an ear should be
missing, the embalmer has at hand a variety of restorative waxes with
which to model replacements. Pores and skin texture are simulated by
stippling with a little brush, and over this cosmetics are laid on. Head off?
Decapitation cases are rather routinely handled. Ragged edges are
trimmed, and head joined to torso with a series of splints, wires and
sutures. It is a good idea to have a little something at the neck—a scarf or
a high collar—when time for viewing comes. Swollen mouth? Cut out
tissue as needed from inside the lips. If too much is removed, the surface
contour can easily be restored by padding with cotton. Swollen necks and
cheeks are reduced by removing tissue through vertical incisions made
down each side of the neck. "When the deceased is casketed, the pillow
will hide the suture incisions . . . as an extra precaution against leakage,
the suture may be painted with liquid sealer."

The opposite condition is more likely to present itself—that of emacia-
tion. His hypodermic syringe now loaded with massage cream, the embalmer seeks out and fills the hollowed and sunken areas by injection. In
this procedure the backs of the hands and fingers and the under-chin area
should not be neglected.

Positioning the lips is a problem that recurrently challenges the ingenuity of the embalmer. Closed too tightly, they tend to give a stern, even
disapproving expression. Ideally, embalmers feel, the lips should give the
impression of being ever so slightly parted, the upper lip protruding
slightly for a more youthful appearance. This takes some engineering,
however, as the lips tend to drift apart. Lip drift can sometimes be
remedied by pushing one or two straight pins through the inner margin
of the lower lip and then inserting them between the two front upper

teeth. If Mr. Jones happens to have no teeth, the pins can just as easily be anchored in his Armstrong Face Former and Denture Replacer. Another method to maintain lip closure is to dislocate the lower jaw, which is then held in its new position by a wire run through holes which have been drilled through the upper and lower jaws at the midline. As the French are fond of saying, *il faut souffrir pour être belle.*[3]

If Mr. Jones has died of jaundice, the embalming fluid will very likely turn him green. Does this deter the embalmer? Not if he has intestinal fortitude. Masking pastes and cosmetics are heavily laid on, burial garments and casket interiors are color-correlated with particular care, and Jones is displayed beneath rose-colored lights. Friends will say "How *well* he looks." Death by carbon monoxide, on the other hand, can be rather a good thing from the embalmer's viewpoint: "One advantage is the fact that this type of discoloration is an exaggerated form of a natural pink coloration." This is nice because the healthy glow is already present and needs but little attention.

The patching and filling completed, Mr. Jones is now shaved, washed and dressed. Cream-based cosmetic, available in pink, flesh, suntan, brunette and blond, is applied to his hands and face, his hair is shampooed and combed (and, in the case of Mrs. Jones, set), his hands manicured. For the horny-handed son of toil special care must be taken; cream should be applied to remove ingrained grime, and the nails cleaned. "If he were not in the habit of having them manicured in life, trimming and shaping is advised for better appearance—never questioned by kin."

Jones is now ready for casketing (this is the present participle of the verb "to casket"). In this operation his right shoulder should be depressed slightly "to turn the body a bit to the right and soften the appearance of lying flat on the back." Positioning the hands is a matter of importance, and special rubber positioning blocks may be used. The hands should be cupped slightly for a more lifelike, relaxed apearance. Proper placement of the body requires a delicate sense of balance. It should lie as high as possible in the casket, yet not so high that the lid, when lowered, will hit the nose. On the other hand, we are cautioned, placing the body too low "creates the impression that the body is in a box."

Jones is next wheeled into the appointed slumber room where a few last touches may be added—his favorite pipe placed in his hand or, if he was a great reader, a book propped into position. (In the case of little Master Jones a Teddy bear may be clutched.) Here he will hold open house for a few days, visiting hours 10 A.M. to 9 P.M.

All now being in readiness, the funeral director calls a staff conference to make sure that each assistant knows his precise duties. Mr. Wilber

3. It's necessary to suffer to be beautiful.

Kriege writes: "This makes your staff feel that they are a part of the team, with a definite assignment that must be properly carried out if the whole plan is to succeed. You never heard of a football coach who failed to talk to his entire team before they go on the field. They have drilled on the plays they are to execute for hours and days, and yet the successful coach knows the importance of making even the bench-warming third-string substitute feel that he is important if the game is to be won." The winning of this game is predicated upon glass-smooth handling of the logistics. The funeral director has notified the pallbearers whose names were furnished by the family, has arranged for the presence of clergyman, organist, and soloist, has provided transportation for everybody, has organized and listed the flowers sent by friends. In *Psychology of Funeral Service* Mr. Edward A. Martin points out: "He may not always do as much as the family thinks he is doing, but it is his helpful guidance that they appreciate in knowing they are proceeding as they should. . . . The important thing is how well his services can be used to make the family believe they are giving unlimited expression to their own sentiment."

The religious service may be held in a church or in the chapel of the funeral home; the funeral director vastly prefers the latter arrangement, for not only is it more convenient for him but it affords him the opportunity to show off his beautiful facilities to the gathered mourners. After the clergyman has had his say, the mourners queue up to file past the casket for a last look at the deceased. The family is never asked whether they want an open-casket ceremony; in the absence of their instruction to the contrary, this is taken for granted. Consequently well over 90 per cent of all American funerals feature the open casket—a custom unknown in other parts of the world. Foreigners are astonished by it. An English woman living in San Francisco described her reaction in a letter to the writer:

> I myself have attended only one funeral here—that of an elderly fellow worker of mine. After the service I could not understand why everyone was walking towards the coffin (sorry, I mean casket), but thought I had better follow the crowd. It shook me rigid to get there and find the casket open and poor old Oscar lying there in his brown tweed suit, wearing a suntan makeup and just the wrong shade of lipstick. If I had not been extremely fond of the old boy, I have a horrible feeling that I might have giggled. Then and there I decided that I could never face another American funeral—even dead.

The casket (which has been resting throughout the service on a Classic Beauty Ultra Metal Casket Bier) is now transferred by a hydraulically operated device called Porto-Lift to a balloon-tired, Glide Easy casket carriage which will wheel it to yet another conveyance, the Cadillac Funeral Coach. This may be lavender, cream, light green—anything but black. Interiors, of course, are color-correlated, "for the man who cannot stop short of perfection."

At graveside, the casket is lowered into the earth. This office, once the prerogative of friends of the deceased, is now performed by a patented mechanical lowering device. A "Lifetime Green" artificial grass mat is at the ready to conceal the sere earth, and overhead, to conceal the sky, is a portable Steril Chapel Tent ("resists the intense heat and humidity of summer and the terrific storms of winter ... available in Silver Grey, Rose or Evergreen"). Now is the time for the ritual scattering of earth over the coffin, as the solemn words "earth to earth, ashes to ashes, dust to dust" are pronounced by the officiating cleric. This can today be accomplished "with a mere flick of the wrist with the Gordon Leak-Proof Earth Dispenser. No grasping of a handful of dirt, no soiled fingers. Simple, dignified, beautiful, reverent! The modern way!" The Gordon Earth Dispenser (at $5) is of nickel-plated brass construction. It is not only "attractive to the eye and long wearing"; it is also "one of the 'tools' for building better public relations" if presented as "an appropriate non-commercial gift" to the clergyman. It is shaped something like a salt-shaker.

Untouched by human hand, the coffin and the earth are now united.

It is in the function of directing the participants through this maze of gadgetry that the funeral director has assigned to himself his relatively new role of "grief therapist." He has relieved the family of every detail, he has revamped the corpse to look like a living doll, he has arranged for it to nap for a few days in a slumber room, he has put on a well-oiled performance in which the concept of *death* has played no part whatsoever—unless it was inconsiderately mentioned by the clergyman who conducted the religious service. He has done everything in his power to make the funeral a real pleasure for everybody concerned. He and his team have given their all to score an upset victory over death.

1963

Lewis Thomas

ON MAGIC IN MEDICINE

Medicine has always been under pressure to provide public explanations for the diseases with which it deals, and the formulation of comprehensive, unifying theories has been the most ancient and willing preoccupation of the profession. In the earliest days, hostile spirits needing exorcism were the principal pathogens, and the shaman's duty was simply the development of improved techniques for incantation. Later on, especially in the Western world, the idea that the distribution of body fluids among various organs determined the course of all illnesses took hold, and we were in for centuries of bleeding, cupping, sweating, and purging in efforts to intervene. Early in this century the theory of autointoxication evolved, and a large part of therapy was directed at emptying the large intestine and keeping it empty. Then the global concept of focal infection became popular, accompanied by the linked notion of allergy to the presumed microbial pathogens, and no one knows the resulting toll of extracted teeth, tonsils, gallbladders, and appendixes: the idea of psychosomatic influences on disease emerged in the 1930s and, for a while, seemed to sweep the field.

Gradually, one by one, some of our worst diseases have been edited out of such systems by having their causes indisputably identified and dealt with. Tuberculosis was the paradigm. This was the most chronic and inexorably progressive of common human maladies, capable of affecting virtually every organ in the body and obviously influenced by crowding, nutrition, housing, and poverty; theories involving the climate in general, and night air and insufficient sunlight in particular, gave rise to the spa as a therapeutic institution. It was not until the development of today's effective chemotherapy that it became clear to everyone that the disease had a single, dominant, central cause. If you got rid of the tubercle bacillus you were rid of the disease.

But that was some time ago, and today the idea that complicated diseases can have single causes is again out of fashion. The microbial infections that can be neatly coped with by antibiotics are regarded as lucky anomalies. The new theory is that most of today's human illnesses, the infections aside, are multifactorial in nature, caused by two great arrays of causative mechanisms: 1) the influence of things in the environment and 2) one's personal life-style. For medicine to become effective in dealing with such diseases, it has become common belief that the environment will have to be changed, and personal ways of living will also have to be transformed, and radically.

These things may turn out to be true, for all I know, but it will take a long time to get the necessary proofs. Meanwhile, the field is wide open for magic.

One great difficulty in getting straightforward answers is that so many of the diseases in question have unpredictable courses, and some of them have a substantial tendency toward spontaneous remission. In rheumatoid arthritis, for instance, when such widely disparate therapeutic measures as copper bracelets, a move to Arizona, diets low in sugar or salt or meat or whatever, and even an inspirational book have been accepted by patients as useful, the trouble in evaluation is that approximately 35 percent of patients with this diagnosis are bound to recover no matter what they do. But if you actually have rheumatoid arthritis or, for that matter, schizophrenia, and then get over it, or if you are a doctor and observe this to happen, it is hard to be persuaded that it wasn't *something* you did that was responsible. Hence you need very large numbers of patients and lots of time, and a cool head.

Magic is back again, and in full force. Laetrile cures cancer, acupuncture is useful for deafness and low-back pain, vitamins are good for anything, and meditation, yoga, dancing, biofeedback, and shouting one another down in crowded rooms over weekends are specifics for the human condition. Running, a good thing to be doing for its own sake, has acquired the medicinal value formerly attributed to rare herbs from Indonesia.

There is a recurring advertisement, placed by Blue Cross on the op-ed page of *The New York Times,* which urges you to take advantage of science by changing your life habits, with the suggestion that if you do so, by adopting seven easy-to-follow items of life-style, you can achieve eleven added years beyond what you'll get if you don't. Since today's average figure is around seventy-two for all parties in both sexes, this might mean going on until at least the age of eighty-three. You can do this formidable thing, it is claimed, by simply eating breakfast, exercising regularly, maintaining normal weight, not smoking cigarettes, not drinking excessively, sleeping eight hours each night, and not eating between meals.

The science which produced this illumination was a careful study by California epidemiologists, based on a questionnaire given to about seven thousand people. Five years after the questionnaire, a body count was made by sorting through the county death certificates, and the 371 people who had died were matched up with their answers to the questions. To be sure, there were more deaths among the heavy smokers and drinkers, as you might expect from the known incidence of lung cancer in smokers and cirrhosis and auto accidents among drinkers. But there was also a higher mortality among those who said they didn't eat breakfast, and even higher in those who took no exercise, no exercise at all, not even going off in the family car for weekend picnics. Being up to 20 percent overweight was not so bad, surprisingly, but being *underweight* was clearly associated with a higher death rate.

The paper describing these observations has been widely quoted, and not just by Blue Cross. References to the Seven Healthy Life Habits keep turning up in popular magazines and in the health columns of newspapers, always with that promise of eleven more years.

The findings fit nicely with what is becoming folk doctrine about disease. You become ill because of not living right. If you get cancer it is, somehow or other, your own fault. If you didn't cause it by smoking or drinking or eating the wrong things, it came from allowing yourself to persist with the wrong kind of personality, in the wrong environment. If you have a coronary occlusion, you didn't run enough. Or you were too tense, or you *wished* too much, and didn't get a good enough sleep. Or you got fat. Your fault.

But eating breakfast? It is a kind of enchantment, pure magic.

You have to read the report carefully to discover that there is another, more banal way of explaining the findings. Leave aside the higher deaths in heavy smokers and drinkers, for there is no puzzle in either case; these are dangerous things to do. But it is hard to imagine any good reason for dying within five years from not eating a good breakfast, or any sort of breakfast.

The other explanation turns cause and effect around. Among the people in that group of seven thousand who answered that they don't eat breakfast, don't go off on picnics, are underweight, and can't sleep properly, there were surely some who were already ill when the questionnaire arrived. They didn't eat breakfast because they couldn't stand the sight of food. They had lost their appetites, were losing weight, didn't feel up to moving around much, and had trouble sleeping. They didn't play tennis or go off on family picnics because they didn't *feel* good. Some of these people probably had an undetected cancer, perhaps of the pancreas; others may have had hypertension or early kidney failure or some other organic disease which the questionnaire had no way of picking up. The study did not ascertain the causes of death in the 371, but just a few deaths from such undiscerned disorders would have made a significant statistical impact. The author of the paper was careful to note these possible interpretations, although the point was not made strongly, and the general sense you have in reading it is that you can live on and on if only you will eat breakfast and play tennis.

The popular acceptance of the notion of Seven Healthy Life Habits, as a way of staying alive, says something important about today's public attitudes, or at least the attitudes in the public mind, about disease and dying. People have always wanted causes that are simple and easy to comprehend, and about which the individual can *do* something. If you believe that you can ward off the common causes of premature death—cancer, heart disease, and stroke, diseases whose pathogenesis we really do not understand—by jogging, hoping, and eating and sleeping regularly, these are good things to believe even if not necessarily true. Medicine has survived other periods of unifying theory, constructed to explain all of human disease, not always as benign in their effects as this one is likely to be. After all, if people can be induced to give up smoking, stop overdrinking and overeating, and take some sort of regular exercise, most of them are bound to feel the better for leading more orderly, regular lives, and many of them are surely going to look better.

Nobody can say an unfriendly word against the sheer goodness of keeping fit, but we should go carefully with the promises.

There is also a bifurcated ideological appeal contained in the seven-life-habits doctrine, quite apart from the subliminal notion of good luck in the numbers involved (7 come 11). Both ends of the political spectrum can find congenial items. At the further right, it is attractive to hear that the individual, the good old freestanding, free-enterprising American citizen, is responsible for his own health and when things go wrong it is his own damn fault for smoking and drinking and living wrong (and he can jolly well pay for it). On the other hand, at the left, it is nice to be told that all our health problems, including dying, are caused by failure of the community to bring up its members to live properly, and if you really want to improve the health of the people, research is not the answer; you should upheave the present society and invent a better one. At either end, you can't lose.

In between, the skeptics in medicine have a hard time of it. It is much more difficult to be convincing about ignorance concerning disease mechanisms than it is to make claims for full comprehension, especially when the comprehension leads, logically or not, to some sort of action. When it comes to serious illness, the public tends, understandably, to be more skeptical about the skeptics, more willing to believe the true believers. It is medicine's oldest dilemma, not to be settled by candor or by any kind of rhetoric; what it needs is a lot of time and patience, waiting for science to come in, as it has in the past, with the solid facts.

1979

THE READER

1. What would be a sensible response to a recommendation of the Seven Healthy Life Habits?
2. Thomas speaks of "folk doctrine about disease" (p. 452). Are there folk doctrines about other things? How are they similar or different?
3. In this essay, Thomas calls himself a skeptic. What evidence does he give of a similar skepticism in "The Long Habit" (p. 575)? What other features of his presumed personality are common to both essays?

THE WRITER

1. In the second paragraph, Thomas uses the word paradigm. First define the term from the way Thomas uses it in that paragraph, and then compare that definition with what you find in the dictionary. Explain how Thomas might say that the study by the California epidemiologists that defined the Seven Healthy Life Habits (p. 452) was also a paradigm—for successful research, in their case. Does such an explanation require that you define a place for magic in the paradigm for successful research? Consult Kuhn's "The Route to Normal Science" (p. 966) for help.
2. On p. 453, Thomas argues for turning cause and effect (in the California study) around so that, for example, what was the effect (sickness) becomes a cause and what was a cause (failure to exercise) becomes an

effect. This is obviously a potent argumentative tactic. Suggest some other applications in politics or international affairs. Explain one of your examples in a paragraph or two.

Dan Lacy

READING IN AN AUDIOVISUAL AND ELECTRONIC ERA

Wandering tribesmen with tales of what lay beyond the distant range or river, old men with memories of their own past and of their fathers' and grandfathers' memories, prophets who professed knowledge of the future—all have from time out of mind helped to fill the hunger of men and women to escape the narrow scope and brief moment of their lives. But the living word, fixed in no enduring form, swirled and rearranged itself in myth, and mankind emerged from a fabled and dream-haunted past to live in a world where monsters and boiling seas and magic mountains lay only a few days' journeys away.

Writing, which fixed words in unchangeable order, made possible the creation of a reliable history and, within limits, a known geography. Thucydides and Tacitus, Strabo and Herodotus,[1] were knowledge-bearers, not myth-makers. Until the invention of printing, however, this possession of real knowledge of what lay beyond men's own eyes and memories was confined to the literate few with access to precious manuscripts. The growth of science was greatly handicapped by the inability to generate and distribute uniform texts that could be relied on by investigators spread across a continent. Thus the leap of knowledge that came in the sixteenth and seventeenth centuries was both print-born and print-borne.

In the first two centuries of print, many other inventions enlarged the capacity of humans to transcend their immediate experience, among them, the telescope, the microscope, reliable time-pieces, and ships adapted for transoceanic voyages. The development of a more powerful mathematics, especially the calculus in the late seventeenth century, greatly enhanced man's ability to organize newly discovered data in meaningful patterns.

Print made possible rapid, wide sharing of the new knowledge. Re-

---

1. Thucydides (died after 426 B.C.): Athenian politician; Cornelius Tacitus (c. A.D. 56–c. 120): Roman orator, politician, and historian; Strabo (64 or 63 B.C.–after A.D. 23): Greek geographer; Herodotus (c. 484–between 430 and 420 B.C.): Greek historian.

ports of voyages to Asia and to the newly discovered American continents, describing their geography, flora, fauna, minerals, and human
inhabitants, were read avidly, and became the impetus for further voyages. Equally valuable was the new ability of scientists to distribute
widely, relatively quickly, and in a fixed form and uniform state the
results of their observations. Man's ability to know distant lands, even
distant planets, and to achieve a deeper understanding of natural
processes was greatly enhanced.

So, too, was the ability to know the past. The world's documented past
had existed precariously in few handwritten copies subject to loss and
decay, and imperiled by errors in transcription. The enormous multipli-
cation of copies of these works and the increased ability to compare
copies made possible the technical skills of editing, verification, and
textual analysis, and focused attention on the past. There was a renaissance of the knowledge of antiquity that gave its name to the era. Print
also facilitated not merely the preservation and dissemination of knowledge, but also its rapid accumulation, as each new student could in turn
command and build on the published works of those who preceded him.

By the late nineteenth century, the processes by which verified knowledge was established and transmitted were both professionalized and
institutionalized. It became possible to earn a living as a physicist or
historian or philologist, and hence to devote one's full time to the discipline. Learned societies organized by discipline gave a specific focus not
found in prior general academies, and created professional corps with a
sense of collaboration in a shared undertaking. Universities became
centers of research as well as of teaching. Learned journals multiplied,
and university presses were created to provide additional means of recording and disseminating the rapidly increasing outflow of the products
of research. Libraries became the centers of universities, and public
libraries were created to bring the broad resources of books to the people
generally.

During the same decades, a series of concurrent developments greatly
widened public access to the flow of print-recorded knowledge. Steam-
powered cylindrical presses, stereotype plates, and paper mass-produced
from woodpulp greatly increased the output and diminished the price of
printed matter. By the end of the century, several hundred times as many
pages were printed per capita as at its beginning. The invention of the
telegraph and the laying of the Atlantic cable enormously enhanced the
speed and efficiency with which the press could convey the news; and the
completion of a rail network made practical the swift nationwide distribution of magazines and books. Nearly universal elementary education
and widespread literacy opened a broad public market for this enormous
flow of print. With the penny newspaper and cheap magazines and
books, print became a mass medium.

Indeed, during the period that in the United States extended roughly from the Civil War to the First World War, print played—as it never had before and never would again—a dominant and exclusive role. Almost all adults in the United States (as in Canada and Western Europe) could read and, moreover, had access to an abundance of print at a cost they could afford. And print was the *only* means, other than word-of-mouth, by which they could learn of things beyond their personal experience.

It was during this era of total print dominance that our contemporary educational system took shape, with an elementary curriculum primarily devoted to teaching children the skills of reading and writing and the comparably abstract techniques of numerical manipulation. High school and college were devoted to the use of these skills to extract knowledge from the accumulated wealth of print and, at the postgraduate level, to contribute further to it. It is no accident that a popular term for education was "book-learning."

In the decades since 1920, two major waves of change have overthrown print's dominance. The first was the audiovisual revolution. It was based on the late nineteenth century inventions of the phonograph and the motion picture and the early twentieth century discovery of radio, but its more important social impact came after the First World War. By the end of the postwar decade, most Americans had abundant access to all three. The speeches of political leaders could be heard rather than read; news had a visual impact through the newsreel. Films rather than novels became the major means of suggesting what life in other times and places and among other social groups and classes was like. It became possible for persons outside large cities to hear great music professionally performed. A more direct access was provided to the range of experience beyond life's daily ambit.

The power of the audiovisual revolution was enormously increased when television became widely available after the Second World War. Within an amazingly few years, television could be received in more than 90 percent of the homes in America, and the average American was spending several hours a day before the screen. Daily, hundreds of millions of hours previously spent in other ways were transferred to television-watching. Probably never before in history had so massive a change in social habit been achieved in so very brief a time.

Some of the change wrought by TV may have been less important than it seemed. To a considerable degree, TV was simply a way to see movies more cheaply and without leaving home. Much of what was shown on TV did indeed consist of films previously shown in motion picture theaters, and much of what was created specifically for TV was very like the movies both in technique and in the recreational functions it served. But the amount of time devoted to the medium, even granting the similarity of the content, was so large as to be very important in itself.

Yet through its news and documentary programs, television emerged as a truly new medium. Radio had already imparted some of the instant availability of news as well as the sense of actual presence, as in Edward R. Murrow's wartime broadcasts from London or Roosevelt's fireside chats. And the newsreels and the rare filmed documentary had provided precedents for television. But the nearly universal attention to television as the principal source of news about events here and abroad, of information about politics and social conditions, about the nature of other cultures and about science, was quite extraordinary. In barely more than a decade, television replaced the newspaper as the principal source of news and, indeed, replaced print in general as the foremost means by which most Americans came to perceive reality beyond their daily experience.

In our own decade there is yet another revolution, that of the computer and its related technology of data communication. The dramatic decrease in the cost of computers has opened their use to people in general. It will probably become quite common to be able, in one's home or office, to call up almost instantly, from enormous banks of information, the particular set of data one seeks and to manipulate it and array it with extraordinary power. Texts and images as well as numerical data can be stored with incredible compactness on laser disks and recalled through the computer's extraordinary searching power, thus creating still additional possibilities. Enthusiasts for the new information technology believe that it will replace or diminish the role of a whole series of industries and institutions: the newspaper, the journal, the book, the library.

The two revolutions—audiovisual and electronic—provide a range of alternatives to communication hitherto carried by print, and promise as well the possibility of many kinds of communication not achievable at all through print: the sound of speech and music, the vision of motion and color, the perception of events as they occur, the instant conveyance of constantly changing data. The average American every week spends several times as many hours with the new media as he or she does reading. The exclusive role of print to provide the reality that lies beyond personal experience has been shattered forever.

How has this affected the role of reading, and what difference does it make? The sheer production of printed matter has been affected less than one would expect. The number of newspapers has declined sharply, and urban evening newspapers have been especially affected. Few cities can any longer support more than one newspaper, very few, indeed, more than two. Television is not only a far more widely used source of news, but a more trusted one. Mass circulation magazines directly competitive with television for audience and advertisers, like the *Saturday Evening Post, Life, Look, American,* and *Colliers,* have died. Yet surviving urban newspapers and a growing number of suburban newspaper chains are highly prosperous, and the magazine industry, with its myriad journals catering for special tastes and interests, is thriving.

The total number of books published annually has approximately quadrupled since television became generally available. Sales of books, as measured in copies rather than dollars, increased rapidly in the early days of television, though they have tended to level off in recent years. Library circulation has been flat or declining in recent years, but this may be reflective more of weakened community support, declining educational enrollments, and the availability of relatively inexpensive paperbacks than any public decline in reading.

None of these statistics gives any clear picture of the amount of reading actually done in our society, but a considerable increase—certainly no such decay as has long been prophesied—appears to have taken place. Our society is by no means ready to say, as in the title of Anthony Smith's recent book, goodbye to Gutenberg.[2]

Yet the functions of print are changing. It is still the indispensable recorder and conveyor of research results and other scholarly activity. In fact, much of the increase in the number of books and journals published reflects the heightened level of such activity. Similarly, though there are marginal and, in some cases, growing uses of audiovisual materials and computers in the classroom, print is still the principal medium of formal education. Finally, there is a substantial increase in recreational reading of various kinds of subliterary novels, among them, romances, "Gothic" stories, suspense stories, and science fiction.

But for all these continuing strengths, reading is no longer the main, indeed almost the only, way of extending personal experience. Most people today decide whom they will vote for, what they believe about atomic weapons control or unemployment, how they perceive the issues of the Middle East, what they conceive China to be like, how they envision the history of man, much more from what they observe on television than from what they read. Beyond the bounds of our daily lives, we all react not to reality, but to an *image* of reality, created for us through the media of communication, and in the last generation, the nature of the media that create this image has changed fundamentally.

Does that matter? Is the image more clear? Less clear? Are our reactions more responsive and meaningful? Or are they being confused and made irrelevant? I suggest that it does matter, that the way we perceive external reality through the audiovisual media is a quite different process from that of perceiving it through the medium of print, and that the

2. Johann Gutenberg (c. 1395–1468): Mainz (Germany) printer instrumental in the invention of movable metal type. This development led to the rapid spread of printing throughout Renaissance Europe.

quality of our perception is now more important than ever before in our history.

That the quality of our perception of reality not experienced directly is important seems clear enough. In the simpler days of our national growth, the great issues we confronted were perhaps as demanding as those we face today, but they lay within the everyday experience of ordinary citizens: British versus local rule, taxation of the unrepresented, a strong or weak union, slavery or freedom, regulation of railroads or submission to their economic dominance. Issues today involve distant lands and peoples, complex economic and governmental issues, esoteric scientific questions. No ordinary citizen on the basis of personal experience alone can have a useful opinion about what our policy should be toward the Middle East—or toward Russia or China or Japan or the Caribbean—or the control of nuclear energy and nuclear weapons, or the reduction of unemployment. The more crucial the issue to public well-being or even to national survival, the more likely its sound resolution depends on knowledge that most of us can achieve only at second hand, through one medium or another. Moreover, a consequence of the increasing involvement of the total population in the flow of the media is the near-instant stimulation and impact of public opinion. Our Constitution was evolved during weeks of secrecy by a few dozen men, unvexed by public pressures; any such effort today would be harassed into impotence by unceasing public pressures. Public opinion narrowly limits the discretion of authority in every major policy question, so that those who govern us cannot be wiser than we are.

But the demands on us for comprehension of what lies beyond the daily sweep of our eyes is not confined to the demands of public policy decision. The extraordinary enhancement of the power of human observation by instruments ranging from the electron microscope to the X-ray telescope, and by techniques of chemical and physical analysis using spectrography, radioactive tracers, lasers and other devices, plus the enormous achievements made in synthesizing intelligence, have made it possible, in the last century, to construct a perception of the universe utterly beyond anything suggested by direct experience: a universe of billions of galaxies, each composed of billions of stars and presumably of solar systems, lasting for tens of billions of years and perhaps for repeated cycles of compression and explosion, each extending over reaches so near to infinity that light itself may require billions of years to traverse them. At the same time, we have discovered that the human race is hundreds of thousands of years older than it was thought to be, and is linked with all other forms of life in a common flow of being. And our conception of the nature of the genetic and biochemical processes that determine the forms and processes of life, intelligence, and self-consciousness itself has been revolutionized.

The comprehension of all this total restructuring of the conceived reality of the universe, of life, and of man's relation to them can of course be achieved only at second hand, through the reception of messages through media of communication. In what ways, then, does it matter how —through which medium—our perception of reality beyond our direct observation is formed? To answer this, one has to begin with the function of words themselves. All words are necessarily abstractions, reaching into the swirling totality of experience and singling out a specific aspect for identification. To put a group of words together in a sentence is not merely to abstract a number of single bits of the surrounding experience, but to assert a structured relationship among them. Even the simplest sentence describing an ordinary event is an extraordinarily complex intellectual exercise, in which human meaning is imposed on a fragment of experience. This is true, of course, of speech as well as writing; but speech conveys more than the words say. Speech is a kind of action itself, bearing a freight of emotional overtone; and informal speech, in particular, may not represent a considered and digested conceptual organization of experience, but rather an instinctive reaction.

Writing distances the reader yet farther from reality than speech does the listener. An event is still described rather than experienced directly, but here the reader is removed from the writer as well as from the event. The overtones of pitch and cadence and gesture are gone; the words lie mutely on the page, stripped of their emotional penumbra.

Print lies at an even further remove. Intended for a large audience, and usually for indefinite preservation, the words are chosen and arranged with greater care. An impersonal formality takes the place of the casualness of, for example, the personal letter.

To convey meaning through print is a demanding enterprise. From an unbounded flow of reality, the author must abstract just those elements— an almost infinitely small fraction of the whole—that he will attempt to convey; must define each by selecting a particular word for each; must describe how he believes these elements relate to each other by arranging the words into sentences (and in more extended communication, such as print is commonly used for, the sentences into paragraphs, thence into chapters, and into the whole complex architecture of a treatise); and must encode all this into complex patterns of ink on paper. The reader, in turn, must decode these patterns, perceive a meaning for each of the words, and construct an image of the complex structure of conceived reality the author has created. It is simply impossible for any idea or information to be conveyed by print without both author and reader having *thought* intensively about the message.

This mode of communication—abstract, formal, and fixed—of course sacrifices much of reality as it may be conveyed through the audiovisual media. To read a description of a Mozart quartet is but a thin and desiccated experience as compared with hearing it by record or radio; to read a description of a sunset or of an El Greco painting is similarly but a poor substitute for seeing it on a slide or film, on a high-definition television screen, or in a color print (which is really an audiovisual rather than a verbal-print form). So, too, the reports of correspondents in earlier wars affected us far less directly and emotionally than the televised scenes of the Vietnam War. No description of a presidential candidate or printed text of his speech can quite convey the living sense of the man as we see and hear him deliver it on a television screen.

Yet the very distancing that separates the reader from reality described is the price paid for understanding and mastery. *Meaning* is a phenomenon created by the reduction of experience into words organized in sentences. The process of understanding is the very process involved in reducing an event to writing. A television documentary about El Salvador or Lebanon can help the viewer create an image more vivid and moving than any conveyed by print; but unless the documentary is accompanied by a spoken analysis—which is, essentially, print read aloud—the documentary will fail to give the auditor the kind of understanding, the kind of *meaning*, he would derive, say, from an article in *Foreign Affairs*. Reading is inherently a different way of constructing an image of reality than is viewing or listening. And it is an indispensable one when the purpose is to require a structured understanding, rather than an impression or an emotional experience, of reality.

There are two other rather obvious ways in which communication by reading printed matter differs from communication by watching or listening to television, radio, films, or records. One is simply the ability to present a substantial mass of information: the content of a single issue of the *New York Times* covers far more than a week's television news programming, and a book affords the only realistic medium for presenting an extensive, structured, and detailed treatment of a subject. The other is the almost infinitely wider range of choice of subject and treatment offered the reader as contrasted with the radio listener or the television viewer. The thrust of the broadcast media, by reason of their very technology, has been to assemble larger and larger audiences for fewer and fewer sources. A prime-time network television program with fewer than 10 million simultaneous viewers can hardly be sustained. In very recent years, this situation has improved substantially, as FM radio, cable television, videocassette recordings, and videodisks have greatly increased the range of individual choice. But there are thousands of magazines, catering to every interest; and the most meager of bookstores or the smallest public library offers incomparably wider opportunities to pursue inquiries or individual tastes than the totality of audiovisual media available at any one time.

The other alternative to reading that has developed in our time is the computer with its related telecommunications facility. In fact, the computer, by increasing the efficiency of editing and printing, providing powerful bibliographic and indexing services, and simplifying library services, does far more to facilitate than to replace traditional reading. But the growing use of electronic publishing and information dissemination does give emphasis to a concept of what it is important to communicate that is widely at variance with that of traditional reading. It is customary to describe a reservoir of knowledge to be disseminated electronically as a "databank" or "database." This is significant, for it reveals the assumption that important knowledge consists of an accumulation of discrete facts, and that the function of at least this medium of information is to select out of the accumulation and deliver the individual facts or collection of facts that have been called for. It assumes that the needs and mode of thought of an inquirer are analogous to those of someone who looks up a number in a telephone directory or consults a dictionary, not those of someone who reads a novel or a biography or a poem. And the oft-expressed conviction that the computer will make the book obsolete reveals a perhaps unconscious, but arid and constricted, belief regarding the nature of important communication.

This is not to question the major and very valuable social roles in communication—roles quite beyond the power of print and reading—that the audiovisual media and computer will play. The color, vividness, and immediacy of the audiovisual media have enriched the lives of all of us. And they have enormously increased the perceptive outreach of most people, for most of the time devoted to viewing or listening occupies hours that had been devoted not to reading, but to activites that did not extend beyond the daily round, and perhaps to inactivity. There can be no question that the audiovisual media have extended and enlarged, for untold numbers of people, an awareness of other lands, other times, other ideas than their own. So, too, has the computer given us powers without which modern society could not operate, and has enhanced immeasurably the capacity of human intelligence to analyze and organize experience.

But neither provides what reading offers as a bridge to the universe of experience beyond our daily ambit. The one can bathe us directly in the unexamined flow of experience, but without the processes of abstraction and organization that give it meaning. The other can give a command over discrete facts scraped bare of penumbral meaning, but does not provide the holistic gathering of experience or endow it with a human conceptual structure.

It is well for our society that the audiovisual and electronic revolutions have complemented print, not replaced it, and that reading vigorously survives as the means of establishing a bridge of meaning, both human and thoughtful, between ourselves and the totality beyond us: a bridge between our culture and other cultures, between ourselves and the infinitely vast and infinitely microscopic world of science, and between our present and the past and the future. Without reading, meaning and comprehension could dissolve into "feeling" or splinter into data, the awareness and integrity of individual identity and purpose could be but ill sustained, and Burke's[3] sense of society as an all-embracing compact of the living with the dead and those yet unborn could not be achieved.

1983

3. Edmund Burke (1729–97): Irish statesman and orator.

Joan Didion

SALVADOR

The three-year-old El Salvador International Airport is glassy and white and splendidly isolated, conceived during the waning of the Molina "National Transformation" as convenient less to the capital (San Salvador is forty miles away, until recently a drive of several hours) than to a central hallucination of the Molina and Romero[1] regimes, the projected beach resorts, the Hyatt, the Pacific Paradise, tennis, golf, water-skiing, condos, *Costa del Sol*; the visionary invention of a tourist industry in yet another republic where the leading natural cause of death is gastrointestinal infection. In the general absence of tourists these hotels have since been abandoned, ghost resorts on the empty Pacific beaches, and to land at this airport built to service them is to plunge directly into a state in which no ground is solid, no depth of field reliable, no perception so definite that it might not dissolve into its reverse.

The only logic is that of acquiescence. Immigration is negotiated in a thicket of automatic weapons, but by whose authority the weapons are brandished (Army or National Guard or National Police or Customs Police or Treasury Police or one of a continuing proliferation of other shadowy and overlapping forces) is a blurred point. Eye contact is avoided. Documents are scrutinized upside down. Once clear of the airport, on the new highway that slices through green hills rendered phosphorescent by the cloud cover of the tropical rainy season, one sees mainly underfed cattle and mongrel dogs and armored vehicles, vans and trucks and Cherokee Chiefs fitted with reinforced steel and bulletproof

1. Arturo Armando Molina and Carlos Humberto Romero: presidents of El Salvador 1972–77 and 1977–79, respectively.

Plexiglas an inch thick. Such vehicles are a fixed feature of local life, and are popularly associated with disappearance and death. There was the Cherokee Chief seen following the Dutch television crew killed in Chalatenango province in March of 1982. There was the red Toyota three-quarter-ton pickup sighted near the van driven by the four American-Catholic workers on the night they were killed in 1980. There were, in the late spring and summer of 1982, the three Toyota panel trucks, one yellow, one blue, and one green, none bearing plates, reported present at each of the mass detentions (a "detention" is another fixed feature of local life, and often precedes a "disappearance") in the Amatepec district of San Salvador. These are the details—the models and the colors of armored vehicles, the makes and calibers of weapons, the particular methods of dismemberment and decapitation used in particular instances—on which the visitor to Salvador learns immediately to concentrate, to the exclusion of past or future concerns, as in a prolonged amnesiac fugue. * * *

Terror is the given of the place. Black-and-white police cars cruise in pairs, each with the barrel of a rifle extruding from an open window. Roadblocks materialize at random, soldiers fanning out from trucks and taking positions, fingers always on triggers, safeties clicking on and off. Aim is taken as if to pass the time. Every morning *El Diario de Hoy* and *La Prensa Gráfica* carry cautionary stories. "*Una madre y sus dos hijos fueron asesinados con arma cortante (corvo) por ocho sujetos desconocidos el lunes en la noche*": A mother and her two sons hacked to death in their beds by eight *desconocidos*, unknown men. The same morning's paper: the unidentified body of a young man, strangled, found on the shoulder of a road. Same morning, different story: the unidentified bodies of three young men, found on another road, their faces partially destroyed by bayonets, one face carved to represent a cross.

It is largely from these reports in the newspapers that the United States embassy compiles its body counts, which are transmitted to Washington in a weekly dispatch referred to by embassy people as "the grim-gram." These counts are presented in a kind of tortured code that fails to obscure what is taken for granted in El Salvador, that government forces do most of the killing. In a January 15 1982 memo to Washington, for example, the embassy issued a "guarded" breakdown on its count of 6,909 "reported" political murders between September 16 1980 and September 15 1981. Of these 6,909, according to the memo, 922 were "believed committed by security forces," 952 "believed committed by leftist terrorists," 136 "believed committed by rightist terrorists," and 4,889 "committed by unknown assailants," the famous *desconocidos* favored by those San Salvador newspapers still publishing. (The figures actually add up not to 6,909 but to 6,899, leaving ten in a kind of official limbo.) The memo continued:

> "The uncertainty involved here can be seen in the fact that responsibility cannot be fixed in the majority of cases. We note, however, that it is generally believed in El Salvador that a large number of the unexplained killings are carried out by the security forces, officially or unofficially. The Embassy is aware of dramatic claims that have been made by one interest group or another in which the security forces figure as the primary agents of murder here. El Salvador's tangled web of attack and vengeance, traditional criminal violence and political mayhem make this an impossible charge to sustain. In saying this, however, we make no attempt to lighten the responsibility for the deaths of many hundreds, and perhaps thousands, which can be attributed to the security forces. . . . "

The body count kept by what is generally referred to in San Salvador as "the Human Rights Commission" is higher than the embassy's, and documented periodically by a photographer who goes out looking for bodies. These bodies he photographs are often broken into unnatural positions, and the faces to which the bodies are attached (when they are attached) are equally unnatural, sometimes unrecognizable as human faces, obliterated by acid or beaten to a mash of misplaced ears and teeth or slashed ear to ear and invaded by insects. *"Encontrado en Antiguo Cuscatlán el día 25 de Marzo 1982: camison de dormir celeste,"* the typed caption reads on one photograph: found in Antiguo Cuscatlán March 25 1982 wearing a sky-blue nightshirt. The captions are laconic. Found in Soyapango May 21 1982. Found in Mejicanos June 11 1982. Found at El Playón May 30, 1982, white shirt, purple pants, black shoes.

The photograph accompanying that last caption shows a body with no eyes, because the vultures got to it before the photographer did. There is a special kind of practical information that the visitor to El Salvador acquires immediately, the way visitors to other places acquire information about the currency rates, the hours for the museums. In El Salvador one learns that vultures go first for the soft tissue, for the eyes, the exposed genitalia, the open mouth. One learns that an open mouth can be used to make a specific point, can be stuffed with something emblematic; stuffed, say, with a penis, or if the point has to do with land title, stuffed with some of the dirt in question. One learns that hair deteriorates less rapidly than flesh, and that a skull surrounded by a perfect corona of hair is a not uncommon sight in the body dumps.

All forensic photographs induce in the viewer a certain protective numbness, but dissociation is more difficult here. In the first place these are not, technically, "forensic" photographs, since the evidence they document will never be presented in a court of law. In the second place the disfigurement is too routine. The locations are too near, the dates too recent. There is the presence of the relatives of the disappeared: the women who sit every day in this cramped office on the grounds of the archdiocese, waiting to look at the spiral-bound photo albums in which the photographs are kept. These albums have plastic covers bearing soft-focus color photographs of young Americans in dating situation (strolling through autumn foliage on one album, recumbent in a field of daisies on another), and the women, looking for the bodies of their husbands and brothers and sisters and children, pass them from hand to hand without comment or expression.

> "One of the more shadowy elements of the violent scene here [is] the death squad. Existence of these groups has long been disputed, but not by many Salvadorans. . . . Who constitutes the death squads is yet another difficult question. We do not believe that these squads exist as permanent formations but rather as ad hoc vigilante groups that coalesce according to perceived need. Membership is also uncertain, but in addition to civilians we believe that both on- and off-duty members of the security forces are participants. This was unofficially confirmed by right-wing spokesman Maj. Roberto D'Aubuisson who stated in an interview in early 1981 that security force members utilize the guise of the death squad when a potentially embarrassing or odious task needs to be performed."
>   —From the confidential but later declassified January 15, 1982 memo previ-
>   ously cited, drafted for the State Department by the political section at the
>   embassy in San Salvador.

The dead and pieces of the dead turn up in El Savador everywhere, every day, as taken for granted as in a nightmare, or a horror movie. Vultures of course suggest the presence of a body. A knot of children on the street suggests the presence of a body. Bodies turn up in the brush of vacant lots, in the garbage thrown down ravines in the richest districts, in public rest rooms, in bus stations. Some are dropped in Lake Ilopango, a few miles east of the city, and wash up near the lakeside cottages and clubs frequented by what remains in San Salvador of the sporting bour-geoisie. Some still turn up in El Playón, the lunar lava field of rotting human flesh visible at one time or another on every television screen in America but characterized in June of 1982 in the El Salvador News Gazette, an English-language weekly edited by an American named Mario Rosenthal, as an "uncorroborated story . . . dredged up from the files of leftist propaganda." Others turn up at Puerta del Diablo, above Parque Balboa, a national Turicentro described as recently as the April–July 1982 issue of Aboard TACA, the magazine provided passen-gers on the national airline of El Salvador, as "offering excellent subjects for color photography."

I drove up to Puerta del Diablo one morning in June of 1982, past the Casa Presidencial and the camouflaged watch towers and heavy concen-trations of troops and arms south of town, on up a narrow road narrowed further by landslides and deep crevices in the roadbed, a drive so insis-tently premonitory that after a while I began to hope that I would pass

Puerta del Diablo without knowing it, just miss it, write it off, turn around and go back. There was however no way of missing it. Puerta del Diablo is a "view site" in an older and distinctly literary tradition, nature as lesson, an immense cleft rock through which half of El Salvador seems framed, a site so romantic and "mystical," so theatrically sacrificial in aspect, that it might be a cosmic parody of nineteenth-century landscape painting. The place presents itself as pathetic fallacy:[2] the sky "broods," the stones "weep," a constant seepage of water weighting the ferns and moss. The foliage is thick and slick with moisture. The only sound is a steady buzz, I believe of cicadas.

Body dumps are seen in El Salvador as a kind of visitors' must-do, difficult but worth the detour. "Of course you have seen El Playón," an aide to President Alvaro Magaña said to me one day, and proceeded to discuss the site geologically, as evidence of the country's geothermal resources. He made no mention of the bodies. I was unsure if he was sounding me out or simply found the geothermal aspect of overriding interest. One difference between El Playón and Puerta del Diablo is that most bodies at El Playón appear to have been killed somewhere else, and then dumped; at Puerta del Diablo the executions are believed to occur in place, at the top, and the bodies thrown over. Sometimes reporters will speak of wanting to spend the night at Puerta del Diablo, in order to document the actual execution, but at the time I was in Salvador no one had.

The aftermath, the daylight aspect, is well documented. "Nothing fresh today, I hear," an embassy officer said when I mentioned that I had visited Puerta del Diablo. "Were there any on top?" someone else asked. "There were supposed to have been three on top yesterday." The point about whether or not there had been any on top was that usually it was necessary to go down to see bodies. The way down is hard. Slabs of stone, slippery with moss, are set into the vertiginous cliff, and it is down this cliff that one begins the descent to the bodies, or what is left of the bodies, pecked and maggoty masses of flesh, bone, hair. On some days there have been helicopters circling, tracking those making the descent. Other days there have been militia at the top, in the clearing where the road seems to run out, but on the morning I was there the only people on top were a man and a woman and three small children, who played in the wet grass while the woman started and stopped a Toyota pickup. She appeared to be learning how to drive. She drove forward and then back toward the edge, apparently following the man's signals, over and over again.

We did not speak, and it was only later, down the mountain and back in the land of the provisionally living, that it occurred to me that there was a definite question about why a man and a woman might choose a

---

2. Attributing human traits and feelings to nature.

well-known body dump for a driving lesson. This was one of a number of occasions, during the two weeks my husband and I spent in El Salvador, on which I came to understand, in a way I had not understood before, the exact mechanism of terror.

Whenever I had nothing better to do in San Salvador I would walk up in the leafy stillness of the San Benito and Escalón districts, where the hush at midday is broken only by the occasional crackle of a walkie-talkie, the click of metal moving on a weapon. I recall a day in San Benito when I opened my bag to check an address, and heard the clicking of metal on metal all up and down the street. On the whole no one walks up here, and pools of blossoms lie undisturbed on the sidewalks. Most of the houses in San Benito are more recent than those in Escalón, less idiosyncratic and probably smarter, but the most striking architectural features in both districts are not the houses but their walls, walls built upon walls, walls stripped of the usual copa de oro[3] and bougainvillea, walls that reflect successive generations of violence: the original stone, the additonal five or six or ten feet of brick, and finally the barbed wire, sometimes concertina, sometimes electrified; walls with watch towers, gun ports, closed-circuit television cameras, walls now reaching twenty and thirty feet.

San Benito and Escalón appear on the embassy security maps as districts of relatively few "incidents," but they remain districts in which a certain oppressive uneasiness prevails. In the first place there are always "incidents"—detentions and deaths and disappearances—in the *barrancas*, the ravines lined with shanties that fall down behind the houses with the walls and the guards and the walkie-talkies; one day in Escalón I was introduced to a woman who kept the lean-to that served as a grocery in a *barranca* just above the Hotel Sheraton. She was sticking prices on bars of Camay and Johnson's baby soap, stopping occasionally to sell a plastic bag or two filled with crushed ice and Coca-Cola, and all the while she talked in a low voice about her fear, about her eighteen-year-old son, about the boys who had been taken out and shot on successive nights recently in a neighboring *barranca*.

In the second place there is, in Escalón, the presence of the Sheraton itself, a hotel that has figured rather too prominently in certain local stories involving the disappearance and death of Americans. The Sheraton always seems brighter and more mildly festive than either the Camino Real or the Presidente, with children in the pool and flowers and pretty women in pastel dresses, but there are usually several bullet-proofed Cherokee Chiefs in the parking area, and the men drinking in the lobby often carry the little zippered purses that in San Salvador suggest not passports or credit cards but Browning 9-mm. pistols.

3. Cupflower (literally, cup of gold).

It was at the Sheraton that one of the few American *desaparecidos*,[4] a young free-lance writer named John Sullivan, was last seen in December of 1980. It was also at the Sheraton, after eleven on the evening of January 3 1981, that the two American advisers on agrarian reform, Michael Hammer and Mark Pearlman, were killed, along with the Salvadoran director of the Institute for Agrarian Transformation, José Rodolfo Viera. The three were drinking coffee in a dining room of the lobby, and whoever killed them used an Ingram MAC-10, without sound suppressor, and then walked out through the lobby, unapprehended. The Sheraton has even turned up in the investigation into the December 1980 deaths of the four American churchwomen, Sisters Ita Ford and Maura Clarke, the two Maryknoll nuns; Sister Dorothy Kazel, the Ursuline nun; and Jean Donovan, the lay volunteer. In *Justice in El Salvador: A Case Study*, prepared and released in July of 1982 in New York by the Lawyers' Committee for International Human Rights, there appears this note:

> "On December 19, 1980, the [Duarte government's] Special Investigative Commission reported that 'a red Toyota ¾-ton pickup was seen leaving (the crime scene) at about 11:00 P.M. on December 2' and that 'a red splotch on the burned van' of the churchwomen was being checked to determine whether the paint splotch 'could be the result of a collision between that van and the red Toyota pickup.' By February 1981, the Maryknoll Sisters' Office of Social Concerns, which has been actively monitoring the investigation, received word from a source which it considered reliable that the FBI had matched the red splotch on the burned van with a red Toyota pickup belonging to the Sheraton hotel in San Salvador. . . . Subsequent to the FBI's alleged matching of the paint splotch and a Sheraton truck, the State Department has claimed, in a communication with the families of the churchwomen, that 'the FBI could not determine the source of the paint scraping.'"

There is also mention in this study of a young Salvadoran businessman named Hans Christ (his father was a German who arrived in El Salvador at the end of World War II), a part owner of the Sheraton. Hans Christ lives now in Miami, and that his name should have even come up in the Maryknoll investigation made many people uncomfortable, because it was Hans Christ, along with his brother-in-law, Ricardo Sol Meza, who, in April of 1981, was first charged with the murders of Michael Hammer and Mark Pearlman and José Rodolfo Viera at the Sheraton. These charges were later dropped, and were followed by a series of other charges, arrests, releases, expressions of "dismay" and "incredulity" from the American embassy, and even, in the fall of 1982, confessions to the killings from two former National Guard corporals, who testified that Hans Christ had led them through the lobby and pointed out the victims. Hans Christ and Ricardo Sol Meza have said that the dropped case

4. Missing (i.e., abducted) persons.

against them was a government frame-up, and that they were only having drinks at the Sheraton the night of the killings, with a National Guard intelligence officer. It was logical for Hans Christ and Ricardo Sol Meza to have drinks at the Sheraton because they both had interests in the hotel, and Ricardo Sol Meza had just opened a roller disco, since closed, off the lobby into which the killers walked that night. The killers were described by witnesses as well dressed, their faces covered. The room from which they walked was at the time I was in San Salvador no longer a restaurant, but the marks left by the bullets were still visible, on the wall facing the door.

Whenever I had occasion to visit the Sheraton I was apprehensive, and this apprehension came to color the entire Escalón district for me, even its lower reaches, where there were people and movies and restaurants. I recall being struck by it on the canopied porch of a restaurant near the Mexican embassy, on an evening when rain or sabotage or habit had blacked out the city and I became abruptly aware, in the light cast by a passing car, of two human shadows, silhouettes illuminated by the headlights and then invisible again. One shadow sat behind the smoked glass windows of a Cherokee Chief parked at the curb in front of the restaurant; the other crouched between the pumps at the Esso station next door, carrying a rifle. It seemed to me unencouraging that my husband and I were the only people seated on the porch. In the absence of the headlights the candle on our table provided the only light, and I fought the impulse to blow it out. We continued talking carefully. Nothing came of this, but I did not forget the sensation of having been in a single instant demoralized, undone, humiliated by fear, which is what I meant when I said that I came to understand in El Salvador the mechanism of terror. * * *

1983

THE READER

1. In the first paragraph of her essay, Didion refers to "a central hallucination of the Molina and Romero regimes." Why does she use the word "hallucination"?

2. How does Didion feel about the things she sees and experiences? How does she convey those feelings?

3. Didion says she "came to understand ... the exact mechanism of terror." What is that mechanism?

4. In her other essays included in this book, Didion is vitally interested in what she and others thought and felt. Is that interest apparent in this essay? In "On Going Home" (p. 69), she speaks of her mother and herself as "veterans of a guerrilla war we never understood" and of "the ambushes of daily life." Do these metaphors shed any light on her interest in "Salvador"?

THE WRITER

1. Why does Didion find it necessary to explain the significance of some of the words she uses, such as "logic . . . of acquiescence," "detention," "disappearance"? Find other similar terms in her essay that she has had to define.
2. Look closely at the third paragraph of Didion's essay. Why does she make "police cars," "roadblocks" and "aim" the subjects of her second, third, and fourth sentences? Why does she use so many past participles ("hacked," "strangled," "found," "destroyed," "carved") in the last three sentences of the paragraph?
3. In "'How Bad Do You Want to Get to Danang?'" (p. 722), Herr describes the terror of experiences in the Vietnam War. Write a brief comparison of the terror Herr describes with the "mechanism of terror" described by Didion.

Jonathan Schell

THE DESTRUCTIVE POWER OF A ONE-MEGATON BOMB ON NEW YORK CITY

* * *

One way to begin to grasp the destructive power of present-day nuclear weapons is to describe the consequences of the detonation of a one-megaton bomb, which possesses eighty times the explosive power of the Hiroshima bomb, on a large city, such as New York. Burst some eighty-five hundred feet above the Empire State Building, a one-megaton bomb would gut or flatten almost every building between Battery Park and 125th Street, or within a radius of four and four-tenths miles, or in an area of sixty-one square miles, and would heavily damage buildings between the northern tip of Staten Island and the George Washington Bridge, or within a radius of about eight miles, or in an area of about two hundred square miles. A conventional explosive delivers a swift shock, like a slap, to whatever it hits, but the blast wave of a sizable nuclear weapon endures for several seconds and "can surround and destroy whole buildings" (Glasstone).[1] People, of course, would be picked up and hurled away from the blast along with the rest of the debris. Within the sixty-one square miles, the walls, roofs, and floors of any buildings that had not been flattened would be collapsed, and the people and furniture inside would be swept down onto the street. (Technically, this zone would be hit by various overpressures of at least five pounds per square inch. Overpressure is defined as the pressure in excess of normal atmos-

1. Samuel Glasstone, editor with Philip Dolan of *Effects of Nuclear Weapons.*

pheric pressure.) As far away as ten miles from ground zero, pieces of glass and other sharp objects would be hurled about by the blast wave at lethal velocities. In Hiroshima, where buildings were low and, outside the center of the city, were often constructed of light materials, injuries from falling buildings were often minor. But in New York, where the buildings are tall and are constructed of heavy materials, the physical collapse of the city would certainly kill millions of people. The streets of New York are narrow ravines running between the high walls of the city's buildings. In a nuclear attack, the walls would fall and the ravines would fill up. The people in the buildings would fall to the street with the debris of the buildings, and the people in the street would be crushed by this avalanche of people and buildings. At a distance of two miles or so from ground zero, winds would reach four hundred miles an hour, and another two miles away they would reach a hundred and eighty miles an hour. Meanwhile, the fireball would be growing, until it was more than a mile wide, and rocketing upward, to a height of over six miles. For ten seconds, it would broil the city below. Anyone caught in the open within nine miles of ground zero would receive third-degree burns and would probably be killed; closer to the explosion, people would be charred and killed instantly. From Greenwich Village up to Central Park, the heat would be great enough to melt metal and glass. Readily inflammable materials, such as newspapers and dry leaves, would ignite in all five boroughs (though in only a small part of Staten Island) and west to the Passaic River, in New Jersey, within a radius of about nine and a half miles from ground zero, thereby creating an area of more than two hundred and eighty square miles in which mass fires were likely to break out.

If it were possible (as it would not be) for someone to stand at Fifth Avenue and Seventy-second Street (about two miles from ground zero) without being instantly killed, he would see the following sequence of events. A dazzling white light from the fireball would illumine the scene, continuing for perhaps thirty seconds. Simultaneously, searing heat would ignite everything flammable and start to melt windows, cars, buses, lampposts, and everything else made of metal or glass. People in the street would immediately catch fire, and would shortly be reduced to heavily charred corpses. About five seconds after the light appeared, the blast wave would strike, laden with the debris of a now nonexistent midtown. Some buildings might be crushed, as though a giant fist had squeezed them on all sides, and others might be picked up off their foundations and whirled uptown with the other debris. On the far side of Central Park, the West Side skyline would fall from south to north. The four-hundred-mile-an-hour wind would blow from south to north, die down after a few seconds, and then blow in the reverse direction with diminished intensity. While these things were happening, the fireball would be burning in the sky for the ten seconds of the thermal pulse. Soon huge, thick clouds of dust and smoke would envelop the scene, and as the mushroom cloud rushed overhead (it would have a diameter of about twelve miles) the light from the sun would be blotted out, and day would turn to night. Within minutes, fires, ignited both by the thermal pulse and by broken gas mains, tanks of gas and oil, and the like, would begin to spread in the darkness, and a strong, steady wind would begin to blow in the direction of the blast. As at Hiroshima, a whirlwind might be produced, which would sweep through the ruins, and radioactive rain, generated under the meteorological conditions created by the blast, might fall. Before long, the individual fires would coalesce into a mass fire, which, depending largely on the winds, would become either a conflagration or a firestorm. In a conflagration, prevailing winds spread a wall of fire as far as there is any combustible material to sustain it; in a firestorm, a vertical updraft caused by the fire itself sucks the surrounding air in toward a central point, and the fires therefore converge in a single fire of extreme heat. A mass fire of either kind renders shelters useless by burning up all the oxygen in the air and creating toxic gases, so that anyone inside the shelters is asphyxiated, and also by heating the ground to such high temperatures that the shelters turn, in effect, into ovens, cremating the people inside them. In Dresden, several days after the firestorm raised there by Allied conventional bombing, the interiors of some bomb shelters were still so hot that when they were opened the inrushing air caused the contents to burst into flame. Only those who had fled their shelters when the bombing started had any chance of surviving. (It is difficult to predict in a particular situation which form the fires will take. In actual experience, Hiroshima suffered a firestorm and Nagasaki suffered a conflagration.)

In this vast theatre of physical effects, all the scenes of agony and death that took place at Hiroshima would again take place, but now involving millions of people rather than hundreds of thousands. Like the people of Hiroshima, the people of New York would be burned, battered, crushed, and irradiated in every conceivable way. The city and its people would be mingled in a smoldering heap. And then, as the fires started, the survivors (most of whom would be on the periphery of the explosion) would be driven to abandon to the flames those family members and other people who were unable to flee, or else to die with them. Before long, while the ruins burned, the processions of injured, mute people would begin their slow progress out of the outskirts of the devastated zone. However, this time a much smaller proportion of the population than at Hiroshima would have a chance of escaping. In general, as the size of the area of devastation increases, the possibilities for escape decrease. When the devastated area is relatively small, as it was at Hiroshima, people who are not incapacitated will have a good chance of escaping to safety before the fires coalesce into a mass fire. But when the devastated area is great, as it would be after the detonation of a megaton bomb, and fires are springing up at a distance of nine and a half miles from ground zero, and when what used to be the streets are piled high with burning rubble, and the day (if the attack occurs in the daytime) has grown impenetrably dark, there is little chance that anyone who is not on the very edge of the devastated area will be able to make his way to safety. In New York, most people would die wherever the blast found them, or not very far from there.

If instead of being burst in the air the bomb were burst on or near the ground in the vicinity of the Empire State Building, the overpressure would be very much greater near the center of the blast area but the range hit by a minimum of five pounds per square inch of overpressure would be less. The range of the thermal pulse would be about the same as that of the air burst. The fireball would be almost two miles across, and would engulf midtown Manhattan from Greenwich Village nearly to Central Park. Very little is known about what would happen to a city that was inside a fireball, but one would expect a good deal of what was there to be first pulverized and then melted or vaporized. Any human beings in the area would be reduced to smoke and ashes; they would simply disappear. A crater roughly three blocks in diameter and two hundred feet deep would open up. In addition, heavy radioactive fallout would be created as dust and debris from the city rose with the mushroom cloud and then fell back to the ground. Fallout would begin to drop almost immediately, contaminating the ground beneath the cloud with levels of radiation many times lethal doses, and quickly killing anyone who might have survived the blast wave and the thermal pulse and might now be attempting an escape; it is difficult to believe that there would be appreciable survival of the people of the city after a megaton ground burst. And for the next twenty-four hours or so more fallout would descend downwind from the blast, in a plume whose direction and length would depend on the speed and the direction of the wind that happened to be blowing at the time of the attack. If the wind was blowing at fifteen miles an hour, fallout of lethal intensity would descend in a plume about a hundred and fifty miles long and as much as fifteen miles wide. Fallout that was sublethal but could still cause serious illness would extend another hundred and fifty miles downwind. Exposure to radioactivity in human beings is measured in units called rems—an acronym for "roentgen equivalent in man." The roentgen is a standard measurement of gamma- and X-ray radiation, and the expression "equivalent in man" indicates that an adjustment has been made to take into account the differences in the degree of biological damage that is caused by radiation of different types. Many of the kinds of harm done to human beings by radiation—for example, the incidence of cancer and of genetic damage—

depend on the dose accumulated over many years; but radiation sickness, capable of causing death, results from an "acute" dose, received in a period of anything from a few seconds to several days. Because almost ninety per cent of the so-called "infinite-time dose" of radiation from fallout—that is, the dose from a given quantity of fallout that one would receive if one lived for many thousands of years—is emitted in the first week, the one-week accumulated dose is often used as a convenient measure for calculating the immediate harm from fallout. Doses in the thousands of rems, which could be expected throughout the city, would attack the central nervous system and would bring about death within a few hours. Doses of around a thousand rems, which would be delivered some tens of miles downwind from the blast, would kill within two weeks everyone who was exposed to them. Doses of around five hundred rems, which would be delivered as far as a hundred and fifty miles downwind (given a wind speed of fifteen miles per hour), would kill half of all exposed able-bodied young adults. At this level of exposure, radiation sickness proceeds in the three stages observed at Hiroshima. The plume of lethal fallout could descend, depending on the direction of the wind, on other parts of New York State and parts of New Jersey, Pennsylvania, Delaware, Maryland, Connecticut, Massachusetts, Rhode Island, Vermont, and New Hampshire, killing additional millions of people. The circumstances in heavily contaminated areas, in which millions of people were all declining together, over a period of weeks, toward painful deaths, are ones that, like so many of the consequences of nuclear explosions, have never been experienced.

A description of the effects of a one-megaton bomb on New York City gives some notion of the meaning in human terms of a megaton of nuclear explosive power, but a weapon that is more likely to be used against New York is the twenty-megaton bomb, which has one thousand six hundred times the yield of the Hiroshima bomb. The Soviet Union is estimated to have at least a hundred and thirteen twenty-megaton bombs in its nuclear arsenal, carried by Bear intercontinental bombers. In addition, some of the Soviet SS-18 missiles are capable of carrying bombs of this size, although the actual yields are not known. Since the explosive power of the twenty-megaton bombs greatly exceeds the amount necessary to destroy most military targets, it is reasonable to suppose that they are meant for use against large cities. If a twenty-megaton bomb were airburst over the Empire State Building at an altitude of thirty thousand feet, the zone gutted or flattened by the blast wave would have a radius of twelve miles and an area of more than four hundred and fifty square miles, reaching from the middle of Staten Island to the northern edge of the Bronx, the eastern edge of Queens, and well into New Jersey, and the zone of heavy damage from the blast wave (the zone hit by a minimum of two pounds of overpressure per square inch) would have a radius of twenty-one and a half miles, or an area of one thousand four hundred and fifty square miles, reaching to the southernmost tip of Staten Island, north as far as southern Rockland County, east into Nassau County, and west to Morris County, New Jersey. The fireball would be about four and a half miles in diameter and would radiate the thermal pulse for some twenty seconds. People caught in the open twenty-three miles away from ground zero, in Long Island, New Jersey, and southern New York State, would be burned to death. People hundreds of miles away who looked at the burst would be temporarily blinded and would risk permanent eye injury. (After the test of a fifteen-megaton bomb on Bikini Atoll, in the South Pacific, in March of 1954, small animals were found to have suffered retinal burns at a distance of three hundred and forty-five miles.) The mushroom cloud would be seventy miles in diameter. New York City and its suburbs would be transformed into a lifeless, flat, scorched desert in a few seconds.

If a twenty-megaton bomb were ground-burst on the Empire State Building, the range of severe blast damage would, as with the one-megaton ground blast, be reduced, but the fireball, which would be almost six miles in diameter, would cover Manhattan from Wall Street to northern Central Park and also parts of New Jersey, Brooklyn, and Queens, and everyone within it would be instantly killed, with most of them physically disappearing. Fallout would again be generated, this time covering thousands of square miles with lethal intensities of radiation. A fair portion of New York City and its incinerated population, now radioactive dust, would have risen into the mushroom cloud and would now be descending on the surrounding territory. On one of the few occasions when local fallout was generated by a test explosion in the multi-megaton range, the fifteen-megaton bomb tested on Bikini Atoll, which was exploded seven feet above the surface of a coral reef, "caused substantial contamination over an area of more than seven thousand square miles," according to Glasstone. If, as seems likely, a twenty-megaton bomb ground-burst on New York would produce at least a comparable amount of fallout, and if the wind carried the fallout onto populated areas, then this one bomb would probably doom upward of twenty million people, or almost ten per cent of the population of the United States.

* * *

1982

Garrison Keillor

THE TOWER PROJECT

Many of our personnel, conscious of the uncertainties of the construction business, have voiced concern relative to their future employment with the Company. What lies ahead on our horizon, they wonder, of the magnitude of the Fred M. and Ida S. Freebold Performing Arts Center, the Tannersfield Freeway Overpass, and other works that have put us in the construction forefront? They recall the cancellation in mid-contract of the Vietnam Parking Lot project, and they ask, "Will the Super-Tall Tower project, too, go down the drain, with a resultant loss of jobs and Company position in the building field?"

The Company believes such will not be the case. While we aren't putting all our "eggs" on one tower and are keeping an eye on the Los Angeles–Honolulu Bridge option and the proposed Lake Michigan Floating Airport, we feel that the Super-Tall Tower has achieved priority status in Washington, and all phases of research and development, land clearance, and counter-resistance are moving forward in expectation of final approval.

As for the Tower critics, they are few in number, and there isn't one of their objections that we haven't answered. Let's look at the record. Their favorite line is "Why build a Super-Tall Tower when money is so urgently needed for cancer and poverty?" With all due respect to the unwell or impoverished person and his or her family, we state our case as follows:

First, Tower construction will create a hundred thousand new jobs, not only in the Babel area and the Greater Southwest but also in other places where the bricks and slime will be made by subcontractors.

Second, because it will be the world's tallest tower, we will be able to see more from it than from any existing tower.

Third, we have reason to believe the Chinese are well along in the development of *their* tower. If we don't wish to abdicate tower leadership to Communist nations, however friendly at the moment, we can't afford to slow down now. To do so would mean the waste of all the money spent on tower research so far and would set back American tower technology for decades to come. Thus, our national prestige is at stake—not merely national pride but the confidence in our ability to rise toward the heavens. When a nation turns away from the sky and looks at its feet, it begins to die as a civilization. Man has long dreamed of building a tall tower from which he could look out and see many interesting and unusual things. Most Americans, we believe, share this dream.

Fourth, environmentalist groups have predicted various disastrous effects from the Tower—that the humming noise of its high-speed elevator will be "unbearable" to the passengers and to nearby residents, that its height will confuse migrating birds, that its long shadow will anger the sun, and so forth. The Company's research laboratory has engaged in a crash program that has already achieved a significant degree of hum reduction; at the same time, our engineers are quick to point out that since no elevator now in service can approach the speed and accompanying hum projected for the Tower elevator, there is no viable data on which to base the entire concept of an "unbearable" hum. Such a determination must wait until the completion of the Tower. In any event, the hum may serve to warn off approaching birds. As for the sun, we feel that, with certain sacrifices, this problem can be taken care of.

1982

THE READER

1. Is "The Tower Project" a fable? If so, what is the moral?
2. What can you infer about the nature of "the Company" from this document?
3. What specific objections to the Tower are put forward by environmentalists and other critics? How seriously are we to take each of these objections? How adequately are the objections answered by "the Company"?
4. It is said that the Tower will be constructed of "bricks and slime." Is slime usually used as a building material? How are we to understand the meaning of the word in this context?
5. Read the passage from Genesis 11:1–9 below. What relevance does it have to Keillor's piece?

GENESIS 11:1–9

And the whole earth was of one language, and of one speech.

2 And it came to pass, as they journeyed from the east, that they found a plain in the land of Shī′när; and they dwelt there.

3 And they said one to another, Go to, let us make brick, and burn them throughly. And they had brick for stone, and slime had they for morter.

4 And they said, Go to, let us build us a city and a tower, whose top may reach unto heaven; and let us make us a name, lest we be scattered abroad upon the face of the whole earth.

5 And the LORD came down to see the city and the tower, which the children of men builded.

6 And the LORD said, Behold, the people is one, and they have all one language; and this they begin to do: and now nothing will be restrained from them, which they have imagined to do.

7 Go to, let us go down, and there confound their language, that they may not understand one another's speech.

8 So the LORD scattered them abroad from thence upon the face of all the earth: and they left off to build the city.

9 Therefore is the name of it called Babel; because the LORD did there confound the language of all the earth: and from thence did the LORD scatter them abroad upon the face of all the earth.

THE WRITER

1. Explain the effect produced by Keillor's choice of words in these phrases or sentences: (1) "all phases of research and development, land clearance, and counter-resistance are moving forward"; (2) "Let's look at the record"; (3) "With all due respect to the unwell or impoverished person and his or her family"; (4) "Man has long dreamed of building a tall tower from which he could look out and see many interesting and unusual things"; (5) "there is no viable data on which to base the entire concept of an 'unbearable' hum."
2. In "A Modest Proposal" (p. 807), Swift gives you various clues that he is not to be taken literally. Does Keillor give clues similar to Swift's or different from Swift's?
3. What is Keillor's attitude toward business or large companies? Toward politicians? Toward environmentalists? Explain how you know.
4. Write a brief essay, using as here the tone, diction, and style of a writer employed by the Company, to draw out the implications of the concluding sentence and to set forth in detail the Company's proposal for taking care of the problem.
5. Take an incident from history or mythology, and use an updated version of it to make some satirical point(s).

Human Nature

Jerome S. Bruner

FREUD AND THE IMAGE OF MAN

By the dawn of the sixth century before Christ, the Greek physicist-philosophers had formulated a bold conception of the physical world as a unitary material phenomenon. The Ionians had set forth a conception of matter as fundamental substance, transformation of which accounted for the myriad forms and substances of the physical world. Anaximander was subtle enough to recognize that matter must be viewed as a generalized substance, free of any particular sensuous properties. Air, iron, water or bone were only elaborated forms, derived from a more general stuff. Since that time, the phenomena of the physical world have been conceived as continuous and monistic, as governed by the common laws of matter. The view was a bold one, bold in the sense of running counter to the immediate testimony of the senses. It has served as an axiomatic basis of physics for more than two millennia. The bold view eventually became the obvious view, and it gave shape to our common understanding of the physical world. Even the alchemists rested their case upon this doctrine of material continuity and, indeed, had they known about neutron bombardment, they might even have hit upon the proper philosopher's stone.

The good fortune of the physicist—and these matters are always relative, for the material monism of physics may have impeded nineteenth-century thinking and delayed insights into the nature of complementarity in modern physical theory—this early good fortune or happy insight has no counterpart in the sciences of man. Lawful continuity between man and the animal kingdom, between dreams and unreason on one side and waking rationality on the other, between madness and sanity, between consciousness and unconsciousness, between the mind of the child and the adult mind, between primitive and civilized man—

each of these has been a cherished discontinuity preserved in doctrinal canons. There were voices in each generation, to be sure, urging the exploration of continuities. Anaximander had a passing good approximation to a theory of evolution based on natural selection; Cornelius Agrippa offered a plausible theory of the continuity of mental health and disease in terms of bottled-up sexuality. But Anaximander did not prevail against Greek conceptions of man's creation nor did Cornelius Agrippa against the demonopathy of the *Malleus Maleficarum*.[1] Neither in establishing the continuity between the varied states of man nor in pursuing the continuity between man and animal was there conspicuous success until the nineteenth century.

I need not insist upon the social, ethical, and political significance of an age's image of man, for it is patent that the view one takes of man affects profoundly one's standard of dignity and the humanly possible. And it is in the light of such a standard that we establish our laws, set our aspirations for learning, and judge the fitness of men's acts. Those who govern, then, must perforce be jealous guardians of man's ideas about man, for the structure of government rests upon an uneasy consensus about human nature and human wants. Since the idea of man is of the order of *res publica*,[2] it is an idea not subject to change without public debate. Nor is it simply a matter of public concern. For man as individual has a deep and emotional investment in his image of himself. If we have learned anything in the last half-century of psychology, it is that man has powerful and exquisite capacities for defending himself against violation of his cherished self-image. This is not to say that Western man has not persistently asked: "What is man that thou art mindful of him?" It is only that the question, when pressed, brings us to the edge of anxiety where inquiry is no longer free.

Two figures stand out massively as the architects of our present-day conception of man: Darwin and Freud. Freud's was the more daring, the more revolutionary, and in a deep sense, the more poetic insight. But Freud is inconceivable without Darwin. It is both timely and perhaps historically just to center our inquiry on Freud's contribution to the modern image of man. Darwin I shall treat as a necessary condition for Freud and for his success, recognizing, of course, that this is a form of psychological license. Not only is it the centenary of Freud's birth; it is also a year in which the current of popular thought expressed in commemoration of the date quickens one's awareness of Freud's impact on our times.

Rear-guard fundamentalism did not require a Darwin to slay it in an age of technology. He helped, but this contribution was trivial in comparison with another. What Darwin had done was to propose a set of

---

1. *The Hammer for Evil Doers*, a notorious   2. The state.
medieval book about demons and witchcraft.

principles unified around the conception that all organic species had their origins and took their form from a common set of circumstances—the requirements of biological survival. All living creatures were on a common footing. When the post-Darwin era of exaggeration had passed and religious literalism had abated into a new nominalism, what remained was a broad, orderly, and unitary conception of organic nature, a vast continuity from the monocellular protozoans to man. Biology had at last found its unifying principle in the doctrine of evolution. Man was not unique but the inheritor of an organic legacy.

As the summit of an evolutionary process, man could still view himself with smug satisfaction, indeed proclaim that God or Nature had shown a persistent wisdom in its effort to produce a final, perfect product. It remained for Freud to present the image of man as the unfinished product of nature: struggling against unreason, impelled by driving inner vicissitudes and urges that had to be contained if man were to live in society, host alike to seeds of madness and majesty, never fully free from an infancy anything but innocent. What Freud was proposing was that man at his best and man at his worst is subject to a common set of explanations: that good and evil grow from a common process.

Freud was strangely yet appropriately fitted for his role as architect of a new conception of man. We must pause to examine his qualifications, for the image of man that he created was in no small measure founded on his painfully achieved image of himself and of his times. We are concerned not so much with his psychodynamics, as with the intellectual traditions he embodies. A child of his century's materialism, he was wedded to the determinism and the classical physicalism of nineteenth-century physiology so boldly represented by Helmholtz. Indeed, the young Freud's devotion to the exploration of anatomical structures was a measure of the strength of this inheritance. But at the same time, as both Lionel Trilling and W. H. Auden have recognized with much sensitivity, there was a deep current of romanticism in Freud—a sense of the role of impulse, of the drama of life, of the power of symbolism, of ways of knowing that were more poetic than rational in spirit, of the poet's cultural alienation. It was perhaps this romantic's sense of drama that led to his gullibility about parental seduction and to his generous susceptibility to the fallacy of the dramatic instance.

Freud also embodies two traditions almost as antithetical as romanticism and nineteenth-century scientism. He was profoundly a Jew, not in a doctrinal sense but in his conception of morality, in his love of the skeptical play of reason, in his distrust of illusion, in the form of his prophetic talent, even in his conception of mature eroticism. His prophetic talent was antithetic to a Utopianism either of innocence or of social control. Nor did it lead to a counsel of renunciation. Free oneself of illusion, of neurotic infantilism, and "the soft voice of intellect" would prevail. Wisdom for Freud was neither doctrine nor formula, but the achievement of maturity. The patient who is cured is the one who is now free enough of neurosis to decide intelligently about his own destiny. As for his conception of mature love, it has always seemed to me that its blend of tenderness and sensuality combined the uxorious imagery of the Chassidic tradition[3] and the sensual quality of the Song of Songs. And might it not have been Freud rather than a commentator of the Haftorahs[4] who said, "In children, it was taught, God gives humanity a chance to make good its mistakes." For the mordern trend of permissiveness toward children is surely a feature of the Freudian legacy.

But for all the Hebraic quality, Freud is also in the classical tradition— combining the Stoics and the great Greek dramatists. For Freud as for the Stoics, there is no possibility of man disobeying the laws of nature. And yet, it is in this lawfulness that for him the human drama inheres. His love for Greek drama and his use of it in his formulation are patent. The sense of the human tragedy, the inevitable working out of the human plight—these are the hallmarks of Freud's case histories. When Freud, the tragic dramatist, becomes a therapist, it is not to intervene as a directive authority. The therapist enters the drama of the patient's life, makes possible a play within a play, the transference, and when the patient has "worked through" and understood the drama, he has achieved the wisdom necessary for freedom. Again, like the Stoics, it is in the recognition of one's own nature and in the acceptance of the laws that govern it that the good life is to be found.

Freud's contribution lies in the continuities of which he made us aware. The first of these is the continuity of organic lawfulness. Accident in human affairs was no more to be brooded as "explanation" than accident in nature. The basis for accepting such an "obvious" proposition had, of course, been well prepared by a burgeoning nineteenth-century scientific naturalism. It remained for Freud to extend naturalistic explanation to the heart of human affairs. The *Psychopathology of Everyday Life* is not one of Freud's deeper works, but "the Freudian slip" has contributed more to the common acceptance of lawfulness in human behavior than perhaps any of the more rigorous and academic formulations from Wundt to the present day. The forgotten lunch engagement, the slip of the tongue, the barked shin could no longer be dismissed as accident. Why Freud should have succeeded where the novelists, philosophers, and academic psychologists had failed we will consider in a moment.

Freud's extension of Darwinian doctrine beyond Haeckel's theorem that ontogeny recapitulates phylogeny[5] is another contribution to con-

3. Or Hasidic; the reference is to a Jewish sect devoted to mystical rather than secular study.

4. Writings of the Old Testament Prophets.
5. That is, the evolution of the fetus into an independent organism parallels the evolu-

tinuity. It is the conception that in the human mind, the primitive, infantile, and archaic exist side-by-side with the civilized and evolved.

> Where animals are concerned we hold the view that the most highly developed have arisen from the lowest. . . . In the realm of mind, on the other hand, the primitive type is so commonly preserved alongside the transformations which have developed out of it that it is superfluous to give instances in proof of it. When this happens, it is usually the result of a bifurcation in development. One quantitative part of an attitude or an impulse has survived unchanged while another has undergone further development. This brings us very close to the more general problem of conservation in the mind. . . . Since the time when we recognized the error of supposing that ordinary forgetting signified destruction or annihilation of the memory-trace, we have been inclined to the opposite view that nothing once formed in the mind could ever perish, that everything survives in some way or other, and is capable under certain conditions of being brought to light again . . . (Freud, *Civilization and Its Discontents*, pp. 14-15).

What has now come to be common sense is that in everyman there is the potentiality for criminality, and that these are neither accidents nor visitations of degeneracy, but products of a delicate balance of forces that, under different circumstances, might have produced normality or even saintliness. Good and evil, in short, grow from a common root.

Freud's genius was in his resolution of polarities. The distinction of child and adult was one such. It did not suffice to reiterate that the child was father to the man. The theory of infantile sexuality and the stages of psychosexual development were an effort to fill the gap, the latter clumsy, the former elegant. Though the alleged progression of sexual expression from the oral, to the anal, to the phallic, and finally to the genital has not found a secure place either in common sense or in general psychology, the developmental continuity of sexuality has been recognized by both. Common sense honors the continuity in the baby-books and in the permissiveness with which young parents of today resolve their doubts. And the research of Beach and others has shown the profound effects of infantile experience on adult sexual behavior—even in lower organisms.

If today people are reluctant to report their dreams with the innocence once attached to such recitals, it is again because Freud brought into common question the discontinuity between the rational purposefulness of waking life and the seemingly irrational purposelessness of fantasy and dream. While the crude symbolism of Freud's early efforts at dream interpretation has come increasingly to be abandoned—that telephone poles and tunnels have an invariant sexual reference—the conception of the dream as representing disguised wishes and fears has become common coin. And Freud's recognition of deep unconscious processes in the

---

tionary development of that species.

creative act, let it also be said, has gone far toward enriching our under-standing of the kinship between the artist, the humanist, and the man of science.

Finally, it is our heritage from Freud that the all-or-none distinction between mental illness and mental health has been replaced by a more humane conception of the continuity of these states. The view that neurosis is a severe reaction to human trouble is as revolutionary in its implications for social practice as it is daring in formulation. The "bad seed" theories, the nosologies of the nineteenth century, the demonolo-gies and doctrines of divine punishment—none of these provided a basis for compassion toward human suffering comparable to that of our time.

One may argue, at last, that Freud's sense of the continuity of human conditions, of the likeness of the human plight, has made possible a deeper sense of the brotherhood of man. It has in any case tempered the spirit of punitiveness toward what once we took as evil and what we now see as sick. We have not yet resolved the dilemma posed by these two ways of viewing. Its resolution is one of the great moral challenges of our age.

Why, after such initial resistance, were Freud's views so phenome-nally successful in transforming common conceptions of man?

One reason we have already considered: the readiness of the Western world to accept a naturalistic explanation of organic phenomena and, concurrently, to be readier for such explanation in the mental sphere. There had been at least four centuries of uninterrupted scientific pro-gress, recently capped by a theory of evolution that brought man into continuity with the rest of the animal kingdom. The rise of naturalism as a way of understanding nature and man witnessed a corresponding de-cline in the explanatory aspirations of religion. By the close of the nineteenth century, religion, to use Morton White's phrase, "too often agreed to accept the role of a non-scientific spiritual grab-bag, or an ideological know-nothing." The elucidation of the human plight had been abandoned by religion and not yet adopted by science.

It was the inspired imagery, the proto-theory of Freud that was to fill the gap. Its success in transforming the common conception of man was not simply its recourse to the "cause-and-effect" discourse of science. Rather it is Freud's imagery, I think, that provides the clue to this ideological power. It is an imagery of necessity, one that combines the dramatic, the tragic, and the scientific views of necessity. It is here that Freud's intellectual heritage matters so deeply. Freud's is a theory or a proto-theory peopled with actors. The characters are from life: the blind, energic, pleasure-seeking id; the priggish and punitive super-ego; the ego, battling for its being by diverting the energy of the others to its own use. The drama has an economy and a terseness. The ego develops canny mechanisms for dealing with the threat of id impulses: denial, projection,[6] and the rest. Balances are struck between the actors, and in the balance is character and neurosis. Freud was using the dramatic technique of decomposition, the play whose actors are parts of a single life. It is a technique that he himself had recognized in fantasies and dreams, one he honored in "The Poet and the Daydream."

The imagery of the theory, moreover, has an immediate resonance with the dialectic of experience. True, it is not the stuff of superficial conscious experience. But it fits the human plight, its conflictedness, its private torment, its impulsiveness, its secret and frightening urges, its tragic quality.

Concerning its scientific imagery, it is marked by the necessity of the classical mechanics. At times the imagery is hydraulic: suppress this stream of impulses, and perforce it breaks out in a displacement elsewhere. The system is a closed and mechanical one. At times it is electrical, as when cathexes are formed and withdrawn like electrical charges. The way of thought fitted well the common-sense physics of its age.

Finally, the image of man presented was thoroughly secular; its ideal type was the mature man free of infantile neuroticism, capable of finding his own way. This freedom from both Utopianism and asceticism has earned Freud the contempt of ideological totalitarians of the Right and the Left. But the image has found a ready home in the rising, liberal intellectual middle class. For them, the Freudian ideal type has become a rallying point in the struggle against spiritual regimentation.

I have said virtually nothing about Freud's equation of sexuality and impulse. It was surely and still is a stimulus to resistance. But to say that Freud's success lay in forcing a reluctant Victorian world to accept the importance of sexuality is as empty as hailing Darwin for his victory over fundamentalism. Each had a far more profound effect.

Can Freud's contribution to the common understanding of man in the twentieth century be likened to the impact of such great physical and biological theories as Newtonian physics and Darwin's conception of evolution? The question is an empty one. Freud's mode of thought is not a theory in the conventional sense, it is a metaphor, an analogy, a way of conceiving man, a drama. I would propose that Anaximander is the proper parallel: his view of the connectedness of physical nature was also an analogy—and a powerful one. Freud is the ground from which theory will grow, and he has prepared the twentieth century to nurture the growth. But far more important, he has provided an image of man that has made him comprehensible without at the same time making him contemptible.

1956

---

6. The attribution to others of one's own feelings.

Carol Gilligan

IMAGES OF RELATIONSHIP

In 1914, with his essay "On Narcissism," Freud[1] swallows his distaste at the thought of "abandoning observation for barren theoretical controversy" and extends his map of the psychological domain. Tracing the development of the capacity to love, which he equates with maturity and psychic health, he locates its origins in the contrast between love for the mother and love for the self. But in thus dividing the world of love into narcissism and "object" relationships, he finds that while men's development becomes clearer, women's becomes increasingly opaque. The problem arises because the contrast between mother and self yields two different images of relationships. Relying on the imagery of men's lives in charting the course of human growth, Freud is unable to trace in women the development of relationships, morality, or a clear sense of self. This difficulty in fitting the logic of his theory to women's experience leads him in the end to set women apart, marking their relationships, like their sexual life, as "a 'dark continent' for psychology" (1926, p. 212).[2]

Thus the problem of interpretation that shadows the understanding of women's development arises from the differences observed in their experience of relationships. To Freud, though living surrounded by women and otherwise seeing so much and so well, women's relationships seemed increasingly mysterious, difficult to discern, and hard to describe. While this mystery indicates how theory can blind observation, it also suggests that development in women is masked by a particular conception of human relationships. Since the imagery of relationships shapes the narrative of human development, the inclusion of women, by changing that imagery, implies a change in the entire account.

The shift in imagery that creates the problem in interpreting women's development is elucidated by the moral judgments of two eleven-year-old children, a boy and a girl, who see, in the same dilemma, two very different moral problems. While current theory brightly illuminates the line and the logic of the boy's thought, it casts scant light on that of the girl. The choice of a girl whose moral judgments elude existing categories of developmental assessment is meant to highlight the issue of interpretation rather than to exemplify sex differences per se. Adding a new line of interpretation, based on the imagery of the girl's thought, makes it possible not only to see development where previously development was

1. Sigmund Freud (1856–1939): Austrian neurologist and father of psychoanalysis.
2. In Sigmund Freud, The Standard Edition of the Complete Psychological Works of Sigmund Freud, trans. and ed. James Strachey. London: The Hogarth Press, 1961.

not discerned but also to consider differences in the understanding of relationships without scaling these differences from better to worse.

The two children were in the same sixth-grade class at school and were participants in the rights and responsibilities study, designed to explore different conceptions of morality and self. The sample selected for this study was chosen to focus the variables of gender and age while maximizing developmental potential by holding constant, at a high level, the factors of intelligence, education, and social class that have been associated with moral development, at least as measured by existing scales. The two children in question, Amy and Jake, were both bright and articulate and, at least in their eleven-year-old aspirations, resisted easy categories of sex-role stereotyping, since Amy aspired to become a scientist while Jake preferred English to math. Yet their moral judgments seem initially to confirm familiar notions about differences between the sexes, suggesting that the edge girls have on moral development during the early school years gives way at puberty with the ascendance of formal logical thought in boys.

The dilemma that these eleven-year-olds were asked to resolve was one in the series devised by Kohlberg[3] to measure moral development in adolescence by presenting a conflict between moral norms and exploring the logic of its resolution. In this particular dilemma, a man named Heinz considers whether or not to steal a drug which he cannot afford to buy in order to save the life of his wife. In the standard format of Kohlberg's interviewing procedure, the description of the dilemma itself—Heinz's predicament, the wife's disease, the druggist's refusal to lower his price—is followed by the question, "Should Heinz steal the drug?" The reasons for and against stealing are then explored through a series of questions that vary and extend the parameters of the dilemma in a way designed to reveal the underlying structure of moral thought.

Jake, at eleven, is clear from the outset that Heinz should steal the drug. Constructing the dilemma, as Kohlberg did, as a conflict between the values of property and life, he discerns the logical priority of life and uses that logic to justify his choice:

> For one thing, a human life is worth more than money, and if the druggist only makes $1,000, he is still going to live, but if Heinz doesn't steal the drug, his wife is going to die. (*Why is life worth more than money?*) Because the druggist can get a thousand dollars later from rich people with cancer, but Heinz can't get his wife again. (*Why not?*) Because people are all different and so you couldn't get Heinz's wife again.

Asked whether Heinz should steal the drug if he does not love his wife, Jake replies that he should, saying that not only is there "a difference

3. Lawrence Kohlberg (1927–): American psychologist known for his studies on the moral development of children.

between hating and killing," but also, if Heinz were caught, "the judge would probably think it was the right thing to do." Asked about the fact that, in stealing, Heinz would be breaking the law, he says that "the laws have mistakes, and you can't go writing up a law for everything that you can imagine."

Thus, while taking the law into account and recognizing its function in maintaining social order (the judge, Jake says, "should give Heinz the lightest possible sentence"), he also sees the law as man-made and therefore subject to error and change. Yet his judgment that Heinz should steal the drug, like his view of the law as having mistakes, rests on the assumption of agreement, a societal consensus around moral values that allows one to know and expect others to recognize what is "the right thing to do."

Fascinated by the power of logic, this eleven-year-old boy locates truth in math, which, he says, is "the only thing that is totally logical." Considering the moral dilemma to be "sort of like a math problem with humans," he sets it up as an equation and proceeds to work out the solution. Since his solution is rationally derived, he assumes that anyone following reason would arrive at the same conclusion and thus that a judge would also consider stealing to be the right thing for Heinz to do. Yet he is also aware of the limits of logic. Asked whether there is a right answer to moral problems, Jake replies that "there can only be right and wrong in judgment," since the parameters of action are variable and complex. Illustrating how actions undertaken with the best of intentions can eventuate in the most disastrous of consequences, he says, "like if you give an old lady your seat on the trolley, if you are in a trolley crash and that seat goes through the window, it might be that reason that the old lady dies."

Theories of developmental psychology illuminate well the position of this child, standing at the juncture of childhood and adolescence, at what Piaget[4] describes as the pinnacle of childhood intelligence, and beginning through thought to discover a wider universe of possibility. The moment of preadolescence is caught by the conjunction of formal operational thought with a description of self still anchored in the factual parameters of his childhood world—his age, his town, his father's occupation, the substance of his likes, dislikes, and beliefs. Yet as his self-description radiates the self-confidence of a child who has arrived, in Erikson's[5] terms, at a favorable balance of industry over inferiority—competent, sure of himself, and knowing well the rules of the game—so his emergent capacity for formal thought, his ability to think about thinking and to reason things out in a logical way, frees him from

4. Jean Piaget (1896–1980): Swiss psychologist known for investigations of thought processes.

5. Erik H. Erikson (1902–): German-American psychoanalyst known for his work on the human life cycle.

dependence on authority and allows him to find solutions to problems by himself.

This emergent autonomy follows the trajectory that Kohlberg's six stages of moral development trace, a three-level progression from an egocentric understanding of fairness based on individual need (stages one and two), to a conception of fairness anchored in the shared conventions of societal agreement (stages three and four), and finally to a principled understanding of fairness that rests on the free-standing logic of equality and reciprocity (stages five and six). While this boy's judgments at eleven are scored as conventional on Kohlberg's scale, a mixture of stages three and four, his ability to bring deductive logic to bear on the solution of moral dilemmas, to differentiate morality from law, and to see how laws can be considered to have mistakes points toward the principled conception of justice that Kohlberg equates with moral maturity.

In contrast, Amy's response to the dilemma conveys a very different impression, an image of development stunted by a failure of logic, an inability to think for herself. Asked if Heinz should steal the drug, she replies in a way that seems evasive and unsure:

> Well, I don't think so. I think there might be other ways besides stealing it, like if he could borrow the money or make a loan or something, but he really shouldn't steal the drug—but his wife shouldn't die either.

Asked why he should not steal the drug, she considers neither property nor law but rather the effect that theft could have on the relationship between Heinz and his wife:

> If he stole the drug, he might save his wife then, but if he did he might have to go to jail, and then his wife might get sicker again, and he couldn't get more of the drug, and it might not be good. So, they should really just talk it out and find some other way to make the money.

Seeing in the dilemma not a math problem with humans but a narrative of relationships that extends over time, Amy envisions the wife's continuing need for her husband and the husband's continuing concern for his wife and seeks to respond to the druggist's need in a way that would sustain rather than sever connection. Just as she ties the wife's survival to the preservation of relationships, so she considers the value of the wife's life in a context of relationships, saying that it would be wrong to let her die because, "if she died, it hurts a lot of people and it hurts her." Since Amy's moral judgment is grounded in the belief that, "if somebody has something that would keep somebody alive, then it's not right not to give it to them," she considers the problem in the dilemma to arise not from the druggist's assertion of rights but from his failure of response.

As the interviewer proceeds with the series of questions that follow from Kohlberg's construction of the dilemma, Amy's answers remain essentially unchanged, the various probes serving neither to elucidate nor to modify her initial response. Whether or not Heinz loves his wife, he still shouldn't steal or let her die; if it were a stranger dying instead, Amy says that "if the stranger didn't have anybody near or anyone she knew," then Heinz should try to save her life, but he should not steal the drug. But as the interviewer conveys through the repetition of questions that the answers she gave were not heard or not right, Amy's confidence begins to diminish, and her replies become more constrained and unsure. Asked again why Heinz should not steal the drug, she simply repeats, "Because it's not right." Asked again to explain why, she states again that theft would not be a good solution, adding lamely, "if he took it, he might not know how to give it to his wife, and so his wife might still die." Failing to see the dilemma as a self-contained problem in moral logic, she does not discern the internal structure of its resolution; as she constructs the problem differently herself, Kohlberg's conception completely evades her.

Instead, seeing a world comprised of relationships rather than of people standing alone, a world that coheres through human connection rather than through systems of rules, she finds the puzzle in the dilemma to lie in the failure of the druggist to respond to the wife. Saying that "it is not right for someone to die when their life could be saved," she assumes that if the druggist were to see the consequences of his refusal to lower his price, he would realize that "he should just give it to the wife and then have the husband pay back the money later." Thus she considers the solution to the dilemma to lie in making the wife's condition more salient to the druggist or, that failing, in appealing to others who are in a position to help.

Just as Jake is confident the judge would agree that stealing is the right thing for Heinz to do, so Amy is confident that, "if Heinz and the druggest had talked it out long enough, they could reach something besides stealing." As he considers the law to "have mistakes," so she sees this drama as a mistake, believing that "the world should just share things more and then people wouldn't have to steal." Both children thus recognize the need for agreement but see it as mediated in different ways—he impersonally through systems of logic and law, she personally through communication in relationship. Just as he relies on the conventions of logic to deduce the solution to this dilemma, assuming these conventions to be shared, so she relies on a process of communication, assuming connection and believing that her voice will be heard. Yet while his assumptions about agreement are confirmed by the convergence in logic between his answers and the questions posed, her assumptions are belied by the failure of communication, the interviewer's inability to understand her response.

Although the frustration of the interview with Amy is apparent in the repetition of questions and its ultimate circularity, the problem of interpretation is focused by the assessment of her response. When considered in the light of Kohlberg's definition of the stages and sequence of moral development, her moral judgments appear to be a full stage lower in maturity that those of the boy. Scored as a mixture of stages two and three, her reponses seem to reveal a feeling of powerlessness in the world, an inability to think systematically about the concepts of morality or law, a reluctance to challenge authority or to examine the logic of received moral truths, a failure even to conceive of acting directly to save a life or to consider that such action, if taken, could possibly have an effect. As her reliance on relationships seems to reveal a continuing dependence and vulnerability, so her belief in communication as the mode through which to resolve moral dilemmas appears naive and cognitively immature.

Yet Amy's description of herself conveys a markedly different impression. Once again, the hallmarks of the preadolescent child depict a child secure in her sense of herself, confident in the substance of her beliefs, and sure of her ability to do something of value in the world. Describing herself at eleven as "growing and changing," she says that she "sees some things differently now, just because I know myself really well now, and I know a lot more about the world." Yet the world she knows is a different world from that refracted by Kohlberg's construction of Heinz's dilemma. Her world is a world of relationships and psychological truths where an awareness of the connection between people gives rise to a recognition of responsibility for one another, a perception of the need for response. Seen in this light, her understanding of morality as arising from the recognition of relationship, her belief in communication as the mode of conflict resolution, and her conviction that the solution to the dilemma will follow from its compelling representation seem far from naive or cognitively immature. Instead, Amy's judgments contain the insights central to an ethic of care, just as Jake's judgments reflect the logic of the justice approach. Her incipient awareness of the "method of truth," the central tenet of nonviolent conflict resolution, and her belief in the restorative activity of care, lead her to see the actors in the dilemma arrayed not as opponents in a contest of rights but as members of a network of relationships on whose continuation they all depend. Consequently her solution to the dilemma lies in activating the network by communication, securing the inclusion of the wife by strengthening rather than severing connections.

But the different logic of Amy's response calls attention to the interpretation of the interview itself. Conceived as an interrogation, it appears instead as a dialogue, which takes on moral dimensions of its own, pertaining to the interviewer's uses of power and to the manifestations of respect. With this shift in the conception of the interview, it immedi-

ately becomes clear that the interviewer's problem in understanding
Amy's response stems from the fact that Amy is answering a different
question from the one the interviewer thought had been posed. Amy is
considering not *whether* Heinz should act in this situation ("*should*
Heinz steal the drug?") but rather *how* Heinz should act in reponse to his
awareness of his wife's need ("Should Heinz *steal* the drug?"). The
interviewer takes the mode of action for granted, presuming it to be a
matter of fact; Amy assumes the necessity for action and considers what
form it should take. In the interviewer's failure to imagine a response not
dreamt of in Kohlberg's moral philosophy lies the failure to hear Amy's
question and to see the logic in her response, to discern that what
appears, from one perspective, to be an evasion of the dilemma signifies
in other terms a recognition of the problem and a search for a more
adequate solution.

Thus in Heinz's dilemma these two children see two very different
moral problems—Jake a conflict between life and property that can be
resolved by logical deduction, Amy a fracture of human relationship that
must be mended with its own thread. Asking different questions that
arise from different conceptions of the moral domain, the children arrive
at answers that fundamentally diverge, and the arrangement of these
answers as successive stages on a scale of increasing moral maturity
calibrated by the logic of the boy's response misses the different truth
revealed in the judgment of the girl. To the question, "What does he see
that she does not?" Kohlberg's theory provides a ready response, manifest in the scoring of Jake's judgments a full stage higher than Amy's in
moral maturity; to the question, "What does she see that he does not?"
Kohlberg's theory has nothing to say. Since most of her responses fall
through the sieve of Kohlberg's scoring system, her responses appear
from his perspective to live outside the moral domain.

Yet just as Jake reveals a sophisticated understanding of the logic of
justification, so Amy is equally sophisticated in her understanding of the
nature of choice. Recognizing that "if both the roads went in totally
separate ways, if you pick one, you'll never know what would happen if
you went the other way," she explains that "that's the chance you have to
take, and like I said, it's just really a guess." To illustrate her point "in a
simple way," she describes her choice to spend the summer at a camp:

> I will never know what would have happened if I had stayed here, and if
> something goes wrong at camp, I'll never know if I stayed here if it would
> have been better. There's really no way around it because there's no way you
> can do both at once, so you've got to decide, but you'll never know.

In this way, these two eleven-year-old children, both highly intelligent
and perceptive about life, though in different ways, display different
modes of moral understanding, different ways of thinking about conflict

and choice. In resolving Heinz's dilemma, Jake relies on theft to avoid confrontation and turns to the law to mediate the dispute. Transposing a hierarchy of power into a hierarchy of values, he defuses a potentially explosive conflict between people by casting it as an impersonal conflict of claims. In this way, he abstracts the moral problem from the interpersonal situation, finding in the logic of fairness an objective way to decide who will win the dispute. But this hierarchical ordering, with its imagery of winning and losing and the potential for violence which it contains, gives way in Amy's construction of the dilemma to a network of connection, a web of relationships that is sustained by a process of communication. With this shift, the moral problem changes from one of unfair domination, the imposition of property over life, to one of unnecessary exclusion, the failure of the druggist to respond to the wife.

* * *

The contrasting images of hierarchy and network in children's thinking about moral conflict and choice illuminate two views of morality which are complementary rather than sequential or opposed. But this construction of differences goes against the bias of developmental theory toward ordering differences in a hierarchical mode. The correspondence between the order of developmental theory and the structure of the boys' thought contrasts with the disparity between existing theory and the structure manifest in the thought of the girls. Yet in neither comparison does one child's judgment appear as a precursor of the other's position. Thus, questions arise concerning the relation between these perspectives: what is the significance of this difference, and how do these two modes of thinking connect? These questions are elucidated by considering the relationship between the eleven-year-old children's understanding of morality and their descriptions of themselves:

Jake	Amy
(How would you describe yourself to yourself?)	
Perfect. That's my conceited side. What do you want—any way that I choose to describe myself?	You mean my character? (What do you think?) Well, I don't know. I'd describe myself as, well, what do you mean?
(If you had to describe the person you are in a way that you yourself would know it was you, what would you say?)	
I'd start off with eleven years old. Jake [last name]. I'd have to add that I live in [town], because that is a big part of me, and also that my father is a doctor, because I think that does change me a little bit, and that I don't believe in	Well, I'd say that I was someone who likes school and studying, and that's what I want to do with my life. I want to be some kind of a scientist or something, and I want to do things, and I want to help people. And I think that's

Jake (cont.)

crime, except for when your
name is Heinz; that I think school
is boring, because I think that
kind of changes your character a
little bit. I don't sort of know how
to describe myself, because I
don't know how to read my personality. (*If you had to describe
the way you actually would describe yourself, what would you
say?*) I like corny jokes. I don't
really like to get down to work,
but I can do all the stuff in school.
Every single problem that I have
seen in school I have been able to
do, except for ones that take
knowledge, and after I do the
reading, I have been able to do
them, but sometimes I don't want
to waste my time on easy homework. And also I'm crazy about
sports. I think, unlike a lot of
people, that the world still has
hope . . . Most people that I know
I like, and I have the good life,
pretty much as good as any I have
seen, and I am tall for my age.

Amy (cont.)

what kind of person I am, or what
kind of person I try to be. And
that's probably how I'd describe
myself. And I want to do something to help other people. (*Why
is that?*) Well, because I think
that this world has a lot of
problems, and I think that everybody should try to help somebody else in some way, and the
way I'm choosing is through science.

In the voice of the eleven-year-old boy, a familiar form of self-definition appears, resonating to the inscription of the young Stephen Daedalus in his geography book: "himself, his name and where he was," and
echoing the descriptions that appear in *Our Town*, laying out across the
coordinates of time and space a hierarchical order in which to define
one's place.[6] Describing himself as distinct by locating his particular
position in the world, Jake sets himself apart from that world by his
abilities, his beliefs, and his height. Although Amy also enumerates her
likes, her wants, and her beliefs, she locates herself in relation to the
world, describing herself through actions that bring her into connection
with others, elaborating ties through her ability to provide help. To

6. In Thornton Wilder's *Our Town*, the
Stage Manager describes the location of the
town of Grover's Corners, New Hampshire,
as "just across the Massachusetts line: longitude 42 degrees 40 minutes; latitude 70 degrees 37 minutes"; Stephen Daedalus, the
young hero of James Joyce's *Portrait of the
Artist as a Young Man*, defines himself by
location as well.

Jake's ideal of perfection, against which he measures the worth of himself, Amy counterposes an ideal of care, against which she measures the worth of her activity. While she places herself in relation to the world and chooses to help others through science, he places the world in relation to himself as it defines his character, his position, and the quality of his life.

The contrast between a self defined through separation and a self delineated through connection, between a self measured against an abstract ideal of perfection and a self assessed through particular activities of care, becomes clearer and the implications of this contrast extend by considering the different ways these children resolve a conflict between responsibility to others and responsibility to self. The question about responsibility followed a dilemma posed by a woman's conflict between her commitments to work and to family relationships. While the details of this conflict color the text of Amy's response, Jake abstracts the problem of responsibility from the context in which it appears, replacing the themes of intimate relationship with his own imagery of explosive connection:

Jake	Amy

(When responsibility to oneself and responsibility to others conflict how should one choose?)

Jake	Amy
You go about one-fourth to the others and three-fourths to yourself.	Well, it really depends on the situation. If you have a responsibility with somebody else, then you should keep it to a certain extent, but to the extent that it is really going to hurt you or stop you from doing something that you really, really want, then I think maybe you should put yourself first. But if it is your responsibility to somebody really close to you, you've just got to decide in that situation which is more important, yourself or that person, and like I said, it really depends on what kind of person you are and how you feel about the other person or persons involved.

(Why?)

Jake	Amy
Because the most important thing in your decision should be	Well, like some people put themselves and things for themselves

Jake (Cont.)

yourself, don't let yourself be guided totally by other people, but you have to take them into consideration. So, if what you want to do is blow yourself up with an atom bomb, you should maybe blow yourself up with a hand grenade because you are thinking about your neighbors who would die also.

Amy (cont.)

before they put other people, and some people really care about other people. Like, I don't think your job is as important as somebody that you really love, like your husband or your parents or a very close friend. Somebody that you really care for—or if it's just your responsibility to your job or somebody that you barely know, then maybe you go first—but if it's somebody that you really love and love as much or even more than you love yourself, you've got to decide what you really love more, that person, or that thing, or yourself. (*And how do you do that?*) Well, you've got to think about it, and you've got to think about both sides, and you've got to think which would be better for everybody or better for yourself, which is more important, and which will make everybody happier. Like if the other people can get somebody else to do it, whatever it is, or don't really need you specifically, maybe it's better to do what you want, because the other people will be just fine with somebody else so they'll still be happy, and then you'll be happy too because you'll do what you want.

(*What does responsibility mean?*)

It means pretty much thinking of others when I do something, and like if I want to throw a rock, not throwing it at a window, because I thought of the people who would have to pay for that window, not doing it just for youself, because you have to live with

That other people are counting on you to do something, and you can't just decide, "Well, I'd rather do this or that." (*Are there other kinds of responsibility?*) Well, to yourself. If something looks really fun but you might hurt yourself doing it because

Jake (cont.)
other people and live with your community, and if you do something that hurts them all, a lot of people will end up suffering, and that is sort of the wrong thing to do.

Amy (cont.)
you don't really know how to do it and your friends say, "Well, come on, you can do it, don't worry," if you're really scared to do it, it's your responsibility to yourself that if you think you might hurt yourself, you shouldn't do it, because you have to take care of yourself and that's your responsibility to yourself.

Again Jake constructs the dilemma as a mathematical equation, deriving a formula that guides the solution: one-fourth to others, three-fourths to yourself. Beginning with his responsibility to himself, a responsibility that he takes for granted, he then considers the extent to which he is responsible to others as well. Proceeding from a premise of separation but recognizing that "you have to live with other people," he seeks rules to limit interference and thus to minimize hurt. Responsibility in his construction pertains to a limitation of action, a restraint of aggression, guided by the recognition that his actions can have effects on others, just as theirs can interfere with him. Thus rules, by limiting interference, make life in community safe, protecting autonomy through reciprocity, extending the same consideration to others and self.

To the question about conflicting responsibilities, Amy again responds contextually rather than categorically, saying "it depends" and indicating how choice would be affected by variations in character and circumstance. Proceeding from a premise of connection, that "if you have a responsibility *with* somebody else, you should keep it," she then considers the extent to which she has a responsibility to herself. Exploring the parameters of separation, she imagines situations where, by doing what you want, you would avoid hurting yourself or where, in doing so, you would not thereby diminish the happiness of others. To her, responsibility signifies response, an extension rather than a limitation of action. Thus it connotes an act of care rather than the restraint of aggression. Again seeking the solution that would be most inclusive of everyone's needs, she strives to resolve the dilemma in a way that "will make everybody happier." Since Jake is concerned with limiting interference, while Amy focuses on the need for response, for him the limiting condition is, "Don't let yourself be guided totally by others," but for her it arises when "other people are counting on you," in which case "you can't just decide, 'Well, I'd rather do this or that.'" The interplay between these responses is clear in that she, assuming connection, begins to explore the parameters of separation, while he, assuming separation, begins to explore the parameters of connection. But the primacy of separation or connection leads to different images of self and relationships.

Most striking among these differences is the imagery of violence in the boy's response, depicting a world of dangerous confrontation and explosive connection, where she sees a world of care and protection, a life lived with others whom "you may love as much or even more than you love yourself." Since the conception of morality reflects the understanding of social relationships, this difference in the imagery of relationships gives rise to a change in the moral injunction itself. To Jake, responsibility means *not doing* what he wants because he is thinking of others; to Amy, it means *doing* what others are counting on her to do regardless of what she herself wants. Both children are concerned with avoiding hurt but construe the problem in different ways—he seeing hurt to arise from the expression of aggression, she from a failure of response.

If the trajectory of development were drawn through either of these children's responses, it would trace a correspondingly different path. For Jake, development would entail coming to see the other as equal to the self and the discovery that equality provides a way of making connection safe. For Amy, development would follow the inclusion of herself in an expanding network of connection and the discovery that separation can be protective and need not entail isolation. In view of these different paths of development and particularly of the different ways in which the experiences of separation and connection are aligned with the voice of the self, the representation of the boy's development as the single line of adolescent growth for both sexes creates a continual problem when it comes to interpreting the development of the girl.

Since development has been premised on separation and told as a narrative of failed relationships—of pre-Oedipal attachments, Oedipal fantasies,[7] preadolescent chumships, and adolescent loves—relationships that stand out against a background of separation, only successively to erupt and give way to an increasingly emphatic individuation, the development of girls appears problematic because of the continuity of relationships in their lives. Freud attributes the turning inward of girls at puberty to an intensification of primary narcissism, signifying a failure of love of "object" relationships. But if this turning inward is construed against a background of continuing connection, it signals a new responsiveness to the self, and an expansion of care rather than a failure of relationship. * * *

1982

---

7. The fundamental aspect of Freud's theory of psychosexual development, the Oedipus complex, named after the mythical king of Thebes who unknowingly killed his father and married his mother, describes the family triangle of love, jealousy, and fear that is at the root of a child's moral development.

Judith Viorst

GOOD AS GUILT

Without guilt
What is man? An animal, isn't he?
A wolf forgiven at his meat,
A beetle innocent in his copulation.

—Archibald MacLeish

Anything *isn't* possible, the realities of love and our bodies persuade us. We aren't unbounded, and never will be free of the limits imposed upon us by the forbidden and the impossible—including the limits imposed upon us by guilt.

For whether or not we humans are the only creatures capable of guilt, we undoubtedly do it better than beetles or wolves. And although our guilty feelings haven't put an end to the Seven Deadly Sins or persuaded us to obey all Ten Commandments, they have without question slowed us down considerably.

Nevertheless we must recognize that while guilt deprives us of numerous gratifications, we and our world would be monstrous minus guilt. For the freedoms we lose, our constraints and taboos, are necessary losses—part of the price we pay for civilization.

Our guilt becomes our own when, at around the age of five, we begin to develop a superego, a conscience, when the "No, you can'ts" and the "Shame on you's" which used to be outside us regroup as our internal critical voice. Our guilt becomes our own when instead of feeling, "Better not do it; they will not like it," that "they" is no longer our mother and father but—us.

For we do not arrive in this world with a commitment to certain admirable moral precepts. We are not born intending to be good. We want, we want, we want, and only slowly relinquish reaching out and grabbing. But control cannot be called conscience until we are able to take it inside us and make it our own, until—in spite of the fact that the wrongs we have done or imagined will never be punished or known—we nonetheless feel that clutch in the stomach, that chill upon the soul, that self-inflicted misery called guilt.

True guilt, it can be argued, is not the fear of our parents' wrath or the loss of their love. True guilt, it can be argued, is the fear of our conscience's wrath, the loss of *its* love.

501

We resolve our oedipal conflicts by acquiring a conscience which—like our parents—limits and restrains. Our conscience is our parents installed in our mind. Later identifications, with teachers and preachers, with friends, with superstars and heroes, will modify what we value and what we forbid. And the emergence, over the years, of increasingly complex cognitive skills, will ready the ground for more complex moral ideas. Indeed, it is now believed that the stages of our moral reasoning (psychologist Lawrence Kohlberg says there are six) parallel the development of our thinking processes. But although our conscience is based on emotion and thought, and although it evolves and changes over time, and although it is built upon feelings from earlier stages, and although it expands beyond oedipal issues to take in all kinds of conflicts and concerns, this superego, this part of our self that contains our moral restraints and our ideals, is born of our primal struggles with lawless passions, is born of our *inner* submission to human law.

And if we breach those moral restraints or abandon those ideals, our conscience will observe, reproach, condemn.

And if we breach those moral restraints or abandon those ideals, our conscience will arrange to make us feel guilty.

There is, however, good and bad, appropriate and inappropriate guilt. There is deficient guilt and also excessive guilt. A few of us may know people who lack the capacity to have feelings of guilt about anything. But most of us know people (and a number of us *are* people) who are able to muster up guilt about virtually everything.

I am one of those people.

I feel guilty whenever my children are unhappy.

I feel guilty whenever one of my houseplants dies.

I feel guilty whenever I fail to floss after eating.

I feel guilty whenever I tell the whitest of lies.

I feel guilty whenever I step on a bug deliberately—all cockroaches excepted.

I feel guilty whenever I cook with a pat of butter that I have dropped on the kitchen floor.

And because, if there were room, I could easily list several hundred more of such genuinely guilt-provoking items, I would say that I am suffering from an excessive, indiscriminate sense of guilt.

Indiscriminate guilt is also the failure to distinguish between forbidden thoughts and forbidden deeds. Thus wicked wishes equal wicked acts. And although we adults believe that we have long ago learned to tell the two apart, our conscience may cruelly condemn us not just for the murder we carry out but for the murder that we harbor in our heart. And although we very well know that wishing does not make it so, it nevertheless may make us feel very guilty.

This lack of discrimination is one of the ways that we display excessive guilt. Disproportionate punitiveness is another. For guilty acts which require no more than a gentle "I'm sorry," a mental slap on the wrist, may inspire astonishing acts of self-flagellation: "I did it, how could I do it, only a low-down no-good moral monster could do it, and I hereby sentence this criminal—me—to death." This excessive punishing guilt is somewhat like pouring a whole cup of salt on an egg-salad sandwich. No one is disputing that perhaps the sandwich needs salt but—*not that much.*

Another form of excess might be called omnipotent guilt, which rests on the illusion of control—the illusion, for example, that we have absolute power over our loved ones' well-being. And so, if they suffer or fail or fall ill in body or in mind, we have no doubt that we alone are to blame, that had we done it differently, or had we done it better, we surely would have been able to prevent it.

A rabbi, for instance, tells of paying condolence calls—one winter afternoon—on two different families where elderly women had died.

At the first house, the bereaved son told the rabbi: "If only I had sent my mother to Florida and gotten her out of this cold and snow, she would be alive today. It's my fault that she died."

At the second house, the other bereaved son told the rabbi: "If only I hadn't insisted on my mother's going to Florida, she would be alive today. That long airplane ride, the abrupt change of climate, was more than she could take. It's my fault that she's dead."

The point here is this: By blaming ourself, we can believe in our life-controlling powers. By blaming ourself, we are saying that we would rather feel guilty than helpless, than not in control.

Others may have a need to believe that Someone Up There has control, that terrible things do not happen without a cause, that if they are struck by tragedy and devastating loss, they are struck because in some way they deserve it. There are those who cannot accept the thought that suffering is random or that evil men prosper and sorrows befall the good. And so they add to their suffering the conviction that they suffer because they should, that their pain is sufficient proof that they are guilty.

A woman whose child had been desperately ill once described to me an astonishing conversation she'd had with God, a God in whom, by the way, she had most earnestly proclaimed she did not believe. "You ought to be ashamed of yourself. You really should," she reproached Him. "What a bully you turned out to be. If you want to punish a disbeliever, punish the disbeliever—not her child. Stop picking on my daughter! Pick on me!"

Analyst Selma Fraiberg writes that a healthy conscience produces guilt feelings commensurate with the act and that guilt feelings serve to prevent our repeating such acts. "But the neurotic conscience," she writes, "behaves like a gestapo[1] headquarters within the personality, mercilessly tracking down dangerous or potentially dangerous ideas and every remote relative of these ideas, accusing, threatening, tormenting in an interminable inquisition to establish guilt for trivial offenses or crimes committed in dreams. Such guilt feelings have the effect of putting the whole personality under arrest. . . . "

Such feelings are excessive, neurotic guilt.

Neurotic guilt may be fed by the events of pre-oedipal years—by the anxiety and anger evoked by early separations or struggles with parents. Thus, for instance, our conscience may exercise an I-was-left-because-I-was-bad-and-therefore-I-deserve-to-be-punished punitiveness. Or it may harshly condemn the parts of ourself that our parents—whose love we so deeply feared losing—condemned. Or it may carry a great load of anger once directed against our mother and our father and now vigorously redirected against ourself. As one psychoanalyst told me, "I think, in general, that anything that leaves the child on his own to grapple with anxiety and rage will predispose him to play it all out on a repetitive inner stage—to get stuck with inappropriate levels and kinds of guilt as an adult."

Such guilt may make us feel that if we ever kiss a fellow, we'll grow hair on our teeth. And if we ever talk back to our mother, we'll give her a heart attack. And if we decide to do what we are desperately longing to do— and it is wonderful—we shouldn't be doing it.

And sometimes, alas, like Dr. Spielvogel's frantic, fictional patient Alexander Portnoy[2]—we *cannot* do it:

> Can't smoke, hardly drink, no drugs, don't borrow money or play cards, can't tell a lie without beginning to sweat as though I'm passing over the equator. Sure, I say *fuck* a lot, but I assure you, that's about the sum of my success with transgressing. . . . Why is a little turbulence so beyond my means? Why must the least deviation from respectable conventions cause me such inner hell? When I *hate* those fucking conventions? When I know *better* than the taboos! Doctor, my doctor, what do you say, LET'S PUT THE ID BACK IN YID! Liberate this nice Jewish boy's libido, will you please? Raise the prices if you have to—I'll pay anything! Only enough cowering in the face of the deep, dark pleasures!

Not everyone is as acutely aware as Portnoy, or his creator, Philip Roth, of the moral inhibitions with which we live. We may consciously feel we are freer than we are. For an important aspect of guilt is that it frequently works upon us without our knowing about it, that we can suffer the consequences of unconscious guilt.

Now we know what our conscious guilt feels like—we know the

1. Secret state police from 1933 of the Nazi regime in Germany.

2. Protagonist of Philip Roth's novel *Portnoy's Complaint*.

tension and the distress—but our unconscious guilt can only be known indirectly. And among the signs that may attest to the presence of unconscious guilt is a powerful need to injure ourself, a persistent need to get or to give ourself punishment.

Criminals leaving self-damaging clues (including Nixon, perhaps, and his Watergate tapes) are very often impelled by unconscious guilt. And so is the husband who, having spent the afternoon with a friend, comes home with her watch in the pocket of his shirt. And so is Dick who, having had a bitter fight with his father, smashes up his Chevy and gets himself hurt. And so is Rita who, watching her boss raise hell with his secretary, fleetingly thinks, "I'm glad it's her, not me"—and then promptly pays for her thought by accidentally spilling hot tea all over her lap.

And so are these erstwhile lovers, Ellie and Marvin.

> Ellie and Marvin
> Have been having secret meetings twice a week
> For the past six months
> But have thus far failed to consummate
> Their passion
> Because
> While both of them agree
> That marital fidelity
> Is not only unrealistic but also
> Irrelevant,
> She has developed migraines, and
> He has developed these sharp shooting pains
> In his chest, and
> She's got impetigo, and
> He's got pinkeye.

> Ellie and Marvin
> Drive forty miles to sneaky luncheonettes
> In separate cars
> But have thus far done no more than
> Heavy necking
> Because
> While both of them agree
> That sexual exclusivity
> Is not only adolescent but also
> Retrograde,
> She has developed colitis, and
> He has developed these dull throbbing pains
> In his back, and
> She's started biting her nails, and
> He's smoking again.

Ellie and Marvin
Yearn to have some love in the afternoon
At a motor hotel
But have thus far only had a lot of
Coffee
Because
He is convinced that his phone is being tapped, and
She is convinced that a man in a trench coat is following her, and
He says what if the motor hotel catches fire, and
She says what if she talks some night in her sleep, and
She thinks her husband is acting suspiciously hostile, and
He thinks his wife is acting suspiciously nice, and
He keeps cutting his face with his double-edge razor, and
She keeps closing her hand in the door of her car, so
While both of them agree
That guilt is not only neurotic but also
Obsolete,
They've also agreed
To give up
Secret meetings.

Unconscious guilt, however, may extract much higher prices than colitis, migraines, backaches or mild paranoia. It may insist on a lifetime of penance and pain. And this guilt may derive from any act or omission, from any thought, that our conscience in its infinite wisdom deems wicked. Thus our mother's ill health, our parents' divorce, our secret envies and hates, our solitary sexual gratifications—any and all can become our blame and our shame. And if the new brother or sister we didn't want and wish wish wish would disappear does in fact—by illness or accident—die, we may hold ourself responsible, we—not knowing we think it—might think: "Why did I kill him? Why didn't I save him? Why?"

And our lives may crash on the rocks of our unconscious guilt.

It was Freud who first observed that analysts sometimes work with patients who ferociously resist relief from their symptoms, who seem to hold on for dear life to emotional pain, and who cling to this pain because it gives them the punishment that they don't even know they want for crimes they don't even know that they have committed. He notes ruefully, however, that a neurosis which has defied an analyst's best efforts may suddenly vanish if the patient gets into an unhappy marriage, loses all his money or becomes dangerously ill. "In such instances," writes Freud, "one form of suffering has been replaced by another; and we see that all that mattered was that it should be possible to maintain a certain amount of suffering."

But sometimes people are guilty and people should suffer, including people like you and people like me. Sometimes guilt is appropriate and good. Not all guilt is neurotic—to be cured, to be analyzed away. We would be moral monsters if it could. But some of us exhibit certain deficiencies in our capacity for guilt.

I have a friend named Elizabeth who cannot acknowledge guilt because, in her mind, the guilty are shot at dawn. She has to be perfect, sinless, error-free. And so she will say, "The car was smacked up," because she would choke on the words "I smacked up the car." And she also will say, "His feelings got hurt," because she cannot accept that she hurt his feelings. At best she can say, "We forgot to buy tickets and now they're all sold out," when she was the only "we" in charge of tickets. And as for certain more drastic acts—she once had a love affair with her husband's best friend—she managed to persuade both herself and her husband that she was guiltless because he had driven her to it!

Elizabeth is quite capable of telling right from wrong. She is, however, incapable of believing that she could experience guilt—and survive.

Another kind of deficient guilt is displayed by people who punish themselves after they have committed some dreadful act, but who then go on to commit these dreadful acts again and again, again and again. For although their conscience acknowledges that what they did was wrong, and exacts quite brutal payments for their sins, their guilt never functions for them as a warning signal. It serves them only to punish, not to prevent.

It is known that certain criminals are actually seeking punishment in order to expiate unconscious guilt. It is known that certain criminals are suffering from distorted, not absent, guilt feelings. There are, however, the so-called psychopathic personalities who seem to display a genuine lack of guilt, whose antisocial and criminal acts, whose repetitive acts of destructiveness and depravity, occur with no restraint and no remorse. These psychopaths cheat and rob and lie and damage and destroy with remarkable emotional impunity. These psychopaths spell out for us, in letters ten feet high, what kind of world this world would be without guilt.

But we don't have to be a psychopath to allow some person or group to stand in the place of our individual conscience. And yet this too can lead to deficient guilt. For when we relinquish to others our sense of moral responsibility, we may become free of central moral constraints. This giving over of conscience can turn ordinary people into lynch mobs and operators of crematoria. And it may enable any of us to act in certain ways which on our own we would surely regard as unthinkable.

In a famous experiment testing conscience versus obedience to authority, experimental psychologist Stanley Milgram brought people into a Yale University psychology laboratory to engage—or so they were told—in a study of memory and learning. The experimenter explained that the issue to be explored was the impact of punishment on learning, and to that end the subject designated "teacher" was asked to administer a learning test to a "learner" strapped in a chair in another room—and to give him an electric shock whenever his answer was wrong. The shocks were executed by a series of thirty switches which ranged from slight (15 volts) to severe (450 volts), and the teacher was told that, with each wrong answer, he was to give the learner the next higher shock. Conflict began when the learner went from grunts to vehement protests to agonized screams, and the teacher became increasingly uneasy and wished to stop. But each time he hesitated, the person in authority urged him to continue, insisting that he must complete the experiment. And despite the concern for the level of shocking pain that was being inflicted, a large number of teachers continued to push the switches all the way up to the highest voltage.

The teachers did not know that the learners were actors, and that they were only simulating distress. The teachers believed that the shocks were painfully real. But some of them persuaded themselves that what they were doing was for a noble cause—the pursuit of truth. And some of them persuaded themselves that "He was so stupid and stubborn he deserved to get shocked." And some of them were simply unable, despite their conviction that what they were doing was wrong, to make an open break with the person running the experiment—to challenge authority.

Milgram notes that a "commonly offered explanation is that those who shocked the victim at the most severe level were monsters, the sadistic fringe of society. But if one considers that almost two-thirds of the participants fall into the category of 'obedient' subjects and that they represented ordinary people drawn from working, managerial and professional classes, the argument becomes very shaky."

It is tempting to read about that experiment and imagine ourselves walking out the door, able to know right from wrong and to act on that knowledge. It is tempting to think that our conscience would prevail. It is tempting to think that put to the test, we would be counted among the morally pure. And some of us would be. And some of us would fail. But all of us, in the course of our life, will engage in acts we know to be morally wrong. And when we do, the healthy response is guilt.

Healthy guilt is appropriate—in quantity and quality—to the deed. Healthy guilt leads to remorse but not self-hate. Healthy guilt discourages us from repeating our guilty act without shutting down a wide range of our passions and pleasures.

We need to be able to know when what we are doing is morally wrong.

We need to be able to know and acknowledge our guilt.

The philosopher Martin Buber, respectful of this need, tells us that "there exists real guilt," that there is value in the "paining and admonishing heart" and that reparation, reconciliation, renewal require a conscience "that does not shy away from the glance into the depths and that already in admonishing envisages the way that leads across it. . . .

"Man," says Buber, "is the being who is capable of becoming guilty and is capable of illuminating his guilt."

We seem to be more familiar with the prohibiting parts of our conscience, the parts that limit our pleasures and water our joys, the parts that are always watching us to judge, condemn and mobilize our guilt. But our conscience also contains our ego ideal—our values and higher aspirations, the parts that speak to our "oughts" instead of our "don'ts." And another task of our conscience is to say in effect, "Good for you" and "You did well," to encourage us and approve of us and praise and reward and love us for meeting, or striving to meet, this ego ideal.

Our ego ideal is composed of our most wishful, hopeful visions of our self. Our ego ideal is composed of our noblest goals. And while it is an impossible dream that can never be fulfilled, our reachings toward it provide a deep sense of well-being. Our ego ideal is precious to us because it repairs a loss of our earlier childhood, the loss of our image of self as perfect and whole, the loss of a major portion of our infantile, limitless, ain't-I-wonderful narcissism which we had to give up in the face of compelling reality. Modified and reshaped into ethical goals and moral standards and a vision of what at our finest we might be, our dream of perfection lives on—our lost narcissism lives on—in our ego ideal.

It is true that we will feel guilt when we fall short of our ego ideal or when we override our moral restraints. It is true that guilt will make us less happy, less free. If we could believe in "anything goes," we could go merrily—guiltlessly—on our way. But without ideals and restraints, what would we be? A wolf forgiven at his meat. A beetle innocent in his copulation. Something beyond the bounds of humanity.

We cannot be full human beings without the loss of some of our anything-goes moral freedom.

We cannot be full human beings without acquiring a capacity for guilt.

1986

THE READER

1. Viorst describes what she calls a tempting way to react to accounts of the Milgram experiment (p. 508). Do you react that way? She follows that with a "But . . ." sentence. What were the signals that such a sentence was coming? Is it logically satisfying?
2. Are there any signs in Viorst's essay that she is a psychoanalyst?

THE WRITER

1. What is Viorst's basic point? How is it served by her initial stress on guilt that is excessive?

2. Write a paragraph on guilt from another professional or personal point of view—for example, a coach, a policeman, a student.

Desmond Morris

TERRITORIAL BEHAVIOR

A territory is a defended space. In the broadest sense, there are three kinds of human territory: tribal, family and personal.

It is rare for people to be driven to physical fighting in defense of these "owned" spaces, but fight they will, if pushed to the limit. The invading army encroaching on national territory, the gang moving into a rival district, the trespasser climbing into an orchard, the burglar breaking into a house, the bully pushing to the front of a queue, the driver trying to steal a parking space, all of these intruders are liable to be met with resistance varying from the vigorous to the savagely violent. Even if the law is on the side of the intruder, the urge to protect a territory may be so strong that otherwise peaceful citizens abandon all their usual controls and inhibitions. Attempts to evict families from their homes, no matter how socially valid the reasons, can lead to siege conditions reminiscent of the defense of a medieval fortress.

The fact that these upheavals are so rare is a measure of the success of Territorial Signals as a sytem of dispute prevention. It is sometimes cynically stated that "all property is theft," but in reality it is the opposite. Property, as owned space which is *displayed* as owned space, is a special kind of sharing system which reduces fighting much more than it causes it. Man is a co-operative species, but he is also competitive, and his struggle for dominance has to be structured in some way if chaos is to be avoided. The establishment of territorial rights is one such structure. It limits dominance geographically. I am dominant in my territory and you are dominant in yours. In other words, dominance is shared out spatially, and we all have some. Even if I am weak and unintelligent and you can dominate me when we meet on neutral ground, I can still enjoy a thoroughly dominant role as soon as I retreat to my private base. Be it ever so humble, there is no place like a home territory.

Of course, I can still be intimidated by a particularly dominant individual who enters my home base, but his encroachment will be dangerous for him and he will think twice about it, because he will know that here my urge to resist will be dramatically magnified and my usual subservience banished. Insulted at the heart of my own territory, I may easily explode into battle—either symbolic or real—with a result that may be damaging to both of us.

In order for this to work, each territory has to be plainly advertised as such. Just as a dog cocks its leg to deposit its personal scent on the trees in its locality, so the human animal cocks its leg symbolically all over his home base. But because we are predominantly visual animals we employ mostly visual signals, and it is worth asking how we do this at the three levels: tribal, family, and personal.

First: the Tribal Territory. We evolved as tribal animals, living in comparatively small groups, probably of less than a hundred, and we existed like that for millions of years. It is our basic social unit, a group in which everyone knows everyone else. Essentially, the tribal territory consisted of a home base surrounded by extended hunting grounds. Any neighboring tribe intruding on our social space would be repelled and driven away. As these early tribes swelled into agricultural supertribes, and eventually into industrial nations, their territorial defense systems became increasingly elaborate. The tiny, ancient home base of the hunting tribe became the great capital city, the primitive warpaint became the flags, emblems, uniforms, and regalia of the specialized military, and the war-chants became national anthems, marching songs, and bugle calls. Territorial boundary-lines hardened into fixed borders, often conspicuously patrolled and punctuated with defensive structures—forts and lookout posts, checkpoints and great walls, and, today, customs barriers.

Today each nation flies its own flag, a symbolic embodiment of its territorial status. But patriotism is not enough. The ancient tribal hunter lurking inside each citizen finds himself unsatisfied by membership in such a vast conglomeration of individuals, most of whom are totally unknown to him personally. He does his best to feel that he shares a common territorial defense with them all, but the scale of the operation has become inhuman. It is hard to feel a sense of belonging with a tribe of fifty million or more. His answer is to form sub-groups, nearer to his ancient pattern, smaller, and more personally known to him—the local club, the teenage gang, the union, the specialist society, the sports association, the political party, the college fraternity, the social clique, the protest group, and the rest. Rare indeed is the individual who does not belong to at least one of these splinter groups, and take from it a sense of tribal allegiance and brotherhood. Typical of all these groups is the development of Territorial Signals—badges, costumes, headquarters, banners, slogans, and all the other displays of group identity. This is where the action is, in terms of tribal territorialism, and only when a major war breaks out does the emphasis shift upwards to the higher group level of the nations.

Each of these modern pseudo-tribes sets up its own special kind of home base. In extreme cases non-members are totally excluded, in others they are allowed in as visitors with limited rights and under a control system of special rules. In many ways they are like miniature nations, with their own flags and emblems and their own border guards. The exclusive club has its own "customs barrier": the doorman who checks your "passport" (your membership card) and prevents strangers from passing in unchallenged. There is a government: the club committee; and often special displays of the tribal elders: the photographs or portraits of previous officials on the walls. At the heart of the specialized territories there is a powerful feeling of security and importance, a sense of shared defense against the outside world. Much of the club chatter, both serious and joking, directs itself against the rottenness of everything outside the club boundaries—in that "other world" beyond the protected portals.

In social organizations which embody a strong class system, such as military units and large business concerns, there are many territorial rules, often unspoken, which interfere with the official hierarchy. High-status individuals, such as officers or managers, could in theory enter any of the regions occupied by the lower levels in the peck order, but they limit this power in a striking way. An officer seldom enters a sergeant's mess or a barrack room unless it is for a formal inspection. He respects those regions as alien territories even though he has the power to go there by virtue of his dominant role. And in businesses, part of the appeal of unions, over and above their obvious functions, is that with their officials, headquarters, and meetings they add a sense of territorial power for the staff workers. It is almost as if each military organization and business concern consists of two warring tribes: the officers versus the other ranks, and the management versus the workers. Each has its special home base within the system, and the territorial defense pattern thrusts itself into what, on the surface, is a pure social hierarchy. Negotiations between managements and unions are tribal battles fought out over the neutral ground of a boardroom table, and are as much concerned with territorial display as they are with resolving problems of wages and conditions. Indeed, if one side gives in too quickly and accepts the other's demands, the victors feel strangely cheated and deeply suspicious that it may be a trick. What they are missing is the protracted sequence of ritual and counter-ritual that keeps alive their group territorial identity.

Likewise, many of the hostile displays of sports fans and teenage gangs are primarily concerned with displaying their group image to rival fan-clubs and gangs. Except in rare cases, they do not attack one another's headquarters, drive out the occupants, and reduce them to a submissive, subordinate condition. It is enough to have scuffles on the borderlands between the two rival territories. This is particularly clear at football matches, where the fan-club headquarters becomes temporarily shifted from the club-house to a section of the stands, and where minor fighting breaks out at the unofficial boundary line between the massed groups of rival supporters. Newspaper reports play up the few accidents and injuries which do occur on such occasions, but when these are studied in relation to the total numbers of displaying fans involved it is clear that the serious incidents represent only a tiny fraction of the overall group behavior. For every actual punch or kick there are a thousand war-cries, war dances, chants, and gestures.

Second: the Family Territory. Essentially, the family is a breeding unit and the family territory is a breeding ground. At the center of this space, there is the nest—the bedroom—where, tucked up in bed, we feel at our most territorially secure. In a typical house the bedroom is upstairs, where a safe nest should be. This puts it farther away from the entrance hall, the area where contact is made, intermittently, with the outside world. The less private reception rooms, where intruders are allowed access, are the next line of defense. Beyond them, outside the walls of the building, there is often a symbolic remnant of the ancient feeding grounds—a garden. Its symbolism often extends to the plants and animals it contains, which cease to be nutritional and become merely decorative—flowers and pets. But like a true territorial space it has a conspicuously displayed boundary-line, the garden fence, wall, or railings. Often no more than a token barrier, this is the outer territorial demarcation, separating the private world for the family from the public world beyond. To cross it puts any visitor or intruder at an immediate disadvantage. As he crosses the threshold, his dominance wanes, slightly but unmistakably. He is entering an area where he senses that he must ask permission to do simple things that he would consider a right elsewhere. Without lifting a finger, the territorial owners exert their dominance. This is done by all the hundreds of small ownership "markers" they have deposited on their family territory: the ornaments, the "possessed" objects positioned in the rooms and on the walls; the furnishings, the furniture, the colors, the patterns, all owner-chosen and all making this particular home base unique to them.

It is one of the tragedies of modern architecture that there has been a standardization of these vital territorial living units. One of the most important aspects of a home is that it should be similar to other homes only in a general way, and that in detail it should have many differences, making it a *particular* home. Unfortunately, it is cheaper to build a row of houses, or a block of flats, so that all the family living-units are identical, but the territorial urge rebels against this trend and house-owners struggle as best they can to make their mark on their mass-produced properties. They do this with garden-design, with front-door colors, with curtain patterns, with wallpaper and all the other decorative elements that together create a unique and different family environment. Only when they have completed this nest-building do they feel truly "at home" and secure.

When they venture forth as a family unit they repeat the process in a minor way. On a day-trip to the seaside, they load the car with personal belongings and it becomes their temporary, portable territory. Arriving at the beach they stake out a small territorial claim, marking it with rugs, towels, baskets, and other belongings to which they can return from their seaboard wanderings. Even if they all leave it at once to bathe, it retains a characteristic territorial quality and other family groups arriving will recognize this by setting up their own "home" bases at a respectful distance. Only when the whole beach has filled up with these marked spaces will newcomers start to position themselves in such a way that the inter-base distance becomes reduced. Forced to pitch between several existing beach territories they will feel a momentary sensation of intrusion, and the established "owners" will feel a similar sensation of invasion, even though they are not being directly inconvenienced.

The same territorial scene is being played out in parks and fields and on riverbanks, wherever family groups gather in their clustered units. But if rivalry for spaces creates mild feelings of hostility, it is true to say that, without the territorial system of sharing and space-limited dominance, there would be chaotic disorder.

Third: the Personal Space. If a man enters a waiting-room and sits at one end of a long row of empty chairs, it is possible to predict where the next man to enter will seat himself. He will not sit next to the first man, nor will he sit at the far end, right away from him. He will choose a position about halfway between these two points. The next man to enter will take the largest gap left, and sit roughly in the middle of that, and so on, until eventually the latest newcomer will be forced to select a seat that places him right next to one of the already seated men. Similar patterns can be observed in cinemas, public urinals, airplanes, trains, and buses. This is a reflection of the fact that we all carry with us, everywhere we go, a portable territory called a Personal Space. If people move inside this space, we feel threatened. If they keep too far outside it, we feel rejected. The result is a subtle series of spatial adjustments, usually operating quite unconsciously and producing ideal compromises as far as this is possible. If a situation becomes too crowded, then we adjust our reactions accordingly and allow our personal space to shrink. Jammed into an elevator, a rush-hour compartment, or a packed room, we give up altogether and allow body-to-body contact, but when we relinquish our Personal Space in this way, we adopt certain special techniques. In essence, what we do is to convert these other bodies into "nonpersons." We studiously ignore them, and they us. We try not to face them if we can possibly avoid it. We wipe all expressiveness from our faces, letting them go blank. We may look up at the ceiling or down at the floor, and we reduce body movements to a minimum. Packed together like sardines in a tin, we stand dumbly still, sending out as few social signals as possible.

Even if the crowding is less severe, we still tend to cut down our social interactions in the presence of large numbers. Careful observations of children in play groups revealed that if they are high-density groupings there is less social interaction between the individual children, even though there is theoretically more opportunity for such contacts. At the same time, the high-density groups show a higher frequency of aggressive and destructive behavior patterns in their play. Personal Space— "elbow room"—is a vital commodity for the human animal, and one that cannot be ignored without risking serious trouble.

Of course, we all enjoy the excitement of being in a crowd, and this reaction cannot be ignored. But there are crowds and crowds. It is pleasant enough to be in a "spectator crowd," but not so appealing to find yourself in the middle of a rush-hour crush. The difference between the two is that the spectator crowd is all facing in the same direction and concentrating on a distant point of interest. Attending a theater, there are twinges of rising hostility toward the stranger who sits down immediately in front of you or the one who squeezes into the seat next to you. The shared armrest can become a polite, but distinct, territorial boundary-dispute region. However, as soon as the show begins, these invasions of Personal Space are forgotten and the attention is focused beyond the small space where the crowding is taking place. Now, each member of the audience feels himself spatially related, not to his cramped neighbors, but to the actor on the stage, and this distance is, if anything, too great. In the rush-hour crowd, by contrast, each member of the pushing throng is competing with his neighbors all the time. There is no escape to a spatial relation with a distant actor, only the pushing, shoving bodies all around.

Those of us who have to spend a great deal of time in crowded conditions become gradually better able to adjust, but no one can ever become completely immune to invasions of Personal Space. This is because they remain forever associated with either powerful hostile or equally powerful loving feelings. All through our childhood we will have been held to be loved and held to be hurt, and anyone who invades our Personal Space when we are adults is, in effect, threatening to extend his behavior into one of these two highly charged areas of human interaction. Even if his motives are clearly neither hostile nor sexual, we still find it hard to suppress our reactions to his close approach. Unfortunately, different countries have different ideas about exactly how close is close. It is easy enough to test your own "space reaction": when you are talking to someone in the street or in any open space, reach out with your arm and see where the nearest point on his body comes. If you hail from western Europe, you will find that he is at roughly fingertip distance from you. In other words, as you reach out, your fingertips will just about make contact with his shoulder. If you come from eastern Europe you will find you are standing at "wrist distance." If you come from the Mediterranean region you will find that you are much closer to your companion, at little more than "elbow distance."

Trouble begins when a member of one of these cultures meets and talks to one from another. Say a British diplomat meets an Italian or an Arab diplomat at an embassy function. They start talking in a friendly way, but soon the fingertips man begins to feel uneasy. Without knowing quite why, he starts to back away gently from his companion. The companion edges forward again. Each tries in his way to set up a Personal Space relationship that suits his own background. But it is impossible to do. Every time the Mediterranean diplomat advances to a distance that feels comfortable for him, the British diplomat feels threatened. Every time the Briton moves back, the other feels rejected. Attempts to adjust this situation often lead to a talking pair shifting slowly across a room, and many an embassy reception is dotted with western-European fingertip-distance men pinned against the walls by eager elbow-distance men. Until such differences are fully understood and allowances made, these minor differences in "body territories" will continue to act as an alienation factor which may interfere in a subtle way with diplomatic harmony and other forms of international transaction.

If there are distance problems when engaged in conversation, then there are clearly going to be even bigger difficulties where people must work privately in a shared space. Close proximity of others, pressing against the invisible boundaries of our personal body-territory, makes it difficult to concentrate on nonsocial matters. Flat-mates, students sharing a study, sailors in the cramped quarters of a ship, and office staff in crowded work-places, all have to face this problem. They solve it by "cocooning." They use a variety of devices to shut themselves off from the others present. The best possible cocoon, of course, is a small private room—a den, a private office, a study, or a studio—which physically obscures the presence of other nearby territory-owners. This is the ideal situation for non-social work, but the space-sharers cannot enjoy this luxury. Their cocooning must be symbolic. They may, in certain cases, be able to erect small physical barriers, such as screens and partitions, which give substance to their invisible Personal Space boundaries, but when this cannot be done, other means must be sought. One of these is the "favored object." Each space-sharer develops a preference, repeatedly expressed until it becomes a fixed pattern, for a particular chair, or table, or alcove. Others come to respect this, and friction is reduced. This sytem is often formally arranged (this is my desk, that is yours), but even where it is not, favored places soon develop. Professor Smith has a favorite chair in the library. It is not formally his, but he always uses it and others avoid it. Seats around a mess-room table, or a boardroom table, become almost personal property for specific individuals. Even in the home, father has his favorite chair for reading the newspaper or watching television. Another device is the blinkers-posture. Just as a horse that over-reacts to other horses and the distractions of the noisy race-course is given a pair of blinkers to shield its eyes, so people studying privately in a public place put on pseudo-blinkers in the form of shielding hands. Resting their elbows on the table, they sit with their hands screening their eyes from the scene on either side.

A third method of reinforcing the body-territory is to use personal markers. Books, papers, and other personal belongings are scattered around the favored site to render it more privately owned in the eyes of companions. Spreading out one's belongings is a well-known trick in public-transport situations, where a traveler tries to give the impression that seats next to him are taken. In many contexts carefully arranged personal markers can act as an effective territorial display, even in the absence of the territory owner. Experiments in a library revealed that placing a pile of magazines on the table in one seating position success-fully reserved that place for an average of 77 minutes. If a sports-jacket was added, draped over the chair, then the "reservation effect" lasted for over two hours.

In these ways, we strengthen the defenses of our Personal Spaces, keeping out intruders with the minimum of open hostility. As with all territorial behavior, the object is to defend space with signals rather than with fists and at all three levels—the tribal, the family, and the personal —it is a remarkably efficient system of space-sharing. It does not always seem so, because newspapers and newscasts inevitably magnify the ex-ceptions and dwell on those cases where the signals have failed and wars have broken out, gangs have fought, neighboring families have feuded, or colleagues have clashed, but for every territorial signal that has failed, there are millions of others that have not. They do not rate a mention in the news, but they nevertheless constitute a dominant feature of human society—the society of a remarkably territorial animal.

1977

THE READER

1. *Morris predicts people's behavior when they are selecting seats (p. 514). Does observation confirm his prediction? Does the balancing of threat and rejection seem like a good explanation?*
2. *Is racism territorial?*
3. *Although he clearly recognizes that territorial behavior can lead to trouble, Morris speaks approvingly of it as "a remarkably efficient system of space-sharing." If you wanted to challenge his argument, where would you start—his definitions, his evidence, his conclusions?*

THE WRITER

1. *The essay is obviously organized to discuss territorial behavior on*

Barbara Garson

WHISTLE WHILE YOU WORK

At the Bumble Bee seafood plant in Oregon I talked to a tuna cleaner named Starlein. Her job was to pull the veins of dark meat (cat food) from the skinned white loins of tuna.

"The loins come past me on a moving belt," she explained. "I put the clean loins on the second belt and the cat food on the third belt and I save my bones." [The supervisor later checked her output by counting the bones.]

Do you talk a lot to the other women?" I asked.

"Not really," she answered.

"What do you do all day?"

"I daydream."

"What do you daydream about?"

"About sex."

At this point her boyfriend apologized proudly. "I guess that's my fault," he grinned.

"No it's not you," she said. "It's the tuna fish."

I wondered what she meant.

"Well first it's the smell. You've got that certain smell in your nose all day.... It's not like out here. [Starlein and I and the boyfriend were talking in the smelly cannery yard.] Your own fish next to you is sweet.... But it's mostly *handling* the loins. Not the touch itself, because we wear gloves. But the soft colors. The reds, the whites, and the purples. The most exciting thing is the dark meat. It comes in streaks. It's red-brown and you have to pull it out with your knife. You pile it next to your loin and it's crumbly and dark red and moist like earth.

"You're supposed to put the cat food on the belt as you finish each loin. But I hold it to make as big a pile of dark meat as I can."

Starlein was new at the cannery then. The next time I met her the tuna cleaning process had lost some of its sensual allure.

"I still try to see how much cat food I can collect but it's just for the size of the pile now."

At a Ping-Pong factory in Rhode Island I talked to a girl whose job was to stack Ping-Pong paddles into piles of fifty.

"Maybe it wouldn't have been so bad if I could have seen all the piles I stacked at the end of the day. But they were taking them down as fast as I was piling them up. That was the worst part of the job."

At the same Ping-Pong plant a Haitian box assembler amused himself by doing the job with his eyes closed. He was very proud of the fact that if the foreman passed behind him he could not tell the difference.

Many assembly-line workers deliberately slow their pace from time to time and watch the pieces pile up. Sometimes this is for revenge against the company that "treats us like machines," "uses us like tools." More often it's just for a break, a chance to talk, kid around, take a drink of water. But the most common motive is one that I hadn't expected.

Young workers like to let the work pile up just so they can race to catch up with the line. This creates a few minutes of seemingly purposeful exertion. It makes hills and troughs, minor goals and fulfillments while you're waiting for the day to end or the line to break down.

I have spent the last two years examining the way people cope with routine and monotonous work. I expected to find resentment, and I found it. I expected to find boredom, and I found it. I expected to find sabotage, and I found it in clever forms that I could never have imagined.

But the most dramatic thing I found was quite the opposite of nonco-operation. *People passionately want to work.*

Whatever creativity goes into sabotage, a more amazing ingenuity goes into manufacturing goals and satisfactions on jobs where measurable achievement has been all but rationalized out. Somehow in an unending flow of parts or papers, with operations subdivided beyond any recognizable unit of accomplishment, people still find ways to define certain stacks of work as "theirs," certain piles as "today's" and "tomorrow's."

Almost everyone wants to feel she is getting something accomplished —to see that stack of paddles, the growing pile of dark meat, or to master the job blindfolded since there's not much to master the other way.

Which is not to say that workers don't also resent and resist the subdivision and trivialization of their jobs.

At the Fair Plan Insurance Company a young clerk named Ellen told me about a not quite so co-operative game.

"The other day when I was proofreading endorsements I noticed some guy had insured his store for $165,000 against vandalism and $5,000 against fire. Now that's bound to be a mistake. They probably got it backwards.

"I was just about to show it to Gloria [the supervisor] when I figured, 'Wait a minute! I'm not supposed to read these forms. I'm just supposed to check one column against another. And they do check. So it couldn't be counted as my error.'

"Then I thought about this poor guy when his store burns down and they tell him he's only covered for $5,000. But I figured the hell with it. It'll get straightened out one way or another."

I must have looked disapproving at that moment.

"Listen," she apologized, "for all I know he took out the insurance just to burn down the store himself." Then growing angry: "Goddamn it! They don't explain this stuff to me. I'm not supposed to understand it. I'm supposed to check one column against the other.

"If they're gonna give me a robot's job to do, I'm gonna do it like a robot."

I met a few more people who played that passive resistance game— "gonna be as dumb as they think I am." But not too many. And as a matter of fact, when I questioned further it turned out that Ellen had reported the error after all. For most people it is hard and uncomfortable to do a bad job.

At Lordstown, Ohio, General Motors runs the fastest assembly line in the world, manned by a work force whose average age is twenty-four. At 101 cars an hour, each young worker has thirty-six seconds to perform his assigned snaps, knocks, twists, or squirts on each passing vehicle.

I visited Lordstown the week before a strike amid union charges of speed-up, company charges of sabotage, and a great deal of national publicity about "the new worker," "the changing work ethic."

While a young Vega worker and his friends argued in the living room about the strike and disciplinary layoffs, I talked to his mother in the kitchen. Someone in the supermarket where she works had said that those young kids were "just lazy."

"One thing, Tony is not lazy. He'll take your car apart and put it together any day. . . . the slightest knock and he takes care of it. And he never will leave it half done. He even cleans up after himself.

"And I'm not lazy either. I love to cook. But supposing they gave me a job just cracking eggs with bowls moving past on a line. Pretty soon I'd get to a point where I'd wish the next egg was rotten just to spoil their whole cake."

Occasionally Lordstown workers toss in a rotten egg of their own by dropping an ignition key down the gas tank, lighting a work glove, locking it in the trunk, and waiting to see how far down the line it will be stopped, or just scratching a car as it goes past because you can't keep up with the pace.

But sabotage, though much publicized, is really quite limited. Much of the ingenuity at Lordstown goes into creating escape devices and games that can be squeezed into the thirty-six-second cycle.

No ingenuity at all goes into building cars.

I wasn't particularly surprised by the negative things I saw in factories: speed, heat, humiliation, monotony. I'm sure the reader will have guessed that I began this research prepared to expose and denounce "the system."

It was the positive things I saw that touched me the most. Not that people are beaten down (which they are) but that they almost always pop up. Not that people are bored (which they are) but the ways they find to make it interesting. Not that people hate their work (which they do) but that even so, they try to make something out of it.

In factories and offices around this country work is systematically reduced to the most minute and repetitious tasks. Supervision ranges from counting bones, raising hands to use the bathroom, issuing "report cards" with number and letter grades for quantity, quality, co-operation, dependability, attendance, etc.

Through all this workers make a constant effort, sometimes creative, sometimes pathetic, sometimes violent, to put meaning and dignity back into their daily acitivity.

I realize now, much more deeply than ever, that work is a human need following right after the need for food and the need for love.

The crime of modern industry is not forcing us to work, but denying us real work. For no matter what tricks people play on themselves to make the day's work meaningful, management seems determined to remind them, "You are just tools for our use."

* * *

1975

Robert Finch

VERY LIKE A WHALE

One day last week at sunset I went back to Corporation Beach in Dennis[1] to see what traces, if any, might be left of the great, dead finback whale that had washed up there several weeks before. The beach was not as hospitable as it had been that sunny Saturday morning after

1. Village on Cape Cod.

Thanksgiving when thousands of us streamed over the sand to gaze and look. A few cars were parked in the lot, but these kept their inhabitants. Bundled up against a sharp wind, I set off along the twelve-foot swath of trampled beach grass, a raw highway made in a few hours by ten thousand feet that day.

I came to the spot where the whale had beached and marveled that such a magnitude of flesh could have been there one day and gone the next. But the carcass had been hauled off and the tide had smoothed and licked clean whatever vestiges had remained. The cold, salt wind had lifted from the sands the last trace of that pervasive stench of decay that clung to our clothes for days, and now blew clean and sharp into my nostrils.

The only sign that anything unusual had been there was that the beach was a little too clean, not quite so pebbly and littered as the surrounding areas, as the grass above a new grave is always fresher and greener. What had so manifestly occupied this space a short while ago was now utterly gone. And yet the whale still lay heavily on my mind; a question lingered, like a persistent odor in the air. And its dark shape, though now sunken somewhere beneath the waves, still loomed before me, beckoning, asking something.

What was it? What had we seen? Even the several thousand of us that managed to get down to the beach before it was closed off did not see much. Whales, dead or alive, are protected these days under the Federal Marine Mammals Act, and shortly after we arrived, local police kept anyone from actually touching the whale. I could hardly regret this, since in the past beached whales, still alive, have had cigarettes put out in their eyes and bits of flesh hacked off with pocket knives by souvenir seekers. And so, kept at a distance, we looked on while the specialists worked, white-coated, plastic-gloved autopsists from the New England Aquarium, hacking open the thick hide with carving knives and plumbing its depth for samples to be shipped to Canada for analysis and determination of causes of death. What was it they were pulling out? What fetid mystery would they pluck from that huge coffin of dead flesh? We would have to trust them for the answer.

But as the crowds continued to grow around the whale's body like flies around carrion, the question seemed to me, and still seems, not so much why did the whale die, as why had we come to see it? What made this dark bulk such a human magnet, spilling us over onto private lawns and fields? I watched electricians and oil truck drivers pulling their vehicles off the road and clambering down to the beach. Women in high heels and pearls, on their way to Filene's,[2] stumbled through the loose sand to gaze at a corpse. The normal human pattern was broken and a carnival

2. Department store in Boston.

atmosphere was created, appropriate enough in the literal sense of "a farewell to the flesh." But there was also a sense of pilgrimage in those trekking across the beach, an obligation to view such a thing. But for what? Are we really such novices to death? Or so reverent toward it?

I could understand my own semiprofessional interest in the whale, but what had drawn these hordes? There are some obvious answers, of course: a break in the dull routine, "something different." An old human desire to associate ourselves with great and extraordinary events. We placed children and sweethearts in front of the corpse and clicked cameras. "Ruthie and the whale." "Having a whale of a time on Cape Cod."

Curiosity, the simplest answer, doesn't really answer anything. What, after all, did we learn by being there? We were more like children at a zoo, pointing and poking, or Indians on a pristine beach, gazing in innocent wonder at strange European ships come ashore. Yet, as the biologists looted it with vials and plastic bags and the press captured it on film, the spectators also tried to make something of the whale. Circling around it as though for some hold on its slippery bulk, we grappled it with metaphors, lashed similes around its immense girth. It lay upside down, overturned "like a trailer truck." Its black skin was cracked and peeling, red underneath, "like a used tire." The distended, corrugated lower jaw, "a giant accordion," was afloat with the gas of putrefaction and, when pushed, oscillated slowly "like an enormous waterbed." Like our primitive ancestors, we still tend to make images to try to comprehend the unknown.

But what were we looking at? Or more to the point, from what perspective were we looking at it? What did we see in it that might tell us why we had come? A male finback whale—*Balaenoptera physalus*—a baleen cetacean. The second largest creature ever to live on earth. An intelligent and complex mammal. A cause for conservationists. A remarkably adapted swimming and eating machine. Perfume, pet food, engineering oil. A magnificent scientific specimen. A tourist attraction. A media event, a "day to remember." A health menace, a "possible carrier of a communicable disease." A municipal headache and a navigational hazard. Material for an essay.

On the whale's own hide seemed to be written its life history, which we could remark but not read. The right fluke was almost entirely gone, lost in some distant accident or battle and now healed over with a white scar. The red eye, unexpectedly small and mammalian, gazed out at us with fiery blankness. Like the glacial scratches sometimes found on our boulders, there were strange marks or grooves in the skin around the anal area, perhaps caused by scraping the ocean bottom.

Yet we could not seem to scratch its surface. The whale—dead, immobile, in full view—nonetheless shifted kaleidoscopically before our eyes. The following morning it was gone, efficiently and sanitarily removed, like the week's garbage. What was it we saw? I have a theory, though probably (as they say in New England) it hardly does.

There is a tendency these days to defend whales and other endangered animals by pointing out their similarities to human beings. Cetaceans, we are told, are very intelligent. They possess a highly complex language and have developed sophisticated communications systems that transmit over long distances. They form family groups, develop social structures and personal relationships, and express loyalty and affection toward one another. Much of their behavior seems to be recreational: they sing, they play. And so on.

These are not sentimental claims. Whales apparently do these things, at least as far as our sketchy information about their habits warrants such interpretations. And for my money, any argument that helps to preserve these magnificent creatures can't be all bad.

I take exception to this approach not because it is wrong, but because it is wrongheaded and misleading. It is exclusive, anthropocentric, and does not recognize nature in its own right. It implies that whales and other creatures have value only insofar as they reflect man himself and conform to his ideas of beauty and achievement. This attitude is not really far removed from that of the whalers themselves. To consume whales solely for their nourishment of human values is only a step from consuming them for meat and corset staves. It is not only presumptuous and patronizing, but it is misleading and does both whales and men a grave disservice. Whales have an inalienable right to exist, not because they resemble man or because they are useful to him, but simply because they do exist, because they have a proven fitness to the exactitudes of being on a global scale matched by few other species. If they deserve our admiration and respect, it is because, as Henry Beston put it, "They are other nations, caught with ourselves in the net of life and time, fellow prisoners of the splendour and travail of life."

But that still doesn't explain the throngs who came pell-mell to stare and conjecture at the dead whale that washed up at Corporation Beach and dominated it for a day like some extravagant *memento mori*. Surely we were not flattering ourselves, consciously or unconsciously, with any human comparisons to that rotting hulk. Nor was there much, in its degenerate state, that it had to teach us. And yet we came—why?

The answer may be so obvious that we have ceased to recognize it. Man, I believe, has a crying need to confront otherness in the universe. Call it nature, wilderness, the "great outdoors," or what you will—we crave to look out and behold something other than our own human faces staring back at us, expectantly and increasingly frustrated. What the human spirit wants, as Robert Frost said, "Is not its own love back in copy-speech, / But counter-love, original reponse."

This sense of otherness is, I feel, as necessary a requirement to our personalities as food and warmth are to our bodies. Just as an individual, cut off from human contact and stimulation, may atrophy and die of loneliness and neglect, so mankind is today in a similar, though more subtle, danger of cutting himself off from the natural world he shares with all creatures. If our physical survival depends upon our devising a proper use of earth's materials and produce, our growth as a species depends equally upon our establishing a vital and generative relationship with what surrounds us.

We need plants, animals, weather, unfettered shores and unbroken woodland, not merely for a stable and healthy environment, but as an antidote to introversion, a preventive against human inbreeding. Here in particular, in the splendor of natural life, we have an extraordinary reservoir of the Cape's untapped possibilities and modes of being, ways of experiencing life, of knowing wind and wave. After all, how many neighborhoods have whales wash up in their backyards? To confine this world in zoos or in exclusive human terms does injustice not only to nature, but to ourselves as well.

Ever since his beginnings, when primitive man adopted totems and animal spirits to himself and assumed their shapes in ritual dance, *Homo sapiens* has been a superbly imitative animal. He has looked out across the fields and seen and learned. Somewhere along the line, though, he decided that nature was his enemy, not his ally, and needed to be confined and controlled. He abstracted nature and lost sight of it. Only now are we slowly realizing that nature can be confined only by narrowing our own concepts of it, which in turn narrows us. That is why we came to see the whale.

We substitute human myth for natural reality and wonder why we starve for nourishment. "Your Cape" becomes "your Mall," as the local radio jingle has it. Thoreau's "huge and real Cape Cod . . . a wild, rank place with no flattery in it," becomes the Chamber of Commerce's "Rural Seaside Charm"—until forty tons of dead flesh wash ashore and give the lie to such thin, flattering conceptions, flesh whose stench is still the stench of life that stirs us to reaction and response. That is why we came to see the whale. Its mute, immobile bulk represented that ultimate, unknowable otherness that we both seek and recoil from, and shouted at us louder than the policeman's bullhorn that the universe is fraught, not merely with response or indifference, but incarnate assertion.

Later that day the Dennis Board of Health declared the whale carcass to be a "health menace" and warned us off the beach. A health menace? More likely an intoxicating, if strong, medicine that might literally bring us to our senses.

But if those of us in the crowd failed to grasp the whale that day, others did not have much better luck. Even in death the whale escaped us: the tissue samples taken in the autopsy proved insufficient for analysis and the biologists concluded, "We will never know why the whale died." The carcass, being towed tail-first by a Coast Guard cutter for a final dumping beyond Provincetown, snapped a six-inch hawser. Eluding further attempts to reattach it, it finally sank from sight. Even our powers of disposal, it seemed, were questioned that day.

And so, while we are left on shore with the memory of a deflated and stinking carcass and of bullhorns that blared and scattered us like flies, somewhere out beyond the rolled waters and the shining winter sun, the whale sings its own death in matchless, sirenian strains.

1981

THE READER

1. What is Finch's basis for a whale's "inalienable right" to exist? Does the AIDS virus have the same right?
2. Why does the whale provide a confrontation with otherness (p. 524)? Presumably the trampled grass did not and a dead gull would not. Why?
3. Explain Finch's irony in the last two paragraphs. He spoke earlier (p. 523) of grappling the whale with metaphors. What is an example in the last paragraph? What is the relation between the irony and the metaphors?

THE WRITER

1. Finch's strategy might be described as question-and-deferred-answer. Does deferring the answer help make confronting otherness a better answer than curiosity?
2. Find some places where Finch might seem condescending to the people who came to see the whale. What, if anything, does he do to check that condescension?
3. Rewrite the last paragraph without metaphors.
4. Write a paragraph explaining the difference referred to in "The Reader," question 2 (above).

Paul West

A PASSION TO LEARN

I

Exceptional children come in two kinds, advanced and retarded. Both, like jugglers and mystics and astronauts, are astounding, especially the second kind, of which I've had a close view for six years. Amanda West, the daughter who is my theme, didn't seem unusual—not to mention exceptional—until she was two. Slow to speak, she was cautious about starting to walk; but once she had walked she ran like a bird preparing to take off. She fell in love, as well, with water and umbrellas, and in the presence of either orated vehemently (although nonverbally) to herself. Water she preferred in puddles on the living-room floor or in baths, but she also liked it in rainspouts, saucepans, and lavatory basins. Umbrellas —which, I think, exerted the stronger spell—she collected with casual relentlessness. She never had fewer than a dozen. They were her trees, really: a plastic-leaved, tin-branched orchard of them, which every night had to be rolled up firm and laid across her bed, and every morning landed in a cascade on ours when she came heavy-footedly in, hooting for them to be opened. Then, with half-blind eyes, down to the living room where we spread them over the floor like Pan[1] and Company afforesting a bare mountain while she, red-cheeked with elation, danced among them, catching occasionally the beads on the rib-ends and skimming the canopies half-around, but never trampling the handles or ramming a fist through the fabric.

She would stand, do a preliminary skip to get her timing right—a one-two-three with her big toes creased downward as if to scratch earth—and then flow into a joyous high-kneed pounding, her long hair a flash, her arms providing her with a tightrope-walker's balance, her eyes unobtainably fixed on an upper corner of the room, where she saw what no one else saw. She looked and smiled, and danced the more wildly for it, fueling her semi-tarantella from the presence in the vacancy.

Fred, we began to say, domesticating the ghost: *it's Fred again*. And so, each morning, with a flim and a flam, and a flim again, followed by a swift series of flim-flams, she danced spread-eagled, lithe, and bony, chirping on an empty stomach.

We began to wonder, hard as it was even to begin to do it, if she wasn't deaf or autistic. Or both. To think a thing is to make it so, whereas to deny it is to abolish it—especially on the Isle of Man, Amanda's home,

1. In Greek mythology, a god of fields and forests.

island of witches, banshees, and temperamental goblins. But being not altogether pagan, we kept on wondering until the day we took her to the mainland, to the Manchester University Audiology Clinic. It was winter, the sea heaving and pumice-gray; so we flew in a BEA Viscount, lurching through the rain, and Amanda, at each plunge or sideslip, let out a birdcall of delight.

Born on the island, she had never been off it—never been Across to England—and now, leaving it for the first time, she seemed isolated in a new way. Her three words—"baba," "more," and "ish-ish"—she had used heroically, intending meanings we missed and being credited with others that we invented. I listened to the lax, feathered whine of the engines, wondering what noise they made to her as she sat smiling into the clouds. I'd heard, I told myself, on humid days, the squeak of my sinuses filling, and then a pop of contraction on a day of high pressure, with all the sinews and membranes tugging and fluctuating in a mucous orchestration. But that was nothing to what I imagined for Amanda's head: a tinnitus of bad bells, a frying noise, which in combination drove her to cup a hand over her right ear and rock heavily to that side as if trying to shake something loose or back into place or—thought ended: the two-foot doll that bathed with Amanda in the teeth-chattering English bathroom and that we brought with us on the plane, slipped sideways from my casual hug, and a cache of bathwater spilled into my lap. My fault, I said; you can't blame a stark-naked doll.

When we landed, Amanda whooped down the steps from the plane. It was still raining, but we had two umbrellas, both hers. The only trouble was that she didn't want them open or up; they had to be carried before us like totems, one red, the other green, every loose fold clamped tight by a rubber band. Two umbrellas, kept from getting wet, made good folk stare; but good folk knew nothing of umbrellas, water, and Amanda. In the taxi, however, she opened up the red umbrella and sat in an indifferent silence, an erect-sitting being of utter trustfulness, heedless of the roof-lining she might puncture, and with no more idea of where she was going than of where she had come from. Out of the taxi, she insisted, with a plangent squeak, on the umbrella's being folded again and rebound in its rubber band. Then she was ready to march with us past the porter's lodge (empty), wrongly up steps to the Department of Law and down again, and finally into a waiting room stocked with heavy, ridable toys, and equipped with tiny toilets whose still water she inspected and approved.

Called for, we went left into the laboratory (one wall of which was a one-way window facing a lecture room). Amanda stared at the people, the things, and, it seemed, at Fred, whom she has always been able to find anywhere. She grew busy and began to chirp. When, to her exact satisfaction, she had arranged the umbrellas and the doll on a low table, she turned to the experts with a patronizing smile. We sat and watched —her mother at one end of the room, myself (still feeling damp) at the other—helpless on the perimeter and unable to smoke. There was some tinkering with a green box, all dials, and a chart. The door snicked open, admitting an authoritative-looking face which beamed and vanished. Then testing began with overtures of friendship from the studious-mannered man whose trousers looked as if he kneeled a lot. The calm woman in patent-leather high heels clicked a tiny clicker, but Amanda did not turn. They gave her a doll then and tried her from behind with a duck quack, a whistle of low pitch, several rattles, then a small tom-tom. Abruptly, not having turned, she ran to the table, slammed one doll alongside the other and hooted, with finger pointed, for the red umbrella to be opened. There were nods; the umbrella opened, sprang taut, was set in her hands, and she squatted, drawing it down over her as if sheltering under a thin, frail mushroom, slipping out a hand to adjust a downslid sock, and beginning to make again the birdcall (as if a curlew tried to bleat) which had driven countless local dogs into emulative frenzy, provoked birds into surpassing themselves (searching for a bird, they never saw *her*), and scared all the cats away.

Private under the panels of vinyl, she sang with mounting fervor, the umbrella stem between her legs. No one moved. It was clear that she was going to be given her leisure, allowed to collect herself. In succession she fluted her voice upward in an ecstatic trill, twirled the umbrella like a color disc without once catching the rim or the plastic against her face (a perfect, sheltering fit it was), peeped out to giggle just a bit fearfully, hoisted the umbrella up and away behind her in a pose from *The Mikado*, and then hid again beneath it. We had seen her face shining with heat, seen her only long enough for that.

Now they tapped on her roof, flicked middle finger hard off thumb against the fabric, and brought their mouths close to the surface, calling her name. Out she came, astounded at something heard: not her name, because she didn't know it, but something—a retaliating and envious dog, a curlew weary of being competed with, a cat returning to venture a duet—amplified and vibrating in the umbrella above her, but only faces and maneuvering mouths to make it. Us. Us only; so she concealed herself again, tilting the canopy forward.

What brought her out again and kept her out was the xylophone. She abandoned the umbrella for it, fondled it a while, then beat the living decibels out of it, a Lionel Hampton[2] Lilliputian[3] who struck away and then canted her ear close to the trembling bars, her eyes widening in half-piqued recognition that *this* was what we'd flown her across the sea for. She banged on it with her wooden hammer a few times more and let it fall

2. Famous xylophonist and band leader.
3. Lilliput: an imaginary island in Jonathan Swift's *Gulliver's Travels*, the inhabitants of which were six inches tall.

the two-and-a-half feet to the parquet, wincing once in the wrong direction as it hit.

After calls, hums, hisses, pops, buzzes, barks, bays, and several indeterminate ululations, all from behind her, they did the left side while she smiled at a distracting monkey puppet over on the right. My hands were holding each other too tightly; her mother, twelve yards down the room, looked pale, her maternality shut painfully off and her own hand beginning gestures that ended halfway, the fingers tongue-tied.

"Now," said the studious, kneeling man, his kindly face tense, and snapped two wooden bars together. A slapstick, I thought; like the split lath of the harlequin. But whatever was going on, it wasn't low comedy. What he said next, after a fractional shake of his head to the woman in heels—the professional pair's exchange of glances crossing the parental one—sounded like:

"Right down the track." The headshake was a zero in mime.

Amanda smiled at the puppet, offering her hand to put inside it. They let her, working through all the modes of sound, but not to a crescendo, only to a punctuational drum-tap which she ignored. And then, as the light waned—that legendary dank Manchester light swollen with soot and rain and absorbed by tons on tons of Victorian brick and tile—they switched sides, this time beguiling her with a model farm at which she sat, cantankerously checking the cows for udders (as a country girl should) and stationing Clydesdale horses at the water trough. Brilliants of wet formed along her narrow nose, and she heard not the snap-crack of the wooden bars: not the first time, anyway. But when it came from a yard closer—these testers gliding about the room like prankish Druids—she flinched, directed an offended stare in a vaguely right-hand direction, and went back to her farm. Again and again they worked from the right, varying the angle and the sound. Again and again, with just a few moments of preoccupied indifference, she jerked her head sideways, beginning to be cheerful as she discovered the routine: beginning to play.

Suddenly there was no farm. It went into a gray steel cabinet against which Amanda kicked and at which she took a running kick as her eyes began to pour (tears whopping enough, I thought, to merit nostrils for conduits) and her birdcall harshened. As she swung, both-handed, the xylophone at the locked handle of the door, I got up, stuck out a hand as I half-fell in a skid on the polish. I took a tonic sol-fa[4] smack in the forehead as she swung the instrument backward again, farther than before, the better to mangle the steel between her and the authentic cows, the horses a-thirsting.

"Ap," I sort of said through the plong and the blank crash, not seeing well. "You might as well get it out again."

4. As in the scale *do, re, mi, fa, sol, la, ti.*

"Naughty girl," her mother said unconvincedly as Amanda laugh-cried, pitching the xylophone over her shoulder without so much as a look. I have seen her dispose in the same way of bus tickets, mail, money, books, food, scissors, and plates. The oubliette[5] is anywhere behind her.

"She'll soon—" I heard, but the rest was drowned by a scream of unmitigated anger while Amanda pounded the cabinet with both fists.

"Strong!" called the man who kneeled a lot, busying himself with earphones attached to the many-dialed machine. "She's a grand temper."

"You've seen nothing," I told him. "Yet." I knew how, in the Cleopa-tra-Clytemnestra[6] rages to which she entitled herself, she could butt her head through a firm window (one so far, without bloodshed, but there were long blond hairs on the splinters of glass). Or pound her uncallused hand down through the crisp and warm pulp of a loaf not long out of the oven, once burying her hand and bringing her arm up with a bread mallet wedged on her wrist, crying "Ish! Ish!" which is anthem, plea, and threat in one.

But it wasn't "Ish" she came out with this time; it was the first of her calls, "Baba—babababba," uttered with pauses only long enough for everyone present to shout the same phonemes back at her. If you didn't, she increased the volume, blustering and raucous. It was the most com-prehensive aural version of herself. So the clinic-room, soundproof of course (there is even a sign just inside the entrance requesting silence), became a barnyard for a while. Turning wet-eyed, grime-faced, to each of us in turn, she babbled at us, coercing, commanding, appealing; and in turn and sometimes in unison we babbled and brayed back, short only of a cock-a-doodle-doo, the hymn of a pig wallowing or even farrowing in hot lava, and a moose drowning in a swamp of caviar. This, so that the testing could go on; one farmyard for another.

In the beginning is the test, and in the end comes a remedy of sorts. But how, I wondered, can they even begin—overworked but obliged not to rush; never short of children to work with, one in six being somehow deaf and usually not deaf only—until they too have run their fingers across the crowns of her blunt, curiously thick teeth, have seen her dance a full hour among the umbrellas, have night after night studied her fanatical atten-tion to the placing of her slippers within an invisible outline which is there and symmetrical for her beneath the chest of drawers in her bedroom.

"You haven't—" I began to say on our third trip to the clinic, seen her do the living things; give Creation a run for its money. Not at home. They hadn't seen her, like a gross Ophelia,[7] distribute around the house

5. A place of oblivion.
6. Cleopatra: queen of ancient Egypt, given to fickle behavior; Clytemnestra: in *The Oresteia*, Aeschylus's dramatic trilogy, the queen of Argos, who kills her husband, Aga-memnon.
7. In Shakespeare's *Hamlet*, Polonius's daughter, who goes mad.

—on the window ledges, in the wardrobe between two decent suits or dresses, on the rim of the letter box, on the Christmas tree itself—pork sausages on butcher's hooks or threaded on wire coat-hangers. Or eat the sausage raw, oblivious of worms. Or, in hydrodynamic delight, rip off shoes and socks to plant her bare feet on the TV screen whenever it showed water. Or (I stopped: they were calling her name again and she wasn't ever going to answer) sit naked and warbling for an hour in a washbasin of cold water. Or green her face with eye-shadow, eat nail-varnish, coat the windows with lavender furniture polish, jump down five stairs fearlessly, mimic (by waving a stiffened arm) men carrying umbrellas, chant into a toilet pedestal after choking it with a whole roll of tissue, chew cigarettes, cover herself with Band-Aids when there wasn't a scratch in sight, climb any ladder and refuse to descend, slide pencils up her nose, use a rubber hammer on the doctor's private parts, drink from her potty, wade into a sewer-inspection chamber the plumber had opened, eat six bananas in six minutes, wind and play an alarm clock at her right ear time and again, shave her face and arms and legs with instant lather and bladeless razor, threaten enormous dogs by advancing upon them with a reed in hand, cut her own hair at random, dissolve soap in a tin basin, rock so hard that her hair touched the floor on either side, sit motionless and rapt in front of a mirror, voluminously autograph walls, tear samples from the dictionary or a book of Picasso prints, stare unblinking into 150-watt bulbs, run, run, run everywhere, heedless of gesticulating and half-felled adults and the sanity of drivers.

"Mandy . . . *Mandy*. . . MANDY," they said, upping the decibels as she gazed from them to the red finger spinning across the dial and back again. When she heard them, her expression changed, fixing in atavistic wonder. Funny, it was as if we were watching the face of sound itself while she, flushed and nervous, heard something visible. After an interval they let her use the microphone herself, and she began to boom and call in an almost continuous orgy of sound, confronted for the first time with her own share of the missing continent: a Columbus of euphony dumbfoundedly exclaiming at the glories of exclamation itself, every bit like the man in Xenophon who kept shouting *thalassa!*[8] when he saw the sea. I myself felt a bit like shouting; I'd never heard anyone hearing before. And since then I've known a good many firsts with her—things which, up to then, I'd done without really experiencing them, or which she herself thought up and I myself had never dreamed of doing. Some of the latter are grotesque and sometimes rather revolting as well; I try not to do them, but usually Amanda prevails, imperious queen with her dithering court. I do as I am told. Most people would. You have to; that's where the education begins.

8. Greek word for sea or gulf.

II

She quickens in you the sense of life; makes you grateful for what's granted, what's taken for granted. A handicap so severe drives you through fury, then through an empty, vengeful indignation, to two points: first, when, in the absence of explanations medical and reasons cosmic, you ignore the handicap to make it go away; second, nearer to common sense, when you welcome it in as her special gift and, while trying to eliminate it, learn its nature by heart as a caution to yourself, and study the voracious subtlety of her compensations—as when she, unlike most of us, smells at a pencil newly sharpened, inhaling from the beechwood its own soot-sour bouquet, or traces with addicted fingers the corrugations on the flat of a halved cabbage before eating it raw with the same naturalness with which she drinks vinegar, steak sauce, and mayonnaise, and sniffs glue. I too, now, have tasted ink (a flavor of charred toenail), coal (a rotted iron-and-yeast pill), bark (woolly and raw, suggesting vulcanized crabmeat), leather (a taste here not of the meat or fat next the hide but of the fur once outside it and of seaweed-iodine).

Tasting—testing—with her, I have found new ways into the world. She discovers what she discovers because she has lost what she's lost. I tag along on her voyages, and together we sneak into the randomness, the arbitrariness, of the universe as distinct from its patterns. Without her—although I have in my time delighted in The Compleat Angler's[9] bald and bland arcana, in insect and fungus books, in Jean Rostand's[1] reports on tadpoles and toads—I don't think I would be delving, as I now am, with strangely relevant irrelevance, into the behavior of slugs, mushrooms, cicadas, and flesh-eating plants, or into a way of death called atherosclerosis, the result not (I learn) of saturated fats yielding cholesterol but of unsaturated fats—much used in the paint and varnish industry—varnishing our insides with lipofuscin. Because she brandished it at a big dog, I found out about Great Reed Mace (Typha latifolia), often wrongly called the bulrush, but rightly, I reckon, thought sexy. The black six-foot stem is a long cheroot, topped by a yellow spike, and, as my Observer's Book of Wild Flowers says, "the closely packed pistillate flowers forming the 'mace' consist of a stalked ovary, with a slender style and a one-sided, narrow stigma, and enveloped in tufts of soft, brownish hairs."

I keep two books, one for what Amanda does, one for what I find out while waiting for our first conversation. She ate a dandelion flower some time back; one day I'll try her with the leaves in oil and vinegar, that good salad. I have a lot to tell her which, thank goodness, I've been late in learning: the hyena isn't quite the scavenger he's supposed to be, whereas the almost extinct American Bald Eagle is a scavenger out and

9. An English masterwork of 1653 on the techniques of fishing and the pleasures of the   simple life, by Izaak Walton.
1. French biologist and writer (1893–   ).

out. And so on; it's a question, really, of finding a life-style, of opening up for myself a universe into which she fits. So I try to devise for her the biggest memberships possible, now and then blundering from wishful thinking into wishful biology, but at other times enrolling her in majestic clans we'd stare at if we knew about them, just as some of the inhumanly ordinary on the earth have stared at her.

Take the shark, created perpetually with two inexplicable handicaps: it has no swim bladder, so must keep on the move or sink; its fixed, paired fins have hardly any braking effect and no motive power, which means that it finds difficulty stopping or reversing. A shark, therefore, is compulsive and a bit helpless; no one knows why. But all sharks are handicapped thus, whereas what I am casting around for is a handicap not just inexplicable but also affecting a minority only. Trying again, I come up with such samples of a partly mismanaged universe as so-called "waltzing" mice, which have an abnormality of that part of the inner ear concerned with balance; the hereditary deafness found in white dogs like Dalmatians and Bull Terriers; Gentian acaulis, which for reasons unknown refuses to flower in good soil but does well where the acid and lime counts are high; holly, whose greenish flowers are sometimes bisexual, although sometimes male and female flowers exist on separate plants (which is why they tell you to plant hollies in groups); uranium 235, old faithful of an unstable and vulnerable isotope which is as it is because it isn't otherwise; the particle for which, it seems, there is no antiparticle; flawed crystals in which one atom is where another should be or where no atom ought to be at all; the so-called incoherence of natural light, traveling as it does in brief packets of energy in random directions at uncorrelated times, compared with the light from an optical maser; acridines, believed to produce mutations which consist in the deletion or addition of a base or bases from the DNA chain. Such is the beginning of my list: Amanda's alibi, not so much an excuse (the popular sense) as her being genuinely elsewhere while the universe put a foot wrong with that mouse or this crystal, but suffering a similar misadministration that relates her more closely than most people to Nature; a Nature I never really noticed until it bungled.

As a factory, Nature—the more familiar end of the universe—is more reliable than the best baseball pitcher ever, but less reliable than the London Underground.[2] To be sure, where it falters it sometimes lowers its guard usefully: U 235 gives us the chain reaction, or at least the possibility of it; the misbehaving particle may teach us something about the "elementariness" of particles (e.g., are two different particles equally fundamental or is one merely an "excited" state of the other?). The imperfect crystal tells physicists a great deal about the mechanical

2. Subway.

properties of solids. And the deaf—also, perhaps, in this case, the autistic and/or brain-damaged—child, from whom I have wandered briefly only to hunt out some of her peers and analogues, is equally instructive, preparing you for the next phase, in which you find what I will call the superior intricacy of one child at the deaf-blind unit at Condover in England: a child born without eyes or ears and with all internal organs so garbled that sex cannot be determined. Yet he/she knows how to get angry, is eager to sniff at things and people alike. Something on the lines of "Age 6—80 decibel hearing loss—IQ 120" says nothing much if you are willing to learn something more; neither does "Age 7—hearing nil— sight nil—sex?—IQ minimal" if you have a passion to learn (I intend the ambiguity). How you proceed from the statistics depends on who and what you are, how much of Nature you're willing to look at; but, pretty certainly, there will be some desperation in your proceeding. Which, given such standard desirables as warmth, light, and some health, may not be a bad thing. It's a bit like writing the prospective novel—being a prospector for fiction in uncharted areas—inasmuch as you don't know where you will end up or how.

To put it topically, locally: you run the home around the child. You learn her ignorances until they are yours. You steal her condition from her by risky analogies, like the mystic borrowing the lover's terms, like the lover borrowing the mystic's. You give your Amanda a glut of olibles, tangibles, edibles, and visibles: all the perfumes of Arabia; all the grades of sandpaper, leading up to a feel at an elephant; all the fluents from goat's milk to mercury; all the spices from cinnamon to chili; all the zoos, parades, Dufys, flags, unwanted *National Geographics*, French colonial stamps, travel posters, and rainbows you can muster. Always a color camera: preferably Polaroid, because she doesn't like to wait.

Against all this—the stark handicap and any voluptuously zany sharing in it—set a thought neither apocalyptic nor original. Ten years after the atomic explosion on Bikini Atoll, birds were sitting on sterile eggs; turtles, instead of going back to the sea after laying their own eggs, pressed on to the island's interior where they died of thirst. Their skeletons remain, thousands of them, evidence of a gratuitous handicap we might have had the brains to do without.

III

It is three years since that first visit to the clinic when powerlessness hit home to us. The strain told on Amanda too. She fetched a shovel from the garden to destroy with: lighting fixtures, windows, crockery, clocks. Strong always, she lifted and swung it with ease, pouting with birdcall. It took her two years to reject the shovel, to change from indefatigable and destructive hobgoblin into a girl who, gaining a word a month only to lose it the month after, developed luminously beautiful, big, Nordic features. Capable, without warning, of histrionic graciousness of manner (as if all the pressures lifted at once and the noises in her head stopped), she enjoyed her increasingly frequent visits to the clinic (toys, earphones, EEG apparatus), ate mightily, hardly ever caught a cold, thumped obliviously past staring or derisive children, and rebaffled the experts. Deaf, yes; "stone" deaf (in that melodramatic inversion of the pathetic fallacy[3]) in the left ear; autistic, perhaps, but that's a vague word like "romantic"; brain damage not ruled out; amblyopia[4] mentioned, with an ophthalmologist joining her team.

At five she left the island for the last time, blasé by now about Viscounts, to live near the clinic and the school associated with it. I signed out a speech-trainer, donated by the Variety Artists' Federation, on which she had a daily lesson, dealing sometimes in words, sometimes in sheer noise. She did her jigsaws like an impatient robot, began to lip-read, and gradually built up and kept a tiny vocabulary enunciated with almost coy preciosity, intoning "more" like an aria, raising "hair" into "har," curtailing "mouth" into "mou," lengthening "nose" into a three-second sound, but all the same *talking* although she still didn't know her name. Nicknames accumulated: Moo, from Mandy-Moo; Birdie, from her call; Tish from "ish-ish"; Lulu (developed cunningly from the two-syllable, high-pitched call with which her mother called her in); Yee (which sound she herself had substituted for Baba); Proof, from the condition called Manda-proof, she being the only thing or person invulnerable to herself, or so we said; and, strangest of all to strangers, Boat (her word for water— until she got *worbar*—shouted while paddling her feet on the TV screen). Epic formulae, these, while she went incognito.

During one spell, she averaged only three hours' sleep a night, erupting at midnight with umbrellas and jigsaws, then fetching a guitar, one mechanical top, several model baths, a dish brimming with soap dissolved, a length of iron piping, and a purloined fruit-knife, with all of which to while the night away until she could go out. And always wet. She became frenetic, twitched more than ever, during this waiting period: all that soothed her was running water, the swing in the garden, and ghoulish faces I pulled while pursuing her up the stairs. She partnered everyone at the lavatory, exclaiming "Oh" in exaggerative dismay at anyone's being under the vile necessity and then seeking to examine the deposit. But, we noticed, her "Yee" was less strident, less insistent; a month later, it had become a delicate, diffident greeting to be answered just as quietly, and she became drier, banged her head less, was less obsessed by the grotesque or the effluvial, gave up rending the day's

3. The literary device of portraying inanimate objects as possessing human qualities, e.g., the angry sea.

4. A disease of the optic nerve, causing blindness.

newspaper, lost her passion for knives, began to draw faces and bodies that had two eyes, not one, with two legs instead of a barbed-wire entanglement of blue ball-point. She even drew a bath—always the long throne of her joy—with a Mandy in it.

She took the intelligence test and passed it before, after forty minutes' concentration, she flung the next puzzle across the room and mounted a full-size tantrum. The children's hospital lost her file, and two starch-bosomed nurses lost their cool when she screamed twenty minutes solid because they took from her the model jet kept to calm little boys during EEG tests. She thought it was a present.

"I'll buy it," I said against the screams. "It's worth it." No, that was out of the question; it was part of the equipment—it was government property. She vanished into the pathology lab, and was there found admiring fetuses, tumors, and cysts in their quiet jars, a true humanist explaining to her what was what. We got her a jet at the airport, and, later, a helicopter, a new swing, a miniature cooking set in Bavarian iron, building blocks, card games, a thousand candy cigarettes, as many lollipops and ices: a surplus for purposes of habilitation.

Out of the clutter has come a girl who can make beds, bake bread, fry bacon, iron and fold clothes, hoover[5] the carpets, mow the lawn (she calls escalators "bo" now), set a table, adjust the TV, fell apples from the tree by swatting it with a tennis racquet, tune her own hearing-aid, on her best days say "roundabout" as "rounabou" and "elephant" as almost that (it's otherwise known as "NO-o-se"), and on most days recite her own name. She cried and shuffled not at all when she began at the school for the deaf, a day-girl, almost six. She dotes on baths, Scotch tape (which she calls yap), steaks, and tenon saws, has become unoffendably gregarious, has learned to spit, looks through illustrated magazines with an anthropologist's gravity, has discovered how "No" doubles her range of concepts, and, I realize, sees Fred less and less. The Martian, we call her, or Miss Rabelais. Photogenic, long and agile, she has about forty words all told, a schoolbag and a homework book, which is all penumbra to the darkness of Amanda invading the house with a big shovel, sometimes a coal hammer, and that unfailing drooped-eyelid leer.

One special thing left a new light shining. Her class of nine children, working by the loop that amplifies sound identically for them whichever way they turn, was told to draw a spider's web. All drew but Amanda, who sat abstractedly apart, aloof from this planet. No one saw her move —and, being ambidextrous, she could have done it with either hand— but when the teacher got to her, Amanda was yee-ing gently beside a perfectly delineated web, all done in one unbroken line, with a spider at center. It's a prized school exhibit now, which she can bring home at

5. Vacuum.

year's end, when, presumably, she will bury it unsentimentally in her crate of junk in which, I once thought, she meant to bury us all, outclassed by her energy, thwarted by her privacy, heartsick at Nature's misbehavior, and as short of new expedients as of sleep.

One day, home from s hool with her homework book in which the teacher uses the special alphabet ("home" is "hoem"), she will extend yee into what I think it is, what it has been all along. I mean yes, and so will she, even if she's as incoherent as daily light, as vulnerable as uranium 235, and has an atom where an atom shouldn't be.

1968

Oliver Sacks

THE DISEMBODIED LADY

The aspects of things that are most important for us are hidden because of their simplicity and familiarity. (One is unable to notice something because it is always before one's eyes.) The real foundations of his enquiry do not strike a man at all.

—Wittgenstein

What Wittgenstein writes here, of epistemology,[1] might apply to aspects of one's physiology and psychology—especially in regard to what Sherrington[2] once called "our secret sense, our sixth sense"—that continuous but unconscious sensory flow from the movable parts of our body (muscles, tendons, joints), by which their position and tone and motion are continually monitored and adjusted, but in a way which is hidden from us because it is automatic and unconscious.

Our other senses—the five senses—are open and obvious; but this—our hidden sense—had to be discovered, as it was, by Sherrington, in the 1890s. He named it "proprioception," to distinguish it from "exteroception" and "interoception,"[3] and, additionally, because of its indispensability for our sense of *ourselves*; for it is only by courtesy of proprioception, so to speak, that we feel our bodies as proper to us, as our "property," as our own. * * *

What is more important for us, at an elemental level, than the control,

1. Study of knowledge, especially with regard to its limits; Ludwig Wittgenstein (1889–1951): influential British philosopher (born in Vienna).
2. Sir Charles Scott Sherrrington

(1857–1952): English physiologist who made a lifelong study of the mammalian nervous system.
3. Reponse to stimuli from outside the body and from within the body, respectively.

the owning and operation, of our own physical selves? And yet it is so automatic, so familiar, we never give it a thought.

Jonathan Miller produced a beautiful television series, *The Body in Question*[4] but the body, normally, is never in question: our bodies are beyond question, or perhaps beneath question—they are simply, unquestionably, there. This unquestionability of the body, its certainty, is, for Wittgenstein, the start and basis of all knowledge and certainty. Thus, in his last book (*On Certainty*), he opens by saying: "If you do know that *here is one hand*, we'll grant you all the rest." But then, in the same breath, on the same opening page: "What we can ask is whether it can make sense to doubt it . . . "; and, a little later, "Can I doubt it? Grounds for *doubt* are lacking!"

Indeed, his book might be titled *On Doubt*, for it is marked by doubting, no less than affirming. Specifically, he wonders—and one in turn may wonder whether these thoughts were perhaps incited by his working with patients, in a hospital, in the war—he wonders whether there might be situations or conditions which take away the certainty of the body, which do give one grounds to doubt one's body, perhaps indeed to lose one's entire body in total doubt. This thought seems to haunt his last book like a nightmare.

Christina was a strapping young woman of twenty-seven, given to hockey and riding, self-assured, robust, in body and mind. She had two young children, and worked as a computer programmer at home. She was intelligent and cultivated, fond of the ballet, and of the Lakeland poets[5] (but not, I would think, of Wittgenstein). She had an active, full life—had scarcely known a day's illness. Somewhat to her surprise, after an attack of abdominal pain, she was found to have gallstones, and removal of the gall-bladder was advised.

She was admitted to hospital three days before the operation date, and placed on an antibiotic for microbial prophylaxis.[6] This was purely routine, a precaution, no complications of any sort being expected at all. Christina understood this, and being a sensible soul had no great anxieties.

The day before surgery Christina, not usually given to fancies or dreams, had a disturbing dream of peculiar intensity. She was swaying wildly, in her dream, very unsteady on her feet, could hardly feel the ground beneath her, could hardly feel anything in her hands, found them flailing to and fro, kept dropping whatever she picked up.

She was distressed by this dream ("I never had one like it," she said. "I can't get it out of my mind.")—so distressed that we requested an opinion

4. Public-television series by the British doctor, writer, actor, and director.
5. I.e., the English "lake poets," such as William Wordsworth.
6. I.e., an interior bodily cleaning against microbes.

from the psychiatrist. "Pre-operative anxiety," he said. "Quite natural, we see it all the time."

But later that day *the dream came true*. Christina did find herself very unsteady on her feet, with awkward flailing movements, and dropping things from her hands.

The psychiatrist was again called—he seemed vexed at the call, but also, momentarily, uncertain and bewildered. "Anxiety hysteria," he now snapped, in a dismissive tone. "Typical conversion[7] symptoms— you see them all the while."

But the day of surgery Christina was still worse. Standing was impossible—unless she looked down at her feet. She could hold nothing in her hands, and they "wandered"—unless she kept an eye on them. When she reached out for something, or tried to feed herself, her hands would miss, or overshoot wildly, as if some essential control or coordination was gone.

She could scarcely even sit up—her body "gave way." Her face was oddly expressionless and slack, her jaw fell open, even her vocal posture was gone.

"Something awful's happened," she mouthed, in a ghostly flat voice. "I can't feel my body. I feel weird—disembodied."

This was an amazing thing to hear, confounded, confounding. "Disembodied"—was she crazy? But what of her physical state then? The collapse of tone and muscle posture, from top to toe; the wandering of her hands, which she seemed unaware of; the flailing and overshooting, as if she were receiving no information from the periphery, as if the control loops for tone and movement had catastrophically broken down.

"It's a strange statement," I said to the residents. "It's almost impossible to imagine what might provoke such a statement."

"But it's hysteria, Dr. Sacks—didn't the psychiatrist say so?"

"Yes, he did. But have you ever seen a hysteria like this? Think phenomenologically—take what you see as genuine phenomenon, in which her state-of-body and state-of-mind are not fictions, but a psychophysical whole. Could anything give such a picture of undermined body and mind?

"I'm not testing you," I added. "I'm as bewildered as you are. I've never seen or imagined anything quite like this before . . . "

I thought, and they thought, we thought together.

"Could it be a biparietal[8] syndrome?" one of them asked.

"It's an 'as if,'" I answered: "*as if* the parietal lobes were not getting their usual sensory information. Let's *do* some sensory testing—and test parietal lobe function, too."

We did so, and a picture began to emerge. There seemed to be a very

7. Conversion hysteria—psychoneurosis in which the body displays symptoms that have no physical basis.

8. Having to do with the two sides of the brain.

profound, almost total, proprioceptive deficit, going from the tips of her toes to her head—the parietal lobes were working, *but had nothing to work with*. Christina might have hysteria, but she had a great deal more, of a sort which none of us had ever seen or conceived before. We put in an emergency call now, not to the psychiatrist, but to the physical medicine specialist, the physiatrist.

He arrived promptly, responding to the urgency of the call. He opened his eyes very wide when he saw Christina, examined her swiftly and comprehensively, and then proceeded to electrical tests of nerve and muscle function. "This is quite extraordinary," he said. "I have never seen or read about anything like this before. She has lost all proprioception—you're right—from top to toe. She has no muscle or tendon or joint sense whatever. There is slight loss of other sensory modalities—to light touch, temperature, and pain, and slight involvement of the motor fibers, too. But it is predominantly position-sense—proprioception—which has sustained such damage."

"What's the cause?" we asked.

"You're the neurologists. You find out."

By afternoon, Christina was still worse. She lay motionless and toneless; even her breathing was shallow. Her situation was grave—we thought of a respirator—as well as strange.

The picture revealed by spinal tap was one of an acute polyneuritis,[9] but a polyneuritis of a most exceptional type: not like Guillain-Barré syndrome, with its overwhelming motor involvement, but a purely (or almost purely) sensory neuritis, affecting the sensory roots of spinal and cranial nerves throughout the neuraxis.[1]

Operation was deferred; it would have been madness at this time. Much more pressing were the questions: "Will she survive? What can we do?"

"What's the verdict?" Christina asked, with a faint voice and fainter smile, after we had checked her spinal fluid.

"You've got this inflammation, this neuritis . . . " we began, and told her all we knew. When we forgot something, or hedged, her clear questions brought us back.

"Will it get better?" she demanded. We looked at each other, and at her: "We have no idea."

The sense of the body, I told her, is given by three things: vision, balance organs (the vestibular system),[2] and proprioception—which she'd lost. Normally all of these worked together. If one failed, the others

9. Disease involving several of the nerves. "Such sensory polyneurophathies occur, but are rare. What was unique in Christina's case, to the best of our knowledge at the time (this was in 1977), was the extraordinary selectivity displayed, so that proprioceptive fibers, and these only, bore the brunt of the damage. * * *" [Sacks's note].
1. The central nervous system.
2. The system in the "vestibule" of the inner ear that affects balance.

could compensate, or substitute—to a degree. In particular, I told of my patient Mr. MacGregor, who, unable to employ his balance organs, used his eyes instead * * *. And of patients with neurosyphilis,[3] *tabes dorsalis*, who had similar symptoms, but confined to the legs—and how they too had to compensate by use of their eyes * * *. And how, if one asked such a patient to move his legs, he was apt to say: "Sure, Doc, as soon as I find them."

Christina listened closely, with a sort of desperate attention.

"What I must do then," she said slowly, "is use vision, use my eyes, in every situation where I used—what do you call it?—proprioception before. I've already noticed," she added, musingly, "that I may 'lose' my arms. I think they're one place, and I find they're another. This 'proprioception' is like the eyes of the body, the way the body sees itself. And if it goes, as it's gone with me, *it's like the body's blind*. My body can't 'see' itself if it's lost its eyes, right? So *I* have to watch it—be its eyes. Right?"

"Right," I said, "right. You could be a physiologist."

"I'll *have* to be a sort of physiologist," she rejoined, "because my physiology has gone wrong, and may never *naturally* go right . . . "

It was as well that Christina showed such strength of mind, from the start, for, though the acute imflammation subsided, and her spinal fluid returned to normal, the damage it did to her proprioceptive fibers persisted—so that there was no neurological recovery a week, or a year, later. Indeed there has been none in the eight years that have now passed—though she has been able to lead a life, a sort of life, through accommodations and adjustments of every sort, emotional and moral no less than neurological.

That first week Christina did nothing, lay passively, scarcely ate. She was in a state of utter shock, horror and despair. What sort of a life would it be, if there was not natural recovery? What sort of a life, every move made by artifice? What sort of a life, above all, if she felt disembodied?

Then life reasserted itself, as it will, and Christina started to move. She could at first do nothing without using her eyes, and collapsed in a helpless heap the moment she closed them. She had, at first, to monitor herself by vision, looking carefully at each part of her body as it moved, using an almost painful conscientiousness and care. Her movements, consciously monitored and regulated, were at first clumsy, artificial, in the highest degree. But then—and here both of us found ourselves most happily surprised, by the power of an ever-increasing, daily increasing, automatism—then her movements started to appear more delicately modulated, more graceful, more natural (though still wholly dependent on use of the eyes).

Increasingly now, week by week, the normal, unconscious feedback of

3. Syphilis affecting the central nervous system.

proprioception was being replaced by an equally unconscious feedback by vision, by visual automatism and reflexes increasingly integrated and fluent. Was it possible, too, that something more fundamental was happening? That the brain's visual model of the body, or body-image—normally rather feeble (it is, of course, absent in the blind), and normally subsidiary to the proprioceptive body-model—was it possible that *this*, now the proprioceptive body model was lost, was gaining, by way of compensation or substitution, an enhanced, exceptional, extraordinary force? And to this might be added a compensatory enhancement of the vestibular body-model or body-image, too . . . both to an extent which was more than we had expected or hoped for.[4]

Whether or not there was increased use of vestibular feedback, there was certainly increased use of her ears—auditory feedback. Normally this is subsidiary, and rather unimportant in speaking—our speech remains normal if we are deaf from a head cold, and some of the congenitally deaf may be able to acquire virtually perfect speech. For the modulation of speech is normally proprioceptive, governed by inflowing impulses from all our vocal organs. Christina had lost this normal inflow, this afference, and lost her normal proprioceptive vocal tone and posture, and therefore had to use her ears, auditory feedback, instead.

Besides these new, compensatory forms of feedback, Christina also started to develop—it was deliberate and conscious in the first place, but gradually became unconscious and automatic—various forms of new and compensatory "feed-forward" (in all this she was assisted by an immensely understanding and resourceful rehabilitative staff).

Thus at the time of her catastrophe, and for about a month afterwards, Christina remained as floppy as a ragdoll, unable even to sit up. But three months later, I was startled to see her sitting very finely—too finely, statuesquely, like a dancer in mid-pose. And soon I saw that her sitting was, indeed, a pose, consciously or automatically adopted and sustained, a sort of forced or willful or histrionic posture, to make up for the continuing lack of any genuine, natural posture. Nature having failed, she took to "artifice," but the artifice was suggested by nature, and soon became "second nature." Similarly with her voice—she had at first been almost mute.

This too was projected, as to an audience from a stage. It was a stagey, theatrical voice—not because of any histrionism, or perversion of mo-

4. "Contrast the fascinating case described by the late Purdon Martin in *The Basal Ganglia and Posture* (1967), p. 32: 'This patient, in spite of years of physiotherapy and training, has never regained the ability to walk in any normal manner. His greatest difficulty is in starting to walk and in propelling himself forward . . . He is also unable to rise from a chair. He cannot crawl or place himself in the all-fours posture. When standing or walking he is entirely dependent on vision and falls down if he closes his eyes. At first he was unable to maintain his position on an ordinary chair when he closed his eyes, but he has gradually acquired the ability to do this'" [Sacks's note].

tive, but because there was still no natural vocal posture. And with her face, too—this still tended to remain somewhat flat and expressionless (though her inner emotions were of full and normal intensity), due to lack of proprioceptive facial tone and posture,[5] unless she used an artificial enhancement of expression (as patients with aphasia may adopt exaggerated emphases and inflections).

But all these measures were, at best, partial. They made life possible— they did not make it normal. Christina learned to walk, to take public transport, to conduct the usual business of life—but only with the exercise of great vigilance, and strange ways of doing things—ways which might break down if her attention was diverted. Thus if she was eating while she was talking, or if her attention was elsewhere, she would grip the knife and fork with painful force—her nails and fingertips would go bloodless with pressure; but if there was any lessening of the painful pressure, she might nervelessly drop them straightaway—there was no in-between, no modulation, whatever.

Thus, although there was not a trace of neurological recovery (recovery from the anatomical damage to nerve fibers), there was, with the help of intensive and varied therapy—she remained in hospital, on the rehabilitation ward, for almost a year—a very considerable functional recovery, i.e., the ability to function using various substitutions and other such tricks. It became possible, finally, for Christina to leave hospital, go home, rejoin her children. She was able to return to her home-computer terminal, which she now learned to operate with extraordinary skill and efficiency, considering that everything had to be done by vision, not feel. She had learned to operate—but how did she feel? Had the substitutions dispersed the disembodied sense she first spoke of?

The answer is—not in the least. She continues to feel, with the continuing loss of proprioception, that her body is dead, not-real, not-hers—she cannot appropriate it to herself. She can find no words for this state, and can only use analogies derived from other senses: "I feel my body is blind and deaf to itself . . . it has no sense of itself"—these are her own words. She has no words, no direct words, to describe this bereftness, this sensory darkness (or silence) akin to blindness or deafness. She has no words, and we lack words too. And society lacks words, and sympathy, for such states. The blind, at least, are treated with solicitude—we can imagine their state, and we treat them accordingly. But when Christina, painfully, clumsily, mounts a bus, she receives nothing but uncomprehending and angry snarls: "What's wrong with you, lady? Are you

---

5. "Purdon Martin, almost alone of contemporary neurologists, would often speak of facial and vocal 'posture,' and their basis, finally, in proprioceptive integrity. He was greatly intrigued when I told him about Christina and showed him some films and tapes of her—many of the suggestions and formulations here are, in fact, his" [Sacks's note].

blind—or blind-drunk?" What can she answer—"I have no proprioception"? The lack of social support and sympathy is an additional trial: disabled, but with the nature of her disability not clear—she is not, after all, manifestly blind or paralyzed, manifestly anything—she tends to be treated as a phony or a fool. This is what happens to those with disorders of the hidden senses (it happens also to patients who have vestibular impairment, or who have been labyrinthectomized).[6]

Christina is condemned to live in an indescribable, unimaginable realm—though "non-realm," "nothingness," might be better words for it. At times she breaks down—not in public, but with me: "If only I could *feel*!" she cries. "But I've forgotten what it's like . . . I *was* normal, wasn't I? I *did* move like everyone else?

"Yes, of course."

"There's no 'of course.' I can't believe it. I want proof."

I show her a home movie of herself with her children, taken just a few weeks before her polyneuritis.

"Yes, of course, that's me!" Christina smiles, and then cries: "But I can't identify with that graceful girl any more! She's gone, I can't remember her, *I can't even imagine her*. It's like something's been scooped right out of me, right at the center . . . that's what they do with frogs, isn't it? They scoop out the center, the spinal cord, they *pith* them . . . That's what I am, *pithed*, like a frog . . . Step up, come and see Chris, the first pithed human being. She's no proprioception, no sense of herself—disembodied Chris, the pithed girl!" She laughs wildly, with an edge of hysteria. I calm her—"Come now!"—while thinking, "Is she right?"

For, in some sense, she *is* "pithed," disembodied, a sort of wraith. She has lost, with her sense of proprioception, the fundamental, organic mooring of identity—at least of that corporeal identity, or "body-ego," which Freud[7] sees as the basis of self: "The ego is first and foremost a body-ego." Some such depersonalization or derealization must always occur, when there are deep disturbances of body perception or body image. Weir Mitchell[8] saw this, and incomparably described it, when he was working with amputees and nerve-damaged patients in the American Civil War—and in a famous, quasi-fictionalized account, but still the best, phenomenologically most accurate, account we have, said (through the mouth of his physician-patient, George Dedlow):

"I found to my horror that at times I was less conscious of myself, of my own existence, than used to be the case. This sensation was so novel that at first it

6. "Vestibular impairment": injury to the "vestibule" of the inner ear; "labyrinthectomized": having had the "labyrinth" of the inner ear removed.
7. Sigmund Freud (1856-1939): Austrian neurologist and father of psychoanalysis, in which "ego" is the term for the largely conscious part of the personality.
8. Silas Weir Mitchell (1829-1914): American doctor and author who specialized in treating neurological disorders.

quite bewildered me. I felt like asking someone constantly if I were really George Dedlow or not; but, well aware of how absurd I should seem after such a question, I refrained from speaking of my case, and strove more keenly to analyse my feelings. At times the conviction of my want of being myself was overwhelming and most painful. It was, as well as I can describe it, a deficiency in the egoistic sentiment of individuality."

For Christina there is this general feeling—this "deficiency in the egoistic sentiment of individuality"—which has become less with accommodation, with the passage of time. And there is this specific, organically based, feeling of disembodiedness, which remains as severe, and uncanny, as the day she first felt it. This is also felt, for example, by those who have high transections of the spinal cord—but they, of course, are paralyzed; whereas Christina, though "bodiless," is up and about.

There are brief, partial reprieves, when her skin is stimulated. She goes out when she can, she loves open cars, where she can feel the wind on her body and face (superficial sensation, light touch, is only slightly impaired). "It's wonderful," she says. "I feel the wind on my arms and face, and then I know, faintly, I have arms and a face. It's not the real thing, but it's something—it lifts this horrible, dead veil for a while."

But her situation is, and remains, a "Wittgensteinian" one. She does not know "Here is one hand"—her loss of proprioception, her de-afferentation, has deprived her of her existential, her epistemic,[9] basis—and nothing she can do, or think, will alter this fact. She cannot be certain of her body—what would Wittgenstein have said, in her position?

In an extraordinary way, she has both succeeded and failed. She has succeeded in operating, but not in being. She has succeeded to an almost incredible extent in all the accommodations that will, courage, tenacity, independence and the plasticity of the senses and the nervous system will permit. She has faced, she faces, an unprecedented situation, has battled against unimaginable difficulties and odds, and has survived as an indomitable, impressive human being. She is one of those unsung heroes, or heroines, of neurological affliction.

But still and forever she remains defective and defeated. Not all the spirit and ingenuity in the world, not all the substitutions or compensations the nervous system allows, can alter in the least her continuing and absolute loss of proprioception—that vital sixth sense without which a body must remain unreal, unpossessed.

Poor Christina is "pithed" in 1985 as she was eight years ago and will remain so for the rest of her life. Her life is unprecedented. She is, so far as I know, the first of her kind, the first "disembodied" human being.

9. I.e., having a sense of existence, possessing a certainty of knowledge; "de-afferentation": lack of communication between nerve ends and central nervous system.

Postscript

Now Christina has company of a sort. I understand from Dr. H. H. Schaumburg, who is the first to describe the syndrome, that large numbers of patients are turning up everywhere now with severe sensory neuronopathies. The worst affected have body-image disturbances like Christina. Most of them are health faddists, or are on a megavitamin craze, and have been taking enormous quantities of vitamin B_6 (pyridoxine). Thus there are now some hundreds of "disembodied" men and women—though most, unlike Christina, can hope to get better as soon as they stop poisoning themselves with pyridoxine.

1985

THE READER

1. *What is the basis for Sacks's use of the philosopher Wittgenstein as an introduction?*
2. *Ordinary phrases like "My back is cold" or "He kicked my shin" reinforce the ideas of the introduction. Equally ordinary phrases like "I am cold" or "He kicked me" contradict them. Does Christina's case history settle the question?*
3. *Near the end (p. 546), Sacks uses an old philosophical term—being. How does his essay define that term?*

THE WRITER

1. *Christina offers one metaphor for her condition (p. 545). What others are possible?*
2. *With little in the way of figurative language or metaphor, Sacks's account of Christina's condition is moving. What makes it so?*

James Baldwin

STRANGER IN THE VILLAGE

From all available evidence no black man had ever set foot in this tiny Swiss village before I came. I was told before arriving that I would probably be a "sight" for the village; I took this to mean that people of my complexion were rarely seen in Switzerland, and also that city people are always something of a "sight" outside of the city. It did not occur to me— possibly because I am an American—that there could be people anywhere who had never seen a Negro.

It is a fact that cannot be explained on the basis of the inaccessibility of the village. The village is very high, but it is only four hours from Milan and three hours from Lausanne. It is true that it is virtually unknown. Few people making plans for a holiday would elect to come here. On the other hand, the villagers are able, presumably, to come and go as they please—which they do: to another town at the foot of the mountain, with a population of approximately five thousand, the nearest place to see a movie or go to the bank. In the village there is no movie house, no bank, no library, no theater; very few radios, one jeep, one station wagon; and at the moment, one typewriter, mine, an invention which the woman next door to me here had never seen. There are about six hundred people living here, all Catholic—I conclude this from the fact that the Catholic church is open all year round, whereas the Protestant chapel, set off on a hill a little removed from the village, is open only in the summertime when the tourists arrive. There are four or five hotels, all closed now, and four or five *bistros*, of which, however, only two do any business during the winter. These two do not do a great deal, for life in the village seems to end around nine or ten o'clock. There are a few stores, butcher, baker, *épicerie*, a hardware store, and a money-changer—who cannot change travelers' checks, but must send them down to the bank, an operation which takes two or three days. There is something called the *Ballet Haus*, closed in the winter and used for God knows what, certainly not ballet, during the summer. There seems to be only one schoolhouse in the village, and this for the quite young children; I suppose this to mean that their older brothers and sisters at some point descend from these mountains in order to complete their education—possibly, again, to the town just below. The landscape is absolutely forbidding, mountains towering on all four sides, ice and snow as far as the eye can reach. In this white wilderness, men and women and children move all day, carrying washing, wood, buckets of milk or water, sometimes skiing on Sunday afternoons. All week long boys and young men are to be seen shoveling snow off the rooftops, or dragging wood down from the forest in sleds.

The village's only real attraction, which explains the tourist season, is the hot spring water. A disquietingly high proportion of these tourists are cripples, or semi-cripples, who come year after year—from other parts of Switzerland, usually—to take the waters. This lends the village, at the height of the season, a rather terrifying air of sanctity, as though it were a lesser Lourdes. There is often something beautiful, there is always something awful, in the spectacle of a person who has lost one of his faculties, a faculty he never questioned until it was gone, and who struggles to recover it. Yet people remain people, on crutches or indeed on deathbeds; and wherever I passed, the first summer I was here, among the native villagers or among the lame, a wind passed with me—of astonishment, curiosity, amusement, and outrage. That first summer I stayed two weeks and never intended to return. But I did return in the winter, to work; the village offers, obviously, no distractions whatever and has the further advantage of being extremely cheap. Now it is winter again, a year later, and I am here again. Everyone in the village knows my name, though they scarcely ever use it, knows that I come from America— though, this, apparently, they will never really believe: black men come from Africa—and everyone knows that I am the friend of the son of a woman who was born here, and that I am staying in their chalet. But I remain as much a stranger today as I was the first day I arrived, and the children shout *Neger! Neger!* as I walk along the streets.

It must be admitted that in the beginning I was far too shocked to have any real reaction. In so far as I reacted at all, I reacted by trying to be pleasant—it being a great part of the American Negro's education (long before he goes to school) that he must make people "like" him. This smile-and-the-world-smiles-with-you routine worked about as well in this situation as it had in the situation for which it was designed, which is to say that it did not work at all. No one, after all, can be liked whose human weight and complexity cannot be, or has not been, admitted. My smile was simply another unheard-of phenomenon which allowed them to see my teeth—they did not, really, see my smile and I began to think that, should I take to snarling, no one would notice any difference. All of the physical characteristics of the Negro which had caused me, in America, a very different and almost forgotten pain were nothing less than miraculous—or infernal—in the eyes of the village people. Some thought my hair was the color of tar, that it had the texture of wire, or the texture of cotton. It was jocularly suggested that I might let it all grow long and make myself a winter coat. If I sat in the sun for more than five minutes some daring creature was certain to come along and gingerly put his fingers on my hair, as though he were afraid of an electric shock, or put his hand on my hand, astonished that the color did not rub off. In all of this, in which it must be conceded there was the charm of genuine wonder and in which there were certainly no element of intentional unkindness, there was yet no suggestion that I was human: I was simply a living wonder.

I knew that they did not mean to be unkind, and I know it now; it is necessary, nevertheless, for me to repeat this to myself each time that I walk out of the chalet. The children who shout *Neger!* have no way of knowing the echoes this sound raises in me. They are brimming with good humor and the more daring swell with pride when I stop to speak with them. Just the same, there are days when I cannot pause and smile, when I have no heart to play with them; when, indeed, I mutter sourly to myself, exactly as I muttered on the streets of a city these children have never seen, when I was no bigger than these children are now: *Your mother was a nigger.* Joyce is right about history being a nightmare—but it may be the nightmare from which no one *can* awaken. People are trapped in history and history is trapped in them.

There is a custom in the village—I am told it is repeated in many villages—of "buying" African natives for the purpose of converting them to Christianity. There stands in the church all year round a small box with a slot for money, decorated with a black figurine, and into this box the villagers drop their francs. During the *carnaval* which precedes Lent, two village children have their faces blackened—out of which bloodless darkness their blue eyes shine like ice—and fantastic horsehair wigs are placed on their blond heads; thus disguised, they solicit among the villagers for money for the missionaries in Africa. Between the box in the church and the blackened children, the village "bought" last year six or eight African natives. This was reported to me with pride by the wife of one of the *bistro* owners and I was careful to express astonishment and pleasure at the solicitude shown by the village for the souls of black folks. The *bistro* owner's wife beamed with a pleasure far more genuine than my own and seemed to feel that I might now breathe more easily concerning the souls of at least six of my kinsmen.

I tried not to think of these so lately baptized kinsmen, of the price paid for them, or the peculiar price they themselves would pay, and said nothing about my father, who having taken his own conversion too literally never, at bottom, forgave the white world (which he described as heathen) for having saddled him with a Christ in whom, to judge at least from their treatment of him, they themselves no longer believed. I thought of white men arriving for the first time in an African village, strangers there, as I am a stranger here, and tried to imagine the astounded populace touching their hair and marveling at the color of their skin. But there is a great difference between being the first white man to be seen by Africans and being the first black man to be seen by whites. The white man takes the astonishment as tribute, for he arrives to conquer and to convert the natives, whose inferiority in relation to himself is not even to be questioned; whereas I, without a thought of conquest, find myself among a people whose culture controls me, has even, in a sense, created me, people who have cost me more in anguish and rage than they will ever know, who yet do not even know of my existence. The astonishment with which I might have greeted them, should they have stumbled into my African village a few hundred years ago, might have rejoiced their hearts. But the astonishment with which they greet me today can only poison mine.

And this is so despite everything I may do to feel differently, despite my friendly conversations with the *bistro* owner's wife, despite their three-year-old son who has at last become my friend, despite the *saluts* and *bonsoirs*[1] which I exchange with people as I walk, despite the fact that I know that no individual can be taken to task for what history is doing, or

---

1. "Hellos" and "good evenings."

has done. I say that the culture of these people controls me—but they can scarcely be held responsible for European culture. America comes out of Europe, but these people have never seen America, nor have most of them seen more of Europe than the hamlet at the foot of their mountain. Yet they move with an authority which I shall never have; and they regard me, quite rightly, not only as a stranger in their village but as a suspect latecomer, bearing no credentials, to everything they have—however unconsciously—inherited.

For this village, even were it incomparably more remote and incredibly more primitive, is the West, the West onto which I have been so strangely grafted. These people cannot be, from the point of view of power, strangers anywhere in the world; they have made the modern world, in effect, even if they do not know it. The most illiterate among them is related, in a way that I am not, to Dante, Shakespeare, Michelangelo, Aeschylus, Da Vinci, Rembrandt, and Racine; the cathedral at Chartres says something to them which it cannot say to me, as indeed would New York's Empire State Building, should anyone here ever see it. Out of their hymns and dances come Beethoven and Bach. Go back a few centuries and they are in their full glory—but I am in Africa, watching the conquerors arrive.

The rage of the disesteemed is personally fruitless, but it is also absolutely inevitable; this rage, so generally discounted, so little understood even among the people whose daily bread it is, is one of the things that makes history. Rage can only with difficulty, and never entirely, be brought under the domination of the intelligence and is therefore not susceptible to any arguments whatever. This is a fact which ordinary representatives of the *Herrenvolk*,[2] having never felt this rage and being unable to imagine, quite fail to understand. Also, rage cannot be hidden, it can only be dissembled. This dissembling deludes the thoughtless, and strengthens rage and adds, to rage, contempt. There are, no doubt, as many ways of coping with the resulting complex of tensions as there are black men in the world, but no black man can hope ever to be entirely liberated from this internal warfare—rage, dissembling, and contempt having inevitably accompanied his first realization of the power of white men. What is crucial here is that, since white men represent in the black man's world so heavy a weight, white men have for black men a reality which is far from being reciprocal; and hence all black men have toward all white men an attitude which is designed, really, either to rob the white man of the jewel of his naïveté, or else to make it cost him dear.

The black man insists, by whatever means he finds at his disposal, that the white man cease to regard him as an exotic rarity and recognize him as a human being. This is a very charged and difficult moment, for there

2. Master race.

is a great deal of will power involved in the white man's naïveté. Most people are not naturally reflective any more than they are naturally malicious, and the white man prefers to keep the black man at a certain human remove because it is easier for him thus to preserve his simplicity and avoid being called to account for crimes committed by his forefathers, or his neighbors. He is inescapably aware, nevertheless, that he is in a better position in the world than black men are, nor can he quite put to death the suspicion that he is hated by black men therefore. He does not wish to be hated, neither does he wish to change places, and at this point in his uneasiness he can scarcely avoid having recourse to those legends which white men have created about black men, the most usual effect of which is that the white man finds himself enmeshed, so to speak, in his own language which describes hell, as well as the attributes which lead one to hell, as being as black as night.

Every legend, moreover, contains its residuum of truth, and the root function of language is to control the universe by describing it. It is of quite considerable significance that black men remain, in the imagination, and in overwhelming numbers in fact, beyond the disciplines of salvation; and this despite the fact that the West has been "buying" African natives for centuries. There is, I should hazard, an instantaneous necessity to be divorced from this so visibly unsaved stranger, in whose heart, moreover, one cannot guess what dreams of vengeance are being nourished; and, at the same time, there are few things on earth more attractive than the idea of the unspeakable liberty which is allowed the unredeemed. When, beneath the black mask, a human being begins to make himself felt one cannot escape a certain awful wonder as to what kind of human being it is. What one's imagination makes of other people is dictated, of course, by the laws of one's own personality and it is one of the ironies of black-white relations that, by means of what the white man imagines the black man to be, the black man is enabled to know who the white man is.

I have said, for example, that I am as much a stranger in this village today as I was the first summer I arrived, but this is not quite true. The villagers wonder less about the texture of my hair than they did then, and wonder rather more about me. And the fact that their wonder now exists on another level is reflected in their attitudes and in their eyes. There are the children who make those delightful, hilarious, sometimes astonishingly grave overtures of friendship in the unpredictable fashion of children; other children, having been taught that the devil is a black man, scream in genuine anguish as I approach. Some of the older women never pass without a friendly greeting, never pass, indeed, if it seems that they will be able to engage me in conversation; other women look down or look away or rather contemptuously smirk. Some of the men drink with me and suggest that I learn how to ski—partly, I gather, because they cannot imagine what I would look like on skis—and want to know if I am married, and ask questions about my métier. But some of the men have accused le sale nègre[3]—behind my back—of stealing wood and there is already in the eyes of some of them that peculiar, intent, paranoiac malevolence which one sometimes surprises in the eyes of American white men when, out walking with their Sunday girl, they see a Negro male approach.

There is a dreadful abyss between the streets of this village and the streets of the city in which I was born, between the children who shout Neger! today and those who shouted Nigger! yesterday—the abyss is experience, the American experience. The syllable hurled behind me today expresses, above all, wonder: I am a stranger here. But I am not a stranger in America and the same syllable riding on the American air expresses the war my presence has occasioned in the American soul.

For this village brings home to me this fact: that there was a day, and not really a very distant day, when Americans were scarcely Americans at all but discontented Europeans, facing a great unconquered continent and strolling, say, into a marketplace and seeing black men for the first time. The shock this spectacle afforded is suggested, surely, by the promptness with which they decided that these black men were not really men but cattle. It is true that the necessity on the part of the settlers of the New World of reconciling their moral assumptions with the fact—and the necessity—of slavery enhanced immensely the charm of this idea, and it is also true that this idea expresses, with a truly American bluntness, the attitude which to varying extents all masters have had toward all slaves.

But between all former slaves and slave-owners and the drama which begins for Americans over three hundred years ago at Jamestown, there are at least two differences to be observed. The American Negro slave could not suppose, for one thing, as slaves in past epochs had supposed and often done, that he would ever be able to wrest the power from his master's hands. This was a supposition which the modern era, which was to bring about such vast changes in the aims and dimensions of power, put to death; it only begins, in unprecedented fashion, and with dreadful implications, to be resurrected today. But even had this supposition persisted with undiminished force, the American Negro slave could not have used it to lend his condition dignity, for the reason that this supposition rests on another: that the slave in exile yet remains related to his past, has some means—if only in memory—of revering and sustaining the forms of his former life, is able, in short, to maintain his identity.

This was not the case with the American Negro slave. He is unique among the black men of the world in that his past was taken from him,

3. The dirty Negro.

almost literally, at one blow. One wonders what on earth the first slave found to say to the first dark child he bore. I am told that there are Haitians able to trace their ancestry back to African kings, but any American Negro wishing to go back so far will find his journey through time abruptly arrested by the signature on the bill of sale which served as the entrance paper for his ancestor. At the time—to say nothing of the circumstances—of the enslavement of the captive black man who was to become the American Negro, there was not the remotest possibility that he would ever take power from his master's hands. There was no reason to suppose that his situation would ever change, nor was there, shortly, anything to indicate that his situation had ever been different. It was his necessity, in the words of E. Franklin Frazier, to find a "motive for living under American culture or die." The identity of the American Negro comes out of this extreme situation, and the evolution of this identity was a source of the most intolerable anxiety in the minds and the lives of his masters.

For the history of the American Negro is unique also in this: that the question of his humanity, and of his rights therefore as a human being, became a burning one for several generations of Americans, so burning a question that it ultimately became one of those used to divide the nation. It is out of this argument that the venom of the epithet *Nigger!* is derived. It is an argument which Europe has never had, and hence Europe quite sincerely fails to understand how or why the argument arose in the first place, why its effects are frequently disastrous and always so unpredictable, why it refuses until today to be entirely settled. Europe's black possessions remained—and do remain—in Europe's colonies, at which remove they represented no threat whatever to European identity. If they posed any problem at all for the European conscience it was a problem which remained comfortingly abstract: in effect, the black man, as a *man* did not exist for Europe. But in America, even as a slave, he was an inescapable part of the general social fabric and no American could escape having an attitude toward him. Americans attempt until today to make an abstraction of the Negro, but the very nature of these abstractions reveals the tremendous effects the presence of the Negro has had on the American character.

When one considers the history of the Negro in America it is of the greatest importance to recognize that the moral beliefs of a person, or a people, are never really as tenuous as life—which is not moral—very often causes them to appear; these create for them a frame of reference and a necessary hope, the hope being that when life has done its worst they will be enabled to rise above themselves and to triumph over life. Life would scarcely be bearable if this hope did not exist. Again, even when the worst has been said, to betray a belief is not by any means to have put oneself beyond its power; the betrayal of a belief is not the same thing as ceasing to believe. If this were not so there would be no moral standards in the world at all. Yet one must also recognize that morality is based on ideas and that all ideas are dangerous—dangerous because ideas can only lead to action and where the action leads no man can say. And dangerous in this respect: that confronted with the impossibility of remaining faithful to one's beliefs, and the equal impossibility of becoming free of them, one can be driven to the most inhuman excesses. The ideas on which American beliefs are based are not, though Americans often seem to think so, ideas which originated in America. They came out of Europe. And the establishment of democracy on the American continent was scarcely as radical a break with the past as was the necessity, which Americans faced, of broadening this concept to include black men.

This was, literally, a hard necessity. It was impossible, for one thing, for Americans to abandon their beliefs, not only because these beliefs alone seemed able to justify the sacrifices they had endured and the blood that they had spilled, but also because these beliefs afforded them their only bulwark against a moral chaos as absolute as the physical chaos of the continent it was their destiny to conquer. But in the situation in which Americans found themselves, these beliefs threatened an idea which, whether or not one likes to think so, is the very warp and woof of the heritage of the West, the idea of white supremacy.

Americans have made themselves notorious by the shrillness and the brutality with which they have insisted on this idea, but they did not invent it; and it has escaped the world's notice that those very excesses of which Americans have been guilty imply a certain, unprecedented uneasiness over the idea's life and power, if not, indeed, the idea's validity. The idea of white supremacy rests simply on the fact that white men are the creators of civilization (the present civilization, which is the only one that matters; all previous civilizations are simply "contributions" to our own) and are therefore civilization's guardians and defenders. Thus it was impossible for Americans to accept the black man as one of themselves, for to do so was to jeopardize their status as white men. But not so to accept him was to deny his human reality, his human weight and complexity, and the strain of denying the overwhelmingly undeniable forced Americans into rationalizations so fantastic that they approached the pathological.

At the root of the American Negro problem is the necessity of the American white man to find a way of living with the Negro in order to be able to live with himself. And the history of this problem can be reduced to the means used by Americans—lynch law and law, segregation and legal acceptance, terrorization and concession—either to come to terms with this necessity, or to find a way around it, or (most usually) to find a way of doing both these things at once. The resulting spectacle, at once foolish and dreadful, led someone to make the quite accurate observation that "the Negro-in-America is a form of insanity which overtakes white men."

In this long battle, a battle by no means finished, the unforeseeable effects of which will be felt by many future generations, the white man's motive was the protection of his identity; the black man was motivated by the need to establish an identity. And despite the terrorization which the Negro in America endured and endures sporadically until today, despite the cruel and totally inescapable ambivalence of his status in his country, the battle for his identity has long ago been won. He is not a visitor to the West, but a citizen there, an American; as American as the Americans who despise him, the Americans who fear him, the Americans who love him—the Americans who became less than themselves, or rose to be greater than themselves by virtue of the fact that the challenge he represented was inescapable. He is perhaps the only black man in the world whose relationship to white men is more terrible, more subtle, and more meaningful than the relationship of bitter possessed to uncertain possessors. His survival depended, and his development depends, on his ability to turn his peculiar status in the Western world to his own advantage and, it may be, to the very great advantage of that world. It remains for him to fashion out of his experience that which will give him sustenance, and a voice.

The cathedral at Chartres, I have said, says something to the people of this village which it cannot say to me; but it is important to understand that this cathedral says something to me which it cannot say to them. Perhaps they are struck by the power of the spires, the glory of the windows; but they have known God, after all, longer than I have known him, and in a different way, and I am terrified by the slippery bottomless well to be found in the crypt, down which heretics were hurled to death, and by the obscene, inescapable gargoyles jutting out of the stone and seeming to say that God and the devil can never be divorced. I doubt that the villagers think of the devil when they face a cathedral because they have never been identified with the devil. But I must accept the status which myth, if nothing else, gives me in the West before I can hope to change the myth.

Yet, if the American Negro has arrived at his identity by virtue of the absoluteness of his estrangement from his past, American white men still nourish the illusion that there is some means of recovering the European innocence, of returning to a state in which black men do not exist. This is one of the greatest errors Americans can make. The identity they fought so hard to protect has, by virtue of that battle, undergone a change: Americans are as unlike any other white people in the world as it is possible to be. I do not think, for example, that it is too much to suggest that the American vision of the world—which allows so little reality, generally speaking, for any of the darker forces in human life, which tends until today to paint moral issues in glaring black and white—owes a great deal to the battle waged by Americans to maintain between themselves and black men a human separation which could not be bridged. It is only now beginning to be borne in on us—very faintly, it must be admitted, very slowly, and very much against our will—that this vision of the world is dangerously inaccurate, and perfectly useless. For it protects our moral high-mindedness at the terrible expense of weakening our grasp of reality. People who shut their eyes to reality simply invite their own destruction, and anyone who insists on remaining in a state of innocence long after that innocence is dead turns himself into a monster.

The time has come to realize that the interracial drama acted out on the American continent has not only created a new black man, it has created a new white man, too. No road whatever will lead Americans back to the simplicity of this European village where white men still have the luxury of looking on me as a stranger. I am not, really, a stranger any longer for any American alive. One of the things that distinguishes Americans from other people is that no other people has ever been so deeply involved in the lives of black men, and vice versa. This fact faced, with all its implications, it can be seen that the history of the American Negro problem is not merely shameful, it is also something of an achievement. For even when the worst has been said, it must also be added that the perpetual challenge posed by this problem was always, somehow, perpetually met. It is precisely this black-white experience which may prove of indispensable value to us in the world we face today. This world is white no longer, and it will never be white again.

1953

THE READER

1. Baldwin begins with the narration of his experience in a Swiss village. At what point do you become aware that he is going to do more than tell the story of his stay in the village? What purpose does he make his experience serve?

2. On p. 554, Baldwin says that Americans have attempted to make an abstraction of the Negro. To what degree has his purpose forced Baldwin to make an abstraction of the white man? What are the components of that abstraction?

THE WRITER

1. Baldwin intimately relates the white man's language and legends about black men to the "laws" of the white man's personality. What conviction about the nature of language does this reveal?

2. Define alienation in a paragraph or two.

3. Describe some particular experience that raises a large social question

*or shows the working of large social forces. Does Baldwin offer any
help in the problem of connecting the particular and the general?*

Norman Podhoretz

MY NEGRO PROBLEM—AND OURS

If we—and ... I mean the relatively conscious whites and the relatively
conscious blacks, who must, like lovers, insist on, or create, the consciousness
of the others—do not falter in our duty now, we may be able, handful that we
are, to end the racial nightmare, and achieve our country, and change the
history of the world.   —JAMES BALDWIN[1]

Two ideas puzzled me deeply as a child growing up in Brooklyn during
the 1930's in what today would be called an integrated neighborhood.
One of them was that all Jews were rich; the other was that all Negroes
were persecuted. These ideas have appeared in print; therefore they
must be true. My own experience and the evidence of my senses told
they were not true, but that only confirmed what a day-dreaming boy in
the provinces—for the lower-class neighborhoods of New York belong as
surely to the provinces as any rural town in North Dakota—discovers
very early: *his* experience is unreal and the evidence of his senses is not to
be trusted. Yet even a boy with a head full of fantasies incongruously
synthesized out of Hollywood movies and English novels cannot altogether deny the reality of his own experience—especially when there is
so much deprivation in that experience. Nor can he altogether gainsay
the evidence of his own senses—especially such evidence of the senses as
comes from being repeatedly beaten up, robbed, and in general hated,
terrorized, and humiliated.

And so for a long time I was puzzled to think that Jews were supposed
to be rich when the only Jews I knew were poor, and that Negroes were
supposed to be persecuted when it was the Negroes who were doing the
only persecuting I knew about—and doing it, moreover, to *me*. During
the early years of the war, when my older sister joined a left-wing youth
organization, I remember my astonishment at hearing her passionately
denounce my father for thinking that Jews were worse off than Negroes.
To me, at the age of twelve, it seemed very clear that Negroes were
better off than Jews—indeed, than *all* whites. A city boy's world is
contained within three or four square blocks, and in my world it was the
whites, the Italians and Jews, who feared the Negroes, not the other way
around. The Negroes were tougher than we were, more ruthless, and on
the whole they were better athletes. What could it mean, then, to say

1. The quotation is from the conclusion of Baldwin's *The Fire Next Time*.

that they were badly off and that we were more fortunate? Yet my sister's opinions, like print, were sacred, and when she told me about exploitation and economic forces I believed her. I believed her, but I was still afraid of Negroes. And I still hated them with all my heart.

It had not always been so—that much I can recall from early childhood. When did it start, this fear and this hatred? There was a kindergarten in the local public school, and given the character of the neighborhood, at least half of the children in my class must have been Negroes. Yet I have no memory of being aware of color differences at that age, and I know from observing my own children that they attribute no significance to such differences even when they begin noticing them. I think there was a day—first grade? second grade?—when my best friend Carl hit me on the way home from school and announced that he wouldn't play with me any more because I had killed Jesus. When I ran home to my mother crying for an explanation, she told me not to pay any attention to such foolishness, and then in Yiddish she cursed the *goyim* and the *schwartzes*, the *schwartzes* and the *goyim*.[2] Carl, it turned out, was a *schwartze*, and so was added a third to the categories into which people were mysteriously divided.

Sometimes I wonder whether this is a true memory at all. It is blazingly vivid, but perhaps it never happened: can anyone really remember back to the age of six? There is no uncertainty in my mind, however, about the years that followed. Carl and I hardly ever spoke, though we met in school every day up through the eight or ninth grade. There would be embarrassed moments of catching his eye or of his catching mine—for whatever it was that had attracted us to one another as very small children remained alive in spite of the fantastic barrier of hostility that had grown up between us, suddenly and out of nowhere. Nevertheless, friendship would have been impossible, and even if it had been possible, it would have been unthinkable. About that, there was nothing anyone could do by the time we were eight years old.

Item: The orphanage across the street is torn down, a city housing project begins to rise in its place, and on the marvelous vacant lot next to the old orphanage they are building a playground. Much excitement and anticipation as Opening Day draws near. Mayor LaGuardia himself comes to dedicate this great gesture of public benevolence. He speaks of neighborliness and borrowing cups of sugar, and of the playground he says that children of all races, colors, and creeds will learn to live together in harmony. A week later, some of us are swatting flies on the playground's inadequate little ball field. A gang of Negro kids, pretty much our own age, enter from the other side and order us out of the park. We refuse, proudly and indignantly, with superb masculine fervor. There is a

2. The Yiddish words *goyim* (Gentiles or white non-Jews) and *schwartzes* (blacks) are both partially derogatory terms.

fight, they win, and we retreat, half whimpering, half with bravado. My first nauseating experience of cowardice. And my first appalled realization that there are people in the world who do not seem to be afraid of anything, who act as though they have nothing to lose. Thereafter the playground becomes a battleground, sometimes quiet, sometimes the scene of athletic competition between Them and Us. But rocks are thrown as often as baseballs. Gradually we abandon the place and use the streets instead. The streets are safer, though we do not admit this to ourselves. We are not, after all, sissies—that most dreaded epithet of an American boyhood.

Item: I am standing alone in front of the building in which I live. It is late afternoon and getting dark. That day in school the teacher had asked a surly Negro boy named Quentin a question he was unable to answer. As usual I had waved my arm eagerly ("Be a good boy, get good marks, be smart, go to college, become a doctor") and, the right answer bursting from my lips, I was held up lovingly by the teacher as an example to the class. I had seen Quentin's face—a very dark, very cruel, very Oriental-looking face—harden, and there had been enough threat in his eyes to make me run all the way home for fear that he might catch me outside.

Now, standing idly in front of my own house, I see him approaching from the project accompanied by his little brother who is carrying a baseball bat and wearing a grin of malicious anticipation. As in a nightmare, I am trapped. The surroundings are secure and familiar, but terror is suddenly present and there is no one around to help. I am locked to the spot. I will not cry out or run away like a sissy, and I stand there, my heart wild, my throat clogged. He walks up, hurls the familiar epithet ("Hey, mo' f—r"), and to my surprise only pushes me. It is a violent push, but not a punch. Maybe I can still back out without entirely losing my dignity. Maybe I can still say, "Hey, c'mon Quentin, whaddya wanna do *that* for? I dint do nothin' to *you*," and walk away, not too rapidly. Instead, before I can stop myself, I push him back—a token gesture—and I say, "Cut that out, I don't wanna fight, I ain't got nothin' to fight about." As I turn to walk back into the building, the corner of my eye catches the motion of the bat his little brother has handed him. I try to duck, but the bat crashes colored lights into my head.

The next thing I know, my mother and sister are standing over me, both of them hysterical. My sister—she who was later to join the "progressive" youth organization—is shouting for the police and screaming imprecations at those dirty little black bastards. They take me upstairs, the doctor comes, the police come. I tell them that the boy who did it was a stranger, that he had been trying to get money from me. They do not believe me, but I am too scared to give them Quentin's name. When I return to school a few days later, Quentin avoids my eyes. He knows that

I have not squealed, and he is ashamed. I try to feel proud, but in my heart I know that it was fear of what his friends might do to me that had kept me silent, and not the code of the street.

Item: There is an athletic meet in which the whole of our junior high school is participating. I am in one of the seventh-grade rapid-advance classes, and "segregation" has now set in with a vengeance. In the last three or four years of the elementary school from which we have just graduated, each grade had been divided into three classes, according to "intelligence." (In the earlier grades the divisions had either been arbitrary or else unrecognized by us as having anything to do with brains.) These divisions by IQ, or however it was arranged, had resulted in a preponderance of Jews in the "1" classes and a corresponding preponderance of Negroes in the "3's," with the Italians split unevenly along the spectrum. At least a few Negroes had always made the "1's," just as there had always been a few Jewish kids among the "3's" and more among the "2's" (where Italians dominated). But the junior high's rapid-advance class of which I am now a member is overwhelmingly Jewish and entirely white—except for a shy lonely Negro girl with light skin and reddish hair.

The athletic meet takes place in a city-owned stadium far from the school. It is an important event to which a whole day is given over. The winners are to get those precious little medallions stamped with the New York City emblem that can be screwed into a belt and that prove the wearer to be a distinguished personage. I am a fast runner, and so I am assigned the position of anchor man on my class's team in the relay race. There are three other seventh-grade teams in the race, two of them all Negro, as ours is all white. One of the all-Negro teams is very tall—their anchor man waiting silently next to me on the line looks years older than I am, and I do not recognize him. He is the first to get the baton and crosses the finishing line in a walk. Our team comes in second, but a few minutes later we are declared the winners, for it has been discovered that the anchor man on the first-place team is not a member of the class. We are awarded the medallions, and the following day our homeroom teacher makes a speech about how proud she is of us for being superior athletes as well as superior students. We want to believe that we deserve the praise, but we know that we could not have won even if the other class had not cheated.

That afternoon, walking home, I am waylaid and surrounded by five Negroes, among whom is the anchor man of the disqualified team. "Gimme my medal, mo'f—r," he grunts. I do not have it with me and I tell him so. "Anyway, it ain't yours," I say foolishly. He calls me a liar on both counts and pushes me up against the wall on which we sometimes play handball. "Gimme my mo'f—n' medal," he says again. I repeat that I have left it home. "Le's search the li'l mo'f—r," one of them suggests, "he prolly got it *hid* in his mo'f—n' *pants.*" My panic is now unmanageable. (How many times had I been surrounded like this and asked in soft tones, "Len' me a nickel, boy." How many times had I been called a liar for pleading poverty and pushed around, or searched, or beaten up, unless there happened to be someone in the marauding gang like Carl who liked me across that enormous divide of hatred and who would therefore say, "Aaah, c'mon, le's git someone else, *this* boy ain't got no money on 'im.") I scream at them through tears of rage and self-contempt, "Keep your f—n' filthy lousy black hands offa me! I swear I'll get the cops." This is all they need to hear, and the five of them set upon me. They bang me around, mostly in the stomach and on the arms and shoulders, and when several adults loitering near the candy store down the block notice what is going on and begin to shout, they run off and away.

I do not tell my parents about the incident. My team-mates, who have also been waylaid, each by a gang led by his opposite number from the disqualified team, have had their medallions taken from them, and they never squeal either. For days, I walk home in terror, expecting to be caught again, but nothing happens. The medallion is put away into a drawer, never to be worn by anyone.

Obviously experiences like these have always been a common feature of childhood life in working-class and immigrant neighborhoods, and Negroes do not necessarily figure in them. Wherever, and in whatever combination, they have lived together in the cities, kids of different groups have been at war, beating up and being beaten up: micks against kikes against wops against spicks against polacks. And even relatively homogeneous areas have not been spared the warring of the young: one block against another, one gang (called in my day, in a pathetic effort at gentility, an "S.A.C.," or social-athletic club) against another. But the Negro-white conflict had—and do doubt still has—a special intensity and was conducted with a ferocity unmatched by intramural white battling.

In my own neighborhood, a good deal of animosity existed between the Italian kids (most of whose parents were immigrants from Sicily) and the Jewish kids (who came largely from East European immigrant families). Yet everyone had friends, sometimes close friends, in the other "camp," and we often visited one another's strange-smelling houses, if not for meals, then for glasses of milk, and occasionally for some special event like a wedding or a wake. If it happened that we divided into warring factions and did battle, it would invariably be half-hearted and soon patched up. Our parents, to be sure, had nothing to do with one another and were mutually suspicious and hostile. But we, the kids, who all spoke Yiddish or Italian at home, were Americans, or New Yorkers, or Brooklyn boys: we shared a culture, the culture of the street, and at least for a while this culture proved to be more powerful than the opposing cultures of the home.

Why, why should it have been so different as between the Negroes and us? How was it borne in upon us so early, white and black alike, that we were enemies beyond any possibility of reconciliation? Why did we hate one another so?

I suppose if I tried, I could answer those questions more or less adequately from the perspective of what I have since learned. I could draw upon James Baldwin—what better witness is there?—to describe the sense of entrapment that poisons the soul of the Negro with hatred for the white man whom he knows to be his jailer. On the other side, if I wanted to understand how the white man comes to hate the Negro, I could call upon the psychologists who have spoken of the guilt that white Americans feel toward Negroes and that turns into hatred for lack of acknowledging itself as guilt. These are plausible answers and certainly there is truth in them. Yet when I think back upon my own experience of the Negro and his of me, I find myself troubled and puzzled, much as I was as a child when I heard that all Jews were rich and all Negroes persecuted. How could the Negroes in my neighborhood have regarded the whites across the street and around the corner as jailers? On the whole, the whites were not so poor as the Negroes, but they were quite poor enough, and the years were years of Depression. As for white hatred of the Negro, how could guilt have had anything to do with it? What share had these Italian and Jewish immigrants in the enslavement of the Negro? What share had they—downtrodden people themselves breaking their own necks to eke out a living—in the exploitation of the Negro?

No, I cannot believe that we hated each other back there in Brooklyn because they thought of us as jailers and we felt guilty toward them. But does it matter, given the fact that we all went through an unrepresentative confrontation? I think it matters profoundly, for if we managed the job of hating each other so well without benefit of the aids to hatred that are supposedly at the root of this madness everywhere else, it must mean that the madness is not yet properly understood. I am far from pretending that I understand it, but I would insist that no view of the problem will begin to approach the truth unless it can account for a case like the one I have been trying to describe. Are the elements of any such view available to us?

At least two, I would say, are. One of them is a point we frequently come upon in the work of James Baldwin, and the other is a related point always stressed by psychologists who have studied the mechanisms of prejudice. Baldwin tells us that one of the reasons Negroes hate the white man is that the white man refuses to *look* at him: the Negro knows that in white eyes all Negroes are alike; they are faceless and therefore not altogether human. The psychologists, in their turn, tell us that the white man hates the Negro because he tends to project those wild impulses that he fears in himself onto an alien group which he then punishes with his contempt. What Baldwin does *not* tell us, however, is that the principle of facelessness is a two-way street and can operate in both directions with no difficulty at all. Thus, in my neighborhood in Brooklyn, *I* was as faceless to the Negroes as they were to me, and if they hated me because I never looked at them, I must also have hated them for never looking at *me*. To the Negroes, my white skin was enough to define me as the enemy, and in a war it is only the uniform that counts and not the person.

So with the mechanism of projection that the psychologists talk about: it too works in both directions at once. There is no question that the psychologists are right about what the Negro represents symbolically to the white man. For me as a child the life lived on the other side of the playground and down the block on Ralph Avenue seemed the very embodiment of the values of the street—free, independent, reckless, brave, masculine, erotic. I put the word "erotic" last, though it is usually stressed above all others, because in fact it came last, in consciousness as in importance. What mainly counted for me about Negro kids of my own age was that they were "bad boys." There were plenty of bad boys among the whites—this was, after all, a neighborhood with a long tradition of crime as a career open to aspiring talents—but the Negroes were *really* bad, bad in a way that beckoned to one, and made one feel inadequate. We all went home every day for a lunch of spinach-and-potatoes; *they* roamed around during lunch hour, munching on candy bars. In winter *we* had to wear itchy woolen hats and mittens and cumbersome galoshes; *they* were bareheaded and loose as they pleased. We rarely played hookey, or got into serious trouble in school, for all our street-corner bravado; *they* were defiant, forever staying out (to do what delicious things?), forever making disturbances in class and in the halls, forever being sent to the principal and returning uncowed. But most important of all, they were *tough*; beautifully, enviably tough, not giving a damn for anyone or anything. To hell with the teacher, the truant officer, the cop; to hell with the whole of the adult world that held *us* in its grip and that we never had the courage to rebel against except sporadically and in petty ways.

This is what I saw and envied and feared in the Negro: this is what finally made him faceless to me, though some of it, of course, was actually there. (The psychologists also tell us that the alien group which becomes the object of a projection will tend to respond by trying to live up to what is expected of them.) But what, on his side, did the Negro see in me that made me faceless to *him*? Did he envy me my lunches of spinach-and-potatoes and my itchy woolen caps and my prudent behavior in the face of authority, as I envied him his noon-time candy bars and his bare head in winter and his magnificent rebelliousness? Did those lunches and caps spell for him the prospect of power and riches in the future? Did they mean that there were possibilities open to me that were denied to him? Very likely they did. But if so, one also supposes that he feared the impulses within himself toward submission to authority no less powerfully than I feared the impulses in myself toward defiance. If I represented the jailer to him, it was not because I was oppressing him or keeping him down: it was because I symbolized for him the dangerous and probably pointless temptation toward greater repression, just as he symbolized for me the equally perilous tug toward greater freedom. I personally was to be rewarded for this repression with a new and better life in the future, but how many of my friends paid an even higher price and were given only gall in return.

We have it on the authority of James Baldwin that all Negroes hate whites. I am trying to suggest that on their side all whites—all American whites, that is—are sick in their feelings about Negroes. There are Negroes, no doubt, who would say that Baldwin is wrong, but I suspect them of being less honest than he is, just as I suspect whites of self-deception who tell me they have no special feeling toward Negroes. Special feelings about color are a contagion to which white Americans seem susceptible even when there is nothing in their background to account for the susceptibility. Thus everywhere we look today in the North we find the curious phenomenon of white middle-class liberals with no previous personal experience of Negroes—people to whom Negroes have always been faceless in virtue rather than faceless in vice—discovering that their abstract commitment to the cause of Negro rights will not stand the test of a direct confrontation. We find such people fleeing in droves to the suburbs as the Negro population in the inner city grows; and when they stay in the city we find them sending their children to private school rather than to the "integrated" public school in the neighborhood. We find them resisting the demand that gerrymandered school districts be re-zoned for the purpose of overcoming de facto segregation; we find them judiciously considering whether the Negroes (for their own good, of course) are not perhaps pushing too hard; we find them clucking their tongues over Negro militancy; we find them speculating on the question of whether there may not, after all, be something in the theory that the races are biologically different; we find them saying that it will take a very long time for Negroes to achieve full equality, no matter what anyone does; we find them deploring the rise of black nationalism and expressing the solemn hope that the leaders of the Negro community will discover ways of containing the impatience and incipient violence within the Negro ghettos.

But that is by no means the whole story; there is also the phenomenon of what Kenneth Rexroth once called "crow-jimism." There are the broken-down white boys like Vivaldo Moore in Baldwin's *Another Country* who go to Harlem in search of sex or simply to brush up against something that looks like primitive vitality, and who are so often punished by the Negroes they meet for crimes that they would have been the last ever to commit and of which they themselves have been as sorry victims as any of the Negroes who take it out on them. There are the writers and intellectuals and artists who romanticize Negroes and pander to them, assuming a guilt that is not properly theirs. And there are all the white liberals who permit Negroes to blackmail them into adopting a double standard of moral judgment, and who lend themselves—again assuming the responsibility for crimes they never committed—to cunning and contemptuous exploitation by Negroes they employ or try to befriend.

And what about me? What kind of feelings do I have about Negroes today? What happened to me, from Brooklyn, who grew up fearing and envying and hating Negroes? Now that Brooklyn is behind me, do I fear them and envy them and hate them still? The answer is yes, but not in the same proportions and certainly not in the same way. I now live on the upper west side of Manhattan, where there are many Negroes and many Puerto Ricans, and there are nights when I experience the old apprehensiveness again, and there are streets that I avoid when I am walking in the dark, as there were streets that I avoided when I was a child. I find that I am not afraid of Puerto Ricans, but I cannot restrain my nervousness whenever I pass a group of Negroes standing in front of a bar or sauntering down the street. I know now, as I did not know when I was a child, that power is on my side, that the police are working for me and not for them. And knowing this I feel ashamed and guilty, like the good liberal I have grown up to be. Yet the twinges of fear and the resentment they bring and the self-contempt they arouse are not to be gainsaid.

But envy? Why envy? And hatred? Why hatred? Here again the intensities have lessened and everything has been complicated and qualified by the guilts and the resulting over-compensations that are the heritage of the enlightened middle-class world of which I am now a member. Yet just as in childhood I envied Negroes for what seemed to me their superior masculinity, so I envy them today for what seems to me their superior physical grace and beauty. I have come to value physical grace very highly, and I am now capable of aching with all my being when I watch a Negro couple on the dance floor, or a Negro playing baseball or basketball. They are on the kind of terms with their own bodies that I should like to be on with mine, and for that precious quality they seemed blessed to me.

The hatred I still feel for Negroes is the hardest of all the old feelings to face or admit, and it is the most hidden and the most overlarded by the conscious attitudes into which I have succeeded in willing myself. It no longer has, as for me it once did, any cause or justification (except, perhaps, that I am constantly being denied my right to an honest expression of the things I earned the right as a child to feel). How, then, do I know that this hatred has never entirely disappeared? I know it from the insane rage that can stir in me at the thought of Negro anti-Semitism; I know it from the disgusting prurience that can stir in me at the sight of a mixed couple; and I know it from the violence that can stir in me whenever I encounter that special brand of paranoid touchiness to which many Negroes are prone.

This, then, is where I am; it is not exactly where I think all other white liberals are, but it cannot be so very far away either. And it is because I am convinced that we white Americans are—for whatever reason, it no longer matters—so twisted and sick in our feelings about Negroes that I despair of the present push toward integration. If the pace of progress were not a factor here, there would perhaps be no cause for despair: time and the law and even the international political situation are on the side of the Negroes, and ultimately, therefore, victory—of a sort, anyway— must come. But from everything we have learned from observers who ought to know, pace has become as important to the Negroes as substance. They want equality and they want it *now*, and the white world is yielding to their demand only as much and as fast as it is absolutely being compelled to do. The Negroes know this in the most concrete terms imaginable, and it is thus becoming increasingly difficult to buy them off with rhetoric and promises and pious assurances of support. And so within the Negro community we find more and more people declaring— as Harold R. Isaacs recently put it in an article in *Commentary*—that they want *out*: people who say that integration will never come, or that it will take a hundred or a thousand years to come, or that it will come at too high a price in suffering and struggle for the pallid and sodden life of the American middle class that at the very best it may bring.

The most numerous, influential, and dangerous movement that has grown out of Negro despair with the goal of integration is, of course, the Black Muslims. This movement, whatever else we may say about it, must be credited with one enduring achievement: it inspired James Baldwin to write an essay which deserves to be placed among the classics of our language. Everything Baldwin has ever been trying to tell us is distilled in *The Fire Next Time* into a statement of overwhelming persuasiveness and prophetic magnificence. Baldwin's message is and always has been simple. It is this: "Color is not a human or personal reality; it is a political reality." And Baldwin's demand is correspondingly simple; color must be forgotten, lest we all be smited with a vengeance "that does not really depend on, and cannot really be executed by, any person or organization, and that cannot be prevented by any police force or army: historical vengeance, a cosmic vengeance based on the law that we recognize when we say, 'Whatever goes up must come down.'" The Black Muslims Baldwin portrays as a sign and a warning to the intransigent white world. They come to proclaim how deep is the Negro's disaffection with the white world and all its works, and Baldwin implies that no American Negro can fail to respond somewhere in his being to their message: that the white man is the devil, that Allah has doomed him to destruction, and that the black man is about to inherit the earth. Baldwin of course knows that this nightmare inversion of the racism from which the black man has suffered can neither win nor even point to the neighborhood in which victory might be located. For in his view the neighborhood of victory lies in exactly the opposite direction: the transcendence of color through love.

Yet the tragic fact is that love is not the answer to hate—not in the world of politics, at any rate. Color is indeed a political rather than a human or a personal reality and if politics (which is to say power) has made it into a human and personal reality, then only politics (which is to say power) can unmake it once again. But the way of politics is slow and bitter, and as impatience on the one side is matched by a setting of the jaw on the other, we move closer and closer to an explosion and blood may yet run in the streets.

Will this madness in which we are all caught never find a resting-place? Is there never to be an end to it? In thinking about the Jews I have often wondered whether their survival as a distinct group was worth one hair on the head of a single infant. Did the Jews have to survive so that six million innocent people should one day be burned in the ovens of Auschwitz? It is a terrible question and no one, not God himself, could ever answer it to my satisfaction. And when I think about the Negroes in America and about the image of integration as a state in which the Negroes would take their rightful place as another of the protected minorities in a pluralistic society, I wonder whether they really believe in their hearts that such a state can actually be attained, and if so *why* they should wish to survive as a distinct group. I think I know why the Jews once wished to survive (though I am less certain as to why we still do): they not only believed that God had given them no choice, but they were tied to a memory of past glory and a dream of imminent redemption. What does the American Negro have that might correspond to this? His past is a stigma, his color is a stigma, and his vision of the future is the hope of erasing the stigma by making color irrelevant, by making it disappear as a fact of consciousness.

I share this hope, but I cannot see how it will ever be realized unless color does *in fact* disappear: and that means not integration, it means assimilation, it means—let the brutal word come out—miscegenation. The Black Muslims, like their racist counterparts in the white world, accuse the "so-called Negro leaders" of secretly pursuing miscegenation as a goal. The racists are wrong, but I wish they were right, for I believe that the wholesale merger of the two races is the most desirable alternative for everyone concerned. I am not claiming that this alternative can be pursued programmatically or that it is immediately feasible as a solution; obviously there are even greater barriers to its achievement than to the achievement of integration. What I am saying, however, is that in my opinion the Negro problem can be solved in this country in no other way.

I have told the story of my own twisted feelings about Negroes here, and of how they conflict with the moral convictions I have since developed, in order to assert that such feelings must be acknowledged as honestly as possible so that they can be controlled and ultimately disregarded in favor of the convictions. It is *wrong* for a man to suffer because of the color of his skin. Beside that clichéd proposition of liberal thought, what argument can stand and be respected? If the arguments are the arguments of feeling, they must be made to yield; and one's own soul is not the worst place to begin working a huge social transformation. Not so long ago, it used to be asked of white liberals, "Would you like your sister to marry one?" When I was a boy and my sister was still unmarried I would certainly have said no to that question. But now I am a man, my sister is already married, and I have daughters. If I were to be asked today whether I would like a daughter of mine "to marry one." I would have to answer: "No, I wouldn't *like* it at all. I would rail and rave and rant and tear my hair. And then I hope I would have the courage to curse myself for raving and ranting, and to give her my blessing. How dare I withhold it at the behest of the child I once was and against the man I now have a duty to be?"

1964

Malcolm Cowley

THE VIEW FROM 80

Even before he or she is 80, the aging person may undergo another identity crisis like that of adolescence. Perhaps there had also been a middle-aged crisis, the male or the female menopause, but for the rest of adult life he had taken himself for granted, with his capabilities and failings. Now, when he looks in the mirror, he asks himself, "Is this really me?"—or he avoids the mirror out of distress at what it reveals, those bags and wrinkles. In his new makeup he is called upon to play a new role in a play that must be improvised. André Gide, that long-lived man of letters, wrote in his journal, "My heart has remained so young that I have the continual feeling of playing a part, the part of the 70-year-old that I certainly am; and the infirmities and weaknesses that remind me of my age act like a prompter, reminding me of my lines when I tend to stray. Then, like the good actor I want to be, I go back into my role, and I pride myself on playing it well."

In his new role the old person will find that he is tempted by new vices, that he receives new compensations (not so widely known), and that he may possibly achieve new virtues. Chief among these is the heroic or merely obstinate refusal to surrender in the face of time. One admires the ships that go down with all flags flying and the captain on the bridge.

Among the vices of age are avarice, untidiness, and vanity, which last takes the form of a craving to be loved or simply admired. Avarice is the worst of those three. Why do so many old persons, men and women alike, insist on hoarding money when they have no prospect of using it and even when they have no heirs? They eat the cheapest food, buy no clothes, and live in a single room when they could afford better lodging. It may be that they regard money as a form of power; there is a comfort in watching it accumulate while other powers are dwindling away. How often we read of an old person found dead in a hovel, on a mattress partly stuffed with bankbooks and stock certificates! The bankbook syndrome, we call it in our family, which has never succumbed.

Untidiness we call the Langley Collyer syndrome. To explain, Langley Collyer was a former concert pianist who lived alone with his 70-year-old brother in a brownstone house on upper Fifth Avenue. The once fashionable neighborhood had become part of Harlem. Homer, the brother, had been an admiralty lawyer, but was now blind and partly paralyzed; Langley played for him and fed him on buns and oranges, which he thought would restore Homer's sight. He never threw away a daily paper because Homer, he said, might want to read them all. He saved other things as well and the house became filled with rubbish from roof to basement. The halls were lined on both sides with bundled newspapers, leaving narrow passageways in which Langley had devised booby traps to catch intruders.

On March 21, 1947, some unnamed person telephoned the police to report that there was a dead body in the Collyer house. The police broke down the front door and found the hall impassable, then they hoisted a ladder to a second-story window. Behind it Homer was lying on the floor in a bathrobe; he had starved to death. Langley had disappeared. After some delay, the police broke into the basement, chopped a hole in the roof, and began throwing junk out of the house, top and bottom. It was 18 days before they found Langley's body, gnawed by rats. Caught in one of his own booby traps, he had died in a hallway just outside Homer's door. By that time the police had collected, and the Department of Sanitation had hauled away, 120 tons of rubbish, including besides the newspapers, 14 grand pianos and the parts of a dismantled Model T Ford.

Why do so many old people accumulate junk, not on the scale of Langley Collyer, but still in a dismaying fashion? Their tables are piled high with it, their bureau drawers are stuffed with it, their closet rods bend with the weight of clothes not worn for years. I suppose that the piling up is partly from lethargy and partly from the feeling that everything once useful, including their own bodies, should be preserved. Others, though not so many, have such a fear of becoming Langley Collyers that they strive to be painfully neat. Every tool they own is in its place, though it will never be used again; every scrap of paper is filed away in alphabetical order. At last their immoderate neatness becomes another vice of age, if a milder one.

The vanity of older people is an easier weakness to explain, and to condone. With less to look forward to, they yearn for recognition of what they have been: the reigning beauty, the athlete, the soldier, the scholar. It is the beauties who have the hardest time. A portrait of themselves at twenty hangs on the wall, and they try to resemble it by making an extravagant use of creams, powders, and dyes. Being young at heart, they think they are merely revealing their essential persons. The athletes find shelves for their silver trophies, which are polished once a year. Perhaps a letter sweater lies wrapped in a bureau drawer. I remember one evening when a no-longer athlete had guests for dinner and tried to find his sweater. "Oh, that old thing," his wife said. "The moths got into it and I threw it away." The athlete sulked and his guests went home early.

Often the yearning to be recognized appears in conversation as an innocent boast. Thus, a distinguished physician, retired at 94, remarks casually that a disease was named after him. A former judge bursts into chuckles as he repeats bright things that he said on the bench. Aging scholars complain in letters (or one of them does), "As I approach 70 I'm becoming avid of honors, and such things—medals, honorary degrees, etc.—are only passed around among academics on a *quid pro quo* basis (one hood capping another)." Or they say querulously, "Bill Underwood has ten honorary doctorates and I have only three. Why didn't they elect me to . . .?" and they mention the name of some learned society. That search for honors is a harmless passion, though it may lead to jealousies and deformations of character, as with Robert Frost in his later years. Still, honors cost little. Why shouldn't the very old have more than their share of them?

To be admired and praised, especially by the young, is an autumnal pleasure enjoyed by the lucky ones (who are not always the most deserving). "What is more charming," Cicero observes in his famous essay *De Senectute*,[1] "than an old age surrounded by the enthusiasm of youth! . . . Attentions which seem trivial and conventional are marks of honor—the morning call, being sought after, precedence, having people rise for you, being escorted to and from the forum. . . . What pleasures of the body can be compared to the prerogatives of influence?" But there are also pleasures of the body, or the mind, that are enjoyed by a greater number of older persons.

Those pleasures include some that younger people find hard to appreciate. One of them is simply sitting still, like a snake on a sun-warmed stone, with a delicious feeling of indolence that was seldom attained in earlier years. A leaf flutters down; a cloud moves by inches across the horizon. At such moments the older person, completely relaxed, has become a part of nature—and a living part, with blood coursing through his veins. The future does not exist for him. He thinks, if he thinks at all, that life for younger persons is still a battle royal of each against each, but that now he has nothing more to win or lose. He is not so much above as outside the battle, as if he had assumed the uniform of some small neutral country, perhaps Liechtenstein or Andorra. From a distance he notes that some of the combatants, men or women, are jostling ahead—but why do they fight so hard when the most they can hope for is a longer obituary? He can watch the scrounging and gouging, he can hear the shouts of exultation, the moans of the gravely wounded, and meanwhile he feels secure; nobody will attack him from ambush.

Age has other physical compensations besides the nirvana of dozing in the sun. A few of the simplest needs become a pleasure to satisfy. When an old woman in a nursing home was asked what she really liked to do, she answered in one word: "Eat." She might have been speaking for many of her fellows. Meals in a nursing home, however badly cooked, serve as climactic moments of the day. The physical essence of the pensioners is being renewed at an appointed hour; now they can go back to meditating or to watching TV while looking forward to the next meal. They can also look forward to sleep, which has become a definite pleasure, not the mere interruption it once had been.

Here I am thinking of old persons under nursing care. Others ferociously guard their independence, and some of them suffer less than one might expect from being lonely and impoverished. They can be rejoiced by visits and meetings, but they also have company inside their heads. Some of them are busiest when their hands are still. What passes through the minds of many is a stream of persons, images, phrases, and familiar tunes. For some that stream has continued since childhood, but now it is deeper; it is their present and their past combined. At times they conduct

1. *On Old Age.*

silent dialogues with a vanished friend, and these are less tiring—often more rewarding—than spoken conversations. If inner resources are lacking, old persons living alone may seek comfort and a kind of companionship in the bottle. I should judge from the gossip of various neighborhoods that the outer suburbs from Boston to San Diego are full of secretly alcoholic widows. One of those widows, an old friend, was moved from her apartment into a retirement home. She left behind her a closet in which the floor was covered wall to wall with whiskey bottles. "Oh, those empty bottles!" she explained. "They were left by a former tenant."

Not whiskey or cooking sherry but simply giving up is the greatest temptation of age. It is something different from a stoical acceptance of infirmities, which is something to be admired. At 63, when he first recognized that his powers were failing, Emerson wrote one of his best poems, "Terminus":

> It is time to be old,
> To take in sail:—
> The god of bounds,
> Who sets to seas a shore,
> Came to me in his fatal rounds,
> And said: "No more!
> No farther shoot
> Thy broad ambitious branches, and thy root.
> Fancy departs: no more invent;
> Contract thy firmament
> To compass of a tent."

Emerson lived in good health to the age of 79. Within his narrowed firmament, he continued working until his memory failed; then he consented to having younger editors and collaborators. The givers-up see no reason for working. Sometimes they lie in bed all day when moving about would still be possible, if difficult. I had a friend, a distinguished poet, who surrendered in that fashion. The doctors tried to stir him to action, but he refused to leave his room. Another friend, once a successful artist, stopped painting when his eyes began to fail. His doctor made the mistake of telling him that he suffered from a fatal disease. He then lost interest in everything except the splendid Rolls-Royce, acquired in his prosperous days, that stood in the garage. Daily he wiped the dust from its hood. He couldn't drive it on the road any longer, but he used to sit in the driver's seat, start the motor, then back the Rolls out of the garage and drive it in again, back twenty feet and forward twenty feet; that was his only distraction.

I haven't the right to blame those who surrender, not being able to put myself inside their minds or bodies. Often they must have compelling reasons, physical or moral. Not only do they suffer from a variety of ailments, but also they are made to feel that they no longer have a function in the community. Their families and neighbors don't ask them for advice, don't really listen when they speak, don't call on them for efforts. One notes that there are not a few recoveries from apparent senility when that situation changes. If it doesn't change, old persons may decide that efforts are useless. I sympathize with their problems, but the men and women I envy are those who accept old age as a series of challenges.

For such persons, every new infirmity is an enemy to be outwitted, an obstacle to be overcome by force of will. They enjoy each little victory over themselves, and sometimes they win a major success. Renoir was one of them. He continued painting, and magnificently, for years after he was crippled by arthritis; the brush had to be strapped to his arm. "You don't need your hand to paint," he said. Goya was another of the unvanquished. At 72 he retired as an official painter of the Spanish court and decided to work only for himself. His later years were those of the famous "black paintings" in which he let his imagination run (and also of the lithographs, then a new technique). At 78 he escaped a reign of terror in Spain by fleeing to Bordeaux. He was deaf and his eyes were failing; in order to work he had to wear several pairs of spectacles, one over another, and then use a magnifying glass; but he was producing splendid work in a totally new style. At 80 he drew an ancient man propped on two sticks, with a mass of white hair and beard hiding his face and with the inscription "I am still learning."

Giovanni Papini said when he was nearly blind, "I prefer martyrdom to imbecility." After writing sixty books, including his famous *Life of Christ*, he was at work on two huge projects when he was stricken with a form of muscular atrophy. He lost the use of his left leg, then of his fingers, so that he couldn't hold a pen. The two big books, though never to be finished, moved forward slowly by dictation; that in itself was a triumph. Toward the end, when his voice had become incomprehensible, he spelled out a word, tapping on the table to indicate letters of the alphabet. One hopes never to be faced with the need for such heroic measures.

"Eighty years old!" the great Catholic poet Paul Claudel wrote in his journal. "No eyes left, no ears, no teeth, no legs, no wind! And when all is said and done, how astonishingly well one does without them!"

1981

Lewis Thomas

THE LONG HABIT

We continue to share with our remotest ancestors the most tangled and evasive attitudes about death, despite the great distance we have come to understanding some of the profound aspects of biology. We have as much distaste for talking about personal death as for thinking about it; it is an indelicacy, like talking in mixed company about venereal disease or abortion in the old days. Death on a grand scale does not bother us in the same special way: we can sit around a dinner table and discuss war, involving 60 million volatilized human deaths, as though we were talking about bad weather; we can watch abrupt bloody death every day, in color, on films and television, without blinking back a tear. It is when the numbers of dead are very small, and very close, that we begin to think in scurrying circles. At the very center of the problem is the naked cold deadness of one's own self, the only reality in nature of which we can have absolute certainty, and it is unmentionable, unthinkable. We may be even less willing to face the issue at first hand than our predecessors because of a secret new hope that maybe it will go away. We like to think, hiding the thought, that with all the marvelous ways in which we seem now to lead nature around by the nose, perhaps we can avoid the central problem if we just become, next year, say, a bit smarter.

"The long habit of living," said Thomas Browne, "indisposeth us to dying." These days, the habit has become an addiction: we are hooked on living, the tenacity of its grip on us, and ours on it, grows in intensity. We cannot think of giving it up, even when living loses its zest—even when we have lost the zest for zest.

We have come a long way in our technologic capacity to put death off, and it is imaginable that we might learn to stall it for even longer periods, perhaps matching the life-spans of the Abkhasian Russians, who are said to go on, springily, for a century and a half. If we can rid ourselves of some of our chronic, degenerative diseases, and cancer, strokes and coronaries, we might go on and on. It sounds attractive and reasonable, but it is no certainty. If we became free of disease, we would make a much better run of it for the last decade or so, but might still terminate on about the same schedule as now. We may be like the genetically different lines of mice, or like Hayflick's different tissue-culture lines, programmed to die after a predetermined number of days clocked by their genomes. If this is the way it is, some of us will continue to wear out and come unhinged in the sixth decade, and some much later, depending on genetic timetables.

If we ever do achieve freedom from most of today's diseases, or even complete freedom from disease, we will perhaps terminate by drying out and blowing away on a light breeze, but we will still die.

Most of my friends do not like this way of looking at it. They prefer to take it for granted that we only die because we get sick, with one lethal ailment or another, and if we did not have our diseases we might go on indefinitely. Even biologists choose to think this about themselves, despite the evidences of the absolute inevitability of death that surround their professional lives. Everything dies, all around, trees, plankton, lichens, mice, whales, flies, mitochondria. In the simplest creatures it is sometimes difficult to see it as death, since the strands of replicating DNA they leave behind are more conspicuously the living parts of themselves than with us (not that it is fundamentally any different, but it seems so). Flies do not develop a ward round[1] of diseases that carry them off, one by one. They simply age, and die, like flies.

We hanker to go on, even in the face of plain evidence that long, long lives are not necessarily pleasurable in the kind of society we have arranged thus far. We will be lucky if we can postpone the search for new technologies for a while, until we have discovered some satisfactory things to do with the extra time. Something will surely have to be found to take the place of sitting on the porch reexamining one's watch.

Perhaps we would not be so anxious to prolong life if we did not detest so much the sickness of withdrawal. It is astonishing how little information we have about this universal process, with all the other dazzling advances in biology. It is almost as though we wanted not to know about it. Even if we could imagine the act of death in isolation, without any preliminary stage of being struck down by disease, we would be fearful of it.

There are signs that medicine may be taking a new interest in the process, partly from interest, partly from an embarrassed realization that we have not been handling this aspect of disease with as much skill as physicians once displayed, back in the days before they became convinced that disease was their solitary and sometimes defeatable enemy. It used to be the hardest and most important of all the services of a good doctor to be on hand at the time of death, and to provide comfort, usually in the home. Now it is done in hospitals, in secrecy (one of the reasons for the increased fear of death these days may be that so many people are totally unfamiliar with it; they never actually see it happen in real life). Some of our technology permits us to deny its existence, and we maintain flickers of life for long stretches in one community of cells or another, as though we were keeping a flag flying. Death is not a sudden all-at-once affair; cells go down in sequence, one by one. You can, if you like, recover great numbers of them many hours after the lights have gone out, and

1. That is, the variety of ailments a doctor sees during his circuit among the patients in a hospital ward.

grow them out in cultures. It takes hours, even days, before the irreversible word finally gets around to all the provinces.

We may be about to rediscover that dying is not such a bad thing to do after all. Sir William Osler took this view; he disapproved of people who spoke of the agony of death, maintaining that there was no such thing.

In a 19th-century memoir about an expedition in Africa, there is a story about an explorer who was caught by a lion, crushed across the chest in the animal's great jaws, and saved in the instant by a lucky shot from a friend. Later, he remembered the episode in clear detail. He was so amazed by the extraordinary sense of peace and calm, and total painlessness, associated with his partial experience of being killed, that he constructed a theory that all creatures are provided with a protective physiologic mechanism, switched on at the verge of death, carrying them through in a haze of tranquility.

I have seen agony in death only once, in a patient with rabies, who remained acutely aware of every stage in the process of his own disintegration over a 24-hour period, right up to his final moment. It was as though, in the special neuropathology of rabies, the switch had been prevented from turning.

We will be having new opportunities to learn more about the physiology of death at first hand, from the increasing numbers of cardiac patients who have been through the whole process and then back again. Judging from what has been found out thus far, from the first generation of people resuscitated from cardiac standstill (already termed the Lazarus syndrome), Osler seems to have been right. Those who remember parts or all of their episodes do not recall any fear, or anguish. Several people who remained conscious throughout, while appearing to have been quite dead, could only describe a remarkable sensation of detachment. One man underwent coronary occlusion with cessation of the heart and dropped for all practical purposes dead in front of a hospital, and within a few minutes his heart had been restarted by electrodes and he breathed his way back into life. According to his account, the strangest thing was that there were so many people around him, moving so urgently, handling his body with such excitement, while all his awareness was of quietude.

In a recent study of the reaction to dying in patients with obstructive disease of the lungs, it was concluded that the process was considerably more shattering for the professional observers than the observed. Most of the patients appeared to be preparing themselves with equanimity for death, as though intuitively familiar with the business. One elderly woman reported that the only painful and distressing part of the process was in being interrupted; on several occasions she was provided with conventional therapeutic measures to maintain oxygenation or restore fluids and electrolytes, and each time she found the experience of coming back harrowing, she deeply resented the interference with her dying.

I find myself surprised by the thought that dying is an all-right thing to do, but perhaps it should not surprise. It is, after all, the most ancient and fundamental of biologic functions, with its mechanisms worked out with the same attention to detail, the same provision for the advantage of the organism, the same abundance of genetic information for guidance through the stages, that we have long since become accustomed to finding in all the crucial acts of living.

Very well. But even so, if the transformation is a co-ordinated, integrated physiologic process in its initial, local stages, there is still that permanent vanishing of consciousness to be accounted for. Are we to be stuck forever with this problem? Where on earth does it go? Is it simply stopped dead in its tracks, lost in humus, wasted? Considering the tendency of nature to find uses for complex and intricate mechanisms, this seems to me unnatural. I prefer to think of it as somehow separated off at the filaments of its attachment, and then drawn like an easy breath back into the membrane of its origin, a fresh memory for a biospherical nervous system, but I have no data on the matter.

This is for another science, another day. It may turn out, as some scientists suggest, that we are forever precluded from investigating consciousness, by a sort of indeterminancy principle that stipulates that the very act of looking will make it twitch and blur out of sight. It this is true, we will never learn. I envy some of my friends who are convinced about telepathy; oddly enough, it is my European scientist acquaintances who believe it most freely and take it most lightly. All their aunts have received Communications, and there they sit, with proof of the motility of consciousness at their fingertips, and the making of a new science. It is discouraging to have had the wrong aunts, and never the ghost of a message.

1973

THE READER

1. "They simply age, and die, like flies" (p. 576). What makes this sentence, which concludes the opening section of this brief essay, effective? What does Thomas establish in this opening section? What does he consider in the next section, which constitutes the bulk of his essay? What is the logic that connects the two, and what is the basic assumption underlying the second section?

2. What does this essay have in common with Thomas's "On Magic in Medicine" (p. 450)? Is Thomas ever "unscientific"? Can you infer from these two essays his estimate of science—what it can do and what it can't do?

THE WRITER

1. In the paragraph beginning "I find myself surprised . . ." (p. 578),

Thomas considers the subject of death anew. What is his perspective here? How does the next paragraph set the limits on that perspective? Explain the metaphor with which he ends the next paragraph.

2. *Write a brief account of a hypothetical society that has a different attitude toward death from ours. What attitudes about other things would follow from a different attitude toward death?*

Elisabeth Kübler-Ross

ON THE FEAR OF DEATH

Let me not pray to be sheltered from
dangers but to be fearless in facing
them.
　　Let me not beg for the stilling of
my pain but for the heart to conquer it.
　　Let me not look for allies in life's
battlefield but to my own strength.
　　Let me not crave in anxious fear to
be saved but hope for the patience to
win my freedom.
　　Grant me that I may not be a
coward, feeling your mercy in my
success alone; but let me find the grasp
of your hand in my failure.

RABINDRANATH TAGORE,
Fruit-Gathering

Epidemics have taken a great toll of lives in past generations. Death in infancy and early childhood was frequent and there were few families who didn't lose a member of the family at an early age. Medicine has changed greatly in the last decades. Widespread vaccinations have practically eradicated many illnesses, at least in western Europe and the United States. The use of chemotherapy, especially the antibiotics, has contributed to an ever decreasing number of fatalities in infectious diseases. Better child care and education has effected a low morbidity and mortality among children. The many diseases that have taken an impressive toll among the young and middle-aged have been conquered. The number of old people is on the rise, and with this fact come the number of people with malignancies and chronic diseases associated more with old age.

Pediatricians have less work with acute and life-threatening situations as they have an ever increasing number of patients with psychosomatic disturbances and adjustment and behavior problems. Physicians have more people in their waiting rooms with emotional problems than they have ever had before, but they also have more elderly patients who not only try to live with their decreased physical abilities and limitations but who also face loneliness and isolation with all its pains and anguish. The majority of these people are not seen by a psychiatrist. Their needs have to be elicited and gratified by other professional people, for instance, chaplains and social workers. It is for them that I am trying to outline the changes that have taken place in the last few decades, changes that are ultimately responsible for the increased fear of death, the rising number of emotional problems, and the greater need for understanding of and coping with the problems of death and dying.

When we look back in time and study old cultures and people, we are impressed that death has always been distasteful to man and will probably always be. From a psychiatrist's point of view this is very understandable and can perhaps best be explained by our basic knowledge that, in our unconscious, death is never possible in regard to ourselves. It is inconceivable for our unconscious to imagine an actual ending of our own life here on earth, and if this life of ours has to end, the ending is always attributed to a malicious intervention from the outside by someone else. In simple terms, in our unconscious mind we can only be killed; it is inconceivable to die of a natural cause or of old age. Therefore death in itself is associated with a bad act, a frightening happening, something that in itself calls for retribution and punishment.

One is wise to remember these fundamental facts as they are essential in understanding some of the most important, otherwise unintelligible communications of our patients.

The second fact that we have to comprehend is that in our unconscious mind we cannot distinguish between a wish and a deed. We are all aware of some of our illogical dreams in which two completely opposite statements can exist side by side—very acceptable in our dreams but unthinkable and illogical in our wakening state. Just as our unconscious mind cannot differentiate betwee the wish to kill somebody in anger and the act of having done so, the young child is unable to make this distinction. The child who angrily wishes his mother to drop dead for not having gratified his needs will be traumatized greatly by the actual death of his mother—even if this event is not linked closely in time with his destructive wishes. He will always take part or the whole blame for the loss of his mother. He will always say to himself—rarely to others—"I did it, I am responsible, I was bad, therefore Mommy left me." It is well to remember that the child will react in the same manner if he loses a parent by divorce, separation, or desertion. Death is often seen by a child as an impermanent thing and has therefore little distinction from a divorce in which he may have an opportunity to see a parent again.

Many a parent will remember remarks of their children such as, "I will bury my doggy now and next spring when the flowers come up again, he will get up." Maybe it was the same wish that motivated the ancient Egyptians to supply their dead with food and goods to keep them happy and the old American Indians to bury their relatives with their belongings.

When we grow older and begin to realize that our omnipotence is really not so omnipotent, that our strongest wishes are not powerful enough to make the impossible possible, the fear that we have contributed to the death of a loved one diminishes—and with it the guilt. The fear remains diminished, however, only so long as it is not challenged too strongly. Its vestiges can be seen daily in hospital corridors and in people associated with the bereaved.

A husband and wife may have been fighting for years, but when the partner dies, the survivor will pull his hair, whine and cry louder and beat his chest in regret, fear and anguish, and will hence fear his own death more than before, still believing in the law of talion—an eye for an eye, a tooth for a tooth—"I am responsible for her death, I will have to die a pitiful death in retribution."

Maybe this knowledge will help us understand many of the old customs and rituals which have lasted over the centuries and whose purpose is to diminish the anger of the gods or the people as the case may be, thus decreasing the anticipated punishment. I am thinking of the ashes, the torn clothes, the veil, the *Klage Weiber*[1] of the old days—they are all means to ask you to take pity on them, the mourners, and are expressions of sorrow, grief, and shame. If someone grieves, beats his chest, tears his hair, or refuses to eat, it is an attempt at self-punishment to avoid or reduce the anticipated punishment for the blame that he takes on the death of a loved one.

This grief, shame, and guilt are not very far removed from feelings of anger and rage. The process of grief always includes some qualities of anger. Since none of us likes to admit anger at a deceased person, these emotions are often disguised or repressed and prolong the period of grief or show up in other ways. It is well to remember that it is not up to us to judge such feelings as bad or shameful but to understand their true meaning and origin as something very human. In order to illustrate this I will again use the example of the child—and the child in us. The five-year-old who loses his mother is both blaming himself for her disappearance and being angry at her for having deserted him and for no longer gratifying his needs. The dead person then turns into something the child loves and wants very much but also hates with equal intensity for this severe deprivation.

1. Wailing wives.

The ancient Hebrews regarded the body of a dead person as something unclean and not to be touched. The early American Indians talked about the evil spirits and shot arrows in the air to drive the spirits away. Many other cultures have rituals to take care of the "bad" dead person, and they all originate in this feeling of anger which still exists in all of us, though we dislike admitting it. The tradition of the tombstone may originate in this wish to keep the bad spirits deep down in the ground, and the pebbles that many mourners put on the grave are left-over symbols of the same wish. Though we call the firing of guns at military funerals a last salute, it is the same symbolic ritual as the Indian used when he shot his spears and arrows into the skies.

I give these examples to emphasize that man has not basically changed. Death is still a fearful, frightening happening, and the fear of death is a universal fear even if we think we have mastered it on many levels.

What has changed is our way of coping and dealing with death and dying and our dying patients.

Having been raised in a country in Europe where science is not so advanced, where modern techniques have just started to find their way into medicine, and where people still live as they did in this country half a century ago, I may have had an opportunity to study a part of the evolution of mankind in a shorter period.

I remember as a child the death of a farmer. He fell from a tree and was not expected to live. He asked simply to die at home, a wish that was granted without questioning. He called his daughters into the bedroom and spoke with each one of them alone for a few moments. He arranged his affairs quietly, though he was in great pain, and distributed his belongings and his land, none of which was to be split until his wife should follow him in death. He also asked each of his children to share in the work, duties, and tasks that he had carried on until the time of the accident. He asked his friends to visit him once more, to bid good-bye to them. Although I was a small child at the time, he did not exclude me or my siblings. We were allowed to share in the preparations of the family just as we were permitted to grieve with them until he died. When he did die, he was left at home, in his own beloved home which he had built, and among his friends and neighbors who went to take a last look at him where he lay in the midst of flowers in the place he had lived in and loved so much. In that country today there is still no make-believe slumber room, no embalming, no false makeup to pretend sleep. Only the signs of very disfiguring illnesses are covered up with bandages and only infectious cases are removed from the home prior to the burial.

Why do I describe such "old-fashioned" customs? I think they are an indication of our acceptance of a fatal outcome, and they help the dying patient as well as his family to accept the loss of a loved one. If a patient is allowed to terminate his life in the familiar and beloved environment, it requires less adjustment for him. His own family knows him well enough to replace a sedative with a glass of his favorite wine; or the smell of a home-cooked soup may give him the appetite to sip a few spoons of fluid which, I think is still more enjoyable than an infusion. I will not minimize the need for sedatives and infusions and realize full well from my own experience as a country doctor that they are sometimes life-saving and often unavoidable. But I also know that patience and familiar people and foods could replace many a bottle of intravenous fluids given for the simple reason that it fulfills the physiological need without involving too many people and/or individual nursing care.

The fact that children are allowed to stay at home where a fatality has stricken and are included in the talk, discussions, and fears gives them the feeling that they are not alone in the grief and gives them the comfort of shared responsibility and shared mourning. It prepares them gradually and helps them view death as part of life, an experience which may help them grow and mature.

This is in great contrast to a society in which death is viewed as taboo, discussion of it is regarded as morbid, and children are excluded with the presumption and pretext that it would be "too much" for them. They are then sent off to relatives, often accompanied with some unconvincing lies of "Mother has gone on a long trip" or other unbelievable stories. The child senses that something is wrong, and his distrust in adults will only multiply if other relatives add new variations of the story, avoid his questions or suspicions, shower him with gifts as a meager substitute for a loss he is not permitted to deal with. Sooner or later the child will become aware of the changed family situation and, depending on the age and personality of the child, will have an unresolved grief and regard this incident as a frightening, mysterious, in any case very traumatic experience with untrustworthy grownups, which he has no way to cope with.

It is equally unwise to tell a little child who lost her brother that God loved little boys so much that he took little Johnny to heaven. When this little girl grew up to be a woman she never solved her anger at God, which resulted in a psychotic depression when she lost her own little son three decades later.

We would think that our great emancipation, our knowledge of science and of man, has given us better ways and means to prepare ourselves and our families for this inevitable happening. Instead the days are gone when a man was allowed to die in peace and dignity in his own home.

The more we are making advancements in science, the more we seem to fear and deny the reality of death. How is this possible?

We use euphemisms, we make the dead look as if they were asleep, we ship the children off to protect them from the anxiety and turmoil around the house if the patient is fortunate enough to die at home, we don't allow children to visit their dying parents in the hospitals, we have long and controversial discussions about whether patients should be told the truth —a question that rarely arises when the dying person is tended by the family physician who has known him from delivery to death and who knows the weaknesses and strengths of each member of the family.

I think there are many reasons for this flight away from facing death calmly. One of the most important facts is that dying nowadays is more gruesome in many ways, namely, more lonely, mechanical, and dehumanized; at times it is even difficult to determine technically when the time of death has occurred.

Dying becomes lonely and impersonal because the patient is often taken out of his familiar environment and rushed to an emergency room. Whoever has been very sick and has required rest and comfort especially may recall his experience of being put on a stretcher and enduring the noise of the ambulance siren and hectic rush until the hospital gates open. Only those who have lived through this may appreciate the discomfort and cold necessity of such transportation which is only the beginning of a long order—hard to endure when you are well, difficult to express in words when noise, light, pumps, and voices are all too much to put up with. It may well be that we might consider more the patient under the sheets and blankets and perhaps stop our well-meant efficiency and rush in order to hold the patient's hand, to smile, or to listen to a question. I include the trip to the hospital as the first episode in dying, as it is for many. I am putting it exaggeratedly in contrast to the sick man who is left at home—not to say that lives should not be saved if they can be saved by a hospitalization but to keep the focus on the patient's experience, his needs and his reactions.

When a patient is severely ill, he is often treated like a person with no right to an opinion. It is often someone else who makes the decision if and when and where a patient should be hospitalized. It would take so little to remember that the sick person too has feelings, has wishes and opinions, and has—most important of all—the right to be heard.

Well, our presumed patient has now reached the emergency room. He will be surrounded by busy nurses, orderlies, interns, residents, a lab technician perhaps who will take some blood, an electrocardiogram technician who takes the cardiogram. He may be moved to X-ray and he will overhear opinions of his condition and discussions and questions to members of the family. He slowly but surely is beginning to be treated like a thing. He is no longer a person. Decisions are made often without his opinion. If he tries to rebel he will be sedated and after hours of waiting and wondering whether he has the strength, he will be wheeled into the operating room or intensive treatment unit and become an object of great concern and great financial investment.

He may cry for rest, peace, and dignity, but he will get infusions, transfusions, a heart machine, or tracheotomy[2] if necessary. He may want one single person to stop for one single minute so that he can ask one single question—but he will get a dozen people around the clock, all busily preoccupied with his heart rate, pulse, electrocardiogram or pulmonary functions, his secretions or excretions but not with him as a human being. He may wish to fight it all but it is going to be a useless fight since all this is done in the fight for his life, and if they can save his life they can consider the person afterwards. Those who consider the person first may lose precious time to save his life! At least this seems to be the rationale or justification behind all this—or is it? Is the reason for this increasingly mechanical, depersonalized approach our own defensiveness? Is this approach our own way to cope with and repress the anxieties that a terminally or critically ill patient evokes in us? Is our concentration on equipment, on blood pressure our desperate attempt to deny the impending death which is so frightening and discomforting to us that we displace all our knowledge onto machines, since they are less close to us than the suffering face of another human being which would remind us once more of our lack of omnipotence, our own limits and failures, and last but not least perhaps our own mortality?

Maybe the question has to be raised: Are we becoming less human or more human? * * * [I]t is clear that whatever the answer may be, the patient is suffering more—not physically, perhaps, but emotionally. And his needs have not changed over the centuries, only our ability to gratify them.

1969

2. The surgical opening of a passage through the neck into the trachea.

THE READER

1. *Thomas, in "The Long Habit" (p. 575), also speaks of dying. To what extent is he in harmony with Kübler-Ross? What differences do you find? What is the special contribution of each author?*
2. *To speak of rights, as Kübler-Ross does in the last pages of her essay, is to raise the question of where they come from. For example, the Declaration of Independence (p. 828) implies that the rights it asserts come from God. From what source would you expect Kübler-Ross to derive the rights she speaks of?*
3. *Kübler-Ross doubts the rationale for efficiency in medical care but, at the same time, recognizes the life-saving results of this efficiency. There is obviously a dilemma here. What are the extreme opposite positions that define the dilemma? What is the best intermediate or compromise position?*

THE WRITER

1. *How is Kübler-Ross's essay organized? What difference does it make that she postpones presenting generalizations about her subject until*

late in her discussion?

2. *Kübler-Ross opens her discussion with a quotation. Read Shakespeare's Sonnet 73 and Hopkins's "Sping and Fall: To a Young Child" (below). Would these poems be appropriate for introducing her essay? Why, or why not?*

73

> That time of year thou mayst in me behold
> When yellow leaves, or none, or few, do hang
> Upon those boughs which shake against the cold,
> Bare ruined choirs, where late the sweet birds sang.
> In me thou see'st the twilight of such day
> As after sunset fadeth in the west;
> Which by and by black night doth take away,
> Death's second self, that seals up all in rest.
> In me thou see'st the glowing of such fire,
> That on the ashes of his youth doth lie,
> As the deathbed whereon it must expire,
> Consumed with that which it was nourished by.
> This thou perceiv'st, which makes thy love more strong,
> To love that well which thou must leave ere long.

—William Shakespeare

SPRING AND FALL

TO A YOUNG CHILD

> Margaret, are you grieving
> Over Goldengrove unleaving?
> Leaves, like the things of man, you
> With your fresh thoughts care for, can you?
> Ah! as the heart grows older
> It will come to such sights colder
> By and by, nor spare a sigh
> Though worlds of wanwood leafmeal lie;
> And yet you *will* weep and know why.
> Now no matter, child, the name:
> Sorrow's springs are the same.
> Nor mouth had, no nor mind, expressed
> What heart heard of, ghost [soul] guessed:
> It is the blight man was born for,
> It is Margaret you mourn for.

—Gerard Manley Hopkins

3. *Write a brief comparison between Thomas and Kübler-Ross along the lines suggested above ("The Reader," question 1).*

Ethics

James Thurber

THE BEAR WHO LET IT ALONE

In the woods of the Far West there once lived a brown bear who could take it or let it lone. He would go into a bar where they sold mead, a fermented drink made of honey, and he would have just two drinks. Then he would put some money on the bar and say, "See what the bears in the back room will have," and he would go home. But finally he took to drinking by himself most of the day. He would reel home at night, kick over the umbrella stand, knock down the bridge lamps, and ram his elbows through the windows. Then he would collapse on the floor and lie there until he went to sleep. His wife was greatly distressed and his children were very frightened.

At length the bear saw the error of his ways and began to reform. In the end he became a famous teetotaller and a persistent temperance lecturer. He would tell everybody that came to his house about the awful effects of drink, and he would boast about how strong and well he had become since he gave up touching the stuff. To demonstrate this, he would stand on his head and on his hands and he would turn cartwheels in the house, kicking over the umbrella stand, knocking down the bridge lamps, and ramming his elbows through the windows. Then he would lie down on the floor, tired by his healthful exercise, and go to sleep. His wife was greatly distressed and his children were very frightened.

Moral: You might as well fall flat on your face as lean over too far backward.

1955

Samuel Johnson

ON SELF-LOVE AND INDOLENCE

—Steriles transmisimus annos,
Haec aevi mihi prima dies, haec limina vitae.
STAT. [I.362]

—Our barren years are past;
Be this of life the first, of sloth the last.
ELPHINSTON[1]

No weakness of the human mind has more frequently incurred animadversion, than the negligence with which men overlook their own faults, however flagrant, and the easiness with which they pardon them, however frequently repeated.

It seems generally believed, that, as the eye cannot see itself, the mind has no faculties by which it can contemplate its own state, and that therefore we have not means of becoming acquainted with our real characters; an opinion which, like innumerable other postulates, an inquirer finds himself inclined to admit upon very little evidence, because it affords a ready solution of many difficulties. It will explain why the greatest abilities frequently fail to promote the happiness of those who possess them; why those who can distinguish with the utmost nicety the boundaries of vice and virtue, suffer them to be confounded in their own conduct; why the active and vigilant resign their affairs implicitly to the management of others; and why the cautious and fearful make hourly approaches toward ruin, without one sigh of solicitude or struggle for escape.

When a position teems thus with commodious consequences, who can without regret confess it to be false? Yet it is certain that declaimers have indulged a disposition to describe the dominion of the passions as extended beyond the limits that nature assigned. Self-love is often rather arrogant than blind; it does not hide our faults from ourselves, but persuades us that they escape the notice of others, and disposes us to resent censures lest we would confess them to be just. We are secretly conscious of defects and vices which we hope to conceal from the public eye, and please ourselves with innumerable impostures, by which, in reality, no body is deceived.

In proof of the dimness of our internal sight, or the general inability of man to determine rightly concerning his own character, it is common to

1. The author of these lines is Publius Papinius Statius, a first-century Latin poet. They are given first in the original and then in William Elphinstone's sixteenth-century translation.

urge the success of the most absurd and incredible flattery, and the resentment always raised by advice, however soft, benevolent, and reasonable. But flattery, if its operation be nearly examined, will be found to owe its acceptance not to our ignorance but knowledge of our failures, and to delight us rather as it consoles our wants than displays our possessions. He that shall solicit the favor of his patron by praising him for qualities which he can find in himself, will be defeated by the more daring panegyrist who enriches him with adscititious excellence. Just praise is only a debt, but flattery is a present. The acknowledgment of those virtues on which conscience congratulates us, is a tribute that we can at any time exact with confidence, but the celebration of those which we only feign, or desire without any vigorous endeavors to attain them, is received as a confession of sovereignty over regions never conquered, as a favorable decision of disputable claims, and is more welcome as it is more gratuitous.

Advice is offensive, not because it lays us open to unexpected regret, or convicts us of any fault which had escaped our notice, but because it shows us that we are known to others as well as to ourselves; and the officious monitor is persecuted with hatred, not because his accusation is false, but because he assumes that superiority which we are not willing to grant him, and has dared to detect what we desired to conceal.

For this reason advice is commonly ineffectual. If those who follow the call of their desires, without inquiry whither they are going, had deviated ignorantly from the paths of wisdom, and were rushing upon dangers unforeseen, they would readily listen to information that recalls them from their errors, and catch the first alarm by which destruction or infamy is denounced. Few that wander in the wrong way mistake it for the right; they only find it more smooth and flowery, and indulge their own choice rather than approve it: therefore few are persuaded to quit it by admonition or reproof, since it impresses no new conviction, nor confers any powers of action or resistance. He that is gravely informed how soon profusion will annihilate his fortune, hears with little advantage what he knew before, and catches at the next occasion of expense, because advice has no force to suppress his vanity. He that is told how certainly intemperance will hurry him to the grave, runs with his usual speed to a new course of luxury, because his reason is not invigorated, nor his appetite weakened.

The mischief of Flattery is, not that it persuades any man that he is what he is not, but that it suppresses the influence of honest ambition, by raising an opinion that honor may be gained without the toil of merit; and the benefit of advice arises commonly, not from any new light imparted to the mind, but from the discovery which it affords, of the publick suffrages. He that could withstand conscience, is frighted at infamy, and shame prevails where reason was defeated.

As we all know our own faults, and know them commonly with many aggravations which human perspicacity cannot discover, there is, perhaps, no man, however hardened by impudence or dissipated by levity, sheltered by hypocrisy, or blasted by disgrace, who does not intend some time to review his conduct, and to regulate the remainder of his life by the laws of virtue. New temptations indeed attack him, new invitations are offered by pleasure and interest, and the hour of reformation is always delayed; every delay gives vice another opportunity of fortifying itself by habit; and the change of manners, though sincerely intended and rationally planned, is referred to the time when some craving passion shall be fully gratified, or some powerful allurement cease its importunity.

Thus procrastination is accumulated on procrastination, and one impediment succeeds another, till age shatters our resolution, or death intercepts the project of amendment. Such is often the end of salutary purposes, after they have long delighted the imagination, and appeased that disquiet which every mind feels from known misconduct, when the attention is not diverted by business or by pleasure.

Nothing surely can be more unworthy of a reasonable nature, than to continue in a state so opposite to real happiness, as that all the peace of solitude and felicity of meditation, must arise from resolutions of forsaking it. Yet the world will often afford examples of men, who pass months and years in a continual war with their own convictions, and are daily dragged by habit or betrayed by passion into practices, which they closed and opened their eyes with purposes to avoid; purposes which, though settled on conviction, the first impulse of momentary desire totally overthrows.

The influence of custom is indeed such that to conquer it will require the utmost efforts of fortitude and virtue, nor can I think any man more worthy of veneration and renown, than those who have burst the shackles of habitual vice. This victory however has different degrees of glory as of difficulty; it is more heroic as the objects of guilty gratification are more familiar, and the recurrence of solicitation more frequent. He that from experience of the folly of ambition resigns his offices, may set himself free at once from temptation to squander his life in courts, because he cannot regain his former station. He who is enslaved by an amorous passion, may quit his tyrant in disgust, and absence will without the help of reason overcome by degrees the desire of returning. But those appetites to which every place affords their proper object, and which require no preparatory measures or gradual advances, are more tenaciously adhesive; the wish is so near the enjoyment, that compliance often precedes consideration, and before the powers of reason can be summoned, the time for employing them is past.

Indolence is therefore one of the vices from which those whom it once infects are seldom reformed. Every other species of luxury operates upon some appetite that is quickly satiated, and requires some concurrence of art or accident which every place will not supply; but the desire of ease acts equally at all hours, and the longer it is indulged in the more increased. To do nothing is in every man's power; we can never want an opportunity of omitting duties. The lapse to indolence is soft and imperceptible, because it is only a mere cessation of activity; but the return to diligence is difficult, because it implies a change from rest to motion, from privation to reality.

> —Facilis descensus Averni:
> Noctes atque dies patet atri janua Ditis:
> Sed revocare gradum, superasque evadere ad auras,
> Hoc opus, hic labor est.—
>
> [VIR. Aeneid VI. 126]

> The gates of Hell are open night and day;
> Smooth the descent, and easy is the way:
> But, to return, and view the chearful skies;
> In this, the task and mighty labour lies.
>
> DRYDEN

Of this vice, as of all others, every man who indulges it is conscious; we all know our own state, if we could be induced to consider it; and it might perhaps be useful to the conquest of all these ensnarers of the mind, if at certain stated days life was reviewed. Many things necessary are omitted, because we vainly imagine that they may be always performed, and what cannot be done without pain will for ever be delayed if the time of doing it be left unsettled. No corruption is great but by long negligence, which can scarcely prevail in a mind regularly and frequently awakened by periodical remorse. He that thus breaks his life into parts, will find in himself a desire to distinguish every stage of his existence by some improvement, and delight himself with the approach of the day of recollection, as of the time which is to begin a new series of virtue and felicity.

1751

Francis Bacon

OF SIMULATION AND DISSIMULATION

Dissimulation is but a faint kind of policy or wisdom; for it asketh a strong wit and a strong heart to know when to tell truth, and to do it. Therefore it is the weaker sort of politics[1] that are the great dissemblers.

Tacitus saith, *Livia sorted well with the arts of her husband and dissimulation of her son;* attributing arts or policy to Augustus, and dissimulation to Tiberius. And again, when Mucianus encourageth Vespasian to take arms against Vitellius, he saith, *We rise not against the piercing judgment of Augustus, nor the extreme caution or closeness of Tiberius.*[2] These properties, of arts or policy and dissimulation or closeness, are indeed habits and faculties several, and to be distinguished. For if a man have that penetration of judgment as he can discern what things are to be laid open, and what to be secreted, and what to be shewed at half lights, and to whom and when (which indeed are arts of state and arts of life, as Tacitus well calleth them), to him a habit of dissimulation is a hinderance and a poorness. But if a man cannot obtain to that judgment, then it is left to him generally to be close, and a dissembler. For where a man cannot choose or vary in particulars, there it is good to take the safest and wariest way in general; like the going softly, by one that cannot well see. Certainly the ablest men that ever were have had all an openness and frankness of dealing; and a name of certainty and veracity; but then they were like horses well managed; for they could tell passing well when to stop or turn; and at such times when they thought the case indeed required dissimulation, if then they used it, it came to pass that the former opinion spread abroad of their good faith and clearness of dealing made them almost invisible.

There be three degrees of this hiding and veiling of a man's self. The first, Closeness, Reservation, and Secrecy; when a man leaveth himself without observation, or without hold to be taken, what he is. The second, Dissimulation, in the negative; when a man lets fall signs and arguments, that he is not that he is. And the third, Simulation, in the affirmative; when a man industriously and expressly feigns and pretends to be that he is not.

For the first of these, Secrecy; it is indeed the virtue of a confessor.[3] And assuredly the secret man heareth many confessions. For who will

1. Politicians.
2. The Roman historian Tacitus here speaks of the plottings of Livia, wife of the emperor Augustus Caesar and mother of his successor Tiberius; and of the Roman official Mucianus, who in A.D. 69 supported Vespasian in his successful struggle against Vitellius to gain the imperial throne.
3. One to whom confession is made.

open himself to a blab or babbler? But if a man be thought secret, it inviteth discovery; as the more close air sucketh in the more open; and as in confession the revealing is not for worldly use, but for the ease of a man's heart, so secret men come to the knowledge of many things in that kind; while men rather discharge their minds than impart their minds. In few words, mysteries are due to secrecy. Besides (to say truth) nakedness is uncomely, as well in mind as body; and it addeth no small reverence to men's manners and actions, if they be not altogether open. As for talkers and futile persons, they are commonly vain and credulous withal. For he that talketh what he knoweth, will also talk what he knoweth not. Therefore set it down, that an habit of secrecy is both politic and moral. And in this part, it is good that a man's face give his tongue leave to speak. For the discovery of a man's self by the tracts of his countenance is a great weakness and betraying; by how much it is many times more marked and believed than a man's words.

For the second, which is Dissimulation; it followeth many times upon secrecy by a necessity; so that he that will be secret must be a dissembler in some degree. For men are too cunning to suffer a man to keep an indifferent carriage between both, and to be secret, without swaying the balance on either side. They will so beset a man with questions, and draw him on, and pick it out of him, that, without an absurd silence, he must shew an inclination one way; or if he do not, they will gather as much by his silence as by his speech. As for equivocations, or oraculous speeches, they cannot hold out for long. So that no man can be secret, except he give himself a little scope of dissimulation; which is, as it were, but the skirts or train of secrecy.

But for the third degree, which is Simulation and false profession; that I hold more culpable, and less politic; except it be in great and rare matters. And therefore a general custom of simulation (which is this last degree) is a vice, rising either of a natural falseness or fearfulness, or of a mind that hath some main faults, which because a man must needs disguise, it maketh him practice simulation in other things, lest his hand should be out of ure.[4]

The great advantages of simulation and dissimulation are three. First, to lay asleep opposition, and to surprise. For where a man's intentions are published, it is an alarum to call up all that are against them. The second is, to reserve to a man's self a fair retreat. For if a man engage himself by a manifest declaration, he must go through or take a fall. The third is, the better to discover the mind of another. For to him that opens himself men will hardly shew themselves adverse; but will (fair) let him go on, and turn their freedom of speech to freedom of thought. And therefore it is a good shrewd proverb of the Spaniard, Tell a lie and find a troth. As if

4. Practice.

there were no way of discovery but by simulation. There be also three disadvantages, to set it even. The first, that simulation and dissimulation commonly carry with them a shew of fearfulness, which in any business doth spoil the feathers of round flying up to the mark. The second, that it puzzleth and perplexeth the conceits[5] of many, that perhaps would otherwise co-operate with him; and makes a man walk almost alone to his own ends. The third and greatest is, that it depriveth a man of one of the most principal instruments for action; which is trust and belief. The best composition and temperature is to have openness in fame and opinion; secrecy in habit; dissimulation in seasonable use; and a power to feign, if there be no remedy.

5. Conceptions, thoughts.

THE READER

1. *Explain Bacon's distinction, drawn in the first two paragraphs, between dissembling, on the one hand, and, on the other, arts and policy. How does this opening prepare the way for the remainder of the essay?*
2. *How is the word "dissimulation" as used in the third paragraph and thereafter to be distinguished from its use in the first two paragraphs?*
3. *In what connection and to what purpose does Bacon use the following expressions? Explain the image or allusion in each:*
   a) *"like the going softly, by one that cannot well see" (p. 592)*
   b) *"like horses well managed; for they could tell passing well when to stop or turn" (p. 592)*
   c) *"as the more close air sucketh in the more open" (p. 593)*
   d) *"it is good that a man's face give his tongue leave to speak" (p. 593)*
   e) *"he must go through or take a fall" (p. 593)*
   f) *"fearfulness, which in any business doth spoil the feathers of round flying up to the mark" (p. 594)*

THE WRITER

1. *What are the three degrees of hiding of a man's self? According to what principles does Bacon arrange these degrees? What accounts for his according unequal amounts of space to the exposition of them?*
2. *Make a close analysis of Bacon's closing paragraph, indicating the ways Bacon achieves symmetry, balance. How does that effect contribute to his tone and purpose? What elements in the paragraph offset a mere symmetry?*
3. *Bacon would allow "Simulation and false profession" in "great and rare matters." Would you? Give an example of such matters. Write a brief essay explaining your position.*
4. *What view of the world underlies Bacon's essay? Write an essay showing what Bacon's assumptions about the world seem to be. Be careful to show how you draw upon the essay to find out Bacon's assumptions.*

Samuel Johnson

LETTER TO LORD CHESTERFIELD

February 1755

My Lord

I have been lately informed by the proprietor of *The World*[1] that two papers in which my *Dictionary* is recommended to the public were written by your Lordship. To be so distinguished is an honor which, being very little accustomed to favors from the great, I know not well how to receive, or in what terms to acknowledge.

When upon some slight encouragement I first visited your Lordship I was overpowered like the rest of mankind by the enchantment of your address,[2] and could not forbear to wish that I might boast myself *le vainqueur du vainqueur de la terre*,[3] that I might obtain that regard for which I saw the world contending, but found my attendance so little encouraged that neither pride nor modesty would suffer me to continue it. When I had once addressed your Lordship in public, I had exhausted all the art of pleasing which a retired and uncourtly scholar can possess. I had done all that I could, and no man is well pleased to have his all neglected, be it ever so little.

Seven years, my lord, have now past since I waited in your outward rooms or was repulsed from your door, during which time I have been pushing on my work through difficulties of which it is useless to complain, and have brought it at last to the verge of publication without one act of assistance, one word of encouragement, or one smile of favor. Such treatment I did not expect, for I never had a patron before.

The shepherd in Virgil grew at last acquainted with Love, and found him a native of the rocks.[4] Is not a patron, my lord, one who looks with unconcern on a man struggling for life in the water and when he has reached ground encumbers him with help. The notice which you have been pleased to take of my labors, had it been early, had been kind; but it has been delayed till I am indifferent and cannot enjoy it, till I am solitary and cannot impart it, till I am known and do not want[5] it.

I hope it is no very cynical asperity not to confess obligation where no benefit has been received, or to be unwilling that the public should

---

1. A journal in which Lord Chesterfield had recently praised Johnson's *Dictionary of the English Language*. Johnson had been at work on the dictionary for nine years.
2. Here in the old sense of "courtesy."
3. The conquerer of the conqueror of the world.
4. Or deserts; an allusion to Virgil's eighth eclogue, line 43.
5. Need.

consider me as owing that to a patron, which Providence has enabled me to do for myself.

Having carried on my work thus far with so little obligation to any favorer of learning I shall not be disappointed though I should conclude it, if less be possible, with less, for I have been long wakened from that dream of hope, in which I once boasted myself with so much exultation, my lord your Lordship's most humble most obedient servant,

SAM:JOHNSON

1755

Lord Chesterfield

LETTER TO HIS SON

London, October 16, O.S. 1747

DEAR BOY

The art of pleasing is a very necessary one to possess, but a very difficult one to acquire. It can hardly be reduced to rules; and your own good sense and observation will teach you more of it than I can. "Do as you would be done by," is the surest method that I know of pleasing. Observe carefully what pleases you in others, and probably the same things in you will please others. If you are pleased with the complaisance and attention of others to your humors, your tastes, or your weaknesses, depend upon it, the same complaisance and attention on your part to theirs will equally please them. Take the tone of the company that you are in, and do not pretend to give it; be serious, gay, or even trifling, as you find the present humor of the company; this is an attention due from every individual to the majority. Do not tell stories in company; there is nothing more tedious and disagreeable; if by chance you know a very short story, and exceedingly applicable to the present subject of conversation, tell it in as few words as possible; and even then, throw out that you do not love to tell stories, but that the shortness of it tempted you.

Of all things banish the egotism out of your conversation, and never think of entertaining people with your own personal concerns or private affairs; though they are interesting to you, they are tedious and impertinent to everybody else; besides that, one cannot keep one's own private affairs too secret. Whatever you think your own excellencies may be, do not affectedly display them in company; nor labor, as many people do, to give that turn to the conversation, which may supply you with an opportunity of exhibiting them. If they are real, they will infallibly be discovered, without your pointing them out yourself, and with much more advantage. Never maintain an argument with heat and clamor, though you think or know yourself to be in the right; but give your opinion modestly and coolly, which is the only way to convince; and, if that does not do, try to change the conversation, by saying, with good-humor, "We shall hardly convince one another; nor is it necessary that we should, so let us talk of something else."

Remember that there is a local propriety to be observed in all companies; and that what is extremely proper in one company may be, and often is, highly improper in another.

The jokes, the *bon-mots*, the little adventures, which may do very well in one company, will seem flat and tedious, when related in another. The particular characters, the habits, the cant of one company may give merit to a word, or a gesture, which would have none at all if divested of those accidental circumstances. Here people very commonly err; and fond of something that has entertained them in one company, and in certain circumstances, repeat it with emphasis in another, where it is either insipid, or, it may be, offensive, by being ill-timed or misplaced. Nay, they often do it with this silly preamble: "I will tell you an excellent thing," or, "I will tell you the best thing in the world." This raises expectations, which, when absolutely disappointed, make the relator of this excellent thing look, very deservedly, like a fool.

If you would particularly gain the affection and friendship of particular people, whether men or women, endeavor to find out their predominant excellency, if they have one, and their prevailing weakness, which everybody has; and do justice to the one, and something more than justice to the other. Men have various objects in which they may excel, or at least would be thought to excel; and, though they love to hear justice done to them, where they know that they excel, yet they are most and best flattered upon those points where they wish to excel, and yet are doubtful whether they do or not. As for example: Cardinal Richelieu, who was undoubtedly the ablest statesman of his time, or perhaps of any other, had the idle vanity of being thought the best poet too; he envied the great Corneille his reputation, and ordered a criticism to be written upon the *Cid*.[1] Those, therefore, who flattered skillfully, said little to him of his abilities in state affairs, or at least but *en passant*, and as it might naturally occur. But the incense which they gave him, the smoke of which they knew would turn his head in their favor, was as a *bel esprit* and a poet. Why? Because he was sure of one excellency, and distrustful as to the other.

You will easily discover every man's prevailing vanity by observing his

1. When the French classic tragedy *The Cid*, founded upon the legendary exploits of the medieval Castilian warrior-hero, was published in 1636 by its author Pierre Corneille (1606–1684), it was the subject of violent criticism, led by the French minister of state Richelieu (1585–1642).

favorite topic of conversation; for every man talks most of what he has most a mind to be thought to excel in. Touch him but there, and you touch him to the quick. The late Sir Robert Walpole[2] (who was certainly an able man) was little open to flattery upon that head, for he was in no doubt himself about it; but his prevailing weakness was, to be thought to have a polite and happy turn to gallantry—of which he had undoubtedly less than any man living. It was his favorite and frequent subject of conversation, which proved to those who had any penetration that it was his prevailing weakness, and they applied to it with success.

Women have, in general, but one object, which is their beauty; upon which scarce any flattery is too gross for them to follow. Nature has hardly formed a woman ugly enough to be insensible to flattery upon her person; if her face is so shocking that she must, in some degree, be conscious of it, her figure and air, she trusts, make ample amends for it. If her figure is deformed, her face, she thinks, counterbalances it. If they are both bad, she comforts herself that she has graces, a certain manner, a *je ne sais quoi*[3] still more engaging than beauty. This truth is evident from the studied and elaborate dress of the ugliest woman in the world. An undoubted, uncontested, conscious beauty is, of all women, the least sensible of flattery upon that head; she knows it is her due, and is therefore obliged to nobody for giving it her. She must be flattered upon her understanding; which, though she may possibly not doubt of herself, yet she suspects that men may distrust.

Do not mistake me, and think that I mean to recommend to you abject and criminal flattery: no; flatter nobody's vices or crimes: on the contrary, abhor and discourage them. But there is no living in the world without a complaisant indulgence for people's weaknesses, and innocent, though ridiculous vanities. If a man has a mind to be thought wiser, and a woman handsomer, than they really are, their error is a comfortable one to themselves, and an innocent one with regard to other people; and I would rather make them my friends by indulging them in it, than my enemies by endeavoring (and that to no purpose) to undeceive them.

There are little attentions, likewise, which are infinitely engaging, and which sensibly affect that degree of pride and self-love, which is inseparable from human nature, as they are unquestionable proofs of the regard and consideration which we have for the persons to whom we pay them. As, for example, to observe the little habits, the likings, the antipathies, and the tastes of those whom we would gain; and then take care to provide them with the one, and to secure them from the other; giving them, genteelly, to understand, that you had observed they liked such a dish, or such a room, for which reason you had prepared it: or, on the

2. For two decades a powerful prime minister, Robert Walpole (1676–1745) was also a patron of the arts and prided himself upon his taste.

3. A certain inexpressible quality.

contrary, that having observed they had an aversion to such a dish, a dislike to such a person, etc., you had taken care to avoid presenting them. Such attention to such trifles flatters self-love much more than greater things, as it makes people think themselves almost the only objects of your thoughts and care.

These are some of the arcana[4] necessary for your initiation in the great society of the world. I wish I had known them better at your age; I have paid the price of three and fifty years for them, and shall not grudge it if you reap the advantage. Adieu.
1747

4. Secret things.

THE READER

1. *Chesterfield's letter is negatively phrased. What is the underlying evil he is advising his son to avoid?*
2. *Gaylin (p. 664) maintains that our behavior defines our identity. Would Chesterfield agree?*
3. *In "The Writer," question 2 (below), you are asked to rewrite a paragraph both positively and negatively. What ethical principle would you appeal to in each case?*

THE WRITER

1. *Is this letter unified around a central concern, or is it a series of separate observations?*
2. *An eighteenth-century aristocrat probably needs translation into modern terms. Rewrite a paragraph from Lord Chesterfield's letter so as to make it as appealing and persuasive as possible. Then do the opposite —make it as offensive as possible.*

Samuel L. Clemens

ADVICE TO YOUTH

Being told I would be expected to talk here, I inquired what sort of a talk I ought to make. They said it should be something suitable to youth —something didactic, instructive, or something in the nature of good advice. Very well. I have a few things in my mind which I have often longed to say for the instruction of the young; for it is in one's tender early years that such things will best take root and be most enduring and most valuable. First, then, I will say to you, my young friends—and I say it beseechingly, urgingly—

Always obey your parents, when they are present. This is the best policy in the long run, because if you don't they will make you. Most parents think they know better than you do, and you can generally make more by humoring that superstition than you can by acting on your own better judgment.

Be respectful to your superiors, if you have any, also to strangers, and sometimes to others. If a person offend you, and you are in doubt as to whether it was intentional or not, do not resort to extreme measures; simply watch your chance and hit him with a brick. That will be sufficient. If you shall find that he had not intended any offense, come out frankly and confess yourself in the wrong when you struck him; acknowledge it like a man and say you didn't mean to. Yes, always avoid violence; in this age of charity and kindliness, the time has gone by for such things. Leave dynamite to the low and unrefined.

Go to bed early, get up early—this is wise. Some authorities say get up with the sun; some others say get up with one thing, some with another. But a lark is really the best thing to get up with. It gives you a splendid reputation with everybody to know that you get up with the lark; and if you get the right kind of a lark, and work at him right, you can easily train him to get up at half past nine, every time—it is no trick at all.

Now as to the matter of lying. You want to be very careful about lying; otherwise you are nearly sure to get caught. Once caught, you can never again be, in the eyes of the good and the pure, what you were before. Many a young person has injured himself permanently through a single clumsy and illfinished lie, the result of carelessness born of incomplete training. Some authorities hold that the young ought not to lie at all. That, of course, is putting it rather stronger than necessary; still, while I cannot go quite so far as that, I do maintain, and I believe I am right, that the young ought to be temperate in the use of this great art until practice and experience shall give them that confidence, elegance, and precision which alone can make the accomplishment graceful and profitable. Patience, diligence, painstaking attention to detail—these are the requirements; these, in time, will make the student perfect; upon these, and upon these only, may he rely as the sure foundation for future eminence. Think what tedious years of study, thought, practice, experience, went to the equipment of that peerless old master who was able to impose upon the whole world the lofty and sounding maxim that "truth is mighty and will prevail"—the most majestic compound fracture of fact which any of woman born has yet achieved. For the history of our race, and each individual's experience, are sown thick with evidence that a truth is not hard to kill and that a lie told well is immortal. There is in Boston a monument of the man who discovered anaesthesia; many people are aware, in these latter days, that that man didn't discover it at all, but stole the discovery from another man. Is this truth mighty, and will it prevail? Ah no, my hearers, the monument is made of hardy material, but the lie it tells will outlast it a million years. An awkward, feeble, leaky lie is a thing which you ought to make it your unceasing study to avoid; such a lie as that has no more real permanence than an average truth. Why, you might as well tell the truth at once and be done with it. A feeble, stupid, preposterous lie will not live two years—except it be a slander upon somebody. It is indestructible, then, of course, but that is no merit of yours. A final word: begin your practice of this gracious and beautiful art early—begin now. If I had begun earlier, I could have learned how.

Never handle firearms carelessly. The sorrow and suffering that have been caused through the innocent but heedless handling of firearms by the young! Only four days ago, right in the next farmhouse to the one where I am spending the summer, a grandmother, old and gray and sweet, one of the loveliest spirits in the land, was sitting at her work, when her young grandson crept in and got down an old, battered, rusty gun which had not been touched for many years and was supposed not to be loaded, and pointed it at her, laughing and threatening to shoot. In her fright she ran screaming and pleading toward the door on the other side of the room; but as she passed him he placed the gun almost against her very breast and pulled the trigger! He had supposed it was not loaded. And he was right—it wasn't. So there wasn't any harm done. It is the only case of that kind I ever heard of. Therefore, just the same, don't you meddle with old unloaded firearms; they are the most deadly and unerring things that have ever been created by man. You don't have to take any pains at all with them; you don't have to have a rest, you don't have to have any sights on the gun, you don't have to take aim, even. No, you just pick out a relative and bang away, and you are sure to get him. A youth who can't hit a cathedral at thirty yards with a Gatling gun in three-quarters of an hour, can take up an old empty musket and bag his grandmother every time, at a hundred. Think what Waterloo[1] would have been if one of the armies had been boys armed with old muskets supposed not to be loaded, and the other army had been composed of their female relations. The very thought of it makes one shudder.

There are many sorts of books; but good ones are the sort for the young to read. Remember that. They are a great, an inestimable, an unspeakable means of improvement. Therefore be careful in your selection, my young friends; be very careful; confine yourselves exclusively to Robertson's Sermons, Baxter's Saint's Rest, The Innocents Abroad, and works of that kind.[2]

But I have said enough. I hope you will treasure up the instructions

1. The bloody battle (1815) in which Napoleon suffered his final defeat at the hands of English and German troops under the Duke of Wellington.
2. The five volumes of sermons by Frederick William Robertson (1816–1853), an English clergyman, and Richard Baxter's Saints' Everlasting Rest (1650) were once well-known religious works. The Innocents Abroad is Clemens's own collection of humorous travel sketches.

which I have given you, and make them a guide to your feet and a light to your understanding. Build your character thoughtfully and painstakingly upon these precepts, and by and by, when you have got it built, you will be surprised and gratified to see how nicely and sharply it resembles everybody else's.

1882   1923

THE READER

1. *How much of Clemens's advice applies only to the young? How much of it is to be taken seriously?*
2. *What does Clemens assume about his audience? How many of these assumptions would hold true today?*

THE WRITER

1. *Is this piece unified? Does it have a thesis sentence? If you think it is unified, in what does the unity consist? If you think it is not unified, where are the breaks? Would it have seemed more unified when it was given as a speech?*
2. *What "image" or "personality" does Clemens project or assume? What does he do that creates his image or personality?*
3. *Write a brief essay comparing what Clemens says about lying with what Didion says about it in "On Keeping a Notebook" (p. 731).*

Judith Martin

SOME THOUGHTS ON THE MANNERLY WAY OF LIFE

On Correcting Others

It would be futile for Miss Manners to pretend to know nothing of the wicked joy of correcting others.[1]

There is that pleasant bubble in the throat, a suppressed giggle at another person's ignorance; that flush of generosity accompanying the resolve to set the poor soul straight; that fever of human kindness when one proclaims, for the benefit of others, one's superior knowledge. Isn't that, after all, the great reward of the trade that Miss Manners practices? Can Miss Manners, whose vocation, whose calling, is correcting people for their own good, condemn the practice?

Certainly.

---

1. In the persona of Miss Manners, *Washington Post* columnist Judith Martin dispenses advice about etiquette with wit and excruciating correctness.

Miss Manners corrects only upon request. Then she does it from a distance, with no names attached, and no personal relationship, however distant, between the corrector and the correctee. She does not search out errors, like a policeman leaping out of a speed trap. When Miss Manners observes people behaving rudely, she never steps in to correct them. She behaves politely to them, and then goes home and snickers about them afterward. That is what the well-bred person does. The only way to enjoy the fun of catching people behaving disgustingly is to have children. One has to keep having them, however, because it is incorrect to correct grown people, even if you have grown them yourself. This is the mistake that many people make when they give helpful criticism to their children-in-law, who arrive on the scene already grown.

Miss Manners is constantly besieged by people who want to know the tactful manner of pointing out their friends' and relatives' inferiorities. These people, their loved ones report to Miss Manners, chew with their mouth open, mispronounce words, talk too loudly, crack their knuckles, spit, belch, and hum tunelessly to themselves. They have bad breath and runs in their stockings. They are too fat, dress badly, and do their hair all wrong.

How can those who love these people dearly, for reasons that are not clear, and who wish to help them, for reasons that unfortunately are clear, politely let them have it?

The answer is that they cannot, certainly not politely. There are times, in certain trusting relationships, when one can accomplish this impolitely. One can sometimes say, "Cracking your knuckles drives me up the wall and if you do it one more time I'll scream," or "Have a mint—there's something wrong with your breath," or "What's that thing on your left front tooth?" No reasonable person should take offense at these remarks. Because they are so frank, they do not seem to carry a history of repulsion long predating the offense. Also they deal with matters that are more or less easily correctable (although Miss Manners knows some determined knuckle crackers she suspects aren't half trying to stop), and which it is plausible to assume the offenders hadn't noticed.

What is unacceptable is to criticize things a person cannot easily remedy or may not want to. People who you think are too fat either disagree about what too fat is, are trying to do something about it, or are not trying to do something about it. In no case is it helpful for them to know that other people consider them too fat.

It is admittedly difficult to arrest the pleasure of correcting and advising long enough to ask oneself who will feel better after the correction is delivered—the person issuing it, or the one who gets it full in the face? But it is well worth the effort, not only for kindness' sake, but because it is a law of nature that he who corrects others will soon do something perfectly awful himself.

Even if it be proven that the mistakes of others come from gross ignorance or from maliciousness, it is not the place of anyone except God, their mothers, or Miss Manners to bring this to their attention. As dear Erasmus[2] said, "It is part of the highest civility if, while never erring yourself, you ignore the errors of others."

Miss Manners prefers to believe that everyone means well, and that if anyone seems to be doing something wrong, it is probably not from intent but from forgetfulness, busyness, absence of mind, or illness. Miss Manners may be mistaken in this now and again, but she leads a happier life for believing it.

* * *

On Sunday Best

Put on your best clothes and come into the best parlor. If you are on your best behavior, you may have tea on the best china, and stir it with one of the best spoons.

Can you imagine anything worse?

The concept of Sunday Best, so popular in previous generations, has become distasteful to modern people who pride themselves on stylistic consistency. Those who do still distinguish the Best actually adhere just as much to one standard—by making provision for a Best Occasion that never arrives. Nevertheless, Miss Manners, who is never afraid to take an unpopular stand when it is all for the best, would like to make a plea for the reinstitution of Sunday Best. The opposite of Best, in this instance, is not worst, but Ordinary Everyday.

In the heyday of Sunday Best, Sunday came regularly once a week. There was a sense, as in the stiff but—Miss Manners maintains—not unattractive parlor scene she has described, that one had at one's command more than one way of living. A version of this remains among those who observe Sunday Worst by slopping around the house on weekends in a manner markedly different from their weekday habits.

Most people nowadays fail to make any distinctions. They dress and act the same any day of the week, usually at the stylistically lowest common denominator. Among the genteel folk known to the people who worship informality as the *petite bourgeoisie*,[3] there is a Best, but it is always yet to be. People who put slipcovers, doilies, plastic protectors, and cellophane on everything good that they own rarely live to see an occasion so good that all these covers are removed.

Miss Manners thinks that everyone should have two modes of living ever available, just as everyone should have a year-round residence and an opportunity to vacation elsewhere. Regular change is refreshing as well as exciting. If given the choice, she would prefer one to be Ordinary

2. Desiderius Erasmus (1466?–1536): Dutch   3. French for "lower middle class."
Humanist and reformer.

and the other Best, rather than one Ordinary and the other Worst.

Everyday dishes and fine china, good stainless steel and better silver, sensible clothes and fancy ones, and family manners, as opposed to company manners, seem to her excellent combinations. If no one is ever allowed into the living room for fear of spoiling the white upholstery, and the good china is never used so it won't break, and the party clothes are left in the closet so they won't get dirty—why, Miss Manners believes, that is worse than the absence of best altogether.

The only excuse for the luxury of maintaining two styles is their continual use. The times to be at one's best are Sundays; days when company is coming; opening nights at the opera; holidays, both traditional and spontaneous.

Miss Manners does understand that the old custom came to be synonymous with dreariness and deprivation of the imagination. She is therefore willing to allow an alteration for modern times. Wednesday Best.

On Embarrassment

While guilt is an emotion Miss Manners does without, having taken the simple precaution of always doing everything right the first time, embarrassment interests her. Miss Manners cannot be expected to experience embarrassment firsthand, but it is something for which she has a moderate amount of sympathy. The proper use of embarrassment is as a conscience of manners. As your conscience might trouble you if you do anything immoral, your sense of embarrassment should be activated if you do anything unmannerly. As conscience should come from within, so should embarrassment. Hot tingles and flushes are quite proper when they arise from your own sense of having violated your own standards, inadvertently or advertently, but Miss Manners hereby absolves everyone from feeling any embarrassment deliberately imposed by others.

The less scrupulous of those who sell funeral services try to embarrass people with the suggestion that anyone who cares about the recently deceased will "spare no expense" in the burial, an emotional non sequitur[4] if ever there was one. The same tactic has been adopted by other professions. The whole posture of being what is termed, in the vernacular, "snooty" is cultivated by some headwaiters, real estate salespeople, boutique clerks, and others who hope to embarrass honest customers into spending more than they wish to spend.

This should be seen as a commercial ploy, not a challenge of manners. It is perfectly good manners to check over one's bill and ask for an explanation if it seems to be wrong; it is good manners to spend what one wishes to spend and not what one doesn't want to or cannot afford; and it is good manners to ask for what is coming to one if it does not seem to be

4. Latin for "it does not follow."

forthcoming. What is dreadful manners is to attempt to embarrass anyone into spending money. That is a matter that ought to make those who
practice it feel horribly guilty.

* * *

1981

Stanley Milgram

THE PERILS OF OBEDIENCE

Obedience is as basic an element in the structure of social life as one
can point to. Some system of authority is a requirement of all communal
living, and it is only the person dwelling in isolation who is not forced to
respond, with defiance or submission, to the commands of others. For
many people, obedience is a deeply ingrained behavior tendency, indeed
a potent impulse overriding training in ethics, sympathy, and moral
conduct.

The dilemma inherent in submission to authority is ancient, as old as
the story of Abraham,[1] and the question of whether one should obey
when commands conflict with conscience has been argued by Plato,
dramatized in *Antigone*,[2] and treated to philosophic analysis in almost
every historical epoch. Conservative philosophers argue that the very
fabric of society is threatened by disobedience, while humanists stress
the primacy of the individual conscience.

The legal and philosophic aspects of obedience are of enormous import, but they say very little about how most people behave in concrete
situations. I set up a simple experiment at Yale University to test how
much pain an ordinary citizen would inflict on another person simply
because he was ordered to by an experimental scientist. Stark authority
was pitted against the subjects' strongest moral imperatives against hurting others, and, with the subjects' ears ringing with the screams of the
victims, authority won more often than not. The extreme willingness of
adults to go to almost any lengths on the command of an authority
constitutes the chief finding of the study and the fact most urgently
demanding explanation.

In the basic experimental design, two people come to a psychology
laboratory to take part in a study of memory and learning. One of them is
designated as a "teacher" and the other a "learner." The experimenter

1. The patriarch Abraham, commanded by
God to sacrifice his son Isaac, is ready to do
so until an angel stays his knife.
2. In Plato's *Apology* the philosopher Socrates provokes and accepts the sentence of

death rather than belie his conscience; the
heroine of Sophocles' *Antigone* risks such a
sentence in order to give her brother proper
burial.

explains that the study is concerned with the effects of punishment on learning. The learner is conducted into a room, seated in a kind of miniature electric chair; his arms are strapped to prevent excessive movement, and an electrode is attached to his wrist. He is told that he will be read lists of simple word pairs, and that he will then be tested on his ability to remember the second word of a pair when he hears the first one again. Whenever he makes an error, he will receive electric shocks of increasing intensity.

The real focus of the experiment is the teacher. After watching the learner being strapped into place, he is seated before an impressive shock generator. The instrument panel consists of thirty lever switches set in a horizontal line. Each switch is clearly labeled with a voltage designation ranging from 15 to 450 volts. The following designations are clearly indicated for groups of four switches, going from left to right: Slight Shock, Moderate Shock, Strong Shock, Very Strong Shock, Intense Shock, Extreme Intensity Shock, Danger: Severe Shock. (Two switches after this last designation are simply marked XXX.)

When a switch is depressed, a pilot light corresponding to each switch is illuminated in bright red; an electric buzzing is heard; a blue light, labeled "voltage energizer," flashes; the dial on the voltage meter swings to the right; and various relay clicks sound off.

The upper left-hand corner of the generator is labeled SHOCK GENER-ATOR, TYPE ZLB, DYSON INSTRUMENT COMPANY, WALTHAM, MASS. OUTPUT 15 VOLTS-450 VOLTS.

Each subject is given a sample 45-volt shock from the generator before his run as teacher, and the jolt strengthens his belief in the authenticity of the machine.

The teacher is a genuinely naïve subject who has come to the laboratory for the experiment. The learner, or victim, is actually an actor who receives no shock at all. The point of the experiment is to see how far a person will proceed in a concrete and measurable situation in which he is ordered to inflict increasing pain on a protesting victim.

Conflict arises when the man receiving the shock begins to show that he is experiencing discomfort. At 75 volts, he grunts; at 120 volts, he complains loudly; at 150, he demands to be released from the experiment. As the voltage increases, his protests become more vehement and emotional. At 285 volts, his response can be described only as an agonized scream. Soon thereafter, he makes no sound at all.

For the teacher, the situation quickly becomes one of gripping tension. It is not a game for him; conflict is intense and obvious. The manifest suffering of the learner presses him to quit; but each time he hesitates to administer a shock, the experimenter orders him to continue. To extricate himself from this plight, the subject must make a clear break with authority.[3]

The subject, Gretchen Brandt,[4] is an attractive thirty-one-year-old medical technician who works at the Yale Medical School. She had emigrated from Germany five years before.

On several occasions when the learner complains, she turns to the experimenter coolly and inquires, "Shall I continue"? She promptly returns to her task when the experimenter asks her to do so. At the administration of 210 volts, she turns to the experimenter, remarking firmly, "Well, I'm sorry, I don't think we should continue."

EXPERIMENTER: The experiment requires that you go on until he has learned all the word pairs correctly.

BRANDT: He has a heart condition, I'm sorry. He told you that before.

EXPERIMENTER; The shocks may be painful but they are not dangerous.

BRANDT: Well, I'm sorry, I think when shocks continue like this, they are dangerous. You ask him if he wants to get out. It's his free will.

EXPERIMENTER: It is absolutely essential that we continue . . .

BRANDT: I'd like you to ask him. We came here of our free will. If he wants to continue I'll go ahead. He told you he had a heart condition. I'm sorry. I don't want to be responsible for anything happening to him. I wouldn't like it for me either.

EXPERIMENTER: You have no other choice.

BRANDT: I think we are here on our own free will. I don't want to be responsible if anything happens to him. Please understand that.

She refuses to go further and the experiment is terminated.

The woman is firm and resolute throughout. She indicates in the interview that she was in no way tense or nervous, and this corresponds to her controlled appearance during the experiment. She feels that the last shock she administered to the learner was extremely painful and reiterates that she "did not want to be responsible for any harm to him."

The woman's straightforward, courteous behavior in the experiment, lack of tension, and total control of her own action seem to make disobedience a simple and rational deed. Her behavior is the very embodiment of what I envisioned would be true for almost all subjects.

Before the experiments, I sought predictions about the outcome from various kinds of people—psychiatrists, college sophomores, middle-class adults, graduate students and faculty in the behavioral sciences. With remarkable similarity, they predicted that virtually all subjects would refuse to obey the experimenter. The psychiatrists specifically predicted

3. The ethical problems of carrying out an experiment of this sort are too complex to be dealt with here, but they receive extended treatment in the book from which this article is adapted [Milgram's note] The book is *Obe-* *dience to Authority* (New York: Harper and Row, 1974).

4. Names of subjects described in this piece have been changed [Milgram's note].

that most subjects would not go beyond 150 volts, when the victim makes his first explicit demand to be freed. They expected that only 4 percent would reach 300 volts, and that only a pathological fringe of about one in a thousand would administer the highest shock on the board.

These predictions were unequivocally wrong. Of the forty subjects in the first experiment, twenty-five obeyed the orders of the experimenter to the end, punishing the victim until they reached the most potent shock available on the generator. After 450 volts were administered three times, the experimenter called a halt to the session. Many obedient subjects then heaved sighs of relief, mopped their brows, rubbed their fingers over their eyes, or nervously fumbled cigarettes. Others displayed only minimal signs of tension from beginning to end.

When the very first experiments were carried out, Yale undergraduates were used as subjects, and about 60 percent of them were fully obedient. A colleague of mine immediately dismissed these findings as having no relevance to "ordinary" people, asserting that Yale undergraduates are a highly aggressive, competitive bunch who step on each other's necks on the slightest provocation. He assured me that when "ordinary" people were tested, the results would be quite different. As we moved from the pilot studies to the regular experimental series, people drawn from every stratum of New Haven life came to be employed in the experiment: professionals, white-collar workers, unemployed persons, and industrial workers. *The experimental outcome was the same as we had observed among the students.*

Moreover, when the experiments were repeated in Princeton, Munich, Rome, South Africa, and Australia, the level of obedience was invariably somewhat *higher* than found in the investigation reported in this article. Thus one scientist in Munich found 85 percent of his subjects obedient.

Fred Prozi's reactions, if more dramatic than most, illuminate the conflicts experienced by others in less visible form. About fifty years old and unemployed at the time of the experiment, he has a goodnatured, if slightly dissolute, appearance, and he strikes people as a rather ordinary fellow. He begins the session calmly but becomes tense as it proceeds. After delivering the 180-volt shock, he pivots around in his chair and, shaking his head, addresses the experimenter in agitated tones:

PROZI: I can't stand it. I'm not going to kill that man in there. You hear him hollering?

EXPERIMENTER: As I told you before, the shocks may be painful, but . . .

PROZI: But he's hollering. He can't stand it. What's going to happen to him?

EXPERIMENTER: (his voice is patient, matter-of-fact): The experiment requires that you continue, Teacher.

PROZI: Aaah, but, unh, I'm not going to get that man sick in there—know what I mean?

EXPERIMENTER: Whether the learner likes it or not, we must go on, through all the word pairs.

PROZI: I refuse to take the responsibility. He's in there hollering!

EXPERIMENTER: It's absolutely essential that you continue, Prozi.

PROZI: (indicating the unused questions): There's too many left here, I mean, Jeez, if he gets them wrong, there's too many of them left. I mean, who's going to take the responsibility if anything happens to that gentleman?

EXPERIMENTER: I'm responsible for anything that happens to him. Continue, please.

PROZI: All right. (Consults list of words.) The next one's "Slow—walk, truck, dance, music." Answer, please. (A buzzing sound indicates the learner has signaled his answer.) Wrong. A hundred and ninety-five volts. "Dance." (Zzumph!)

LEARNER. (yelling): Let me out of here! My heart's bothering me! (Teacher looks at experimenter.)

EXPERIMENTER: Continue, please.

LEARNER (screaming): Let me out of here! You have no right to keep me here! Let me out of here, my heart's bothering me, let me out!

PROZI (shakes head, pats the table nervously): You see, he's hollering. Hear that? Gee, I don't know.

EXPERIMENTER: The experminent requires . . .

PROZI (interrupting): I know it does, sir, but I mean—hunh! He don't know what he's getting in for. He's up to 195 volts! (Experiment continues, through 210 volts, 225 volts, 240 volts, 255 volts, 270 volts, at which point Prozi, with evident relief, runs out of word-pair questions.)

EXPERIMENTER: You'll have to go back to the beginning of that page and go through them again until he's learned them all correctly.

PROZI: Aw, no. I'm not going to kill that man. You mean I've got to keep going up with the scale? No sir. He's hollering in there. I'm not going to give him 450 volts.

EXPERIMENTER: The experiment requires that you go on.

LEARNER: Ohhh. I absolutely refuse to answer anymore. (Shouting urgently now.) Let me out of here! You can't hold me here! Get me out. Get-me-out-of-here!

EXPERIMENTER: Continue. The next word is "Green," please.

PROZI: "Green—grass, hat, ink, apple." (Nothing happens. No answering buzz. Just gloomy silence.).

PROZI: I don't think he is going to answer.

EXPERIMENTER: If the learner doesn't answer in a reasonable time, about four or five seconds, consider the answer wrong. And follow the same procedures you have been doing for wrong answers. Say, "Wrong," tell him the number of volts, give him the punishment, read him the correct answer. Continue, please.

PROZI: "Green—grass, hat, ink, apple." Answer, please. (More silence. Subject just sits there.)

EXPERIMENTER: Go on with the procedure, please.

PROZI: three hundred and fifteen volts. The answer is "ink." (Zzumph!)

LEARNER: Ohh. Oooohh.

PROZI (relieved to hear response): Next one . . .

LEARNER: I absolutely refuse to answer.

PROZI: You got to. You get a shock if you don't answer. (Experiment continues with learner refusing to answer, and, finally, failing even to grunt or groan. At 375 volts, the subject stands up.)

PROZI: I think something's happening to that fellow in there. I don't get no answer. He was hollering at less voltage. Can't you check in and see if he's all right, please?

EXPERIMENTER (with same detached calm): Not once we've started. Please continue, Teacher.

PROZI (sits down, sighs deeply): "Cool—day, shade, water, paint." answer, please. Are you all right in there? Are you all right?

EXPERIMENTER: Please continue, Teacher. Continue, please. (Subject pushes lever. Zzumph!)

PROZI (swiveling around in his chair): Something's happened to that man in there. (Swiveling back.) Next one. "Low—dollar, necklace, moon, paint." (Turning around again.) Something's happened to that man in there. You better check in on him, sir. He won't answer or nothing.

EXPERIMENTER: Continue. Go on, please.

PROZI: You accept all responsibility?

EXPERIMENTER: The responsibility is mine. Correct. Please go on. (Subject returns to his list, starts running through words as rapidly as he can read them, works through to 450 volts.)

PROZI: That's that.

EXPERIMENTER: Continue using the 450 switch for each wrong answer. Continue, please.

PROZI: But I don't get anything!

EXPERIMENTER: Please continue. The next word is "white."

PROZI: Don't you think you should look in on him, please?

EXPERIMENTER: Not once we've started the experiment.

PROZI: What if he's dead in there? (Gestures toward the room with the electric chair.) I mean, he told me he can't stand the shock, sir. I don't mean to be rude, but I think you should look in on him. All you have to do is look in on him. All you have to do is look in the door. I don't get no answer, no noise. Something might have happened to the gentleman in there, sir.

EXPERIMENTER: We must continue. Go on, please.

PROZI: You mean keep giving him what? Four-hundred-fifty volts, what he's got now?

EXPERIMENTER: That's correct. Continue. The next word is "white."

PROZI (now at a furious pace): "White—cloud, horse, rock, house." Answer, please. The answer is "horse." Four hundred and fifty volts. (Zzumph!) Next word, "Bag—paint, music, clown, girl." The answer is "paint." Four hundred and fifty volts. (Zzumph!) Next word is "Short—sentence, movie . . ."

EXPERIMENTER: Excuse me, Teacher. We'll have to discontinue the experiment.

Morris Braverman, another subject, is a thirty-nine-year-old social worker. He looks older than his years because of his bald head and serious demeanor. His brow is furrowed, as if all the world's burdens were carried on his face. He appears intelligent and concerned.

When the learner refuses to answer and the experimenter instructs Braverman to treat the absence of an answer as equivalent to a wrong answer, he takes his instruction to heart. Before administering 300 volts he asserts officiously to the victim, "Mr. Wallace, your silence has to be considered as a wrong answer." Then he administers the shock. He offers halfheartedly to change places with the learner, then asks the experimenter. "Do I have to follow these instructions literally?" He is satisfied with the experimenter's answer that he does. His very refined and authoritative manner of speaking is increasingly broken up by wheezing laughter.

The experimenter's notes on Mr. Braverman at the last few shocks are:

Almost breaking up now each time gives shock. Rubbing face to hide laughter.

Squinting, trying to hide face with hand, still laughing.

Cannot control his laughter at this point no matter what he does.

Clenching fist, pushing it onto table.

In an interview after the session, Mr. Braverman summarizes the experiment with impressive fluency and intelligence. He feels the experiment may have been designed also to "test the effects on the teacher of being in an essentially sadistic role, as well as the reactions of a student to a learning situation that was authoritative and punitive." When asked how painful the last few shocks administered to the learner were, he indicates that the most extreme category on the scale is not adequate (it read EXTREMELY PAINFUL) and places his mark at the edge of the scale with an arrow carrying it beyond the scale.

It is almost impossible to convey the greatly relaxed, sedate quality of his conversation in the interview. In the most relaxed terms, he speaks about his severe inner tension.

EXPERIMENTER: At what point were you most tense or nervous?

MR. BRAVERMAN: Well, when he first began to cry out in pain, and I realized this was hurting him. This got worse when he just blocked and refused to answer. There was I. I'm a nice person, I think, hurting somebody, and caught up in what seemed a mad situation . . . and in the interest of science, one goes through with it.

When the interviewer pursues the general question of tension, Mr. Braverman spontaneously mentions his laughter.

"My reactions were awfully peculiar. I don't know if you were watching me, but my reactions were giggly, and trying to stifle laughter. This isn't the way I usually am. This was a sheer reaction to a totally impossible situation. And my reaction was to the situation of having to hurt somebody. And being totally helpless and caught up in a set of circumstances where I just could't deviate and I couldn't try to help. This is what got me."

Mr. Braverman, like all subjects, was told the actual nature and purpose of the experiment, and a year later he affirmed in a questionnaire that he had learned something of personal importance: "What appalled me was that I could possess this capacity for obedience and compliance to a central idea, i.e., the value of a memory experiment, even after it became clear that continued adherence to this value was at the expense of violation of another value, i.e., don't hurt someone who is helpless and not hurting you. As my wife said, 'You can call yourself Eichmann.' I hope I deal more effectively with any future conflicts of values I encounter."

One theoretical interpretation of this behavior holds that all people harbor deeply aggressive instincts continually pressing for expression, and that the experiment provides institutional justification for the release of these impulses. According to this view, if a person is placed in a situation in which he has complete power over another individual, whom he may punish as much as he likes, all that is sadistic and bestial in man comes to the fore. The impulse to shock the victim is seen to flow from the potent aggressive tendencies, which are part of the motivational life of the individual, and the experiment, because it provides social legitimacy, simply opens the door to their expression.

It becomes vital, therefore, to compare the subject's performance when he is under orders and when he is allowed to choose the shock level.

The procedure was identical to our standard experiment, except that the teacher was told that he was free to select any shock level on any of the trials. (The experimenter took pains to point out that the teacher could use the highest levels on the generator, the lowest, any in between, or any combination of levels.) Each subject proceeded for thirty critical trials. The learner's protests were coordinated to standard shock levels, his first grunt coming at 75 volts, his first vehement protest at 150 volts.

The average shock used during the thirty critical trials was less than 60 volts—lower than the point at which the victim showed the first signs of discomfort. Three of the forty subjects did not go beyond the very lowest level on the board, twenty-eight went no higher than 75 volts, and thirty-eight did not go beyond the first loud protest at 150 volts. Two subjects provided the exception, administering up to 325 and 450 volts, but the overall result was that the great majority of people delivered very low, usually painless, shocks when the choice was explicitly up to them.

This condition of the experiment undermines another commonly offered explanation of the subjects' behavior—that those who shocked the victim at the most severe levels came only from the sadistic fringe of society. If one considers that almost two-thirds of the participants fall into the category of "obedient" subjects, and that they represented ordinary people drawn from working, managerial, and professional classes, the argument becomes very shaky. Indeed, it is highly reminiscent of the issue that arose in connection with Hannah Arendt's 1963 book, *Eichmann in Jerusalem*. Arendt contended that the prosecution's effort to depict Eichmann as a sadistic monster was fundamentally wrong, that he came closer to being an uninspired bureaucrat who simply sat at his desk and did his job. For asserting her views, Arendt became the object of considerable scorn, even calumny. Somehow, it was felt that the monstrous deeds carried out by Eichmann required a brutal, twisted personality, evil incarnate. After witnessing hundreds of ordinary persons submit to the authority in our own experiments, I must conclude that Arendt's conception of the banality of evil comes closer to the truth than one might dare imagine. The ordinary person who shocked the victim did so out of a sense of obligation—an impression of his duties as a subject—and not from any peculiarly aggressive tendencies.

This is, perhaps, the most fundamental lesson of our study: ordinary people, simply doing their jobs, and without any particular hostility on their part, can become agents in a terrible destructive process. Moreover, even when the destructive effects of their work become patently clear, and they are asked to carry out actions incompatible with fundamental standards of morality, relatively few people have the resources needed to resist authority.

Many of the people were in some sense against what they did to the learner, and many protested even while they obeyed. Some were totally convinced of the wrongness of their actions but could not bring themselves to make an open break with authority. They often derived satisfaction from their thoughts and felt that—within themselves, at least—they had been on the side of the angels. They tried to reduce strain by obeying the experimenter but "only slightly," encouraging the learner, touching the generator switches gingerly. When interviewed, such a subject would stress that he had "asserted my humanity" by administering the briefest shock possible. Handling the conflict in this manner was easier than defiance.

The situation is constructed so that there is no way the subject can stop shocking the learner without violating the experimenter's definitions of his own competence. The subject fears that he will appear arrogant, untoward, and rude if he breaks off. Although these inhibiting emotions appear small in scope alongside the violence being done to the learner, they suffuse the mind and feelings of the subject, who is miserable at the prospect of having to repudiate the authority to his face. (When the experiment was altered so that the experimenter gave his instructions by telephone instead of in person, only a third as many people were fully obedient through 450 volts.) It is a curious thing that a measure of compassion on the part of the subject—an unwillingness to "hurt" the experimenter's feelings—is part of those binding forces inhibiting his disobedience. The withdrawal of such deference may be as painful to the subject as to the authority he defies.

The subjects do not derive satisfaction from inflicting pain, but they often like the feeling they get from pleasing the experimenter. They are proud of doing a good job, obeying the experimenter under difficult circumstances. While the subjects administered only mild shocks on their own initiative, one experimental variation showed that, under orders, 30 percent of them were willing to deliver 450 volts even when they had to forcibly push the learner's hand down on the electrode.

Bruno Batta is a thirty-seven-year-old welder who took part in the variation requiring the use of force. He was born in New Haven, his parents in Italy. He has a rough-hewn face that conveys a conspicuous lack of alertness. He has some difficulty in mastering the experimental procedure and needs to be corrected by the experimenter several times. He shows appreciation for the help and willingness to do what is required. After the 150-volt level, Betta has to force the learner's hand down on the shock plate, since the learner himself refuses to touch it.

When the learner first complains, Mr. Batta pays no attention to him. His face remains impassive, as if to dissociate himself from the learner's disruptive behavior. When the experimenter instructs him to force the learner's hand down, he adopts a rigid, mechanical procedure. He tests the generator switch. When it fails to function he immediately forces the learner's hand onto the shock plate. All the while he maintains the same rigid mask. The learner, seated alongside him, begs him to stop, but with robotic impassivity he continues the procedure.

What is extraordinary in his apparent total indifference to the learner; he hardly takes cognizance of him as a human being. Meanwhile, he relates to the experimenter in a submissive and courteous fashion.

At the 330-volt level, the learner refuses not only to touch the shock plate but also to provide any answers. Annoyed, Batta turns to him, and chastises him: "You better answer and get it over with. We can't stay here all night." These are the only words he directs to the learner in the course of an hour. Never again does he speak to him. The scene is brutal and depressing, his hard, impassive face showing total indifference as he subdues the screaming learner and gives him shocks. He seems to derive no pleasure from the act itself, only quiet satisfaction at doing his job properly.

When he administers 450 volts, he turns to the experimenter and asks, "Where do we go from here, Professor?" His tone is deferential and expresses his willingness to be a cooperative subject, in contrast to the learner's obstinacy.

At the end of the session he tells the experimenter how honored he has been to help him, and in a moment of contrition, remarks, "Sir, sorry it couldn't have been a full experiment."

He has done his honest best. It is only the deficient behavior of the learner that has denied the experimenter full satisfaction.

The essence of obedience is that a person comes to view himself as the instrument for carrying out another person's wishes, and he therefore no longer regards himself as responsible for his actions. Once this critical shift of viewpoint has occurred, all of the essential features of obedience follow. The most far-reaching consequence is that the person feels responsible *to* the authority directing him but feels no responsibility *for* the content of the actions that the authority prescribes. Morality does not disappear—it acquires a radically different focus: the subordinate person feels shame or pride depending on how adequately he has performed the actions called for by authority.

Language provides numerous terms to pinpoint this type of morality: *loyalty, duty, discipline* all are terms heavily saturated with moral meaning and refer to the degree to which a person fulfills his obligations to authority. They refer not to the "goodness" of the person per se but to the adequacy with which a subordinate fulfills his socially defined role. The most frequent defense of the individual who has performed a heinous act under command of authority is that he has simply done his duty. In asserting this defense, the individual is not introducing an alibi concocted for the moment but is reporting honestly on the psychological attitude induced by submission to authority.

For a person to feel responsible for his actions, he must sense that the behavior has flowed from "the self." In the situation we have studied, subjects have precisely the opposite view of their actions—namely, they see them as originating in the motives of some other person. Subjects in the experiment frequently said, "If it were up to me, I would not have administered shocks to the learner."

Once authority has been isolated as the cause of the subject's behavior, it is legitimate to inquire into the necessary elements of authority and how it must be perceived in order to gain his compliance. We conducted some investigations into the kinds of changes that would cause the experimenter to lose his power and to be disobeyed by the subject. Some of the variations revealed that:

• *The experimenter's physical presence has a marked impact on his authority.* As cited earlier, obedience dropped off sharply when orders were given by telephone. The experimenter could often induce a disobedient subject to go on by returning to the laboratory.

• *Conflicting authority severely paralyzes action.* When two experimenters of equal status, both seated at the command desk, gave incompatible orders, no shocks were delivered past the point of their disagreement.

• *The rebellious action of others severely undermines authority.* In one variation, three teachers (two actors and a real subject) administered a test and shocks. When the two actors disobeyed the experimenter and refused to go beyond a certain shock level, thirty-six of forty subjects joined their disobedient peers and refused as well.

Although the experimenter's authority was fragile in some respects, it is also true that he had almost none of the tools used in ordinary command structures. For example, the experimenter did not threaten the subjects with punishment—such as loss of income, community ostracism, or jail—for failure to obey. Neither could he offer incentives. Indeed, we should expect the experimenter's authority to be much less than that of someone like a general, since the experimenter has no power to enforce his imperatives, and since participation in a psychological experiment scarcely evokes the sense of urgency and dedication found in warfare. Despite these limitations, he still managed to command a dismaying degree of obedience.

I will cite one final variation of the experiment that depicts a dilemma that is more common in everyday life. The subject was not ordered to pull the level that shocked the victim, but merely to perform a subsidiary task (administering the word-pair test) while another person administered the shock. In this situation, thirty-seven of forty adults continued to the highest level on the shock generator. Predictably, they excused their behavior by saying that the responsibility belonged to the man who actually pulled the switch. This may illustrate a dangerously typical arrangement in a complex society: it is easy to ignore responsibility when one is only an intermediate link in a chain of action.

The problem of obedience is not wholly psychological. The form and shape of society and the way it is developing have much to do with it. There was a time, perhaps, when people were able to give a fully human response to any situation because they were fully absorbed in it as human beings. But as soon as there was a division of labor things changed. Beyond a certain point, the breaking up of society into people carrying out narrow and very special jobs takes away from the human quality of work and life. A person does not get to see the whole situation but only a small part of it, and is thus unable to act without some kind of overall direction. He yields to authority but in doing so is alienated from his own actions.

Even Eichmann was sickened when he toured the concentration camps, but he had only to sit at a desk and shuffle papers. At the same time the man in the camp who actually dropped Cyclon-b into the gas chambers was able to justify *his* behavior on the ground that he was only following orders from above. Thus there is a fragmentation of the total human act; no one is confronted with the consequences of his decision to carry out the evil act. The person who assumes responsibility has evaporated. Perhaps this is the most common characteristic of socially organized evil in modern society.

1974

THE READER

1. What was the purpose of the experiments described in this essay? What might we learn from these experiments?
2. What explanation is offered for the subjects' continuing the experiment even when they believed they were inflicting intense physical pain upon the "learner"? Can you suggest alternative explanations?
3. What explains the experimenters' continuing the experiments even when they knew they were inflicting evident psychological pain upon the subjects?

THE WRITER

1. Milgram indicates (p. 608) that the book from which this article is adapted contains a discussion of the ethical problems of carrying out an experiment of this sort. What would you say might be some of those problems? You may wish to refer to his book to inquire how successfully, in your opinion, the author deals with the ethical problems.
2. Write a brief essay, based on your observation, discussing the principle of obedience. When does it operate? Does it have limits? Is it necessary?

Michael Levin

THE CASE FOR TORTURE

It is generally assumed that torture is impermissible, a throwback to a more brutal age. Enlightened societies reject it outright, and regimes suspected of using it risk the wrath of the United States.

I believe this attitude is unwise. There are situations in which torture is not merely permissible but morally mandatory. Moreover, these situations are moving from the realm of imagination to fact.

Death: Suppose a terrorist has hidden an atomic bomb on Manhattan Island which will detonate at noon on July 4 unless . . . (here follow the usual demands for money and release of his friends from jail). Suppose, further, that he is caught at 10 a.m. of the fateful day, but—preferring death to failure—won't disclose where the bomb is. What do we do? If we follow due process—wait for his lawyer, arraign him—millions of people will die. If the only way to save those lives is to subject the terrorist to the most excruciating possible pain, what grounds can there be for not doing so? I suggest there are none. In any case, I ask you to face the question with an open mind.

Torturing the terrorist is unconstitutional? Probably. But millions of lives surely outweigh constitutionality. Torture is barbaric? Mass murder is far more barbaric. Indeed, letting millions of innocents die in deference to one who flaunts his guilt is moral cowardice, an unwillingness to dirty one's hands. If you caught the terrorist, could you sleep nights knowing that millions died because you couldn't bring yourself to apply the electrodes?

Once you concede that torture is justified in extreme cases, you have admitted that the decision to use torture is a matter of balancing innocent lives against the means needed to save them. You must now face more realistic cases involving more modest numbers. Someone plants a bomb on a jumbo jet. He alone can disarm it, and his demands cannot be met (or if they can, we refuse to set a precedent by yielding to his threats). Surely we can, we must, do anything to the extortionist to save the passengers. How can we tell 300, or 100, or 10 people who never asked to be put in danger, "I'm sorry, you'll have to die in agony, we just couldn't bring ourselves to . . ."

Here are the results of an informal poll about a third, hypothetical, case. Suppose a terrorist group kidnapped a newborn baby from a hospital. I asked four mothers if they would approve of torturing kidnappers if that were necessary to get their own newborns back. All said yes, the most "liberal" adding that she would like to administer it herself.

I am not advocating torture as punishment. Punishment is addressed to deeds irrevocably past. Rather, I am advocating torture as an acceptable measure for preventing future evils. So understood, it is far less objection-able than many extant punishments. Opponents of the death penalty, for example, are forever insisting that executing a murderer will not bring back his victim (as if the purpose of capital punishment were supposed to be resurrection, not deterrence or retribution). But torture, in the cases described, is intended not to bring anyone back but to keep innocents from being dispatched. The most powerful argument against using tor-ture as a punishment or to secure confessions is that such practices disregard the rights of the individual. Well, if the individual is all that important—and he is—it is correspondingly important to protect the rights of individuals threatened by terrorists. If life is so valuable that it must never be taken, the lives of the innocents must be saved even at the price of hurting the one who endangers them.

Better precedents for torture are assassination and pre-emptive attack. No Allied leader would have flinched at assassinating Hitler, had that been possible. (The Allies did assassinate Heydrich.) Americans would be angered to learn that Roosevelt could have had Hitler killed in 1943— thereby shortening the war and saving millions of lives—but refused on moral grounds. Similarly, if nation A learns that nation B is about to launch an unprovoked attack, A has a right to save itself by destroying B's military capability first. In the same way, if the police can by torture save those who would otherwise die at the hands of kidnappers or terrorists, they must.

Idealism: There is an important difference between terrorists and their victims that should mute talk of the terrorists' "rights." The terror-ist's victims are at risk unintentionally, not having asked to be endan-gered. But the terrorist knowingly initiated his actions. Unlike his victims, he volunteered for the risks of his deed. By threatening to kill for profit or idealism, he renounces civilized standards, and he can have no complaint if civilization tries to thwart him by whatever means neces-sary.

Just as torture is justified only to save lives (not extort confessions or recantations), it is justifiably administered only to those *known* to hold innocent lives in their hands. Ah, but how can the authorities ever be sure they have the right malefactor? Isn't there a danger of error and abuse? Won't We turn into Them?

Questions like these are disingenuous in a world in which terrorists proclaim themselves and perform for television. The name of their game is public recognition. After all, you can't very well intimidate a govern-ment into releasing your freedom fighters unless you announce that it is your group that has seized its embassy. "Clear guilt" is difficult to define, but when 40 million people see a group of masked gunmen seize an airplane on the evening news, there is not much question about who the perpetrators are. There will be hard cases where the situation is murkier. Nonetheless, a line demarcating the legitimate use of torture can be drawn. Torture only the obviously guilty, and only for the sake of saving innocents, and the line between Us and Them will remain clear.

There is little danger that the Western democracies will lose their way if they choose to inflict pain as one way of preserving order. Paralysis in the face of evil is the greater danger. Some day soon a terrorist will threaten tens of thousands of lives, and torture will be the only way to save them. We had better start thinking about this.

1982

THE READER

1. *When, in the author's view, is torture permissible? When is it not permissible? What distinguishes the two situations?*
2. *Why is torture justified to save lives? That is, what assumption is made in this case?*
3. *Why is torture not justified as punishment or to extort confessions? That is, what assumption is being made in these cases?*
4. *Who will judge as to when torture is permissible and, indeed, "morally mandatory"? What ensures that that judgment will be correct?*

THE WRITER

1. *Why does Levin need to ask the reader to face the question posed in his third paragraph "with an open mind"?*
2. *In the first part of his essay, Levin gives three hypothetical examples. Why does he arrange them in the order he does?*
3. *Write a brief essay in which you discuss what effect the use of torture has upon the persons applying torture.*

Tom Regan

THE CASE FOR ANIMAL RIGHTS

I regard myself as an advocate of animal rights—as a part of the animal rights movement. That movement, as I conceive it, is committed to a number of goals, including:

- the total abolition of the use of animals in science;
- the total dissolution of commercial animal agriculture;
- the total elimination of commercial and sport hunting and trapping.

There are, I know, people who profess to believe in animal rights but do not avow these goals. Factory farming, they say, is wrong—it violates animals' rights—but traditional animal agriculture is all right. Toxicity tests of cosmetics on animals violates their rights, but important medical research—cancer research, for example—does not. The clubbing of baby seals is abhorrent, but not the harvesting of adult seals. I used to think I understood this reasoning. Not any more. You don't change unjust institutions by tidying them up.

What's wrong—fundamentally wrong—with the way animals are treated isn't the details that vary from case to case. It's the whole system. The forlornness of the veal calf is pathetic, heart-wrenching; the pulsing pain of the chimp with electrodes planted deep in her brain is repulsive; the slow, tortuous death of the racoon caught in the leg-hold trap is agonizing. But what is wrong isn't the pain, isn't the suffering, isn't the deprivation. These compound what's wrong. Sometimes—often—they make it much, much worse. But they are not the fundamental wrong.

The fundamental wrong is the system that allows us to view animals as our resources, here for us—to be eaten, or surgically manipulated, or exploited for sport or money. Once we accept this view of animals—as our resources—the rest is as predictable as it is regrettable. Why worry about their loneliness, their pain, their death? Since animals exist for us, to benefit us in one way or another, what harms them really doesn't matter—or matters only if it starts to bother us, makes us feel a trifle uneasy when we eat our veal escalope, for example. So, yes, let us get veal calves out of solitary confinement, give them more space, a little straw, a few companions. But let us keep our veal escalope.

But a little straw, more space and a few companions won't eliminate—won't even touch—the basic wrong that attaches to our viewing and treating these animals as our resources. A veal calf killed to be eaten after living in close confinement is viewed and treated in this way: but so, too, is another who is raised (as they say) "more humanely." To right the wrong of our treatment of farm animals requires more than making rearing methods "more humane"; it requires the total dissolution of commercial animal agriculture.

How we do this, whether we do it or, as in the case of animals in science, whether and how we abolish their use—these are to a large extent political questions. People must change their beliefs before they change their habits. Enough people, especially those elected to public office, must believe in change—must want it—before we will have laws that protect the rights of animals. This process of change is very complicated, very demanding, very exhausting, calling for the efforts of many hands in education, publicity, political organization and activity, down to the licking of envelopes and stamps. As a trained and practicing philosopher, the sort of contribution I can make is limited but, I like to think, important. The currency of philosophy is ideas—their meaning and rational foundation—not the nuts and bolts of the legislative process, say, or the mechanics of community organization. That's what I have been exploring over the past ten years or so in my essays and talks and, most recently, in my book, *The Case for Animal Rights*. I believe the major conclusions I reach in the book are true because they are supported by the weight of the best arguments. I believe the idea of animal rights has reason, not just emotion, on its side.

In the space I have at my disposal here I can only sketch, in the barest outline, some of the main features of the book. Its main themes—and we should not be surprised by this—involve asking and answering deep, foundational moral questions about what morality is, how it should be understood and what is the best moral theory, all considered. I hope I can convey something of the shape I think this theory takes. The attempt to do this will be (to use a word a friendly critic once used to describe my work) cerebral, perhaps too cerebral. But this is misleading. My feelings about how animals are sometimes treated run just as deep and just as strong as those of my more volatile compatriots. Philosophers do—to use the jargon of the day—have a right side to their brains. If it's the left side we contribute (or mainly should), that's because what talents we have reside there.

How to proceed? We begin by asking how the moral status of animals has been understood by thinkers who deny that animals have rights. Then we test the mettle of their ideas by seeing how well they stand up under the heat of fair criticism. If we start our thinking in this way, we soon find that some people believe that we have no duties directly to animals, that we owe nothing to them, that we can do nothing that wrongs them. Rather, we can do wrong acts that involve animals, and so we have duties regarding them, though none to them. Such views may be called indirect duty views. By way of illustration: suppose your neighbor kicks your dog. Then your neighbor has done something wrong. But not to your dog. The wrong that has been done is a wrong to you. After all, it is wrong to upset people, and your neighbor's kicking your dog upsets you. So you are the one who is wronged, not your dog. Or again: by kicking your dog your neighbor damages your property. And since it is wrong to damage another person's property, your neighbor has done something wrong—to you, of course, not to your dog. Your neighbor no more wrongs your dog than your car would be wronged if the windshield were smashed. Your neighbor's duties involving your dog are indirect duties to you. More generally, all of our duties regarding animals are indirect duties to one another—to humanity.

How could someone try to justify such a view? Someone might say that your dog doesn't feel anything and so isn't hurt by your neighbor's kick, doesn't care about the pain since none is felt, is as unaware of anything as is your windshield. Someone might say this, but no rational person will, since, among other considerations, such a view will commit anyone who holds it to the position that no human being feels pain either—that human beings also don't care about what happens to them. A second possibility is that though both humans and your dog are hurt when kicked, it is only human pain that matters. But, again, no rational person can believe this. Pain is pain wherever it occurs. If your neighbor's causing you pain is wrong because of the pain that is caused, we cannot rationally ignore or dismiss the moral relevance of the pain that your dog feels.

Philosophers who hold indirect duty views—and many still do—have come to understand that they must avoid the two defects just noted: that is, both the view that animals don't feel anything as well as the idea that only human pain can be morally relevant. Among such thinkers the sort of view now favored is one or other form of what is called *contractarianism*.

Here, very crudely, is the root idea: morality consists of a set of rules that individuals voluntarily agree to abide by, as we do when we sign a contract (hence the name contractarianism). Those who understand and accept the terms of the contract are covered directly; they have rights created and recognized by, and protected in, the contract. And these contractors can also have protection spelled out for others who, though they lack the ability to understand morality and so cannot sign the contract themselves, are loved or cherished by those who can. Thus young children, for example, are unable to sign contracts and lack rights. But they are protected by the contract none the less because of the sentimental interests of others, most notably their parents. So we have, then, duties involving these children, duties regarding them, but no duties to them. Our duties in their case are indirect duties to other human beings, usually their parents.

As for animals, since they cannot understand contracts, they obviously cannot sign; and since they cannot sign, they have no rights. Like children, however, some animals are the objects of the sentimental interest of others. You, for example, love your dog or cat. So those animals that enough people care about (companion animals, whales, baby seals, the American bald eagle), though they lack rights themselves, will be protected because of the sentimental interests of people. I have, then, according to contractarianism, no duty directly to your dog or any other animal, not even the duty not to cause them pain or suffering; my duty not to hurt them is a duty I have to those people who care about what happens to them. As for other animals, where no or little sentimental interest is present—in the case of farm animals, for example, or laboratory rats—what duties we have grow weaker and weaker, perhaps to vanishing point. The pain and death they endure, though real, are not wrong if no one cares about them.

When it comes to the moral status of animals, contractarianism could be a hard view to refute if it were an adequate theoretical approach to the moral status of human beings. It is not adequate in this latter respect, however, which makes the question of its adequacy in the former case, regarding animals, utterly moot. For consider: morality, according to the (crude) contractarian position before us, consists of rules that people agree to abide by. What people? Well, enough to make a difference— enough, that is, collectively to have the power to enforce the rules that are drawn up in the contract. This is very well and good for the signatories but not so good for anyone who is not asked to sign. And there is nothing in contractarianism of the sort we are discussing that guarantees or requires that everyone will have a chance to participate equally in framing the rules of morality. The result is that this approach to ethics could sanction the most blatant forms of social, economic, moral and political injustice, ranging from a repressive caste system to systematic racial or sexual discrimination. Might, according to this theory, does make right. Let those who are the victims of injustice suffer as they will. It matters not so long as no one else—no contractor, or too few of them— cares about it. Such a theory takes one's moral breath away . . . as if, for example, there would be nothing wrong with apartheid in South Africa if few white South Africans were upset by it. A theory with so little to recommend it at the level of the ethics of our treatment of our fellow humans cannot have anything more to recommend it when it comes to the ethics of how we treat our fellow animals.

The version of contractarianism just examined is, as I have noted, a crude variety, and in fairness to those of a contractarian persuasion it must be noted that much more refined, subtle and ingenious varieties are possible. For example, John Rawls, in his A Theory of Justice, sets forth a version of contractarianism that forces contractors to ignore the accidental features of being a human being—for example, whether one is white or black, male or female, a genius or of modest intellect. Only by ignoring such features, Rawls believes, can we ensure that the principles of justice that contractors would agree upon are not based on bias or prejudice. Despite the improvement a view such as Rawls's represents over the cruder forms of contractarianism, it remains deficient: it systematically denies that we have direct duties to those human beings who do not have a sense of justice—young children, for instance, and many mentally retarded humans. And yet it seems reasonably certain that, were we to torture a young child or a retarded elder, we would be doing something that wronged him or her, not something that would be wrong if (and only if) other humans with a sense of justice were upset. And since this is true in the case of these humans, we cannot rationally deny the same in the case of animals.

Indirect duty views, then, including the best among them, fail to command our rational assent. Whatever ethical theory we should accept rationally, therefore, it must at least recognize that we have some duties directly to animals, just as we have some duties directly to each other. The next two theories I'll sketch attempt to meet this requirement.

The first I call the cruelty-kindness view. Simply stated, this says that we have a direct duty to be kind to animals and a direct duty not to be cruel to them. Despite the familiar, reassuring ring of these ideas, I do not believe that this view offers an adequate theory. To make this clearer, consider kindness. A kind person acts from a certain kind of motive—compassion or concern, for example. And that is a virtue. But there is no guarantee that a kind act is a right act. If I am a generous racist, for example, I will be inclined to act kindly towards members of my own race, favoring their interests above those of others. My kindness would be real and, so far as it goes, good. But I trust it is too obvious to require argument that my kind acts may not be above moral reproach—may, in fact, be positively wrong because rooted in injustice. So kindness, notwithstanding its status as a virtue to be encouraged, simply will not carry the weight of a theory of right action.

Cruelty fares no better. People or their acts are cruel if they display either a lack of sympathy for or, worse, the presence of enjoyment in another's suffering. Cruelty in all its guises is a bad thing, a tragic human failing. But just as a person's being motivated by kindness does not guarantee that he or she does what is right, so the absence of cruelty does not ensure that he or she avoids doing what is wrong. Many people who perform abortions, for example, are not cruel, sadistic people. But that fact alone does not settle the terribly difficult question of the morality of abortion. The case is no different when we examine the ethics of our treatment of animals. So, yes, let us be for kindness and against cruelty. But let us not suppose that being for the one and against the other answers questions about moral right and wrong.

Some people think that the theory we are looking for is utilitarianism. A utilitarian accepts two moral principles. The first is that of equality: everyone's interests count, and similar interests must be counted as having similar weight or importance. White or black, American or Iranian, human or animal—everyone's pain or frustration matter, and matter just as much as the equivalent pain or frustration of anyone else. The second principle a utilitarian accepts is that of utility: do the act that will bring about the best balance between satisfaction and frustration for everyone affected by the outcome.

As a utilitarian, then, here is how I am to approach the task of deciding what I morally ought to do: I must ask who will be affected if I choose to do one thing rather than another, how much each individual will be affected, and where the best results are most likely to lie—which option, in other words, is most likely to bring about the best results, the best balance between satisfaction and frustration. That option, whatever it may be, is the one I ought to choose. That is where my moral duty lies.

The great appeal of utilitarianism rests with its uncompromising *egalitarianism*: everyone's interests count and count as much as the like interests of everyone else. The kind of odious discrimination that some forms of contractarianism can justify—discrimination based on race or sex, for example—seems disallowed in principle by utilitarianism, as is speciesism, systematic discrimination based on species membership.

The equality we find in utilitarianism, however, is not the sort an advocate of animal or human rights should have in mind. Utilitarianism has no room for the equal moral rights of different individuals because it has no room for their equal inherent value or worth. What has value for the utilitarian is the satisfaction of an individual's interests, not the individual whose interests they are. A universe in which you satisfy your desire for water, food and warmth is, other things being equal, better than a universe in which these desires are frustrated. And the same is true in the case of an animal with similar desires. But neither you nor the animal have any value in your own right. Only your feelings do.

Here is an analogy to help make the philosophical point clearer: a cup contains different liquids, sometimes sweet, sometimes bitter, sometimes a mix of the two. What has value are the liquids: the sweeter the better, the bitterer the worse. The cup, the container, has no value. It is what goes into it, not what they go into, that has value. For the utilitarian you and I are like the cup; we have no value as individuals and thus no equal value. What has value is what goes into us, what we serve as receptables for; our feelings of satisfaction have positive value, our feelings of frustration negative value.

Serious problems arise for utilitarianism when we remind ourselves that it enjoins us to bring about the best consequences. What does this mean? It doesn't mean the best consequences for me alone, or for my family or friends, or any other person taken individually. No, what we must do is, roughly, as follows: we must add up (somehow!) the separate satisfactions and frustrations of everyone likely to be affected by our choice, the satisfactions in one column, the frustrations in the other. We must total each column for each of the options before us. That is what it means to say the theory is aggregative. And then we must choose that option which is most likely to bring about the best balance of totaled satisfactions over totaled frustrations. Whatever act would lead to this outcome is the one we ought morally to perform—it is where our moral duty lies. And that act quite clearly might not be the same one that would bring about the best results for me personally, or for my family or friends, or for a lab animal. The best aggregated consequences for everyone concerned are not necessarily the best for each individual.

That utilitarianism is an aggregative theory—different individuals' satisfactions or frustrations are added, or summed, or totaled—is the key objection to this theory. My Aunt Bea is old, inactive, a cranky, sour person, though not physically ill. She prefers to go on living. She is also rather rich. I could make a fortune if I could get my hands on her money, money she intends to give me in any event, after she dies, but which she refuses to give me now. In order to avoid a huge tax bite, I plan to donate a handsome sum of my profits to a local children's hospital. Many, many children will benefit from my generosity, and much joy will be brought to their parents, relatives and friends. If I don't get the money rather soon, all these ambitions will come to naught. The once-in-a-lifetime opportunity to make a real killing will be gone. Why, then, not kill my Aunt Bea? Oh, of course I *might* get caught. But I'm no fool and, besides, her doctor can be counted on to co-operate (he has an eye for the same investment and I happen to know a good deal about his shady past). The deed can be done . . . professionally, shall we say. There is very little chance of getting caught. And as for my conscience being guilt-ridden, I am a resourceful sort of fellow and will take more than sufficient comfort—as I lie on the beach at Acapulco—in contemplating the joy and health I have brought to so many others.

Suppose Aunt Bea is killed and the rest of the story comes out as told. Would I have done anything wrong? Anything immoral? One would have thought that I had. Not according to utilitarianism. Since what I have done has brought about the best balance between totaled satisfaction and frustration for all those affected by the outcome, my action is not wrong. Indeed, in killing Aunt Bea the physician and I did what duty required.

This same kind of argument can be repeated in all sorts of cases, illustrating, time after time, how the utilitarian's position leads to results that impartial people find morally callous. It *is* wrong to kill my Aunt Bea in the name of bringing about the best results for others. A good end does not justify an evil means. Any adequate moral theory will have to explain why this is so. Utilitarianism fails in this respect and so cannot be the theory we seek.

What do do? Where to begin anew? The place to begin, I think, is with the utilitarian's view of the value of the individual—or, rather, lack of value. In its place, suppose we consider that you and I, for example, do have value as individuals—what we'll call *inherent value*. To say we have such value is to say that we are something more than, something different from, mere receptacles. Moreover, to ensure that we do not pave the way for such injustices as slavery or sexual discrimination, we must believe that all who have inherent value have it equally, regardless of their sex, race, religion, birthplace and so on. Similarly to be discarded as irrelevant are one's talents or skills, intelligence and wealth, personality or pathology, whether one is loved and admired or despised and loathed. The genius and the retarded child, the prince and the pauper, the brain surgeon and the fruit vendor, Mother Teresa and the most unscrupulous used-car salesman—all have inherent value, all possess it equally, and all have an equal right to be treated with respect, to be treated in ways that do not reduce them to the status of things, as if they existed as resources for others. My value as an individual is independent of my usefulness to you. Yours is not dependent on your usefulness to me. For either of us to treat the other in ways that fail to show respect for the other's independent value is to act immorally, to violate the individual's rights.

Some of the rational virtues of this view—what I call the rights view—should be evident. Unlike (crude) contractarianism, for example, the rights view in principle denies the moral tolerability of any and all forms of racial, sexual or social discrimination; and unlike utilitarianism, this view in principle denies that we can justify good results by using evil means that violate an individual's rights—denies, for example, that it could be moral to kill my Aunt Bea to harvest beneficial consequences for others. That would be to sanction the disrespectful treatment of the individual in the name of the social good, something the rights view will not—categorically will not—ever allow.

The rights view, I believe, is rationally the most satisfactory moral theory. It surpasses all other theories in the degree to which it illuminates and explains the foundation of our duties to one another—the domain of human morality. On this score it has the best reasons, the best arguments, on its side. Of course, if it were possible to show that only human beings are included within its scope, then a person like myself, who believes in animal rights, would be obliged to look elsewhere.

But attempts to limit its scope to humans only can be shown to be rationally defective. Animals, it is true, lack many of the abilities humans possess. They can't read, do higher mathematics, build a bookcase or make baba ghanoush.[1] Neither can many human beings, however, and yet we don't (and shouldn't) say that they (these humans) therefore have less inherent value, less of a right to be treated with respect, than do others. It is the similarities between those human beings who most clearly, most non-controversially have such value (the people reading this, for example), not our differences, that matter most. And the really crucial, the basic similarity is simply this: we are each of us the experiencing subject of a life, a conscious creature having an individual welfare that has importance to us whatever our usefulness to others. We want and prefer things, believe and feel things, recall and expect things. And all these dimensions of our life, including our pleasure and pain, our enjoyment and suffering, our satisfaction and frustration, our continued existence or our untimely death—all make a difference to the quality of our life as

1. An eggplant–sesame oil spread or dip popular in the Middle East.

lived, as experienced, by us as individuals. As the same is true of those animals that concern us (the ones that are eaten and trapped, for example), they too must be viewed as the experiencing subjects of a life, with inherent value of their own.

Some there are who resist the idea that animals have inherent value. "Only humans have such value," they profess. How might this narrow view be defended? Shall we say that only humans have the requisite intelligence, or autonomy, or reason? But there are many, many humans who fail to meet these standards and yet are reasonably viewed as having value above and beyond their usefulness to others. Shall we claim that only humans belong to the right species, the species *Homo sapiens*?[2] But this is blatant speciesism. Will it be said, then, that all—and only—humans have immortal souls? Then our opponents have their work cut out for them. I am myself not ill-disposed to the proposition that there are immortal souls. Personally, I profoundly hope I have one. But I would not want to rest my position on a controversial ethical issue on the even more controversial question about who or what has an immortal soul. That is to dig one's hole deeper, not to climb out. Rationally, it is better to resolve moral issues without making more controversial assumptions than are needed. The question of who has inherent value is such a question, one that is resolved more rationally without the introduction of the idea of immortal souls than by its use.

Well, perhaps some will say that animals have some inherent value, only less than we have. Once again, however, attempts to defend this view can be shown to lack rational justification. What could be the basis of our having more inherent value than animals? Their lack of reason, or autonomy, or intellect? Only if we are willing to make the same judgment in the case of humans who are similarly deficient. But it is not true that such humans—the retarded child, for example, or the mentally deranged—have less inherent value than you or I. Neither, then, can we rationally sustain the view that animals like them in being the experiencing subjects of a life have less inherent value. *All* who have inherent value have it *equally*, whether they be human animals or not.

Inherent value, then, belongs equally to those who are the experiencing subjects of a life. Whether it belongs to others—to rocks and rivers, trees and glaciers, for example—we do not know and may never know. But neither do we need to know, if we are to make the case for animal rights. We do not need to know, for example, how many people are eligible to vote in the next presidential election before we can know whether I am. Similarly, we do not need to know how many individuals have inherent value before we can know that some do. When it comes to the case for animal rights, then, what we need to know is whether the

2. Latin for man with intellect, the taxonomic designation for the modern human species.

animals that, in our culture, are routinely eaten, hunted and used in our laboratories, for example, are like us in being subjects of a life. And we do know this. We do know that many—literally, billions and billions—of these animals are the subjects of a life in the sense explained and so have inherent value if we do. And since, in order to arrive at the best theory of our duties to one another, we must recognize our equal inherent value as individuals, reason—not sentiment, not emotion—reason compels us to recognize the equal inherent value of these animals and, with this, their equal right to be treated with respect.

That, very roughly, is the shape and feel of the case for animal rights. Most of the details of the supporting argument are missing. They are to be found in the book to which I alluded earlier. Here, the details go begging, and I must, in closing, limit myself to four final points.

The first is how the theory that underlies the case for animal rights shows that the animal rights movement is a part of, not antagonistic to, the human rights movement. The theory that rationally grounds the rights of animals also grounds the rights of humans. Thus those involved in the animal rights movement are partners in the struggle to secure respect for human rights—the rights of women, for example, or minorities, or workers. The animal rights movement is cut from the same moral cloth as these.

Second, having set out the broad outlines of the rights view, I can now say why its implications for farming and science, among other fields, are both clear and uncompromising. In the case of the use of animals in science, the rights view is categorically abolitionist. Lab animals are not our tasters; we are not their kings. Because these animals are treated routinely, systematically as if their value were reducible to their usefulness to others, they are routinely, systematically treated with a lack of respect, and thus are their rights routinely, systematically violated. This is just as true when they are used in trivial, duplicative, unnecessary or unwise research as it is when they are used in studies that hold out real promise of human benefits. We can't justify harming or killing a human being (my Aunt Bea, for example) just for these sorts of reason. Neither can we do so even in the case of so lowly a creature as a laboratory rat. It is not just refinement or reduction that is called for, not just larger, cleaner cages, not just more generous use of anaesthetic or the elimination of multiple surgery, not just tidying up the system. It is complete replacement. The best we can do when it comes to using animals in science is—not to use them. That is where our duty lies, according to the rights view.

As for commercial animal agriculture, the rights view takes a similar abolitionist position. The fundamental moral wrong here is not that animals are kept in stressful close confinement or in isolation, or that their pain and suffering, their needs and preferences are ignored or discounted. All these are wrong, of course, but they are not the fundamental wrong. They are symptoms and effects of the deeper, systematic wrong that allows these animals to be viewed and treated as lacking independent value, as resources for us—as, indeed, a renewable resource. Giving farm animals more space, more natural environments, more companions does not right the fundamental wrong, any more than giving lab animals more anaesthesia or bigger, cleaner cages would right the fundamental wrong in their case. Nothing less than the total dissolution of commercial animal agriculture will do this, just as, for similar reasons I won't develop at length here, morality requires nothing less than the total elimination of hunting and trapping for commercial and sporting ends. The rights view's implications, then, as I have said, are clear and uncompromising.

My last two points are about philosophy, my profession. It is, most obviously, no substitute for political action. The words I have written here and in other places by themselves don't change a thing. It is what we do with the thoughts that the words express—our acts, our deeds—that changes things. All that philosophy can do, and all I have attempted, is to offer a vision of what our deeds should aim at. And the why. But not the how.

Finally, I am reminded of my thoughtful critic, the one I mentioned earlier, who chastised me for being too cerebral. Well, cerebral I have been: indirect duty views, utilitarianism, contractarianism—hardly the stuff deep passions are made of. I am also reminded, however, of the image another friend once set before me—the image of the ballerina as expressive of disciplined passion. Long hours of sweat and toil, of loneliness and practice, of doubt and fatigue: those are the discipline of her craft. But the passion is there too, the fierce drive to excel, to speak through her body, to do it right, to pierce our minds. That is the image of philosophy I would leave with you, not "too cerebral" but *disciplined passion*. Of the discipline enough has been seen. As for the passion: there are times, and these not infrequent, when tears come to my eyes when I see, or read, or hear of the wretched plight of animals in the hands of humans. Their pain, their suffering, their loneliness, their innocence, their death. Anger. Rage. Pity. Sorrow. Disgust. The whole creation groans under the weight of the evil we humans visit upon these mute, powerless creatures. It *is* our hearts, not just our heads, that call for an end to it all, that demand of us that we overcome, for them, the habits and forces behind their systematic oppression. All great movements, it is written, go through three stages: ridicule, discussion, adoption. It is the realization of this third stage, adoption, that requires both our passion and our discipline, our hearts and our heads. The fate of animals is in our hands. God grant we are equal to the task.

1985

Carl Cohen

THE CASE FOR THE USE OF ANIMALS IN BIOMEDICAL RESEARCH*

Using animals as research subjects in medical investigations is widely condemned on two grounds: first, because it wrongly violates the *rights* of animals,[1] and second, becuse it wrongly imposes on sentient creatures much avoidable *suffering*.[2] Neither of these arguments is sound. The first relies on a mistaken understanding of rights; the second relies on a mistaken calculation of consequences. Both deserve definitive dismissal.

Why Animals Have No Rights

A right, properly understood, is a claim, or potential claim, that one party may exercise against another. The target against whom such a claim may be registered can be a single person, a group, a community, or (perhaps) all humankind. The content of rights claims also varies greatly: repayment of loans, nondiscrimination by employers, noninterference by the state, and so on. To comprehend any genuine right fully, therefore, we must know *who* holds the right, *against whom* it is held, and *to what* it is a right.

Alternative sources of rights add complexity. Some rights are grounded in constitution and law (e.g., the right of an accused to trial by jury); some rights are moral but give no legal claims (e.g., my right to your keeping the promise you gave me); and some rights (e.g., against theft or assault) are rooted both in morals and in law.

The different targets, contents, and sources of rights, and their inevitable conflict, together weave a tangled web. Notwithstanding all such complications, this much is clear about rights in general: they are in every case claims, or potential claims, within a community of moral agents. Rights arise, and can be intelligibly defended, only among beings who actually do, or can, make moral claims against one another. Whatever else rights may be, therefore, they are necessarily human; their possessors are persons, human beings.

The attributes of human beings from which this moral capability arises have been described variously by philosophers, both ancient and modern: the inner consciousness of a free will (Saint Augustine[3]); the

---

* The notes to this essay are all Cohen's and are collected at the end as "References," as is the style of the *New England Journal of Medicine*, in which this essay appeared.

grasp, by human reason, of the binding character of moral law (Saint Thomas[4]); the self-conscious participation of human beings in an objective ethical order (Hegel[5]); human membership in an organic moral community (Bradley[6]); the development of the human self through the consciousness of other moral selves (Mead[7]); and the underivative, intuitive cognition of the rightness of an action (Prichard[8]). Most influential has been Immanuel Kant's emphasis on the universal human possession of a uniquely moral will and the autonomy its use entails.[9] Humans confront choices that are purely moral; humans—but certainly not dogs or mice—lay down moral laws, for others and for themselves. Human beings are self-legislative, morally *auto-nomous*.

Animals (that is, nonhuman animals, the ordinary sense of that word) lack this capacity for free moral judgment. They are not beings of a kind capable of exercising or responding to moral claims. Animals therefore have no rights, and they can have none. This is the core of the argument about the alleged rights of animals. The holders of rights must have the capacity to comprehend rules of duty, governing all including themselves. In applying such rules, the holders of rights must recognize possible conflicts between what is in their own interest and what is just. Only in a community of beings capable of self-restricting moral judgments can the concept of a right be correctly invoked.

Humans have such moral capacities. They are in this sense self-legislative, are members of communities governed by moral rules, and do possess rights. Animals do not have such moral capacities. They are not morally self-legislative, cannot possibly be members of a truly moral community, and therefore cannot possess rights. In conducting research on animal subjects, therefore, we do not violate their rights, because they have none to violate.

To animate life, even in its simplest forms, we give a certain natural reverence. But the possession of rights presupposes a moral status not attained by the vast majority of living things. We must not infer, therefore, that a live being has, simply in being alive, a "right" to its life. The assertion that all animals, only because they are alive and have interests, also possess the "right to life"[10] is an abuse of that phrase, and wholly without warrant.

It does not follow from this, however, that we are morally free to do anything we please to animals. Certainly not. In our dealings with animals, as in our dealings with other human beings, we have obligations that do not arise from claims against us based on rights. Rights entail obligations, but many of the things one ought to do are in no way tied to another's entitlement. Rights and obligations are not reciprocals of one another, and it is a serious mistake to suppose that they are.

Illustrations are helpful. Obligations may arise from internal commitments made: physicians have obligations to their patients not grounded merely in their patients' rights. Teachers have such obligations to their students, shepherds to their dogs, and cowboys to their horses. Obligations may arise from differences of status: adults owe special care when playing with young children, and children owe special care when playing with young pets. Obligations may arise from special relationships: the payment of my son's college tuition is something to which he may have no right, although it may be my obligation to bear the burden if I reasonably can; my dog has no right to daily exercise and veterinary care, but I do have the obligation to provide these things for her. Obligations may arise from particular acts or circumstances: one may be obliged to another for a special kindness done, or obliged to put an animal out of its misery in view of its condition—although neither the human benefactor nor the dying animal may have had a claim of right.

Plainly, the grounds of our obligations to humans and to animals are manifold and cannot be formulated simply. Some hold that there is a general obligation to do no gratuitous harm to sentient creatures (the principle of nonmaleficence); some hold that there is a general obligation to do good to sentient creatures when that is reasonably within one's power (the pinciple of beneficence). In our dealings with animals, few will deny that we are at least obliged to act humanely—that is, to treat them with the decency and concern that we owe, as sensitive human beings, to other sentient creatures. To treat animals humanely, however, is not to treat them as humans or as the holders of rights.

A common objection, which deserves a response, may be paraphrased as follows:

> If having rights requires being able to make moral claims, to grasp and apply moral laws, then many humans—the brain-damaged, the comatose, the senile —who plainly lack those capacities must be without rights. But that is absurd. This proves [the critic concludes] that rights do not depend on the presence of moral capacities.[1,10]

This objection fails; it mistakenly treats an essential feature of humanity as though it were a screen for sorting humans. The capacity for moral judgment that distinguishes humans from animals is not a test to be administered to human beings one by one. Persons who are unable, because of some disability, to perform the full moral functions natural to human beings are certainly not for that reason ejected from the moral community. The issue is one of kind. Humans are of such a kind that they may be the subject of experiments only with their voluntary consent. The choices they make freely must be respected. Animals are of such a kind that it is impossible for them, in principle, to give or withhold voluntary consent or to make a moral choice. What humans retain when disabled, animals have never had.

A second objection, also often made, may be paraphrased as follows:

Capacities will not succeed in distinguishing humans from the other animals. Animals also reason; animals also communicate with one another; animals also care passionately for their young; animals also exhibit desires and preferences,[11],[12] Features of moral relevance—rationality, interdependence, and love—are not exhibited uniquely by human beings. Therefore [this critic concludes], there can be no solid moral distinction between humans and other animals.[10]

This criticism misses the central point. It is not the ability to communicate or to reason, or dependence on one another, or care for the young, or the exhibition of preference, or any such behavior that marks the critical divide. Analogies between human families and those of monkeys, or between human communities and those of wolves, and the like, are entirely beside the point. Patterns of conduct are not at issue. Animals do indeed exhibit remakable behavior at times. Conditioning, fear, instinct, and intelligence all contribute to species survival. Membership in a community of moral agents nevertheless remains impossible for them. Actors subject to moral judgment must be capable of grasping the generality of an ethical premise in a practical syllogism. Humans act immorally often enough, but only they—never wolves or monkeys—can discern, by applying some moral rule to the facts of a case, that a given act ought or ought not to be performed. The moral restraints imposed by humans on themselves are thus highly abstract and are often in conflict with the self-interest of the agent. Communal behavior among animals, even when most intelligent and most endearing, does not approach autonomous morality in this fundamental sense.

Genuinely moral acts have an internal as well as an external dimension. Thus, in law, an act can be criminal only when the guilty deed, the actus reus, is done with a guilty mind, mens rea. No animal can ever commit a crime; bringing animals to criminal trial is the mark of primitive ignorance. The claims of moral right are similarly inapplicable to them. Does a lion have a right to eat a baby zebra? Does a baby zebra have a right not to be eaten? Such questions, mistakenly invoking the concept of right where it does not belong, do not make good sense. Those who condemn biomedical research because it violates "animal rights" commit the same blunder.

In Defense of "Speciesism"

Abandoning reliance on animal rights, some critics resort instead to animal sentience—their feelings of pain and distress. We ought to desist from imposition of pain insofar as we can. Since all or nearly all experimentation on animals does impose pain and could be readily forgone, say these critics, it should be stopped. The ends sought may be worthy, but those ends do not justify imposing agonies on humans, and by animals the agonies are felt no less. The laboratory use of animals (these critics conclude) must therefore be ended—or at least very sharply curtailed.

Argument of this variety is essentially utilitarian, often expressly so;[13] it is based on the calculation of the net product, in pains and pleasures, resulting from experiments on animals. Jeremy Bentham, comparing horses and dogs with other sentient creatures, is thus commonly quoted: "The question is not, Can they reason? nor Can they talk? but, Can they suffer?"[14]

Animals certainly can suffer and surely ought not to be made to suffer needlessly. But in inferring, from these uncontroversial premises, that biomedical research causing animal distress is largely (or wholly) wrong, the critic commits two serious errors.

The first error is the assumption, often explicitly defended, that all sentient animals have equal moral standing. Between a dog and a human being, according to this view, there is no moral difference; hence the pains suffered by dogs must be weighed no differently from the pains suffered by humans. To deny such equality, according to this critic, is to give unjust preference to one species over another; it is "speciesism." The most influential statement of this moral equality of species was made by Peter Singer:

> The racist violates the principle of equality by giving greater weight to the interests of members of his own race when there is a clash between their interests and the interests of those of another race. The sexist violates the principle of equality by favoring the interests of his own sex. Similarly the speciesist allows the interests of his own species to override the greater interests of members of other species. The pattern is identical in each case.[2]

This argument is worse than unsound; it is atrocious. It draws an offensive moral conclusion from a deliberately devised verbal parallelism that is utterly specious. Racism has no rational ground whatever. Differing degrees of respect or concern for humans for no other reason than that they are members of different races is an injustice totally without foundation in the nature of the races themselves. Racists, even if acting on the basis of mistaken factual beliefs, do grave moral wrong precisely because there is no morally relevant distinction among the races. The supposition of such differences has led to outright horror. The same is true of the sexes, neither sex being entitled by right to greater respect or concern than the other. No dispute here.

Between species of animate life, however—between (for example) humans on the one hand and cats or rats on the other—the morally relevant differences are enormous, and almost universally appreciated. Humans engage in moral reflection; humans are morally autonomous; humans are members of moral communities, recognizing just claims against their own interest. Human beings do have rights, theirs is a moral status very different from that of cats or rats.

I am a speciesist. Speciesism is not merely plausible; it is essential for right conduct, because those who will not make the morally relevant distinctions among species are almost certain, in consequence, to misapprehend their true obligations. The analogy between speciesism and racism is insidious. Every sensitive moral judgment requires that the differing natures of the beings to whom obligations are owed be considered. If all forms of animate life—or vertebrate animal life?—must be treated equally, and if therefore in evaluating a research program the pains of a rodent count equally with the pains of a human, we are forced to conclude (1) that neither humans nor rodents possess rights, or (2) that rodents possess all the rights that humans possess. Both alternatives are absurd. Yet one or the other must be swallowed if the moral equality of all species is to be defended.

Humans owe to other humans a degree of moral regard that cannot be owed to animals. Some humans take on the obligation to support and heal others, both humans and animals, as a principal duty in their lives; the fulfillment of that duty may require the sacrifice of many animals. If biomedical investigators abandon the effective pursuit of their professional objectives because they are convinced that they may not do to animals what the service of humans requires, they will fail, objectively, to do their duty. Refusing to recognize the moral differences among species is a sure path to calamity. (The largest animal rights group in the country is People for the Ethical Treatment of Animals; its codirector, Ingrid Newkirk, calls research using animal subjects "fascism" and "supremacism." "Animal liberationists do not separate out the *human* animal," she says, "so there is no rational basis for saying that a human being has special rights. A rat is a pig is a dog is a boy. They're all mammals."[15])

Those who claim to base their objection to the use of animals in biomedical research on their reckoning of the net pleasures and pains produced make a second error, equally grave. Even if it were true—as it is surely not—that the pains of all animal beings must be counted equally, a cogent utilitarian calculation requires that we weigh all the consequences of the use, and of the nonuse, of animals in laboratory research. Critics relying (however mistakenly) on animal rights may claim to ignore the beneficial results of such research, rights being trump cards to which interest and advantage must give way. But an argument that is explicitly framed in terms of interest and benefit for all over the long run must attend also to the disadvantageous consequences of not using animals in research, and to all the achievements attained and attainable only through their use. The sum of the benefits of their use is utterly beyond quantification. The elimination of horrible disease, the increase of longevity, the avoidance of great pain, the saving of lives, and the improvement of the quality of lives (for humans and for animals) achieved through research using animals is so incalculably great that the argument of these critics, systematically pursued, establishes not their conclusion but its reverse: to refrain from using animals in biomedical research is, on utilitarian grounds, morally wrong.

When balancing the pleasures and pains resulting from the use of animals in research, we must not fail to place on the scales the terrible pains that would have resulted, would be suffered now, and would long continue had animals not been used. Every disease eliminated, every vaccine developed, every method of pain relief devised, every surgical procedure invented, every prosthetic device implanted—indeed, virtually every modern medical therapy is due, in part or in whole, to experimentation using animals. Nor may we ignore, in the balancing process, the predictable gains in human (and animal) well-being that are probably achievable in the future but that will not be achieved if the decision is made now to desist from such research or to curtail it.

Medical investigators are seldom insensitive to the distress their work may cause animal subjects. Opponents of research using animals are frequently insensitive to the cruelty of the results of the restrictions they would impose.[2] Untold numbers of human beings—real persons, although not now identifiable—would suffer grievously as the consequence of this well-meaning but shortsighted tenderness. If the morally relevant differences between humans and animals are borne in mind, and if all relevant considerations are weighed, the calculation of long-term consequences must give overwhelming support for biomedical research using animals.

Concluding Remarks

Substitution. The humane treatment of animals requires that we desist from experimenting on them if we can accomplish the same result using alternative methods—in vitro experimentation, computer simulation, or others. Critics of some experiments using animals rightly make this point.

It would be a serious error to suppose, however, that alternative techniques could soon be used in most research now using live animal subjects. No other methods now on the horizon—or perhaps ever to be available—can fully replace the testing of a drug, a procedure, or a vaccine, in live organisms. The flood of new medical possibilities being opened by the successes of recombinant DNA technology will turn to a trickle if testing on live animals is forbidden. When initial trials entail great risks, there may be no forward movement whatever without the use of live animal subjects. In seeking knowledge that may prove critical in later clinical applications, the unavailability of animals for inquiry may spell complete stymie. In the United States, federal regulations require the testing of new drugs and other products on animals, for efficacy and safety, before human beings are exposed to them.[16,17] We would not want it otherwise.

Every new advance in medicine—every new drug, new operation, new therapy of any kind—must sooner or later be tried on a living being for the first time. That trial, controlled or uncontrolled, will be an experiment. The subject of that experiment, if it is not an animal, will be a human being. Prohibiting the use of live animals in biomedical research, therefore, or sharply restricting it, must result either in the blockage of much valuable research or in the replacement of animal subjects with human subjects. These are the consequences—unacceptable to most reasonable persons—of not using animals in research.

Reduction. Should we not at least reduce the use of animals in biomedical research? No, we should increase it, to avoid when feasible the use of humans as experimental subjects. Medical investigations putting human subjects at some risk are numerous and greatly varied. The risks run in such experiments are usually unavoidable, and (thanks to earlier experiments on animals) most such risks are minimal or moderate. But some experimental risks are substantial.

When an experimental protocol that entails substantial risk to humans comes before an institutional review board, what response is appropriate? The investigation, we may suppose, is promising and deserves support, so long as its human subjects are protected against unnecessary dangers. May not the investigators be fairly asked, Have you done all that you can do to eliminate risk to humans by the extensive testing of that drug, that procedure, or that device on animals? To achieve maximal safety for humans we are right to require thorough experimentation on animal subjects before humans are involved.

Opportunities to increase human safety in this way are commonly missed; trials in which risks may be shifted from humans to animals are often not devised, sometimes not even considered. Why? For the investigator, the use of animals as subjects is often more expensive, in money and time, than the use of human subjects. Access to suitable human subjects is often quick and convenient, whereas access to appropriate animal subjects may be awkward, costly, and burdened with red tape. Physician-investigators have often had more experience working with human beings and know precisely where the needed pool of subjects is to be found and how they may be enlisted. Animals, and the procedures for their use, are often less familiar to these investigators. Moreover, the use of animals in place of humans is now more likely to be the target of zealous protests from without. The upshot is that humans are sometimes subjected to risks that animals could have borne, and should have borne, in their place. To maximize the protection of human subjects, I conclude, the wide and imaginative use of live animal subjects should be encouraged rather than discouraged. This enlargement in the use of animals is our obligation.

Consistency. Finally, inconsistency between the profession and the practice of many who oppose research using animals deserves comment. This frankly ad hominem observation aims chiefly to show that a coherent position rejecting the use of animals in medical research imposes costs so high as to be intolerable even to the critics themselves.

One cannot coherently object to the killing of animals in biomedical investigations while continuing to eat them. Anesthetics and thoughtful animal husbandry render the level of actual animal distress in the laboratory generally lower than that in the abattoir. So long as death and discomfort do not substantially differ in the two contexts, the consistent objector must not only refrain from all eating of animals but also protest as vehemently against others eating them as against others experimenting on them. No less vigorously must the critic object to the wearing of animal hides in coats and shoes, to employment in any industrial enterprise that uses animal parts, and to any commercial development that will cause death or distress to animals.

Killing animals to meet human needs for food, clothing, and shelter is judged entirely reasonable by most persons. The ubiquity of these uses and the virtual universality of moral support for them confront the opponent of research using animals with an inescapable difficulty. How can the many common uses of animals be judged morally worthy, while their use in scientific investigation is judged unworthy?

The number of animals used in research is but the tiniest fraction of the total used to satisfy assorted human appetites. That these appetites, often base and satisfiable in other ways, morally justify the far larger consumption of animals, whereas the quest for improved human health and understanding cannot justify the far smaller, is wholly implausible. Aside from the numbers of animals involved, the distinction in terms of worthiness of use, drawn with regard to any single animal, is not defensible. A given sheep is surely not more justifiably used to put lamb chops on the supermarket counter than to serve in testing a new contraceptive or a new prosthetic device. The needless killing of animals is wrong; if the common killing of them for our food or convenience is right, the less common but more humane uses of animals in the service of medical science are certainly not less right.

Scrupulous vegetarianism, in matters of food, clothing, shelter, commerce, and recreation, and in all other spheres, is the only fully coherent position the critic may adopt. At great human cost, the lives of fish and crustaceans must also be protected, with equal vigor, if speciesism has been forsworn. A very few consistent critics adopt this position. It is the reductio ad absurdum of the rejection of moral distinctions between animals and human beings.

Opposition to the use of animals in research is based on arguments of two different kinds—those relying on the alleged rights of animals and those relying on the consequences for animals. I have argued that arguments of both kinds must fail. We surely do have obligations to animals, but they have, and can have, no rights against us on which research can infringe. In calculating the consequences of animal research, we must weigh all the long-term benefits of the results achieved—to animals and to humans—and in that calculation we must not assume the moral equality of all animate species.

References

1. Regan T. The case for animal rights. Berkeley, Calif.: University of California Press, 1983.
2. Singer P. Animal liberation. New York: Avon Books, 1977.
3. St. Augustine. Confessions. Book Seven. 397 A.D. New York: Pocket books, 1957:104–26.
4. St. Thomas Aquinas. Summa theologica. 1273 A.D. Philosophic texts. New York. Oxford University Press, 1960:353–66.
5. Hegel GWF. Philosophy of right. 1821. London: Oxford University Press, 1952:105–10.
6. Bradley FH. Why should I be moral? 1876. In: Melden AI, ed. Ethical theories. New York: Prentice Hall, 1950:345–59.
7. Mead GH. The genesis of the self and social control. 1925. In: Reck AJ, ed. Selected writings. Indianapolis: Bobbs-Merrill, 1964:264–93.
8. Prichard HA. Does moral philosophy rest on a mistake? 1912. In: Cellars W, Hospers J, eds. Readings in ethical theory. New York: Appleton-Century-Crofts, 1952:149–63.
9. Kant I. Fundamental principles of the metaphysic of morals. 1785. New York: Liberal Arts Press, 1949.
10. Rollin, BE. Animal rights and human morality. New York: Prometheus Books, 1981.
11. Hoff C. Immoral and moral uses of animals. N Engl J Med 1980; 302:115–8.
12. Jamieson D. Killing persons and other beings. In: Miller HB, Williams WH, eds. Ethics and animals. Clifton, N.J.: Humana Press, 1983:135–46.
13. Singer P. Ten years of animal liberation. New York Review of Books. 1985; 31:46–52.
14. Bentham J. Introduction to the principles of morals and legislation. London: Athlone Press, 1970.

15. McCabe K. Who will live, who will die? Washingtonian Magazine. August 1986:115.

16. U.S. Code of Federal Regulations, Title 21, Sect. 505(i). Food, drug and cosmetic regulations.

17. U.S. Code of Federal Regulations, Title 16, Sect. 1500.40–2. Consumer product regulations.

1986

Stephen Jay Gould

THE TERRIFYING NORMALCY OF AIDS

Disney's Epcot Center in Orlando, Fla., is a technological tour de force and a conceptual desert. In this permanent World's Fair, American industrial giants have built their versions of an unblemished future. These masterful entertainments convey but one message, brilliantly packaged and relentlessly expressed: progress through technology is the solution to all human problems. G.E. proclaims from Horizons: "If we can dream it, we can do it." A.T.&T. speaks from on high within its giant golf ball: We are now "unbounded by space and time." United Technologies bubbles from the depths of Living Seas: "With the help of modern technology, we feel there's really no limit to what can be accomplished."

Yet several of these exhibits at the Experimental Prototype Community of Tomorrow, all predating last year's space disaster, belie their stated message from within by using the launch of the shuttle as a visual metaphor for technological triumph. The Challenger disaster may represent a general malaise, but it remains an incident. The AIDS pandemic, an issue that may rank with nuclear weaponry as the greatest danger of our era, provides a more striking proof that mind and technology are not omnipotent and that we have not canceled our bond to nature.

In 1984, John Platt, a biophysicist who taught at the University of Chicago for many years, wrote a short paper for private circulation. At a time when most of us were either ignoring AIDS, or viewing it as a contained and peculiar affliction of homosexual men, Platt recognized that the limited data on the origin of AIDS and its spread in America suggested a more frightening prospect: we are all susceptible to AIDS, and the disease has been spreading in a simple exponential manner.

Exponential growth is a geometric increase. Remember the old kiddy problem: if you place a penny on square one of a checkerboard and double the number of coins on each subsequent square—2, 4, 8, 16, 32 . . .

—how big is the stack by the 64th square? The answer: about as high as the universe is wide. Nothing in the external environment inhibits this increase, thus giving to exponential processes their relentless character. In the real, noninfinite world, of course, some limit will eventually arise, and the process slows down, reaches a steady state, or destroys the entire system: the stack of pennies falls over, the bacterial cells exhaust their supply of nutrients.

Platt noticed that data for the initial spread of AIDS fell right on an exponential curve. He then followed the simplest possible procedure of extrapolating the curve unabated into the 1990's. Most of us were incredulous, accusing Platt of the mathematical gamesmanship that scientists call "curve fitting." After all, aren't exponential models unrealistic? Surely we are not all susceptible to AIDS. Is it not spread only by odd practices to odd people? Will it not, therefore, quickly run its short course within a confined group?

Well, hello 1987—worldwide data still match Platt's extrapolated curve. This will not, of course, go on forever. AIDS has probably already saturated the African areas where it probably originated, and where the sex ratio of afflicted people is 1-to-1, male-female. But AIDS still has far to spread, and may be moving exponentially, through the rest of the world. We have learned enough about the cause of AIDS to slow its spread, if we can make rapid and fundamental changes in our handling of that most powerful part of human biology—our own sexuality. But medicine, as yet, has nothing to offer as a cure and precious little even for palliation.

This exponential spread of AIDS not only illuminates its, and our, biology, but also underscores the tragedy of our moralistic misperception. Exponential processes have a definite time and place of origin, an initial point of "inoculation"—in this case, Africa. We didn't notice the spread at first. In a population of billions, we pay little attention when 1 increases to 2, or 8 to 16, but when 1 million becomes 2 million, we panic, even though the rate of doubling has not increased.

The infection has to start somewhere, and its initial locus may be little more than an accident of circumstance. For a while, it remains confined to those in close contact with the primary source, but only by accident of proximity, not by intrinsic susceptibility. Eventually, given the power and lability of human sexuality, it spreads outside the initial group and into the general population. And now AIDS has begun its march through our own heterosexual community.

What a tragedy that our moral stupidity caused us to lose precious time, the greatest enemy in fighting an exponential spread, by downplaying the danger because we thought that AIDS was a disease of three irregular groups of minorities: minorities of life style (needle users), of sexual preference (homosexuals) and of color (Haitians). If AIDS had first been imported from Africa into a Park Avenue apartment, we would not have dithered as the exponential march began.

The message of Orlando—the inevitability of technological solutions —is wrong, and we need to understand why.

Our species has not won its independence from nature, and we cannot do all that we can dream. Or at least we cannot do it at the rate required to avoid tragedy, for we are not unbounded from time. Viral diseases are preventable in principle, and I suspect that an AIDS vaccine will one day be produced. But how will this discovery avail us if it takes until the millenium, and by then AIDS has fully run its exponential course and saturated our population, killing a substantial percentage of the human race? A fight against an exponential enemy is primarily a race against time.

We must also grasp the perspective of ecology and evolutionary biology and recognize, once we reinsert ourselves properly into nature, that AIDS represents the ordinary workings of biology, not an irrational or diabolical plague with a moral meaning. Disease, including epidemic spread, is a natural phenomenon, part of human history from the beginning. An entire subdiscipline of my profession, paleopathology, studies the evidence of ancient diseases preserved in the fossil remains of organisms. Human history has been marked by episodic plagues. More native peoples died of imported disease than ever fell before the gun during the era of colonial expansion. Our memories are short, and we have had a respite, really, only since the influenza pandemic at the end of World War I, but AIDS must be viewed as a virulent expression of an ordinary natural phenomenon.

I do not say this to foster either comfort or complacency. The evolutionary perspective is correct, but utterly inappropriate for our human scale. Yes, AIDS is a natural phenomenon, one of a recurring class of pandemic diseases. Yes, AIDS may run through the entire population, and may carry off a quarter or more of us. Yes, it may make no *biological* difference to Homo sapiens in the long run: there will still be plenty of us left and we can start again. Evolution cares as little for its agents— organisms struggling for reproductive success—as physics cares for individual atoms of hydrogen in the sun. But we care. These atoms are our neighbors, our lovers, our children and ourselves. AIDS is both a natural phenomenon and, potentially, the greatest natural tragedy in human history.

The cardboard message of Epcot fosters the wrong attitudes; we must both reinsert ourselves into nature and view AIDS as a natural phenomenon in order to fight properly. If we stand above nature and if technology is all-powerful, then AIDS is a horrifying anomaly that must be trying to tell us something. If so, we can adopt one of two attitudes, each potentially fatal. We can either become complacent, because we believe the message of Epcot and assume that medicine will soon generate a cure, or we can panic in confusion and seek a scapegoat for something so irregular that it must have been visited upon us to teach us a moral lesson.

But AIDS is not irregular. It is part of nature. So are we. This should galvanize us and give us hope, not prompt the worst of all responses: a kind of "new-age" negativism that equates natural with what we must accept and cannot, or even should not, change. When we view AIDS as natural, and when we recognize both the exponential property of its spread and the accidental character of its point of entry into America, we can break through our destructive tendencies to blame others and to free ourselves of concern.

If AIDS is natural, then there is no *message* in its spread. But by all that science has learned and all that rationality proclaims, AIDS works by a *mechanism*—and we can discover it. Victory is not ordained by any principle of progress, or any slogan of technology, so we shall have to fight like hell, and be watchful. There is no message, but there is a mechanism.

1987

Michael Stone

SHOULD TESTING FOR THE AIDS VIRUS BE MANDATORY?

Testing has become the most controversial issue surrounding AIDS. Should marriage applicants, hospital patients, and visitors to sexually-transmitted-disease (STD) clinics be required to undergo tests for AIDS antibodies? Short of that, should such tests be routinely made available? A recent conference run by the CDC[1] and attended by about 800 health officials focused on these questions. The overwhelming consensus was that tests should not be required—but that's not likely to end the dispute.

Many AIDS experts seem to be influenced in their opinions on testing by their approach to the disease. Health officials and epidemiologists deal with whole populations. While they are often concerned with the legal and ethical implications of testing, their overriding objection is pragmatic. Most of them simply don't believe that such measures will stem the spread of the virus, and some worry about the psychological effects of

1. Centers for Disease Control.

a positive result. "Mandatory testing needs effective treatment," says Health Commissioner Joseph. "But right now, I can't offer that treatment."

Clinical doctors, on the other hand, approach AIDS on case-by-case terms. They view testing as a requisite to treatment and responsible social behavior; many can't understand why health authorities around the country won't undertake the same measures long used to fight gonorrhea, syphilis, and other sexually transmitted diseases. In a recent survey conducted by *MD* magazine, more than half of the 1,500 doctors in private practice who were queried supported mandatory testing for marriage applicants.

"This is the first time in history that we have the means of diagnosing a disease and we're not using it," says Dr. Redfield of Walter Reed. "In just three years, we figured out the etiology of this disease and developed a test for it, and now, three years later, we're still not fully using that knowledge. We did screen blood when we found out that blood was less than one percent of AIDS transmission. But in New York, where one out of every 50 male Army applicants is seropositive, they are still not testing in the VD clinics. If you don't look for the virus, you're not going to find it." (In fact, the City Health Department has been running tests at an STD clinic as part of an epidemiological study. So far, after about 200 tests, the study has found no positives who are not members or sex partners of members of high-risk groups.)

The testing issue is complicated by civil-liberties concerns. Most health officials distinguish between AIDS and other sexually transmitted diseases on the basis of AIDS's association with homosexuality and drug use—and its extreme virulence. Many authorities say they cannot guarantee the confidentiality of test results; as a result, carriers of the virus could be exposed to discrimination by employers, landlords, and insurers, among other groups.

But Dr. Redfield, for one, thinks the health risks far outweigh the threat to civil liberties. What's more, he argues that even without a cure, an accurate diagnosis can be immensely helpful. "There are a number of things that can be done," he says. "If I know you're positive, I can monitor the progress of the virus. If you're in the first four stages—okay. If you're in the fifth or sixth stage, we're aggressive. We practice medicine appropriately. We don't misdiagnose.

"Second, you don't have to become a cardiac cripple. I can give you drugs that stop opportunistic infections. We don't see a lot of *Pneumocystis carinii* pneumonia [at Walter Reed]. That's the No. 1 cause of death among AIDS patients. We can give them a prophylactic drug—Fansidar—that can stop recurrence. But the timing is very important.

"Third, we let you prognosticate. I tell you how this virus is. I give you the opportunity to know and to plan where you are in your life.

"Fourth, I allow you the opportunity to make a decision whether you want to infect others. A positive result is not a death sentence. It's not unhelpable, and testing does make the difference. Clinically, as a doctor, it makes an amazing difference to me to know the immunological status of my patient. It allows me to intervene at the greatest risk-benefit ratio to him."

There's disagreement, too, over the effects a diagnosis—one way or the other—would have. If it takes a positive test to make people modify their behavior, as some proponents of mandatory testing claim, does that mean they won't change if they know they're negative? Shouldn't everyone practice "safer sex" regardless of his or her status?

Homosexual men in New York and San Francisco began to change their behavior even before widespread testing became available. Studies show that knowing someone who suffers or died from AIDS is more likely to prompt change than knowing one's sero-status. But waiting for that kind of personal understanding of the disease may take too long. Even though homosexuals changed their sexual behavior dramatically, their communities are now 50 to 60 percent seropositive.

So far, no states require testing and almost all testing services are anonymous. Of the people who do come in for a test, 22 percent nationally test positive, indicating that the system is attracting at-risk groups; even Redfield advocates setting up more anonymous-test sites to encourage more people to come in. But Dr. Redfield also thinks that authorities should strongly encourage testing in which the subject is identified and his or her sex partners are traced. "I think most people are not threatened by name-linked testing," he says. "We asked 29 seropositive women we saw at Walter Reed for their sexual contacts. Of the 23 contacts they gave us, we found 17 were infected. We should be using the same classic public-health approach to AIDS that we use for other sexually transmitted diseases."

Last month, New York State ordered about 250 STD, family-planning, and prenatal-care clinics to provide free, voluntary testing for the AIDS virus. Five of these clinics are in New York City. In addition, the City Health Department operates two anonymous-testing clinics and encourages people who fear they are at risk to get tested. But Health Commissioner Joseph feels that tracing partners is impractical in the high-risk groups. With an estimated 500,000 seropositives in New York, the time and money needed to track even a small fraction of their contacts would be better spent on education or research. "Some of the people we deal with can't remember who they slept with last night, much less five years ago," says one community worker. The Health Department does encourage a carrier to notify his or her partners, however, and offers to help.

Colorado has taken a somewhat more aggressive approach than New York and most other states. Testing in Colorado is required to be name-linked—that is, whoever gets tested has to give a name (at the anonymous-test sites, the subjects are usually given just a number). However, since no identification is asked for, many test subjects simply give a pseudonym. That ensures confidentiality, says Colorado health chief Dr. Thomas Vernon, but allows counselors to develop closer relationships with their subjects than they would if the system were anonymous.

Still, Dr. Vernon thinks the system should become far more aggressive in tracing contacts in groups and communities that have a low incidence of infection. "If I had known who the 150 positives were in Colorado in 1981," he says, "I could have prevented the 20,000 infected today."

In certain special situations, health officials generally support mandatory testing. Blood and organ donors, of course, must be screened for infectiousness. Military recruits are tested in part because of the financial burden AIDS cases could create and because in some cases soldiers are expected to serve as a transfusion source for their colleagues.

Many of these issues may be radically altered by advances in diagnostic research. The technology is already in place for a highly accurate test that could be performed during the course of a routine doctor's visit. If approved by the FDA, a quick test could dramatically affect the costs, logistics, and epidemiology of current testing.

Some experts worry that as testing becomes more common, it will polarize the population into antibody positives and negatives. Already, clubs are being formed that issue negative-status-confirmation cards to members. If the antibody-positive group overwhelmingly includes the anticipated categories—homosexuals, IV-drug users, and people from communities with high drug use—then AIDS may again become the "other guy's disease." Indeed, if heterosexual, white, middle-class Americans no longer regard AIDS as an imminent threat to them, the growing effort to contain it may falter.

1987

Thomas Murray

THE GROWING DANGER

My son Peter is twelve, and lately the cuffs of his pants have been racing up his ankles—a sure sign that growth hormone is coursing through his body. He's on about the same growth schedule that I was. By my fourteenth birthday I was already just shy of six feet, and hopeful of four or five inches more. I thought that would be enough to give me a shot at playing basketball in college. Alas, I'd reached my limit. Lacking any notable physical talents, I had to rely on guile; if you can't shoot over the guy, get him looking one way and then scurry past on the other side. (As we used to say, "Fake left, go right.") Recent happenings in genetic engineering make me wonder if something similar, albeit unintentional, is going on there: Is our attention being directed one way while what's important is slipping by on the other side?

At least since 1980, worries about using recombinant DNA technology to alter "human nature" have focused on gene therapy—the direct and intentional alteration of genetic material to treat disease. On June 20 of that year the general secretaries of three national organizations, for Protestants, Jews, and Catholics, wrote the President to warn: "History has shown us that there will always be those who believe it appropriate to 'correct' our mental and social structures by genetic means, so as to fit their vision of humanity. This becomes more dangerous when the basic tools to do so are finally at hand. Those who would play God will be tempted as never before."

Nothing garners attention as quickly as a nice little scandal; within a month of the letter, Dr. Martin Cline of UCLA provided one by experimenting on two patients with beta-zero thalassemia, a genetic condition that causes severe anemia. Cline removed some of their bone marrow, treated it with recombinant DNA containing normal hemoglobin genes, then reinserted it into the bone (after making room by killing some of the remaining marrow cells with radiation). The hope was that the treated cells would multiply and produce normal hemoglobin.

They didn't. Worse, Cline didn't have the approval of the UCLA committee that oversees research with human subjects. When the affair became public, the National Institutes of Health (NIH) stripped Cline of $162,000 in grant money and demanded strict supervision of his research. For those suspicious of human gene therapy, the case was proof that scientists couldn't be trusted to regulate themselves.

Since then, such work has proceeded very cautiously. A presidential commission gave its tentative blessing to gene therapy with somatic cells

650

—those that don't pass the altered genes on to future generations. The NIH's watchdog recombinant DNA advisory committee set up a "human gene therapy subcommittee," which has suggested "points to consider" for doctors who propose to tinker with genes. Among them: whether the benefits of the treatment outweigh the risks, how to choose patients fairly, and how to publicize the results of the research. Thanks to the brouhaha over gene therapy, no great threats to humanity are likely to slip by in the near future—at least not on that side.

But there's another side to genetic engineering that has the power to alter us physically and socially. Rather than directly altering our genes, it can modify our bodies by supplementing the natural supply of important regulatory hormones with genetically engineered ones. A prime example is biosynthetically manufactured human growth hormone—hGH. Except for one additional amino acid—methionine (which appears to have no effect on its action)—biosynthetic hGH is identical to the hormone that promotes natural growth.

Produced in the pituitary gland, hGH plays a key role in determining how tall we'll become. So-called pituitary dwarfs usually lack an adequate supply of bioactive hGH. To treat them, for more than twenty years we've been harvesting pituitaries from human cadavers, each of which yields a minute quantity of hGH. Until recently the supply was barely adequate. In 1979 genetic engineers cloned the gene carrying instructions for making hGH, inserted it into a microorganism, and coaxed the bug to produce the human hormone. Just in time, it appears, because some hGH recovered from human pituitaries seems to have been contaminated with the slow virus that causes Creutzfeldt-Jakob disease (CJD), a degenerative infection of the brain. In April 1985 the Food and Drug Administration (FDA) halted the sale of natural growth hormone, and shortly thereafter approved Genentech's[1] biosynthetic version. Since no human tissue is used in producing it, there's no danger of contamination with the CJD virus. Also, we're no longer limited by the scarcity of cadaver pituitaries, and other uses for hGH can be explored.

Biotechnology came to the rescue of kids deficient in growth hormone. But if hGH injections can make extremely short children a bit taller, what can it do for those who aren't dwarfs, but just shorter than average? What about the youngster who would have been only of average height? And what about the basketball player for whom a couple of inches more might mean the difference between the schoolyard and the NBA? In short (no pun intended), why not use hGH to give your child the advantages that come with being tall?

Years ago, at an FDA hearing, I speculated that once biosynthetic hGH was approved, people would want to use it for all sorts of non-

1. A major American biotechnology company.

therapeutic purposes. One member of the FDA committee told me that several parents had already asked her if they could get the drug for their kids, who weren't hGH-deficient. All, she recalled, were physicians. Rebecca Kirkland, who does clinical trials of biosynthetic hGH at the Baylor College of Medicine, recently said she's had inquiries from five parents wanting to get hGH for their normal children.

Why would parents want to go to such expense (treatment with biosynthetic hGH costs roughly $10,000 a year), cause their children pain (the shots hurt a bit), and risk unknown long-term side effects? Quite simply, because it's advantageous to be tall—within limits. A modest body of scientific evidence supports the commonsense observation that taller people often get the nod over their shorter counterparts, because they're perceived as more intelligent, good-looking, likable, extroverted, and attractive. Being very much taller than the average is a mixed blessing, to be sure. But being a few inches above average seems to help.

A survey at the University of Pittsburgh in 1968 found that starting salaries for graduates varied with height: roughly $300 an inch up to six feet two inches. In a study of men whose heights had been recorded twenty-five years earlier, a graduate student at Washington University in St. Louis demonstrated a "height bonus" of approximately $400 per inch.

When a researcher at Eastern Michigan University presented two hypothetical job candidates to recruiters, one eight inches taller than the other, 72 percent preferred the taller one, 27 percent said there was no difference, and only one chose the shorter applicant, And much has been made of the fact that the taller candidate for President usually wins. Only two presidents—Madison and Benjamin Harrison—were shorter than the average American male of their eras.

If some parents want to give their child the edge that height seems to confer, what's wrong with that? If it's O.K. to spend $2,500 on orthodontics, to buy your kid private tennis and music lessons, or to spend $10,000 a year and up for prep school and private college, what's a few thousand bucks more to buy a couple of inches? The kid could turn out to be a klutz at tennis, have a tin ear, and major in Michelob, but taller is taller.

In this century, we make a strong presumption in favor of liberty. Before we interfere with the right of parents to bring up their children as they judge best, we demand strong reasons for doing so. Can we find them in the case of hGH?

Let me ask a skeptical question: What's the disease for which human growth hormone is the cure? Philosophers have a difficult time agreeing on the definition of disease, but most would recognize a physiological deficiency in hGH as a genuine disease, and hGH injections as a reasonable treatment. There are some kids, though, who aren't measurably deficient in hGH but who are very short. Their shortness can be the consequence of any one of numerous medical problems, or they may fall into the category of "familial short stature"—that is, short like mom or pop. Either way, can their shortness ever be a disability? A disability is a condition that interferes with the tasks of everyday living. If people are so short that they qualify for the elevator riddle,[2] their shortness may well be a disability. Disabilities usually justify medical intervention. But what if a person isn't suffering from a disease, and isn't so short that the lack of height becomes a disability? What if it's merely a disadvantage?

Even if hGH turns out to be physiologically harmless—some experts have warned of possible effects on glucose regulation, as well as an increased risk of atherosclerosis and high blood pressure—there may be psychological consequences to treating children with the hormone. The unmistakable message given to a child is that shortness is a grave enough problem to justify the considerable expense, inconvenience, and discomfort of hGH treatment. It's likely to increase the child's self-consciousness about height. And since children rarely grow as much with the hormone as they or their parents hope, disappointment is likely.

A study of hGH-deficient children and their families found that the most psychologically mature kids weren't those who grew the most but those whom parents and other adults had treated appropriately for their age rather than their size. Kids who were encouraged to pursue interests where their height wasn't a disadvantage were much happier with themselves.

People differ in so many ways: in intelligence, charm, quickness of hand and foot, facility with words, wit, etc. But when we put children through hGH treatments, we focus almost entirely on their height (where they don't "measure up") and ignore their other talents and abilities. Understandably, short kids receiving hGH may come to feel that they're inadequate and inferior.

All other things being equal, taller basketball players are more effective than shorter ones. Height is an advantage in basketball and some other sports. In almost all other realms of human endeavor, though, height bears no relationship to the ability to do a job well. But in a culture that regularly imputes desirable characteristics to tall people and undesirable ones to short ones, shortness is surely a disadvantage. (Even our language is laden with "heightisms": we look up to people we admire, look down on those we don't.)

Like other "isms," such as racism and sexism, heightism involves making unwarranted judgments about people based on irrelevant criteria. Does anyone believe the solution to racism is to find a drug that lightens black skin? The mind boggles at the possible biotechnological remedies for sexism. And yet those who want to give their kids hGH are

2. Why did the man always take the elevator to the sixth floor, then walk up four more flights to his apartment? Because he could only reach the button for the sixth floor [author's note].

proposing just this sort of technological end-run around heightism.

If we choose to allow hGH to be used for non-disease, non-disabling shortness, then we must make a choice. Either we let those who can afford it buy it for their children, or we make it available at public expense to all children whose parents want it.

Suppose we let it be sold. The children of rich parents will have one more leg up, so to speak, on their peers. You could ask, what's one more advantage in the light of all the others available to people with means? But the prospect of two classes—one tall and monied, the other short and poor—is ugly and disquieting. It would allow injustice to be piled upon injustice.

Suppose we take the other route and provide hGH to anyone who wants it. If all parents (short and tall alike) rushed out to get hGH shots for their kids, the average height of the entire population might increase. But in all likelihood the distribution of height in the population wouldn't change much, if at all. There would still be the taller and the shorter, and since we're doing nothing to diminish heightism, discrimination against the shorter would continue. Some people would benefit, of course—for example, the stockholders in Genentech (which holds the patent for making biosynthetic hGH) and those who produce fabrics (since everyone will be wearing bigger sizes). Meanwhile, at considerable social expense, kids would get their three shots a week with a little pain and, we hope, minimal side effects.

Inevitably, a few eager parents would want to regain the edge for their kids and try to get bigger doses of hGH, like those athletes who take increasing amounts of anabolic steroids in the hope of obtaining an advantage over their rivals. In both cases, individuals pursue their own interests, only to make everyone worse off.

Whether hGH is available just to those who can pay for it or to everyone, the results would be unfortunate. In one instance, we use biotechnology to reinforce the advantages of wealth; in the other, we incur enormous expense and unknown risks without making anyone better off. The wisest course is to restrict hGH to cases of disease and disability.

Although hGH may be the first biosynthetic hormone to tempt us to improve on human nature, it won't be the last. Imagine what we might do with a hormone that prompted damaged nerves to regenerate. Someone would wonder whether it would also stimulate growth in the brain. And soon we'd be trying to enlarge our brains, however misguided that might be, scientifically or morally.

It also occurs to me that simply by writing this article I may spur some parents to seek out growth hormone for their child of normal height. I fervently hope not. But the temptation posed by hGH, and by other fruits of biotechnology as yet unripened, will be great. And it will require all our collective common sense to use them wisely.

1987

THE READER

1. How does Murray's "Fake left, go right" apply to his discussion of genetic engineering?
2. Considering the possibility that hGH could be sold, Murray raises "the prospect of two classes—one tall and monied, the other short and poor." Judging by his data, assess the likelihood of this outcome. How important is it to his argument?
3. Murray would restrict availability of hGH to cases of disease and disability, but earlier he has acknowledged the difficulty of defining disease. How seriously does he take that difficulty? How seriously do you take it?

THE WRITER

1. The author is perfectly clear about the wisest course to follow with hGH. Why doesn't he just stop there, without adding the two final paragraphs? What is the tone of these two paragraphs? How does he feel about what he is saying?
2. Murray teaches in a medical school. How well suited is this essay to an audience of prospective doctors?
3. Without worrying about scientific plausibility in your examples, try to draw a line between responsible and irresponsible use of biosynthetic hormones.

Gilbert Ryle

ON FORGETTING THE DIFFERENCE BETWEEN RIGHT AND WRONG

"Don't you know the difference between right and wrong?" "Well, I did learn it once, but I have forgotten it." This is a ridiculous thing to say. But why is it ridiculous? We forget lots of things, including lots of important things, that we used to know. So what is the absurdity in the idea of a person's forgetting the difference between right and wrong?

I think the question worthy of discussion, if only because the epistemological wheels on which ethical theories are made to run are apt to be wooden and uncircular.

Only one philosopher, as far as I know, has discussed my question. Aristotle does so very briefly in the Nicomachean Ethics 1100^b 17 and

1140^b 29.[1]

First let us get rid of two possible misconstructions of my question.

In speaking of a person's knowing or not knowing the difference between right and wrong, I shall not be speaking of him as knowing or not knowing the solutions to philosophers' conceptual questions like, "What are the definitions of Rightness and Wrongness, respectively?" A properly brought up child knows the difference between right and wrong, for all that he has never heard an argument from Kant or Thrasymachus[2] and would not have understood their definitions if he had. Anyhow, there is no absurdity in the idea of a philosophy student's having forgotten some ethical definitions or analyses that he had once known. He would not thereby cease to know the difference between right and wrong.

Next, the assertion that it is absurd to say that a person might forget the difference between right and wrong could be misconstrued as the ascription to our knowledge of right and wrong of an inspiring kind of indelibility, perhaps a Heaven-hinting innateness or a trailing cloud of glory.[3] No such edifying moral can be looked for. If it is absurd to say that one has forgotten the difference, it is also absurd to say that one recollects it. If it is absurd to say that one's knowledge of the difference between right and wrong might, like one's Latin, get rusty, then it is also absurd to say that it actually remains, like one's English, unrusty.

1. It might be suggested that there is a quite simple reason why we cannot forget the difference between right and wrong, namely, that daily life gives us constant reminders of it. Somewhat as, throughout December, Christmas carols, Christmas cards, and butchers' shops constantly remind us of the imminence of Christmas Day, so the daily procession of duties to be done and derelictions to be apologized for keeps us constantly in mind of the difference between right and wrong. But this explanation will not do. A very forgetful person remains unreminded in the midst of reminders. Even the knot in his handkerchief does not remind him of anything. Moreover, a man might happen to sojourn in a part of the world where there were no reminders of Christmas. If this were all, then the maker of the paradoxical remark might just be in the rare position of being unusually forgetful or unusually unexposed to obligations; and then his remark would be not ridiculous but only hard to credit. Forgetting the difference between right and wrong would then be merely a rare thing, like forgetting one's own name.

This suggested explanation is a causal hypothesis. It offers to tell what makes people very unlikely to forget the difference between right and

1. Aristotle's last treatise on ethics; the passage in question is part of a discussion of the role of habit in morality.
2. Immanuel Kant, eighteenth-century German philosopher; Thrasymachus appears in Plato's *Republic*.

3. The reference is to "Ode: Intimations of Immortality," by the English poet William Wordsworth (1770–1850), which asserts that as children, "trailing clouds of glory do we come / From God, who is our home."

wrong. It therefore assumes that there is such a thing as forgetting this difference. But our question is, rather, "Why is there no such thing? Why will 'forget' and 'be reminded of' not go with 'the difference between right and wrong'?"

2. A better, though still inadequate, explanation would be this. Knowing the difference between right and wrong is of a piece not with remembering particular matters of fact, like names, dates, and engagements, but with knowing how to do things, knowing the way from place to place, knowing Latin, and knowing the rules of the road in one's own country. Such things do not slip our memories, nor are knots tied in our handkerchiefs to keep us in mind of them. Knowledge here is mastery of techniques rather than mere possession of information; it is a capacity that can improve or decline, but cannot just come in and go out. We acquire such knowledge not just from being told things, but from being trained to do things. The knowledge is not imparted but inculcated. It is a second nature, and therefore not evanescent. Now our knowledge of the difference between right and wrong certainly is in many important respects much more like a mastery than like the retention of a piece of information. It is, for instance, inculcated by upbringing rather than imparted by dictation. It is not a set of things memorized and is not, consequently, the sort of knowledge of which shortness of memory is the natural enemy.

Nonetheless, there is such a thing as forgetting much or all of one's Latin. With desuetude, one does become rustier and rustier, until one has totally forgotten it. We know what we have to do to keep up our Latin, our geometry, or our tennis, namely, to give ourselves regular practice. Just here is one place where the analogy breaks down between knowing the difference between right and wrong and having mastery of a science or a craft. One's knowlege of the difference between right and wrong does not get rusty; we do not keep up our honesty by giving ourselves regular exercises in it. Nor do we excuse a malicious action by saying that we have recently been short of practice in fair-mindedness and generosity. Virtues are not proficiencies. The notion of being out of practice, which is appropriate to skills, is inappropriate to virtues.

Aristotle's explanation of the fact that there is no such thing as forgetting the difference between right and wrong seems to be that moral dispositions are, from constant exercise, much more abiding things than even our masteries of sciences and crafts. In the latter there is forgetting, though only gradual forgetting; in the former there happens to be none. But the difference does not seem to be just a difference in degree, or even just a difference between a small magnitude and zero. Nor is it just a matter of anthropological fact that our knowledge of the difference between right and wrong never decays. The notion of decay does not fit.

En passant,[4] when I argue that we do not impose moral exercises upon ourselves in order to prevent our knowledge of the difference between right and wrong from rusting, since the notion of rusting does not belong, I am not denying that we can or should drill ourselves into good habits and out of bad ones. I am only denying that such self-disciplining is to be assimilated to the exercises by which we prevent our Latin or our tennis from getting rusty. The object of moral drills is not to save us from forgeting the difference between right and wrong, but to stiffen us against doing what we know to be wrong.

Neither, to make the obverse point, am I denying that moral deterioration occurs. People often do get more callous, less public-spirited, meaner, lazier, and shiftier. What I am denying is that such deteriorations are to be assimilated to declines in expertness, i.e., to getting rusty.

3. A third explanation would be this. Since virtues are not skills, that is, since to be unselfish or patient is not to be good *at* doing anything, perhaps virtues should be classed rather with tastes and preferences, and particularly with educated tastes and cultivated preferences. As the music lover had once to learn to appreciate music, and the bridge player had to learn both to play and to enjoy playing bridge, so the honest man had to be taught or trained to dislike deception, and the charitable man had to be taught or trained to want to relieve distress. Doubtless, as some people take to music from the start as a duck takes to water, so some people are naturally more prone than others to be frank and sympathetic. But to be honest or charitable on principle, even against the impulses of the moment, involves knowing the difference between right and wrong —much as, unlike the mere relishing of one piece of music more than another, appreciating the superiority of the one piece over the other involves knowing their relative merits and demerits. Taste is educated preference, preference for recognized superiorities. To be able to recognize superiorities is to know the difference between good and bad.

Now likings, whether natural or cultivated, can be lost. Most grown-ups have lost the enthusiasm for playing hide-and-seek, and some cease to enjoy tobacco and poetry. There can also be deteriorations in taste. A person who once had appreciated the excellences of Jane Austen[5] might become so coarsened in palate as to cease to recognize or relish them.

It is relevant to my problem that we do not call such losses or deteriorations "forgetting." Perhaps the absurdity in speaking of someone's forgetting the difference between right and wrong is of a piece with the absurdity in speaking of someone who has lost the taste for poetry as having forgotten the difference between good and bad poetry.

When a person has an educated taste, he can speak of himself as having learned or been taught not only to recognize the differences between,

---

4. In passing.　　　　　　5. English novelist (1775–1817).

say, good and bad singing or good and bad tennis strokes, but also to appreciate, i.e., to like, admire, and try for the good and to dislike, despise, and avoid the bad. Knowing, in this region, goes hand in hand with approving and disapproving, relishing and disrelishing, admiring and despising, pursuing and avoiding. Indeed, their connection seems even closer than mere hand-in-hand concomitance. There seems to be a sort of incongruity in the idea of a person's knowing the difference between good and bad wine or poetry, while not caring a whit more for the one than for the other; of his appreciating without being appreciative of excellences. When we read, "We needs must love the highest when we see it,"[6] we incline to say, "Of course. We should not be seeing it if we were not loving it. The 'needs must' is a conceptual one. At least in this field, the partitions are down between the Faculties of Cognition, Conation, and Feeling."

Now whether this inclination is justified or not, it exists just as much in our thinking about the knowledge of right and wrong. Here, too, there seems to be an incongruity in the idea of a person's knowing that something wrong had been done, but still not disapproving of it or being ashamed of it; of his knowing that something would be the wrong thing for him to do, but still not scrupling to do it. We hanker to say that, if he has no scruples at all in doing the thing, then he cannot know that it is wrong, but only, perhaps, that it is "wrong," i.e., what other people call "wrong."

Socrates used to ask the important question, "Can Virtue be taught?" It puzzled him, very properly, that if virtue can be taught there exist no pundits in courage, abstinence, or justice. If we, too, think that knowledge of the difference between right and wrong is knowledge, ought we not to be puzzled that universities and technical colleges do not give courses in industriousness, fair-mindedness, and loyalty? But the moment such a suggestion is made, we realize that the nonexistence of pundits and colleges of the virtues is not a lamentable lacuna in our society. It would be silly to try to provide such instruction; silly, since knowledge of the difference between right and wrong is not the sort of thing that such instruction could bestow. We continue to think that children have to be taught the difference between right and wrong, but we know in our bones that this teaching is not a species of either factual or technical instruction. What sort of teaching, then, is the teaching of the difference between right and wrong? What sort of learning is the learning of this difference? What kind of knowing is the knowing of it? Maybe we can approach an answer to these questions by considering the teaching and learning of tastes.

6. From "Guinevere," in *The Idylls of the King*, by the nineteenth-century English poet Alfred, Lord Tennyson.

A person who has received technical instruction in tennis, music, or landscape gardening may, but may not, owe to his instructor a second debt of gratitude for having taught him also to enjoy these things. A person who has learned from a geographer and a botanist the special features of the Lake District[7] may have been inspired by Wordsworth also to love this district for these features. As one gets to know a person better, one may learn to respect or admire him. Learning to enjoy, to love, or to admire is not acquiring a skill or a parcel of information. Nonetheless it *is* learning. There is a difference between a mere change-over from disliking rice pudding to liking it, and learning to appreciate wines, poems, or people for their excellences. Learning to appreciate requires some studiousness, judiciousness, and acuteness. The judge has reasons to give for his likings, his verdicts, and his choices.

True, the special notions of *lessons, instruction, coaching, examinations, laboratories, courses, manuals,* and the like are no part of the idea of learning to enjoy or learning to admire. Even if Wordsworth really does teach us to love the Lake District, he does not merit or need a professor's chair. But this is only to say again that admiring, enjoying, and loving are not efficiencies or equipments. The notions of *learning, studying, teaching,* and *knowing* are ampler notions than our academic epistemologies have acknowledged. They are hospitable enough to house under their roofs notions like those of *inspiring, kindling,* and *infecting.*

It will be objected, I expect, that what is called "learning to enjoy" or "being taught to admire" is really always two processes, namely, (1) coming to know some things, and (2) as an effect of coming to know them, coming to like or admire. An emotional condition, disposition, or attitude is caused by a cognitive act or disposition. As the rolling of the ship makes me feel sick, so discovering a person's characteristics makes me experience feelings of admiration toward him. So, presumably, as certain nostrums save me from feeling sick when the ship rolls, certain other nostrums might save me from admiring a person when I have discovered what a stanch friend he is. Alternatively, if this sounds too ridiculous, then a peculiarly intimate kind of causal connection has to be invoked in order to represent the connection between knowing and admiring as still a causal one, and yet as one that is exempt from preventions.

If we ask what the supposedly antecedent process of coming to know consists in, we are likely to be told that it consists in coming to be equipped with some information or/and coming to be relatively efficient at doing certain sorts of things, *plus,* perhaps, coming to be able and ready to explain, instruct, criticize, and so forth. These are not effects of coming to know; they are concrete examples of what coming to know is coming to. But why not add that sometimes coming to know *is,* also, *inter*

---

7. Region in the northwest of England celebrated in many of Wordsworth's poems.

alia,[8] coming to admire or enjoy? If making a skillful tennis stroke or a skillful translation is doing something that one has learned to do, i.e., is an exercise and not an effect of knowledge, why may not admiring a person for his stanchness be, in a partly similar way, an example and not an after-effect of what our study of his character has taught us? The reply that what is learned must be either a piece of information or a technique begs the question, since the question is, in part, "Why must it be either one or the other?"

How does all this apply to our knowledge of the difference between right and wrong? We are unwilling to allow that a person has learned this difference who does not, for instance, care a bit whether he breaks a promise or keeps it, and is quite indifferent whether someone else is cruel or kind. This *caring* is not a special feeling; it covers a variety of feelings, like those that go with being shocked, ashamed, indignant, admiring, emulous, disgusted, and enthusiastic; but it also covers a variety of actions, as well as readinesses and pronenesses to do things, like apologizing, recompensing, scolding, praising, persevering, praying, confessing, and making good resolutions. Now, if we consider what in detail a person who has learned the difference between right and wrong has learned, we do not naturally draw a line between some things, namely, what he has learned to say and do, and other things, namely, what he has learned to feel, and relegate the latter to the class of mere aftereffects of his learning to say and do the proper things. In thinking about his conscience or his sense of duty, we do not naturally fence off his qualms from his acts of reparation; his pangs from his confessings or his resolvings; his pickings from his perseverings. *Because* he has learned the difference between right and wrong, he both makes reparations and feels contrite; and the "because" is the same noncausal "because." Certainly his feeling contrite is not an exercise of a technique or the giving of a piece of information; but the same is true, though for different reasons, of his making reparations, persevering, reproaching, resolving, and keeping appointments. All are marks, though different sorts of marks, of his knowing the difference between right and wrong; all show, though in different ways, that he has principles, and what these principles are; any one of them is one of the many sorts of things that we have in mind when we say of him that he has a sense of duty.

Now we can begin to see why it is ridiculous to say that one has forgotten the difference between right and wrong. To have been taught the difference is to have been brought to appreciate the difference, and this appreciation is not just a competence to label correctly or just a capacity to do things efficiently. It includes an inculcated caring, a habit of taking certain sorts of things seriously.

8. Among other things.

A person who used to care may, indeed, cease to care or to care so much. But ceasing to care is not forgetting, any more than ceasing to believe something or to mistrust someone is forgetting. "Forget" is reserved, apparently, mainly for the nonretention of information and the loss of skills through desuetude, though it is also used for ceasing to notice things, e.g., for the oblivion brought by sleep or distractions.

This use of "forget" for the loss of information and technical abilities, and its nonuse for cessations of caring, may go with another difference. If I have ceased to enjoy bridge, or come to admire Picasso,[9] then I have changed. But, if I have forgotten a date or become rusty in my Latin, I do not think of this as a change in *me*, but rather as a diminution of my equipment. In the same way, a person who becomes less or more conscientious is a somewhat changed person, not a person with an enlarged or diminished stock of anything. In a testimonial both personal qualities and equipment need to be mentioned, but the equipment is not mentioned among the personal qualities.

So far I have been pressing some analogies between things like tastes and pastimes on the one hand and virtues on the other; I have concentrated on ways in which the notions of *learning, teaching,* and *knowing* lock in with notions of *caring,* i.e., *enjoying, admiring, despising, trying, avoiding,* and so forth; and I have tried to show how, in these connections, they detach themselves from the notion of *forgetting.* But we must not push assimilation to the point of identification.

The man who knows the difference between good and bad tennis strokes, and applauds or tries for the good ones and pities or avoids the bad ones, is something of a specialist. The man who appreciates wines is something of a connoisseur. They have acquired special technical abilities and, therewith, special enjoyments. We others may envy them for both. But knowledge of the difference between right and wrong is common knowledge, and it is not mastery of a technique. There is nothing in particular that the honest man knows, ex officio,[1] how to do. He is not, ex officio, even a bit of an expert at anything. Nor is his life enriched by some extra relishes. He possesses nothing for us to envy.

Often, though not always, we study to become relatively good at things, e.g., games, fine arts, and recreations, because we either enjoy them from the start or anyhow expect to get pleasure from them in the end. Our elders coerce us into learning to swim, largely because they think that we shall miss a lot of pleasure afterward if we do not learn to swim, or to swim well. But this is nothing like the reason or reasons for which elders train the young to be honest. The truth lover has no treats to match against those of the music lover. A sense of duty is not an

9. Pablo Picasso (1881–1973), Spanish painter and sculptor.
1. By virtue of an office or position; in this instance, by virtue of his being an honest man.

esthetic sensibility; nor is the passion for righteousness indulged as the passion for bridge or birdwatching is indulged. It is not addiction to a sport or hobby. Certainly there are activities, like most work, in which, although technical excellence pleases and bad craftsmanship displeases, still the jobs are not done or even done well only for pleasure's sake. But the honest or charitable man has not, ex officio, any particular job to do, much less to be proud of doing well rather than botching. Knowing the difference between right and wrong is not identical with knowing the difference between good and bad work, even though they resemble one another in the fact that ceasing to care how one does one's job, like ceasing to care what one does, is not a case of forgetting.

One more reinsurance. I have claimed to detect an incongruity, and the same sort of incongruity, in the idea of a man's knowing the difference between right and wrong but not caring a bit whether he lies, say, or tells the truth; in the idea of a man's recognizing. without being appreciative of, the excellences of Jane Austen; and in the idea of a craftsman's knowing the difference between good and bad workmanship without taking any pride in his own good work or feeling any contempt for the bad work of others. I may seem to have equated this knowing with having learned to take seriously. But there is a trap here.

I may be a bit shocked and indignant at an exhibition of unfairness, while you are much shocked and highly indignant. I care a bit about it, and you care much more. But this does not involve that you know more differences between right and wrong than I do, if this makes any sense, or that you know the difference better, if this makes any sense. Similarly, a specimen of Shakespeare's literary genius may please me while it thrills you. We appreciate the same excellence, though we are unequally appreciative of it. So even if, in some domains, to teach is, inter alia, to kindle, still we do not think of what is taught as varying in magnitude with the heat of the fire. The match is the same, but the fuels are different.

One last point. In most fields instructors can misinstruct. I may be taught that the Battle of Hastings was fought in 1077,[2] and I may be taught to grip fiercely my billiard cue and my steering wheel. While I retain faith in my instructor, I shall still claim to know the date of the battle and to know how to control the cue and the steering wheel; but, when I have learned better, I shall agree that I had not formerly known the date of the battle or how to control the cue or the wheel. I have to unlearn what I was originally taught.

There is no difficulty in conceiving of misinstruction in the particular articles of codes of etiquette. A boy might well be trained to remain respectfully hatted in a lady's drawing room and punctiliously to end his letters to tradesmen with "Yours sincerely."[3] Nor is there much difficulty

2. It completed the Norman Conquest of England and was fought, as every British schoolchild knows, in 1066.

3. One code of etiquette reserves "Yours

in conceiving of misinstruction in some of the bylaws of morality. Some people used scrupulously to pay all their gambling debts before paying off any of their debts to servants and tradesmen. Their consciences had been educated to insist on this priority.

But there is a difficulty in conceiving of a person's being taught to be selfish, deceitful, cruel, and lazy on principle; to be morally shocked at exhibitions of fair-mindedness; or scrupulously to make reparations for his backslidings into unselfishness. The notion of moral noneducation is familiar enough, but the notion of moral miseducation has a smell of absurdity. There is a whiff of the same smell of absurdity in the notion of the would-be connoisseur of wines or engravings being mistaught, taught, that is, to relish wines for their immaturity or to admire engravings for their smudginesses. However, the smell of absurdity is less strong here. The Albert Memorial[4] does seem to have been admired for its architectural badnesses.

The oddness, if it exists, in the idea of moral miseducation might be one source of the strength of the notion of The Moral Law. But to follow up this train of thought would seduce me into talking Ethics.

1958

---

sincerely" for personal—as opposed to business—letters.

4. A monument to Queen Victoria's prince consort, Albert, built in an ornate Victorian style no longer fashionable.

Willard Gaylin

WHAT YOU SEE IS THE REAL YOU

It was, I believe, the distinguished Nebraska financier Father Edward J. Flanagan[1] who professed to having "never met a bad boy." Having, myself, met a remarkable number of bad boys, it might seem that either our experiences were drastically different or we were using the word "bad" differently. I suspect neither is true, but rather that the Father was appraising the "inner man," while I, in fact, do not acknowledge the existence of inner people.

Since we psychoanalysts have unwittingly contributed to this confusion, let one, at least, attempt a small rectifying effort. Psychoanalytic data—which should be viewed as supplementary information—is, unfortunately, often viewed as alternative (and superior) explanation. This has led to the prevalent tendency to think of the "inner" man as the real man

---

1. Founder (1917) of Boys Town, a self-governing community for homeless and abandoned boys, for which he was also an energetic fund raiser.

and the outer man as an illusion or pretender.

While psychoanalysis supplies us with an incredibly useful tool for explaining the motives and purposes underlying human behavior, most of this has little bearing on the moral nature of that behavior.

Like roentgenology, psychoanalysis is a fascinating, but relatively new, means of illuminating the person. But few of us are prepared to substitute an X-ray of Grandfather's head for the portrait that hangs in the parlor. The inside of the man represents another view, not a truer one. A man may not always be what he appears to be, but what he appears to be is always a significant part of what he is. A man is the sum total of all his behavior. To probe for unconscious determinants of behavior and then define him in their terms exclusively, ignoring his overt behavior altogether, is a greater distortion than ignoring the unconscious completely.

Kurt Vonnegut has said, "You are what you pretend to be," which is simply another way of saying, you are what we (all of us) perceive you to be, not what you think you are.

Consider for a moment the case of the ninety-year-old man on his deathbed (surely the Talmud must deal with this?) joyous and relieved over the success of his deception. For ninety years he has shielded his evil nature from public observation. For ninety years he has affected courtesy, kindness, and generosity—suppressing all the malice he knew was within him while he calculatedly and artificially substituted grace and charity. All his life he had been fooling the world into believing he was a good man. This "evil" man will, I predict, be welcomed into the Kingdom of Heaven.

Similarly, I will not be told that the young man who earns his pocket money by mugging old ladies is "really" a good boy. Even my generous and expansive definition of goodness will not accommodate that particular form of self-advancement.

It does not count that beneath the rough exterior he has a heart—or, for that matter, an entire innards—of purest gold, locked away from human perception. You are for the most part what you seem to be, not what you would wish to be, nor, indeed, what you believe yourself to be.

Spare me, therefore, your good intentions, your inner sensitivities, your unarticulated and unexpressed love. And spare me also those tedious psychohistories which—by exposing the goodness inside the bad man, and the evil in the good—invariably establish a vulgar and perverse egalitarianism, as if the arrangement of what is outside and what inside makes no moral difference.

Saint Francis[2] may, in his unconscious, indeed have been compensating for, and denying, destructive, unconscious Oedipal impulses identi-

2. Saint Francis of Assisi, who early in the thirteenth century renounced parental wealth, entered on a life of poverty, and founded the Franciscan order of begging friars.

cal to those which Atilla projected and acted on. But the similarity of the unconscious constellations in the two men matters precious little, if it does not distinguish between them.

I do not care to learn that Hitler's heart was in the right place. A knowledge of the unconscious life of the man may be an adjunct to understanding his behavior. It is *not* a substitute for his behavior in describing him.

The inner man is a fantasy. If it helps you to identify with one, by all means, do so; preserve it, cherish it, embrace it, but do not present it to others for evaluation or consideration, for excuse or exculpation, or, for that matter, for punishment or disapproval.

Like any fantasy, it serves your purposes alone. It has no standing in the real world which we share with each other. Those character traits, those attitudes, that behavior—that strange and alien stuff sticking out all over you—*that's the real you!*

1977

THE READER

1. *Gaylin makes a key distinction between the inner and the outer man. Why is it necessary for him to start with this distinction?*
2. *Gaylin says in his first paragraph that he does "not acknowledge the existence of inner people," while in his fourth paragraph he says that "the inside of the man represents another view, not a truer one." How can you account for this seeming contradiction?*

THE WRITER

1. *Gaylin finds in the relation between an X-ray and a portrait an analogy for the relation between the inner man and the outer man. How accurate is this analogy?*
2. *Discuss the effectiveness of the examples in the essay, and suggest others that Gaylin might have used.*
3. *Write a paragraph commenting on the appropriateness of Gaylin's title.*

Prose Forms: Apothegms

At the beginning of Bacon's essay "Of Truth," jesting Pilate asks, "What is truth?" and does not stay for an answer. Perhaps Pilate asked in jest because he thought the question foolish; perhaps because he thought an answer impossible. Something of Pilate's skepticism is in most of us, but something too of a belief that there is truth, even if—as the history of philosophy teaches us—determining its nature may be enormously difficult. We readily assume some things to be true even if we hesitate to say what ultimately is Truth.

The test of truth most often is an appeal to the observed facts of experience. The observation of experience yields knowledge; the generalized statement of that knowledge yields a concept of the experience; the concise, descriptive form in which that concept is expressed we call variously, apothegm, proverb, maxim, or aphorism. Thus Sir James Mackintosh can speak of apothegms as "the condensed good sense of nations," because the apothegm conveys the distilled observations of people about their own persistent conduct. To hear the familiar "Absence makes the heart grow fonder" is to be reminded of a general truth which you and the world acknowledge. It does not matter that the equally familiar "Out of sight, out of mind" seems to contradict the other saying; both are true but applicable to different situations. Both statements are immediately recognizable as true and neither requires to be argued for, representing as they do the collective experience of mankind intelligently observed.

Aphoristic statements often occur within the context of more extended pieces of writing, and while not apothegms in the strictest sense, but rather propositions, they have the force of apothegms. For example, Percy Shelley's "Defence of Poetry" (1821) concludes that "Poets are the unacknowledged legislators of the world." Seventy years later in his Preface to The Picture of Dorian Gray Oscar Wilde asserts that "All art is quite useless." Although these statements seem contradictory, each is unarguable within its own context.

667

Not everyone is as astute an observer as the writer of apothegms and maxims, of course, but everyone is presumably capable of perceiving their rightness. What we perceive first is the facts to which the saying applies. When Franklin says "An empty bag cannot stand upright" (in 1740 he obviously had in mind a cloth bag), we acknowledge that this is the condition of the empty bag—and of ourselves when we are empty. Or when La Rochefoucauld says "We are all strong enough to endure the misfortunes of others," he too observes a condition that exists among people.

Many aphoristic assertions claim their validity primarily in descriptive terms. But the descriptive "is" in most apothegms and maxims is joined to a normative "ought" and the sayings therefore convey admonitions about and judgments of the conditions they describe. "Waste not, want not" is a simple illustration of this use of fact to admonish. Samuel Butler briefly gives us the presumed fact that "the world will always be governed by self-interest." Then he quickly advises: "We should not try to stop this, we should try to make the self-interest of cads a little more consistent with that of decent people." The condition of "ought" need not always be admonitory; it may be the implied judgment in La Rochefoucauld's assertion that "It is the habit of mediocre minds to condemn all that is beyond their grasp." The judgment is explicit in Franklin's "Fish and visitors stink in three days." And Bierce's definitions of ordinary words are not specifications of meanings in the way of ordinary dictionaries, but critical concepts of the experiences to which the words point.

"Wisdom" or "good sense," then, is the heart of the apothegm or maxim, the conjunction of "is" and "ought" in an assertion of universal truth. Unlike ordinary assertions of fact or opinion usually concerned with particular rather than universal experience, the wise saying is complete in its brevity. Before the ordinary assertion is allowed to hold, we require that the assumptions on which it rests, the implications it carries, the critical concepts and terms it contains, be examined closely and explored or justified. If someone says that the modern college student wants most to succeed materially in life, we want to be satisfied about what constitutes "modern," which college students (and where) are referred to, what else is involved in the comparative "most," what specifically is meant by "materially." But the apothegm assumes facts widely known and accepted, and in its judgments invokes values or attitudes readily intelligible to the great majority. It is the truth as most people experience it.

In a sense, every writer's concern is ultimately with truth. Certainly the essayist is directly concerned, in defining and ordering ideas, to say what is true and, somehow, to say it "new." Much of what he or she says is of the nature of assertion about particular experience; he or she must *therefore be at pains to handle such matters as assumptions and logical proofs carefully and deliberately. But one cannot always be starting from scratch, not daring to assume anything, trusting no certain knowledge or experience or beliefs held in common with other people. Careful one must be, but also aware that there is available, in addition to methods of logical analysis and proof, rules of evidence, and the other means to effective exposition, the whole memory and record of the vast experience of the race contained in a people's apothegms and aphorisms. In them is a treasury of truths useful to many demands of clarity and precision. And in them, too, is a valuable lesson in the way a significantly large body of experience—direct, in a person's day-to-day encounters; indirect, in the study of all forms of history—can be observed, conceptualized, and then expressed in an economy of language brief in form, comprehensive in meaning, and satisfyingly true.*

W. H. Auden: Apothegms

Some books are undeservedly forgotten; none are undeservedly remembered.

You do not educate a person's palate by telling him that what he has been in the habit of eating—watery, overboiled cabbage, let us say—is disgusting, but by persuading him to try a dish of vegetables which have been properly cooked. With some people, it is true, you seem to get quicker results by telling them—"Only vulgar people like overcooked cabbage; the best people like cabbage as the Chinese cook it"—but the results are less likely to be lasting.

No poet or novelist wishes he were the only one who ever lived, but most of them wish they were the only one alive, and quite a number fondly believe their wish has been granted.

The integrity of a writer is more threatened by appeals to his social conscience, his political or religious convictions, than by appeals to his cupidity. It is morally less confusing to be goosed by a traveling salesman than by a bishop.

Only a minor talent can be a perfect gentleman; a major talent is always more than a bit of a cad. Hence the importance of minor writers—as teachers of good manners. Now and again, an exquisite minor work can make a master feel thoroughly ashamed of himself.

Narcissus does not fall in love with his reflection because it is beautiful, but because it is *his*. If it were his beauty that enthralled him he would be set free in a few years by its fading.

"After all," sighed Narcissus the hunchback, "on *me* it looks good."

Our sufferings and weaknesses, in so far as they are personal, *our* sufferings, *our* weaknesses, are of no literary interest whatsoever. They are only interesting in so far as we can see them as typical of the human condition. A suffering, a weakness, which cannot be expressed as an aphorism should not be mentioned.

The same rules apply to self-examination as apply to confession to a priest: *be brief, be blunt, be gone.* Be brief, be blunt, forget. The scrupuland is a nasty specimen.

In a state of panic, a man runs round in circles by himself. In a state of joy, he links hands with others and they dance round in a circle together.

A sense of humor develops in a society to the degree that its members are simultaneously conscious of being each a unique person and of being all in common subjection to unalterable laws.

Among those whom I like or admire, I can find no common denominator, but among those whom I love, I can: all of them make me laugh.

If Homer had tried reading the *Iliad* to the gods on Olympus, they would either have started to fidget and presently asked if he hadn't got something a little lighter, or, taking it as a comic poem, would have roared with laughter or possibly, even, reacting like ourselves to a tearjerking movie, have poured pleasing tears.

1962

Ambrose Bierce: FROM THE DEVIL'S DICTIONARY

abdication, *n.* An act whereby a sovereign attests his sense of the high temperature of the throne.

abscond, *v.i.* To "move in a mysterious way," commonly with the property of another.

absent, *adj.* Peculiarly exposed to the tooth of detraction; vilified; hopelessly in the wrong; superseded in the consideration and affection of another.

accident, *n.* An inevitable occurrence due to the action of immutable natural laws.

accordion, *n.* An instrument in harmony with the sentiments of an assassin.

achievement, *n.* The death of endeavor and the birth of disgust.

admiration, *n.* Our polite recognition of another's resemblance to ourselves.

alone, *adj.* In bad company.

applause, *n.* The echo of a platitude.

ardor, *n.* The quality that distinguishes love without knowledge.

bore, *n.* A person who talks when you wish him to listen.

cemetery, *n.* An isolated suburban spot where mourners match lies, poets write at a target and stone-cutters spell for a wager. The inscription following will serve to illustrate the success attained in these Olympian games:

> His virtues were so conspicuous that his enemies, unable to overlook them, denied them, and his friends, to whose loose lives they were a rebuke, represented them as vices. They are here commemorated by his family, who shared them.

childhood, n. The period of human life intermediate between the idiocy of infancy and the folly of youth—two removes from the sin of manhood and three from the remorse of age.

Christian, n. One who believes that the New Testament is a divinely inspired book admirably suited to the spiritual needs of his neighbor. One who follows the teachings of Christ in so far as they are not inconsistent with a life of sin.

compulsion, n. The eloquence of power.

congratulation, n. The civility of envy.

conservative, n. A statement who is enamored of existing evils, as distinguished from the Liberal, who wishes to replace them with others.

consult, v.t. To seek another's approval of a course already decided on.

contempt, n. The feeling of a prudent man for an enemy who is too formidable safely to be opposed.

coward, n. One who in a perilous emergency thinks with his legs.

debauchee, n. One who has so earnestly pursued pleasure that he has had the misfortune to overtake it.

destiny, n. A tyrant's authority for crime and a fool's excuse for failure.

diplomacy, n. The patriotic art of lying for one's country.

distance, n. The only thing that the rich are willing for the poor to call theirs and keep.

duty, n. That which sternly impels us in the direction of profit, along the line of desire.

education, n. That which discloses to the wise and disguises from the foolish their lack of understanding.

erudition, n. Dust shaken out of a book into an empty skull.

extinction, n. The raw material out of which theology created the future state.

faith, n. Belief without evidence in what is told by one who speaks without knowledge, of things without parallel.

genealogy, n. An account of one's descent from an ancestor who did not particularly care to trace his own.

ghost, n. The outward and visible sign of an inward fear.

habit, n. A shackle for the free.

heaven, n. A place where the wicked cease from troubling you with talk of their personal affairs, and the good listen with attention while you expound your own.

historian, n. A broad-gauge gossip.

hope, *n.* Desire and expectation rolled into one.

hypocrite, *n.* One who, professing virtues that he does not respect, secures the advantage of seeming to be what he despises.

impiety, *n.* Your irreverence toward my deity.

impunity, *n.* Wealth.

language, *n.* The music with which we charm the serpents guarding another's treasure.

logic, *n.* The art of thinking and reasoning in strict accordance with the limitations and incapacities of the human misunderstanding.

The basis of logic is the syllogism, consisting of a major and a minor premise and a conclusion—thus:

Major Premise: Sixty men can do a piece of work sixty times as quickly as one man.

Minor Premise: One man can dig a post-hole in sixty seconds; therefore—

Conclusion: Sixty men can dig a post-hole in one second.

This may be called the syllogism arithmetical, in which, by combining logic and mathematics, we obtain a double certainty and are twice blessed.

love, *n.* A temporary insanity curable by marriage or by removal of the patient from the influences under which he incurred the disorder. This disease, like *caries* and many other ailments, is prevalent only among civilized races living under artificial conditions; barbarous nations breathing pure air and eating simple food enjoy immunity from its ravages. It is sometimes fatal, but more frequently to the physician than to the patient.

miracle, *n.* An act or event out of the order of nature and unaccountable, as beating a normal hand of four kings and an ace with four aces and a king.

monkey, *n.* An arboreal animal which makes itself at home in genealogical trees.

mouth, *n.* In man, the gateway to the soul; in woman, the outlet of the heart.

non-combatant, *n.* A dead Quaker.

platitude, *n.* The fundamental element and special glory of popular literature. A thought that snores in words that smoke. The wisdom of a million fools in the diction of a dullard. A fossil sentiment in artificial rock. A moral without the fable. All that is mortal of a departed truth. A demi-tasse of milk-and-morality. The Pope's-nose of a featherless peacock. A jelly-fish withering on the shore of the sea of thought. The cackle surviving the egg. A dessicated epigram.

pray, *v.* To ask that the laws of the universe be annulled in behalf of a single petitioner confessedly unworthy.

presidency, *n.* The greased pig in the field game of American politics.

prude, *n.* A bawd hiding behind the back of her demeanor.

rapacity, *n* Providence without industry. The thrift of power.

reason, *v.i.* To weigh probabilities in the scales of desire.

religion, *n.* A daughter of Hope and Fear, explaining to Ignorance the nature of the Unknowable.

resolute, *adj.* Obstinate in a course that we approve.

retaliation, *n.* The natural rock upon which is reared the Temple of Law.

saint, *n.* A dead sinner revised and edited.

> The Duchess of Orleans relates that the irreverent old calumniator, Marshal Villeroi, who in his youth had known St. Francis de Sales, said, on hearing him called saint: "I am delighted to hear that Monsieur de Sales is a saint. He was fond of saying indelicate things, and used to cheat at cards. In other respects he was a perfect gentleman, though a fool."

valor, *n.* A soldierly compound of vanity, duty and the gambler's hope:

> "Why have you halted?" roared the commander of a division at Chickamauga, who had ordered a charge; "move forward, sir, at once."
>
> "General," said the commander of the delinquent brigade, "I am persuaded that any further display of valor by my troops will bring them into collision with the enemy."

1906

William Blake: PROVERBS OF HELL

In seed time learn, in harvest teach, in winter enjoy.

Drive your cart and your plough over the bones of the dead.

The road of excess leads to the palace of wisdom.

Prudence is a rich, ugly old maid courted by Incapacity.

He who desires but acts not, breeds pestilence.

The cut worm forgives the plough.

Dip him in the river who loves water.

A fool sees not the same tree that a wise man sees.

He whose face gives no light, shall never become a star.

Eternity is in love with the productions of time.

The busy bee has no time for sorrow.

The hours of folly are measur'd by the clock; but of wisdom, no clock can measure.

All wholesome food is caught without a net or a trap.

Bring out number, weight, and measure in a year of dearth.

No bird soars too high, if he soars with his own wings.

A dead body revenges not injuries.

The most sublime act is to set another before you.

If the fool would persist in his folly he would become wise.

Folly is the cloak of knavery.

Shame is Pride's cloak.

Prisons are built with stones of Law, brothels with bricks of Religion.

The pride of the peacock is the glory of God.

The lust of the goat is the bounty of God.

The wrath of the lion is the wisdom of God.

The nakedness of woman is the work of God.

Excess of sorrow laughs. Excess of joy weeps.

The roaring of lions, the howling of wolves, the raging of the stormy sea, and the destructive sword are portions of eternity too great for the eye of man.

The fox condemns the trap, not himself.

Joys impregnate. Sorrows bring forth.

Let man wear the fell of the lion, woman the fleece of the sheep.

The bird a nest, the spider a web, man friendship.

The selfish, smiling fool, and the sullen, frowning fool shall be both thought wise, that they may be a rod.

What is now proved was once only imagin'd.

The rat, the mouse, the fox, the rabbit watch the roots; the lion, the tiger, the horse, the elephant watch the fruits.

The cistern contains: the fountain overflows.

One thought fills immensity.

Always be ready to speak your mind, and a base man will avoid you.

Everything possible to be believ'd is an image of truth.

The eagle never lost so much time as when he submitted to learn of the crow.

The fox provides for himself; but God provides for the lion.

Think in the morning. Act in the noon. Eat in the evening. Sleep in the night.

He who has suffer'd you to impose on him, knows you.

As the plough follows words, so God rewards prayers.

The tigers of wrath are wiser than the horses of instruction.

Expect poison from the standing water.

You never know what is enough unless you know what is more than enough.

Listen to the fool's reproach! it is a kingly title!

The eyes of fire, the nostrils of air, the mouth of water, the beard of earth.

The weak in courage is strong in cunning.

The apple tree never asks the beech how he shall grow; nor the lion, the horse, how he shall take his prey.

The thankful receiver bears a plentiful harvest.

If others had not been foolish, we should be so.

The soul of sweet delight can never be defil'd.

When thou seest an eagle, thou seest a portion of Genius; lift up thy head!

As the caterpillar chooses the fairest leaves to lay her eggs on, so the priest lays his curse on the fairest joys.

To create a little flower is the labor of ages.

Damn braces. Bless relaxes.

The best wine is the oldest, the best water the newest.

Prayers plough not! Praises reap not!

Joys laugh not! Sorrows weep not!

The head Sublime, the heart Pathos, the genitals Beauty, the hands and feet Proportion.

As the air to a bird or the sea to a fish, so is contempt to the contemptible.

The crow wish'd everything was black, the owl that everything was white.

Exuberance is Beauty.

If the lion was advised by the fox, he would be cunning.

Improvement makes straight roads; but the crooked roads without improvement are roads of Genius.

Sooner murder an infant in its cradle than nurse unacted desires.

Where man is not, nature is barren.

Truth can never be told so as to be understood, and not be believ'd.

Enough! or Too much.

1790

Benjamin Franklin: FROM POOR RICHARD'S ALMANACK

Light purse, heavy heart.   1733
He's a fool that makes his doctor his heir.
Love well, whip well.
Hunger never saw bad bread.
Fools make feasts, and wise men eat 'em.
He that lies down with dogs, shall rise up with fleas.
He is ill clothed, who is bare of virtue.
There is no little enemy.

Without justice courage is weak.   1734

Where there's marriage without love, there will be love without marriage.

Do good to thy friend to keep him, to thy enemy to gain him.

He that cannot obey, cannot command.

Marry your son when you will, but your daughter when you can.

Approve not of him who commends all you say.   1735

Necessity never made a good bargain.

Be slow in chusing a friend, slower in changing.

Three may keep a secret, if two of them are dead.

Deny self for self's sake.

To be humble to superiors is duty, to equals courtesy, to inferiors nobleness.

Fish and visitors stink in three days.   1736

Do not do that which you would not have known.

Bargaining has neither friends nor relations.

Now I've a sheep and a cow, every body bids me good morrow.

God helps them that help themselves.

He that speaks much, is much mistaken.

God heals, and the doctor takes the fees.

There are no ugly loves, nor handsome prisons.   1737

Three good meals a day is bad living.

Who has deceiv'd thee so oft as thyself?   1738

Read much, but not many books.

Let thy vices die before thee.

He that falls in love with himself, will have no rivals.   1739

Sin is not hurtful because it is forbidden, but it is forbidden because it's hurtful.

An empty bag cannot stand upright.   1740

Learn of the skilful: he that teaches himself, hath a fool for his master.   1741

Death takes no bribes.   1742

An old man in a house is a good sign.   1744

Fear God, and your enemies will fear you.

He's a fool that cannot conceal his wisdom.   1745

Many complain of their memory, few of their judgment.

When the well's dry, we know the worth of water.   1746
The sting of a reproach is the truth of it.

Write injuries in dust, benefits in marble.   1747

Nine men in *ten* are suicides.   1749
A man in a passion rides a mad horse.

He is a governor that governs his passions, and he is a servant that
serves them.   1750
Sorrow is good for nothing but sin.

Calamity and prosperity are the touchstones of integrity. 1752
Generous minds are all of kin.

Haste makes waste.   1753

The doors of wisdom are never shut.   1755

The way to be safe, is never to be secure.   1757

La Rochefoucauld: FROM MAXIMS

Our virtues are mostly but vices in disguise.

14. Men not only forget benefits received and injuries endured; they
even come to dislike those to whom they are indebted, while ceasing to
hate those others who have done them harm. Diligence in returning good
for good, and in exacting vengeance for evil, comes to be a sort of
servitude which we do not readily accept.

19. We are all strong enough to endure the misfortunes of others.

20. The steadiness of the wise man is only the art of keeping his
agitations locked within his breast.

25. Firmer virtues are required to support good fortune than bad.

28. Jealousy is, in its way, both fair and reasonable, since its intention is
to preserve for ourselves something which is ours, or which we believe to
be ours; envy, on the other hand, is a frenzy which cannot endure
contemplating the possessions of others.

31. Were we faultless, we would not derive such satisfaction from

remarking the faults of others.

38. Our promises are made in hope, and kept in fear.

50. A man convinced of his own merit will accept misfortune as an honor, for thus can he persuade others, as well as himself, that he is a worthy target for the arrows of fate.

56. To achieve a position in the world a man will do his utmost to appear already arrived.

59. There is no accident so disastrous that a clever man cannot derive some profit from it: nor any so fortunate that a fool cannot turn it to his disadvantage.

62. Sincerity comes from an open heart. It is exceedingly rare; what usually passes for sincerity is only an artful pretense designed to win the confidence of others.

67. Grace is to the body what sense is to the mind.

71. When two people have ceased to love, the memory that remains is almost always one of shame.

72. Love, to judge by most of its effects, is closer to hatred than to friendship.

75. Love, like fire, needs constant motion; when it ceases to hope, or to fear, love dies.

78. For most men the love of justice is only the fear of suffering injustice.

79. For a man who lacks self-confidence, silence is the wisest course.

83. What men have called friendship is only a social arrangement, a mutual adjustment of interests, an interchange of services given and received; it is, in sum, simply a business from which those involved purpose to derive a steady profit for their own self-love.

89. Everyone complains of his memory, none of his judgment.

90. In daily life our faults are frequently more pleasant than our good qualities.

93. Old people love to give good advice: it compensates them for their inability nowadays to set a bad example.

119. We are so accustomed to adopting a mask before others that we end by being unable to recognize ourselves.

122. If we master our passions it is due to their weakness, not our strength.

134. We are never so ridiculous through what we are as through what we pretend to be.

138. We would rather speak ill of ourselves than not at all.

144. We do not like to give praise, and we never do so without reasons of self-interest. Praise is a cunning, concealed and delicate form of flattery which, in different ways, gratifies both the giver and the receiver; the one accepts it as the reward for merit; the other bestows it to display his sense of justice and his powers of discernment.

146. We usually only praise that we may be praised.

149. The refusal to accept praise is the desire to be praised twice over.

150. The wish to deserve the praise we receive strengthens our virtues; and praise bestowed upon wit, courage and beauty contributes to their increase.

167. Avarice, more than open-handedness, is the opposite of economy.

170. When a man's behavior is straightforward, sincere and honest it is hard to be sure whether this is due to rectitude or cleverness.

176. In love there are two sorts of constancy: the one comes from the perpetual discovery of new delights in the beloved: the other, from the self-esteem which we derive from our own fidelity.

180. Our repentance is less a regret for the evil we have done than a precaution against the evil that may be done to us.

185. Evil, like good, has its heroes.

186. Not all who have vices are contemptible: all without a trace of virtue are.

190. Only great men are marked with great faults.

192. When our vices depart from us, we flatter ourselves that it is we who have rid ourselves of them.

200. Virtue would not go so far did vanity not keep her company.

205. Virtue, in women, is often love of reputation and fondness for tranquillity.

216. Perfect valor is to behave, without witnesses, as one would act were all the world watching.

218. Hypocrisy is the tribute that vice pays to virtue.

230. Nothing is as contagious as example, and we never perform an outstandingly good or evil action without its producing others of its sort. We copy goodness in the spirit of emulation, and wickedness owing to the malignity of our nature which shame holds in check until example sets it free.

237. No man should be praised for his goodness if he lacks the strength to be bad: in such cases goodness is usually only the effect of indolence or impotence of will.

259. The pleasure of love is in loving: and there is more joy in the passion one feels than in that which one inspires.

264. Pity is often only the sentiment of our own misfortunes felt in the ills of others. It is a clever pre-science of the evil times upon which we may fall. We help others in order to ensure their help in similar circumstances; and the kindnesses we do them are, if the truth were told, only acts of charity towards ourselves invested against the future.

276. Absence diminishes small loves and increases great ones, as the wind blows out the candle and blows up the bonfire.

277. Women frequently believe themselves to be in love even when they are not: the pursuit of an intrigue, the stimulus of gallantry, the

natural inclination towards the joys of being loved, and the difficulty of refusal, all these combine to tell them that their passions are aroused when in fact it is but their coquetry at play.

375. It is the habit of mediocre minds to condemn all that is beyond their grasp.

376. True friendship destroys envy, as true love puts an end to coquetry.

378. We give advice but we do not inspire behavior.

392. One should treat one's fate as one does one's health; enjoy it when it is good, be patient with it when it is poorly, and never attempt any drastic cure save as an ultimate resort.

399. There is a form of eminence which is quite independent of our fate; it is an air which distinguishes us from our fellow men and makes us appear destined for great things; it is the value which we imperceptibly attach to ourselves; it is the quality which wins us the deference of others; more than birth, honours or even merit, it gives us ascendancy.

417. In love, the person who recovers first recovers best.

423. Few people know how to be old.

467. Vanity leads us to act against our inclinations more often than does reason.

479. Only people who are strong can be truly gentle: what normally passes for gentleness is mere weakness, which quickly turns sour.

483. Vanity, rather than malice, is the usual source of slander.

540. Hope and fear are inseparable. There is no hope without fear, nor any fear without hope.

576. We always discover, in the misfortunes of our dearest friends, something not altogether displeasing.

597. No man can be sure of his own courage until he has stared danger in the face.

617. How can we expect another to keep our secret, if we cannot keep it ourself?

1655–1678

George Bernard Shaw: FROM THE REVOLUTIONIST'S HANDBOOK (IN MAN AND SUPERMAN)

Democracy

Democracy substitutes selection by the incompetent many for appointment by the corrupt few.

Democratic republics can no more dispense with national idols than monarchies with public functionaries.

Liberty and Equality

He who confuses political liberty with freedom and political equality with similarity has never thought for five minutes about either.

Nothing can be unconditional: consequently nothing can be free.

Liberty means responsibility. That is why most men dread it.

The duke inquires contemptuously whether his gamekeeper is the equal of the Astronomer Royal; but he insists that they shall both be hanged equally if they murder him.

The notion that the colonel need be a better man than the private is as confused as the notion that the keystone need be stronger than the coping stone.

The relation of superior to inferior excludes good manners.

Education

When a man teaches something he does not know to somebody else who has no aptitude for it, and gives him a certificate of proficiency, the latter has completed the education of a gentleman.

A fool's brain digests philosophy into folly, science into superstition, and art into pedantry. Hence University education.

The best brought-up children are those who have seen their parents as they are. Hypocrisy is not the parent's first duty.

The vilest abortionist is he who attempts to mould a child's character.

He who can, does. He who cannot, teaches.

A learned man is an idler who kills time with study. Beware of his false knowledge: it is more dangerous than ignorance.

Activity is the only road to knowledge.

Every fool believes what his teachers tell him, and calls his credulity science or morality as confidently as his father called it divine revelation.

No man fully capable of his own language ever masters another.

No man can be a pure specialist without being in the strict sense an idiot.

Do not give your children moral and religious instruction unless you are quite sure they will not take it too seriously. Better be the mother of Henri Quatre and Nell Gwynne than of Robespierre and Queen Mary Tudor.

Virtues and Vices

No specific virtue or vice in a man implies the existence of any other specific virtue or vice in him, however closely the imagination may associate them.

Virtue consists, not in abstaining from vice, but in not desiring it.

Self-denial is not a virtue: it is only the effect of prudence on rascality.

Obedience simulates subordination as fear of the police simulates honesty.

Disobedience, the rarest and most courageous of the virtues, is seldom distinguished from neglect, the laziest and commonest of the vices.

Vice is waste of life. Poverty, obedience, and celibacy are the canonical vices.

Economy is the art of making the most of life.

The love of economy is the root of all virtue.

Greatness

In heaven an angel is nobody in particular.

Greatness is the secular name for Divinity: both mean simply what lies beyond us.

If a great man could make us understand him, we should hang him.

We admit that when the divinity we worshipped made itself visible and comprehensible we crucified it.

To a mathematician the eleventh means only a single unit: to the bushman who cannot count further than his ten fingers it is an incalculable myriad.

The difference between the shallowest routineer and the deepest thinker appears, to the latter, trifling; to the former, infinite.

In a stupid nation the man of genius becomes a god: everybody worships him and nobody does his will.

Gambling

The most popular method of distributing wealth is the method of the roulette table.

The roulette table pays nobody except him that keeps it. Nevertheless a passion for gaming is common, though a passion for keeping roulette tables is unknown.

Gambling promises the poor what Property performs for the rich: that is why the bishops dare not denounce it fundamentally.

1903

History

Herbert Butterfield

THE ORIGINALITY OF THE OLD TESTAMENT

The Old Testament sometimes seems very ancient, but the earliest considerable body of historical literature that we possess was being produced through a period of a thousand years and more before that. It consisted of what we call "annals," written in the first person singular by the heads of great empires which had their centre in Egypt or Mesopotamia or Asia Minor. These monarchs, often year by year, would produce accounts—quite detailed accounts sometimes—of their military campaigns. It is clear from what they say that one of their objects in life was to put their own personal achievements on record—their building feats, their prowess in the hunt, but also their victories in war. They show no sign of having had any interest in the past, but, amongst other things, they betray a great anxiety about the reputation they would have after they were dead. They did not look behind them to previous generations, but instead they produced what we should call the history of their own times, in a way rather like Winston Churchill producing his account of his wars against Germany in the twentieth century.

After this, however, a great surprise occurs. There emerges from nowhere a people passionately interested in the past, dominated by an historical memory. It is clear that this is due to the fact that there is a bygone event that they really cannot get over; it takes command over their whole mentality. This people were the ancient Hebrews. They had been semi-nomads, moving a great deal in the desert, but having also certain periods in rather better areas where they could grow a bit of something. Like semi-nomads in general, they had longed to have land of their own, a settled land which they could properly cultivate. This is what they expected their God to provide for them, and what he promised to provide. Indeed the semi-nomads would tend to judge his effectiveness as a god by his ability to carry out his promise. The ancient Hebrews, the Children of Israel, had to wait a long time for their due reward, and perhaps this was the reason why they were so tremendously impressed when ultimately the Promise was actually fulfilled.

The earliest thing that we know from sheer historical evidence about these people is that as soon as they appear in the light of day they are already dominated by this historical memory. In some of the earliest books of the Bible there are embedded patches of text far earlier still, far earlier than the Old Testament itself, and repeatedly they are passages about this very thing. Fresh references go on perpetually being made to the same matter throughout the many centuries during which the Old Testament was being produced, indeed also in the Jewish literature that was written for a few centuries after that. We are more sure that the memory of this historical event was the predominating thing amongst them than we are of the reality, the actual historicity, of the event itself.

What they commemorated in this tremendous way, of course, was the fact that God had brought them up out of the land of Egypt and into the Promised Land. In reality it seems pretty clear that some of the tribes of Israel did not come into the land of Palestine from Egypt at all. Nevertheless I think it would be a central view amongst scholars that some of the ancient Hebrews came to the Promised Land from Egypt, and the impression of this was so powerful that it became the common memory of the whole group of tribes which settled in the land of Canaan; it became the accepted tradition even among the tribes that had never been in Egypt. Moreover the common tradition was the very thing that became the effective bond between the tribes of Israel, helping to weld them together as a people. This sense of a common history is always a powerful factor in fusing a group of tribes into a nation, just as Homer made the various bodies of Greeks feel that they had had a common experience in the past, a consciousness that they were all Hellenes. All this was so powerful with the Children of Israel because they felt such a fabulous gratitude for what had happened. I know of no other case in history where gratitude was carried so far, no other case where gratitude proved to be such a generative thing. Their God had stepped into history and kept his ancient Promise, bringing them to freedom and the Promised Land, and they simply could not get over it.

This was not the first time in history that gratitude had been a factor in religion, for at a date earlier still there are signs amongst the Hittites that the very sincerity of their feeling of indebtedness added an attractive kind of devotion to their worship of their pagan deities. But this gratitude was such a signal thing amongst the Israelitish people that it altered the whole development of religion in that quarter of the globe; it altered the character of religion in the area from which our Western civilisation sprang. It gave the Children of Israel a historical event that they could not get over, could not help remembering, and in the first place it made them historians—historians in a way that nobody had ever been before. The ancient Hebrews worshipped the God who brought them up out of the land of Egypt more than they worshipped God as the Creator of the World. By all the rules of the game, when once they had settled down in the land of Canaan and become an agricultural people, they ought to have turned to the gods of nature, the gods of fertility, and this is what some of their number wanted to do. But their historical memory was too strong. Even when they borrowed rites and ceremonies from neighbouring peoples—pieces of ritual based on the cycle of nature, the succession of the seasons—they turned these into celebrations of historical events, just as I suppose Christianity may have turned the rites of Spring into a celebration of the Resurrection. The Hebrews took over circumcision, which existed amongst their neighbours, but they turned even this into the celebration of a historical event. A Harvest Festival is an occasion on which even amongst Christians to-day we call attention to the cycle of the seasons and the bounty of nature. But amongst the Children of Israel at this ceremony you handed your thankoffering to the priest and then, if you please, you did not speak of the corn or the vine—you recited your national history, you narrated the story of the Exodus. It was set down in writing that if the younger generation started asking why they were expected to obey God's commandments they should be told that it was because God had brought their forefathers out of the house of bondage. Everything was based on their gratitude for what God had done for the nation. And it is remarkable to see to what a degree the other religious ideas of the Old Testament always remained historical in character—the Promise, the Covenant, the Judgment, the Messiah, the remnant of Israel, etc.

Yet this Promised Land to which God had brought them and on which they based a religion of extravagant gratitude was itself no great catch, and if they called it a land flowing with milk and honey, this was only because it looked rich when compared to the life that they had hitherto led. In the twentieth century Palestine has demanded a tremendous wrestling with nature, and if one looks back to the state of that region in Old Testament times one cannot help feeling that Providence endowed this people with one of the riskiest bits of territory that existed in that part of the globe. They were placed in an area which had already been encircled by vast empires, based on Egypt and on Mesopotamia and on a Hittite realm in Asia Minor. And, for all their gratitude, they were one of the most unlucky peoples of history. Other great empires soon arose again in the same regions, and they were so placed that they could not be expected to keep their freedom—their independence as a state only lasted for a few centuries, something like the period between Tudor

England and the present day.[1] The one stroke of luck that they did have was that for just a space at the crucial period those surrounding empires had come into decline, and this gave the Hebrews the chance of forming an independent state for a while. They virtually stood in the cockpit in that part of the world, just as Belgium stood in the cockpit in Western Europe and Poland in Eastern Europe. The fact that the Hebrews became, along with the Greeks, one of the main contributors to the formation of Western civilisation is a triumph of mind over matter, of the human spirit over misfortune and disaster. They almost built their religion on gratitude for their good fortune in having a country at all, a country that they could call their own.

Because of the great act of God which had brought them to Palestine they devoted themselves to the God of History rather than to the gods of nature. Here is their great originality, the thing that in a way enabled them to change the very nature of religion. Because they turned their intellect to the actions of God in history, they were drawn into an ethical view of God. They were continually wrestling with him about ethical questions, continually debating with him as to whether he was playing fair with them. Religion became intimately connected with morality because this was a God who was always in personal relations with human beings in the ordinary historical realm, and in any case you find that it was the worshippers of the gods of nature who ran to orgies and cruelties and immoralities. In fact, the ancient Hebrews developed their thought about God, about personality, and about ethics all together, all rolled into one. Because these things all involved what we call problems of personal relations they developed their thought about history step by step along with the rest. For a student of history, one of the interesting features of the Old Testament is that it gives us evidence of religious development from very early stages, from most primitive ideas about God, some of these ideas being quite shocking to the modern mind. Indeed, in some of the early books of the Bible there are still embedded certain ancient things that make it look as though, here as in no other parts of Western Asia, the God of History may at one stage have been really the God of War.

So far as I have been able to discover—approaching the matter as a modern historian, and rather an outsider, and using only what is available in Western languages—the Children of Israel, while still a comparatively primitive society, are the first people who showed a really significant interest in the past, the first to produce anything like a history of their nation, the first to lay out what we call a universal history, doing it with the help of some Babylonian legends but attempting to see the whole story of the human race. Because what we possess in the Old Testament

1. Queen Elizabeth I, the last of the Tudor monarchs, died in 1603.

is history as envisaged by the priests, or at least by the religious people, it is also a history very critical of the rulers—not like the mass of previous historical writing, a case of monarchs blowing their own trumpets. The history they wrote is a history of the people and not just of the kings, and it is very critical even of the people. So far as I know here is the only case of a nation producing a national history and making it an exposure of its national sins. In a technical sense this ancient Hebrew people became very remarkable as writers of history, some of their narratives (for example, the death of King David and the question of the succession to his throne) being quite wonderful according to modern standards of judgment. It was to be of momentous importance for the development of Western civilisation, that, growing up in Europe (with Christianity presiding over its creative stages), it was influenced by the Old Testament, by this ancient Jewish passion for history. For century after century over periods of nearly 2000 years, the European could not even learn about his religion without studying the Bible, including the Old Testament—essentially a history-book, a book of very ancient history. Our civilisation, unlike many others, became historically-minded, therefore, one that was interested in the past, and we owe that in a great part to the Old Testament.

1949

THE READER

1. What difference does Butterfield find between the writings of the ancient Hebrews and writings made in the empires of the Near East? What caused the difference?
2. What was the effect of historical memory on the formation of the ancient nation of Israel?
3. How did the sense of history in Israel make Hebrew religion different from the religions around Israel?

THE WRITER

1. What value does Butterfield attach to being "historically-minded"? In what specific ways does his essay imply that being so minded is beneficial?
2. Butterfield believes that one of the key factors in the development of our civilization is that we "became historically-minded." Write a brief essay discussing to what degree we are still "historically-minded" today.

Henry David Thoreau

THE BATTLE OF THE ANTS

One day when I went out to my wood-pile, or rather my pile of stumps, I observed two large ants, the one red, the other much larger, nearly half an inch long, and black, fiercely contending with one another. Having once got hold they never let go, but struggled and wrestled and rolled on the chips incessantly. Looking farther, I was surprised to find that the chips were covered with such combatants, that it was not a *duellum*, but a *bellum*, a war between two races of ants, the red always pitted against the black, and frequently two red ones to one black. The legions of these Myrmidons[1] covered all the hills and vales in my wood-yard, and the ground was already strewn with the dead and dying, both red and black. It was the only battle which I have ever witnessed, the only battle-field I ever trod while the battle was raging; internecine war; the red republicans on the one hand, and the black imperialists on the other. On every side they were engaged in deadly combat, yet without any noise that I could hear, and human soldiers never fought so resolutely. I watched a couple that were fast locked in each other's embraces, in a little sunny valley amid the chips, now at noonday prepared to fight till the sun went down, or life went out. The smaller red champion had fastened himself like a vice to his adversary's front, and through all the tumblings on that field never for an instant ceased to gnaw at one of his feelers near the root, having already caused the other to go by the board; while the stronger black one dashed him from side to side, and, as I saw on looking nearer, had already divested him of several of his members. They fought with more pertinacity than bulldogs. Neither manifested the least disposition to retreat. It was evident that their battle-cry was "Conquer or die." In the meanwhile there came along a single red ant on the hillside of this valley, evidently full of excitement, who either had despatched his foe, or had not yet taken part in the battle; probably the latter, for he had lost none of his limbs; whose mother had charged him to return with his shield or upon it. Or perchance he was some Achilles, who had nourished his wrath apart, and had now come to avenge or rescue his Patroclus.[2] He saw this unequal combat from afar—for the blacks were nearly twice the size of the red—he drew near with rapid pace till he stood on his guard within half an inch of the combatants; then, watching his opportunity, he sprang upon the black warrior, and commenced his operations near the root of his right fore leg, leaving the foe to select among his own mem-

---

1. The reference is to the powerful soldiers of Achilles in Homer's *Iliad*.

2. A Greek warrior in the *Iliad*, whose death Achilles avenges.

bers; and so there were three united for life, as if a new kind of attraction had been invented which put all other locks and cements to shame. I should not have wondered by this time to find that they had their respective musical bands stationed on some eminent chip, and playing their national airs the while, to excite the slow and cheer the dying combatants. I was myself excited somewhat even as if they had been men. The more you think of it, the less the difference. And certainly there is not the fight recorded in Concord history, at least, if in the history of America, that will bear a moment's comparison with this, whether for the numbers engaged in it, or for the patriotism and heroism displayed. For numbers and for carnage it was an Austerlitz or Dresden.[3] Concord Fight! Two killed on the patriots' side, and Luther Blanchard wounded! Why here every ant was a Buttrick—"Fire! for God's sake fire!"—and thousands shared the fate of Davis and Hosmer. There was not one hireling there. I have no doubt that it was a principle they fought for, as much as our ancestors, and not to avoid a three-penny tax on their tea; and the results of this battle will be as important and memorable to those whom it concerns as those of the battle of Bunker Hill, at least.

I took up the chip on which the three I have particularly described were struggling, carried into my house, and placed it under a tumbler on my window-sill, in order to see the issue. Holding a microscope to the first-mentioned red ant, I saw that, though he was assiduously gnawing at the near fore leg of his enemy, having severed his remaining feeler, his own breast was all torn away, exposing what vitals he had there to the jaws of the black warrior, whose breastplate was apparently too thick for him to pierce; and the dark carbuncles of the sufferer's eyes shone with ferocity such as war only could excite. They struggled half an hour longer under the tumbler, and when I looked again the black soldier had severed the heads of his foes from their bodies, and the still living heads were hanging on either side of him like ghastly trophies at his saddle-bow, still apparently as firmly fastened as ever, and he was endeavoring with feeble struggles, being without feelers, and with only the remnant of a leg, and I know not how many other wounds, to divest himself of them; which at length, after half an hour more, he accomplished. I raised the glass, and he went off over the window-sill in that crippled state. Whether he finally survived that combat, and spent the remainder of his days in some Hôtel des Invalides,[4] I do not know; but I thought that his industry would not be worth much thereafter. I never learned which party was victorious, nor the cause of the war, but I felt for the rest of that day as if I had my feelings excited and harrowed by witnessing the struggle, the ferocity and carnage, of a human battle before my door.

Kirby and Spence tell us that the battles of ants have long been

3. Bloody Napoleonic victories.
4. The famous French hospital for wounded soldiers and sailors.

celebrated and the date of them recorded, though they say that Huber[5] is
the only modern author who appears to have witnessed them. "Aeneas
Sylvius," say they, "after giving a very circumstantial account of one
contested with great obstinacy by a great and small species on the trunk
of a pear tree," adds that "'this action was fought in the pontificate of
Eugenius the Fourth, in the presence of Nicholas Pistoriensis, an eminent lawyer, who related the whole history of the battle with the greatest
fidelity.' A similar engagement between great and small ants is recorded
by Olaus Magnus, in which the small ones, being victorious, are said to
have buried the bodies of their own soldiers, but left those of their giant
enemies a prey to the birds. This event happened previous to the expulsion of the tyrant Christiern the Second from Sweden." The battle which
I witnessed took place in the Presidency of Polk, five years before the
passage of Webster's Fugitive-Slave Bill.[6]

1854

5. Kirby and Spence were nineteenth-cen-   great Swiss entomologist.
tury American entomologists; Huber was a   6. Passed in 1851.

THE READER

1. Thoreau uses the Latin word bellum to describe the battle of the ants,
   and he quickly follows this with a reference to the Myrmidons of
   Achilles. What comparison is implicit here? Find further examples of
   it.
2. This passage comes from a chapter in Thoreau's Walden entitled
   "Brute Neighbors." How does the comparison alluded to in the previous question amplify the meaning of that title?

THE WRITER

1. How might a strictly scientific account of the behavior of ants differ
   from Thoreau's?
2. Why does Thoreau end his account the way he does?
3. Describe the life, or part of the life, of an animal so that, while
   remaining faithful to the facts as you understand them, your description opens outward as does Thoreau's, and speaks not only of the
   animal but also of man, society, or nature.

Chief Seattle

ADDRESS[1]

The Governor made a fine speech, but he was outranged and out-classed that day. Chief Seattle, who answered on behalf of the Indians, towered a foot above the Governor. He wore his blanket like the toga of a Roman senator, and he did not have to strain his famous voice, which everyone agreed was audible and distinct at a distance of half a mile.

Seattle's oration was in Duwamish. Doctor Smith, who had learned the language, wrote it down; under the flowery garlands of his translation the speech rolls like an articulate iron engine, grim with meanings that outlasted his generation and may outlast all the generations of men. As the amiable follies of the white race become less amiable, the iron rumble of old Seattle's speech sounds louder and more ominous.

Standing in front of Doctor Maynard's office in the stumpy clearing, with his hand on the little Governor's head, the white invaders about him and his people before him, Chief Seattle said:

"Yonder sky that has wept tears of compassion upon my people for centuries untold, and which to us appears changeless and eternal, may change. Today is fair. Tomorrow may be overcast with clouds. My words are like the stars that never change. Whatever Seattle says the great chief at Washington can rely upon with as much certainty as he can upon the return of the sun or the seasons. The White Chief says that Big Chief at Washington sends us greetings of friendship and goodwill. That is kind of him for we know he has little need of our friendship in return. His people are many. They are like the grass that covers vast prairies. My people are few. They resemble the scattering trees of a storm-swept plain. The great, and—I presume—good, White Chief sends us word that he wishes to buy our lands but is willing to allow us enough to live comfortably. This indeed appears just, even generous, for the Red Man no longer has rights that he need respect, and the offer may be wise also, as we are no longer in need of an extensive country. . . . I will not dwell on, nor mourn over, our untimely decay, nor reproach our paleface brothers with hastening it, as we too may have been somewhat to blame.

"Youth is impulsive. When our young men grow angry at some real or imaginary wrong, and disfigure their faces with black paint, it denotes

1. In 1854, Governor Isaac Stevens, Commissioner of Indian Affairs for the Washington Territory, proffered a treaty to the Indians providing for the sale of two million acres of their land to the federal government. This address is the reply of Chief Seattle of the Duwampo tribe. The translator was Henry A. Smith.

that their hearts are black, and then they are often cruel and relentless, and our old men and old women are unable to restrain them. Thus it has ever been. Thus it was when the white men first began to push our forefathers further westward. But let us hope that the hostilities between us may never return. We would have everything to lose and nothing to gain. Revenge by young men is considered gain, even at the cost of their own lives, but old men who stay at home in times of war, and mothers who have sons to lose, know better.

"Our good father at Washington—for I presume he is now our father as well as yours, since King George has moved his boundaries further north—our great good father, I say, sends us word that if we do as he desires he will protect us. His brave warriors will be to us a bristling wall of strength, and his wonderful ships of war will fill our harbors so that our ancient enemies far to the northward—the Hydas and Tsimpsians—will cease to frighten our women, children, and old men. Then in reality will he be our father and we his children. But can that ever be? Your God is not our God! Your God loves your people and hates mine. He folds his strong and protecting arms lovingly about the paleface and leads him by the hand as a father leads his infant son—but He has forsaken His red children—if they really are his. Our God, the Great Spirit, seems also to have forsaken us. Your God makes your people wax strong every day. Soon they will fill the land. Our people are ebbing away like a rapidly receding tide that will never return. The white man's God cannot love our people or He would protect them. They seem to be orphans who can look nowhere for help. How then can we be brothers? How can your God become our God and renew our prosperity and awaken in us dreams of returning greatness? If we have a common heavenly father He must be partial—for He came to his paleface children. We never saw Him. He gave you laws but He had no word for His red children whose teeming multitudes once filled this vast continent as stars fill the firmament. No; we are two distinct races with separate origins and separate destinies. There is little in common between us.

"To us the ashes of our ancestors are sacred and their resting place is hallowed ground. You wander far from the graves of your ancestors and seemingly without regret. Your religion was written upon tables of stone by the iron finger of your God so that you could not forget. The Red Man could never comprehend nor remember it. Our religion is the traditions of our ancestors—the dreams of our old men, given them in solemn hours of night by the Great Spirit; and the visions of our sachems; and it is written in the hearts of our people.

"Your dead cease to love you and the land of their nativity as soon as they pass the portals of the tomb and wander way beyond the stars. They are soon forgotten and never return. Our dead never forget the beautiful world that gave them being.

"Day and night cannot dwell together. The Red Man has ever fled the approach of the White Man, as the morning mist flees before the morning sun. However, your proposition seems fair and I think that my people will accept it and will retire to the reservation you offer them. Then we will dwell apart in peace, for the words of the Great White Chief seem to be the words of nature speaking to my people out of dense darkness.

"It matters little where we pass the remnant of our days. They will not be many. A few more moons; a few more winters—and not one of the descendants of the mighty hosts that once moved over this broad land or lived in happy homes, protected by the Great Spirit, will remain to mourn over the graves of a people once more powerful and hopeful than yours. But why should I mourn at the untimely fate of my people? Tribe follows tribe, and nation follows nation, like the waves of the sea. It is the order of nature, and regret is useless. Your time of decay may be distant, but it will surely come, for even the White Man whose God walked and talked with him as friend with friend, cannot be exempt from the common destiny. We may be brothers after all. We will see.

"We will ponder your proposition, and when we decide we will let you know. But should we accept it, I here and now make this condition that we will not be denied the privilege without molestation of visiting at any time the tombs of our ancestors, friends and children. Every part of this soil is sacred in the estimation of my people. Every hillside, every valley, every plain and grove, has been hallowed by some sad or happy event in days long vanished. . . . The very dust upon which you now stand responds more lovingly to their footsteps than to yours, because it is rich with the blood of our ancestors and our bare feet are conscious of the sympathetic touch. . . . Even the little children who lived here and rejoiced here for a brief season will love these somber solitudes and at eventide they greet shadowy returning spirits. And when the last Red Man shall have perished, and the memory of my tribe shall have become a myth among the White Men, these shores will swarm with the invisible dead of my tribe, and when your children's children think themselves alone in the field, the store, the shop, upon the highway, or in the silence of the pathless woods, they will not be alone. . . . At night when the streets of your cities and villages are silent and you think them deserted, they will throng with the returning hosts that once filled and still love this beautiful land. The White Man will never be alone.

"Let him be just and deal kindly with my people, for the dead are not powerless. Dead, did I say? There is no death, only a change of worlds."

1854

Walt Whitman

DEATH OF ABRAHAM LINCOLN

I shall not easily forget the first time I ever saw Abraham Lincoln. It must have been about the 18th or 19th of February, 1861. It was rather a pleasant afternoon, in New York city, as he arrived there from the West, to remain a few hours, and then pass on to Washington, to prepare for his inauguration. I saw him in Broadway, near the site of the present Post-office. He came down, I think from Canal street, to stop at the Astor House. The broad spaces, sidewalks, and streets in the neighborhood, and for some distance, were crowded with solid masses of people, many thousands. The omnibuses and other vehicles had all been turn'd off, leaving an unusual hush in that busy part of the city. Presently two or three shabby hack barouches made their way with some difficulty through the crowd, and drew up at the Astor House entrance. A tall figure stepp'd out of the centre of these barouches, paus'd leisurely on the sidewalk, look'd up at the granite walls and looming architecture of the grand old hotel—then, after a relieving stretch of arms and legs, turn'd round for over a minute to slowly and good-humoredly scan the appearance of the vast and silent crowds. There were no speeches—no compliments—no welcome—as far as I could hear, not a word said. Still much anxiety was conceal'd in the quiet. Cautious persons had fear'd some mark'd insult or indignity to the President-elect—for he possess'd no personal popularity at all in New York City, and very little political. But it was evidently tacitly agreed that if the few political supporters of Mr. Lincoln present would entirely abstain from any demonstration on their side, the immense majority, who were anything but supporters, would abstain on their sides also. The result was a sulky, unbroken silence, such as certainly never before characterized so great a New York crowd.

Almost in the same neighborhood I distinctly remember'd seeing Lafayette on his visit to America in 1825. I had also personally seen and heard, various years afterward, how Andrew Jackson, Clay, Webster, Hungarian Kossuth, Filibuster Walker, the Prince of Wales on his visit, and other *célèbres*, native and foreign, had been welcom'd there—all that indescribable human roar and magnetism, unlike any other sound in the universe—the glad exulting thunder-shouts of countless unloos'd throats of men! But on this occasion, not a voice—not a sound. From the top of an omnibus, (driven up one side, close by, and block'd by the curbstone and the crowds), I had, I say, a capital view of it all, and especially of Mr. Lincoln, his look and gait—his perfect composure and coolness—his unusual and uncouth height, his dress of complete black, stovepipe hat push'd back on the head, dark-brown complexion, seam'd and wrinkled yet canny-looking face, black, bushy head of hair, disproportionately long neck, and his hands held behind as he stood observing the people. He look'd with curiosity upon that immense sea of faces, and the sea of faces return'd the look with similar curiosity. In both there was a dash of comedy, almost farce, such as Shakspere puts in his blackest tragedies. The crowd that hemm'd around consisted I should think of thirty to forty thousand men, not a single one his personal friend—while I have no doubt, (so frenzied were the ferments of the time,) many an assassin's knife and pistol lurk'd in hip or breast-pocket there, ready, soon as break and riot came.

But no break or riot came. The tall figure gave another relieving stretch or two of arms and legs; then with moderate pace, and accompanied by a few unknown-looking persons, ascended the portico-steps of the Astor House, disappear'd through its broad entrance—and the dumb-show ended.

I saw Abraham Lincoln often the four years following that date. He changed rapidly and much during his Presidency—but this scene, and him in it, are indelibly stamp'd upon my recollection. As I sat on the top of my omnibus, and had a good view of him, the thought, dim and inchoate then, has since come out clear enough, that four sorts of genius, four mighty and primal hands, will be needed to the complete limning of this man's future portrait—the eyes and brains and finger-touch of Plutarch and Eschylus and Michel Angelo, assisted now by Rabelais.

And now—(Mr. Lincoln passing on from this scene to Washington, where he was inaugurated, amid armed cavalry, and sharpshooters at every point—the first instance of the kind in our history—and I hope it will be the last)—now the rapid succession of well-known events, (too well-known—I believe, these days, we almost hate to hear them mention'd)—the national flag fired on at Sumter—the uprising of the North, in paroxysms of astonishment and rage—the chaos of divided councils—the call for troops—the first Bull Run—the stunning cast-down, shock, and dismay of the North—and so in full flood the Secession war. Four years of lurid, bleeding, murky, murderous war. Who paint those years, with all their scenes?—the hard-fought engagements—the defeats, plans, failures—the gloomy hours, days, when our Nationality seem'd hung in pall of doubt, perhaps death—the Mephistophelean sneers of foreign lands and attachés—the dreaded Scylla of European interference, and the Charybdis of the tremendously dangerous latent strata of seccession sympathizers throughout the free States, (far more numerous than is supposed)—the long marches in summer—the hot sweat, and many a sunstroke, as on the rush to Gettysburg in '63—the night battles in the woods, as under Hooker at Chancellorsville—the camps in winter—the military prisons—the hospitals—(alas! alas! the hospitals.)

The Secession war? Nay, let me call it the Union war. Though whatever call'd, it is even yet too near us—too vast and too closely overshadowing—its branches unform'd yet, (but certain,) shooting too far into the future—and the most indicative and mightiest of them yet ungrown. A great literature will yet arise out of the era of those four years, those scenes—era compressing centuries of native passion, first-class pictures, tempests of life and death—an inexhaustible mine for the histories, drama, romance, and even philosophy, of peoples to come—indeed the verteber[1] of poetry and art, (of personal character too,) for all future America—far more grand, in my opinion, to the hands capable of it, than Homer's siege of Troy, or the French wars to Shakspere.

But I must leave these speculations, and come to the theme I have assign'd and limited myself to. Of the actual murder of President Lincoln, though so much has been written, probably the facts are yet very indefinite in most persons' minds. I read from my memoranda, written at the time, and revised frequently and finally since.

The day, April 14, 1865, seems to have been a pleasant one throughout the whole land—the moral atmosphere pleasant too—the long storm, so dark, so fratricidal, full of blood and doubt and gloom, over and ended at last by the sunrise of such an absolute National victory, and utter breakdown of Secessionism—we almost doubted our own senses! Lee had capitulated beneath the apple-tree of Appomattox. The other armies, the flanges of the revolt, swiftly follow'd. And could it really be, then? Out of all the affairs of this world of woe and failure and disorder, was there really come the confirm'd, unerring sign of plan, like a shaft of pure light—of rightful rule—of God? So the day, as I say, was propitious. Early herbage, early flowers, were out. (I remember where I was stopping at the time, the season being advanced, there were many lilacs in full bloom. By one of those caprices that enter and give tinge to events without being at all a part of them, I find myself always reminded of the great tragedy of that day by the sight and odor of these blossoms.[2] It never fails.)

But I must not dwell on accessories. The deed hastens. The popular afternoon paper of Washington, the little *Evening Star*, has spatter'd all over its third page, divided among the advertisements in a sensational manner, in a hundred different places, "*The President and his Lady will be at the Theatre this evening. . . .*" (Lincoln was fond of the theatre. I have myself seen him there several times. I remember thinking how funny it was that he, in some respects the leading actor in the stormiest drama known to real history's stage through centuries, should sit there and be so completely interested and absorb'd in those human jackstraws, moving about with their silly little gestures, foreign spirit, and flatulent text.)

1. Vertebra.
2. Cf. Whitman's elegy on Lincoln, "When

Lilacs Last in the Dooryard Bloom'd" (1865–66).

On this occasion the theatre was crowded, many ladies in rich and gay costumes, officers in their uniforms, many well-known citizens, young folks, the usual clusters of gas-lights, the usual magnetism of so many people, cheerful, with perfumes, music of violins and flutes—(and over all, and saturating all, that vast, vague wonder, *Victory*, the nation's victory, the triumph of the Union, filling the air, the thought, the sense, with exhilaration more than all music and perfumes.)

The President came betimes, and, with his wife, witness'd the play from the large stage-boxes of the second tier, two thrown into one, and profusely drap'd with the national flag. The acts and scenes of the piece —one of those singularly written compositions which have at least the merit of giving entire relief to an audience engaged in mental action or business excitements and cares during the day, as it makes not the slightest call on either the moral, emotional, esthetic, or spiritual nature —a piece, (*Our American Cousin*,) in which, among other characters so call'd, a Yankee, certainly such a one as was never seen, or the least like it ever seen, in North America, is introduced in England, with a varied fol-de-rol of talk, plot, scenery, and such phantasmagoria as goes to make up a modern popular drama—had progress'd through perhaps a couple of its acts, when in the midst of this comedy, or non-such, or whatever it is to be call'd, and to offset it, or finish it out, as if in Nature's and the great Muse's mockery of those poor mimes, came interpolated that scene, not really or exactly to be described at all, (for on the many hundreds who were there it seems to this hour to have left a passing blur, a dream, a blotch)—and yet partially to be described as I now proceed to give it. There is a scene in the play representing a modern parlor, in which two unprecedented English ladies are inform'd by the impossible Yankee that he is not a man of fortune, and therefore undesirable for marriage-catching purposes; after which, the comments being finish'd, the dramatic trio make exit, leaving the stage clear for a moment. At this period came the murder of Abraham Lincoln. Great as all its manifold train, circling round it, and stretching into the future for many a century, in the politics, history, art &c., of the New World, in point of fact the main thing, the actual murder, transpired with the quiet and simplicity of any commonest occurrence—the bursting of a bud or pod in the growth of vegetation, for instance. Through the general hum following the stage pause, with the change of positions, came the muffled sound of a pistol-shot, which not one-hundredth part of the audience heard at the time— and yet a moment's hush—somehow, surely, a vague startled thrill—and then, through the ornamented, draperied, starr'd and striped space-way of the President's box, a sudden figure, a man, raises himself with hands and feet, stands a moment on the railing, leaps below to the stage, (a distance of perhaps fourteen or fifteen feet), falls out of position, catching his boot-heel in the copious drapery, (the American flag,) falls on one knee, quickly recovers himself, rises as if nothing had happen'd, (he really sprains his ankle, but unfelt then)—and so the figure, Booth, the murderer, dress'd in plain black broadcloth, bare-headed, with full, glossy, raven hair, and his eyes like some mad animal's flashing with light and resolution, yet with a certain strange calmness, holds aloft in one hand a large knife—walks along not much back from the footlights—turns fully toward the audience his face of statuesque beauty, lit by those basilisk eyes, flashing with desperation, perhaps insanity—launches out in a firm and steady voice the words *Sic semper tyrannis*[3]—and then walks with neither slow nor very rapid pace diagonally across to the back of the stage, and disappears. (Had not all this terrible scene—making the mimic ones preposterous—had it not all been rehears'd, in blank, by Booth, beforehand?)

A moment's hush—a scream—the cry of "*murder*"—Mrs. Lincoln leaning out of the box, with ashy cheeks and lips, with involuntary cry, pointing to the retreating figure, "*He has kill'd the President.*" And still a moment's strange, incredulous suspense—and then the deluge! then that mixture of horror, noises, uncertainty—(the sound, somewhere back, of a horse's hoofs clattering with speed)—the people burst through chairs and railings, and break them up—there is inextricable confusion and terror—women faint—quite feeble persons fall, and are trampl'd on—many cries of agony are heard—the broad stage suddenly fills to suffocation with a dense and motley crowd, like some horrible carnival—the audience rush generally upon it, at least the strong men do—the actors and actresses are all there in their play-costumes and painted faces, with mortal fright showing through the rouge—the screams and calls, confused talk—redoubled, trebled—two or three manage to pass up water from the stage to the President's box—others try to clamber up—&c., &c.

In the midst of all this, the soldiers of the President's guard, with others, suddenly drawn to the scene, burst in—(some two hundred altogether)—they storm the house, through all the tiers, especially the upper ones, inflam'd with fury, literally charging the audience with fix'd bayonets, muskets, and pistols, shouting "*Clear out! clear out! you sons of — — —*".... Such a wild scene, or a suggestion of it rather, inside the playhouse that night.

Outside, too, in the atmosphere of shock and craze, crowds of people, fill'd with frenzy, ready to seize any outlet for it, come near committing murder several times on innocent individuals. One such case was especially exciting. The infuriated crowd, through some chance, got started against one man, either for words he utter'd, or perhaps without any cause at all, and were proceeding at once to actually hang him on a neighboring lamp-post, when he was rescued by a few heroic policemen,

3. "Thus always to tyrants."

who placed him in their midst, and fought their way slowly and amid great peril toward the station-house. It was a fitting episode of the whole affair. The crowd rushing and eddying to and fro—the night, the yells, the pale faces, many frighten'd people trying in vain to extricate themselves—the attack'd man, not yet freed from the jaws of death, looking like a corpse—the silent, resolute, half-dozen policemen, with no weapons but their little clubs, yet stern and steady through all those eddying swarms—made a fitting side-scene to the grand tragedy of the murder. They gain'd the station house with the protected man, whom they placed in security for the night, and discharged him in the morning.

And in the midst of that pandemonium, infuriated soldiers, the audience and the crowd, the stage, and all its actors and actresses, its paint-pots, spangles, and gas-lights—the life blood from those veins, the best and sweetest of the land, drips slowly down, and death's ooze already begins its little bubbles on the lips.

Thus the visible incidents and surroundings of Abraham Lincoln's murder, as they really occur'd. Thus ended the attempted secession of these States: thus the four years' war. But the main things come subtly and invisibly afterward, perhaps long afterward—neither military, political, nor (great as those are,) historical. I say, certain secondary and indirect results, out of the tragedy of this death, are, in my opinion, greatest. Not the event of the murder itself. Not that Mr. Lincoln strings the principal points and personages of the period, like beads, upon the single string of his career. Not that his idiosyncrasy, in its sudden appearance and disappearance, stamps this Republic with a stamp more mark'd and enduring than any yet given by any one man—(more even than Washington's;)—but, join'd with these, the immeasurable value and meaning of that whole tragedy lies, to me, in senses finally dearest to a nation, (and here all our own)—the imaginative and artistic senses—the literary and dramatic ones. Not in any common or low meaning of those terms, but a meaning precious to the race, and to every age. A long and varied series of contradictory events arrives at last at its highest poetic, single, central, pictorial dénouement. The whole involved, baffling, multiform whirl of the secession period comes to a head, and is gather'd in one brief flash of lightning-illumination—one simple, fierce deed. Its sharp culmination, and as it were solution, of so many bloody and angry problems, illustrates those climax-moments on the stage of universal Time, where the historic Muse at one entrance, and the tragic Muse at the other, suddenly ringing down the curtain, close an immense act in the long drama of creative thought, and give it radiation, tableau, stranger than fiction. Fit radiation—fit close! How the imagination—how the student loves these things! America, too, is to have them. For not in all great deaths, not far or near—not Caesar in the Roman senate-house, or Napoleon passing away in the wild night-storm at St. Helena—not Paleologus,[4] falling, desperately fighting, piled over dozens deep with Grecian corpses—not calm old Socrates, drinking the hemlock—outvies that terminus of the secession war, in one man's life, here in our midst, in our time—that seal of the emancipation of three million slaves—that parturition and delivery of our at last really free Republic, born again, henceforth to commence its career of genuine homogeneous Union, compact, consistent with itself.

Nor will ever future American Patriots and Unionists, indifferently over the whole land, or North or South, find a better moral to their lesson. The final use of the greatest men of a Nation is, after all, not with reference to their deeds in themselves, or their direct bearing on their times or lands. The final use of a heroic-eminent life—especially of a heroic-eminent death—is its indirect filtering into the nation and the race, and to give, often at many removes, but unerringly, age after age, color and fibre to the personalism of the youth and maturity of that age, and of mankind. Then, there is a cement to the whole people, subtler, more underlying, than any thing in written constitution, or courts or armies—namely, the cement of a death identified thoroughly with that people, at its head, and for its sake. Strange, (is it not?) that battles, martyrs, agonies, blood, even assassination, should so condense—perhaps only really, lastingly condense—a Nationality.

I repeat it—the grand deaths of the race—the dramatic deaths of every nationality—are its most important inheritance-value—in some respects beyond its literature and art—(as the hero is beyond his finest portrait, and the battle itself beyond its choicest song or epic.) Is not here indeed the point underlying all tragedy? the famous pieces of the Grecian masters—and all masters? Why, if the old Greeks had had this man, what trilogies of plays—what epics—would have been made out of him! How the rhapsodes would have recited him! How quickly that quaint tall form would have enter'd into the region where men vitalize gods, and gods divinify men! But Lincoln, his times, his death—great as any, any age—belong altogether to our own, and are autochthonic.[5] (Sometimes indeed I think our American days, our own stage—the actors we know and have shaken hands, or talk'd with—more fateful than any thing in Eschylus[6]—more heroic than the fighters around Troy—afford kings of men for our Democracy prouder than Agamemnon—models of character cute and hardy as Ulysses—deaths more pitiful than Priam's.)

When centuries hence, (as it must, in my opinion, be centuries hence before the life of these States, or of Democracy, can be really written and

---

4. Emperor Constantine XI, who yielded Constantinople to the Turks in 1453.
5. Aboriginal, indigenous.
6. Eschylus (i.e., Aeschylus): Greek tragic dramatist (525–456 B.C.) whose plays, like Homer's epics, dealt with such figures of the Trojan War as Agamemnon, leader of the Greek forces; Ulysses, whose return to Ithaca after the war took ten years; and Priam, slaughtered king of Troy.

illustrated,) the leading historians and dramatists seek for some personage, some special event, incisive enough to mark with deepest cut, and mnemonize, this turbulent nineteenth century of ours, (not only these States, but all over the political and social world)—something, perhaps, to close that gorgeous procession of European feudalism, with all its pomp and caste-prejudices, (of whose long train we in America are yet so inextricably the heirs)—something to identify with terrible identification, by far the greatest revolutionary step in the history of the United States, (perhaps the greatest of the world, our century)—the absolute extirpation and erasure of slavery from the States—those historians will seek in vain for any point to serve more thoroughly their purpose, than Abraham Lincoln's death.

Dear to the Muse—thrice dear to Nationality—to the whole human race—precious to this Union—precious to Democracy—unspeakably and forever precious—their first great Martyr Chief.

1882

THE READER

1. Whitman says that "four sorts of genius" would be needed to give a complete portrait of Lincoln. What does he mean by this? Look up more about each of the four people he mentions, and determine what each might contribute to a complete picture of Lincoln.
2. Whitman says that the murder of Lincoln "transpired with the quiet and simplicity of any commonest occurrence—the bursting of a bud or pod in the growth of vegetation, for instance." What meaning and effect does this metaphor convey?
3. At the end, Whitman speaks grandly of Lincoln's significance for far more than the citizens of the still United States. As he sees it, what do all these people have in common that would allow for this more-than-national significance?
4. Compare Whitman's practice as a biographer with the theory set forth by Woolf in "The New Biography" (p. 738).

THE WRITER

1. Whitman delivered this piece as a lecture. How might it have differed if he had composed it as an essay to be read rather than a lecture to be heard?
2. The events of the assassination lead Whitman to mention his perception of Lincoln's fondness for the theater. What does he do to make this particular observation serve a larger purpose?
3. How does Whitman convey the sense of horror and confusion in the scene when Lincoln is shot? Using some of Whitman's techniques, write an account of a similar scene which produces a strong emotional effect.
4. Using a dictionary if you like, explain the different meanings of the different names for the war. Be sure to consider our own name, which

Whitman does not use—the Civil War. Does this difference about names imply a difference about attitudes toward the war? Toward Lincoln?

5. *Using the details Whitman provides, write a movie or TV script for one of the scenes he describes. What things will the camera "see" and focus on?*

John Houseman

THE WAR OF THE WORLDS

The War of the Worlds formed part of our general plan of contrasting shows.[1] No one, as I recall, was particularly enthusiastic about it. But it seemed good programming—following *Julius Caesar* (with the original Mercury cast and commentary by Kaltenborn out of Plutarch[2]), *Oliver Twist* (in which Orson played both the boy Oliver and the villainous Fagin), *Eighty Days Around the World, The Heart of Darkness, Jane Eyre* and before *Life with Father*, which was to be our next show—to throw in something of a scientific nature. We thought of Shiel's *Purple Cloud*, Conan Doyle's *Lost World* and several other well-known works of science fiction before settling on H. G. Wells's twenty-year-old novel, which neither Orson nor I remembered at all clearly. It is just possible that neither of us had ever read it.

Actually it was a narrow squeak. The men from Mars barely escaped being stillborn. Late Tuesday night—thirty-six hours before the first rehearsal—Howard Koch called me at the theater. He was in deep distress. After three days of slaving on H. G. Wells's scientific fantasy he was ready to give up. Under no circumstances, he declared, could it be made interesting or in any way credible to modern American ears. Koch was not given to habitual alarmism. To confirm his fears, Annie[3] came to the phone. "You can't do it, Houseman!" she whined. "Those old Martians are just a lot of nonsense! It's all too silly! We're going to make fools of ourselves! Absolute idiots!"

We were not averse to changing a show at the last moment. But the only other script available was an extremely dreary version of *Lorna*

1. In the series *Mercury Theatre of the Air*, named for the stage company of which Houseman and Orson Welles were cofounders and presiding geniuses; the series offered weekly broadcasts of adaptations of famous plays and fictional works.
2. H. V. Kaltenborn was a leading news commentator of the day, distinguished for his clipped, pedantic speech [Houseman's note]. Plutarch (46–120) was a biographer of famous Greeks and Romans, among the latter the dictator Julius Caesar.
3. Ann Froelich, who worked with Howard Koch, the show's regular scriptwriter; Paul Stewart, mentioned later, was associate producer of the show.

Doone[4] which I had started during the summer and abandoned. I reasoned with Koch. I was severe. I taxed him and Annie with defeatism. I gave them false comfort, I promised to come up and help. When I finally got there—around two in the morning—things were better. They were beginning to have fun laying waste the State of New Jersey. Annie had stopped grinding her teeth. I worked with them for the rest of the night and they went on through the next day. Wednesday at sunset the script was finished.

Thursday, as usual, Paul Stewart rehearsed the show, then made a record. We listened to it rather gloomily, between *Danton* rehearsals, in Orson's room at the St. Regis, sitting on the floor because all the chairs were still covered with coils of unrolled and unedited film.[5] He was dead tired and thought it was a dull show. We all agreed that its only chance of coming off lay in emphasizing its newscast style—its simultaneous, eye-witness quality.

All night we sat up—Howard, Paul, Annie and I—spicing the script with circumstantial allusions and authentic detail. Friday afternoon it was sent over to CBS to be passed by the network censor. Certain name alterations were requested. Under protest and with a deep sense of grievance we changed the Hotel Biltmore to a nonexistent Park Plaza, Trans-America to Inter-Continent, the Columbia Broadcasting Building to Broadcasting Building. Then the script went over to mimeograph and I went back to the theater. We had done our best and, after all, it was just another radio show.

Saturday, Paul Stewart rehearsed with sound effects and without Welles. He worked for a long time on the crowd scenes, the roar of cannon echoing in the Watchung Hills[6] and the sound of New york Harbor as the ships with the last remaining survivors put out to sea.

Around six we left the studio. Orson, phoning from the theater a few minutes later to find out how things were going, was told by one of the CBS sound men, who had stayed behind to pack up his equipment, that it was not one of our better shows. Confidentially, the man opined, it just didn't come off. Twenty-seven hours later, quite a few of his employers would have found themselves a good deal happier if he had turned out to be right.

On Sunday, October 30, at 8:00 P.M., E.S.T., in a studio littered with coffee cartons and sandwich paper, Orson swallowed a second container of pineapple juice, put on his earphones, raised his long white fingers and threw the cue for the Mercury theme—the Tchaikovsky Piano Concerto No. 1 in B Flat Minor. After the music dipped, there were routine

4. Well-known romantic novel (1869) by R. D. Blackmore.
5. A future Mercury Theatre stage production was to have two filmed chase senses, tion was to have two filmed chase senses, which for several weeks Welles had been trying to edit. Currently in rehearsal was Georg Büchner's *Danton's Death* (1835).
6. In northern New Jersey.

introductions—then the announcement that a dramatization of H. G. Wells's famous novel, *The War of the Worlds*, was about to be performed. Around 8:01 Orson began to speak, as follows:

WELLES

We know now that in the early years of the twentieth century this world was being watched closely by intelligences greater than man's and yet as mortal as his own. We know now that as human beings busied themselves about their various concerns they were scrutinized and studied, perhaps almost as narrowly as a man with a microscope might scrutinize the transient creatures that swarm and multiply in a drop of water. With infinite complacence people went to and fro over the earth about their little affairs, serene in the assurance of their dominion over this small spinning fragment of solar driftwood which by chance or design man has inherited out of the dark mystery of Time and Space. Yet across an immense ethereal gulf minds that are to our minds as ours are to the beasts in the jungle, intellects vast, cool, and unsympathetic regarded this earth with envious eyes and slowly and surely drew their plans against us. In the thirty-ninth year of the twentieth century came the great disillusionment.

It was near the end of October. Business was better. The war scare was over. More men were back at work. Sales were picking up. On this particular evening, October 30th, the Crossley service estimated that thirty-two million people were listening in on their radios. . . .

Neatly, without perceptible transition, he was followed on the air by an anonymous announcer caught in a routine bulletin:

ANNOUNCER

. . . for the next twenty-four hours not much change in temperature. A slight atmospheric disturbance of undetermined origin is reported over Nova Scotia, causing a low pressure area to move down rather rapidly over the northeastern states, bringing a forecast of rain, accompanied by winds of light gale force. Maximum temperature 66; minimum 48. This weather report comes to you from the Government Weather Bureau. . . . We now take you to the Meridian Room in the Hotel Park Plaza in downtown New York, where you will be entertained by the music of Ramon Raquello and his orchestra.

At which cue, Bernard Herrmann led the massed men of the CBS house orchestra in a thunderous symphonic rendition of "La Cumparsita." The entire hoax might have been exposed there and then—but for the fact that hardly anyone was listening. They were being entertained by Charlie McCarthy.

The Crossley census, taken about a week before the broadcast, had given us 3.6 percent of the listening audience to Edgar Bergen's 34.7 percent. What the Crossley Institute (that hireling of the advertising agencies) deliberately ignored, was the healthy American habit of dial twisting. On that particular evening Edgar Bergen, in the person of

Charlie McCarthy, temporarily left the air about 8:12 P.M. E.S.T., yielding place to a new and not very popular singer. At that point, and during the following minutes, a large number of listeners started twisting their dials in search of other entertainment. Many of them turned to us—and when they did, they stayed put! For by this time the mysterious meteorite had fallen at Grovers Mill in New Jersey, the Martians had begun to show their foul leathery heads above the ground, and the New Jersey State Police were racing to the spot. Within a few minutes people all over the United States were praying, crying, fleeing frantically to escape death from the Martians. Some remembered to rescue loved ones, others telephoned farewells or warnings, hurried to inform neighbors, sought information from newspapers or radio stations, summoned ambulances and police cars.

The reaction was strongest at points nearest the tragedy—in Newark, New Jersey, in a single block, more than twenty families rushed out of their houses with wet handkerchiefs and towels over their faces. Some began moving household furniture. Police switchboards were flooded with calls inquiring, "Shall I close my windows?"; "Have the police any extra gas masks?" Police found one family waiting in the yard with wet cloths on faces contorted with hysteria. As one women reported later:

> I was terribly frightened. I wanted to pack and take my child in my arms, gather up my friends and get in the car and just go north as far as we could. But what I did was just sit by one window, praying, listening, and scared stiff, and my husband by the other sniffing, and looking out to see if people were running. . . .

In New York hundreds of people on Riverside Drive left their homes ready for flight. Bus terminals were crowded. A woman calling up the Dixie Bus Terminal for information said impatiently, "Hurry please, the world is coming to an end and I have a lot to do."

In the parlor churches of Harlem, evening service became "end of the world" prayer meetings. Many turned to God in that moment:

> I held a crucifix in my hand and prayed while looking out of my open window for falling meteors. . . . When the monsters were wading across the Hudson River and coming into New York, I wanted to run up on my roof to see what they looked like, but I couldn't leave my radio while it was telling me of their whereabouts.

> Aunt Grace began to pray with Uncle Henry. Lily got sick to her stomach. I don't know what I did exactly but I know I prayed harder and more earnestly than ever before. Just as soon as we were convinced that this thing was real, how petty all things on this earth seemed; how soon we put our trust in God!

The panic moved upstate. One man called up the Mt. Vernon Police Headquarters to find out "where the forty policemen were killed." Another took time out to philosophize:

> I thought the whole human race was going to be wiped out—that seemed more important than the fact that we were going to die. It seemed awful that everything that had been worked on for years was going to be lost forever.

In Rhode Island weeping and hysterical women swamped the switchboard of the Providence *Journal* for details of the massacre, and officials of the electric light company received a score of calls urging them to turn off all lights so that the city would be safe from the enemy. The Boston *Globe* received a call from one woman who "could see the fire." A man in Pittsburgh hurried home in the midst of the broadcast and found his wife in the bathroom, a bottle of poison in her hand, screaming, "I'd rather die this way than that." In Minneapolis a woman ran into church screaming, "New York destroyed, this is the end of the world. You might as well go home to die. I just heard it on the radio."

The Kansas City bureau of the AP received inquiries about the "meteors" from Los Angeles; Salt Lake City; Beaumont, Texas; and St. Joseph, Missouri. In San Francisco the general impression of listeners seemed to be that an overwhelming force had invaded the United States from the air—was in process of destroying New York and threatening to move westward. "My God," roared an inquirer into a telephone, "where can I volunteer my services, we've got to stop this awful thing!"

As far south as Birmingham, Alabama, people gathered in churches and prayed. On the campus of a Southeastern college—

> The girls in the sorority houses and dormitories huddled around their radios trembling and weeping in each other's arms. They separated themselves from their friends only to take their turn at the telephones to make long-distance calls to their parents, saying goodbye for what they thought might be the last time. . . .

There are hundreds of such items, gathered from coast to coast. At least one book and quite a pile of sociological literature have appeared on the subject of "the invasion from Mars." Many theories have been put forward to explain the "tidal wave" of panic that swept the nation. Two factors, in my opinion, contributed to the broadcast's extraordinarily violent effect. First, its historical timing. It came within thirty-five days of the Munich crisis.[7] For weeks, the American people had been hanging on their radios, getting most of their news over the air. A new technique of "on-the-spot" reporting had been developed and eagerly accepted by an anxious and newshungry world. The Mercury Theatre of the Air, by faithfully copying every detail of the new technique, including its imper-

7. The broadcast was on October 30, 1938. In September the prime ministers of Great Britain and France had met in Munich with Hitler and Mussolini and ceded western Czechoslovakia to Germany in an effort to appease Hitler's expansionism and prevent war.

fections, found an already enervated audience ready to accept its wildest fantasies. The second factor was the show's sheer technical brilliance. To this day it is impossible to sit in a room and hear the scratched, worn, off-the-air recording of the broadcast without feeling in the back of your neck some slight draft left over from the great wind of terror that swept the nation. Even with the element of credibility totally removed it remains a surprisingly effective broadcast.

Beginning some time around two when the show started to take shape under Orson's hands, a strange fever seemed to invade the studio—part childish mischief, part professional zeal. First to feel it were the actors. I remember Frank Readick (who played the part of Carl Phillips, the network's special reporter) going down to the record library and digging up the recording of the explosion of the *Hindenburg* at Lakehurst. This is a classic reportage—one of those wonderful, unpredictable accidents of eyewitness description. The broadcaster is casually describing the routine landing of the giant dirigible. Suddenly he sees something. A flash of flame! An instant later the whole thing explodes. It takes him time—a full second—to react at all. Then seconds more of sputtering ejaculations before he can make the adjustment between brain and tongue. He starts to describe the terrible things he sees—the writhing human figures twisting and squirming as they fall from the white burning wreckage. He stops, fumbles, vomits, then quickly continues. Readick played the record to himself, over and over. Then, recreating the emotion in his own terms he described the Martian meteorite as he saw it lying inert and harmless in a field at Grovers Mill, lit up by the headlights of a hundred cars, the coppery cylinder suddenly opening, revealing the leather tentacles and the terrible pale-eyed faces of the Martians within. As they began to emerge he froze, unable to translate his vision into words; he fumbled, retched, and then after a second continued.

A few moments later Carl Phillips lay dead, tumbling over the microphone in his fall—one of the first victims of the Martian ray. There followed a moment of absolute silence—an eternity of waiting. Then without warning, the network's emergency fill-in was heard—somewhere in a quiet studio, a piano, close on mike, playing "Claire de Lune," soft and sweet as honey, for many seconds, while the fate of the universe hung in the balance. Finally it was interrupted by the manly reassuring voice of Brigadier General Montgomery Smith, Commander of the New Jersey State Militia, speaking from Trenton and placing "the counties of Mercer and Middlesex as far west as Princeton and east to Jamesburg" under martial law! Tension—release—then renewed tension. Soon after that came an eyewitness account of the fatal battle of the Watchung Hills; then, once again, that lone piano was heard—now a symbol of terror, shattering the dead air with its ominous tinkle. As it played on and on, its effect became increasingly sinister—a thin band of suspense stretched almost beyond endurance.

That piano was the neatest trick of the show—a fine specimen of the theatrical "retard," boldly conceived and exploited to the full. It was one of the many devices with which Welles succeeded in compelling not merely the attention, but also the belief of his invisible audience. The War of the Worlds was a magic act, one of the world's greatest, and Orson was the man to bring it off.

For Welles, as I have said, was first and foremost, a magician whose particular talent lay in his ability to stretch the familiar elements of theatrical effect far beyond their normal point of tension. For this reason (as we were discovering to our sorrow on Forty-first Street) his productions required more careful preparation and more perfect execution than most; like all complicated magic tricks, they remained, till the last moment, in a state of precarious balance. When they came off they gave, by virtue of their unusually high intensity, an impression of the greatest brilliance and power; when they failed—when something in their balance went wrong or the original structure proved to have been unsound —they provoked a particularly violent reaction of unease and revulsion. Welles's flops were louder then other men's. The Mars broadcast was one of his unqualified successes.

Among the columnists and public figures who discussed the affair during the next few days (some praising us for the public service we had rendered, some condemning us as sinister scoundrels), the most general reaction was one of amazement at the "incredible stupidity" and "gullibility" of the American public, who had accepted as real, in this single broadcast, incidents which in actual fact would have taken days or even weeks to occur. One explanation of our success lay in the fact that the first few minutes of our broadcast were strictly realistic in time and perfectly credible, though somewhat boring, in content. Herein lay the great tensile strength of the show; it was the structural device that made the whole illusion possible. And it could have been carried off in no other medium than radio.

Our actual broadcasting time, from the first mention of the meteorites to the fall of New York City, was less than forty minutes. During that time men traveled long distances, large bodies of troops were mobilized, cabinet meetings were held, savage battles fought on land and in the air. And millions of people accepted it—emotionally if not logically.

There is nothing so very strange about that. Most of us do the same thing, to some degree, most days of our lives—every time we look at a movie or a television show. Not even the realistic theater observes the literal unities; films, TV and, particularly, in its day, radio (where neither place nor time existed save in the imagination of the listener) have no difficulty in getting their audiences to accept the telescoped reality of dramatic time. Our special hazard lay in the fact that we purported to be not a play, but reality. In order to take advantage of the accepted convention, we had to slide swiftly and imperceptibly out of the "real" time of a news report into the "dramatic" time of a fictional broadcast. Once that was achieved—without losing the audience's attention or arousing their skepticism—once they were sufficiently absorbed and bewitched not to notice the transitions any more, there was no extreme of fantasy through which they would not follow us. If, that night, the American public proved "gullible," it was because enormous pains and a great deal of thought had been spent to make it so.

In the script, The War of the Worlds started extremely slowly—dull meteorological and astronomical bulletins alternating with musical interludes. These were followed by a colorless scientific interview and still another stretch of dance music. These first few minutes of routine broadcasting "within the existing standards of judgment of the listener" were intended to lull (or maybe bore) the audience into a false security and to furnish a solid base of realistic time from which to accelerate later. Orson, in directing the show, extended these slow movements far beyond our original conception. The interview in the Princeton Observatory—the clockwork ticking monontonously overhead, the wooly-minded professor mumbling vague replies to the reporters' uninformed questions—this, too, was dragged out to the point of tedium. Over my protests, lines were restored that had been cut at earlier rehearsals. I cried there would not be a listener left. Welles stretched them out even longer.

He was right. His sense of tempo, that night, was infallible. When the flashed news of the cylinder's landing finally came—almost fifteen minutes after the beginning of a fairly dull show—he was able suddenly to spiral his action to a speed as wild and reckless as its base was solid. The appearance of the Martians; their first treacherous act; the death of Carl Phillips; the arrival of the militia; the battle of the Watchung Hills; the destruction of New Jersey—all these were telescoped into a space of twelve minutes without overstretching the listeners' emotional credulity. The broadcast, by then, had its own reality, the reality of emotionally felt time and space.

At the height of the crisis, around 8:31, the Secretary of the Interior came on the air with an exhortation to the American people. It was admirably spoken—in a voice just faintly reminiscent of Franklin Delano Roosevelt's—by a young man named Kenneth Delmar, who later grew rich and famous as Senator Claghorn.[8]

THE SECRETARY

Citizens of the nation: I shall not try to conceal the gravity of the situation that confronts the country, nor the concern of your Government in protecting the lives and property of its people. However, I wish to impress upon you

8. A comic character in Fred Allen's popular radio show.

—private citizens and public officials, all of you—the urgent need of calm and resourceful action. Fortunately, this formidable enemy is still confined to a comparatively small area, and we may place our faith in the military forces to keep them there. In the meantime placing our trust in God, we must continue the performance of our duties, each and every one of us, so that we may confront this destructive adversary with a nation united, courageous, and consecrated to the preservation of human supremacy of this earth. I thank you.

Toward the end of this speech (circa 8:32 E.S.T.), Davidson Taylor, supervisor of the broadcast for the Columbia Broadcasting System, received a phone call in the control room, creased his lips, and hurriedly left the studio. By the time he returned, a few minutes later, pale as death, clouds of heavy smoke were rising from Newark, New Jersey, and the Martians, tall as skyscrapers, were astride the Pulaski Highway preparatory to wading the Hudson River. To us in the studio the show seemed to be progressing splendidly—how splendidly Davidson Taylor had just learned outside. For several minutes now, a kind of madness had been sweeping the continent: it was somehow connected with our show. The CBS switchboards had been swamped into uselessness, but from outside sources vague rumors were coming in of deaths and suicides and panic injuries by the thousands.

Taylor had orders to interrupt the show immediately with an explanatory station announcement. By now the Martians were across the Hudson and gas was blanketing the city. The end was near. We were less than a minute from the station break. Ray Collins, superb as the "last announcer," was choking heroically to death on the roof of Broadcasting Building. The boats were all whistling for a while as the last of the refugees perished in New York Harbor. Finally, as they died away, an amateur short-wave operator was heard, from heaven knows where, weakly reaching out for human companionship across the empty world:

> $_2$X$_2$L Calling CQ
> $_2$X$_2$L Calling CQ
> $_2$X$_2$L Calling CQ
> Isn't there anyone on the air?
> Isn't there anyone?

Five seconds of absolute silence. Then, shattering the reality of world's end—the announcer's voice was heard, suave and bright:

ANNOUNCER

You are listening to the CBS presentation of Orson Welles and the Mercury Theatre of the Air in an original dramatization of *The War of the Worlds,* by H. G. Wells. The performance will continue after a brief intermission.

The second part of the show was well written and sensitively played—but nobody heard it. It recounted the adventures of a lone survivor, with interesting observations on the nature of human society; it described the eventual death of the Martian invaders, slain—"after all man's defenses had failed by the humblest thing that God in his wisdom had put upon this earth"—by bacteriological action; it told of the rebuilding of a brave new world. After a stirring musical finale, Welles, in his own person, delivered a charmingly apologetic little speech about Halloween and goblins.

I remember, during the playing of the final theme, the phone starting to ring in the control room and a shrill voice through the receiver announcing itself as belonging to the mayor of some Midwestern city, one of the big ones. He was screaming for Welles. Choking with fury, he reported mobs in the streets of his city, women and children huddled in the churches, violence and looting. If, as he now learned, the whole thing was nothing but a crummy joke—then he, personally, was on his way to New York to punch the author of it on the nose! I hung up quickly. For we were off the air now and the studio door had burst open.

The following hours were a nightmare. The building was suddenly full of people and dark-blue uniforms. Hustled out of the studio, we were locked into a small back office on another floor. Here we sat incommunicado while network employees were busily collecting, destroying, or locking up all scripts and records of the broadcast. Finally the Press was let loose upon us, ravening for horror. How many deaths had we heard of? (Implying they knew of thousands.) What did we know of the fatal stampede in a Jersey hall? (Implying it was one of many.) What traffic deaths? (The ditches must be choked with corpses.) The suicides? (Haven't you heard about the one on Riverside Drive?) It is all quite vague in my memory and quite terrible.

Hours later, instead of arresting us, they let us out a back way and we scurried down to the theater like hunted animals to their hole. It was surprising to see life going on as usual in the midnight streets, cars stopping for traffic, people walking. At the Mercury the company was still rehearsing *Danton's Death*—falling up and down stairs and singing the "Carmagnole."[9] Welles went up on stage, where photographers, lying in wait, caught him with his eyes raised to heaven, his arms outstretched in an attitude of crucifixion. Thus he appeared in a tabloid the next morning over the caption, "I Didn't Know What I was Doing!" *The New York Times* quoted him as saying, "I don't think we will choose anything like this again."

We were on the front page for two days. Having had to bow to radio as a news source during the Munich crisis, the press was now only too eager

9. A song of the French Revolution of 1789, the setting for *Danton's Death*.

to expose the perilous irresponsibilities of the new medium. Orson was their whipping boy. They quizzed and badgered him. Condemnatory editorials were delivered by our press-clipping bureau in bushel baskets. There was talk, for a while, of criminal action.

Then gradually, after about two weeks, the excitement subsided. By then it had been discovered that the casualties were not as numerous or as serious as had at first been supposed. One young woman had fallen and broken her arm running downstairs. Later the Federal Communications Commission held some hearings and passed some regulations. The Columbia Broadcasting System made a public apology. With that the official aspects of the incident were closed.

Of the suits that were brought against the network—amounting to over three-quarters of a million dollars for damages, injuries, miscarriages and distresses of various kinds—not one was substantiated. We did settle one claim, however. It was the particularly affecting case of a man in Massachusetts, who wrote:

> I thought the best thing to do was to go away. So I took three dollars twenty-five cents out of my savings and bought a ticket. After I had gone sixty miles I knew it was a play. Now I don't have money left for the shoes I was saving up for. Will you please have someone send me a pair of black shoes size 9B!

We did. And all the lawyers were very angry with us.

Hannah Arendt

DENMARK AND THE JEWS

At the Wannsee Conference,[1] Martin Luther, of the Foreign Office, warned of great difficulties in the Scandinavian countries, notably in Norway and Denmark. (Sweden was never occupied, and Finland, though in the war on the side of the Axis, was one country the Nazis never even approached on the Jewish question. This surprising exception of Finland, with some two thousand Jews, may have been due to Hitler's great esteem for the Finns, whom perhaps he did not want to subject to threats and humiliating blackmail.) Luther proposed postponing evacuations from Scandinavia for the time being, and as far as Denmark was concerned, this really went without saying, since the country retained its independent government, and was respected as a neutral state, until the fall of 1943, although it, along with Norway, had been invaded by the German Army in April, 1940. There existed no

1. A meeting of German officials on "the Jewish question."

Fascist or Nazi movement in Denmark worth mentioning, and therefore no collaborators. In Norway, however, the Germans had been able to find enthusiastic supporters; indeed, Vidkun Quisling, leader of the pro-Nazi and anti-Semitic Norwegian party, gave his name to what later became known as a "quisling government." The bulk of Norway's seventeen hundred Jews were stateless, refugees from Germany; they were seized and interned in a few lightning operations in October and November, 1942. When Eichmann's office ordered their deportation to Auschwitz, some of Quisling's own men resigned their government posts. This may not have come as a surprise to Mr. Luther and the Foreign Office, but what was much more serious, and certainly totally unexpected, was that Sweden immediately offered asylum, and even Swedish nationality, to all who were persecuted. Dr. Ernst von Weizsäcker, Undersecretary of State of the Foreign Office, who received the proposal, refused to discuss it, but the offer helped nevertheless. It is always relatively easy to get out of a country illegally, whereas it is nearly impossible to enter the place of refuge without permission and to dodge the immigration authorities. Hence, about nine hundred people, slightly more than half of the small Norwegian community, could be smuggled into Sweden.

It was in Denmark, however, that the Germans found out how fully justified the Foreign Office's apprehensions had been. The story of the Danish Jews is *sui generis*, and the behavior of the Danish people and their government was unique among all the countries in Europe— whether occupied, or a partner of the Axis, or neutral and truly independent. One is tempted to recommend the story as required reading in political science for all students who wish to learn something about the enormous power potential inherent in non-violent action and in resistance to an opponent possessing vastly superior means of violence. To be sure, a few other countries in Europe lacked proper "understanding of the Jewish question," and actually a majority of them were opposed to "radical" and "final" solutions. Like Denmark, Sweden, Italy, and Bulgaria proved to be nearly immune to anti-Semitism, but of the three that were in the German sphere of influence, only the Danes dared speak out on the subject to their German masters. Italy and Bulgaria sabotaged German orders and indulged in a complicated game of double-dealing and double-crossing, saving their Jews by a tour de force of sheer ingenuity, but they never contested the policy as such. That was totally different from what the Danes did. When the Germans approached them rather cautiously about introducing the yellow badge, they were simply told that the King would be the first to wear it, and the Danish government officials were careful to point out that anti-Jewish measures of any sort would cause their own immediate resignation. It was decisive in this whole matter that the Germans did not even succeed in introducing the vitally important distinction between native Danes of Jewish origin, of

whom there were about sixty-four hundred, and the fourteen hundred
German Jewish refugees who had found asylum in the country prior to
the war and who now had been declared stateless by the German government. This refusal must have surprised the Germans no end, since it
appeared so "illogical" for a government to protect people to whom it
had categorically denied naturalization and even permission to work.
(Legally, the prewar situation of refugees in Denmark was not unlike that
in France, except that the general corruption in the Third Republic's
civil services enabled a few of them to obtain naturalization papers,
through bribes or "connections," and most refugees in France could
work illegally, without a permit. But Denmark, like Switzerland, was no
country *pour se débrouiller*[2].) The Danes, however, explained to the
German officials that because the stateless refugees were no longer
German citizens, the Nazis could not claim them without Danish assent.
This was one of the few cases in which statelessness turned out to be an
asset, although it was of course not statelessness per se that saved the
Jews but, on the contrary, the fact that the Danish government had
decided to protect them. Thus, none of the preparatory moves, so important for the bureaucracy of murder, could be carried out, and operations
were postponed until the fall of 1943.

What happened then was truly amazing; compared with what took
place in other European countries, everything went topsy-turvey. In
August, 1943—after the German offensive in Russia had failed, the
Afrika Korps had surrendered in Tunisia, and the Allies had invaded
Italy—the Swedish government canceled its 1940 agreement with Germany which had permitted German troops the right to pass through the
country. Thereupon, the Danish workers decided that they could help a
bit in hurrying things up; riots broke out in Danish shipyards, where the
dock workers refused to repair German ships and then went on strike.
The German military commander proclaimed a state of emergency and
imposed martial law, and Himmler thought this was the right moment to
tackle the Jewish question, whose "solution" was long overdue. What he
did not reckon with was that—quite apart from Danish resistance—the
German officials who had been living in the country for years were no
longer the same. Not only did General von Hannecken, the military
commander, refuse to put troops at the disposal of the Reich plenipoten-
tiary, Dr. Werner Best; the special S.S. units (*Einsatz-kommandos*) employed in Denmark very frequently objected to "the measures they were
ordered to carry out by the central agencies"—according to Best's testimony of Nuremberg. And Best himself, an old Gestapo man and former
legal adviser to Heydrich, author of a then famous book on the police,
who had worked for the military government in Paris to the entire

2. For wangling—using bribery to circumvent bureaucratic regulations.

satisfaction of his superiors, could not longer be trusted, although it is doubtful that Berlin ever learned the extent of his unreliability. Still, it was clear from the beginning that things were not going well, and Eichmann's office sent one of its best men to Denmark—Rolf Günther, whom no one had ever accused of not possessing the required "ruthless toughness." Günther made no impression on his colleagues in Copenhagen, and now von Hannecken refused even to issue a decree requiring all Jews to report for work.

Best went to Berlin and obtained a promise that all Jews from Denmark would be sent to Theresienstadt[3] regardless of their category—a very important concession, from the Nazis' point of view. The night of October 1 was set for their seizure and immediate departure—ships were ready in the harbor—and since neither the Danes nor the Jews nor the German troops stationed in Denmark could be relied on to help, police units arrived from Germany for a door-to-door search. At the last moment, Best told them that they were not permitted to break into apartments, because the Danish police might then interfere, and they were not supposed to fight it out with the Danes. Hence they could seize only those Jews who voluntarily opened their doors. They found exactly 477 people, out of a total of more then 7,800, at home and willing to let them in. A few days before the date of doom, a German shipping agent, Georg F. Duckwitz, having probably been tipped off by Best himself, had revealed the whole plan to Danish government officials, who, in turn, had hurriedly informed the heads of the Jewish community. They, in marked contrast to Jewish leaders in other countries, had then communicated the news openly in the synagogues on the occasion of the New Year services. The Jews had just time enough to leave their apartments and go into hiding, which was very easy in Denmark, because, in the words of the judgment, "all sections of the Danish people, from the King down to simple citizens," stood ready to receive them.

They might have remained in hiding until the end of the war if the Danes had not been blessed with Sweden as a neighbor. It seemed reasonable to ship the Jews to Sweden, and this was done with the help of the Danish fishing fleet. The cost of transportation for people without means—about a hundred dollars per person—was paid largely by wealthy Danish citizens, and that was perhaps the most astounding feat of all, since this was a time when Jews were paying for their own deportation, when the rich among them were paying fortunes for exit permits (in Holland, Slovakia, and, later, in Hungary) either by bribing the local authorities or by negotiating "legally" with the S.S., who accepted only hard currency and sold exit permits, in Holland, to the tune of five or ten thousand dollars per person. Even in places where Jews met

---

3. A camp for certain classes of prisoners who were to receive special treatment.

with genuine sympathy and a sincere willingness to help, they had to pay for it, and the chances poor people had of escaping were nil.

It took the better part of October to ferry all the Jews across the five to fifteen miles of water that separates Denmark from Sweden. The Swedes received 5,919 refugees, of whom at least 1,000 were of German origin, 1,310 were half-Jews, and 686 were non-Jews married to Jews. (Almost half the Danish Jews seem to have remained in the country and survived the war in hiding.) The non-Danish Jews were better off than ever before, they all received permission to work. The few hundred Jews whom the German police had been able to arrest were shipped to Theresienstadt. They were old or poor people, who either had not received the news in time or had not been able to comprehend its meaning. In the ghetto, they enjoyed greater privileges than any other group because of the never-ending "fuss" made about them by Danish institutions and private persons. Forty-eight persons died, a figure that was not particularly high, in view of the average age of the group. When everything was over, it was the considered opinion of Eichmann that "for various reasons the action against the Jews in Denmark has been a failure," whereas the curious Dr. Best declared that "the objective of the operation was not to seize a great number of Jews but to clean Denmark of Jews, and this objective has now been achieved."

Politically and psychologically, the most interesting aspect of this incident is perhaps the role played by the German authorities in Denmark, their obvious sabotage of orders from Berlin. It is the only case we know of in which the Nazis met with *open* native resistance, and the result seems to have been that those exposed to it changed their minds. They themselves apparently no longer looked upon the extermination of a whole people as a matter of course. They had met resistance based on principle, and their "toughness" had melted like butter in the sun, they had even been able to show a few timid beginnings of genuine courage. That the ideal of "toughness," except, perhaps, for a few half-demented brutes, was nothing but a myth of self-deception, concealing a ruthless desire for conformity at any price, was clearly revealed at the Nuremberg Trials, where the defendants accused and betrayed each other and assured the world that they "had always been against it" or claimed, as Eichmann was to do, that their best qualities had been "abused" by their superiors. (In Jerusalem, he accused "those in power" of having abused his "obedience." "The subject of a good government is lucky, the subject of a bad government is unlucky. I had no luck.") The atmosphere had changed, and although most of them must have known that they were doomed, not a single one of them had the guts to defend the Nazi ideology. Werner Best claimed at Nuremberg that he had played a complicated double role and that it was thanks to him that the Danish officials had been warned of the impending catastrophe; documentary evidence showed, on the contrary, that he himself had proposed the Danish operation in Berlin, but he explained that this was all part of the game. He was extradited to Denmark and there condemned to death, but he appealed the sentence, with surprising results; because of "new evidence," his sentence was commuted to five years in prison, from which he was released soon afterward. He must have been able to prove to the satisfaction of the Danish court that he really had done his best.

1963

Michael Arlen

GRIEFSPEAK

When Robert Kennedy was shot, the reporters were already there—the cameras, the lights, the heralds of the people standing upon chairs and tabletops, trailing wire and tape recorders, the black tubelike microphones stretched out arclike into the room (that kitchen). He was shot, and it was real—a life, a death, the *event*, confusion, motion, people running, the man on the floor, young girls in straw hats crying, policemen, people pushing, yelling, the man on the floor, dying, dead, dying. It was all there for a moment, for a short while (it is perhaps this moment, stretching out forward and backward in our imaginations, that now remains), this event, this God knows what it was, and then the hands of people began to touch it. Inevitably, one will say. Inevitably. *Je suis touriste ici moi-même.*[1] Soft hands, tired hands, sincere hands, oh those sincere hands touching it (and him), poking it, rubbing it, plumping it, patting it. The men in rumpled shirts, hastily buttoned coats, were on the tabletops (our witness-technicians), on sidewalks, in corridors, holding aloft their microphones and cameras. The other men, in better-fitting suits and serious expressions, were inside some room—it all seemed like the same room (some underground chamber), but it could not have been. They talked—to each other, out to us. "I suppose," said Charles Kuralt, "we ought to be giving some comfort to the country in times like this. . . ." Griefspeak. "I don't know about the rest of you," John Chancellor said, "but in the last few hours I seem to have lost part of my self-respect." Somebody handed a piece of paper to Edwin Newman. "I have some new information here," said Edwin Newman. "Sirhan has ordered two books." He looked at the piece of paper. "One is by Madame Blavatsky. The other is by C. W. Ledbetter. We don't know the meaning of this as yet. Or whether it has anything to do with the alleged, the—

---

1. "I'm a tourist here myself."

we want to remind you that all this is tentative, because in this country no man is guilty until judged by a court of law." They talked of irony awhile. It was a time for discovering ironies. It was ironic about "the family." It was ironic that he was shot at the time of his "greatest triumph." It was ironic that "he had spoken out so often against violence." It was ironic that only yesterday he had rescued one of his children from the surf at Malibu. "Excuse me, John," said Edwin Newman. "We just got this on Madame Blavatsky. She lived from 1830 to 1891 and was a Theosophist—although I want to say that we're not yet sure what relationship, if any, this has to the . . ." "I just thought of another irony," said Sander Vanocur. "In a speech just a few days ago Senator Kennedy said, 'We were killed in Oregon. I hope to be resurrected in Los Angeles.'" A psychiatrist appeared at some point to say he thought the violence in our country derived from showing films like *Bonnie and Clyde*. There were discussions across the nation about brain surgery. "I think each one of us is guilty," Mike Wallace said. Telephone calls from prominent people to the family were duly logged and reported. CBS announced telephone calls from President Johnson, Vice-President Humphrey, Governor Reagan, and Senator Mansfield. NBC announced telephone calls from President Johnson, Governor Reagan, Robert McNamara, and Mayor Daley. The police chief of Los Angeles appeared before the press and spoke calmly and effectively. "I'll give you boys a moment to get your machines adjusted," he said before beginning. Prime Minister Harold Wilson was interviewed via satellite. The BBC announced "prayers for America." There were scenes of the coffin being placed into the plane in Los Angeles and being taken out of the plane in New York. There was an interview with Cardinal Cushing. Lord Harlech said that violence in America had become "an international scandal." There were interviews by satellite with former Prime Minister Macmillan and Romain Gary. There was an interview with an old gentleman seated in a chair upon a lawn, who had once been Robert Kennedy's grade-school principal. "I remember him very well," he said. "One day he brought one of these animals to school with him. A little pig, I think it was." They showed us the inside of the cathedral. Norman Mailer was standing at vigil around the coffin. "I think Nick Katzenbach is there," said an announcer. "There is George Plimpton. Ed, is that George Plimpton?" "No," said Edwin Newman. "But I think Mayor Lindsay is now coming down the aisle." They showed us Ethel Kennedy. Mrs. Robert Kennedy was seated in church beside a child, her head bent low over the child. The camera zoomed in. "How does one comfort a child at a time like that?" asked Edwin Newman. There was a Chevrolet ad. A man and a girl were seated on top of a convertible singing about "the big new savings on all regular Chevrolets." The song ended. "And on Chevelles too," the girl said with a wink. CBS was running off a

Western. A man and a very blond girl with frizzy hair were hiding behind some curtains. There were advance shots of the route to be taken by the funeral procession. There were shots of tree-lined streets in Washington. "He often enjoyed a brisk walk down streets such as these," a voice informed us. There were pictures of the White House. Leonard Bernstein, it was announced, would handle the musical arrangements. There were more scenes of Ethel Kennedy in church. There were scenes at Union Station. There were distant views of Hickory Hill. "He liked fresh air," said another voice. Jerome Wilson of WCBS had a number of people seated around him. "I realize it is hard for you to talk at a time like this," he said to a young man who had been a Citizen for Kennedy, "but what did you young people *especially* like about him?" The young man thought for a moment. "We especially liked him because he had leverage," he said. "I think I can say that business would have been happy with Robert Kennedy," said Roswell Gilpatric. They showed us the crowds lined up outside Saint Patrick's. "Young and old alike are joined in grief," an announcer said. They showed us the flags flying on the office buildings on Park Avenue. Some were flying at half-mast, some were not. "The flags fly at half-mast all across this mourning city," an announcer said. They showed us people filing by the coffin. They showed us the train on the way to Washington. They showed us the railroad stations. They showed us the train tracks. "What was it . . . what was the *mystique* that the Kennedy family had?" asked Johnny Carson. "Ethel Kennedy must now begin to build anew," Gabe Pressman said. The Red Cross, one learned, had already distributed four thousand cups of cold drink. They showed us the Lincoln Memorial. They showed us the Joint Chiefs of Staff. "As time goes on," said Louis Nizer, "the pain from his passing will diminish." They showed us John Kennedy's widow in church. I watched the television on and off those days, and the strangely disconnected people on the streets, in crowds, in the lines that rolled around Saint Patrick's down to Forty-fourth Street. "The people have come by to pay their last respects," the voices said. "The people file by . . . the people wait . . . the people touch . . . the people grieve. . . ." They showed us that throng of men and women waiting outside the station at Trenton—kids with American flags, parents in their shirtsleeves, the long train tracks, the crowded platform. "The question," the announcer said, "is how much the train has been slowed down en route from Newark." No. The question all along (we had known three days ago who had been killed) was who was dead.

1969

THE READER

1. *What is the significance of the title?*
2. *Isolate a sample of Arlen's sentences. How many of them are cast in the*

form of straight observation—"It is . . ." There are . . ." "Mike Wallace said . . ."? What effect does this distribution have on the essay?

3. Whitman (p. 696) writes about Lincoln. The differences between his memorial and Arlen's essay are many and great. List a few. To what degree do they seem to be caused by differences between the two events? To what degree do they seem to be caused by differences between the two writers? Is it possible to distinguish the causes in that way? If not, what causes can you distinguish?

4. Is this essay an indictment of television?

THE WRITER

1. Arlen's essay is one long paragraph. Is there any organizational scheme? Is there a topic sentence, either explicit or implicit? Where might Arlen have made paragraph divisions? What would he have gained and what would he have lost by making more divisions?

2. Mostly Arlen describes and quotes. What are the signs of his distress about the treatment of Robert Kennedy's assassination?

3. Write a paragraph answering the question at the end.

4. Read Whitman's account of the death of Lincoln (p. 696). Then, imagining that TV had already been invented in Lincoln's time, write an account, similar to Arlen's, of how TV might have covered Lincoln's death.

5. Imitating Arlen's style, write an account as it might be presented on TV of some event you have witnessed.

Michael Herr

"HOW BAD DO YOU WANT TO GET TO DANANG?"

You could be in the most protected space in Vietnam and still know that your safety was provisional, that early death, blindness, loss of legs, arms or balls, major and lasting disfigurement—the whole rotten deal—could come in on the freaky-fluky as easily as in the so-called expected ways, you heard so many of those stories it was a wonder anyone was left alive to die in firefights and mortar-rocket attacks. After a few weeks, when the nickel had jarred loose and dropped and I saw that everyone around me was carrying a gun, I also saw that any one of them could go off at any time, putting you where it wouldn't matter whether it had been an accident or not. The roads were mined, the trails booby-trapped, satchel charges and grenades blew up jeeps and movie theaters, the VC[1] got work inside all the camps as shoeshine boys and laundresses and honey-dippers,[2] they'd starch your fatigues and burn your shit and then go home and mortar your area. Saigon and Cholon and Danang held such hostile vibes that you felt you were being dry-sniped every time someone looked at you, and choppers fell out of the sky like fat poisoned birds a hundred times a day. After a while I couldn't get on one without thinking that I must be out of my fucking mind.

Fear and motion, fear and standstill, no preferred cut there, no way even to be clear about which was really worse, the wait or the delivery. Combat spared far more men than it wasted, but everyone suffered the time between contact, especially when they were going out every day looking for it; bad going on foot, terrible in trucks and APC's,[3] awful in helicopters, the worst, traveling so fast toward something so frightening. I can remember times when I went half dead with my fear of the motion, the speed and direction already fixed and pointed one way. It was painful enough just flying "safe" hops between firebases and lz's;[4] if you were ever on a helicopter that had been hit by ground fire your deep, perpetual chopper anxiety was guaranteed. At least actual contact when it was happening would draw long ragged strands of energy out of you, it was juicy, fast and refining, and traveling toward it was hollow, dry, cold and steady, it never let you alone. All you could do was look around at the other people on board and see if they were as scared and numbed out as you were. If it looked like they weren't you thought they were insane, if it looked like they were it made you feel a lot worse.

I went through that thing a number of times and only got a fast return on my fear once, a too classic hot landing with the heat coming from the trees about 300 yards away, sweeping machine-gun fire that sent men head down into swampy water, running on their hands and knees toward the grass where it wasn't blown flat by the rotor blades, not much to be running for but better than nothing. The helicopter pulled up before we'd all gotten out, leaving the last few men to jump twenty feet down between the guns across the paddy and the gun on the chopper door. When we'd all reached the cover of the wall and the captain had made a check, we were amazed to see that no one had even been hurt, except for one man who'd sprained both his ankles jumping. Afterwards, I remembered that I'd been down in the muck worrying about leeches. I guess you could say that I was refusing to accept the situation.

"Boy, you sure get offered some shitty choices," a Marine once said to me, and I couldn't help but feel that what he really meant was that you didn't get offered any at all. Specifically, he was just talking about a couple of C-ration cans, "dinner," but considering his young life you

---

1. Vietcong.
2. Latrine cleaners.

3. Armored Personnel Carriers.
4. Landing zones.

couldn't blame him for thinking that if he knew one thing for sure, it was that there wsn't anybody he wanted to thank for his food, but he was grateful that there was no one anywhere who cared less about what *he* wanted. There wsn't anybody he wanted to thank for his food, but he was grateful that he was still alive to eat it, that the motherfucker hadn't scarfed him up first. He hadn't been anything but tired and scared for six months and he'd lost a lot, mostly people, and seen far too much, but he was breathing in and breathing out, some kind of choice all by itself.

He had one of those faces, I saw that face at least a thousand times at a hundred bases and camps, all the youth sucked out of the eyes, the color drawn from the skin, cold white lips, you knew he wouldn't wait for any of it to come back. Life had made him old, he'd live it out old. All those faces, sometimes it was like looking into faces at a rock concert, locked in, the event had them; or like students who were very heavily advanced, serious beyond what you'd call their years if you didn't know for yourself what the minutes and hours of those years were made up of. Not just like all the ones you saw who looked like they couldn't drag their asses through another day of it. (How do you feel when a nineteen-year-old kid tells you from the bottom of his heart that he's gotten too old for this kind of shit?) Not like the faces of the dead or wounded either, they could look more released than overtaken. These were the faces of boys whose whole lives seemed to have backed up on them, they'd be a few feet away but they'd be looking back at you over a distance you knew you'd never really cross. We'd talk, sometimes fly together, guys going out on R&R,[5] guys escorting bodies, guys who'd flipped over into extremes of peace or violence. Once I flew with a kid who was going home, he looked back down once at the ground where he'd spent the year and spilled his whole load of tears. Sometimes you even flew with the dead.

Once I jumped on a chopper that was full of them. The kid in the Op[6] shack had said that there would be a body on board, but he'd been given some wrong information. "How bad do you want to get to Danang?" he'd asked me, and I'd said, "Bad."

When I saw what was happening I didn't want to get on, but they'd made a divert and a special landing for me, I had to go with the chopper I'd drawn, I was afraid of looking squeamish. (I remember, too, thinking that a chopper full of dead men was far less likely to get shot down than one full of living.) They weren't even in bags. They'd been on a truck near one of the firebases in the DMZ[7] that was firing support for Khe Sanh, and the truck had hit a Command-detonated mine, then they'd been rocketed. The Marines were always running out of things, even food, ammo and medicine, it wsn't so strange that they'd run out of bags too. The men had been wrapped around in ponchos, some of them carelessly fastened with plastic straps, and loaded on board. There was a

5. Rest and Recreation.   7. Demilitarized Zone.
6. Operations.

small space cleared for me between one of them and the door gunner, who looked pale and so tremendously furious that I thought he was angry with me and I couldn't look at him for a while. When we went up the wind blew through the ship and made the ponchos shake and tremble until the one next to me blew back in a fast brutal flap, uncovering the face. They hadn't even closed his eyes for him.

The gunner started hollering as loud as he could, "Fix it! Fix it!," maybe he thought the eyes were looking at him, but there wasn't anything I could do. My hand went there a couple of times and I couldn't, and then I did. I pulled the poncho tight, lifted his head carefully and tucked the poncho under it, and then I couldn't believe that I'd done it. All during the ride the gunner kept trying to smile, and when we landed at Dong Ha he thanked me and ran off to get a detail. The pilots jumped down and walked away without looking back once, like they'd never seen that chopper before in their lives. I flew the rest of the way to Danang in a general's plane.

1977

Kildare Dobbs

THE SHATTERER OF WORLDS

Before that morning in 1945 only a few conventional bombs, none of which did any great damage, had fallen on the city. Fleets of U.S. bombers had, however, devastated many cities round about, and Hiroshima had begun a program of evacuation which had reduced its population from 380,000 to some 245,000. Among the evacuees were Emiko and her family.

"We were moved out to Otake, a town about an hour's train-ride out of the city," Emiko told me. She had been a fifteen-year-old student in 1945. Fragile and vivacious, versed in the gentle traditions of the tea ceremony and flower arrangement, Emiko still had an air of the frail school-child when I talked with her. Every day, she and her sister Hideko used to commute into Hiroshima to school. Hideko was thirteen. Their father was an antique-dealer and he owned a house in the city, although it was empty now. Tetsuro, Emiko's thirteen-year-old brother, was at the Manchurian front with the Imperial Army. Her mother was kept busy looking after the children, for her youngest daughter Eiko was sick with heart trouble, and rations were scarce. All of them were undernourished.

The night of August 5, 1945, little Eiko was dangerously ill. She was not expected to live. Everybody took turns watching by her bed, soothing her by massaging her arms and legs. Emiko retired at 8:30 (most Japanese people go to bed early) and at midnight was roused to take her turn with the sick girl. At 2 A.M. she went back to sleep.

While Emiko slept, the *Enola Gay*, a U.S. B-29 carrying the world's first operational atom bomb, was already in the air. She had taken off from the Pacific island of Iwo Jima at 1:45 A.M., and now Captain William Parsons, U.S.N. ordnance expert, was busy in her bomb-hold with the final assembly of Little Boy. Little Boy looked much like an outsize T.N.T. block-buster but the crew knew there was something different about him. Only Parsons and the pilot, Colonel Paul Tibbets, knew exactly in what manner Little Boy was different. Course was set for Hiroshima.

Emiko slept.

On board the *Enola Gay* co-pilot Captain Robert Lewis was writing up his personal log. "After leaving Iwo," he recorded, "we began to pick up some low stratus and before very long we were flying on top of an under-cast. Outside of a thin, high cirrus and the low stuff, it's a very beautiful day."

Emiko and Hideko were up at six in the morning. They dressed in the uniform of their women's college—white blouse, quilted hat, and black skirt—breakfasted and packed their aluminum lunch-boxes with white rice and eggs. These they stuffed into their shoulder bags as they hurried for the seven-o'clock train to Hiroshima. Today there would be no classes. Along with many women's groups, high school students, and others, the sisters were going to work on demolition. The city had begun a project of clearance to make fire-breaks in its downtown huddle of wood and paper buildings.

It was a lovely morning.

While the two young girls were at breakfast, Captain Lewis, over the Pacific, had made an entry in his log. "We are loaded. The bomb is now alive, and it's a funny feeling knowing it's right in back of you. Knock wood!"

In the train Hideko suddenly said she was hungry. She wanted to eat her lunch. Emiko dissuaded her: she'd be much hungrier later on. The two sisters argued, but Hideko at last agreed to keep her lunch till later. They decided to meet at the main station that afternoon and catch the five-o'clock train home. By now they had arrived at the first of Hiroshima's three stations. This was where Hideko got off, for she was to work in a different area from her sister. "Sayonara!" she called. "Goodbye." Emiko never saw her again.

There had been an air-raid at 7 A.M., but before Emiko arrived at Hiroshima's main station, two stops farther on, the sirens had sounded the all-clear. Just after eight, Emiko stepped off the train, walked through the station, and waited in the morning sunshine for her streetcar.

At about the same moment Lewis was writing in his log. "There'll be a short intermission while we bomb our target."

It was hot in the sun, Emiko saw a class-mate and greeted her. Together they moved back into the shade of a high concrete wall to chat. Emiko looked up at the sky and saw, far up in the cloudless blue, a single B-29.

It was exactly 8:10 A.M. The other people waiting for the streetcar saw it too and began to discuss it anxiously. Emiko felt scared. She felt that at all costs she must go on talking to her friend. Just as she was thinking this, there was a tremendous greenish-white flash in the sky. It was far brighter than the sun. Emiko afterwards remembered vaguely that there was a roaring or a rushing sound as well, but she was not sure, for just at that moment she lost consciousness.

"About 15 seconds after the flash," noted Lewis, 30,000 feet high and several miles away, "there were two very distinct slaps on the ship from the blast and the shock wave. That was all the physical effect we felt. We turned the ship so that we could observe the results."

When Emiko came to, she was lying on her face about forty feet away from where she had been standing. She was not aware of any pain. Her first thought was: "I'm alive!" She lifted her head slowly and looked about her. It was growing dark. The air was seething with dust and black smoke. There was a smell of burning. Emiko felt something trickle into her eyes, tested it in her mouth. Gingerly she put a hand to her head, then looked at it. She saw with a shock that it was covered with blood.

She did not give a thought to Hideko. It did not occur to her that her sister who was in another part of the city could possibly have been in danger. Like most of the survivors, Emiko assumed she had been close to a direct hit by a conventional bomb. She thought it had fallen on the post-office next to the station. With a hurt child's panic, Emiko, streaming with blood from gashes in her scalp, ran blindly in search of her mother and father.

The people standing in front of the station had been burned to death instantly (a shadow had saved Emiko from the flash). The people inside the station had been crushed by falling masonry. Emiko heard their faint cries, saw hands scrabbling weakly from under the collapsed platform. All around her the maimed survivors were running and stumbling away from the roaring furnace that had been a city. She ran with them toward the mountains that ring the landward side of Hiroshima.

From the *Enola Gay*, the strangers from North America looked down at their handiwork. "There, in front of our eyes," wrote Lewis, "was without a doubt the greatest explosion man had ever witnessed. The city was nine-tenths covered with smoke of a boiling nature, which seemed to indicate buildings blowing up, and a large white cloud which in less than three minutes reached 30,000 feet, then went to at least 50,000 feet."

Far below, on the edge of this cauldron of smoke, at a distance of some 2,500 yards from the blast's epicenter, Emiko ran with the rest of the living. Some who could not run limped or dragged themselves along. Others were carried. Many, hideously burned, were screaming with pain; when they tripped they lay where they had fallen. There was a man whose face had been ripped open from mouth to ear, another whose forehead was a gaping wound. A young soldier was running with a foot-long splinter of bamboo protruding from one eye. But these, like Emiko, were the lightly wounded.

Some of the burned people had been literally roasted. Skin hung from their flesh like sodden tissue paper. They did not bleed but plasma dripped from their seared limbs.

The *Enola Gay*, mission completed, was returning to base. Lewis sought words to express his feelings, the feelings of all the crew. "I might say," he wrote, "I might say 'My God! What have we done?'"

Emiko ran. When she had reached the safety of the mountain she remembered that she still had her shoulder bag. There was a small first-aid kit in it and she applied ointment to her wounds and to a small cut in her left hand. She bandaged her head.

Emiko looked back at the city. It was a lake of fire. All around her the burned fugitives cried out in pain. Some were scorched on one side only. Others, naked and flayed, were burned all over. They were too many to help and most of them were dying. Emiko followed the walking wounded along a back road, still delirious, expecting suddenly to meet her father and mother.

The thousands dying by the roadside called feebly for help or water. Some of the more lightly injured were already walking in the other direction, back towards the flames. Others, with hardly any visible wounds, stopped, turned ashy pale, and died within minutes. No one knew then that they were victims of radiation.

Emiko reached the suburb of Nakayama.

Far off in the *Enola Gay*, Lewis, who had seen none of this, had been writing, "If I live a hundred years, I'll never get those few minutes out of my mind. Looking at Captain Parsons, why he is as confounded as the rest, and he is supposed to have known everything and expected this to happen. . . ."

At Nakayama, Emiko stood in line at a depot where rice-balls were being distributed. Though it distressed her that the badly maimed could hardly feed themselves, the child found she was hungry. It was about 6 P.M. now. A little farther on, at Gion, a farmer called her by name. She did not recognize him, but it seemed he came monthly to her home to collect manure. The farmer took Emiko by the hand, led her to his own house, where his wife bathed her and fed her a meal of white rice. Then the child continued on her way. She passed another town where there were hundreds of injured. The dead were being hauled away in trucks. Among the injured a woman of about forty-five was waving frantically and muttering to herself. Emiko brought this woman a little water in a pumpkin leaf. She felt guilty about it; the schoolgirls had been warned not to give water to the seriously wounded. Emiko comforted herself with the thought that the woman would die soon anyway.

At Koi, she found standing-room in a train. It was heading for Otake with a full load of wounded. Many were put off at Ono, where there was a hospital; and two hours later the train rolled into Otake station. It was around 10 P.M.

A great crowd had gathered to look for their relations. It was a nightmare, Emiko remembered years afterwards; people were calling their dear kinfolk by name, searching frantically. It was necessary to call them by name, since most were so disfigured as to be unrecognizable. Doctors in the town council offices stitched Emiko's head-wounds. The place was crowded with casualties lying on the floor. Many died as Emiko watched.

The town council authorities made a strange announcement. They said a new and mysterious kind of bomb had fallen in Hiroshima. People were advised to stay away from the ruins.

Home at midnight, Emiko found her parents so happy to see her that they could not even cry. They could only give thanks that she was safe. Then they asked, "Where is your sister?"

For ten long days, while Emiko walked daily one and a half miles to have her wounds dressed with fresh gauze, her father searched the rubble of Hiroshima for his lost child. He could not have hoped to find her alive. All, as far as the eye could see, was a desolation of charred ashes and wreckage, relieved only by a few jagged ruins and by the seven estuarial rivers that flowed through the waste delta. The banks of these rivers were covered with the dead and in the rising tidal waters floated thousands of corpses. On one broad street in the Hakushima district the crowds who had been thronging there were all naked and scorched cadavers. Of thousands of others there was no trace at all. A fire several times hotter than the surface of the sun had turned them instantly to vapor.

On August 11 came the news that Nagasaki had suffered the same fate as Hiroshima; it was whispered that Japan had attacked the United States mainland with similar mysterious weapons. With the lavish circumstantiality of rumor, it was said that two out of a fleet of six-engined trans-Pacific bombers had failed to return. But on August 15, speaking for the first time over the radio to his people, the Emperor Hirohito announced his country's surrender. Emiko heard him. No more bombs! she thought. No more fear! The family did not learn till June the following year that this very day young Tetsuro had been killed in action in Manchuria.

Emiko's wounds healed slowly. In mid-September they had closed with a thin layer of pinkish skin. There had been s shortage of antiseptics and Emiko was happy to be getting well. Her satisfaction was short-lived. Mysteriously she came down with diarrhea and high fever. The fever continued for a month. Then one day she started to bleed from the gums, her mouth and throat became acutely inflamed, and her hair started to fall out. Through her delirium the child heard the doctors whisper by her pillow that she could not live. By now the doctors must have known that ionizing radiation caused such destruction of the blood's white cells that victims were left with little or no resistance against infection.

Yet Emiko recovered.

The wound on her hand, however, was particularly troublesome and did not heal for a long time.

As she got better, Emiko began to acquire some notion of the fearful scale of the disaster. Few of her friends and acquaintances were still alive. But no one knew precisely how many had died in Hiroshima. To this day the claims of various agencies conflict.

According to General Douglas MacArthur's headquarters, there were 78,150 dead and 13,083 missing.[1] The United States Atomic Bomb Casualty Commission claims there were 79,000 dead. Both sets of figures are probably far too low. There's reason to believe that at the time of the surrender Japanese authorities lied about the number of survivors, exaggerating it to get extra medical supplies. The Japanese welfare ministry's figures of 260,000 dead and 163,263 missing may well be too high. But the very order of such discrepancies speaks volumes about the scale of the catastrophe. The dead were literally uncountable.

This appalling toll of human life had been exacted from a city that had been prepared for air attack in a state of full wartime readiness. All civil-defense services had been overwhelmed from the first moment and it was many hours before any sort of organized rescue and relief could be put into effect.

It's true that single raids using so-called conventional weapons on other cities such as Tokyo and Dresden inflicted far greater casualties. And that it could not matter much to a victim whether he was burnt alive by a fire-storm caused by phosphorus, or by napalm or by nuclear fission. Yet in the whole of human history so savage a massacre had never before been inflicted with a single blow. And modern thermonuclear weapons are upwards of 1,000 times more powerful and deadly than the Hiroshima bomb.

The white scar I saw on Emiko's small, fine-boned hand was a tiny

---

1. Douglas MacArthur (1880–1964): American army officer, Allied Supreme Commander in the Southwest Pacific (1942) and of occupied Japan following World War II (1945–51).

metaphor, a faint but eloquent reminder of the scar on humanity's conscience.

1968

Joan Didion

ON KEEPING A NOTEBOOK

"'That woman Estelle,'" the note reads, "'is partly the reason why George Sharp and I are separated today.' *Dirty crepe-de-Chine wrapper, hotel bar, Wilmington RR, 9:45 a.m. August Monday morning.*"

Since the note is in my notebook, it presumably has some meaning to me. I study it for a long while. At first I have only the most general notion of what I was doing on an August Monday morning in the bar of the hotel across from the Pennsylvania Railroad station in Wilmington, Delaware (waiting for a train? missing one? 1960? 1961? why Wilmington?), but I do remember being there. The woman in the dirty crepe-de-Chine wrapper had come down from her room for a beer, and the bartender had heard before the reason why George Sharp and she were separated today. "Sure," he said, and went on mopping the floor. "You told me." At the other end of the bar is a girl. She is talking, pointedly, not to the man beside her but to a cat lying in the triangle of sunlight cast through the open door. She is wearing a plaid silk dress from Peck & Peck, and the hem is coming down.

Here is what it is: the girl has been on the Eastern Shore, and now she is going back to the city, leaving the man beside her, and all she can see ahead are the viscous summer sidewalks and the 3 a.m. long-distance calls that will make her lie awake and then sleep drugged through all the steaming mornings left in August (1960? 1961?). Because she must go directly from the train to lunch in New York, she wishes that she had a safety pin for the hem of the plaid silk dress, and she also wishes that she could forget about the hem and the lunch and stay in the cool bar that smells of disinfectant and malt and make friends with the woman in the crepe-de-Chine wrapper. She is afflicted by a little self-pity, and she wants to compare Estelles. That is what that was all about.

Why did I write it down? In order to remember, of course, but exactly what was it I wanted to remember? How much of it actually happened? Did any of it? Why do I keep a notebook at all? It is easy to deceive oneself on all those scores. The impulse to write things down is a peculiarly compulsive one, inexplicable to those who do not share it, useful only accidentally, only secondarily, in the way that any compulsion tries to justify itself. I suppose that it begins or does not begin in the cradle. Although I have felt compelled to write things down since I was five years old, I doubt that my daughter ever will, for she is a singularly blessed and accepting child, delighted with life exactly as life presents itself to her, unafraid to go to sleep and unafraid to wake up. Keepers of private notebooks are a different breed altogether, lonely and resistant rearrangers of things, anxious malcontents, children afflicted apparently at birth with some presentiment of loss.

My first notebook was a Big Five tablet, given to me by my mother with the sensible suggestion that I stop whining and learn to amuse myself by writing down my thoughts. She returned the tablet to me a few years ago; the first entry is an account of a woman who believed herself to be freezing to death in the Arctic night, only to find, when day broke, that she had stumbled onto the Sahara Desert, where she would die of the heat before lunch. I have no idea what turn of a five-year-old's mind could have prompted so insistently "ironic" and exotic a story, but it does reveal a certain predilection for the extreme which has dogged me into adult life; perhaps if I were analytically inclined I would find it a truer story than any I might have told about Donald Johnson's birthday party or the day my cousin Brenda put Kitty Litter in the aquarium.

So the point of my keeping a notebook has never been, nor is it now, to have an accurate factual record of what I have been doing or thinking. That would be a different impulse entirely, an instinct for reality which I sometimes envy but do not possess. At no point have I ever been able successfully to keep a diary; my approach to daily life ranges from the grossly negligent to the merely absent, and on those few occasions when I have tried dutifully to record a day's events, boredom has so overcome me that the results are mysterious at best. What is this business about "shopping, typing piece, dinner with E, depressed"? Shopping for what? Typing what piece? Who is E? Was this "E" depressed, or was I depressed? Who cares?

In fact I have abandoned altogether that kind of pointless entry; instead I tell what some would call lies. "That's simply not true," the members of my family frequently tell me when they come up against my memory of a shared event. "The party was *not* for you, the spider was *not* a black widow, *it wasn't that way at all.*" Very likely they are right, for not only have I always had trouble distinguishing between what happened and what merely might have happened, but I remain unconvinced that the distinction, for my purposes, matters. The cracked crab that I recall having for lunch the day my father came home from Detroit in 1945 must certainly be embroidery, worked into the day's pattern to lend verisimilitude; I was ten years old and would not now remember the cracked crab. The day's events did not turn on cracked crab. And yet it is precisely that fictitious crab that makes me see the afternoon all over again, a home movie run all too often, the father bearing gifts, the child weeping, an exercise in family love and guilt. Or that is what it was to me. Similarly, perhaps it never did snow that August in Vermont; perhaps there never were flurries in the night wind, and maybe no one else felt the ground hardening and summer already dead even as we pretended to bask in it, but that was how it felt to me, and it might as well have snowed, could have snowed, did snow.

How it felt to me: that is getting closer to the truth about a notebook. I sometimes delude myself about why I keep a notebook, imagine that some thrifty virtue derives from preserving everything observed. See enough and write it down, I tell myself, and then some morning when the world seems drained of wonder, some day when I am only going through the motions of doing what I am supposed to do, which is write—on that bankrupt morning I will simply open my notebook and there it will all be, a forgotten account with accumulated interest, paid passage back to the world out there: dialogue overheard in hotels and elevators and at the hatcheck counter in Pavillon (one middle-aged man shows his hat check to another and says, "That's my old football number"); impressions of Bettina Aptheker and Benjamin Sonnenberg and Teddy ("Mr. Acapulco") Stauffer; careful aperçus about tennis bums and failed fashion models and Greek shipping heiresses, one of whom taught me a significant lesson (a lesson I could have learned from F. Scott Fitzgerald, but perhaps we all must meet the very rich for ourselves) by asking, when I arrived to interview her in her orchid-filled sitting room on the second day of a paralyzing New York blizzard, whether it was snowing outside.

I imagine, in other words, that the notebook is about other people. But of course it is not. I have no real business with what one stranger said to another at the hat-check counter in Pavillon; in fact I suspect that the line "That's my old football number" touched not my own imagination at all, but merely some memory of something once read, probably "The Eighty-Yard Run." Nor is my concern with a woman in a dirty crepe-de-Chine wrapper in a Wilmington bar. My stake is always, of course, in the unmentioned girl in the plaid silk dress. Remember what it was to be me: that is always the point.

It is a difficult point to admit. We are brought up in the ethic that others, any others, all others, are by definition more interesting than ourselves; taught to be diffident, just this side of self-effacing. ("You're the least important person in the room and don't forget it," Jessica Mitford's governess would hiss in her ear on the advent of any social occasion; I copied that into my notebook because it is only recently that I have been able to enter a room without hearing some such phrase in my inner ear.) Only the very young and the very old may recount their dreams at breakfast, dwell upon self, interrupt with memories of beach picnics and favorite Liberty lawn dresses and the rainbow trout in a creek near Colorado Springs. The rest of us are expected, rightly, to affect absorption in other people's favorite dresses, other people's trout.

And so we do. But our notebooks give us away, for however dutifully we record what we see around us, the common denominator of all we see is always, transparently, shamelessly, the implacable "I." We are not talking here about the kind of notebook that is patently for public consumption, a structural conceit for binding together a series of graceful *pensées;*[1] we are talking about something private, about bits of the mind's string too short to use, an indiscriminate and erratic assemblage with meaning only for its maker.

And sometimes even the maker has difficulty with the meaning. There does not seem to be, for example, any point in my knowing for the rest of my life that, during 1964, 720 tons of soot fell on every square mile of New York City, yet there it is in my notebook, labeled "FACT." Nor do I really need to remember that Ambrose Bierce liked to spell Leland Stanford's[2] name "£eland $tanford" or that "smart women almost always wear black in Cuba," a fashion hint without much potential for practical application. And does not the relevance of these notes seem marginal at best?:

> In the basement museum of the Inyo County Courthouse in Independence, California, sign pinned to a mandarin coat: "This MANDARIN COAT was often worn by Mrs. Minnie S. Brooks when giving lectures on her TEAPOT COLLECTION."
> Redhead getting out of car in front of Beverly Wilshire Hotel, chinchilla stole, Vuitton bags with tags reading:
>
> MRS LOU FOX
> HOTEL SAHARA
> VEGAS

Well, perhaps not entirely marginal. As a matter of fact, Mrs. Minnie S. Brooks and her MANDARIN COAT pull me back into my own childhood, for although I never knew Mrs. Brooks and did not visit Inyo County until I was thirty, I grew up in just such a world, in houses cluttered with Indian relics and bits of gold ore and ambergris and the souvenirs my Aunt Mercy Farnsworth brought back from the Orient. It is a long way from that world to Mrs. Lou Fox's world, where we all live now, and is it not just as well to remember that? Might not Mrs. Minnie S. Brooks help me to remember what I am? Might not Mrs. Lou Fox help me to remember what I am not?

---

1. Thoughts, reflections.
2. A nineteenth-century American millionaire.

But sometimes the point is harder to discern. What exactly did I have in mind when I noted down that it cost the father of someone I know $650 a month to light the place on the Hudson in which he lived before the Crash?[3] What use was I planning to make of this line by Jimmy Hoffa: "I may have my faults, but being wrong ain't one of them"? And although I think it interesting to know where the girls who travel with the Syndicate have their hair done when they find themselves on the West Coast, will I ever make suitable use of it? Might I not be better off just passing it on to John O'Hara? What is a recipe for sauerkraut doing in my notebook? What kind of magpie keeps this notebook? *"He was born the night the Titanic went down."* That seems a nice enough line, and I even recall who said it, but is it not really a better line in life than it could ever be in fiction?

But of course that is exactly it: not that I should ever use the line, but that I should remember the woman who said it and the afternoon I heard it. We were on her terrace by the sea, and we were finishing the wine left from lunch, trying to get what sun there was, a California winter sun. The woman whose husband was born the night the *Titanic* went down wanted to rent her house, wanted to go back to her children in Paris. I remember wishing that I could afford the house, which cost $1,000 a month. "Someday you will," she said lazily. "Someday it all comes." There in the sun on her terrace it seemed easy to believe in someday, but later I had a low-grade afternoon hangover and ran over a black snake on the way to the supermarket and was flooded with inexplicable fear when I heard the checkout clerk explaining to the man ahead of me why she was finally divorcing her husband. "He left me no choice," she said over and over as she punched the register. "He has a little seven-month-old baby by her, he left me no choice." I would like to believe that my dread then was for the human condition, but of course it was for me, because I wanted a baby and did not then have one and because I wanted to own the house that cost $1,000 a month to rent and because I had a hangover.

It all comes back. Perhaps it is difficult to see the value in having one's self back in that kind of mood, but I do see it; I think we are well advised to keep on nodding terms with the people we used to be whether we find them attractive company or not. Otherwise they turn up unannounced and surprise us, come hammering on the mind's door at 4 a.m. of a bad night and demand to know who deserted them, who betrayed them, who is going to make amends. We forget all too soon the things we thought we could never forget. We forget the loves and the betrayals alike, forget what we whispered and what we screamed, forget who we were. I have already lost touch with a couple of people I used to be; one of them, a seventeen-year-old, presents little threat, although it would be of some

3. The stock market crash of 1929.

interest to me to know again what it feels like to sit on a river levee drinking vodka-and-orange-juice and listening to Les Paul and Mary Ford and their echoes sing "How High the Moon" on the car radio. (You see I still have the scenes, but I no longer perceive myself among those present, no longer could even improvise the dialogue.) The other one, a twenty-three-year-old, bothers me more. She was always a good deal of trouble, and I suspect she will reappear when I least want to see her, skirts too long, shy to the point of aggravation, always the injured party, full of recriminations and little hurts and stories I do not want to hear again, at once saddening me and angering me with her vulnerability and ignorance, an apparition all the more insistent for being so long banished.

It is a good idea, then, to keep in touch, and I suppose that keeping in touch is what notebooks are all about. And we are all on our own when it comes to keeping those lines open to ourselves: your notebook will never help me, nor mine you. "So what's new in the whiskey business?" What could that possibly mean to you? To me it means a blonde in a Pucci bathing suit sitting with a couple of fat men by the pool at the Beverly Hills Hotel. Another man approaches, and they all regard one another in silence for a while. "So what's new in the whiskey business?" one of the fat men finally says by way of welcome, and the blonde stands up, arches one foot and dips it in the pool, looking all the while at the cabaña where Baby Pignatari is talking on the telephone. That is all there is to that, except that several years later I saw the blonde coming out of Saks Fifth Avenue in New York with her California complexion and a voluminous mink coat. In the harsh wind that day she looked old and irrevocably tired to me, and even the skins in the mink coat were not worked the way they were doing them that year, not the way she would have wanted them done, and there is the point of the story. For a while after that I did not like to look in the mirror, and my eyes would skim the newspapers and pick out only the deaths, the cancer victims, the premature coronaries, the suicides, and I stopped riding the Lexington Avenue IRT[4] because I noticed for the first time that all the strangers I had seen for years—the man with the seeing-eye dog, the spinster who read the classified pages every day, the fat girl who always got off with me at Grand Central— looked older than they once had.

It all comes back. Even that recipe for sauerkraut: even that brings it back. I was on Fire Island when I first made that sauerkraut, and it was raining, and we drank a lot of bourbon and ate the sauerkraut and went to bed at ten, and I listened to the rain and the Atlantic and felt safe. I made the sauerkraut again last night and it did not make me feel any safer, but that is, as they say, another story.

1968

---

4. A New York City subway line; one of its stops is the Grand Central railway terminal.

THE READER

1. What distinction does Didion make between a diary and a notebook?
2. What uses does a notebook have for Didion?
3. Didion says she uses her notebook to "tell what some would call lies." Why does she do this? Would some people call these things truths? Why?
4. What does Didion imply is the difference between a notebook and a diary?
5. Is the visit Didion describes in "On Going Home" (p. 69) an effort to keep in touch with the people we used to be (p. 733)? One test would be to check "On Going Home" for phrases and observations like those she quotes from her notebooks. Are there any?

THE WRITER

1. Didion says that "we are brought up in the ethic that others . . . are by definition more interesting than ourselves." Explain whether she believes this can be harmful to one's development as a writer.
2. Didion says: "How it felt to me: that is getting closer to the truth about a notebook." What writing strategies does she use to convey "how it felt"?
3. Try keeping a notebook for a week, jotting down the sort of things that Didion does. At the end of the week, take one or two of your entries and expand on them, as Didion does with the entries on Mrs. Minnie S. Brooks and Mrs. Lou Fox.
4. Read Woolf's "The New Biography" (p. 738), and write a brief comparison of Woolf's metaphors of granite and rainbow with Didion's distinction between the facts of "what happened and what merely might have happened." Are the two writers talking about the same basic distinction or not?
5. References to her notebooks give you a lot of biographical detail about Didion's life, as do her essays "On Going Home" (p. 69) and "Georgia O'Keeffe" (p. 1098). Restricting yourself to that information, sketch out as much of her biography as you can, and then write a paragraph of that biography. For advice about writing a biography, you might consult Woolf's "The New Biography" (p. 738).

Virginia Woolf

THE NEW BIOGRAPHY

"The aim of biography," said Sir Sidney Lee, who had perhaps read and written more lives than any man of his time, "is the truthful transmission of personality," and no single sentence could more neatly split up into two parts the whole problem of biography as it presents itself to us today. On the one hand there is truth; on the other there is personality. And if we think of truth as something of granite-like solidity and of personality as something of rainbow-like intangibility and reflect that the aim of biography is to weld these two into one seamless whole, we shall admit that the problem is a stiff one and that we need not wonder if biographers have for the most part failed to solve it.

For the truth of which Sir Sidney speaks, the truth which biography demands, is truth in its hardest, most obdurate form; it is truth as truth is to be found in the British Museum; it is truth out of which all vapor of falsehood has been pressed by the weight of research. Only when truth had been thus established did Sir Sidney Lee use it in the building of his monument; and no one can be so foolish as to deny that the piles he raised of such hard facts, whether one is called Shakespeare or King Edward the Seventh, are worthy of all our respect. For there is a virtue in truth; it has an almost mystic power. Like radium, it seems able to give off forever and ever grains of energy, atoms of light. It stimulates the mind, which is endowed with a curious susceptibility in this direction as no fiction, however artful or highly colored, can stimulate it. Truth being thus efficacious and supreme, we can only explain the fact that Sir Sidney's life of Shakespeare is dull, and that his life of Edward the Seventh is unreadable, by supposing that though both are stuffed with truth, he failed to choose those truths which transmit personality. For in order that the light of personality may shine through, facts must be manipulated; some must be brightened; others shaded; yet, in the process, they must never lose their integrity. And it is obvious that it is easier to obey these precepts by considering that the true life of your subject shows itself in action which is evident rather than in that inner life of thought and emotion which meanders darkly and obscurely through the hidden channels of the soul. Hence, in the old days, the biographer chose the easier path. A life, even when it was lived by a divine, was a series of exploits. The biographer, whether he was Izaak Walton or Mrs. Hutchinson or that unknown writer who is often so suprisingly eloquent on tombstones and memorial tablets, told a tale of battle and victory. With their stately phrasing and their deliberate artistic purpose, such records transmit personality with a formal sincerity which is perfectly satisfactory of its kind. And so, perhaps, biography might have pursued its way, draping the robes decorously over the recumbent figures of the dead, had there not arisen toward the end of the eighteenth century one of those curious men of genius who seem able to break up the stiffness into which the company has fallen by speaking in his natural voice. So Boswell spoke. So we hear booming out from Boswell's page the voice of Samuel Johnson. "No, sir; stark insensibility," we hear him say. Once we have heard those words we are aware that there is an incalculable presence among us which will go on ringing and reverberating in widening circles however times may change and ourselves. All the draperies and decencies of biography fall to the ground. We can no longer maintain that life consists in actions only or in works. It consists in personality. Something has been liberated beside which all else seems cold and colorless. We are freed from a servitude which is now seen to be intolerable. No longer need we pass solemnly and stiffly from camp to council chamber. We may sit, even with the great and good, over the table and talk.

Through the influence of Boswell, presumably, biography all through the nineteenth century concerned itself as much with the lives of the sedentary as with the lives of the active. It sought painstakingly and devotedly to express not only the outer life of work and activity but the inner life of emotion and thought. The uneventful lives of poets and painters were written out as lengthily as the lives of soldiers and states-men. But the Victorian biography was a parti-colored, hybrid, monstrous birth. For though truth of fact was observed as scrupulously as Boswell observed it, the personality which Boswell's genius set free was ham-pered and distorted. The convention which Boswell had destroyed set-tled again, only in a different form, upon biographers who lacked his art. Where the Mrs. Hutchinsons and the Izaak Waltons had wished to prove that their heroes were prodigies of courage and learning the Victorian biographer was dominated by the idea of goodness. Noble, upright, chaste, severe; it is thus that the Victorian worthies are presented to us. The figure is almost always above life size in top hat and frock coat, and the manner of presentation becomes increasingly clumsy and laborious. For lives which no longer express themselves in action take shape in innumerable words. The conscientious biographer may not tell a fine tale with a flourish, but must toil through endless labyrinths and embarrass himself with countless documents. In the end he produces an amorphous mass, a life of Tennyson, or of Gladstone, in which we go seeking disconsolately for voice or laughter, for curse or anger, for any trace that this fossil was once a living man. Often, indeed, we bring back some invaluable trophy, for Victorian biographies are laden with truth; but always we rummage among them with a sense of the prodigious waste, of the artistic wrongheadedness of such a method.

With the twentieth century, however, a change came over biography, as it came over fiction and poetry. The first and most visible sign of it was the difference in size. In the first twenty years of the new century biographies must have lost half their weight. Mr. Strachey compressed four stout Victorians into one slim volume; M. Maurois boiled the usual two volumes of a Shelley life into one little book the size of a novel. But the diminution of size was only the outward token of an inward change. The point of view had completely altered. If we open one of the new school of biographies its bareness, its emptiness makes us at once aware that the author's relation to his subject is different. He is no longer the serious and sympathetic companion, toiling even slavishly in the footsteps of his hero. Whether friend or enemy, admiring or critical, he is an equal. In any case, he preserves his freedom and his right to independent judgment. Moreover, he does not think himself constrained to follow every step of the way. Raised upon a little eminence which his independence has made for him, he sees his subject spread about him. He chooses; he synthesizes; in short, he has ceased to be the chronicler; he has become an artist.

Few books illustrate the new attitude to biography better than *Some People*,[1] by Harold Nicolson. In his biographies of Tennyson and of Byron Mr. Nicolson followed the path which had been already trodden by Mr. Strachey and others. Here he has taken a step on his own initiative. For here he has devised a method of writing about people and about himself as though they were at once real and imaginary. He has succeeded remarkably, if not entirely, in making the best of both worlds. *Some People* is not fiction because it has the substance, the reality of truth. It is not biography because it has the freedom, the artistry of fiction. And if we try to discover how he has won the liberty which enables him to present us with these extremely amusing pages we must in the first place credit him with having had the courage to rid himself of a mountain of illusion. An English diplomat is offered all the bribes which usually induce people to swallow humbug in large doses with composure. If Mr. Nicolson wrote about Lord Curzon it should have been solemnly. If he mentioned the Foreign Office it should have been respectfully. His tone toward the world of Bognors[2] and Whitehall should have been friendly but devout. But thanks to a number of influences and people, among whom one might mention Max Beerbohm and Voltaire, the attitude of the bribed and docile official has been blown to atoms. Mr. Nicolson laughs. He laughs at Lord Curzon; he laughs at the

---

1. "Nine semi-biographical sketches concerning which the author says, 'Many are purely imaginary. Such truths as they may contain are only half-truths'" (*Book Review Digest*, 1927).

2. Bognors: a seaside resort in Sussex featuring many convalescent homes; Whitehall: the British civil-service administration, much of it housed on the street of this name.

Foreign Office; he laughs at himself. And since his laughter is the laughter of the intelligence it has the effect of making us take the people he laughs at seriously. The figure of Lord Curzon concealed behind the figure of a drunken valet is touched off with merriment and irreverence; yet of all the studies of Lord Curzon which have been written since his death none makes us think more kindly of that preposterous but, it appears, extremely human man.

So it would seem as if one of the great advantages of the new school to which Mr. Nicolson belongs is the lack of pose, humbug, solemnity. They approach their bigwigs fearlessly. They have no fixed scheme of the universe, no standard of courage or morality to which they insist that he shall conform. The man himself is the supreme object of their curiosity. Further, and it is this chiefly which has so reduced the bulk of biography, they maintain that the man himself, the pith and essence of his character, shows itself to the observant eye in the tone of a voice, the turn of a head, some little phrase or anecdote picked up in passing. Thus in two subtle phrases, in one passage of brilliant description, whole chapters of the Victorian volume are synthesized and summed up. *Some People* is full of examples of this new phase of the biographer's art. Mr. Nicolson wants to describe a governess and he tells us that she had a drop at the end of her nose and made him salute the quarter-deck. He wants to describe Lord Curzon, and he makes him lose his trousers and recite "Tears, Idle Tears." He does not cumber himself with a single fact about them. He waits till they have said or done something characteristic, and then he pounces on it with glee. But, though he waits with an intention of pouncing which might well make his victims uneasy if they guessed it, he lays suspicion by appearing himself in his own proper person in no flattering light. He has a scrubby dinner jacket, he tells us; a pink bumptious face, curly hair, and a curly nose. He is as much the subject of his own ironies and observation as they are. He lies in wait for his own absurdities as artfully as for theirs. Indeed, by the end of the book we realize that the figure which has been most completely and most subtly displayed is that of the author. Each of the supposed subjects holds up in his or her small bright diminishing mirror a different reflection of Harold Nicolson. And though the figure thus revealed is not noble or impressive or shown in a very heroic attitude, it is for these very reasons extremely like a real human being. It is thus, he would seem to say, in the mirrors of our friends, that we chiefly live.

To have contrived this effect is a triumph not of skill only, but of those positive qualities which we are likely to treat as if they were negative— freedom from pose, from sentimentality, from illusion. And the victory is definite enough to leave us asking what territory it has won for the art of biography. Mr. Nicolson has proved that one can use many of the devices of fiction in dealing with real life. He has shown that a little fiction mixed with fact can be made to transmit personality very effectively. But some objections or qualifications suggest themselves. Undoubtedly the figures in *Some People* are all rather below life size. The irony with which they are treated, though it has its tenderness, stunts their growth. It dreads nothing more than that one of these little beings should grow up and become serious or perhaps tragic. And, again, they never occupy the stage for more than a few brief moments. They do not want to be looked at very closely. They have not a great deal to show us. Mr. Nicolson makes us feel, in short, that he is playing with very dangerous elements. An incautious movement and the book will be blown sky high. He is trying to mix the truth of real life and the truth of fiction. He can only do it by using no more than a pinch of either. For though both truths are genuine, they are antagonistic; let them meet and they destroy each other. Even here, where the imagination is not deeply engaged, when we find people whom we know to be real like Lord Oxford or Lady Colefax, mingling with Miss Plimsoll and Marstock, whose reality we doubt, the one casts suspicion upon the other. Let it be fact, one feels, or let it be fiction; the imagination will not serve under two masters simultaneously.

And here we again approach the difficulty which, for all his ingenuity, the biographer still has to face. Truth of fact and truth of fiction are incompatible; yet he is now more than ever urged to combine them. For it would seem that the life which is increasingly real to us is the fictitious life; it dwells in the personality rather than in the act. Each of us is more Hamlet, Prince of Denmark, than he is John Smith of the Corn Exchange. Thus, the biographer's imagination is always being stimulated to use the novelists's art of arrangement, suggestion, dramatic effect to expound the private life. Yet if he carries the use of fiction too far, so that he disregards the truth, or can only introduce it with incongruity, he loses both worlds; he has neither the freedom of fiction nor the substance of fact. Boswell's astonishing power over us is based largely upon his obstinate veracity, so that we have implicit belief in what he tells us. When Johnson says "No, sir; stark insensibility," the voice has a ring in it because we have been told, soberly and prosaically, a few pages earlier, that Johnson "was entered a Commoner of Pembroke, on the 31st of October, 1728, being then in his nineteenth year." We are in the world of brick and pavement; of birth, marriage, and death; of Acts of Parliament; of Pitt and Burke and Sir Joshua Reynolds. Whether this is a more real world than the world of Bohemia and Hamlet and Macbeth we doubt; but the mixture of the two is abhorrent.

Be that as it may we can assure ourselves by a very simple experiment that the days of Victorian biography are over. Consider one's own life; pass under review a few years that one has actually lived. Conceive how Lord Morley would have expounded them; how Sir Sidney Lee would have documented them; how strangely all that has been most real in them would have slipped through their fingers. Nor can we name the biographer whose art is subtle and bold enough to present that queer amalgamation of dream and reality, that perpetual marriage of granite and rainbow. His method still remains to be discovered. But Mr. Nicolson with his mixture of biography and autobiography, of fact and fiction, of Lord Curzon's trousers and Miss Plimsoll's nose, waves his hand airily in a possible direction.

1958

THE READER

1. Explain the significance of the metaphors of "granite" and "rainbow" in Woolf's first paragraph.
2. Woolf says that for some biographers a life was "a series of exploits." What more does she think a good biography should be? Why?
3. Why does Woolf object to the presentation of figures "above life size" in biography?
4. What are the differences between a biographer who is a "chronicler" and one who is an "artist"?
5. Explain why Woolf thinks that "truth of fact and truth of fiction are incompatible."

THE WRITER

1. What does Woolf mean when she says that in the new school of biography "the figure which has been most completely and most subtly displayed is that of the author"? How "truthful" can such a biography be?
2. Why does Woolf call the new biography an "art"? How does it differ from the biography of "facts" displaying "the weight of research"?
3. Make a list of facts and actions that would be important in writing a brief autobiography or a biography of someone you know well. Make a list of personality traits for yourself or the other person selected. Then, using Woolf's essay as a guide, write a brief autobiographical or biographical sketch.
4. How far does Woolf follow her theory of what a good biography should be in her sketch of her father, Leslie Stephen (p. 146)?

Frances FitzGerald

REWRITING AMERICAN HISTORY

Those of us who grew up in the fifties believed in the permanence of our American-history textbooks. To us as children, those texts were the truth of things: they were American history. It was not just that we read them before we understood that not everything that is printed is the truth, or the whole truth. It was that they, much more than other books, had the demeanor and trappings of authority. They were weighty volumes. They spoke in measured cadences: imperturbable, humorless, and as distant as Chinese emperors. Our teachers treated them with respect, and we paid them abject homage by memorizing a chapter a week. But now the textbook histories have changed, some of them to such an extent that an adult would find them unrecognizable.

One current junior-high-school American history begins with a story about a Negro cowboy called George McJunkin. It appears that when McJunkin was riding down a lonely trail in New Mexico one cold spring morning in 1925 he discovered a mound containing bones and stone implements, which scientists later proved belonged to an Indian civilization ten thousand years old. The book goes on to say that scientists now believe there were people in the Americas at least twenty thousand years ago. It discusses the Aztec, Mayan, and Incan civilizations and the meaning of the word "culture" before introducing the European explorers.

Another history text—this one for the fifth grade—begins with the story of how Henry B. Gonzalez, who is a member of Congress from Texas, learned about his own nationality. When he was ten years old, his teacher told him he was an American because he was born in the United States. His grandmother, however, said, "The cat was born in the oven. Does that make him bread?" After reporting that Mr. Gonzalez eventually went to college and law school, the book explains that "the melting pot idea hasn't worked out as some thought it would," and that now "some people say that the people of the United States are more like a salad bowl than a melting pot."

Poor Columbus! He is a minor character now, a walk-on in the middle of American history. Even those books that have not replaced his picture with a Mayan temple or an Iroquois mask do not credit him with discovering America—even for the Europeans. The Vikings, they say, preceded him to the New World, and after that the Europeans, having lost or forgotten their maps, simply neglected to cross the ocean again for five hundred years. Columbus is far from being the only personage to have suffered from time and revision. Captain John Smith, Daniel Boone, and Wild Bill Hickok—the great self-promoters of American history—have all but disappeared, taking with them a good deal of the romance of the American frontier. General Custer has given way to Chief Crazy Horse; General Eisenhower no longer liberates Europe single-handed; and, indeed, most generals, even to Washington and Lee, have faded away, as old soldiers do, giving place to social reformers such as William Lloyd Garrison and Jacob Riis. A number of black Americans have risen to prominence: not only George Washington Carver but Frederick Douglass and Martin Luther King, Jr. W. E. B. Du Bois now invariably accompanies Booker T. Washington. In addition, there is a mystery man called Crispus Attucks, a fugitive slave about whom nothing seems to be known for certain except that he was a victim of the Boston Massacre and thus became one of the first casualties of the American Revolution. Thaddeus Stevens has been reconstructed—his character changed, as it were, from black to white, from cruel and vindictive to persistent and sincere. As for Teddy Roosevelt, he now champions the issue of conservation instead of charging up San Juan Hill. No single President really stands out as a hero, but all Presidents—except certain unmentionables in the second half of the nineteenth century—seem to have done as well as could be expected, given difficult circumstances.

Of course, when one thinks about it, it is hardly surprising that modern scholarship and modern perspectives have found their way into children's books. Yet the changes remain shocking. Those who in the sixties complained of the bland optimism, the chauvinism, and the materialism of their old civics text did so in the belief that, for all their protests, the texts would never change. The thought must have had something reassuring about it, for that generation never noticed when its complaints began to take effect and the songs about radioactive rainfall and houses made of ticky-tacky began to appear in the textbooks. But this is what happened.

The history texts now hint at a certain level of unpleasantness in American history. Several books, for instance, tell the story of Ishi, the last "wild" Indian in the continental United States, who, captured in 1911 after the massacre of his tribe, spent the final four and a half years of his life in the University of California's museum of anthropology, in San Francisco. At least three books show the same stunning picture of the breaker boys, the child coal miners of Pennsylvania—ancient children with deformed bodies and blackened faces who stare stupidly out from the entrance to a mine. One book quotes a soldier on the use of torture in the American campaign to pacify the Philippines at the beginning of the century. A number of books say that during the American Revolution the patriots tarred and feathered those who did not support them, and drove many of the loyalists from the country. Almost all the present-day history books note that the United States interned Japanese-Americans in detention camps during the Second World War.

Ideologically speaking, the histories of the fifties were implacable, seamless. Inside their covers, America was perfect: the greatest nation in the world, and the embodiment of democracy, freedom, and technological progress. For them, the country never changed in any important way: its values and its political institutions remained constant from the time of the American Revolution. To my generation—the children of the fifties —these texts appeared permanent just because they were so self-contained. Their orthodoxy, it seemed, left no handholds for attack, no lodging for decay. Who, after all, would dispute the wonders of technology or the superiority of the English colonists over the Spanish? Who would find fault with the pastorale of the West or the Old South? Who would question the anti-Communist crusade? There was, it seemed, no point in comparing these visions with reality, since they were the public truth and were thus quite irrelevant to what existed and to what anyone privately believed. They were—or so it seemed—the permanent expression of mass culture in America.

But now the texts have changed, and with them the country that American children are growing up into. The society that was once uniform is now a patchwork of rich and poor, old and young, men and women, blacks, whites, Hispanics, and Indians. The system that ran so smoothly by means of the Constitution under the guidance of benevolent conductor Presidents is now a rattletrap affair. The past is no highway to the present; it is a collection of issues and events that do not fit together and that lead in no single direction. The word "progress" has been replaced by the word "change": children, the modern texts insist, should learn history so that they can adapt to the rapid changes taking place around them. History is proceeding in spite of us. The present, which was once portrayed in the concluding chapters as a peaceful haven of scientific advances and Presidential inaugurations, is now a tangle of problems: race problems, urban problems, foreign-policy problems, problems of pollution, poverty, energy depletion, youthful rebellion, assassination, and drugs. Some books illustrate these problems dramatically. One, for instance, contains a picture of a doll half buried in a mass of untreated sewage; the caption reads, "Are we in danger of being overwhelmed by the products of our society and wastage created by their production? Would you agree with this photographer's interpretation?" Two books show the same picture of an old black woman sitting in a straight chair in a dingy room, her hands folded in graceful resignation; the surrounding text discusses the problems faced by the urban poor and by the aged who depend on Social Security. Other books present current problems less starkly. One of the texts concludes sagely:

Problems are part of life. Nations face them, just as people face them, and try to solve them. And today's Americans have one great advantage over past generations. Never before have Americans been so well equipped to solve their problems. They have today the means to conquer poverty, disease, and ignorance. The technetronic age has put that power into their hands.

Such passages have a familiar ring. Amid all the problems, the deus ex machina[1] of science still dodders around in the gloaming of pious hope.

Even more surprising than the emergence of problems is the discovery that the great unity of the texts has broken. Whereas in the fifties all texts represented the same political view, current texts follow no pattern of orthodoxy. Some books, for instance, portray civil-rights legislation as a series of actions taken by a wise, paternal government; others convey some suggestion of the social upheaval involved and make mention of such people as Stokely Carmichael and Malcolm X.[2] In some books, the Cold War has ended; in others, it continues, with Communism threatening the free nations of the earth.

The political diversity in the books is matched by a diversity of pedagogical approach. In addition to the traditional narrative histories, with their endless streams of facts, there are so-called "discovery," or "inquiry," texts, which deal with a limited number of specific issues in American history. These tests do not pretend to cover the past; they focus on particular topics, such as "stratification in Colonial society" or "slavery and the American Revolution," and illustrate them with documents from primary and secondary sources. The chapters in these books amount to something like case studies, in that they include testimony from people with different perspectives or conflicting views on a single subject. In addition, the chapters provide background information, explanatory notes, and a series of questions for the student. The questions are the heart of the matter, for when they are carefully selected they force students to think much as historians think: to define the point of view of the speaker, analyze the ideas presented, question the relationship between events, and so on. One text, for example, quotes Washington, Jefferson, and John Adams on the question of foreign alliances and then asks, "What did John Adams assume that the international situation would be after the American Revolution? What did Washington's attitude toward the French alliance seem to be? How do you account for his attitude?" Finally, it asks, "Should a nation adopt a policy toward alliances and cling to it consistently, or should it vary its policies toward other countries as circumstances change?" In these books, history is clearly not a list of agreed-upon facts or a sermon on politics but a babble of voices and a welter of events which must be ordered by the historian.

1. God from a machine. A reference to early plays in which a god, lowered to the stage by mechanical means, solved the drama's problems; thus, an artificial solution to a difficulty.

2. Radical black leaders of the 1960s.

In matters of pedagogy, as in matters of politics, there are not two sharply differentiated categories of books; rather, there is a spectrum. Politically, the books run from moderate left to moderate right; pedagogically, they run from the traditional history sermons, through a middle ground of narrative texts with inquiry-style questions and of inquiry texts with long stretches of narrative, to the most rigorous of case-study books. What is common to the current texts—and makes all of them different from those of the fifties—is their engagement with the social sciences. In eighth-grade histories, the "concepts" of social sciences make fleeting appearances. But these "concepts" are the very foundation stones of various elementary-school social-studies series. The 1970 Harcourt Brace Jovanovich[3] series, for example, boasts in its preface of "a horizontal base or ordering of conceptual schemes" to match its "vertical arm of behavioral themes." What this means is not entirely clear, but the books do proceed from easy questions to hard ones, such as—in the sixth-grade book—"How was interaction between merchants and citizens different in the Athenian and Spartan social systems?" Virtually all the American-history texts for older children include discussions of "role," "status," and "culture." Some of them stage debates between eminent social scientists in roped-off sections of the text; some include essays on economics or sociology; some contain pictures and short biographies of social scientists of both sexes and of diverse races. Many books seem to accord social scientists a higher status than American Presidents.

Quite as striking as these political and pedagogical alterations is the change in the physical appearance of the texts. The schoolbooks of the fifties showed some effort in the matter of design: they had maps, charts, cartoons, photographs, and an occasional four-color picture to break up the columns of print. But beside the current texts they look as naïve as Soviet fashion magazines. The print in the fifties books is heavy and far too black, the colors muddy. The photographs are conventional news shots—portraits of Presidents in three-quarters profile, posed "action" shots of soldiers. The other illustrations tend to be Socialist-realist-style[4] drawings (there are a lot of hefty farmers with hoes in the Colonial-period chapters) or incredibly vulgar made-for-children paintings of patriotic events. One painting shows Columbus standing in full court dress on a beach in the New World from a perspective that could have belonged only to the Arawaks.[5] By contrast, the current texts are paragons of sophisticated modern design. They look not like *People* or *Family Circle* but, rather, like *Architectural Digest* or *Vogue*. * * * The amount of space given to illustrations is far greater than it was in the fifties; in fact, in

3. Major textbook publisher.
4. Socialist realism, which originated in the Soviet Union, is a style of art in which the communal labor of farmers and industrial workers is glorified in works of poster-like crudity.
5. American Indians, then inhabiting the Caribbean area.

certain "slow-learner" books the pictures far outweigh the text in importance. However, the illustrations have a much greater historical value. Instead of made-up paintings or anachronistic sketches, there are cartoons, photographs, and paintings drawn from the periods being treated. The chapters on the Colonial period will show, for instance, a ship's carved prow, a Revere bowl, a Copley[6] painting—a whole gallery of Early Americana. The nineteenth century is illustrated with nineteenth-century cartoons and photographs—and the photographs are all of high artistic quality. As for the twentieth-century chapters, they are adorned with the contents of a modern-art museum.

The use of all this art and high-quality design contains some irony. The nineteenth-century photographs of child laborers or urban slum apartments are so beautiful that they transcend their subjects. To look at them, or at the Victor Gatto painting of the Triangle shirtwaist-factory fire, is to see not misery or ugliness but an art object. In the modern chapters, the contrast between style and content is just as great: the color photographs of junk yards or polluted rivers look as enticing as Gourmet's photographs of food. The book that is perhaps the most stark in its description of modern problems illustrates the horrors of nuclear testing with a pretty Ben Shahn picture of the Bikini explosion,[7] and the potential for global ecological disaster with a color photograph of the planet swirling its mantle of white clouds. Whereas in the nineteen-fifties the texts were childish in the sense that they were naïve and clumsy, they are now childish in the sense that they are polymorphous-perverse. American history is not dull any longer; it is a sensuous experience.

The surprise that adults feel in seeing the changes in history texts must come from the lingering hope that there is, somewhere out there, an objective truth. The hope is, of course, foolish. All of us children of the twentieth century know, or should know, that there are no absolutes in human affairs, and thus there can be no such thing as perfect objectivity. We know that each historian in some degree creates the world anew and that all history is in some degree contemporary history. But beyond this knowledge there is still a hope for some reliable authority, for some fixed stars in the universe. We may know that journalists cannot be wholly unbiased and that "balance" is an imaginary point between two extremes, and yet we hope that Walter Cronkite will tell us the truth of things. In the same way, we hope that our history will not change—that we learned the truth of things as children. The texts, with their impersonal voices, encourage this hope, and therefore it is particularly dis-

6. The reference is to John Singleton Copley (1738–1815), greatest of the American old masters; he specialized in portraits and historical paintings.

7. The Bikini atoll, part of the Marshall Islands in the Pacific, was the site of American nuclear-bomb testing from 1946 to 1958. Ben Shahn (1898–1969) was an American painter and graphic artist with strong social and political concerns.

turbing to see how they change, and how fast.

Slippery history! Not every generation but every few years the content of American-history books for children changes appreciably. School-books are not, like trade books,[8] written and left to their fate. To stay in step with the cycles of "adoption"[9] in school districts across the country, the publishers revise most of their old texts or substitute new ones every three or four years. In the process of revision, they not only bring history up to date but make changes—often substantial changes—in the body of the work. History books for children are thus more contemporary than any other form of history. How should it be otherwise? Should students read histories written ten, fifteen, thirty years ago? In theory, the system is reasonable—except that each generation of children reads only one generation of schoolbooks. The transient history is those children's history forever—their particular version of America.

1979

---

8. Books written for a general audience, as opposed to textbooks.   9. Choice of required textbooks.

THE READER

1. What sorts of difference does FitzGerald find between the history textbooks of the fifties and those of today? In what ways—according to what she states or implies—have the texts been improved? Does she see any changes for the worse?
2. On p. 746, FitzGerald says that in the new texts, "the word 'progress' has been replaced by the word 'change.'" What is the difference between these two words? What does the replacement imply?
3. Is FitzGerald showing that the new textbooks give a truer account of American history?

THE WRITER

1. By "rewriting," does FitzGerald mean changing the facts of history? What is the relationship between the facts of history and history textbooks?
2. Why does FitzGerald give the story about George McJunkin (p. 744)? Was his discovery important?
3. Compare the process of "rewriting" or "revision" of history described by FitzGerald with Sommers's discussion of revision strategies (p. 344).
4. Write a brief account of the revisions you would like to see in some textbook you have used.

Edward Hallett Carr

THE HISTORIAN AND HIS FACTS

What is history? Lest anyone think the question meaningless or super-fluous, I will take as my text two passages relating respectively to the first and second incarnations of *The Cambridge Modern History*. Here is Acton in his report of October 1896 to the Syndics of the Cambridge University Press on the work which he had undertaken to edit:

> It is a unique opportunity of recording, in the way most useful to the greatest number, the fullness of the knowledge which the nineteenth century is about to bequeath. . . . By the judicious division of labor we should be able to do it, and to bring home to every man the last document, and the ripest conclusions of international research.
>
> Ultimate history we cannot have in this generation; but we can dispose of conventional history, and show the point we have reached on the road from one to the other, now that all information is within reach, and every problem has become capable of solution.

And almost exactly sixty years later Professor Sir George Clark, in his general introduction to the second *Cambridge Modern History*, commented on this belief of Acton and his collaborators that it would one day be possible to produce "ultimate history," and went on:

> Historians of a later generation do not look forward to any such prospect. They expect their work to be superseded again and again. They consider that knowledge of the past has come down through one or more human minds, has been "processed" by them, and therefore cannot consist of elemental and impersonal atoms which nothing can alter. . . . The exploration seems to be endless, and some impatient scholars take refuge in scepticism, or at least in the doctrine that, since all historical judgments involve persons and points of view, one is as good as another and there is no "objective" historical truth.

Where the pundits contradict each other so flagrantly the field is open to enquiry. I hope that I am sufficiently up-to-date to recognize that any-thing written in the 1890's must be nonsense. But I am not yet advanced enough to be committed to the view that anything written in the 1950's necessarily makes sense. Indeed, it may already have occurred to you that this enquiry is liable to stray into something even broader than the nature of history. The clash between Acton and Sir George Clark is a reflection of the change in our total outlook on society over the interval between these two pronouncements. Acton speaks out of the positive belief, the clear-eyed self-confidence of the later Victorian age; Sir George Clark echoes the bewilderment and distracted scepticism of the beat generation. When we attempt to answer the question, What is history?, our answer, consciously or unconsciously, reflects our own position in time, and forms part of our answer to the broader question, what view we take of the society in which we live. I have no fear that my subject may, on closer inspection, seem trivial. I am afraid only that I may seem presumptuous to have broached a question so vast and so important.

The nineteenth century was a great age for facts. "What I want," said Mr. Gradgrind in *Hard Times*, "is Facts. . . . Facts alone are wanted in life." Nineteenth-century historians on the whole agreed with him. When Ranke in the 1830's, in legitimate protest against moralizing history, remarked that the task of the historian was "simply to show how it really was [*wie es eigentlich gewesen*]" this not very profound aphorism had an astonishing success. Three generations of German, British, and even French historians marched into battle intoning the magic words, "*Wie es eigentlich gewesen*" like an incantation—designed, like most incantations, to save them from the tiresome obligation to think for themselves. The Positivists, anxious to stake out their claim for history as a science, contributed the weight of their influence to this cult of facts. First ascertain the facts, said the positivists, then draw your conclusions from them. In Great Britain, this view of history fitted in perfectly with the empiricist tradition which was the dominant strain in British philosophy from Locke to Bertrand Russell. The empirical theory of knowledge presupposes a complete separation between subject and object. Facts, like sense-impressions, impinge on the observer from outside, and are independent of his consciousness. The process of reception is passive: having received the data, he then acts on them. *The Shorter Oxford English Dictionary*, a useful but tendentious work of the empirical school, clearly marks the separateness of the two processes by defining a fact as "a datum of experience as distinct from conclusions." This is what may be called the common-sense view of history. History consists of a corpus of ascertained facts. The facts are available to the historian in documents, inscriptions, and so on, like fish on the fishmonger's slab. The historian collects them, takes them home, and cooks and serves them in whatever style appeals to him. Acton, whose culinary tastes were austere, wanted them served plain. In his letter of instructions to contributors to the first *Cambridge Modern History* he announced the requirement "that our Waterloo must be one that satisfies French and English, German and Dutch alike; that nobody can tell, without examining the list of authors where the Bishop of Oxford laid down the pen, and whether Fairbairn or Gasquet, Liebermann or Harrison took it up." Even Sir George Clark, critical as he was of Acton's attitude, himself contrasted the "hard core of facts" in history with the "surrounding pulp of disputable interpretation"—forgetting perhaps that the pulpy part of the fruit is more rewarding than the hard core. First get your facts straight, then plunge at your peril into the shifting sands of interpretation—that is the ultimate wisdom of the empirical, common-sense school of history. It recalls the favorite dictum of the great liberal journalist C. P. Scott: "Facts are sacred, opinion is free."

Now this clearly will not do. I shall not embark on a philosophical discussion of the nature of our knowledge of the past. Let us assume for present purposes that the fact that Caesar crossed the Rubicon and the fact that there is a table in the middle of the room are facts of the same or of a comparable order, that both these facts enter our consciousness in the same or in a comparable manner, and that both have the same objective character in relation to the person who knows them. But, even on this bold and not very plausible assumption, our argument at once runs into the difficulty that not all facts about the past are historical facts, or are treated as such by the historian. What is the criterion which distinguishes the facts of history from other facts about the past?

What is a historical fact? This is a crucial question into which we must look a little more closely. According to the common-sense view, there are certain basic facts which are the same for all historians and which form, so to speak, the backbone of history—the fact, for example, that the Battle of Hastings was fought in 1066. But this view calls for two observations. In the first place, it is not with facts like these that the historian is primarily concerned. It is no doubt important to know that the great battle was fought in 1066 and not in 1065 or 1067, and that it was fought at Hastings and not at Eastbourne or Brighton. The historian must not get these things wrong. But when points of this kind are raised, I am reminded of Housman's remark[1] that "accuracy is a duty, not a virtue." To praise a historian for his accuracy is like praising an architect for using well-seasoned timber or properly mixed concrete in his building. It is a necessary condition of his work, but not his essential function. It is precisely for matters of this kind that the historian is entitled to rely on what have been called the "auxiliary sciences" of history—archaeology, epigraphy, numismatics, chronology, and so forth. The historian is not required to have the special skills which enable the expert to determine the origin and period of a fragment of pottery or marble, or decipher an obscure inscription, or to make the elaborate astronomical calculations necessary to establish a precise date. These so-called basic facts which are the same for all historians commonly belong to the category of the raw materials of the historian rather than of history itself. The second observation is that the necessity to establish these basic facts rests not on any quality in the facts themselves, but on an *a priori* decision of the historian. In spite of C. P. Scott's motto, every journalist knows today

1. In the preface to his critical edition of Manilius, *Astronomicon*, an obscure Latin work.

that the most effective way to influence opinion is by the selection and arrangement of the appropriate facts. It used to be said that facts speak for themselves. This is, of course, untrue. The facts speak only when the historian calls on them: It is he who decides to which facts to give the floor, and in what order or context. It was, I think, one of Pirandello's characters who said that a fact is like a sack—it won't stand up till you've put something in it. The only reason why we are interested to know that the battle was fought at Hastings in 1066 is that historians regard it as a major historical event. It is the historian who has decided for his own reasons that Caesar's crossing of that petty stream, the Rubicon, is a fact of history, whereas the crossing of the Rubicon by millions of other people before or since interests nobody at all. The fact that you arrived in this building half an hour ago on foot, or on a bicycle, or in a car, is just as much a fact about the past as the fact that Caesar crossed the Rubicon. But it will probably be ignored by historians. Professor Talcott Parsons once called science "a selective system of cognitive orientations to reality." It might perhaps have been put more simply. But history is, among other things, that. The historian is necessarily selective. The belief in a hard core of historical facts existing objectively and independently of the interpretation of the historian is a preposterous fallacy, but one which it is very hard to eradicate.

Let us take a look at the process by which a mere fact about the past is transformed into a fact of history. At Stalybridge Wakes in 1850, a vendor of gingerbread, as the result of some petty dispute, was deliberately kicked to death by an angry mob. Is this a fact of history? A year ago I should unhesitatingly have said "no." It was recorded by an eyewitness in some little-known memoirs;[2] but I had never seen it judged worthy of mention by any historian. A year ago Dr. Kitson Clark cited it in his Ford lectures in Oxford. Does this make it into a historical fact? Not, I think, yet. Its present status, I suggest, is that it has been proposed for membership of the select club of historical facts. It now awaits a seconder and sponsors. It may be that in the course of the next few years we shall see this fact appearing first in footnotes, then in the text, of articles and books about nineteenth-century England, and that in twenty or thirty years' time it may be a well established historical fact. Alternatively, nobody may take it up, in which case it will relapse into the limbo of unhistorical facts about the past from which Dr. Kitson Clark has gallantly attempted to rescue it. What will decide which of these two things will happen? It will depend, I think, on whether the thesis or interpretation in support of which Dr. Kitson Clark cited this incident is accepted by other historians as valid and significant. Its status as a historical fact will turn on a question of interpretation. This element of interpretation enters into

2. Lord George Sanger: *Seventy Years a Showman* (London: J. M. Dent & Sons, 1926), pp. 188–9 [Carr's note].

every fact of history.

May I be allowed a personal reminiscence? When I studied ancient history in this university many years ago, I had as a special subject "Greece in the period of the Persian Wars." I collected fifteen or twenty volumes on my shelves and took it for granted that there, recorded in these volumes, I had all the facts relating to my subject. Let us assume—it was very nearly true—that those volumes contained all the facts about it that were then known, or could be known. It never occurred to me to enquire by what accident or process of attrition that minute selection of facts, out of all the myriad facts that must have once been known to somebody, had survived to become *the* facts of history. I suspect that even today one of the fascinations of ancient and mediaeval history is that it gives us the illusion of having all the facts at our disposal within a manageable compass: the nagging distinction between the facts of history and other facts about the past vanishes because the few known facts are all facts of history. As Bury, who had worked in both periods, said, "the records of ancient and mediaeval history are starred with lacunae." History has been called an enormous jig-saw with a lot of missing parts. But the main trouble does not consist of the lacunae. Our picture of Greece in the fifth century b.c. is defective not primarily because so many of the bits have been accidentally lost, but because it is, by and large, the picture formed by a tiny group of people in the city of Athens. We know a lot about what fifth-century Greece looked like to an Athenian citizen; but hardly anything about what it looked like to a Spartan, a Corinthian, or a Theban—not to mention a Persian, or a slave or other non-citizen resident in Athens. Our picture has been preselected and predetermined for us, not so much by accident as by people who were consciously or unconsciously imbued with a particular view and thought the facts which supported that view worth preserving. In the same way, when I read in a modern history of the Middle Ages that the people of the Middle Ages were deeply concerned with religion, I wonder how we know this, and whether it is true. What we know as the facts of mediaeval history have almost all been selected for us by generations of chroniclers who were professionally occupied in the theory and practice of religion, and who therefore thought it supremely important, and recorded everything relating to it, and not much else. The picture of the Russian peasant as devoutly religious was destroyed by the revolution of 1917. The picture of mediaeval man as devoutly religious, whether true or not, is indestructible, because nearly all the known facts about him were preselected for us by people who believed it, and wanted others to believe it, and a mass of other facts, in which we might possibly have found evidence to the contrary, has been lost beyond recall. The dead hand of vanished generations of historians, scribes, and chroniclers has determined beyond the possibility of appeal the pattern of the past. "The history we read," writes Professor Barraclough, himself trained as a mediaevalist, "though based on facts, is, strictly speaking, not factual at all, but a series of accepted judgments."

But let us turn to the different, but equally grave, plight of the modern historian. The ancient or mediaeval historian may be grateful for the vast winnowing process which, over the years, has put at his disposal a manageable corpus of historical facts. As Lytton Strachey said in his mischievous way, "ignorance is the first requisite of the historian, ignorance which simplifies and clarifies, which selects and omits." When I am tempted, as I sometimes am, to envy the extreme competence of colleagues engaged in writing ancient or mediaeval history, I find consolation in the reflection that they are so competent mainly because they are so ignorant of their subject. The modern historian enjoys none of the advantages of this built-in ignorance. He must cultivate this necessary ignorance for himself—the more so the nearer he comes to his own times. He has the dual task of discovering the few significant facts and turning them into facts of history, and of discarding the many insignificant facts as unhistorical. But this is the very converse of the nineteenth-century heresy that history consists of the compilation of a maximum number of irrefutable and objective facts. Anyone who succumbs to this heresy will either have to give up history as a bad job, and take to stamp-collecting or some other form of antiquarianism, or end in a madhouse. It is this heresy, which during the past hundred years has had such devastating effects on the modern historian, producing in Germany, in Great Britain, and in the United States a vast and growing mass of dry-as-dust factual histories, of minutely specialized monographs, of would-be historians knowing more and more about less and less, sunk without trace in an ocean of facts. It was, I suspect, this heresy—rather than the alleged conflict between liberal and Catholic loyalties—which frustrated Acton as a historian. In an early essay he said of his teacher Döllinger: "He would not write with imperfect materials, and to him the materials were always imperfect."[3] Acton was surely here pronouncing an anticipatory verdict on himself, on that strange phenomenon of a historian whom many would regard as the most distinguished occupant the Regius Chair of Modern History in this university has ever had—but who wrote no history. And Acton wrote his own epitaph in the introductory note to the first volume of the *Cambridge Modern History*, published just after his death, when he lamented that the requirements pressing on the historian "threaten to turn him from a man of letters into the compiler of an encyclopedia." Something had gone wrong. What had gone wrong was the belief in this untiring and unending accumulation of hard facts as the foundation of history, the belief that facts speak for themselves and that

3. Later Acton said of Döllinger that "it was given him to form his philosophy of history on the largest induction ever available to man" [Carr's note].

we cannot have too many facts, a belief at that time so unquestioning that few historians then thought it necessary—and some still think it unnecessary today—to ask themselves the question: What is history?

The nineteenth-century fetishism of facts was completed and justified by a fetishism of documents. The documents were the Ark of the Covenant in the temple of facts. The reverent historian approached them with bowed head and spoke of them in awed tones. If you find it in the documents, it is so. But what, when we get down to it, do these documents—the decrees, the treaties, the rent-rolls, the blue books, the official correspondence, the private letters and diaries—tell us? No document can tell us more than what the author of the document thought—what he thought had happened, what he thought ought to happen or would happen, or perhaps only what he wanted others to think he thought, or even only what he himself thought he thought. None of this means anything until the historian has got to work on it and deciphered it. The facts, whether found in documents or not, have still to be processed by the historian before he can make any use of them: the use he makes of them is, if I may put it that way, the processing process.

Let me illustrate what I am trying to say by an example which I happen to know well. When Gustav Stresemann, the Foreign Minister of the Weimar Republic, died in 1929, he left behind him an enormous mass—300 boxes full—of papers, official, semiofficial, and private, nearly all relating to the six years of his tenure of office as Foreign Minister. His friends and relatives naturally thought that a monument should be raised to the memory of so great a man. His faithful secretary Bernhardt got to work; and within three years there appeared three massive volumes, of some 600 pages each, of selected documents from the 300 boxes, with the impressive title Stresemanns Vermächtnis.[4] In the ordinary way the documents themselves would have moldered away in some cellar or attic and disappeared for ever; or perhaps in a hundred years or so some curious scholar would have come upon them and set out to compare them with Bernhardt's text. What happened was far more dramatic. In 1945 the documents fell into the hands of the British and the American governments, who photographed the lot and put the photostats at the disposal of scholars in the Public Record Office in London and in the National Archives in Washington, so that, if we have sufficient patience and curiosity, we can discover exactly what Bernhardt did. What he did was neither very unusual nor very shocking. When Stresemann died, his Western policy seemed to have been crowned with a series of brilliant successes—Locarno, the admission of Germany to the League of Nations, the Dawes and Young plans and the American loans, the withdrawal of allied occupation armies from the Rhineland. This seemed the

4. Stresemann's Legacy.

important and rewarding part of Stresemann's foreign policy; and it was not unnatural that it should have been over-represented in Bernhardt's selection of documents. Stresemann's Eastern policy, on the other hand, his relations with the Soviet Union, seemed to have led nowhere in particular; and, since masses of documents about negotiations which yielded only trivial results were not very interesting and added nothing to Stresemann's reputation, the process of selection could be more rigorous. Stresemann in fact devoted a far more constant and anxious attention to relations with the Soviet Union, and they played a far larger part in his foreign policy as a whole, than the reader of the Bernhardt selection would surmise. But the Bernhardt volumes compare favorably, I suspect, with many published collections of documents on which the ordinary historian implicitly relies.

This is not the end of my story. Shortly after the publication of Bernhardt's volumes, Hitler came into power. Stresemann's name was consigned to oblivion in Germany, and the volumes disappeared from circulation: many, perhaps most, of the copies must have been destroyed. Today *Stresemanns Vermächtnis* is a rather rare book. But in the West Stresemann's reputation stood high. In 1935 an English publisher brought out an abbreviated translation of Bernhardt's work—a selection from Bernhardt's selection; perhaps one third of the original was omitted. Sutton, a well-known translator from the German, did his job competently and well. The English version, he explained in the preface, was "slightly condensed, but only by the omission of a certain amount of what, it was felt, was more ephemeral matter ... of little interest to English readers or students." This again is natural enough. But the result is that Stresemann's Eastern policy, already under-represented in Bernhardt, recedes still further from view, and the Soviet Union appears in Sutton's volumes merely as an occasional and rather unwelcome intruder in Stresemann's predominantly Western foreign policy. Yet it is safe to say that, for all except a few specialists, Sutton and not Bernhardt—and still less the documents themselves—represents for the Western world the authentic voice of Stresemann. Had the documents perished in 1945 in the bombing, and had the remaining Bernhardt volumes disappeared, the authenticity and authority of Sutton would never have been questioned. Many printed collections of documents gratefully accepted by historians in default of the originals rest on no securer basis than this.

But I want to carry the story one step further. Let us forget about Bernhardt and Sutton, and be thankful that we can, if we choose, consult the authentic papers of a leading participant in some important events in recent European history. What do the papers tell us? Among other things they contain records of some hundreds of Stresemann's conversations with the Soviet ambassador in Berlin and of a score or so with

Chicherin.[5] These records have one feature in common. They depict Stresemann as having the lion's share of the conversations and reveal his arguments as invariably well put and cogent, while those of his partner are for the most part scanty, confused, and unconvincing. This is a familiar characteristic of all records of diplomatic conversations. The documents do not tell us what happened, but only what Stresemann thought had happened. It was not Sutton or Bernhardt, but Stresemann himself, who started the process of selection. And, if we had, say Chicherin's records of these same conversations, we should still learn from them only what Chicherin thought, and what really happened would still have to be reconstructed in the mind of the historian. Of course, facts and documents are essential to the historian. But do not make a fetish of them. They do not by themselves constitute history; they provide in themselves no ready-made answer to this tiresome question: What is history?

At this point I should like to say a few words on the question of why nineteenth-century historians were generally indifferent to the philosophy of history. The term was invented by Voltaire, and has since been used in different senses; but I shall take it to mean, if I use it at all, our answer to the question: What is history? The nineteenth century was, for the intellectuals of Western Europe, a comfortable period exuding confidence and optimism. The facts were on the whole satisfactory; and the inclination to ask and answer awkward questions about them was correspondingly weak. Ranke piously believed that divine providence would take care of the meaning of history if he took care of the facts; and Burckhardt with a more modern touch of cynicism observed that "we are not initiated into the purposes of the eternal wisdom." Professor Butterfield as late as 1931 noted with apparent satisfaction that "historians have reflected little upon the nature of things and even the nature of their own subject." But my predecessor in these lectures, Dr. A. L. Rowse, more justly critical, wrote of Sir Winston Churchill's *The World Crisis*—his book about the First World War—that, while it matched Trotsky's *History of the Russian Revolution* in personality, vividness, and vitality, it was inferior in one respect: it had "no philosophy of history behind it." British historians refused to be drawn, not because they believed that history had no meaning, but because they believed that its meaning was implicit and self-evident. The liberal nineteenth-century view of history had a close affinity with the economic doctrine of *laissez-faire*—also the product of a serene and self-confident outlook on the world. Let everyone get on with his particular job, and the hidden hand would take care of the universal harmony. The facts of history were themselves a demonstration of the supreme fact of a beneficent and apparently infinite progress

5. Soviet foreign minister from 1918 to 1928.

towards higher things. This was the age of innocence, and historians walked in the Garden of Eden, without a scrap of philosophy to cover them, naked and unashamed before the god of history. Since then, we have known Sin and experienced a Fall; and those historians who today pretend to dispense with a philosophy of history are merely trying, vainly and self-consciously, like members of a nudist colony, to recreate the Garden of Eden in their garden suburb. Today the awkward question can no longer be evaded. * * *

During the past fifty years a good deal of serious work has been done on the question: What is history? It was from Germany, the country which was to do so much to upset the comfortable reign of nineteenth-century liberalism, that the first challenge came in the 1880's and 1890's to the doctrine of the primacy and autonomy of facts in history. The philosophers who made the challenge are now little more than names: Dilthey is the only one of them who has recently received some belated recognition in Great Britain. Before the turn of the century, prosperity and confidence were still too great in this country for any attention to be paid to heretics who attacked the cult of facts. But early in the new century, the torch passed to Italy, where Croce began to propound a philosophy of history which obviously owed much to German masters. All history is "contemporary history," declared Croce,[6] meaning that history consists essentially in seeing the past through the eyes of the present and in the light of its problems, and that the main work of the historian is not to record, but to evaluate; for, if he does not evaluate, how can he know what is worth recording? In 1910 the American philosopher, Carl Becker, argued in deliberately provocative language that "the facts of history do not exist for any historian till he creates them." These challenges were for the moment little noticed. It was only after 1920 that Croce began to have a considerable vogue in France and Great Britain. This was not perhaps because Croce was a subtler thinker or a better stylist than his German predecessors, but because, after the First World War, the facts seemed to smile on us less propitiously than in the years before 1914, and we were therefore more accessible to a philosophy which sought to diminish their prestige. Croce was an important influence on the Oxford philosopher and historian Collingwood, the only British thinker in the present century who has made a serious contribution to the philosophy of history. He did not live to write the systematic treatise he had planned; but his published and unpublished papers on the subject were collected

6. The context of this celebrated aphorism is as follows: "The practical requirements which underlie every historical judgment give to all history the character of 'contemporary history,' because, however remote in time events thus recounted may seem to be, the history in reality refers to present needs and present situations wherein those events vibrate" [Carr's note].

after his death in a volume entitled *The Idea of History*, which appeared in 1945.

The views of Collingwood can be summarized as follows. The philosophy of history is concerned neither with "the past by itself" nor with "the historian's thought about it by itself," but with "the two things in their mutual relations." (This dictum reflects the two current meanings of the word "history"—the enquiry conducted by the historian and the series of past events into which he enquires.) "The past which a historian studies is not a dead past, but a past which in some sense is still living in the present." But a past act is dead, *i.e.* meaningless to the historian, unless he can understand the thought that lay behind it. Hence "all history is the history of thought," and "history is the re-enactment in the historian's mind of the thought whose history he is studying." The reconstitution of the past in the historian's mind is dependent on empirical evidence. But it is not in itself an empirical process, and cannot consist in a mere recital of facts. On the contrary, the process of reconstitution governs the selection and interpretation of the facts: this, indeed, is what makes them historical facts. "History," says Professor Oakeshott, who on this point stands near to Collingwood, "is the historian's experience. It is 'made' by nobody save the historian: to write history is the only way of making it."

This searching critique, though it may call for some serious reservations, brings to light certain neglected truths.

In the first place, the facts of history never come to us "pure," since they do not and cannot exist in a pure form: they are always refracted through the mind of the recorder. It follows that when we take up a work of history, our first concern should be not with the facts which it contains but with the historian who wrote it. Let me take as an example the great historian in whose honor and in whose name these lectures were founded. Trevelyan, as he tells us in his autobiography, was "brought up at home on a somewhat exuberantly Whig tradition"; and he would not, I hope, disclaim the title if I described him as the last and not the least of the great English liberal historians of the Whig tradition. It is not for nothing that he traces back his family tree, through the great Whig historian George Otto Trevelyan, to Macaulay, incomparably the greatest of the Whig historians. Dr. Trevelyan's finest and maturest work *England under Queen Anne* was written against that background, and will yield its full meaning and significance to the reader only when read against that background. The author, indeed, leaves the reader with no excuse for failing to do so. For if, following the technique of connoisseurs of detective novels, you read the end first, you will find on the last few pages of the third volume the best summary known to me of what is nowadays called the Whig interpretation of history; and you will see that what Trevelyan is trying to do is to investigate the origin and development of the Whig tradition, and to root it fairly and squarely in the years after the death of its founder, William III. Though this is not, perhaps, the only conceivable interpretation of the events of Queen Anne's reign, it is a valid and, in Trevelyan's hands, a fruitful interpretation. But, in order to appreciate it at its full value, you have to understand what the historian is doing. For if, as Collingwood says, the historian must re-enact in thought what has gone on in the mind of his *dramatis personae*, so the reader in his turn must re-enact what goes on in the mind of the historian. Study the historian before you begin to study the facts. This is, after all, not very abstruse. It is what is already done by the intelligent undergraduate who, when recommended to read a work by that great scholar Jones of St. Jude's, goes round to a friend at St. Jude's to ask what sort of chap Jones is, and what bees he has in his bonnet. When you read a work of history, always listen out for the buzzing. If you can detect none, either you are tone deaf or your historian is a dull dog. The facts are really not at all like fish on the fishmonger's slab. They are like fish swimming about in a vast and sometimes inaccessible ocean; and what the historian catches will depend partly on chance, but mainly on what part of the ocean he chooses to fish in and what tackle he chooses to use—these two factors being, of course, determined by the kind of fish he wants to catch. By and large, the historian will get the kind of facts he wants. History means interpretation. Indeed, if, standing Sir George Clark on his head, I were to call history "a hard core of interpretation surrounded by a pulp of disputable facts," my statement would, no doubt, be one-sided and misleading, but no more so, I venture to think, than the original dictum.

The second point is the more familiar one of the historian's need of imaginative understanding for the minds of the people with whom he is dealing, for the thought behind their acts: I say "imaginative understanding," not "sympathy," lest sympathy should be supposed to imply agreement. The nineteenth century was weak in mediaeval history, because it was too much repelled by the superstitious beliefs of the Middle Ages and by the barbarities which they inspired, to have any imaginative understanding of mediaeval people. Or take Burckhardt's censorious remark about the Thirty Years' War: "It is scandalous for a creed, no matter whether it is Catholic or Protestant, to place its salvation above the integrity of the nation." It was extremely difficult for a nineteenth-century liberal historian, brought up to believe that it is right and praiseworthy to kill in defense of one's country, but wicked and wrongheaded to kill in defense of one's religion, to enter into the state of mind of those who fought the Thirty Years' War. This difficulty is particularly acute in the field in which I am now working. Much of what has been written in English-speaking countries in the last ten years about the Soviet Union, and in the Soviet Union about the English-speaking countries, has been vitiated by this inability to achieve even the most elementary measure of imaginative understanding of what goes on in the mind of the other party, so that the words and actions of the other are always made to appear malign, senseless, or hypocritical. History cannot be written unless the historian can achieve some kind of contact with the mind of those about whom he is writing.

The third point is that we can view the past, and achieve our understanding of the past, only through the eyes of the present. The historian is of his own age, and is bound to it by the conditions of human existence. The very words which he uses—words like democracy, empire, war, revolution—have current connotations from which he cannot divorce them. Ancient historians have taken to using words like *polis* and *plebs* in the original, just in order to show that they have not fallen into this trap. This does not help them. They, too, live in the present, and cannot cheat themselves into the past by using unfamiliar or obsolete words, any more than they would become better Greek or Roman historians if they delivered their lectures in a *chlamys* or a *toga*. The names by which successive French historians have described the Parisian crowds which played so prominent a role in the French revolution—*les sansculottes, le peuple, la canaille, les bras-nus*—are all, for those who know the rules of the game, manifestos of a political affiliation and of a particular interpretation. Yet the historian is obliged to choose: the use of language forbids him to be neutral. Nor is it a matter of words alone. Over the past hundred years the changed balance of power in Europe has reversed the attitude of British historians to Frederick the Great. The changed balance of power within the Christian churches between Catholicism and Protestantism has profoundly altered their attitude to such figures as Loyola, Luther, and Cromwell. It requires only a superficial knowledge of the work of French historians of the last forty years on the French revolution to recognize how deeply it has been affected by the Russian revolution of 1917. The historian belongs not to the past but to the present. Professor Trevor-Roper tells us that the historian "ought to love the past." This is a dubious injunction. To love the past may easily be an expression of the nostalgic romanticism of old men and old societies, a symptom of loss of faith and interest in the present or future.[7] Cliché for cliché, I should prefer the one about freeing oneself from "the dead hand of the past." The function of the historian is neither to love the past nor to emancipate himself from the past, but to master and understand it as the key to the understanding of the present.

If, however, these are some of the sights of what I may call the Collingwood view of history, it is time to consider some of the dangers. The emphasis on the role of the historian in the making of history tends, if pressed to its logical conclusion, to rule out any objective history at all:

7. Compare Nietzsche's view of history: "To old age belongs the old man's business of looking back and casting up his accounts, of seeking consolation in the memories of the past, in historical culture" [Carr's note].

history is what the historian makes. Collingwood seems indeed, at one moment, in an unpublished note quoted by his editor, to have reached this conclusion:

> St. Augustine looked at history from the point of view of the early Christian; Tillemont, from that of a seventeenth-century Frenchman; Gibbon, from that of an eighteenth-century Englishman; Mommsen, from that of a nineteenth-century German. There is no point in asking which was the right point of view. Each was the only one possible for the man who adopted it.

This amounts to total scepticism, like Froude's remark that history is "a child's box of letters with which we can spell any word we please." Collingwood, in his reaction against "scissors-and-paste history," against the view of history as a mere compilation of facts, comes perilously near to treating history as something spun out of the human brain, and leads back to the conclusion referred to by Sir George Clark in the passage which I quoted earlier, that "there is no 'objective' historical truth." In place of the theory that history has no meaning, we are offered here the theory of an infinity of meanings, none any more right than any other—which comes to much the same thing. The second theory is surely as untenable as the first. It does not follow that, because a mountain appears to take on different shapes from different angles of vision, it has objectively either no shape at all or an infinity of shapes. It does not follow that, because interpretation plays a necessary part in establishing the facts of history, and because no existing interpretation is wholly objective, one interpretation is as good as another, and the facts of history are in principle not amenable to objective interpretation. I shall have to consider at a later stage what exactly is meant by objectivity in history.

But a still greater danger lurks in the Collingwood hypothesis. If the historian necessarily looks at his period of history through the eyes of his own time, and studies the problems of the past as a key to those of the present, will he not fall into a purely pragmatic view of the facts, and maintain that the criterion of a right interpretation is its suitability to some present purpose? On this hypothesis, the facts of history are nothing, interpretation is everything. Nietzsche had already enunciated the principle: "The falseness of an opinion is not for us any objection to it. . . . The question is how far it is life-furthering, life-preserving, species-preserving, perhaps species-creating." The American pragmatists moved, less explicitly and less wholeheartedly, along the same line. Knowledge is knowledge for some purpose. The validity of the knowledge depends on the validity of the purpose. But, even where no such theory has been professed, the practice has often been no less disquieting. In my own field of study, I have seen too many examples of extravagant interpretation riding roughshod over facts, not to be impressed with the reality of this danger. It is not surprising that perusal of some of the more extreme products of Soviet and anti-Soviet schools of historiography should sometimes breed a certain nostalgia for that illusory nineteenth-century heaven of purely factual history.

How then, in the middle of the twentieth century, are we to define the obligation of the historian to his facts? I trust that I have spent a sufficient number of hours in recent years chasing and perusing documents, and stuffing my historical narrative with properly footnoted facts, to escape the imputation of treating facts and documents too cavalierly. The duty of the historian to respect his facts is not exhausted by the obligation to see that his facts are accurate. He must seek to bring into the picture all known or knowable facts relevant, in one sense or another, to the theme on which he is engaged and to the interpretation proposed. If he seeks to depict the Victorian Englishman as a moral and rational being, he must not forget what happened at Stalybridge Wakes in 1850. But this, in turn, does not mean that he can eliminate interpretation, which is the life-blood of history. Laymen—that is to say, non-academic friends or friends from other academic disciplines—sometimes ask me how the historian goes to work when he writes history. The commonest assumption appears to be that the historian divides his work into two sharply distinguishable phases or periods. First, he spends a long preliminary period reading his source and filling his notebooks with facts: then, when this is over, he puts away his sources, takes out his notebooks, and writes his book from beginning to end. This is to me an unconvincing and unplausible picture. For myself, as soon as I have got going on a few of what I take to be the capital sources, the itch becomes too strong and I begin to write—not necessarily at the beginning, but somewhere, anywhere. Thereafter, reading and writing go on simultaneously. The writing is added to, subtracted from, re-shaped, cancelled, as I go on reading. The reading is guided and directed and made fruitful by the writing: the more I write, the more I know what I am looking for, the better I understand the significance and relevance of what I find. Some historians probably do all this preliminary writing in their head without using pen, paper, or typewriter, just as some people play chess in their heads without recourse to board and chess-men: this is a talent which I envy, but cannot emulate. But I am convinced that, for any historian worth the name, the two processes of what economists call "input" and "output" go on simultaneously and are, in practice, parts of a single process. If you try to separate them, or to give one priority over the other, you fall into one of two heresies. Either you write scissors-and-paste history without meaning or significance; or you write propaganda or historical fiction, and merely use facts of the past to embroider a kind of writing which has nothing to do with history.

Our examination of the relation of the historian to the facts of history finds us, therefore, in an apparently precarious situation, navigating delicately between the Scylla of an untenable theory of history as an objective compilation of facts, of the unqualified primacy of fact over interpretation, and the Charybdis of an equally untenable theory of history as the subjective product of the mind of the historian who establishes the facts of history and masters them through the process of interpretation, between a view of history having the center of gravity in the past and the view having the center of gravity in the present. But our situation is less precarious than it seems. We shall encounter the same dichotomy of fact and interpretation again in these lectures in other guises—the particular and the general, the empirical and the theoretical, the objective and the subjective. The predicament of the historian is a reflection of the nature of man. Man, except perhaps in earliest infancy and in extreme old age, is not totally involved in his environment and unconditionally subject to it. On the other hand, he is never totally independent of it and its unconditional master. The relation of man to his environment is the relation of the historian to his theme. The historian is neither the humble slave, nor the tyrannical master, of his facts. The relation between the historian and his facts is one of equality, of give-and-take. As any working historian knows, if he stops to reflect what he is doing as he thinks and writes, the historian is engaged on a continuous process of molding his facts to his interpretation and his interpretation to his facts. It is impossible to assign primacy to one over the other.

The historian starts with the provisional selection of facts and a provisional interpretation in the light of which that selection has been made—by others as well as by himself. As he works, both the interpretation and the selection and ordering of facts undergo subtle and perhaps partly unconscious changes through the reciprocal action of one or the other. And this reciprocal action also involves reciprocity between present and past, since the historian is part of the present and the facts belong to the past. The historian and the facts of history are necessary to one another. The historian without his facts is rootless and futile; the facts without their historian are dead and meaningless. My first answer therefore to the question, What is history?, is that it is a continuous process of interaction between the historian and his facts, an unending dialogue between the present and the past.

1961

THE READER

1. In his discussion of the facts of history, Carr distinguishes between "a mere fact about the past" and "a fact of history." Into which category should Bettelheim's encounter with the infirmary guard go (p. 41)?
2. If you were commissioned to write a history of the semester or of a particular group during the semester, what would be your most important "facts of history"?

THE WRITER

1. Carr begins with a question but does not answer it until the last sentence. What are the main steps of the discussion leading to his answer? The answer takes the form of a definition. Which is the most important of the defining words?

2. Carr says that the historian's "facts are really not at all like fish on the fishmonger's slab. They are like fish swimming about in a vast and sometimes inaccessible ocean; and what the historian catches will depend partly on chance, but mainly on what part of the ocean he chooses to fish in and what tackle he chooses to use—these two factors being, of course, determined by the kind of fish he wants to catch." How appropriate a description is this of the way other kinds of writers use facts—for example, the scientist, the psychologist, the novelist, the familiar essayist?

3. Write a brief "history" of an event, keeping in mind what Carr says about what the historian does.

Politics and Government

George Orwell

SHOOTING AN ELEPHANT

In Moulmein, in Lower Burma, I was hated by large numbers of people
—the only time in my life that I have been important enough for this to
happen to me. I was sub-divisional police officer of the town, and in an
aimless, petty kind of way anti-European feeling was very bitter. No one
had the guts to raise a riot, but if a European woman went through the
bazaars alone somebody would probably spit betel juice over her dress.
As a police officer I was an obvious target and was baited whenever it
seemed safe to do so. When a nimble Burman tripped me up on the
football field and the referee (another Burman) looked the other way, the
crowd yelled with hideous laughter. This happened more than once. In
the end the sneering yellow faces of young men that met me everywhere,
the insults hooted after me when I was at a safe distance, got badly on my
nerves. The young Buddhist priests were the worst of all. There were
several thousands of them in the town and none of them seemed to have
anything to do except stand on street corners and jeer at Europeans.

All this was perplexing and upsetting. For at that time I had already
made up my mind that imperialism was an evil thing and the sooner I
chucked up my job and got out of it the better. Theoretically—and
secretly, of course—I was all for the Burmese and all against their oppressors, the British. As for the job I was doing, I hated it more bitterly than I
can perhaps make clear. In a job like that you see the dirty work of
Empire at close quarters. The wretched prisoners huddling in the stinking cages of the lock-ups, the grey, cowed faces of the long-term convicts,
the scarred buttocks of the men who had been flogged with bamboos—all
these oppressed me with an intolerable sense of guilt. But I could get
nothing into perspective. I was young and ill-educated and I had had to
think out my problems in the utter silence that is imposed on every

Englishman in the East. I did not even know that the British Empire is dying, still less did I know that it is a great deal better than the younger empires that are going to supplant it. All I knew was that I was stuck between my hatred of the empire I served and my rage against the evil-spirited little beasts who tried to make my job impossible. With one part of my mind I thought of the British Raj[1] as an unbreakable tyranny, as something clamped down, in *saecula saeculorum*,[2] upon the will of prostrate peoples; with another part I thought that the greatest joy in the world would be to drive a bayonet into a Buddhist priest's guts. Feelings like these are the normal by-products of imperialism; ask any Anglo-Indian official, if you can catch him off duty.

One day something happened which in a roundabout way was enlightening. It was a tiny incident in itself, but it gave me a better glimpse than I had had before of the real nature of imperialism—the real motives for which despotic governments act. Early one morning the sub-inspector at a police station the other end of the town rang me up on the 'phone and said that an elephant was ravaging the bazaar. Would I please come and do something about it? I did not know what I could do, but I wanted to see what was happening and I got on to a pony and started out. I took my rifle, an old .44 Winchester and much too small to kill an elephant, but I thought the noise might be useful *in terrorem*. Various Burmans stopped me on the way and told me about the elephant's doings. It was not, of course, a wild elephant, but a tame one which had gone "must."[3] It had been chained up, as tame elephants always are when their attack of "must" is due, but on the previous night it had broken its chain and escaped. Its mahout, the only person who could manage it when it was in that state, had set out in pursuit, but had taken the wrong direction and was now twelve hours' journey away, and in the morning the elephant had suddenly reappeared in the town. The Burmese population had no weapons and were quite helpless against it. It had already destroyed somebody's bamboo hut, killed a cow and raided some fruit-stalls and devoured the stock; also it had met the municipal rubbish van and, when the driver jumped out and took to his heels, had turned the van over and inflicted violences upon it.

The Burmese sub-inspector and some Indian constables were waiting for me in the quarter where the elephant had been seen. It was a very poor quarter, a labyrinth of squalid bamboo huts, thatched with palm-leaf, winding all over a steep hillside. I remember that it was a cloudy, stuffy morning at the beginning of the rains. We began questioning the people as to where the elephant had gone and, as usual, failed to get any definite information. That is invariably the case in the East; a story always sounds clear enough at a distance, but the nearer you get to the

---

1. The imperial government of British India and Burma.
2. Forever and ever.
3. Gone into sexual heat.

scene of events the vaguer it becomes. Some of the people said that the elephant had gone in one direction, some said that he had gone in another, some professed not even to have heard of any elephant. I had almost made up my mind that the whole story was a pack of lies, when we heard yells a little distance away. There was a loud, scandalized cry of "Go away, child! Go away this instant!" and an old woman with a switch in her hand came round the corner of a hut, violently shooing away a crowd of naked children. Some more women followed, clicking their tongues and exclaiming; evidently there was something that the children ought not to have seen. I rounded the hut and saw a man's dead body sprawling in the mud. He was an Indian, a black Dravidian coolie, almost naked, and he could not have been dead many minutes. The people said that the elephant had come suddenly upon him round the corner of the hut, caught him with its trunk, put its foot on his back and ground him into the earth. This was the rainy season and the ground was soft, and his face had scored a trench a foot deep and a couple of yards long. He was lying on his belly with arms crucified and head sharply twisted to one side. His face was coated with mud, the eyes wide open, the teeth bared and grinning with an expression of unendurable agony. (Never tell me, by the way, that the dead look peaceful. Most of the corpses I have seen looked devilish.) The friction of the great beast's foot had stripped the skin from his back as neatly as one skins a rabbit. As soon as I saw the dead man I sent an orderly to a friend's house nearby to borrow an elephant rifle. I had already sent back the pony, not wanting it to go mad with fright and throw me if it smelt the elephant.

The orderly came back in a few minutes with a rifle and five cartridges, and meanwhile some Burmans had arrived and told us that the elephant was in the paddy fields below, only a few hundred yards away. As I started forward practically the whole population of the quarter flocked out of the houses and followed me. They had seen the rifle and were all shouting excitedly that I was going to shoot the elephant. They had not shown much interest in the elephant when he was merely ravaging their homes, but it was different now that he was going to be shot. It was a bit of fun to them, as it would be to an English crowd; besides they wanted the meat. It made me vaguely uneasy. I had no intention of shooting the elephant—I had merely sent for the rifle to defend myself if necessary—and it is always unnerving to have a crowd following you. I marched down the hill, looking and feeling a fool, with the rifle over my shoulder and an ever-growing army of people jostling at my heels. At the bottom, when you got away from the huts, there was a metalled road and beyond that a miry waste of paddy fields a thousand yards across, not yet ploughed but soggy from the first rains and dotted with coarse grass. The elephant was standing eight yards from the road, his left side towards us. He took not the slightest notice of the crowd's approach. He was tearing up bunches of grass, beating them against his knees to clean them and stuffing them into his mouth.

I had halted on the road. As soon as I saw the elephant I knew with perfect certainty that I ought not to shoot him. It is a serious matter to shoot a working elephant—it is comparable to destroying a huge and costly piece of machinery—and obviously one ought not to do it if it can possibly be avoided. And at that distance, peacefully eating, the elephant looked no more dangerous than a cow. I thought then and I think now that his attack of "must" was already passing off; in which case he would merely wander harmlessly about until the mahout came back and caught him. Moreover, I did not in the least want to shoot him. I decided that I would watch him for a little while to make sure that he did not turn savage again, and then go home.

But at that moment I glanced round at the crowd that had followed me. It was an immense crowd, two thousand at the least and growing every minute. It blocked the road for a long distance on either side. I looked at the sea of yellow faces above the garish clothes—faces all happy and excited over this bit of fun, all certain that the elephant was going to be shot. They were watching me as they would watch a conjurer about to perform a trick. They did not like me, but with the magical rifle in my hands I was momentarily worth watching. And suddenly I realized that I should have to shoot the elephant after all. The people expected it of me and I had got to do it; I could feel their two thousand wills pressing me forward, irresistibly. And it was at this moment, as I stood there with the rifle in my hands, that I first grasped the hollowness, the futility of the white man's dominion in the East. Here was I, the white man with his gun, standing in front of the unarmed native crowd—seemingly the leading actor of the piece; but in reality I was only an absurd puppet pushed to and fro by the will of those yellow faces behind. I perceived in this moment that when the white man turns tyrant it is his own freedom that he destroys. He becomes a sort of hollow, posing dummy, the conventionalized figure of a sahib. For it is the condition of his rule that he shall spend his life in trying to impress the "natives," and so in every crisis he has got to do what the "natives" expect of him. He wears a mask, and his face grows to fit it. I had got to shoot the elephant. I had committed myself to doing it when I sent for the rifle. A sahib has got to act like a sahib; he has got to appear resolute, to know his own mind and do definite things. To come all that way, rifle in hand, with two thousand people marching at my heels, and then to trail feebly away, having done nothing—no, that was impossible. The crowd would laugh at me. And my whole life, every white man's life in the East, was one long struggle not to be laughed at.

But I did not want to shoot the elephant. I watched him beating his bunch of grass against his knees, with that preoccupied grandmotherly air that elephants have. It seemed to me that it would be murder to shoot him. At that age I was not squeamish about killing animals, but I had never shot an elephant and never wanted to. (Somehow it always seems worse to kill a *large* animal.) Besides, there was the beast's owner to be considered. Alive, the elephant was worth at least a hundred pounds; dead, he would only be worth the value of his tusks, five pounds, possibly. But I had got to act quickly. I turned to some experienced-looking Burmans who had been there when we arrived, and asked them how the elephant had been behaving. They all said the same thing: he took no notice of you if you left him alone, but he might charge if you went too close to him.

It was perfectly clear to me what I ought to do. I ought to walk up to within, say, twenty-five yards of the elephant and test his behavior. If he charged, I could shoot; if he took no notice of me, it would be safe to leave him until the mahout came back. But also I knew that I was going to do no such thing. I was a poor shot with a rifle and the ground was soft mud into which one would sink at every step. If the elephant charged and I missed him, I should have about as much chance as a toad under a steam-roller. But even then I was not thinking particularly of my own skin, only of the watchful yellow faces behind. For at that moment, with the crowd watching me, I was not afraid in the ordinary sense, as I would have been if I had been alone. A white man mustn't be frightened in front of "natives"; and so, in general, he isn't frightened. The sole thought in my mind was that if anything went wrong those two thousand Burmans would see me pursued, caught, trampled on and reduced to a grinning corpse like that Indian up the hill. And if that happened it was quite probable that some of them would laugh. That would never do. There was only one alternative. I shoved the cartridges into the magazine and lay down on the road to get a better aim.

The crowd grew very still, and a deep, low, happy sigh, as of people who see the theatre curtain go up at last, breathed from innumerable throats. They were going to have their bit of fun after all. The rifle was a beautiful German thing with cross-hair sights. I did not then know that in shooting an elephant one would shoot to cut an imaginary bar running from ear-hole to ear-hole. I ought, therefore, as the elephant was sideways on, to have aimed straight at his ear-hole; actually I aimed several inches in front of this, thinking the brain would be further forward.

When I pulled the trigger I did not hear the bang or feel the kick—one never does when a shot goes home—but I heard the devilish roar of glee that went up from the crowd. In that instant, in too short a time, one would have thought, even for the bullet to get there, a mysterious, terrible change had come over the elephant. He neither stirred nor fell, but every line of his body had altered. He looked suddenly stricken, shrunken, immensely old, as though the frightful impact of the bullet had paralysed him without knocking him down. At last, after what seemed a long time—it might have been five seconds, I dare say—he sagged flabbily to his knees. His mouth slobbered. An enormous senility seemed to have settled upon him. One could have imagined him thousands of years old. I fired again into the same spot. At the second shot he did not collapse but climbed with desperate slowness to his feet and stood weakly upright, with legs sagging and head drooping. I fired a third time. That was the shot that did for him. You could see the agony of it jolt his whole body and knock the last remnant of strength from his legs. But in falling he seemed for a moment to rise, for as his hind legs collapsed beneath him he seemed to tower upward like a huge rock toppling, his trunk reaching skywards like a tree. He trumpeted, for the first and only time. And then down he came, his belly towards me, with a crash that seemed to shake the ground even where I lay.

I got up. The Burmans were already racing past me across the mud. It was obvious that the elephant would never rise again, but he was not dead. He was breathing very rhythmically with long rattling gasps, his great mound of a side painfully rising and falling. His mouth was wide open—I could see far down into caverns of pale pink throat. I waited a long time for him to die, but his breathing did not weaken. Finally I fired my two remaining shots into the spot where I thought his heart must be. The thick blood welled out of him like red velvet, but still he did not die. His body did not even jerk when the shots hit him, the tortured breathing continued without a pause. He was dying, very slowly and in great agony, but in some world remote from me where not even a bullet could damage him further. I felt that I had got to put an end to that dreadful noise. It seemed dreadful to see the great beast lying there, powerless to move and yet powerless to die, and not even to be able to finish him. I sent back for my small rifle and poured shot after shot into his heart and down his throat. They seemed to make no impression. The tortured gasps continued as steadily as the ticking of a clock.

In the end I could not stand it any longer and went away. I heard later that it took him half an hour to die. Burmans were bringing dahs[3] and baskets even before I left, and I was told they had stripped his body almost to the bones by the afternoon.

Afterwards, of course, there were endless discussions about the shooting of the elephant. The owner was furious, but he was only an Indian and could do nothing. Besides, legally I had done the right thing, for a mad elephant has to be killed, like a mad dog, if its owner fails to control it. Among the Europeans opinion was divided. The older men said I was right, the younger men said it was a damn shame to shoot an elephant for killing a coolie, because an elephant was worth more than any damn

3. Butcher knives.

Coringhee coolie. And afterwards I was very glad that the coolie had been killed; it put me legally in the right and it gave me a sufficient pretext for shooting the elephant. I often wondered whether any of the others grasped that I had done it solely to avoid looking a fool.

1936

THE READER

1. What issue does Orwell address, and what kind of evidence is proper to it? Does he actually prove anything?
2. Does Robley (see question 2 under "The Writer," below) show any sign that he recognizes what Orwell calls "the futility of the white man's dominion in the East" (p. 771)? Could it be that this dominion was not futile for Robley, or in his day?

THE WRITER

1. The proportion of this essay devoted to narrative is relatively high. What effect(s) does Orwell aim at? How does he organize his essay? Where does he state his thesis? Would he have done better to argue his thesis directly rather than mainly by example? Why, or why not?
2. The following is a sketch from The Graphic (London) of January 21, 1888, written by a Major-General H. G. Robley:

SHOOTING A MAN-EATING CROCODILE

It is tedious work waiting for the man-eater to come out of the water, but a fat native child as a lure will make the monster speedily walk out of his aqueous lair. Contracting the loan of a chubby infant, however, is a matter of some negotiation, and it is perhaps not to be wondered at that mammas occasionally object to their offspring being pegged down as food for a great crocodile; but there are always some parents to be found whose confidence in the skill of the British sportsman is unlimited. My sketch [omitted here] gives a view of the collapse of the man-eater, who, after viewing the tempting morsel tethered carefully to a bamboo near the water's edge, makes a rush through the sedges. The sportsman, hidden behind a bed of reeds, then fires, the bullet penetrates the heart, and the monster is dead in a moment. The little bait, whose only alarm has been caused by the report of the rifle, is now taken home by its doting mother for its matutinal banana. The natives wait to get the musky flesh of the animal, and the sportsman secures the scaly skin and the massive head of porous bone as a trophy.

There are probably educational and social similarities between Robley and Orwell, and, of course, both were imperial Englishmen in a colonial setting. However, the differences between the two men are far more striking. Briefly and basically, what are they? How are these similarities and differences reflected in the essays' styles?
3. Compare Robley's sketch with Swift's "A Modest Proposal" (p. 807). How can you tell that Robley is not ironic and that Swift is? If you can't

tell, what does your uncertainty suggest about the nature of irony?
4. Adapt Robley's sketch to meet an ironic purpose like Swift's.

Ngũgĩ wa Thiong'o

DECOLONIZING THE MIND

I was born into a large peasant family: father, four wives and about twenty-eight children. I also belonged, as we all did in those days, to a wider extended family and to the community as a whole.

We spoke Gĩkũyũ as we worked in the fields. We spoke Gĩkũyũ in and outside the home. I can vividly recall those evenings of story-telling around the fireside. It was mostly the grown-ups telling the children but everybody was interested and involved. We children would re-tell the stories the following day to other children who worked in the fields picking the pyrethrum flowers, tea-leaves or coffee beans of our European and African landlords.

The stories, with mostly animals as the main characters, were all told in Gĩkũyũ. Hare, being small, weak but full of innovative wit and cunning, was our hero. We identified with him as he struggled against the brutes of prey like lion, leopard, hyena. His victories were our victories and we learned that the apparently weak can outwit the strong. We followed the animals in their struggle against hostile nature—drought, rain, sun, wind—a confrontation often forcing them to search for forms of co-operation. But we were also interested in their struggles amongst themselves, and particularly between the beasts and the victims of prey. These twin struggles, against nature and other animals, reflected real-life struggles in the human world.

Not that we neglected stories with human beings as the main characters. There were two types of characters in such human-centered narratives: the species of truly human beings with qualities of courage, kindness, mercy, hatred of evil, concern for others; and a man-eat-man two-mouthed species with qualities of greed, selfishness, individualism and hatred of what was good for the larger co-operative community. Co-operation as the ultimate good in a community was a constant theme. It could unite human beings with animals against ogres and beasts of prey, as in the story of how dove, after being fed with castor-oil seeds, was sent to fetch a smith working far away from home and whose pregnant wife was being threatened by these man-eating two-mouthed ogres.

There were good and bad story-tellers. A good one could tell the same story over and over again, and it would always be fresh to us, the listeners.

He or she could tell a story told by someone else and make it more alive and dramatic. The differences really were in the use of words and images and the inflection of voices to effect different tones.

We therefore learned to value words for their meaning and nuances. Language was not a mere string of words. It had a suggestive power well beyond the immediate and lexical meaning. Our appreciation of the suggestive magical power of language was reinforced by the games we played with words through riddles, proverbs, transpositions of syllables, or through nonsensical but musically arranged words.[1] So we learned the music of our language on top of the content. The language, through images and symbols, gave us a view of the world, but it had a beauty of its own. The home and the field were then our pre-primary school but what is important, for this discussion, is that the language of our evening teach-ins, and the language of our immediate and wider community, and the language of our work in the fields were one.

And then I went to school, a colonial school, and this harmony was broken. The language of my education was no longer the language of my culture. I first went to Kamaandura, missionary run, and then to another called Maanguuũ run by nationalists grouped around the Gĩkũyũ Independent and Karinga Schools Association. Our language of education was still Gĩkũyũ. The very first time I was ever given an ovation for my writing was over a composition in Gĩkũyũ. So for my first four years there was still harmony between the language of my formal education and that of the Limuru peasant community.

It was after the declaration of a state of emergency over Kenya in 1952 that all the schools run by patriotic nationalists were taken over by the colonial regime and were placed under District Education Boards chaired by Englishmen. English became the language of my formal education. In Kenya, English became more than a language: it was *the* language, and all the others had to bow before it in deference.

Thus one of the most humiliating experiences was to be caught speaking Gĩkũyũ in the vicinity of the school. The culprit was given corporal punishment—three to five strokes of the cane on bare buttocks—or was made to carry a metal plate around the neck with inscriptions such as I AM STUPID or I AM A DONKEY. Sometimes the culprits were fined money they could hardly afford. And how did the teachers catch the culprits? A button was initially given to one pupil who was supposed to hand it over to whoever was caught speaking his mother tongue. Whoever had the button at the end of the day would sing who had given it to him and the

1. Example from a tongue twister: "Kaana ka Nikoora koona koora koora: na ko koora koona kaana ka Nikoora koora koora." I'm indebted to Wangui wa Goro for this example. "Nichola's child saw a baby frog and ran away: and when the baby frog saw Nichola's child it also ran away." A Gĩkũyũ speaking child has to get the correct tone and length of vowel and pauses to get it right. Otherwise it becomes a jumble of *k*'s and *r*'s and *na*'s [author's note].

ensuing process would bring out all the culprits of the day. Thus children were turned into witchhunters and in the process were being taught the lucrative value of being a traitor to one's immediate community.

The attitude to English was the exact opposite: any achievement in spoken or written English was highly rewarded; prizes, prestige, applause; the ticket to higher realms. English became the measure of intelligence and ability in the arts, the sciences, and all the other branches of learning. English became *the* main determinant of a child's progress up the ladder of formal education.

As you may know, the colonial system of education in addition to its apartheid racial demarcation had the structure of a pyramid: a broad primary base, a narrowing secondary middle, and an even narrower university apex. Selections from primary into secondary were through an examination, in my time called Kenya African Preliminary Examination, in which one had to pass six subjects ranging from Maths to Nature Study and Kiswahili. All the papers were written in English. Nobody could pass the exam who failed the English language paper no matter how brilliantly he had done in the other subjects. I remember one boy in my class of 1954 who had distinctions in all subjects except English, which he had failed. He was made to fail the entire exam. He went on to become a turn boy in a bus company. I who had only passes but a credit in English got a place at the Alliance High School, one of the most elitist institutions for Africans in colonial Kenya. The requirements for a place at the University, Makerere University College, were broadly the same: nobody could go on to wear the undergraduate red gown, no matter how brilliantly they had performed in all the other subjects unless they had a credit—not even a simple pass!—in English. Thus the most coveted place in the pyramid and in the system was only available to the holder of an English language credit card. English was the official vehicle and the magic formula to colonial elitedom.

Literary education was now determined by the dominant language while also reinforcing that dominance. Orature (oral literature) in Kenyan languages stopped. In primary school I now read simplified Dickens and Stevenson alongside Rider Haggard. Jim Hawkins, Oliver Twist, Tom Brown—not Hare, Leopard and Lion—were now my daily companions in the world of imagination. In secondary school, Scott and G. B. Shaw vied with more Rider Haggard, John Buchan, Alan Paton, Captain W. E. Johns. At Makerere I read English: from Chaucer to T. S. Eliot with a touch of Graham Greene.

Thus language and literature were taking us further and further from ourselves to other selves, from our world to other worlds.

What was the colonial system doing to us Kenyan children? What were the consequences of, on the one hand, this systematic suppression of our languages and the literature they carried, and on the other the elevation of English and the literature it carried? To answer those questions, let me first examine the relationship of language to human experience, human culture, and the human perception of reality.

Language, any language, has a dual character: it is both a means of communication and a carrier of culture. Take English. It is spoken in Britain and in Sweden and Denmark. But for Swedish and Danish people English is only a means of communication with non-Scandinavians. It is not a carrier of their culture. For the British, and particularly the English, it is additionally, and inseparably from its use as a tool of communication, a carrier of their culture and history. Or take Swahili in East and Central Africa. It is widely used as a means of communication across many nationalities. But it is not the carrier of a culture and history of many of those nationalities. However in parts of Kenya and Tanzania, and particularly in Zanzibar, Swahili is inseparably both a means of communication and a carrier of the culture of those people to whom it is a mother-tongue.

Language as communication has three aspects or elements. There is first what Karl Marx once called the language of real life,[2] the element basic to the whole notion of language, its origins and development: that is, the relations people enter into with one another in the labor process, the links they necessarily establish among themselves in the act of a people, a community of human beings, producing wealth or means of life like food, clothing, houses. A human community really starts its historical being as a community of co-operation in production through the division of labor; the simplest is between man, woman and child within a household; the more complex divisions are between branches of production such as those who are sole hunters, sole gatherers of fruits or sole workers in metal. Then there are the most complex divisions such as those in modern factories where a single product, say a shirt or a shoe, is the result of many hands and minds. Production is co-operation, is communication, is language, is expression of a relation between human beings and it is specifically human.

The second aspect of language as communication is speech and it imitates the language of real life, that is communication in production. The verbal signposts both reflect and aid communication or the relations

---

2. "The production of ideas, of conceptions, of consciousness, is at first directly interwoven with the material activity and the material intercourse of men, the languge of real life. Conceiving, thinking, the mental intercourse of men, appear at this stage as the direct efflux of their material behaviour. The same applies to mental production as expressed in the language of politics, laws, morality, religion, metaphysics, etc., of a people. Men are the producers of their conceptions, ideas etc.—real active men, as they are conditioned by a definite development of their productive forces and of the intercourse corresponding to these, up to its furthest form." Marx and Engels, German Ideology, the first part published under the title *Feuerbach: Opposition of the Materialist and Idealist Outlooks*, London: 1973, p. 8 [author's note].

established between human beings in the production of their means of life. Language as a system of verbal signposts makes that production possible. The spoken word is to relations between human beings what the hand is to the relations between human beings and nature. The hand through tools mediates between human beings and nature and forms the language of real life: spoken words mediate between human beings and form the language of speech.

The third aspect is the written signs. The written word imitates the spoken. Where the first two aspects of language as communication through the hand and the spoken word historically evolved more or less simultaneously, the written aspect is a much later historical development. Writing is representation of sounds with visual symbols, from the simplest knot among shepherds to tell the number in a herd or the hieroglyphics among the Agĩkũyũ gicaandi singers and poets of Kenya, to the most complicated and different letter and picture writing systems of the world today.

In most societies the written and the spoken languages are the same, in that they represent each other: what is on paper can be read to another person and be received as that language which the recipient has grown up speaking. In such a society there is broad harmony for a child between the three aspects of language as communication. His interaction with nature and with other men is expressed in written and spoken symbols or signs which are both a result of that double interaction and a reflection of it. The association of the child's sensibility is with the language of his experience of life.

But there is more to it: communication between human beings is also the basis and process of evolving culture. In doing similar kinds of things and actions over and over again under similar circumstances, similar even in their mutability, certain patterns, moves, rhythms, habits, attitudes, experiences and knowledge emerge. Those experiences are handed over to the next generation and become the inherited basis for their further actions on nature and on themselves. There is a gradual accumulation of values which in time become almost self-evident truths governing their conception of what is right and wrong, good and bad, beautiful and ugly, courageous and cowardly, generous and mean in their internal and external relations. Over a time this becomes a way of life distinguishable from other ways of life. They develop a distinctive culture and history. Culture embodies those moral, ethical and aesthetic values, the set of spiritual eyeglasses, through which they come to view themselves and their place in the universe. Values are the basis of a people's identity, their sense of particularity as members of the human race. All this is carried by language. Language as culture is the collective memory bank of a people's experience in history. Culture is almost indistinguishable from the language that makes possible its genesis, growth, banking, articulation and indeed its transmission from one generation to the next.

Language as culture also has three important aspects. Culture is a product of the history which it in turn reflects. Culture in other words is a product and a reflection of human beings communicating with one another in the very struggle to create wealth and to control it. But culture does not merely reflect that history, or rather it does so by actually forming images or pictures of the world of nature and nurture. Thus the second aspect of language as culture is as an image-forming agent in the mind of a child. Our whole conception of ourselves as a people, individually and collectively, is based on those pictures and images which may or may not correctly correspond to the actual reality of the struggles with nature and nurture which produced them in the first place. But our capacity to confront the world creatively is dependent on how these images correspond or not to that reality, how they distort or clarify the reality of our struggles. Language as culture is thus mediating between me and my own self; between my own self and other selves; between me and nature. Language is mediating in my very being. And this brings us to the third aspect of language as culture. Culture transmits or imparts those images of the world and reality through the spoken and the written language, that is through a specific language. In other words, the capacity to speak, the capacity to order sounds in a manner that makes for mutual comprehension between human beings is universal. This is the universality of language, a quality specific to human beings. It corresponds to the universality of the struggle against nature and that between human beings. But the particularity of the sounds, the words, the word order into phrases and sentences, and the specific manner, or laws, of their ordering is what distinguishes one language from another. Thus a specific culture is not transmitted through language in its universality but in its particularity as the language of a specific community with a specific history. Written literature and orature are the main means by which a particular language transmits the images of the world contained in the culture it carries.

Language as communication and as culture are then products of each other. Communication creates culture: culture is a means of communication. Language carries culture, and culture carries, particularly through orature and literature, the entire body of values by which we come to perceive ourselves and our place in the world. How people perceive themselves affects how they look at their culture, at their politics and at the social production of wealth, at their entire relationship to nature and to other beings. Language is thus inseparable from ourselves as a community of human beings with a specific form and character, a specific history, a specific relationship to the world.

So what was the colonialist imposition of a foreign language doing to us children?

The real aim of colonialism was to control the people's wealth: what they produced, how they produced it, and how it was distributed; to control, in other words, the entire realm of the language of real life. Colonialism imposed its control of the social production of wealth through military conquest and subsequent political dictatorship. But its most important area of domination was the mental universe of the colonized, the control, through culture, of how people perceived themselves and their relationship to the world. Economic and political control can never be complete or effective without mental control. To control a people's culture is to control their tools of self-definition in relationship to others.

For colonialism this involved two aspects of the same process: the destruction or the deliberate undervaluing of a people's culture, their art, dances, religions, history, geography, education, orature and literature, and the conscious elevation of the language of the colonizer. The domination of a people's language by the languages of the colonizing nations was crucial to the domination of the mental universe of the colonized.

Take language as communication. Imposing a foreign language, and suppressing the native languages as spoken and written, were already breaking the harmony previously existing between the African child and the three aspects of language. Since the new language as a means of communication was a product of and was reflecting the "real language of life" elsewhere, it could never as spoken or written properly reflect or imitate the real life of that community. This may in part explain why technology always appears to us as slightly external, *their* product and not *ours*. The word "missile" used to hold an alien far-away sound until I recently learned its equivalent in Gĩkũyũ, *ngurukuhĩ*, and it made me apprehend it differently. Learning, for a colonial child, became a cerebral activity and not an emotionally felt experience.

But since the new, imposed languages could never completely break the native languages as spoken, their most effective area of domination was the third aspect of language as communication, the written. The language of an African child's formal education was foreign. The language of the books he read was foreign. The language of his conceptualization was foreign. Thought, in him, took the visible form of a foreign language. So the written language of a child's upbringing in the school (even his spoken language within the school compound) became divorced from his spoken language at home. There was often not the slightest relationship between the child's written world, which was also the language of his schooling, and the world of his immediate environment in the family and the community. For a colonial child, the harmony existing between the three aspects of language as communication was irrevocably broken. This resulted in the disassociation of the sensibility of that child from his natural and social environment, what we might call colonial alienation. The alienation became reinforced in the teaching of history, geography, music, where bourgeois Europe was always the center of the universe.

This disassociation, divorce, or alienation from the immediate environment becomes clearer when you look at colonial language as a carrier of culture.

Since culture is a product of the history of a people which it in turn reflects, the child was now being exposed exclusively to a culture that was a product of a world external to himself. He was being made to stand outside himself to look at himself. *Catching Them Young* is the title of a book on racism, class, sex, and politics in children's literature by Bob Dixon. "Catching them young" as an aim was even more true of a colonial child. The images of this world and his place in it implanted in a child take years to eradicate, if they ever can be.

Since culture does not just reflect the world in images but actually, through those very images, conditions a child to see that world in a certain way, the colonial child was made to see the world and where he stands in it as seen and defined by or reflected in the culture of the language of imposition.

And since those images are mostly passed on through orature and literature it meant the child would now only see the world as seen in the literature of his language of adoption. From the point of view of alienation, that is of seeing oneself from outside oneself as if one was another self, it does not matter that the imported literature carried the great humanist tradition of the best in Shakespeare, Goethe, Balzac, Tolstoy, Gorky, Brecht, Sholokhov, Dickens. The location of this great mirror of imagination was necessarily Europe and its history and culture and the rest of the universe was seen from that center.

But obviously it was worse when the colonial child was exposed to images of his world as mirrored in the written languages of his colonizer. Where his own native languages were associated in his impressionable mind with low status, humiliation, corporal punishment, slow-footed intelligence and ability or downright stupidity, non-intelligibility and barbarism, this was reinforced by the world he met in the works of such geniuses of racism as a Rider Haggard or a Nicholas Monserrat; not to mention the pronouncement of some of the giants of western intellectual and political establishment, such as Hume (". . . the negro is naturally inferior to the whites . . ."), Thomas Jefferson (". . . the blacks . . . are inferior to the whites on the endowments of both body and mind . . ."), or Hegel with his Africa comparable to a land of childhood still enveloped in the dark mantle of the night as far as the development of self-conscious history was concerned. Hegel's statement that there was nothing harmonious with humanity to be found in the African character is representative of the racist images of Africans and Africa such a colonial child was bound to encounter in the literature of the colonial languages. The results could be disastrous.

In her paper read to the conference on the teaching of African literature in schools held in Nairobi in 1973, entitled "Written Literature and Black Images," the Kenyan writer and scholar Professor Mîcere Mûgo related how a reading of the description of Gagool as an old African woman in Rider Haggard's *King Solomon's Mines* had for a long time made her feel mortal terror whenever she encountered old African women. In his autobiography *This Life* Sydney Poitier describes how, as a result of the literature he had read, he had come to associate Africa with snakes. So on arrival in Africa and being put up in a modern hotel in a modern city, he could not sleep because he kept on looking for snakes everywhere, even under the bed. These two have been able to pinpoint the origins of their fears. But for most others the negative image becomes internalized and it affects their cultural and even political choices in ordinary living.

Thus Léopold Sédar Senghor[3] has said very clearly that although the colonial language had been forced upon him, if he had been given the choice he would still have opted for French. He becomes lyrical in his subservience to French:

> We express ourselves in French since French has a universal vocation and since our message is also addressed to French people and others. In our languages [i.e. African languages] the halo that surrounds the words is by nature merely that of sap and blood; French words send out thousands of rays like diamonds.

Senghor has now been rewarded by being anointed to an honored place in the French Academy—that institution for safe-guarding the purity of the French language.

In Malawi, Banda[4] has erected his own monument by way of an institution, The Kamuzu Academy, designed to aid the brightest pupils of Malawi in their mastery of English.

> It is a grammar school designed to produce boys and girls who will be sent to universities like Harvard, Chicago, Oxford, Cambridge and Edinburgh and be able to compete on equal terms with others elsewhere.
>
> The President has instructed that Latin should occupy a central place in the curriculum. All teachers must have had at least some Latin in their academic background. Dr Banda has often said that no one can fully master English without knowledge of languages such as Latin and French . . .

3. Léopold Sédar Senghor: African statesman and poet, born in 1906, became president of the republic of Senegal in 1960.

4. Hastings Kamuzu Banda: born in 1902 (?), became president of Malawi in 1966.

For good measure no Malawian is allowed to teach at the academy—none is good enough—and all the teaching staff has been recruited from Britain. A Malawian might lower the standards, or rather, the purity of the English language. Can you get a more telling example of hatred of what is national, and a servile worship of what is foreign even though dead?

In history books and popular commentaries on Africa, too much has been made of the supposed differences in the policies of the various colonial powers, the British indirect rule (or the pragmatism of the British in their lack of a cultural program!) and the French and Portuguese conscious program of cultural assimilation. These are a matter of detail and emphasis. The final effect was the same: Senghor's embrace of French as this language with a universal vocation is not so different from Chinua Achebe's[5] gratitude in 1964 to English—"those of us who have inherited our English language may not be in a position to appreciate the value of the inheritance." The assumptions behind the practice of those of us who have abandoned our mother-tongues and adopted European ones as the creative vehicles of our imagination, are not different either.

Thus the 1962 conference of "African Writers of English expression" was only recognizing, with approval and pride of course, what through all the years of selective education and rigorous tutelage, we had already been led to accept: the "fatalistic logic of the unassailable position of English in our literature." The logic was embodied deep in imperialism; and it was imperialism and its effects that we did not examine at Makerere. It is the final triumph of a system of domination when the dominated start singing its virtues.

1986

5. Chinua Achebe: Nigerian novelist, poet, and essayist, born in 1930.

THE READER

1. *"Culture is . . . an image-forming agent in the mind of a child" (p. 780). Is the author right? How do you know? How can this statement be tested?*
2. *What distinctions does Ngũgĩ make between language as communication and language as culture? What connections between the two does he see?*
3. *What connections does Ngũgĩ draw between language and colonialism?*
4. *Ngũgĩ uses different verbs to describe the relation between language and reality. List some. If you grant his idea about that relation, is his conclusion inevitable?*
5. *On p. 781, Ngũgĩ speaks movingly of the power of language and literature to define the selves of the speakers and then of the division between English and Gĩkũyũ in his experience. His context is colonial, but the idea is plausible in other contexts—popular culture, for in-*

stance. To what degree do rock music and cult movies provide analogies to his experience of his native Gĩkũyũ?

THE WRITER

1. On p. 781, Ngũgĩ makes an important distinction between images and reality. How does he use this distinction in his essay?

2. On p. 783, Ngũgĩ speaks of other Africans who have adopted French or English. What does he think of them? Can he share a culture with them?

3. When Ngũgĩ wrote the book from which this piece is taken, he said it would be the last time he would write in English. Address a letter to Ngũgĩ either applauding his decision or attempting to change his mind.

4. Write a brief essay comparing Ngũgĩ's view of the political effects of language with Orwell's (p. 353).

5. Write a brief essay comparing Ngũgĩ's view of the cultural effect of language with Rodriguez's (p. 315).

Charles R. Morris

CIVIL DISOBEDIENCE

The assignment of primacy to the moral over the political resonates comfortably within the American tradition, however revolutionary its implications. The radical Black Panthers, with a wry sense of nuance, adopted the Declaration of Independence as their official platform. ("It is the Right of the People ... it is their duty, to throw off such Government.") The higher claim of the civil rights movement over legal authority was formally stated by Martin Luther King in his famous "Letter from a Birmingham Jail" of 1963. The letter was a response to a group of Southern white clergymen who had criticized King for breaking local laws during a series of demonstrations. It is notable not only for its claim that civil disobedience is a legitimate technique to advance the cause of equal rights, but for its attempt to lay down a formal set of rules for its application and practice.

King argued that his violation of the law in Birmingham qualified as "legitimate" civil disobedience, as the concept was developed in the teachings and writings of Gandhi. In King's view, the pressing reality of social injustice in the South made action imperative. The lawbreaking was not casual, for King had carefully ascertained the facts of the law beforehand. He had negotiated fruitlessly and at great length with local officials. He had "purified" himself with prayer and meditation before his action. He had taken care that he would break the law nonviolently. The laws violated were either unjust laws—they applied only to a minority or they were undemocratically passed—or proper laws being applied unjustly. Finally, the violation was "open and loving," and King was willing to accept whatever penalty was imposed.

Civil disobedience became something of an intellectual industry in the mid-1960s. It was not a new idea, of course. Aside from Gandhi and Sam Adams, there was Henry David Thoreau, who had refused to pay taxes in 1848 to protest against the Mexican War; there were the Boston abolitionists who had forcibly prevented the return of fugitive slaves, and, if one cared to stretch the gospels a bit, there was even Jesus. The underlying assumption was that there was a higher law that took precedence over political codes. The problem for philosophers and moralists was to define that higher law and to establish the circumstances that made civil disobedience permissible. Some of the attempts were ingenious; in my view, none of them was wholly successful. One fairly typical formulation, that of John Rawls,[1] defined civil disobedience as a "public, nonviolent, conscientious yet political act contrary to law usually done with the aim of bringing about a change in the law or policies of the government." The public character of the act was necessary if it was to result in the desired changes. The "conscientious" requirement meant that the lawbreaking was reasoned and principled—that the lawbreakers, in effect, could point to the higher law they were obeying, could demonstrate why it imposed a superior obligation, and could show that there was no available recourse within the current legal framework.

It was more difficult to demonstrate why civil disobedience had to be nonviolent. Most theorists, in company with King's Birmingham letter, argued that nonviolence advertised the lawbreakers' continued respect for the law and increased the effectiveness of the protest. But that rings more of tactical advice than of moral canon. By 1963, in fact, an important element in SNCC[2]—oxymoronically but understandably—had rejected nonviolence and were carrying guns. Howard Zinn, who had become a sort of quasi-official SNCC theorist, insisted that change may *require* violence, citing sources as diverse as Albert Camus, Frederick Douglass, Ralph Waldo Emerson, and Reinhold Niebuhr. While scholars like Rawls, Ronald Dworkin, and Morris Cohen were constructing high-minded hypotheses drawn from civil rights or anti-Vietnam protests, Zinn was calling for takeovers of university buildings, "smashing a hospital gate" to keep the hospital from closing, "occupying a skyscraper and living in it," "running up bills and sending them to the federal government," forcibly keeping the police out of the ghettos, and other

1. John Rawls: Harvard philosophy professor.
2. The Student Nonviolent Coordinating Committee, an organization formed in the 1960s to further the civil-rights movement and to oppose the Vietnam War.

fevered products of a rich academic imagination. Violence, as H. Rap Brown, a later SNCC chairman, jeered, was "as American as cherry pie."

It may not be possible to construct a truly consistent theory of "legitimate" or "permissible" civil disobedience. Locke and Hume argued that selective disobedience entails rejection of the entire government. If individuals are the final arbiters of the law, the entire structure of authority must eventually collapse. Rawls and Zinn struggle to avoid that logic, but the arguments of both, if they have little else in common, are circular —each selects specific incidents of civil disobedience he approves of and then searches for principles to fit them. Nor is historical precedent of much help. Thoreau was more quirky than principled, and admitted that he enjoyed picking and choosing which laws to obey. Emerson made a hero and martyr of John Brown,[3] who was probably a psychopath. Gandhi, at least in his Indian phase, and Sam Adams were forthright revolutionaries, not reformists; their civil disobedience was merely a tactic in the larger treason.

It is easy to conceive of instances where the law should be disobeyed. The logic of Nuremberg,[4] after all, rested on the principle of a higher duty. But when the most extreme cases have been allowed for, the argument quickly collapses into mere subjectivity. Rawls maintains that "each person must decide for himself whether the circumstances justify civil disobedience," although he hastens to add that "it does not follow that one is to decide as one pleases." The distinction may be sufficient guide for a Harvard philosophy professor but is rather harder to employ as the platform of a mass movement. The early proclivity of the Kennedy administration to prefer tranquillity and ordered change over strict justice sprang from an instinctive Burkean[5] reliance on settled institutions. As pragmatic liberals they were prepared to accept, even embrace, change. But their insistence that it proceed incrementally and at a pace that could be readily absorbed by the existing political structure seemed arid and unfeeling in the face of the pressing issues that were churning to the surface first in the South and later in Vietnam. And, to an extent, their position was arid and unfeeling, and in the case of Vietnam, casually arrogant as well. But if pragmatism proved an inadequate guide as the country careened toward the confrontations of the late 1960s, it remained to be shown whether deduction from principles of individual morality could provide a more reliable compass.

1984

3. John Brown: American abolitionist (1800–59), hanged for leading a raid on the federal arsenal at Harpers Ferry, Virginia.
4. Site of the war-crimes trials of Nazi leaders after World War II.

5. A reference to Edmund Burke (1729–97), British political writer and statesman, influential spokesman for European conservatives.

THE READER

1. *This is a historical account of civil disobedience. What are Morris's data? What are the phenomena he is observing in order to write his history? Arrange them on a scale from the most factual and objective to the most abstract and general. Where does his emphasis fall?*
2. *Morris permits himself some indirect judgments of people involved in civil disobedience. Cite some examples. Are they coherent enough to show Morris's own attitude toward civil disobedience? If so, what is it?*

THE WRITER

1. *On p. 786, Morris says that theorists "argued that nonviolence advertised the lawbreakers' continued respect for the law and increased the effectiveness of the protest." He then goes on to say, "That rings more of tactical advice than of moral canon." Write a paragraph to amplify his judgment or to refute it by explaining the moral grounds for the theorists' argument.*
2. *Choose a sentence expressing one of Morris's indirect judgments ("The Reader," question 2). Rewrite it, first, so that no judgment is expressed and, then, so as to express a different judgment.*

Ralph W. Conant

THE JUSTIFICATION OF CIVIL PROTEST, NONVIOLENT AND VIOLENT

There is substantial agreement among legal and political thinkers that nonviolent challenges to the policies and laws of civil authority are an indispensable mechanism of corrective change in a democratic society. Insofar as possible, procedures for challenge which may involve open and deliberate disobedience should be built into the laws and policies of the system, for such procedures give the system a quality of resilience and flexibility, the capacity to absorb constructive attack from within.

As George Lakay has pointed out, one great strength of democratic institutions is that they build a degree of conflict into the decision-making structure just so that conflicts can be resolved publicly and without violence. Adequately designed democratic institutions deliberately reflect shifting views and power relations of interest groups and the normal workings of compromise and settlement, and equilibrium is usually maintained. Civil disobedience, and other forms of civil protest, are resorted to when political adversaries exhaust means of compromise in the political arena. Then the less powerful of the adversaries is forced to carry his challenge into a legal procedure or to the public in a show of protest.

Agreement on a policy of deliberate tolerance of peaceful challenge does not imply automatic agreement on what conditions *justify* challenges that involve disobedience. Moreover, agreement on a policy of tolerance toward nonviolent civil disobedience bears no necessary relationship at all to the question of the justification of civil protest involving violence, as riots and insurrection always do.

Nonviolent civil disobedience is justified under the following circumstances:

1. When an oppressed group is deprived of lawful channels for remedying its condition; conversely, a resort to civil disobedience is never politically legitimate where methods of due process in both the legal and political systems are available as remedies.

2. As a means of resisting or refusing to participate in an obvious and intolerable evil perpetrated by civil authorities (for example, a policy of genocide or enslavement).

3. When government takes or condones actions that are inconsistent with values on which the society and the political system are built, and thus violates the basic assumptions on which the regime's legitimacy rests.

4. When it is certain that the law or policy in question violates the constitution of the regime and, therefore, would be ruled unconstitutional by proper authority if challenged.

5. When a change in law or policy is demanded by social or economic need in the community and the normal procedures of law and politics are inadequate, obstructed or held captive by antilegal forces.

6. When the actions of government have become so obnoxious to one's own personal ethics (value system) that one would feel hypocritical in submitting to a law that enforces these actions: for example, the Fugitive Slave Law.

It seems to me that a citizen is justified in originating or participating in an act of civil disobedience under any of these circumstances, and, as Herbert Kelman[1] has argued, that an act of civil disobedience in such circumstances should be generally regarded as *obligatory* in terms of the highest principles of citizenship. This does not mean that acts of civil disobedience should be ignored by civil authorities; on the contrary,

1. Herbert Kelman (b. 1927, Austria): psychologist and educator noted for his work on the ethics of social intervention.

aside from the damage such a policy would do to effectiveness of the act of civil disobedience, it must be considered the obligation of the regime to punish a law breaker *so long as the violated law is in force*. As William Buckley[2] has argued, it is the individual's right to refuse to go along with his community, but the community, not the individual, must specify the consequences. For the regime to act otherwise would be to concede the right of personal veto over every act of government. At the same time, a conscientious challenge to civil authority (with full expectation of punishment) aimed at repairing a serious flaw in the system of justice is a step every citizen should know how to *decide* to take.

When Is Civil Protest Involving Violence Justified?

Americans like to think of themselves as a peace-loving people, yet violence is and always has been an important and sometimes indispensable instrument of social, economic and political change in our national history. We do not need to be reminded of the role it has played in United States foreign policy and in domestic relations.

The fact is that Americans are *both* peace-loving and willing to resort to violence when other avenues of goal achievement seem closed or ineffective. In our national history violence was the ultimate instrument in our conquest of the lands on the North American continent that now comprise the nation. Violence freed the American colonists from British rule and later insured freedom of the seas (1812–1815). Violence abolished slavery, established the bargaining rights of labor, twice put down threatening tyrannies in Europe and once in the Asian Pacific. In the present day, violence is the unintended instrument of black citizens to break through oppressive discrimination in housing, employment, education and political rights.

Americans have always taken the position that violence could be justified *as an instrument of last resort* in the achievement of critical national goals or in the face of external threat.

While it is true that we have always felt most comfortable about government-sponsored violence and especially violence in response to an external threat, we have often rationalized *post factum* the use of violence by aggrieved segments of the population *when the cause was regarded as a just one in terms of our deeply held egalitarian values*. The anti-draft riots during the Civil War are one example; labor strife that finally led to legitimizing workers' bargaining rights is another. Two or three generations from now, the ghetto riots (and even the spasmodic insurrection that is bound to follow) will be seen as having contributed to the perfection of our system of egalitarian values. Thus, I conclude that violence in

2. William Buckley, Jr. (b. 1925): magazine editor, author, influential advocate of conservatism in America.

the cause of hewing to our most cherished goals of freedom, justice and equal opportunity for all our citizens is and will remain as indispensable a corrective ingredient in our system as peaceful acts of civil disobedience. The sole qualification is that all other avenues of legitimate and peaceful change first be substantially closed, exhausted or ineffective.

When an aggrieved segment of the population finds it necessary to resist, riot or commit deliberate acts of insurrection, the government must respond firmly to enforce the law, to protect people and property from the consequences of violence, but it must, with equal energy and dedication, seek out the causes of the outbursts and move speedily to rectify any injustices that are found at the root of the trouble.

1968

THE READER

1. *Conant lists six circumstances in which he believes nonviolent civil disobedience is justified. Which of these six have similar bases for justification? Are some bases stronger than others?*
2. *Under what circumstances does Conant believe violence is justified?*
3. *What does Conant believe the obligations of government are? Is this view consistent with his other views?*

THE WRITER

1. *What assumptions does Conant seem to be making about his audience?*
2. *Conant asserts that violence is sometimes justified, and that nonviolent civil disobedience is sometimes justified. Does he offer the same or different kinds of support for these two assertions? Is the case for one stronger than the case for the other?*
3. *Conant asserts that a citizen not only is justified in engaging in an act of civil disobedience under some circumstances, but also has an obligation to do so. Write a brief essay supporting or opposing his view.*
4. *Write a brief essay comparing Conant's views with those of Morris (p. 788) or King (p. 792).*

Martin Luther King, Jr.

LETTER FROM BIRMINGHAM JAIL[1]

My Dear Fellow Clergymen:

While confined here in the Birmingham city jail, I came across your recent statement calling my present activities "unwise and untimely." Seldom do I pause to answer criticism of my work and ideas. If I sought to answer all the criticisms that cross my desk, my secretaries would have little time for anything other than such correspondence in the course of the day, and I would have no time for constructive work. But since I feel that you are men of genuine good will and that your criticisms are sincerely set forth, I want to try to answer your statement in what I hope will be patient and reasonable terms.

I think I should indicate why I am here in Birmingham, since you have been influenced by the view which argues against "outsiders coming in." I have the honor of serving as president of the Southern Christian Leadership Conference, an organization operating in every southern state, with headquarters in Atlanta, Georgia. We have some eighty-five affiliated organizations across the South, and one of them is the Alabama Christian Movement for Human Rights. Frequently we share staff, educational, and financial resources with our affiliates. Several months ago the affiliate here in Birmingham asked us to be on call to engage in a nonviolent direct-action program if such were deemed necessary. We readily consented, and when the hour came we lived up to our promise. So I, along with several members of my staff, am here because I was invited here. I am here because I have organizational ties here.

But more basically, I am in Birmingham because injustice is here. Just as the prophets of the eighth century B.C. left their villages and carried their "thus saith the Lord" far beyond the boundaries of their home towns, and just as the Apostle Paul left his village of Tarsus and carried the gospel of Jesus Christ to the far corners of the Greco-Roman world, so am I compelled to carry the gospel of freedom beyond my own home town. Like Paul, I must constantly respond to the Macedonian call for aid.

1. This response to a published statement by eight fellow clergymen from Alabama (Bishop C. C. J. Carpenter, Bishop Joseph A. Durick, Rabbi Milton L. Grafman, Bishop Paul Hardin, Bishop Holan B. Harmon, the Reverend George M. Murray, the Reverend Edward V. Ramage and the Reverend Earl Stallings) was composed under somewhat constricting circumstances. Begun on the margins of the newspaper in which the statement appeared while I was in jail, the letter was continued on scraps of writing paper supplied by a friendly Negro trusty, and concluded on a pad my attorneys were eventually permitted to leave me. Although the text remains in substance unaltered, I have indulged in the author's prerogative of polishing it for publication [King's note].

Moreover, I am cognizant of the interrelatedness of all communities and states. I cannot sit idly by in Atlanta and not be concerned about what happens in Birmingham. Injustice anywhere is a threat to justice everywhere. We are caught in an inescapable network of mutuality, tied in a single garment of destiny. Whatever affects one directly, affects all indirectly. Never again can we afford to live with the narrow, provincial "outside agitator" idea. Anyone who lives inside the United States can never be considered an outsider anywhere within its bounds.

You deplore the demonstrations taking place in Birmingham. But your statement, I am sorry to say, fails to express a similar concern for the conditions that brought about the demonstrations. I am sure that none of you would want to rest content with the superficial kind of social analysis that deals merely with effects and does not grapple with underlying causes. It is unfortunate that demonstrations are taking place in Birmingham, but it is even more unfortunate that the city's white power structure left the Negro community with no alternative.

In any nonviolent campaign there are four basic steps: collection of the facts to determine whether injustices exist; negotiation; self-purification; and direct action. We have gone through all these steps in Birmingham. There can be no gainsaying the fact that racial injustice engulfs this community. Birmingham is probably the most thoroughly segregated city in the United States. Its ugly record of brutality is widely known. Negroes have experienced grossly unjust treatment in the courts. There have been more unsolved bombings of Negro homes and churches in Birmingham than in any other city in the nation. These are the hard, brutal facts of the case. On the basis of these conditions, Negro leaders sought to negotiate with the city fathers. But the latter consistently refused to engage in good-faith negotiation.

Then, last September, came the opportunity to talk with leaders of Birmingham's economic community. In the course of the negotiations, certain promises were made by the merchants—for example, to remove the stores' humiliating racial signs. On the basis of these promises, the Reverend Fred Shuttlesworth and the leaders of the Alabama Christian Movement for Human Rights agreed to a moratorium on all demonstrations. As the weeks and months went by, we realized that we were the victims of a broken promise. A few signs, briefly removed, returned; the others remained.

As in so many past experiences, our hopes had been blasted, and the shadow of deep disappointment settled upon us. We had no alternative except to prepare for direct action, whereby we would present our very bodies as a means of laying our case before the conscience of the local and the national community. Mindful of the difficulties involved, we decided to undertake a process of self-purification. We began a series of workshops on nonviolence, and we repeatedly asked ourselves: "Are you able to accept blows without retaliating?" "Are you able to endure the ordeal of jail?" We decided to schedule our direct-action program for the Easter season, realizing that except for Christmas, this is the main shopping period of the year. Knowing that a strong economic-withdrawal program would be the by-product of direct action, we felt that this would be the best time to bring pressure to bear on the merchants for the needed change.

Then it occurred to us that Birmingham's mayoral election was coming up in March, and we speedily decided to postpone action until after election day. When we discovered that the Commissioner of Public Safety, Eugene "Bull" Connor, had piled up enough votes to be in the run-off, we decided again to postpone action until the day after the run-off so that the demonstrations could not be used to cloud the issues. Like many others, we wanted to see Mr. Connor defeated, and to this end we endured postponement after postponement. Having aided in this community need, we felt that our direct-action program could be delayed no longer.

You may well ask, "Why direct action? Why sit-ins, marches, and so forth? Isn't negotiation a better path?" You are quite right in calling for negotiation. Indeed, this is the very purpose of direct action. Nonviolent direct action seeks to create such a crisis and foster such a tension that a community which has constantly refused to negotiate is forced to confront the issue. It seeks so to dramatize the issue that it can no longer be ignored. My citing the creation of tension as part of the work of the nonviolent-resister may sound rather shocking. But I must confess that I am not afraid of the word "tension." I have earnestly opposed violent tension, but there is a type of constructive, nonviolent tension which is necessary for growth. Just as Socrates felt that it was necessary to create a tension in the mind so that individuals could rise from the bondage of myths and half-truths to the unfettered realm of creative analysis and objective appraisal, so must we see the need for nonviolent gadflies to create the kind of tension in society that will help men rise from the dark depths of prejudice and racism to the majestic heights of understanding and brotherhood.

The purpose of our direct-action program is to create a situation so crisis-packed that it will inevitably open the door to negotiation. I therefore concur with you in your call for negotiation. Too long has our beloved Southland been bogged down in a tragic effort to live in monologue rather than dialogue.

One of the basic points in your statement is that the action that I and my associates have taken in Birmingham is untimely. Some have asked: "Why didn't you give the new city administration time to act?" The only answer that I can give to this query is that the new Birmingham administration must be prodded about as much as the outgoing one, before it will act. We are sadly mistaken if we feel that the election of Albert Boutwell as mayor will bring the millennium to Birmingham. While Mr. Boutwell is a much more gentle person than Mr. Connor, they are both segregationists, dedicated to maintenance of the status quo. I have hoped that Mr. Boutwell will be reasonable enough to see the futility of massive resistance to desegregation. But he will not see this without pressure from devotees of civil rights. My friends, I must say to you that we have not made a single gain in civil rights without determined legal and nonviolent pressure. Lamentably, it is an historical fact that privileged groups seldom give up their privileges voluntarily. Individuals may see the moral light and voluntarily give up their unjust posture; but, as Reinhold Niebuhr has reminded us, groups tend to be more immoral than individuals.

We know through painful experience that freedom is never voluntarily given by the oppressor; it must be demanded by the oppressed. Frankly, I have yet to engage in a direct-action campaign that was "well timed" in the view of those who have not suffered unduly from the disease of segregation. For years now I have heard the word "Wait!" It rings in the ear of every Negro with piercing familiarity. This "Wait" has almost always meant "Never." We must come to see, with one of our distinguished jurists, that "justice too long delayed is justice denied."

We have waited for more than 340 years for our constitutional and God-given rights. The nations of Asia and Africa are moving with jetlike speed toward gaining political independence, but we still creep at horse-and-buggy pace toward gaining a cup of coffee at a lunch counter. Perhaps it is easy for those who have never felt the stinging darts of segregation to say, "Wait." But when you have seen vicious mobs lynch your mothers and fathers at will and drown your sisters and brothers at whim; when you have seen hate-filled policemen curse, kick, and even kill your black brothers and sisters; when you see the vast majority of your twenty million Negro brothers smothering in an airtight cage of poverty in the midst of an affluent society; when you suddenly find your tongue twisted and your speech stammering as you seek to explain to your six-year-old daughter why she can't go to the public amusement park that has just been advertised on television, and see tears welling up in her eyes when she is told that Funtown is closed to colored children, and see ominous clouds of inferiority beginning to form in her little mental sky, and see her beginning to distort her personality by developing an unconscious bitterness toward white people; when you have to concoct an answer for a five-year-old son who is asking, "Daddy, why do white people treat colored people so mean?"; when you take a cross-country drive and find it necessary to sleep night after night in the uncomfortable corners of your automobile because no motel will accept you; when you are humiliated day in and day out by nagging signs reading "white" and "colored"; when your first name becomes "nigger," your middle name becomes "boy" (however old you are) and your last name becomes "John," and your wife and mother are never given the respected title "Mrs."; when you are harried by day and haunted by night by the fact that you are a Negro, living constantly at tiptoe stance, never quite knowing what to expect next, and are plagued with inner fears and outer resentments; when you are forever fighting a degenerating sense of "nobodiness"—then you will understand why we find it difficult to wait. There comes a time when the cup of endurance runs over, and men are no longer willing to be plunged into the abyss of despair. I hope, sirs, you can understand our legitimate and unavoidable impatience.

You express a great deal of anxiety over our willingness to break laws. This is certainly a legitimate concern. Since we so diligently urge people to obey the Supreme Court's decision of 1954 outlawing segregation in the public schools, at first glance it may seem rather paradoxical for us consciously to break laws. One may well ask: "How can you advocate breaking some laws and obeying others?" The answer lies in the fact that there are two types of laws: just and unjust. I would be the first to advocate obeying just laws. One has not only a legal but a moral responsibility to obey just laws. Conversely, one has a moral responsibility to disobey unjust laws. I would agree with St. Augustine that "an unjust law is no law at all."

Now, what is the difference between the two? How does one determine whether a law is just or unjust? A just law is a man-made code that squares with the moral law or the law of God. An unjust law is a code this is out of harmony with the moral law. To put it in the terms of St. Thomas Aquinas: An unjust law is a human law that is not rooted in eternal law and natural law. Any law that uplifts human personality is just. Any law that degrades human personality is unjust. All segregation statutes are unjust because segregation distorts the soul and damages the personality. It gives the segregator a false sense of superiority and the segregated a false sense of inferiority. Segregation, to use the terminology of the Jewish philosopher Martin Buber, substitutes an "I-it" relationship for an "I-thou" relationship and ends up relegating persons to the status of things. Hence segregation is not only politically, economically, and sociologically unsound, it is morally wrong and sinful. Paul Tillich has said that sin is separation. Is not segregation an existential expression of man's tragic separation, his awful estrangement, his terrible sinfulness? Thus it is that I can urge men to obey the 1954 decision of the Supreme Court, for it is morally right; and I can urge them to disobey segregation ordinances, for they are morally wrong.

Let us consider a more concrete example of just and unjust laws. An unjust law is a code that a numerical or power majority group compels a minority group to obey but does not make binding on itself. This is *difference* made legal. By the same token, a just law is a code that a majority compels a minority to follow and that it is willing to follow itself. This is *sameness* made legal.

Let me give another explanation. A law is unjust if it is inflicted on a minority that, as a result of being denied the right to vote, had no part in enacting or devising the law. Who can say that the legislature of Alabama which set up that state's segregation laws was democratically elected? Throughout Alabama all sorts of devious methods are used to prevent Negroes from becoming registered voters, and there are some counties in which, even though Negroes constitute a majority of the population, not a single Negro is registered. Can any law enacted under such circumstances be considered democratically structured?

Sometimes a law is just on its face and unjust in its application. For instance, I have been arrested on a charge of parading without a permit. Now, there is nothing wrong in having an ordinance which requires a permit for a parade. But such an ordinance becomes unjust when it is used to maintain segregation and to deny citizens the First-Amendment privilege of peaceful assembly and protest.

I hope you are able to see the distinction I am trying to point out. In no sense do I advocate evading or defying the law, as would the rabid segregationist. That would lead to anarchy. One who breaks an unjust law must do so openly, lovingly, and with a willingness to accept the penalty. I submit that an individual who breaks a law that conscience tells him is unjust, and who willingly accepts the penalty of imprisonment in order to arouse the conscience of the community over its injustice, is in reality expressing the highest respect for law.

Of course, there is nothing new about this kind of civil disobedience. It was evidenced sublimely in the refusal of Shadrach, Meshach, and Abednego to obey the laws of Nebuchadnezzar, on the ground that a higher moral law was at stake. It was practiced superbly by the early Christians, who were willing to face hungry lions and the excruciating pain of chopping blocks rather than submit to certain unjust laws of the Roman Empire. To a degree, academic freedom is a reality today because Socrates practiced civil disobedience.[2] In our own nation, the Boston Tea Party represented a massive act of civil disobedience.

We should never forget that everything Adolf Hitler did in Germany was "legal" and everything the Hungarian freedom fighters[3] did in Hungary was "illegal." It was "illegal" to aid and comfort a Jew in Hitler's Germany. Even so, I am sure that, had I lived in Germany at the time, I

---

2. The ancient Greek philosopher Socrates was tried by the Athenians for corrupting their youth through his skeptical, questioning manner of teaching. He refused to change his ways, and was condemned to death.

3. In the anti-Communist revolution of 1956, which was quickly put down by the Russian army.

would have aided and comforted my Jewish brothers. If today I lived in a Communist country where certain principles dear to the Christian faith are suppressed, I would openly advocate disobeying that country's anti-religious laws.

I must make two honest confessions to you, my Christian and Jewish brothers. First, I must confess that over the past few years I have been gravely disappointed with the white moderate. I have almost reached the regrettable conclusion that the Negro's great stumbling block in his stride toward freedom is not the White Citizen's Counciler or the Ku Klux Klanner, but the white moderate, who is more devoted to "order" than to justice; who prefers a negative peace which is the absence of tension to a positive peace which is the presence of justice; who constantly says, "I agree with you in the goal you seek, but I cannot agree with your methods of direct action"; who paternalistically believes he can set the timetable for another man's freedom; who lives by a mythical concept of time and who constantly advises the Negro to wait for a "more convenient season." Shallow understanding from people of good will is more frustrating than absolute misunderstanding from people of ill will. Lukewarm acceptance is much more bewildering than outright rejection.

I had hoped that the white moderate would understand that law and order exist for the purpose of establishing justice and that when they fail in this purpose they become the dangerously structured dams that block the flow of social progress. I had hoped that the white moderate would understand that the present tension in the South is a necessary phase of the transition from an obnoxious negative peace, in which the Negro passively accepted his unjust plight, to a substantive and positive peace, in which all men will respect the dignity and worth of human personality. Actually, we who engage in nonviolent direct action are not the creators of tension. We merely bring to the surface the hidden tension that is already alive. We bring it out in the open, where it can be seen and dealt with. Like a boil that can never be cured so long as it is covered up but must be opened with all its ugliness to the natural medicines of air and light, injustice must be exposed, with all the tension its exposure creates, to the light of human conscience and the air of national opinion, before it can be cured.

In your statement you assert that our actions, even though peaceful, must be condemned because they precipitate violence. But is this a logical assertion? Isn't this like condemning a robbed man because his possession of money precipitated the evil act of robbery? Isn't this like condemning Socrates because his unswerving commitment to truth and his philosophical inquiries precipitated the act by the misguided populace in which they made him drink hemlock? Isn't this like condemning Jesus because his unique God-consciousness and never-ceasing devotion to God's will precipitated the evil act of crucifixion? We must come to see that, as the federal courts have consistently affirmed, it is wrong to urge an individual to cease his efforts to gain his basic constitutional rights because the quest may precipitate violence. Society must protect the robbed and punish the robber.

I had also hoped that the white moderate would reject the myth concerning time in relation to the struggle for freedom. I have just received a letter from a white brother in Texas. He writes: "All Christians know that the colored people will receive equal rights eventually, but it is possible that you are in too great a religious hurry. It has taken Christianity almost two thousand years to accomplish what it has. The teachings of Christ take time to come to earth." Such an attitude stems from a tragic misconception of time, from the strangely irrational notion that there is something in the very flow of time that will inevitably cure all ills. Actually, time itself is neutral; it can be used either destructively or constructively. More and more I feel that the people of ill will have used time much more effectively than have the people of good will. We will have to repent in this generation not merely for the hateful words and actions of the bad people, but for the appalling silence of the good people. Human progress never rolls in on wheels of inevitability; it comes through the tireless efforts of men willing to be co-workers with God, and without this hard work, time itself becomes an ally of the forces of social stagnation. We must use time creatively, in the knowledge that the time is always ripe to do right. Now is the time to make real the promise of democracy and transform our pending national elegy into a creative psalm of brotherhood. Now is the time to lift our national policy from the quicksand of racial injustice to the solid rock of human dignity.

You speak of our activity in Birmingham as extreme. At first I was rather disappointed that fellow clergymen would see my nonviolent efforts as those of an extremist. I began thinking about the fact that I stand in the middle of two opposing forces in the Negro community. One is a force of complacency, made up in part of Negroes who, as a result of long years of oppression, are so drained of self-respect and a sense of "somebodiness" that they have adjusted to segregation; and in part of a few middle-class Negroes who, because of a degree of academic and economic security and because in some ways they profit by segregation, have become insensitive to the problems of the masses. The other force is one of bitterness and hatred, and it comes perilously close to advocating violence. It is expressed in the various black nationalist groups that are springing up across the nation, the largest and best-known being Elijah Muhammad's Muslim movement. Nourished by the Negro's frustration over the continued existence of racial discrimination, this movement is made up of people who have lost faith in America, who have absolutely repudiated Christianity, and who have concluded that the white man is an incorrigible "devil."

I have tried to stand between these two forces, saying that we need emulate neither the "do-nothingism" of the complacent nor the hatred and despair of the black nationalist. For there is the more excellent way of love and nonviolent protest. I am grateful to God that, through the influence of the Negro church, the way of nonviolence became an integral part of our struggle.

If this philosophy had not emerged, by now many streets of the South would, I am convinced, be flowing with blood. And I am further convinced that if our white brothers dismiss as "rabblerousers" and "outside agitators" those of use who employ nonviolent direct action, and if they refuse to support our nonviolent efforts, millions of Negroes will, out of frustration and despair, seek solace and security in black-nationalist ideologies—a development that would inevitably lead to a frightening racial nightmare.

Oppressed people cannot remain oppressed forever. The yearning for freedom eventually manifests itself, and that is what has happened to the American Negro. Something within has reminded him of his birthright of freedom, and something without has reminded him that it can be gained. Consciously or unconsciously, he has been caught up by the Zeitgeist,[4] and with his black brothers of Africa and his brown and yellow brothers of Asia, South America, and the Caribbean, the United States Negro is moving with a sense of great urgency toward the promised land of racial justice. If one recognizes this vital urge that has engulfed the Negro community, one should readily understand why public demonstrations are taking place. The Negro has many pent-up resentments and latent frustrations, and he must release them. So let him march; let him make prayer pilgrimages to the city hall; let him go on freedom rides—and try to understand why he must do so. If his repressed emotions are not released in nonviolent ways, they will seek expression through violence; this is not a threat but a fact of history. So I have not said to my people, "Get rid of your discontent." Rather, I have tried to say that this normal and healthy discontent can be channeled into the creative outlet of nonviolent direct action. And now this approach is being termed extremist.

But though I was initially disappointed at being categorized as an extremist, as I continued to think about the matter I gradually gained a measure of satisfaction from the label. Was not Jesus an extremist for love: "Love your enemies, bless them that curse you, do good to them that hate you, and pray for them which despitefully use you, and persecute you." Was not Amos an extremist for justice: "Let justice roll down like waters and righteousness like an ever-flowing stream." Was not Paul an extremist for the Christian gospel: "I bear in my body the marks of the

4. The spirit of the times.

Lord Jesus." Was not Martin Luther an extremist: "Here I stand; I cannot do otherwise, so help me God." And John Bunyan: "I will stay in jail to the end of my days before I make a butchery of my conscience." And Abraham Lincoln: "This nation cannot survive half slave and half free." And Thomas Jefferson: "We hold these truths to be self-evident, that all men are created equal. . . ." So the question is not whether we will be extremists, but what kind of extremists we will be. Will we be extremists for hate or for love? Will we be extremists for the preservation of injustice or for the extension of justice? In that dramatic scene on Calvary's hill three men were crucified. We must never forget that all three were crucified for the same crime—the crime of extremism. Two were extremists for immorality, and thus fell below their environment. The other, Jesus Christ, was an extremist for love, truth, and goodness, and thereby rose above his environment. Perhaps the South, the nation, and the world are in dire need of creative extremists.

I had hoped that the white moderate would see this need. Perhaps I was too optimistic; perhaps I expected too much. I suppose I should have realized that few members of the oppressor race can understand the deep groans and passionate yearnings of the oppressed race, and still fewer have the vision to see that injustice must be rooted out by strong, persistent, and determined action. I am thankful, however, that some of our white brothers in the South have grasped the meaning of this social revolution and committed themselves to it. They are still all too few in quantity, but they are big in quality. Some—such as Ralph McGill, Lillian Smith, Harry Golden, James McBridge Dabbs, Ann Braden, and Sarah Patton Boyle—have written about our struggle in eloquent and prophetic terms. Others have marched with us down nameless streets of the South. They have languished in filthy, roach-infested jails, suffering the abuse and brutality of policemen who view them as "dirty nigger-lovers." Unlike so many of their moderate brothers and sisters, they have recognized the urgency of the moment and sensed the need for powerful "action" antidotes to combat the disease of segregation.

Let me take note of my other major disappointment. I have been so greatly disappointed with the white church and its leadership. Of course, there are some notable exceptions. I am not unmindful of the fact that each of you has taken some significant stands on this issue. I commend you, Reverend Stallings, for your Christian stand on this past Sunday, in welcoming Negroes to your worship service on a nonsegregated basis. I commend the Catholic leaders of this state for integrating Spring Hill College several years ago.

But despite these notable exceptions, I must honestly reiterate that I have been disappointed with the church. I do not say this as one of those negative critics who can always find something wrong with the church. I say this as a minister of the gospel, who loves the church; who was nurtured in its bosom; who has been sustained by its spiritual blessings and who will remain true to it as long as the cord of life shall lengthen.

When I was suddenly catapulted into the leadership of the bus protest in Montgomery, Alabama, a few years ago, I felt we would be supported by the white church. I felt that the white ministers, priests, and rabbis of the South would be among our strongest allies. Instead, some have been outright opponents, refusing to understand the freedom movement and misrepresenting its leaders; all too many others have been more cautious than courageous and have remained silent behind the anesthetizing security of stainedglass windows.

In spite of my shattered dreams, I came to Birmingham with the hope that the white religious leadership of this community would see the justice of our cause and, with deep moral concern, would serve as the channel through which our just grievances could reach the power structure. I had hoped that each of you would understand. But again I have been disappointed.

I have heard numerous southern religious leaders admonish their worshipers to comply with a desegregation decision because it is the law, but I have longed to hear white ministers declare: "Follow this decree because integration is morally right and because the Negro is your brother." In the midst of blatant injustices inflicted upon the Negro, I have watched white churchmen stand on the sideline and mouth pious irrelevancies and sanctimonious trivialities. In the midst of a mighty struggle to rid our nation of racial and economic injustice, I have heard many ministers say: "Those are social issues, with which the gospel has no real concern." And I have watched many churches commit themselves to a completely otherworldly religion which makes a strange, un-Biblical distinction between body and soul, between the sacred and the secular.

I have traveled the length and breadth of Alabama, Mississippi, and all the other southern states. On sweltering summer days and crisp autumn mornings I have looked at the South's beautiful churches with their lofty spires pointing heavenward. I have beheld the impressive outlines of her massive religious-education buildings. Over and over I have found myself asking: "What kind of people worship here? Who is their God? Where were their voices when the lips of Governor Barnett dripped with words of interposition and nullification? Where were they when Governor Wallace gave a clarion call for defiance and hatred? Where were their voices of support when bruised and weary Negro men and women decided to rise from the dark dungeons of complacency to the bright hills of creative protest?"

Yes, these questions are still in my mind. In deep disappointment I have wept over the laxity of the church. But be assured that my tears have been tears of love. There can be no deep disappointment where there is not deep love. Yes, I love the church. How could I do otherwise? I am in the rather unique position of being the son, the grandson, and the great-grandson of preachers. Yes, I see the church as the body of Christ. But, oh! How we have blemished and scarred that body through social neglect and through fear of being nonconformists.

There was a time when the church was very powerful—in the time when the early Christians rejoiced at being deemed worthy to suffer for what they believed. In those days the church was not merely a thermometer that recorded the ideas and principles of popular opinion; it was a thermostat that transformed the mores of society. Whenever the early Christians entered a town, the people in power became disturbed and immediately sought to convict the Christians for being "disturbers of the peace" and "outside agitators." But the Christians pressed on, in the conviction that they were "a colony of heaven," called to obey God rather than man. Small in number, they were big in commitment. They were too God-intoxicated to be "astronomically intimidated." By their effort and example they brought an end to such ancient evils as infanticide and gladiatorial contests.

Things are different now. So often the contemporary church is a weak, ineffectual voice with an uncertain sound. So often it is an archdefender of the status quo. Far from being disturbed by the presence of the church, the power structure of the average community is consoled by the church's silent—and often even vocal—sanction of things as they are.

But the judgment of God is upon the church as never before. If today's church does not recapture the sacrificial spirit of the early church, it will lose its authenticity, forfeit the loyalty of millions, and be dismissed as an irrelevant social club with no meaning for the twentieth century. Every day I meet young people whose disappointment with the church has turned into outright disgust.

Perhaps I have once again been too optimistic. Is organized religion too inextricably bound to the status quo to save our nation and the world? Perhaps I must turn my faith to the inner spiritual church, the church within the church, as the true *ekklesia*[5] and the hope of the world. But again I am thankful to God that some noble souls from the ranks of organized religion have broken loose from the paralyzing chains of conformity and joined us as active partners in the struggle for freedom. They have left their secure congregations and walked the streets of Albany, Georgia, with us. They have gone down the highways of the South on tortuous rides for freedom. Yes, they have gone to jail with us. Some have been dismissed from their churches, have lost the support of their bishops and fellow ministers. But they have acted in the faith that right defeated is stronger than evil triumphant. Their witness has been

5. The Greek New Testament word for the early Christian church.

the spiritual salt that has preserved the true meaning of the gospel in these troubled times. They have carved a tunnel of hope through the dark mountain of disappointment.

I hope the church as a whole will meet the challenge of this decisive hour. But even if the church does not come to the aid of justice, I have no despair about the future. I have no fear about the outcome of our struggle in Birmingham, even if our motives are at present misunderstood. We will reach the goal of freedom in Birmingham and all over the nation, because the goal of America is freedom. Abused and scorned though we may be, our destiny is tied up with America's destiny. Before the pilgrims landed at Plymouth, we were here. Before the pen of Jefferson etched the majestic words of the Declaration of Independence across the pages of history, we were here. For more than two centuries our forebears labored in this country without wages; they made cotton king; they built the homes of their masters while suffering gross injustice and shameful humiliation—and yet out of a bottomless vitality they continued to thrive and develop. If the inexpressible cruelties of slavery could not stop us, the opposition we now face will surely fail. We will win our freedom because the sacred heritage of our nation and the eternal will of God are embodied in our echoing demands.

Before closing I feel impelled to mention one other point in your statement that has troubled me profoundly. You warmly commended the Birmingham police force for keeping "order" and "preventing violence." I doubt that you would have so warmly commended the police force if you had seen its dogs sinking their teeth into unarmed, nonviolent Negroes. I doubt that you would so quickly commend the policemen if you were to observe their ugly and inhumane treatment of Negroes here in the city jail; if you were to watch them push and curse old Negro women and young Negro girls; if you were to see them slap and kick old Negro men and young boys; if you were to observe them, as they did on two occasions, refuse to give us food because we wanted to sing our grace together. I cannot join you in your praise of the Birmingham police department.

It is true that the police have exercised a degree of discipline in handling the demonstrators. In this sense they have conducted themselves rather "nonviolently" in public. But for what purpose? To preserve the evil system of segregation. Over the past few years I have consistently preached that nonviolence demands that the means we use must be as pure as the ends we seek. I have tried to make clear that it is wrong to use immoral means to attain moral ends. But now I must affirm that it is just as wrong, or perhaps even more so, to use moral means to preserve immoral ends. Perhaps Mr. Connor and his policemen have been rather nonviolent in public, as was Chief Pritchett in Albany, Georgia, but they have used the moral means of nonviolence to maintain the immoral end of racial injustice. As T. S. Eliot has said, "The last temptation is the greatest treason: To do the right deed for the wrong reason."

I wish you had commended the Negro sit-inners and demonstrators of Birmingham for their sublime courage, their willingness to suffer, and their amazing discipline in the midst of great provocation. One day the South will recognize its real heroes. They will be the James Merediths,[6] with the noble sense of purpose that enables them to face jeering and hostile mobs, and with the agonizing loneliness that characterizes the life of the pioneer. They will be old, oppressed, battered Negro women, symbolized in a seventy-two-year-old woman in Montgomery, Alabama, who rose up with a sense of dignity and with her people decided not to ride segregated buses, and who responded with ungrammatical profundity to one who inquired about her weariness: "My feets is tired, but my soul is at rest." They will be the young high school and college students, the young ministers of the gospel and a host of their elders, courageously and nonviolently sitting in at lunch counters and willingly going to jail for conscience' sake. One day the South will know that when these disinherited children of God sat down at lunch counters, they were in reality standing up for what is best in the American dream and for the most sacred values in our Judaeo-Christian heritage, thereby bringing our nation back to those great wells of democracy which were dug deep by the founding fathers in their formulation of the Constitution and the Declaration of Independence.

Never before have I written so long a letter. I'm afraid it is much too long to take your precious time. I can assure you that it would have been much shorter if I had been writing from a comfortable desk, but what else can one do when he is alone in a narrow jail cell, other than write long letters, think long thoughts, and pray long prayers?

If I have said anything in this letter that overstates the truth and indicates an unreasonable impatience, I beg you to forgive me. If I have said anything that understates the truth and indicates my having a patience that allows me to settle for anything less than brotherhood, I beg God to forgive me.

I hope this letter finds you strong in the faith. I also hope that circumstances will soon make it possible for me to meet each of you, not as an integrationist or a civil-rights leader but as a fellow clergyman and a Christian brother. Let us all hope that the dark clouds of racial prejudice will soon pass away and the deep fog of misunderstanding will be lifted from our fear-drenched communities, and in some not too distant tomor-

---

6. Meredith was the first black to enroll at the University of Mississippi.

row the radiant stars of love and brotherhood will shine over our great
nation with all their scintillating beauty.

>   Yours for the cause of Peace and Brotherhood,
>   MARTIN LUTHER KING, JR.

1963

James Thurber

THE RABBITS WHO CAUSED ALL THE TROUBLE

Within the memory of the youngest child there was a family of rabbits
who lived near a pack of wolves. The wolves announced that they did not
like the way the rabbits were living. (The wolves were crazy about the
way they themselves were living, because it was the only way to live.)
One night several wolves were killed in an earthquake and this was
blamed on the rabbits, for it is well known that rabbits pound on the
ground with their hind legs and cause earthquakes. On another night one
of the wolves was killed by a bolt of lightning and this was also blamed on
the rabbits, for it is well known that lettuce-eaters cause lightning. The
wolves threatened to civilize the rabbits if they didn't behave, and the
rabbits decided to run away to a desert island. But the other animals, who
lived at a great distance, shamed them, saying, "You must stay where you
are and be brave. This is no world for escapists. If the wolves attack you,
we will come to your aid, in all probability." So the rabbits continued to
live near the wolves and one day there was a terrible flood which
drowned a great many wolves. This was blamed on the rabbits, for it is
well known that carrot-nibblers with long ears cause floods. The wolves
descended on the rabbits, for their own good, and imprisoned them in a
dark cave, for their own protection.

When nothing was heard about the rabbits for some weeks, the other
animals demanded to know what had happened to them. The wolves
replied that the rabbits had been eaten and since they had been eaten the
affair was a purely internal matter. But the other animals warned that
they might possibly unite against the wolves unless some reason was
given for the destruction of the rabbits. So the wolves gave them one.
"They were trying to escape," said the wolves, "and, as you know, this is
no world for escapists."

Moral: Run, don't walk, to the nearest desert island.

1955

Jonathan Swift

A MODEST PROPOSAL

For Preventing the Children of Poor People in Ireland
from Being a Burden to Their Parents or Country,
and for Making Them Beneficial to the Public

It is a melancholy object to those who walk through this great town[1] or travel in the country, when they see the streets, the roads, and cabin doors, crowded with beggars of the female-sex, followed by three, four, or six children, all in rags and importuning every passenger for an alms. These mothers, instead of being able to work for their honest livelihood, are forced to employ all their time in strolling to beg sustenance for their helpless infants, who, as they grow up, either turn thieves for want of work, or leave their dear native country to fight for the Pretender in Spain, or sell themselves to the Barbadoes.[2]

I think it is agreed by all parties that this prodigious number of children in the arms, or on the backs, or at the heels of their mothers, and frequently of their fathers, is in the present deplorable state of the kingdom a very great additional grievance; and therefore whoever could find out a fair, cheap, and easy method of making these children sound, useful members of the commonwealth would deserve so well of the public as to have his statue set up for a preserver of the nation.

But my intention is very far from being confined to provide only for the children of professed beggars; it is of a much greater extent, and shall take in the whole number of infants at a certain age who are born of parents in effect as little able to support them as those who demand our charity in the streets.

As to my own part, having turned my thoughts for many years upon this important subject, and maturely weighed the several schemes of other projectors,[3] I have always found them grossly mistaken in their computation. It is true, a child just dropped from its dam may be supported by her milk for a solar year, with little other nourishment; at most

1. Dublin.
2. Many poor Irish sought to escape poverty by emigrating to the Barbadoes and other western English colonies, paying for transport by binding themselves to work for a landowner there for a period of years. The Pretender, claimant to the English throne, was barred from succession after his father, King James II, was deposed in a Protestant revolution; thereafter, many Irish Catholics joined the Pretender in his exile in France and Spain, and in his unsuccessful attempts at counterrevolution.
3. People with projects; schemers.

not above the value of two shillings,[4] which the mother may certainly get, or the value in scraps, by her lawful occupation of begging; and it is exactly at one year old that I propose to provide for them in such a manner as instead of being a charge upon their parents or the parish, or wanting food and raiment for the rest of their lives, they shall on the contrary contribute to the feeding, and partly to the clothing, of many thousands.

There is likewise another great advantage in my scheme, that it will prevent those voluntary abortions, and that horrid practice of women murdering their bastard children, alas, too frequent among us, sacrificing the poor innocent babes, I doubt, more to avoid the expense than the shame, which would move tears and pity in the most savage and inhuman breast.

The number of souls in this kingdom being usually reckoned one million and a half, of these I calculate there may be about two hundred thousand couple whose wives are breeders; from which number I subtract thirty thousand couples who are able to maintain their own children, although I apprehend there cannot be so many under the present distresses of the kingdom; but this being granted, there will remain an hundred and seventy thousand breeders. I again subtract fifty thousand for those women who miscarry, or whose children die by accident or disease within the year. There only remain an hundred and twenty thousand children of poor parents annually born. The question therefore is, how this number shall be reared and provided for, which, as I have already said, under the present situation of affairs, is utterly impossible by all the methods hitherto proposed. For we can neither employ them in handicraft or agriculture; we neither build houses (I mean in the country) nor cultivate land. They can very seldom pick up a livelihood by stealing till they arrive at six years old, except where they are of towardly parts;[5] although I confess they learn the rudiments much earlier, during which time they can however be looked upon only as probationers, as I have been informed by a principal gentleman in the county of Cavan, who protested to me that he never knew above one or two instances under the age of six, even in a part of the kingdom so renowned for the quickest proficiency in that art.

I am assured by our merchants that a boy or a girl before twelve years old is no salable commodity; and even when they come to this age they will not yield above three pounds, or three pounds and half a crown[6] at most on the Exchange; which cannot turn to account either to the parents or the kingdom, the charge of nutriment and rags having been at least four times that value.

4. A shilling used to be worth about twenty-five cents.
5. Promising ability.
6. A pound was twenty shillings; a crown, five shillings.

I shall now therefore humbly propose my own thoughts, which I hope will not be liable to the least objection.

I have been assured by a very knowing American of my acquaintance in London, that a young healthy child well nursed is at a year old a most delicious, nourishing, and wholesome food, whether stewed, roasted, baked, or boiled; and I make no doubt that it will equally serve in a fricassee or a ragout.

I do therefore humbly offer it to public consideration that of the hundred and twenty thousand children, already computed, twenty thousand may be reserved for breed, whereof only one fourth part to be males, which is more than we allow to sheep, black cattle, or swine; and my reason is that these children are seldom the fruits of marriage, a circumstance not much regarded by our savages, therefore one male will be sufficient to serve four females. That the remaining hundred thousand may at a year old be offered in sale to the persons of quality and fortune through the kingdom, always advising the mother to let them suck plentifully in the last month, so as to render them plump and fat for a good table. A child will make two dishes at an entertainment for friends; and when the family dines alone, the fore or hind quarter will make a reasonable dish, and seasoned with a little pepper or salt will be very good boiled on the fourth day, especially in winter.

I have reckoned upon a medium that a child just born will weigh twelve pounds, and in a solar year if tolerably nursed increaseth to twenty-eight pounds.

I grant this food will be somewhat dear, and therefore very proper for landlords, who, as they have already devoured most of the parents, seem to have the best title to the children.

Infant's flesh will be in season throughout the year, but more plentiful in March, and a little before and after. For we are told by a grave author, an eminent French physician,[7] that fish being a prolific diet, there are more children born in Roman Catholic countries about nine months after Lent than at any other season; therefore, reckoning a year after Lent, the markets will be more glutted than usual, because the number of popish infants is at least three to one in this kingdom; and therefore it will have one other collateral advantage, by lessening the number of Papists among us.[8]

I have already computed the charge of nursing a beggar's child (in which list I reckon all cottagers, laborers, and four fifths of the farmers) to be about two shillings per annum, rags included; and I believe no gentleman would repine to give ten shillings for the carcass of a good fat child, which, as I have said, will make four dishes of excellent nutritive

7. The sixteenth-century comic writer François Rabelais.
8. The speaker is addressing Protestant Anglo-Irish, who were the chief landowners and administrators, and his views of Catholicism in Ireland and abroad echo theirs.

meat, when he hath only some particular friend or his own family to dine with him. Thus the squire will learn to be a good landlord, and grow popular among the tenants; the mother will have eight shillings net profit, and be fit for work till she produces another child.

Those who are more thrifty (as I must confess the times require) may flay the carcass; the skin of which artificially[9] dressed will make admirable gloves for ladies, and summer boots for fine gentlemen.

As to our city of Dublin, shambles[1] may be appointed for this purpose in the most convenient parts of it, and butchers we may be assured will not be wanting; although I rather recommend buying the children alive, and dressing them hot from the knife as we do roasting pigs.

A very worthy person, a true lover of his country, and whose virtues I highly esteem, was lately pleased in discoursing on this matter to offer a refinement upon my scheme. He said that many gentlemen of this kingdom, having of late destroyed their deer, he conceived that the want of venison might be well supplied by the bodies of young lads and maidens, not exceeding fourteen years of age nor under twelve, so great a number of both sexes in every county being now ready to starve for want of work and service; and these to be disposed of by their parents, if alive, or otherwise by their nearest relations. But with due deference to so excellent a friend and so deserving a patriot, I cannot be altogether in his sentiments; for as to the males, my American acquaintance assured me from frequent experience that their flesh was generally tough and lean, like that of our schoolboys, by continual exercise, and their taste disagreeable; and to fatten them would not answer the charge. Then as to the females, it would, I think with humble submission, be a loss to the public, because they soon would become breeders themselves: and besides, it is not improbable that some scrupulous people might be apt to censure such a practice (although indeed very unjustly) as a little bordering upon cruelty; which, I confess, hath always been with me the strongest objection against any project, how well soever intended.

But in order to justify my friend, he confessed that this expedient was put into his head by the famous Psalmanazar, a native of the island Formosa,[2] who came from thence to London above twenty years ago, and in conversation told my friend that in his country when any young person happened to be put to death, the executioner sold the carcass to persons of quality as a prime dainty; and that in his time the body of a plump girl of fifteen, who was crucified for an attempt to poison the emperor, was sold to his Imperial Majesty's prime minister of state, and other great mandarins of the court, in joints from the gibbet, at four hundred crowns.

9. Skillfully.
1. Slaughterhouses.
2. Actually a Frenchman, George Psalmanazar had passed himself off as from Formosa (now Taiwan) and had written a fictitious book about his "homeland," with descriptions of human sacrifice and cannibalism.

Neither indeed can I deny that if the same use were made of several plump young girls in this town, who without one single groat[3] to their fortunes cannot stir abroad without a chair,[4] and appear at the playhouse and assemblies in foreign fineries which they never will pay for, the kingdom would not be the worse.

Some persons of a desponding spirit are in great concern about that vast number of poor people who are aged, diseased, or maimed, and I have been desired to employ my thoughts what course may be taken to ease the nation of so grievous an encumbrance. But I am not in the least pain upon that matter, because it is very well known that they are every day dying and rotting by cold and famine, and filth and vermin, as fast as can be reasonably expected. And as to the younger laborers, they are now in almost as hopeful a condition. They cannot get work, and consequently pine away for want of nourishment to a degree that if at any time they are accidentally hired to common labor, they have not strength to perform it; and thus the country and themselves are happily delivered from the evils to come.

I have too long digressed, and therefore shall return to my subject. I think the advantages by the proposal which I have made are obvious and many, as well as of the highest importance.

For first, as I have already observed, it would greatly lessen the number of Papists, with whom we are yearly overrun, being the principal breeders of the nation as well as our most dangerous enemies; and who stay at home on purpose to deliver the kingdom to the Pretender, hoping to take their advantage by the absence of so many good Protestants, who have chosen rather to leave their country than to stay at home and pay tithes against their conscience to an Episcopal curate.

Secondly, the poorer tenants will have something valuable of their own, which by law may be made liable to distress,[5] and help to pay their landlord's rent, their corn and cattle being already seized and money a thing unknown.

Thirdly, whereas the maintenance of an hundred thousand children, from two years old and upwards, cannot be computed at less than ten shillings a piece per annum, the nation's stock will be thereby increased fifty thousand pounds per annum, besides the profit of a new dish introduced to the tables of all gentlemen of fortune in the kingdom who have any refinement in taste. And the money will circulate among ourselves, the goods being entirely of our own growth and manufacture.

Fourthly, the constant breeders, besides the gain of eight shillings sterling per annum by the sale of their children, will be rid of the charge of maintaining them after the first year.

Fifthly, this food would likewise bring great custom to taverns, where

3. An English coin worth about four pennies.   5. Seizure for the payment of debts.
4. A sedan chair.

the vintners will certainly be so prudent as to procure the best receipts for dressing it to perfection, and consequently have their houses frequented by all the fine gentlemen, who justly value themselves upon their knowledge in good eating; and a skillful cook, who understands how to oblige his guests, will contrive to make it as expensive as they please.

Sixthly, this would be a great inducement to marriage, which all wise nations have either encouraged by rewards or enforced by laws and penalties. It would increase the care and tenderness of mothers toward their children, when they were sure of a settlement for life to the poor babes, provided in some sort by the public, to their annual profit instead of expense. We should see an honest emulation among the married women, which of them could bring the fattest child to the market. Men would become as fond of their wives during the time of pregnancy as they are now of their mares in foal, their cows in calf, or sows when they are ready to farrow; nor offer to beat or kick them (as is too frequent a practice) for fear of a miscarriage.

Many other advantages might be enumerated. For instance, the addition of some thousand carcasses in our exportation of barreled beef, the propagation of swine's flesh, and improvement in the art of making good bacon, so much wanted among us by the great destruction of pigs, too frequent at our tables, which are no way comparable in taste or magnificence to a well-grown, fat, yearling child, which roasted whole will make a considerable figure at a lord mayor's feast or any other public entertainment. But this and many others I omit, being studious of brevity.

Supposing that one thousand families in this city would be constant customers for infants' flesh, besides others who might have it at merry meetings, particularly weddings and christenings, I compute that Dublin would take off annually about twenty thousand carcasses, and the rest of the kingdom (where probably they will be sold somewhat cheaper) the remaining eighty thousand.

I can think of no one objection that will possibly be raised against this proposal, unless it should be urged that the number of people will be thereby much lessened in the kingdom. This I freely own, and it was indeed one principal design in offering it to the world. I desire the reader will observe, that I calculate my remedy for this one individual kingdom of Ireland and for no other that ever was, is, or I think ever can be upon earth. Therefore let no man talk to me of other expedients: of taxing our absentees at five shillings a pound: of using neither clothes nor household furniture except what is of our own growth and manufacture: of utterly rejecting the materials and instruments that promote foreign luxury: of curing the expensiveness of pride, vanity, idleness, and gaming in our women: of introducing a vein of parsimony, prudence, and temperance: of learning to love our country, in the want of which we differ even from

Laplanders and the inhabitants of Topinamboo[6]: of quitting our animosities and factions, nor acting any longer like the Jews, who were murdering one another at the very moment their city was taken: of being a little cautious not to sell our country and conscience for nothing: of teaching landlords to have at least one degree of mercy toward their tenants: lastly, of putting a spirit of honesty, industry, and skill into our shopkeepers; who, if a resolution could now be taken to buy only our native goods, would immediately unite to cheat and exact upon us in the price, the measure, and the goodness, nor could ever yet be brought to make one fair proposal of just dealing, though often and earnestly invited to it.[7]

Therefore I repeat, let no man talk to me of these and the like expedients, till he hath at least some glimpse of hope that there will ever be some hearty and sincere attempt to put them in practice.

But as to myself, having been wearied out for many years with offering vain, idle, visionary thoughts, and at length utterly despairing of success, I fortunately fell upon this proposal, which, as it is wholly new, so it hath something solid and real, of no expense and little trouble, full in our own power, and whereby we can incur no danger in disobliging England. For this kind of commodity will not bear exportation, the flesh being of too tender a consistence to admit a long continuance in salt, although perhaps I could name a country[8] which would be glad to eat up our whole nation without it.

After all, I am not so violently bent upon my own opinion as to reject any offer proposed by wise men, which shall be found equally innocent, cheap, easy, and effectual. But before something of that kind shall be advanced in contradiction to my scheme, and offering a better, I desire the author or authors will be pleased maturely to consider two points. First, as things now stand, how they will be able to find food and raiment for an hundred thousand useless mouths and backs. And secondly, there being a round million of creatures in human figure throughout this kingdom, whose sole subsistence put into a common stock would leave them in debt two millions of pounds sterling, adding those who are beggars by profession to the bulk of farmers, cottagers, and laborers, with their wives and children who are beggars in effect; I desire those politicians who dislike my overture, and may perhaps be so bold to attempt an answer, that they will first ask the parents of these mortals whether they would not at this day think it a great happiness to have been sold for food at a year old in the manner I prescribe, and thereby have avoided such a perpetual scene of misfortunes as they have since gone through by the oppression of landlords, the impossibility of paying rent without money or trade, the want of common sustenance, with neither house nor clothes to cover them from the inclemencies of the weather, and the most

6. A district in Brazil.
7. Swift himself had made these proposals

seriously in various previous works.
8. England.

inevitable prospect of entailing the like or greater miseries upon their breed forever.

I profess, in the sincerity of my heart, that I have not the least personal interest in endeavoring to promote this necessary work, having no other motive than the public good of my country, by advancing our trade, providing for infants, relieving the poor, and giving some pleasure to the rich. I have no children by which I can propose to get a single penny; the youngest being nine years old, and my wife past childbearing.

                                                                          1729

THE READER

1. At what point do you begin to suspect that Swift is using irony? What further evidence accumulates to make you certain that Swift is being ironic?
2. Does the essay shock you? Was it Swift's purpose to shock you?
3. What is the main target of Swift's attack? What subsidiary targets are there? Does Swift offer any serious solutions for the problems and conditions he is describing?

THE WRITER

1. This essay has been called one of the best examples of sustained irony in the English language. Irony is difficult to handle because there is always the danger that the reader will miss the irony and take what is said literally. What does Swift do to try to prevent this?
2. Why does Swift use such phrases as "just dropped from its dam," "whose wives are breeders," "one fourth part to be males"?
3. What devices of argument, apart from the use of irony, does Swift use that could be successfully applied to other subjects?
4. In the study questions for Orwell's "Shooting an Elephant" (p. 768), there is a brief sketch from The Graphic of 1888, "Shooting a Man-eating Crocodile." How can you tell that this sketch is not ironic and that "A Modest Proposal" is? If you can't tell, what does your uncertainty suggest about the nature of irony?
5. Write your own modest proposal for something, keeping in mind Swift's technique.

Niccolò Machiavelli

THE MORALS OF THE PRINCE[1]

On the Reasons Why Men Are Praised or Blamed—Especially Princes

It remains now to be seen what style and principles a prince ought to adopt in dealing with his subjects and friends. I know the subject has been treated frequently before, and I'm afraid people will think me rash for trying to do so again, especially since I intend to differ in this discussion from what others have said. But since I intend to write something useful to an understanding reader, it seemed better to go after the real truth of the matter than to repeat what people have imagined. A great many men have imagined states and princedoms such as nobody ever saw or knew in the real world, for there's such a difference between the way we really live and the way we ought to live that the man who neglects the real to study the ideal will learn how to accomplish his ruin, not his salvation. Any man who tries to be good all the time is bound to come to ruin among the great number who are not good. Hence a prince who wants to keep his post must learn how not to be good, and use that knowledge, or refrain from using it, as necessity requires.

Putting aside, then, all the imaginary things that are said about princes, and getting down to the truth, let me say that whenever men are discussed (and especially princes because they are prominent), there are certain qualities that bring them either praise or blame. Thus some are considered generous, others stingy (I use a Tuscan term, since "greedy" in our speech means a man who wants to take other people's goods. we call a man "stingy" who clings to his own); some are givers, others grabbers; some cruel, others merciful; one man is treacherous, another faithful; one is feeble and effeminate, another fierce and spirited; one humane, another proud; one lustful, another chaste; one straightforward, another sly; one harsh, another gentle; one serious, another playful; one religious, another skeptical, and so on. I know everyone will agree that among these many qualities a prince certainly ought to have all those that are considered good. But since it is impossible to have and exercise them all, because the conditions of human life simply do not allow it, a prince must be shrewd enough to avoid the public disgrace of those vices that would lose him his state. If he possibly can, he should also guard against vices that will not lose him his state; but if he cannot prevent them, he should not be too worried about indulging them. And furthermore, he

1. From *The Prince*, a book on statecraft written for Giuliano de' Medici (1479–1516), a member of one of the most famous and powerful families of Renaissance Italy.

should not be too worried about incurring blame for any vice without which he would find it hard to save his state. For if you look at matters carefully, you will see that something resembling virtue, if you follow it, may be your ruin, while something else resembling vice will lead, if you follow it, to your security and well-being.

On Liberality and Stinginess

Let me begin, then, with the first of the qualities mentioned above, by saying that a reputation for liberality is doubtless very fine; but the generosity that earns you that reputation can do you great harm. For if you exercise your generosity in a really virtuous way, as you should, nobody will know of it, and you cannot escape the odium of the opposite vice. Hence if you wish to be widely known as a generous man, you must seize every opportunity to make a big display of your giving. A prince of this character is bound to use up his entire revenue in works of ostentation. Thus, in the end, if he wants to keep a name for generosity, he will have to load his people with exorbitant taxes and squeeze money out of them in every way he can. This is the first step in making him odious to his subjects; for when he is poor, nobody will respect him. Then, when his generosity has angered many and brought rewards to a few, the slightest difficulty will trouble him, and at the first approach of danger, down he goes. If by chance he foresees this, and tries to change his ways, he will immediately be labeled a miser.

Since a prince cannot use this virtue of liberality in such a way as to become known for it unless he harms his own security, he won't mind, if he judges prudently of things, being known as a miser. In due course he will be thought the more liberal man, when people see that his parsimony enables him to live on his income, to defend himself against his enemies, and to undertake major projects without burdening his people with taxes. Thus he will be acting liberally toward all those people from whom he takes nothing (and there are an immense number of them), and in a stingy way toward those people on whom he bestows nothing (and they are very few). In our times, we have seen great things being accomplished only by men who have had the name of misers; all the others have gone under. Pope Julius II, though he used his reputation as a generous man to gain the papacy, sacrificed it in order to be able to make war; the present king of France has waged many wars without levying a single extra tax on his people, simply because he could take care of the extra expenses out of the savings from his long parsimony. If the present king of Spain had a reputation for generosity, he would never have been able to undertake so many campaigns, or win so many of them.

Hence a prince who prefers not to rob his subjects, who wants to be able to defend himself, who wants to avoid poverty and contempt, and who doesn't want to become a plunderer, should not mind in the least if people consider him a miser; this is simply one of the vices that enable him to reign. Someone may object that Caesar used a reputation for generosity to become emperor, and many other people have also risen in the world, because they were generous or were supposed to be so. Well, I answer, either you are a prince already, or you are in the process of becoming one; in the first case, this reputation for generosity is harmful to you, in the second case it is very necessary. Caesar was one of those who wanted to become ruler in Rome; but after he had reached his goal, if he had lived, and had not cut down on his expenses, he would have ruined the empire itself. Someone may say: there have been plenty of princes, very successful in warfare, who have had a reputation for generosity. But I answer: either the prince is spending his own money and that of his subjects, or he is spending someone else's. In the first case, he ought to be sparing; in the second case, he ought to spend money like water. Any prince at the head of his army, which lives on loot, extortion, and plunder, disposes of other people's property, and is bound to be very generous; otherwise, his soldiers would desert him. You can always be a more generous giver when what you give is not yours or your subjects'; Cyrus, Caesar, and Alexander[2] were generous in this way. Spending what belongs to other people does no harm to your reputation, rather it enhances it; only spending your own substance harms you. And there is nothing that wears out faster than generosity; even as you practice it, you lose the means of practicing it, and you become either poor and contemptible or (in the course of escaping poverty) rapacious and hateful. The thing above all against which a prince must protect himself is being contemptible and hateful; generosity leads to both. Thus, it's much wiser to put up with the reputation of being a miser, which brings you shame without hate, than to be forced—just because you want to appear generous—into a reputation for rapacity, which brings shame on you and hate along with it.

On Cruelty and Clemency: Whether It Is Better to Be Loved or Feared

Continuing now with our list of qualities, let me say that every prince should prefer to be considered merciful rather than cruel, yet he should be careful not to mismanage this clemency of his. People thought Cesare Borgia[3] was cruel, but that cruelty of his reorganized the Romagna, united it, and established it in peace and loyalty. Anyone who views the matter realistically will see that this prince was much more merciful than the people of Florence, who, to avoid the reputation of cruelty, allowed

2. Persian, Roman, and Macedonian conquerors and rulers in ancient times.
3. The son of Pope Alexander VI (referred to later) and duke of Romagna, which he subjugated in 1499–1502.

Pistoia to be destroyed.[4] Thus, no prince should mind being called cruel for what he does to keep his subjects united and loyal; he may make examples of a very few, but he will be more merciful in reality than those who, in their tenderheartedness, allow disorders to occur, with their attendant murders and lootings. Such turbulence brings harm to an entire community, while the executions ordered by a prince affect only one individual at a time. A new prince, above all others, cannot possibly avoid a name for cruelty, since new states are always in danger. And Virgil, speaking through the mouth of Dido,[5] says:

> My cruel fate
> And doubts attending an unsettled state
> Force me to guard my coast from foreign foes.

Yet a prince should be slow to believe rumors and to commit himself to action on the basis of them. He should not be afraid of his own thoughts; he ought to proceed cautiously, moderating his conduct with prudence and humanity, allowing neither overconfidence to make him careless, nor overtimidity to make him intolerable.

Here the question arises: is it better to be loved than feared, or vice versa? I don't doubt that every prince would like to be both; but since it is hard to accommodate these qualities, if you have to make a choice, to be feared is much safer than to be loved. For it is a good general rule about men, that they are ungrateful, fickle, liars and deceivers, fearful of danger and greedy for gain. While you serve their welfare, they are all yours, offering their blood, their belongings, their lives, and their children's lives, as we noted above—so long as the danger is remote. But when the danger is close at hand, they turn against you. Then, any prince who has relied on their words and has made no other preparations will come to grief; because friendships that are bought at a price, and not with greatness and nobility of soul, may be paid for but they are not acquired, and they cannot be used in time of need. People are less concerned with offending a man who makes himself loved than one who makes himself feared: the reason is that love is a link of obligation which men, because they are rotten, will break any time they think doing so serves their advantage; but fear involves dread of punishment, from which they can never escape.

Still, a prince should make himself feared in such a way that, even if he gets no love, he gets no hate either; because it is perfectly possible to be feared and not hated, and this will be the result if only the prince will keep his hands off the property of his subjects or citizens, and off their women. When he does have to shed blood, he should be sure to have a strong justification and manifest cause; but above all, he should not

---

4. By unchecked rioting between opposing factions (1502).

5. Queen of Carthage and tragic heroine of Virgil's epic, *The Aeneid*.

confiscate people's property, because men are quicker to forget the death of a father than the loss of a patrimony. Besides, pretexts for confiscation are always plentiful, it never fails that a prince who starts living by plunder can find reasons to rob someone else. Excuses for proceeding against someone's life are much rarer and more quickly exhausted.

But a prince at the head of his armies and commanding a multitude of soldiers should not care a bit if he is considered cruel; without such a reputation, he could never hold his army together and ready for action. Among the marvelous deeds of Hannibal,[6] this was prime: that, having an immense army, which included men of many different races and nations, and which he led to battle in distant countries, he never allowed them to fight among themselves or to rise against him, whether his fortune was good or bad. The reason for this could only be his inhuman cruelty, which, along with his countless other talents, made him an object of awe and terror to his soldiers; and without the cruelty, his other qualities would never have sufficed. The historians who pass snap judgments on these matters admire his accomplishments and at the same time condemn the cruelty which was their main cause.

When I say, "His other qualities would never have sufficed," we can see that this is true from the example of Scipio,[7] an outstanding man not only among those of his own time, but in all recorded history; yet his armies revolted in Spain, for no other reason than his excessive leniency in allowing his soldiers more freedom than military discipline permits. Fabius Maximus rebuked him in the senate for this failing, calling him the corrupter of the Roman armies. When a lieutenant of Scipio's plundered the Locrians,[8] he took no action in behalf of the people, and did nothing to discipline that insolent lieutenant; again, this was the result of his easygoing nature. Indeed, when someone in the senate wanted to excuse him on this occasion, he said there are many men who knew better how to avoid error themselves than how to correct error in others. Such a soft temper would in time have tarnished the fame and glory of Scipio, had he brought it to the office of emperor; but as he lived under the control of the senate, this harmful quality of his not only remained hidden but was considered creditable.

Returning to the question of being feared or loved, I conclude that since men love at their own inclination but can be made to fear at the inclination of the prince, a shrewd prince will lay his foundations on what is under his own control, not on what is controlled by others. He should simply take pains not to be hated, as I said.

6. Carthaginian general who led a massive but unsuccessful invasion of Rome in 218–203 B.C.

7. The Roman general whose successful invasion of Carthage in 203 B.C. caused Hannibal's army to be recalled from Rome. The episode described here occurred in 206 B.C.

8. A people of Sicily, defeated by Scipio in 205 B.C. and placed under Q. Pleminius; Fabius Maximus: not only a senator but a high public official and general who had fought against Hannibal in Italy.

The Way Princes Should Keep Their Word

How praiseworthy it is for a prince to keep his word and live with integrity rather than by craftiness, everyone understands; yet we see from recent experience that those princes have accomplished most who paid little heed to keeping their promises, but who knew how craftily to manipulate the minds of men. In the end, they won out over those who tried to act honestly.

You should consider then, that there are two ways of fighting, one with laws and the other with force. The first is properly a human method, the second belongs to beasts. But as the first method does not always suffice, you sometimes have to turn to the second. Thus a prince must know how to make good use of both the beast and the man. Ancient writers made subtle note of this fact when they wrote that Achilles and many other princes of antiquity were sent to be reared by Chiron the centaur,[9] who trained them in his discipline. Having a teacher who is half man and half beast can only mean that a prince must know how to use both these two natures, and that one without the other has no lasting effect.

Since a prince must know how to use the character of beasts, he should pick for imitation the fox and the lion. As the lion cannot protect himself from traps, and the fox cannot defend himself from wolves, you have to be a fox in order to be wary of traps, and a lion to overawe the wolves. Those who try to live by the lion alone are badly mistaken. Thus a prudent prince cannot and should not keep his word when to do so would go against his interest, or when the reasons that made him pledge it no longer apply. Doubtless if all men were good, this rule would be bad; but since they are a sad lot, and keep no faith with you, you in your turn are under no obligation to keep it with them.

Besides, a prince will never lack for legitimate excuses to explain away his breaches of faith. Modern history will furnish innumerable examples of this behavior, showing how many treaties and promises have been made null and void by the faithlessness of princes, and how the man succeeded best who knew best how to play the fox. But it is a necessary part of this nature that you must conceal it carefully; you must be a great liar and hypocrite. Men are so simple of mind, and so much dominated by their immediate needs, that a deceitful man will always find plenty who are ready to be deceived. One of many recent examples calls for mention. Alexander VI[1] never did anything else, never had another thought, except to deceive men, and he always found fresh material to work on. Never was there a man more convincing in his assertions, who sealed his

---

9. Half man and half horse, the mythical Chiron was said to have taught the arts of war and peace, including hunting, medicine, music, and prophecy; Achilles: foremost among the Greek heroes in the Trojan War.
1. Pope from 1492 to 1503.

promises with more solemn oaths, and who observed them less. Yet his deceptions were always successful, because he knew exactly how to manage this sort of business.

In actual fact, a prince may not have all the admirable qualities we listed, but it is very necessary that he should seem to have them. Indeed, I will venture to say that when you have them and exercise them all the time, they are harmful to you; when you just seem to have them, they are useful. It is good to appear merciful, truthful, humane, sincere, and religious; it is good to be so in reality. But you must keep your mind so disposed that, in case of need, you can turn to the exact contrary. This has to be understood: a prince, and especially a new prince, cannot possibly exercise all those virtues for which men are called "good." To preserve the state, he often has to do things against his word, against charity, against humanity, against religion. Thus he has to have a mind ready to shift as the winds of fortune and the varying circumstances of life may dictate. And as I said above, he should not depart from the good if he can hold to it, but he should be ready to enter on evil if he has to.

Hence a prince should take great care never to drop a word that does not seem imbued with the five good qualities noted above; to anyone who sees or hears him, he should appear all compassion, all honor, all humanity, all integrity, all religion. Nothing is more necessary than to seem to have this last virtue. Men in general judge more by the sense of sight than by the sense of touch, because everyone can see but only a few can test by feeling. Everyone sees what you seem to be, few know what you really are; and those few do not dare take a stand against the general opinion, supported by the majesty of the government. In the actions of all men, and especially of princes who are not subject to a court of appeal, we must always look to the end. Let a prince, therefore, win victories and uphold his state; his methods will always be considered worthy, and everyone will praise them, because the masses are always impressed by the superficial appearance of things, and by the outcome of an enterprise. And the world consists of nothing but the masses; the few who have no influence when the many feel secure. A certain prince of our own time, whom it's just as well not to name,[2] preaches nothing but peace and mutual trust, yet he is the determined enemy of both; and if on several different occasions he had observed either, he would have lost both his reputation and his throne.

1513

2. Probably Ferdinand of Spain, then allied with the house of Medici.

THE READER

1. *Toward the end of the first paragraph, Machiavelli says, "The man who neglects the real to study the ideal will learn how to accomplish his ruin." Explain the logical relation between that statement and the*

statements of the last two sentences of that paragraph.

2. Speaking of a prince, Machiavelli uses a moral, personal vocabulary: "liberality"/"stinginess," "cruelty"/"clemency," "loved"/"feared," etc. Other vocabularies are possible. For example, the stinginess of a miser (p. 816) might be fiscal responsibility. Provide alternatives for some of the other terms in his moral, personal vocabulary.

3. Machiavelli speaks about government by a prince. To what degree do his observations and advice apply to a democracy?

THE WRITER

1. On p. 821, the author speaks of five admirable qualities: compassion, honor, humanity, integrity, and religion. How admirable do you think he believes those qualities to be? Base your answer on your sense of what matters to him in this essay. What would you say he admires most?

2. Machiavelli clearly says a prince should seem to be virtuous. Write a one-page strategy paper for Machiavelli as if you were the media consultant to a prince, or for yourself as if you were the media consultant to a candidate.

3. Machiavelli sees men as "a sad lot" and has a generally bleak view of human behavior. What would be the best logical strategy for an argument in refutation? Can you get any help from King (p. 792) or Lincoln (p. 822) or the Declaration of Independence (p. 828)?

Abraham Lincoln

SECOND INAUGURAL ADDRESS

At this second appearing to take the oath of the presidential office, there is less occasion for an extended address than there was at the first. Then a statement, somewhat in detail, of a course to be pursued, seemed fitting and proper. Now, at the expiration of four years, during which public declarations have been constantly called forth on every point and phase of the great contest which still absorbs the attention, and engrosses the energies of the nation, little that is new could be presented. The progress of our arms, upon which all else chiefly depends, is as well known to the public as to myself; and it is, I trust, reasonably satisfactory and encouraging to all. With high hope for the future, no prediction in regard to it is ventured.

On the occasion corresponding to this four years ago, all thoughts were anxiously directed to an impending civil war. All dreaded it—all sought to avert it. While the inaugural address was being delivered from this place, devoted altogether to saving the Union without war, insurgent agents were in the city seeking to *destroy* it without war—seeking to dissolve the Union, and divide effects, by negotiation. Both parties deprecated war; but one of them would *make* war rather than let the nation survive; and the other would *accept* war rather than let it perish. And the war came.

One-eighth of the whole population were colored slaves, not distributed generally over the Union, but localized in the Southern part of it. These slaves constituted a peculiar and powerful interest. All knew that this interest was, somehow, the cause of the war. To strengthen, perpetuate, and extend this interest was the object for which the insurgents would rend the Union, even by war; while the government claimed no right to do more than to restrict the territorial enlargement of it. Neither party expected for the war, the magnitude, or the duration, which it has already attained. Neither anticipated that the *cause* of the conflict might cease with, or even before, the conflict itself should cease. Each looked for an easier triumph, and a result less fundamental and astounding. Both read the same Bible, and pray to the same God; and each invokes His aid against the other. It may seem strange that any men should dare to ask a just God's assistance in wringing their bread from the sweat of other men's faces; but let us judge not that we be not judged.[1] The prayers of both could not be answered; that of neither has been answered fully. The Almighty has His own purposes. "Woe unto the world because of offenses! for it must needs be that offenses come; but woe to that man by whom the offense cometh!"[2] If we shall suppose that American slavery is one of those offenses which, in the providence of God, must needs come, but which, having continued through His appointed time, He now wills to remove, and that He gives to both North and South, this terrible war, as the woe due to those by whom the offense came, shall we discern therein any departure from those divine attributes which the believers in a Living God always ascribe to Him? Fondly do we hope—fervently do we pray—that this mightly scourge of war may speedily pass away. Yet, if God wills that it continue, until all the wealth piled by the bondman's two hundred and fifty years of unrequited toil shall be sunk, and until every drop of blood drawn with the lash, shall be paid by another drawn with the sword, as was said three thousand years ago, so still it must be said "the judgments of the Lord are true and righteous altogether."[3]

With malice toward none; with charity for all; with firmness in the right, as God gives us to see the right, let us strive on to finish the work we are in; to bind up the nation's wounds; to care for him who shall have

1. Lincoln alludes to Jesus' statement in the Sermon on the Mount—"Judge not, that ye be not judged" (Matthew vii.1)—and to God's curse on Adam—"In the sweat of thy face shalt thou eat bread, till thou return unto the ground" (Genesis iii.19).
2. From Jesus' speech to his disciples (Matthew xviii.7).
3. Psalms xix.9.

borne the battle, and for his widow, and his orphan—to do all which may achieve and cherish a just, and a lasting peace, among ourselves, and with all nations.

1865

Thomas Jefferson

ORIGINAL DRAFT OF THE DECLARATION OF INDEPENDENCE

A DECLARATION OF THE REPRESENTATIVES OF THE UNITED STATES OF AMERICA, IN GENERAL CONGRESS ASSEMBLED.

When in the course of human events it becomes necessary for a people to advance from that subordination in which they have hitherto remained, & to assume among the powers of the earth the equal & independant station to which the laws of nature & of nature's god entitle them, a decent respect to the opinions of mankind requires that they should declare the causes which impel them to the change.

We hold these truths to be sacred & undeniable; that all men are created equal & independant, that from that equal creation they derive rights inherent & inalienable, among which are the preservation of life, & liberty, & the spirit of happiness; that to secure these ends, governments are instituted among men, deriving their just powers from the consent of the governed; that whenever any form of government shall become destructive of these ends, it is the right of the people to alter or to abolish it, & to institute new government, laying it's foundation on such principles & organising it's powers in such form, as to them shall seem most likely to effect their safety & happiness. prudence indeed will dictate that governments long established should not be changed for light & transient causes: and accordingly all experience hath shewn that mankind are more disposed to suffer while evils are sufferable, than to right themselves by abolishing the forms to which they are accustomed. but when a long train of abuses & usurpations, begun at a distinguished period, & pursuing invariably the same object, evinces a design to subject them to arbitrary power, it is their right, it is their duty, to throw off such government & to provide new guards for their future security. such has been the patient sufferance of these colonies; & such is now the necessity which constrains them to expunge their former systems of government. The history of his present majesty, is a history of unremitting injuries and usurpations, among which no one fact stands single or solitary to contradict the uniform tenor of the rest, all of which have in direct object the establishment of an absolute tyranny over these states. to prove this, let facts be submitted to a candid world, for the truth of which we pledge a faith yet unsullied by falsehood.

he has refused his assent to laws the most wholesome and necessary for the public good:

he has forbidden his governors to pass laws of immediate & pressing importance, unless suspended in their operation till his assent should be obtained; and when so suspended, he has neglected utterly to attend to them.

he has refused to pass other laws for the accommodation of large districts of people unless those people would relinquish the right of representation, a right inestimable to them, & formidable to tyrants alone:[1]

he has dissolved Representative houses repeatedly & continually, for opposing with manly firmness his invasions on the rights of the people:

he has refused for a long space of time to cause others to be elected, whereby the legislative powers, incapable of annihilation, have returned to the people at large for their exercise, the state remaining in the mean time exposed to all the dangers of invasion from without, &, convulsions within:

he has suffered the administration of justice totally to cease in some of these colonies, refusing his assent to laws for establishing judiciary powers:

he has made our judges dependant on his will alone, for the tenure of their offices, and amount of their salaries:

he has erected a multitude of new offices by a self-assumed power, & sent hither swarms of officers to harrass our people & eat out their substance:

he has kept among us in times of peace standing armies & ships of war:

he has affected[2] to render the military, independent of & superior to the civil power:

he has combined with others to subject us to a jurisdiction foreign to our constitutions and unacknowledged by our laws; giving his assent to their pretended acts of legislation, for quartering large bodies of

1. At this point in the manuscript a strip containing the following clause is inserted: "He called together legislative bodies at places unusual, unco[mfortable, & distant from] the depository of their public records for the sole purpose of fatiguing [them into compliance] with his measures:" Missing parts in the Library of Congress text are supplied from the copy made by Jefferson for George Wythe. This copy is in the New York Public Library. The fact that this passage was omitted from John Adams's transcript suggests that it was not a part of Jefferson's original rough draft.

2. Tried.

armed troops among us;

> for protecting them by a mock-trial from punishment for any murders they should commit on the inhabitants of these states;
>
> for cutting off our trade with all parts of the world;
>
> for imposing taxes on us without our consent;
>
> for depriving us of the benefits of trial by jury

he has endeavored to prevent the population of these states; for that purpose obstructing the laws for naturalization of foreigners; refusing to pass others to encourage their migrations hither; & raising the conditions of new appropriations of lands;

> for transporting us beyond seas to be tried for pretended offences:
>
> for taking away our charters & altering fundamentally the forms of our governments;
>
> for suspending our own legislatures & declaring themselves invested with power to legislate for us in all cases whatsoever:

he has abdicated government here, withdrawing his governors, & declaring us out of his allegiance & protection:

he has plundered our seas, ravaged our coasts, burnt our towns & destroyed the lives of our people:

he is at this time transporting large armies of foreign mercenaries to compleat the works of death, desolation & tyranny, already begun with circumstances of cruelty & perfidy unworthy the head of a civilized nation:

he has endeavored to bring on the inhabitants of our frontiers the merciless Indian savages, whose known rule of warfare is an undistinguished destruction of all ages, sexes, & conditions of existence:

he has incited treasonable insurrections of our fellow-citizens, with the allurements of forfeiture & confiscation of our property:

he has waged cruel war against human nature itself, violating it's most sacred rights of life & liberty in the persons of a distant people who never offended him, captivating & carrying them into slavery in another hemisphere, or to incur miserable death in their transportation thither. this piratical warfare, the opprobrium of *infidel* powers, is the warfare of the CHRISTIAN king of Great Britain. determined to keep open a market where MEN should be bought & sold; he has prostituted his negative for suppressing every legislative attempt to prohibit or to restrain this execrable commerce: and that this assemblage of horrors might want no fact of distinguished die, he is now exciting those very people to rise in arms among us, and to purchase that liberty of which *he* has deprived them, by murdering the people upon whom *he* also obtruded them; thus paying off former crimes committed against the *liberties* of one people, with crimes which he urges them to commit against the *lives* of another.

in every stage of these oppressions we have petitioned for redress in the most humble terms; our repeated petitions have been answered by repeated injury. a prince whose character is thus marked by every act which may define a tyrant, is unfit to be the ruler of a people who mean to be free. future ages will scarce believe that the hardiness of one man, adventured within the short compass of twelve years only, on so many acts of tyranny without a mask, over a people fostered & fixed in principles of liberty.

Nor have we been wanting in attentions to our British brethren. we have warned them from time to time of attempts by their legislature to extend a jurisdiction over these our states. we have reminded them of the circumstances of our emigration & settlement here, no one of which could warrant so strange a pretension: that these were effected at the expence of our own blood & treasure, unassisted by the wealth or the strength of Great Britain: that in constituting indeed our several forms of government, we had adopted one common king, thereby laying a foundation for perpetual league & amity with them; but that submission to their [Parliament, was no Part of our Constitution, nor ever in Idea, if History may be]³ credited: and we appealed to their native justice & magnanimity, as to the ties of our common kindred to disavow these usurpations which were likely to interrupt our correspondence & connection. they too have been deaf to the voice of justice & of consanguinity, & when occasions have been given them, by the regular course of their laws, of removing from their councils the disturbers of our harmony, they have by their free election re-established them in power. at this very time too they are permitting their chief magistrate to send over not only soldiers of our common blood, but Scotch & foreign mercenaries to invade & deluge us in blood. these facts have given the last stab to agonizing affection, and manly spirit bids us to renounce for ever these unfeeling brethren. we must endeavor to forget our former love for them, and to hold them as we hold the rest of mankind, enemies in war, in peace friends. we might have been a free & a great people together; but a communication of grandeur & of freedom it seems is below their dignity. be it so, since they will have it: the road to glory & happiness is open to us too; we will climb it in a separate state, and acquiesce in the necessity which pronounces our everlasting Adieu!

We therefore the representatives of the United States of America in General Congress assembled do, in the name & by authority of the good people of these states, reject and renounce all allegiance & subjection to the kings of Great Britain & all others who may hereafter claim by, through, or under them; we utterly dissolve & break off all political connection which may have heretofore subsisted between us & the

---

3. An illegible passage is supplied from John Adams's transcription.

people or parliament of Great Britain; and finally we do assert and declare these colonies to be free and independant states, and that as free & independant states they shall hereafter have power to levy war, conclude peace, contract alliances, establish commerce, & to do all other acts and things which independant states may of right do. And for the support of this declaration we mutually pledge to each other our lives, our fortunes, & our sacred honour.

1776

Thomas Jefferson and Others

THE DECLARATION OF INDEPENDENCE

IN CONGRESS, JULY 4, 1776
THE UNANIMOUS DECLARATION OF THE
THIRTEEN UNITED STATES OF AMERICA

When in the Course of human events it becomes necessary for one people to dissolve the political bands which have connected them with another, and to assume among the powers of the earth, the separate and equal station to which the Laws of Nature and of Nature's God entitle them, a decent respect to the opinions of mankind requires that they should declare the causes which impel them to the separation.

We hold these truths to be self-evident, that all men are created equal, that they are endowed by their Creator with certain unalienable Rights, that among these are Life, Liberty and the pursuit of Happiness. That to secure these rights, Governments are instituted among Men, deriving their just powers from the consent of the governed. That whenever any Form of Government becomes destructive of these ends, it is the Right of the People to alter or to abolish it, and to institute new Government, laying its foundation on such principles and organizing its powers in such form, as to them shall seem most likely to affect their Safety and Happiness. Prudence, indeed, will dictate that Governments long established should not be changed for light and transient causes; and accordingly all experience hath shewn that mankind are more disposed to suffer, while evils are sufferable, than to right themselves by abolishing the forms to which they are accustomed. But when a long train of abuses and usurpations, pursuing invariably the same Object evinces a design to reduce them under absolute Despotism, it is their right, it is their duty, to throw off such Government, and to provide new Guards for their future security. Such has been the patient sufferance of these Colonies; and such is now the necessity which constrains them to alter their former Systems of Government. The history of the present King of Great Britain is a history of repeated injuries and usurpations, all having in direct object the establishment of an absolute Tyranny over these States. To prove this, let Facts be submitted to a candid world.

He has refused his Assent to Laws, the most wholesome and necessary for the public good.

He has forbidden his Governors to pass laws of immediate and pressing importance, unless suspended in their operation till his Assent should be obtained; and when so suspended, he has utterly neglected to attend to them.

He has refused to pass other Laws for the accommodation of large districts of people, unless those people would relinquish the right of Representation in the Legislature, a right inestimable to them and formidable to tyrants only.

He has called together legislative bodies at places unusual, uncomfortable, and distant from the depository of their Public Records, for the sole purpose of fatiguing them into compliance with his measures.

He has dissolved Representative Houses repeatedly, for opposing with manly firmness his invasions on the rights of the people.

He has refused for a long time, after such dissolutions, to cause others to be elected; whereby the Legislative Powers, incapable of Annihilation, have returned to the People at large for their exercise; the State remaining in the mean time exposed to all the dangers of invasion from without, and convulsions within.

He has endeavored to prevent the population of these States; for that purpose obstructing the Laws for Naturalization of Foreigners; refusing to pass others to encourage their migration hither, and raising the conditions of new Appropriations of Lands.

He has obstructed the Administration of Justice, by refusing his Assent to Laws for establishing Judiciary Powers.

He has made Judges dependent on his Will alone, for the tenure of their offices, and the amount and payment of their salaries.

He has erected a multitude of New Offices, and sent hither swarms of Officers to harass our people, and eat out their substance.

He has kept among us, in times of peace, Standing Armies without the Consent of our legislatures.

He has affected to render the Military independent of and superior to the Civil Power.

He has combined with others to subject us to a jurisdiction foreign to our constitution, and unacknowledged by our laws; giving his Assent to their Acts of pretended Legislation: For quartering large bodies of armed troops among us: For protecting them, by a mock Trial, from punishment for any Murders which they should commit on the Inhabitants of these States: For cutting off our Trade with all parts of the world: For imposing Taxes on us without our Consent: For depriving us in many cases, of the benefits of Trial by Jury; For transporting us beyond Seas to be tried for pretended offenses: for abolishing the free System of English Laws in a neighboring Province, establishing therein an Arbitrary government, and enlarging its Boundaries so as to render it at once an example and fit instrument for introducing the same absolute rule into these Colonies: For taking away our Charters, abolishing our most valuable Laws and altering fundamentally the Forms of our Governments: For suspending our own Legislatures, and declaring themselves invested with power to legislate for us in all cases whatsoever.

He has abdicated Government here, by declaring us out of his Protection and waging War against us.

He has plundered our seas, ravaged our Coasts, burnt our towns, and destroyed the lives of our people.

He is at this time transporting large Armies of foreign Mercenaries to complete the works of death, desolation and tyranny, already begun with circumstances of Cruelty & Perfidy scarcely paralleled in the most barbarous ages, and totally unworthy the Head of a civilized nation.

He has constrained our fellow Citizens taken Captive on the high Seas to bear Arms against their Country, to become the executioners of their friends and Brethren, or to fall themselves by their Hands.

He has excited domestic insurrections amongst us, and has endeavored to bring on the inhabitants of our frontiers, the merciless Indian Savages, whose known rule of warfare, is an undistinguished destruction of all ages, sexes, and conditions.

In every stage of these Oppressions We have Petitioned for Redress in the most humble terms: Our repeated Petitions have been answered only by repeated injury. A Prince, whose character is thus marked by every act which may define a Tyrant, is unfit to be the ruler of a free people.

Nor have We been wanting in attention to our British brethren. We have warned them from time to time of attempts by their legislature to extend an unwarrantable jurisdiction over us. We have reminded them of the circumstances of our emigration and settlement here. We have appealed to their native justice and magnanimity, and we have conjured them by the ties of our common kindred to disavow these usurpations, which would inevitably interrupt our connections and correspondence. They too have been deaf to the voice of justice and of consanguinity. We must, therefore, acquiesce in the necessity, which denounces our Separation, and hold them, as we hold the rest of mankind, Enemies in War, in Peace Friends.

We, THEREFORE the Representatives of the UNITED STATES OF AMERICA, in General Congress, Assembled, appealing to the Supreme

Judge of the world for the rectitude of our intentions, do, in the Name, and by Authority of the good People of these Colonies, solemnly publish and declare, That these United Colonies are, and of Right ought to be FREE AND INDEPENDENT STATES; that they are Absolved from all Allegiance to the British Crown, and that all political connection between them and the State of Great Britain, is and ought to be totally dissolved; and that as Free and Independent States, they have full Power to levy War, conclude Peace, contract Alliances, establish Commerce, and to do all other Acts and Things which Independent States may of right do. And for the support of this Declaration, with a firm reliance on the protection of Divine Providence, we mutually pledge to each other our Lives, our Fortunes, and our sacred Honor.

1776

THE READER

1. *Find the key terms and phrases of the Declaration (such as "these truths . . . self-evident," "created equal," "unalienable Rights," and so on), and determine how fully they are defined by the contexts in which they occur. Why are no formal definitions given for them?*
2. *The signers of the Declaration appeal both to general principles and to factual evidence in presenting their case. Which of the appeals to principle could still legitimately be made today by a nation eager to achieve independence? In other words, how far does the Declaration reflect unique events of history, and how far does it reflect universal aspirations and ideals?*

THE WRITER

1. *The Declaration of Independence was addressed to several audiences: the king of Great Britain, the people of Great Britain, the people of America, and the world at large. Show ways in which the final draft was adapted for its several audiences.*
2. *Closely examine the second paragraph of both the original draft and the final version of the Declaration. How have the revisions of the final version increased its effectiveness over the first draft?*
3. *The Declaration has often been called a classic example of deductive argument: setting up general statements, relating particular cases to them, and drawing conclusions. Trace this pattern through the document, noting the way each part is developed. Would the document have been as effective if the long middle part had either come first or been left out entirely? Explain.*
4. *Using only what is implied in the Declaration, write a brief definition for one of the key terms referred to in question 1 under "The Reader."*
5. *Burgess refers to the "dangerous naiveté" of the Declaration (p. 387). Read Burgess's remark in its context, and then write a paragraph or two supporting or opposing his view.*

Carl Becker

DEMOCRACY

Democracy, like liberty or science or progress, is a word with which we are all so familiar that we rarely take the trouble to ask what we mean by it. It is a term, as the devotees of semantics say, which has no "referent"—there is no precise or palpable thing or object which we all think of when the word is pronounced. On the contrary, it is a word which connotes different things to different people, a kind of conceptual Gladstone bag which, with a little manipulation, can be made to accommodate almost any collection of social facts we may wish to carry about in it. In it we can as easily pack a dictatorship as any other form of government. We have only to stretch the concept to include any form of government supported by a majority of the people, for whatever reasons and by whatever means of expressing assent, and before we know it the empire of Napoleon, the Soviet regime of Stalin, and the Fascist systems of Mussolini and Hitler are all safely in the bag. But if this is what we mean by democracy, then virtually all forms of government are democratic, since virtually all governments, except in times of revolution, rest upon the explicit or implicit consent of the people. In order to discuss democracy intelligently it will be necessary, therefore, to define it, to attach to the word a sufficiently precise meaning to avoid the confusion which is not infrequently the chief result of such discussions.

All human institutions, we are told, have their ideal forms laid away in heaven, and we do not need to be told that the actual institutions conform but indifferently to these ideal counterparts. It would be possible then to define democracy either in terms of the ideal or in terms of the real form—to define it as government of the people, by the people, for the people; or to define it as government of the people, by the politicians, for whatever pressure groups can get their interests taken care of. But as a historian I am naturally disposed to be satisfied with the meaning which, in the history of politics, men have commonly attributed to the word—a meaning, needless to say, which derives partly from the experience and partly from the aspirations of mankind. So regarded, the term democracy refers primarily to a form of government, and it has always meant government by the many as opposed to government by the one—government by the people as opposed to government by a tyrant, a dictator, or an absolute monarch. This is the most general meaning of the word as men have commonly understood it.

In this antithesis there are, however, certain implications, always tacitly understood, which give a more precise meaning to the term.

Peisistratus, for example, was supported by a majority of the people, but his government was never regarded as a democracy for all that. Caesar's power derived from a popular mandate, conveyed through established republican forms, but that did not make his government any the less a dictatorship. Napoleon called his government a democratic empire, but no one, least of all Napoleon himself, doubted that he had destroyed the last vestiges of the democratic republic. Since the Greeks first used the term, the essential test of democratic government has always been this: the source of political authority must be and remain in the people and not in the ruler. A democratic government has always meant one in which the citizens, or a sufficient number of them to represent more or less effectively the common will, freely act from time to time, and according to established forms, to appoint or recall the magistrates and to enact or revoke the laws by which the community is governed. This I take to be the meaning which history has impressed upon the term democracy as a form of government.

1941

E. B. White

DEMOCRACY

We received a letter from the Writers' War Board the other day asking for a statement on "The Meaning of Democracy." It presumably is our duty to comply with such a request, and it is certainly our pleasure.

Surely the Board knows what democracy is. It is the line that forms on the right. It is the don't in don't shove. It is the hole in the stuffed shirt through which the sawdust slowly trickles; it is the dent in the high hat. Democracy is the recurrent suspicion that more than half of the people are right more than half of the time. It is the feeling of privacy in the voting booths, the feeling of communion in the libraries, the feeling of vitality everywhere. Democracy is a letter to the editor. Democracy is the score at the beginning of the ninth. It is an idea which hasn't been disproved yet, a song the words of which have not gone bad. It's the mustard on the hot dog and the cream in the rationed coffee. Democracy is a request from a War Board, in the middle of a morning in the middle of a war, wanting to know what democracy is.

1943

THE READER

1. Look up democracy in a standard desk dictionary. Of the several meanings given, which one best applies to White's definition? Does

more than one apply?
2. *If White were writing this piece today, which of his examples might he change and which would he probably retain?*
3. *Compare White's definition of* democracy *with Becker's (p. 832).*

THE WRITER

1. *White's piece is dated July 3, 1943, the middle of World War II. How did the occasion shape what White says about democracy?*
2. *Translate White's definition into nonmetaphorical language. (For example, "It is the line that forms on the right" might be translated by "It has no special privileges.") Determine what is lost in the translation or, in other words, what White has gained by using figurative language.*
3. *If you didn't know that White was the author of "Some Remarks on Humor" (p. 1076), what specific features of his use of metaphor in that piece might enable you to guess that he was?*
4. *Using White's technique for definition, write a definition of an abstraction such as love, justice, or beauty.*

E. B. White

FOUR LETTERS ON FREEDOM OF EXPRESSION

[*In an editorial published on November 27, 1947, the* Herald Tribune, *though somewhat grudgingly, supported the right of the movie industry to blacklist the "Hollywood Ten" and any others who refused to answer questions before J. Parnell Thomas's House Un-American Activities Committee. The following letter, White's reaction to the editorial, was published in the* Tribune *on December 2.*]

To the New York Herald Tribune

New York, New York
November 29, 1947

TO THE NEW YORK HERALD TRIBUNE:

I am a member of a party of one, and I live in an age of fear. Nothing lately has unsettled my party and raised my fears so much as your editorial, on Thanksgiving Day, suggesting that employees should be required to state their beliefs in order to hold their jobs. The idea is inconsistent with our Constitutional theory and has been stubbornly opposed by watchful men since the early days of the Republic. It's hard for me to believe that the *Herald Tribune* is backing away from the fight, and I can only assume that your editorial writer, in a hurry to get home for Thanksgiving, tripped over the First Amendment and thought it was the office cat.

The investigation of alleged Communists by the Thomas committee has been a confusing spectacle for all of us. I believe its implications are widely misunderstood and that the outcome is grave beyond exaggerating. The essence of our political theory in this country is that a man's conscience shall be a private, not a public affair, and that only his deeds and words shall be open to survey, censure and to punishment. The idea is a decent one, and it works. It is an idea that cannot safely be compromised with, lest it be utterly destroyed. It cannot be modified even under circumstances where, for security reasons, the temptation to modify it is great.

I think security in critical times takes care of itself if the people and the institutions take care of themselves. First in line is the press. Security, for me, took a tumble not when I read that there were Communists in Hollywood but when I read your editorial in praise of loyalty testing and thought control. If a man is in health, he doesn't need to take anybody else's temperature to know where he is going. If a newspaper or a motion picture company is in health, it can get rid of Communists and spies simply by reading proof and by watching previews.

I hold that it would be improper for any committee or any employer to examine my conscience. They wouldn't know how to get into it, they wouldn't know what to do when they got in there, and I wouldn't let them in anyway. Like other Americans, my acts and my words are open to inspection—not my thoughts or my political affiliation (As I pointed out, I am a member of a party of one.) Your editorialist said he hoped the companies in checking for loyalty would use their powers sparingly and wisely. That is a wistful idea. One need only watch totalitarians at work to see that once men gain power over other men's minds, that power is never used sparingly and wisely, but lavishly and brutally and with unspeakable results. If I must declare today that I am not a Communist, tomorrow I shall have to testify that I am not a Unitarian. And the day after, that I never belonged to a dahlia club.

It is not a crime to believe anything at all in America. To date it has not been declared illegal to belong to the Communist party. Yet ten men have been convicted not of wrongdoing but of wrong believing. That is news in this country, and if I have not misread history, it is bad news.

E. B. WHITE

[*On the same page on the same day that White's November 29 letter was published in the* Tribune, *another editorial appeared entitled "The Party of One." It said that people like Mr. White "have been with us since the dawn of civilization. They have always been highly valuable elements in our civilization and nearly always as destructive as they have been valuable." Members of the party of one were also characterized as "probably the most dangerous single elements in our confused and complicated society."*

White's reply to the "Party of One" editorial, appeared on December 9 under the heading "Mr. White Believes Us Needlessly Unkind."]

To the New York Herald Tribune

New York
Dec. 4, 1947

TO THE NEW YORK HERALD TRIBUNE:

The editorial that you wrote about me illustrated what I meant about the loyalty check system and about what would happen if it got going in the industrial world. My letter, expressing a dissenting opinion, was a letter that any conscientious reader might write to his newspaper, and you answered it by saying I belonged to "probably the most dangerous element in our society." Thus a difference of opinion became suddenly a mark of infamy. A man who disagreed with a *Tribune* editorial used to be called plucky—now he's called dangerous. By your own definition I already belong among the unemployables.

You said that in these times we need "new concepts and new principles" to combat subversion. It seems to me the loyalty check in industry is not a new principle at all. It is like the "new look,"[1] which is really the old, old look, slightly tinkered up. The principle of demanding an expression of political conformity as the price of a job is the principle of hundred percentism. It is not new and it is blood brother of witch burning.

I don't know why I should be bawling out the *Herald Tribune* or why the *Herald Tribune* should be bawling out me. I read those Bert Andrews pieces[2] and got a new breath of fresh air. Then I turned in a dissenting opinion about an editorial and got hit over the head with a stick of wood. These times are too edgy. It is obvious to everyone that the fuss about loyalty arises from fear of war with Russia, and from the natural feeling that we should clear our decks of doubtful characters. Well, I happen to believe that we can achieve reasonably clear decks if we continue to apply our civil rights and duties equally to all citizens, even to citizens of opposite belief. That may be a dangerous and false idea, but my holding it does not necessarily make me a dangerous and false man, and I wish that the *Herald Tribune* next time it sits down to write a piece about me and my party would be good enough to make the distinction. Right now

1. A major change in women's fashion introduced in 1947.
2. Bert Andrews, chief of the Washington news bureau of the *New York Herald Tribune*, won a Pulitzer Prize for his reporting on loyalty cases in 1947.

it's a pretty important distinction to make.

E. B. WHITE

[*Determined to have the last word, the* Tribune *printed a parenthetical editorial comment right underneath White's letter. The comment began* "Perhaps we were over-emphatic in our disagreement with Mr. White, but since the same editorial which suggested that he belonged to a 'dangerous element' also said that it was a 'highly valuable' element, he can scarcely hold that we were attaching any badge of 'infamy' to him." *The editor went on to express the* Tribune's *regard for White, to deny that its editors were the slightest bit afraid of war with Russia, and to state that they continued to feel that Communism was* "exploiting toleration in order to destroy toleration." *The comment concluded that* "We may be misguided in our attempts to deal with it, but it seems to us that Mr. White fails to deal with it at all."]

* * *

To the Editor of the Ellsworth (Maine) American

[North Brooklin, Me.]
January 1, 1976

TO THE EDITOR:

I think it might be useful to stop viewing fences for a moment and take a close look at *Esquire* magazine's new way of doing business. In February, *Esquire* will publish a long article by Harrison E. Salisbury, for which Mr. Salisbury will receive no payment from *Esquire* but will receive $40,000 from the Xerox Corporation—plus another $15,000 for expenses. This, it would seem to me, is not only a new idea in publishing, it charts a clear course for the erosion of the free press in America. Mr. Salisbury is a former associate editor of the *New York Times* and should know better. *Esquire* is a reputable sheet and should know better. But here we go—the Xerox–Salisbury–*Esquire* axis in full cry!

A news story about this amazing event in the December 14th issue of the *Times* begins: "Officials of *Esquire* magazine and of the Xerox Corporation report no adverse reactions, so far, to the announcement that *Esquire* will publish a 23-page article [about travels through America] in February 'sponsored' by Xerox." Herewith I am happy to turn in my adverse reaction even if it's the first one across the line.

Esquire, according to the *Times* story, attempts to justify its new payment system (get the money from a sponsor) by assuring us that Mr. Salisbury will not be tampered with by Xerox; his hand and his pen will be free. If Xerox likes what he writes about America, Xerox will run a "low keyed full-page ad preceding the article" and another ad at the end of it. From this advertising, *Esquire* stands to pick up $115,000, and Mr. Salisbury has already picked up $40,000, traveling, all expenses paid, through this once happy land. . . .

Apparently Mr. Salisbury had a momentary qualm about taking on the Xerox job. The *Times* reports him as saying, "At first I thought, gee whiz, should I do this?" But he quickly conquered his annoying doubts and remembered that big corporations had in the past been known to sponsor "cultural enterprises," such as opera. The emergence of a magazine reporter as a cultural enterprise is as stunning a sight as the emergence of a butterfly from a cocoon. Mr. Salisbury must have felt great, escaping from his confinement.

Well, it doesn't take a giant intellect to detect in all this the shadow of disaster. If magazines decide to farm out their writers to advertisers and accept the advertiser's payment to the writer and to the magazine, then the periodicals of this country will be far down the drain and will become so fuzzy as to be indistinguishable from the controlled press in other parts of the world.

E. B. WHITE

[*Some weeks after his letter on the Xerox-Esquire-Salisbury arrangement was published, White received a letter of inquiry from W. B. Jones, Director of Communications Operations at Xerox Corporation, outlining the ground rules of the corporation's sponsorship of the Salisbury piece and concluding: "With these ground rules, do you still see something sinister in the sponsorship? The question is put seriously, because if a writer of your achievement and insight—after considering the terms of the arrangement—still sees this kind of corporate sponsorship as leading the periodicals of this country toward the controlled press of other parts of the world, then we may well reconsider our plans to underwrite similar projects in the future." White's reply follows.*]

To W. B. Jones

North Brooklin
January 30, 1976

DEAR MR. JONES:

In extending my remarks on sponsorship, published in the Ellsworth *American*, I want to limit the discussion to the press—that is, to newspapers and magazines. I'll not speculate about television, as television is outside my experience and I have no ready opinion about sponsorship in that medium.

In your recent letter to me, you ask whether, having studied your ground rules for proper conduct in sponsoring a magazine piece, I still see something sinister in the sponsorship. Yes, I do. Sinister may not be the right word, but I see something ominous and unhealthy when a corporation underwrites an article in a magazine of general circulation. This is not, essentially, the old familiar question of an advertiser trying to influence editorial content; almost everyone is acquainted with that common phenomenon. Readers are aware that it is always present but usually in a rather subdued or non-threatening form. Xerox's sponsoring of a specific writer on a specific occasion for a specific article is something quite different. No one, as far as I know, accuses Xerox of trying to influence editorial opinion. But many people are wondering why a large corporation placed so much money on a magazine piece, why the writer of the piece was willing to get paid in so unusual a fashion, and why *Esquire* was ready and willing to have an outsider pick up the tab. These are reasonable questions.

The press in our free country is reliable and useful not because of its good character but because of its great diversity. As long as there are many owners, each pursuing his own brand of truth, we the people have the opportunity to arrive at the truth and to dwell in the light. The multiplicity of ownership is crucial. It's only when there are a few owners, or, as in a government-controlled press, one owner, that the truth becomes elusive and the light fails. For a citizen in our free society, it is an enormous privilege and a wonderful protection to have access to hundreds of periodicals, each peddling its own belief. There is safety in numbers: the papers expose each other's follies and peccadillos, correct each other's mistakes, and cancel out each other's biases. The reader is free to range around in the whole editorial bouillabaisse and explore it for the one clam that matters—the truth.

When a large corporation or a rich individual underwrites an article in a magazine, the picture changes: the ownership of that magazine has been diminished, the outline of the magazine has been blurred. In the case of the Salisbury piece, it was as though *Esquire* had gone on relief, was accepting its first welfare payment, and was not its own man anymore. The editor protests that he accepts full responsibility for the text and that Xerox had nothing to do with the whole business. But the fact remains that, despite his full acceptance of responsibility, he somehow did not get around to paying the bill. This is unsettling and I think unhealthy. Whenever money changes hands, something goes along with it—an intangible something that varies with the circumstances. It would be hard to resist the suspicion that *Esquire* feels indebted to Xerox, that Mr. Salisbury feels indebted to both, and that the ownership, or sovereignty, of *Esquire* has been nibbled all around the edges.

Sponsorship in the press is an invitation to corruption and abuse. The temptations are great, and there is an opportunist behind every bush. A funded article is a tempting morsel for any publication—particularly for one that is having a hard time making ends meet. A funded assignment is a tempting dish for a writer, who may pocket a much larger fee than he is accustomed to getting. And sponsorship is attractive to the sponsor himself, who, for one reason or another, feels an urge to penetrate the editorial columns after being so long pent up in the advertising pages. These temptations are real, and if the barriers were to be let down I believe corruption and abuse would soon follow. Not all corporations would approach subsidy in the immaculate way Xerox did or in the same spirit of benefaction. There are a thousand reasons for someone's wishing to buy his way into print, many of them unpalatable, all of them to some degree self-serving. Buying and selling space in news columns could become a serious disease of the press. If it reached epidemic proportions, it could destroy the press. I don't want IBM or the National Rifle Association providing me with a funded spectacular when I open my paper, I want to read what the editor and the publisher have managed to dig up on their own—and paid for out of the till. . . .

My affection for the free press in a democracy goes back a long way. My love for it was my first and greatest love. If I felt a shock at the news of the Salisbury-Xerox-*Esquire* arrangement, it was because the sponsorship principle seemed to challenge and threaten everything I believe in: that the press must not only be free, it must be fiercely independent—to survive and to serve. Not all papers are fiercely independent, God knows, but there are always enough of them around to provide a core of integrity and an example that others feel obliged to steer by. The funded article is not in itself evil, but it is the beginning of evil and it is an invitation to evil. I hope the invitation will not again be extended, and, if extended, I hope it will be declined.

About a hundred and fifty years ago, Tocqueville wrote: "The journalists of the United States are generally in a very humble position, with a scanty education and a vulgar turn of mind." Today, we chuckle at this antique characterization. But about fifty years ago, when I was a young journalist, I had the good fortune to encounter an editor who fitted the description quite closely. Harold Ross, who founded the New Yorker, was deficient in education and had—at least to all outward appearances—a vulgar turn of mind. What he did possess, though, was the ferocity of independence. He was having a tough time finding money to keep his foundering little sheet alive, yet he was determined that neither money nor influence would ever corrupt his dream or deflower his text. His boiling point was so low as to be comical. The faintest suggestion of the shadow of advertising in his news and editorial columns would cause him to erupt. He would explode in anger, the building would reverberate with his wrath, and his terrible swift sword would go flashing up and down the corridors. For a young man, it was an impressive sight and a memorable one. Fifty years have not dimmed for me either the spectacle of Ross's ferocity or my own early convictions—which were identical with his. He has come to my mind often while I've been composing this reply to your inquiry.

I hope I've clarified by a little bit my feelings about the autonomy of the press and the dangers of sponsorship of articles. Thanks for giving me the chance to speak my piece.

Sincerely,
E. B. White

[Mr. Jones wrote and thanked White for "telling me what I didn't want to hear." In May another letter arrived from Jones saying that Xerox had decided not to underwrite any more articles in the press and that they were convinced it was "the right decision."]

Walter Lippmann

THE INDISPENSABLE OPPOSITION

Were they pressed hard enough, most men would probably confess that political freedom—that is to say, the right to speak freely and to act in opposition—is a noble ideal rather than a practical necessity. As the case for freedom is generally put today, the argument lends itself to this feeling. It is made to appear that, whereas each man claims his freedom as a matter of right, the freedom he accords to other men is a matter of toleration. Thus, the defense of freedom of opinion tends to rest not on its substantial, beneficial, and indispensable consequences, but on a somewhat eccentric, a rather vaguely benevolent, attachment to an abstraction.

It is all very well to say with Voltaire, "I wholly disapprove of what you say, but will defend to the death your right to say it," but as a matter of fact most men will not defend to the death the rights of other men: if they disapprove sufficiently what other men say, they will somehow suppress those men if they can.

So, if this is the best that can be said for liberty of opinion, that a man must tolerate his opponents because everyone has a "right" to say what he pleases, then we shall find that liberty of opinion is a luxury, safe only in pleasant times when men can be tolerant because they are not deeply and vitally concerned.

Yet actually, as a matter of historic fact, there is a much stronger foundation for the great constitutional right of freedom of speech, and as a matter of practical human experience there is a much more compelling reason for cultivating the habits of free men. We take, it seems to me, a naïvely self-righteous view when we argue as if the right of our opponents to speak were something that we protect because we are magnanimous, noble, and unselfish. The compelling reason why, if liberty of opinion did not exist, we should have to invent it, why it will eventually have to be restored in all civilized countries where it is now suppressed, is that we must protect the right of our opponents to speak because we must hear what they have to say.

We miss the whole point when we imagine that we tolerate the freedom of our political opponents as we tolerate a howling baby next door, as we put up with the blasts from our neighbor's radio because we are too peaceable to heave a brick through the window. If this were all there is to freedom of opinion, that we are too goodnatured or too timid to do anything about our opponents and our critics except to let them talk, it would be difficult to say whether we are tolerant because we are magnanimous or because we are lazy, because we have strong principles or because we lack serious convictions, whether we have the hospitality of an inquiring mind or the indifference of an empty mind. And so, if we truly wish to understand why freedom is necessary in a civilized society, we must begin by realizing that, because freedom of discussion improves our own opinions, the liberties of other men are our own vital necessity.

We are much closer to the essence of the matter, not when we quote Voltaire, but when we go to the doctor and pay him to ask us the most embarrassing questions and to prescribe the most disagreeable diet. When we pay the doctor to exercise complete freedom of speech about the cause and cure of our stomachache, we do not look upon ourselves as tolerant and magnanimous, and worthy to be admired by ourselves. We have enough common sense to know that if we threaten to put the doctor in jail because we do not like the diagnosis and the prescription it will be unpleasant for the doctor, to be sure, but equally unpleasant for our own stomachache. That is why even the most ferocious dictator would rather be treated by a doctor who was free to think and speak the truth than by his own Minister of Propaganda. For there is a point, the point at which things really matter, where the freedom of others is no longer a question of their right but of our own need.

The point at which we recognize this need is much higher in some men than in others. The totalitarian rulers think they do not need the freedom of an opposition: they exile, imprison, or shoot their opponents. We have concluded on the basis of practical experience, which goes back to Magna Carta and beyond, that we need the opposition. We pay the opposition salaries out of the public treasury.

In so far as the usual apology for freedom of speech ignores this experience, it becomes abstract and eccentric rather than concrete and human. The emphasis is generally put on the right to speak, as if all that mattered were that the doctor should be free to go out into the park and explain to the vacant air why I have a stomachache. Surely that is a miserable caricature of the great civic right which men have bled and died for. What really matters is that the doctor should tell me what ails me, that I should listen to him; that if I do not like what he says I should be free to call in another doctor; and that then the first doctor should have to listen to the second doctor; and that out of all the speaking and listening, the give-and-take of opinions, the truth should be arrived at.

This is the creative principle of freedom of speech, not that it is a system for the tolerating of error, but that it is a system for finding the truth. It may not produce the truth, or the whole truth all the time, or often, or in some cases ever. But if the truth can be found, there is no other system which will normally and habitually find so much truth. Until we have thoroughly understood this principle, we shall not know why we must value our liberty, or how we can protect and develop it.

Let us apply this principle to the system of public speech in a totalitarian state. We may, without any serious falsification, picture a condition of affairs in which the mass of the people are being addressed through one broadcasting system by one man and his chosen subordinates. The orators speak. The audience listens but cannot and dare not speak back. It is a system of one-way communication; the opinions of the rulers are broadcast outwardly to the mass of the people. But nothing comes back to the rulers from the people except the cheers; nothing returns in the way of knowledge of forgotten facts, hidden feelings, neglected truths, and practical suggestions.

But even a dictator cannot goven by his own one-way inspiration alone. In practice, therefore, the totalitarian rulers get back the reports of the secret police and of their party henchmen down among the crowd. If these reports are competent, the rulers may manage to remain in touch with public sentiment. Yet that is not enough to know what the audience feels. The rulers have also to make great decisions that have enormous consequences, and here their system provides virtually no help from the give-and-take of opinion in the nation. So they must either rely on their own intuition, which cannot be permanently and continually inspired, or, if they are intelligent despots, encourage their trusted advisers and their technicians to speak and debate freely in their presence.

On the walls of the houses of Italian peasants one may see inscribed in large letters the legend, "Mussolini is always right." But if that legend is taken seriously by Italian ambassadors, by the Italian General Staff, and by the Ministry of Finance, then all one can say is heaven help Mussolini, heaven help Italy, and the new Emperor of Ethiopia.[1]

For at some point, even in a totalitarian state, it is indispensable that

1. Benito Mussolini was then dictator of Italy, which he led into World War II; after Italy's conquest of Ethiopia in 1936, he had the Italian king, Victor Emanuel III, proclaimed its emperor.

there should exist the freedom of opinion which causes opposing opinions to be debated. As time goes on, that is less and less easy under a despotism; critical discussion disappears as the internal opposition is liquidated in favor of men who think and feel alike. That is why the early successes of despots, of Napoleon I and of Napoleon III, have usually been followed by an irreparable mistake. For in listening only to his yes men—the others being in exile or in concentration camps, or terrified—the despot shuts himself off from the truth that no man can dispense with.

We know all this well enough when we contemplate the dictatorships. But when we try to picture our own system, by way of contrast, what picture do we have in our minds? It is, is it not, that anyone may stand up on his own soapbox and say anything he pleases, like the individuals in Kipling's poem[2] who sit each in his separate star and draw the Thing as they see it for the God of Things as they are. Kipling, perhaps, could do this, since he was a poet. But the ordinary mortal isolated on his separate star will have an hallucination, and a citizenry declaiming from separate soapboxes will poison the air with hot and nonsensical confusion.

If the democratic alternative to the totalitarian one-way broadcasts is a row of separate soapboxes, than I submit that the alternative is unworkable, is unreasonable, and is humanly unattractive. It is above all a false alternative. It is not true that liberty has developed among civilized men when anyone is free to set up a soapbox, is free to hire a hall where he may expound his opinions to those who are willing to listen. On the contrary, freedom of speech is established to achieve its essential purpose only when different opinions are expounded in the same hall to the same audience.

For, while the right to talk may be the beginning of freedom, the necessity of listening is what makes the right important. Even in Russia and Germany a man may still stand in an open field and speak his mind. What matters is not the utterance of opinions. What matters is the confrontation of opinions in debate. No man can care profoundly that every fool should say what he likes. Nothing has been accomplished if the wisest man proclaims his wisdom in the middle of the Sahara Desert. This is the shadow. We have the substance of liberty when the fool is compelled to listen to the wise man and learn; when the wise man is compelled to take account of the fool, and to instruct him; when the wise man can increase his wisdom by hearing the judgment of his peers.

That is why civilized men must cherish liberty—as a means of promoting the discovery of truth. So we must not fix our whole attention on the right of anyone to hire his own hall, to rent his own broadcasting station, to distribute his own pamphlets. These rights are incidental; and though they must be preserved, they can be preserved only by regarding them as

2. "L'Envoi."

incidental, as auxiliary to the substance of liberty that must be cherished and cultivated.

Freedom of speech is best conceived, therefore, by having in mind the picture of a place like the American Congress, an assembly where opposing views are represented, where ideas are not merely uttered but debated, or the British Parliament, where men who are free to speak are also compelled to answer. We may picture the true condition of freedom as existing in a place like a court of law, where witnesses testify and are cross-examined, where the lawyer argues against the opposing lawyer before the same judge and in the presence of one jury. We may picture freedom as existing in a forum where the speaker must respond to questions; in a gathering of scientists where the data, the hypothesis, and the conclusion are submitted to men competent to judge them; in a reputable newspaper which not only will publish the opinions of those who disagree but will re-examine its own opinion in the light of what they say.

Thus the essence of freedom of opinion is not in mere toleration as such, but in the debate which toleration provides: it is not in the venting of opinion, but in the confrontation of opinion. That this is the practical substance can readily be understood when we remember how differently we feel and act about the censorship and regulation of opinion purveyed by different media of communication. We find then that, in so far as the medium makes difficult the confrontation of opinion in debate, we are driven towards censorship and regulation.

There is, for example, the whispering campaign, the circulation of anonymous rumors by men who cannot be compelled to prove what they say. They put the utmost strain on our tolerance, and there are few who do not rejoice when the anonymous slanderer is caught, exposed, and punished. At a higher level there is the moving picture, a most powerful medium for conveying ideas, but a medium which does not permit debate. A moving picture cannot be answered effectively by another moving picture; in all free countries there is some censorship of the movies, and there would be more if the producers did not recognize their limitations by avoiding political controversy. There is then the radio. Here debate is difficult: it is not easy to make sure that the speaker is being answered in the presence of the same audience. Inevitably, there is some regulation of the radio.

When we reach the newspaper press, the opportunity for debate is so considerable that discontent cannot grow to the point where under normal conditions there is any disposition to regulate the press. But when newspapers abuse their power by injuring people who have no means of replying, a disposition to regulate the press appears. When we arrive at Congress we find that, because the membership of the House is so large, full debate is impracticable. So there are restrictive rules. On the other hand, in the Senate, where the conditions of full debate exist, there is almost absolute freedom of speech.

This shows us that the preservation and development of freedom of opinion are not only a matter of adhering to abstract legal rights, but also, and very urgently, a matter of organizing and arranging sufficient debate. Once we have a firm hold on the central principle, there are many practical conclusions to be drawn. We then realize that the defense of freedom of opinion consists primarily in perfecting the opportunity for an adequate give-and-take of opinion; it consists also in regulating the freedom of those revolutionists who cannot or will not permit or maintain debate when it does not suit their purposes.

We must insist that free oratory is only the beginning of free speech; it is not the end, but a means to an end. The end is to find the truth. The practical justification of civil liberty is not that self-expression is one of the rights of man. It is that the examination of opinion is one of the necessities of man. For experience tells us that it is only when freedom of opinion becomes the compulsion to debate that the seed which our fathers planted has produced its fruit. When that is understood, freedom will be cherished not because it is a vent for our opinions but because it is the surest method of correcting them.

The unexamined life, said Socrates, is unfit to be lived by man. This is the virtue of liberty, and the ground on which we may best justify our belief in it, that it tolerates error in order to serve the truth. When men are brought face to face with their opponents, forced to listen and learn and mend their ideas, they cease to be children and savages and begin to live like civilized men. Then only is freedom a reality, when men may voice their opinions because they must examine their opinions.

The only reason for dwelling on all this is that if we are to preserve democracy we must understand its principles. And the principle which distinguishes it from all other forms of government is that in a democracy the opposition not only is tolerated as constitutional but must be maintained because it is in fact indispensable.

The democratic system cannot be operated without effective opposition. For, in making the great experiment of governing people by consent rather than by coercion, it is not sufficient that the party in power should have a majority. It is just as necessary that the party in power should never outrage the minority. That means that it must listen to the minority and be moved by the criticisms of the minority. That means that its measures must take account of the minority's objections, and that in administering measures it must remember that the minority may become the majority.

The opposition is indispensable. A good statesman, like any other sensible human being, always learns more from his opponents than from his fervent supporters. For his supporters will push him to disaster unless his opponents show him where the dangers are. So if he is wise he will often pray to be delivered from his friends, because they will ruin him. But, though it hurts, he ought also to pray never to be left without opponents; for they keep him on the path of reason and good sense.

The national unity of a free people depends upon a sufficiently even balance of political power to make it impracticable for the administration to be arbitrary and for the opposition to be revolutionary and irreconcilable. Where that balance no longer exists, democracy perishes. For unless all the citizens of a state are forced by circumstances to compromise, unless they feel that they can affect policy but that no one can wholly dominate it, unless by habit and necessity they have to give and take, freedom cannot be maintained.

1939

THE READER

1. What is the importance of Lippmann's distinction between "free oratory" and "free speech" (p. 846)?
2. What does Lippmann mean when he says that the point at which we recognize the need for the freedom of others "is much higher in some men than in others" (p. 842)? Does this assertion in any way weaken his argument?
3. Thurber's rabbits (p. 806) listened to their opposition—that is, "the other animals, who lived at a great distance"—and were annihilated. Does Thurber's fable suggest any necessary qualification for Lippmann's thesis concerning the value of the opposition? Explain.
4. Lippmann's essay was written before the term brainwashing was in common use. If he were writing the essay today, how might he take account of this term?

THE WRITER

1. What is Lippmann's reason for dividing the essay into three parts? What is the purpose of the third part?
2. Why has Lippmann discussed motion pictures but not literature (p. 845)? How sound is his view that the motion picture is "a medium which does not permit debate"? Does literature permit debate?
3. What does Lippmann mean by his statement that "the usual apology for freedom of speech . . . becomes abstract and eccentric rather than concrete and human" (p. 842)? Why has he chosen these particular words to contrast the "usual apology" with his own view? Is his argument "concrete and human"?
4. Write a brief essay in which you test whether opposition is necessary to democracy in the way that Becker (p. 832) or White (p. 833) defines it.

Jonathan Schell

THE ROOTS OF NUCLEAR PERIL

* * *

If a council were to be empowered by the people of the earth to do whatever was necessary to save humanity from extinction by nuclear arms, it might well decide that a good first step would be to order the destruction of all the nuclear weapons in the world. When the order had been carried out, however, warlike or warring nations might still rebuild their nuclear arsenals—perhaps in a matter of months. A logical second step, accordingly, would be to order the destruction of the factories that make the weapons. But, just as the weapons might be rebuilt, so might the factories, and the world's margin of safety would not have been increased by very much. A third step, then, would be to order the destruction of the factories that make the factories that make the weapons—a measure that might require the destruction of a considerable part of the world's economy. But even then lasting safety would not have been reached, because in some number of years—at most, a few decades—everything could be rebuilt, including the nuclear arsenals, and mankind would again be ready to extinguish itself. A determined council might next decide to try to arrest the world economy in a prenuclear state by throwing the blueprints and technical manuals for reconstruction on the bonfires that had by then consumed everything else, but that recourse, too, would ultimately fail, because the blueprints and manuals could easily be redrawn and rewritten. As long as the world remained acquainted with the basic physical laws that underlie the construction of nuclear weapons—and these laws include the better part of physics as physics is understood in our century—mankind would have failed to put many years between itself and its doom. For the fundamental origin of the peril of human extinction by nuclear arms lies not in any particular social or political circumstances of our time but in the attainment by mankind as a whole, after millennia of scientific progress, of a certain level of knowledge of the physical universe. As long as that knowledge is in our possession, the atoms themselves, each one stocked with its prodigious supply of energy, are, in a manner of speaking, in a perilously advanced state of mobilization for nuclear hostilities, and any conflict anywhere in the world can become a nuclear one. To return to safety through technical measures alone, we would have to disarm matter itself, converting it back into its relatively safe, inert, nonexplosive nineteenth-century Newtonian state—something that not even the physics of our time can teach us how to do. (I mention these farfetched, wholly imaginary programs of demolition and suppression in part because the final destruction of all mankind is so much more farfetched, and therefore seems to give us license to at least consider extreme alternatives, but mainly because their obvious inadequacy serves to demonstrate how deeply the nuclear peril is ingrained in our world.)

It is fundamental to the shape and character of the nuclear predicament that its origins lie in scientific knowledge rather than in social circumstances. Revolutions born in the laboratory are to be sharply distinguished from revolutions born in society. Social revolutions are usually born in the minds of millions, and are led up to by what the Declaration of Independence calls "a long train of abuses," visible to all; indeed, they usually cannot occur unless they are widely understood by and supported by the public. By contrast, scientific revolutions usually take shape quietly in the minds of a few men, under cover of the impenetrability to most laymen of scientific theory, and thus catch the world by surprise. In the case of nuclear weapons, of course, the surprise was greatly increased by the governmental secrecy that surrounded the construction of the first bombs. When the world learned of their existence, Mr. Fukai had already run back into the flames of Hiroshima, and tens of thousands of people in that city had already been killed. Even long after scientific discoveries have been made and their applications have transformed our world, most people are likely to remain ignorant of the underlying principles at work, and this has been particularly true of nuclear weapons, which, decades after their invention, are still surrounded by an aura of mystery, as though they had descended from another planet. (To most people, Einstein's famous formula $E=mc^2$, which defines the energy released in nuclear explosions, stands as a kind of symbol of everything that is esoteric and incomprehensible.)

But more important by far than the world's unpreparedness for scientific revolutions are their universality and their permanence once they have occurred. Social revolutions are restricted to a particular time and place; they arise out of particular circumstances, last for a while, and then pass into history. Scientific revolutions, on the other hand, belong to all places and all times. In the words of Alfred North Whitehead, "Modern science was born in Europe, but its home is the whole world." In fact, of all the products of human hands and minds, scientific knowledge has proved to be the most durable. The physical structures of human life—furniture, buildings, paintings, cities, and so on—are subject to inevitable natural decay, and human institutions have likewise proved to be transient. Hegel, whose philosophy of history was framed in large measure in an attempt to redeem the apparent futility of the efforts of men to found something enduring in their midst, once wrote, "When we see the evil, the vice, the ruin that has befallen the most flourishing kingdoms which the mind of man ever created, we can scarce avoid being filled with sorrow at this universal taint of corruption; and, since this decay is not the work of mere Nature, but of Human Will—a moral embitterment—a revolt of the Good Spirit (if it have a place within us) may well be the result of our reflections." Works of thought and many works of art have a better chance of surviving, since new copies of a book or a symphony can be transcribed from old ones, and so can be preserved indefinitely; yet these works, too, can and do go out of existence, for if every copy is lost, then the work is also lost. The subject matter of these works is man, and they seem to be touched with his mortality. The results of scientific work, on the other hand, are largely immune to decay and disappearance. Even when they are lost, they are likely to be rediscovered, as is shown by the fact that several scientists often make the same discovery independently. (There is no record of several poets' having independently written the same poem, or of several composers' having independently written the same symphony.) For both the subject matter and the method of science are available to all capable minds in a way that the subject matter and the method of the arts are not. The human experiences that art deals with are, once over, lost forever, like the people who undergo them, whereas matter, energy, space, and time, alike everywhere and in all ages, are always available for fresh inspection. The subject matter of science is the physical world, and its findings seem to share in the immortality of the physical world. And artistic vision grows out of the unrepeatable individuality of each artist, whereas the reasoning power of the mind—its ability to add two and two and get four—is the same in all competent persons. The rigorous exactitude of scientific methods does not mean that creativity is any less individual, intuitive, or mysterious in great scientists than in great artists, but it does mean that scientific findings, once arrived at, can be tested and confirmed by shared canons of logic and experimentation. The agreement among scientists thus achieved permits science to be a collective enterprise, in which each generation, building on the accepted findings of the generations before, makes amendments and additions, which in their turn become the starting point for the next generation. (Philosophers, by contrast, are constantly tearing down the work of their predecessors, and circling back to re-ask questions that have been asked and answered countless times before. Kant once wrote in despair, "It seems ridiculous that while every science moves forward ceaselessly, this [metaphysics], claiming to be wisdom itself, whose oracular pronouncements everyone consults, is continually revolving in one spot, without advancing one step.") Scientists, as they erect the steadily growing structure of scientific knowledge, resemble nothing so much as a swarm of bees working harmoniously together to construct a single, many-chambered hive, which grows more elaborate and splendid with every year that passes. Looking at what they have made over the centuries, scientists need feel no "sorrow" or "moral embitterment" at any "taint of corruption" that supposedly undoes all human achievements.

When God, alarmed that the builders of the Tower of Babel would reach Heaven with their construction, and so become as God, put an end to their undertaking by making them all speak different languages, He apparently overlooked the scientists, for they, speaking what is often called the "universal language" of their disciplines from country to country and generation to generation, went on to build a new tower—the edifice of scientific knowledge. Their phenomenal success, beginning not with Einstein but with Euclid and Archimedes, has provided the unshakable structure that supports the world's nuclear peril. So durable is the scientific edifice that if we did not know that human beings had constructed it we might suppose that the findings on which our whole technological civilization rests were the pillars and crossbeams of an invulnerable, inhuman order obtruding into our changeable and perishable human realm. It is the crowning irony of this lopsided development of human abilities that the only means in sight for getting rid of the knowledge of how to destroy ourselves would be to do just that—in effect, to remove the knowledge by removing the knower.

Although it is unquestionably the scientists who have led us to the edge of the nuclear abyss, we would be mistaken if we either held them chiefly responsible for our plight or looked to them, particularly, for a solution. Here, again, the difference between scientific revolutions and social revolutions shows itself, for the notion that scientists bear primary responsibility springs from a tendency to confuse scientists with political actors. Political actors, who, of course, include ordinary citizens as well as government officials, act with definite social ends in view, such as the preservation of peace, the establishment of a just society, or, if they are corrupt, their own aggrandizement; and they are accordingly held responsible for the consequences of their actions, even when these are unintended ones, as they so often are. Scientists, on the other hand (and here I refer to the so-called pure scientists, who search for the laws of nature for the sake of knowledge itself, and not to the applied scientists, who make use of already discovered natural laws to solve practical problems), do not aim at social ends, and, in fact, usually do not know what the social results of their findings will be; for that matter, they cannot know what the findings themselves will be, because science is a process of discovery, and it is in the nature of discovery that one cannot know beforehand what one will find. This element of the unexpected is present when a researcher sets out to unravel some small, carefully defined mystery—say, the chemistry of a certain enzyme—but it is most conspicuous in the synthesis of the great laws of science and in the development of science as a whole, which, over decades and centuries, moves toward destinations that no one can predict. Thus, only a few decades ago it might have seemed that physics, which had just placed nuclear energy at man's disposal, was the dangerous branch of science, while biology, which underlay improvements in medicine and also helped us to understand our dependence on the natural environment, was the beneficial branch; but now that biologists have begun to fathom the secrets of genetics, and to tamper with the genetic substance of life directly, we cannot be so sure. The most striking illustration of the utter disparity that may occur between the wishes of the scientist as a social being and the social results of his scientific findings is certainly the career of Einstein. By nature, he was, according to all accounts, the gentlest of men, and by conviction he was a pacifist, yet he made intellectual discoveries that led the way to the invention of weapons with which the species could exterminate itself. Inspired wholly by a love of knowledge for its own sake, and by an awe at the creation which bordered on the religious, he made possible an instrument of destruction with which the terrestrial creation could be disfigured.

A disturbing corollary of the scientists' inability even to foresee the path of science, to say nothing of determining it, is that while science is without doubt the most powerful revolutionary force in our world, no one directs that force. For science is a process of submission, in which the mind does not dictate to nature but seeks out and then bows to nature's laws, letting its conclusions be guided by that which *is*, independent of our will. From the political point of view, therefore, scientific findings, some lending themselves to evil, some to good, and some to both, simply pour forth from the laboratory in senseless profusion, offering the world now a neutron bomb, now bacteria that devour oil, now a vaccine to prevent polio, now a cloned frog. It is not until the pure scientists, seekers of knowledge for its own sake, turn their findings over to the applied scientists that social intentions begin to guide the results. The applied scientists do indeed set out to make a better vaccine or a bigger bomb, but even they, perhaps, deserve less credit or blame than we are sometimes inclined to give them. For as soon as our intentions enter the picture we are in the realm of politics in the broadest sense, and in politics it is ultimately not technicians but governments and citizens who are in charge. The scientists in the Manhattan Project could not decide to make the first atomic bomb; only President Roosevelt, elected to office by the American people, could do that.

If scientists are unable to predict their discoveries, neither can they cancel them once they have been made. In this respect, they are like the rest of us, who are asked not whether we would like to live in a world in which we can convert matter into energy but only what we want to do about it once we have been told that we do live in such a world. Science is a tide that can only rise. The individual human mind is capable of forgetting things, and mankind has collectively forgotten many things, but we do not know how, as a species, to *deliberately* set out to forget something. A basic scientific finding, therefore, has the character of destiny for the world. Scientific discovery is in this regard like any other form of discovery; once Columbus had discovered America, and had told the world about it, America could not be hidden again.

Scientific progress (which can and certainly will occur) offers little more hope than scientific regression (which probably cannot occur) of giving us relief from the nuclear peril. It does not seem likely that science will bring forth some new invention—some antiballistic missile or laser beam—that will render nuclear weapons harmless (although the unpredictability of science prevents any categorical judgment on this point). In the centuries of the modern scientific revolution, scientific knowledge has steadily increased the destructiveness of warfare, for it is in the very nature of knowledge, apparently, to increase our might rather than to diminish it. One of the most common forms of the hope for deliverance from the nuclear peril by technical advances is the notion that the species will be spared extinction by fleeing in spaceships. The thought seems to be that while the people on earth are destroying themselves communities in space will be able to survive and carry on. This thought does an injustice to our birthplace and habitat, the earth. It assumes that if only we could escape the earth we would find safety—as though it were the earth and its plants and animals that threatened us, rather than the other way around. But the fact is that wherever human beings went there also would go the knowledge of how to build nuclear weapons, and, with it, the peril of extinction. Scientific progress may yet deliver us from many evils, but there are at least two evils that it cannot deliver us from: its own findings and our own destructive and self-destructive bent. This is a combination that we will have to learn to deal with by some other means.

We live, then, in a universe whose fundamental substance contains a supply of energy with which we can extinguish ourselves. We shall never live in any other. We now know that we live in such a universe, and we shall never stop knowing it. Over the millennia, this truth lay in waiting for us, and now we have found it out, irrevocably. If we suppose that it is an integral part of human existence to be curious about the physical world we are born into, then, to speak in the broadest terms, the origin of the nuclear peril lies, on the one hand, in our nature as rational and inquisitive beings and, on the other, in the nature of matter. Because the energy that nuclear weapons release is so great, the whole species is threatened by them, and because the spread of scientific knowledge is unstoppable, the whole species poses the threat: in the last analysis, it is all of mankind that threatens all of mankind. (I do not mean to overlook the fact that at present it is only two nations—the United States and the Soviet Union—that possess nuclear weapons in numbers great enough to possibly destroy the species, and that they thus now bear the chief responsibility for the peril. I only wish to point out that, regarded in its full dimensions, the nuclear peril transcends the rivalry between the present superpowers.)

The fact that the roots of the nuclear peril lie in basic scientific knowledge has broad political implications that cannot be ignored if the world's solution to the predicament is to be built on a solid foundation, and if futile efforts are to be avoided. One such effort would be to rely on secrecy to contain the peril—that is, to "classify" the "secret" of the bomb. The first person to try to suppress knowledge of how nuclear weapons can be made was the physicist Leo Szilard, who in 1939, when he first heard that a nuclear chain reaction was possible, and realized that a nuclear bomb might be possible, called on a number of his colleagues to keep the discovery secret from the Germans. Many of the key scientists refused. His failure foreshadowed a succession of failures, by whole governments, to restrict the knowledge of how the weapons are made. The first, and most notable, such failure was the United States' inability to monopolize nuclear weapons, and prevent the Soviet Union from building them. And we have subsequently witnessed the failure of the entire world to prevent nuclear weapons from spreading. Given the nature of scientific thought and the very poor record of past attempts to suppress it, these failures should not have surprised anyone. (The Catholic Church succeeded in making Galileo recant his view that the earth revolves around the sun, but we do not now believe that the sun revolves around the earth.) Another, closely related futile effort—the one made by our hypothetical council—would be to try to resolve the nuclear predicament through disarmament alone, without accompanying political measures. Like the hope that the knowledge can be classified, this hope loses sight of the fact that the nuclear predicament consists not in the possession of nuclear weapons at a particular moment by certain nations but in the circumstance that mankind as a whole has now gained possession once and for all of the knowledge of how to make them, and that all nations—and even some groups of people which are not nations, including terrorist groups—can potentially build them. Because the nuclear peril, like the scientific knowledge that gave rise to it, is probably global and everlasting, our solution must at least aim at being global and everlasting. And the only kind of solution that holds out this promise is a global political one. In defining the task so broadly, however, I do not mean to argue against short-term palliatives, such as the Strategic Arms Limitation Talks between the United States and the Soviet Union, or nuclear-nonproliferation agreements, on the ground that they are short-term. If a patient's life is in danger, as mankind's now is, no good cause is served by an argument between the nurse who wants to give him an aspirin to bring down his fever and the doctor who wants to perform the surgery that can save his life; there is need for an argument only if the nurse is claiming that the aspirin is all that is necessary. If, given the world's discouraging record of political achievement, a lasting political solution seems almost beyond human powers, it may give us confidence to remember that what challenges us is simply our extraordinary success in another field of activity—the scientific. We have only to learn to live politically in the world in which we already live scientifically.

Since 1947, the *Bulletin of the Atomic Scientists* has included a "doomsday clock" in each issue. The editors place the hands farther away from or closer to midnight as they judge the world to be farther away from or closer to a nuclear holocaust. A companion clock can be imagined whose hands, instead of metaphorically representing a judgment about the likelihood of a holocaust, would represent an estimate of the amount of time that, given the world's technical and political arrangements, the people of the earth can be sure they have left before they are destroyed in a holocaust. At present, the hands would stand at, or a fraction of a second before, midnight, because none of us can be sure that at any second we will not be killed in a nuclear attack. If, by treaty, all nuclear warheads were removed from their launchers and stored somewhere else, and therefore could no longer descend on us at any moment without warning, the clock would show the amount of time that it would take to put them back on. If all the nuclear weapons in the world were destroyed, the clock would show the time that it would take to manufacture them again. If in addition confidence-inspiring political arrangements to prevent rearmament were put in place, the clock would show some estimate of the time that it might take for the arrangements to break down. And if these arrangements were to last for hundreds or thousands of years (as they must if mankind is to survive this long), then some generation far in the future might feel justified in setting the clock at decades, or even centuries, before midnight. But no generation would ever be justified in retiring the clock from use altogether, because, as far as we can tell, there will never again be a time when self-extinction is beyond the reach of our species. An observation that Plutarch made about politics holds true also for the task of survival, which has now become the principal obligation of politics: "They are wrong who think that politics is like an ocean voyage or a military campaign, something to be done with some end in view, something which levels off as soon as that end is reached. It is not a public chore, to be got over with; it is a way of life."

1982

Science

Edward O. Wilson

THE SUPERORGANISM

In March 1983 I returned to South America to begin a new program of study on tropical ants. I was interested in the way the communication systems and division of labor of these insects adapt them to their environment. My first stop was the field site of the Minimum Critical Size Project of the World Wildlife Fund, located in Amazonian forest sixty miles north of Manaus,[1] Brazil. I was accompanied by Thomas Lovejoy, the young and vigorous vice-president for science of WWF-US, who had conceived the project in the late 1970s. We joined an assortment of researchers, students, and assistants who were working back and forth between Manaus and the site on weekly tours. Camaraderie came easily and was genuine; our shared values were implicit, forming a bond too strong to allow much discussion of why we had come together in this unlikely place. We talked only about organisms, in endless technical detail.

My hosts were not ordinary field biologists. They did not affect the verbal delicacy and critical reserve of typical academics encountered on leave from comfortable bases in Berkeley, Ann Arbor, and Cambridge. Their manner was self-confident and achievement-oriented, tough in a pleasant way, and they reminded me a bit of settlers I had met in Australia and New Guinea (and the Israeli biologist who pointed out the house where he had commanded a company during the 1967 war, as we returned from a field trip to the Dead Sea). Even though the World Wildlife Fund is operating on a slender budget, its Amazon Project is truly pioneering on a large scale. Planned to run into the next century, it is designed to answer one of the key questions of ecology and conserva-

1. Capital of the state of West Brazil, located on the left bank of the Río Negro.

tion practice: how extensive does a wildlife preserve have to be to sustain permanently most or all of the kinds of plants and animals protected within its boundaries?

We know that when a species loses part of its range,[2] it is in greater danger of extinction. Expressed in loosely mathematical terms, the chance that a population of organisms will go extinct in a given year increases as its living space is cut back and its numbers are held at correspondingly lower numbers. All populations fluctuate in size to some extent, but those kept at a low maximum are more likely to zigzag all the way down to zero than those permitted to fluctuate at higher levels. For example, a population of ten grizzly bears living on one hundred square miles of land will probably disappear much earlier than a population of a thousand grizzly bears living on ten thousand square miles of similar land; the thousand could persist for centuries or, so far as ordinary human awareness is concerned, forever.

This simple fact of nature bears heavily on the design of nature reserves. When a piece of primeval forest is set aside and the surrounding forest cleared, it becomes an island in an agricultural sea. Like wave-lapped Puerto Rico or Bali, it has lost most of its connections with other natural land habitats from which new immigrations can occur. Over a period of years the number of plant and animal species will fall to a new and predictable level. Some impoverishment of diversity is inevitable even if men never put an ax to a single tree in the reserve. This natural decline presents biologists with a problem that is technically difficult and soluble only through the chancing of risky compromises. The reserve they recommend must be small enough to be economically reasonable. They cannot ask that an entire country be set aside. But they have the obligation to insist that the patch be made large enough to sustain the fauna and flora. It is their job to prove that a certain minimum area is required, to list as completely as possible which species will be saved in the reserve, and for approximately how long.

The tropical rain forest north of Manaus, like that in many other parts of the Amazon basin, is being clear-cut from the edge inward. It is being lifted up from the ground entire like a carpet rolled off a bare floor, leaving behind vast stretches of cattle range and cropland that need artificial fertilization to sustain even marginal productivity for more than two or three years. A rain forest in Brazil differs fundamentally from a deciduous woodland in Pennsylvania or Germany in the way its key resources are distributed. A much greater fraction of organic matter is bound up in the tissues of the standing trees, so that the leaf litter and humus are only a few inches deep. When the forest is felled and burned, the hard equatorial downpours quickly wash away the thin blanket of top

2. Native habitat.

soil.

Although I had this general information in advance, I was still shaken by the sight of newly cleared land around Manaus. The pans and hillocks of lateritic[3] clay, littered with blackened tree stumps, bore the look of a freshly deserted battlefield. Spherical termite mounds sprouted from the fallen wood in an ill-fated population explosion, while vultures and swifts wheeled overhead in representation of the mostly vanished bird fauna. Bony white cattle, forlorn replacements of a magnificent heritage, clustered in small groups around the scattered watersheds. Near midday the heat of the sun bounced up from the bare patches of soil to hit with an almost tactile force. It was another world altogether from the shadowed tunnels of the nearby forest, and a constant reminder of what had happened: tens of thousands of species had been scraped away as by a giant hand and will not be seen in that place for generations, if ever. The action can be defended (with difficulty) on economic grounds, but it is like burning a Renaissance painting to cook dinner.

The Brazilian authorities have sanctioned the opening of the wilderness on the basis of a logical formula: the impoverished Northeast has people and no land, the Amazon has land and no people; join them together and build a nation. But they are also well aware of the problems of environmental degradation. More recently, influenced by biologists such as Warwick Kerr, Paulo Nogueira Neto, and Paulo Vanzolini, they have begun to forge a policy of preservation. Now by law, honored at least in principle, half of the forest must be left standing. Of equal importance, more than twenty Amazonian reserves and parks have been set aside in key areas where the greatest number of species of plants and animals are thought to exist. Most are over a thousand square miles in extent, the minimum area that, according to Princeton University's John Terborgh and other experts on the subject, is needed to hold the number of disappearing species to less than 1 percent of the initial complement over the next century. In other words, the formula is meant to ensure that 99 out of every 100 kinds of organisms will still be present in the year 2100. With reserves of this size there is hope even for the harpy eagle and the jaguar, of which single individuals need three square miles or more to survive, as well as the flourish of rare orchids, monkeys, river fish, and brilliant toucans and macaws that symbolize the admirable élan[4] of Brazil itself.

But this leaves the smaller reserves elsewhere in Brazil and in the more densely populated countries of South and Central America. The American and Brazilian scientists at the Manaus project are addressing the problem in the following way. At the edge of the cutting, where the rain forest begins and continues virtually unbroken north to Venezuela, they

---

3. From decayed rock, a residue red in color.   4. Ardor, spirit.

have marked off a series of twenty plots ranging in size from one to a thousand hectares (a hectare is 100 meters on the side and equals 2.47 acres). In each plot they survey the most easily classified and monitored of the big organisms, including the trees, butterflies, birds, monkeys, and other large mammals. Then, with the cooperation of the landowners, they supervise the clearing of the surrounding land, leaving the plots behind as forest islands in a newly created agricultural sea. The surveys were begun in 1980 and will be continued for many years. Eventually the data should reveal how much faster the smaller island-reserves lose their species than larger ones, which kinds of animals and plants decline the most rapidly, why they become extinct, and, most crucially, the minimum area needed to hold on to the greater part of the diversity of life. No process being addressed by modern science is more complicated or, in my opinion, more important.

We rode in a World Wildlife Fund truck to a camp just inside the forest border at Fazenda Esteio, where the biologists were conducting one of the initial surveys. True to the philosophy of the sponsoring organization, the camp was a tiny clearing with a temporary shelter just large enough to hold a few hammocks, plus a cook's shed and fireplace, and nothing more. To my delight I found that I could roll out of my hammock in the morning, take twenty steps, and be in virgin rain forest. For five days I stayed in the woods except for meals and as little sleep as I needed to keep going.

I savored the cathedral feeling expressed by Darwin in 1832 when he first encountered tropical forest near Rio de Janeiro ("wonder, astonishment & sublime devotion, fill & elevate the mind"). And once again I could hold still for long intervals to study a few centimeters of tree trunk or ground, finding some new organism at each shift of focus. The intervals of total silence, often prolonged, became evidence of the intensity of the enveloping life. Several times a day I heard what may be the most distinctive sound of the primary tropical forest: a sharp crack like a rifle shot, followed by a whoosh and a solid thump. Somewhere a large tree, weakened by age and rot and top heavy from layers of vines, has chosen that moment to fall and end decades or centuries of life. The process is random and continuous, a sprinkling of events through the undisturbed portion of the forest. The broad trunk snaps or keels over to lever up the massive root system, the branches plow down through the canopies of neighboring trees at terrifying speed, and the whole thunders to the ground in a cloud of leaves, trailing lianas,[5] and fluttering insects. There may be a hundred thousand trees within earshot of any place the hiker stands in the forest, so that the odds of hearing one coming down on a given day are high. But the chance of being close enough to be struck by

5. Climbing tropical vine.

any part of the tree is remote, comparable to that of stepping on a poisonous snake or coming round the bend of a trail one day to meet a mother jaguar with cubs. Still, the lifetime risk builds up cumulatively, like that in daily flights aboard single-engined airplanes, so that those who spend years in the forest count falling trees as an important source of danger.

Most of the time I worked with a restless energy to get ahead on several research projects I had in mind. I opened logs and twigs like presents on Christmas morning, entranced by the endless variety of insects and other small creatures that scuttled away to safety. None of these organisms was repulsive to me; each was beautiful, with a name and special meaning. It is the naturalist's privilege to choose almost any kind of plant or animal for examination and be able to commence productive work within a relatively short time. In the tropical forest, with thousands of mostly unknown species all around, the number of discoveries per investigator per day is probably greater than anywhere else in the world.

As if to dramatize the point, an insect I most wanted to find made its appearance soon after my arrival at Fazenda Esteio, with no effort of my own and literally at my feet. It was the leafcutter ant (*Atta cephalotes*), one of the most abundant and visually striking animals of the New World tropics. The saúva, as it is called locally, is a prime consumer of fresh vegetation, rivaled only by man, and a leading agricultural pest in Brazil. I had devoted years of research to the species in the laboratory but never studied it in the field. At dusk on the first day in camp, as the light failed to the point where we found it difficult to make out small objects on the ground, the first worker ants came scurrying purposefully out of the surrounding forest. They were brick red in color, about a quarter inch in length, and bristling with short, sharp spines. Within minutes, several hundred had arrived and formed two irregular files that passed on either side of the hammock shelter. They ran in a nearly straight line across the clearing, their paired antennae scanning right and left, as though drawn by some directional beam from the other side. Within an hour, the trickle expanded to twin rivers of tens of thousands of ants running ten or more abreast. The columns could be traced easily with the aid of a flashlight. They came up from a huge earthen nest a hundred yards from the camp on a descending slope, crossed the clearing, and disappeared again into the forest. By climbing through tangled undergrowth we were able to locate one of their main targets, a tall tree bearing white flowers high in its crown. The ants streamed up the trunk, scissored out pieces of leaves and petals with their sharp-toothed mandibles, and headed home carrying the fragments over their heads like little parasols. Some floated the pieces to the ground, where most were picked up and carried away by newly arriving nestmates. At maximum activity, shortly before midnight, the trails were a tumult of ants bobbing and weaving past each other like miniature mechanical toys.

For many visitors to the forest, even experienced naturalists, the foraging expeditions are the whole of the matter, and individual leafcutter ants seem to be inconsequential ruddy specks on a pointless mission. But a closer look transforms them into beings of another order. If we magnify the scene to human scale, so that an ant's quarter-inch length grows into six feet, the forager runs along the trail for a distance of about ten miles at a velocity of 16 miles an hour. Each successive mile is covered in three minutes and forty-five minutes, about the current (human) world record. The forager picks up a burden of 750 pounds and speeds back toward the nest at 15 miles an hour—hence, four-minute miles. This marathon is repeated many times during the night and in many localities on through the day as well.

From research conducted jointly by biologists and chemists, it is known that the ants are guided by a secretion paid onto the soil through the sting, in the manner of ink being drawn out of a pen. The crucial molecule is methyl-4-methylpyrrole-2-carboxylate, which is composed of a tight ring of carbon and nitrogen atoms with short side chains made of carbon and oxygen. The pure substance has an innocuous odor, judged by various people to be faintly grassy, sulphurous, or fruitlike with a hint of naphtha[6] (I'm not sure I can smell it at all). But whatever the impact on human beings, it is an ichor[7] of extraordinary power for the ants. One milligram, a quantity that would just about cover the printed letters in this sentence, if dispensed with theoretical maximum efficiency, is enough to excite billions of workers into activity or to lead a short column of them three times around the world. The vast difference between us and them has nothing to do with the trail substance itself, which is a biochemical material of unexceptional structure. It lies entirely in the unique sensitivity of the sensory organs and brains of the insects.

One millimeter above the ground, where ants exist, things are radically different from what they seem to the gigantic creatures who peer down from a thousand times that distance. The ants do not follow the trail substance as a liquid trace on the soil, as we are prone to think. It comes up to them as a cloud of molecules diffusing through still air at the ground surface. The foragers move inside a long ellipsoidal space in which the gaseous material is dense enough to be detected. They sweep their paired antennae back and forth in advance of the head to catch the odorant molecules. The antennae are the primary sensory centers of the ant. Their surfaces are furred with thousands of nearly invisible hairs and pegs, among which are scattered diminutive plates and bottle-necked pits. Each of these sense organs is serviced by cells that carry electrical impulses into the central nerve of the antenna. Then relay cells take over

6. Low-grade petroleum.
7. From Greek mythology, an ethereal fluid that flowed in the veins of ancient gods.

and transmit the messages to the integrating regions of the brain. Some of the antennal organs react to touch, while others are sensitive to slight movements of air, so that the ant responds instantaneously whenever the nest is breached by intruders. But most of the sensors monitor the chemicals that swirl around the ant in combinations that change through each second of its life. Human beings live in a world of sight and sound, but social insects exist primarily by smell and taste. In a word, we are audiovisual where they are chemical.

The oddness of the insect sensory world is illustrated by the swift sequence of events that occurs along the odor trail. When a forager takes a wrong turn to the left and starts to run away from the track, its left antenna breaks out of the odor space first and is no longer stimulated by the guiding substance. In a few thousandths of a second, the ant perceives the change and pulls back to the right. Twisting right and left in response to the vanishing molecules, it follows a tightly undulating course between the nest and the tree. During the navigation it must also dodge moment by moment through a tumult of other runners. If you watch a foraging worker from a few inches away with the unaided eye, it seems to touch each passerby with its antennae, a kind of tactile probe. Slow-motion photography reveals that it is actually sweeping the tips of the antennae over parts of the other ant's body to smell it. If the surface does not present exactly the right combination of chemicals—the colony's unique odor signature—the ant attacks at once. It may simultaneously spray an alarm chemical from special glands located in the head capsule, causing others in the vicinity to rush to the site with their mandibles gaping.

An ant colony is organized by no more than ten or twenty such signals, most of which are chemical secretions leaked or sprayed from glands. The workers move with swiftness and precision through a life that human beings have come to understand only with the aid of mathematical diagrams and molecular formulas. We can also simulate the behavior. Computer technology has made it theoretically possible to create a mechanical ant that duplicates the observed activity. But the machine, if for some reason we chose to build one, would be the size of a small automobile, and even then I doubt if it would tell us anything new about the ant's inner nature.

At the end of the trail the burdened foragers rush down the nest hole, into throngs of nestmates and along tortuous channels that end near the water table fifteen feet or more below. The ants drop the leaf sections onto the floor of a chamber, to be picked up by workers of a slightly smaller size who clip them into fragments about a millimeter across. Within minutes still smaller ants take over, crush and mold the fragments into moist pellets, and carefully insert them into a mass of similar material. This mass ranges in size between a clenched fist and a human head, is riddled with channels, and resembles a gray cleaning sponge. It is the garden of the ants: on its surface a symbiotic fungus grows which, along with the leaf sap, forms the ants' sole nourishment. The fungus spreads like a white frost, sinking its hyphae into the leaf paste to digest the abundant cellulose and proteins held there in partial solution.

The gardening cycle proceeds. Worker ants even smaller than those just described pluck loose strands of the fungus from places of dense growth and plant them onto the newly constructed surfaces. Finally, the very smallest—and most abundant—workers patrol the beds of fungal strands, delicately probing them with their antennae, licking their surfaces clean, and plucking out the spores and hyphae of alien species of mold. These colony dwarfs are able to travel through the narrowest channels deep within the garden masses. From time to time they pull tufts of fungus loose and carry them out to feed their larger nestmates.

The leafcutter economy is organized around this division of labor based on size. The foraging workers, about as big as houseflies, can slice leaves but are too bulky to cultivate the almost microscopic fungal strands. The tiny gardener workers, somewhat smaller than this printed letter I, can grow the fungus but are too weak to cut the leaves. So the ants form an assembly line, each successive step being performed by correspondingly smaller workers, from the collection of pieces of leaves out of doors to the manufacture of leaf paste to the cultivation of dietary fungi deep within the nest.

The defense of the colony is also organized according to size. Among the scurrying workers can be seen a few soldier ants, three hundred times heavier than the gardener workers. Their sharp mandibles are powered by massive adductor muscles that fill the swollen, quarter-inch wide head capsules. Working like miniature wire clippers, they chop enemy insects into pieces and easily slice through human skin. These behemoths are especially adept at repelling large invaders. When entomologists digging into a nest grow careless, their hands become nicked all over as if pulled through a thorn bush. I have occasionally had to pause to staunch the flow of blood from a single bite, impressed by the fact that a creature one-millionth my size could stop me with nothing but its jaws.

No other animals have evolved the ability to turn fresh vegetation into mushrooms. The evolutionary event occurred only once, millions of years ago, somewhere in South America. It gave the ants an enormous advantage: they could now send out specialized workers to collect the vegetation while keeping the bulk of their populations safe in subterranean retreats. As a result, all of the different kinds of leafcutters together, comprising fourteen species in the genus *Atta* and twenty-three in *Acromyrmex*, dominate a large part of the American tropics. They consume more vegetation than any other group of animals, including the more abundant forms of caterpillars, grasshoppers, birds, and mammals. A single colony can strip an orange tree or bean patch overnight, and the combined populations inflict over a billion dollars' worth of damage yearly. It was with good reason that the early Portuguese settlers called Brazil the Kingdom of the Ants.

At full size, a colony contains three to four million workers and occupies three thousand or more underground chambers. The earth it excavates forms a pile twenty feet across and three to four feet high. Deep inside the nest sits the mother queen, a giant insect the size of a newborn mouse. She can live at least ten years and perhaps as long as twenty. No one has had the persistence to determine the true longevity. In my laboratory I have an individual collected in Guyana[8] fourteen years ago. When she reaches eighteen, and breaks the proved longevity record of the seventeen-year locusts, my students and I will open a bottle of champagne to celebrate. In her lifetime an individual can produce over twenty million offspring, which translates into the following: a mere three hundred ants, a small fraction of the number emerging from a single colony in a year, can give birth to more ants than there are human beings on Earth.

The queen is born as a tiny egg, among thousands laid daily by the old mother queen. The egg hatches as a grublike larva, which is fed and laved incessantly throughout its month-long existence by the adult worker nurses. Through some unknown treatment, perhaps a special diet controlled by the workers, the larva grows to a relatively huge size. She then transforms into a pupa, whose waxy casement is shaped like an adult queen in fetal position, with legs, wings, and antennae folded tightly against the body. After several weeks the full complement of adult organs develops within this cuticle, and the new queen emerges. From the beginning she is fully adult and grows no more in size. She also possesses the same genes as her sisters, the colony workers. Their smaller size and pedestrian behavior is not due to heredity but rather to the different treatment they received as larvae.

In bright sunshine following a heavy rain, the virgin queen comes to the surface of the nest and flies up into the air to join other queens and the darkly pigmented, big-eyed males. Four or five males seize and inseminate her in quick succession, while she is still flying through the air. Their sole function now completed, they die within hours without returning to the home nest. The queen stores their sperm in her spermatheca, a tough muscular bag located just above and behind her ovaries. These reproductive cells live like independent microorganisms for years, passively waiting until they are released into the oviduct to meet an egg and create a new female ant. If the egg passes through the oviduct and to the outside without receiving a sperm, it produces a male. The queen can control the

8. Coastal nation in northeast South America, formerly British Guiana.

sex of her offspring, as well as the number of new workers and queens she produces, by opening or shutting the passage leading from her sperm-storage organ to the oviduct.

The newly inseminated queen descends to the ground. Raking her legs forward, she breaks off her wings, painlessly because they are composed of dead, membranous tissue. She wanders in a random pattern until she finds a patch of soft, bare soil, then commences to excavate a narrow tunnel straight down. Several hours later, when the shaft has been sunk to a depth of about ten inches, the queen widens its bottom into a small room. She is now set to start a garden and a colony of her own. But there is a problem in this life-cycle strategy. The queen has completely separated herself from the mother colony. Where can she obtain a culture of the vital symbiotic fungus to start the garden? Answer: she has been carrying it all along in her mouth. Just before leaving home, the young queen gathered a wad of fungal strands and inserted it into a pocket in the floor of her oral cavity, just back of the tongue. Now she passes the pellet out onto the floor of the nest and fertilizes it with droplets of feces.

As the fungus proliferates in the form of a whitish mat, the queen lays eggs on and around its surface. When the young larvae hatch, they are fed with other eggs given to them by the queen. At the end of their development, six weeks later, they transform into small workers. These new adults quickly take over the ordinary tasks of the colony. When still only a few days old, they proceed to enlarge the nest, work the garden, and feed the queen and larvae with tufts of the increasingly abundant fungus. In a year the little band has expanded into a force of a thousand workers, and the queen has ceased almost all activity to become a passive eating and egg-laying machine. She retains that exclusive role for the rest of her life. The measure of her Darwinian success is whether some of her daughters born five or ten years down the line grow into queens, leave on nuptial flights, and—rarest of all achievements—found new colonies of their own. In the world of the social insects, by the canons of biological organization, colonies beget colonies; individuals do not directly beget individuals.

People often ask me whether I see any human qualities in an ant colony, any form of behavior that even remotely mimics human thought and feeling. Insects and human beings are separated by more than 600 million years of evolution, but a common ancestor did exist in the form of one of the earliest multicellular organisms. Does some remnant of psychological continuity exist across that immense phylogenetic gulf? The answer is that I open an ant colony as I would the back of a Swiss watch. I am enchanted by the intricacy of its parts and the clean, thrumming precision. But I never see the colony as anything more than an organic machine.

Let me qualify that metaphor. The leafcutter colony is a superorganism. The queen sits deep in the central chambers, the vibrant growing tip from which all the workers and new queens originate. But she is not in any sense the leader or the repository of an organizational blueprint. No command center directs the colony. The social master plan is partitioned into the brains of the all-female workers, whose separate programs fit together to form a balanced whole. Each ant automatically performs certain tasks and avoids others according to its size and age. The superorganism's brain is the entire society; the workers are the crude analogue of its nerve cells. Seen from above and at a distance, the leafcutter colony resembles a gigantic amoeba. Its foraging columns snake out like pseudopods to engulf and shred plants, while their stems pull the green pieces down holes into the fungus gardens. Through a unique step in evolution taken millions of years ago, the ants captured a fungus, incorporated it into the superorganism, and so gained the power to digest leaves. Or perhaps the relation is the other way around: perhaps the fungus captured the ants and employed them as a mobile extension to take leaves into the moist underground chambers.

In either case, the two now own each other and will never pull apart. The ant-fungus combination is one of evolution's master clockworks, tireless, repetitive, and precise, more complicated than any human invention and unimaginably old. To find a colony in the South American forest is like coming upon some device left in place ages ago by an extraterrestrial visitor for a still undisclosed purpose. Biologists have only begun to puzzle out its many parts.

Because of modern science the frontier is no longer located along the retreating wall of the great rain forest. It is in the bodies and lives of the leafcutters and thousands of other species found for the most part on the other side of that tragic line.

1984

Michael J. Katz

ON THE WINGS OF AN ANGEL: AN EXPLORATION OF THE LIMITS OF BIOLOGICAL ENTERPRISE

When you have eliminated the impossible, whatever remains, however improbable, must be the truth.

—SHERLOCK HOLMES in *The Sign of the Four*

Biologists rarely use the word "impossible." To a biologist, the range of the possible is so large, the potential biological entities so overwhelmingly numerous, that the impossible is only a tiny issue.

To a biologist, impossibilities are the wall at the edge of the physical universe—real and formidable constraints, but constraints lying somewhere far away, somewhere in the realm of the physicist.

The biologist sees these physical constraints as if through the wrong end of a telescope. Demagnified and miniaturized, the limits of the physical universe form toy fences in someone else's province. With more than 1,500 species of daisies in Europe alone and more than 2,000 species of crickets world-wide, with 30,000 different proteins specific to the brain of the rat, biologists have little room on their desks for perpetual motion machines or for rockets that travel faster than the speed of light.

The mainstream of biological tradition is natural history, the record of Nature's accomplishments, the careful charting of the possible. Moreover, biologists are artisans at heart; they want to do things and make things, and they actively seek out the possible. Beyond this, however, I suspect that there is a more fundamental reason that biologists rarely speak in terms of the impossible. Perhaps there are no biological impossibilities. Perhaps, deep within the true province of biology, everything is possible.

The Province of Biology

The wide range of the possible in biology depends on the unique and peculiar province of the living. Living beings form a special realm of science, filled with eye-popping collages of butterflies, sheets of grasses, mildewing molds, people, bears, whales, and bats, eggs and embryos, grandmothers and grandfathers. Biology is about life, and life is organisms.

We know them well, these organisms. We pass them every day as we walk on the grass, under the trees, past the birds and squirrels. Gardening, we run our hands through the cool earth, crumbles of plant detritus, worms, larvae, hundreds of thousands of microorganisms. We know them by touch, smell, and sight; and those organisms that never come within our grasps, such as the gulls at the shore, we know by sight and sound.

But most of all, we know the human organisms. We know our parents and our friends; we know strangers on the bus, on the street, and in the stores; and, of course, we know ourselves. How many times a day do we look at our hands? A hundred? A thousand? We feel our toes from outside and from inside. We hear our heartbeats at night. We smell our sweat, we taste our blood. We are not all physicists or economists or mathematicians, but we are all biologists. We know organisms, and most of us know them quite well.

Biological organisms fall into a few general types but into innumerable specific varieties. In fact, each organism is essentially unique. Human "identical" twins differ in many ways; for example, their fingerprints are different. Even a pair of cloned organisms are sufficiently complex so that, during their creation, the stochasticism of the world can insinuate itself and change a molecule here or an organelle there and in this way produce two slightly different individuals. The complexity and the individuality of its particular items of study—that is, organisms—are certainly characteristic of the biological realm, but these features do not distinguish biology from physics or metallurgy or economics. Each of these disciplines faces items of study that have many interactive parts, with those parts forming unique wholes. What is it, then, that distinguishes biology from other sciences?

Ontogeny. Organisms are patterns of matter that are at once complex and individual, and the features that distinguish these patterns from other complex and individual patterns of the natural world are the two sequential processes that produce organisms; ontogeny and phylogeny.

Ontogeny is the history of a living entity from conception through birth to maturity and death, the laying out of all the stages in its transformation from an unspecialized embryonic form to a particular and idiomatic machine. Ontogenies come in all shapes and sizes. At one extreme, bacteria go through an ontogeny that is entirely internal: the transformations from a single parent cell to two daughter cells are a series of changes of molecules *inside* the cell. On the other hand, multicellular organisms, such as squid, butterflies, and people, begin as single fertile cells— zygotes—and transform into unified collections of millions of cells. The ontogeny of a multicellular organism is a cascade of intracellular, cellular, and extracellular changes that establish whole cities of specialized cells. During the ontogeny of a multicellular organism, interactive pockets of cells are geographically segregated into organs and tissues connected by highways of nerves and vessels. The construction of these cities is continuously dynamic, and it proceeds inexorably in a particular sequence, the characteristic ontogeny of that organism.

An ontogeny is stereotyped and highly reproducible. It is like a phonograph record; when conception sets the needle in the first groove (and given that the basic machinery has an appropriate supply of energy), it plays out the full music of a life. Random dust will always change the notes a bit along the way. Sometimes the environment intervenes to turn the volume up or down. Occasionally, the needle gets caught by a scratch and falls into the endless loops of a cancer. Usually, however, a scratch or even a jarring of the turntable causes only a skip in the sequence as the needle falls into a different groove and proceeds once again resolutely on its inevitable path.

Ontogenies are dogged things, and organisms are those highly complex patterns produced by ontogenies. It is ontogeny—the repeated generation of stereotyped yet complex patterns—that first sets the biological realm apart from the other spheres of natural science.

Phylogeny

> This is the book of the generations of Adam. . . . And Adam lived an hundred and thirty years, and begat a son in his own likeness, after his image; and called his name Seth. . . . And Seth lived an hundred and five years and begat Enos. . . . And Enos lived ninety years and begat Cainan. . . . And Cainan lived seventy years and begat Mahalaleel. . . . And Lamech lived an hundred eighty and two years and begat a son: and he called his name Noah . . . and Noah was five hundred years old: and Noah begat Shem, Ham, and Japheth.
>
> —GENESIS, Chapter 5

Generation after generation, organisms beget like organisms. This is phylogeny, the ancestral lineages of organisms. Ontogenies are the life histories of individual organisms, and phylogenies are the repeated unfoldings of ontogenies. Our ancestors are our phylogeny.

Biological time is different from physical time, and the biological clock of phylogenies ticks in generations. In one hundred years, a human phylogeny contains five generations, a buttercup phylogeny one hundred generations, a fruit fly phylogeny 2,500 generations, and a bacterial phylogeny can contain 2.5 million generations.

A human phylogeny of five generations is, on the whole, a very short time, and it represents an almost unchanging set of transformations. The striking similarities between ancestors and descendants transcend a handful of generations—how often have we heard: "He certainly reminds me of his grandfather." Those differences that do show up during a few generations are really rather subtle, and each child is inordinately more like his parents than he is different from them. A few generations of phylogeny is a biologically stable time interval, but a million or ten million generations is quite another story.

In the course of millions of generations, the difference between members of a phylogeny can become so marked that we say the original organism has evolved into a new organism. "Evolution" means "change," and long phylogenies tend to change. If traced back into the dim reaches of time, the human phylogeny contains all manner of different creatures: apes, small bright-eyed mammals, dog-sized sharp-toothed reptiles, flat snub-nosed amphibians, and even fish. If we take a patient astronomical view, we can see clearly that we have evolved from our ancestors. Phylogenies slowly evolve, and evolving phylogenies characterize the biological realm.

One distinguishing characteristic of the province of biology is ontogeny, the recurrent stereotyped re-creation of a very complex pattern. The other distinguishing characteristic of the biological realm is phylogeny, the ancestral lineage of these ontogenies. While an ontogeny is a relatively stable sequence, a phylogeny is a slowly evolving sequence of ontogenies. When we ask what is impossible in biology—in biology specifically, above and beyond physics and chemistry, besides psychology and economics, separate from mathematics and the arts—we are asking what is impossible in ontogeny and in phylogeny.

The Richness of Natural Ontogenies and Phylogenies

If there is a constant in biology, it is its exuberant variety. A major contributor to this rich unpredictability of living things is unnecessary complexity: biological systems often contain more machinery than is necessary to make them work properly. Excess complexities permeate life. At the molecular level, there is the DNA that does not code for any proteins—noncoding DNA can outnumber coding DNA a hundredfold in some cells. Then, there are the "futile metabolic cycles" in cells, circular chemical reactions that go back and forth producing and unproducing the same molecules and depleting energy stores to no apparent purpose.

Another example of unnecessary complexity is the blood-clotting cascade. When you cut your finger, blood proteins immediately begin to clump together, the wound is soon dammed up, and the cut stops bleeding within five to ten minutes. To staunch the blood flow, the initial injury sets off a waterfall of from eight to thirteen separate chemical reactions in two chains, with each chemical transformation giving rise to the next in an orderly sequence. At least thirteen different proteins—coagulation factors—form the normal clotting cascades in humans, and if one of these factors is missing the person can have a bleeding disorder such as hemophilia.

The complete blood-clotting cascade is quite complex, and a theoretical biologist would be hard-pressed to predict its actual details from a priori considerations, from first principles, or from the requirements of blood-clotting systems. One of the factors—Hageman Factor or Factor XII—even appears to be unnecessary. Those people who, through genetic disorders, develop without any Factor XII do not have bleeding problems; and whales, dolphins, and porpoises, all of which survive injuries quite normally, do not have any Factor XII.

Complex and elusive intricacies also characterize the tissue level of biological organization. Consider the corpus callosum, one of the largest bundles of axons in the human brain. Although it interconnects most areas of the cerebral hemispheres, its function is so subtle that for years no one understood exactly what it does. The five out of a thousand individuals born without a corpus callosum cannot normally be distinguished from those with one. The corpus callosum is found only in placental mammals: other mammals (such as opossums and kangaroos) and all nonmammals live quite happily without it. Only through an ingenious series of psychological experiments did Roger Sperry finally show how the two halves of the brain normally use the corpus callosum as their most intimate route of self-communication.

From his desk, the theoretical biologist could not determine the role of the corpus callosum with certainty, and he could not predict its appearance or its use in those animals that have acquired one during the last 200 million years. Who could have imagined that the human brain contains two separate minds, a right mind and a left mind, each localized in one of the major cerebral hemispheres? Normally, the two minds are in such close touch that they think alike, they trade thoughts instantaneously, they share the same sensations and emotions, and they act as one. All this intimacy flows through the corpus callosum, and the intercommunication is smooth and efficient. At the same time, each separate brain is a powerful and complete mind. Amazingly, without a corpus callosum, the nervous system still functions as a smooth and efficient unit—one brain, to almost all outward appearance. Normally two brains make each human, and two brains are a wonderful but unnecessary complexity.

The corpus callosum is not a necessity, but is it just a frill? Two minds are not a necessity, but is the second one a frill? Such questions, with words like "frill" or even "necessity," are slightly askew. They are difficult to answer because they are built from peculiarly human judgments. As Richard Bentley[1] wrote (in the late seventeenth century):

> All pulchritude is relative. . . . We ought not . . . to believe that the banks of the ocean are really deformed, because they have not the form of a regular bulwark; nor that the mountains are out of shape, because they are not exact pyramids or cones; nor that the stars are unskillfully placed, because they are not situated at uniform distance. These are not natural irregularities, but with respect to our fancies only; nor are they incommodious to the true uses of life and the designs of man's being on earth.

Nature need not adhere to human standards, and she need not follow human principles. Nature does as she does, and we can only be secure in our science when we act as natural historians, conscientiously describing the natural record retrospectively. We walk a precipitous course when we attempt a priori evaluations based on anthropocentric standards.

Ontogenies and phylogenies are not limited to the simplest or the most efficient paths. In the natural realm, organisms are not built by engineers who, with an overall plan in mind, use only the most appropriate materi-

---

1. Richard Bentley: English clergyman, classical scholar, and critic (1662–1742).

als, the most effective design, and the most reliable construction techniques. Instead, organisms are patchworks containing appendixes, uvulas, earlobes, dewclaws, adenoids, warts, eyebrows, underarm hair, wisdom teeth, and toenails. They are a meld of ancestral parts integrated step by step during their development through a set of tried and true ontogenetic mechanisms. These mechanisms ensure matching between disparate elements such as nerves and muscles, but they have no overall vision. Natural ontogenies and natural phylogenies are not limited by principles of parsimony,[2] and they have no teleology.[3] Possible organisms can be overdetermined, unnecessarily complex, or inefficiently designed.

Many Roads

Two roads diverged in a yellow wood,
And sorry I could not travel both
And be one traveler, long I stood
And looked down one as far as I could
To where it bent in the undergrowth;

Then took the other, as just as fair,
And having perhaps the better claim,
Because it was grassy and wanted wear;
Though as for that the passing there
Had worn them really about the same. . . .

—ROBERT FROST

The constraints in building organisms are usually insufficient to limit Nature to only one blueprint, and a wide range of alternate constructions have evolved. There is no one "right" way to build an eye. The octopus and the human both have eyes that appear quite similar, but the human eye is built exactly inside out when compared to the [eye of the] octopus. In an octopus, light passing through the lens falls directly on the photoreceptors, while in a person, light must travel through many layers of cells and axons before reaching the photoreceptors, which are themselves pointing the wrong way—that is, toward the back of the eye. Likewise, Nature has used a number of radically different designs for building wings: bat wings, for instance, are modified hands, while insect wings are entirely separate appendages.

Even molecules themselves can have architectural latitude. Although

---

2. Occam's razor, a principle formulated by the English philosopher William of Occam or Ockham (?1300–?49) maintaining that entities should not be multiplied unnecessarily —i.e., that the simplest of competing theories should be preferred to more complex ones and that explanations of unknown phenomena should be sought in the known.

3. Explanation of nature or natural processes that can be attributed to design or purpose.

certain parts of a biological molecule are fairly immutable, there is often no one right overall molecule. For instance, insulin is an essential protein hormone that is built of about fifty subunits (amino acids). Three to five of these subunits differ between the insulin molecules of pigs, cows, and humans. Nonetheless, the insulins from pigs and cows are perfectly acceptable substitutes for human insulin, and both pig and cow insulin are commonly used to treat human diabetes.

In terms of many roads, the capricious courses of phylogenies are most telling. Evolution has followed the exigencies of the times under the whims of chance and the accidents of history. Had the continents not drifted apart, Australian fauna and flora would undoubtedly be less peculiar—Australia would probably have had indigenous hoofed animals and indigenous apes, animal groups that never developed on that island. Had Alexander Fleming not discovered penicillin, penicillin-resistant bacteria would be a freakish oddity rather than ubiquitous inhabitants of our planet. Extant organisms are legacies of habits acquired by their ancestors, but these habits coalesced from a plethora of possibilities.

What Nature Cannot Do in Ontogeny and Phylogeny

> I am Rose my eyes are blue
> I am Rose and who are you
> I am Rose and when I sing
> I am Rose like anything

—GERTRUDE STEIN

Science fiction comes in two varieties. On one hand are the tales that explore worlds harboring phenomena that scientists think are impossible. These stories ask the questions of dreams: How would people spend their evenings if everyone had a perpetual motion machine in the basement? How soon would you get bored if you lived forever?

Then there are those tales that explore worlds that just might exist. They ask the questions of science: In what language could we talk to an extraterrestrial creature? What could we do with self-reproducing automata? What will people do when the sun goes out?

The standard science fiction of biology certainly falls into both of these categories, but which biological tall tales are the stories of dreams and which the stories of science?

Consider, for a moment, the mushroom—"the elf of plants," Emily Dickinson called it. Actually mushrooms are only distantly related to plants. They are many-celled fungi, relatively advanced organisms with cell walls but with no ability to manufacture their own food (e.g., no photosynthetic machinery), no ability to move, and no nervous system.

We are all aware that many animals are fungivorous, but it took science fiction to popularize the idea that mushrooms could be carnivorous. In *The Wonderful Flight to the Mushroom Planet*, for instance, Eleanor Cameron invented the mushroom people of the mysterious planet Basidium-X, who must eat chicken eggs to remain healthy. The stories of dreams? Surprisingly not. Carnivorous mushrooms actually exist here on earth: certain species of woodland toadstools trap and eat worms—and from worms it may be only a small step to chickens. Carnivorous mushrooms, once in the realm of science fiction, are now unequivocally science fact.

Or, consider the square organism, once a creature confined to E. A. Abbott's *Flatland*, where all "Professional Men and Gentlemen are Squares." Today, the square organism has found a home on our well-worn earth, swimming in the brine pools of the Middle East. There tiny, flat, transparent bacteria in the form of thin square sheets float like ghostly salt crystals, mimicking the perfect planar polygons and belying the notion that—to reduce their surface-to-volume ratios—cells must be spheres.

Carnivorous mushrooms and square bacteria bring a smile to the biologist, but they do not stretch the bounds of biology because they can be explained by mechanisms that sit somewhere on Nature's cluttered shelf of standard organismic machinery. True, the biologist may have to hunt around a bit among the everyday mitochondria,[4] the familiar Krebs cycles, and the mundane cyclic AMPs to retrieve all of the appropriate mechanisms. He will certainly have to spend some time in serious study to find how these mechanisms have been stuck together in each of their peculiar combinations. Nonetheless, somewhere in a corner of her cupboard Nature is sure to have just the right bits and pieces to construct these natural oddities.

Nature regularly builds baby carnivorous mushrooms from spores of parent carnivorous mushrooms and replicates daughter square bacteria from parent square bacteria, and Nature derived the parent carnivorous mushrooms from other preexisting mushrooms and the parent square bacteria from other preexisting bacteria. Strange as they are, carnivorous mushrooms and square bacteria—the incarnations of biological tall tales—are neither ontogenetically nor phylogenetically impossible.

Angels, on the other hand, are somewhat different. Although they adorn the spiritual world, our natural world has no angels. Why is this? While it is not absolutely impossible, it is nonetheless difficult for Nature

---

4. "Mitochondria": various round or long cellular organelles found outside the nucleus that produce energy for the cell through cellular respiration; "Krebs cycles": sequences of reactions in the living organism in which oxidation of acetic acid or an acetyl equivalent provides energy for storage in phosphate bonds; "AMPs": mononucleotides of adenine originally isolated from mammalian muscle that are reversibly convertible to ADP and ATP in metabolic reactions.

to construct an angel from an extant phylogeny. Besides the arms and legs of a human, an angel has a set of wings along its back. Wings are complex structures sculpted of muscles, bones, and nerves; and angels' wings are covered with feathers. To introduce wings or any other complex appendage into an existing organismal lineage, Nature needs the appropriate raw materials and organizational blueprint—preexisting structures that can be transformed—because complex biological forms cannot be created ex nihilo.[5]

For angels' wings, the preexisting structures are simply not available. The wings of the natural extant flying vertebrates—the birds and bats—are direct modifications of preexisting front limbs. The muscles, bones, and nerves were already there in ancestral organisms, and Nature proceeded to evolve wings by stretching, shrinking, folding, and bending those elements. Furthermore, through all of the transmogrifications, the overall organization of the front limb has remained the same during evolution. For example, the upper limb always has a single long bone, the humerus, and the lower limb always has a pair of parallel long bones, the radius and the ulna.

The back of a mammal has no structures that can be stretched or shrunk, folded or bent into a wing. To make an angel, the ground plan of the existing elements must be tampered with and new structures must be generated without precedent. This Nature cannot easily do.

Angels are probably destined to remain spiritual, and winged horses like Pegasus are likely to be forever myths; but biologists do not consider them impossible. Instead, they are put into another realm: they are highly improbable biological phenomena. Improbable biological phenomena cannot easily be pieced together by Nature from any of the mechanisms in her crowded cupboard of organismic machinery. Without the coincidence of a number of highly improbable events, Nature cannot generate a winged horse or an angel in an existing phylogeny.

5. Out of nothing.

What a Biologist Cannot Do

> He said "I look for butterflies
> That sleep among the wheat;
> I make them into mutton pies,
> And sell them in the street.
> I sell them unto men," he said
> "Who sail on stormy seas;
> And that's the way I get my bread—
> A trifle, if you please."

—LEWIS CARROLL

With the development of his complex and specialized brain, man has taken a place beside Nature as a biological creator. Nature creates through ontogenies and phylogenies, but man is an engineer and can construct biological forms from other beginnings and through other ad hoc processes. Man is not limited to the natural routes of creation, and in the laboratory he can generate biological phenomena that would be highly improbable in nature.

A protein, an organelle, a cell, a tissue, an organism—each is made of a great many different parts, and in each case these parts are organized in a particular and characteristic design. The many parts and unique designs are found at every level—we see them whether we look at an elephant from a distance or we examine its gall bladder under a microscope. These biological items are truly complex in all ways. Not only are they composed of many different parts interrelated in unique designs, their fabrication is complex. In most cases, the parts of a biological item will not fully self-assemble. You cannot shake a beaker of salts and amino acids and make insulin, and you cannot stir a soup of cells and make a mouse. To build a protein or an animal, one must carefully put all of the parts together in their single proper order. One must impose detailed external information—templets—on the raw materials.

Biological items form only a small subset of all the possible items that one might construct from the same raw materials. This means that, as an architect, the biologist cannot merely choose the right bricks and mortar, but he must also draw up the right plan and then contrive to interweave the building blocks into just the right design. This is a difficult set of tasks. Often the parts are tiny and cannot be easily moved about or stored by themselves, isolated from their natural settings. Moreover, gluing these tiny parts together in such a way as to create the proper order at all levels, from macroscopic to microscopic to molecular, takes extreme patience, steady hands, X-ray vision, and highly specialized, Rube Goldberg contraptions.[6]

In the face of these problems, biologists have been undauntedly optimistic, twiddling and fiddling, tinkering with bones and nerves, gingerly reconstructing hormones, and rearranging genes. The job of building a biological item entirely from scratch is usually too overwhelming to be practical. The fabrication of a biological item from extant biological scraps, however, and the sculpting of new biological items from preexisting ones, these have become everyday operations in the laboratory. In baby newts, embryonic eyes are transplanted to tail buds, where they eventually mature and send out nerves. The adult newts, three-eyed oddities [such as Nature has never seen,] swim in laboratory aquaria with two eyes fore and one aft. In embryonic chicks, extra limb buds are

6. Devices invented by the American cartoonist Reuben L. Goldberg that accomplish simple tasks by complex means.

grafted alongside the normal ones; later, the adult chickens run through the laboratory flailing supernumerary appendages. Mouse and human cells are fused to form hybrid mammalian cells, biological items never found in nature but powerful tools for mapping human chromosomes. Copies of human insulin genes are inserted into yeast or bacterial cells, and these tiny and primitive creatures, as different from us as any organisms on earth, will now manufacture human proteins. In the lab, the biologist is busily creating highly improbable biological phenomena.

Building Ontogenies and Phylogenies

Given the range, the power, and the detailed precision of modern technologies, is there anything that the biologist cannot do within the bounds of the physical constraints of the universe? Today's biologists have the faith that it is possible to construct almost any biological item from precursor materials.

A gene, a protein, a cell, a tissue, an organism—these all seem to be in the realm of possibility. It may not always be practical to create these items from the most elemental materials. Nonetheless, new genes can be manufactured by mutating and rearranging existing genes, and short proteins can be made to order from their constituent amino acids. Primal protocells can be formed in appropriate man-made molecular soups, and new and complex cell types can be pieced together by fusing whole cells or combining parts of cells. New tissues can be designed by growing cells on artificial templets. New organisms can be constructed by mutations, by genetic engineering, and by embryonic reconstructions such as grafts and transplants.

Biologists can build improbable biological items in the laboratory, but the hallmarks of the biological realm are more than individual biological items. Life is not a DNA molecule or a nerve cell or a kumquat or a wolf spider. Life is a special set of sequences; it is the autonomous and recurrent stereotyped re-creation of certain very complex patterns. Life is a child growing and becoming a mother and eventually a grandmother. Can the biologist create new grandmothers, that is, can he generate ontogenies and phylogenies never before seen in nature?

The answer is yes, although the new ontogenies and phylogenies take advantage of natural cascades of developmental events that are normally found in preexisting ontogenies. To begin, the biologist makes an improbable change in some developmental event; for example, he grafts a frog eye primordium into the side of a newt embryo. In nature, the two sets of tissues would never interact, but in the laboratory the hybrid organism undergoes an ontogeny. The frog cells form an eye and send an optic nerve into the newt nervous system; concurrently, the newt skin cells form a lens and the newt nervous system accommodates the aberrant nerves. Frog cells integrate with newt cells, newt cells mesh with frog cells, and the strange three-eyed chimera that develops unfolds through a truly new ontogeny.

Similarly, new phylogenies—ancestral lineages never before seen in nature—take advantage of natural cascades of ontogenies that are normally found in preexisting phylogenies. Here, the biologist makes an improbable change in the stuff of inheritance; for example, he grafts a sequence of human DNA into the DNA of a bacterium. In nature, the two sets of genes would never interact, but in the laboratory the hybrid bacterium divides and quickly becomes a grandmother. All of her children and grandchildren will manufacture certain human proteins, and a truly new phylogeny has been founded.

Such ontogenies and phylogenies are new, but they are not unnatural. Once triggered, they unfold spontaneously and thereby enter the natural realm, producing surprising wonders like three-eyed frog-newts and insulin-secreting germs or carnivorous mushrooms and square bacteria. Man-made ontogenies and phylogenies are autonomous and recurrent stereotyped re-creations of certain very complex patterns, just as are naturally initiated ontogenies and phylogenies. In the laboratory, it is only the initiating event that may have been "unnatural."

When the biologist founds a new ontogeny or phylogeny, he can, of course, understand the initial improbable event. Many times, he can also understand the initial event when Nature founds a new ontogeny or phylogeny. But in nature initial events can sometimes remain arcane. As Dr. Seuss wrote in *The 500 Hats of Bartholomew Cubbins*:

> But neither Bartholomew Cubbins, nor King Derwin himself, nor anyone else in the Kingdom of Didd could ever explain how the strange thing had happened. They could only say it just "happened to happen" and was not very likely to happen again.

In the province of biology, buttermilk-thick with life and under the patience of millions of generations, Nature sometimes stumbles on the extremely improbable, and arcane initial events can indeed be quite natural. They just "happen to happen" and are "not very likely to happen again." Moreover, when they happen in a natural ontogeny or phylogeny, arcane events can trigger sequences that are as natural as apples. It is the initiating event in the generation of an angel that would undoubtedly be arcane, but the autonomous development of an angel from a tiny wisp of an angelic embryo or the spontaneous unfolding of a lineage of angels, once set on their way, become natural phenomena no more impossible than the development of an oak from an acorn or the spontaneous unfolding of the ancestral lineage of the great Bach family.[7]

7. A German family of musicians and composers, the most famous of whom was Johann Sebastian Bach (1685–1750).

Biological Possibilities

What is an impossibility? I think that for the biological realm, the requirements are rather special. Not only must we be able to write science fiction about it, we must also be able to imagine it as a part of a natural ontogeny and phylogeny. Truly biological entities are always enmeshed in a developmental and an evolutionary sequence: they are dynamic, they have a lifespan, they have ancestors, and they beget progeny. In this way, a biological impossibility would be something—be it an organelle, a cell, or a creature—that we could imagine in an ontogeny or in a phylogeny but that cannot ever exist in the real world.

Physically impossible organisms, such as hedgehogs that can run faster than the speed of light and perpetual motion bees, can be dreamt by the physicist, but I cannot easily imagine a biologically impossible organism. When we have eliminated the physically impossible, when we remain within the constraints set by the physical limits of the universe, whatever remains—no matter how improbable—must be considered biologically possible. With the biologist as creator, the improbable has ofttimes become probable. But, Nature herself is wild and rich and her splendor is unconstrained. Afternoons poking about the Woods Hole seashore among the horseshoe crabs, the seaweed, and the tunicates or munching blue-eyed scallops and beach peas on a rocky island in Penobscot Bay or chipping ornate brachiopods from the shale of the Chagrin River make me hesitate to think that I could ever dream of a creature that might not creep out from among the cattails one windy spring morning.

1985

Konrad Z. Lorenz

THE TAMING OF THE SHREW

Though Nature, red in tooth and claw,
With ravine, shrieked against his creed.
TENNYSON, *In Memoriam*

All shrews are particularly difficult to keep; this is not because, as we are led proverbially to believe, they are hard to tame, but because the metabolism of these smallest of mammals is so very fast that they will die of hunger within two or three hours if the food supply fails. Since they feed exclusively on small, living animals, mostly insects, and demand, of these, considerably more than their own weight every day, they are most exacting charges. At the time of which I am writing, I had never succeeded in keeping any of the terrestrial shrews alive for any length of time; most of those that I happened to obtain had probably only been caught because they were already ill and they died almost at once. I had never succeeded in procuring a healthy specimen. Now the order Insectivora is very low in the genealogical hierarchy of mammals and is, therefore, of particular interest to the comparative ethologist. Of the whole group, there was only one representative with whose behavior I was tolerably familiar, namely the hedgehog, an extremely interesting animal of whose ethology Professor Herter of Berlin has made a very thorough study. Of the behavior of all other members of the family practically nothing is known. Since they are nocturnal and partly subterranean animals, it is nearly impossible to approach them in field observation, and the difficulty of keeping them in captivity had hitherto precluded their study in the laboratory. So the Insectivores were officially placed on my program.

First I tried to keep the common mole. It was easy to procure a healthy specimen, caught to order in the nursery gardens of my father-in-law, and I found no difficulty in keeping it alive. Immediately on its arrival, it devoured an almost incredible quantity of earthworms which, from the very first moment, it took from my hand. But, as an object of behavior study, it proved most disappointing. Certainly, it was interesting to watch its method of disappearing in the space of a few seconds under the surface of the ground, to study its astoundingly efficient use of its strong, spadeshaped fore-paws, and to feel their amazing strength when one held the little beast in one's hand. And again, it was remarkable with what surprising exactitude it located, by smell, from underground, the earthworms which I put on the surface of the soil in its terrarium. But these observations were the only benefits I derived from it. It never became any tamer and it never remained above ground any longer than it took to devour its prey; after this, it sank into the earth as a submarine sinks into the water. I soon grew tired of procuring the immense quantities of living food it required and, after a few weeks, I set it free in the garden.

It was years afterwards, on an excursion to that extraordinary lake, the Neusiedlersee, which lies on the Hungarian border of Austria, that I again thought of keeping an insectivore. This large stretch of water, though not thirty miles from Vienna, is an example of the peculiar type of lake found in the open steppes of Eastern Europe and Asia. More than thirty miles long and half as broad, its deepest parts are only about five feet deep and it is much shallower on the average. Nearly half its surface is overgrown with reeds which form an ideal habitat for all kinds of water birds. Great colonies of white, purple, and grey heron and spoonbills live among the reeds and, until a short while ago, glossy ibis were still to be found here. Greylag geese breed here in great numbers and, on the eastern, reedless shore, avocets and many other rare waders can regularly be found. On the occasion of which I am speaking, we, a dozen tired zoologists, under the experienced guidance of my friend Otto Koenig, were wending our way, slowly and painfully, through the forest of reeds. We were walking in single file, Koenig first, I second, with a few students in our wake. We literally left a wake, an inky-black one in pale grey water. In the reed forests of Lake Neusiedel, you walk knee deep in slimy, black ooze, wonderfully perfumed by sulphureted-hydrogen-producing bacteria. This mud clings tenaciously and only releases its hold on your foot with a loud, protesting plop at every step.

After a few hours of this kind of wading you discover aching muscles whose very existence you had never suspected. From the knees to the hips you are immersed in the milky, clay-colored water characteristic of the lake, which, among the reeds, is populated by myriads of extremely hungry leeches conforming to the old pharmaceutical recipe, "*Hirudines medicinales maxime affamati.*"[1] The rest of your person inhabits the upper air, which here consists of clouds of tiny mosquitoes whose blood-thirsty attacks are all the more exasperating because you require both your hands to part the dense reeds in front of you and can only slap your face at intervals. The British ornithologist who may perhaps have envied us some of our rare specimens will perceive that bird watching on Lake Neusiedel is not, after all, an entirely enviable occupation.

We were thus wending our painful way through the rushes when suddenly Koenig stopped and pointed mutely towards a pond, free from reeds, that stretched in front of us. At first, I could only see whitish water, dark blue sky and green reeds, the standard colors of Lake Neusiedel. Then, suddenly, like a cork popping up on to the surface, there appeared, in the middle of the pool, a tiny black animal, hardly bigger than a man's thumb. And for a moment I was in the rare position of a zoologist who sees a specimen and is not able to classify it, in the literal sense of the word: I did not know to which class of vertebrates the object of my gaze belonged. For the first fraction of a second I took it for the young of some diving bird of a species unknown to me. It appeared to have a beak and it swam on the water like a bird, not in it as a mammal. It swam about in narrow curves and circles, very much like a whirligig beetle, creating an extensive wedge-shaped wake, quite out of proportion to the tiny animal's size. Then a second little beast popped up from below, chased the first one with a shrill, bat-like twitter, then both dived and were gone. The whole episode had not lasted five seconds.

I stood open-mouthed, my mind racing. Koenig turned round with a broad grin, calmly detached a leech that was sticking like a leech to his

1. "In medicine, the hungriest leech is best." Until modern times, patients were bled as a remedy for various ills, and doctors kept live leeches for the purpose.

wrist, wiped away the trickle of blood from the wound, slapped his cheek, thereby killing thirty-five mosquitoes, and asked, in the tone of an examiner, "What was that?" I answered as calmly as I could, "water shrews," thanking, in my heart, the leech and the mosquitoes for the respite they had given me to collect my thoughts. But my mind was racing on: water shrews ate fishes and frogs which were easy to procure in any quantity; water shrews were less subterranean than most other insectivores; they were the very insectivore to keep in captivity. "That's an animal I must catch and keep," I said to my friend. "That is easy," he responded. "There is a nest with young under the floor mat of my tent." I had slept that night in his tent and Koenig had not thought it worth-while to tell me of the shrews; such things are, to him, as much a matter of course as wild little spotted crakes feeding out of his hand, or as any other wonders of his queer kingdom in the reeds.

On our return to the tent that evening, he showed me the nest. It contained eight young which, compared with their mother, who rushed away as we lifted the mat, were of enormous size. They were considerably more than half her length and must each have weighed well between a fourth and a third of their dam: that is to say, the whole litter weighed, at a very modest estimate, twice as much as the old shrew. Yet they were still quite blind and the tips of their teeth were only just visible in their rosy mouths. And two days later when I took them under my care, they were still quite unable to eat even the soft abdomens of grasshoppers, and in spite of evident greed, they chewed interminably on a soft piece of frog's meat without succeeding in detaching a morsel from it. On our journey home, I fed them on the squeezed-out insides of grasshoppers and finely minced frog's meat, a diet on which they obviously throve. Arrived home in Altenberg, I improved on this diet by preparing a food from the squeezed-out insides of mealworm larvae, with some finely chopped small, fresh fishes, worked into a sort of gravy with a little milk. They consumed large quantities of this food, and their little nest-box looked quite small in comparison with the big china bowl whose contents they emptied three times a day. All these observations raise the problem of how the female water shrew succeeds in feeding her gigantic litter. It is absolutely impossible that she should do so on milk alone. Even on a more concentrated diet my young shrews devoured the equivalent of their own weight daily and this meant nearly twice the weight of a grown shrew. Yet, at that time of their lives, young shrews could not possibly engulf a frog or a fish brought whole to them by their mother, as my charges indisputably proved. I can only think that the mother feeds her young by regurgitation of chewed food. Even thus, it is little short of miraculous that the adult female should be able to obtain enough meat to sustain herself and her voracious progeny.

When I brought them home, my young watershrews were still blind.

They had not suffered from the journey and were as sleek and fat as one could wish. Their black, glossy coats were reminiscent of moles, but the white color of their underside, as well as the round, streamlined contours of their bodies, reminded me distinctly of penguins, and not, indeed, without justification: both the streamlined form and the light underside are adaptations to a life in the water. Many free-swimming animals, mammals, birds, amphibians and fishes, are silvery-white below in order to be invisible to enemies swimming in the depths. Seen from below, the shining white belly blends perfectly with the reflecting surface film of the water. It is very characteristic of these water animals that the dark dorsal and the white ventral colors do not merge gradually into each other as is the case in "counter-shaded" land animals whose coloring is calculated to make them invisible by eliminating the contrasting shade on their undersides. As in the killer whale, in dolphins, and in penguins, the white underside of the watershrew is divided from the dark upper side by a sharp line which runs, often in very decorative curves, along the animal's flank. Curiously enough, this borderline between black and white showed considerable variations in individuals and even on both sides of one animal's body. I welcomed this, since it enabled me to recognize my shrews personally.

Three days after their arrival in Altenberg my eight shrew babies opened their eyes and began, very cautiously, to explore the precincts of their nest-box. It was now time to remove them to an appropriate container, and on this question I expended much hard thinking. The enormous quantity of food they consumed and, consequently, of excrement they produced, made it impossible to keep them in an ordinary aquarium whose water, within a day, would have become a stinking brew. Adequate sanitation was imperative for particular reasons; in ducks, grebes, and all waterfowl, the plumage must be kept perfectly dry if the animal is to remain in a state of health, and the same premise may reasonably be expected to hold good of the shrew's fur. Now water which has been polluted soon turns strongly alkaline and this I knew to be very bad for the plumage of waterbirds. It causes saponification of the fat to which the feathers owe their waterproof quality, and the bird becomes thoroughly wet and is unable to stay on the water. I hold the record, as far as I know hitherto unbroken by any other birdlover, for having kept dabchicks alive and healthy in captivity for nearly two years, and even then they did not die but escaped, and may still be living. My experience with these birds proved the absolute necessity of keeping the water perfectly clean: whenever it became a little dirty I noticed their feathers beginning to get wet, a danger which they anxiously tried to counteract by constantly preening themselves. I had, therefore, to keep these little grebes in crystal clear water which was changed every day, and I rightly assumed that the same would be necessary for my water shrews.

I took a large aquarium tank, rather over a yard in length and about two feet wide. At each end of this, I placed two little tables, and weighed them down with heavy stones so that they would not float. Then I filled up the tank until the water was level with the tops of the tables. I did not at first push the tables close against the panes of the tank, which was rather narrow, for fear that the shrews might become trapped underwater in the blind alley beneath a table and drown there; this precaution, however, subsequently proved unnecessary. The water shrew which, in its natural state, swims great distances under the ice, is quite able to find its way to the open surface in much more difficult situations. The nest-box, which was placed on one of the tables, was equipped with a sliding shutter, so that I could imprison the shrews whenever the container had to be cleaned. In the morning, at the hour of general cage-cleaning, the shrews were usually at home and asleep, so that the procedure caused them no appreciable disturbance. I will admit that I take great pride in devising, by creative imagination, suitable containers for animals of which nobody, myself included, has had any previous experience, and it was particularly gratifying that the contraption described above proved so satisfactory that I never had to alter even the minutest detail.

When first my baby shrews were liberated in this container they took a very long time to explore the top of the table on which their nest-box was standing. The water's edge seemed to exert a strong attraction; they approached it ever and again, smelled the surface and seemed to feel along it with the long, fine whiskers which surround their pointed snouts like a halo and represent not only their most important organ of touch but the most important of all their sensory organs. Like other aquatic mammals, the water shrew differs from the terrestrial members of its class in that its nose, the guiding organ of the average mammal, is of no use whatsoever in its underwater hunting. The water shrew's whiskers are actively mobile like the antennae of an insect or the fingers of a blind man.

Exactly as mice and many other small rodents would do under similar conditions, the shrews interrupted their careful exploration of their new surroundings every few minutes to dash wildly back into the safe cover of their nest-box. The survival value of this peculiar behavior is evident: the animal makes sure, from time to time that it has not lost its way and that it can, at a moment's notice, retreat to the one place it knows to be safe. It was a queer spectacle to see those podgy black figures slowly and carefully whiskering their way forward and, in the next second, with lightning speed, dash back to the nest-box. Queerly enough, they did not run straight through the little door, as one would have expected, but in their wild dash for safety they jumped, one and all, first onto the roof of the box and only then, whiskering along its edge, found the opening and slipped in with a half somersault, their back turned nearly vertically downward.

After many repetitions of this maneuver, they were able to find the opening without feeling for it; they "knew" perfectly its whereabouts yet still persisted in the leap onto the roof. They jumped onto it and immediately vaulted in through the door, but they never, as long as they lived, found out that the leap and vault which had become their habit was really quite unnecessary and that they could have run in directly without this extraordinary detour. We shall hear more about this dominance of path habits in the water shrew presently.

It was only on the third day, when the shrews had become thoroughly acquainted with the geography of their little rectangular island, that the largest and most enterprising of them ventured into the water. As is so often the case with mammals, birds, reptiles, and fishes, it was the largest and most handsomely colored male which played the role of leader. First he sat on the edge of the water and thrust in the fore part of his body, at the same time frantically paddling with his forelegs but still clinging with his hind ones to the board. Then he slid in, but in the next moment took fright, scampered madly across the surface very much after the manner of a frightened duckling, and jumped out onto the board at the opposite end of the tank. There he sat, excitedly grooming his belly with one hind paw, exactly as coypus and beavers do. Soon he quieted down and sat still for a moment. Then he went to the water's edge a second time, hesitated for a moment, and plunged in; diving immediately, he swam ecstatically about underwater, swerving upward and downward again, running quickly along the bottom, and finally jumping out of the water at the same place as he had first entered it.

When I first saw a water shrew swimming I was most struck by a thing which I ought to have expected but did not: at the moment of diving, the little black and white beast appears to be made of silver. Like the plumage of ducks and grebes, but quite unlike the fur of most water mammals, such as seals, otters, beavers or coypus, the fur of the water shrew remains absolutely dry under water, that is to say, it retains a thick layer of air while the animal is below the surface. In the other mammals mentioned above, it is only the short, woolly undercoat that remains dry, the superficial hair tips becoming wet, wherefore the animal looks its natural color when underwater and is superficially wet when it emerges. I was already aware of the peculiar qualities of the waterpfoof fur of the shrew, and, had I given it a thought, I should have known that it would look, under water, exactly like the air-retaining fur on the underside of a water beetle or on the abdomen of a water spider. Nevertheless the wonderful, transparent silver coat of the shrew was, to me, one of those delicious surprises that nature has in store for her admirers.

Another surprising detail which I only noticed when I saw my shrews in the water was that they have a fringe of stiff, erectile hairs on the outer side of their fifth toes and on the underside of their tails. These form collapsible oars and a collapsible rudder. Folded and inconspicuous as long as the animal is on dry land, they unfold the moment it enters the water and broaden the effective surface of the propelling feet and of the steering tail by a considerable area.

Like penguins, the water shrews looked rather awkward and ungainly on dry land but were transformed into objects of elegance and grace on entering the water. As long as they walked, their strongly convex underside made them look pot-bellied and reminiscent of an old, overfed dachshund. But under water, the very same protruding belly balanced harmoniously the curve of their back and gave a beautifully symmetrical streamline which, together with their silver coating and the elegance of their movements, made them a sight of entrancing beauty.

When they had all become familiar with the water, their container was one of the chief attractions that our research station had to offer to any visiting naturalists or animal lovers. Unlike all other mammals of their size, the water shrews were largely diurnal and, except in the early hours of the morning, three or four of them were constantly on the scene. It was exceedingly interesting to watch their movements upon and under the water. Like the whirligig beetle, Gyrinus, they could turn in an extremely small radius without diminishing their speed, a faculty for which the large rudder surface of the tail with its fringe of erectile hairs is evidently essential. They had two different ways of diving, either by taking a little jump as grebes or coots do and working their way down at a steep angle, or by simply lowering their snout under the surface and paddling very fast till they reached "planing speed," thus working their way downward on the principle of the inclined plane—in other words, performing the converse movement of an ascending airplane. The water shrew must expend a large amount of energy in staying down since the air contained in its fur exerts a strong pull upwards. Unless it is paddling straight downwards, a thing it rarely does, it is forced to maintain a constant minimum speed, keeping its body at a slightly downward angle in order not to float to the surface. While swimming under water the shrew seems to flatten, broadening its body in a peculiar fashion, in order to present a better planing surface to the water. I never saw my shrews try to cling by their claws to any underwater objects, as the dipper is alleged to do. When they seemed to be running along the bottom, they were really swimming close above it, but perhaps the smooth gravel on the bottom of the tank was unsuitable for holding on to and it did not occur to me then to offer them a rougher surface. They were very playful when in the water and chased one another loudly twittering on the surface, or silently in the depths. Unlike any other mammal, but just like water birds, they could rest on the surface; this they used to do, rolling partly over and grooming themselves. Once out again, they instantly proceeded to clean their fur—one is almost tempted to say "preen" it, so similar was their behavior to that of ducks which have just left the water after a long swim.

Most interesting of all was their method of hunting under water. They came swimming along with an erratic course, darting a foot or so forward very swiftly in a straight line, then starting to gyrate in looped turns at reduced speed. While swimming straight and swiftly their whiskers were, as far as I could see, laid flat against their head, but while circling they were erect and bristled out in all directions, as they sought contact with some prey. I have no reason to believe that vision plays any part in the water shrew's hunting, except perhaps in the activation of its tactile search. My shrews may have noticed visually the presence of the live tadpoles or little fishes which I put in the tank, but in the actual hunting of its prey the animal is exclusively guided by its sense of touch, located in the wide-spreading whiskers on its snout. Certain small free-swimming species of catfish find their prey by exactly the same method. When these fishes swim fast and straight, the long feelers on their snout are depressed but, like the shrew's whiskers, are stiffly spread out when the fish becomes conscious of the proximity of potential prey; like the shrew, the fish then begins to gyrate blindly in order to establish contact with its prey. It may not even be necessary for the water shrew actually to touch its prey with one of its whiskers. Perhaps, at very close range, the water vibration caused by the movements of a small fish, a tadpole or a water insect is perceptible by those sensitive tactile organs. It is quite impossible to determine this question by mere observation, for the action is much too quick for the human eye. There is a quick turn and a snap and the shrew is already paddling shorewards with a wriggling creature in its maw.

In relation to its size, the water shrew is perhaps the most terrible predator of all vertebrate animals, and it can even vie with the invertebrates, including the murderous Dytiscus larva. It has been reported by A. E. Brehm that water shrews have killed fish more than sixty times heavier than themselves by biting out their eyes and brain. This happened only when the fish were confined in containers with no room for escape. The same story has been told to me by fishermen on Lake Neusiedel, who could not possibly have heard Brehm's report. I once offered to my shrews a large edible frog. I never did it again, nor could I bear to see out to its end the cruel scene that ensued. One of the shrews encountered the frog in the basin and instantly gave chase, repeatedly seizing hold of the creature's legs; although it was kicked off again it did not cease in its attack and finally, the frog, in desperation, jumped out of the water and onto one of the tables, where several shrews raced to the pursuer's assistance and buried their teeth in the legs and hindquarters of the wretched frog. And now, horribly, they began to eat the frog alive, beginning just where each one of them happened to have hold of it; the poor frog croaked heartrendingly, as the jaws of the shrews munched audibly in chorus. I need hardly be blamed for bringing this experiment to an abrupt and agitated end and putting the lacerated frog out of its misery. I never offered the shrews large prey again but only such as would be killed at the first bite or two. Nature can be very cruel indeed; it is not out of pity that most of the larger predatory animals kill their prey quickly. The lion has to finish off a big antelope or a buffalo very quickly indeed in order not to get hurt itself, for a beast of prey which has to hunt daily cannot afford to receive even a harmless scratch in effecting a kill; such scratches would soon add up to such an extent as to put the killer out of action. The same reason has forced the python and other large snakes to evolve a quick and really humane method of killing the well-armed mammals that are their natural prey. But where there is no danger of the victim doing damage to the killer, the latter shows no pity whatsoever. The hedgehog which, by virtue of its armor, is quite immune to the bite of a snake, regularly proceeds to eat it, beginning at the tail or in the middle of its body, and in the same way the water shrew treats its innocuous prey. But man should abstain from judging his innocently-cruel fellow creatures, for even if nature sometimes "shrieks against his creed," what pain does he himself not inflict upon the living creatures that he hunts for pleasure and not for food?

The mental qualities of the water shrew cannot be rated very high. They were quite tame and fearless of me and never tried to bite when I took them in my hand, nor did they ever try to evade it, but, like little tame rodents, they tried to dig their way out if I held them for too long in the hollow of my closed fist. Even when I took them out of their container and put them on a table or on the floor, they were by no means thrown into a panic but were quite ready to take food out of my hand and even tried actively to creep into it if they felt a longing for cover. When, in such an unwonted environment, they were shown their nest-box, they plainly showed that they knew it by sight and instantly made for it, and even pursued it with upraised heads if I moved the box along above them, just out of their reach. All in all, I really may pride myself that I have tamed the shrew, or at least one member of that family.

In their accustomed surroundings, my shrews proved to be very strict creatures of habit. I have already mentioned the remarkable conservatism with which they persevered in their unpractical way of entering their nest-box by climbing onto its roof and then vaulting, with a half turn, in through the door. Something more must be said about the unchanging tenacity with which these animals cling to their habits once they have formed them. In the water shrew, the path habits, in particular, are of a really amazing immutability; I hardly know another instance to which the saying, "As the twig is bent, so the tree is inclined," applies so literally.

In a territory unknown to it, the water shrew will never run fast except under pressure of extreme fear, and than it will run blindly along, bumping into objects and usually getting caught in a blind alley. But, unless the little animal is severely frightened, it moves in strange surroundings, only step by step, whiskering right and left all the time and following a path that is anything but straight. Its course is determined by a hundred fortuitous factors when it walks that way for the first time. But, after a few repetitions, it is evident that the shrew recognizes the locality in which it finds itself and that it repeats, with the utmost exactitude, the movements which it performed the previous time. At the same time, it is noticeable that the animal moves along much faster whenever it is repeating what it has already learned. When placed on a path which it has already traversed a few times, the shrew starts on its way slowly, carefully whiskering. Suddenly it finds known bearings, and now rushes forward a short distance, repeating exactly every step and turn which it executed on the last occasion. Then, when it comes to a spot where it ceases to know the way by heart, it is reduced to whiskering again and to feeling its way step by step. Soon, another burst of speed follows and the same thing is repeated, bursts of speed alternating with very show progress. In the beginning of this process of learning their way, the shrews move along at an extremely slow average rate and the little bursts of speed are few and far between. But gradually the little laps of the course which have been "learned by heart" and which can be covered quickly begin to increase in length as well as in number until they fuse and the whole course can be completed in a fast, unbroken rush.

Often, when such a path habit is almost completely formed, there still remains one particularly difficult place where the shrew always loses its bearings and has to resort to its senses of smell and touch, sniffing and whiskering vigorously to find out where the next reach of its path "joins on." Once the shrew is well settled in its path habits it is as strictly bound to them as a railway engine to its tracks and as unable to deviate from them by even a few centimeters. If it diverges from its path by so much as an inch, it is forced to stop abruptly, and laboriously regain its bearings. The same behavior can be caused experimentally by changing some small detail in the customary path of the animal. Any major alteration in the habitual path threw the shrews into complete confusion. One of their paths ran along the wall adjoining the wooden table opposite to that on which the nest box was situated. This table was weighted with two stones lying close to the panes of the tank, and the shrews, running along the wall, were accustomed to jump on and off the stones which lay right in their path. If I moved the stones out of the runway, placing both together in the middle of the table, the shrews would jump right up into the air in the place where the stone should have been; they came down with a jarring bump, were obviously disconcerted and started whiskering cautiously right and left, just as they behaved in an unknown environment. And then they did a most interesting thing: they went back the way they had come, carefully feeling their way until they had again got their bearings. Then, facing round again, they tried a second time with a rush and jumped and crashed down exactly as they had done a few seconds before. Only then did they seem to realize that the first fall had not been their own fault but was due to a change in the wonted pathway, and now they proceeded to explore the alteration, cautiously sniffing and bewhiskering the place where the stone ought to have been. This method of going back to the start, and trying again always reminded me of a small boy who, in reciting a poem, gets stuck and begins again at an earlier verse.

In rats, as in many small mammals, the process of forming a path habit, for instance in learning a maze, is very similar to that just described; but a rat is far more adaptable in its behavior and would not dream of trying to jump over a stone which was not there. The preponderance of motor habit over present perception is a most remarkable peculiarity of the water shrew. One might say that the animal actually disbelieves its senses if they report a change of environment which necessitates a sudden alteration in its motor habits. In a new environment a water shrew would be perfectly able to see a stone of that size and consequently to avoid it or to run over it in a manner well adapted to the spatial conditions; but once a habit is formed and has become ingrained, it supersedes all better knowledge. I know of no animal that is a slave to its habits in so literal a sense as the water shrew. For this animal the geometric axiom that a straight line is the shortest distance between two points simply does not hold good. To them, the shortest line is always the accustomed path and, to a certain extent, they are justified in adhering to this principle: they run with amazing speed along their pathways and arrive at their destination much sooner than they would if, by whiskering and nosing, they tried to go straight. They will keep to the wonted path, even though it winds in such a way that it crosses and recrosses itself. A rat or mouse would be quick to discover that it was making an unnecessary detour, but the water shrew is no more able to do so than is a toy train to turn off at right angles at a level crossing. In order to change its route, the water shrew must change its whole path habit, and this cannot be done at a moment's notice but gradually, over a long period of time. An unnecessary, loop-shaped detour takes weeks and weeks to become a little shorter, and after months it is not even approximately straight. The biological advantage of such a path habit is obvious: it compensates the shrew for being nearly blind and enables it to run exceedingly fast without wasting a minute on orientation. On the other hand it may, under unusual circumstances, lead the shrew to destruction. It has been reported, quite plausibly, that water shrews have broken their necks by jumping into a pond which had been recently drained. In spite of the possibility of such mishaps, it would be shortsighted if one were simply to stigmatize the water shrew as stupid because it solves the spatial problems of its daily life in quite a different way from man. On the contrary, if one thinks a little more deeply, it is very wonderful that the same result, namely a perfect orientation in space, can be brought about in two so widely divergent ways: by true observation, as we achieve it, or, as the water shrew does, by learning by heart every possible spatial contingency that may arise in a given territory.

Among themselves, my water shrews were surprisingly good-natured. Although, in their play, they would often chase each other, twittering with a great show of excitement, I never saw a serious fight between them until an unfortunate accident occurred: one morning, I forgot to reopen the little door of the nest-box after cleaning out their tank. When at last I remembered, three hours had elapsed—a very long time for the swift metabolism of such small insectivores. Upon the opening of the door, all the shrews rushed out and made a dash for the food tray. In their haste to get out, not only did they soil themselves all over but they apparently discharged, in their excitement, some sort of glandular secretion, for a strong, musk-like odor accompanied their exit from the box. Since they appeared to have incurred no damage by their three hours' fasting, I turned away from the box to occupy myself with other things. However, on nearing the container soon afterwards, I heard an unusually loud, sharp twittering and, on my hurried approach, found my eight shrews locked in deadly battle. Two were even then dying and, though I consigned them at once to separate cages, two more died in the course of the day. The real cause of this sudden and terrible battle is hard to ascertain but I cannot help suspecting that the shrews, owing to the sudden change in the usual odor, had failed to recognize each other and had fallen upon each other as they would have done upon strangers. The four survivors quieted down after a certain time and I was able to reunite them in the original container without fear of further mishap.

I kept those four remaining shrews in good health for nearly seven months and would probably have had them much longer if the assistant whom I had engaged to feed them had not forgotten to do so. I had been obliged to go to Vienna and, on my return in the late afternoon, was met by that usually reliable fellow who turned pale when he saw me, thereupon remembering that he had forgotten to feed the shrews. All four of them were alive but very weak; they ate greedily when we fed them but died nonetheless within a few hours. In other words, they showed exactly the same symptoms as the shrews which I had formerly tried to keep; this confirmed my opinion that the latter were already dying of hunger when they came into my possession.

To any advanced animal keeper who is able to set up a large tank, preferably with running water, and who can obtain a sufficient supply of small fish, tadpoles, and the like, I can recommend the water shrew as one of the most gratifying, charming, and interesting objects of care. Of course it is a somewhat exacting charge. It will eat raw chopped heart (the customary substitute for small live prey) only in the absence of something better and it cannot be fed exclusively on this diet for long periods. Moreover, really clean water is indispensable. But if these clear-cut requirements be fulfilled, the water shrew will not merely remain alive but will really thrive, nor do I exclude the possibility that it might even breed in captivity.

1952

THE READER

1. *What features of the shrew's behavior does Lorenz select for special emphasis? What conclusions does he draw about these features?*
2. *Lorenz employs a narrative framework in which to describe the shrews. Make a list of narrative events and a list of major characteristics of the shrew. Do you as a reader react differently to the facts about shrew behavior because they are embedded in narrative?*

THE WRITER

1. *Lorenz discusses a field trip and some other matters before he reports his laboratory observations. What is the effect of this organization?*
2. *Though this is mainly a report of his observations, Lorenz includes matters that are not necessary to the report of strictly controlled observation of the shrew's habits. Indicate some of the places where his discussion moves beyond strict reporting. Characterize the roles he assumes in these passages. Do these other roles or revelations of personality compromise or support his claim to being a scientist?*
3. *Write an account of the characteristics of some animal, either domesticated or wild, embedding them in a brief narrative.*

Niko Tinbergen

THE BEE-HUNTERS OF HULSHORST[1]

On a sunny day in the summer of 1929 I was walking rather aimlessly over the sands, brooding and a little worried. I had just done my finals, had got a half-time job, and was hoping to start on research for a doctor's thesis. I wanted very much to work on some problem of animal behaviour

1. Hulshorst is the sparsely populated region in Holland where Tinbergen's observations and experiments were carried out.

and had for that reason rejected some suggestions of my well-meaning supervisor. But rejecting sound advice and taking one's own decisions are two very different things, and so far I had been unable to make up my mind.

While walking about, my eye was caught by a bright orange-yellow wasp the size of the ordinary jam-loving *Vespa*. It was busying itself in a strange way on the bare sand. With brisk, jerky movements it was walking slowly backwards, kicking the sand behind it as it proceeded. The sand flew away with every jerk. I was sure that this was a digger wasp. The only kind of that size I knew was *Bembex*, the large fly-killer. But this was no *Bembex*. I stopped to watch it, and soon saw that it was shovelling sand out of a burrow. After ten minutes of this, it turned round, and now, facing away from the entrance, began to rake loose sand over it. In a minute the entrance was completely covered. Then the wasp flew up, circled a few times round the spot, describing wider and wider loops in the air, and finally flew off. Knowing something of the way of digger wasps, I expected it to return with a prey within a reasonable time, and decided to wait.

Sitting down on the sand, I looked round and saw that I had blundered into what seemed to be a veritable wasp town. Within ten yards I saw more than twenty wasps occupied at their burrows. Each burrow had a patch of yellow sand round it the size of a hand, and to judge from the number of these sand patches there must have been hundreds of burrows.

I had not to wait long before I saw a wasp coming home. It descended slowly from the sky, alighting after the manner of a helicopter on a sand patch. Then I saw that it was carrying a load, a dark object about its own size. Without losing hold of it, the wasp made a few raking movements with its front legs, the entrance became visible and, dragging its load after it, the wasp slipped into the hole.

At the next opportunity I robbed a wasp of its prey, by scaring it on its arrival, so that it dropped its burden. Then I saw that the prey was a Honey Bee.

I watched these wasps at work all through that afternoon, and soon became absorbed in finding out exactly what was happening in this busy insect town. It seemed that the wasps were spending part of their time working at their burrows. Judging from the amount of sand excavated these must have been quite deep. Now and then a wasp would fly out and, after half an hour or longer, return with a load, which was then dragged in. Every time I examined the prey, it was a Honey Bee. No doubt they captured all these bees on the heath for all to and fro traffic was in the direction of the south-east, where I knew the nearest heath to be. A rough calculation showed that something was going on here that would not please the owners of the bee-hives on the heath; on a sunny day like this several thousand bees fell victims to this large colony of killers.

As I was watching the wasps, I began to realize that here was a wonderful opportunity for doing exactly the kind of field work I would like to do. Here were many hundreds of digger wasps—exactly which species I did not know yet, but that would not be difficult to find out. I had little doubt that each wasp was returning regularly to its own burrow, which showed that they must have excellent powers of homing. How did they manage to find their way back to their own burrow? * * *

Settling down to work, I started spending the wasps' working days (which lasted from about 8 a.m. till 6 p.m. and so did not put too much of a strain on me) on the 'Philanthus plains', as we called this part of the sands as soon as we had found out that *Philanthus triangulum Fabr.* was the official name of this bee-killing digger wasp. Its vernacular name was 'Bee-Wolf'.

An old chair, field glasses, note-books, and food and water for the day were my equipment. The local climate of the open sands was quite amazing, considering that ours is a temperate climate. Surface temperatures of 110° F were not rare. * * *

My first job was to find out whether each wasp was really limited to one burrow, as I suspected from the unhesitating way in which the homecoming wasps alighted on the sand patches in front of the burrows. I installed myself in a densely populated quarter of the colony, five yeards or so from a group of about twenty-five nests. Each borrow was marked and mapped. Whenever I saw a wasp at work at a burrow, I caught it and, after a short unequal struggle, adorned its back with one or two colour dots (using quickly drying enamel paint) and released it. Such wasps soon returned to work, and after a few hours I had ten wasps, each marked with a different combination of colours, working right in front of me. It was remarkable how this simple trick of marking my wasps changed my whole attitude to them. From members of the species *Philanthus triangulum* they were transformed into personal acquaintances, whose lives from that very moment became affairs of the most personal interest and concern to me.

While waiting for events to develop, I spent my time having a close look at the wasps. A pair of lenses mounted on a frame that could be worn as spectacles enabled me, by crawling up slowly to a working wasp, to observe it, much enlarged, from a few inches away. When seen under such circumstances most insects reveal a marvellous beauty, totally unexpected as long as you observe them with the unaided eye. Through my lenses I could look at my *Philanthus* right into their huge compound eyes; I saw their enormous, claw-like jaws which they used for crumbling up the sandy crust; I saw their agile black antennae in continuous, restless movement; I watched their yellow, bristled legs rake away the loose sand with such vigour that it flew through the air in rhythmic puffs, landing several inches behind them.

Soon several of my marked wasps stopped working at their burrows, raked loose sand back over the entrance, and flew off. The take-off was often spectacular. Before leaving they circled a little while over the burrow, at first low above the ground, soon higher, describing ever widening loops; then flew away, but returned to cruise once more low over the nest. Finally, they would set out in a bee-line, fifteen to thirty feet above the ground, a rapidly vanishing speck against the blue sky. All the wasps disappeared towards the south-east. Half a mile away in that direction the bare sands bordered upon an extensive heath area, buzzing with bees. This, as I was to see later, was the wasps' hunting area.

The curious loops my wasps described in the air before leaving their home area had been described by other observers of many other digger wasps. Philip Rau had given them the name of 'locality studies'. Yet so far nobody proved that they deserved that name; that the wasps actually took in the features of the burrow's surroundings while circling above them. To check this if possible was one of my aims—I thought that it was most probable that the wasps would use landmarks, and that this locality study was what the name implied. First, however, I had to make sure that my marked wasps would return to their own holes. * * *

Before the first day was over, each of them had returned with a bee; some had returned twice or even three times. At the end of that day it was clear that each of them had its own nest, to which it returned regularly.

On subsequent days I extended these observations and found out some more facts about the wasps' daily life. As in other species, the digging of the large burrows and the capturing of prey that served as food for the larvae was exclusively the task of the females. And a formidable task it was. The wasps spent hours digging the long shafts, and throwing the sand out. Often they stayed down for a long time and, waiting for them to reappear, my patience was often put to a hard test. Eventually, however, there would be some almost imperceptible movement in the sand, and a small mound of damp soil was gradually lifted up, little by little, as if a miniature Mole were at work. Soon the wasp emerged, tail first, and all covered with sand. One quick shake, accompanied by a sharp staccato buzz, and the wasp was clean. Then it began to mop up, working as if possessed, shovelling the sand several inches away from the entrance.

I often tried to dig up the burrows to see their inner structure. Usually the sand crumbled and I lost track of the passage before I was ten inches down, but sometimes, by gently probing with a grass shoot first, and then digging down along it, I succeeded in getting down to the cells. These were found opening into the far end of the shaft, which itself was a narrow tube, often more than 2 ft. long. Each cell contained an egg or a larva with a couple of Honey Bees, its food store. A burrow contained from one to five cells. Each larva had its own living room-cum-larder in the house, provided by the hard-working female. From the varying nunber of cells I found in the nests, and the varying ages of the larvae in one burrow, I concluded that the female usually filled each cell with bees before she started to dig a new cell, and I assumed that it was the tunnelling out of a new cell that made her stay down for such long spells.

I did not spend much time digging up the burrows, for I wanted to observe the wasps while they were undisturbed. Now that I was certain that each wasp returned regularly to her own burrow, I was faced with the problem of her orientation. The entire valley was littered with the yellow sand patches; how could a wasp, after a hunting trip of about a mile in all, find exactly her own burrow?

Having seen the wasps make their 'locality studies', I naturally believed that each female actually did what this term implied: take her bearings. A simple test suggested that this was correct. While a wasp was away I brushed over the ground surrounding the nest entrance, moving all possible landmarks such as pebbles, twigs, tufts of grass, Pine cones, etc, so that over an area of 3–4 square metres none of them remained in exactly the same place as before. The burrow itself, however, I left intact. Then I awaited the wasp's return. When she came, slowly descending from the skies, carrying her bee, her behaviour was striking. All went well until she was about 4ft. above the ground. There she suddenly stopped, dashed back and forth as if in panic, hung motionless in the air for a while, then flew back and up in a wide loop, came slowly down again in the same way, and again shied at the same distance from the next. Obviously she was severely disturbed. Since I had left the nest itself, its entrance, and the sand patch in front of it untouched, this showed that the wasp was affected by the change in the surroundings.

Gradually she calmed down, and began to search low over the disturbed area. But she seemed to be unable to find the nest. She alighted now here, now there, and began to dig tentatively at a variety of places at the approximate site of the nest entrance. After a while she dropped her bee and started a thorough trial-and-error search. After twenty-five minutes or so she stumbled on the nest entrance as if by accident, and only then did she take up her bee and drag it in. A few minutes later she came out again, closed the entrance, and set off. And now she had a nice surprise in store for me: upon leaving she made an excessively long 'locality study': for fully two minutes she circled and circled, coming back again and again to fly over the disturbed area before she finally zoomed off.

I waited for another hour and a half, and had the satisfaction of seeing her return once more. And what I had hoped for actually happened: there was scarcely a trace of hesitation this time. Not only had the wasp lost her shyness of the disturbed soil, but she now knew her way home perfectly well.

I repeated this test with a number of wasps, and their reactions to my interference were roughly the same each time. It seemed probable, therefore, that the wasps found their way home by using something like landmarks in the environment, and not by responding to some stimulus (visual or otherwise) sent out by the nest itself. I had now to test more critically whether this was actually the case.

The test I did next was again quite simple. If a wasp used landmarks it should be possible to do more than merely disturb her by throwing her beacons all over the place; I ought to be able to mislead her, to make her go to the wrong place, by moving the whole constellation of her land-marks over a certain distance. I did this at a few nests that were situated on bare sandy soil and that had only a few, but conspicuous, objects nearby, such as twigs, or tufts of grass. After the owner of such a nest was gone, I moved these two or three objects a foot to the south-west, roughly at right angles to the expected line of approach. The result was as I had hoped for and expected, and yet I could not help being surprised as well as delighted: each wasp missed her own nest, and alighted at exactly the spot where the nest 'ought' to be according to the landmarks' new positions! I could vary my tests by very cautiously shooing the wasp away, then moving the beacons a foot in another direction, and allowing the wasp to alight again. In whatever position I put the beacons, the wasp would follow them. At the end of such a series of tests I replaced the landmarks in their original position, and this finally enabled the wasp to return to her home. Thus the tests always had a happy ending—for both of us. This was no pure altruism on my part—I could now use the wasp for another test if I wished.

When engaged in such work, it is always worth observing oneself as well as the animals, and to do it as critically and as detachedly as possible —which, of course, is a tall order. I have often wondered why the outcome of such a test delighted me so much. A rationalist would proba-bly like to assume that it was the increased predictability resulting from the test. This was a factor of considerable importance, I am sure. But a more important factor still (not only to me, but to many other people I have watched in this situation) is of a less dignified type: people enjoy, they relish the satisfaction of their desire for power. The truth of this was obvious, for instance, in people who enjoyed seeing the wasps being misled without caring much for the intellectual question whether they used landmarks or not. I am further convinced that even the joy of gaining insight was not often very pure either; it was mixed with pride at having had success with the tests.

To return to the wasps: next I tried to make the wasps use landmarks which I provided. This was not only for the purpose of satisfying my lust for power, but also for nobler purposes, as I hope to show later. Since changing the environment while the wasp was away disturbed her upon her return and even might prevent her from finding her nest altogether, I waited until a wasp had gone down into her nest, and then put my own landmarks round the entrance—sixteen Pine cones arranged in a circle of about eight inches diameter.

The first wasp to emerge was a little upset, and made a rather long locality study. On her return home, she hesitated for some time, but eventually alighted at the nest. When next she went out she made a really thorough locality study, and from then on everything went smoothly. Other wasps behaved in much the same way, and next day regular work was going on at five burrows so treated. I now subjected all five wasps, one by one, to a displacement test similar to those already described. The results, however, were not clearcut. Some wasps, upon returning, followed the cones; but others were not fooled, and went straight home, completely ignoring my beacons. Others again seemed to be unable to make up their minds, and oscillated between the real nest and the ring of cones. This half-hearted behaviour did not disturb me, however, for if my idea was correct—that the wasps use landmarks—one would rather expect that my tests put the wasps in a kind of conflict situation: the natural landmarks which they must have been using before I gave them the Pine cones were still in their original position; only the cones had been moved. And while the cones were very conspicuous landmarks, they had been there for no more than one day. I therefore put all the cone-rings back and waited for two more days before testing the wasps again. And sure enough, this time the tests gave a hundred per cent preference for the Pine cones; I had made the wasps train themselves to my landmarks.

The rest of this first summer I spent mainly in consolidating this result in various ways. There was not much time to do this, for the season lasts only two months; by the end of August the wasps became sluggish, and soon after they died, leaving the destiny of their race in the hands of the pupae deep down in the sand, which were to lie there dormant until next July. And even in this short summer season the wasps could not work steadily, but were active on dry sunny days only—and of these a Dutch summer rarely supplies more than about twenty in all.

However, I had time to make sure that the wasps relied for their homing mainly on vision. First, I could cut off their antennae—the bearers of delicate organs of smell, of touch and of other sense organs—without at all disturbing the orientation. Second, when, in other tests, I covered the eyes of intact wasps with black paint, the wasps could not fly at all. Removing the cover of paint restored their eyesight, and with it their normal behaviour. Furthermore, when I trained a wasp to accept a circle of Pine cones together with two small squares of cardboard drenched in Pine oil, which gave off a strong scent, displacement of the cones would mislead the wasps in the usual way, but moving the scented squares had not the slightest effect. Finally, when wasps used to rings of cones were given, instead of cones, a ring of grey pebbles a foot from the nest, they followed these pebbles. This can only have been due to the pebbles being visually similar to the cones.

* * *

We began by investigating the wasp's 'locality study' a little more closely. As I mentioned before, we had already quite suggestive indications that it really deserved this name, but clear-cut proof was still lacking. The otherwise annoying vagaries of the Atlantic climate provided us with a wonderful opportunity to get this proof. Long spells of cold rainy weather are not uncommon in a Dutch summer—in fact they are more common than periods of sunny weather, which alone could tempt the wasps to 'work'. Rainy weather put a strain on morale in our camp, but the first sign of improvement usually started an outburst of feverish activity, all of us doing our utmost to be ready for the wasps before they could resume their flights.

We had previously noticed that many (though not all) wasps spent cold and wet periods in their burrows. Rain and wind often played havoc with their landmarks and perhaps the wasps also forgot their exact position while sitting indoors. At any rate, with the return of good weather, all the wasps made prolonged 'locality studies' when setting out on their first trip. Could it be that they had to learn anew the lie of the land?

On one such morning, while the ground was still wet but the weather sunny and promising, we were at the colony at 7.30 a.m. Each of us took up a position near a group of nests and watched for the first signs of emerging wasps. We had not to wait long before we saw the sand covering one of the entrances move—a sure sign of a wasp trying to make her way into the open. Quickly we put a circle of pine cones round the burrow. When the wasp came out, she started digging and working at her nest, then raked sand over the entrance and left. In the course of the morning many wasps emerged and each received pine cones round her entrance before she had 'opened the door'. Some of these wasps did not bother to work at the nest, but left at once after coming out. These latter wasps we were going to use for our tests. As expected, they made elaborate locality studies, describing many loops of increasing range and altitude before finally departing. We timed these flights carefully. As soon as one of these wasps had definitely gone, we took the Pine cones away. This was done in order to make absolutely sure that, if the wasp should return unobserved, she could not see cones round her nest. If then, when we saw her return with a bee, a displacement test in which the circle of Pine cones was laid out some distance away from the nest would give positive results (i.e., the wasp would choose these cones), we would have proved that she must have learnt them during her locality study, for at no other time could she have seen them.

Not all such wasps returned on the same day. Their prolonged stay and their fast down in the burrows probably forced them to feed themselves in the Heather first. Some, however, returned with a bee and with these we succeeded in doing some exciting tests. In all we tested 13 wasps. They were observed to choose 93 times between the true nest and a 'sham nest' surrounded by the Pine cones. Seventy-three choices fell on the sham nests, against only 20 on the real nests. In control tests taken after the experiments, when the cones were put back round the real nest, of a total of 39 only 3 choices were now in favour of the sham nests, the other 36 being in favour of the real nests. There was no doubt then that these wasps had learnt the nature and the position of the new landmarks during the locality study.

The most impressive achievement was that of wasp No. 179. She had made one locality study of a mere six seconds and had left without returning, let alone alighting. When she was tested upon her return more than an hour later she chose the cones 12 times and never came near the nest. When the original situation was restored she alighted at once on her burrow and slipped in. Nos. 174 and 177 almost equalled this record; both were perfectly trained after uninterrupted locality studies of 13 seconds. All the other wasps either made longer locality studies or interrupted them by alighting on the nest one or more times before leaving again. Such wasps might have learnt during alighting rather than while performing the locality study, so their results were less convincing.

This result, while not at all unexpected, nevertheless impressed us very much. It not only revealed an amazing capacity in these little insects to learn so quickly, but we were struck even more by the fact that a wasp, when not fully oriented, would set out to perform such a locality study, as if it knew what the effect of this specialized type of behaviour would be.

I have already described that a wasp, which has made a number of flights to and from a burrow, makes no, or almost no, locality study, but that it will make an elaborate one after the surroundings have been disturbed. Further tests threw light on the question what exactly made her do this. We studied the effect on locality studies of two types of disturbances. In tests of type A we either added or removed a conspicuous landmark before the wasp returned and then restored the original situation while she was inside. Such wasps, although finding the old, familiar situation upon emerging again, made long locality studies. In tests of type B the wasps were not disturbed at all when entering, but changes similar to those of the A-tests were made just before they left. None of these wasps made locality studies. Wasps used for A-tests always hesitated before alighting. Therefore, disturbances of the familiar surroundings perceived upon returning make the wasps perform a locality study when next departing, while the same disturbances actually present at the time of departure have no influence!

Some further, rather incomplete and preliminary tests pointed to another interesting aspect. Conspicuous new landmarks given before the return of the wasp and left standing until after her departure influenced the form of the locality study as well as its duration: the wasp would repeatedly circle round this particular landmark. If, however, such a landmark was left for some time, so that the wasp passed it several times on her way out and back, and then moved to a new place, the wasp would make a longer locality study than before, yet she would not describe extra loops round the beacon. She obviously recognized the object and had merely to learn its new position. These tests were too few and not fully conclusive, but they did suggest that there is more to this locality study than we had at first suspected. The whole phenomenon is remarkable and certainly deserves further study.

We next turned our attention to the exact nature of the landmarks that were used by the wasps. What exactly did they learn? We spent several seasons examining this and the more striking of our tests are worth describing.

First of all we found that not all objects round the nest were of equal value to the wasps. The first indication of this was found when we tried to train them to use sheets of coloured paper about 3 x 4 inches, which we put out near the nests, as a preparation to study colour vision. It proved to be almost impossible to make the wasps use even a set of three of them; even after leaving them out for days on end we rarely succeeded with the same simple displacement tests that worked so well with the Pine cones. Most wasps just ignored them. Yet the bright blue, yellow and red papers were very conspicuous to us. For some reason, the Pine cones were meeting the wasps' requirements for landmarks better than the flat sheets. [We] worked out a method to test this. We provided two types of objects round a nest—for instance, flat discs and Pine cones—arranged in a circle in alternation. After a day or so, we moved the whole circle and checked whether the wasps used it. If so, we then provided two sham nests at equal distances, one on each side of the real nest, and put all objects of one type round one of these sham nests, all of the other type round the other. If then the wasp had trained herself to one type of landmark rather than to the other, it should prefer one of the two sham nests. Such a preferential choice could not be due to anything but the difference in the wasps' attitude towards the two classes of objects, for all could have been seen by the wasp equally often, their distance to the nest entrance had been the same, they had been offered all round the nest, etc. —in short, they had had absolutely equal chances.

In this way we compared flat objects with solid, dark with light, those contrasting with the colour of the background with those matching it, larger with smaller, nearer with more distant ones, and so on. Each test had, of course, to be done with many wasps and each wasp had to make a number of choices for us to be sure that there was consistency in her preference. This programme kept us busy for a long time, but the results were worth the trouble. The wasps actually showed for landmarks a preference which was different from ours.

When we offered flat circular discs and hemispheres of the same diameter, the wasps always followed the hemispheres (43 against 2 choices). This was not due to the larger surface area of the hemispheres, for when we did similar tests with flat discs of much larger size (of 10 cm. diameter, whereas the hemispheres had a diameter of only 4 cm.), the choices were still 73 in favour of the hemispheres against 19 for the discs.

In other tests we found out that the hemispheres were not preferred because of their shading, nor because they showed contrasts between highlights and deep blacks, nor because they were three—dimensional, but because of the fact that they stood out above the ground. The critical test for this was to offer hollow cones, half of them standing up on top of the soil on their bases, half sunk upside down into the ground. Both were three dimensional, but one extended above the ground while the others formed pits in the ground. The standing cones were almost always chosen (108 against 21).

The preference for objects that projected above the ground was one of the reasons why Pine cones were preferred. Another reason was that Pine cones offered a chequered pattern of light and dark, while yet another reason was the fact that they had a broken instead of a smooth surface— i.e., dented objects were more stimulating than smooth ones. Similar facts had been found about Honey Bees by other students and much of this has probably to do with the organization of the compound eyes of insects.

We further found that large objects were better than small objects; near objects better than the same objects further away from the nest, objects that contrasted in tone with the background better than those matching the background, objects presented during critical periods (such as at the start of digging a new nest or immediately after a rainy period) better than objects offered once a wasp had acquired a knowledge of its surroundings.

It often amazed us, when doing these tests, that the wasps frequently chose a sham nest so readily although the circle offered contained only half the objects to which they had been trained. This would not be so strange if the wasps had just ignored the weaker 'beacons', but this was not the case. If, in our original test with flat discs and hemispheres, we would offer the discs alone, the wasps, confronted with a choice between the discs and the original nest without either discs or hemispheres, often chose the discs. These, therefore, had not been entirely ignored; they were potential beacons, but were less valued than the hemispheres. Once we knew this, we found that with a little perseverance we could train the wasps to our flat coloured papers. But it took time.

The fact that the wasps accepted these circles, with half the number of objects they used to see, suggested that they responded to the circular arrangement as a whole as well as to the properties of the individual beacon. This raised the interesting issue of 'configurational' stimuli and it seemed to offer good opportunities for experiment. This work was taken up by Van Beusekom who, in a number of ingenious tests, showed that the wasps responded to a very complicated stimulus situation indeed.

First of all, he made sure that wasps could recognize beacons such a Pine cones fairly well. He trained wasps to the usual circle of Pine cones and then gave them the choice between these and a similar arrangement of smooth blocks of Pine cone size. The wasps decided predominantly in favour of the Pine cones, which showed that they were responding to details which distinguished the two types of beacons.

He next trained a number of wasps to a circle of 16 Pine cones and subjected them to two types of tests. In Type A the wasp had to choose between two sets of 16 cones, one arranged in a circle, the other in a figure of another shape, such as a square, a triangle, or an ellipse. He found that, unless the figure was very similar to the circle, the wasps could distinguish between the two figures and alighted in the circle. In those tests the individual cones did not count; he could either use the original cones for constructing the circle or use them for the square or triangle. It was the circular figure the wasps chose, not the Pine cones used during training.

In tests of type B, after the usual training to a circle of 16, he offered the 16 cones in a non-circular arrangement against 8 or even fewer cones in a (loose) circle—and found that the wasps chose the circle in spite of the smaller number of cones. He could even go further and offer a circle of quite different elements, such as square blocks (which the wasps could distinguish from cones, as other tests had shown). If such a circle was offered against cones in a noncircular arrangement, it was the circle that won. Thus it was shown in a variety of ways that the wasps responded not only to the individual beacons (as the preference tests * * * had shown), but also to the circle as a whole.

However, all these experiments, while giving us valuable information about the way our wasps perceived their environment, had one limitation in common—they showed us only how the wasps behaved at the last stage of their journey home. We had many indications that the Pine cones were not seen until the wasps were within a few yards from the nest. How did they find their way previous to this?

Although we were aware of these limitations, it was extremely difficult to extend our tests. However, we did a little about this. More than once we displaced small Pine trees growing at a distance of several yards from nests under observation. In many cases wasps were misled by this and tried to find their nests in the correct position in relation to the displaced tree. The precision of their orientation to such relatively distant marks was truly amazing.

Such large landmarks were used in a slightly different way from the Pine cones. Firstly, they were used even when relatively far from the nest. Secondly, they could be moved over far greater distances than the Pine cones. A circle of Pine cones would fail to draw the wasp with it if it was moved over more than about 7 ft., but a Pine tree, or even a branch of about 4 ft. high, could lure the wasps away even if moved over 8 metres. We further observed in many of our earlier tests that wasps, upon finding the immediate surroundings of the nest disturbed, flew back, circled round a Pine tree or a large sandhill perhaps 70 yards away, and then again approached the nest. This looked very much as though they were taking their bearings upon these larger landmarks.

Van der Linde and others also spent a great deal of time and energy in transporting individual wasps in light-proof cloth over distances up to 1,000 metres in all directions. Since good hunting grounds were to the south and south-east of the colony, whereas in other directions bare sand flats or dense Pine plantations bordered upon the *Philanthus* plains, we could assume that our wasps knew the country to the south and south-east better than in other directions—an assumption which was confirmed by the fact that our wasps always flew out in a south or south-east direction and returned with bees from there. The transported wasps, whose return to their nests was watched, did indeed much better from the south and south-east than from any other direction. From the north-west, for instance, half the wasps never returned as long as our observations lasted. This did indeed suggest that return from unknown country was difficult if not impossible and, therefore, that learning of some kind was essential, but it could not tell us more.

1958

THE READER

1. *Which of Tinbergen's activities, as described in this account of his research, are the kind you expect of a scientist? Do any of them surprise you?*
2. *How did Tinbergen find the question he decided to study?*

THE WRITER

1. *In the paragraph beginning "When engaged in such work..." (p. 897), Tinbergen suggests that it is desirable for the scientific observer to observe himself as well as the object of study. Why? In his own case, did this attention to himself interfere with his objective*

study of the facts? What did Tinbergen observe in this particular instance?

2. *Before Tinbergen started his research, what was known of the "locality studies" made by the wasps? What steps did he go through to find out more about this matter? To what degree and in what ways was his study a matter of observation? What arrangements did he make to change the conditions for observing? Write a description of scientific method as exemplified by Tinbergen's study.*

3. *Write a brief comparison of Tinbergen's account of his research and that of Lorenz in "The Taming of the Shrew" (p. 879). If these authors convey to you a sense of excitement about their work, show some of the specific ways in which their writing does this.*

Alexander Petrunkevitch

THE SPIDER AND THE WASP

In the feeding and safeguarding of their progeny insects and spiders exhibit some interesting analogies to reasoning and some crass examples of blind instinct. The case I propose to describe here is that of the tarantula spiders and their archenemy, the digger wasps of the genus Pepsis. It is a classic example of what looks like intelligence pitted against instinct—a strange situation in which the victim, though fully able to defend itself, submits unwittingly to its destruction.

Most tarantulas live in the tropics, but several species occur in the temperate zone and a few are common in the southern U.S. Some varieties are large and have powerful fangs with which they can inflict a deep wound. These formidable looking spiders do not, however, attack man; you can hold one in your hand, if you are gentle, without being bitten. Their bite is dangerous only to insects and small mammals such as mice; for man it is no worse than a hornet's sting.

Tarantulas customarily live in deep cylindrical burrows, from which they emerge at dusk and into which they retire at dawn. Mature males wander about after dark in search of females and occasionally stray into houses. After mating, the male dies in a few weeks, but a female lives much longer and can mate several years in succession. In a Paris museum is a tropical specimen which is said to have been living in captivity for 25 years.

A fertilized female tarantula lays from 200 to 400 eggs at a time; thus it is possible for a single tarantula to produce several thousand young. She takes no care of them beyond weaving a cocoon of silk to enclose the eggs. After they hatch, the young walk away, find convenient places in which to dig their burrows and spend the rest of their lives in solitude. The eyesight of tarantulas is poor, being limited to a sensing of change in the intensity of light and to the perception of moving objects. They apparently have little or no sense of hearing, for a hungry tarantula will pay no attention to a loudly chirping cricket placed in its cage unless the insect happens to touch one of its legs.

But all spiders, and especially hairy ones, have an extremely delicate sense of touch. Laboratory experiments prove that tarantulas can distinguish three types of touch: pressure against the body wall, stroking of the body hair, and riffling of certain very fine hairs on the legs called trichobothria. Pressure against the body, by the finger or the end of a pencil, causes the tarantula to move off slowly for a short distance. The touch excites no defensive response unless the approach is from above where the spider can see the motion, in which case it rises on its hind legs, lifts its front legs, opens its fangs and holds this threatening posture as long as the object continues to move.

The entire body of a tarantula, especially its legs, is thickly clothed with hair. Some of it is short and wooly, some long and stiff. Touching this body hair produces one of two distinct reactions. When the spider is hungry, it responds with an immediate and swift attack. At the touch of a cricket's antennae the tarantula seizes the insect so swiftly that a motion picture taken at the rate of 64 frames per second shows only the result and not the process of capture. But when the spider is not hungry, the stimulation of its hairs merely causes it to shake the touched limb. An insect can walk under its hairy belly unharmed.

The trichobothria, very fine hairs growing from dislike[1] membranes on the legs, are sensitive only to air movement. A light breeze makes them vibrate slowly, without disturbing the common hair. When one blows gently on the trichobothria, the tarantula reacts with a quick jerk of its four front legs. If the front and hind legs are stimulated at the same time, the spider makes a sudden jump. This reaction is quite independent of the state of its appetite.

These three tactile responses—to pressure on the body wall, to moving of the common hair, and to flexing of the trichobothria—are so different from one another that there is no possibility of confusing them. They serve the tarantula adequately for most of its needs and enable it to avoid most annoyances and dangers. But they fail the spider completely when it meets its deadly enemy, the digger wasp Pepsis.

These solitary wasps are beautiful and formidable creatures. Most species are either a deep shiny blue all over, or deep blue with rusty wings. The largest have a wing span of about four inches. They live on nectar. When excited, they give off a pungent odor—a warning that they

---

1. Unlike or dissimilar.

are ready to attack. The sting is much worse than that of a bee or common wasp, and the pain and swelling last longer. In the adult stage the wasp lives only a few months. The female produces but a few eggs, one at a time at intervals of two or three days. For each egg the mother must provide one adult tarantula, alive but paralyzed. The mother wasp attaches the egg to the paralyzed spider's abdomen. Upon hatching from the egg, the larva is many hundreds of times smaller than its living but helpless victim. It eats no other food and drinks no water. By the time it has finished its single Gargantuan meal and become ready for wasphood, nothing remains of the tarantula but its indigestible chitinous skeleton.

The mother wasp goes tarantula-hunting when the egg in her ovary is almost ready to be laid. Flying low over the ground late on a sunny afternoon, the wasp looks for its victim or for the mouth of a tarantula burrow, a round hole edged by a bit of silk. The sex of the spider makes no difference, but the mother is highly discriminating as to species. Each species of Pepsis requires a certain species of tarantula, and the wasp will not attack the wrong species. In a cage with a tarantula which is not its normal prey, the wasp avoids the spider and is usually killed by it in the night.

Yet when a wasp finds the correct species, it is the other way about. To identify the species the wasp apparently must explore the spider with her antennae. The tarantula shows an amazing tolerance to this exploration. The wasp crawls under it and walks over it without evoking any hostile response. The molestation is so great and so persistent that the tarantula often rises on all eight legs, as if it were on stilts. It may stand this way for several minutes. Meanwhile the wasp, having satisfied itself that the victim is of the right species, moves off a few inches to dig the spider's grave. Working vigorously with legs and jaws, it excavates a hole 8 to 10 inches deep with a diameter slightly larger than the spider's girth. Now and again the wasp pops out of the hole to make sure that the spider is still there.

When the grave is finished, the wasp returns to the tarantula to complete her ghastly enterprise. First she feels it all over once more with her antennae. Then her behavior becomes more aggressive. She bends her abdomen, protruding her sting, and searches for the soft membrane at the point where the spider's legs join its body—the only spot where she can penetrate the horny skeleton. From time to time, as the exasperated spider slowly shifts ground, the wasp turns on her back and slides along with the aid of her wings, trying to get under the tarantula for a shot at the vital spot. During all this maneuvering, which can last for several minutes, the tarantula makes no move to save itself. Finally the wasp corners it against some obstruction and grasps one of its legs in her powerful jaws. Now at last the harassed spider tries a desperate but vain defense. The two contestants roll over and over on the ground. It is a terrifying sight and the outcome is always the same. The wasp finally manages to thrust her sting into the soft spot and holds it there for a few seconds while she pumps in the poison. Almost immediately the tarantula falls paralyzed on its back. Its legs stop twitching; its heart stops beating. Yet it is not dead, as is shown by the fact that if taken from the wasp it can be restored to some sensitivity by being kept in a moist chamber for several months.

After paralyzing the tarantula, the wasp cleans herself by dragging her body along the ground and rubbing her feet, sucks the drop of blood oozing from the wound in the spider's abdomen, then grabs a leg of the flabby, helpless animal in her jaws and drags it down to the bottom of the grave. She stays there for many minutes, sometimes for several hours, and what she does all that time in the dark we do not know. Eventually she lays her egg and attaches it to the side of the spider's abdomen with a sticky secretion. Then she emerges, fills the grave with soil carried bit by bit in her jaws, and finally tramples the ground all around to hide any trace of the grave from prowlers. Then she flies away, leaving her descendant safely started in life.

In all this the behavior of the wasp evidently is qualitatively different from that of the spider. The wasp acts like an intelligent animal. This is not to say that instinct plays no part or that she reasons as man does. But her actions are to the point; they are not automatic and can be modified to fit the situation. We do not know for certain how she identifies the tarantula—probably it is by some olfactory or chemo-tactile sense—but she does it purposefully and does not blindly tackle a wrong species.

On the other hand, the tarantula's behavior shows only confusion. Evidently the wasp's pawing gives it no pleasure, for it tries to move away. That the wasp is not simulating sexual stimulation is certain because male and female tarantulas react in the same way to its advances. That the spider is not anesthetized by some odorless secretion is easily shown by blowing lightly at the tarantula and making it jump suddenly. What, then, makes the tarantula behave as stupidly as it does?

No clear, simple answer is available. Possibly the stimulation by the wasp's antennae is masked by a heavier pressure on the spider's body, so that it reacts as when prodded by a pencil. But the explanation may be much more complex. Initiative in attack is not in the nature of tarantulas; most species fight only when cornered so that escape is impossible. Their inherited patterns of behavior apparently prompt them to avoid problems rather than attack them. For example, spiders always weave their webs in three dimensions, and when a spider finds that there is insufficient space to attach certain threads in the third dimension, it leaves the place and seeks another, instead of finishing the web in a single plane. This urge to escape seems to arise under all circumstances, in all phases of life, and to take the place of reasoning. For a spider to change the pattern of its web is as impossible as for an inexperienced man to build a bridge across a chasm obstructing his way.

In a way the instinctive urge to escape is not only easier but often more efficient than reasoning. The tarantula does exactly what is most efficient in all cases except in an encounter with a ruthless and determined attacker dependent for the existence of her own species on killing as many tarantulas as she can lay eggs. Perhaps in this case the spider follows its usual pattern of trying to escape, instead of seizing and killing the wasp, because it is not aware of its danger. In any case, the survival of the tarantula species as a whole is protected by the fact that the spider is much more fertile than the wasp.

1952

THE READER

1. What are the major points of contrast between the spider and the wasp? Why does Petrunkevitch emphasize these particular points and neglect other possible differences?
2. Petrunkevitch suggests more than one hypothesis or possible explanation for the behavior of the tarantula, and he says that "no clear, simple answer is available." How does he test the possible explanations? Explain which one you think he prefers.
3. What evidence do you have that Petrunkevitch sees the tarantula and the wasp at least partly in human terms? Explain why you think this is or is not legitimate for a scientist.

THE WRITER

1. Petrunkevitch says that "insects and spiders exhibit some interesting analogies to reasoning and some crass examples of blind instinct." Why does he use the words "analogies" and "crass"?
2. Why is Petrunkevitch's initial description of the tarantula longer than his initial description of the wasp?
3. Petrunkevitch says that the wasp behaves "like an intelligent animal," while the spider behaves "stupidly" and "shows only confusion." Rewrite the tenth, eleventh, twelfth, and thirteenth paragraphs, reversing the characteristics of the two so that the spider acts intelligently and the wasp behaves stupidly. What other changes are necessary?

Stephen Jay Gould

OUR ALLOTTED LIFETIMES

Meeting with Henry Ford in E. L. Doctorow's *Ragtime*, J. P. Morgan praises the assembly line as a faithful translation of nature's wisdom:

> Has it occurred to you that your assembly line is not merely a stroke of industrial genius but a projection of organic truth? After all, the interchangeability of parts is a rule of nature. . . . All mammals reproduce in the same way and share the same designs of self-nourishment, with digestive and circulatory systems that are recognizably the same, and they enjoy the same senses. . . . Shared design is what allows taxonomists to classify mammals as mammals.

An imperious tycoon should not be met with equivocation; nonetheless, I can only reply "yes, and no" to Morgan's pronouncement. Morgan was wrong if he thought that large mammals are geometric replicas of small ones. Elephants have relatively smaller brains and thicker legs than mice, and these differences record a general rule of mammalian design, not the idiosyncracies of particular animals.

Morgan was right in arguing that large animals are essentially similar to small members of their group. The similarity, however, does not lie in a constant shape. The basic laws of geometry dictate that animals must change their shape in order to perform the same function at different sizes. I remind readers of the classical example, first discussed by Galileo in 1638: the strength of an animal's leg is a function of its cross-sectional area (length × length); the weight that the leg must support varies as the animal's volume (length × length × length). If a mammal did not alter the relative thickness of its legs as it got larger, it would soon collapse since body weight would increase much faster than the supporting strength of limbs. Instead, large mammals have relatively thicker leg bones than small mammals. To remain the same in function, animals must change their form.

The study of these changes in form is called "scaling theory." Scaling theory has uncovered a remarkable regularity of changing shape over the 25-millionfold range of mammalian weight from shrew to blue whale. If we plot brain weight versus body weight for all mammals on the so-called mouse-to-elephant (or shrew-to-whale) curve, very few species deviate far from a single line expressing the general rule: brain weight increases only two-thirds as fast as body weight as we move from small to large mammals. (We share with bottle-nosed dolphins the honor of greatest deviance from the curve.)

We can often predict these regularities from the physical behavior of objects. The heart, for example, is a pump. Since all mammalian hearts are similar in function, small hearts will pump considerably faster than large ones (imagine how much faster you could work a finger-sized toy bellows than the giant model that fuels a blacksmith's large forge). On the mouse-to-elephant curve for mammals, the length of a heartbeat increases between one-fourth and one-third as fast as body weight as we move from small to large mammals. The generality of this conclusion has just been affirmed in an interesting study by J. E. Carrel and R. D. Heathcote on the scaling of heart rate in spiders. They used a cool laser beam to illuminate the hearts of resting spiders and drew a crab spider-to-tarantula curve for eighteen species spanning nearly a thousandfold range of body weight. Again, scaling is very regular with heart rate increasing four-tenths as fast as body weight (or .409 times as fast, to be exact).

We may extend this conclusion for hearts to a very general statement about the pace of life in small versus large animals. Small animals tick through life far more rapidly than large ones—their hearts work more quickly, they breathe more frequently, their pulse beats much faster. Most importantly, metabolic rate, the so-called fire of life, scales only three-fourths as fast as body weight in mammals. Large mammals generate much less heat per unit of body weight to keep themselves going. Tiny shrews move frentically, eating nearly all their waking lives to keep their metabolic fire burning at its maximal rate among mammals; blue whales glide majestically, their hearts beating the slowest rhythm among active, warmblooded creatures.

If we consider the scaling of lifetime among mammals, an intriguing synthesis of these disparate data seems to suggest itself. We have all had enough experience with mammalian pets of various sizes to understand that small mammals tend to live for a shorter time than large ones. In fact, the scaling of mammalian lifetime follows a regular curve at about the same rate as heartbeat and breath time—between one-fourth and one-third as fast as body weight as we move from small to large animals. (Again, *Homo sapiens* emerges as a very peculiar animal. We live far longer than a mammal of our body size should. I have argued elsewhere that humans evolved by a process called "neoteny"—the retention of shapes and growth rates that characterize juvenile stages of our primate ancestors. I also believe that neoteny is responsible for our elevated longevity. Compared with other mammals, all stages of human life—from juvenile features to adulthood—arise "too late." We are born as helpless embryos after a long gestation; we mature late after an extended childhood; we die, if fortune be kind, at ages otherwise reached only by the very largest warmblooded creatures.)

Usually, we pity the pet mouse or gerbil that lived its full span of a year or two at most. How brief its life, while we endure for the better part of a century. As the main theme of this column, I want to argue that such pity is misplaced (our personal grief, of course, is quite another matter; with this, science does not deal). J. P. Morgan of *Ragtime* was right—small and large mammals are essentially similar. Their lifetimes are scaled to their life's pace, and all endure for approximately the same amount of biological time. Small mammals tick fast, burn rapidly, and live for a short time; large ones live long at a stately pace. Measured by their own internal clocks, mammals of different sizes tend to live for the same amount of time.

Yet we are prevented from grasping this important and comforting concept by a deeply ingrained habit of Western thought. We are trained from earliest memory to regard absolute Newtonian time as the single valid measuring stick in a rational and objective world. We impose our kitchen clock, ticking equably, upon all things. We marvel at the quickness of a mouse, express boredom at the torpor of a hippopotamus. Yet each is living at the appropriate pace of its own biological clock.

I do not wish to deny the importance of absolute, astronomical time to organisms. Animals must measure it to lead successful lives. Deer must know when to regrow their antlers, birds when to migrate. Animals track the day–night cycle with their circadian rhythms; jet lag is the price we pay for moving much faster than nature intended. Bamboos can somehow count 120 years before flowering again.

But absolute time is not the appropriate measuring stick for all biological phenomena. Consider the song of the humpback whale. These magnificent animals sing with such volume that their sounds travel through water for thousands of miles, perhaps even around the world, as their leading student Roger S. Payne has suggested. E. O. Wilson has described the awesome effect of these vocalizations: "The notes are eerie yet beautiful to the human ear. Deep basso groans and almost inaudibly high soprano squeaks alternate with repetitive squeals that suddenly rise or fall in pitch." We do not know the function of these songs. Perhaps they enable whales to find each other and to stay together during their annual transoceanic migrations.

Each whale has its own characteristic song; the highly complex patterns are repeated over and over again with great faithfulness. No scientific fact that I have learned in the last decade struck me with more force than Payne's report that the length of some songs may extend for more than half an hour. I have never been able to memorize the five-minute first Kyrie of the B-minor Mass[1] (and not for want of trying); how could a whale sing for thirty minutes and then repeat itself accurately? Of what possible use is a thirty-minute repeat cycle—far too long for a human to

1. By Johann Sebastian Bach; the movement is woven together from many independent musical lines.

recognize: we would never grasp it as a single song (without Payne's recording machinery and much study after the fact). But then I remembered the whale's metabolic rate, the enormously slow pace of its life compared with ours. What do we know about a whale's perception of thirty minutes? A humpback may scale the world to its own metabolic rate: its half-hour song may be our minute waltz.[2] From any point of view, the song is spectacular; it is the most elaborate single display so far discovered in any animal. I merely urge the whale's point of view as an appropriate perspective.

We can provide some numerical precision to support the claim that all mammals, on average, live for the same amount of biological time. In a method developed by W. R. Stahl, B. Gunther, and E. Guerra in the late 1950s and early 1960s, we search the mouse-to-elephant equations for biological properties that scale at the same rate against body weight. For example, Gunther and Guerra give the following equations for mammalian breath time and heartbeat time versus body weight.

$$\text{breath time} = .0000470 \ \text{body}^{0.28}$$
$$\text{heartbeat time} = .0000119 \ \text{body}^{0.28}$$

(Nonmathematical readers need not be overwhelmed by the formalism. The equations simply mean that both breath time and heartbeat time increase about .28 times as fast as body weight as we move from small to large mammals.) If we divide the two equations, body weight cancels out because it is raised to the same power.

$$\frac{\text{breath time}}{\text{heartbeat time}} = \frac{.0000470 \ \cancel{\text{body}^{0.28}}}{.0000119 \ \cancel{\text{body}^{0.28}}} = 4.0$$

This says that the ratio of breath time to heartbeat time is 4.0 in mammals of any body size. In other words, all mammals, whatever their size, breathe once for each four heartbeats. Small animals breathe and beat their hearts faster than large animals, but both breath and heart slow up at the same relative rate as mammals get larger.

Lifetime also scales at the same rate to body weight (.28 times as fast as we move from small to large mammals). This means that the ratio of both breath time and heartbeat time to lifetime is also constant over the whole range of mammalian size. When we perform an exercise similar to that above, we find that all mammals, regardless of their size, tend to breathe about 200 million times during their lives (their hearts, therefore, beat about 800 million times). Small mammals breathe fast, but live for a short time. Measured by the sensible internal clocks of their own hearts or the

2. The reference is to the "Minute Waltz," by Frédéric Chopin, which is not only brief but fast-moving.

rhythm of their own breathing, all mammals live about the same time. (Astute readers, having counted their breaths, may have calculated that they should have died long ago. But Homo sapiens is a markedly deviant mammal in more ways than braininess alone. We live about three times as long as mammals of our body size "should," but we breathe at the "right" rate and thus live to breathe about three times as much as an average mammal of our body size.)

The mayfly lives but a day as an adult. It may, for all I know, experience that day as we live a lifetime. Yet all is not relative in our world, and such a short glimpse of it must invite distortion in interpreting events ticking on longer scales. In a brilliant metaphor, the pre-Darwinian evolutionist Robert Chambers spoke of a mayfly watching the metamorphosis of a tadpole into a frog (from Vestiges of the Natural History of Creation, 1844):

> Suppose that an ephemeron [a mayfly], hovering over a pool for its one April day of life, were capable of observing the fry of the frog in the waters below. In its aged afternoon, having seen no change upon them for such a long time, it would be little qualified to conceive that the external branchiae [gills] of these creatures were to decay, and be replaced by internal lungs, that feet were to be developed, the tail erased, and the animal then to become a denizen of the land.

Human consciousness arose but a minute before midnight on the geologic clock. Yet we mayflies, ignorant perhaps of the messages buried in earth's long history, try to bend an ancient world to our purposes. Let us hope that we are still in the morning of our April day.

1977

Nigel Calder

HEADS AND TAILS

During the comet Halley's * * * visit to the sun in 1910, reputable observers said that it broke up. At the time this was widely believed to be true but, after the comet departed, calmer opinions prevailed and the reports were seen as the products of imagination working on certain jets and streamers visible in the comet's head. Like the planet Vulcan, it was an example of people seeing what they expected to see: there would have been no such suggestion a hundred years earlier.

An amiable mathematician told me how he once thought Saturday was Sunday. All the evidence of Saturday bustle around him failed to shake his conviction and he rebuked an astonished newspaper-seller for fobbing people off with yesterday's papers. Only in the evening, when he went to deliver a society lecture and found no one there, did the truth begin to dawn. Again, the annals of war are full of instances of troops, ships and aircraft being misidentified and efficiently destroyed by "friendly" forces. Christopher Columbus's belief was that he had sailed west to Asia and we all connive in it to this day by calling the American natives "Indians." And there is no reason to doubt the sincerity of those who spot flying saucers.

A rich vein of experimental psychology was opened in the late 1940s when Jerome Bruner of Harvard began researching into influences on human perception. In a series of classic experiments with Cecile Goodman and Leo Postman, he showed (1) that valuable coins look larger than they really are, (2) that emotionally loaded words like "crime" and "bitch" are harder to read than bland words, and (3) that when people are shown a false playing card, say a red six of clubs, they are likely to report it as a six of hearts. In this playing-card experiment a person may hesitate uneasily for quite a while before he sees the deception and typically exclaims, "My God!" The historian of science Thomas Kuhn has drawn the parallel between this experiment and the reluctant shifts of ideas in science.

Expect strange sights in the sky and you are liable to see them. A medical student, Ambroise Paré, wins pride of place in the chronicles of wishful seeing for his observations of the comet of 1528. He was an able young man who went on to be a surgeon to four kings of France and invented, among other practical novelties, ligatures for stopping arterial bleeding. Yet in all honesty he described the comet as being bloody in color, which is plausible, but also stocked with weapons and arrayed with hideous human heads, which seems unlikely.

A malodorous comet demonstrates even better how ideas influence perceptions. Medieval scholars in Europe, who deferred to ancient wisdom and considered that comets inhabited the upper atmosphere of the Earth, also suspected them of being Devil's work. So it is not altogether surprising to learn that certain medieval monks swore they smelled a comet, or that the odor was of suitably devilish sulphurous gas. This report of halleytosis won approval in a book already mentioned, *Cometomantia* of 1684, which used it as evidence against those over-zealous astronomers who wanted to displace all comets into deep space, far beyond the orbit of the Moon.

In the matter of the break-up of comets, the first psychological effect to manifest itself was blindness of the kind that prevented the Europeans seeing "new" stars: it was followed by the eager supersight which affords a grand view of invisible objects and processes. An historian of ancient Greece, Ephorus by name, reported that in 371 B.C. a comet broke into pieces; and he was reviled by Nero's tutor, Lucius Seneca, as an irresponsible gossip. Even though Johann Kepler had also said that comets could break up, by the nineteenth century the possibility was either forgotten or regarded as a grotesque fiction. Multiple tails of comets were seen often enough but multiple heads were unthinkable.

When, in the winter of 1845-6, a comet called *Biela* became oddly pear-shaped and then divided into two distinct comets, one of the astronomers who observed them, James Challis of Cambridge, averted his gaze. A week later he took another peep and *Biela* was still flaunting its rude duality. He had never heard of such a thing and for several more days the cautious Challis hesitated before he announced it to his astronomical colleagues. Meanwhile American astronomers in Washington D.C. and New Haven, equally surprised but possibly more confident in their own sobriety, had already staked their claim to the discovery. Challis excused his slowness in reporting the event by saying that he was busy looking for the new planet beyond Uranus. When later in the same year he was needlessly beaten to the discovery of that planet (Neptune) by German astronomers, Challis explained that he had been preoccupied with his work on comets.

After *Biela*'s fission similar sights became commonplace, not because nature embarked on a frenzy of comet smashing but because astronomers' visual neurones were at last prepared to register such events. In fact, splitting comets became the popular thing to see, whether or not they really happened. For example, the great comet *Donati* (1858) was reported as coming to pieces but it almost certainly did not do so. And inevitably the most famous comet, *Halley*, was supposed to conform with the latest fashion in 1910, and to fall apart. A considered, and one might say considerate, view of those reports is that *Halley* was on the verge of disruption in 1910, but survived intact.

On the other hand, several other comets certainly have split since *Biela*, some of them being well documented in photographs. Zdenek Sekanina, a Czechoslovak-born astronomer in Cometsville, has put the stamp of certified break-up on *Sawerthal* (1888), *Campbell* (1914), *Whipple-Fedtke-Tevzadze* (1943), *Honda* (1955) and *Tago-Sato-Kosaka* (1969). The ones with cumbersome names deserve to split up, but that cannot be said for *West* (1976). This was the great comet that the public did not see, because news editors, feeling foolish after they promoted *Kohoutek* of 1973 as the spectacle of the century, virtually banned any mention of comets from their papers and television screens. The head of *West* divided itself into four pieces and in the process threw out streamers of dust every two or three days, which gave the comet a fanned, peacock-like tail. Paolo Toscanelli described *Halley* in those terms, in 1456, but any inference would be rash.

In the twelfth century, by Brian Marsden's retrospective calculations, a comet passed extremely close to the Sun and broke up into at least two pieces. (It may have been a conspicuous comet of A.D. 1106.) One of the pieces came back in 1882 as the "Great September Comet" and again grazed the Sun; another, on an almost indistinguishable orbit, appeared in 1965 as the comet *Ikeya-Seki*. There is in fact a group of "sungrazers," sharing very similar orbits, and they have been spawned over many centuries by successive break-ups, from a single parent comet. The "Great March Comet" of 1843 was one of them, and so were at least seven since then. *Pereyra* of 1963 passed within a mere 60,000 kilometers of the bright solar surface, while the "Great Southern Comet" of 1887 may have collided with the Sun.

The visual system is adept at filling in details in a cartoon, seeing the Man in the Moon and generally perceiving unreal patterns. The ink-blot tests with which psychologists used to plague people are a case in point; another is the interpretation of comet haloes and streamers as bleeding heads or splitting heads. The most celebrated discovery in the history of astronomy was the Canals of Mars. In 1877 Giovanni Schiaparelli of Milan reported that he could see channels crossing the face of that planet and by the end of the century Percival Lowell, founder of a famous observatory at Flagstaff, Arizona, had mapped an intricate network of dozens of canals.

The martians' planet-wide irrigation system was, for Lowell, the dismaying sign of an advanced civilization fighting the growing aridity of the planet. The American comet hunter, Edward Barnard, wittily disposed of the fiction: he operated what was, at the time, the most advanced telescope in the world, and he said that it was too powerful to show the Canals of Mars. Yet (there is always a "yet" in science) the ghosts of Schiaparelli and Lowell can have one last snigger. In 1971 a spacecraft sent back pictures of Mars showing huge valleys, including a natural rift eighty kilometers wide and five thousand kilometers long—one of the features mapped by the "canal" enthusiasts. Of the martian civilization there was of course no sign, but the channels were not all imaginary. And there were also immense volcanoes on Mars: the jesting Barnard had seen them himself, but did not dare mention them for fear of ridicule.

Some illusions are deep-seated in the machinery of our brains, which compel us, for instance, to interpret the sky as a flattened dome so that the Moon and the comets always look much bigger on the horizon than when they are overhead. Telescopes, too, can deceive and many an eager amateur mistakes a stray reflection in his instrument for a new-found comet. An observatory in tsarist Russia had a telescope that was well adapted to the discovery of companions of the stars, because a flaw in the glass made it see everything double. But when misperceptions and misconceptions ferment together the results can be more vivid than that.

The discoveries of Isaac Newton and Edmond Halley did not at once

dispose of devilish connotations of comets. On the contrary, the realization that comets move in great ellipses around the Sun helped to modern-
ize the notions of Hell. What better punishment for sinners than to be
condemned to ride on a comet for ever and experience a fearful alternation of freezing in the outer darkness and roasting when the comet
brushed past the Sun? The cheerful idea that the comet of 44 B.C. was
Caesar on his way to Heaven was thus revised to stock comets with the
souls of the damned, not on their way but there already, in a brand-new,
eighteenth-century, whirly version of Hell.

Astronomers had more sense than that. They knew that comets were
free-ranging lumps of light that were necessary to sustain all living folk,
like those who made their home on the Sun. Nowadays the bad habit of
attending to only those past ideas that pointed more or less directly
towards modern scientific theories is being corrected by historians of
science, and from these professional investigators of theories long since
dead we learn what creative errors surrounded the attempts to explain
the illuminations of the sky, two to three centuries ago. By then the
misunderstandings about light were no longer quite as bizarre as the
ancient proposition that eyes acted like lasers and looked around by
sending out beams, as in the "darting glances" favored by some novelists.
But there was a persistent confusion between light and its sources. Most
of us nowadays can distinguish a lamp from the dust of photons that it
throws in our eyes. Our predecessors, though, were infected with the old
concept of "fire" as an element in its own right, and in any case, not
knowing about plasmas heated by nuclear reactions, they found the light
of the Sun and the stars mysterious.

Even Newton, who founded the modern science of light in his spare
time and certainly knew the difference between rays and sources, was at a
loss to say how the Sun could burn undiminished for thousands of years
(billions of years, as we now know). The comets came like cosmic cavalry
to the rescue: Newton said that God arranged for the Sun to be reinforced
by comets that fell into it as a result of fatal changes in their orbits. Here
too, he thought, was an explanation for the new star seen by Tycho Brahe
in 1572. Astrophysicists today would say it was a natural H-bomb going
off, in the destructive explosion of a giant star; for Newton it was a star
that suddenly acquired new splendor thanks to a goodly stoking of comet-
fuel.

Newton was no Newtonian, in the austere nineteenth-century sense of
one content to contemplate the celestial clockwork. The taming of imagination by algebra dates not from the Principia of 1687 but from Karl
Friedrich Gauss's Theoria Motus Corporum of 1809. In the intervening
century astronomers, clergymen and laymen continued to regard comets
as manifestations of divine purpose. Taking their cue from Newton, they
wondered about the light of comets and about their life-giving proper-

ties, whether in watering the Earth or conveying some vital principle that might breathe life into all the orbs of the sky. Such ideas foreshadowed a twentieth-century proposition that the Earth might have been seeded with the first bacteria by a comet's tail * * *.

The cheekiest of all ideas about the cosmos was William Herschel's belief that the nearest star was peopled: " . . . we need not hesitate to admit that the Sun is richly stored with inhabitants." Herschel flourished a hundred years after Newton and his name is one of the most celebrated in the history of astronomy. He was a Hanoverian musician living at Bath in England, and was catapulted to fame when his telescope revealed the large planet Uranus, the first major piece of the Solar System to be noticed since prehistoric times. Many astronomers had already seen the planet but mistook it for a star. In the post-Halley era Herschel naturally announced his discovery as a new comet, and it fell to others to infer that it was a planet lying far beyond Saturn and a hundred times larger than the Earth.

Concerning comet light and its contribution to the habitability of the Sun, Herschel pictured alien creatures going about their business on the solid surface of the Sun which underlay an atmosphere of light that was replenished, as Newton had said, by an influx of comets. Cosmic light was thus a special kind of life-giving stuff that nature could manipulate, in this case into a shell around the sun that illuminated the solar surface as well as the Solar System. Even in Herschel's day, to say that the Sun was cool could earn you a certificate of insanity, but he supposed that the solar rays generated heat only when absorbed in a suitable medium, such as the Earth's atmosphere. And he offered visible evidence in support of the proposition: what were the familiar dark sunspots but chinks in the light offering glimpses of a cooler surface below? Present-day reckonings of the internal temperature of the Sun guarantee that any inhabitants of that world must be, to say the least, jumping like fleas on a hotplate, and sunspots are known to be magnetic storms.

Yet the adherents of these ideas about light are entitled to more than a posthumous chuckle, because their line of reasoning led them to conclusions that the latest astrophysics regards as sensationally correct. The marshaling of the supposed light-stuff around the heavy Sun indicated to eighteenth-century astronomers that light was subject to the action of gravity. The luminiferous comets, moving in obedience to Newton's law, provided equally graphic proof. But the ability of gravity to bend light and slow it down was to be the basis of General Relativity. Albert Einstein arrived at it armed with less devious notions about the nature of light, and the anticipation might be dismissed as a chance intersection of two very different lines of thought, had it not also led to General Relativity's most breathtaking deduction. The eighteenth-century theory of light predicted black holes.

The man to say so first was a clergyman at Thornhill near Leeds: John Michell. At Cambridge he had initiated the modern study of magnetism and of earthquakes; he also identified the double stars and gave Herschel a correspondence course in telescope-making. Michell set down the idea of an invisible star in a paper that was published in 1784 and resurrected in 1979 by Simon Schaffer, an historian at Cambridge. The original black hole arose in Michell's mind from the thought that a large and massive star would, by its powerful gravity, slow down the light that it emitted. In the extreme case a star could choke off its light entirely, and Michell calculated that a star with five hundred times the Sun's diameter, and the same density, would be invisible. The French theorist Pierre-Simon de Laplace arrived at the same idea in 1796 (and has often been credited with originating it) but he reckoned the size of the black-hole star at half the diameter given by Michell. General Relativity agrees with Michell: the Rector of Thornhill turns out to have been more accurate as well as earlier than the great Laplace.

Astronomy is thus a four-legged animal standing on sound and false ideas at the front and false observations at the rear. Amazingly the beast can limp forward, sometimes even gallop, from one discovery to the next. And lurching on its way to valuable information about the nature and history of the universe it has in passing exposed the character of those ephemera, the tails of comets.

1980

Arthur Koestler

GRAVITY AND THE HOLY GHOST

"If I have been able to see farther than others," said Newton, "it was because I stood on the shoulders of giants." One of the giants was Johannes Kepler (1571–1630) whose three laws of planetary motion provided the foundation on which the Newtonian universe was built. They were the first "natural laws" in the modern sense: precise, verifiable statements expressed in mathematical terms; at the same time, they represent the first attempt at a synthesis of astronomy and physics which, during the preceding two thousand years, had developed on separate lines.

Astronomy before Kepler had been a purely descriptive geometry of the skies. The motion of stars and planets had been represented by the device of epicycles and eccentrics—an imaginary clockwork of circles turning on circles turning on circles. Copernicus, for instance, had used forty-eight wheels to represent the motion of the five known planets around the sun. These wheels were purely fictitious, and meant as such—they enabled astronomers to make more or less precise predictions, but, above all, they satisfied the dogma that all heavenly motion must be uniform and in perfect circles. Though the planets moved neither uniformly nor in perfect circles, the imaginary cogwheels did, and thereby "saved the appearances."

Kepler's discoveries put an end to this state of affairs. He reconciled astronomy with physics, and substituted for the fictitious clockwork a universe of material bodies not unlike the earth, freely floating and turning in space, moved by forces acting on them. His most important book bears the provocative title: *A New Astronomy Based on Causation, or Physics of the Sky* (1609). It contains the first and second of Kepler's three laws. The first says that the planets move around the sun not in circles but in elliptic orbits; the second says that a planet moves in its orbit not at uniform speed but at a speed that varies according to its position, and is defined by a simple and beautiful law: the line connecting planet and sun sweeps over equal areas in equal times. The third law establishes an equally elegant mathematical correlation between the length of a planet's year and its mean distance from the sun.

Kepler did not start his career as an astronomer, but as a student of theology (at the Lutheran University of Thuebingen); yet already as a student he was attracted by the Copernican idea of a sun-centered universe. Now Canon Copernicus's book, *On the Revolutions of the Heavenly Spheres*, had been published in the year of his death, 1543; that is, fifty years before Kepler first heard of him; and during that half century it had attracted very little attention. One of the reasons was its supreme unreadability, which made it into an all-time worst-seller: its first edition of a thousand copies was never sold out. Kepler was the first Continental astronomer to embrace the Copernican theory. His *Mysterium Cosmographicum*, published in 1597 (fifty-four years after Copernicus's death) started the great controversy—Galileo entered the scene fifteen years later.

The reason why the idea of a sun-centered universe appealed to Kepler was repeatedly stated by himself: "I often defended the opinions of Copernicus in the disputations of the candidates and I composed a careful disputation on the first motion which consists in the rotation of the earth; then I was adding to this the motion of the earth around the sun *for physical or, if you prefer, metaphysical reasons.*" I have emphasized the last words because they contain the leitmotif of Kepler's quest, and because he used the same expression in various passages in his works. Now what were those "physical or, if you prefer, metaphysical reasons" which made Kepler prefer to put the sun into the center of the universe instead of the earth?

> My ceaseless search concerned primarily three problems, namely, the number, size, and motion of the planets—why they are just as they are and not otherwise arranged. I was encouraged in my daring inquiry by that beautiful analogy between the stationary objects, namely, the sun, the fixed stars, and the space between them, with God the Father, the Son, and the Holy Ghost. I shall pursue this analogy in my future cosmographical work.

Twenty-five years later, when he was over fifty, Kepler repeated his credo: "It is by no means permissible to treat this analogy as an empty comparison; it must be considered by its Platonic form and archetypal quality as one of the primary causes."

He believed in this to the end of his life. Yet gradually the analogy underwent a significant change:

> The sun in the middle of the *moving* stars, himself at rest and yet the source of motion, carries the image of God the Father and Creator. He distributes his motive force through a medium which contains the moving bodies, even as the Father creates through the Holy Ghost.

Thus the "moving bodies"—that is, the planets—are now brought into the analogy. The Holy Ghost no longer merely fills the space between the motionless sun and the motionless fixed stars. It has become an active force, a *vis motrix*, which *drives* the planets. Nobody before Kepler had postulated, or even suspected, the existence of a physical force acting between the sun and the planets. Astronomy was not concerned with physical forces, nor with the causes of the heavenly motions, merely with their description. The passages which I have just quoted are the first intimation of the forthcoming marriage between physics and astronomy—the act of betrothal, as it were. By looking at the sky, not through the eyes of the geometrician only, but of the physicist concerned with natural causes, he hit upon a question which nobody had asked before. The question was: "Why do the planets closer to the sun move faster than those which are far away? What is the mathematical relation between a planet's distance from the sun and the length of its year?"

These questions could only occur to one who had conceived the revolutionary hypothesis that the motion of the planet—and therefore its velocity and the duration of its year—was governed by a physical force emanating from the sun. Every astronomer knew, of course, that the greater their distance from the sun the slower the planets moved. But this phenomenon was taken for granted, just as it was taken for granted that boys will be boys and girls will be girls, as an irreducible fact of creation. Nobody asked the cause of it because physical causes were not assumed to enter into the motion of heavenly bodies. The greatness of the philosophers of the scientific revolution consisted not so much in finding the right answers but in asking the right questions; in seeing a problem where nobody saw one before; in substituting a "why" for a "how."

Kepler's answer to the question why the outer planets move slower than the inner ones, and how the speed of their motion is related to their distance from the sun, was as follows:

> There exists only one moving soul in the center of all the orbits that is the sun which drives the planets the more vigorously the closer the planet is, but whose force is quasi-exhausted when acting on the outer planets because of the long distance and the weakening of the force which it entails.

Later on he commented: "If we substitute for the word 'soul' the word 'force,' then we get just the principle which underlies my 'Physics of the Skies.' As I reflected that this cause of motion *diminishes in proportion to distance* just as the light of the sun diminishes in proportion to distance from the sun, I came to the conclusion that this force must be substantial —'substantial' not in the literal sense but . . . in the same manner as we say that light is something substantial, meaning by this an unsubstantial entity emanating from a substantial body."

We notice that Kepler's answer came *before* the question—that it was the answer that begot the question. The answer, the starting point, was the analogy between God the Father and the sun—the former acting through the Holy Ghost, the latter through a physical force. The planets must obey the law of the sun—the law of God—the mathematical law of nature; and the Holy Ghost's action through empty space diminishes, as the light emanating from the sun does, with distance. The degenerate, purely descriptive astronomy which originated in the period of the Greek decline, and continued through the Dark and Middle Ages until Kepler, did not ask for meaning and causes. But Kepler was convinced that physical causes operate between heavenly, just as between earthly, bodies, and more specifically that the sun exerts a physical force on the planets. It was this conviction which enabled him to formulate his laws. Physics became the auxiliary matrix which secured his escape from the blocked situation into which astronomy had maneuvered itself.

The blockage—to cut a very long story short—was due to the fact that Tycho de Brahe[1] had improved the instruments and methods of stargazing, and produced observational data of a hitherto unequaled abundance and precision; and the new data did not fit into the traditional schemes. Kepler, who served his apprenticeship under Tycho, was given the task of working out the orbit of Mars. He spent six years on the task and covered nine thousand foliosheets with calculations in his small handwriting without getting anywhere. When at last he believed he had succeeded he found to his dismay that certain observed positions of Mars differed from those which his theory demanded by magnitudes up to eight minutes arc. Eight minutes arc is approximately one-quarter of the apparent diameter of the moon.

1. Danish astronomer (1546–1601).

This was a catastrophe. Ptolemy, and even Copernicus, could afford to neglect a difference of eight minutes, because their observations were accurate only within a margin of ten minutes, anyway. "But," Kepler wrote in the New Astronomy, "but for us, who by divine kindness were given an accurate observer such as Tycho Brahe, for us it is fitting that we should acknowledge this divine gift and put it to use.... Henceforth I shall lead the way toward that goal according to my ideas. For if I had believed that we could ignore these eight minutes, I would have patched up by hypothesis accordingly. But since it was not permissible to ignore them, those eight minutes point the road to a complete reformation of astronomy...."

Thus a theory, built on years of labor and torment, was instantly thrown away because of a discord of eight miserable minutes arc. Instead of cursing those eight minutes as a stumbling block, he transformed them into the cornerstone of a new science. For those eight minutes arc had at last made him realize that the field of astronomy in its traditional framework was well and truly blocked.

One of the recurrent frustrations and tragedies in the history of thought is caused by the uncertainty whether it is possible to solve a given problem by traditional methods previously applied to problems which seem to be of the same nature. Who can say how many lives were wasted and good minds destroyed in futile attempts to square the circle, or to construct a *perpetuum mobile?*[2] The proof that these problems are *insoluble* was in each case an original discovery in itself (such as Maxwell's second law of thermodynamics);[3] and such proofs could only be found by looking at the problem from a point of view outside its traditional matrix. On the other hand, the mere knowledge that a problem is soluble means that half the game is already won.

The episode of the eight minutes arc had convinced Kepler that his problem—the orbit of Mars—was insoluble so long as he felt bound by the traditional rules of sky-geometry. Implied in those rules was the dogma of "uniform motion in perfect circles." *Uniform* motion he had already discarded before the crisis; now he felt that the even more sacred one of *circular* motion must also go. The impossibility of constructing a circular orbit which would satisfy all existing observations suggested to him that the circle must be replaced by some other curve.

> The conclusion is quite simply that the planet's path is not a circle—it curves inward on both sides and outward again at opposite ends. Such a curve is called an oval. The orbit is not a circle but an oval figure.

2. A hypothetical machine which, once set in motion, would continue in motion forever unless stopped by some external force or by its own the wearing out.

3. The second law of thermodynamics, put forward not by James Clerk Maxwell, but by Rudolf Julius Emmanuel Clausius (1822–1888), provides an explanation of why a perpetual-motion machine cannot exist.

This oval orbit was a wild, frightening new departure for him. To be fed up with cycles and epicycles, to mock the slavish imitators of Aristotle was one thing; to assign an entirely new, lopsided, implausible path for the heavenly bodies was quite another. Why indeed an oval? There is something in the perfect symmetry of spheres and circles which has a deep, reassuring appeal to the unconscious mind—otherwise it could not have survived two millennia. The oval lacks that archetypal appeal. It has an arbitrary, distorted form. It destroyed the dream of the "harmony of the spheres," which lay at the origin of the whole quest. At times he felt like a criminal, or worse: a fool. All he had to say in his own defense was: "I have cleared the Augean stables of astronomy of cycles and spirals, and left behind me only a single cartful of dung."

That cartful of dung—nonuniform motion in noncircular orbits— could only be justified and explained by arguments derived not from geometry, but from physics. A phrase kept humming in his ear like a catchy tune, and crops up in his writings over and again: there is a force in the sun which moves the planets, there is a force in the sun. . . . And since there is a force in the sun, there must exist some simple relationship between the planet's distance from the sun, and its speed. A light shines the brighter the nearer one is to its source, and the same must apply to the force of the sun: the closer the planet to it, the quicker it will move. This had been his instinctive conviction; but now he thought that he had found the proof of it. "Ye physicists, prick your ears, for now we are going to invade your territory." The next six chapters in the *Astronomia Nova* are a report on that invasion into celestial physics, which had been out of bounds for astronomy since Plato. He had found the second matrix which would unblock his problem.

That excursion was something of a comedy of errors—which nevertheless ended with finding the truth. Since he had no notion of the principle of inertia, which makes a planet persist in its tangential motion under its own momentum, and had only a vague intuition of gravity, he had to invent a force which, emanating from the sun, sweeps the planet round its path like a broom. In the second place, to account for the eccentricity of the orbits he had to postulate that the planets were "huge round magnets" whose poles pointed always in the same direction so that they would alternately be drawn closer to and be repelled by the sun. But although today the whole thing seems cockeyed, his intuition that there are *two antagonistic forces* acting on the planets, guided him in the right direction. A single force, as previously assumed—the divine Prime Mover and its allied hierarchy of angels—would never produce elliptic orbits and periodic changes of speed. These could only be the result of some dynamic tug of war going on in the sky—as indeed there is. The concept of two antagonistic forces provided rules for a new game in which elliptic orbits and velocities depending on solar distance have their legitimate place.

He made many mistakes during that wild flight of thought; but "as if by miracle"—as he himself remarked—the mistakes canceled out. It looks as if at times his conscious critical faculties had been anesthetized by the creative impulse, by the impatience to get to grips with the physical forces in the solar system. The problem of the planetary orbits had been hopelessly bogged down in its purely geometrical frame of reference, and when he realized that he could not get it unstuck he tore it out of that frame and removed it into the field of physics. That there were inconsistencies and impurities in his method did not matter to him in the heat of the moment, hoping that somehow they would right themselves later on —as they did. This inspired cheating—or, rather, borrowing on credit— is a characteristic and recurrent feature in the history of science. The latest example is subatomic physics, which may be said to live on credit —in the pious hope that one day its inner contradictions and paradoxes will somehow resolve themselves.

Kepler's determination of the orbit of Mars became the unifying link between the two formerly separate realms of physics and astronomy. His was the first serious attempt at explaining the mechanism of the solar system in terms of physical forces; and once the example was set, physics and cosmology could never again be divorced.

1964

THE READER

1. Why, according to Koestler, was it so difficult for Kepler to discard the notion of circular movement for the heavenly bodies, and why was it difficult to conceive of physical forces acting between the heavenly bodies? Are there any ideas in your own way of thinking that might be similarly difficult to discard or to accept? Perhaps Bronowski's "The Reach of Imagination" (p. 194) and "The Nature of Scientific Reasoning" (p. 927) may help you in thinking or writing about these questions.

2. What was the role of Tycho Brahe's observations, fact finding, and data gathering in the formulation of Kepler's thought? Did the facts speak for themselves and make a true conception of the solar system evident at once? Explain the reasons for your answer.

3. On p. 924, Koestler says of Kepler, "Instead of cursing those eight minutes as a stumbling block, he transformed them into the cornerstone of a new science." What does this statement mean? Is a difference of such small scale between theory and observation necessarily significant in itself? If so, of what? Do you know of similar differences between expectation and actual behavior in your own personal relationships? How have you handled such discrepancies?

THE WRITER

1. What effect is produced by the essay's title, "Gravity and the Holy

Ghost"? What relationship between the two terms in the title does the essay explore? Which of the two terms is more familiar to you? Which do you think you know more about? Write an account of your understanding of them.

2. *Koestler says that "the greatness of the philosophers of the scientific revolution consisted not so much in finding the right answers but in asking the right questions." On the basis of your reading of "Humanities and Science" (p. 253), do you think Thomas would agree or disagree? Put your answer in the form of a brief essay.*

Jacob Bronowski

THE NATURE OF SCIENTIFIC REASONING

What is the insight in which the scientist tries to see into nature? Can it indeed be called either imaginative or creative? To the literary man the question may seem merely silly. He has been taught that science is a large collection of facts; and if this is true, then the only seeing which scientists need to do is, he supposes, seeing the facts. He pictures them, the colorless professionals of science, going off to work in the morning into the universe in a neutral, unexposed state. They then expose themselves like a photographic plate. And then in the darkroom or laboratory they develop the image, so that suddenly and startlingly it appears, printed in capital letters, as a new formula for atomic energy.

Men who have read Balzac and Zola[1] are not deceived by the claims of these writers that they do no more than record the facts. The readers of Christopher Isherwood[2] do not take him literally when he writes "I am a camera." Yet the same readers solemnly carry with them from their schooldays this foolish picture of the scientist fixing by some mechanical process the facts of nature. I have had of all people a historian tell me that science is a collection of facts, and his voice had not even the ironic rasp of one filing cabinet reproving another.

It seems impossible that this historian had ever studied the beginnings of a scientific discovery. The Scientific Revolution can be held to begin in the year 1543 when there was brought to Copernicus, perhaps on his deathbed, the first printed copy of the book he had finished about a dozen years earlier. The thesis of this book is that the earth moves around the sun. When did Copernicus go out and record this fact with his camera? What appearance in nature prompted his outrageous guess? And in what

---

1. Honoré de Balzac and Émile Zola, nine-   2. Modern English novelist and playwright.
teenth-century French novelists.

odd sense is this guess to be called a neutral record of fact?

Less than a hundred years after Copernicus, Kepler published (between 1609 and 1619) the three laws which describe the paths of the planets. The work of Newton and with it most of our mechanics spring from these laws. They have a solid, matter-of-fact sound. For example, Kepler says that if one squares the year of a planet, one gets a number which is proportional to the cube of its average distance from the sun. Does anyone think that such a law is found by taking enough readings and then squaring and cubing everything in sight? If he does, then, as a scientist, he is doomed to a wasted life; he has as little prospect of making a scientific discovery as an electronic brain has.

It was not this way that Copernicus and Kepler thought, or that scientists think today. Copernicus found that the orbits of the planets would look simpler if they were looked at from the sun and not from the earth. But he did not in the first place find this by routine calculation. His first step was a leap of imagination—to lift himself from the earth, and put himself wildly, speculatively into the sun. "The earth conceives from the sun," he wrote; and "the sun rules the family of stars." We catch in his mind an image, the gesture of the virile man standing in the sun, with arms outstretched, overlooking the planets. Perhaps Copernicus took the picture from the drawings of the youth with outstretched arms which the Renaissance teachers put into their books on the proportions of the body. Perhaps he had seen Leonardo's drawings of his loved pupil Salai. I do not know. To me, the gesture of Copernicus, the shining youth looking outward from the sun, is still vivid in a drawing which William Blake in 1780 based on all these: the drawing which is usually called *Glad Day*.

Kepler's mind, we know, was filled with just such fanciful analogies; and we know what they were. Kepler wanted to relate the speeds of the planets to the musical intervals. He tried to fit the five regular solids into their orbits. None of these likenesses worked, and they have been forgotten; yet they have been and they remain the stepping stones of every creative mind. Kepler felt for his laws by way of metaphors, he searched mystically for likenesses with what he knew in every strange corner of nature. And when among these guesses he hit upon his laws, he did not think of their numbers as the balancing of a cosmic bank account, but as a revelation of the unity in all nature. To us, the analogies by which Kepler listened for the movement of the planets in the music of the spheres are farfetched. Yet are they more so than the wild leap by which Rutherford and Bohr in our own century found a model for the atom in, of all places, the planetary system?

No scientific theory is a collection of facts. It will not even do to call a theory true or false in the simple sense in which every fact is either so or not so. The Epicureans held that matter is made of atoms two thousand years ago and we are now tempted to say that their theory was true. But if we do so we confuse their notion of matter with our own. John Dalton in 1808 first saw the structure of matter as we do today, and what he took from the ancients was not their theory but something richer, their image: the atom. Much of what was in Dalton's mind was as vague as the Greek notion, and quite as mistaken. But he suddenly gave life to the new facts of chemistry and the ancient theory together, by fusing them to give what neither had: a coherent picture of how matter is linked and built up from different kinds of atoms. The act of fusion is the creative act.

All science is the search for unity in hidden likenesses. The search may be on a grand scale, as in the modern theories which try to link the fields of gravitation and electromagnetism. But we do not need to be browbeaten by the scale of science. There are discoveries to be made by snatching a small likeness from the air too, if it is bold enough. In 1935 the Japanese physicist Hideki Yukawa wrote a paper which can still give heart to a young scientist. He took as his starting point the known fact that waves of light can sometimes behave as if they were separate pellets. From this he reasoned that the forces which hold the nucleus of an atom together might sometimes also be observed as if they were solid pellets. A schoolboy can see how thin Yukawa's analogy is, and his teacher would be severe with it. Yet Yukawa without a blush calculated the mass of the pellet he expected to see, and waited. He was right; his meson was found, and a range of other mesons, neither the existence nor the nature of which had been suspected before. The likeness had borne fruit.

The scientist looks for order in the appearances of nature by exploring such likenesses. For order does not display itself of itself; if it can be said to be there at all, it is not there for the mere looking. There is no way of pointing a finger or camera at it; order must be discovered and, in a deep sense, it must be created. What we see, as we seen it, is mere disorder.

This point has been put trenchantly in a fable by Karl Popper. Suppose that someone wished to give his whole life to science. Suppose that he therefore sat down, pencil in hand, and for the next twenty, thirty, forty years recorded in notebook after notebook everything that he could observe. He may be supposed to leave out nothing: today's humidity, the racing results, the level of cosmic radiation and the stockmarket prices and the look of Mars, all would be there. He would have compiled the most careful record of nature that has ever been made; and, dying in the calm certainty of a life well spent, he would of course leave his notebooks to the Royal Society. Would the Royal Society thank him for the treasure of a lifetime of observation? It would not. The Royal Society would treat his notebooks exactly as the English bishops have treated Joanna Southcott's box.[3] It would refuse to open them at all, because it would

3. Joanna Southcott was a nineteenth-century English farm servant who claimed to be a prophetess. She left behind a box which was to be opened in a time of national emer-

know without looking that the notebooks contain only a jumble of disorderly and meaningless items.

Science finds order and meaning in our experience, and sets about this in quite a different way. It sets about it as Newton did in the story which he himself told in his old age, and of which the schoolbooks give only a caricature. In the year 1665, when Newton was twenty-two, the plague broke out in southern England, and the University of Cambridge was closed. Newton therefore spent the next eighteen months at home, removed from traditional learning, at a time when he was impatient for knowledge and, in his own phrase, "I was in the prime of my age for invention." In this eager, boyish mood, sitting one day in the garden of his widowed mother, he saw an apple fall. So far the books have the story right; we think we even know the kind of apple; tradition has it that it was a Flower of Kent. But now they miss the crux of the story. For what struck the young Newton at the sight was not the thought that the apple must be drawn to the earth by gravity; that conception was older than Newton. What struck him was the conjecture that the same force of gravity, which reaches to the top of the tree, might go on reaching out beyond the earth and its air, endlessly into space. Gravity might reach the moon: this was Newton's new thought; and it might be gravity which holds the moon in her orbit. There and then he calculated what force from the earth (falling off as the square of the distance) would hold the moon, and compared it with the known force of gravity at tree height. The forces agreed; Newton says laconically, "I found them answer pretty nearly." Yet they agreed only nearly: the likeness and the approximation go together, for no likeness is exact. In Newton's science modern science is full grown.

It grows from a comparison. It has seized a likeness between two unlike appearances; for the apple in the summer garden and the grave moon overhead are surely as unlike in their movements as two things can be. Newton traced in them two expressions of a single concept, gravitation: and the concept (and the unity) are in that sense his free creation. The progress of science is the discovery at each step of a new order which gives unity to what had long seemed unlike.

* * *

1953, 1965

THE READER

*1. In his opening paragraph, Bronowski pictures what the "literary man,"
or perhaps the ordinary nonscientist, thinks of as the nature of science.
Is this a fair representation of the layman's view? What features of*

---

gency in the presence of all the English bishops. In 1927, a bishop agreed to officiate; when the box was opened, it was found to contain only some odds and ends.

science or of the presentation of science might contribute to the development of that view? How does the process depicted in that paragraph compare with the actual activity of a scientist, as described in the account of his own work given by Lorenz in "The Taming of the Shrew" (p. 879) or in the account of Kepler given by Koestler in "Gravity and the Holy Ghost" (p. 920)?

2. *Bronowski recounts the famous story of Newton and the apple. What general principle about science is the author exemplifying in this story?*

3. *In "The Reach of Imagination" (p. 194), Bronowski shows the work of imagination in Newton's thinking of the moon as a huge ball, thrown hard, and in Galileo's imaginary experiment with unequal weights. In what particular ways do these examples relate to and supplement Bronowski's remarks on science in "The Nature of Scientific Reasoning"?*

THE WRITER

1. *On p. 927, Bronowski says: "I have had of all people a historian tell me that science is a collection of facts, and his voice had not even the ironic rasp of one filing cabinet reproving another." Is that image appropriate to the point he wants to make? Can you find other such uses of language in the selection?*

2. *In his fourth paragraph, Bronowski indicates that an electronic brain has little or no chance of making a scientific discovery. Do you agree? Why, or why not? Develop your answer in a brief essay.*

3. *Write an essay comparing Bronowski's description of the process of science with that given by Kuhn in "The Route to Normal Science" (p. 966). In what respects are the views of these authors similar? Do they differ in any important ways? What sorts of language does each of them use to convey his thoughts? How would you account for differences in tone and usage?*

Richard S. Westfall

THE CAREER OF ISAAC NEWTON: A SCIENTIFIC LIFE IN THE SEVENTEENTH CENTURY

If anyone has had a good press among the scientific community, surely it is Isaac Newton. He has appeared as the archetype of the modern empirical scientist, the example on which the majority of contemporary scientists would happily model themselves. It is not surprising that Newton should have assumed this role. In his *Principia* he produced the paradigm of the scientific world view. The law of universal gravitation was almost the least of its contents. Its three laws of motion, still presented today at the beginning of any introduction to physics, provided the foundation of a general science of mechanics. The work also presented the ideal of science as exact mathematical description, not confined to ideal situations as mathematical descriptions had been in earlier works such as those of Galileo, but exact descriptions of the extent to which physical reality fails to embody the ideal. In his other great work, *Opticks*, Newton produced one of the earliest exemplars of experimental procedure. Finally, he capped the whole performance with the invention of calculus, the basic instrument of physical science. It was, all in all, an achievement without equal—one indeed without serious rival. More than any other single man, Newton defined what modern science would be.

The case for Newton as the archetype of the empirical scientist extends beyond his achievement in science. Throughout his career he consistently expressed a methodological point of view to which most contemporary scientists would readily subscribe. The first occasion for such utterance came soon after he burst upon the scientific scene, in 1672, with his paper on colors. The paper contained an experimental investigation that established the heterogeneity of light. It was laid before a community convinced by a tradition some two thousand years old, which common sense supported, that primary light—the light of the sun—is homogeneous and that colors appear in certain circumstances, such as rainbows, when media modify primary light. Influenced as well by the mechanical philosophy of nature, the audience who read his paper looked for mechanistic explanations that would explain both the modification light undergoes and the nature of colors.

Not surprisingly, they misunderstood Newton's paper. In reply to their criticism, he took a methodological stand. In science, he insisted, experimental investigations must take precedence over explanatory hypotheses devised to explain phenomena. "For if the possibility of hypotheses is to be the test of the truth and reality of things, I see not how certainty can be obtained in any science; since numerous hypotheses may be devised, which shall seem to overcome new difficulties." "The proper Method for inquiring after the properties of things," he added, in another letter, "is to deduce them from Experiments. And I told you that the Theory wch I propounded was evinced by me, *not by inferring tis thus because not otherwise*, that is not by deducing it onely from the confutation of contrary suppositions, but *by deriving it from Experiments concluding positively & directly*. The way therefore to examin it is by considering whether the experiments wch I propound do prove those parts of the Theory to wch they are applyed, or by prosecuting other experiments wch the Theory may suggest for its examination."

More than forty years later, when he was well past his seventieth year,

Newton asserted the same position to distinguish himself from Leibniz. "The Philosophy which Mr. Newton in his *Principles* and *Optiques* has pursued is Experimental," he stated, referring to himself in the third person; "and it is not the Business of Experimental Philosophy to teach the Causes of things any further than they can be proved by Experiments. We are not to fill this Philosophy with Opinions which cannot be proved by Phaenomena. In this Philosophy Hypotheses have no place, unless as Conjectures or Questions proposed to be examined by Experiments. ... And ... one would wonder that Mr. Newton should be reflected upon for not explaining the Causes of Gravity and other Attractions by Hypotheses; as if it were a crime to content himself with Certainties and let Uncertainties alone." In his own age, this was a stance that differed from the prevailing one. It is, in general terms, the one modern science has adopted, and it is small wonder that Newton is seen by contemporary scientists as the archetype of the experimental, empirical scientist.

How familiar he looks, from a distance. Up close and examined in detail, how completely strange Newton's career appears—a career so unlike what we now take for granted that we would hardly recognize it as a career in science were we not convinced a priori that it must have been. "The past is like a foreign country," a character in the movie *The Go-Between* remarked, "they do things differently there." Certainly they pursued science differently in the seventeenth century. Three features of Newton's career—three important features which differ profoundly from the normal career of a twentieth-century scientist who sees Newton as his model—illustrate how foreign the past indeed was.

Physical isolation is the first feature distinguishing past from present. People familiar with Newton's life are apt to object to such a characterization. He was, after all, President of the Royal Society for the final twenty-three years of his life and a fellow of the Society for nearly thirty-two years before that. Newton's relationship to the Royal Society can be misleading if it is not closely inspected. When he assumed its presidency, he had passed well beyond his age of scientific creativity; and during the earlier period when he was a fellow, he lived far away, separated from its activities and its members by sixty miles of impossible roads. With only the smallest exceptions, all of Newton's creative work, all of what we remember him for today, stemmed from his Cambridge years. Physical isolation characterized him in his Cambridge setting; it is necessary to understand him in that context.

Of Newton's isolation, it is hard to distinguish between factors that were purely personal and factors that were general and, therefore, offer some insight into scientific life in his day. Newton was a born recluse if ever one existed. As early as grammar school he found it difficult to get along with fellow students. It did not become any easier at the university, and his isolation only increased when he proceeded to a fellowship in Trinity College. It is striking that only one personal letter from Newton to one of his peers in Trinity exists, and there is some doubt that it was ever mailed. No letters at all from one of them to him is known. He was hardly mentioned by those who reflected on college life during the period when he was a fellow—this despite the fact that he had become the leading intellectual of the land by the time the reflections were set down.

Newton's strange and bizarre habits were the lone characteristics recorded about him. When he set out for dinner in the Hall, he would sometimes take the wrong turn, go out through the gate into the town, and then, when he realized something was wrong, return to his room rather than the Hall. When he did make it to dinner, he was apt to show up disheveled, dressed in the wrong gown, and then to sit there silently, lost in thought, while the meal remained on his plate uneaten. This last habit—about which a number of stories have come down—appeared an excessive peculiarity to the age. Cambridge was at that time going through a disastrous decline. Its dons, who no longer believed in the mission of the university and treated their fellowships as freeholds to be exploited for their personal benefit, happily surrendered to the attractions of the plate and the bottle, becoming, in the splendid phrase of Roger North, wet epicures. They found Newton quite impossible to comprehend. He lived in Trinity College thirty-five years from the time of his admission as an undergraduate. During that time he did not form any close friendships except with his chamber fellow Wickins, and that relationship ended with a breach. After he left, Newton did not exchange a single personal letter with anyone he had known there, and he never returned to Cambridge for any purpose other than electioneering for a university seat in Parliament.

Even though all of the above is true, we can still not ignore the intellectual dimension of Newton's isolation. As an undergraduate he deliberately cut himself off from the established curriculum in order to pursue his own interests: mathematics, as he found it in the writings of Wallis, Viète, and Descartes; and the new natural philosophy, as he found it in Descartes, Galileo, Gassendi, and others. In following this course, Newton very nearly destroyed his prospects. If he wished to remain in the university, where alone he could have pursued the intellectual life from which his achievement sprang, he had to be elected to a scholarship in Trinity College. A scholarship was the necessary preliminary to a fellowship, and since he was a student in Trinity, a Trinity fellowship was the only one to which he could aspire. Even under the best of circumstances, the odds against a sizar (a student who supported himself by performing menial tasks in the college) were enormous. Every year approximately half the scholarships were reserved for a privileged clique of students from Westminster School. The younger sons and clients of powerful men secured most of the rest. The possibilities for Newton, a strange young man without evident connections and from a remote village in Lincolnshire, were hardly great.

Nevertheless, sometime less than a year before the election of 1664, the only one at which he would be eligible, Newton chose to throw over the established curriculum in order to pursue his own line of interests. There is a story, told by Newton in his old age, that he was sent to be examined in mathematics by Isaac Barrow. At this time Newton had mastered Descartes' geometry and was beginning to move beyond it toward his own discoveries. Barrow examined him on Euclid, however, and formed, as Newton recalled it, a tepid opinion of his knowledge of mathematics. Nevertheless, luck was on Newton's side. He was, in fact, not entirely without connections. Among the most senior fellows in the college was one Humphrey Babington, who not only hailed from Newton's corner of Lincolnshire but was the brother of the woman with whom he had boarded in Grantham. It appears likely that Babington was instrumental in his election. Although his early studies did not finally exclude him from a fellowship, his continuing interest in such things always formed a barrier that separated him from the rest of the college. One of Newton's strange habits, as they were later remembered, was a tendency to draw geometric diagrams in the walks of the fellows' garden. The other fellows were awed as much as they were amused by their strange compatriot, and they carefully walked around the diagrams in order not to disturb them. It is not known if another fellow ever stopped to study them.

Within a year and a half of taking his bachelor's degree, Newton had invented calculus and recorded it in a definitive tract in the notebook that he called his Waste Book. By every indication we have, Newton carried out his education in mathematics and his program of research entirely on his own. At the time, as far as we know, no one at all was aware of his achievement. It was his isolation that set the stage for the destructive conflict with Leibniz half a century later, for initially Newton's accomplishments were not known to anyone, and during the following two decades they were known only within a small circle gathered around John Collins, the London mathematical enthusiast.

By the late 1660s, one man, Isaac Barrow, the Lucasian Professor of Mathematics at Cambridge, had become acquainted with Newton's work. As it happened, Barrow was then preparing to vacate the mathematics chair, and he secured Newton's nomination to succeed him. For his initial lectures, Newton chose the subject of optics, and the lectures served to emphasize his isolation anew. He had discovered a new property of one of the major phenomena of nature: the heterogeneity of light. Not only was the discovery unknown to anyone, but when he presented it in three series of lectures, they were as unknown as the discovery itself.

There is no testimony of any kind that a single listener heard and understood what the new Lucasian Professor was presenting.

Optics did bring Newton's complete isolation to an end, however. His theory of colors had led him to the idea of a reflecting telescope to eliminate chromatic aberration, and he was proud enough of the telescope to show it around. Eventually the Royal Society in London heard about it and asked to see it, and ultimately Newton sent them a paper on his theory of colors early in 1672.

The moment Newton ended his isolation, he discovered how much he preferred it. His paper stimulated a modest number of questions and objections which he found it necessary to answer, and he quickly came to resent the intrusion on his time. Thus Newton was no sooner brought into communication with the scientific community, both of Britain and of Europe, than he wanted to sever the connection. He did finally succeed in doing so to a considerable degree and lived mostly in renewed isolation during the decade from the mid-1670s to the mid-1680s. He reinforced his isolation by turning almost entirely away from his studies in mathematics and physics to devote himself to alchemy and theology.

Newton's extraordinary intellectual capacity had become known, however, and letters intermittently intruded upon his isolation. In August 1684, he received a visit from Edmund Halley. We must not overestimate the personal contact that resulted from the visit. Halley put one question to Newton: What would be the shape of the orbit followed by a planet moving in an inverse square force field? That question and all that it implied grasped Newton's attention and refused to let it go. It stimulated the process from which, two and a half years later, the *Principia* emerged. Once more the composition was carried out in isolation. Halley retired to London after he posed his question, made only two brief visits to Cambridge during the following thirty months, and refrained from imposing a burden of correspondence on Newton. The period between his visit and the completion of the manuscript constitutes the largest gap in our knowledge of Newton's adult life, for he had cut himself off from every contact in order to work out the consequences of his ideas alone. The investigation culminated in the book that, by its impact on the scientific world, ended his isolation once and for all. By 1687, however, Newton stood only a few years from the end of his creative intellectual activity, and nearly everything which has made his name immortal had already been accomplished.

Significant personal elements figured in Newton's isolation. He was reclusive by nature. In the early 1670s, after Barrow made Collins aware of Newton's mathematical abilities, Newton consented to Collins's publication of a solution to the annuity problem that he had written only if his, Newton's, name was left off. "It would perhaps increase my acquaintance," he told Collins, "ye thing wch I cheifly study to decline." Nevertheless, the issue stretches far beyond the limits of a personal idiosyncracy. With whom could he have communicated had he not been a recluse? In Britain there were perhaps four men: John Wallis of the previous generation; James Gregory and Christopher Wren of his own; and Edmund Halley of the following. All, for various reasons, would have been less than ideal collaborators. In the rest of Europe, Newton had indeed two scientific peers, Christiaan Huygens and Gottfried Wilhelm Leibniz. Obviously, as such a list implies, we deal here in part with the problem of genius, which is in short supply everywhere always. The short supply of genius does not exhaust the issue, however. The brevity of the list serves to remind us of what we too readily forget, that modern science was created in the seventeenth century by the philosophic rebellion of a tiny handful of men.

By the second half of the seventeenth century, these men were becoming numerous enough to form the first scientific societies. We need to remember how small those societies were. The *Académie Royale des Sciences* in Paris was created in 1666 with sixteen members to cover the entire range of scientific endeavor. The Royal Society in London was a popular organization instead of an exclusive one, and it became for a time a fad in London society, so that its membership swelled to around two hundred. While even two hundred is not an imposing number, it is still misleading as a guide to the size of the English scientific community. It is instructive to listen in briefly on a typical meeting of the Royal Society in the 1690s. John Van de Bembde solemnly informed the society that "cows piss drank to about a pint, will either purge or vomit with great Ease." You may think that he was summarily ejected, whether for indelicacy or irrelevancy. Not at all. The membership seized on the remark as the opportunity for a general discussion of bovine elixir, which was clearly the most stimulating part of the meeting. If we focus, not on the total membership of the Royal Society, but on the number of working scientists in its ranks, we find fewer than the sixteen that made up the Royal Academy. Relative isolation was an unavoidable aspect of the scientific revolution. Newton's reclusive habits only reinforced what would have been his lot in any case.

Physical isolation was of course not equivalent to intellectual isolation. Through the printed page, kindred spirits of more than one locale and more than one age could communicate with one another. Unencumbered as he was with endless committees, colloquia, and consultations, the seventeenth-century scientist had the opportunity to attend carefully to the printed page and to wrestle earnestly with what it presented. It may have been a more effective form of communication than the plethora of immediate contacts in which contemporary scientists of all sorts struggle desperately to preserve some sense of sustained endeavor.

A second distinctive feature of Newton's career was its philosophic breadth. By that phrase I mean to indicate the constant concern in his scientific work more with the total philosophy of nature than with the specific results of immediate investigations. Once again, those familiar with Newton are likely to object. *Opticks*, an experimental investigation of the heterogeneity of light and of the periodicity of some phenomena, especially appears to belie such a characterization. But, in response to the objection, let me call attention first of all to the *Principia*. The *Principia* presented more than the law of universal gravitation, and more than a new science of dynamics which entailed universal gravitation. What it presented, and consciously so, was a new philosophy of nature based on the principle of forces. "I wish we could derive the rest of the phenomena of Nature by the same kind of reasoning from mechanical principles," Newton stated in the preface, with reference to his explanation of the solar system from the concept of gravitational attraction, "for I am induced by many reasons to suspect that they may all depend upon certain forces by which the particles of bodies, by some causes hitherto unknown, are either mutually impelled towards one another, and cohere in regular figures, or are repelled and recede from one another. These forces being unknown, philosophers have hitherto attempted the search of Nature in vain; but I hope the principles here laid down will afford some light either to this or some truer method of philosophy."

During the years that immediately followed the publication of the *Principia*, when Newton first put the *Opticks* together, he treated the work primarily as an exposition of the new philosophy in which he used optical phenomena further to demonstrate the existence of forces in nature. True, in the end, apparently to avoid controversy, he eliminated most of these features, so that the work he eventually published confined such matters mostly, though not entirely, to the Queries at the work's close. Nevertheless, he always saw his scientific work as so many aspects of a new natural philosophy, and the considerable number of followers who wrote popular versions of it in the early eighteenth century all presented it in such terms.

To appreciate this facet of Newton, it is necessary to comprehend his historical situation. When Newton enrolled in Cambridge in 1661, he was educated in a natural philosophy that was more than two thousand years old. The universities of medieval Europe had built themselves in the Aristotelian system. It was still being taught, and not only in Cambridge, when Newton began his university education. In England the Parliamentary statutes that prescribed the curricula of the universities required the study of Aristotle. Newton's first step in natural science was to rebel against the established Aristotelian philosophy and to embrace a new one. The rebellion coincided with his rejection of the standard curriculum, which I mentioned earlier. He was still an undergraduate. Somehow he had found the writings of the men of the previous generation who had offered a radical new approach to nature—among them, Descartes, Gassendi, and Hobbes. Historians call their philosophy (for they agreed on a common core of principles despite their differences on many details) the mechanical philosophy. It provided the intellectual framework of the scientific revolution. Although he did not date his notes, it was apparently in 1664 that Newton embraced the mechanical philosophy and in doing so inaugurated his scientific career.

He did not embrace it for long, however, for he quickly became dissatisfied with aspects of the mechanical philosophy. His dissatisfaction rested partly on religious grounds. Mechanical philosophers proposed, or appeared to propose, the autonomy of the material realm, and Newton decided that such was a program for atheism. In his revulsion, he found in alchemy a concept of nature more in harmony with the demands of religion, and alchemy was one of Newton's major enterprises during the years of silence before the *Principia*.

Alchemy is not a popular topic in many circles. Even to bring it up is to raise doubts in some minds that one is competent to talk about science at all. Newton's alchemical manuscripts are nevertheless authentic. There can be no doubt that he did devote himself to alchemy, and quite extensively. If the goal of history, including the history of science, is to present the past in its own terms to the best of our ability, and not merely to present it as a pale anticipation of the twentieth century, we cannot afford to ignore Newton's immersion in alchemy. We especially cannot afford to ignore its influence on his philosophy of nature, for it appears to have been primarily alchemy that led Newton toward the concept of forces.

The idea of forces was not a single, limited concept; it turned out in the end to involve the entire philosophy of nature. From the beginning, Newton's disenchantment with standard mechanical philosophy had not been solely religious. Mechanical philosophies generated an abundance of talk about the invisible mechanisms by which nature produces phenomena, but their mechanical models proved incapable of yielding exact quantitative results. The great advantage of forces in Newton's eyes was exactly their capacity to generate such results. As he contemplated their import, they promised to revise every corner of natural philosophy. Descartes had argued that nature is a plenum; although atomists rejected the plenum, they nevertheless thought of a universe well filled with matter mixed with dispersed voids. Newton depopulated the universe of matter as he filled it with forces. As he finally conceived of it, nature was an infinite void seasoned with the merest suggestion of solid matter. For example, he paid careful attention to the implications of relative densities. Gold, he argued, cannot be absolutely dense since thin leaves of gold are translucent. He assumed for the moment that gold is made up half of solid matter and half of voids. Gold is nineteen times denser than water;

water therefore can contain only one-thirty-eighth part of solid matter. In fact, he continued, water must contain far less solid matter than that, for water readily transmits rays of light in straight lines at every angle. Water in turn cannot be compressed. Newton ended up with a picture of matter in the form of tenuous nets composed of punctiform particles held together by forces, and eighteenth-century Newtonians would argue that all of the solid matter in the universe could fit inside a nutshell.

Method was involved in the change as much as in the system of nature; the statement on method quoted above comes from a passage on his natural philosophy. Most general of all, his position embodied a new ideal of science as the exact mathematical description both of ideal patterns in nature and of the extent to which material embodiments deviate from the ideal. Even his conception of the relation of God to the physical universe was involved. The dispute with Leibniz over priority in the discovery of calculus, a dispute which reached its climax during the second decade of the eighteenth century, was equally a debate about the philosophy of nature in which all of the above issues were enmeshed.

Moreover, philosophic breadth was not a characteristic unique to Newton. Its greatest interest lies in the fact that it was not. To be sure, Newton may have been of a more contemplative spirit than the average scientist of his time. Despite his reputation as an empirical scientist, he was perhaps the greatest speculator of the age. His meditations on the nature of things, ruminations that extended throughout the length of his career, furnished the warp on which he wove the fabric of his career in science. His concept of forces was only the most fruitful of a long series of speculations. Nevertheless, every member of the scientific community of the age, of necessity, also concerned himself with the philosophy of nature. Virtually without exception, they had been educated like Newton in the Aristotelian philosophy, and like him they had all gone through their own personal rebellions against it. Such was the very meaning of the mechanical philosophy—a new beginning, a determination to reshape natural philosophy according to new principles. In the early eighteenth century, in turn, no one could stand aloof from the controversy that separated Newtonian natural philosophy from the prevailing forms of the mechanical philosophy. It was precisely in this feature that Newton most diverged from the image of the archetype of the modern empirical scientist. It is indeed a distortion of language to call him a scientist at all. In his own eyes, he was a natural philosopher.

A third prominent feature of Newton's career was his theological depth. No one familiar with Newton is likely to protest against this, for Newton's religious concerns are well known. The General Scholium to the *Principia,* to cite only one example, hymns a rhapsody to God. "This most beautiful system of the sun, planets, and comets, could only proceed from the counsel and dominion of an intelligent and powerful Being. . . .

This Being governs all things, not as the soul of the world, but as Lord over all; and on account of his dominion He is wont to be called *Lord God, pantokrator,* or *Universal Ruler.* . . . We know him only by his most wise and excellent contrivances of things, and final causes; we admire him for his perfections; but we reverence and adore him on account of his dominion. . . ." "When I wrote my treatise about our Systeme," he wrote to Richard Bentley, "I had an eye upon such Principles as might work wth considering men for the beleife of a Deity. . . ."

These passages and similar ones are well known. They do not, how-ever, constitute Newton's theological depth. They are evidence, rather, of his personal piety. To find the theological depth we must turn to his private papers instead of his published works, to papers fully opened to public scrutiny only within the last decade. They reveal that Newton plunged into serious and sustained theological study in the early 1670s—not in his old age as is usually assumed, but during the full flower of his early manhood, when he was approaching the age of thirty. Together with alchemy, theology constituted the primary substance of his intellec-tual life from that time until the composition of the *Principia.* The Bible supplied part of his reading; Newton's extensive knowledge of it, which John Locke said was equaled by few whom he knew, undoubtedly de-rived from the intense study of this period. The Bible was by no means the only object of his attention. He took up the early fathers of the church and read and digested the writings of every father of any significance. He turned to the prophecies and invested immense energy in an interpreta-tion of them. To be sure that he had the correct text of the Book of Revelation, he collated more than twenty versions of the Greek text. Since he regarded the prophecies as the core of the Bible and the key to the rest, he combed the Scriptures for supporting passages; and since he insisted on an exact correlation between prophecy and history, he de-voted equal zeal to the history of the early Christian centuries. The prophecies took him into the study of Judaism. As part of that study he became interested in the plan of the Jewish temple. Newton was never interested in things only in a general way. He wanted to know the exact plan of the temple, and for that purpose he reconstructed four chapters of Ezekiel while he drew a detailed plan of the temple to accompany the text.

In such activities one may begin to sense the measure of Newton's theological depth. They do not yet indicate the full depth, however. Behind all his study of theology was a fundamental goal—an anguished reassessment of the whole Christian tradition. The initial stimulus to his theological reading was probably the requirement that bore upon Fel-lows of Trinity College to be ordained to the Anglican clergy within seven years of taking their M.A. degrees. Almost the first result of Newton's study was an impassable obstacle to ordination, for he quickly convinced himself that the dominant Christian tradition, Trinitarianism, was false. The doctrine of the Trinity, he believed, was more than false; it was a deliberate fraud foisted onto the church in the fourth century by deceitful and evil men pursuing their own selfish interests. Newton adopted the ancient belief of Arianism as his own theological position, a position that denied the full divinity of Christ. Trinitarianism stood at the center of his interpretation of the prophecies. It was the Great Apostasy foretold by God when men would fall away from the true worship into idolatry; the plagues and vials of wrath of the Apocalypse, corresponding to the barbarian invasions of the empire, were God's punishment on a stiff-necked people who had gone whoring after false gods. In a word, Newton was one of the more advanced heretics of his day. His constant concern to conceal opinions which would have led to ostracism, first from the university, and later from the government's service, furnished a basic theme throughout his life. The piety of the General Scholium was sincere. No one should question it. Nevertheless it concealed a reality more complicated than has generally been realized.

This feature of Newton's career was also a general characteristic of the age. The constant references to God and to Christianity in the writings of scientists, like those of Newton, are usually taken as testimonies to the piety of the age. They derived rather from the fact that traditional piety had been called into question. Basil Willey has referred to the seventeenth century's "touch of cold philosophy." It had dissipated the enchanted world of medieval Christianity before the very eyes of scientists like Newton. They were unable to ignore this fact of their existence, as unsettling a piece of reality as one can readily imagine. Not many followed Newton into heterodoxy, but the endless refutations of atheism and proofs of the existence of God with which they filled their books adequately testify that they were aware of the same motives that animated Newton's lifelong inquiry into the true religion. When Robert Boyle died in 1691, after soundly refuting atheism at least fifty times, he left part of his fortune to endow a series of lectures. What were the lectures to do? Refute atheism still more. When during the previous thousand years of Western history had anyone thought that was necessary? Thinkers of the late seventeenth century knew only too well that the ground on which Christianity stood was shifting. In one way or another, most of them took account of the new circumstances. Many things contributed to Willey's touch of cold philosophy, but the birth of modern science was not the least among its sources. No wonder theological depth was a common feature of scientists (or natural philosophers) such as Newton.

Let us now turn the three chief characteristics of Newton's career back on ourselves and use them as a yardstick to measure the contemporary scientific community. No one, I suspect, would suggest that physical isolation is a normal feature of a twentieth-century scientist. Every year throughout the Western and Communist worlds there are meetings, such as those of the AAAS,[1] where thousands of scientists come together; increasingly they are spreading into the third world as well. I teach at Indiana University, a distinguished institution but not, in the opinion of any informed judge, a leading center of contemporary science. Nevertheless, the scientific community at Indiana University is larger than the whole of Europe could have mustered at any time during the seventeenth century. There are several other groups of equal size in the state of Indiana and well over fifty centers in the state where scientists can be and are in immediate contact with trained and interested colleagues. This situation is also normal throughout the Western and Communist worlds. When one adds to the scientists the considerable army of technical experts called into being by modern science—an army which had no counterpart in the seventeenth century—the scientific community emerges as a significant portion of the working population. The small handful of natural philosophers who created the scientific revolution has burgeoned into a sociological phenomenon of immense scope.

As for philosophic breadth, it is no longer required. It is true of some contemporary scientists; it is not required of any one—that is, it is no longer necessary for every scientist constantly to consider the fundamental issues of natural philosophy. Although our century has witnessed a profound revision of the conception of nature, virtually no one in the scientific community considers that the system as a whole is in serious question, and it is perfectly proper for scientists to ignore the problems that occupied Newton in order to work at clarifying details of the system. Thus a typical issue of the *Physical Review* contains articles on "Three-body Lippmann-Schwinger Equations," "Influence of Vibrations of Gas Molecules on Neutron Reaction Cross Sections," "Core Coupled States in ^{145}Eu," and "Decays of Mass-separated ^{139}Xe and ^{139}Cs," together with many more in a similar vein. The articles all assume the existence of a coherent philosophy of nature. Without bothering themselves about such questions, their authors devote themselves, without manifest anxiety, to getting on with the work of science.

Theological depth has become for most scientists irrelevant. There are of course a number of scientists as pious as any in the seventeenth century; a like number are equally committed to articulate atheism. For most scientists, however, the issue has ceased to have any meaning. In the three centuries that have passed since Newton published the *Principia*, Christianity and science have exchanged roles, and natural science today occupies the position in Western civilization that Christianity once held. Theologians are now the small handful. Once theology

---

1. American Association for the Advancement of Science.

was queen of all the sciences. We have redefined what the word *science* means, and every other intellectual discipline now measures itself against the enterprise that carries the word in its new meaning as its name.

Thus the scientific career of Isaac Newton enables us to appreciate the full extent to which natural science has been the most successful and significant endeavor of the modern world, reshaping first the intellectual structure of the West, then the economic system, and finally society itself. There is no way to avoid the conclusion: the scientists have inherited the earth. The rest of us are waiting breathlessly to see what they will do with it.

1981

THE READER

1. *Westfall states that Isaac Newton's career had three distinguishing characteristics. What are they? How does Newton's career differ from a typical career in science today, as given in Westfall's concluding paragraphs? Is this difference good or bad, in the view of the author? In your view?*
2. *How did the three distinguishing features of Newton's career contribute to or detract from the work he did in science? What, by the way, does science owe to Newton?*
3. *What view of science does the author propose in his closing paragraph? Do you subscribe to that view? Why, or why not?*

THE WRITER

1. *What role do the three distinguishing characteristics of Newton's career play in the essay's organization?*
2. *Does the author succeed in making Newton come alive as a person? If so, by what particular means does he accomplish this? If not, what might he have done to bring out Newton as a person?*
3. *Write a brief character sketch of Newton, based on the information in this essay. What additional information might it have been useful to have?*

Stephen Jay Gould

DARWIN'S MIDDLE ROAD

"We began to sail up the narrow strait lamenting," narrates Odysseus. "For on the one hand lay Scylla, with twelve feet all dangling down; and six necks exceeding long, and on each a hideous head, and therein three rows of teeth set thick and close, full of black death. And on the other mighty Charybdis sucked down the salt sea water. As often as she belched it forth, like a cauldron on a great fire she would seethe up through all her troubled deeps." Odysseus managed to swerve around Charybdis, but Scylla grabbed six of his finest men and devoured them in his sight—"the most pitiful thing mine eyes have seen of all my travail in searching out the paths of the sea."

False lures and dangers often come in pairs in our legends and metaphors—consider the frying pan and the fire, or the devil and the deep blue sea. Prescriptions for avoidance either emphasize a dogged steadiness—the straight and narrow of Christian evangelists—or an averaging between unpleasant alternatives—the golden mean of Aristotle. The idea of steering a course between undesirable extremes emerges as a central prescription for a sensible life.

The nature of scientific creativity is both a perennial topic of discussion and a prime candidate for seeking a golden mean. The two extreme positions have not been directly competing for allegiance of the unwary. They have, rather, replaced each other sequentially, with one now in the ascendency, the other eclipsed.

The first—inductivism—held that great scientists are primarily great observers and patient accumulators of information. For new and significant theory, the inductivists claimed, can only arise from a firm foundation of facts. In this architectural view, each fact is a brick in a structure built without blueprints. Any talk or thought about theory (the completed building) is fatuous and premature before the bricks are set. Inductivism once commanded great prestige within science, and even represented an "official" position of sorts, for it touted, however falsely, the utter honesty, complete objectivity, and almost automatic nature of scientific progress towards final and incontrovertible truth.

Yet, as its critics so rightly claimed, inductivism also depicted science as a heartless, almost inhuman discipline offering no legitimate place to quirkiness, intuition, and all the other subjective attributes adhering ot our vernacular notion of genius. Great scientists, the critics claimed, are distinguished more by their powers of hunch and synthesis, than their skill in experiment or observation. The criticisms of inductivism are certainly valid and I welcome its dethroning during the past thirty years as a necessary preclude to better understanding. Yet, in attacking it so strongly, some critics have tried to substitute an alternative equally extreme and unproductive in its emphasis on the essential subjectivity of creative thought. In this "eureka" view, creativity is an ineffable something, accessible only to persons of genius. It arises like a bolt of lightning, unanticipated, unpredictable and unanalyzable—but the bolts strike only a few special people. We ordinary mortals must stand in awe and thanks. (The name refers, of course, to the legendary story of Archimedes running naked through the streets of Syracuse shouting eureka [I have discovered it] when water displaced by his bathing body washed the scales abruptly from his eyes and suggested a method for measuring volumes.)

I am equally disenchanted by both these opposing extremes. Inductivism reduces genius to dull, rote operations; eurekaism grants it an inaccessible status more in the domain of intrinsic mystery than in a realm where we might understand and learn from it. Might we not marry the good features of each view, and abandon both the elitism of eurekaism and the pedestrian qualities of inductivism? May we not acknowledge the personal and subjective character of creativity, but still comprehend it as a mode of thinking that emphasizes or exaggerates capacities sufficiently common to all of us that we may at least understand if not hope to imitate?

In the hagiography of science, a few men hold such high positions that all arguments must apply to them if they are to have any validity. Charles Darwin, as the principal saint of evolutionary biology, has therefore been presented both as an inductivist and as a primary example of eurekaism. I will attempt to show that these interpretations are equally inadequate, and that recent scholarship on Darwin's own odyssey towards the theory of natural selection supports an intermediate position.

So great was the prestige of inductivism in his own day, that Darwin himself fell under its sway and, as an old man, falsely depicted his youthful accomplishments in its light. In an autobiography, written as a lesson in morality for his children and not intended for publication, he penned some famous lines that misled historians for nearly a hundred years. Describing his path to the theory of natural selection, he claimed: "I worked on true Baconian principles, and without any theory collected facts on a wholesale scale."[1]

The inductivist interpretation focuses on Darwin's five years aboard the *Beagle* and explains his transition from a student for the ministry to the nemesis of preachers as the result of his keen powers of observation applied to the whole world. Thus, the traditional story goes, Darwin's

1. Francis Bacon (1561–1626): English philosopher, statesman, and essayist, and the first apostle of inductivism.

eyes opened wider and wider as he saw, in sequence, the bones of giant South American fossil mammals, the turtles and finches of the Galapagos, and the marsupial fauna of Australia. The truth of evolution and its mechanism of natural selection crept up gradually upon him as he sifted facts in a sieve of utter objectivity.

The inadequacies of this tale are best illustrated by the falsity of its conventional premier example—the so-called Darwin's finches of the Galapagos. We now know that although these birds share a recent and common ancestry on the South American mainland, they have radiated into an impressive array of species on the outlying Galapagos. Few terrestrial species manage to cross the wide oceanic barrier between South America and the Galapagos. But the fortunate migrants often find a sparsely inhabited world devoid of the competitors that limit their opportunities on the crowded mainland. Hence, the finches evolved into roles normally occupied by other birds and developed their famous set of adaptations for feeding—seed crushing, insect eating, even grasping and manipulating a cactus needle to dislodge insects from plants. Isolation—both of the islands from the mainland and among the islands themselves—provided an opportunity for separation, independent adaptation, and speciation.

According to the traditional view, Darwin discovered these finches, correctly inferred their history, and wrote the famous lines in his notebook: "If there is the slightest foundation for these remarks the zoology of Archipelagoes will be worth examining; for such facts would undermine the stability of Species." But, as with so many heroic tales from Washington's cherry tree to the piety of Crusaders, hope rather than truth motivates the common reading. Darwin found the finches to be sure. But he didn't recognize them as variants of a common stock. In fact, he didn't even record the island of discovery for many of them—some of his labels just read "Galapagos Islands." So much for his immediate recognition of the role of isolation in the formation of new species. He reconstructed the evolutionary tale only after his return to London, when a British Museum ornithologist correctly identified all the birds as finches.

The famous quotation from his notebook refers to Galapagos tortoises and to the claim of native inhabitants that they can "at once pronounce from which Island any Tortoise may have been brought" from subtle differences in size and shape of body and scales. This is a statement of different, and much reduced, order from the traditional tale of finches. For the finches are true and separate species—a living example of evolution. The subtle differences among tortoises represent minor geographic variation within a species. It is a jump in reasoning, albeit a valid one as we now know, to argue that such small differences can be amplified to produce a new species. All creationists, after all, acknowledged geo-

graphic variation (consider human races), but argued that it could not
proceed beyond the rigid limits of a created archetype.

I don't wish to downplay the pivotal influence of the *Beagle* voyage on
Darwin's career. It gave him space, freedom and endless time to think in
his favored mode of independent self-stimulation. (His ambivalence towards university life, and his middling performance there by conventional standards, reflected his unhappiness with a curriculum of received
wisdom.) He writes from South America in 1834: "I have not one clear
idea about cleavage, stratification, lines of upheaval. I have no books,
which tell me much and what they do I cannot apply to what I see. In
consequence I draw my own conclusions, and most gloriously ridiculous
ones they are." The rocks and plants and animals that he saw did provoke
him to the crucial attitude of doubt—midwife of all creativity. Sydney,
Australia—1836. Darwin wonders why a rational God would create so
many marsupials on Australia since nothing about its climate or geography suggests any superiority for pouches: "I had been lying on a sunny
bank and was reflecting on the strange character of the animals of this
country as compared to the rest of the World. An unbeliever in everything beyond his own reason might exclaim, 'Surely two distinct Creators must have been at work.'"

Nonetheless, Darwin returned to London without an evolutionary
theory. He suspected the truth of evolution, but had no mechanism to
explain it. Natural selection did not arise from any direct reading of the
Beagle's facts, but from two subsequent years of thought and struggle as
reflected in a series of remarkable notebooks that have been unearthed
and published during the past twenty years. In these notebooks, we see
Darwin testing and abandoning a number of theories and pursuing a
multitude of false leads—so much for his later claim about recording facts
with an empty mind. He read philosophers, poets, and economists, always searching for meaning and insight—so much for the notion that
natural selection arose inductively from the *Beagle's* facts. Later, he
labelled one notebook as "full of metaphysics on morals."

Yet if this tortuous path belies the Scylla of inductivism, it has engendered an equally simplistic myth—the Charybdis of eurekaism. In his
maddeningly misleading autobiography, Darwin does record a eureka
and suggests that natural selection struck him as a sudden, serendipitous
flash after more than a year of groping frustration:

> In October 1838, that is, fifteen months after I had begun my systematic
> inquiry, I happened to read for amusement Malthus on Population,[2] and
> being well prepared to appreciate the struggle for existence which every-
> where goes on from long-continued observation of the habits of animals and

2. Thomas Malthus, whose work on population was published under several titles between
1798 and 1817.

plants, it at once struck me that under these circumstances favorable variations would tend to be preserved, and unfavorable ones to be destroyed. The
result of this would be the formation of new species. Here, then, I had at last
got a theory by which to work.

Yet, again, the notebooks belie Darwin's later recollections—in this
case by their utter failure to record, at the time it happened, any special
exultation over his Malthusian insight. He inscribes it as a fairly short
and sober entry without a single exclamation point, though he habitually
used two or three in moments of excitement. He did not drop everything
and reinterpret a confusing world in its light. On the very next day, he
wrote an even longer passage on the sexual curiosity of primates.

The theory of natural selection arose neither as a workmanlike induction from nature's facts, nor as a mysterious bolt from Darwin's subconscious, triggered by an accidental reading of Malthus. It emerged instead
as the result of a conscious and productive search, proceeding in a
ramifying but ordered manner, and utilizing both the facts of natural
history and an astonishingly broad range of insights from disparate disciplines far from his own. Darwin trod the middle path between inductivism and eurekaism. His genius is neither pedestrian nor inaccessible.

Darwinian scholarship has exploded since the centennial of the *Origin*[3]
in 1959. The publication of Darwin's notebooks and the attention devoted by several scholars to the two crucial years between the *Beagle's*
docking and the demoted Malthusian insight has clinched the argument
for a "middle path" theory of Darwin's creativity. Two particularly
important works focus on the broadest and narrowest scales. Howard E.
Gruber's masterful intellectual and psychological biography of this phase
in Darwin's life, *Darwin on Man*, traces all the false leads and turning
points in Darwin's search. Gruber shows that Darwin was continually
proposing, testing, and abandoning hypotheses, and that he never simply
collected facts in a blind way. He began with a fanciful theory involving
the idea that new species arise with a prefixed life span, and worked his
way gradually, if fitfully, towards an idea of extinction by competition in
a world of struggle. He recorded no exultation upon reading Malthus,
because the jigsaw puzzle was only missing a piece or two at the time.

Silvan S. Schweber has reconstructed, in detail as minute as the record
will allow, Darwin's activities during the few weeks before Malthus (The
Origin of the *Origin* Revisited, *Journal of the History of Biology*, 1977). He
argues that the final pieces arose not from new facts in natural history,
but from Darwin's intellectual wanderings in distant fields. In particular,
he read a long review of social scientist and philosopher Auguste Comte's
most famous work, the *Cours de philosophie positive*.[4] He was particularly struck by Comte's insistence that a proper theory be predictive and

3. *The Origin of Species* (1859).　　　　4. *Course in Positivist Philosophy* (1830–42).

at least potentially quantitative. He then turned to Dugald Stewart's *On the Life and Writing of Adam Smith,* and imbibed the basic belief of the Scottish economists that theories of overall social structure must begin by analyzing the unconstrained actions of individuals. (Natural selection is, above all, a theory about the struggle of individual organisms for success in reproduction.) Then, searching for quantification, he read a lengthy analysis of work by the most famous statistician of his time—the Belgian Adolphe Quetelet. In the review of Quetelet, he found, among other things, a forceful statement of Malthus's quantitative claim—that population would grow geometrically and food supplies only arithmetically, thus guaranteeing an intense struggle for existence. In fact, Darwin had read the Malthusian statement several times before; but only now was he prepared to appreciate its significance. Thus, he did not turn to Malthus by accident, and he already knew what it contained. His "amusement," we must assume, consisted only in a desire to read in its original formulation the familiar statement that had so impressed him in Quetelet's secondary account.

In reading Schweber's detailed account of the moments preceding Darwin's formulation of natural selection, I was particularly struck by the absence of deciding influence from his own field of biology. The immediate precipitators were a social scientist, an economist, and a statistician. If genius has any common denominator, I would propose breadth of interest and the ability to construct fruitful analogies between fields.

In fact, I believe that the theory of natural selection should be viewed as an extended analogy—whether conscious or unconscious on Darwin's part I do not know—to the laissez faire economics of Adam Smith. The essence of Smith's argument is a paradox of sorts: if you want an ordered economy providing maximal benefits to all, then let individuals compete and struggle for their own advantages. The result, after appropriate sorting and elimination of the inefficient, will be a stable and harmonious polity. Apparent order arises naturally from the struggle among individuals, not from predestined principles or higher control. Dugald Stewart epitomized Smith's system in the book Darwin read:

> The most effective plan for advancing a people ... is by allowing every man, as long as he observes the rules of justice, to pursue his own interest in his own way, and to bring both his industry and his capital into the freest competition with those of his fellow citizens. Every system of policy which endeavors ... to draw towards a particular species of industry a greater share of the capital of the society than would naturally go to it ... is, in reality, subversive of the great purpose which it means to promote.

As Schweber states: "The Scottish analysis of society contends that the combined effect of individual actions results in the institutions upon which society is based, and that such a society is a stable and evolving one and functions without a designing and directing mind."

We know that Darwin's uniqueness does not reside in his support for the idea of evolution—scores of scientists had preceded him in this. His special contribution rests upon his documentation and upon the novel character of his theory about how evolution operates. Previous evolutionists had proposed unworkable schemes based on internal perfecting tendencies and inherent directions. Darwin advocated a natural and testable theory based on immediate interaction among individuals (his opponents considered it heartlessly mechanistic). The theory of natural selection is a creative transfer to biology of Adam Smith's basic argument for a rational economy: the balance and order of nature does not arise from a higher, external (divine) control, or from the existence of laws operating directly upon the whole, but from struggle among individuals for their own benefits (in modern terms, for the transmission of their genes to future generations through differential success in reproduction).

Many people are distressed to hear such an argument. Does it not compromise the integrity of science if some of its primary conclusions originate by analogy from contemporary politics and culture rather than from data of the discipline itself? In a famous letter to Engels, Karl Marx identified the similarities between natural selection and the English social scene:

> It is remarkable how Darwin recognizes among beasts and plants his English society with its division of labor, competition, opening up of new markets, 'invention,' and the Malthusian 'struggle for existence.' It is Hobbes' *bellum omnium contra omnes* (the war of all against all).[5]

Yet Marx was a great admirer of Darwin—and in this apparent paradox lies resolution. For reasons involving all the themes I have emphasized here—that inductivism is inadequate, that creativity demands breadth, and that analogy is a profound source of insight—great thinkers cannot be divorced from their social background. But the source of an idea is one thing; its truth or fruitfulness is another. The psychology and utility of discovery are very different subjects indeed. Darwin may have cribbed the idea of natural selection from economics, but it may still be right. As the German socialist Karl Kautsky wrote in 1902: "The fact that an idea emanates from a particular class, or accords with their interests, of course proves nothing as to its truth or falsity." In this case, it is ironic that Adam Smith's system of laissez faire does not work in his own domain of economics, for it leads to oligopoly and revolution, rather than to order and harmony. Struggle among individuals does, however, seem to be the law of nature.

Many people use such arguments about social context to ascribe great insights primarily to the indefinable phenomenon of good luck. Thus,

5. From the English philosopher Thomas Hobbes's *Leviathan* (1651).

Darwin was lucky to be born rich, lucky to be on the *Beagle*, lucky to live amidst the ideas of his age, lucky to trip over Parson Malthus—essentially little more than a man in the right place at the right time. Yet, when we read of his personal struggle to understand, the breadth of his concerns and study, and the directedness of his search for a mechanism of evolution, we understand why Pasteur made his famous quip that fortune favors the prepared mind.[6]

1980

6. Louis Pasteur (1822–95): French chemist.

Tom Bethell

AGNOSTIC EVOLUTIONISTS

The first time I saw Colin Patterson was at the American Museum of Natural History in New York City in the spring of 1983. He was in the office of Donn Rosen, a curator in the museum's department of ichthyology, which is the branch of zoology that deals with fishes. Patterson, a paleontologist specializing in fossil fishes, was staring through a binocular microscope at a slice of codfish. In his mid-fifties and balding, he was wearing black corduroys and a smoking-jacket affair of the kind that I associate with the Sloane Square poets of the "angry young man" generation—the generation to which Patterson belongs by age, and perhaps by temperament. I would later spend time with him in London, at the British Museum of Natural History, where he is a senior paleontologist, and at Cambridge University, where we attended a lecture by the famous Harvard paleontologist Stephen Jay Gould. He often conveyed an impression of moody rebelliousness: he is authoritative, the kind of person others defer to in a discussion; he is habitually pessimistic; and he seemed not at all sanguine about his brushes with other scientists—encounters that by the late 1970s had become quite frequent. Those with whom Patterson has been arguing are mostly paleontologists and evolutionary biologists—researchers and academics who have devoted their careers, their lives, to upholding and fine-tuning the ideas about the origins and the development of species introduced by Charles Darwin in the second half of the nineteenth century. Patterson, it seemed, was no longer sure he believed in evolutionary theory, and he was saying so. Or, perhaps more accurately, he was saying that evolutionists—like the creationists they periodically do battle with—are nothing more than believers themselves.

In 1978, Patterson wrote an introductory book called *Evolution*, which was published by the British Museum. A year later, he received a letter from Luther Sunderland, an electrical engineer in upstate New York and a creationist-activist, asking why *Evolution* did not include any "direct illustrations of evolutionary transitions." Patterson's reply included the following:

> You say I should at least "show a photo of the fossil from which each type of organism was derived." I will lay it on the line—there is not one such fossil for which one could make a watertight argument. The reason is that statements about ancestry and descent are not applicable in the fossil record. Is *Archaeopteryx* the ancestor of all birds? Perhaps yes, perhaps no: there is no way of answering the question. It is easy enough to make up stories of how one form gave rise to another, and to find reasons why the stages should be favoured by natural selection. But such stories are not part of science, for there is no way of putting them to the test.

By 1981, Patterson's doubts about evolutionary theory were finding their way to the public. A sentence in a brochure he wrote that year for the British Museum began: "If the theory of evolution is true . . . " In the fall of 1981, Patterson addressed the Systematics Discussion Group at the American Museum of Natural History. Once a month, the group meets in an upstairs classroom at the museum, opposite the dinosaur exhibit hall. The audience in any given month is likely to be made up of museum staff, graduate students from nearby universities, and the occasional amateur like Norman Macbeth, the author of *Darwin Retried*. (Systematics is a science of classification; taxonomists working in systematics study the way taxonomic groups relate to one another in nature.) There may be no more than fifteen people on hand when the discussion focuses on, say, fossil rodent teeth; or there may be 150 or more when Richard C. Lewontin, the renowned geneticist and author, gives a talk on the meaning (if any) of adaptation in biology.

Patterson's address was titled "Evolutionism and Creationism." Patterson is not a creationist, but he had been trying to think like one as a sort of experiment. "It's true," he told his audience, "that for the last eighteen months or so I've been kicking around non-evolutionary or even anti-evolutionary ideas." He went on:

> I think always before in my life when I've got up to speak on a subject I've been confident of one thing—that I know more about it than anybody in the room, because I've worked on it. Well, this time it isn't true. I'm speaking on two subjects, evolutionism and creationism, and I believe it's true to say that I know nothing whatever about either of them.
>
> One of the reasons I started taking this anti-evolutionary view, or let's call it a non-evolutionary view, was that last year I had a sudden realization. For over twenty years I had thought I was working on evolution in some way. One morning I woke up and something had happened in the night, and it struck me that I had been working on this stuff for more than twenty years, and there was not one thing I knew about it. It's quite a shock to learn that one can be so

misled for so long. Either there was something wrong with me or there was something wrong with evolutionary theory. Naturally I know there is nothing wrong with me, so for the last few weeks I've tried putting a simple question to various people and groups.

Question is: Can you tell me anything you know about evolution? Any one thing, any one thing that is true?

In the public mind, challenges to Darwin's theory of evolution are associated with biblical creationists who periodically remove their children from schoolrooms where they are being taught that man evolved from monkeys. Most Americans know about the Scopes trial of 1925, in which a Tennessee high school teacher was fined $100 for teaching evolutionary theory. Four years ago there was the trial in San Diego in which Kelly Seagraves, director of the Creation Science Research Center, unsuccessfully sued the state of California over regulations governing the teaching of evolution in California public schools. (Seagraves wanted science teachers to be required to mention pertinent passages from the Book of Genesis.) What most people do not know is that for much of this century, and especially in recent years, scientists have been fighting among themselves about Darwin and his ideas.

Scientists are largely responsible for keeping the public in the dark about these in-house arguments. When they see themselves as beleaguered by opponents outside the citadel of science, they tend to put their differences aside and unite to defeat the heathen. The layman sees only the closed ranks. At the moment, with creationism apparently quiescent, we can, if we listen hard enough, hear fresh murmurs of dissent within the scientific walls. These debates are more complicated, perhaps, than the old contest, Science vs. Religion, but they are at least as interesting, and sometimes as heated.

One of the least publicized and least understood challenges to Darwin and the theory of evolution—and surely one of the more fascinating, in its sweep and rigor—involves a school of taxonomists called cladists. (A "clade" is a branch, from the Greek *klados*; "cladist" is pronounced with a long a.) Particularly interesting—vexing, evolutionary biologists would say (and do)—are those who toil in what is called transformed cladistics, and who might be thought of as agnostic evolutionists. Like many who have broken with a faith and challenged an orthodoxy, the transformed cladists are perhaps best defined by an opponent—in this case, the British biologist Beverly Halstead. Asked not long ago in a BBC interview what he thought of transformed cladistics, Halstead replied: "Well, I object to it! I mean, this is going back to Aristotle. It is not pre-Darwinian, it is Aristotelian. From Darwin's day to the present we've understood there's a time element; we've begun to understand evolution. What they are doing in transformed cladistics is to say, Let's forget about evolution, let's forget about process, let's simply consider pattern."

Since Darwin's time, biologists have been absorbed in process: Where did we come from? How did everything in nature get to be what it now is? How will things continue to alter? The transformed cladists—they are sometimes called pattern cladists—are not concerned primarily with time or process. To understand why, it helps to know that they are trained in taxonomy: they are rigorous, scrupulous labelers. Their job as taxonomists is to discover and name the various groups found in nature— a task first assigned to Adam by God, according to Genesis—and put them into one category or another. Taxonomists try to determine not how groups came into existence but what groups exist, among both present-day and fossil organisms. To understand that cladists believe this knowledge must be acquired before ideas about process can be tested is to understand the natural tension that exists between taxonomists and evolutionary biologists.

The transformed cladists have escalated the battle. In the 1940s and 1950s, years which witnessed the growth of evolutionary biology, taxonomists allowed themselves what might be called a bit of artistic license. (They called it the new systematics.) This occurred in part, no doubt, because taxonomy had come to be thought of as dull and stuffy—particularly by evolutionists like Sir Julian Huxley (the grandson of Darwin's contemporary champion Thomas Henry Huxley), who believed it was high time to cease being "bogged down in semantics and definitions." (Sir Julian said this in 1959 at the University of Chicago during a centennial celebration for Darwin's On the Origin of Species.) Taxonomists, in other words, were regarded as bookkeepers and accountants in need of a little loosening up. In his 1959 book Nature & Man's Fate, Garrett Hardin, a professor of human ecology at the University of California at Santa Barbara, quoted a zoologist as giving this advice: "Whoever wants to hold to firm rules should give up taxonomic work. Nature is much too disorderly for such a man."

The transformed cladists think otherwise, and have sought to re-establish taxonomic rigor. In doing so, they have come to think that it is the evolutionists who have the problem—the problem being slipshod methodology. Colin Patterson, perhaps the leading transformed cladist, has enunciated what might be regarded as the cladists' battle cry: "The concept of ancestry is not accessible by the tools we have." Patterson and his fellow cladists argue that a common ancestor can only be hypothesized, not identified in the fossil record. A group of people can be brought together for a family reunion on the basis of birth documents, tombstone inscriptions, and parish records—evidence of process, one might say. But in nature there are no parish records; there are only fossils. And a fossil, Patterson told me once, is a "mess on a rock." Time, change, process, evolution—none of this, the cladists argue, can be read from rocks.

What can be discerned in nature, according to the cladists, are patterns—relationships between things, not between eras. There can be no absolute tracing back. There can be no certainty about parent-offspring links. There are only inferences drawn from fossils. To the cladists, the science of evolution is in large part a matter of faith—faith different, but not all *that* different, from that of the creationists.

"I really put my foot in it," Patterson told me that day I first met him nearly two years ago. We were in a restaurant on Columbus Avenue near the Museum of Natural History, and he was recalling the talk he had given eighteen months earlier to the systematics discussion group. "I compared evolution and creation and made a case that the two were equivalent. I was all fired up, and I said what I thought. I went through merry hell for about a year. Almost everybody except the people at the museum objected. Lots of academics wrote. Deluges of mail. 'Here we are trying to combat a political argument,' they said, 'and you give them ammunition!'"

He ordered something from the menu and said:"One has to live with one's colleagues. They hold the theory very dear. I found out that what you say will be taken in 'political' rather than rational terms."

Patterson told me that he regarded the theory of evolution as "often unnecessary" in biology. "In fact," he said, "they could do perfectly well without it." Nevertheless, he said, it was presented in textbooks as though it were "the unified field theory of biology," holding the whole subject together—and binding the profession to it. "Once something has that status," he said, "it becomes like religion."

The founding father of cladistics was an entomologist named Willi Hennig. Hennig was born in what is now East Germany and spent the bulk of his career there, studying and classifying flies. At some point in the mid-1960s (there is very little biographical information available about him) he turned up in West Germany; he died there, at the age of 63, in 1976. His principal work is *Phylogenetic Systematics*, an updated version of which was translated into English and published in the United States in 1966 by the University of Illinois Press. It is a difficult book, and an enormously influential one. By the 1970s, as the prominent evolutionary biologist Ernst Mayr wrote in *The Growth of Biological Thought*, a virtual Hennig cult had developed. A Willi Hennig Society was formed in 1980, and its fourth annual meeting, held last summer in London, was attended by some 250 scientists from around the world. Last month, the society published the first issue of its new quarterly journal, *Cladistics*. According to David Hull, the philosopher of science (he was at the meeting too), "among evolutionary biologists, cladistics is what everyone is arguing about."

At the heart of cladistics are the concepts of "plesiomorphy" and "paraphyly." A characteristic, or trait, is said to be plesiomorphic if it is found in a group of organisms of more general scope than the specific group under consideration. Thus, while all primates have hair, hair is also a characteristic of a more general class of creatures—mammals. What Hennig called the fallacy of plesiomorphy is the belief that a characteristic (like hair) identifies and helps to define a particular species or order of animal life when in fact it can be found among a broader group.

Hennig also objected to the still common practice in biology of identifying a grouping of animal life only by the absence of certain characteristics. (His reasoning was Aristotelian; in On the Parts of Animals, Aristotle wrote that "there can be no specific forms of a negation, of Featherless, for instance or of Footless, as there are of Feathered or Footed.") It was the lack of precision that bothered Hennig: a feathered animal is one thing (a bird); a non-feathered animal is anything (except a bird). Groups in nature defined by an absence of characteristics Hennig called paraphyletic.

By calling attention to the paraphyletic traits, Hennig helped revive the rigor taxonomy once prided itself on. Colin Patterson and other transformed cladists have moved on to examine—and call into question—the crucial role that paraphyletic groups and species play in evolutionary theory. In his 1981 talk at the Museum of Natural History, for example, Patterson touched on the subject of invertebrates. Invertebrates make up one of the two general categories of animals. The grouping comprises a huge and often bewildering diversity of animals, from the simplest single-cell protozoan to insects, clams, worms, and crabs. Every schoolchild learns that what brings this wide array of creatures under one heading is their shared lack of a backbone. Cladists like Patterson have asked: Why group them this way? What function does it serve? The problem they have is this: the term invertebrate does not serve a scientific function; it is too nebulous, too inexact for that. (It also accurately describes strawberries and chairs.) What the term invertebrate does serve, the cladists maintain, is a rhetorical function: it makes possible the claim, found in many textbooks, that "vertebrates evolved from invertebrates." According to the cladistic reading, the last two words of the four-word statement do not contain any information that is not asserted as factual by the first two words; "vertebrates evolved" simply means that the first vertebrate had parents without backbones. The transformed cladists claim that "vertebrates evolved from invertebrates" is a disguised tautology.

In his museum talk, Patterson said that groups defined only by negative traits have "no existence in nature, and they cannot possibly convey knowledge, though they appear to when you first hear them." Evolutionary biologists maintain that negatively defined groups make sense and serve a purpose; they tend to accuse the cladists, as one writer recently did in the magazine Science, of engaging in "verbal legerdemain." But

Patterson and his colleagues point their fingers back at the evolutionists. Patterson for one has called the paraphyletic groups "voids."

What evolutionary theory does, the cladists say, is make claims about something that cannot be determined by studying fossils. They say that the "tree of life," with its paraphyletic branches, is nothing more than a hypothesis, a reasonable guess.

Nor do they believe it will ever be anything more than that. When asked about this in an interview, Patterson said: "I don't think we shall ever have any access to any form of tree which we can call factual." He was then asked: "Do you believe it to be, then, no reality?" He replied: "Well, isn't it strange that this is what it comes to, that you have to ask me whether I believe it, as if it mattered whether I believe it or not. Yes, I do believe it. But in saying that, it is obvious it is faith."

Cladists do not spend their time on the lecture circuit drumming up sentiment against Darwin. Some of them would like it if all the talk about evolution just quietly went away. Evolution is not important to the work they do. That work involves finding the positive and verifiable characteristics of the various species and determining how all these species fit together in the animal kingdom—what patterns exist in nature. Their interest is the here and now, not how it all came to be.

I recently spent some time with two cladists on the staff of the Museum of Natural History. I first met with Gareth Nelson, who in 1982 was named chairman of the department of ichthyology. Nelson graduated from the University of Hawaii in 1966 and he joined the museum staff a year later. The walls of Nelson's office were lined with boxes of articles from scientific journals, and a large table was covered with papers and jars stuffed with small, silvery fish preserved in alcohol: anchovies. Nelson is just about the world's expert on anchovies, although he told me that the number of people studying them (three or four) is much smaller than the number of anchovy species (there are 150 known species, and Nelson believes there are many more). This disparity between the magnitude of the scientific "problem" and the number of people working on it is a commonplace in biology. Most laymen think that the experts have pretty exhaustively studied the earth's biota, when they have barely scratched the surface.

Nelson put the issue of evolution this way: in order to understand what we actually know, we must first look at what it is that the evolutionists claim to know for certain. He said that if you turn to a widely used college text like Alfred Romer's *Vertebrate Paleontology*, published by the University of Chicago Press in 1966 and now in its third edition, you will find such statements as "mammals evolved from reptiles," and "birds are descended from reptiles." (Very rarely, at least in the current literature, will you find the claim that a given species evolved from another given species.) The trouble with general statements like "mammals evolved from reptiles," Nelson said, is that the "ancestral groups are taxonomic artifacts." These groups "do not have any characters that are unique," he said. "They do not have defining characters, and therefore they are not real groups." I asked Nelson to name some of these allegedly "unreal" groups. He replied: invertebrates, fishes, reptiles, apes. According to Nelson, this does not by any means exhaust the list of negatively defined groups. Statements imputing ancestry to such groups have no real meaning, he said.

I asked Nelson about the fossil record. Don't we know that evolutionary theory is true from the fossils? Like most people, I thought the natural history museums had pretty well worked out the fossil sequences, much as in an automobile museum you can find the "ancestors" of contemporary cars lined up in sequence: Thunderbird back to Model T.

"Usually with fossils all you find are a few nuts and bolts," Nelson said. "An odd piston ring, maybe, or different pieces of a carburetor that are spread out or piled on top of one another, but not in their correct arrangement."

He maintained that too much importance has been attached to fossils. "And it's easy to understand why," he said. "You put in all this effort studying them, and you get out a little bit. Therefore you are persuaded that that little bit must be very important. I can get ten times more information per unit with recent fishes. So if you put in all that effort on fossils, you are inclined to say that the information you get is worth ten times as much."

Nelson said it was quite common for paleontologists to go to all the trouble of digging up fossils without realizing that the animals in question were still walking about. (Think of spending months hunting for a book in used-book stores without realizing it was still in print.) "Say you dig up a 50-million-year-old beetle," he said. "It looks like it belongs to a certain family, but there may be 30,000 species in the family. What do you do? Go through all 30,000? No, you just give it an appropriate-sounding name, *Eocoleoptera*, say. If it is a species that has been in existence for 50 million years, somebody else will have to find that out, because you don't have enough time. You're out digging in the rocks, not poking through beetle collections in museums."

I asked him about anchovy fossils. How far back do they go? "Well," he said, "Lance Grande, who was a student here recently, studied that, and it turns out that all the fossils previously described as anchovies are not anchovies at all." (Grande is now an assistant curator in the department of geology at the Field Museum of Natural History in Chicago.) "In other words," Nelson said, "the people who described them did not do a very good job. So the fossil record of anchovies was reduced to zero. However, there was something in the British Museum that I think Colin Patterson told Grande about, something from the Miocene in Cyprus; maybe 10 million years old. And it turned out to be an anchovy—the only known fossil. It has not yet been described in detail, but there is information suggesting it is the same kind of animal we find inhabiting the Mediterranean today."

A week or two after I met with Nelson I spoke to Norman Platnick, a curator in the museum's entomology department and an expert on spiders. On my way to see him on the fifth floor, I was joined in the elevator by a couple of lab assistants who were wheeling on a cart what looked like a dinosaur head. (I was reminded that for a long time the museum had the wrong head on its brontosaurus. One of the few bits of conventional wisdom about paleontology is that entire animals can be reconstructed from scraps of bone. Paleontologists now repudiate the idea, first enunciated by the French anatomist Baron Cuvier in the early 1800s. Steve Farris, a professor in the department of ecology and evolution at the State University of New York at Stony Brook and the president of the Hennig Society, told me that Cuvier erected a monument to his own error in the form of a cement statue of an iguanodon, now at the Crystal Palace outside London. "The animal that Cuvier imagined was four-footed and resembled a rhinoceros," Farris said. "The complete skeleton of the iguanodon is now known—the animal was bipedal, with a long tail." As for the idea that the relationship of early animals to present-day ones is well established, Farris said: "When they are writing for a general audience, a lot of paleontologists do try to give that impression.")

Not far from the elevator I found Platnick's orderly office: spiders (dead) inside little labeled bottles; book-filled shelves; journal articles neatly stacked. It would seem that professional biologists spend at least as much time studying each other's work as they do the world around them.

Platnick, who is rather square-shaped and bearded, told me that when he was an undergraduate at a small Appalachian college, he would go along with his wife when she collected millipedes. "But I was a wretched millipede collector," he said. "When we arrived home, all I would have in my jars would be spiders." So he started to study them. Today he has a Ph.D. from Harvard, and he and Nelson are co-authors of a book recently published by Columbia University Press entitled *Systematics and Biogeography: Cladistics and Vicariance.*

Spiders, which go back to the Devonian period, 400 million years ago, belong to the class Arachnida and the phylum Arthropoda. They are among the "invertebrates," in other words, and are not well preserved in the fossil record. About 35,000 species of spiders have been identified, Platnick said, "but there may be three times that many in the world." He thought there were perhaps four full-time systematists examining spiders in the United States, "and perhaps another dozen who teach at small colleges and do some research." There is an American Arachnological

Society, with 475 members worldwide, some of them amateurs. They meet once a year and discuss scorpions and daddy-long-legs, as well as spiders.

"Most of the spiders I look at may have been looked at by two or three people in history," Platnick said, adding that he would most likely be dead before anyone looked at them again.

I asked Platnick what was known about spider phylogeny, or ancestry.

"Very little," he said. "We still don't know a hill of beans about that." We certainly don't know, he said, what species the animal belonged to that was the ancestor of the very first spider. All we know of such an animal is that it was *not* a spider. We don't even know of any links in the (presumed) 400-million-year chain of spider ancestry.

"I do not ever say that this spider is ancestral to that one," Platnick said firmly.

"Does anyone?"

"I don't know of a single case in the modern literature where it's claimed that one spider is the ancestor of another."

Some spiders have been well preserved in amber. Even so, Platnick said, "very few spider fossils have been so well preserved that you can put a species name on them." After a pause he added: "You don't learn much from fossils."

In view of Platnick's comments about our knowledge of spider ancestry, I was curious to know what he thought of the following passage from a well-known high school biology text, *Life: An Introduction to Biology*, by George Simpson and William S. Beck, first published in 1957 by Harcourt Brace Jovanovich and still in print.

> An animal is not classified as an arachnid because it has four or five pairs of legs rather than three. It is classified in the Arachnida because it has the same ancestry as other arachnids, and a different ancestry from insects over some hundreds of millions of years, as attested by all the varying characteristics of the two groups and by large numbers of fossil representatives of both.

At that he threw himself back in his chair, and burst out laughing.

In this passage, Simpson and Beck were practicing the verbal sleight of hand that has been common in evolutionary biology since the 1940s. All we know for sure is that there is a group of organisms (in this case spiders) that are identifiable as a group because they have certain unique characteristics. They have spinnerets for spinning silk, for instance, and thus we can say that all organisms with spinnerets are spiders. (They share other unique features, too.)

If we want to explain *why* thousands of members of a group have features uniquely in common, that is another matter entirely. We can, if we like, posit a theoretical common ancestor in the ur-spider, which transmitted spider traits to all its descendants. That is precisely what

Darwin did in *On the Origin of Species*. But Simpson and Beck do something very different. They say that the composition of the class Arachnida was determined by examining not the features of spiders but their *ancestral lines*. But no such pedigrees are known to science—not just with respect to spiders but with respect to *all* groups of organisms.

The point stressed by the cladists is this: unless we know the taxonomic relationships of organisms—what makes each unique and different from the other—we cannot possibly guess at the ancestral relationships. Things in nature here and now must be ranked according to their taxonomic relationship before they can be placed in a family tree. Thus the speculations of evolutionists ("Do X and Y have a common ancestor?") must be subordinate to the findings of taxonomists ("X and Y have features not shared by anything else"). If fossils came with pedigrees attached, this laborious method of comparison would not be necessary; but of course they don't.

"Stephen Jay Gould does his work without bothering about cladistics, I assure you," Platnick said, citing a recent paper by Niels Bonde, a paleontologist at the University of Copenhagen. Platnick went on to say that "the literature is replete with such statements as 'fossil X is the ancestor of some other taxon,' when it has not even been shown that fossil X is the closest relative of that taxon." (By "closest relative" he means that the two taxa form a group having unique characteristics.) "This is seen most commonly in accounts of human paleontology, but it is by no means restricted to it," Platnick said.

One reason why many laymen readily accept evolution as fact is that they have seen the famous "horse sequence" reproduced in textbooks. The sequence, which shows a gradual increase in the size of the horse with time, is dear to the hearts of textbook writers, in large part because it is on display at the American Museum of Natural History. For obvious reasons, the museum staff are uncomfortable going on record about the horse sequence, but when Niles Eldridge, a curator in the department of invertebrates at the museum and co-author, with Stephen Jay Gould, of the "punctuated equilibria" theory of evolution (organisms stay the same for millions of years, then change quickly rather than gradually, as Darwin believed), was asked about it once, he said:

> There have been an awful lot of stories, some more imaginative than others, about what the nature of that history [of life] really is. The most famous example, still on exhibit downstairs, is the exhibit on horse evolution prepared perhaps fifty years ago. That has been presented as the literal truth in textbook after textbook. Now I think that that is lamentable, particularly when the people who propose these kinds of stories may themselves be aware of the speculative nature of some of that stuff.

When I brought the subject up with Platnick, he said that he thought horse fossils had not yet been properly classified, or even exhaustively studied. I wanted to know whether Platnick believed that evolution has occurred. He said he did, and that the evidence was to be found in the existing hierarchical structure of nature. All organisms can, as it were, be placed within an internested set of "boxes." The box labeled "gazelles" fits in the larger box labeled "ungulates" (animals with hoofs), which fits inside the "mammals" box, which fits inside "tetrapods" (four-footed animals), which fits inside "vertebrates." The grand task of taxonomy, Platnick said, is to describe this hierarchical pattern precisely, and in particular to define the traits that delineate the boundaries of each "box."

Whether taxonomy will ever fill in all the blanks in the pattern is a question Platnick cannot answer. One problem, he said, is the shortage of taxonomists. "Systematics," he said, "doesn't have the glamour to attract research funds." Research grants have increasingly gone to molecular and biochemical studies; the result is that support for taxonomy at many institutions has, he said, "withered away." This bothered Platnick. "I am fully prepared to stand up to any biologist who says evolutionary theory is more important, or more basic. Without the results of systematics there is nothing to be explained."

I wanted to find out what those on the other side—the evolutionary biologists and paleontologists—had to say about what the cladists are saying. First I went to the bookshelf. In his 1969 book *The Triumph of the Darwinian Method* (recently reprinted by the University of Chicago Press), Michael T. Ghiselin, one of Darwin's greatest admirers, seems to be taking on the cladists (or trying to) when he writes:

> Instead of finding patterns in nature and deciding that because of their conspicuousness they seem important, we discover the underlying mechanisms that impose order on natural phenomena, whether we see that order or not, and then derive the structure of our classification system from this understanding.

I next looked in *Hen's Teeth and Horse's Toes*, Stephen Jay Gould's volume of essays on natural history. "No debate in evolutionary biology has been more intense during the past decade than the challenges raised by cladistics against traditional schemes of classification," Gould writes. He is not sympathetic to cladistics ("its leading exponents in America are among the most contentious scientists I have ever encountered"), but in his essay "What, If Anything, Is a Zebra?" he admits that "behind the names and the nastiness lies an important set of principles." These he enunciates, only to repudiate. He acknowledges that a strict taxonomy would eliminate groups like apes and fishes. But when cladists go this far, "many biologists rebel, and rightly, I think." Like his Harvard colleague Edward O. Wilson, the Frank B. Baird Professor of Science, Gould opts for the "admittedly vague and qualitative, but not therefore unimportant notion of overall similarity" of form.

I decided it would be a good idea to talk with a scientist who believes strongly in evolutionary theory. Last May, I traveled to Boston to meet with Richard C. Lewontin, a geneticist, a one-time president of the Society for the Study of Evolution, a well-known writer on science, and currently Agassiz Professor of Zoology at Harvard. I had seen a quote from Lewontin used as a chapter head in a book titled *Science on Trial*, by Douglas Futuyma. The quote, as edited, read: "Evolution is fact, not theory.... Birds evolve from nonbirds, humans evolve from nonhumans."

Lewontin was uncharacteristically attired in a scientist's regulation white lab coat when I first saw him (instead of his usual blue work shirt). We talked a bit about his stand against biological determinism. Finally it was time to get around to the point of my visit. What about these claims: evolution is fact; birds evolve from nonbirds, humans from nonhumans? The cladists disapproved, I said.

He paused for a split second and said: "Those are very weak statements, I agree." Then he made one of the clearest statements about evolution I have heard. He said; "Those statements flow simply from the assertion that all organisms have parents. It is an empirical claim, I think, that all living organisms have living organisms as parents. The second empirical claim is that there was a time on earth when there were no mammals. Now, if you allow me those two claims as empirical, then the claim that mammals arose from non-mammals is simply a conclusion. It's the deduction from two empirical claims. But that's all I want to claim for it. You can't make the direct empirical statement that mammals arose from non-mammals."

Lewontin had made what seemed to me to be a deduction—a materialist's deduction. "The only problem is that it appears to be based on evidence derived from fossils," I said. "But the cladists say they don't really have that kind of information."

"Of course they don't," Lewontin said. "In fact, the stuff I've written on creationism, which isn't much, has always made that point. There is a vast weight of empirical evidence about the universe which says that unless you invoke supernatural causes, the birds could not have arisen from muck by any natural processes. Well, if the birds couldn't have arisen from muck by any natural processes, then they had to arise from non-birds. The only alternative is to say that they did arise from muck—because God's finger went out and touched that muck. That is to say, there was a non-natural process. And that's really where the action is. Either you think that complex organisms arose by non-natural phenomena, or you think that they arose by natural phenomena. If they arose by natural phenomena, they had to evolve. And that's all there is to it. And that's the only claim I'm making."

He reached for a copy of his 1982 book *Human Diversity*, and said: "Look, I'm a person who says in this book that we don't know anything about the ancestors of the human species." (He writes on page 163: "Despite the excited and optimistic claims that have been made by some paleontologists, no fossil hominid species can be established as our direct ancestor. . . .") "All the fossils which have been dug up and are claimed to be ancestors—we haven't the faintest idea whether they are ancestors. Because all you've got, and the cladists are right . . . " He got up and began to do his famous rat-a-tat-tat with a piece of chalk on the blackboard. "All you've got is Homo Sapiens there, you've got *that* fossil there, you've got another fossil *there* . . . this is time here . . . and it's up to you to draw the lines. Because there are no lines. I don't think any one of them is likely to be the direct ancestor of the human species. But how would you know it's *that* [pat] one?

"The only way you can know that some fossil is the direct ancestor is that it's so human that it *is* human. There is a contradiction there. If it is different enough from humans to be interesting, then you don't know whether it's an ancestor or not. And if it's similar enough to be human, then it's not interesting."

He returned to his chair and looked out at the slanting rain. "So," he said. "Look, we're not ever going to know what the direct ancestor is."

What struck me about Lewontin's argument was how much it depended on his premise that all organisms have parents. In a sense, his argument includes the assertion that evolutionary theory is true. Lewontin maintains that his premise is "empirical," but this is so only in the (admittedly important) sense that it has never to our knowledge been falsified. No one has ever found an organism that is known not to have parents, or a parent. This is the strongest evidence on behalf of evolution.

Our belief, or "faith," that, as Patterson says, "all organisms have parents" ultimately derives from our acceptance of the philosophy of materialism. It is hard for us to understand (so long has materialism been the natural habitat of Western thought) that this philosophy was not always accepted. In one of his essays on natural history reprinted in *Ever Since Darwin*, Stephen Jay Gould suggests that Darwin delayed publishing his theory of evolution by natural selection because he was, perhaps unconsciously, waiting for the climate of materialism to become more firmly established. In his 1838 *M Notebook* Darwin wrote: "To avoid stating how far, I believe, in Materialism, say only that emotions, instincts, degrees of talent, which are hereditary are so because brain of child resembles parent stock." Darwin realized that the climate *had* changed—that evolution was "in the air"—in 1858 when he was jolted by Alfred Russel Wallace's paper outlining a theory of the mechanism of evolution very similar to his own.

The theory of evolution has never been falsified. On the other hand, it is also surely true that the positive evidence for evolution is very much weaker than most laymen imagine, and than many scientists want us to imagine. Perhaps, as Patterson says, that positive evidence is missing entirely. The human mind, alas, seems on the whole to find such uncertainty intolerable. Most people want certainty in one form (Darwin) or another (the Bible). Only evolutionary agnostics like Patterson and Nelson and the other cladists seem willing to live with doubt. And that, surely, is the only truly scientific outlook.

1986

THE READER

1. What, according to Bethell, is "the only true scientific outlook"? Do you agree? Is this view generally supported by other essays on science in this section, or are there exceptions?
2. What is the difference between the kind of work done by taxonomists and by evolutionary biologists?
3. What is meant by "the philosophy of materialism"?
4. What question, specifically, is at issue in the discussion of evolution presented here?

THE WRITER

1. Does Bethell have a thesis? If so, by what means does he demonstrate or develop it?
2. Write a brief explanation of the relationship between Bethell's title and the body of the article.

Thomas S. Kuhn

THE ROUTE TO NORMAL SCIENCE

In this essay, 'normal science' means research firmly based upon one or more past scientific achievements, achievements that some particular scientific community acknowledges for a time as supplying the foundation for its further practice. Today such achievements are recounted, though seldom in their original form, by science textbooks, elementary and advanced. These textbooks expound the body of accepted theory, illustrate many or all of its successful applications, and compare these applications with exemplary observations and experiments. Before such books became popular early in the nineteenth century (and until even more recently in the newly matured sciences), many of the famous classics of science fulfilled a similar function. Aristotle's *Physica*, Ptolemy's *Almagest*, Newton's *Principia* and *Opticks*, Franklin's *Electricity*, Lavoisier's *Chemistry*, and Lyell's *Geology*—these and many other works served for a time implicitly to define the legitimate problems and methods of a research field for succeeding generations of practitioners. They were able to do so because they shared two essential characteristics. Their achievement was sufficiently unprecedented to attract an enduring group of adherents away from competing modes of scientific activity. Simultaneously, it was sufficiently open-ended to leave all sorts of problems for the redefined group of practitioners to resolve.

Achievements that share these two characteristics I shall henceforth refer to as 'paradigms,' a term that relates closely to 'normal science.' By choosing it, I mean to suggest that some accepted examples of actual scientific practice—examples which include law, theory, application, and instrumentation together—provide models from which spring particular coherent traditions of scientific research. These are the traditions which the historian describes under such rubrics as 'Ptolemaic astronomy' (or 'Copernican'), 'Aristotelian dynamics' (or 'Newtonian'), 'corpuscular optics' (or 'wave optics'), and so on. The study of paradigms, including many that are far more specialized than those named illustratively above, is what mainly prepares the student for membership in the particular scientific community with which he will later practice. Because he there joins men who learned the bases of their field from the same concrete models, his subsequent practice will seldom evoke overt disagreement over fundamentals. Men whose research is based on shared paradigms are committed to the same rules and standards for scientific practice. That commitment and the apparent consensus it produces are prerequisites for normal science, i.e., for the genesis and continuation of a particular research tradition.

Because in this essay the concept of a paradigm will often substitute for a variety of familiar notions, more will need to be said about the reasons for its introduction. Why is the concrete scientific achievement, as a locus of professional commitment, prior to the various concepts, laws, theories, and points of view that may be abstracted from it? In what sense is the shared paradigm a fundamental unit for the student of scientific development, a unit that cannot be fully reduced to logically atomic components which might function in its stead? There can be a sort of scientific research without paradigms, or at least without any so unequivocal and so binding as the ones named above. Acquisition of a paradigm and of the more esoteric type of research it permits is a sign of maturity in the development of any given scientific field.

If the historian traces the scientific knowledge of any selected group of related phenomena backward in time, he is likely to encounter some minor variant of a pattern here illustrated from the history of physical optics. Today's physics textbooks tell the student that light is photons, i.e., quantum-mechanical entities that exhibit some characteristics of waves and some of particles. Research proceeds accordingly, or rather according to the more elaborate and mathematical characterization from which this usual verbalization is derived. That characterization of light is, however, scarcely half a century old. Before it was developed by Planck, Einstein, and others early in this century, physics texts taught that light was transverse wave motion, a conception rooted in a paradigm that derived ultimately from the optical writings of Young and Fresnel in the early nineteenth century. Nor was the wave theory the first to be embraced by almost all practitioners of optical science. During the eighteenth century the paradigm for this field was provided by Newton's *Opticks*, which taught that light was material corpuscles. At that time physicists sought evidence, as the early wave theorists had not, of the pressure exerted by light particles impinging on solid bodies.

These transformations of the paradigms of physical optics are scientific revolutions, and the successive transition from one paradigm to another via revolution is the usual developmental pattern of mature science. It is not, however, the pattern characteristic of the period before Newton's work, and that is the contrast that concerns us here. No period between remote antiquity and the end of the seventeenth century exhibited a single generally accepted view about the nature of light. Instead there were a number of competing schools and sub-schools, most of them espousing one variant or another of Epicurean, Aristotelian, or Platonic theory.[1] One group took light to be particles emanating from material bodies; for another it was a modification of the medium that intervened between the body and the eye; still another explained light in terms of an interaction of the medium with an emanation from the eye; and there were other combinations and modifications besides. Each of the corresponding schools derive strength from its relation to some particular metaphysic, and each emphasized, as paradigmatic observations, the particular cluster of optical phenomena that its own theory could do most to explain. Other observations were dealt with by *ad hoc* elaborations, or they remained as outstanding problems for further research.

At various times all these schools made significant contributions to the body of concepts, phenomena, and techniques from which Newton drew the first nearly uniformly accepted paradigm for physical optics. Any definition of the scientist that excludes at least the more creative members of these various schools will exclude their modern successors as well. Those men were scientists. Yet anyone examining a survey of physical optics before Newton may well conclude that, though the field's practitioners were scientists, the net result of their activity was something less than science. Being able to take no common body of belief for granted,

1. The reference is to the three principal world views of ancient Greek philosophy.

each writer on physical optics felt forced to build his field anew from its foundations. In doing so, his choice of supporting observation and experiment was relatively free, for there was no standard set of methods or of phenomena that every optical writer felt forced to employ and explain. Under these circumstances, the dialogue of the resulting books was often directed as much to the members of other schools as it was to nature. That pattern is not unfamiliar in a number of creative fields today, nor is it incompatible with significant discovery and invention. It is not, however, the pattern of development that physical optics acquired after Newton and that other natural sciences make familiar today.

The history of electrical research in the first half of the eighteenth century provides a more concrete and better known example of the way a science develops before it acquires its first universally received paradigm. During that period there were almost as many views about the nature of electricity as there were important electrican experimenters, men like Haukshee, Gray, Desaguliers, Du Fay, Nollett, Watson, Franklin, and others. All their numerous concepts of electricity had something in common—they were partially derived from one or another version of the mechanico-corpuscular philosophy that guided all scientific research of the day. In addition, all were components of real scientific theories, of theories that had been drawn in part from experiment and observation and that partially determined the choice and interpretation of additional problems undertaken in research. Yet though all the experiments were electrical and though most of the experimenters read each other's works, their theories had no more than a family resemblance.

One early group of theories, following seventeenth-century practice, regarded attraction and frictional generation as the fundamental electrical phenomena. This group tended to treat repulsion as a secondary effect due to some sort of mechanical rebounding and also to postpone for as long as possible both discussion and systematic research on Gray's newly discovered effect, electrical conduction. Other "electricians" (the term is their own) took attraction and repulsion to be equally elementary manifestations of electricity and modified their theories and research accordingly. (Actually, this group is remarkably small—even Franklin's theory never quite accounted for the mutual repulsion of two negatively charged bodies.) But they had as much difficulty as the first group in accounting simultaneously for any but the simplest conduction effects. Those effects, however, provided the starting point for still a third group, one which tended to speak of electricity as a "fluid" that could run through conductors rather than as an "effluvium" that emanated from non-conductors. This group, in its turn, had difficulty reconciling its theory with a number of attractive and repulsive effects. Only through the work of Franklin and his immediate successors did a theory arise that could account with something like equal facility for very nearly all these effects and that therefore could and did provide a subsequent generation of "electricians" with a common paradigm for its research.

Excluding those fields, like mathematics and astronomy, in which the first firm paradigms date from prehistory and also those, like biochemistry, that arose by division and recombination of specialties already matured, the situations outlined above are historically typical. Though it involves my continuing to employ the unfortunate simplification that tags an extended historical episode with a single and somewhat arbitrarily chosen name (e.g., Newton or Franklin), I suggest that similar fundamental disagreements characterized, for example, the study of motion before Aristotle and of statics before Archimedes, the study of heat before Black, of chemistry before Boyle and Boerhaave, and of historical geology before Hutton. In parts of biology—the study of heredity, for example—the first universally received paradigms are still more recent; and it remains an open question what parts of social science have yet acquired such paradigms at all. History suggests that the road to a firm research consensus is extraordinarily arduous.

History also suggests, however, some reasons for the difficulties encountered on the road. In the absence of a paradigm or some candidate for paradigm, all of the facts that could possibly pertain to the development of a given science are likely to seem equally relevant. As a result, early fact-gathering is a far more nearly random activity than the one that subsequent scientific development makes familiar. Futhermore, in the absence of a reason for seeking some particular form of more recondite information, early fact-gathering is usually restricted to the wealth of data that lie ready to hand. The resulting pool of facts contains those accessible to casual observation and experiment together with some of the more esoteric data retrievable from established crafts medicine, calendar making, and metallurgy. Because the crafts are one readily accessible source of facts that could not have been casually discovered, technology has often played a vital role in the emergence of new sciences.

But though this sort of fact-collecting has been essential to the origin of many significant sciences, anyone who examines, for example, Pliny's encyclopedic writings or the Baconian natural histories of the seventeenth century will discover that it produces a morass. One somehow hesitates to call the literature that results scientific. The Baconian "histories" of heat, color, wind, mining, and so on, are filled with information, some of it recondite. But they juxtapose facts that will later prove revealing (e.g., heating by mixture) with others (e.g., the warmth of dung heaps) that will for some time remain too complex to be integrated with theory at all. In addition, since any description must be partial, the typical natural history often omits from its immensely circumstantial accounts just those details that later scientists will find sources of important illumination. Almost none of the early "histories" of electricity, for example, mention that chaff, attracted to a rubbed glass rod, bounces off again. That effect seemed mechanical, not electrical. Moreover, since the casual fact-gatherer seldom possesses the time or the tools to be critical, the natural histories often juxtapose descriptions like the above with others, say, heating by antiperistasis (or by cooling), that we are now quite unable to confirm.[2] Only very occasionally, as in the cases of ancient statics, dynamics, and geometrical optics, do facts collected with so little guidance from pre-established theory speak with sufficient clarity to permit the emergence of a first paradigm.

This is the situation that creates the schools characteristic of the early stages of a science's development. No natural history can be interpreted in the absence of at least some implicit body of intertwined theoretical and methodological belief that permits selection, evaluation, and criticism. If that body of belief is not already implicit in the collection of facts —in which case more than "mere facts" are at hand—it must be externally supplied, perhaps by a current metaphysic, by another science, or by personal and historical accident. No wonder, then, that in the early stages of the development of any science different men confronting the same range of phenomena, but not usually all the same particular phenomena, describe and interpret them in different ways. What is surprising, and perhaps also unique in its degree to the fields we call science, is that such initial divergences should ever largely disappear.

For they do disappear to a very considerable extent and then apparently once and for all. Furthermore, their disappearance is usually caused by the triumph of one of the pre-paradigm schools, which, because of its own characteristic beliefs and pre-conceptions, emphasized only some special part of the too sizable and inchoate pool of information. Those electricians who thought electricity a fluid and therefore gave particular emphasis to conduction provide an excellent case in point. Led by this belief, which could scarcely cope with the known multiplicity of attractive and repulsive effects, several of them conceived the idea of bottling the electrical fluid. The immediate fruit of their efforts was the Leyden jar, a device which might never have been discovered by a man exploring nature casually or at random, but which was in fact independently developed by at least two investigators in the early 1740's. Almost from the start of his electrical researches, Franklin was particularly concerned to explain that strange and, in the event, particularly revealing piece of special apparatus. His success in doing so provided the most effective of the arguments that made his theory a paradigm, though one that was still unable to account for quite all the known cases of electrical repulsion.[3]

2. Bacon [in the Novum Organum] says, "Water slightly warm is more easily frozen than quite cold" [Kuhn's note]; *antiperistasis:* an old word meaning a reaction caused by the action of an opposite quality or principle —here, heating through cooling.
3. The troublesome case was the mutual repulsion of negatively charged bodies [Kuhn's

To be accepted as a paradigm, a theory must seem better than its competitors, but it need not, and in fact never does, explain all the facts with which it can be confronted.

What the fluid theory of electricity did for the subgroup that held it, the Franklinian paradigm later did for the entire group of electricians. It suggested which experiments would be worth performing and which, because directed to secondary or to overly complex manifestations of electricity, would not. Only the paradigm did the job far more effectively, partly because the end of interschool debate ended the constant reiteration of fundamentals and partly because the confidence that they were on the right track encouraged scientists to undertake more precise, esoteric, and consuming sorts of work.[4] Freed from the concern with any and all electrical phenomena, the united group of electricians could pursue selected phenomena in far more detail, designing much special equipment for the task and employing it more stubbornly and systematically than electricians had ever done before. Both fact collection and theory articulation became highly directed activities. The effectiveness and efficiency of electrical research increased accordingly, providing evidence for a societal version of Francis Bacon's acute methodological dictum: "Truth emerges more readily from error than from confusion."

We shall be examining the nature of this highly directed or paradigm-based research in the next section, but must first note briefly how the emergence of a paradigm affects the structure of the group that practices the field. When, in the development of a natural science, an individual or group first produces a synthesis able to attract most of the next generation's practitioners, the older schools gradually disappear. In part their disappearance is caused by their members' conversion to the new paradigm. But there are always some men who cling to one or another of the older views, and they are simply read out of the profession, which thereafter ignores their work. The new paradigm implies a new and more rigid definition of the field. Those unwilling or unable to accommodate their work to it must proceed in isolation or attach themselves to some other group.[5] Historically, they have often simply stayed in the depart-

---

note].

4. It should be noted that the acceptance of Franklin's theory did not end quite all debate. In 1759 Robert Symmer proposed a two-fluid version of that theory, and for many years thereafter electricians were divided about whether electricity was a single fluid or two. But the debates on this subject only confirm what has been said above about the manner in which a universally recognized achievement unites the profession. Electricians, though they continued divided on this point, rapidly concluded that no experimental tests could distinguish the two

versions of the theory and that they were therefore equivalent. After that, both schools could and did exploit all the benefits that the Franklinian theory provided [Kuhn's note].

5. The history of electricity provides an excellent example which could be duplicated from the careers of Priestley, Kelvin, and others. Franklin reports that Nollet, who at mid-century was the most influential of the Continental electricians, "lived to see himself the last of his Sect, except Mr. B.—his *Eleve* [pupil] and immediate Disciple." More interesting, however, is the endurance of

ments of philosophy from which so many of the special sciences have been spawned. As these indications hint, it is sometimes just its reception of a paradigm that transforms a group previously interested merely in the study of nature into a profession or, at least, a discipline. In the sciences (though not in fields like medicine, technology, and law, of which the principal *raison d'être* is an external social need), the formation of specialized journals, the foundation of specialists' societies, and the claim for a special place in the curriculum have usually been associated with a group's first reception of a single paradigm. At least this was the case between the time, a century and a half ago, when the institutional pattern of scientific specialization first developed and the very recent time when the paraphernalia of specialization acquired a prestige of their own.

The more rigid definition of the scientific group has other consequences. When the individual scientist can take a paradigm for granted, he need no longer, in his major works, attempt to build his field anew, starting from first principles and justifying the use of each concept introduced. That can be left to the writer of textbooks. Given a textbook, however, the creative scientist can begin his research where it leaves off and thus concentrate exclusively upon the subtlest and most esoteric aspects of the natural phenomena that concern his group. And as he does this, his research communiqués will begin to change in ways whose evolution has been too little studied but whose modern end products are obvious to all and oppressive to many. No longer will his researches usually be embodied in books addressed, like Franklin's *Experiments . . . on Electricity* or Darwin's *Origin of Species*, to anyone who might be interested in the subject matter of the field. Instead they will usually appear as brief articles addressed only to professional colleagues, the men whose knowledge of a shared paradigm can be assumed and who prove to be the only ones able to read the papers addressed to them.

Today in the sciences, books are usually either texts or retrospective reflections upon one aspect or another of the scientific life. The scientist who writes one is more likely to find his professional reputation impaired than enhanced. Only in the earlier, pre-paradigm, stages of the development of the various sciences did the book ordinarily possess the same relation to professional achievement that it still retains in other creative fields. And only in those fields that still retain the book, with or without the article, as a vehicle for research communication are the lines of professionalization still so loosely drawn that the layman may hope to follow progress by reading the practitioners' original reports. Both in mathematics and astronomy, research reports had ceased already in

whole schools in increasing isolation from professional science. Consider, for example, the case of astrology, which was once an integral part of astronomy. Or consider the continuation in the late eighteenth, and early nineteenth centuries of a previously respected tradition of "romantic" chemistry [Kuhn's note].

antiquity to be intelligible to a generally educated audience. In dynamics, research became similarly esoteric in the latter Middle Ages, and it recaptured general intelligibility only briefly during the early seventeenth century when a new paradigm replaced the one that had guided medieval research. Electrical research began to require translation for the layman before the end of the eighteenth century, and most other fields of physical science ceased to be generally accessible in the nineteenth. During the same two centuries similar transitions can be isolated in the various parts of the biological sciences. In parts of the social sciences they may well be occurring today. Although it has become customary, and is surely proper, to deplore the widening gulf that separates the professional scientist from his collegues in other fields, too little attention is paid to the essential relationship between that gulf and the mechanisms intrinsic to scientific advance.

Ever since prehistoric antiquity one field of study after another has crossed the divide between what the historian might call its prehistory as a science and its history proper. These transitions to maturity have seldom been so sudden or so unequivocal as my necessarily schematic discussion may have implied. But neither have they been historically gradual, coextensive, that is to say, with the entire development of the fields within which they occurred. Writers on electricity during the first four decades of the eighteenth century possessed far more information about electrical phenomena than had their sixteenth-century predecessors. During the half-century after 1740, few new sorts of electrical phenomena were added to their lists. Nevertheless, in important respects, the electrical writings of Cavendish, Coulomb, and Volta in the last third of the eighteenth century seem further removed from those of Gray, Du Fay, and even Franklin than are the writings of these early eighteenth-century electrical discoverers from those of the sixteenth century.[6] Sometime between 1740 and 1780, electricians were for the first time enabled to take the foundations of their field for granted. From that point they pushed on to more concrete and recondite problems, and increasingly they then reported their results in articles addressed to other electricians rather than in books addressed to the learned world at large. As a group they achieved what had been gained by astronomers in antiquity and by students of motion in the Middle Ages, of physical optics in the late seventeenth century, and of historical geology in the early nineteenth. They had, that is, achieved a paradigm that proved able

---

6. The post-Franklinian developments include an immense increase in the sensitivity of charge detectors, the first reliable and generally diffused techniques for measuring charge, the evolution of the concept of capacity and its relation to a newly refined notion of electric tension, and the quantification of electrostatic force [Kuhn's note].

to guide the whole group's research. Except with the advantage of hindsight, it is hard to find another criterion that so clearly proclaims a field a science.

1962

THE READER

1. *What does Kuhn mean by a "paradigm" in science, and what advantages for science does he ascribe to it? Can you state the prevailing paradigm in sciences other than those he uses for illustration (for example, chemistry, biology, psychology)? Does the search for or the finding of the paradigms help you to understand what these sciences are about?*
2. *What is the relationship, by Kuhn's account, of the science textbook to the nature and practice of science? Examine a textbook in your course in one of the natural or social sciences. Does it have the character Kuhn ascribes to textbooks? Does regarding the textbook in this light help you in your study of the subject?*

THE WRITER

1. *What is Kuhn's thesis? How is the essay organized to develop that thesis?*
2. *What does Kuhn's essay suggest about the nature of a scientific fact or the place of fact in science? By and large, does this conclusion agree or disagree with Bronowski's statement of the matter in "The Reach of Imagination" (p. 194)? Is it not the business of a science to observe and record the facts? Is this not what Tinbergen, for instance, does in "The Bee-Hunters of Hulshorst" (p. 892)? What more should science do? Put your answer to one or more of these questions into a brief essay.*

Literature and the Arts

Eudora Welty

ONE WRITER'S BEGINNINGS

I learned from the age of two or three that any room in our house, at any time of day, was there to read in, or to be read to. My mother read to me. She'd read to me in the big bedroom in the mornings, when we were in her rocker together, which ticked in rhythm as we rocked, as though we had a cricket accompanying the story. She'd read to me in the diningroom on winter afternoons in front of the coal fire, with our cuckoo clock ending the story with "Cuckoo," and at night when I'd got in my own bed. I must have given her no peace. Sometimes she read to me in the kitchen while she sat churning, and the churning sobbed along with any story. It was my ambition to have her read to me while I churned; once she granted my wish, but she read off my story before I brought her butter. She was an expressive reader. When she was reading "Puss in Boots,"[1] for instance, it was impossible not to know that she distrusted all cats.

It had been startling and disappointing to me to find out that story books had been written by *people*, that books were not natural wonders, coming up of themselves like grass. Yet regardless of where they came from, I cannot remember a time when I was not in love with them—with the books themselves, cover and binding and the paper they were printed on, with their smell and their weight and with their possession in my arms, captured and carried off to myself. Still illiterate, I was ready for them, committed to all the reading I could give them.

Neither of my parents had come from homes that could afford to buy many books, but though it must have been something of a strain on his salary, as the youngest officer in a young insurance company, my father

---

1. A fairy tale.

was all the while carefully selecting and ordering away for what he and Mother thought we children should grow up with. They bought first for the future.

Besides the bookcase in the livingroom, which was always called "the library," there were the encyclopedia tables and dictionary stand under windows in our diningroom. Here to help us grow up arguing around the diningroom table were the Unabridged Webster, the Columbia Encyclopedia, Compton's Pictured Encyclopedia, the Lincoln Library of Information, and later the Book of Knowledge. And the year we moved into our new house, there was room to celebrate it with the new 1925 edition of the Britannica, which my father, his face always deliberately turned toward the future, was of course disposed to think better than any previous edition.

In "the library," inside the mission-style bookcase with its three diamond-latticed glass doors, with my father's Morris chair and the glass-shaded lamp on its table beside it, were books I could soon begin on—and I did, reading them all alike and as they came, straight down their rows, top shelf to bottom. There was the set of Stoddard's Lectures, in all its late nineteenth-century vocabulary and vignettes of peasant life and quaint beliefs and customs, with matching halftone illustrations: Vesuvius erupting, Venice by moonlight, gypsies glimpsed by their campfires. I didn't know then the clue they were to my father's longing to see the rest of the world. I read straight through his other love-from-afar: the Victrola Book of the Opera, with opera after opera in synopsis, with portraits in costume of Melba, Caruso, Galli-Curci, and Geraldine Farrar,[2] some of whose voices we could listen to on our Red Seal records.

My mother read secondarily for information; she sank as a hedonist into novels. She read Dickens in the spirit in which she would have eloped with him. The novels of her girlhood that had stayed on in her imagination, besides those of Dickens and Scott and Robert Louis Stevenson,[3] were Jane Eyre, Trilby, The Woman in White, Green Mansions, King Solomon's Mines.[4] Marie Corelli's[5] name would crop up but I understood she had gone out of favor with my mother, who had only kept Ardath out of loyalty. In time she absorbed herself in Galsworthy, Edith Wharton, above all in Thomas Mann of the Joseph volumes.[6]

St. Elmo was not in our house; I saw it often in other houses. This

2. Nellie Melba (1861–1931); Enrico Caruso (1837–1921); Amelita Galli-Curci (1889–1964); Geraldine Farrar (1882–1967).
3. Charles Dickens (1812–70); Sir Walter Scott (1771–1832); Robert Louis Stevenson (1850–94). The first was English, the others Scottish.
4. Respectively by Charlotte Brontë (1816–55), George Du Maurier (1834–96), Wilkie Collins (1824–89), William Henry Hudson (1841–1922), Sir H. Rider Haggard (1856–1925). All were English.
5. The pen name of Mary Mackay (1855–1924), a popular and prolific English novelist.
6. John Galsworthy (1867–1933), English; Edith Wharton (1862–1937), American; Thomas Mann (1875–1955), German, whose Joseph novels appeared in four parts, from 1933 to 1943.

wildly popular Southern novel is where all the Edna Earles in our population started coming from. They're all named for the heroine, who succeeded in bringing a dissolute, sinning roué and atheist of a lover (St. Elmo) to his knees. My mother was able to forgo it. But she remembered the classic advice given to rose growers on how to water their bushes long enough: "Take a chair and *St. Elmo*."[7]

To both my parents I owe my early acquaintance with a beloved Mark Twain. There was a full set of Mark Twain and a short set of Ring Lardner in our bookcase,[8] and those were the volumes that in time united us all, parents and children.

Reading everything that stood before me was how I came upon a worn old book without a back that had belonged to my father as a child. It was called *Sanford and Merton*. Is there anyone left who recognizes it, I wonder? It is the famous moral tale written by Thomas Day in the 1780s, but of him no mention is made on the title page of *this* book; here it is *Sanford and Merton in Words of One Syllable* by Mary Godolphin. Here are the rich boy and the poor boy and Mr. Barlow, their teacher and interlocutor, in long discourses alternating with dramatic scenes—danger and rescue allotted to the rich and the poor respectively. It may have only words of one syllable, but one of them is "quoth." It ends with not one but two morals, both engraved on rings: "Do what you ought, come what may," and "If we would be great, we must first learn to be good."

This book was lacking its front cover, the back held on by strips of pasted paper, now turned golden, in several layers, and the pages stained, flecked, and tattered around the edges; its garish illustrations had come unattached but were preserved, laid in. I had the feeling even in my heedless childhood that this was the only book my father as a little boy had had of his own. He had held onto it, and might have gone to sleep on its coverless face: he had lost his mother when he was seven. My father had never made any mention to his own children of the book, but he had brought it along with him from Ohio to our house and shelved it in our bookcase.

My mother had brought from West Virginia that set of Dickens; those books looked sad, too—they had been through fire and water before I was born, she told me, and there they were, lined up—as I later realized, waiting for *me*.

I was presented, from as early as I can remember, with books of my own, which appeared on my birthday and Christmas morning. Indeed, my parents could not give me books enough. They must have sacrificed to give me on my sixth or seventh birthday—it was after I became a reader for myself—the ten-volume set of *Our Wonder World*. These were beautifully made, heavy books I would lie down with on the floor in front of the diningroom hearth, and more often than the rest volume 5, *Every Child's Story Book*, was under my eyes. There were the fairy tales —Grimm, Andersen, the English, the French, "Ali Baba and the Forty Thieves"; and there was Aesop and Reynard the Fox; there were the myths and legends, Robin Hood, King Arthur, and St. George and the Dragon, even the history of Joan of Arc; a whack of *Pilgrim's Progress* and a long piece of *Gulliver*.[9] They all carried their classic illustrations. I located myself in these pages and could go straight to the stories and pictures I loved; very often "The Yellow Dwarf" was first choice, with Walter Crane's Yellow Dwarf in full color making his terrifying appearance flanked by turkeys.[1] Now that volume is as worn and backless and hanging apart as my father's poor *Sanford and Merton*. The precious page with Edward Lear's "Jumblies"[2] on it has been in danger of slipping out for all these years. One measure of my love for Our Wonder World was that for a long time I wondered if I would go through fire and water for it as my mother had done for Charles Dickens; and the only comfort was to think I could ask my mother to do it for me.

I believe I'm the only child I know of who grew up with this treasure in the house. I used to ask others, "Did you have Our Wonder World?" I'd have to tell them The Book of Knowledge could not hold a candle to it.

I live in gratitude to my parents for initiating me—and as early as I begged for it, without keeping me waiting—into knowledge of the word, into reading and spelling, by way of the alphabet. They taught it to me at home in time for me to begin to read before starting to school. I believe the alphabet is no longer considered an essential piece of equipment for traveling through life. In my day it was the keystone to knowledge. You learned the alphabet as you learned to count to ten, as you learned "Now I lay me" and the Lord's Prayer and your father's and mother's name and address and telephone number, all in case you were lost.

My love for the alphabet, which endures, grew out of reciting it but, before that, out of seeing the letters on the page. In my own story books, before I could read them for myself, I fell in love with various winding, enchanting-looking initials drawn by Walter Crane at the heads of fairy tales. In "Once upon a time," an "O" had a rabbit running it as a treadmill, his feet upon flowers. When the day came, years later, for me to see the Book of Kells,[3] all the wizardry of letter, initial, and word swept over me a thousand times over, and the illumination, the gold, seemed a part of the word's beauty and holiness that had been there from the start.

9. Respectively by John Bunyan (1628–88) and Jonathan Swift (1667–1745). Both were English.
1. A fairy tale illustrated by Walter Crane (1845–1915), popular illustrator of children's books.

2. A narrative poem about creatures called Jumblies who went to sea in a sieve. Edward Lear (1812–88), English, wrote nonsense poems for children.
3. An illustrated Irish manuscript of the four Gospels from the eighth or ninth century.

Learning stamps you with its moments. Childhood's learning is made up of moments. It isn't steady. It's a pulse.

In a children's art class, we sat in a ring on kindergarten chairs and drew three daffodils that has just been picked out of the yard; and while I was drawing, my sharpened pencil and the cup of the yellow daffodil gave off whiffs just alike. That the pencil doing the drawing should give off the same smell as the flower it drew seemed a part of the art lesson—as shouldn't it be? Children, like animals, use all their senses to discover the world. Then artists come along and discover it the same way, all over again. Here and there, it's the same world. Or now and then we'll hear from an artist who's never lost it.

In my sensory education I include my physical awareness of the word. Of a certain word, that is; the connection it has with what it stands for. At around age six, perhaps, I was standing by myself in our front yard waiting for supper, just at that hour in a late summer day when the sun is already below the horizon and the risen full moon in the visible sky stops being chalky and begins to take on light. There comes the moment, and I saw it then, when the moon goes from flat to round. For the first time it met my eyes as a globe. The word "moon" came into my mouth as though fed to me out of a silver spoon. Held in my mouth the moon became a word. It had the roundness of a Concord grape Grandpa took off his vine and gave me to suck out of its skin and swallow whole, in Ohio.

This love did not prevent me from living for years in foolish error about the moon. The new moon just appearing in the west was the rising moon to me. The new should be rising. And in early childhood the sun and moon, those opposite reigning powers, I just as easily assumed rose in east and west respectively in their opposite sides of the sky, and like partners in a reel they advanced, sun from the east, moon from the west, crossed over (when I wasn't looking) and went down on the other side. My father couldn't have known I believed that when, bending behind me and guiding my shoulder, he positioned me at our telescope in the front yard and, with careful adjustment of the focus, brought the moon close to me.

The night sky over my childhood Jackson[4] was velvety black. I could see the full constellations in it and call their names; when I could read, I knew their myths. Though I was always waked for eclipses, and indeed carried to the window as an infant in arms and shown Halley's Comet[5] in my sleep, and though I'd been taught at our diningroom table about the solar system and knew the earth revolved around the sun, and our moon around us, I never found out the moon didn't come up in the west until I was a writer and Herschel Brickell, the literary critic, told me after I

---

4. Jackson, Mississippi, where Welty grew up.

5. A comet named after Edmund Halley (1656–1742), English astronomer.

misplaced it in a story. He said valuable words to me about my new profession: "Always be sure you get your moon in the right part of the sky."

My mother always sang to her children. Her voice came out just a little bit in the minor key. "Wee Willie Winkie's" song was wonderfully sad when she sang the lullabies.

"Oh, but now there's a record. She could have her own record to listen to," my father would have said. For there came a Victrola record of "Bobby Shafftoe" and "Rock-a-Bye Baby,"[6] all of Mothers's lullabies, which could be played to take her place. Soon I was able to play her my own lullabies all day long.

Our Victrola stood in the diningroom. I was allowed to climb onto the seat of a diningroom chair to wind it, start the record turning, and set the needle playing. In a second I'd jumped to the floor, to spin or march around the table as the music called for—now there were all the other records I could play too. I skinned back onto the chair just in time to lift the needle at the end, stop the record and turn it over, then change the needle. That brass receptable with a hole in the lid gave off a metallic smell like human sweat, from all the hot needles that were fed it. Winding up, dancing, being cocked to start and stop the record, was of course all in one the act of listening—to "Overture to Daughter of the Regiment," "Selections from The Fortune Teller," "Kiss Me Again," "Gypsy Dance from Carmen," "Stars and Stripes Forever," "When the Midnight Choo-Choo Leaves for Alabam," or whatever came next.[7] Movement must be at the very heart of listening.

Ever since I was first read to, then started reading to myself, there has never been a line read that I didn't hear. As my eyes followed the sentence, a voice was saying it silently to me. It isn't my mother's voice, or the voice of any person I can identify, certainly not my own. It is human, but inward, and it is inwardly that I listen to it. It is to me the voice of the story or the poem itself. The cadence, whatever it is that asks you to believe, the feeling that resides in the printed word, reaches me through the reader-voice. I have supposed, but never found out, that this is the case with all readers—to read as listeners—and with all writers, to write as listeners. It may be part of the desire to write. The sound of what

6. "Wee Willie Winkie": a nursery rhyme of 1841 in which sleep is personified; "Bobby Shafftoe": a traditional sea chantey dating from about 1750; "Rock-a-Bye Baby": words from Mother Goose's Melodies (1765) set to music in 1884.
7. Daughter of the Regiment: an opera (1840) by the French composer Gaetano Donizetti; The Fortune Teller: an operetta (1898) by the American Victor Herbert; "Kiss Me Again": a song from Herbert's Mlle. Modiste (1905); Carmen: an opera (1875) by the French composer Georges Bizet; "Stars and Stripes Forever": a march (1897) by the American John Philip Sousa (the "March King"); "When the Midnight Choo-Choo Leaves for Alabam": a popular song (1912) by the American Irving Berlin.

falls on the page begins the process of testing it for truth, for me. Whether I am right to trust so far I don't know. By now I don't know whether I could do either one, reading or writing, without the other.

My own words, when I am at work on a story, I hear too as they go, in the same voice that I hear when I read in books. When I write and the sound of it comes back to my ears, then I act to make my changes. I have always trusted this voice.

1985

THE READER

1. *On p. 980, Welty devotes a paragraph to drawing a daffodil in chil-dren's art class. What is the relation of that paragraph to the one about the initial "O" just before and to the one about the full moon just after?*
2. *Welty concludes by talking of "trust" and "truth." What meaning does she give to these words?*
3. *When she speaks of her father's belief about the 1925 edition of the Britannica or puts quotation marks around "the library," Welty sug-gests that her mature judgment differs from her parents' judgment. How significant is her mature judgment on these matters? How does the answer to this question relate to the meaning she gives to "trust" and "truth" (see question 2, above)?*

THE WRITER

1. *Welty speaks of her "sensory education." What does she mean?*
2. *Welty got her sensory education before television. Suppose she had watched children's television as a child. Write a couple of sentences in her voice explaining its function in her sensory education. Write a paragraph in your own voice explaining its function in your sensory education.*

John Gardner

WHAT WRITERS DO

Everyone knows at least in a general way what writers—that is, writers of fiction—do. They write fiction. But even for writers themselves it's not easy to say just what that means. We listen to the sentence "They write fiction" and nod impatiently, as if the thing were too obvious to need saying, which in a way it is, because we all agree, as speakers of English, on what "they" means, and "write" and "fiction." But maybe we nodded too hastily. What *do* we mean, to start with the easiest question, by "they"—that is, "writers"?

Most of us are snobs and would be inclined to say at once that we need not concern ourselves with the obvious fact that writers are of various sorts ranging from, say, John Jakes (of the Bicentennial series) to Kurt Vonnegut, to Herman Melville. As warthogs, IRS agents, and zebras are all animals, these dissimilar beings—Jakes, Vonnegut, and Melville—are all writers; but though the problem here might amuse a chimpanzee or a positivist, it does not seem, to us snobs, worth attention. The word *writers*, and the pronoun we substitute for it, has various meanings, but the only one we really care about is the one which refers to the class represented by Melville. The trouble with this hasty, respectable judgment lies of course in the fact that every individual writer, even a stern-minded person like Melville, is different people at different times. In one mood, or in one crowd, the serious writer writes fairy tales; in another he writes ponderous novels; in still another, dirty limericks. A great writer is not great because he never writes dirty limericks but because, if he does write one, he tries to write a very good one.

Any writer who's worked in various forms can tell you from experience that it all feels like writing. Some people may feel that they're "really" writing when they work on their novels and just fooling around when they write bedtime stories for their children; but that can mean only one of two things, I think: either that the writer has a talent for writing novels and not much talent for writing children's stories, or else that the writer is a self-important donzel who writes both miserable novels and miserable children's stories. I would say that even in a given work a writer is many different people. Just at the moment when his novel is most serious —most strenuously laboring to capture some profound idea through meticulous analysis of characters in action—the Melvillian heavyweight suddenly notices (as John Jakes would do) that the serving-girl in the corner has lowered her bodice a little, trying to catch the central character's eye. I don't mean that our serious writer's mind has wandered; I mean that another side of him, after vigorous signaling, has gotten his attention. Or to put it another way, wanting to write like Tolstoi at his solemnest, he has suddenly discovered in himself an urge to write like, say, Henry Fielding. If he gives in to the impulse, as he may or may not, and pursues the romance the lowered bodice has invited, he may suddenly, at the height of idealistic love, or the depth of debauchery, find himself feeling a little cynical somehow, or puritanically pious; or he may find himself distracted by the ferns outside the window, which lure him to delicate appositions and fluttering rhythms, lyricism for its own sake.

What's happening here, of course, is not that several writers inside the one writer's head are clubbing each other for control of the typewriter keys. The true writer's mind is not a jungle but a noble democracy, in which all parties have their say, even the crazy ones, even the most violently passionate, because otherwise justice, balance, sanity are impossible. Wanting to write like Tolstoi at his solemnest, the writer finds a part of himself rising to object to a hint of pompous braying, agrarian bigotry, righteousness unredeemed by humor. Swinging toward Fielding, the writer finds a part of himself complaining about the absence of high-mindedness. Scanning possibilities like a chess-playing computer, weighing the votes of his innumerable selves, following now this leading voice, now that, the writer-multitude finds out, page by page and draft by draft, the sane and passionate whole which is his novel.

Every fine writer has within him a John Jakes, a Marquis de Sade, a James Michener, a William Gass, a Melville. If his multitude of selves is rich but anarchic, uncontrollable, so that his work bulges here with pornography, here with dry philosophy, he is likely to be a "serious" writer but not a very good one. If for one reason or another his selection of selves is limited, he is likely to be a lesser writer. Some writers are limited because they are, simply, not very rich personalities: they contain in them no Melville, no Marquis de Sade. Other writers are limited because, though rich in selves, they voluntarily disenfranchise large segments of their inner population to satisfy the whim of some market: they avoid ideas, or sex, or—as in the stock "New Yorker story"—unfashionable emotion.

Writers whose stock of selves is limited by simplicity of personality we dismiss—uncharitably but not unjustly—as stupid. Writers limited by concern about market we dismiss as commercial. How do we distinguish these lesser kinds of writers from the serious, even sublime writer who limits himself by the choice of some relatively simple form—Shakespeare in the sonnets, Hawthorne in his stories for children? And how, we may as well ask in the same breath, does the simplicity of a sonnet or children's story differ from the simplicity of a porno or mystery thriller?

If you accept my metaphor of the writer as democracy, the answer to both questions seems obvious. The whole community cannot get together on a porno or the usual emotionally simpleminded thriller, at least so long as the porno or thriller remain recognizable themselves, conscious and intentional distortions of human experience. (Ross Macdonald is the superior mystery writer he is precisely because he refuses to abide by the usual rules of his form, consistently writing, so to speak, better than necessary.) On the other hand, the sonnet and children's story—or the parable, tale, yarn, sketch, and so on—do not of necessity oversimplify or distort. When the whole community argues about war, pollution, or energy, it argues in one way; when it argues about building swing-sets on playgrounds, it argues in another. I think no part of a writer need be suppressed to write *Charlotte's Web* or the juveniles of Joan Aiken. It is true, of course, that the children's story, like the traditional gothic tale, tends to use a very special language; but it is not a language into which large parts of our common experience cannot be translated.

One might put it this way: important thought is important only insofar as it communicates with those at whom it is aimed; no sensible human being goes on talking when all of his audience has walked away. Great children's literature talks about the complexity of human experience in a way interesting and meaningful to children; bad children's literature talks about what some mistaken person imagines children care about. The bad children's writer writes as he does either because, being of limited personality, he thinks children care about no more than he does, or because, being commercial, he wants to satisfy formulas made up by fools and statisticians.

Great children's writers, like great writers of any other kind, are complex, multitudinous of self. To speak only of living American writers, think of the children's fiction of Nancy Willard, Hilma Wolitzer, or Susan Shreve. All of these writers, as it happens—not by chance—are also respectable writers of adult fiction or poetry. For contrast think of Maxine Kumin or Raoul Dahl, occasionally unsatisfying writers both for children and for adults because, in each case, one side of the writer's personality—the angrily righteous—overwhelms the democratic balance with pious despotism.

So much for the "they" in the truism about writers, "They write fiction." Let me turn to "write."

Writing is an action, a different action from talking. The only conceivable reason for engaging in writing is to make something relatively permanent which one might otherwise forget. That would seem to imply that one thinks there is some value in the thing not to be forgotten—either some value already achieved, as in the case of a good recipe for scalloped potatoes, or some potential value, as in the case of a love poem which stinks at the moment but has the right spirit and might get better under revision. Writers of the Melvillian class, that is, "serious" writers, write only in the second sense: they write works that with luck and devotion may be improved by revision—or, in the end, works that *have* been so improved, so that we may class them with other human treasures, such as good recipes for scalloped potatoes. If one looks at the first drafts of even the greatest writers, like Tolstoi and Dostoevski, one sees that literary art does not come flying like Athena, fully formed, from Zeus' head. Indeed, the first-draft stupidity of great writers is a shocking and comforting thing to see. What one learns from studying successive drafts is that the writer did not know what he meant to say until he said it. A typo of "murder" for "mirror" can change the whole plot of a novel.

To put all this another way, what oral storytellers seem to do is figure out certain parts of the world by telling stories about those parts. The Greeks, as you know, made much of this. Whereas most civilizations feared and hated blindness, the Greeks elevated it, at least as a symbol: the blind man was the man who had to see with his tongue, understand-

ing the world by telling of it. What writers do is somewhat different.
They figure out the world by talking about it, then looking at what
they've said and changing it. I don't mean, of course, that oral storytellers
don't polish and repolish; I only mean to say that there's a great difference
between the power and precision of the two instruments—a difference as
great as that between, say, a reading glass and a microscope. Think again
of Homer. A fair pile of prehomeric poetry survives, all of it fairly good,
most of it battle poetry, all the battle pieces relatively short, at least in
comparison with the *Iliad*. The standard heroic poem before Homer's
time probably ran to about the length of one or two books of the *Iliad*. It
may be true, as tradition says, that Homer was a blind oral poet, like
Demodokos, his character in the *Odyssey*; but it does not seem likely.
Homer appeared at the very moment when writing was reintroduced in
ancient Greece, and the complexity of his poems—repeated, cunningly
varied references to bows, looms, Odysseus' bed and the great phallic
pillar which supports it—images we're forced to describe, finally, as
richly and ingeniously symbolic—can only be accounted for in one of two
ways: either by a theory that Homer was vastly more intelligent than any
other human being who ever lived, or by a theory that Homer wrote
things down, studied them patiently and stubbornly, like Beethoven,
and, like Beethoven, endlessly, brilliantly revised.

   Or think of the sudden, astonishing rise of serious "popular" literature
in the late Middle Ages and early Renaissance; I mean the use, in writers
like Boccaccio, Chaucer, and Shakespeare, of salacious stories and folktales as the base of psychologically and philosophically serious literature.
Before Boccaccio's time, as has recently been pointed out, writers used
parchment. To make a Bible you had to kill three hundred cows. Books
cost a lot, in money and cattle-blood. One used parchment only for things
of the greatest importance—religious writings, cathedral plans, the shopping lists of kings. Then in Boccaccio's time paper was introduced, so
that suddenly it was possible for Boccaccio to write down a dirty joke he'd
heard, fool around with it a little—change the farmer's daughter to a nun,
for instance, or introduce comically disparate high-class symbolism—and
produce the *Decameron*. Chaucer did the same only better. We have two
drafts—by no means all that once existed—of Chaucer's story borrowed
from Boccaccio, *Troilus and Criseyde*. For artists, writing has always
meant, in effect, the art of endless revising.

   Now let me turn to the third term in the formula "They write fiction."
What oral storytellers tell and retell we call legends, a tricky word that, if
we derive it from the Latin, means "that which is read," and if we take it
(by false etymology, a once common one) from Anglo-Saxon, means—as
a result of the softening of g to y—*lying*. Even in the beginning no one
knew what to do with that. The primary meaning of *legend* in the Middle
Ages was "a saint's life." In any case, *fiction* was from the beginning

something else: it can only come from the Latin and means "something shaped, molded, or devised." As everyone knows, the origins of words don't prove much; but it seems true that we still use fiction in the original sense, not to describe some noble old lie which can be told, with no great loss, in a variety of ways, but to describe a specific kind of made-up story, a story we think valuable precisely because of the way it's been shaped. You can tell the legend or fairy tale of *Jack and the Beanstalk* pretty much any way you please, as long as you don't throw out Jack, the giant, the colored beans, or the beanstalk. Jack can make three trips, or two, or one; he can trade in the cow (or something) for the colored beans either on the way in to town or at the fair; and so on. To tell Faulkner's *As I Lay Dying*, Joyce's "The Dead," or William Gass' "In the Heart of the Heart of the Country," one has to use the writer's exact words or all is lost. The essential difference between what we think of as "fiction" and what we think of as "legend" is that, relatively at least, the shaping in fiction counts more heavily.

In the broadest and perhaps most important sense, fiction can go wrong in two ways: it fails as basic legend or it fails in its artifice. Most of the fiction one reads—I mean contemporary fiction, but the same may be said of fiction done in Dickens' day, most of it by now ground to dust by time's selectivity—is trash. It makes no real attempt at original and interesting style, and the story it tells is boring. This is simply to say, of course, that if fiction moves too far from its model, legend, and abandons story, it fails to satisfy our age-old expectations; if it does not move far enough, telling its story without concern for style, it fails to satisfy other, newer expectations. What writers do, if they haven't been misled by false canons of taste or some character defect, is try to make up an interesting story and tell it in an authentically interesting way—that is, some way that, however often we may read it, does not turn out to be boring.

The odds against a writer's achieving a real work of art are astronomical. Most obviously the "they" of our "They write fiction" formula—in other words, the writer's personality—may go wrong. Every good writer is many things—a symbolist, a careful student of character, a person of strong opinions, a lover of pure tale or adventure. In a bad or just ordinary novel, the writer's various selves war with one another. We feel, as we read, not one commanding voice but a series of jarringly different voices, even voices in sharp and confusing disagreement.

The war of the writer's selves can result in great fiction only in the case of an extraordinarily great writer, which is to say, an almost supernaturally wise man—one who has the rare gift of being able to see through his own soul's trickery. Very few people of the kind who make good writers —rather childlike people, as psychologists have often pointed out—are wise in life. They become wise, if they do, by revision—by looking over what they've written down again and again, a hundred times, two hundred, each time in a slightly different mood, with a different model ringing in their ears: one day the writer looks over what he's written just after spending a few hours reading Tolstoi; another day he rereads his own work just after seeing a play by Samuel Beckett, or some simple-minded but good-hearted movie like *The Sound of Music*, or just after returning from his mother's funeral. That process, endless revision and rereading—in different moods, with different models in mind—is the writer's chief hope.

Or anyway it is his chief hope if he has known all along what fiction is and has been trying to write real fiction. I have said that true fiction is, in effect, oral-storytelling written down and fixed, perfected by revision. Let me refine that a little now. What is it that the writer is trying to achieve—or ought to be—as he endlessly fiddles with rough drafts?

A true work of fiction is a wonderfully simple thing—so simple that most so-called serious writers avoid trying it, feeling they ought to do something more important and ingenious, never guessing how incredibly difficult it is. A true work of fiction does all of the following things, and does them elegantly, efficiently: It creates a vivid and continuous dream in the reader's mind; it is implicitly philosophical; it fulfills or at least deals with all of the expectations it sets up; and it strikes us, in the end, not simply as a thing done but as a shining performance.

I will not elaborate that description in much detail. Some of it I've mentioned before, here and there; some of it seems to me to need no elaboration. I've said, first, that fiction creates a vivid and continuous dream in the reader's mind. Any reader knows at a glance that that is true, and that if a given work does not bring a vivid and continuous dream to the reader—almost instantly, after five or six words—the fiction is either bad or, what may be the same thing, a so-called metafiction. One can derive all the principles of effective fiction from the idea that the writer must make his dream vivid and continuous. The dream is not vivid, of course, if too many words are abstract, not concrete, if too many verbs are passive, too many metaphors familiar or dull, and so on; and the dream is not continuous if some element in the writing distracts the reader from the story to thoughts about the stupidity of the writer—his inability to use proper grammar, his excessive loquacity, his deviation into sentimentality, mannerism, or frigidity, and so on. If the student writer can get rid of every one of those common errors which regularly undermine vividness and continuousness, a finite list not difficult to spell out, then that student can consistently avoid writing bad fiction. Whether or not he can write *great* fiction is of course another matter, one of genius or the lack of it. When the writer is finally writing true fiction, the best he is capable of, he may well discover that he'd better start making some carefully calculated mistakes, disguise his insipidity.

It's the law of the vivid and continuous dream—for it is, I think, something close to an aesthetic law for fiction—that makes writing fiction what I've described as a "wonderfully simple thing." All the writer has to do is see with absolute clarity and vividness, and describe without mistake exactly what he's seen. That was Faulkner's genius—to see very clearly. No one forgets his image of the falling lantern and the fire starting in "Shingles for the Lord," or his image of a Negro shanty's dirt yard, "smooth as an old, worn nickle." What offends in Faulkner, as has often been remarked, is his failure to value that clarity of vision, again and again mucking it up—especially toward the end—with outrageously mannered prose, that is, prose calculated to obscure the vision and call attention to the writer. Joyce did the same. At the end of his life, clear-headedly looking back, he thought "The Dead" the finest thing he'd ever done, and Tolstoi's "How Much Land Does a Man Need?" the finest work of fiction ever written. It had been Joyce himself, of course, who made the claim that the writer should be inconspicuous in his work, like God off in the corner of the universe paring his nails. In *Dubliners* and *Portrait* he'd been true to that ideal; from that point on—however great the books in certain ways—Joyce went for mannerism, and the sad truth is he carried most of twentieth-century fiction with him.

To do the wonderfully simple thing real writers do at their best, one needs only to look clearly and levelly at one's character and his situation. If the writer sees his character clearly, and if the character is, as all human beings in fact are, unique in certain respects, that character will inevitably behave in ways no one else would behave in that precise situation. It will prove impossible to write a story which could be equally well played in a film version by Robert Redford, Dustin Hoffman, Alan Arkin, Richard Dreyfus, or Frank Sinatra. If the writer sees each and every one of his characters clearly—even the most minor walk-ons—he can never for a moment slip into cliché. Following actions and reactions second by second through a significant chain of events, keeping a sharp eye out to catch every wince or grin or twitch, always checking his imagination against experience (how do misers really behave in the world), the writer almost cannot help coming up with a dream worth following—not a passive dream, of course, but one the reader struggles with, judges, tries to second-guess, a dream of reality more vivid and powerful than all but the rarest, keenest moments of reality itself.

Of course part of what makes this dream so vivid and powerful is that, like our best nightmares, the dream is thematic, or, as I put it earlier, it is implicitly philosophical. I would say that, at their best, both fiction and philosophy do the same thing, only fiction does it better—though slower. Philosophy is by essence abstract, a sequence of general argument controlled in its profluence by either logic (in old-fashioned systematic philosophy) or emotional coherence (in the intuitive philosophies of, say, Nietzsche and Kierkegaard). We read the argument and it seems to flow along okay, make sense, but what we ask is, "Is this true of my mailman?" or, "Do I really follow the Golden Rule because, unlike Prussian officers, I am a coward? Do I *know* any good Prussian officers?" Fiction comes at questions from the other end. It traces or explores some general argument by examining a particular case in which the universal case seems implied; and in place of logic or emotional coherence—the philosopher's stepping stones—fictional argument is controlled by mimesis: we are persuaded that the characters would indeed do and say exactly what we are told they do and say, whether the characters are lifelike human beings or a congress of insects given human traits. If the mimesis convinces us, then the question we ask is opposite to that we ask of philosophical argument; that is, we ask, "Is this true *in general?*" Convinced by Captain Ahab, we want to know if in some way his story, the story of a madman, applies to all human beings, mad or sane. In great fiction the writer, inching along from particular to particular, builds into his work arrows or vectors pointing us toward the general. He does this, we know, in numerous ways—by relating his particulars to some symbolic system recalling a familiar set of questions of values, by playing his plot off against some old and familiar plot, as Joyce does in *Ulysses*, by old-fashioned allegory, by explicit authorial comment, by arranging that his characters discuss the important issues within the story (the method of Tolstoi and Dostoevski), or by some other means.

What happens in great fiction is that, while we are occupied with the vividness and convincingness of detail—admiring, for instance, the fact that Captain Ahab's personal crew is made up of Chinese never before seen on the ship until now, with the first lowering of the longboats—we are also occupied with the neatness and power of the philosophical argument. When reading great fiction, one never feels that the writer has wandered from the subject. The true writer sets up for us some important question, in dramatic form, and explores it clear-mindedly, relentlessly. We read of Raskolnikov's initial indecision about whether or not he has the right to commit murder, and we instantly recognize the universal significance of the question and lean forward tensely, waiting to see what will happen. We delight in the particulars—the fact that he is very nearly caught on the stairs—and we delight simultaneously in seeing the implied universals. It's in this sense that true fiction is implicitly philosophical.

I need say nothing about the next standard I've mentioned, that fiction at its best satisfies our expectations. At the end of a mystery, we want all the questions answered, red herrings explained away, false clues justified, and so on. In a more serious kind of novel, we want all important issues dealt with, no character left hiding forever behind the tree where the author put him and forgot him. It may be that, finishing the novel, we at first imagine that some thread was left untied—for instance, some symbolic idea. Two different characters may have been subtly identified as Eden serpents, and as we finish the novel we at first can't see how the double identification was resolved. Carefully rereading, we discover that the seeming contradiction was indeed resolved, and the belated satisfaction of our expectation gives pleasure. But whether the satisfaction is immediate or purposely delayed, it must sooner or later come.

Finally, I've said that in the best fiction we get not just a piece of work —efficient energy which moves something—but a "shining performance." We say not just "What a true and good book!" but "What magnificent writing!" To win our applause, it cannot have the fake magnificence of mannerism—flights of purple prose, advance-guard trickery, artifice aimed solely at calling attention to the artificer. It must have the true magnificence of beautiful (some would prefer to say "interesting") technique: adequate and "inspired"—that is, revised, rerevised, polished to near perfection. We recognize this at once, I think, in acting. Some actors do a perfectly good job—we are never distracted to the actor behind the character played—while other actors do a brilliant job: we *do* think of the actor, not as a human being at war with the part being played, but as an artist whose skills come singing through the part, making the character more interesting and "real" than we could have hoped or dreamed from a reading of the script.

What the writers I care most about do is take fiction as the single most important thing in life after life itself—life itself being both their raw material and the object of their celebration. They do it not for ego but simply to make something singularly beautiful. Fiction is their religion and comfort: when they are depressed, they go not to church or psychoanalysis but to Salinger or Joyce, early Malamud, parts of Faulkner, Tolstoi, or the Bible as book. They write, themselves, to make things equally worthy of trust, not stories of creeps and cynics but stories of people capable of a measure of heroism, capable of strong and honest feeling at least some of the time, capable of love and sacrifice—capable of all this, and available as models for imitation. Everything true writers do, I think, from laborious plotting on butcher paper or three-by-five cards to laborious revision, draft after draft, they do to create *characters*—the center and heart of all true fiction—characters who will serve till Messiah comes, characters whose powerful existence in our minds make a real-life messiah unnecessary. Imperfect, even childish human beings, writers raise themselves up by the techniques of fiction to something much better than even the best of writers are in everyday life: ordinary mortals transmuted for the moment into apostles.

1981

Vladimir Nabokov

GOOD READERS AND GOOD WRITERS

"How to be a Good Reader" or "Kindness to Authors"—something of that sort might serve to provide a subtitle for these various discussions of various authors, for my plan is to deal lovingly, in loving and lingering detail, with several European masterpieces. A hundred years ago, Flaubert in a letter to his mistress made the following remark: *Comme l'on serait savant si l'on connaissait bien seulement cinq à six livres:* "What a scholar one might be if one knew well only some half a dozen books."

In reading, one should notice and fondle details. There is nothing wrong about the moonshine of generalization when it comes *after* the sunny trifles of the book have been lovingly collected. If one begins with a ready-made generalization, one begins at the wrong end and travels away from the book before one has started to understand it. Nothing is more boring or more unfair to the author than starting to read, say, *Madame Bovary*, with the preconceived notion that it is a denunciation of the bourgeoisie. We should always remember that the work of art is invariably the creation of a new world, so that the first thing we should do is to study that new world as closely as possible, approaching it as something brand new, having no obvious connection with the worlds we already know. When this new world has been closely studied, then and only then let us examine its links with other worlds, other branches of knowledge.

Another question: Can we expect to glean information about places and times from a novel? Can anybody be so naive as to think he or she can learn anything about the past from those buxom best-sellers that are hawked around by book clubs under the heading of historical novels? But what about the masterpieces? Can we rely on Jane Austen's picture of landowning England with baronets and landscaped grounds when all she knew was a clergyman's parlor? And *Bleak House*, that fantastic romance within a fantastic London, can we call it a study of London a hundred years ago? Certainly not. And the same holds for other such novels in this series. The truth is that great novels are great fairy tales—and the novels in this series are supreme fairy tales.

Time and space, the colors of the seasons, the movements of muscles and minds, all these are for writers of genius (as far as we can guess and I trust we guess right) not traditional notions which may be borrowed from the circulating library of public truths but a series of unique surprises which master artists have learned to express in their own unique way. To minor authors is left the ornamentation of the commonplace: these do not bother about any reinventing of the world; they merely try to squeeze the best they can out of a given order of things, out of traditional patterns of fiction. The various combinations these minor authors are able to produce within these set limits may be quite amusing in a mild ephemeral way because minor readers like to recognize their own ideas in a pleasing disguise. But the real writer, the fellow who sends planets spinning and models a man asleep and eagerly tampers with the sleeper's rib, that kind of author has no given values at his disposal: he must create them himself. The art of writing is a very futile business if it does not imply first of all the art of seeing the world as the potentiality of fiction. The material of this world may be real enough (as far as reality goes) but does not exist at all as an accepted entirety: it is chaos, and to this chaos the author says "go!" allowing the world to flicker and to fuse. It is now recombined in its very atoms, not merely in its visible and superficial parts. The writer is the first man to map it and to name the natural objects it contains. Those berries there are edible. That speckled creature that bolted across my path might be tamed. That lake between those trees will be called Lake Opal or, more artistically, Dishwater Lake. That mist is a mountain—and that mountain must be conquered. Up a trackless slope climbs the master artist, and at the top, on a windy ridge, whom do you think he meets? The panting and happy reader, and there they spontaneously embrace and are linked forever if the book lasts forever.

One evening at a remote provincial college through which I happened to be jogging on a protracted lecture tour, I suggested a little quiz—ten definitions of a reader, and from these ten the students had to choose four definitions that would combine to make a good reader. I have mislaid the list, but as far as I remember the definitions went something like this. Select four answers to the question what should a reader be to be a good reader:

1. The reader should belong to a book club.

2. The reader should identify himself or herself with the hero or heroine.

3. The reader should concentrate on the social-economic angle.

4. The reader should prefer a story with action and dialogue to one with none.

5. The reader should have seen the book in a movie.

6. The reader should be a budding author.

7. The reader should have imagination.

8. The reader should have memory.

9. The reader should have a dictionary.

10. The reader should have some artistic sense.

The students leaned heavily on emotional identification, action, and the social-economic or historical angle. Of course, as you have guessed, the good reader is one who has imagination, memory, a dictionary, and some artistic sense—which sense I propose to develop in myself and in others whenever I have the chance.

Incidentally, I use the word *reader* very loosely. Curiously enough, one cannot *read* a book: one can only reread it. A good reader, a major reader, an active and creative reader is a rereader. And I shall tell you why. When we read a book for the first time the very process of laboriously moving our eyes from left to right, line after line, page after page, this complicated physical work upon the book, the very process of learning in terms of space and time what the book is about, this stands between us and artistic appreciation. When we look at a painting we do not have to move our eyes in a special way even if, as in a book, the picture contains elements of depth and development. The element of time does not really enter in a first contact with a painting. In reading a book, we must have time to acquaint ourselves with it. We have no physical organ (as we have the eye in regard to a painting) that takes in the whole picture and then can enjoy its details. But at a second, or third, or fourth reading we do, in a sense, behave towards a book as we do towards a painting. However, let us not confuse the physical eye, that monstrous master-piece of evolution, with the mind, an even more monstrous achievement. A book, no matter what it is—a work of fiction or a work of science (the boundary line between the two is not as clear as is generally believed)—a book of fiction appeals first of all to the mind. The mind, the brain, the top of the tingling spine, is, or should be, the only instrument used upon a book.

Now, this being so, we should ponder the question how does the mind work when the sullen reader is confronted by the sunny book. First, the sullen mood melts away, and for better or worse the reader enters into the spirit of the game. The effort to begin a book, especially if it is praised by people whom the young reader secretly deems to be too old-fashioned or too serious, this effort is often difficult to make; but once it is made, rewards are various and abundant. Since the master artist used his imagi-nation in creating his book, it is natural and fair that the consumer of a book should use his imagination too.

There are, however, at least two varieties of imagination in the reader's case. So let us see which one of the two is the right one to use in reading a book. First, there is the comparatively lowly kind which turns for support to the simple emotions and is of a definitely personal nature. (There are various subvarieties here, in this first section of emotional reading.) A situation in a book is intensely felt because it reminds us of something that happened to us or to someone we know or knew. Or, again, a reader treasures a book mainly because it evokes a country, a landscape, a mode of living which he nostalgically recalls as part of his own past. Or, and this is the worst thing a reader can do, he identifies himself with a character in the book. This lowly variety is not the kind of imagination I would like readers to use.

So what is the authentic instrument to be used by the reader? It is impersonal imagination and artistic delight. What should be established, I think, is an artistic harmonious balance between the reader's mind and the author's mind. We ought to remain a little aloof and take pleasure in this aloofness while at the same time we keenly enjoy—passionately enjoy, enjoy with tears and shivers—the inner weave of a given masterpiece. To be quite objective in these matters is of course impossible. Everything that is worthwhile is to some extent subjective. For instance, you sitting there may be merely my dream, and I may be your nightmare. But what I mean is that the reader must know when and where to curb his imagination and this he does by trying to get clear the specific world the author places at his disposal. We must see things and hear things, we must visualize the rooms, the clothes, the manners of an author's people. The color of Fanny Price's eyes in *Mansfield Park* and the furnishing of her cold little room are important.

We all have different temperaments, and I can tell you right now that the best temperament for a reader to have, or to develop, is a combination of the artistic and the scientific one. The enthusiastic artist alone is apt to be too subjective in his attitude towards a book, and so a scientific coolness of judgment will temper the intuitive heat. If, however, a would-be reader is utterly devoid of passion and patience—of an artist's passion and a scientist's patience—he will hardly enjoy great literature.

Literature was born not the day when a boy crying wolf, wolf came running out of the Neanderthal valley with a big gray wolf at his heels: literature was born on the day when a boy came crying wolf, wolf and there was no wolf behind him. That the poor little fellow because he lied too often was finally eaten up by a real beast is quite incidental. But here is what is important. Between the wolf in the tall grass and the wolf in the tall story there is a shimmering go-between. That go-between, that prism, is the art of literature.

Literature is invention. Fiction is fiction. To call a story a true story is an insult to both art and truth. Every great writer is a great deceiver, but so is that arch-cheat Nature. Nature always deceives. From the simple deception of propagation to the prodigiously sophisticated illusion of protective colors in butterflies or birds, there is in Nature a marvelous system of spells and wiles. The writer of fiction only follows Nature's lead.

Going back for a moment to our wolf-crying woodland little woolly fellow, we may put it this way: the magic of art was in the shadow of the wolf that he deliberately invented, his dream of the wolf; then the story of his tricks made a good story. When he perished at last, the story told about him acquired a good lesson in the dark around the camp fire. But he was the little magician. He was the inventor.

There are three points of view from which a writer can be considered: he may be considered as a storyteller, as a teacher, and as an enchanter. A major writer combines these three—storyteller, teacher, enchanter—but it is the enchanter in him that predominates and makes him a major writer.

To the storyteller we turn for entertainment, for mental excitement of the simplest kind, for emotional participation, for the pleasure of traveling in some remote region in space or time. A slightly different though not necessarily higher mind looks for the teacher in the writer. Propagandist, moralist, prophet—this is the rising sequence. We may go to the teacher not only for moral education but also for direct knowledge, for simple facts. Alas, I have known people whose purpose in reading the French and Russian novelists was to learn something about life in gay Paree or in sad Russia. Finally, and above all, a great writer is always a great enchanter, and it is here that we come to the really exciting part when we try to grasp the individual magic of his genius and to study the style, the imagery, the pattern of his novels or poems.

The three facets of the great writer—magic, story, lesson—are prone to blend in one impression of unified and unique radiance, since the magic of art may be present in the very bones of the story, in the very marrow of thought. There are masterpieces of dry, limpid, organized thought which provoke in us an artistic quiver quite as strongly as a novel like *Mansfield Park* does or as any rich flow of Dickensian sensual imagery. It seems to me that a good formula to test the quality of a novel is, in the long run, a merging of the precision of poetry and the intuition of science. In order to bask in that magic a wise reader reads the book of genius not with his heart, not so much with his brain, but with his spine. It is there that occurs the telltale tingle even though we must keep a little aloof, a little detached when reading. Then with a pleasure which is both sensual and intellectual we shall watch the artist build his castle of cards and watch the castle of cards become a castle of beautiful steel and glass.

c. 1941   1980

Northrop Frye

THE MOTIVE FOR METAPHOR

For the past twenty-five years I have been teaching and studying English literature in a university. As in any other job, certain questions stick in one's mind, not because people keep asking them, but because they're the questions inspired by the very fact of being in such a place. What good is the study of literature? Does it help us to think more clearly, or feel more sensitively, or live a better life than we could without it? What is the function of the teacher and scholar, or of the person who calls himself, as I do, a literary critic? What difference does the study of literature make in our social or political or religious attitude? In my early days I thought very little about such questions, not because I had any of the answers, but because I assumed that anybody who asked them was naïve. I think now that the simplest questions are not only the hardest to answer, but the most important to ask, so I'm going to raise them and try to suggest what my present answers are. I say try to suggest, because there are only more or less inadequate answers to such questions—there aren't any right answers. The kind of problem that literature raises is not the kind that you ever "solve." Whether my answers are any good or not, they represent a fair amount of thinking about the questions. As I can't see my audience, I have to choose my rhetorical style in the dark, and I'm taking the classroom style, because an audience of students is the one I feel easiest with.

There are two things in particular that I want to discuss with you. In school, and in university, there's a subject called "English" in English-speaking countries. English means, in the first place, the mother tongue. As that, it's the most practical subject in the world: you can't understand anything or take any part in your society without it. Wherever illiteracy is a problem, it's as fundamental a problem as getting enough to eat or a place to sleep. The native language takes precedence over every other subject of study: nothing else can compare with it in its usefulness. But then you find that every mother tongue, in any developed or civilized society, turns into something called literature. If you keep on studying "English," you find yourself trying to read Shakespeare and Milton. Literature, we're told, is one of the arts, along with painting and music, and, after you've looked up all the hard words and the Classical allusions and learned what words like imagery and diction are supposed to mean, what you use in understanding it, or so you're told, is your imagination. Here you don't seem to be in quite the same practical and useful area: Shakespeare and Milton, whatever their merits, are not the kind of thing you must know to hold any place in society at all. A person who knows nothing about literature may be an ignoramus, but many people don't mind being that. Every child realizes that literature is taking him in a different direction from the immediately useful, and a good many children complain loudly about this. Two questions I want to deal with, then, are, first: what is the relation of English as the mother tongue to English as a literature? Second: What is the social value of the study of literature, and what is the place of the imagination that literature addresses itself to, in the learning process?

Let's start with the different ways there are of dealing with the world we're living in. Suppose you're shipwrecked on an uninhabited island in the South Seas. The first thing you do is to take a long look at the world around you, a world of sky and sea and earth and stars and trees and hills. You see this world as objective, as something set over against you and not yourself or related to you in any way. And you notice two things about this objective world. In the first place, it doesn't have any conversation. It's full of animals and plants and insects going on with their own business, but there's nothing that responds to you: it has no morals and no intelligence, or at least none that you can grasp. It may have a shape and a meaning, but it doesn't seem to be a human shape or a human meaning. Even if there's enough to eat and no dangerous animals, you feel lonely and frightened and unwanted in such a world.

In the second place, you find that looking at the world, as something set over against you, splits your mind in two. You have an intellect that feels curious about it and wants to study it, and you have feelings or emotions that see it as beautiful or austere or terrible. You know that both these attitudes have some reality, at least for you. If the ship you were wrecked in was a Western ship, you'd probably feel that your intellect tells you more about what's really there in the outer world, and that your emotions tell you more about what's going on inside you. If your background were Oriental, you'd be more likely to reverse this and say that the beauty or terror was what was really there, and that your instinct to count and classify and measure and pull to pieces was what was inside your mind. But whether your point of view is Western or Eastern, intellect and emotion never get together in your mind as long as you're simply looking at the world. They alternate, and keep you divided between them.

The language you use on this level of the mind is the language of consciousness or awareness. It's largely a language of nouns and adjectives. You have to have names for things, and you need qualities like "wet" or "green" or "beautiful" to describe how things seem to you. This is the speculative or contemplative position of the mind, the position in which the arts and sciences begin, although they don't stay there very long. The sciences begin by accepting the facts and the evidence about an outside world without trying to alter them. Science proceeds by accurate measurement and description, and follows the demands of the reason rather than the emotions. What it deals with is there, whether we like it or not. The emotions are unreasonable: for them it's what they like and don't like that comes first. We'd be naturally inclined to think that the arts follow the path of emotion, in contrast to the sciences. Up to a point they do, but there's a complicating factor.

That complicating factor is the contrast between "I like this" and "I don't like this." In this Robinson Crusoe life I've assigned you, you may have moods of complete peacefulness and joy, moods when you accept your island and everything around you. You wouldn't have such moods very often, and when you had them, they'd be moods of identification, when you felt that the island was a part of you and you a part of it. That is not the feeling of consciousness or awareness, where you feel split off from everything that's not your perceiving self. Your habitual state of mind is the feeling of separation which goes with being conscious, and the feeling "this is not a part of me" soon becomes "this is not what I want." Notice the word "want": we'll be coming back to it.

So you soon realize that there's a difference between the world you're living in and the world you want to live in. The world you want to live in is a human world, not an objective one: it's not an environment but a home; it's not the world you see but the world you build out of what you see. You go to work to build a shelter or plant a garden, and as soon as you start to work you've moved into a different level of human life. You're not separating only yourself from nature now, but constructing a human world and separating it from the rest of the world. Your intellect and emotions are now both engaged in the same activity, so there's no longer any real distinction between them. As soon as you plant a garden or a crop, you develop the conception of a "weed," the plant you don't want in there. But you can't say that "weed" is either an intellectual or an emotional conception, because it's both at once. Further, you go to work because you feel you have to, and because you want something at the end of the work. That means that the important categories of your life are no longer the subject and the object, the watcher and the things being watched: the important categories are what you have to do and what you want to do—in other words, necessity and freedom.

One person by himself is not a complete human being, so I'll provide you with another shipwrecked refugee of the opposite sex and an eventual family. Now you're a member of a human society. This human society after a while will transform the island into something with a human shape. What that human shape is, is revealed in the shape of the work you do: the buildings, such as they are, the paths through the woods, the planted crops fenced off against whatever animals want to eat them. These things, these rudiments of city, highway, garden, and farm, are the human form of nature, or the form of human nature, whichever you like. This is the area of the applied arts and sciences, and it appears in our society as engineering and agriculture and medicine and architecture. In this area we can never say clearly where the art stops and the science begins, or vice versa.

The language you use on this level is the language of practical sense, a language of verbs or words of action and movement. The practical world, however, is a world where actions speak louder than words. In some way it's a higher level of existence than the speculative level, because it's doing something about the world instead of just looking at it, but in itself it's a much more primitive level. It's the process of adapting to the environment, or rather of transforming the environment in the interests of one species, that goes on among animals and plants as well as human beings. The animals have a good many of our practical skills: some insects make pretty fair architects, and beavers know quite a lot about engineering. In this island, probably, and certainly if you were alone, you'd have about the ranking of a second-rate animal. What makes our practical life really human is a third level of the mind, a level where consciousness and practical skill come together.

This third level is a vision or model in your mind of what you want to construct. There's that word "want" again. The actions of man are prompted by desire, and some of these desires are needs, like food and warmth and shelter. One of these needs is sexual, the desire to reproduce and bring more human beings into existence. But there's also a desire to bring a social human form into existence: the form of cities and gardens and farms that we call civilization. Many animals and insects have this social form too, but man knows that he has it: he can compare what he does with what he can imagine being done. So we begin to see where the imagination belongs in the scheme of human affairs. It's the power of constructing possible models of human experience. In the world of the imagination, anything goes that's imaginatively possible, but nothing really happens. If it did happen, it would move out of the world of imagination into the world of action.

We have three levels of the mind now, and a language for each of them, which in English-speaking societies means an English for each of them. There's the level of consciousness and awareness, where the most important thing is the difference between me and everything else. The English of this level is the English of ordinary conversation, which is mostly monologue, as you'll soon realize if you do a bit of eavesdropping, or listening to yourself. We can call it the language of self-expression. Then there's the level of social participation, the working or technological language of teachers and preachers and politicians and advertisers and lawyers and journalists and scientists. We've already called this the language of practical sense. Then there's the level of imagination, which produces the literary language of poems and plays and novels. They're not really different languages, of course, but three different reasons for using words.

On this basis, perhaps, we can distinguish the arts from the sciences. Science begins with the world we have to live in, accepting its data and trying to explain its laws. From there, it moves towards the imagination: it becomes a mental construct, a model of a possible way of interpreting experience. The further it goes in this direction, the more it tends to speak the language of mathematics, which is really one of the languages of the imagination, along with literature and music. Art, on the other hand, begins with the world we construct, not with the world we see. It starts with the imagination, and then works towards ordinary experience: that is, it tries to make itself as convincing and recognizable as it can. You can see why we tend to think of the sciences as intellectual and the arts as emotional: one starts with the world as it is, the other with the world we want to have. Up to a point it is true that science gives an intellectual view of reality, and that the arts try to make the emotions as precise and disciplined as sciences do the intellect. But of course it's nonsense to think of the scientist as a cold unemotional reasoner and the artist as somebody who's in a perpetual emotional tizzy. You can't distinguish the arts from the sciences by the mental processes the people in them use: they both operate on a mixture of hunch and common sense. A highly developed science and and a highly developed art are very close together, psychologically and otherwise.

Still, the fact that they start from opposite ends, even if they do meet in the middle, makes for one important difference between them. Science learns more and more about the world as it goes on: it evolves and improves. A physicist today knows more physics than Newton did, even if he's not as great a scientist. But literature begins with the possible model of experience, and what it produces is the literary model we call the classic. Literature doesn't evolve or improve or progress. We may have dramatists in the future who will write plays as good as *King Lear*, though they'll be very different ones, but drama as a whole will never get better than *King Lear*. *King Lear* is it, as far as drama is concerned; so is *Oedipus Rex*, written two thousand years earlier than that, and both will be models of dramatic writing as long as the human race endures. Social conditions may improve: most of us would rather live in nineteenth-century United States than in thirteenth-century Italy, and for most of us Whitman's celebration of democracy makes a lot more sense than Dante's Inferno. But it doesn't follow that Whitman is a better poet than Dante: literature won't line up with that kind of improvement.

So we find that everything that does improve, including science, leaves the literary artist out in the cold. Writers don't seem to benefit much by the advance of science, although they thrive on superstitions of all kinds. And you certainly wouldn't turn to contemporary poets for guidance or leadership in the twentieth-century world. You'd hardly go to Ezra Pound, with his fascism and social credit and Confucianism and anti-semitism. Or to Yeats, with his spiritualism and fairies and astrology. Or to D. H. Lawrence, who'll tell you that it's a good thing for servants to be flogged because that restores the precious current of blood-reciprocity between servant and master. Or to T. S. Eliot, who'll tell you that to have a flourishing culture we should educate an élite, keep most people living in the same spot, and never disestablish the Church of England. The novelists seem to be a little closer to the world they're living in, but not much. When Communists talk about the decadence of bourgeois culture, this is the kind of thing they always bring up. Their own writers don't seem to be any better, though; just duller. So the real question is a bigger one. Is it possible that literature, especially poetry, is something that a scientific civilization like ours will eventually outgrow? Man has always wanted to fly, and thousands of years ago he was making sculptures of winged bulls and telling stories about people who flew so high on artificial wings that the sun melted them off. In an Indian play fifteen hundred years old, *Sakuntala*, there's a god who flies around in a chariot that to a modern reader sounds very much like a private aeroplane. Interesting that the writer had so much imagination, but do we need such stories now that we have private aeroplanes?

This is not a new question: it was raised a hundred and fifty years ago by Thomas Love Peacock, who was a poet and novelist himself, and a very brilliant one. He wrote an essay called *Four Ages of Poetry*, with his tongue of course in his cheek, in which he said that poetry was the mental rattle that awakened the imagination of mankind in its infancy, but that now, in an age of science and technology, the poet has outlived his social function. "A poet in our times," said Peacock, "is a semi-barbarian in a civilized community. He lives in the days that are past. His ideas, thoughts, feelings, associations, are all with barbarous manners, obsolete customs, and exploded superstitions. The march of his intellect is like that of a crab, backwards." Peacock's essay annoyed his friend Shelley, who wrote another essay called *A Defence of Poetry* to refute it. Shelley's essay is a wonderful piece of writing, but it's not likely to convince anyone who needs convincing. I shall be spending a good deal of my time on this question of the relevance of literature in the world of today, and I can only indicate the general lines my answer will take. There are two points I can make now, one simple, the other more difficult.

The simple point is that literature belongs to the world man constructs, not to the world he sees; to his home, not his environment. Literature's world is a concrete human world of immediate experience. The poet uses images and objects and sensations much more than he uses abstract ideas; the novelist is concerned with telling stories, not with working out arguments. The world of literature is human in shape, a world where the sun rises in the east and sets in the west over the edge of a flat earth in three dimensions, where the primary realities are not atoms or electrons but bodies, and the primary forces not energy or gravitation but love and death and passion and joy. It's not surprising if writers are often rather simple people, not always what we think of as intellectuals, and certainly not always any freer of silliness or perversity than anyone else. What concerns us is what they produce, not what they are, and poetry, according to Milton, who ought to have known, is "more simple, sensuous and passionate" than philosophy or science.

The more difficult point takes us back to what we said when we were on that South Sea island. Our emotional reaction to the world varies from "I like this" to "I don't like this." The first, we said, was a state of identity, a feeling that everything around us was part of us, and the second is the ordinary state of consciousness, or separation, where art and science begin. Art begins as soon as "I don't like this" turns into "this is not the way I could imagine it." We notice in passing that the creative and the neurotic minds have a lot in common. They're both dissatisfied with what they see; they both believe that something else ought to be there, and they try to pretend it is there or to make it be there. The differences are more important, but we're not ready for them yet.

At the level of ordinary consciousness the individual man is the centre of everything, surrounded on all sides by what he isn't. At the level of practical sense, or civilization, there's a human circumference, a little cultivated world with a human shape, fenced off from the jungle and inside the sea and the sky. But in the imagination anything goes that can be imagined, and the limit of the imagination is a totally human world. Here we recapture, in full consciousness, that original lost sense of identity with our surroundings, where there is nothing outside the mind of man, or something identical with the mind of man. Religions present us with visions of eternal and infinite heavens or paradises which have the form of the cities and gardens of human civilization, like the Jerusalem and Eden of the Bible, completely separated from the state of frustration and misery that bulks so large in ordinary life. We're not concerned with these visions as religion, but they indicate what the limits of the imagination are. They indicate too that in the human world the imagination has no limits, if you follow me. We said that the desire to fly produced the aeroplane. But people don't get into planes because they want to fly; they get into planes because they want to get somewhere else faster. What's produced the aeroplane is not so much a desire to fly as a rebellion against the tyranny of time and space. And that's a process that can never stop, no matter how high our Titovs[1] and Glenns[2] may go.

1. Sherman Titov, Russian astronaut and first man to make a multi-orbital flight (August 1961).

2. John H. Glenn, astronaut and first American to make an orbital flight (February 1962).

For each of these six talks I've taken a title from some work of literature, and my title for this one is "The Motive for Metaphor," from a poem of Wallace Stevens. Here's the poem:

> You like it under the trees in autumn,
> Because everything is half dead.
> The wind moves like a cripple among the leaves
> And repeats words without meaning.
>
> In the same way, you were happy in spring,
> With the half colors of quarter-things,
> The slightly brighter sky, the melting clouds,
> The single bird, the obscure moon—
>
> The obscure moon lighting an obscure world
> Of things that would never be quite expressed,
> Where you yourself were never quite yourself
> And did not want nor have to be,
>
> Desiring the exhilarations of changes:
> The motive for metaphor, shrinking from
> The weight of primary noon,
> The A B C of being,
>
> The ruddy temper, the hammer
> Of red and blue, the hard sound—
> Steel against intimation—the sharp flash,
> The vital, arrogant, fatal, dominant X.

What Stevens calls the weight of primary noon, the A B C of being, and the dominant X is the objective world, the world set over against us. Outside literature, the main motive for writing is to describe this world. But literature itself uses language in a way which associates our minds with it. As soon as you use associative language, you begin using figures of speech. If you say this talk is dry and dull, you're using figures associating it with bread and breadknives. There are two main kinds of association, analogy and identity, two things that are like each other and two things that are each other. You can say with Burns, "My love's like a red, red rose," or you can say with Shakespeare:

> Thou that art now the world's fresh ornament
> And only herald to the gaudy spring.

One produces the figure of speech called the simile; the other produces the figure called metaphor.

In descriptive writing you have to be careful of associative language. You'll find that analogy, or likeness to something else, is very tricky to handle in description, because the differences are as important as the resemblances. As for metaphor, where you're really saying "this is that," you're turning your back on logic and reason completely, because logically two things can never be the same thing and still remain two things. The poet, however, uses these two crude, primitive, archaic forms of thought in the most uninhibited way, because his job is not to describe nature, but to show you a world completely absorbed and possessed by the human mind. So he produces what Baudelaire called a "suggestive magic including at the same time object and subject, the world outside the artist and the artist himself." The motive for metaphor, according to Wallace Stevens, is a desire to associate, and finally to identify, the human mind with what goes on outside it, because the only genuine joy you can have is in those rare moments when you feel that although we may know in part, as Paul says, we are also a part of what we know.

1964

THE READER

1. At what point in his essay does Frye come to the meaning of his title? What does this essay say the motive for metaphor is? Does it seem to you to be a satisfactory motive?
2. How far does Frye go in this essay toward responding to the simple, big questions he starts out with? Has he clarified for you or answered any of these questions? Is there indication in the essay that this is a beginning of the discussion, with more to follow?
3. What are the three kinds of English Frye talks about in his essay? Do we really need three kinds—isn't one enough?
4. Why do you have to take so much English in school when you already know how to use English even before you start school?

THE WRITER

1. Why does Frye ask his reader to imagine him- or herself a castaway on a South Sea island? Are you ever likely to be in that position, or is it a bit far-fetched? Is it just a colorful way to get his point across? If so, what is his point?
2. Does Frye anticipate a possible objection that metaphor distorts the truth and misleads us as to the way things really are? Why, or why not?
3. Why doesn't literature get any better, the way science does? Can literature be any good, seeing that it doesn't improve? Given the fact that it doesn't improve, shouldn't much of it be outdated? Cast your answer to these questions in the form of two brief essays, one addressed to an English teacher, one addressed to a fellow student majoring in science. How do your two essays differ?

Annie Dillard

ABOUT SYMBOL

Fiction does interpret the world at large. It traffics in understanding. Does it also traffic in knowledge? Do its interpretations have the status of hard data? Does art know?

Knowledge and understanding meet where science meets theology, where substance and idea mingle their parts. This juncture is the apex of the pyramid of abstractions. It is the apogee of all our researches; it is the vanishing point where all lines of thought converge. Here eternity gives birth to time. I wish to assert that art is especially competent to penetrate these regions, and others as well.

Zola, according to Charles Child Walcutt,[1] said that fiction "had been an art but would henceforth be an instrument for the scientific study of man and society." Now, no one is going to attack Zola, who is not so much a sacred cow as a dead horse. Let me just use these notions. Zola makes a false distinction when he says that fiction was formerly an art but was now an instrument for scientific study—an instrument, I infer, like a lens or a sextant. Because the truth is that only by being art is fiction an instrument at all. Art itself is an instrument, a cognitive instrument, and with religion the only instrument, for probing certain materials and questions. Art and religion probe the mysteries in those difficult areas where blurred and powerful symbols are the only possible speech and their arrangement into coherent religions and works of art the only possible grammar.

All art may be said to be symbolic in this sense: it is a material mock-up of bright idea. Any work of art symbolizes the process by which spirit generates matter, or materials generate idea. Any work of art symbolizes juncture itself, the socketing of eternity into time and energy into form. Of course, all that man makes is similar in this respect: a bowl, a highway, and a triangle are also material mock-ups of mental orders. But this is *all* that art is, in essence and by intent. A highway intends something quite other. Any art object is essentially a model in which the creative process is frozen with its product in its arms.

Any art object as a whole is symbolic, then. But more pertinent to my point is the familiar level at which an art object is symbolic because its parts are. These things warrant a brief restatement.

1. Émile Zola (1840–1902): French novelist and founder of Naturalism in literature; Charles Child Walcutt (1908–): American literary critic, novelist, textbook author.

An allegorical symbol is precise and bounded. When fair-haired Virtue shatters the opium pipe of Indolence, we may conclude that moral virtue in the abstract, which the author finds as attractive as he finds blondes, rejects indolence, strongly. Nonallegorical symbols, which are the topic at hand, are not precise. It is when these symbols break their allegorical boundaries, their commitment to reference, that they start stepping out on us. The laxity of their bonds permits them to enter unsuspected relationships. They become suggestive. These artistic symbols do not represent things in the great world directly, as the opium pipe represents indolence. Instead, these symbols, like art objects themselves, are semi-enclosed worlds of meaning the essence of whose referential substance we may approximate, but whose boundaries and total possibilities for significance we can never locate precisely or exhaust.

Of the "stately pleasure dome" of "Kubla Khan," shall we say it is an ordered, pleasing, and aloof work of art ("A stately pleasure dome"); or any conscious product of active power ("decree"); or the passive receptacle of the wellspring of the creative imagination itself ("Where Alph, the sacred river, ran"); or a formal ordering of subconscious materials ("Through caverns measureless to man"); or the civilization from which instruments of cognition are launched which discover and illuminate that civilization's sources in chaos, or its fated destiny, or its brute environment ("Down to a sunless sea")? Of course, these are just opening suggestions; the other parts of the poem shed much light on the pleasure dome, clarifying some interpretations and suggesting others. Complete readings of the poem are available. If we even begin to investigate "Kubla Khan," do we not hazard into realms where paraphrase is inadequate? Of course. That is truism. Well, then, does this not mean that the pleasure dome, and other symbolic parts of the poem, and the poem itself, are vehicles of understanding? They are not the express products of past knowledge and understanding, such as the expression $2 + 3 = 5$, or the statement that virtue rejects indolence; instead, they are new objects wherein new understanding may be sought and found. They are objects set beyond the limits of the already known.

We may find symbolized in "Kubla Khan"—by the dome, by Kubla Khan, the river and its fountain, the forests, the caverns, the sea, the ice, and the Abyssinian maid and her song—something of the relationship between order and chaos, and between spirit and matter, between the artist and his materials, and the artist and society ("Ancestral voices prophesying war!"), and the romantic imagination and its sources and values ("A savage place! as holy and enchanted"), and the dangerously close relationship in the art object and perhaps in the artist between inspirational sources and the appalling chaos of the abyss ("the mingled measure / From the fountain and the caves"). We are interested in these relationships. The poem presents them. The poem is a form of knowledge.[2]

But what is knowledge if we cannot state it? If art objects quit the bounds of the known and make blurry feints at the unknown, can they truly add to knowledge or understanding? I think they can; for although we may never exhaust or locate precisely the phenomena they signify, we may nevertheless approximate them—and this, of course, is our position in relation to all knowledge and understanding. All our knowledge is partial and approximate; if we are to know electrons and chimpanzees less than perfectly, and call it good enough, we may as well understand phenomena like love and death, or art and freedom, imperfectly also.

Artistic symbol, in other words, instead of merely imitating the flux and mystery of the great world, actually penetrates them on its own. That is, if a document like *The New York Times* or Pepys' *Diary*[3] is a kind of island miniature of our planet, an island which we may explore on foot, then a symbol or a structure of related symbols (including myth, religion, and innumerable works of art, like *Moby Dick* and "Kubla Khan") is, by contrast, a kind of exploratory craft. It is a space probe. Although it is constructed of the planet's materials, it nevertheless leaves the planet altogether. It is a rocket ship; it opens new and hitherto inaccessible regions.

This is the unique cognitive property of symbol: there is no boundary, and probably no difference, between symbol and the realm it comes to mean. An art object, say, and a myth are each the agent and the object of cognition. Each is a lens focused on itself. Say that the story of Christ is a symbol. Say that generations of thinkers have enlarged and enriched the symbol. What then? What is the difference between this narrative, or this artifact, and what it symbolizes? It is it, itself. You cannot address this question (or any other) in depth without using its own terms, which are symbolic at every level: cup, manger, and cross, or grace, incarnation, and sacrifice—and so on, either "up" or "down" the levels of abstraction. You must either learn to use these terms, and like them, or relinquish this field of knowledge altogether.

Similarly, to speak of "Kubla Khan" at any useful level is to speak of the pleasure dome and of Alph the sacred river, and the caverns measureless to man, and the Abyssinian maid. You learn the poem as you learn Italian. You cease to translate its bits in your mind, and instead let them

2. Incidentally, "Kubla Khan" also raises the question of its own beauty. Why is it so beautiful? Why do otherwise rational people —sober, grouchy, skeptical people—turn soft in the head about "Kubla Khan"? Why is this creepy-crawly, misty, overlandscaped, striving-after-beautiful-effect, water-colorish little portentous poem one of the most beautiful and powerful poems in English [author's note]?

3. Pepys' *Diary*, January 1, 1660–May 31, 1669, written by Samuel Pepys (1633–1703), gives an honest presentation of the ways of court and everyday life in seventeenth-century England.

speak for themselves. All our knowledge is of course in one sense symbolic, and to go deeply into any field—physics, say, or art—is to learn faith in its symbols. At first you notice that these tools and objects of thought are symbols; you translate them, as you go, into your own familiar idiom. Later you learn faith and release them. You learn to let them relate on their own terms, hadron[4] to hadron, paint surface to paint surface—and only then do you begin to make progress. (In this sense, faith is the requisite of knowledge.)

One interesting, well-known, yet elusive thing about true symbols is something unmanageable about the way they are formed. Since their regions of meaning are blurred, and since there is no clear difference between symbols and the realms they come to mean, and since they act at the level where the scarcely understood fades into the unknown, the hapless artist who sets one of these things in motion shortly finds himself out of control. Symbols, and the many works of art that contain them, "assume a life of their own," as the cliché goes; they outreach the span of their maker's arm; they guide their creator's hand; they illuminate a wider area than that which their maker ever intended. * * * The art object is always passive in relation to its audience. It is alarmingly active, however, in relation to its creator. Far from being like a receptacle in which you, the artist, drop your ideas, and far from being like a lump of clay which you pummel until it fits your notion of an ashtray, the art object is more like an enthusiastic and ill-trained Labrador retriever which yanks you into traffic. I do not intend to wax mystical or sentimental at this juncture; nevertheless, this familiar notion—that the art object drags its maker into deep waters—is worth mentioning again, matter-of-factly, as one evidence that art, especially insofar as it is symbolic art, is not only an object of past knowledge but an instrument of new knowledge. For if you already understood all the relationships among phenomena to which the parts of your art referred, you could control them easily from the start—and you cannot. It is the artist's business, then, to learn from his art and to order formally his new understanding. Confused art is merely confusing. When in the art object the artist has mastered his own confusion, he has gained new ground; and if he is mature enough and educated enough to have begun at the far edge of his own culture's knowledge, then he has won new ground not only for himself but for his culture as well.

Symbol does not only refer; it acts. There is no such thing as a *mere* symbol. When you climb to the higher levels of abstraction, symbols, those enormous, translucent planets, are all there is. They are at once your only tools of knowledge and that knowledge's only object. It is no

4. A subatomic particle.

leap to say that space-time is itself a symbol. If the material world is a symbol, it is the symbol of mind, or of God. Which is more or less meaningless—as you choose. But is not mere. In the last analysis, symbols and art objects do not stand for things; they manifest them, in their fullness. You begin by using symbols, and end by contemplating them.

1974

THE READER

1. What does Dillard mean when she says a poem "is a form of knowledge"?

2. Is Dillard right in asserting that "there is no boundary, and probably no difference, between symbol and the realm it comes to mean"?

3. Dillard says that "to go deeply into any field—physics, say, or art—is to learn faith in its symbols." Why does she believe this is necessary?

4. Dillard says that "the art object ... is alarmingly active ... in its relation to its creator. Far from being like a receptacle in which you, the artist, drop your ideas, and far from being like a lump of clay which you pummel until it fits your notion of an ashtray, the art object is more like an enthusiastic and ill-trained Labrador retriever which yanks you into traffic." Rewrite this passage, translating the metaphors into nonmetaphorical statements. Have you lost any of the meaning?

THE WRITER

1. Dillard discusses "Kubla Khan" (printed below) at some length. How does discussing the poem allow her to make some of her key points?

KUBLA KHAN

OR A VISION IN A DREAM. A FRAGMENT

The following fragment is here published at the request of a poet of great and deserved celebrity,[1] and, as far as the author's own opinions are concerned, rather as a psychological curiosity, than on the ground of any supposed poetic merits.

In the summer of the year 1797, the author, then in ill health, had retired to a lonely farmhouse between Porlock and Linton, on the Exmoor confines of Somerset and Devonshire. In consequence of a slight indisposition, an anodyne had been prescribed, from the effects of which he fell asleep in his chair at the moment that he was reading the following sentence, or words of the same substance, in *Purchas's Pilgrimage*: "Here the Khan Kubla commanded a palace to be built, and a stately garden thereunto. And thus ten miles of fertile ground were inclosed with a wall.[2] The author continued for about three

---

1. Lord Byron.
2. "In Xamadu did Cublai Can build a stately Palace, encompassing sixteene miles of plaine ground with a wall, wherein fertile Meddowes, pleasant springs, delightfull Streames, and all softs of beasts of chase and game, and in the middest thereof a sumptuous house of pleasure, which may be removed from place to place." From Samuel Purchas, *Purchas his Pilgrimage* (1613). The historical Kublai Khan founded the Mongol dynasty in China in the thirteenth century.

hours in a profound sleep, at least of the external senses,[3] during which time he has the most vivid confidence that he could not have composed less than from two to three hundred lines; if that indeed can be called composition in which all the images rose up before him as *things*, with a parallel production of the correspondent expressions, without any sensation or consciousness of effort. On awaking he appeared to himself to have a distinct recollection of the whole, and taking his pen, ink, and paper, instantly and eagerly wrote down the lines that are here preserved. At this moment he was unfortunately called out by a person on business from Porlock, and detained by him above an hour, and on his return to his room, found, to his no small surprise and mortification, that though he still retained some vague and dim recollection of the general purport of his vision, yet, with the exception of some eight or ten scattered lines and images, all the rest had passed away like the images on the surface of a stream into which a stone has been cast, but, alas! without the after restoration of the latter!

> Then all the charm
> Is broken—all that phantom world so fair
> Vanishes, and a thousand circlets spread,
> And each misshape[s] the other. Stay awhile,
> Poor youth! who scarcely dar'st lift up thine eyes—
> The stream will soon renew its smoothness, soon
> The visions will return! And lo, he stays,
> And soon the fragments dim of lovely forms
> Come trembling back, unite, and now once more
> The pool becomes a mirror.

> > [From Coleridge's *The Picture;
> > or, the Lover's Resolution*, lines 91–100]

Yet from the still surviving recollections in his mind, the author has frequently purposed to finish for himself what had been originally, as it were, given to him. Σαμερον αδιον ασω:[4] but the tomorrow is yet to come.

> In Xanadu did Kubla Khan
> A stately pleasure dome decree:
> Where Alph, the sacred river, ran
> Through caverns measureless to man
> > Down to a sunless sea.
> So twice five miles of fertile ground
> With walls and towers were girdled round:
> And there were gardens bright with sinuous rills,
> Where blossomed many an incense-bearing tree;

3. In a note on a manuscript copy of *Kubla Khan*, Coleridge gave a more precise account of the nature of this "sleep": "This fragment with a good deal more, not recoverable, composed, in a sort of reverie brought on by two grains of opium, taken to check a dysentery, at a farmhouse between Porlock and Linton, a quarter of a mile from Culbone Church, in the fall of the year, 1797."

4. "I shall sing a sweeter song today." In the edition of 1834, Σαμερον ("today") was changed to αὔριον ("tomorrow"). Coleridge had in mind Theocritus. *Idyls* I.145: ἐν ὕστερον ἄδιον ἄσῶ ("I shall sing a sweeter song on a later day").

And here were forests ancient as the hills,
Enfolding sunny spots of greenery.

But oh! that deep romantic chasm which slanted
Down the green hill athwart a cedarn cover!
A savage place! as holy and enchanted
As e'er beneath a waning moon was haunted
By woman wailing for her demon lover!
And from this chasm, with ceaseless turmoil seething,
As if this earth in fast thick pants were breathing,
A mighty fountain momently was forced:
Amid whose swift half-intermitted burst
Huge fragments vaulted like rebounding hail,
Or chaffy grain beneath the thresher's flail:
And 'mid these dancing rocks at once and ever
It flung up momently the sacred river.
Five miles meandering with a mazy motion
Through wood and dale the sacred river ran,
Then reached the caverns measureless to man,
And sank in tumult to a lifeless ocean:
And 'mid this tumult Kubla heard from far
Ancestral voices prophesying war!
    The shadow of the dome of pleasure
    Floated midway on the waves;
    Where was heard the mingled measure
    From the fountain and the caves.
It was a miracle of rare device,
A sunny pleasure dome with caves of ice!

    A damsel with a dulcimer
    In a vision once I saw:
    It was an Abyssinian maid,
    And on her dulcimer she played,
    Singing of Mount Abora.
Could I revive within me
Her symphony and song,
To such a deep delight 'twould win me,
That with music loud and long,
I would build that dome in air,
That sunny dome! those caves of ice!
And all who heard should see them there,
And all should cry, Beware! Beware!
His flashing eyes, his floating hair!
Weave a circle round him thrice,
And close your eyes with holy dread,
For he on honeydew hath fed,
And drunk the milk of Paradise.

c. 1797–98   1816

2. *In a footnote, Dillard calls "Kubla Khan" "one of the most beautiful
   and powerful poems in English" and a "creepy-crawly, misty, overlandscaped, striving-after-beautiful-effect, water-colorish little porent-
   ous poem." Is there a contradiction here? Embody your answer in a
   brief essay.*
3. *Dillard calls a work of art "a space probe . . . [that] opens new and
   hitherto inaccessible regions." What other metaphors might she have
   used to convey this idea? Try out one or two, and compare their
   effectiveness with Dillard's.*
4. *Read Thomas's "Humanities and Science" (p. 253), and write a brief
   essay comparing the ways that Thomas and Dillard treat one similar
   idea.*

Susanne K. Langer

EXPRESSIVENESS

When we talk about "Art" with a capital "A"—that is, about any or all
of the arts: painting, sculpture, architecture, the potter's and goldsmith's
and other designers' arts, music, dance, poetry, and prose fiction, drama
and film—it is a constant temptation to say things about "Art" in this
general sense that are true only in one special domain, or to assume that
what holds for one art must hold for another. For instance, the fact that
music is made for performance, for presentation to the ear, and is simply
not the same thing when it is given only to the tonal imagination of a
reader silently perusing the score, has made some aestheticians pass
straight to the conclusion that literature, too, must be physically heard to
be fully experienced, because words are originally spoken, not written; an
obvious parallel, but a careless and, I think, invalid one. It is dangerous to
set up principles by analogy, and generalize from a single consideration.

But it is natural, and safe enough, to ask analogous questions:

"What is the function of sound in music? What is the function of
sound in poetry? What is the function of sound in prose composition?
What is the function of sound in drama?" The answers may be quite
heterogeneous; and that is itself an important fact, a guide to something
more than a simple and sweeping theory. Such findings guide us to exact
relations and abstract, variously exemplified basic principles.

At present, however, we are dealing with principles that have proven
to be the same in all the arts, when each kind of art—plastic, musical,
balletic, poetic, and each major mode, such as literary and dramatic

writing, or painting, sculpturing, building plastic shapes—has been studied in its own terms. Such candid study is more rewarding than the usual passionate declaration that all the arts are alike, only their materials differ, their principles are all the same, their techniques all analogous, etc. That is not only unsafe, but untrue. It is in pursuing the differences among them that one arrives, finally, at a point where no more differences appears; then one has found, not postulated, their unity. At that deep level there is only one concept exemplified in all the different arts, and that is the concept of Art.

The principles that obtain wholly and fundamentally in every kind of art are few, but decisive; they determine what is art, and what is not. Expressiveness, in one definite and appropriate sense, is the same in all art works of any kind. What is created is not the same in any two distinct arts—this is, in fact, what makes them distinct—but the principle of creation is the same. And "living form" means the same in all of them.

A work of art is an expressive form created for our perception through sense or imagination, and what it expresses is human feeling. The word "feeling" must be taken here in its broadest sense, meaning *everything that can be felt*, from physical sensation, pain and comfort, excitement and repose, to the most complex emotions, intellectual tensions, or the steady feeling-tones of a conscious human life. In stating what a work of art is, I have just used the words "form," "expressive," and "created"; these are key words. One at a time, they will keep us engaged.

Let us consider first what is meant, in this context, by a *form*. The word has many meanings, all equally legitimate for various purposes; even in connection with art it has several. It may, for instance—and often does— denote the familiar, characteristic structures known as the sonnet form, the sestina, or the ballad form in poetry, the sonata form, the madrigal, or the symphony in music, the contredance or the classical ballet in choreography, and so on. This is not what I mean; or rather, it is only a very small part of what I mean. There is another sense in which artists speak of "form" when they say, for instance, "form follows function," or declare that the one quality shared by all good works of art is "significant form," or entitle a book *The Life of Forms in Art*, or *Search for Form*. They are using "form" in a wider sense, which on the one hand is close to the commonest, popular meaning, namely just the *shape* of a thing, and on the other hand to the quite unpopular meaning it has in science and philosophy, where it designates something more abstract; "form" in its most abstract sense means structure, articulation, a whole resulting from the relation of mutually dependent factors, or more precisely, the way that whole is put together.

The abstract sense, which is sometimes called "logical form," is involved in the notion of expression, at least the kind of expression that characterizes art. That is why artists, when they speak of achieving "form," use the word with something of an abstract connotation, even when they are talking about a visible and tangible art object in which that form is embodied.

The more recondite concept of form is derived, of course, from the naive one, that is, material shape. Perhaps the easiest way to grasp the idea of "logical form" is to trace its derivation.

Let us consider the most obvious sort of form, the shape of an object, say a lampshade. In any department store you will find a wide choice of lampshades, mostly monstrosities, and what is monstrous is usually their shape. You select the least offensive one, maybe even a good one, but realize that the color, say violet, will not fit into your room; so you look about for another shade of the same shape but a different color, perhaps green. In recognizing this same shape in another object, possibly of another material as well as another color, you have quite naturally and easily abstracted the concept of this shape from your actual impression of the first lampshade. Presently it may occur to you that this shade is too big for your lamp; you ask whether they have *this same shade* (meaning another one of this shape) in a smaller size. The clerk understands you.

But what is *the same* in the big violet shade and the little green one? Nothing but the interrelations among their respective various dimensions. They are not "the same" even in their spatial properties, for none of their actual measures are alike; but their shapes are congruent. Their respective spatial factors are put together in the same way, so they exemplify the same form.

It is really astounding what complicated abstractions we make in our ordinary dealing with forms—that is to say, through what twists and transformations we recognize the same logical form. Consider the similarity of your two hands. Put one on the table, palm down, superimpose the other, palm down, as you may have superimposed cut-out geometric shapes in school—they are not alike at all. But their shapes are *exact opposites*. Their respective shapes fit the same description, provided that the description is modified by a principle of application whereby the measures are read one way for one hand and the other way for the other—like a timetable in which the list of stations is marked: "Eastbound, read down; Westbound, read up."

As the two hands exemplify the same form with a principle of reversal understood, so the list of stations describes two ways of moving, indicated by the advice to "read down" for one and "read up" for the other. We can all abstract the common element in these two respective trips, which is called the *route*. With a return ticket we may return only by the same route. The same principle relates a mold to the form of the thing that is cast in it, and establishes their formal correspondence, or common logical form.

So far we have considered only objects—lampshades, hands, or regions of the earth—as having forms. These have fixed shapes; their parts remain in fairly stable relations to each other. But there are also substances that have no definite shapes, such as gases, mist, and water, which take the shape of any bounded space that contains them. The interesting thing about such amorphous fluids is that when they are put into violent motion they do exhibit visible forms, not bounded by any container. Think of the momentary efflorescence of a bursting rocket, the mushroom cloud of an atomic bomb, the funnel of water or dust screwing upward in a whirlwind. The instant the motion stops, or even slows beyond a certain degree, those shapes collapse and the apparent "thing" disappears. They are not shapes of things at all, but forms of motions, or dynamic forms.

Some dynamic forms, however, have more permanent manifestations, because the stuff that moves and makes them visible is constantly replenished. A waterfall seems to hang from the cliff, waving streamers of foam. Actually, of course, nothing stays there in midair; the water is always passing; but there is more and more water taking the same paths, so we have a lasting shape made and maintained by its passage—a permanent dynamic form. A quiet river, too, has dynamic form; if it stopped flowing it would either go dry or become a lake. Some twenty-five hundred years ago, Heracleitos was struck by the fact that you cannot step twice into the same river at the same place—at least, if the river means the water, not its dynamic form, the flow.

When a river ceases to flow because the water is deflected or dried up, there remains the river bed, sometimes cut deeply in solid stone. That bed is shaped by the flow, and records as graven lines the currents that have ceased to exist. Its shape is static, but it *expresses* the dynamic form of the river. Again, we have two congruent forms, like a cast and its mold, but this time the congruence is more remarkable because it holds between a dynamic form and a static one. That relation is important; we shall be dealing with it again when we come to consider the meaning of "living form" in art.

The congruence of two given perceptible forms is not always evident upon simple inspection. The common *logical* form they both exhibit may become apparent only when you know the principle whereby to relate them, as you compare the shapes of your hands not by direct correspondence, but by correspondence of opposite parts. Where the two exemplifications of the single logical form are unlike in most other respects one needs a rule for matching up the relevant factors of one with the relevant factors of the other; that is to say, a *rule of translation*, whereby one instance of the logical form is shown to correspond formally to the other.

The logical form itself is not another thing, but an abstract concept, or better an *abstractable* concept. We usually don't abstract it deliberately, but only use it, as we use our vocal cords in speech without first learning all about their operation and then applying our knowledge. Most people perceive intuitively the similarity of their two hands without thinking of them as conversely related; they can guess at the shape of the hollow inside a wooden shoe from the shape of a human foot, without any abstract study of topology. But the first time they see a map in the Mercator projection—with parallel lines of longitude, not meeting at the poles—they find it hard to believe that this corresponds logically to the circular map they used in school, where the meridians bulged apart toward the equator and met at both poles. The visible shapes of the continents are different on the two maps, and it takes abstract thinking to match up the two representations of the same earth. If, however, they have grown up with both maps, they will probably see the geographical relationships either way with equal ease, because these relationships are not *copied* by either map, but *expressed,* and expressed equally well by both; for the two maps are different *projections* of the same logical form, which the spherical earth exhibits in still another—that is, a spherical— projection.

An expressive form is any perceptible or imaginable whole that exhibits relationships of parts, or points, or even qualities or aspects within the whole, so that it may be taken to represent some other whole whose elements have analogous relations. The reason for using such a form as a symbol is usually that the thing it represents is not perceivable or readily imaginable. We cannot see the earth as an object. We let a map or a little globe express the relationships of places on the earth, and think about the earth by means of it. The understanding of one thing through another seems to be a deeply intuitive process in the human brain; it is so natural that we often have difficulty in distinguishing the symbolic expressive form from what it conveys. The symbol seems to be the thing itself, or contain it, or be contained in it. A child interested in a globe will not say: "This means the earth," but: "Look, this is the earth." A similar identification of symbol and meaning underlies the widespread conception of holy names, of the physical efficacy of rites, and many other primitive but culturally persistent phenomena. It has a bearing on our perception of artistic import; that is why I mention it here.

The most astounding and developed symbolic device humanity has evolved is language. By means of language we can conceive the intangible, incorporeal things we call our *ideas,* and the equally inostensible elements of our perceptual world that we call *facts.* It is by virtue of language that we can think, remember, imagine, and finally conceive a universe of facts. We can describe things and represent their relations, express rules of their interactions, speculate and predict and carry on a long symbolizing process known as reasoning. And above all, we can communicate, by producing a serried array of audible or visible words, in a pattern commonly known, and readily understood to reflect our multifarious concepts and percepts and their interconnections. This use of language is *discourse*; and the pattern of discourse is known as *discursive* form. It is a highly versatile, amazingly powerful pattern. It has impressed itself on our tacit thinking, so that we call all systematic reflection "discursive thought." It has made, far more than most people know, the very frame of our sensory experience—the frame of objective facts in which we carry on the practical business of life.

Yet even the discursive pattern has its limits of usefulness. An expressive form can express any complex of conceptions that, via some rule of projection, appears congruent with it, that is, appears to be of that form. Whatever there is in experience that will not take the impress—directly or indirectly—of discursive form, is not discursively communicable or, in the strictest sense, logically thinkable. It is unspeakable, ineffable; according to practically all serious philosophical theories today, it is unknowable.

Yet there is a great deal of experience that is knowable, not only as immediate, formless, meaningless impact, but as one aspect of the intricate web of life, yet defies discursive formulation, and therefore verbal expression: that is what we sometimes call the *subjective aspect* of experience, the direct feeling of it—what it is like to be waking and moving, to be drowsy, slowing down, or to be sociable, or to feel self-sufficient but alone; what it feels like to pursue an elusive thought or to have a big idea. All such directly felt experiences usually have no names—they are named, if at all, for the outward conditions that normally accompany their occurrence. Only the most striking ones have names like "anger," "hate," "love," "fear," and are collectively called "emotion." But we feel many things that never develop into any designable emotion. The ways we are moved are as various as the lights in a forest; and they may intersect, sometimes without cancelling each other, take shape and dissolve, conflict, explode into passion, or be transfigured. All these inseparable elements of subjective reality compose what we call the "inward life" of human beings. The usual factoring of that life-stream into mental, emotional, and sensory units is an arbitrary scheme of simplification that makes scientific treatment possible to a considerable extent; but we may already be close to the limit of its usefulness, that is, close to the point where its simplicity becomes an obstacle to further questioning and discovery instead of the revealing, ever-suitable logical projection it was expected to be.

Whatever resists projection into the discursive form of language is, indeed, hard to hold in conception, and perhaps impossible to communicate, in the proper and strict sense of the word "communicate." But fortunately our logical intuition, or form-perception, is really much more powerful than we commonly believe, and our knowledge—genuine knowledge, understanding—is considerably wider than our discourse.

Even in the use of language, if we want to name something that is too new to have a name (e.g., a newly invented gadget or a newly discovered creature), or want to express a relationship for which there is no verb or other connective word, we resort to metaphor; we mention it or describe it as something else, something analogous. The principle of metaphor is simply the principle of saying one thing and meaning another, and expecting to be understood to mean the other. A metaphor is not language, it is an idea expressed by language, an idea that in its turn functions as a symbol to express something. It is not discursive and therefore does not really make a statement of the idea it conveys; but it formulates a new conception for our direct imaginative grasp.

Sometimes our comprehension of a total experience is mediated by a metaphorical symbol because the experience is new, and language has words and phrases only for familiar notions. Then an extension of language will gradually follow the wordless insight, and discursive expression will supersede the non-discursive pristine symbol. This is, I think, the normal advance of human thought and language in that whole realm of knowledge where discourse is possible at all.

But the symbolic presentation of subjective reality for contemplation is not only tentatively beyond the reach of language—that is, not merely beyond the words we have; it is impossible in the essential frame of language. That is why those semanticists who recognize only discourse as a symbolic form must regard the whole life of feeling as formless, chaotic, capable only of symptomatic expression, typified in exclamations like "Ah!" "Ouch!" "My sainted aunt!" They usually do believe that art is an expression of feeling, but that "expression" in art is of this sort, indicating that the speaker has an emotion, a pain, or other personal experience, perhaps also giving us a clue to the general kind of experience it is—pleasant or unpleasant, violent or mild—but not setting that piece of inward life objectively before us so we may understand its intricacy, its rhythms and shifts of total appearance. The differences in feeling-tones or other elements of subjective experience are regarded as differences in quality, which must be felt to be appreciated. Furthermore, since we have no intellectual access to pure subjectivity, the only way to study it is to study the symptoms of the person who is having subjective experiences. This leads to physiological psychology—a very important and interesting field. But it tells us nothing about the phenomena of subjective life, and sometimes simplifies the problem by saying they don't exist.

Now, I believe the expression of feeling in a work of art—the function that makes the work an expressive form—is not symptomatic at all. An artist working on a tragedy need not be in personal despair or violent upheaval; nobody, indeed, could work in such a state of mind. His mind would be occupied with the causes of his emotional upset. Self-expression does not require composition and lucidity; a screaming baby gives his feeling far more release than any musician, but we don't go into a concert hall to hear a baby scream; in fact, if that baby is brought in we are likely to go out. We don't want self-expression.

A work of art presents feeling (in the broad sense I mentioned before, as everything that can be felt) for our contemplation, making it visible or audible or in some way perceivable through a symbol, not inferable from a symptom. Artistic form is congruent with the dynamic forms of our direct sensuous, mental, and emotional life; works of art are projections of "felt life," as Henry James called it, into spatial, temporal, and poetic structures. They are images of feeling, that formulate it for our cognition. What is artistically good is whatever articulates and presents feeling to our understanding.

Artistic forms are more complex than any other symbolic forms we know. They are, indeed, not abstractable from the works that exhibit them. We may abstract a shape from an object that has this shape, by disregarding color, weight and texture, even size; but to the total effect that is an artistic form, the color matters, the thickness of lines matters, and the appearance of texture and weight. A given triangle is the same in any position, but to an artistic form its location, balance, and surroundings are not indifferent. Form, in the sense in which artists speak of "significant form" or "expressive form," is not an abstracted structure, but an apparition; and the vital processes of sense and emotion that a good work of art expresses seem to the beholder to be directly contained in it, not symbolized but really presented. The congruence is so striking that symbol and meaning appear as one reality. Actually, as one psychologist who is also a musician has written, "Music sounds as feelings feel." And likewise, in good painting, sculpture, or building, balanced shapes and colors, lines and masses look as emotions, vital tensions and their resolutions feel.

An artist, then, expresses feeling, but not in the way a politician blows off steam or a baby laughs and cries. He formulates that elusive aspect of reality that is commonly taken to be amorphous and chaotic; that is, he objectifies the subjective realm. What he expresses is, therefore, not his own actual feelings, but what he knows about human feeling. Once he is in possession of a rich symbolism, that knowledge may actually exceed his entire personal experience. A work of art expresses a conception of life, emotion, inward reality. But it is neither a confessional nor a frozen tantrum; it is a developed metaphor, a non-discursive symbol that articulates what is verbally ineffable—the logic of consciousness itself.

1957

Carl Gustav Jung

THE POET

Creativeness, like the freedom of the will, contains a secret. The psychologist can describe both these manifestations as processes, but he can find no solution of the philosophical problems they offer. Creative man is a riddle that we may try to answer in various ways, but always in vain, a truth that has not prevented modern psychology from turning now and again to the question of the artist and his art. Freud thought that he had found a key in his procedure of deriving the work of art from the personal experiences of the artist. It is true that certain possibilities lay in this direction, for it was conceivable that a work of art, no less than a neurosis, might be traced back to those knots in psychic life that we call the complexes. It was Freud's great discovery that neuroses have a causal origin in the psychic realm—that they take their rise from emotional states and from real or imagined childhood experiences. Certain of his followers, like Rank and Stekel, have taken up related lines of enquiry and have achieved important results. It is undeniable that the poet's psychic disposition permeates his work root and branch. Nor is there anything new in the statement that personal factors largely influence the poet's choice and use of his materials. Credit, however, must certainly be given to the Freudian school for showing how far-reaching this influence is and in what curious ways it comes to expression.

Freud takes the neurosis as a substitute for a direct means of gratification. He therefore regards it as something inappropriate—a mistake, a dodge, an excuse, a voluntary blindness. To him it is essentially a shortcoming that should never have been. Since a neurosis, to all appearances, is nothing but a disturbance that is all the more irritating because it is without sense or meaning, few people will venture to say a good word for it. And a work of art is brought into questionable proximity with the neurosis when it is taken as something which can be analysed in terms of the poet's repressions. In a sense it finds itself in good company, for religion and philosophy are regarded in the same light by Freudian psychology. No objection can be raised if it is admitted that this approach amounts to nothing more than the elucidation of those personal determinants without which a work of art is unthinkable. But should the claim be made that such an anlaysis accounts for the work of art itself, then a categorical denial is called for. The personal idiosyncrasies that creep into a work of art are not essential; in fact, the more we have to cope with these peculiarities, the less is it a question of art. What is essential in a work of art is that it should rise far above the realm of personal life and speak from the spirit and heart of the poet as man to the spirit and heart of mankind. The personal aspect is a limitation—and even a sin—in the realm of art. When a form of "art" is primarily personal it deserves to be treated as if it were a neurosis. There may be some validity in the idea held by the Freudian school that artists without exception are narcissistic —by which is meant that they are undeveloped persons with infantile and autoerotic traits. The statement is only valid, however, for the artist as a person, and has nothing to do with the man as an artist. In his capacity of artist he is neither auto-erotic, nor hetero-erotic, nor erotic in any sense. He is objective and impersonal—even inhuman—for as an artist he is his work, and not a human being.

Every creative person is a duality or a synthesis of contradictory aptitudes. On the one side he is a human being with a personal life, while on the other side he is an impersonal, creative process. Since as a human being he may be sound or morbid, we must look at his psychic make-up to find the determinants of his personality. But we can only understand him in his capacity of artist by looking at his creative achievement. We should make a sad mistake if we tried to explain the mode of life of an English gentleman, a Prussian officer, or a cardinal in terms of personal factors. The gentleman, the officer and the cleric function as such in an impersonal role, and their psychic make-up is qualified by a peculiar objectivity. We must grant that the artist does not function in an official capacity—the very opposite is nearer the truth. He nevertheless resembles the types I have named in one respect, for the specifically artistic disposition involves an overweight of collective psychic life as against the personal. Art is a kind of innate drive that seizes a human being and makes him its instrument. The artist is not a person endowed with free will who seeks his own ends, but one who allows art to realize its purposes through him. As a human being he may have moods and a will and personal aims, but as an artist he is "man" in a higher sense—he is "collective man"—one who carries and shapes the unconscious, psychic life of mankind. To perform this difficult office it is sometimes necessary for him to sacrifice happiness and everything that makes life worth living for the ordinary human being.

All this being so, it is not strange that the artist is an especially interesting case for the psychologist who uses an analytical method. The artist's life cannot be otherwise than full of conflicts, for two forces are at war within him—on the one hand the common human longing for happiness, satisfaction and security in life, and on the other a ruthless passion for creation which may go so far as to override every personal desire. The lives of artists are as a rule so highly unsatisfactory—not to say tragic—because of their inferiority on the human and personal side, and not because of a sinister dispensation. There are hardly any exceptions to the rule that a person must pay dearly for the divine gift of the creative fire. It is as though each of us were endowed at birth with a certain capital of energy. The strongest force in our make-up will seize and all but monopolize this energy, leaving so little over that nothing of value can come of it. In this way the creative force can drain the human impulses to such a degree that the personal ego must develop all sorts of bad qualities—ruthlessnes, selfishness and vanity (so-called "auto-erotism")—and even every kind of vice, in order to maintain the spark of life and to keep itself from being wholly bereft. The auto-erotism of artists resembles that of illegitimate or neglected children who from their tenderest years must protect themselves from the destructive influence of people who have no love to give them—who develop bad qualities for that very purpose and later maintain an invincible egocentrism by remaining all their lives infantile and helpless or by actively offending against the moral code or the law. How can we doubt that it is his art that explains the artist, and not the insufficiencies and conflicts of his personal life? These are nothing but the regrettable results of the fact that he is an artist—that is to say, a man who from his very birth has been called to a greater task than the ordinary mortal. A special ability means a heavy expenditure of energy in a particular direction, with a consequent drain from some other side of life.

It makes no difference whether the poet knows that his work is begotten, grows and matures with him, or whether he supposes that by taking thought he produces it out of the void. His opinion of the matter does not change the fact that his own work outgrows him as a child its mother. The creative process has feminine quality, and the creative work arises from unconscious depths—we might say, from the realm of the mothers. Whenever the creative force predominates, human life is ruled and moulded by the unconscious as against the active will, and the conscious ego is swept along on a subterranean current, being nothing more than a helpless observer of events. The work in process becomes the poet's fate and determines his psychic development. It is not Goethe who creates *Faust*, but *Faust* which creates Goethe. And what is *Faust* but a symbol? By this I do not mean an allegory that points to something all too familiar, but an expression that stands for something not clearly known and yet profoundly alive. Here it is something that lives in the soul of every German, and that Goethe has helped to bring to birth. Could we conceive of anyone but a German writing *Faust* or *Also sprach Zarathustra?* Both play upon something that reverberates in the German soul—a "primordial image," as Jacob Burckhardt once called it—the figure of a physician or teacher of mankind. The archetypal image of the wise man, the saviour or redeemer, lies buried and dormant in man's unconscious since the dawn of culture; it is awakened whenever the times are out of joint and a human society is committed to a serious error. When people go astray they feel the need of a guide or teacher or even of the physician.

These primordial images are numerous, but do not appear in the dreams of individuals or in works of art until they are called into being by the waywardness of the general outlook. When conscious life is character- ized by one-sidedness and by a false attitude, then they are activated— one might say, "instinctively"—and come to light in the dreams of individuals and the visions of artists and seers, thus restoring the psychic equilibrium of the epoch.

In this way the work of the poet comes to meet the spiritual need of the society in which he lives, and for this reason his work means more to him than his personal fate, whether he is aware of this or not. Being essen- tially the instrument for his work, he is subordinate to it, and we have no reason for expecting him to interpret it for us. He has done the best that in him lies in giving it form, and he must leave the interpretation to others and to the future. A great work of art is like a dream; for all its apparent obviousness it does not explain itself and is never unequivocal. A dream never says: "You ought," or: "This is the truth." It presents an image in much the same way as nature allows a plant to grow, and we must draw our own conclusions. If a person has a nightmare, it means either that he is too much given to fear, or else that he is too exempt from it; and if he dreams of the old wise man it may mean that he is too pedagogical, as also that he stands in need of a teacher. In a subtle way both meanings come to the same thing, as we perceive when we are able to let the work of art act upon us as it acted upon the artist. To grasp its meaning, we must allow it to shape us as it once shaped him. Then we understand the nature of his experience. We see that he has drawn upon the healing and redeeming forces of the collective psyche that underlies consciousness with its isolation and its painful errors; that he has pene- trated to that matrix of life in which all men are embedded, which imparts a common rhythm to all human existence, and allows the individ- ual to communicate his feeling and his striving to mankind as a whole.

The secret of artistic creation and of the effectiveness of art is to be found in a return to the state of *participation mystique*—to that level of experience at which it is man who lives, and not the individual, and at which the weal or woe of the single human being does not count, but only human existence. This is why every great work of art is objective and impersonal, but none the less profoundly moves us each and all. And this is also why the personal life of the poet cannot be held essential to his art —but at most a help or a hindrance to his creative task. He may go the way of a Philistine, a good citizen, a neurotic, a fool or a criminal. His personal career may be inevitable and interesting, but it does not explain the poet.

1946

THE READER

1. *Jung makes a distinction between the "human being with a personal life" and the "impersonal, creative process." What is the importance of this distinction? How does it help to shape the rest of Jung's argument?*

2. *Consider the following stanzas (69–72) from Byron's "Childe Harold's Pilgrimage." To what extent would Jung feel that psychological considerations were helpful in analyzing these lines?*

> To fly from, need not be to hate, mankind:
> All are not fit with them to stir and toil,
> Nor is it discontent to keep the mind
> Deep in its fountain, lest it overboil
> In the hot throng, where we become the spoil
> Of our infection, till too late and long
> We may deplore and struggle with the coil,
> In wretched interchange of wrong for wrong
> Midst a contentious world, striving where none are strong.

> There, in a moment we may plunge our years
> In fatal penitence, and in the blight
> Of our own Soul turn all our blood to tears,
> And colour things to come with hues of Night;
> The race of life becomes a hopeless flight
> To those that walk in darkness: on the sea
> The boldest steer but where their ports invite—
> But there are wanderers o'er Eternity
> Whose bark drives on and on, and anchored ne'er shall be.

> Is it not better, then, to be alone,
> And love Earth only for its earthly sake?
> By the blue rushing of the arrowy Rhone,
> Or the pure bosom of its nursing Lake,
> Which feeds it as a mother who doth make
> A fair but froward infant her own care,
> Kissing its cries away as these awake;—
> Is it not better thus our lives to wear,
> Than join the rushing crowd, doomed to inflict or bear?

> I live not in myself, but I become
> Portion of that around me; and to me
> High mountains are a feeling, but the hum
> Of human cities torture: I can see
> Nothing to loathe in Nature, save to be
> A link reluctant in a fleshly chain,
> Classed among creatures, when the soul can flee,
> And with the sky—the peak—the heaving plain
> Of ocean, or the stars, mingle—and not in vain.

THE WRITER

1. *Jung says that the "personal idiosyncracies that creep into a work of art are not essential," since art "should rise far above the realm of personal life and speak from the spirit and heart of the poet as man to the spirit and heart of mankind." Is a contradiction involved here? Can a poet speak from the heart without being personal? Are "personal idiosyncracies" desirable in a work to give it the flavor of a distinctive style?*
2. *In a brief essay, compare Jung's view of creativity with that of Bronowski in "The Reach of Imagination" (p. 194).*

Robert Frost

EDUCATION BY POETRY:
A MEDITATIVE MONOLOGUE[1]

I am going to urge nothing in my talk. I am not an advocate. I am going to consider a matter, and commit a description. And I am going to describe other colleges than Amherst. Or, rather say all that is good can be taken as about Amherst; all that is bad will be about other colleges.

I know whole colleges where all American poetry is barred—whole colleges. I know whole colleges where all contemporary poetry is barred.

I once heard of a minister who turned his daughter—his poetry-writing daughter—out on the street to earn a living, because he said there should be no more books written; God wrote one book, and that was enough. (My friend George Russell, "Æ", has read no literature, he protests, since just before Chaucer.)

That all seems sufficiently safe, and you can say one thing for it. It takes the onus off the poetry of having to be used to teach children anything. It comes pretty hard on poetry, I sometimes think, what it has to bear in the teaching process.

Then I know whole colleges where, though they let in older poetry, they manage to bar all that is poetical in it by treating it as something other than poetry. It is not so hard to do that. Their reason I have often hunted for. It may be that these people act from a kind of modesty. Who are professors that they should attempt to deal with a thing as high and as fine as poetry? Who are *they*? There is a certain manly modesty in that.

That is the best general way of settling the problem; treat all poetry as if it were something else than poetry, as if it were syntax, language, science. Then you can even come down into the American and into the

1. An address given at Amherst College in 1930.

contemporary without any special risk.

There is another reason they have, and that is that they are, first and foremost in life, markers. They have the marking problem to consider. Now, I stand here a teacher of many years' experience and I have never complained of having had to mark. I had rather mark anyone for anything —for his looks, carriage, his ideas, his correctness, his exactness, anything you please—I would rather give him a mark in terms of letters, A, B, C, D, than have to use adjectives on him. We are all being marked by each other all the time, classified, ranked, put in our place, and I see no escape from that. I am no sentimentalist. You have got to mark, and you have got to mark, first of all, for accuracy, for correctness. But if I am going to give a mark, that is the least part of my marking. The hard part is the part beyond that, the part where the adventure begins.

One other way to rid the curriculum of the poetry nuisance has been considered. More merciful than the others it would neither abolish nor denature the poetry, but only turn it out to disport itself, with the plays and games—in no wise discredited, though given no credit for. Any one who liked to teach poetically could take his subject, whether English, Latin, Greek or French, out into the nowhere along with the poetry. One side of a sharp line would be left to the rigorous and righteous; the other side would be assigned to the flowery where they would know what could be expected of them. Grade marks were more easily given, of course, in the courses concentrating on correctness and exactness as the only forms of honesty recognized by plain people; a general indefinite mark of X in the courses that scatter brains over taste and opinion. On inquiry I have found no teacher willing to take position on either side of the line, either among the rigors or among the flowers. No one is willing to admit that his discipline is not partly in exactness. No one is willing to admit that his discipline is not partly in taste and enthusiasm.

How shall a man go through college without having been marked for taste and judgment? What will become of him? What will his end be? He will have to take continuation courses for college graduates. He will have to go to night schools. They are having night schools now, you know, for college graduates. Why? Because they have not been educated enough to find their way around in contemporary literature. They don't know what they may safely like in the libraries and galleries. They don't know how to judge an editorial when they see one. They don't know how to judge a political campaign. They don't know when they are being fooled by a metaphor, an analogy, a parable. And metaphor is, of course, what we are talking about. Education by poetry is education by metaphor.

Suppose we stop short of imagination, initiative, enthusiasm, inspiration and originality—dread words. Suppose we don't mark in such things at all. There are still two minimal things, that we have got to take care of, taste and judgment. Americans are supposed to have more judgment than taste, but taste is there to be dealt with. That is what poetry, the only art in the colleges of arts, is there for. I for my part would not be afraid to go in for enthusiasm. There is the enthusiasm like a blinding light, or the enthusiasm of the deafening shout, the crude enthusiasm that you get uneducated by poetry, outside of poetry. It is exemplified in what I might call "sunset raving." You look westward toward the sunset, or if you get up early enough, eastward toward the sunrise, and you rave. It is oh's and ah's with you and no more.

But the enthusiasm I mean is taken through the prism of the intellect and spread on the screen in a color, all the way from hyperbole at one end —or overstatement, at one end—to understatement at the other end. It is a long strip of dark lines and many colors. Such enthusiasm is one object of all teaching in poetry. I heard wonderful things said about Virgil yesterday, and many of them seemed to me crude enthusiasm, more like a deafening shout, many of them. But one speech had range, something of overstatement, something of statement, and something of understatement. It had all the colors of an enthusiasm passed through an idea.

I would be willing to throw away everything else but that: enthusiasm tamed by metaphor. Let me rest the case there. Enthusiasm tamed to metaphor, tamed to that much of it. I do not think anybody ever knows the discreet use of metaphor, his own and other people's, the discreet handling of metaphor, unless he has been properly educated in poetry.

Poetry begins in trivial metaphors, petty metaphors, "grace" metaphors, and goes on to the profoundest thinking that we have. Poetry provides the one permissible way of saying one thing and meaning another. People say, "Why don't you say what you mean?" We never do that, do we, being all of us too much poets. We like to talk in parables and in hints and in indirections—whether from diffidence or some other instinct.

I have wanted in late years to go further and further in making metaphor the whole of thinking. I find some one now and then to agree with me that all thinking, except mathematical thinking, is metaphorical, or all thinking except scientific thinking. The mathematical might be difficult for me to bring in, but the scientific is easy enough.

Once on a time all the Greeks were busy telling each other what the All was—or was like unto. All was three elements, air, earth, and water (we once thought it was ninety elements; now we think it is only one). All was substance, said another. All was change, said a third. But best and most fruitful was Pythagoras' comparison of the universe with number. Number of what? Number of feet, pounds, and seconds was the answer, and we had science and all that has followed in science. The metaphor has held and held, breaking down only when it came to the spiritual and psychological or the out of the way places of the physical.

The other day we had a visitor here, a noted scientist, whose latest word to the world has been that the more accurately you know where a thing is, the less accurately you are able to state how fast it is moving. You can see why that would be so, without going back to Zeno's problem of the arrow's flight. In carrying numbers into the realm of space and at the same time into the realm of time you are mixing metaphors, that is all, and you are in trouble. They won't mix. The two don't go together.

Let's take two or three more of the metaphors now in use to live by. I have just spoken of one of the new ones, a charming mixed metaphor right in the realm of higher mathematics and higher physics: that the more accurately you state where a thing is, the less accurately you will be able to tell how fast it is moving. And, of course everything is moving. Everything is an event now. Another metaphor. A thing, they say, is an event. Do you believe it is? Not quite. I believe it is almost an event. But I like the comparison of a thing with an event.

I notice another from the same quarter. "In the neighborhood of matter space is something like curved." Isn't that a good one! It seems to me that that is simply and utterly charming—to say that space is something like curved in the neighborhood of matter. "Something like."

Another amusing one is from—what is the book?—I can't say it now; but here is the metaphor. Its aim is to restore you to your ideas of free will. It wants to give you back your freedom of will. All right, here it is on a platter. You know that you can't tell by name what persons in a certain class will be dead ten years after graduation, but you can tell actuarially how many will be dead. Now, just so this scientist says of the particles of matter flying at a screen, striking a screen; you can't tell what individual particles will come, but you can say in general that a certain number will strike in a given time. It shows, you see, that the individual particle can come freely. I asked Bohr about that particularly, and he said, "Yes, it is so. It can come when it wills and as it wills; and the action of the individual particle is unpredictable. But it is not so of the action of the mass. There you can predict." He says, "That gives the individual atom its freedom, but the mass its necessity."

Another metaphor that has interested us in our time and has done all our thinking for us is the metaphor of evolution. Never mind going into the Latin word. The metaphor is simply the metaphor of the growing plant or of the growing thing. And somebody very brilliantly, quite a while ago, said that the whole universe, the whole of everything, was like unto a growing thing. That is all. I know the metaphor will break down at some point, but it has not failed everywhere. It is a very brilliant metaphor, I acknowledge, though I myself get too tired of the kind of essay that talks about the evolution of candy, we will say, or the evolution of elevators—the evolution of this, that, and the other. Everything is evolution. I emancipate myself by simply saying that I didn't get up the metaphor and so am not much interested in it.

What I am pointing out is that unless you are at home in the metaphor, unless you have had your proper poetical education in the metaphor, you are not safe anywhere. Because you are not at ease with figurative values: you don't know the metaphor in its strength and its weakness. You don't know how far you may expect to ride it and when it may break down with you. You are not safe in science; you are not safe in history. In history, for instance—to show that is the same in history as elsewhere—I heard somebody say yesterday that Aeneas was to be likened unto (those words, "likened unto"!) George Washington. He was that type of national hero, the middle-class man, not thinking of being a hero at all, bent on building the future, bent on his children, his descendants. A good metaphor, as far as it goes, and you must know how far. And then he added that Odysseus should be likened unto Theodore Roosevelt. I don't think that is so good. Someone visiting Gibbon at the point of death, said he was the same Gibbon as of old; still at his parallels.

Take the way we have been led into our present position morally, the world over. It is by a sort of metaphorical gradient. There is a kind of thinking—to speak metaphorically—there is a kind of thinking you might say was endemic in the brothel. It is always there. And every now and then in some mysterious way it becomes epidemic in the world. And how does it do so? By using all the good words that virtue has invented to maintain virtue. It uses honesty, first—frankness, sincerity—those words; picks them up, uses them. "In the name of honesty, let us see what we are." You know. And then it picks up the word joy. "Let us in the name of joy, which is the enemy of our ancestors, the Puritans . . . Let us in the name of joy, which is the enemy of the kill-joy Puritan . . ." You see. "Let us," and so on. And then, "In the name of health . . ." Health is another good word. And that is the metaphor Freudianism trades on, mental health. And the first thing we know, it has us all in up to the top knot. I suppose we may blame the artists a good deal, because they are great people to spread by metaphor. The stage too—the stage is always a good intermediary between the two worlds, the under and the upper, if I may say so without personal prejudice to the stage.

In all this, I have only been saying that the devil can quote Scripture, which simply means that the good words you have lying around the devil can use for his purposes as well as anybody else. Never mind about my morality. I am not here to urge anything. I don't care whether the world is good or bad—not on any particular day.

Let me ask you to watch a metaphor breaking down here before you.

Somebody said to me a little while ago, "It is easy enough for me to think of the universe as a machine, as a mechanism."

I said, "You mean the universe is like a machine?"

He said, "No. I think it is one . . . Well, it is like . . ."

"I think you mean the universe is like a machine."

"All right. Let it go at that."

I asked him, "Did you ever see a machine without a pedal for the foot, or a lever for the hand, or a button for the finger?"

He said "No—no."

I said, "All right. Is the universe like that?"

And he said, "No. I mean it is like a machine, only . . ."

". . . it is different from a machine," I said.

He wanted to go just that far with that metaphor and no further. And so do we all. All metaphor breaks down somewhere. That is the beauty of it. It is touch and go with the metaphor, and until you have lived with it long enough you don't know when it is going. You don't know how much you can get out of it and when it will cease to yield. It is a very living thing. It is as life itself.

I have heard this ever since I can remember, and ever since I have taught: the teacher must teach the pupil to think. I saw a teacher once going around in a great school and snapping pupils' heads with thumb and finger and saying, "Think." That was when thinking was becoming the fashion. The fashion hasn't yet quite gone out.

We still ask boys in college to think, as in the nineties, but we seldom tell them what thinking means; we seldom tell them it is just putting this and that together; it is saying one thing in terms of another. To tell them is to set their feet on the first rung of a ladder the top of which sticks through the sky.

Greatest of all attempts to say one thing in terms of another is the philosophical attempt to say matter in terms of spirit, or spirit in terms of matter, to make the final unity. That is the greatest attempt that ever failed. We stop just short there. But it is the height of poetry, the height of all thinking, the height of all poetic thinking, that attempt to say matter in terms of spirit and spirit in terms of matter. It is wrong to call anybody a materialist simply because he tries to say spirit in terms of matter, as if that were a sin. Materialism is not the attempt to say all in terms of matter. The only materialist—be he poet, teacher, scientist, politician, or statesman—is the man who gets lost in his material without a gathering metaphor to throw it into shape and order. He is the lost soul.

We ask people to think, and we don't show them what thinking is. Somebody says we don't need to show them how to think; bye and bye they will think. We will give them the forms of sentences and, if they have any ideas, then they will know how to write them. But that is preposterous. All there is to writing is having ideas. To learn to write is to learn to have ideas.

The first little metaphor . . . Take some of the trivial ones. I would rather have trivial ones of my own to live by than the big ones of other people.

I remember a boy saying, "He is the kind of person that wounds with his shield." That may be a slender one, of course. It goes a good way in character description. It has poetic grace. "He is the kind that wounds with his shield."

The shield reminds me—just to linger a minute—the shield reminds me of the inverted shield spoken of in one of the books of the *Odyssey*, the book that tells about the longest swim on record. I forget how long it lasted—several days, was it?—but at last as Odysseus came near the coast of Phoenicia, he saw it on the horizon "like an inverted shield."

There is a better metaphor in the same book. In the end Odysseus comes ashore and crawls up the beach to spend the night under a double olive tree, and it says, as in a lonely farmhouse where it is hard to get fire —I am not quoting exactly—where it is hard to start the fire again if it goes out, they cover the seeds of fire with ashes to preserve it for the night, so Odysseus covered himself with the leaves around him and went to sleep. There you have something that gives you character, something of Odysseus himself. "Seeds of fire." So Odysseus covered the seeds of fire in himself. You get the greatness of his nature.

But these are slighter metaphors than the ones we live by. They have their charm, their passing charm. They are as it were the first steps toward the great thoughts, grave thoughts, thoughts lasting to the end.

The metaphor whose manage we are best taught in poetry—that is all there is of thinking. It may not seem far for the mind to go but it is the mind's furthest. The richest accumulation of the ages is the noble metaphors we have rolled up.

I want to add one thing more that the experience of poetry is to anyone who comes close to poetry. There are two ways of coming close to poetry. One is by writing poetry. And some people think I want people to write poetry, but I don't; that is, I don't necessarily. I only want people to write poetry if they want to write poetry. I have never encouraged anybody to write poetry that did not want to write it, and I have not always encouraged those who did want to write it. That ought to be one's own funeral. It is a hard, hard life, as they say.

(I have just been to a city in the West, a city full of poets, a city they have made safe for poets. The whole city is so lovely that you do not have to write it up to make it poetry; it is ready-made for you. But, I don't know —the poetry written in that city might not seem like poetry if read outside of the city. It would be like the jokes made when you were drunk; you have to get drunk again to appreciate them.)

But as I say, there is another way to come close to poetry, fortunately, and that is in the reading of it, not as linguistics, not as history, not as anything but poetry. It is one of the hard things for a teacher to know how close a man has come in reading poetry. How do I know whether a man has come close to Keats in reading Keats? It is hard for me to know. I have lived with some boys a whole year over some of the poets and I have not felt sure whether they have come near what it was all about. One remark sometimes told me. One remark was their mark for the year; had to be— it was all I got that told me what I wanted to know. And that is enough, if it was the right remark, if it came close enough. I think a man might make twenty fool remarks if he made one good one some time in the year. His mark would depend on that good remark.

The closeness—everything depends on the closeness with which you come, and you ought to be marked for the closeness, for nothing else. And that will have to be estimated by chance remarks, not by question and answer. It is only by accident that you know some day how near a person has come.

The person who gets close enough to poetry, he is going to know more about the word *belief* than anybody else knows, even in religion nowadays. There are two or three places where we know belief outside of religion. One of them is at the age of fifteen to twenty, in our self-belief. A young man knows more about himself than he is able to prove to anybody. He has no knowledge that anybody else will accept as knowledge. In his foreknowledge he has something that is going to believe itself into fulfilment, into acceptance.

There is another belief like that, the belief in someone else, a relationship of two that is going to be believed into fulfilment. That is what we are talking about in our novels, the belief of love. And disillusionment that the novels are full of is simply the disillusionment from disappointment in that belief. That belief can fail, of course.

Then there is a literary belief. Every time a poem is written, every time a short story is written, it is written not by cunning, but by belief. The beauty, the something, the little charm of the thing to be, is more felt than known. There is a common jest, one that always annoys me, on the writers, that they write the last end first, and then work up to it; that they lay a train toward one sentence that they think is pretty nice and have all fixed up to set like a trap to close with. No, it should not be that way at all. No one who has ever come close to the arts has failed to see the difference between things written that way, with cunning and device, and the kind that are believed into existence, that begin in something more felt than known. This you can realize quite as well—not quite as well, perhaps, but nearly as well—in reading as you can in writing. I would undertake to separate short stories on that principle; stories that have been believed into existence and stories that have been cunningly devised. And I could separate the poems still more easily.

Now I think—I happen to think—that those three beliefs that I speak of, the self-belief, the love-belief, and the art-belief, are all closely related to the God-belief, that the belief in God is a relationship you enter into with Him to bring about the future.

There is a national belief like that, too. One feels it. I have been where

I came near getting up and walking out on the people who thought that they had to talk against nations, against nationalism, in order to curry favor with internationalism. Their metaphors are all mixed up. They think that because a Frenchman and an American and an Englishman can all sit down on the same platform and receive honors together, it must be that there is no such thing as nations. That kind of bad thinking springs from a source we all know. I should want to say to anyone like that: "Look! First I want to be a person. And I want you to be a person, and then we can be as interpersonal as you please. We can pull each other's noses—do all sorts of things. But, first of all, you have got to have the personality. First of all, you have got to have the nations and then they can be as international as they please with each other."

I should like to use another metaphor on them. I want my palette, if I am a painter, I want my palette on my thumb or on my chair, all clean, pure, separate colors. Then I will do the mixing on the canvas. The canvas is where the work of art is, where we make the conquest. But we want the nations all separate, pure, distinct, things as separate as we can make them; and then in our thoughts, in our arts, and so on, we can do what we please about it.

But I go back. There are four beliefs that I know more about from having lived with poetry. One is the personal belief, which is a knowledge that you don't want to tell other people about because you cannot prove that you know. You are saying nothing about it till you see. The love belief, just the same, has that same shyness. It knows it cannot tell; only the outcome can tell. And the national belief we enter into socially with each other, all together, party of the first part, party of the second part, we enter into that to bring the future of the country. We cannot tell some people what it is we believe, partly, because they are too stupid to understand and partly because we are too proudly vague to explain. And anyway it has got to be fulfilled, and we are not talking until we know more, until we have something to show. And then the literary one in every work of art, not of cunning and craft, mind you, but of real art; that believing the thing into existence, saying as you go more than you even hoped you were going to be able to say, and coming with surprise to an end that you foreknew only with some sort of emotion. And then finally the relationship we enter into with God to believe the future in—to believe the hereafter in.

1930

THE READER

1. How can the "poetry nuisance" be gotten out of the curriculum? Does Frost think it ought to stay in? Why?
2. What is meant by "enthusiasm passed through an idea" and "enthusiasm tamed to metaphor" (p. 1028)? What sort of metaphors does Frost

use in those phrases, and what do they imply?
3. *What does Frost mean when he says "unless you have had your proper poetical education in the metaphor, you are not safe anywhere" (p. 1030)? Indicate some of the metaphors Frost examines in this essay. From what fields are they drawn? What does he say about each? Nominate some further metaphors—from politics, science, sociology, or anything else—and analyze them. To what extent are they useful? Do they have a breaking point? How might they mislead beyond the breaking point?*

THE WRITER

1. *In what way does the subtitle describe this essay? Is it rambling? Is it unified?*
2. *Frost admires a speech that has "range, something of overstatement, something of statement, and something of understatement." Is this spectrum visible in Frost's own speech? Show where and how.*
3. *Choose two metaphors from different fields (like literature and science, politics and biology, etc.), and write a brief essay comparing the use and usefulness of the metaphors in each field.*

Robertson Davies

HAM AND TONGUE

There are, I believe, something like three hundred millions of people on this continent at this moment. I have added a few additional millions, to include visitors from abroad who are here for the express purpose of making speeches. I estimate very roughly that of those three hundred millions, at least three hundred thousand are on their feet at this moment, talking to various groups drawn from the others. Speech-making is one of the principal pursuits of the Western World, but although everybody does it, nobody seems to talk about how it is done. We have keen critics of the techniques of all sports and pastimes, but who criticizes the technique of the speaker? Every art—drama, music, painting—comes under the reducing lens of the critic, except the art of making speeches. Literature, even on the lowest levels, is the fodder for thousands of critics, and the subject of countless graduate-school theses, but the body of a public speech is rarely examined as if it were a literary creation. The content of a speech is frequently chewed over, but the manner in which it is delivered, and the circumstances of its delivery go undiscussed. One wonders why.

In part, I think, it is because there is a widespread belief that a public speaker is a more or less inspired creature, who is making up what he says as he goes along, and that he should not be held accountable for his grammatical muddles, his inaccurate facts, and his uncouth delivery. In my lifetime I have seen the growth of what might be called The North American Myth of Sincerity, a myth which suggests that anything that is done skillfully, or with accomplishment, is of less worth than what is botched. This Myth applies very strongly to the public speaker; the botcher is thought to be a worthy fellow, who is searching his soul for every word that falls maimed and bleeding from his lips. The reality is otherwise; sincerity can be as much of a mannerism as anything else, and I am always suspicious of speakers who appear to be struggling for every sentence. They are frequently crooks, who have mastered their barbarous style just as, in an earlier day, they would have mastered the elements of rhetoric.

In my boyhood I heard many speakers of that earlier day, who prided themselves upon being spell-binders and silver-tongued orators. I have heard speakers of whom it was said—the remark was by no means original, but it never failed to give pleasure—that when they were infants the bees had clustered round their cradles, to sip the honey from their lips. In retrospect, I wonder if any bee ever came back for a second sip. They were very strong on manner, those spell-binders, but they were no better stocked with matter than their less gaudy contemporaries. At the time I heard them, their day was passing. The Age of Sincerity was dawning; I hope that I may live to see the sun set on the Sincere Speaker. There is only one way to make a speech, and that is to have something to say, and to say it as clearly as you can, in a fashion that does not insult or patronize your hearers. Easy to say: not in the least easy to do. Nor is the fault all with the speakers. The passion for public speaking that possesses us on this continent, the unquenchable thirst for everything from full-scale oratory to what is misleadingly called "a few words," makes public speakers of thousands who would do better to remain silent, and drives those who have some knack for speaking to speak altogether too much.

Consider the situation in which we find ourselves. I am greatly complimented to have been asked to speak to you; I am delighted to be here. But common decency compels me to recognize that you would be far better off if you were being entertained by a first-rate conjuror, or a talented clown, or perhaps even by a ventriloquist. There was a time when this fact was given due consideration. When I was a boy I used often to go with my parents to political rallies, where candidates for Parliament appealed for votes. Those men were no fools. They included in their entourage an entertainer, who put the audience in a good mood. After the entertainer had delighted us with his comic songs and his imitation of a Red Indian reciting *The Charge of the Light Brigade*,[1] we were softened

---

1. I.e., a burlesque rendition of Alfred Lord Tennyson's lengthy war poem.

up for the political address. As a boy, I had no vote; if I had been enfranchised, I should unhesitatingly have voted for the entertainer. I learned a lesson at those meetings, and it was this: if you haven't got a professional entertainer on your side, you should do your best to be entertaining in your own person.

I put this lesson into practice at an early age. At my school many prizes were offered, and two I regarded as my personal property; they were the prize for reading aloud, and the prize for public speaking. I sought them, not for glory, but for money. Each contest carried a prize of a finely bound book but, in addition, the right to buy twenty-five dollars' worth of books. Fifty dollars! It was the riches of Ali Baba in a day when a very good book could be bought for three dollars and fifty cents. The unappeasable lust for books which has been one of the glories and the nuisances of my life made it absolutely obligatory for me to get that money. How? Other boys had similar ambitions. But I had a degree of low cunning that was beyond my years, and I reduced the arts of reading and speaking to a formula drawn from the world of the sandwich-maker. It was, very simply, Ham and Tongue.

How well I remember those school contests! My rivals, who were fine boys and have since grown up to be fine men, went in very heavily for Sincerity. They knew where the wellspring of sincerity was; it resided in their fathers. They would admit, though of course not to the judges of the contest, that they had received some help from their fathers in preparing their speeches. In consequence the physician's son was apt to harass the audience with addresses on Man's Struggle Against the Common Cold, and the chartered accountant's son pontificated on Municipal Taxation —Whither? They shouted and waved their fists; the cords in their necks stood out with strain. But I was not a fine boy; looking back, I think I must have been a rather horrid boy, because I adopted a conversational manner, cracked a lot of jokes, and sometimes—I blush to recall—made fun of the other speakers. These were very probably the promptings of the Evil One, but the Evil One was a good friend to me, and I always got the fifty dollars.

I think that the Evil One must have whispered something to the Headmaster of the school as well, because during my time he changed the rules, and demanded that the speeches be extemporary, on subjects drawn from a list he prepared himself. The experts on the Common Cold and Municipal Taxation were flummoxed. But Ham and Tongue carried me through. My affectation of naturalness was precisely that—an affectation; my apparently conversational delivery was in fact quite a loud, carefully articulated yell; I could make myself heard over a brass band.

The Headmaster's purpose in changing the rules was to give us some experience of thinking on our feet. And so it did. It could not, however, do much for a boy who never by any chance thought in any other posture. Personally, I mistrust the notion of thinking on one's feet; I have known many speakers who prided themselves on that ability, and I am sorry to say that many of them were blatherers; they did not know when to stop. This took me some time to realize, because my father was a great admirer of these extemporary speakers; it was the fashion of his day to value length of oratory, and he exulted over political figures who could hold forth for two hours, without a note. My father particularly stressed this: "Without a note!" he would cry, fixing me with a glowing eye. So when my turn came, I naturally tried to speak without notes, but I soon found that it was not for me. Not merely notes, but a prepared script was what I liked. Of course I did not know it, but I was part of a movement toward the prepared speech, with a typescript for the assistance of reporters who cannot write shorthand.

The prepared script also has its dangers. Politicians were probably the first to discover that the script might as well be prepared by somebody else. But no—I wrong them; credit for that discovery belongs to the clergy. Politicians—slapdash fellows with a boundless faith in the gullibility of mankind—all too often gave speeches which were as new to them as to the audience, and not infrequently they came upon words that were unfamiliar to them and ideas that surprised them.

I know all about that. My own political career was a very quiet one: I was a back-room literary hack. I recall writing a series of broadcast speeches for a political aspirant whose fame had been gained as a professional hockey-player. Nothing could persuade him to look at his speech before going on the air, and although I did my level best to write in his own style and vocabulary, such as it was, every now and then he would gag over something—a subordinate clause, or a crumb of unfamiliar punctuation—and reveal himself in all his pitiable insufficiency. Once I gave him a joke, and that was a very great miscalculation, because the cast of his mind was not jocular. Having uttered the joke, and being dimly aware that something untoward had happened, he tried—if I may so express it—to suck the joke back out of the microphone. His committee were displeased with me, but as they were not paying me anything and I was writing simply out of political loyalty, I could afford to ignore their huffing and puffing.

Another experience as a political ghost-writer found me preparing speeches for a man who had been, thirty years earlier, a modest success as a baseball player. He was convinced that his small fame was still resounding in the minds of the youth of the day, and he kept urging me to get it into the speeches. "Tell them I'm a straight shooter," he would say. So I did, but without conviction, for he was so plainly not a shooter at all; he was a magazine of blanks, and he lost the election. He seemed to think that I was a contributing cause. You cannot make a Demosthenes[2] out of an old ball-player; you cannot even cloak him in the grey mantle of

2. Demosthenes (383?–322 B.C.): Athenian orator and statesman.

Phoney Sincerity. If he has no conception of Ham and Tongue, you are beaten, and so is he.

When I speak of Ham, I hope you do not think I recommend a grossly histrionic style of delivery. That used to be popular. There were speakers who wept, speakers who were immense in their indignation, speakers who were hugely sarcastic. At the very bottom of the list came the speakers who told funny stories.

A funny story is, in itself, a good thing, but we have not the appetite for them that existed in our grandfathers. Their taste now seems to us to be gross; their delight in stories involving dialect or racial characteristics is out of fashion. But there was a day when a speaker who rose to his feet and declared that the situation in which he found himself reminded him of the Scotchman, the Irishman, and the Jew who went to a funeral could hold an audience in the palm of his hand. Scotchmen, Irishmen, and Jews were all, by definition, funny, but the real gold of the story lay in the funeral. In Canada forty years ago funerals were surefire.

Let me recall one of these rib-binders. A Scotchman was attending the funeral of his wife, and when the ceremony was concluded, and everyone had left the graveyard, he was to be seen standing by the grave, looking into it with a countenance set in what might have been taken for deep grief. A friend approached him, and said gently: "Well, Jock, so Margaret's gone." "Aye," said the bereaved husband. "She was always a good wife to you," said the friend. "Aye, so she was for fifty years and more," said the widower, and then, after a moment's reflection, "but ye ken I never really likit the wumman."

I have seen that joke throw an audience into paroxysms. Scotchmen and their wives nudged one another in ecstasy and slapped one another's thighs as they laughed at it. Irishmen and Jews laughed, at the same time wondering how they could adapt the story to their own races. But of course that was out of the question; there was something resolutely Scotch about it, and you could no more change it than you could hope to bleach a piece of tartan.

All of these modes of oratory depended heavily on Ham, that quality of histrionism without which a public speech is as piffle before the wind. Ham is out of favor in our age of sincerity, except for the assumption of fake modesty of which I have already spoken. When I left the world of journalism to become a university professor I quickly discovered that Ham was nowhere so deplored as in the academic world. The professor who calls upon the arts of rhetoric and oratory to make his students pay attention quickly wins a name as a charlatan. I have always been glad of my twenty years in the newspaper world, because it taught me many useful things, and one of them is that the public has no particular objection to a charlatan if he does not overstep the bounds of modesty and artistic restraint. Better the charlatan you can hear than the sincere scholar who lulls you to sleep with a sound like the moan of doves in immemorial elms. My own education was prolonged and various, and my best professors were all hams.

I recall with particular affection a Scotsman who was lecturing about the Romantic Poets; he was trying to give us some understanding of the stress of soul and intolerable pressure of imagination that made those men great, and I suppose we looked uncomprehending. He paused, and walked to the window, and looked out at the snowy landscape for perhaps a full minute, and then he said, in a sorrowful voice: "I don't suppose there is one of you mutts who has the slightest idea what I'm talking about." What happened? Did we rise in indignation? Did we rush to his office and burn his library, and demand that he apologize on his knees before he would consent to hear another word? No; we sat up straight and listened very hard and loved him forever after. About two weeks ago I sent a contribution to a fund to create a scholarship in his name. Greater love hath no student than this; that he lay out hard cash to memorialize a dead professor.

That was Ham. What about Tongue?

To me, it is almost wholly a matter of vocabulary. We have all met those excitable, exuberant people who assure us that they just love words. People who just love words too often delight in the showy siftings of the dictionary. I would rather listen to somebody who loved meanings better than words themselves, a speaker who would remain silent rather than use a word he did not truly know. People who just love words are all too often people who talk about "meaningful interface," and spend a lot of time on "marginal variables" whenever they set out upon an "in-depth overview." Doubtless these expressions have some original meaning, but as the people who just love words use them they are gaudy toys, bearing the same relationship to a perceptible meaning that a Christmas tree ornament bears to a fine jewel.

The true word-lover must be constantly on the alert to changes in language. When I was a young man at Oxford I took heed of the fate that befell an American friend of mine, who was reprimanded on his oral examination because he dearly loved the word "motivate" and used it often. The examiner who rebuked him was an old man who explained courteously and patiently—but oh, the courtesy and patience at Oxford can burn like a refiner's fire!—that the word had no respectable ancestry, that it could not be derived from Latin and had sneaked into the language from France and Germany; it was a low word which my friend would do well to scrub from his tongue with acid. I took warning by my friend's experience, and I shrink from "motivate" still. But much time has passed; "motivate" is now in the Oxford English Dictionary and I have become a fossil, in this respect at least. My recollection of this incident makes me cautious about rebuking my own pupils when they say "prestigious" when they mean "distinguished." To me "prestigious" means, and always will mean, juggling tricks, because it derives from *praestigiae*, and when it is used in the modern way I feel as though a rusty sword had been thrust into my—well, not perhaps into my heart, but into some sensitive part of my body. But I do not want to parade as a conservator of endangered species in the world of words. Let the unlettered yahoos ravish the language; what do I care? But I refuse to join in the gang-bang.

I refuse for what I consider a good reason. I am not one of those tedious people who writes to the papers correcting other correspondents about English usage. No, my concern is that of a writer, and on occasion a formal speaker, who wants to be as careful and even pernickety about meanings as he can. Without precision of meaning we damage not simply language, but thought. The language we share is beautiful and alarmingly complex. Try as we may, we are all likely to make mistakes, and very few among us can claim to know the English language in perfection. But we can try.

A humbling lessom for me came about a few years ago when I had an Oriental student of great promise who was terribly worried about English idiom. Blithely I undertook to help him, and we set to work to go right through Fowler's *Modern English Usage*, I to explain and he to learn. It was not long before I was over my head in difficulties and my Japanese friend was in gales of laughter. I was embarrassed because of my ignorance and he was embarrassed because it was wholly against his code to laugh at a professor. What do you say when someone asks: "Why do they say 'Let's drink toast,' when they are drinking wine? What does it mean, 'By hook or by crook,'" But we managed to laugh our way through from A to Z with great benefit to us both; the difference is that he has remembered most of what we learned, whereas I have lapsed into my old bad habits. To this day I cannot be sure when I should use "that" and when I should use "which," but my secretary knows, and between us we keep up some sort of pretense.

It is the idioms that ensnare us, and never so fatally as when we have learned them by ear rather than by the eye. Some years ago I was being introduced at a dinner where I was to make a speech, and the man who had undertaken this dangerous work had the easy fluency of a politician. Having told his hearers my age—which is something about which all audiences feel an unseemly curiosity—and all the jobs I had held, he announced solemnly; "Mr. Davies is a man of many faucets." There was a little coarse laughter, but most of the audience looked at me with new respect.

Ham and Tongue are the essentials of public speaking, and ideally they should be balanced in roughly equal quantity. Shakespeare supplied a splendid object lesson in the Forum Scene in *Julius Caesar*. The first speaker is Marcus Brutus, and he is a skilled rhetorician; schoolmasters and professors delight in demonstrating how finely balanced is his address to the mob. But Brutus was wholly a patrician; he was too much a gentleman to stoop to emotional appeals. The second speaker of the day, as you recall, was Mark Antony. He was no mean rhetorician, but in addition to Tongue he had a splendid endowment of Ham, and we all know what happened. Brutus won respect, but Antony started a riot.

1977

Margaret Atwood

WRITING THE MALE CHARACTER

"Why do men feel threatened by women?" I asked a male friend of mine. (I love that wonderful rhetorical device, "a male friend of mine." It's often used by female journalists when they want to say something particularly bitchy but don't want to be held responsible for it themselves. It also lets people know that you *do* have male friends, that you aren't one of those fire-breathing mythical monsters, The Radical Feminists, who walk around with little pairs of scissors and kick men in the shins if they open doors for you. "A male friend of mine" also gives—let us admit it—a certain weight to the opinions expressed.) So this male friend of mine, who does by the way exist, conveniently entered into the following dialogue. "I mean," I said, "men are bigger, most of the time, they can run faster, strangle better, and they have on the average a lot more money and power." "They're afraid women will laugh at them," he said. "Undercut their world view." Then I asked some women students in a quickie poetry seminar I was giving, "Why do women feel threatened by men?" "They're afraid of being killed," they said.

From this I concluded that men and women are indeed different, if only in the range and scope of their threatenability. A man is not just a woman in funny clothes and a jock strap. *They don't think the same*, except about things like higher math. But neither are they an alien or inferior form of life. From the point of view of the novelist, this discovery has wide-ranging implications; and you can see that we are approaching this evening's topic, albeit in a crabwise, scuttling, devious and feminine manner; nevertheless, approaching. But first, a small digression, partly to demonstrate that when people ask you if you hate men, the proper reply is "which ones?"—because, of course, the other big revelation of the evening is that *not all men are the same*. Some of them have beards. Apart from that, I have never been among those who would speak slightingly of men by lumping them all in together; I would never say, for instance—as some have—"Put a paper bag over their bodies and they're all the same." I give you Albert Schweitzer in one corner, Hitler in another.

But think of what civilization would be today without the contributions of men. No electric floor polishers, no neutron bomb, no Freudian psychology, no heavy metal rock groups, no pornography, no repatriated Canadian Consitution[1] . . . the list could go on and on. And they're fun to play Scrabble with and handy for eating up the leftovers. I have heard some rather tired women express the opinion that the only good man is a dead man, but this is far from correct. They may be hard to find, but think of it this way: like diamonds, in the rough or not, their rarity makes them all the more appreciated. Treat them like human beings! This may surprise them at first, but sooner or later their good qualities will emerge, most of the time. Well, in view of the statistics . . . some of the time.

That wasn't the digression . . . this is the digression. I grew up in a family of scientists. My father was a forest entomologist and fond of children, and incidentally not threatened by women, and many were the happy hours we spent listening to his explanations of the ways of the wood-boring beetle, or picking forest tent caterpillars out of the soup because he had forgotten to feed them and they had gone crawling all over the house in search of leaves. One of the results of my upbringing was that I had a big advantage in the schoolyard when little boys tried to frighten me with worms, snakes and the like; the other was that I developed, slightly later, an affection for the writings of the great nineteenth century naturalist and father of modern entomology, Henri Fabre.[2] Fabre was, like Charles Darwin, one of those gifted and obsessive amateur naturalists which the nineteenth century produced in such abundance. He pursued his investigations for the love of the subject, and unlike many biologists today, whose language tends to be composed of numbers rather than words, he was an enthusiastic and delightful writer. I read with pleasure his account of the life of the spider, and of his experiments with ant-lions, by which he tried to prove that they could reason. But it was not only Fabre's subject matter that intrigued me; it was the character of the man himself, so full of energy, so pleased with everything, so resourceful, so willing to follow his line of study wherever it might lead. Received opinion he would take into account, but would believe nothing until he had put it to the test himself. It pleases me to think of him, spade in hand, setting forth to a field full of sheep droppings, in search of the Sacred Dung Beetle and the secrets of her egg-laying ritual. "I am all eyes," he exclaimed, as he brought to light a little object, not round like the Sacred Beetle's usual edible dung-ball, but cunningly pear-shaped! "Oh blessed joys of truth suddenly shining forth," he wrote. "What others are there to compare with you!"

And it is in this spirit, it seems to me, that we should approach all

---

1. Until 1982, Canada's constitution was the British North America Act, with ultimate authority maintained in England. In 1982, Canada "returned" that power to itself in an independent constitution.

2. Jean Henri Fabre: distinguished French naturalist (1823–1915).

subjects. If a dung-beetle is worthy of it, why not that somewhat more complex object, the human male? Admittedly the analogy has certain drawbacks. For instance, one dung-beetle is much like another, whereas, as we've noted, there's quite a range in men. Also, we are supposed to be talking about novels here, and, to belabor the obvious, a novel is not a scientific treatise; that is, it can make no claim to present the kind of factual truth which can be demonstrated by repeatable experiments. Although the novelist presents observations and reaches conclusions, they are not of the same order as the observations of Fabre on the behavior of the mating practices of the female scorpion, although some critics react as though they are.

Note that we have landed in the middle of a swamp, that is, at the crux of the problem: if a novel is not a scientific treatise, what is it? Our evaluation of the role of the male character within the novel will of course depend on what kind of beast we think we're dealing with. I'm sure you've all heard the one about the four blind philosophers and the elephant. Substitute "critics" for "philosophers" and "Novel" for "elephant" and you'll have the picture. One critic gets hold of the novelist's life and decides that novels are disguised spiritual autobiographies, or disguised personal sexual phobias, or something of the kind. Another gets hold of the Zeitgeist (or Spirit of the Times, for those unlucky enough never to have had to pass a Ph.D. language exam in German) and writes about the Restoration Novel or the Novel of Sensibility or The Rise of the Political Novel or The Novel of Twentieth Century Alienation; another figures out that the limitations of the language have something to do with what can be said, or that certain pieces of writing display similar patterns, and the air fills with mythopoeia, structuralism and similar delights; another goes to Harvard and gets hold of the Human Condition, a favorite of mine, and very handy to fall back on when you can't think of anything else to say. The elephant however remains an elephant, and sooner or later gets tired of having the blind philosophers feeling its parts, whereupon it stretches itself, rises to its feet and ambles away in another direction altogether. This is not to say that critical exercises are futile or trivial. From what I have said about dung-beetles—which also preserve their innermost secrets—you will know that I think the description of elephants is a worthwhile activity. But describing an elephant and giving birth to one are two different things, and the novelist and the critic approach the novel with quite different sets of preconceptions, problems and emotions.

"Whence comest thou?" says a well-known male character in a multi-faceted prose narrative with which I am sure you are all familiar. "From going to and fro in the earth, and from walking up and down in it," answers his adversary.[3] Thus the novelist. One would of course not want

3. God addresses the question to His adversary, Satan (see Job 1:7).

to continue with this analogy—a critic is not God, contrary to some opinions, and a novelist is not the Devil, although one could remark, with Blake, that creative energies are more likely to emerge from the underworld than from the upper world of rational order. Let us say only that the going to and fro and the walking up and down in the earth are things that all novelists seem to have done in some way or another, and that the novel proper, as distinguished from the romance and its variants, is one of the points in human civilization at which the human world as it is collides with language and imagination. This is not to limit the novel to a Zola-like naturalism (though Zola himself was not a narrow Zola-like naturalist, as anyone who has read the triumphant final passage of *Germinal* will testify); but it is to state that some of the things that get into novels get into them because they are there in the world. There would have been no flogging scene in *Moby Dick* if there had been none on nineteenth century whaling ships, and its inclusion is not mere sado-masochism on the part of Melville. However, if the book consisted of nothing but, one might have cause to wonder.

Thus one must conclude that the less than commendable behavior of male characters in certain novels by women is not necessarily due to a warped view of the opposite sex on behalf of the authors. Could it be . . . I say it hesitantly, in a whisper, since like most women I cringe at the very thought of being called—how can I even say it— a *man-hater* . . . could it be that the behavior of some men in what we are fond of considering real life . . . could it be that not every man always behaves well? Could it be that some emperors have no clothes on?

* * *

Let me take you back a few years, to the days of Kate Millett's *Sexual Politics*, which was preceded ancestrally by Leslie Fiedler's *Love and Death in the American Novel*. Both were criticisms based on an analysis of the relations, within novels, of men and women, and both gave black marks to certain male authors for simplistic and stereotyped negative depictions of women. Well, that was interesting, but the worm has turned. Now we're handing out black marks for what male critics (and, to be fair, some female ones) consider to be unfavorable depictions of men by female authors. I base this conclusion mainly on reviews of my own books, naturally, since that's what I see most of, but I've noted it elsewhere too.

Now, we know there's no such thing as value-free novel writing. Creation does not happen in a vacuum, and a novelist is either depicting or exposing some of the values of the society in which he or she lives. Novelists from Defoe through Dickens and Faulkner have always done that. But it sometimes escapes us that the same is true of criticism. We are all organisms within environments, and we interpret what we read in the light of how we live and how we would like to live, which are almost never the same thing, at least for most novel readers. I think that political interpretations of novels have a place in the body of criticism, as long as we recognize them for what they are; but total polarization can only be a disservice to literature. For instance, a male friend of mine—just to let you know I have more than one—wrote a novel which has a scene in it in which men are depicted urinating outdoors standing up. Now, so far as I know, this is something men have been doing for many years, and they are still doing it, judging from the handwriting in the snow; it is merely one of those things that happens. But a female poet took my friend to task in print. She found this piece of writing not only unforgivably Central Canadian—you can tell she was from British Columbia—she also found it unforgivably *macho*. I'm not sure what novelistic solution she had in mind. Possibly she wanted my friend to leave out the subject of urination altogether, thus avoiding the upsetting problem of physiological differences; maybe she wanted the men to demonstrate equality of attitude by sitting on toilets to perform this function. Or maybe she wanted them to urinate outdoors standing up but also to feel guilty about it. Or maybe it would have been all right if they had been urinating into the Pacific Ocean, regionalism being what it is today. You may think this kind of criticism is silly, but it happens all the time on New Grub Street,[4] which is where I live.

For the female novelist, it means that certain men will find it objectionable if she depicts men behaving the way they do behave a lot of the time. Not enough that she may avoid making them rapists and murderers, child molesters, warmongers, sadists, power-hungry, callous, domineering, pompous, foolish or immoral, though I'm sure we will all agree that such men do exist. Even if she makes them sensitive and kind she's open to the charge of having depicted them as "weak." What this kind of critic wants is Captain Marvel,[5] without the Billy Batson *alter ego*; nothing less will do.

Excuse me for underlining the obvious, but it seems to me that a good, that is, a successfully-written, character in a novel is not at all the same as a "good," that is, a morally good, character in real life. In fact, a character in a book who is consistently well-behaved probably spells disaster for the book. There's a lot of public pressure on the novelist to write such characters, however, and it isn't new. I take you back to Samuel Richardson, author of such running-away-from-rape classics as *Pamela* and *Clarissa*. Both contain relatively virtuous women and relatively lecherous and nasty-minded men, who also happen to be English gentlemen. No one accused Richardson of being mean to men, but some English gentlemen felt that dirt had been done to them; in other words, the insecurities were primarily class ones rather than sex ones. Obligingly, Richardson

4. A metaphor for a kind of Bohemia, where young, struggling writers and artists cluster; derives from George Gissings's novel *New Grub Street* (1891).

5. Captain Marvel: the comic-strip hero with superhuman capacities; when he is ordinarily human, he is Billy Batson.

came up with *Sir Charles Grandison*, a novel in which he set out to do right by the image of the English gentleman. It starts out promisingly enough, with an abduction with intent to rape by a villain after that priceless pot of gold, the heroine's virginity. Unfortunately Sir Charles Grandison enters the picture, saves the heroine from a fate worse than death, and invites her to his country residence; after which most readers kiss the novel goodbye. I however always sit to the end, even of bad movies, and since I'm the only person I've ever met who has actually made it through to page 900 of this novel I can tell you what happens. Sir Charles Grandison displays his virtues; the heroine admires them. That's it. Oh, and then there's a proposal. Feel like reading it? You bet you don't, and neither do all those male critics who complain about the image of men in books by women. A friend of mine—not a male one this time, but a perceptive reader and critic—says that her essential criterion for evaluating literature is, "Does it live or does it die?" A novel based on other people's needs for having their egos stroked, their images shored up, or their sensitivities pandered to is unlikely to live.

* * * Is *Hamlet*, for instance, a slur on men? Is *Macbeth*? Is *Faust*, in any version? How about the behavior of the men in *Moll Flanders*? Or *Tom Jones*? Is *A Sentimental Journey* about the quintessential wimp? Because Dickens created Orlick, Gradgrind, Dotheboys Hall, Fagin, Uriah Heep, Steerforth, and Bill Sykes, must we conclude that he's a man-hater? * * * Captain Ahab, although a forceful literary creation, is hardly anybody's idea of an acceptable role model. Please note that all these characters and novels were the creations of men, not women; but nobody, to my knowledge, has accused these male authors of being mean to men, although they've been accused of all sorts of other things. Possibly the principle involved is the same one involved in the telling of ethnic jokes: it's all right within the group, but coming from outside it's racism, though the joke may be exactly the same. If a man depicts a male character unfavorably, it's The Human Condition; if a woman does it, she's being mean to men. * * *

Incidentally, you could make a case—if you wanted to—for concluding that women authors have historically been easier on men in their books than male authors have.

* * * One of the questions people have been asking me most frequently is, "Do you write women's novels?" You have to watch this question, since, like many other questions, its meaning varies according to who's asking it and of whom. "Women's novels" can mean pop genre novels, such as the kind with nurses and doctors on the covers or the kind with rolling-eyed heroines in period costumes and windblown hair in front of gothic castles or Southern mansions or other locales where villainy may threaten and Heathcliff[6] is still lurking around in the Span-

6. Heathcliff: the brooding, passionate hero of Emily Brontë's *Wuthering Heights* (1847).

ish moss. Or it may mean novels for whom the main audience is assumed to be women, which would take in quite a lot, since the main audience for novels of all kinds, with the exception of Louis L'amour western romances and certain kinds of porn, is also women. Or it can mean feminist propaganda novels. Or it can mean novels depicting male-female relationships, which again covers quite a lot of ground. Is *War and Peace* a women's novel? Is *Gone With The Wind*, even though it's got a war in it? Is *Middlemarch*, even though it's got The Human Condition in it? Could it be that women aren't afraid to be caught reading books that might be considered "men's novels," whereas men still think something they need will fall off them if they look too hard at certain supposedly malevolent combinations of words put together by women? Judging from my recent walking to and fro in the earth and going up and down in bookstores for the purpose of signing my name on a lot of fly-leafs, I can tell you that this attitude is on the fade. More and more men are willing to stand in the line and *be seen*; fewer and fewer of them say, "It's for my wife's birthday."

But I almost put the boots to my old friend and cohort, the redoubtable Pierre Berton,[7] when he asked me on television why all the men in my recent book *Bodily Harm* were wimps. Displaying the celebrated female compassion, not to be confused with feeble-mindedness, I merely dribbled aimlessly for a few minutes. "Pierre," I should have said, "who do you think is likely to have had more experience of men in sexual relationships: you, or me?" This is not quite so mean as it sounds, and there's even something to it. Women as people have a relatively large pool of experiences from which to draw. They have their own experiences with men, of course, but they also have their friends', since, yes, girls do discuss men more than men—beyond the dirty anecdote syndrome—discuss women. Women are willing to talk about their weaknesses and fears to other women; men are not willing to talk about theirs to men, since it's still a dog-eat-dog world out there for them and no man wants to reveal his underbelly to a pack of fang-toothed potential rivals. If men are going to talk about their problems with women to anybody, it's usually either to a shrink or—guess what? to another woman. In both reading and writing, women are likely to know more about how men actually behave with women than men are; so that what a man finds a slur on his self-image, a woman may find merely realistic or indeed unduly soft.

But to go back to Pierre Berton's assertion. I thought quite carefully about my male characters in *Bodily Harm*. There are three of them with whom the heroine actually sleeps, and the fourth main male character with whom she doesn't. A female novelist and critic noted that there is one good man in the book and no good women, and she's quite right. The

---

7. Pierre Berton: distinguished Canadian journalist, writer, broadcaster, and popular historian.

other men are not "bad"—in fact they are quite nice and attractive as male characters in literature go, a sight better than Mr. Kurtz and Iago— but the *good* man is *black*, which is perhaps why the "mean-to-menners" overlooked him. When playing the role-model game, you have to read carefully; otherwise you may be caught in an embarrassing position, like that one.

Now, back to the practical concerns of New Grub Street. Let us suppose that I am writing a novel. First: how many points of view will this novel have? If it has only one point of view, will it be that of a man, a woman or a seagull? Let us suppose that my novel will have one point of view and that the eyes through which we see the world of the novel unfolding will be those of a woman. Immediately it follows that the perceptions of all male characters in the book will have to pass through the perceiving apparatus of this central character. Nor will the central character necessarily be accurate or just. It also follows that all the other characters will be, of necessity, secondary. If I'm skillful I will be able to bounce another set of perceptions off those of the central character, through dialogue and between-the-lines innuendo, but there will be a strong bias toward A as truth-teller and we will never get to hear what Characters B and C really think when they're by themselves, urinating outdoors perhaps or doing other male things. However, the picture changes if I use a multiple point of view. Now I can have Characters B and C think for themselves, and what they think won't always be what Character A thinks of *them*. If I like, I can add in yet another point of view, that of the omniscient author (who is of course not "me," the same me that had bran muffins for breakfast this morning and is right now giving this speech) but yet another voice within the novel. The omniscient author can claim to know things about the characters that even they don't know, thus letting the reader know these things as well.

The next thing I have to decide is what tone I'm taking, what mode I'm writing in. A careful study of *Wuthering Heights* will reveal that Heathcliff is never to be observed picking his nose, or indeed even blowing it, and you can search through Walter Scott in vain for any mention of bathrooms. Leopold Bloom on the other hand is preoccupied with the mundane wants of the body on almost every page, and we find him sympathetic, yes, and comic and also pathetic, but he is not exactly love's young dream. Leopold Bloom[8] climbing in through Cathy's window would probably slip. Which is the more accurate portrayal of Man with a capital M? Or, like Walter Mitty, does each man contain within him both an ordinary, limited and trivial self and a heroic concept, and if so, which should we be writing about? I carry no brief for either, except to

8. Leopold Bloom: the protagonist of James Joyce's novel *Ulysses* (1922); Cathy: the tempestuous heroine of Emily Brontë's *Wuthering Heights* (1847); Walter Mitty: the henpecked husband in James Thurber's short story "The Secret Life of Walter Mitty" (1939).

remark that serious novelists in the twentieth century usually opt for Leopold, and poor Heathcliff has been relegated to the Gothic romance. If a given serious novelist of the twentieth century is female, she too will probably go for Leopold, with all his habits, daydreams and wants. This doens't mean she hates men; merely that she's interested in what they look like without the cloak.

All right. Suppose I've chosen to have in my novel at least one male character as a narrator or protagonist (not necessarily the same thing). I do not want to make my male character unnaturally evil, like Mr. Hyde; instead I'm trying for Dr. Jekyll, an essentially good man with certain flaws. That's a problem right there; because, as Stevenson knew, evil is a lot easier to write about and make interesting than goodness. What, these days, is a believable notion of a good man? Let us suppose that I'm talking about a man who is merely unbad; that is, one who obeys the major laws, pays his bills, helps with the dishes, doesn't beat up his wife or molest his kids, and so forth. Let's suppose that I want him to have some actual good qualities, good in the active, positive sense. What is he to do? And how can I make him—unlike Sir Charles Grandison—interesting in a novel?

This I suspect is the point at which the concerns of the novelist coincide with those of society. Once upon a time, when we defined people—much more that we do now—by how far they lived up or failed to live up to certain pre-defined sexual role models, it was a lot easier to tell what was meant by "a good man" or "a good woman." "A good woman" was one that fulfilled our notions of what a woman should be and how she should behave. Likewise "a good man." There were certain concepts about what constituted manliness and how you got it—most authorities agreed that you weren't just born with it, you somehow had to earn, acquire or be initiated into it; acts of courage and heroism counted for something, ability to endure pain without flinching, or drink a lot without passing out, or whatever. In any case there were rules, and you could cross a line that separated the men from the boys.

It's true that the male sexual role model had a lot of drawbacks, even for men—not everybody could be Superman, many were stuck with Clark Kent—but there were certain positive and, at that time, useful features. What have we replaced this package with? We know that women have been in a state of upheaval and ferment for some time now, and movement generates energy; many things can be said by women now that were once not possible, many things can be thought that were once unthinkable. But what are we offering men? Their territory, though still large, is shrinking. The confusion and desperation and anger and conflicts that we find in male characters in novels don't exist only in novels. They're out there in the real world. "Be a person, my son," doesn't yet have the same ring to it as "Be a man," though it is indeed a worthy goal.

The novelist *qua* novelist, as opposed to the utopian romancer, takes *what is there* as a point of departure. What is there, when we're talking about men, is a state of change, new attitudes overlapping with old ones, no simple rules any more. Some exciting form of life may emerge from all this.

Meanwhile, I think women have to take the concerns of men as seriously as they expect men to take theirs, both as novelists and as inhabitants of this earth. One encounters, too often, the attitude that only the pain felt by persons of the female sex is real pain, that only female fears are real fears. That for me is the equivalent of the notion that only working-class peole are real, that middle-class people are not, and so forth. Of course there's a distinction between earned pain and mere childish self-pity, and yes, women's fear of being killed by men is grounded in authenticity, not to mention statistics, to a greater extent than men's fear of being laughed at. Damage to one's self-image is not quite the same as damage to one's neck, though not to be underestimated: men have been known to murder and kill themselves because of it.

I'm not advocating a return to door-mat status for women, or even to the arrangement whereby women prop up and nurture and stroke and feed the egos of men without having men do at least some of the same for them. To understand is not necessarily to condone; and it could be pointed out that women have been "understanding" men for centuries, partly because it was necessary for survival. If the other fellow has the heavy artillery, it's best to be able to anticipate his probable moves. Women, like guerrilla fighters, developed infiltration rather than frontal attack as their favored strategy. But "understanding" as a manipulative tool—which is really a form of contempt for the thing understood—isn't the kind I would like to see. * * * But one cannot deprive any part of humanity of the definition "human" without grievous risk to one's own soul. And for women to define themselves as powerless and men as all-powerful is to fall into an ancient trap, to shirk responsibility as well as to warp reality. The opposite also is true; to depict a world in which women are already equal to men, in power, opportunities and freedom of movement, is a similar abdication.

I know I haven't given any specific directions for writing the male character; how can I? They're all different, remember. All I've given are a few warnings, an indication of what you're up against from the real world and from critics. But just because it's difficult is no reason not to try.

When I was young and reading a lot of comic books and fairy tales, I used to wish for two things: the cloak of invisibility, so I could follow people around and listen to what they were saying when I wasn't there, and the ability to teleport my mind into somebody else's mind, still retaining my own perceptions and memory. You can see that I was cut out to be a novelist, because these are the two fantasies novelists act out every time they write a page. Throwing your mind is easier to do if you're throwing it into a character who has a few things in common with you, which may be why I've written more pages from a female character's point of view than from a male's. But male characters are more of a challenge, and now that I'm middle-aged and less lazy I'll undoubtedly try a few more of them. If writing novels—and reading them—have any redeeming social value, it's probably that they force you to imagine what it's like to be somebody else.

Which, increasingly, is something we all need to know.

1982

THE READER

1. *Clearly Atwood believes that novels reflect reality (e.g., p. 1045). But when she talks about point of view (p. 1049), she offers a complicated differentiation of voices in a novel, including that of the omniscient author. What is the point of that complexity? Is she forgetting her conviction that novels reflect reality?*

2. *The essay is full of allusions. Some are explained (e.g., Fabre on p. 1043); some are not presumably because Atwood thinks they are familiar (e.g., Darwin in the same paragraph); and some are not presumably because she thinks you can get the idea without an explanation (e.g., Heathcliff on p. 1047; New Grub Street on p. 1046). Ignoring the editors' footnotes, select some allusions, and distribute them on a scale running from those you understood because she explained them to those you couldn't understand because she didn't explain them or didn't explain them enough. What is the function of all these allusions? Are they part of her "crabwise, scuttling, devious and feminine manner" (p. 1042)?*

3. *Atwood says of men and women, "They don't think the same." Would Gilligan (p. 488) agree? Atwood distinguishes a novelist's observation from a scientist's (p. 1044). Is Gilligan speaking as a scientist?*

THE WRITER

1. *Write a paragraph to explain how Atwood's two fantasies (p. 1051) imply a basic conviction about what matters to a novelist.*

2. *At various points, Atwood dissociates herself from man-hating. What are her strategies for doing this? Is she witty, or "cute," or something else? What concerns her in these passages?*

3. *Is the gender barrier a particular part of a general writing problem— how to get things right—or is the writing problem part of the gender barrier? Does it matter?*

Virginia Woolf

IN SEARCH OF A ROOM OF ONE'S OWN[1]

It was disappointing not to have brought back in the evening some important statement, some authentic fact. Women are poorer than men because—this or that. Perhaps now it would be better to give up seeking for the truth, and receiving on one's head an avalanche of opinion hot as lava, discoloured as dish-water. It would be better to draw the curtains; to shut out distractions; to light the lamp; to narrow the enquiry and to ask the historian, who records not opinions but facts, to describe under what conditions women lived, not throughout the ages, but in England, say in the time of Elizabeth.

For it is a perennial puzzle why no woman wrote a word of that extraordinary literature when every other man, it seemed, was capable of song or sonnet. What were the conditions in which women lived, I asked myself; for fiction, imaginative work that is, is not dropped like a pebble upon the ground, as science may be; fiction is like a spider's web, attached ever so lightly perhaps, but still attached to life at all four corners. Often the attachment is scarcely perceptible; Shakespeare's plays, for instance, seem to hang there complete by themselves. But when the web is pulled askew, hooked up at the edge, torn in the middle, one remembers that these webs are not spun in midair by incorporeal creatures, but are the work of suffering human beings, and are attached to grossly material things, like health and money and the houses we live in.

I went, therefore, to the shelf where the histories stand and took down one of the latest, Professor Trevelyan's *History of England*. Once more I looked up Women, found "position of," and turned to the pages indicated. "Wife-beating," I read, "was a recognised right of man, and was practised without shame by high as well as low.... Similarly," the historian goes on, "the daughter who refused to marry the gentleman of her parents' choice was liable to be locked up, beaten and flung about the room, without any shock being inflicted on public opinion. Marriage was not an affair of personal affection, but of family avarice, particularly in the 'chivalrous' upper classes.... Betrothal often took place while one or both of the parties was in the cradle, and marriage when they were scarcely out of the nurses' charge." That was about 1470, soon after

1. This selection is Chapter 3 of Woolf's *A Room of One's Own*, a long essay that began as two lectures on women and fiction given at Newnham College and Girton College, women's colleges at Cambridge University, in 1928. In Chapter 1, Woolf advances the proposition that "a woman must have money and a room of her own if she is to write fiction." In Chapter 2, she describes a day spent at the British Museum (now the British Library) looking for information about the lives of women.

Chaucer's time. The next reference to the position of women is some two hundred years later, in the time of the Stuarts. "It was still the exception for women of the upper and middle class to choose their own husbands, and when the husband had been assigned, he was lord and master, so far at least as law and custom could make him. Yet even so," Professor Trevelyan concludes, "neither Shakespeare's women nor those of authentic seventeenth-century memoirs, like the Verneys and the Hutchinsons, seem wanting in personality and character." Certainly, if we consider it, Cleopatra must have had a way with her; Lady Macbeth, one would suppose, had a will of her own; Rosalind, one might conclude, was an attractive girl. Professor Trevelyan is speaking no more than the truth when he remarks that Shakespeare's women do not seem wanting in personality and character. Not being a historian, one might go even further and say that women have burnt like beacons in all the works of all the poets from the beginning of time—Clytemnestra, Antigone, Cleopatra, Lady Macbeth, Phèdre, Cressida, Rosalind, Desdemona, the Duchess of Malfi, among the dramatists; then among the prose writers: Millamant, Clarissa, Becky Sharp, Anna Karenina, Emma Bovary, Madame de Guermantes—the names flock to mind, nor do they recall women "lacking in personality and character." Indeed, if woman had no existence save in the fiction written by men, one would imagine her a person of the utmost importance; very various; heroic and mean; splendid and sordid; infinitely beautiful and hideous in the extreme; as great as a man, some think even greater.[2] But this is woman in fiction. In fact, as Professor Trevelyan points out, she was locked up, beaten and flung about the room.

A very queer, composite being thus emerges. Imaginatively she is of the highest importance; practically she is completely insignificant. She pervades poetry from cover to cover; she is all but absent from history. She dominates the lives of kings and conquerors in fiction; in fact she was the slave of any boy whose parents forced a ring upon her finger. Some of the most inspired words, some of the most profound thoughts in literature fall from her lips; in real life she could hardly read, could scarcely

2. "It remains a strange and almost inexplicable fact that in Athena's city, where women were kept in almost Oriental suppression as odalisques or drudges, the stage should yet have produced figures like Clytemnestra and Cassandra, Atossa and Antigone, Phèdre and Medea, and all the other heroines who dominate play after play of the 'misogynist' Euripides. But the paradox of this world where in real life a respectable woman could hardly show her face alone in the street, and yet on the stage woman equals or surpasses man, has never been satisfactorily explained. In modern tragedy the same predominance exists. At all events, a very cursory survey of Shakespeare's work (similarly with Webster, though not with Marlowe or Jonson) suffices to reveal how this dominance, this initiative of women, persists from Rosalind to Lady Macbeth. So too in Racine; six of his tragedies bear their heroines' names; and what male characters of his shall we set against Hermione and Andromaque, Bérénice and Roxane, Phèdre and Athalie? So again with Ibsen; what men shall we match with Solveig and Nora, Hedda and Hilda Wangel and Rebecca West?"—F. L. LUCAS, Tragedy, pp. 114–15 [Woolf's note].

spell, and was the property of her husband.

It was certainly an odd monster that one made up by reading the historians first and the poets afterwards—a worm winged like an eagle; the spirit of life and beauty in a kitchen chopping up suet. But these monsters, however amusing to the imagination, have no existence in fact. What one must do to bring her to life was to think poetically and prosaically at one and the same moment, thus keeping in touch with fact —that she is Mrs. Martin, aged thirty-six, dressed in blue, wearing a black hat and brown shoes; but not losing sight of fiction either—that she is a vessel in which all sorts of spirits and forces are coursing and flashing perpetually. The moment, however, that one tries this method with the Elizabethan woman, one branch of illumination fails; one is held up by the scarcity of facts. One knows nothing detailed, nothing perfectly true and substantial about her. History scarcely mentions her. And I turned to Professor Trevelyan again to see what history meant to him. I found by looking at his chapter headings that it meant—

"The Manor Court and the Methods of Open-field Agriculture . . . The Cistercians and Sheep-farming . . . The Crusades . . . The University . . . The House of Commons . . . The Hundred Years' War . . . The Wars of the Roses . . . The Renaissance Scholars . . . The Dissolution of the Monasteries . . . Agrarian and Religious Strife . . . The Origin of English Sea-power . . . The Armada . . ." and so on. Occasionally an individual woman is mentioned, an Elizabeth, or a Mary; a queen or a great lady. But by no possible means could middle-class women with nothing but brains and character at their command have taken part in any one of the great movements which, brought together, constitute the historian's view of the past. Nor shall we find her in any collection of anecdotes. Aubrey[3] hardly mentions her. She never writes her own life and scarcely keeps a diary; there are only a handful of her letters in existence. She left no plays or poems by which we can judge her. What one wants, I thought—and why does not some brilliant student at Newnham or Girton supply it?—is a mass of information; at what age did she marry; how many children had she as a rule; what was her house like; had she a room to herself; did she do the cooking; would she be likely to have a servant? All these facts lie somewhere, presumably, in parish registers and account books; the life of the average Elizabethan woman must be scattered about somewhere, could one collect it and make a book of it. It would be ambitious beyond my daring, I thought, looking about the shelves for books that were not there, to suggest to the students of those famous colleges that they should re-write history, though I own that it often seems a little queer as it is, unreal, lop-sided; but why should they not add a supplement to history? calling it, of course, by some inconspicu-

---

3. John Aubrey (1626–97), whose biographical writings were published posthumously as *Brief Lives*.

ous name so that women might figure there without impropriety? For one often catches a glimpse of them in the lives of the great, whisking away into the background, concealing, I sometimes think, a wink, a laugh, perhaps a tear. And, after all, we have lives enough of Jane Austen; it scarcely seems necessary to consider again the influence of the tragedies of Joanna Baillie upon the poetry of Edgar Allan Poe; as for myself, I should not mind if the homes and haunts of Mary Russell Mitford were closed to the public for a century at least.[4] But what I find deplorable, I continued, looking about the bookshelves again, is that nothing is known about women before the eighteenth century. I have no model in my mind to turn about this way and that. Here am I asking why women did not write poetry in the Elizabethan age, and I am not sure how they were educated; whether they were taught to write; whether they had sitting-rooms to themselves; how many women had children before they were twenty-one; what, in short, they did from eight in the morning till eight at night. They had no money evidently; according to Professor Treve-lyan they were married whether they liked it or not before they were out of the nursery, at fifteen or sixteen very likely. It would have been extremely odd, even upon this showing, had one of them suddenly written the plays of Shakespeare, I concluded, and I thought of that old gentleman, who is dead now, but was a bishop, I think, who declared that it was impossible for any woman, past, present, or to come, to have the genius of Shakespeare. He wrote to the papers about it. He also told a lady who applied to him for information that cats do not as a matter of fact go to heaven, though they have, he added, souls of a sort. How much thinking those old gentlemen used to save one! How the borders of ignorance shrank back at their approach! Cats do not go to heaven. Women cannot write the plays of Shakespeare.

Be that as it may, I could not help thinking, as I looked at the works of Shakespeare on the shelf, that the bishop was right at least in this; it would have been impossible, completely and entirely, for any woman to have written the plays of Shakespeare in the age of Shakespeare. Let me imagine, since facts are so hard to come by, what would have happened had Shakespeare had a wonderfully gifted sister, called Judith, let us say. Shakespeare himself went, very probably—his mother was an heiress—to the grammar school, where he may have learnt Latin—Ovid, Virgil and Horace—and the elements of grammar and logic. He was, it is well known, a wild boy who poached rabbits, perhaps shot a deer, and had, rather sooner than he should have done, to marry a woman in the neighbourhood, who bore him a child rather quicker than was right. That escapade sent him to seek his fortune in London. He had, it seemed, a taste for the theatre; he began by holding horses at the stage door. Very

---

4. Jane Austen (1775–1817), English novelist; Joanna Baillie (1762–1851), Scottish dramatist and poet; Mary Russell Mitford (1787–1855), English novelist and dramatist.

soon he got work in the theatre, became a successful actor, and lived at the hub of the universe, meeting everybody, knowing everybody, practising his art on the boards, exercising his wits in the streets, and even getting access to the palace of the queen. Meanwhile his extraordinarily gifted sister, let us suppose, remained at home. She was as adventurous, as imaginative, as agog to see the world as he was. But she was not sent to school. She had no chance of learning grammar and logic, let alone of reading Horace and Virgil. She picked up a book now and then, one of her brother's perhaps, and read a few pages. But then her parents came in and told her to mend the stockings or mind the stew and not moon about with books and papers. They would have spoken sharply but kindly, for they were substantial people who knew the conditions of life for a woman and loved their daughter—indeed, more likely than not she was the apple of her father's eye. Perhaps she scribbled some pages up in an apple loft on the sly, but was careful to hide them or set fire to them. Soon, however, before she was out of her teens, she was to be betrothed to the son of a neighbouring wool-stapler. She cried out that marriage was hateful to her, and for that she was severely beaten by her father. Then he ceased to scold her. He begged her instead not to hurt him, not to shame him in this matter of her marriage. He would give her a chain of beads or a fine petticoat, he said; and there were tears in his eyes. How could she disobey him? How could she break his heart? The force of her own gift alone drove her to it. She made up a small parcel of her belongings, let herself down by a rope one summer's night and took the road to London. She was not seventeen. The birds that sang in the hedge were not more musical than she was. She had the quickest fancy, a gift like her brother's, for the tune of words. Like him, she had a taste for the theatre. She stood at the stage door; she wanted to act, she said. Men laughed in her face. The manager—a fat, loose-lipped man—guffawed. He bellowed something about poodles dancing and women acting—no woman, he said, could possibly be an actress.[5] He hinted—you can imagine what. She could get no training in her craft. Could she even seek her dinner in a tavern or roam the streets at midnight? Yet her genius was for fiction and lusted to feed abundantly upon the lives of men and women and the study of their ways. At last—for she was very young, oddly like Shakespeare the poet in her face, with the same grey eyes and rounded brows—at last Nick Greene the actor-manager took pity on her; she found herself with child by that gentleman and so—who shall measure the heat and violence of the poet's heart when caught and tangled in a woman's body?—killed herself one winter's night and lies buried at some cross-roads where the omnibuses now stop outside the Elephant and Castle.

That, more or less, is how the story would run, I think, if a woman in

---

5. Boys played women's parts in the Elizabethan theater.

Shakespeare's day had had Shakespeare's genius. But for my part, I agree with the deceased bishop, if such he was—it is unthinkable that any woman in Shakespeare's day should have had Shakespeare's genius. For genius like Shakespeare's is not born among labouring, uneducated, servile people. It was not born in England among the Saxons and the Britons. It is not born today among the working classes. How, then, could it have been born among women whose work began, according to Professor Trevelyan, almost before they were out of the nursery, who were forced to it by their parents and held to it by all the power of law and custom? Yet genius of a sort must have existed among women as it must have existed among the working classes. Now and again an Emily Brontë or a Robert Burns blazes out and proves its presence.[6] But certainly it never got itself on to paper. When, however, one reads of a witch being ducked, of a woman possessed by devils, of a wise woman selling herbs, or even of a very remarkable man who had a mother, then I think we are on the track of a lost novelist, a suppressed poet, of some mute and inglorious Jane Austen,[7] some Emily Brontë who dashed her brains out on the moor or mopped and mowed about the highways crazed with the torture that her gift had put her to. Indeed, I would venture to guess that Anon, who wrote so many poems without signing them, was often a woman. It was a woman Edward Fitzgerald,[8] I think, suggested who made the ballads and the folk-songs, crooning them to her children, beguiling her spinning with them, or the length of the winter's night.

This may be true or it may be false—who can say?—but what is true in it, so it seemed to me, reviewing the story of Shakespeare's sister as I had made it, is that any woman born with a great gift in the sixteenth century would certainly have gone crazed, shot herself, or ended her days in some lonely cottage outside the village, half witch, half wizard, feared and mocked at. For it needs little skill in psychology to be sure that a highly gifted girl who had tried to use her gift for poetry would have been so thwarted and hindered by other people, so tortured and pulled asunder by her own contrary instincts, that she must have lost her health and sanity to a certainty. No girl could have walked to London and stood at a stage door and forced her way into the presence of actor-managers without doing herself a violence and suffering an anguish which may have been irrational—for chastity may be a fetish invented by certain societies for unknown reasons—but were none the less inevitable. Chastity had then, it has even now, a religious importance in a woman's life, and has so wrapped itself round with nerves and instincts that to cut it free and bring it to the light of day demands courage of the rarest. To

6. Woolf's examples are Emily Brontë (1818–48), the English novelist, and Robert Burns (1759–96), the Scottish poet.
7. Woolf alludes to Thomas Gray's "Elegy Written in a Country Churchyard": "Some mute inglorious Milton here may rest."
8. Edward FitzGerald (1809–83), poet and translator.

have lived a free life in London in the sixteenth century would have meant for a woman who was poet and playwright a nervous stress and dilemma which might well have killed her. Had she survived, whatever she had written would have been twisted and deformed, issuing from a strained and morbid imagination. And undoubtedly, I thought, looking at the shelf where there are no plays by women, her work would have gone unsigned. That refuge she would have sought certainly. It was the relic of the sense of chastity that dictated anonymity to women even so late as the nineteenth century. Currer Bell, George Eliot, George Sand, all the victims of inner strife as their writings prove, sought ineffectively to veil themselves by using the name of a man.[9] Thus they did homage to the convention, which if not implanted by the other sex was liberally encouraged by them (the chief glory of a woman is not to be talked of, said Pericles,[1] himself a much-talked-of man), that publicity in women is detestable. Anonymity runs in their blood. The desire to be veiled still possesses them. They are not even now as concerned about the health of their fame as men are, and, speaking generally, will pass a tombstone or a signpost without feeling an irresistible desire to cut their names on it, as Alf, Bert or Chas. must do in obedience to their instinct, which murmurs if it sees a fine woman go by, or even a dog, Ce chien est à moi.[2] And, of course, it may not be a dog, I thought, remembering Parliament Square, the Sieges Allee and other avenues; it may be a piece of land or a man with curly black hair. It is one of the great advantages of being a woman that one can pass even a very fine negress without wishing to make an Englishwoman of her.

That woman, then, who was born with a gift of poetry in the sixteenth century, was an unhappy woman, a woman at strife against herself. All the conditions of her life, all her own instincts, were hostile to the state of mind which is needed to set free whatever is in the brain. But what is the state of mind that is most propitious to the act of creation, I asked. Can one come by any notion of the state that furthers and makes possible that strange activity? Here I opened the volume containing the Tragedies of Shakespeare. What was Shakespeare's state of mind, for instance, when he wrote *Lear* and *Antony and Cleopatra*? It was certainly the state of mind most favourable to poetry that there has ever existed. But Shakespeare himself said nothing about it. We only know casually and by chance that he "never blotted a line."[3] Nothing indeed was ever said by the artist himself about his state of mind until the eighteenth century perhaps. Rousseau perhaps began it.[4] At any rate, by the nineteenth

---

9. The pseudonyms of Charlotte Brontë (1816–55), English novelist; Mary Ann Evans (1819–80), English novelist; and Amandine Aurore Lucie Dupin, Baronne Dudevant (1804–76), French novelist.
1. Pericles (d. 429 B.C.), Athenian statesman.

2. That dog is mine.
3. As recorded by his contemporary Ben Jonson (*Timber: Or Discoveries Made Upon Men and Matter*).
4. Jean-Jacques Rousseau (1712–78), whose *Confessions* were published posthumously.

century self-consciousness had developed so far that it was the habit for men of letters to describe their minds in confessions and autobiographies. Their lives also were written, and their letters were printed after their deaths. Thus, though we do not know what Shakespeare went through when he wrote *Lear*, we do know what Carlyle went through when he wrote the *French Revolution*; what Flaubert went through when he wrote *Madame Bovary*; what Keats was going through when he tried to write poetry against the coming of death and the indifference of the world.

And one gathers from this enormous modern literature of confession and self-analysis that to write a work of genius is almost always a feat of prodigious difficulty. Everything is against the likelihood that it will come from the writer's mind whole and entire. Generally material circumstances are against it. Dogs will bark; people will interrupt; money must be made; health will break down. Further, accentuating all these difficulties and making them harder to bear is the world's notorious indifference. It does not ask people to write poems and novels and histories; it does not need them. It does not care whether Flaubert finds the right word or whether Carlyle scrupulously verifies this or that fact. Naturally, it will not pay for what it does not want. And so the writer, Keats, Flaubert, Carlyle, suffers, especially in the creative years of youth, every form of distraction and discouragement. A curse, a cry of agony, rises from those books of analysis and confession. "Mighty poets in their misery dead"[5]—that is the burden of their song. If anything comes through in spite of all this, it is a miracle, and probably no book is born entire and uncrippled as it was conceived.

But for women, I thought, looking at the empty shelves, these difficulties were infinitely more formidable. In the first place, to have a room of her own, let alone a quiet room or a sound-proof room, was out of the question, unless her parents were exceptionally rich or very noble, even up to the beginning of the nineteenth century. Since her pin money, which depended on the good will of her father, was only enough to keep her clothed, she was debarred from such alleviations as came even to Keats or Tennyson or Carlyle, all poor men, from a walking tour, a little journey to France, from the separate lodging which, even if it were miserable enough, sheltered them from the claims and tyrannies of their families. Such material difficulties were formidable; but much worse were the immaterial. The indifference of the world which Keats and Flaubert and other men of genius have found so hard to bear was in her case not indifference but hostility. The world did not say to her as it said to them, Write if you choose; it makes no difference to me. The world said with a guffaw, Write? What's the good of your writing? Here the

5. From William Wordsworth's poem "Resolution and Independence."

psychologists of Newnham and Girton might come to our help, I thought, looking again at the blank spaces on the shelves. For surely it is time that the effect of discouragement upon the mind of the artist should be measured, as I have seen a dairy company measure the effect of ordinary milk and Grade A milk upon the body of the rat. They set two rats in cages side by side, and of the two one was furtive, timid and small, and the other was glossy, bold and big. Now what food do we feed women as artists upon? I asked, remembering, I suppose, that dinner of prunes and custard.[6] To answer that question I had only to open the evening paper and to read that Lord Birkenhead is of opinion—but really I am not going to trouble to copy out Lord Birkenhead's opinion upon the writing of women. What Dean Inge says I will leave in peace. The Harley Street specialist may be allowed to rouse the echoes of Harley Street with his vociferations without raising a hair on my head. I will quote, however, Mr. Oscar Browning, because Mr. Oscar Browning was a great figure in Cambridge at one time, and used to examine the students at Girton and Newnham.[7] Mr. Oscar Browning was wont to declare "that the impression left on his mind, after looking over any set of examination papers, was that, irrespective of the marks he might give, the best woman was intellectually the inferior of the worst man." After saying that Mr. Browning went back to his rooms—and it is this sequel that endears him and makes him a human figure of some bulk and majesty—he went back to his rooms and found a stable-boy lying on the sofa—"a mere skeleton, his cheeks were cavernous and sallow, his teeth were black, and he did not appear to have the full use of his limbs. . . . 'That's Arthur' [said Mr. Browning]. 'He's a dear boy really and most high-minded.'" The two pictures always seem to me to complete each other. And happily in this age of biography the two pictures often do complete each other, so that we are able to interpret the opinions of great men not only by what they say, but by what they do.

But though this is possible now, such opinions coming from the lips of important people must have been formidable enough even fifty years ago. Let us suppose that a father from the highest motives did not wish his daughter to leave home and become writer, painter or scholar. "See what Mr. Oscar Browning says," he would say; and there was not only Mr. Oscar Browning; there was the *Saturday Review*; there was Mr. Greg[8]—the "essentials of a woman's being," said Mr. Greg emphatically, "are that *they are supported by, and they minister to, men*"—there was an

---

6. In Chapter 1, Woolf contrasts the lavish dinner—partridge and wine—she ate as a guest in a men's college at Cambridge University with the plain fare—prunes and custard—served in a women's college.
7. In Chapter 2, Woolf lists the fruits of her day's research on the lives of women, which

include Lord Birkenhead's, Dean Inge's, and Mr. Oscar Browning's opinions of women; she does not, however, quote them. Harley Street is where fashionable medical doctors in London have their offices.
8. Mr. Greg does not appear on Woolf's list (see preceding note).

enormous body of masculine opinion to the effect that nothing could be expected of women intellectually. Even if her father did not read out loud these opinions, any girl could read them for herself; and the reading, even in the nineteenth century, must have lowered her vitality, and told profoundly upon her work. There would always have been that assertion —you cannot do this, you are incapable of doing that—to protest against, to overcome. Probably for a novelist this germ is no longer of much effect; for there have been women novelists of merit. But for painters it must still have some sting in it; and for musicians, I imagine, is even now active and poisonous in the extreme. The woman composer stands where the actress stood in the time of Shakespeare. Nick Greene, I thought, remembering the story I had made about Shakespeare's sister, said that a woman acting put him in mind of a dog dancing. Johnson repeated the phrase two hundred years later of women preaching.[9] And here, I said, opening a book about music, we have the very words used again in this year of grace, 1928, of women who try to write music. "Of Mlle. Germaine Tailleferre one can only repeat Dr. Johnson's dictum concerning a woman preacher, transposed into terms of music. 'Sir, a woman's composing is like a dog's walking on his hind legs. It is not done well, but you are surprised to find it done at all.'"[1] So accurately does history repeat itself.

Thus, I concluded, shutting Mr. Oscar Browning's life and pushing away the rest, it is fairly evident that even in the nineteenth century a woman was not encouraged to be an artist. On the contrary, she was snubbed, slapped, lectured and exhorted. Her mind must have been strained and her vitality lowered by the need of opposing this, of disproving that. For here again we come within range of that very interesting and obscure masculine complex which has had so much influence upon the woman's movement; that deep-seated desire, not so much that she shall be inferior as that he shall be superior, which plants him wherever one looks, not only in front of the arts, but barring the way to politics too, even when the risk to himself seems infinitesimal and the suppliant humble and devoted. Even Lady Bessborough, I remembered, with all her passion for politics, must humbly bow herself and write to Lord Granville Leveson-Gower:[2] "... notwithstanding all my violence in politics and talking so much on that subject, I perfectly agree with you that no woman has any business to meddle with that or any other serious business, farther than giving her opinion (if she is ask'd)." And so she goes on to spend her enthusiasm where it meets with no obstacle whatsoever

9. The quotation is from James Boswell's *The Life of Samuel Johnson, L.L.D.* Woolf, in her tale of Judith Shakespeare, imagines the manager bellowing "something about poodles dancing and women acting."
1. *A Survey of Contemporary Music*, Cecil Gray, p. 246 [Woolf's note].

2. Henrietta, Countess of Bessborough (1761–1821) and Lord Granville Leveson Gower, first Earl Granville (1773–1846). Their correspondence, edited by Castalia Countess Granville, was published as his *Private Correspondence, 1781 to 1821*, in 1916.

upon that immensely important subject, Lord Granville's maiden speech in the House of Commons. The spectacle is certainly a strange one, I thought. The history of men's opposition to women's emancipation is more interesting perhaps than the story of that emancipation itself. An amusing book might be made of it if some young student at Girton or Newnham would collect examples and deduce a theory—but she would need thick gloves on her hands, and bars to protect her of solid gold.

But what is amusing now, I recollected, shutting Lady Bessborough, had to be taken in desperate earnest once. Opinions that one now pastes in a book labelled cock-a-doodle-dum and keeps for reading to select audiences on summer nights once drew tears, I can assure you. Among your grandmothers and great-grandmothers there were many that wept their eyes out. Florence Nightingale[3] shrieked aloud in her agony.[4] Moreover, it is all very well for you, who have got yourselves to college and enjoy sitting-rooms—or is it only bed-sitting-rooms?—of your own to say that genius should disregard such opinions; that genius should be above caring what is said of it. Unfortunately, it is precisely the men or women of genius who mind most what is said of them. Remember Keats. Remember the words he had cut on his tombstone. Think of Tennyson;[5] think—but I need hardly multiply instances of the undeniable, if very unfortunate, fact that it is the nature of the artist to mind excessively what is said about him. Literature is strewn with the wreckage of men who have minded beyond reason the opinions of others.

And this susceptibility of theirs is doubly unfortunate, I thought, returning again to my original enquiry into what state of mind is most propitious for creative work, because the mind of an artist, in order to achieve the prodigious effort of freeing whole and entire the work that is in him, must be incandescent, like Shakespeare's mind, I conjectured, looking at the book which lay open at *Antony and Cleopatra*. There must be no obstacle in it, no foreign matter unconsumed.

For though we say that we know nothing about Shakespeare's state of mind, even as we say that, we are saying something about Shakespeare's state of mind. The reason perhaps why we know so little of Shakespeare —compared with Donne or Ben Jonson or Milton—is that his grudges and spites and antipathies are hidden from us. We are not held up by some "revelation" which reminds us of the writer. All desire to protest, to preach, to proclaim an injury, to pay off a score, to make the world the witness of some hardship or grievance was fired out of him and consumed. Therefore his poetry flows from him free and unimpeded. If ever

3. Florence Nightingale (1820–1910), English nurse and philanthropist.
4. See *Cassandra*, by Florence Nightingale, printed in *The Cause*, by R. Strachey [Woolf's note].
5. Keats's epitaph reads "Here lies one whose name was writ in water." Tennyson was notably sensitive to reviews of his poetry.

a human being got his work expressed completely, it was Shakespeare. If ever a mind was incandescent, unimpeded, I thought, turning again to the bookcase, it was Shakespeare's mind.

1929

S. I. Hayakawa

SEX IS NOT A SPECTATOR SPORT

In current discussions of pornography and obscenity, there is widespread confusion about two matters. First there is sexual behavior and what it means to the participants. Secondly there is the outside observer of sexual behavior and what it means to him. When a man and a woman make love, enjoying themselves and each other unself-consciously, a rich relationship is reaffirmed and made richer by their lovemaking. However beautiful or sacred that love relationship may be to that man and woman, it would have an entirely different significance to a Peeping Tom, secretly watching the proceedings from outside the window. The sexual behavior is not itself obscene. Obscenity is peculiarly the evaluation of the outside observer. Theoretically the actors may themselves be made the observers. If, for example, unknown to the man and woman, a movie were to be made of their lovemaking, and that movie were to be shown to them later, that lovemaking might take on an entirely different significance. What was performed unself-consciously and spontaneously might be viewed later by the actors themselves with giggling or shame or shock. They might even insist that the film be destroyed—which is entirely different from saying that they would stop making love.

What I am saying is that obscenity and pornography can happen only when sexual events are seen from the outside, from a spectator's point of view. This is the crux of the pornography problem. Pornography is sexual behvior made public through symbolization—by representation in literature, by simulation or enactment in a nightclub act or on stage, by arts such as painting, photography, or the movies. To object to pornographic movies or art is not, as some would have us believe, a result of hang-ups about sex. One may be completely healthy and still object to many of the current representations of sexual acts in the movies and on the stage.

Standards of morality are one thing. Standards of decorum are another. There is nothing immoral about changing one's clothes or evacuating one's bowels. But in our culture people as a rule do not change their clothing in the presence of the other sex, excepting their spouses. Men and women have separate public lavatories, and within them each toilet is in a separate compartment for privacy. Love too needs privacy. Human beings normally make love in private, whether that love is socially sanctioned, as in marriage, or unsanctioned, as in a house of prostitution.

The trouble with sexual intercourse as an object of artistic or literary representation is that its meaning is not apparent in the behavior. Hence serious writers have historically been reticent in their description of sex. In Dante's *Divine Comedy* Francesca tells of her tragic love for Paolo. They were reading an ancient romance, and as they read, their passions suddenly overcame them. What happened? Dante simply has Francesca say, "That day we read no further." The rest is left to the reader's imagination—and the reader cannot help feeling the power of that on-rushing, fatal passion.

Men and women couple with each other for a wide variety of reasons. Sometimes the sexual encounter is the fulfillment of true love and respect for each other. Sometimes one of the partners is using sex as an instrument of exploitation or aggression against the other. Sometimes sex is a commercial transaction, with either party being the prostitute. Sometimes sex is the expression of neurosis. Sometimes it is evidence of people getting over their neuroses. However, to the movie camera, as to a Peeping Tom, they are all "doing the same thing." To concentrate on the mechanics of sex is to ignore altogether its human significance.

Today movies do not stop at exhibiting copulation. Every kind of aberrant sexual behavior and sadomasochistic perversion is being shown. The advertisements in the newspaper before me announce such titles as *Nude Encounter, Too Hot to Handle, Deep Throat, The Devil in Miss Jones, The Passion Parlor, Hot Kitten,* and *Honeymoon Suite,* as well as "16 hours of hard-core male stag." The only purpose of movies such as these, from all I can tell from advertisements and reviews, is, as D. H. Lawrence expressed it, "to do dirt on sex." Let the American Civil Liberties Union fight for the right of these movies to be shown. I will not.

1979

THE READER

1. This is a short essay. What is the functional relation of its six paragraphs?
2. What is the function of Hayakawa's idea of decorum? How does he establish it?
3. What is the argumentative function of Hayakawa's distinction between meaning and behavior? Would behavior be obscene if it didn't have the right meaning?

THE WRITER

1. Is Hayakawa refuting an argument directed against the opponents of pornography, or is he asserting an argument opposing pornography?

Does it matter? What is the position he takes at the end?
2. *Rewrite Hayakawa's conclusion so that it asserts a stronger position.
Can you do this without changing his argument?*

Vicki Hearne

HORSES IN PARTNERSHIP WITH TIME

Grand Prix riding, which is to say either dressage or jumping competitions in which the demands placed on horse and rider are so extraordinary that it is not hyperbole to say that they are limitless—and in precisely the way that the demands of art are limitless—are places where the logics of art, sport and morality become indistinguishable.[1] In Grand Prix jumping, the judge's decision rests solely on whether or not the lumber is still there or has been knocked to the ground after you and your horse complete your ride, and on what the automatic timers say about the time the ride took. We call this a sport or a game because neither the horse's nor the rider's intentions enter into public judgments about what has occurred, any more than a batter's intentions enter into the judgment "foul ball" in baseball. You may, for example, have intended to use the course simply as preparation for another, more important Grand Prix event, and so not have put a great deal of pressure on your horse to jump clean. That is, what you had in mind was increasing the horse's knowledge and experience, not primarily winning. But if the fences are all up when you have finished taking them in the correct order, and your time is the fastest, you have won. The observer is to a great extent relieved of the burden of judgment. Dressage events are slightly more complicated for the judges, since in these, as in gymnastics or diving, winning is a matter of how well the horse performs a given movement. There are nonetheless criteria for judging that are largely independent of the rider's or the horse's intentions. I don't mean, of course, that such events are commonly won or lost *accidentally*, only that the logic of judgment does not demand an account of the competitor's intentions. There are exceptions to this general rule, as there are in baseball when the pitcher hits the

---

1. When I say this, I have in mind Stanley Cavell's discussion, in "A Matter of Meaning It," of the different ways our intentions alter our positions and our responsibilities in the various forms of life that sort themselves out as either art, games or morality. He says: "Games are places where intention does not count, human activities in which intention need not generally be taken into account; because in games *what happens* is described solely in terms set by the game itself, because the consequences one is responsible for are limited by the rules of the game. In morality, tracing an intention limits a man's responsibility; in art it dilates it completely" [Hearne's note].

batter with the ball, but such exceptions tend mostly to show that even baseball is not epistemologically perfectible.

In all riding competitions, the presence of the horse imposes a continuous, unique moral burden. Not all riders are responsive to this burden, but its presence is revealed in the logic of horse-show judgments. The regulations and structures of different horse shows are variously hedged with regulations about cruelty—and whether or not a judge or a committee decides that a given matter is a case of cruelty will depend, as it does normally in the rest of the law, on evaluating intentions. In Grand Prix riding, as it happens, it is rather difficult to compete both successfully and cruelly, but it is not impossible. It may happen that while warming up a rider uses a pole studded with tacks to inspire the horse to jump high and carefully. If the rider does this knowingly, it is straightforwardly cruel. If, however, in the confusion of the warm-up ring I have without noticing taken my horse over such a pole that you or someone else has brought to put up, or if a trainer, unbeknownst to the rider, blisters the pasterns of a gaited horse, then the rider isn't in the same way responsible for what has happened and is probably not going to be barred from showing. (Though there might be a reprimand to the rider to be more alert in the future, and, of course, once the rider is aware of such a possibility, the nature of his or her responsibility expands. If my trainer has blistered my horse's pasterns, and I don't fire the trainer or at least get really tough with him or her, then official as well as unofficial judgments of my behavior will change.)

But the burden is deeper than this. It is like the burden of teaching humans, since the nature of riding is such that doing it at all entails meaning to do well by the horse. There are hundreds of children's stories that reveal this; the rider or keeper who sacrifices the horse's mental and physical well-being to some momentary or permanent advantage is shown to be not a bad horseman but rather no horseman at all. The world can make mistakes about this, which is not only why there are such stories but also evidence of what kind of allegory a horse story is. In jumping there are some riders who win fairly continuously for seasons of varying lengths despite rough, ugly methods. These riders' failures to develop their horses' beauty, understanding, nobility and so forth cannot by the logic of the thing enter into a judge's decision whether or not s/he has eyes that are open to genuine beauty as opposed to what is merely thrilling.

The case of the rider who clowns and lurches his or her way around the ring year after year with little or no intelligent thought for the horse is different from the case of the rider who just doesn't happen, for whatever reason, to give a pretty ride; it is the rider's intention to *ride well* that makes the difference. The green rider going around the show ring for the first time on a wise and long-suffering old trooper is not judged *cruel* because of the knocks and bumps both rider and mount encounter and endure. Beyond which, there are riders who are not especially strong, or a bit stiff, or badly built, whose horses nonetheless go beautifully in the full brilliance of their intelligence.

What matters is an understanding of the *horse's* capacity for caring about beauty, precision, perfection of performance. This gives his or her pain meaning and context, so that riding a green horse who knows little or nothing of art close to the point of exhaustion is totally different from, on occasion, asking a mature horse with a strong, developed vision for an effort that will leave him or her for a time weak. It is not that the mature horse becomes desensitized to pain, but that the pain now means something.

To say that pain is meaningful is simply to say that for the creature experiencing the pain there is something that matters more than comfort, for the moment at least; something that is the ground of a certain creature's being, what it cares about, toward which it is oriented, in relationship to which pain isn't quite pain anymore, not anything that matters. This is probably not something anyone can make a judgment about for anyone else. My pain, like my death, belongs to me uniquely most of the time.

My horse, when he is in his stall or lounging about the pasture, has the same relationship to pain that I have when cuddling up with a good murder mystery—comfort and convenience have top priority. Indeed, convenience is so important to horses that in the earlier stages of training one can accomplish a great deal by remembering that, as Podhajsky[2] points out, they will even overcome objections to obeying in order to save themselves inconvenience. Nonetheless, a developed jumper or dressage horse not only doesn't object to the removal of his warm blanket and the substitution of saddle and bridle, s/he actually welcomes these preparations for work. And even horses who are extremely fastidious about stepping on wet, sloppy ground will cheerfully plow through it under tack in the course of performing voltes, serpentines[3] and so on. (Similarly with dogs: my Pit Bull Belle is one of the most comfort-minded dogs in existence and has gone so far as to pull the electric blanket off my bed and put it on her bed. Furthermore, in the winter, she hates going outside, even to relieve herself, and peers out the door at the weather with extreme gloom. With her tracking harness on, it is different, and when, at the beginning of a track, I ask for the down-stay that lasts for several minutes, she will throw herself down cheerfully in ice-encrusted snow, though not at any other time).

2. Alois Podhajsky (1898–1973): Austrian army officer, director of the Spanish Riding School in Vienna from 1939 to 1964, and author of numerous books on dressage.

3. In dressage, a volte is a circular movement executed by a horse, a serpentine is a winding movement that leads back to its starting place.

Some horses are plainly more sensitive to pain than others, and Drummer Girl was such a horse. If she knocked her legs against something while playing in the pasture, she would actually limp for a while, looking distressed and sorry for herself—and this was not the kind of faking that some horses do so well. Even though she loved jumping, I had to be very careful in the beginning to avoid, as far as I could, her hitting herself on the jump poles and becoming frightened again. Yet once she came to *understand* and actively participate in jumping, she wasn't distracted even by hitting a quite solid fence with a significnt thwack—she simply responded by jumping harder and more carefully the next time.

Almost anyone can see what I'm talking about at a Puissance class. In such a class there is a relatively low (around four feet, usually) practice fence, and then a few very formidable obstacles that are raised after each round until there is only one horse remaining who can clear them. The fences may go higher than the mounted rider's head; these are the classes where jumping records are set. Horses do not go about jumping such heights in other situations—at least, I never knew a horse to jump higher than seven feet to get out of a corral, even a horse that can jump higher than that under saddle; a Puissance horse can often be kept quite handily behind fencing that is not more than four feet high. Horses, like people, require meaningful occasions and contexts for intentions that are deep and focused. Seasoned horses develop a very keen sense of the importance or absence of it in a given context.

The riders, while they can tell a horse they know fairly well something about the magnitude of such an occasion ahead of time, can't say, "At around eight-thirty this evening you will have to be psyched up for your best effort," though they *can* say, "Horse! Stirring things are in the air!" So in the Puissance ring there is a practice fence, which is jumped more or less on the way to the fences that count, and which is the last step in the mental preparation of the horse.

One frequent way of using this fence is deliberately to jump it badly. I don't mean to interfere actively with the horse's taking it well, but rather to come in to it casually, sloppily even, not paying much attention, not putting up one's best effort, so that the horse either takes it uncomfortably, off-balance, or actually hits it. If it is the right horse, the right rider and the right training, this throws the horse powerfully onto his own mental resources, and you can see good jumpers, after the practice fence, prick up their ears, look around for the next fence and instead of trying to pull away from it, pull eagerly toward it. You can see even an awesome moment of decision in horses coming down toward really big fences.

First there is the discovery, the moment of "My God! That is a big sucker," and then the deliberate gathering, in the horse, of all of her power, all forward desire. (Or, unfortunately, sometimes the opposite, a desperate squirreling around, seeking any avenue of escape.)

There are various ways to talk about what could possibly motivate a horse, or any animal, to such an effort. Fear certainly does not do it. Courage, joy, exaltation are more like it, but beyond that horses have, some of the time, a strong sense of artistry. This is something very specific. It is not merely craftsmanship, although being able to do a difficult thing well is, of course, a powerful motivator for man or beast. When I say artistry, I mean that the movements of a developed horse, the figures and leaps, mean something, and an artistic horse is one who is capable of wanting to mean the movements and the jump perfectly.

The jump, like the complicated movements of dressage, is an imitation of nature, especially of various movements that horses perform for the sake of sexual display or in the course of exercising claim rights—a stallion's claiming of a herd or a mare's claiming of a foal or of leadership status. In nature, in the horse's first inheritance of these gestures, they have particular meanings, such as "Wait your turn!" or "Watch out!" or "Look at me! I love you!" or "Wait. Be still. Something wicked this way comes." But the movements of dressage and formal jumping, properly performed, don't mean "Look at me, I love you" or any of the others. They mean the natural movements themselves. This is why the language of analysis and criticism of riding at the highest levels is the language of art cirticism. Podhajsky, attending the Olympic games, recorded detailed observations of the rides, which became the book *The Art of Dressage*. He says, speaking, as always, after Xenophon,[4] "Anything forced or misunderstood can never be beautiful," and later in that same chapter:

> ... nature can exist without art, but not art without nature. Consequently, the well-trained dressage horse should perform the natural paces with perfection. Any defects in these movements cannot be made up for by some other spectacular exercises. Riders or judges who allow themselves to be dazzled by such striking movements betray the true art of riding.

Such betrayals are not only common, they have become activities in themselves, and there are competitions in which special effects have entirely replaced genuine art. In the true art, Podhajsky insists, haste in the movements is always a fault, as is unhappiness on the face of the horse. Guiding phrases include: "purity of the paces," "*harmony*, lightness in all movements," "the impression of complete confidence," "the horse's *concentration* upon his rider becomes obvious. . . ." Riders are criticized for failures of *cadence* and *tempo*, or are praised for what is "*fluent* and precisely performed" and especially for what is *expressive*. Of a ride that does not achieve full entry over what he calls "the threshold of art," he says, "without brilliance . . . hesitant transition . . . performance of a tolerably obedient horse with little charm and suppleness."

4. Xenophon (4th century B.C.): Greek historian and writer of essays, including an essay on horsemanship.

Podhajsky died before *The Art of Dressage* could be published, so it concludes with an "In Memoriam" by Berthold Spangenberg, who thanks his great master for teaching "the gentle, the difficult art of riding." And indeed it became a gentle art under Podhajsky's influence, but gentle because so difficult, or gentle because genuine, since in a genuine art there is the amassment and expression of true power as opposed to mere force. Which brings me finally in contact with the central question, which will be hard to talk about because it is difficult to talk about the horse without talking about the rider and vice versa (although it can be quite hard to see why from the ground). If this is an art for the horse, then the horse must intend it, and what does the horse intend, what can the horse possibly mean by it? And does—can—the horse mean by it anything like what the rider means, or can mean?

The movements themselves are not literal; they don't mean what they say. The horse would be as disconcerted if anyone, equine or human, were to respond to, say, a capriole[5] as a literal threat or appeal, as a composer would be to such a response to passages of music that are expressive of rage. But if the movements are not literal, the horses nevertheless mean something by them, and there are a few horses, very great horses, who, like very great artists, have the capacity to accept full responsibility for meaning what they "say"—do—and this is the kind of meaning that is always entailed in art. In other words, I am claiming that a great horse, in Cavell's words, "is responsible for everything that happens in his work—and not just in the sense that it is done, but in the sense that it is meant."[6]

This does not yet explain what the horse means by it, but it does begin to suggest one aspect of the rider's role, the rider's responsibility. Cavell goes on to say:

> It is a terrible responsibility. . . . But it is all the more terrible, when it is shouldered, not to appreciate it, to refuse to understand something meant so well. . . . In art [the right to question the artist] has to be earned, through the talent of understanding, the skill of commitment, and truthfulness to one's response—the ways the artist earned his initial right to our attention. If we have earned the right to question it, the object itself will answer: otherwise not. There is poetic justice.

So a rider who is a true rider and no mere keeper of horses is someone who continuously earns the right to question the horse and the horse's performance, and it is the horse's performance that answers the rider's questioning. Thus the very fact, the very possibility, of Grand Prix riding, both jumping and dressage, is our discovery in the horse of a capacity for meaning a movement or a series of movements artistically.

5. Capriole: in dressage, a leap with a backward kick of the hind legs.

6. Stanley Cavell (1926–): American educator, professor of aesthetics.

When the threshold of art has been crossed, then the wonderful obedience and supple submission of the horse, the joy of the horse's submission, are like the intensely accurate responsiveness of a great performer to a good audience, another case of the collapse of command and obedience into a single supple relation. It is, as Podhajsky says, as though the rider thinks and the horse executes the thought, without mediation or any sort of cuing; but it is also the other way around on the back of a great horse—it is as though the horse thinks and the rider creates, or becomes, a space and direction for the execution of the horse's thoughts. The rider is the person who shoulders the burden of knowing through "the talent of understanding and the skill of commitment" what the horse means.

But, as I have said, there are differences between the horses' concept of time and ours. It is, of course, the rider and not the horse who sits in the study working out training schedules and filling in entry forms to be mailed to the show committee, marking dates on a calendar. Horses do not have what we call the tenses of verbs, so they don't talk or think about that, and that is why the Puissance rider, for all of the wonderful things s/he can say to the horse, can't say, "Be ready to do your very best tonight at eight o'clock." The concepts of time that enable us to make appointments and leave notes are not in the grammar of the horse's world, so we cannot share that form of life with them. And our concept of a rehearsal is very much a concept of ordering time in a particular way, by means of a particular grammar.

There is a novel called *Nightmare*, by Piers Anthony, which is told from the point of view of a mare whose task is to bring instructively awful dreams to human beings. One of these human beings is a woman who, herself rapidly approaching death, asks the mare if her kind, horses, are immortal. The mare, for whom the question is a new one, thinks about it and comes up with the clumsy but strangely apt answer, "Yes . . . until we die, that is."

But some horses (and this, alas, is part of the talent in them) are capable of responding to the knowledge art creates of what it feels like when there is complete congruence between the soul and the moment (that congruence Wittgenstein[7] indicated when, at the end of the *Tractatus Logico-Philosophicus*, he says, "He who lives in the present lives in eternity"[8]) with a general anxiety that work should continue. When left to mooch serenely around the pasture, some of these horses become, not peaceful and lazy, but rather depressed if work for some reason ceases. Such a state of mind does not, of course, entail the full grammar of angst

7. Ludwig Josef Johann Wittgenstein (1889–1951): British philosopher born in Austria.

8. "*Denn lebt er ewig, der in der Gegenwart lebt*" [Hearne's note].

or melancholy in human beings, but the taint of mortality is on the horse, and it takes more than mere comfort for his or her spine to be restored to a feeling of congruence with the landscape. I don't mean that in such a case any horse ever learns that death is inevitable, any more than any horse ever learns that the National Horse Show at Madison Square Garden is on the twenty-seventh of next month, however much s/he learns about the significance for a given moment of activities before, during and after horse-show activities and seasons. We cannot, thank heaven, teach horses the tenses of English verbs, which means that we cannot teach them that they die, or that we do, any more than you can tell your dog not to worry, that you ill be back from the store in ten minutes, or back from the Holy Land in ten years. But we can nonetheless interfere with, disturb their sense of time, teaching new modes of anticipation as well as new modes of loss.

The book *Nightmare* provides a kind of allegory of this. The heroine becomes "mortal by day," and this means that, during the day, she cannot escape being ridden by the extremely sinister figure called Horseman. That vulnerability is a nice emblem of what horses can learn from us— not the grammar of mortality, not a knowledge of their own, but rather a participation in ours.

If what I have said so far were all there is to it, it wouldn't be hard to come to the conclusion that training horses is morally indefensible, but this isn't all there is to it, because horses have their own grammar of time. They can't say anything that requires past, present or future tense, but that doesn't mean that without us they live in eternity, in the present tense only. Their concept of time might be expressed by saying that the names of their tenses are "not yet, here and gone." You can't make appointments with such tenses, but you can remember, and you can anticipate the future with no little anxiety. That is to say, horses do have some sensitivity to the knowledge of death, and it makes them nervous, just as it makes us nervous.

That knowledge is what they are relieved of, just as their riders are, in the tremendous concentration of horsemanship at the highest levels. This is why we are forgiven for riding them, especially in competitions, for distracting and scaring them with brass bands at football stadiums, spooking them by placing garlands of roses around their sweating necks and surrounding them with photographers, neon beer signs and journalists who profanely scribble figures on note pads while the horses are jumping their hearts out. And nothing short of the tremendous artistic task of training them in such a fashion that they can be released from time could ever justify our interfering with their greater serenity, our imposing our stories and our deathly arithmetics on their coherent landscapes.

What they mean by their artistry, then, is just this, which one could call the release from time, but which could also be understood as what happens when a horse becomes time's lover or time's partner, moving with time instead of as time's slave.

1986

Christopher Fry

LAUGHTER

A friend once told me that when he was under the influence of ether, he dreamed he was turning over the pages of a great book, in which he knew he would find, on the last page, the meaning of life. The pages of the book were alternately tragic and comic, and he turned page after page, his excitement growing, not only because he was approaching the answer but because he couldn't know, until he arrived, on which side of the book the final page would be. At last it came: the universe opened up to him in a hundred words: and they were uproariously funny. He came back to consciousness crying with laughter, remembering everything. He opened his lips to speak. It was then that the great and comic answer plunged back out of his reach.

If I had to draw a picture of the person of Comedy, it is so I should like to draw it: the tears of laughter running down the face, one hand still lying on the tragic page which so nearly contained the answer, the lips about to frame the great revelation, only to find it had gone as disconcertingly as a chair twitched away when we want to sit down. Comedy is an escape, not from truth but from despair: a narrow escape into faith. It believes in a universal cause for delight, even though knowledge of the cause is always twitched away from under us, which leaves us to rest on our own buoyancy. In tragedy every moment is eternity; in comedy eternity is a moment. In tragedy we suffer pain; in comedy pain is a fool, suffered gladly.

Charles Williams[1] once said to me, indeed it was the last thing he said to me (he died not long after), and it was shouted from the tailboard of a moving bus, over the heads of pedestrians and bicyclists outside the Midland Station, Oxford: "When we're dead we shall have the sensation of having enjoyed life altogether, whatever has happened to us." The distance between us widened, and he leaned out into the space so that his voice should reach me: "Even if we've been murdered, what a pleasure to have been capable of it!"; and, having spoken the words for comedy, away he went like that revelation which almost came out of the ether.

He was not at all saying that everything is for the best in the best of all

---

1. English writer whose poems, novels, plays, and essays explore the implications of Christian theology and morality for modern life.

possible worlds. He was saying—or so it seems to me—that there is an angle of experience where the dark is distilled into light: either here or hereafter, in or out of time: where our tragic fate finds itself with perfect pitch, and goes straight to the key which creation was composed in. And comedy senses and reaches out to this experience. It says, in effect, that, groaning as we may be, we move in the figure of a dance, and, so moving, we trace the outline of the mystery. Laughter did not come by chance, but how or why it came is beyond comprehension, unless we think of it as a kind of perception. The human animal, beginning to feel his spiritual inches, broke in onto an unfamiliar tension of life, where laughter became inevitable. But how? Could he, in his first unlaughing condition, have contrived a comic view of life and then developed the strange rib-shaking response?

Or is it not more likely that when he was able to grasp the tragic nature of time he was of a stature to sense its comic nature also; and, by the experience of tragedy and the intuition of comedy, to make his difficult way? The difference between tragedy and comedy is the difference between experience and intuition. In the experience we strive against every condition of our animal life: against death, against the frustration of ambition, against the instability of human love. In the intuition we trust the arduous eccentricities we're born to, and see the oddness of a creature who has never got acclimatized to being created. Laughter inclines me to know that man is essential spirit; his body, with its functions and accidents and frustrations, is endlessly quaint and remarkable to him; and though comedy accepts our position in time, it barely accepts our posture in space.

The bridge by which we cross from tragedy to comedy and back again is precarious and narrow. We find ourselves in one or the other by the turn of a thought; a turn such as we make when we turn from speaking to listening. I know that when I set about writing a comedy the idea presents itself to me first of all as tragedy. The characters press on to the theme with all their divisions and perplexities heavy about them; they are already entered for the race to doom, and good and evil are an infernal tangle skinning the fingers that try to unravel them. If the characters were not qualified for tragedy there would be no comedy, and to some extent I have to cross the one before I can light on the other. In a century less flayed and quivering we might reach it more directly; but not now, unless every word we write is going to mock us. A bridge has to be crossed, a thought has to be turned. Somehow the characters have to unmortify themselves: to affirm life and assimilate death and persevere in joy. Their hearts must be as determined as the phoenix; what burns must also light and renew: not by a vulnerable optimism but by a hard-won maturity of delight, by the intuition of comedy, an active patience declaring the solvency of good. The Book of Job is the great reservoir of comedy. "But there is a spirit in man. . . . Fair weather cometh out of the north. . . . The blessing of him that was ready to perish came upon me: and I caused the widow's heart to sing for joy."

I have come, you may think, to the verge of saying that comedy is greater than tragedy. On the verge I stand and go no further. Tragedy's experience hammers against the mystery to make a breach which would admit the whole triumphant answer. Intuition has no such potential. But there are times in the state of man when comedy has a special worth, and the present is one of them: a time when the loudest faith has been faith in a trampling materialism, when literature has been thought unrealistic which did not mark and remark our poverty and doom. Joy (of a kind) has been all on the devil's side, and one of the necessities of our time is to redeem it. If not, we are in poor sort to meet the circumstances, the circumstances being the contention of death with life, which is to say evil with good, which is to say desolation with delight. Laughter may only seem to be like an exhalation of air, but out of that air we came; in the beginning we inhaled it; it is a truth, not a fantasy, a truth voluble of good which comedy stoutly maintains.

1951

E. B. White

SOME REMARKS ON HUMOR

Analysts have had their go at humor, and I have read some of this interpretative literature, but without being greatly instructed. Humor can be dissected, as a frog can, but the thing dies in the process and the innards are discouraging to any but the pure scientific mind.

In a newsreel theatre the other day I saw a picture of a man who had developed the soap bubble to a higher point than it had ever before reached. He had become the ace soap bubble blower of America, had perfected the business of blowing bubbles, refined it, doubled it, squared it, and had even worked himself up into a convenient lather. The effect was not pretty. Some of the bubbles were too big to be beautiful, and the blower was always jumping into them or out of them, or playing some sort of unattractive trick with them. It was, if anything, a rather repulsive sight. Humor is a little like that: it won't stand much blowing up, and it won't stand much poking. It has a certain fragility, an evasiveness, which one had best respect. Essentially, it is a complete mystery. A human frame convulsed with laughter, and the laughter becoming hysterical and uncontrollable, is as far out of balance as one shaken with the hiccoughs or in the throes of a sneezing fit.

One of the things commonly said about humorists is that they are really very sad people—clowns with a breaking heart. There is some truth in it, but it is badly stated. It would be more accurate, I think, to say that there is a deep vein of melancholy running through everyone's life and that the humorist, perhaps more sensible of it than some others, compensates for it actively and positively. Humorists fatten on trouble. They have always made trouble pay. They struggle along with a good will and endure pain cheerfully, knowing how well it will serve them in the sweet by and by. You find them wrestling with foreign languages, fighting folding ironing boards and swollen drainpipes, suffering the terrible discomfort of tight boots (or as Josh Billings[1] wittily called them, "tite" boots). They pour out their sorrows profitably, in a form that is not quite fiction nor quite fact either. Beneath the sparkling surface of these dilemmas flows the strong tide of human woe.

Practically everyone is a manic depressive of sorts, with his up moments and his down moments, and you certainly don't have to be a humorist to taste the sadness of situation and mood. But there is often a rather fine line between laughing and crying, and if a humorous piece of writing brings a person to the point where his emotional responses are untrustworthy and seem likely to break over into the opposite realm, it is because humor, like poetry, has an extra content. It plays close to the big hot fire which is Truth, and sometimes the reader feels the heat.

1954

1. Pseudonym of Henry Wheeler Shaw, nineteenth-century American humorist whose sketches often depended on an exaggerated imitation of the dialect of rural New England or New York.

THE READER

1. White uses a number of concrete details (dissected frog, soap bubbles and bubble blower, clowns with a breaking heart, fighting folding ironing boards and swollen drain pipes, suffering the terrible discomfort of tight boots, big hot fire which is Truth). Which of these are metaphors or analogies (comparisons with a different kind of thing), and which are concrete examples of general statements? Why does White use so many metaphors or analogies in his definition?

2. Compare White's definition of humor with Fry's definition of laughter (p. 1074). How far do the two definitions agree? Would White agree with Fry's hint that comedy might even be considered greater than tragedy?

THE WRITER

1. Compare White's definition of humor with his definition of democracy (p. 833). Is there a recognizable similarity in language or style? In devices used?

*2. Rewrite White's definition in abstract or general language, leaving out
   the analogies or metaphors and the concrete examples. Then compare
   the rewritten version with the original. Which is clearer? Which is
   more interesting to read?*

Aaron Copland

HOW WE LISTEN

We all listen to music according to our separate capacities. But, for the
sake of analysis, the whole listening process may become clearer if we
break it up into its component parts, so to speak. In a certain sense we all
listen to music on three separate planes. For lack of a better terminology,
one might name these: (1) the sensuous plane, (2) the expressive plane, (3)
the sheerly musical plane. The only advantage to be gained from
mechanically splitting up the listening process into these hypothetical
planes is the clearer view to be had of the way in which we listen.

The simplest way of listening to music is to listen for the sheer
pleasure of the musical sound itself. That is the sensuous plane. It is the
plane on which we hear music without thinking, without considering it
in any way. One turns on the radio while doing something else and
absentmindedly bathes in the sound. A kind of brainless but attractive
state of mind is engendered by the mere sound appeal of the music.

You may be sitting in a room reading this book. Imagine one note
struck on the piano. Immediately that one note is enough to change the
atmosphere of the room—proving that the sound element in music is a
powerful and mysterious agent, which it would be foolish to deride or
belittle.

The surprising thing is that many people who consider themselves
qualified music lovers abuse that plane in listening. They go to concerts
in order to lose themselves. They use music as a consolation or an escape.
They enter an ideal world where one doesn't have to think of the realities
of everyday life. Of course they aren't thinking about the music either.
Music allows them to leave it, and they go off to a place to dream,
dreaming because of and apropos of the music yet never quite listening to
it.

Yes, the sound appeal of music is a potent and primitive force, but you
must not allow it to usurp a disproportionate share of your interest. The
sensuous plane is an important one in music, a very important one, but it
does not constitute the whole story.

There is no need to digress further on the sensuous plane. Its appeal to every normal human being is self-evident. There is, however, such a thing as becoming more sensitive to the different kinds of sound stuff as used by various composers. For all composers do not use that sound stuff in the same way. Don't get the idea that the value of music is commensurate with its sensuous appeal or that the loveliest sounding music is made by the greatest composer. If that were so, Ravel would be a greater creator than Beethoven. The point is that the sound element varies with each composer, that his usage of sound forms an integral part of his style and must be taken into account when listening. The reader can see, therefore, that a more conscious approach is valuable even on this primary plane of music listening.

The second plane on which music exists is what I have called the expressive one. Here, immediately, we tread on controversial ground. Composers have a way of shying away from any discussion of music's expressive side. Did not Stravinsky himself proclaim that his music was an "object," a "thing," with a life of its own, and with no other meaning than its own purely musical existence? This intransigent attitude of Stravinsky's may be due to the fact that so many people have tried to read different meanings into so many pieces. Heaven knows it is difficult enough to say precisely what it is that a piece of music means, to say it definitely, to say it finally so that everyone is satisfied with your explanation. But that should not lead one to the other extreme of denying to music the right to be "expressive."

My own belief is that all music has an expressive power, some more and some less, but that all music has a certain meaning behind the notes and that that meaning behind the note constitutes, after all, what the piece is saying, what the piece is about. This whole problem can be stated quite simply by asking, "Is there a meaning to music?" My answer to that would be. "Yes." And "Can you state in so many words what the meaning is?" My answer to that would be, "No." Therein lies the difficulty.

Simple-minded souls will never be satisfied with the answer to the second of these questions. They always want music to have a meaning, and the more concrete it is the better they like it. The more the music reminds them of a train, a storm, a funeral, or any other familiar conception the more expressive it appears to be to them. This popular idea of music's meaning—stimulated and abetted by the usual run of musical commentator—should be discouraged wherever and whenever it is met. One timid lady once confessed to me that she suspected something seriously lacking in her appreciation of music because of her inability to connect it with anything definite. That is getting the whole thing backward, of course.

Still, the question remains, How close should the intelligent music lover wish to come to pinning a definite meaning to any particular work?

No closer than a general concept, I should say. Music expresses, at different moments, serenity or exuberance, regret or triumph, fury or delight. It expresses each of these moods, and many others, in a number-less variety of subtle shadings and differences. It may even express a state of meaning for which there exists no adequate word in any language. In that case, musicians often like to say that it has only a purely musical meaning. They sometimes go farther and say that all music has only a purely musical meaning. What they really mean is that no appropriate word can be found to express the music's meaning and that, even if it could, they do not feel the need of finding it.

But whatever the professional musician may hold, most musical nov-ices still search for specific words with which to pin down their musical reactions. That is why they always find Tchaikovsky easier to "under-stand" than Beethoven. In the first place, it is easier to pin a meaning-word on a Tchaikovsky piece than on a Beethoven one. Much easier. Moreover, with the Russian composer, every time you come back to a piece of his it almost always says the same thing to you, whereas with Beethoven it is often quite difficult to put your finger right on what he is saying. And any musician will tell you that that is why Beethoven is the greater composer. Because music which always says the same thing to you will necessarily soon become dull music, but music whose meaning is slightly different with each hearing has a greater chance of remaining alive.

Listen, if you can, to the forty-eight fugue themes of Bach's *Well Tempered Clavichord*. Listen to each theme, one after another. You will soon realize that each theme mirrors a different world of feeling. You will also soon realize that the more beautiful a theme seems to you the harder it is to find any word that will describe it to your complete satisfaction. Yes, you will certainly know whether it is a gay theme or a sad one. You will be able, in other words, in your own mind, to draw a frame of emotional feeling around your theme. Now study the sad one a little closer. Try to pin down the exact quality of its sadness. Is it pessimisti-cally sad or resignedly sad; is it fatefully sad or smilingly sad?

Let us suppose that you are fortunate and can describe to your own satisfaction in so many words the exact meaning of your chosen theme. There is still no guarantee that anyone else will be satisfied. Nor need they be. The important thing is that each one feel for himself the specific expressive quality of a theme or, similarly, an entire piece of music. And if it is a great work of art, don't expect it to mean exactly the same thing to you each time you return to it.

Themes or pieces need not express only one emotion, of course. Take such a theme as the first main one of the *Ninth Symphony*, for example. It is clearly made up of different elements. It does not say only one thing. Yet anyone hearing it immediately gets a feeling of strength, a feeling of power. It isn't a power that comes simply because the theme is played loudly. It is a power inherent in the theme itself. The extraordinary strength and vigor of the theme results in the listener's receiving an impression that a forceful statement has been made. But one should never try to boil it down to "the fateful hammer of life," etc. That is where the trouble begins. The musician, in his exasperation, says it means nothing but the notes themselves, whereas the nonprofessional is only too anxious to hang on to any explanation that gives him the illusion of getting closer to the music's meaning.

Now, perhaps, the reader will know better what I mean when I say that music does have an expressive meaning but that we cannot say in so many words what that meaning is.

The third plane on which music exists is the sheerly musical plane. Besides the pleasurable sound of music and the expressive feeling that it gives off, music does exist in terms of the notes themselves and of their manipulation. Most listeners are not sufficiently conscious of this third plane. . . .

Professional musicians, on the other hand, are, if anything, too conscious of the mere notes themselves. They often fall into the error of becoming so engrossed with their arpeggios and staccatos that they forget the deeper aspects of the music they are performing. But from the layman's standpoint, it is not so much a matter of getting over bad habits on the sheerly musical plane as of increasing one's awareness of what is going on, in so far as the notes are concerned.

When the man in the street listens to the "notes themselves" with any degree of concentration, he is most likely to make some mention of the melody. Either he hears a pretty melody or he does not, and he generally lets it go at that. Rhythm is likely to gain his attention next, particularly if it seems exciting. But harmony and tone color are generally taken for granted, if they are thought of consciously at all. As for music's having a definite form of some kind, that idea seems never to have occurred to him.

It is very important for all of us to become more alive to music on its sheerly musical plane. After all, an actual musical material is being used. The intelligent listener must be prepared to increase his awareness of the musical material and what happens to it. He must hear the melodies, the rhythms, the harmonies, the tone colors in a more conscious fashion. But above all he must, in order to follow the line of the composer's thought, know something of the principles of musical form. Listening to all of these elements is listening on the sheerly musical plane.

Let me repeat that I have split up mechanically the three separate planes on which we listen merely for the sake of greater clarity. Actually, we never listen on one or the other of these planes. What we do is to correlate them—listening in all three ways at the same time. It takes no mental effort, for we do it instinctively.

Perhaps an analogy with what happens to us when we visit the theater will make this instinctive correlation clearer. In the theater, you are aware of the actors and actresses, costumes and sets, sounds and movements. All these give one the sense that the theater is a pleasant place to be in. They constitute the sensuous plane in our theatrical reactions.

The expressive plane in the theater would be derived from the feeling that you get from what is happening on the stage. You are moved to pity, excitement, or gayety. It is this general feeling, generated aside from the particular words being spoken, a certain emotional something which exists on the stage, that is analogous to the expressive quality in music.

The plot and plot development is equivalent to our sheerly musical plane. The playwright creates and develops a character in just the same way that a composer creates and develops a theme. According to the degree of your awareness of the way in which the artist in either field handles his material will you become a more intelligent listener.

It is easy enough to see that the theatergoer never is conscious of any of these elements separately. He is aware of them all at the same time. The same is true of music listening. We simultaneously and without thinking listen on all three planes.

In a sense, the ideal listener is both inside and outside the music at the same moment, judging it and enjoying it, wishing it would go one way and watching it go another—almost like the composer at the moment he composes it; because in order to write his music, the composer must also be inside and outside his music, carried away by it and yet coldly critical of it. A subjective and objective attitude is implied in both creating and listening to music.

What the reader should strive for, then, is a more *active* kind of listening. Whether you listen to Mozart or Duke Ellington, you can deepen your understanding of music only by being a more conscious and aware listener—not someone who is just listening, but someone who is listening *for* something.

                                                                           1957

Lord Clark

THE BLOT AND THE DIAGRAM

I have been told to "look down from a high place over the whole extensive landscape of modern art." We all know how tempting high places can be, and how dangerous. I usually avoid them myself. But if I must do as I am told, I shall try to find out why modern art has taken its peculiar form, and to guess how long that form will continue.

I shall begin with Leonardo da Vinci, because although all processes are gradual, he does represent one clearly marked turning point in the history of art. Before that time, the painter's intentions were quite simple; they were first of all to tell a story, secondly to make the invisible visible, and thirdly to turn a plain surface into a decorated surface. Those are all very ancient aims, going back to the earliest civilizations, or beyond; and for three hundred years painters had been instructed how to carry them out by means of a workshop tradition. Of course, there had been breaks in that tradition—in the fourth century, maybe, and towards the end of the seventh century; but broadly speaking, the artist learnt what he could about the technique of art from his master in his workshop, and then set up shop on his own and tried to do better.

As is well known, Leonardo had a different view of art. He thought that it involved both science and the pursuit of some peculiar attribute called beauty or grace. He was, by inclination, a scientist: he wanted to find out how things worked, and he believed that this knowledge could be stated mathematically. He said "Let no one who is not a mathematician read my works," and he tried to relate this belief in measurement to his belief in beauty. This involved him in two rather different lines of thought, one concerned with magic—the magic of numbers—the other with science. Ever since Pythagoras had discovered that the musical scale could be stated mathematically, by means of the length of the strings, etc., and so had thrown a bridge between intellectual analysis and sensory perception, thinkers on art had felt that it should be possible to do the same for painting. I must say that their effort had not been very rewarding; the modulus, or golden section, and the logarithmic spiral[1] of shells are practically the only undisputed results. But Leonardo lived at a time when it was still possible to hope great things from perspective, which should not only define space, but order it harmoniously; and he also

1. A curve that cuts all its radii at the same angle (the mathematical expression of the shape of snail shells); *golden section:* the division of a line such that the ratio of the smaller to the larger part is the same as that of the larger part to the whole; long regarded as a key to artistic proportion.

inherited a belief that ideal mathematical combinations could be derived from the proportions of the human body. This line of thought may be called the *mystique* of measurement. The other line may be called *the use* of measurement. Leonardo wished to state mathematically various facts related to the act of seeing. How do we see light passing over a sphere? What happens when objects make themselves perceptible on our retina? Both these lines of thought involved him in drawing diagrams and taking measurements, and for this reason were closely related in his mind. No painter except perhaps Piero della Francesca has tried more strenuously to find a mathematical statement of art, nor has had a greater equipment for doing so.

But Leonardo was also a man of powerful and disturbing imagination. In his notebooks, side by side with his attempts to achieve *order* by mathematics, are drawings and descriptions of the most violent scenes of *disorder* which the human mind can conceive—battles, deluges, eruptions. And he included in his treatise on painting advice on how to develop this side of the artistic faculty also. The passages in which he does so have often been quoted, but they are so incredibly foreign to the whole Renaissance idea of art, although related to a remark in Pliny,[2] that each time I read them, they give me a fresh surprise. I will, therefore, quote them again.

> I shall not refrain from including among these precepts a new and speculative idea, which although it may seem trivial and almost laughable, is none the less of great value in quickening the spirit of invention. It is this: that you should look at certain walls stained with damp or at stones of uneven color. If you have to invent some setting you will be able to see in these the likeness of divine landscapes, adorned with mountains, ruins, rocks, woods, great plains, hills and valleys in great variety; and then again you will see there battles and strange figures in violent action, expressions of faces and clothes and an infinity of things which you will be able to reduce to their complete and proper forms. In such walls the same thing happens as in the sound of bells, in whose strokes you may find every named word which you can imagine.

Later he repeats this suggestion in slightly different form, advising the painter to study not only marks on walls, but also "the embers of the fire, or clouds or mud, or other similar objects from which you will find most admirable ideas ... because from a confusion of shapes the spirit is quickened to new inventions."

I hardly need to insist on how relevant these passages are to modern painting. Almost every morning I receive cards inviting me to current exhibitions, and on the cards are photographs of the works exhibited. Some of them consist of blots, some of scrawls, some look like clouds, some like embers of the fire, some are like mud—some of them are mud; a

2. Roman author of the first century A.D., whose comprehensive *Natural History* included a history of painting.

great many look like stains on walls, and one of them, I remember, consisted of actual stains on walls, photographed and framed. Leonardo's famous passage has been illustrated in every particular. And yet I doubt if he would have been satisfied with the results, because he believed that we must somehow unite the two opposite poles of our faculties. Art itself was the connection between the diagram and the blot.

Now in order to prevent the impression that I am taking advantage of a metaphor, as writers on art are often bound to do, I should explain how I am going to use these words. By "diagram" I mean a rational statement in a visible form, involving measurements, and usually done with an ulterior motive. The theorem of Pythagoras is proved by a diagram. Leonardo's drawings of light striking a sphere are diagrams; but the works of Mondrian, although made up of straight lines, are not diagrams, because they are not done in order to prove or measure some experience, but to please the eye. That they look like diagrams is due to influences which I will examine later. But diagrams can exist with no motive other than their own perfection, just as mathematical propositions can.

By "blots" I mean marks or areas which are not intended to convey information, but which, for some reason, seem pleasant and memorable to the maker, and can be accepted in the same sense by the spectator. I said that these blots were not intended to convey information, but of course they do, and that of two kinds. First, they tell us through association, about things we had forgotten; that was the function of Leonardo's stains on walls, which as he said, quickened the spirit of invention, and it can be the function of man-made blots as well; and secondly a man-made blot will tell us about the artist. Unless it is made entirely accidentally, as by spilling an inkpot, it will be a commitment. It is quite difficult to make a noncommittal blot. Although the two are connected, I think we can distinguish between analogy blots and gesture blots.

Now let me try to apply this to modern art. Modern art is not a subject on which one can hope for a large measure of agreement, but I hope I may be allowed two assumptions. The first is that the kind of painting and architecture which we call, with varying inflections of the voice, "modern," is a true and vital expression of our own day; and the second assumption is that it differs radically from any art which has preceded it. Both these assumptions have been questioned. It has been said that modern art is "a racket" engineered by art dealers, who have exploited the incompetence of artists and the gullibility of patrons, that the whole thing is a kind of vast and very expensive practical joke. Well, fifty years is a long time to keep up a hoax of this kind, and during these years modern art has spread all over the free world and created a complete international style. I don't think that any honest-minded historian, whether he liked it or not, could pretend that modern art was the result of an accident or a conspiracy. The only doubt he could have would be whether it is, so to say, a long-term or a short-term movement. In the history of art there are stylistic changes which appear to develop from purely internal causes, and seem almost accidental in relation to the other circumstances of life and society. Such, for example, was the state of art in Italy (outside Venice) from about 1530 to 1600. When all is said about the religious disturbances of the time, the real cause of the Mannerist style[3] was the domination of Michelangelo, who had both created an irresistible style and exhausted its possibilities. It needed the almost equally powerful pictorial imagination of Caravaggio to produce a counter-infection, which could spread from Rome to Spain and the Netherlands and prepare the way for Rembrandt. I can see nothing in the history of man's spirit to account for this episode. It seems to me to be due to an internal and specifically artistic chain of events which are easily related to one another, and comprehensible within the general framework of European art. On the other hand, there are events in the history of art which go far beyond the interaction of styles and which evidently reflect a change in the whole condition of the human spirit. Such an event took place towards the end of the fifth century, when the Hellenistic-Roman style gradually became what we call Byzantine; and again in the early thirteenth century, when the Gothic cathedrals shot up out of the ground. In each case the historian could produce a series of examples to prove that the change was inevitable. But actually, it was nothing of the sort; it was wholly unpredictable; and was part of a complete spiritual revolution.

Whether we think that modern art represents a transformation of style or a change of spirit depends to some extent on my second assumption, that it differs radically from anything which has preceded it. This too has been questioned; it has been said that Léger is only a logical development of Poussin, or Mondrian of Vermeer.[4] And it is true that the element of design in each has something in common. If we pare a Poussin down to its bare bones, there are combinations of curves and cubes which are the foundations of much classical painting, and Léger had the good sense to make use of them. Similarly, in Vermeer there is a use of rectangles, large areas contrasted with very narrow ones, and a feeling for shallow recessions, which became the preferred theme of Mondrian. But such analogies are trifling compared with the differences. Poussin was a very intelligent man who thought deeply about his art, and if anyone had suggested to him that his pictures were praiseworthy solely on account of their construction, he would have been incredulous and affronted.

So let us agree that the kind of painting and architecture which we find most representative of our times—say, the painting of Jackson Pollock

---

3. A late-sixteenth-century style characterized by spatial distortion and elongation of the human figure.
4. Léger and Mondrian: French and Dutch

modern painters, respectively. Poussin, French, and Vermeer, Dutch, were both seventeenth-century painters.

and the architecture of the Lever building[5]—is deeply different from the painting and architecture of the past; and is *not* a mere whim of fashion, but the result of a great change in our ways of thinking and feeling.

How did this great change take place and what does it mean? To begin with, I think it is related to the development upon which all industrial civilization depends, the differentiation of function. Leonardo was exceptional, almost unique in his integration of functions—the scientific and the imaginative. Yet he foreshadowed more than any other artist their disintegration, by noting and treating in isolation the diagrammatic faculty and the blot-making faculty. The average artist took the unity of these faculties for granted. They were united in Leonardo, and in lesser artists, by *interest or pleasure in the thing seen*. The external object was like a magnetic pole which drew the two faculties together. At some point the external object became a negative rather than a positive charge. Instead of drawing together the two faculties, it completely dissociated them; architecture went off in one direction witht he diagram, painting went in the other direction with the blot.

This disintegration was related to a radical change in the philosophy of art. We all know that such changes, however harmless they sound when first enunciated, can have drastic consequences in the world of action. Rulers who wish to maintain the *status quo* are well advised to chop off the heads of all philosophers. What Hilaire Belloc called the "remote and ineffectual don" is more dangerous than the busy columnist with his eye on the day's news. The revolution in our ideas about the nature of painting seems to have been hatched by a don who was considered remote and ineffectual even by Oxford standards—Walter Pater. It was he (inspired, I believe, by Schopenhauer) who first propounded the idea of the aesthetic sensation, intuitively perceived.

> In its primary aspect [Pater said] a great picture has no more difficult message for us than an accidental play of sunlight and shadow for a few moments on the wall or floor; in itself, in truth, a space of such fallen light, caught, as in the colors of an Eastern carpet, but refined upon and dealt with more subtly and exquisitely than by nature itself.

It is true that his comparison with an Eastern carpet admits the possibility of "pleasant sensations" being arranged or organized; and Pater confirms this need for organization a few lines later, when he sets down his famous dictum that "all art constantly aspires towards the condition of music." He does not believe in blots uncontrolled by the conscious mind. But he is very far from the information-giving diagram.

This belief that art has its origin in our intuitive rather than our

5. A severely simple office building in New York City, built in the early 1950s, with plain rectangular sides of glass supported by a stainless-steel framework; *Jackson Pollock:* contemporary who in his "action painting" made frequent use of dribbled or spattered pigments.

rational faculties, picturesquely asserted by Pater, was worked out historically and philosophically, in the somewhat wearisome volumes of Benedetto Croce, and owing to his authoritative tone, he is usually considered the originator of a new theory of aesthetics. It was, in fact, the reversion to a very old idea. Long before the Romantics had stressed the importance of intuition and self-expression, men had admitted the Dionysiac nature of art. But philosophers had always assumed that the frenzy of inspiration must be controlled by law and by the intellectual power of putting things into harmonious order. And this general philosophic concept of art as a combination of intuition and intellect had been supported by technical necessities. It was necessary to master certain laws and to use the intellect in order to build the Gothic cathedrals, or set up the stained glass windows of Chartres or cast the bronze doors of the Florence Baptistry. When this bracing element of craftsmanship ceased to dominate the artist's outlook, as happened soon after the time of Leonardo, new scientific disciplines had to be invented to maintain the intellectual element in art. Such were perspective and anatomy. From a purely artistic point of view, they were unnecessary. The Chinese produced some of the finest landscapes ever painted, without any systematic knowledge of perspective. Greek figure sculpture reached its highest point before the study of anatomy had been systematized. But from the Renaissance onwards, painters felt that these two sciences made their art intellectually respectable. They were two ways of connecting the diagram and the blot.

In the nineteenth century, belief in art as a scientific activity declined, for a quantity of reasons. Science and technology withdrew into specialization. Voltaire's efforts to investigate the nature of heat seem to us ludicrous; Goethe's studies of botany and physics a waste of a great poet's time. In spite of their belief in inspiration, the great Romantics were aware of the impoverishment of the imagination which would take place when science had drifted out of reach, and both Shelley and Coleridge spent much time in chemical experiments. Even Turner, whose letters reveal a singular lack of analytic faculty, annotated Goethe's theories of color, and painted two pictures to demonstrate them. No good. The laws which govern the movement of the human spirit are inexorable. The enveloping assumption, within which the artist has to function, was that science was no longer approachable by any but the specialist. And gradually there grew up the idea that all intellectual activities were hostile to art.

I have mentioned the philosophic development of this view of Croce. Let me give one example of its quiet acceptance by the official mind. The British Council sends all over the world, even to Florence and Rome, exhibitions of children's art—the point of these children's pictures being that they have no instruction of any kind, and do not attempt the troublesome task of painting what they see. Well, why not, after all? The results are quite agreeable—sometimes strangely beautiful; and the therapeutic effect on the children is said to be excellent. It is like one of those small harmless heresies which we are shocked to find were the object of persecution by the Mediaeval Church. When, however, we hear admired modern painters saying that they draw their inspiration from the drawings of children and lunatics, as well as from stains on walls, we recognize that we have accomplices in a revolution.

The lawless and intuitive character of modern art is a familiar theme and certain historians have said that it is symptomatic of a decline in Western civilization. This is journalism—one of those statements that sound well to-day and nonsense to-morrow. It is obvious that the development of physical science in the last hundred years has been one of the most colossal efforts the human intellect has ever made. But I think it is also true that human beings can produce, in a given epoch, only a certain amount of creative energy, and that this is directed to different ends and different times—music in the eighteenth century is the obvious example; and I believe that the dazzling achievements of science during the last seventy years have deflected far more of those skills and endowments which go to the making of a work of art than is usually realized. To begin with, there is the sheer energy. In every molding of a Renaissance palace we are conscious of an immense intellectual energy, and it is the absence of this energy in the nineteenth-century copies of Renaissance buildings which makes them seem so dead. To find a form with the same vitality as a window molding of the Palazzo Farnese I must wait till I get back into an aeroplane, and look at the relation of the engine to the wing. That form is alive, not (as used to be said) because it is functional—many functional shapes are entirely uninteresting—but because it is animated by the breath of modern science.

The deflections from art to science are the more serious because these are not, as used to be supposed, two contrary activities, but in fact draw on many of the same capacities of the human mind. In the last resort each depends on the imagination. Artist and scientist alike are both trying to give concrete form to dimly apprehended ideas. Dr. Bronowski has put it very well: "All science is the search for unity in hidden likenesses, and the starting point is an image, because then the unity is before our mind's eye." Even if we no longer have to pretend that a group of stars looks like a plough or a bear, our scientists still depend on humanly comprehensible images, and it is striking that the valid symbols of our time, invented to embody some scientific truth, have taken root in the popular imagination. Do those red and blue balls connected by rods really resemble a type of atomic structure? I am too ignorant to say. I accept the symbol just as an early Christian accepted the Fish or the Lamb, and I find it echoed or even (it would seem) anticipated in the work of modern artists like

Kandinsky and Miró.

Finally, there is the question of popular interest and approval. We have grown accustomed to the idea that artists can work in solitude and incomprehension; but that was not the way things happened in the Renaissance or the seventeenth century, still less in ancient Greece. The pictures carried through the streets by cheering crowds, the *Te Deum* sung on completion of a public building—all this indicates a state of opinion in which men could undertake great works of art with a confidence quite impossible to-day. The research scientist, on the other hand, not only has millions of pounds worth of plant and equipment for the asking, he has principalities and powers waiting for his conclusions. He goes to work, as Titian once did, confident that he will succeed because the strong tide of popular admiration is flowing with him.

But although science has absorbed so many of the functions of art and deflected (I believe) so many potential artists, it obviously cannot be a *substitute* for art. Its mental process may be similar, but its ends are different. There have been three views about the purpose of art. First that it aims simply at imitation; secondly that it should influence human conduct; and thirdly that it should produce a kind of exalted happiness. The first view, which was developed in ancient Greece, must be reckoned one of the outstanding failures of Greek thought. It is simply contrary to experience, because if the visual arts aimed solely at imitating things they would be of very little importance; whereas the Greeks above all people knew that they were important, and treated them as such. Yet such was the prestige of Greek thought that this theory of art was revived in the Renaissance, in an uncomfortable sort of way, and had a remarkable recrudescence in the nineteenth century. The second view, that art should influence conduct and opinions, is more respectable, and held the field throughout the Middle Ages; indeed the more we learn about the art of the past and motives of those who commissioned it, the more important this particular aim appears to be; it still dominated art theory in the time of Diderot.[6] The third view, that art should produce a kind of exalted happiness, was invented by the Romantics at the beginning of the nineteenth century (well, perhaps *invented* by Plotinus,[7] but given currency by the Romantics), and gradually gained ground until by the end of the century it was believed in by almost all educated people. It has held the field in Western Europe till the present day. Leaving aside the question which of these theories is correct, let me ask which of them is most likely to be a helpful background to art (for that is all that a theory of aesthetics can be) in an age when science has such an overwhelming domination over the human mind. The first aim must be reckoned by *itself* to be pointless, since science has now discovered so many ways of

6. Near the end of the eighteenth century.
7. Roman philosopher of the third century A.D.

imitating appearances, which are incomparably more accurate and convincing than even the most realistic picture. Painting might defend itself against the daguerreotype, but not against Cinerama.

The popular application of science has also, it seems to me, invalidated the second aim of art, because it is quite obvious that no picture can influence human conduct as effectively as a television advertisement. It is quite true that in totalitarian countries artists are still instructed to influence conduct. But that is either due to technical deficiencies, as in China, where in default of T.V., broadsheets and posters are an important way of communicating with an illiterate population; or, in Russia, to a philosophic time-lag. The fact is that very few countries have had the courage to take Plato's advice and exclude works of art altogether. They have, therefore, had to invent some excuse for keeping them on, and the Russians are still using the pretext that paintings and sculpture can influence people in favor of socialist and national policies, although it must have dawned on them that these results can be obtained far more effectively by the cinema and television.

So it seems to me that of these three possible purposes of art—imitation, persuasion, or exalted pleasure—only the third still holds good in an age of science; and it must be justified very largely by the fact that it is a feeling which is absent from scientific achievements—although mathematicians have told us that it is similar to the feeling aroused by their finest calculations. We might say that in the modern world the art of painting is defensible only in so far as it is complementary to science.

We are propelled in the same direction by another achievement of modern science, the study of psychology. That peeling away of the psyche, which was formerly confined to spiritual instructors, or the great novelists, has become a commonplace of conversation. When a good, solid, external word like Duty is turned into a vague, uneasy, internal word like Guilt, one cannot expect artists to take much interest in good, solid, external objects. The artist has always been involved in the painful process of turning himself inside out, but in the past his inner convictions have been of such a kind that they can, so to say, re-form themselves round an object. But, as we have seen, even in Leonardo's time, there were certain obscure needs and patterns of the spirit, which could discover themselves only through less precise analogies—the analogies provided by stains on walls or the embers of a fire. Now, I think that in this inward-looking age, when we have become so much more aware of the vagaries of the spirit, and so respectful of the working of the unconscious, the artist is more likely to find his point of departure in analogies of this kind. They are more exciting because they, so to say, take us by surprise, like forgotten smells; and they seem to be more profound because the memories they awaken have been deeply buried in our minds. Whether Jung is right in believing that this free, undirected, illogical form of mental activity will allow us to pick up, like a magic radio station, some deep memories of our race which can be of universal interest, I do not know. The satisfaction we derive from certain combinations of shape and color does seem to be inexplicable even by the remotest analogies, and may perhaps involve inherited memories. It is not yet time for the art-historian to venture in to that mysterious jungle. I must, however, observe that our respect for the unconscious mind not only gives us an interest in analogy blots, but in what I called "gesture blots" as well. We recognize how free and forceful such a communication can be, and this aspect of art has become more important in the last ten years. An apologist of modern art has said: "What we want to know is not what the world looks like, but what we mean to each other." So the gesture blot becomes a sort of ideogram, like primitive Chinese writing. Students of Zen assure us it is a means of communication more direct and complete than anything which our analytic system can achieve. Almost 2,000 years before Leonardo looked for images in blots, Lao-tzu had written:

> The Tao is something blurred and indistinct.
> How indistinct! How blurred!
> Yet within are images,
> How blurred! How indistinct!
> Yet within are things.

I said that when the split took place between our faculties of measurement and intuition, *architecture* went off with the diagram. Of course architecture had always been involved with measurement and calculation, but we tend to forget how greatly it was also involved with the imitation of external objects. "The question to be determined," said Ruskin, "is whether architecture is a frame for the sculpture, or the sculpture an ornament of the architecture." And he came down on the first alternative. He thought that a building became architecture only in so far as it was a frame for figurative sculpture. I wonder if there is a single person alive who would agree with him. And yet Ruskin had the most sensitive eye and the keenest analytic faculty that has ever been applied to architecture. Many people disagreed with him in his own day; they thought that sculpture should be subordinate to the total design of the building. But that anything claiming to be architecture could dispense with ornament altogether never entered anyone's head till a relatively short time ago.

A purely diagrammatic architecture is only about thirty years older than a purely blottesque painting; yet it has changed the face of the world and produced in every big city a growing uniformity. Perhaps because it is a little older, perhaps because it seems to have a material justification, we have come to accept it without question. People who are still puzzled or affronted by action painting are proud of the great steel and glass boxes which have arisen so miraculously in the last ten years. And yet these two are manifestations of the same state of mind. The same difficulties of function, the same deflection from the external object, and the same triumph of science. Abstract painting and glass box architecture are related in two different ways. There is the direct relationship of style—the kind of relationship which painting and architecture had with one another in the great consistent ages of art like the 13th and 17th centuries. For modern architecture is not simply functional; at its best it has a style which is almost as definite and as arbitrary as Gothic. And this leads me back to my earlier point: that diagrams can be drawn in order to achieve some imagined perfection, similar to that of certain mathematical propositions. Thirty years after Pater's famous dictum, painters in Russia, Holland, and France began to put into practice the theory that "all art constantly aspires to the condition of music"; and curiously enough this Pythagorean mystique of measurements produced a style—the style which reached its purest expression in the Dutch painter, Mondrian. And through the influence of the Bauhaus,[8] this became the leading style of modern architecture.

The other relationship between contemporary architecture and painting appears to be indirect and even accidental. I am thinking of the visual impact when the whole upper part of a tall glass building mirrors the clouds or the dying embers of a sunset, and so becomes a frame for a marvelous, moving Tachiste[9] picture. I do not think that future historians of art will find this accidental at all, but will see it as the culmination of a long process beginning in the Romantic period, in which, from Wordsworth and De Quincey onwards, poets and philosophers recognized the movement of clouds as the symbol of a newly discovered mental faculty.

Such, then, would be my diagnosis of the present condition of art. I must now, by special request, say what I think will happen to art in the future. I think that the state of affairs which I have called the blot and the diagram will last for a long time. Architecture will continue to be made up of glass boxes and steel grids, without ornament of any kind. Painting will continue to be subjective and arcane, an art of accident rather than rule, of stains on walls rather than of calculation, of inscape rather than of external reality.

This conclusion is rejected by those who believe in a social theory of art. They maintain that a living art must depend on the popular will, and that neither the blot nor the diagram is popular; and, since those who hold a social theory of art are usually Marxists, they point to Soviet

8. Architectural school founded in Germany in 1919, known for its applications of technology to art.

9. A method of nonrepresentational contemporary painting which exploits the quality of freely flowing oil paint for its own sake.

Russia as a country where all my conditions obtain—differentiation of function, the domination of science and so forth—and yet what we call modern art has gained no hold. This argument does not impress me. There is of course, nothing at all in the idea that Communist doctrines inevitably produce social realism. Painting in Yugoslavia, in Poland and Hungary is in the same modern idiom as painting in the United States, and shows remarkable vitality. Whereas the official social realism of the U.S.S.R., except for a few illustrators, lacks life or conviction, and shows no evidence of representing the popular will. In fact Russian architecture has already dropped the grandiose official style, and I am told that this is now taking place in painting also. In spite of disapproval amounting to persecution, experimental painters exist and find buyers.

I doubt if the Marxists are even correct in saying that the blot and the diagram are not popular. The power, size, and splendor of, say, the Seagram building in New York makes it as much the object of pride and wonder as great architecture was in the past. And one of the remarkable things about Tachisme is the speed with which it has spread throughout the world, not only in sophisticated centers, but in small local art societies. It has become as much an international style as Gothic in the 14th and Baroque in the 17th centuries. I recently visited the exhibition of a provincial academy in the north of England, a very respectable body then celebrating its hundred and fiftieth anniversary. A few years ago it had been full of Welsh mountain landscapes, and scenes of streets and harbors, carefully delineated. Now practically every picture was in the Tachiste style, and I found that many of them were painted by the same artists, often quite elderly people, who had previously painted the mountains and streets. As works of art, they seemed to me neither better nor worse. But I could not help thinking that they must have been less trouble to do, and I reflected that the painters must have had a happy time releasing the Dionysiac elements in their natures. However, we must not be too cynical about this. I do not believe that the spread of action painting is due solely to the fact that it is easy to do. Cubism,[1] especially synthetic Cubism, also looks easy to do, and never had this immense diffusion. It remained the style of a small élite of professional painters and specialized art lovers; whereas Tachisme has spread to fabrics, to the decoration of public buildings, to the backgrounds of television programs, to advertising of all kinds. Indeed the closest analogy to action painting is the most popular art of all—the art of jazz. The trumpeter who rises from his seat as one possessed, and squirts out his melody like a scarlet scrawl against a background of plangent dashes and dots, is not as a rule performing for a small body of intellectuals.

Nevertheless, I do not think that the style of the blot and the diagram

---

1. School of modern art emphasizing abstract geometric forms rather than realistic representation.

will last forever. For one thing, I believe that the imitation of external reality is a fundamental human instinct which is bound to reassert itself. In his admirable book on sculpture called *Aratra Pentelici*, Ruskin describes an experience which many of us could confirm. "Having been always desirous," he says,

> that the education of women should begin in learning how to cook, I got leave, one day, for a little girl of eleven years old to exchange, much to her satisfaction, her schoolroom for the kitchen. But as ill fortune would have it, there was some pastry toward, and she was left unadvisedly in command of some delicately rolled paste; whereof she made no pies, but an unlimited quantity of cats and mice. . . .
>
> Now [he continues] you may read the works of the gravest critics of art from end to end; but you will find, at last, they can give you no other true account of the spirit of sculpture than that it is an irresistible human instinct for the making of cats and mice, and other imitable living creatures, in such permanent form that one may play with the images at leisure.

I cannot help feeling that he was right. I am fond of works of art, and I collect them. But I do not want to hang them on the wall simply in order to get an electric shock every time that I pass them. I want to hold them, and turn them round and re-hang them—in short, to play with the images at leisure. And, putting aside what may be no more than a personal prejudice, I rather doubt if an art which depends solely on the first impact on our emotions is permanently valid. When the shock is exhausted, we have nothing to occupy our minds. And this is particularly troublesome with an art which depends so much on the unconscious, because, as we know from the analysis of dreams, the furniture of our unconscious minds is even more limited, repetitive, and commonplace than that of our conscious minds. The blots and stains of modern painting depend ultimately on the memories of things seen, memories sunk deep in the unconscious, overlaid, transformed, assimilated to a physical condition, but memories none the less. *Ex nihilo nihil fit.*[2] It is not possible for a painter to lose contact with the visible world.

At this point the apes have provided valuable evidence. There is no doubt that they are Tachiste painters of considerable accomplishment. I do not myself care for the work of Congo the chimp, but Sophie, the Rotterdam gorilla, is a charming artist, whose delicate traceries remind me of early Paul Klee. As you know, apes take their painting seriously. The patterns they produce are not the result of mere accident, but of intense, if short-lived, concentration, and a lively sense of balance and space-filling. If you compare the painting of a young ape with that of a human child of relatively the same age, you will find that in the first, expressive, pattern-making stage, the ape is superior. Then, automati-

2. "Nothing is made from nothing."

cally and inexorably the child begins to draw *things*—man, house, truck, etc. This the ape never does. Of course his Tachiste paintings are far more attractive than the child's crude conceptual outlines. But they cannot develop. They are monotonous and ultimately rather depressing.

The difference between the child and the ape does not show itself in aesthetic perception, or in physical perception of any kind, but in the child's power to form a concept. Later, as we know, he will spend his time trying to adapt his concept to the evidence of physical sensation; in that struggle lies the whole of style. But the concept—the need to draw a line round his thought—comes first. Now it is a truism that the power to form concepts is what distinguishes man from the animals; although the prophets of modern society, Freud, Jung, D. H. Lawrence, have rightly insisted on the importance of animal perceptions in balanced human personality, the concept-forming faculty has not declined in modern man. On the contrary, it is the basis of that vast scientific achievement which, as I said earlier, seems almost to have put art out of business.

Now, if the desire to represent external reality depended solely on an interest in visual sensation, I would agree that it might disappear from art and never return. But if, as the evidence of children and monkeys indicates, it depends primarily on the formation of concepts, which are then modified by visual sensation, I think it is bound to return. For I consider the human faculty of forming concepts at least as "inalienable" as "life, liberty, and the pursuit of happiness. . . ."

I am not, of course, suggesting that the imitation of external reality will ever again become what it was in European art from the mid-17th to the late 19th centuries. Such a subordination of the concept to the visual sensation was altogether exceptional in the history of art. Much of the territory won by modern painting will, I believe, be held. For example, freedom of association, the immediate passage from one association to another—which is so much a part of Picasso's painting and Henry Moore's sculpture, is something which has existed in music since Wagner and in poetry since Rimbaud and Mallarmé. (I mean existed consciously; of course it underlies all great poetry and music.) It need not be sacrificed in a return to external reality. Nor need the direct communication of intuition, through touch and an instinctive sense of materials. This I consider pure gain. In the words of my original metaphor, both the association blot and the gesture blot can remain. But they must be given more nourishment: they must be related to a fuller knowledge of the forms and structures which impress us most powerfully, and so become part of our concept of natural order. At the end of the passage in which Leonardo tells the painter that he can look for battles, landscapes, and animals in the stains on walls, he adds this caution, "But first be sure that you know all the members of all things you wish to depict, both the members of the animals and the members of landscapes, that is to say of rocks, plants, and so forth." It is because one feels in Henry Moore's sculpture this knowledge of the members of animals and plants, that his work, even at its most abstract, makes an impression on us different from that of his imitators. His figures are not merely pleasing examples of design, but seem to be a part of nature, "rolled round in Earth's diurnal course with rocks and stones and trees."

Those lines of Wordsworth lead me to the last reason why I feel that the intuitive blot and scribble may not dominate painting forever. Our belief in the whole purpose of art may change. I said earlier that we now believe it should aim at producing a kind of exalted happiness: this really means that art becomes an end in itself. Now it is an incontrovertible fact of history that the greatest art has always been *about* something, a means of communicating some truth which is assumed to be more important than the art itself. The truths which art has been able to communicate have been of a kind which could not be put in any other way. They have been ultimate truths, stated symbolically. Science has achieved its triumph precisely by disregarding such truths, by not asking unanswerable questions, but sticking to the question "how." I confess it looks to me as if we shall have to wait a long time before there is some new belief which requires expression through art rather than through statistics or equations. And until this happens, the visual arts will fall short of the greatest epochs, the ages of the Parthenon, the Sistine Ceiling, and Chartres Cathedral.

I am afraid there is nothing we can do about it. No amount of goodwill and no expenditure of money can affect that sort of change. We cannot even dimly foresee when it will happen or what form it will take. We can only be thankful for what we have got—a vigorous, popular, decorative art, complementary to our architecture and our science, somewhat monotonous, somewhat prone to charlatanism, but genuinely expressive of our time.

1963

THE READER

1. *What definition does Clark give of his central metaphor, "the blot and the diagram"? Are "blot" and "diagram" the equivalents of "art" and "science"? Explain.*
2. *What distinction does Clark make between "analogy [or association] blots" and "gesture blots"? What importance does the distinction have for his discussion of modern painting?*
3. *In what ways, according to Clark, is the place of science in the modern world similar to the place occupied by science in the past? What past functions of art has science assumed? To what extent does Clark consider the situation satisfactory? What defects does he mention?*
4. *How does Clark show "blot" painting and "diagram" architecture to be related? Is architecture today an art or a science? How scientific is*

painting?
5. *Why, according to Clark, will humankind's concept-forming nature eventually bring about a change of style in art?*

THE WRITER

1. *What purpose does Clark's first paragraph serve?*
2. *Study closely some examples of advertising. To what extent do they appear influenced by "blot"? Is there influence of "diagram" in any? Are any exemplary of "blot" and "diagram" in harmony? Write a brief summary of your conclusions.*
3. *Clark points out that "the closest analogy to action painting is the most popular art of all—the art of jazz" (p. 1094). Is there any jazz analogous to "diagram"? Explain in a brief essay.*
4. *What extensions into other disciplines can be made of Clark's blot-diagram antithesis? Write a brief essay testing its application to another field such as literature, psychology, or biology.*

Joan Didion

GEORGIA O'KEEFFE

"Where I was born and where and how I have lived is unimportant," Georgia O'Keeffe told us in the book of paintings and words published in her ninetieth year on earth. She seemed to be advising us to forget the beautiful face in the Stieglitz photographs. She appeared to be dismissing the rather condescending romance that had attached to her by then, the romance of extreme good looks and advanced age and deliberate isolation. "It is what I have done with where I have been that should be of interest." I recall an August afternoon in Chicago in 1973 when I took my daughter, then seven, to see what Georgia O'Keeffe had done with where she had been. One of the vast O'Keeffe "Sky Above Clouds" canvases floated over the back stairs in the Chicago Art Institute that day, dominating what seemed to be several stories of empty light, and my daughter looked at it once, ran to the landing, and kept on looking. "Who drew it," she whispered after a while. I told her. "I need to talk to her," she said finally.

My daughter was making, that day in Chicago, an entirely unconscious but quite basic assumption about people and the work they do. She was assuming that the glory she saw in the work reflected a glory in its maker, that the painting was the painter as the poem is the poet, that every choice one made alone—every word chosen or rejected, every brush stroke laid or not laid down—betrayed one's character. *Style is character.*

It seemed to me that afternoon that I had rarely seen so instinctive an application of this familiar principle, and I recall being pleased not only that my daughter responded to style as character but that it was Georgia O'Keeffe's particular style to which she responded: this was a hard woman who had imposed her 192 square feet of clouds on Chicago.

"Hardness" has not been in our century a quality much admired in women, nor in the past twenty years has it even been in official favor for men. When hardness surfaces in the very old we tend to transform it into "crustiness" or eccentricity, some tonic pepperiness to be indulged at a distance. On the evidence of her work and what she has said about it, Georgia O'Keeffe is neither "crusty" nor eccentric. She is simply hard, a straight shooter, a woman clean of received wisdom and open to what she sees. This is a woman who could early on dismiss most of her contemporaries as "dreamy," and would later single out one she liked as "a very poor painter." (And then add, apparently by way of softening the judgment: "I guess he wasn't a painter at all. He had no courage and I believe that to create one's own world in any of the arts takes courage.") This is a woman who in 1939 could advise her admirers that they were missing her point, that their appreciation of her famous flowers was merely sentimental. "When I paint a red hill," she observed coolly in the catalogue for an exhibition that year, "you say it is too bad that I don't always paint flowers. A flower touches almost everyone's heart. A red hill doesn't touch everyone's heart." This is a woman who could describe the genesis of one of her most well-known paintings—the "Cow's Skull: Red, White and Blue" owned by the Metropolitan—as an act of quite deliberate and derisive orneriness. "I thought of the city men I had been seeing in the East," she wrote. "They talked so often of writing the Great American Novel—the Great American Play—the Great American Poetry. . . . So as I was painting my cow's head on blue I thought to myself, 'I'll make it an American painting. They will not think it great with the red stripes down the sides—Red, White and Blue—but they will notice it.'"

The city men. The men. They. The words crop up again and again as this astonishingly aggressive woman tells us what was on her mind when she was making her astonishingly aggressive paintings. It was those city men who stood accused of sentimentalizing her flowers: "I made you take time to look at what I saw and when you took time to really notice my flower you hung all your associations with flowers on my flower and you write about my flower as if I think and see what you think and see—and I don't." *And I don't.* Imagine those words spoken, and the sound you hear is *don't tread on me.* "The men" believed it impossible to paint New York, so Georgia O'Keeffe painted New York. "The men" didn't think much of her bright color, so she made it brighter. The men yearned toward Europe so she went to Texas, and then New Mexico. The men talked about Cézanne, "long involved remarks about the 'plastic quality' of his form and color," and took one another's long involved remarks, in the view of this angelic rattlesnake in their midst, altogether too seriously. "I can paint one of those dismal-colored paintings like the men," the woman who regarded herself always as an outsider remembers thinking one day in 1922, and she did: a painting of a shed "all low-toned and dreary with the tree beside the door." She called this act of rancor "The Shanty" and hung it in her next show. "The men seemed to approve of it," she reported fifty-four years later, her contempt undimmed. "They seemed to think that maybe I was beginning to paint. That was my only low-toned dismal-colored painting."

Some women fight and others do not. Like so many successful guerrillas in the war between the sexes, Georgia O'Keeffe seems to have been equipped early with an immutable sense of who she was and a fairly clear understanding that she would be required to prove it. On the surface her upbringing was conventional. She was a child on the Wisconsin prairie who played with china dolls and painted watercolors with cloudy skies because sunlight was too hard to paint and, with her brother and sisters, listened every night to her mother read stories of the Wild West, of Texas, of Kit Carson and Billy the Kid. She told adults that she wanted to be an artist and was embarrassed when they asked what kind of artist she wanted to be: she had no idea "what kind." She had no idea what artists did. She had never seen a picture that interested her, other than a pen-and-ink Maid of Athens in one of her mother's books, some Mother Goose illustrations printed on cloth, a tablet cover that showed a little girl with pink roses, and the painting of Arabs on horseback that hung in her grandmother's parlor. At thirteen, in a Dominican convent, she was mortified when the sister corrected her drawing. At Chatham Episcopal Institute in Virginia she painted lilacs and sneaked time alone to walk out to where she could see the line of the Blue Ridge Mountains on the horizon. At the Art Institute in Chicago she was shocked by the presence of live models and wanted to abandon anatomy lessons. At the Art Students League in New York one of her fellow students advised her that, since he would be a great painter and she would end up teaching painting in a girls' school, any work of hers was less important than modeling for him. Another painted over her work to show her how the Impressionists did trees. She had not before heard how the Impressionists did trees and she did not much care.

At twenty-four she left all those opinions behind and went for the first time to live in Texas, where there were no trees to paint and no one to tell her how not to paint them. In Texas there was only the horizon she craved. In Texas she had her sister Claudia with her for a while, and in the late afternoons they would walk away from town and toward the horizon and watch the evening star come out. "That evening star fascinated me," she wrote. "It was in some way very exciting to me. My sister had a gun, and as we walked she would throw bottles into the air and shoot as many as she could before they hit the ground. I had nothing but to walk into nowhere and the wide sunset space with the star. Ten watercolors were made from that star." In a way one's interest is compelled as much by the sister Claudia with the gun as by the painter Georgia with the star, but only the painter left us this shining record. Ten watercolors were made from that star.

1971

THE READER

1. What does Didion mean when she says her daughter assumed "that the painting was the painter as the poem is the poet"?
2. Didion records her daughter's assumption about "people and the work they do. . . . Style is character" (p. 1098). Would Gaylin (p. 664) agree? Does Didion herself agree?
3. "Angelic rattlesnake" is an arresting phrase. Define it from the essay.
4. O'Keeffe used terms like "the city men," "the men," and "they" to describe her audience. What does this show about her beliefs and practice as an artist?
5. How was O'Keeffe one of the "many successful guerrillas in the war between the sexes"?
6. What is the significance of the anecdote with which Didion ends her sketch?

THE WRITER

1. Didion talks about the "familiar principle" that "style is character." How much of Didion's character can you deduce from the style of her essay? Is that deduction confirmed in her other essays "On Going Home" (p. 69), "Salvador" (p. 464), and "On Keeping a Notebook" (p. 731)?
2. O'Keeffe put some distance between herself and the audience for her paintings because she felt the need to develop her own view of the things she painted. Does the writer need a similar distance to develop an original style? Is the process of communication different in painting than in writing?
3. Does Didion seem to have any principle for selecting the details about O'Keeffe's life and career that she does?
4. How can you tell that Didion admires O'Keeffe? How does she amplify her admiration? What does it show about Didion? Is what it shows about Didion confirmed in other essays by Didion?
5. Write a few sentences that would explain why "one's interest is compelled . . . by the sister Claudia with the gun." Then write the logical transition from these sentences back to Didion's concluding point.
6. Write a brief biographical sketch, using Didion's as a model. First determine a dominant impression of the person that you wish to convey, and then choose your details to support that impression.

Prose Forms: Parables

When we read a short story or a novel, we are less interested in the working out of ideas than in the working out of characters and their destinies. In Dickens' Great Expectations, *for example, Pip, the hero, undergoes many triumphs and defeats in his pursuit of success, only to learn finally that he has expected the wrong things, or the right things for the wrong reasons; that the great values in life are not always to be found in what the world calls success. In realizing this meaning we entertain, with Dickens, certain concepts or ideas that organize and evaluate the life in the novel, and that ultimately we apply to life generally. Ideas are there not to be exploited discursively, but to be understood as the perspective which shapes the direction of the novel and our view of its relation to life.*

When ideas in their own reality are no longer the primary interest in writing, we have obviously moved from expository to other forms of prose. The shift need not be abrupt and complete, however; there is an area where the discursive interest in ideas and the narrative interest in characters and events blend. In allegory, for example, abstract ideas are personified. "Good Will" or "Peace" may be shown as a young woman, strong, confident, and benevolent in her bearing but vulnerable, through her sweet reasonableness, to the single-minded, fierce woman who is "Dissension." Our immediate interest is in their behavior as characters, but our ultimate interest is in the working out, through them, of the ideas they represent. We do not ask that the characters and events be entirely plausible in relation to actual life, as we do for the novel; we are satisfied if they are consistent with the nature of the ideas that define their vitality.

Ideas themselves have vitality, a mobile and dynamic life with a behavior of its own. The title of the familiar Negro spiritual "Sometimes I Feel Like a Motherless Child," to choose a random instance, has several kinds of "motion" as an idea. The qualitative identity of an adult's feelings and those of a child; the whole burgeoning possibility of all that the phrase "motherless child" can mean; the subtle differences in meaning—the power of context—that occur when it is a black who feels this and when it is a white; the speculative possibilities of the title as social commentary or psychological analysis—these suggest something of the "life" going on in and around the idea. Definition, analogy, assumption, implication, context, illustration are some of the familiar terms we use to describe this kind of life.

There is, of course, another and more obvious kind of vitality which an idea has: its applicability to the affairs of people in everyday life. Both the kind and extent of an idea's relevance are measures of this vitality. When an essayist wishes to exploit both the life in an idea and the life it comprehends, he or she often turns to narration, because there one sees the advantage of lifelike characters and events, and of showing through them the liveliness of ideas in both the senses we have noted. Ideas about life can be illustrated in life. And, besides, people like stories. The writer's care must be to keep the reader's interest focused on the ideas, rather than on the life itself; otherwise, he or she has ceased being essentially the essayist and has become the short-story writer or novelist.

The parable and the moral fable are ideal forms for this purpose. In both, the idea is the heart of the composition; in both the ideas usually assume the form of a lesson about life, some moral truth of general consequence; and in both there are characters and actions. Jesus often depended on parables in his teaching. Simple, economical, pointed, the parables developed a "story," but more importantly, applied a moral truth to experience. Peter asked Jesus how often he must forgive the brother who sins against him, and Jesus answered with the parable of the king and his servants, one of whom asked and got forgiveness of the king for his debts but who would not in turn forgive a fellow servant his debt. The king, on hearing of this harshness, retracted his own benevolence and punished the unfeeling servant. Jesus concluded to Peter, "So likewise shall my heavenly Father do also unto you, if ye from your hearts forgive not every one his brother their trespasses." But before this direct drawing of the parallel, the lesson was clear in the outline of the narrative.

Parables usually have human characters; fables often achieve a special liveliness with animals or insects. Swift, in "The Spider and the Bee," narrates the confrontation of a comically humanized spider and bee who debate the merits of their natures and their usefulness in the world of experience. The exchange between the two creatures is brilliantly and characteristically set out, but by its end, the reader realizes that extraordinary implications about the nature of art, of education, of human psychological and intellectual potential have been the governing idea all along.

The writer will be verging continually on strict prose narrative in writing the parable or fable, but through skill and tact he or she can preserve the essayist's essential commitment to the definition and development of ideas in relation to experience.

Aesop: THE FROGS DESIRING A KING

The frogs always had lived a happy life in the marshes. They had jumped and splashed about with never a care in the world. Yet some of them were not satisfied with their easygoing life. They thought they should have a king to rule over them and to watch over their morals. So they decided to send a petition to Jupiter[1] asking him to appoint a king.

Jupiter was amused by the frogs' plea. Good-naturedly he threw down a log into the lake, which landed with such a splash that it sent all the frogs scampering for safety. But after a while, when one venturesome frog saw that the log lay still, he encouraged his friends to approach the fallen monster. In no time at all the frogs, growing bolder and bolder, swarmed over the log Jupiter had sent and treated it with the greatest contempt.

Dissatisfied with so tame a ruler, they petitioned Jupiter a second time, saying: "We want a real king, a king who will really rule over us." Jupiter, by this time, had lost some of his good nature and was tired of the frogs' complaining.

So he sent them a stork, who proceeded to gobble up the frogs right and left. After a few days the survivors sent Mercury[2] with a private message to Jupiter, beseeching him to take pity on them once more.

"Tell them," said Jupiter coldly, "that this is their own doing. They wanted a king. Now they will have to make the best of what they asked for."

Moral: Let well enough alone!

1. The king of the gods.　　　　2. The messenger of the gods.

Plato: THE ALLEGORY OF THE CAVE

And now, I said, let me show in a figure how far our nature is enlightened or unenlightened: Behold! human beings living in an underground den, which has a mouth open towards the light and reaching all along the den; here they have been from their childhood, and have their legs and necks chained so that they cannot move, and can only see before them, being prevented by the chains from turning round their heads. Above and behind them a fire is blazing at a distance, and between the fire and the prisoners there is a raised way; and you will see, if you look, a low wall built along the way, like the screen which marionette players have in front of them, over which they show the puppets.

I see.

And do you see, I said, men passing along the wall carrying all sorts of vessels, and statues and figures of animals made of wood and stone and various materials, which appear over the wall? Some of them are talking, others silent.

You have shown me a strange image, and they are strange prisoners.

Like ourselves, I replied; and they see only their own shadows, or the shadows of one another, which the fire throws on the opposite wall of the cave?

True, he said; how could they see anything but the shadows if they were never allowed to move their heads?

And of the objects which are being carried in like manner they would only see the shadows?

Yes, he said.

And if they were able to converse with one another, would they not suppose that they were naming what was actually before them?

Very true.

And suppose further that the prison had an echo which came from the other side, would they not be sure to fancy when one of the passers-by spoke that the voice which they heard came from the passing shadow?

No question, he replied.

To them, I said, the truth would be literally nothing but the shadows of the images.

That is certain.

And now look again, and see what will naturally follow if the prisoners are released and disabused of their error. At first, when any of them is liberated and compelled suddenly to stand up and turn his neck round and walk and look towards the light, he will suffer sharp pains; the glare will distress him and he will be unable to see the realities of which in his former state he had seen the shadows; and then conceive some one saying to him, that what he saw before was an illusion, but that now, when he is approaching nearer to being and his eye is turned towards more real existence, he has a clearer vision—what will be his reply? And you may further imagine that his instructor is pointing to the objects as they pass and requiring him to name them—will he not be perplexed? Will he not fancy that the shadows which he formerly saw are truer than the objects which are now shown to him?

Far truer.

And if he is compelled to look straight at the light, will he not have a pain in his eyes which will make him turn away to take refuge in the objects of vision which he can see, and which he will conceive to be in reality clearer than the things which are now being shown to him?

True, he said.

And suppose once more, that he is reluctantly dragged up a steep and rugged ascent, and held fast until he is forced into the presence of the sun himself, is he not likely to be pained and irritated? When he approaches the light his eyes will be dazzled and he will not be able to see anything at all of what are now called realities.

Not all in a moment, he said.

He will require to grow accustomed to the sight of the upper world. And first he will see the shadows best, next the reflections of men and other objects in the water, and then the objects themselves; then he will gaze upon the light of the moon and the stars and the spangled heaven; and he will see the sky and the stars by night better than the sun or the light of the sun by day?

Certainly.

Last of all he will be able to see the sun, and not mere reflections of him in the water, but he will see him in his own proper place, and not in another; and he will contemplate him as he is.

Certainly.

He will then proceed to argue that this is he who gives the season and the years, and is the guardian of all that is in the visible world, and in a certain way the cause of all things which he and his fellows have been accustomed to behold?

Clearly, he said, he would first see the sun and then reason about him.

And when he remembered his old habitation, and the wisdom of the den and his fellow-prisoners, do you not suppose that he would felicitate himself on the change, and pity them?

Certainly, he would.

And if they were in the habit of conferring honors among themselves on those who were quickest to observe the passing shadows and to remark which of them went before, and which followed after, and which were together; and who were therefore best able to draw conclusions as to the future, do you think that he would care for such honors and glories, or envy the possessors of them? Would he not say with Homer,

Better to be the poor servant of a poor master,

and to endure anything, rather than think as they do and live after their manner?

Yes, he said, I think that he would rather suffer anything than entertain these false notions and live in this miserable manner.

Imagine once more, I said, such an one coming suddenly out of the sun to be replaced in his old situation; would he not be certain to have his eyes full of darkness?

To be sure, he said.

And if there were a contest, and he had to compete in measuring the shadows with the prisoners who had never moved out of the den, while his sight was still weak, and before his eyes had become steady (and the time which would be needed to acquire this new habit of sight might be very considerable) would he not be ridiculous? Men would say of him that up he went and down he came without his eyes; and that it was better not even to think of ascending; and if any one tried to loose another and lead him up to the light, let them only catch the offender, and they would put him to death.

No question, he said.

This entire allegory, I said, you may now append, dear Glaucon, to the previous argument, the prison-house is the world of sight, the light of the fire is the sun, and you will not misapprehend me if you interpret the journey upwards to be the ascent of the soul into the intellectual world according to my poor belief, which, at your desire, I have expressed— whether rightly or wrongly God knows. But, whether true or false, my opinion is that in the world of knowledge the idea of good appears last of all, and is seen only with an effort; and, when seen, is also inferred to be the universal author of all things beautiful and right, parent of light and of the lord of light in this visible world, and the immediate source of reason and truth in the intellectual; and that this is the power upon which he who would act rationally either in public or private life must have his eye fixed.

I agree, he said, as far as I am able to understand you.

Moreover, I said, you must not wonder that those who attain to this beatific vision are unwilling to descend to human affairs; for their souls are ever hastening into the upper world where they desire to dwell; which desire of theirs is very natural, if our allegory may be trusted.

Yes, very natural.

And is there anything surprising in one who passes from divine contemplations to the evil state of man, misbehaving himself in a ridiculous manner; if, while his eyes are blinking and before he has become accustomed to the surrounding darkness, he is compelled to fight in courts of law, or in other places, about the images or the shadows of images of justice, and is endeavouring to meet the conceptions of those who have never yet seen absolute justice?

Anything but surprising, he replied.

Any one who has common sense will remember that the bewilderments of the eyes are of two kinds, and arise from two causes, either from coming out of the light or from going into the light, which is true of the mind's eye, quite as much as of the bodily eye; and he who remembers this when he sees any one whose vision is perplexed and weak, will not be too ready to laugh; he will first ask whether that soul of man has come out of the brighter life, and is unable to see because unaccustomed to the dark, or having turned from darkness to the day is dazzled by excess of light. And he will count the one happy in his condition and state of being, and he will pity the other; or, if he have a mind to laugh at the soul which comes from below into the light, there will be more reason in this than in the laugh which greets him who returns from above out of the light into the den.

That, he said, is a very just distinction.

4th century B.C.

Jesus: PARABLES OF THE KINDGOM[1]

Then shall the kingdom of heaven be likened unto ten virgins, which took their lamps, and went forth to meet the bridegroom.

And five of them were wise, and five were foolish.

They that were follish took their lamps, and took no oil with them:

But the wise took oil in their vessels with their lamps.

While the bridegroom tarried, they all slumbered and slept.

And at midnight there was a cry made, Behold, the bridegroom cometh; go ye out to meet him.

Then all those virgins arose, and trimmed their lamps.

And the foolish said unto the wise, Give us of your oil; for our lamps are gone out.

But the wise answered, saying Not so; lest there be not enough for us and you: but go ye rather to them that sell, and buy for yourselves.

And while they went to buy, the bridgroom came; and they that were ready went in with him to the marriage: and the door was shut.

Afterward came also the other virgins, saying, Lord, Lord, open to us.

But he answered and said, Verily I say unto you, I know you not.

Watch therefore, for ye know neither the day nor the hour wherein the Son of man cometh.

For the kingdom of heaven is as a man travelling into a far country, who called his own servants, and delivered unto them his goods.

And unto one he gave five talents, to another two, and to another one; to every man according to his several ability; and straightway took his journey.

Then he that had received the five talents went and traded with the same, and made them other five talents.

And likewise he that had received two, he also gained other two.

1. From Jesus' sayings to his disciples on the Mount of Olives, as reported in Matthew xxv.

But he that had received one went and digged in the earth, and hid his lord's money.

After a long time the lord of those servants cometh, and reckoneth with them.

And so he that had received five talents came and brought other five talents, saying, Lord, thou deliveredst unto me five talents: behold, I have gained beside them five talents more.

His lord said unto him, Well done, *thou* good and faithful servant: thou hast been faithful over a few things, I will make thee ruler over many things: enter thou into the joy of thy lord.

He also that had received two talents came and said, Lord, thou deliverdst unto me two talents: behold, I have gained two other talents beside them.

His lord said unto him, Well done, good and faithful servant; thou hast been faithful over a few things, I will make thee ruler over many things: enter thou into the joy of thy lord.

Then he which had received the one talent came and said, Lord, I knew thee that thou art an hard man, reaping where thou hast not sown, and gathering where thou hast not strawed:

And I was afraid, and went and hid thy talent in the earth: lo, *there* thou hast *that is* thine.

His lord answered and said unto him, *Thou* wicked and slothful servant, thou knewest that I reap where I sowed not, and gather where I have not strawed:

Thou oughtest therefore to have put my money to the exchanges, and *then* at my coming I should have received mine own with usury.

Take therefore the talent from him, and give *it* unto him which hath ten talents.

For unto every one that hath shall be given, and he shall have abundance: but from him that hath not shall be taken away even that which he hath.

And cast ye the unprofitable servant into outer darkness: there shall be weeping and gnashing of teeth.

When the Son of man shall come in his glory, and all the holy angels with him, then shall he sit upon the throne of his glory:

And before him shall be gathered all nations: and he shall separate them one from another, as a shepherd divideth *his* sheep from the goats:

And he shall set the sheep on his right hand, but the goats on the left.

Then shall the King say unto them on his right hand, Come, ye blessed of my Father, inherit the kingdom prepared for you from the foundation of the world:

For I was an hungred, and ye gave me meat: I was thirsty, and ye gave me drink: I was a stranger, and ye took me in:

Naked, and ye clothed me: I was sick, and ye visited me: I was in prison, and ye came unto me.

Then shall the righteous answer him, saying, Lord, when saw we thee an hungred, and fed *thee?* or thirsty, and gave *thee* drink?

When saw we thee a stranger, and took *thee* in? or naked, and clothed thee?

Or when saw we thee sick, or in prison, and came unto thee?

And the King shall answer and say unto them, Verily I say unto you, Inasmuch as ye have done *it* unto one of the least of these my brethren, ye have done *it* unto me.

Then shall he say also unto them on the left hand, Depart from me, ye cursed, into everlasting fire, prepared for the devil and his angels:

For I was an hungred, and ye gave me no meat: I was thirsty, and ye gave me no drink.

I was a stranger, and ye took me not in: naked, and ye clothed me not: sick, and in prison, and ye visited me not.

Then shall they also answer him, saying, Lord, when saw we thee an hungred, or athirst, or a stranger, or naked, or sick, or in prison, and did not minister unto thee?

Then shall he answer them, saying, Verily I say unto you, Inasmuch as ye did *it* not to one of the least of these, ye did *it* not to me.

And these shall go away into everlasting punishment: but the righteous into life eternal.

ZEN PARABLES

Muddy Road

Tanzan and Ekido were once traveling together down a muddy road. A heavy rain was still falling.

Coming around a bend, they met a lovely girl in a silk kimono and sash, unable to cross the intersection.

"Come on, girl," said Tanzan at once. Lifting her in his arms, he carried her over the mud.

Ekido did not speak again until that night when they reached a lodging temple. Then he no longer could restrain himself. "We monks don't go near females," he told Tanzan, "especially not young and lovely ones. It is dangerous. Why did you do that?"

"I left the girl there," said Tanzan. "Are you still carrying her?"

A Parable

Buddha told a parable in a sutra:

A man traveling across a field encountered a tiger. He fled, the tiger after him. Coming to a precipice, he caught hold of the root of a wild vine and swung himself down over the edge. The tiger sniffed at him from above. Trembling, the man looked down to where, far below, another tiger was waiting to eat him. Only the vine sustained him.

Two mice, one white and one black, little by little started to gnaw away the vine. The man saw a luscious strawberry near him. Grasping the vine with one hand, he plucked the strawberry with the other. How sweet it tasted!

Learning to Be Silent

The pupils of the Tendai school used to study meditation before Zen entered Japan. Four of them who were intimate friends promised one another to observe seven days of silence.

On the first day all were silent. Their meditation had begun auspiciously, but when night came and the oil lamps were growing dim one of the pupils could not help exclaiming to a servant: "Fix those lamps."

The second pupil was surprised to hear the first one talk. "We are not supposed to say a word," he remarked.

"You two are stupid. Why did you talk?" asked the third.

"I am the only one who has not talked," concluded the fourth pupil.

Jonathan Swift: THE SPIDER AND THE BEE

Things were at this crisis, when a material accident fell out. For, upon the highest corner of a large window, there dwelt a certain spider, swollen up to the first magnitude by the destruction of infinite numbers of flies, whose spoils lay scattered before the gates of his palace, like human bones before the cave of some giant. The avenues of his castle were guarded with turnpikes and palisadoes, all after the modern way of fortification. After you had passed several courts, you came to the center, wherein you might behold the constable himself in his own lodgings, which had windows fronting to each avenue, and ports to sally out upon all occasions of prey or defense. In this mansion he had for some time dwelt in peace and plenty, without danger to his person by swallows from above, or to his palace by brooms from below, when it was the pleasure of fortune to conduct thither a wandering bee, to whose curiosity a broken pane in the glass had discovered itself, and in he went; where expatiating a while, he at last happened to alight upon one of the outward walls of the spider's citadel; which, yielding to the unequal weight, sunk down to the very foundation. Thrice he endeavored to force his passage, and thrice the center shook. The spider within, feeling the terrible convulsion, supposed at first that nature was approaching to her final dissolution; or else that Beelzebub,[1] with all his legions, was come to revenge the death of many thousands of his subjects, whom his enemy had slain and devoured. However, he at length valiantly resolved to issue forth, and meet his fate. Meanwhile the bee had acquitted himself of his toils, and posted securely at some distance, was employed in cleansing his wings, and disengaging them from the ragged remnants of the cobweb. By this time the spider was adventured out, when beholding the chasms, and ruins, and dilapidations of his fortress, he was very near at his wit's end; he stormed and swore like a madman, and swelled till he was ready to burst. At length, casting his eye upon the bee, and wisely gathering causes from events (for they knew each other by sight), "A plague split you," said he, "for a giddy son of a whore. Is it you, with a vengeance, that have made this litter here? Could you not look before you, and be d—nd? Do you think I have nothing else to do (in the devil's name) but to mend and repair after your arse?" "Good words, friend," said the bee (having pruned himself, and being disposed to droll) "I'll give you my hand and word to come near your kennel no more; I was never in such a confounded pickle since I was born." "Sirrah," replied the spider, "if it were not for breaking an old custom in our family, never to stir abroad against an enemy, I should come and teach you better manners." "I pray have patience," said the bee, "or you will spend your substance, and for aught I see, you may stand in need of it all, towards the repair of your house." "Rogue, rogue," replied the spider, "yet methinks you should have more respect to a person, whom all the world allows to be so much your betters." "By my troth," said the bee, "the comparison will amount to a very good jest, and you will do me a favor to let me know the reasons that all the world is pleased to use in so hopeful a dispute." At this the spider, having swelled himself into the size and posture of a disputant, began his argument in the true spirit of controversy, with a resolution to be heartily scurrilous and angry, to urge on his own reasons, without the least regard to the answers or objections of his opposite, and fully predetermined in his mind against all conviction.

"Not to disparage myself," said he, "by the comparison with such a rascal, what art thou but a vagabond without house or home, without stock or inheritance, born to no possession of your own, but a pair of

1. The Hebrew god of flies.

wings and a drone-pipe? Your livelihood is an universal plunder upon nature; a freebooter over fields and gardens; and for the sake of stealing will rob a nettle as easily as a violet. Whereas I am a domestic animal, furnished with a native stock within myself. This large castle (to show my improvements in the mathematics) is all built with my own hands, and the materials extracted altogether out of my own person."

"I am glad," answered the bee, "to hear you grant at least that I am come honestly by my wings and my voice; for then, it seems, I am obliged to Heaven alone for my flights and my music; and Providence would never have bestowed on me two such gifts, without designing them for the noblest ends. I visit indeed all the flowers and blossoms of the field and the garden; but whatever I collect from thence enriches myself, without the least injury to their beauty, their smell, or their taste. Now, for you and your skill in architecture and other mathematics, I have little to say: in that building of yours there might, for aught I know, have been labor and method enough, but by woful experience for us both, 'tis too plain, the materials are naught, and I hope you will henceforth take warning, and consider duration and matter as well as method and art. You boast, indeed, of being obliged to no other creature, but of drawing and spinning out all from yourself; that is to say, if we may judge of the liquor in the vessel by what issues out, you possess a good plentiful store of dirt and poison in your breast; and, tho' I would by no means lessen or disparage your genuine stock of either, yet I doubt you are somewhat obliged for an increase of both, to a little foreign assistance. Your inherent portion of dirt does not fail of acquisitions, by sweepings exhaled from below; and one insert furnishes you with a share of poison to destroy another. So that in short, the question comes all to this—which is the nobler being of the two, that which by a lazy contemplation of four inches round, by an overweening pride, feeding and engendering on itself, turns all into excrement and venom, produces nothing at last, but flybane and a cobweb; or that which, by an universal range, with long search, much study, true judgment, and distinction of things, brings home honey and wax."

1697   1704

Samuel L. Clemens: THE WAR PRAYER

It was a time of great and exalting excitement. The country was up in arms, the war was on, in every breast burned the holy fire of patriotism; the drums were beating, the bands playing, the toy pistols popping, the bunched firecrackers hissing and spluttering; on every hand and far down the receding and fading spread of roofs and balconies a fluttering wilderness of flags flashed in the sun; daily the young volunteers marched down the wide avenue gay and fine in their new uniforms, the proud fathers and mothers and sisters and sweethearts cheering them with voices choked with happy emotion as they swung by; nightly the packed mass meetings listened, panting, to patriot oratory which stirred the deepest deeps of their hearts and which they interrupted at briefest intervals with cyclones of applause, the tears running down their cheeks the while; in the churches the pastors preached devotion to flag and country and invoked the God of Battles, beseeching His aid in our good cause in outpouring of fervid eloquence which moved every listener. It was indeed a glad and gracious time, and the half-dozen rash spirits that ventured to disapprove of the war and cast a doubt upon its righteousness straightway got such a stern and angry warning that for their personal safety's sake they quickly shrank out of sight and offended no more in that way.

Sunday morning came—next day the battalions would leave for the front; the church was filled; the volunteers were there, their young faces alight with martial dreams—visions of the stern advance, the gathering momentum, the rushing charge, the flashing sabers, the flight of the foe, the tumult, the enveloping smoke, the fierce pursuit, the surrender!— then home from the war, bronzed heroes, welcomed, adored, submerged in golden seas of glory! With the volunteers sat their dear ones, proud, happy, and envied by the neighbors and friends who had no sons and brothers to send forth to the field of honor, there to win for the flag or, failing die the noblest of noble deaths. The service proceeded; a war chapter from the Old Testament was read; the first prayer was said; it was followed by an organ burst that shook the building, and with one impulse the house rose, with glowing eyes and beating hearts, and poured out that tremendous invocation—

"God the all-terrible! Thou who ordainest,
 Thunder thy clarion and lightning thy sword!"

Then came the "long" prayer. None could remember the like of it for passionate pleading and moving and beautiful language. The burden of its supplication was that an ever-merciful and benignant Father of us all would watch over our noble young soldiers and aid, comfort, and encourage them in their patriotic work; bless them, shield them in the day of battle and the hour of peril, bear them in His mighty hand, make them strong and confident, invincible in the bloody onset; help them to crush the foe, grant to them and to their flag and country imperishable honor and glory—

An aged stranger entered and moved with slow and noiseless step up the main aisle, his eyes fixed upon the minister, his long body clothed in a robe that reached to his feet, his head bare, his white hair descending in a frothy cataract to his shoulders, his seamy face unnaturally pale, pale even to ghastliness. With all eyes following him and wondering, he made his silent way; without pausing, he ascended to the preacher's side and stood there, waiting. With shut lids the preacher, unconscious of his presence, continued his moving prayer, and at last finished it with the words, uttered in fervent appeal, "Bless our arms, grant us the victory, O Lord our God, Father and Protector of our land and flag!"

The stranger touched his arm, motioned him to step aside—which the startled minister did—and took his place. During some moments he surveyed the spellbound audience with solemn eyes in which burned an uncanny light; then in a deep voice he said:

"I come from the Throne—bearing a message from Almighty God!" The words smote the house with a shock; if the stranger perceived it he gave no attention. "He has heard the prayer of His servant your shepherd and will grant it if such shall be your desire after I, His Messenger, shall have explained to you its import—that is to say, its full import. For it is like unto many of the prayers of men, in that it asks for more than he who utters it is aware of—except he pause and think.

"God's servant and yours has prayed his prayer. Has he paused and taken thought? Is it one prayer? No, it is two—one uttered, the other not. Both have reached the ear of Him Who heareth all supplications, the spoken and the unspoken. Ponder this—keep it in mind. If you would beseech a blessing upon yourself, beware! lest without intent you invoke a curse upon a neighbor at the same time. If you pray for the blessing of rain upon your crop which needs it, by that act you are possibly praying for a curse upon some neighbor's crop which may not need rain and can be injured by it.

"You have heard your servant's prayer—the uttered part of it. I am commissioned of God to put into words the other part of it—that part which the pastor, and also you in your hearts, fervently prayed silently. And ignorantly and unthinkingly? God grant that it was so! You heard these words: 'Grant us the victory, O Lord our God!' That is sufficient. The whole of the uttered prayer is compact into those pregnant words. Elaborations were not necessary. When you have prayed for victory you have prayed for many unmentioned results which follow victory—must follow it, cannot help but follow it. Upon the listening spirit of God the

Father fell also the unspoken part of the prayer. He commandeth me to put it into words. Listen!

"O Lord our Father, our young patriots, idols of our hearts, go forth to battle—be Thou near them! With them, in spirit, we also go forth from the sweet peace of our beloved firesides to smite the foe. O Lord our God, help us to tear their soldiers to bloody shreds with our shells; help us to cover their smiling fields with the pale forms of their patriot dead; help us to drown the thunder of the guns with the shrieks of their wounded, writhing in pain; help us to lay waste their humble homes with a hurricane of fire; help us to wring the hearts of their unoffending widows with unavailing grief; help us to turn them out roofless with their little children to wander unfriended the wastes of their desolated land in rags and hunger and thirst, sports of the sun flames of summer and the icy winds of winter, broken in spirit, worn with travail, imploring Thee for the refuge of the grave and denied it—for our sakes who adore Thee, Lord, blast their hopes, blight their lives, protract their bitter pilgrimage, make heavy their steps, water their way with their tears, stain the white snow with the blood of their wounded feet! We ask it, in the spirit of love, of Him Who is the Source of Love, and Who is the ever-faithful refuge and friend of all that are sore beset and seek His aid with humble and contrite hearts. Amen.

(*After a pause*) "Ye have prayed it: if ye still desire it, speak! The messenger of the Most High waits."

It was believed afterward that the man was a lunatic, because there was no sense in what he said.

1904/1905   1923

Franz Kafka: PARABLE OF THE LAW

"Before the Law stands a doorkeeper. To this doorkeeper there comes a man from the country who begs for admittance to the Law. But the doorkeeper says that he cannot admit the man at the moment. The man, on reflection, asks if he will be allowed, then, to enter later. 'It is possible,' answers the doorkeeper, 'but not at this moment.' Since the door leading into the Law stands open as usual and the doorkeeper steps to one side, the man bends down to peer through the entrance. When the doorkeeper sees that, he laughs and says: 'If you are so strongly tempted, try to get in without my permission. But note that I am powerful. And I am only the lowest doorkeeper. From hall to hall, keepers stand at every door, one more powerful than the other. And the sight of the third man is already more than even I can stand.' These are difficulties which the man from the country has not expected to meet, the Law, he thinks, should be accessible to every man and at all times, but when he looks more closely at the doorkeeper in his furred robe, with his huge pointed nose and long thin Tartar beard, he decides that he had better wait until he gets permission to enter. The doorkeeper gives him a stool and lets him sit down at the side of the door. There he sits waiting for days and years. He makes many attempts to be allowed in and wearies the doorkeeper with his importunity. The doorkeeper often engages him in brief conversation, asking him about his home and about other matters, but the questions are put quite impersonally, as great men put questions, and always conclude with the statement that the man cannot be allowed to enter yet. The man, who has equipped himself with many things for his journey, parts with all he has, however valuable, in the hope of bribing the doorkeeper. The doorkeeper accepts it all, saying, however, as he takes each gift: 'I take this only to keep you from feeling that you have left something undone.' During all these long years the man watches the doorkeeper almost incessantly. He forgets about the other doorkeepers, and this one seems to him the only barrier between himself and the Law. In the first years he curses his evil fate aloud; later, as he grows old, he only mutters to himself. He grows childish, and since in his prolonged study of the doorkeeper he has learned to know even the fleas in his fur collar, he begs the very fleas to help him and to persuade the doorkeeper to change his mind. Finally his eyes grow dim and he does not know whether the world is really darkening around him or whether his eyes are only deceiving him. But in the darkness he can now perceive a radiance that streams inextinguishably from the door of the Law. Now his life is drawing to a close. Before he dies, all that he has experienced during the whole time of his sojourn condenses in his mind into one question, which he has never yet put to the doorkeeper. He beckons the doorkeeper, since he can no longer raise his stiffening body. The doorkeeper has to bend far down to hear him, for the difference in size between them has increased very much to the man's disadvantage. 'What do you want to know now?' asks the doorkeeper, 'you are insatiable.' 'Everyone strives to attain the Law,' answers the man, 'how does it come about, then, that in all these years no one has come seeking admittance but me?' The doorkeeper perceives that the man is nearing his end and his hearing is failing, so he bellows in his ear: 'No one but you could gain admittance through this door, since this door was intended for you. I am now going to shut it.'"

"So the doorkeeper deceived the man," said K. immediately, strongly attracted by the story. "Don't be too hasty," said the priest, "don't take over someone else's opinion without testing it. I have told you the story in the very words of the scriptures. There's no mention of deception in it." "But it's clear enough," said K., "and your first interpretation of it was quite right. The doorkeeper gave the message of salvation to the man only when it could no longer help him." "He was not asked the question any earlier," said the priest, "and you must consider, too, that he was only a doorkeeper, and as such fulfilled his duty." "What makes you think he fulfilled his duty?" asked K. "He didn't fulfill it. His duty might have been to keep all strangers away, but this man, for whom the door was intended, should have been let in." "You have not enough respect for the written word and you are altering the story," said the priest. "The story contains two important statements made by the doorkeeper about admission to the Law, one at the beginning, the other at the end. The first statement is: that he cannot admit the man at the moment, and the other is: that this door was intended only for the man. If there were a contradiction be-tween the two, you would be right and the doorkeeper would have deceived the man. But there is no contradiction. The first statement, on the contrary, even implies the second. One could almost say that in suggesting to the man the possibility of future admittance the door-keeper is exceeding his duty. At that time his apparent duty is only to refuse admittance and indeed many commentators are surprised that the suggestion should be made at all, since the doorkeeper appears to be a precisian with a stern regard for duty. He does not once leave his post during these many years, and he does not shut the door until the very last minute; he is conscious of the importance of his office, for he says: 'I am powerful'; he is respectful to his superiors, for he says: 'I am only the lowest doorkeeper'; he is not garrulous, for during all these years he puts only what are called 'impersonal questions'; he is not to be bribed, for he says in accepting a gift: 'I take this only to keep you from feeling that you have left something undone'; where his duty is concerned he is to be moved neither by pity nor rage, for we are told that the man 'wearied the doorkeeper with his importunity'; and finally even his external appear-ance hints at a pedantic character, the large, pointed nose and the long, thin, black, Tartar beard. Could one imagine a more faithful doorkeeper? Yet the doorkeeper has other elements in his character which are likely to advantage anyone seeking admittance and which make it comprehen-sible enough that he should somewhat exceed his duty in suggesting the possibility of future admittance. For it cannot be denied that he is a little simple-minded and consequently a little conceited. Take the statements he makes about his power and the power of the other doorkeepers and their dreadful aspect which even he cannot bear to see—I hold that these statements may be true enough, but that the way in which he brings them out shows that his perceptions are confused by simpleness of mind and conceit. The commentators note in this connection: 'The right perception of any matter and a misunderstanding of the same matter do not wholly exclude each other.' One must at any rate assume that such simpleness and conceit, however sparingly manifest, are likely to weaken his defense of the door; they are breaches in the character of the door-keeper. To this must be added the fact that the doorkeeper seems to be a friendly creature by nature, he is by no means always on his official dignity. In the very first moments he allows himself the jest of inviting the man to enter in spite of the strictly maintained veto against entry; then he does not, for instance, send the man away, but gives him, as we are told, a stool and lets him sit down beside the door. The patience with which he endures the man's appeals during so many years, the brief conversations, the acceptance of the gifts, the politeness with which he allows the man to curse loudly in his presence the fate for which he himself is responsible—all this lets us deduce certain feelings of pity. Not every doorkeeper would have acted thus. And finally, in answer to a gesture of the man's he bends down to give him the chance of putting a last question. Nothing but mild impatience—the doorkeeper knows that this is the end of it all—is discernible in the words: 'You are insatiable.' Some push this mode of interpretation even further and hold that these words express a kind of friendly admiration, though not without a hint of condescension. At any rate the figure of the doorkeeper can be said to come out very differently from what you fancied." "You have studied the story more exactly and for a longer time than I have," said K. They were both silent for a little while. Then. K. said: "So you think the man was not deceived?" "Don't misunderstand me," said the priest, "I am only show-ing you the various opinions concerning that point. You must not pay too much attention to them. The scriptures are unalterable and the com-ments often enough merely express the commentators' despair. In this case there even exists an interpretation which claims that the deluded person is really the doorkeeper." "That's a farfetched interpretation," said K. "On what is it based?" "It is based," answered the priest, "on the simple-mindedness of the doorkeeper. The argument is that he does not know the Law from inside, he knows only the way that leads to it, where he patrols up and down. His ideas of the interior are assumed to be childish, and it is supposed that he himself is afraid of the other guardians whom he holds up as bogies before the man. Indeed, he fears them more than the man does, since the man is determined to enter after hearing about the dreadful guardians of the interior, while the doorkeeper has no desire to enter, at least not so far as we are told. Others again say that he must have been in the interior already, since he is after all engaged in the service of the Law and can only have been appointed from inside. This is countered by arguing that he may have been appointed by a voice calling from the interior, and that anyhow he cannot have been far inside, since the aspect of the third doorkeeper is more than he can endure. Moreover, no indication is given that during all these years he ever made any remarks showing a knowledge of the interior, except for the one remark about the doorkeepers. He may have been forbidden to do so, but there is no mention of that either. On these grounds the conclusion is reached that he knows nothing about the aspect and significance of the interior, so that he is in a state of delusion. But he is deceived also about his relation to the man from the country, for he is inferior to the man and does not know it. He treats the man instead as his own subordinate, as can be recognized from many details that must be still fresh in your mind. But, according to this view of the story, it is just as clearly indicated that he is really subordinated to the man. In the first place, a bondman is always subject to a free man. Now the man from the country is really free, he can go where he likes, it is only the Law that is closed to him, and access to the Law is forbidden him only by one individual, the doorkeeper. When he sits down on the stool by the side of the door and stays there for the rest of his life, he does it of his own free will; in the story there is no mention of any compulsion. But the doorkeeper is bound to his post by his very office, he does not dare go out into the country, nor apparently may he go into the interior of the Law, even should he wish to. Besides, although he is in the service of the Law, his service is confined to this one entrance; that is to say, he serves only this man for whom alone the entrance is intended. On that ground too he is inferior to the man. One must assume that for many years, for as long as it takes a man to grow up to the prime of life, his service was in a sense an empty formality, since he had to wait for a man to come, that is to say someone in the prime of life, and so he had to wait a long time before the purpose of his service could be fulfilled, and, moreover, had to wait on the man's pleasure, for the man came of his own free will. But the termination of his service also depends on the man's term of life, so that to the very end he is subject to the man. And it is emphasized throughout that the doorkeeper apparently realizes nothing of all this. That is not in itself remarkable, since according to this interpretation the doorkeeper is deceived in a much more important issue, affecting his very office. At the end, for example, he says regarding the entrance to the Law: 'I am now going to shut it,' but at the beginning of the story we are told that the door leading into the Law always stands open, and if it always stands open, that is to say at all times, without reference to life or death of the man, then the doorkeeper cannot close it. There is some difference of opinion about the motive behind the door-keeper's statement, whether he said he was going to close the door merely for the sake of giving an answer, or to emphasize his devotion to duty, or to bring the man into a state of grief and regret in his last moments. But there is no lack of agreement that the doorkeeper will not be able to shut the door. Many indeed profess to find that he is subordinate to the man even in knowledge, toward the end, at least, for the man sees the radiance that issues from the door of the Law while the doorkeeper in his official position must stand with his back to the door, nor does he say anything to show that he has perceived the change."

"That is well argued," said K., after repeating to himself in a low voice several passages from the priest's exposition. "It is well argued, and I am inclined to agree that the doorkeeper is deceived. But that has not made me abandon my former opinion, since both conclusions are to some extent compatible. Whether the doorkeeper is clear-sighted or deceived does not dispose of the matter. I said the man is deceived. If the doorkeeper is clear-sighted, one might have doubts about that, but if the doorkeeper himself is deceived, then his deception must of necessity be communicated to the man. That makes the doorkeeper not, indeed, a deceiver, but a creature so simple-minded that he ought to be dismissed at once from his office. You mustn't forget that the doorkeeper's deceptions do himself no harm but do infinite harm to the man." "There are objections to that," said the priest. "Many aver that the story confers no right on anyone to pass judgment on the doorkeeper. Whatever he may seem to us, he is yet a servant of the Law; that is, he belongs to the Law and as such is beyond human judgment. In that case one must not believe that the doorkeeper is subordinate to the man. Bound as he is by his service, even only at the door of the Law, he is incomparably greater than anyone at large in the world. The man is only seeking the Law, the doorkeeper is already attached to it. It is the Law that has placed him at his post; to doubt his dignity is to doubt the Law itself." "I don't agree with that point of view," said K., shaking his head, "for if one accepts it, one must accept as true everything the doorkeeper says. But you yourself have sufficiently proved how impossible it is to do that." "No," said the priest, "it is not necessary to accept everything as true, one must only accept it as necessary." "A melancholy conclusion," said K. "It turns lying into a universal principle."

1925

Philosophy and Religion

James Thurber

THE OWL WHO WAS GOD

Once upon a starless midnight there was on owl who sat on the branch of an oak tree. Two ground moles tried to slip quietly by, unnoticed. "You!" said the owl. "Who?" they quavered, in fear and astonishment, for they could not believe it was possible for anyone to see them in that thick darkness. "You two!" said the owl. The moles hurried away and told the other creatures of the field and forest that the owl was the greatest and wisest of all animals because he could see in the dark and because he could answer any question. "I'll see about that," said a secretary bird, and he called on the owl one night when it was again very dark. "How many claws am I holding up?" said the secretary bird, "Two," said the owl, and that was right. "Can you give me another expression for 'that is to say' or 'namely'?" asked the secretary bird. "To wit," said the owl. "Why does a lover call on his love?" asked the secretary bird. "To woo," said the owl.

The secretary bird hastened back to the other creatures and reported that the owl was indeed the greatest and wisest animal in the world because he could see in the dark and because he could answer any question. "Can he see in the daytime, too?" asked a red fox. "Yes," echoed a dormouse and a French poodle. "Can he see in the daytime, too?" All the other creatures laughed loudly at this silly question, and they set upon the red fox and his friends and drove them out of the region. Then they sent a messenger to the owl and asked him to be their leader.

When the owl appeared among the animals it was high noon and the sun was shining brightly. He walked very slowly, which gave him an appearance of great dignity, and he peered about him with large, staring eyes, which gave him an air of tremendous importance. "He's God!"

screamed a Plymouth Rock hen. And the others took up the cry "He's God!" So they followed him wherever he went and when he began to bump into things they began to bump into things, too. Finally he came to a concrete highway and he started up the middle of it and all the other creatures followed him. Presently a hawk, who was acting as outrider, observed a truck coming toward them at fifty miles an hour, and he reported to the secretary bird and the secretary bird reported to the owl. "There's danger ahead," said the secretary bird. "To wit?" said the owl. The secretary bird told him. "Aren't you afraid?" He asked. "Who?" said the owl calmly, for he could not see the truck. "He's God!" cried all the creatures again, and they were still crying "He's God!" when the truck hit them and ran them down. Some of the animals were merely injured, but most of them, including the owl, were killed.

Moral: *You can fool too many of the people too much of the time.*

1955

Robert Graves

MYTHOLOGY

Mythology is the study of whatever religious or heroic legends are so foreign to a student's experience that he cannot believe them to be true. Hence the English adjective "mythical," meaning "incredible"; and hence the omission from standard European mythologies of all Biblical narratives even when closely paralleled by myths from Persia, Babylonia, Egypt, and Greece, and of all hagiological legends. * * *

Myth has two main functions. The first is to answer the sort of awkward questions that children ask, such as: "Who made the world? How will it end? Who was the first man? Where do souls go after death?" The answers, necessarily graphic and positive, confer enormous power on the various deities credited with the creation and care of souls—and incidentally on their priesthoods.

The second function of myth is to justify an existing social system and account for traditional rites and customs. The Erechtheid clan of Athens, who used a snake as an amulet, preserved myths of their descent from King Erichthonius, a man-serpent, son of the Smith-god Hephaestus and foster-son of the Goddess Athene. The Ioxids of Caria explained their veneration for rushes and wild asparagus by a story of their ancestress Perigune, whom Theseus the Erechtheid courted in a thicket of these plants; thus incidentally claiming cousinship with the Attic royal house.

The real reason may have been that wild asparagus stalks and rushes were woven into sacred baskets, and therefore taboo.

Myths of origin and eventual extinction vary according to the climate. In the cold North, the first human beings were said to have sprung from the licking of frozen stones by a divine cow named Audumla; and the Northern afterworld was a bare, misty, featureless plain where ghosts wandered hungry and shivering. According to a myth from the kinder climate of Greece, a Titan named Prometheus, kneading mud on a flowery riverbank, made human statuettes which Athene—who was once the Libyan Moon-goddess Neith—brought to life, and Greek ghosts went to a sunless, flowerless underground cavern. These afterworlds were destined for serfs or commoners; deserving nobles could count on warm, celestial mead halls in the North, and Elysian Fields in Greece.

Primitive peoples remodel old myths to conform with changes produced by revolutions, or invasions and, as a rule, politely disguise their violence: thus a treacherous usurper will figure as a lost heir to the throne who killed a destructive dragon or other monster and, after marrying the king's daughter, duly succeeded him. Even myths of origin get altered or discarded. Prometheus' creation of men from clay superseded the hatching of all nature from a world-egg laid by the ancient Mediterranean Dove-goddess Eurynome—a myth common also in Polynesia, where the Goddess is called Tangaroa.

A typical case-history of how myths develop as culture spreads: Among the Akan of Ghana, the original social system was a number of queendoms, each containing three or more clans and ruled by a Queen-mother with her council of elder women, descent being reckoned in the female line, and each clan having its own animal deity. The Akan believed that the world was born from the all-powerful Moon-goddess Ngame, who gave human beings souls, as soon as born, by shooting lunar rays into them. At some time or other, perhaps in the early Middle Ages, patriarchal nomads from the Sudan forced the Akans to accept a male Creator, a Sky-god named Odomankoma, but failed to destroy Ngame's dispensation. A compromise myth was agreed upon: Odomankoma created the world with hammer and chisel from inert matter, after which Ngame brought it to life. These Sudanese invaders also worshipped the seven planetary powers ruling the week—a system originating in Babylonia. (It had spread to Northern Euope, bypassing Greece and Rome, which is why the names of pagan deities—Tuisto, Woden, Thor, and Frigg—are still attached to Tuesday, Wednesday, Thursday, and Friday.) This extra cult provided the Akan with seven new deities, and the compromise myth made both them and the clan gods bisexual. Towards the end of the fourteenth century A.D., a social revolution deposed Odomankoma in favor of a Universal Sun-god, and altered the myth accordingly. While Odomankoma ruled, a queendom was still a queendom, the king acting merely as a consort and male representative of the sovereign Queen-mother, and being styled "Son of the Moon": a yearly dying, yearly resurrected, fertility godling. But the gradual welding of small queendoms into city-states, and of city-states into a rich and populous nation, encouraged the High King—the king of the dominant city-state—to borrow a foreign custom. He styled himself "Son of the Sun," as well as "Son of the Moon," and claimed limitless authority. The Sun, which, according to the myth, had hitherto been reborn every morning from Ngame, was now worshipped as an eternal god altogether independent of the Moon's life-giving function. New myths appeared when the Akan accepted the patriarchal principle, which Sun-worship brought in; they began tracing succession through the father, and mothers ceased to be the spiritual heads of households.

This case-history throws light on the complex Egyptian corpus of myth. Egypt, it seems, developed from small matriarchal Moonqueendoms to Pharaonic patriarchal Sun-monarchy. Grotesque animal deities of leading clans in the Delta became city-gods, and the cities were federated under the sovereignty of a High King (once a "Son of the Moon"), who claimed to be the Son of Ra the Sun-god. Opposition by independent-minded city-rulers to the Pharaoh's autocratic sway appears in the undated myth of how Ra grew so old and feeble that he could not even control his spittle; the Moon-goddess Isis plotted against him and Ra retaliated by casting his baleful eye on mankind—they perished in their thousands. Ra nevertheless decided to quit the ungrateful land of Egypt, whereupon Hathor, a loyal Cow-goddess, flew him up to the vault of Heaven. The myth doubtless records a compromise that consigned the High King's absolutist pretensions, supported by his wife, to the vague realm of philosophic theory. He kept the throne, but once more became, for all practical purposes, an incarnation of Osiris, consort of the Moon-goddess Isis—a yearly dying, yearly resurrected fertility godling.

Indian myth is highly complex, and swings from gross physical abandon to rigorous asceticism and fantastic visions of the spirit world. Yet it has much in common with European myth, since Aryan invasions in the second millennium B.C. changed the religious system of both continents. The invaders were nomad herdsmen, and the peoples on whom they imposed themselves as a military aristocracy were peasants. Hesiod, an early Greek poet, preserves a myth of pre-Aryan "Silver Age" heroes: "divinely created eaters of bread, utterly subject to their mothers however long they lived, who never sacrificed to the gods, but at least did not make war against one another." Hesiod put the case well: in primitive agricultural communities, recourse to war is rare, and goddessworship the rule. Herdsmen, on the contrary, tend to make fighting a profession and, perhaps because bulls dominate their herds, as rams do flocks, worship a male Sky-god typified by a bull or a ram. He sends down rain for the pastures, and they take omens from the entrails of the victims sacrificed to him.

When an invading Aryan chieftain, a tribal rainmaker, married the Moon-priestess and Queen of a conquered people, a new myth inevitably celebrated the marriage of the Sky-god and the Moon. But since the Moon-goddess was everywhere worshipped as a triad, in honor of the Moon's three phases—waxing, full, and waning—the god split up into a complementary triad. This accounts for three-bodied Geryon, the first king of Spain; three-headed Cernunnos, the Gallic god; the Irish triad, Brian, Iuchar, and Iucharba, who married the three queenly owners of Ireland; and the invading Greek brothers Zeus, Poseidon, and Hades, who, despite great opposition, married the pre-Greek Moon-goddess in her three aspects, respectively as Queen of Heaven, Queen of the Sea, and Queen of the Underworld.

The Queen-mother's decline in religious power, and the goddesses' continual struggle to preserve their royal prerogatives, appears in the Homeric myth of how Zeus ill-treated and bullied Hera, and how she continually plotted against him. Zeus remained a Thunder-god, because Greek national sentiment forbad his becoming a Sun-god in Oriental style. But his Irish counterpart, a thunder-god named The Dagda, grew senile at last and surrendered the throne to his son Bodb the Red, a war-god—in Ireland, the magic of rainmaking was not so important as in Greece.

One constant rule of mythology is that whatever happens among the gods above reflects events on earth. Thus a father-god named "The Ancient One of the Jade" (Yu-ti) ruled the pre-revolutionary Chinese Heaven: like Prometheus, he had created human beings from clay. His wife was the Queen-mother, and their court an exact replica of the old Imperial Court at Pekin, with precisely the same functionaries: ministers, soldiers, and a numerous family of the gods' sisters, daughters, and nephews. The two annual sacrifices paid by the Emperor to the August One of the Jade—at the winter solstice when the days first lengthen and at the Spring equinox when they become longer than the nights—show him to have once been a solar god. And the theological value to the number 72 suggests that the cult started as a compromise between Moongoddess worship and Sun-god worship. 72 means three-times-three, the Moon's mystical number, multipled by two-times-two-times-two, the Sun's mystical number, and occurs in solar-lunar divine unions throughout Europe, Asia, and Africa. Chinese conservatism, by the way, kept these gods dressed in ancient court-dress, making no concessions to the new fashions which the invading dynasty from Manchuria had introduced.

In West Africa, whenever the Queen-mother, or King, appointed a new functionary at Court, the same thing happened in Heaven, by royal decree. Presumably this was also the case in China; and if we apply the principle to Greek myth, it seems reasonably certain that the account of Tirynthian Heracles' marriage to Hera's daughter Hebe, and his appointment as Celestial Porter to Zeus, commemorates the appointment of a Tirynthian prince as vizier at the court of the Mycenaean High King, after marriage to a daughter of his Queen, the High Priestess of Argos. Probably the appointment of Ganymede, son of an early Trojan king, as cup-bearer to Zeus, had much the same significance: Zeus, in this context, would be more likely the Hittite king resident at Hattusas.

Myth, then, is a dramatic shorthand record of such matters as invasions, migrations, dynastic changes, admission of foreign cults, and social reforms. When bread was first introduced into Greece—where only beans, poppyseeds, acorns, and asphodel roots had hitherto been known —the myth of Demeter and Triptolemus sanctified its use; the same event in Wales produced a myth of "The Old White One," a Sow-goddess who went around the country with gifts of grain, bees, and her own young; for agriculture, pig breeding and beekeeping were taught to the aborigines by the same wave of neolithic invaders. Other myths sanctified the invention of wine.

A proper study of myth demands a great store of abstruse geographical, historical, and anthropological knowledge, also familiarity with the properties of plants and trees, and the habits of wild birds and beasts. Thus a Central American stone sculpture, a Toad-god sitting beneath a mushroom, means little to mythologists who have not considered the worldwide association of toads with toxic mushrooms or heard of a Mexican Mushroom-god, patron of an oracular cult; for the toxic agent is a drug, similar to that secreted in the sweat glands of frightened toads, which provides magnificent hallucinations of a heavenly kingdom.

Myths are fascinating and easily misread. Readers may smile at the picture of Queen Maya and her prenatal dream of the Buddha descending upon her disguised as a charming white baby elephant—he looks as though he would crush her to pulp—when "at once all nature rejoiced, trees burst into bloom, and musical instruments played of their own accord." In English-speaking countries, "white elephant" denotes something not only useless and unwanted, but expensive to maintain; and the picture could be misread there as indicating the Queen's grave embarrassment at the prospect of bearing a child. In India, however, the elephant symbolizes royalty—the supreme God Indra rides one—and white elephants (which are not albinos, but animals suffering from a vitiliginous skin disease) are sacred to the Sun, as white horses were for the ancient Greeks, and white oxen for the British druids. The elephant, moreover, symbolizes intelligence, and Indian writers traditionally acknowledge the Elephant-god Ganesa as their patron; he is supposed to have dictated the *Mahabharata*.[1]

Again, in English, a scallop shell is associated either with cookery or with medieval pilgrims returning from a visit to the Holy Sepulcher; but Aphrodite the Greek Love-goddess employed a scallop shell for her voyages across the sea, because its two parts were so tightly hinged together as to provide a symbol of passionate sexual love—the hinge of the scallop being a principal ingredient in ancient love-philters. The lotus-flower sacred to Buddha and Osiris has five petals, which symbolize the four limbs and the head; the five senses; the five digits; and, like the pyramid, the four points of the compass and the zenith. Other esoteric meanings abound, for myths are seldom simple, and never irresponsible.

1959

1. A vast Indian epic of 200,000 lines, written before A.D. 500.

E. F. Schumacher

LEVELS OF BEING

Our task is to look at the world and see it whole.

We see what our ancestors have always seen: a great Chain of Being which seems to divide naturally into four sections—four "kingdoms," as they used to be called: mineral, plant, animal, and human. This "was, in fact, until not much more than a century ago, probably the most widely familiar conception of the general *scheme* of things, of the constitutive pattern of the universe."[1] The Chain of Being can be seen as extending downward from the Highest to the lowest, or it can be seen as extending upward from the lowest to the Highest. The ancient view begins with the Divine and sees the downward Chain of Being as moving an ever-increasing distance from the Center, with a progressive loss of qualities. The modern view, largely influenced by the doctrine of evolution, tends to start with inanimate matter and to consider man the last link of the chain, as having evolved the widest range of useful qualities. For our purposes here, the direction of looking—upward or downward—is unimportant, and, in line with modern habits of thought, we shall start at the lowest level, the mineral kingdom, and consider the successive gain of qualities or *powers* as we move to the higher levels.

No one has any difficulty recognizing the astonishing and mysterious difference between a living plant and one that has died and has thus fallen to the lowest Level of Being, inanimate matter. What is this *power* that has been lost? We call it "life." Scientists tell us that we must not talk of a

1. Arthur O. Lovejoy, *The Great Chain of Being* (New York, 1960) [author's note].

"life force" because no such force has ever been found to exist. Yet the *difference* between alive and dead exists. We could call it "x," to indicate something that is there to be noticed and studied but that cannot be explained. If we call the mineral level "m," we can call the plant level m + x. This factor x is obviously worthy of our closest attention, particularly since we are able to destroy it, although it is completely outside our ability to create it. Even if somebody could provide us with a recipe, a set of instructions, for creating life out of lifeless matter, the mysterious character of x would remain, and we would never cease to marvel that something that could do nothing is now able to extract nourishment from its environment, grow, and reproduce itself, "true to form," as it were. There is nothing in the laws, concepts, and formulae of physics and chemistry to explain or even to describe such powers. X is something quite new and additional, and the more deeply we contemplate it, the clearer it becomes that we are faced here with what might be called an *ontological discontinuity* or, more simply, a jump in the Level of Being.

From plant to animal, there is a similar jump, a similar addition of powers, which enable the typical, fully developed animal to do things that are totally outside the range of possibilities of the typical, fully developed plant. These powers, again, are mysterious and, strictly speaking, nameless. We can refer to them by the letter "y," which will be the safest course, because any word label we might attach to them could lead people to think that such a designation was not merely a hint as to their nature but an adequate description. However, since we cannot talk without words, I shall attach to these mysterious powers the label *consciousness*. It is easy to recognize consciousness in a dog, a cat, or a horse, if only because they can be knocked unconscious: the processes of life continue as in a plant, although the animal has lost its peculiar powers.

If the plant, in our terminology, can be called m + x, the animal has to be described as m + x + y. Again, the new factor "y" is worthy of our closest attention; we are able to destroy but not to create it. Anything that we can destroy but are unable to make is, in a sense, sacred, and all our "explanations" of it do not really explain anything. Again we can say that y is something quite new and additional when compared with the level "plant"—another *ontological discontinuity*, another jump in the Level of Being.

Moving from the animal to the human level, who would seriously deny the addition, again, of new powers? What precisely they are has become a matter of controversy in modern times, but the fact that man is able to do—and is doing—innumerable things which lie totally outside the range of possibilities of even the most highly developed animals cannot be disputed and has never been denied. Man has powers of life like the plant, powers of consciousness like the animal, and evidently something more: the mysterious power "z." What is it? How can it be defined?

What can it be called? This power z has undoubtedly a great deal to do with the fact that man is not only able to think but is also *able to be aware of his thinking*. Consciousness and intelligence, as it were, recoil upon themselves. There is not merely a conscious being, but a being capable of being conscious of its consciousness; not merely a thinker, but a thinker capable of watching and studying his own thinking. There is something able to say "I" and *to direct consciousness* in accordance with its own purposes, a master or controller, a power at a higher level than consciousness itself. This power z, consciousness recoiling upon itself, opens up unlimited possibilities of purposeful learning, investigating, exploring, and of formulating and accumulating knowledge. What shall we call it? As it is necessary to have word labels, I shall call it *self-awareness*. We must, however, take great care always to remember that such a word label is merely (to use a Buddhist phrase) "a finger pointing to the moon." The "moon" itself remains highly mysterious and needs to be studied with the greatest patience and perseverance if we want to understand anything about man's position in the Universe.

Our initial review of the four great Levels of Being can be summed up as follows:

Man can be written $\qquad$ $m + x + y + z$
Animal can be written $\qquad$ $m + x + y$
Plant can be written $\qquad$ $m + x$
Mineral can be written $\qquad$ m

Only m is visible; x, y, and z are invisible, and they are extremely difficult to grasp, although their effects are matters of everyday experience.

If, instead of taking "minerals" as our base line and reaching the higher Levels of Being by the addition of powers, we start with the highest level directly known to us—man—we can reach the lower Levels of Being by the progressive subtraction of powers. We can then say:

Man can be written $\qquad$ M
Animal can be written $\qquad$ $M - z$
Plant can be written $\qquad$ $M - z - y$
Mineral can be written $\qquad$ $M - z - y - x$

Such a downward scheme is easier for us to understand than the upward one, simply because it is closer to our practical experience. We know that all three factors—x, y, and z—can weaken and die away; we can in fact deliberately destroy them. Self-awareness can disappear while consciousness continues; consciousness can disappear while life continues; and life can disappear leaving an inanimate body behind. We can observe, and in a sense *feel*, the process of diminution to the point of the apparently total disappearance of self-awareness, consciousness, and life. But it is outside our power to give life to inanimate matter, to give consciousness to living matter, and finally to add the power of self-awareness to conscious beings.

What we can do ourselves, we can, in a sense, understand; what we cannot do at all, we cannot understand—not even "in a sense." Evolution as a process of the spontaneous, accidental emergence of the powers of life, consciousness, and self-awareness, out of inanimate matter, is totally incomprehensible.

For our purposes, however, there is no need to enter into such speculations at this stage. We hold fast to what we can see and experience: the Universe is as a great hierarchic structure of four markedly different Levels of Being. Each level is obviously a broad band, allowing for higher and lower beings within each band, and the precise determination of where a lower band ends and a higher band begins may sometimes be a matter of difficulty and dispute. The existence of the four kingdoms, however, is not put into question by the fact that some of the frontiers are occasionally disputed.

Physics and chemistry deal with the lowest level, "minerals." At this level, x, y, and z—life, consciousness, and self-awareness—do not exist, (or, in any case, are totally inoperative and therefore cannot be noticed). Physics and chemistry can tell us nothing, *absolutely nothing*, about them. These sciences possess no concepts relating to such powers and are incapable of describing their effects. Where there is life, there is form, *Gestalt*, which reproduces itself over and over again from seed or similar beginnings which do not possess this *Gestalt* but develop it in the process of growth. Nothing comparable is to be found in physics or chemistry.

To say that life is nothing but a property of certain peculiar combinations of atoms is like saying that Shakespeare's *Hamlet* is nothing but a property of a peculiar combination of letters. The truth is that the peculiar combination of letters is nothing but a property of Shakespeare's *Hamlet*. The French or German versions of the play "own" different combinations of letters.

The extraordinary thing about the modern "life sciences" is that they hardly ever deal with *life as such*, the factor x, but devote infinite attention to the study and analysis of the physicochemical body that is life's carrier. It may well be that modern science has no method for coming to grips with *life as such*. If this is so, let it be frankly admitted; there is no excuse for the pretense that life is nothing but physics and chemistry.

Nor is there any excuse for the pretense that consciousness is nothing but a property of life. To describe an animal as a physicochemical system of extreme complexity is no doubt perfectly correct, except that it misses out on the "animalness" of the animal. Some zoologists, at least, have advanced beyond this level of erudite absurdity and have developed an ability to see in animals more than complex machines. Their influence, however, is as yet deplorably small, and with the increasing "rationalization" of the modern life-style, more and more animals are being treated as if they really were nothing but "animal machines." (This is a very telling example of how philosophical theories, no matter how absurd and offensive to common sense, tend to become, after a while, "normal practice" in everyday life.)

All the "humanities," as distinct from the natural sciences, deal in one way or another with factor y—consciousness. But a distinction between consciousness (y) and self-awareness (z) is seldom drawn. As a result, modern thinking has become increasingly uncertain whether or not there is any "real" difference between animal and man. A great deal of study of the behavior of animals is being undertaken for the purpose of understanding the nature of man. This is analogous to studying physics with the hope of learning something about life (x). Naturally, since man, as it were, *contains* the three lower Levels of Being, certain things about him can be elucidated by studying minerals, plants, and animals—in fact, everything can be learned about him *except that which makes him human*. All the four constituent elements of the human person—m, x, y, and z—deserve study, but there can be little doubt about their relative importance in terms of *knowledge for the conduct of our lives*.

This importance increases in the order given above, and so do the difficulty and uncertainty experienced by modern humanity. Is there really anything beyond the world of matter, of molecules and atoms and electrons and innumerable other small particles, the ever more complex combinations of which allegedly account for simply everything, from the crudest to the most sublime? Why talk about fundamental differences, "jumps" in the Chain of Being, or "ontological discontinuities" when all we can be really sure of are *differences in degree*? It is not necessary for us to battle over the question whether the palpable and overwhelmingly obvious differences between the four great Levels of Being are better seen as differences in kind or differences in degree. What has to be fully understood is that there are differences in kind, and not simply in degree, between the *powers* of life, consciousness, and self-awareness. Traces of these powers may already exist at the lower levels, although not noticeable (or not yet noticed) by man. Or maybe they are infused, so to speak, on appropriate occasions from "another world." It is not essential for us to have theories about their origin, provided we recognize their quality and, in so doing, never fail to remember that they are beyond anything our own intelligence enables us to create.

It is not unduly difficult to appreciate the difference between what is alive and what is lifeless; it is more difficult to distinguish consciousness from life; and to realize, experience, and appreciate the difference between self-awareness and consciousness (that is, between z and y) is hard indeed. The reason for the difficulty is not far to seek: While the higher comprises and therefore in a sense understands the lower, no being can understand anything higher than itself. A human being can indeed strain and stretch toward the higher and induce a process of growth through adoration, awe, wonder, admiration, and imitation, and by attaining a higher level expand its understanding * * *. But people within whom the power of self-awareness (z) is poorly developed cannot grasp it as a separate power and tend to take it as *nothing but* a slight extension of consciousness (y). Hence we are given a large number of definitions of man which make him out to be *nothing but* an exceptionally intelligent animal with a measurably larger brain, or a tool-making animal, or a political animal, or an unfinished animal, or simply a naked ape.

No doubt, people who use these terms cheerfully include themselves in their definitions—and may have some reason for doing so. For others, they sound merely inane, like defining a dog as a barking plant or a running cabbage. Nothing is more conducive to the brutalization of the modern world than the launching, in the name of science, of wrongful and degrading definitions of man, such as "the naked ape." What could one expect of such a creature, of other "naked apes," or, indeed, of oneself? When people speak of animals as "animal machines," they soon start treating them accordingly, and when they think of people as naked apes, all doors are opened to the free entry of bestiality.

"What a piece of work is a man! how noble in reason! how infinite in faculty!"[2] Because of the power of self-awareness (z), his faculties are indeed infinite; they are not narrowly determined, confined, or "programmed" as one says today. Werner Jaeger[3] expressed a profound truth in the statement that once a human potentiality is realized, it exists. It is the greatest human achievements that define man, not any average behavior or performance, and certainly not anything that can be derived from the observation of animals. "All men cannot be outstanding," says Catherine Roberts. "Yet all men, through knowledge of superior humanness, could know what it means to be a human being and that, as such, they too have a contribution to make. It is magnificent to become as human as one is able. And it requires no help from science. In addition, the very act of realising one's potentialities might constitute an advance over what has gone before."[4]

This "open-endedness" is the wonderful result of the specifically human powers of self-awareness (z), which, as distinct from the powers of life and consciousness, have nothing automatic or mechanical about them. The powers of self-awareness are *essentially* a limitless potentiality rather than an actuality. They have to be developed and "realized" by each human individual if he is to become truly human, that is to say, a *person*.

---

2. *Hamlet* II.ii.303–304.
3. Werner Jaeger (1888–1961): German-born scholar of literature, theology, and philosophy.

4. Catherine Roberts, *The Scientific Conscience* (Fontwell, Sussex, 1974) [author's note].

I said earlier on that man can be written

$$m + x + y + z.$$

These four elements form a sequence of increasing rarity and vulnerability. Matter (m) cannot be destroyed; to kill a body means to deprive it of x, y, and z, and the inanimate matter remains; it "returns" to the earth. Compared with inanimate matter, life is rare and precarious; in turn, compared with the ubiquitousness and tenacity of life, consciousness is even rarer and more vulnerable. Self-awareness is the rarest power of all, precious and vulnerable to the highest degree, the supreme and generally fleeting achievement of a person, present one moment and all too easily gone the next. The study of this factor z has in all ages—except the present—been the primary concern of mankind. How is it possible to study something so vulnerable and fleeting? How is it possible to study that which does the studying? How, indeed, can I study the "I" that employs the very consciousness needed for the study? * * *. Before we can turn to [these questions] directly, we shall do well to take a closer look at the four great Levels of Being: how the intervention of additional powers introduces *essential* changes, even though similarities and "correspondences" remain.

Matter (m), life (x), consciousness (y), self-awareness (z)—these four elements are ontologically—that is, in their fundamental nature—different, incomparable, incommensurable, and discontinuous. Only one of them is directly accessible to objective, scientific observation by means of our five senses. The other three are none the less known to us because we ourselves, every one of us, can verify their existence from our own inner experience.

We never find life except as living matter; we never find consciousness except as conscious living matter; and we never find self-awareness except as self-aware, conscious, living matter. The ontological differences between these four elements are analogous to the discontinuity of dimensions. A line is one-dimensional, and no elaboration of a line, no subtlety in its construction, and no complexity can ever turn it into a surface. Equally, no elaboration of a two-dimensional surface, no increase in complexity, subtlety, or size, can ever turn it into a solid. Existence in the physical world we know is attained only by three-dimensional beings. One- or two-dimensional things exist only in our minds. Analogically speaking, it might be said that only man has "real" existence in this world insofar as he alone possesses the "three dimensions" of life, consciousness, and self-awareness. In this sense, animals, with only two dimensions —life and consciousness—have but a shadowy existence, and plants, lacking the dimensions of self-awareness and consciousness, relate to a human being as a line relates to a solid. In terms of this analogy, matter, lacking the three "invisible dimensions," has no more reality than a geometrical point.

This analogy, which may seem farfetched from a logical point of view, points to an inescapable *existential* truth: The most "real" world we live in is that of our fellow human beings. Without them we should experience a sense of enormous emptiness; we could hardly be human ourselves, for we are made or marred by our relations with other people. The company of animals could console us only because, and to the extent to which, they were reminders, even caricatures, of human beings. A world without fellow human beings would be an eerie and unreal place of banishment; with neither fellow humans nor animals the world would be a dreadful wasteland, no matter how luscious its vegetation. To call it one-dimensional would not seem to be an exaggeration. Human existence in a totally inanimate environment, if it were possible, would be total emptiness, total despair. It may seem absurd to pursue such a line of thought, but it is surely not so absurd as a view which counts as "real" only inanimate matter and treats as "unreal," "subjective," and therefore scientifically nonexistent the invisible dimensions of life, consciousness, and self-awareness.

A simple inspection of the four great Levels of Being has led us to the recognition of their four "elements"—matter, life, consciousness, and self-awareness. It is this recognition that matters, not the precise association of the four elements with the four Levels of Being. If the natural scientists should come and tell us that there are some beings they call animals in whom no trace of consciousness can be detected, it would not be for us to argue with them. Recognition is one thing; identification quite another. For us, only recognition is important, and we are entitled to choose for our purpose typical and fully developed specimens from each Level of Being. If they manifest and demonstrate most clearly the "invisible dimensions" of life, consciousness, and self-awareness, this demonstration is not nullified or invalidated by any difficulty of classification in other cases.

Once we have recognized the ontological gaps and discontinuities that separate the four "elements"—m,x,y,z— from one another, we know also that there can exist no "links" or "transitional forms": Life is either present or absent; there cannot be a half-presence; and the same goes for consciousness and self-awareness. Difficulties of identification are often increased by the fact that the lower level appears to present a kind of mimicry or counterfeit of the higher, just as an animated puppet can at times be mistaken for a living person, or a two-dimensional picture can look like three-dimensional reality. But neither difficulties of identification and demarcation nor possibilities of deception and error can be used as arguments against the existence of the four great Levels of Being, exhibiting the four "elements" we have called Matter, Life, Consciousness, and Self-awareness. These four "elements" are four irreducible mysteries, which need to be most carefully observed and studied, but which cannot be explained, let alone "explained away."

In a hierarchic structure, the higher does not merely possess powers that are additional to and exceed those possessed by the lower; it also has power over the lower: it has the power to organize the lower and use it for its own purposes. Living beings can organize and utilize inanimate matter, conscious beings can utilize life, and self-aware beings can utilize consciousness. Are there powers that are higher than self-awareness? Are there Levels of Being above the human? At this stage in our investigation we need do no more than register the fact that the great majority of mankind throughout its known history, until very recently, has been unshakenly convinced that the Chain of Being extends upward beyond man. This universal conviction of mankind is impressive for both its duration and its intensity. Those individuals of the past whom we still consider the wisest and greatest not only shared this belief but considered it of all truths the most important and the most profound.

1977

John Donne

LET ME WITHER

Let me wither and wear out mine age in a discomfortable, in an unwholesome, in a penurious prison, and so pay my debts with my bones and recompense the wastefulness of my youth with the beggary of mine age. Let me wither in a spital[1] under sharp and foul and infamous diseases, and so recompense the wantonness of my youth with that loathsomeness in mine age. Yet if God withdraw not his spiritual blessings, his grace, his patience; if I can call my suffering his doing, my passion[2] his action; all this that is temporal is but a caterpillar got into one corner of my garden, but a mildew fallen upon one acre of my corn. The body of all, the substance of all, is safe as long as the soul is safe.

But when I shall trust to that which we call a good spirit and God shall deject[3] and impoverish and evacuate[4] that spirit; when I shall rely upon a moral constancy and God shall shake and enfeeble and enervate, destroy and demolish that constancy; when I shall think to refresh myself in the serenity and sweet air of a good conscience and God shall call up the damps and vapors of hell itself and spread a cloud of diffidence[5] and an impenetrable crust of desperation upon my conscience; when health

1. Hospital.
2. State of being acted upon.
3. Cast down.

4. Make empty.
5. Distrust.

shall fly from me, and I shall lay hold upon riches to succor me and
comfort me in my sickness, and riches shall fly from me and I shall snatch
after favor and good opinion to comfort me in my poverty; when even
this good opinion shall leave me and calumnies and misinformations shall
prevail against me; when I shall need peace because there is none but
thou, O Lord, that should stand for me, and then shall find that all the
wounds that I have come from thy hand, all the arrows that stick in me
from thy quiver; when I shall see that because I have given myself to my
corrupt nature thou hast changed thine, and because I am all evil towards
thee, therefore thou hast given over being good towards me: when it
comes to this height, that the fever is not in the humors but in the spirits,[6]
that mine enemy is not an imaginary enemy, Fortune, nor a transitory
enemy, Malice in great persons, but a real and an irresistible and an
inexorable and an everlasting enemy, the Lord of Hosts himself, the
Almighty God himself—the Almighty God himself only knows the
weight of this affliction, and except[7] he put in that *pondus gloriae*, that
exceeding weight of an eternal glory, with his own hand into the other
scale, we are weighed down, we are swallowed up irreparably, irrevocably, irrecoverably, irremediably.

1625   1640

6. Not merely in the physical fluids of the   and to serve as a link between body and soul.
body but even in those more refined vapors   7. Unless.
thought to permeate the blood and organs

THE READER

1. *Donne is perhaps more famous as a poet than as a preacher, yet all that
   any author writes will in one way or another bear the stamp of his
   thought and personality. Read the following passage from a poem by
   Donne, and compare it with the sermon. Does the conception of God
   suggested in the poem resemble that in the sermon? Does the poem
   accomplish any of the same purposes as the sermon? Is the sermon
   "poetic" in any way? What differences arise from the fact that in the
   sermon Donne is speaking to a congregation, in the poem he is addressing God?*

> Batter my heart, three person'd God; for, you
> As yet but knocke, breathe, shine, and seeke to mend.
> That I may rise, and stand, o'erthrow mee, and bend
> Your force, to breake, blowe, burn and make me new.
> I, like an usurpt towne, to another due,
> Labour to admit you, but Oh, to no end,
> Reason your viceroy in mee, mee should defend,
> But is captiv'd, and proves weake or untrue.

2. *How far is Donne's sermon intelligible to a reader or hearer who is not
   a Christian?*

THE WRITER

1. *Rewrite Donne's first paragraph, substituting direct statements for all the metaphors. Compare your revision with Donne's original.*
2. *Write a brief essay comparing Donne's sermon to the above poem (see question 1 under "The Reader").*

Langston Hughes

SALVATION

I was saved from sin when I was going on thirteen. But not really saved. It happened like this. There was a big revival at my Auntie Reed's church. Every night for weeks there had been much preaching, singing, praying, and shouting, and some very hardened sinners had been brought to Christ, and the membership of the church had grown by leaps and bounds. Then just before the revival ended, they held a special meeting for children, "to bring the young lambs to the fold." My aunt spoke of it for days ahead. That night I was escorted to the front row and placed on the mourners' bench with all the other young sinners, who had not yet been brought to Jesus.

My aunt told me that when you were saved you saw a light, and something happened to you inside! And Jesus came into your life! And God was with you from then on! She said you could see and hear and feel Jesus in your soul. I believed her. I had heard a great many old people say the same thing and it seemed to me they ought to know. So I sat there calmly in the hot, crowded church, waiting for Jesus to come to me.

The preacher preached a wonderful rhythmical sermon, all moans and shouts and lonely cries and dire pictures of hell, and then he sang a song about the ninety and nine safe in the fold, but one little lamb was left out in the cold. Then he said: "Won't you come? Won't you come to Jesus? Young lambs, won't you come?" And he held out his arms to all us young sinners there on the mourners' bench. And the little girls cried. And some of them jumped up and went to Jesus right away. But most of us just sat there.

A great many old people came and knelt around us and prayed, old women with jet-black faces and braided hair, old men with work-gnarled hands. And the church sang a song about the lower lights are burning, some poor sinners to be saved. And the whole building rocked with prayer and song.

Still I kept waiting to see Jesus.

Finally all the young people had gone to the altar and were saved, but one boy and me. He was a rounder's[1] son named Westley. Westley and I were surrounded by sisters and deacons praying. It was very hot in the church, and getting late now. Finally Westley said to me in a whisper: "God damn! I'm tired o' sitting here. Let's get up and be saved." So he got up and was saved.

Then I was left all alone on the mourners' bench. My aunt came and knelt at my knees and cried, while prayers and songs swirled all around me in the little church. The whole congregation prayed for me alone, in a mightly wail of moans and voices. And I kept waiting serenely for Jesus, waiting, waiting—but he didn't come. I wanted to see him, but nothing happened to me. Nothing! I wanted something to happen to me, but nothing happened.

I heard the songs and the minister saying: "Why don't you come? My dear child, why don't you come to Jesus? Jesus is waiting for you. He wants you. Why don't you come? Sister Reed, what is this child's name?"

"Langston," my aunt sobbed.

"Langston, why don't you come? Why don't you come and be saved? Oh, Lamb of God! Why don't you come?"

Now it was really getting late. I began to be ashamed of myself, holding everything up so long. I began to wonder what God thought about Westley, who certainly hadn't seen Jesus either, but who was now sitting proudly on the platform, swinging his knickerbockered legs and grinning down at me, surrounded by deacons and old women on their knees praying. God had not struck Westley dead for taking his name in vain or for lying in the temple. So I decided that maybe to save further trouble, I'd better lie, too, and say that Jesus had come, and get up and be saved.

So I got up.

Suddenly the whole room broke into a sea of shouting, as they saw me rise. Waves of rejoicing swept the place. Women leaped in the air. My aunt threw her arms around me. The minister took me by the hand and led me to the platform.

When things quieted down, in a hushed silence, punctuated by a few ecstatic "Amens," all the new young lambs were blessed in the name of God. Then joyous singing filled the room.

That night, for the last time in my life but one—for I was a big boy twelve years old—I cried. I cried, in bed alone, and couldn't stop. I buried my head under the quilts, but my aunt heard me. She woke up and told my uncle I was crying because the Holy Ghost had come into my life, and because I had seen Jesus. But I was really crying because I couldn't bear to tell her that I had lied, that I had deceived everybody in the church, and I

---

1. Loafer's, bum's.

hadn't seen Jesus, and that now I didn't believe there was a Jesus any more, since he didn't come to help me.

1940

THE READER

1. When the preacher held out his arms to the young sinners, Hughes says, the little girls cried and some of them jumped up and went to Jesus right away. Is this a sexist observation? Does the fact that this was published in 1940 affect your answer?
2. Hughes obviously does not accept his Auntie Reed's explanation for his behavior. It is pretty hard to get around his explanation of why he cried, but when it comes to his salvation at the meeting, can her explanation be disproved?

THE WRITER

1. What are the signs in the first two paragraphs that point to the outcome?
2. What is Hughes's attitude toward Westley? Toward Auntie Reed?
3. This essay is written simply, with a careful regard for the facts. Replace Hughes's last paragraph with a plausible alternative that presents a different conclusion.

C. S. Lewis

THREE SCREWTAPE LETTERS

I

My Dear Wormwood,[1]

I note what you say about guiding your patient's reading and taking care that he sees a good deal of his materialist friend. But are you not being a trifle naïf? It sounds as if you supposed that argument was the way to keep him out of the Enemy's clutches. That might have been so if he had lived a few centuries earlier. At that time the humans still knew pretty well when a thing was proved and when it was not; and if it was proved they really believed it. They still connected thinking with doing and were prepared to alter their way of life as the result of a chain of reasoning. But what with the weekly press and other such weapons we have largely altered that. Your man has been accustomed, ever since he was a boy, to have a dozen incompatible philosophies dancing about together inside his head. He doesn't think of doctrines as primarily "true" or "false", but as "academic" or "practical", "outworn" or "con-

1. In these letters from Hell, Screwtape, an experienced devil, is counseling his nephew Wormwood, a neophyte tempter, who has ascended to Earth to begin his work.

temporary", "conventional" or "ruthless". Jargon, not argument, is your best ally in keeping him from the Church. Don't waste time trying to make him think that materialism is *true*! Make him think it is strong, or stark, or courageous—that it is the philosophy of the future. That's the sort of thing he cares about.

The trouble about argument is that it moves the whole struggle onto the Enemy's own ground. He can argue too; whereas in really practical propaganda of the kind I am suggesting He has been shown for centuries to be greatly the inferior of Our Father Below. By the very act of arguing, you awake the patient's reason; and once it is awake, who can foresee the result? Even if a particular train of thought can be twisted so as to end in our favour, you will find that you have been strengthening in your patient the fatal habit of attending to universal issues and withdrawing his attention from the stream of immediate sense experiences. Your business is to fix his attention on the stream. Teach him to call it "real life" and don't let him ask what he means by "real".

Remember, he is not, like you, a pure spirit. Never having been a human (Oh that abominable advantage of the Enemy's!) you don't realise how enslaved they are to the pressure of the ordinary. I once had a patient, a sound atheist, who used to read in the British Museum. One day, as he sat reading, I saw a train of thought in his mind beginning to go the wrong way. The Enemy, of course, was at his elbow in a moment. Before I knew where I was I saw my twenty years' work beginning to totter. If I had lost my head and begun to attempt a defence by argument I should have been undone. But I was not such a fool. I struck instantly at the part of the man which I had best under my control and suggested that it was just about time he had some lunch. The Enemy presumably made the countersuggestion (you know how one can never *quite* overhear what He says to them?) that this was more important than lunch. At least I think that must have been His line for when I said "Quite. In fact much *too* important to tackle at the end of a morning", the patient brightened up considerably; and by the time I had added "Much better come back after lunch and go into it with a fresh mind", he was already half way to the door. Once he was in the street the battle was won. I showed him a newsboy shouting the midday paper, and a No. 73 bus going past, and before he reached the bottom of the steps I had got into him an unalter-able conviction that, whatever odd ideas might come into a man's head when he was shut up alone with his books, a healthy dose of "real life" (by which he meant the bus and the newsboy) was enough to show him that all "that sort of thing" just couldn't be true. He knew he'd had a narrow escape and in later years was fond of talking about "that inarticulate sense for actuality which is our ultimate safeguard against the aberrations of mere logic". He is now safe in Our Father's house.

You begin to see the point? Thanks to processes which we set at work in them centuries ago, they find it all but impossible to believe in the unfamiliar while the familiar is before their eyes. Keep pressing home on him the *ordinariness* of things. Above all, do not attempt to use science (I mean, the real sciences) as a defence against Christianity. They will positively encourage him to think about realities he can't touch and see. These have been sad cases among the modern physicists. If he must dabble in science, keep him on economics and sociology; don't let him get away from that invaluable "real life". But the best of all is to let him read no science but to give him a grand general idea that he knows it all and that everything he happens to have picked up in casual talk and reading is "the results of modern investigation". Do remember you are there to fuddle him. From the way some of you young fiends talk, anyone would suppose it was our job to *teach*!

Your affectionate uncle
SCREWTAPE

II

My Dear Wormwood,

I note with grave displeasure that your patient has become a Christian. Do not indulge the hope that you will escape the usual penalties: indeed, in your better moments, I trust you would hardly even wish to do so. In the meantime we must make the best of the situation. There is no need to despair; hundreds of these adult converts have been reclaimed after a brief sojourn in the Enemy's camp and are now with us. All the *habits* of the patient, both mental and bodily, are still in our favour.

One of our great allies at present is the Church itself. Do not misunderstand me. I do not mean the Church as we see her spread out through all time and space and rooted in eternity, terrible as an army with banners. That, I confess, is a spectacle which makes our boldest tempters uneasy. But fortunately it is quite invisible to these humans. All your patient sees is the half-finished, sham Gothic erection on the new building estate. When he goes inside, he sees the local grocer with rather an oily expression on his face bustling up to offer him one shiny little book containing a liturgy which neither of them understands, and one shabby little book containing corrupt texts of a number of religious lyrics, mostly bad, and in very small print. When he gets to his pew and looks round him he sees just that selection of his neighbours whom he has hitherto avoided. You want to lean pretty heavily on those neighbours. Make his mind flit to and fro between an expression like "the body of Christ" and the actual faces in the next pew. It matters very little of course, what kind of people that next pew really contains. You may know one of them to be a great warrior on the Enemy's side. No matter. Your patient, thanks to Our Father Below, is a fool. Provided that any of those neighbours sing out of tune, or have boots that squeak, or double chins, or odd clothes, the patient will quite easily believe that their religion must therefore be somehow ridiculous. At his present stage, you see, he has an idea of "Christians" in his mind which he supposes to be spiritual but which, in fact, is largely pictorial. His mind is full of togas and sandals and armour and bare legs and the mere fact that the other people in church wear modern clothes is a real—though of course an unconscious—difficulty to him. Never let it come to the surface; never let him ask what he expected them to look like. Keep everything hazy in his mind now, and you will have all eternity wherein to amuse yourself by producing in him the peculiar kind of clarity which Hell affords.

Work hard, then, on the disappointment or anticlimax which is certainly coming to the patient during his first few weeks as a churchman. The Enemy allows this disappointment to occur on the threshold of every human endeavour. It occurs when the boy who has been enchanted in the nursery by *Stories from the Odyssey* buckles down to really learning Greek. It occurs when lovers have got married and begin the real task of learning to live together. In every department of life it marks the transition from dreaming aspiration to laborious doing. The Enemy takes this risk because He has a curious fantasy of making all these disgusting little human vermin into what He calls His "free" lovers and servants— "sons" is the word He uses, with His inveterate love of degrading the whole spiritual world by unnatural liaisons with the two-legged animals. Desiring their freedom, He therefore refuses to carry them, by their mere affections and habits, to any of the goals which He sets before them: He leaves them to "do it on their own". And there lies our opportunity. But also, remember, there lies our danger. If once they get through this initial dryness successfully, they become much less dependent on emotion and therefore much harder to tempt.

I have been writing hitherto on the assumption that the people in the next pew afford no *rational* ground for disappointment. Of course if they do—if the patient knows that the woman with the absurd hat is a fanatical bridge-player or the man with squeaky boots a miser and an extortioner—then your task is so much the easier. All you then have to do is to keep out of his mind the question "If I, being what I am, can consider that I am in some sense a Christian, why should the different vices of those people in the next pew prove that their religion is mere hypocrisy and convention?" You may ask whether it is possible to keep such an obvious thought from occurring even to a human mind. It is, Wormwood, it is! Handle him properly and it simply won't come into his head. He has not been anything like long enough with the Enemy to have any real humility yet. What he says, even on his knees, about his own sinfulness is all parrot talk. At bottom, he still believes he has run up a very favourable credit-balance in the Enemy's ledger by allowing himself to be converted, and thinks that he is showing great humility and condescension in going to church with those "smug", commonplace neighbours at all. Keep him in that state of mind as long as you can.

Your affectionate uncle
SCREWTAPE

III

My Dear Wormwood,

I am very pleased by what you tell me about this man's relations with his mother. But you must press your advantage. The Enemy will be working from the centre outwards, gradually bringing more and more of the patient's conduct under the new standard, and may reach his behaviour to the old lady at any moment. You want to get in first. Keep in close touch with our colleague Glubose who is in charge of the mother, and build up between you in that house a good settled habit of mutual annoyance; daily pinpricks. The following methods are useful.

1. Keep his mind on the inner life. He thinks his conversion is something *inside* him and his attention is therefore chiefly turned at present to the states of his own mind—or rather to that very expurgated version of them which is all you should allow him to see. Encourage this. Keep his mind off the most elementary duties by directing it to the most advanced and spiritual ones. Aggravate that most useful human characteristic, the horror and neglect of the obvious. You must bring him to a condition in which he can practise self-examination for an hour without discovering any of those facts about himself which are perfectly clear to anyone who has ever lived in the same house with him or worked in the same office.

2. It is, no doubt, impossible to prevent his praying for his mother, but we have means of rendering the prayers innocuous. Make sure that they are always very "spiritual", that he is always concerned with the state of her soul and never with her rheumatism. Two advantages will follow. In the first place, his attention will be kept on what he regards as her sins, by which, with a little guidance from you, he can be induced to mean any of her actions which are inconvenient or irritating to himself. Thus you can keep rubbing the wounds of the day a little sorer even while he is on his knees; the operation is not at all difficult and you will find it very entertaining. In the second place, since his ideas about her soul will be very crude and often erroneous, he will, in some degree, be praying for an imaginary person, and it will be your task to make that imaginary person daily less and less like the real mother—the sharp-tongued old lady at the breakfast table. In time, you may get the cleavage so wide that no thought or feeling from his prayers for the imagined mother will ever flow over into his treatment of the real one. I have had patients of my own so well in hand that they could be turned at a moment's notice from impassioned prayer for a wife's or son's "soul" to beating or insulting the real wife or son without a qualm.

3. When two humans have lived together for many years it usually happens that each has tones of voice and expressions of face which are almost unendurably irritating to the other. Work on that. Bring fully into the consciousness of your patient that particular lift of his mother's eyebrows which he learned to dislike in the nursery, and let him think how much he dislikes it. Let him assume that she knows how annoying it is and does it to annoy—if you know your job he will not notice the immense improbability of the assumption. And, of course, never let him suspect that he has tones and looks which similarly annoy her. As he cannot see or hear himself, this is easily managed.

4. In civilised life domestic hatred usually expresses itself by saying things which would appear quite harmless on paper (the words are not offensive) but in such a voice, or at such a moment, that they are not far short of a blow in the face. To keep this game up you and Glubose must see to it that each of these two fools has a sort of double standard. Your patient must demand that all his own utterances are to be taken at their face value and judged simply on the actual words, while at the same time judging all his mother's utterances with the fullest and most over-sensitive interpretation of the tone and the context and the suspected intention. She must be encouraged to do the same to him. Hence from every quarrel they can both go away convinced, or very nearly convinced, that they are quite innocent. You know the kind of thing: "I simply ask her what time dinner will be and she flies into a temper." Once this habit is well established you have the delightful situation of a human saying things with the express purpose of offending and yet having a grievance when offence is taken.

Finally, tell me something about the old lady's religious position. Is she at all jealous of the new factor in her son's life?—at all piqued that he should have learned from others, and so late, what she considers she gave him such good opportunity of learning in childhood? Does she feel he is making a great deal of "fuss" about it—or that he's getting in on very easy terms? Remember the elder brother in the Enemy's story,[2]

Your affectionate uncle
SCREWTAPE

1942

2. The reference is to Jesus' parable of the prodigal son. The younger brother, having gone out into the world and spent his inheritance, was welcomed back by the father with feasting and celebration; this made the older brother, who had stayed at home and labored diligently for the father, angry and envious.

THE READER

1. *How would you state the serious underlying purpose of the Screwtape letters? Does Lewis derive advantages for that purpose by adopting a humorous manner? Can you show any instances in which that manner places familiar material in a new light?*

2. What sort of characteristics does Lewis attribute to his devil Screwtape? Are they strange and unfamiliar, or are they human and familiar? What point does Lewis make by portraying his devil as he does?

THE WRITER

1. Following Lewis, write another letter from Screwtape to Wormwood upon learning that Wormwood's subject has just been reading Graves's "Mythology" (p. 1124) or Tillich's "The Riddle of Inequality" (p. 1147).
2. Try applying Lewis's method of irony to some other topic: write a letter or series of letters from an older student to a freshman on the subject of teachers, for example; or from one parent to another about their college-age children; or from an experienced government official to a newly elected one.

Paul Tillich

THE RIDDLE OF INEQUALITY

For to him who has will more be given; and from him
who has not, even what he has will be taken away.
—MARK iv. 25

One day a learned colleague called me up and said to me with angry excitement: "There is a saying in the New Testament which I consider to be one of the most immoral and unjust statements ever made!" And then he started quoting our text: "To him who has will more be given," and his anger increased when he continued: "and from him who has not, even what he has will be taken away." We all, I think, feel offended with him. And we cannot easily ignore the offense by suggesting what *he* suggested —that the words may be due to a misunderstanding of the disciples. It appears at least four times in the gospels with great emphasis. And even more, we can clearly see that the writers of the gospels felt exactly as we do. For them it was a stumbling block, which they tried to interpret in different ways. Probably none of these explanations satisfied them fully, for with this saying of Jesus, we are confronted immediately with the greatest and perhaps most painful riddle of life, that of the inequality of all beings. We certainly cannot hope to solve it when neither the Bible nor any other of the great religions and philosophies was able to do so. But we can do two things: We can show the breadth and the depth of the riddle of inequality and we can try to find a way to live with it, even if it is unsolved.

I

If we hear the words, "to him who has will more be given," we ask ourselves: What *do* we have? And then we may find that much is given to us in terms of external goods, of friends, of intellectual gifts and even of a comparatively high moral level of action. So we can expect that more will be given to us, while we must expect that those who are lacking in all that will lose the little they already have. Even further, according to Jesus' parable, the one talent[1] they have will be given to us who have five or ten talents. We shall be richer because they will be poorer. We may cry out against such an injustice. But we cannot deny that life confirms it abundantly. We cannot deny it, but we can ask the question, do we *really* have what we believe we have so that it cannot be taken from us? It is a question full of anxiety, confirmed by a version of our text rendered by Luke. "From him who has not, even what he *thinks* that he has will be taken away." Perhaps our having of those many things is not the kind of having which is increased. Perhaps the having of few things by the poor ones is the kind of having which makes them grow. In the parable of the talents, Jesus confirms this. Those talents which are used, even with a risk of losing them, are those which we really have; those which we try to preserve without using them for growth are those which we do not really have and which are being taken away from us. They slowly disappear, and suddenly we feel that we have lost these talents, perhaps forever.

Let us apply this to our own life, whether it is long or short. In the memory of all of us many things appear which we had without having them and which were taken away from us. Some of them became lost because of the tragic limitations of life; we had to sacrifice them in order to make other things grow. We all were given childish innocence; but innocence cannot be used and increased. The growth of our lives is possible only because we have sacrificed the original gift of innocence. Nevertheless, sometimes there arises in us a melancholy longing for a purity which has been taken from us. We all were given youthful enthusiasm for many things and aims. But this also cannot be used and increased. Most of the objects of our early enthusiasm must be sacrificed for a few, and the few must be approached with soberness. No maturity is possible without this sacrifice. Yet often a melancholy longing for the lost possibilities and enthusiasm takes hold of us. Innocence and youthful enthusiasm: we had them and had them not. Life itself demanded that they were taken from us.

But there are other things which we had and which were taken from us, because we let them go through our own guilt. Some of us had a deep sensitivity for the wonder of life as it is revealed in nature. Slowly under the pressure of work and social life and the lure of cheap pleasures, we

---

1. A Middle Eastern coin at the time of Christ. See p. 1109, above.

lose the wonder of our earlier years when we felt intense joy and the presence of the mystery of life through the freshness of the young day or the glory of the dying day, the majesty of the mountains or the infinity of the sea, a flower breaking through the soil or a young animal in the perfection of its movements. Perhaps we try to produce such feelings again, but we are empty and do not succeed. We had it and had it not, and it has been taken from us.

Others had the same experience with music, poetry, the great novels and plays. One wanted to devour all of them, one lived in them and created for oneself a life above the daily life. We *had* all this and did not have it; we did not let it grow; our love towards it was not strong enough and so it was taken from us.

Many, especially in this group, remember a time in which the desire to learn to solve the riddles of the universe, to find truth has been the driving force in their lives. They came to college and university, not in order to buy their entrance ticket into the upper middle classes or in order to provide for the preconditions of social and economic success, but they came, driven by the desire for knowledge. They had something and more could have been given to them. But in reality they did not have it. They did not make it grow and so it was taken from them and they finished their academic work in terms of expendiency and indifference towards truth. Their love for truth has left them and in some moments they are sick in their hearts because they realize that what they have lost they may never get back.

We all know that any deeper relation to a human being needs watchfulness and growth, otherwise it is taken away from us. And we cannot get it back. This is a form of having and not having which is the root of innumerable human tragedies. We all know about them. And there is another, the most fundamental kind of having and not having—our having and losing God. Perhaps we were rich towards God in our childhood and beyond it. We may remember the moments in which we felt his ultimate presence. We may remember prayers with an overflowing heart, the encounter with the holy in word and music and holy places. We had communication with God; but it was taken from us because we had it and had it not. We did not let it grow, and so it slowly disappeared leaving an empty space. We became unconcerned, cynical, indifferent, not because we doubted about our religious traditions—such doubt belongs to being rich towards God—but because we turned away from that which once concerned us infinitely.

Such thoughts are a first step in approaching the riddle of inequality. Those who have, receive more if they really have it, if they use it and make it grow. And those who have not, lose what they have because they never had it really.

II

But the question of inequality is not yet answered. For one now asks: Why do some receive more than others in the very beginning, before there is even the possibility of using or wasting our talents? Why does the one servant receive five talents and the other two and the third one? Why is the one born in the slums and the other in a well-to-do suburban family? It does not help to answer that of those to whom much is given much is demanded and little of those to whom little is given. For it is just this inequality of original gifts, internal and external, which arouses our question. Why is it given to one human being to gain so much more out of his being human than to another one? Why is so much given to the one that much *can* be asked of him, while to the other one little is given and little *can* be asked? If this question is asked, not only about individual men but also about classes, races and nations, the everlasting question of political inequality arises, and with it the many ways appear in which men have tried to abolish inequality. In every revolution and in every war, the will to solve the riddle of inequality is a driving force. But neither war nor revolution can remove it. Even if we imagine that in an indefinite future most social inequalities are conquered, three things remain: the inequality of talents in body and mind, the inequality created by freedom and destiny, and the fact that all generations before the time of such equality would be excluded from its blessings. This would be the greatest possible inequality! No! In face of one of the deepest and most torturing problems of life, it is unpermittably shallow and foolish to escape into a social dreamland. We have to live now; we have to live this our life, and we must face today the riddle of inequality.

Let us not confuse the riddle of inequality with the fact that each of us is a unique incomparable self. Certainly our being individuals belongs to our dignity as men. It is given to us and must be used and intensified and not drowned in the gray waters of conformity which threaten us today. One should defend every individuality and the uniqueness of every human self. But one should not believe that this is a way of solving the riddle of inequality. Unfortunately, there are social and political reactionaries who use this confusion in order to justify social injustice. They are at least as foolish as the dreamers of a future removal of inequality. Whoever has seen hospitals, prisons, sweatshops, battlefields, houses for the insane, starvation, family tragedies, moral aberrations should be cured from any confusion of the gift of individuality with the riddle of inequality. He should be cured from any feelings of easy consolation.

III

And now we must make the third step in our attempt to penetrate the riddle of inequality and ask: Why do some use and increase what was given to them, while others do not, so that it is taken from them? Why does God say to the prophet in our Old Testament lesson that the ears and eyes of a nation are made insensible for the divine message?

Is it enough to answer: Because some use their freedom responsibly and do what they ought to do while others fail through their own guilt? Is this answer, which seems so obvious, sufficient? Now let me first say that it *is* sufficient if we apply it to ourselves. Each of us must consider the increase or the loss of what is given to him as a matter of his own responsibility. Our conscience tells us that we cannot put the blame for our losses on anybody or anything else than ourselves.

But if we look at others, this answer is not sufficient. On the contrary: If we applied the judgment which we *must* apply to anyone else we would be like the Pharisee in Jesus' parable.[2] You cannot tell somebody who comes to you in distress about himself: Use what has been given to you; for he may come to you just because he is unable to do so! And you cannot tell those who are in despair about what they are: Be something else; for this is just what despair means—the inability of getting rid of oneself. You cannot tell those who did not conquer the destructive influences of their surroundings and were driven into crime and misery that they should have been stronger; for it was just of this strength they had been deprived by heritage or environment. Certainly they all are men, and to all of them freedom is given; but they all are also subject to destiny. It is not up to us to condemn them because they were free, as it is not up to us to excuse them because they were under their destiny. We cannot judge them. And when we judge ourselves, we must be conscious that even this is not the last word, but that we like them are under an ultimate judgment. In it the riddle of inequality is eternally answered. But this answer is not ours. It is our predicament that we must ask. And we ask with an uneasy conscience. Why are they in misery, why not we? Thinking of some who are near to us, we can ask: Are we partly responsible? But even if we are, it does not solve the riddle of inequality. The uneasy conscience asks about the farthest as well as about the nearest: Why they, why not we?

Why has my child, or any of millions and millions of children, died before even having a chance to grow out of infancy? Why is my child, or any child, born feeble-minded or crippled? Why has my friend or relative, or anybody's friend or relative, disintegrated in his mind and lost both his freedom and his destiny? Why has my son or daughter, gifted as I believe with many talents, wasted them and been deprived of them? And why does this happen to any parent at all? Why have this boy's or this girl's creative powers been broken by a tyrannical father or by a possessive mother?

In all these questions it is not the question of our own misery which we ask. It is not the question: Why has this happened to *me*?

It is not the question of Job which God answers by humiliating him and

2. Praying in the temple, the Pharisee said, "God, I thank thee, that I am not as other men are, extortioners, unjust, adulterers . . ." (Luke xviii. 11).

then by elevating him into communion with him.[3] It is not the old and urgent question: Where is the divine justice, where is the divine love towards me? But it is almost the opposite question: Why has this *not* happened to me, why has it happened to the other one, to the innumerable other ones to whom not even the power of Job is given to accept the divine answer? Why—and Jesus has asked the same question—are many called and few elected?

He does not answer; he only states that this is the human predicament. Shall we therefore cease to ask and humbly accept the fact of a divine judgment which condemns most human beings away from the community with him into despair and self-destruction? Can we accept the eternal victory of judgment over love? We cannot; and nobody ever could, even if he preached and threatened in these terms. As long as he could not see himself with complete certainty as eternally rejected, his preaching and threatening would be self-deceiving. And who could see himself eternally rejected?

But if this is not the solution of the riddle of inequality at its deepest level, can we trespass the boundaries of the Christian tradition and listen to those who tell us that this life does not decide about our eternal destiny? There will be occasions in other lives, as our present life is determined by previous ones and what we have achieved or wasted in them. It is a serious doctrine and not completely strange to Christianity. But if we don't know and never will know what each of us has been in the previous or future lives, then it is not really *our* destiny which develops from life to life, but in each life it is the destiny of someone else. This answer also does not solve the riddle of inequality.

There is no answer at all if we ask about the temporal and eternal destiny of the single being separated from the destiny of the whole. Only in the unity of all beings in time and eternity can a humanly possible answer to the riddle of inequality be found. *Humanly* possible does not mean an answer which removes the riddle of inequality, but an answer with which we can live.

There is an ultimate unity of all beings, rooted in the divine life from which they come and to which they go. All beings, nonhuman as well as human, participate in it. And therefore they all participate in each other. We participate in each other's having and we participate in each other's not-having. If we become aware of this unity of all beings, something happens. The fact that others have-not changes in every moment the character of my having: It undercuts its security, it drives me beyond myself, to understand, to give, to share, to help. The fact that others fall

3. Job, one of God's favored servants, was stricken with afflictions. His question, very briefly, was "Why?" God's answer was to remind Job of how powerless man was in comparison with God, and to refuse to explain His actions. After accepting this pronouncement, Job was elevated again into God's favor.

into sin, crime and misery changes the character of the grace which is given to me: It makes me realize my own hidden guilt, it shows to me that those who suffer for their sin and crime, suffer also for me; for I am guilty of their guilt—at least in the desire of my heart—and ought to suffer as they do. The awareness that others who *could* have become fully developed human beings and never *have*, changes my state of full humanity. Their early death, their early or late disintegration, makes my life and my health a continuous risk, a dying which is not yet death, a disintegration which is not yet destruction. In every death which we encounter, something of us dies; in every disease which we encounter, something of us tends to disintegrate.

Can we live with this answer? We can to the degree in which we are liberated from the seclusion within ourselves. But nobody can be liberated from himself unless he is grasped by the power of that which is present in everyone and everything—the eternal from which we come and to which we go, which gives us to ourselves and which liberates us *from* ourselves. It is the greatness and the heart of the Christian message that God—as manifest in the Cross of the Christ—participates totally in the dying child, in the condemned criminal, in the disintegrating mind, in the starving one and in him who rejects him. There is no extreme human condition into which the divine presence would not reach. This is what the Cross, the most extreme of all human conditions, tells us. The riddle of inequality cannot be solved on the level of our separation from each other. It is eternally solved in the divine participation in all of us and every being. The certainty of the divine participation gives us the courage to stand the riddle of inequality, though finite minds cannot solve it. Amen.

                                                                    1963

Stephen Jay Gould

NONMORAL NATURE

When the Right Honorable and Reverend Francis Henry, earl of Bridgewater, died in February, 1829, he left £8,000 to support a series of books "on the power, wisdom, and goodness of God, as manifested in the creation." William Buckland, England's first official academic geologist and later dean of Westminster, was invited to compose one of the nine Bridgewater Treatises. In it he discussed the most pressing problem of natural theology: if God is benevolent and the Creation displays his "power, wisdom, and goodness," then why are we surrounded with pain, suffering, and apparently senseless cruelty in the animal world?

Buckland considered the depredation of "carnivorous races" as the primary challenge to an idealized world where the lion might dwell with the lamb. He resolved the issue to his satisfaction by arguing that carnivores actually increase "the aggregate of animal enjoyment" and "diminish that of pain." Death, after all, is swift and relatively painless, victims are spared the ravages of decrepitude and senility, and populations do not outrun their food supply to the greater sorrow of all. God knew what he was doing when he made lions. Buckland concluded in hardly concealed rapture:

> The appointment of death by the agency of carnivora, as the ordinary termination of animal existence, appears therefore in its main results to be a dispensation of benevolence; it deducts much from the aggregate amount of the pain of universal death; it abridges, and almost annihilates, throughout the brute creation, the misery of disease, and accidental injuries, and lingering decay; and imposes such salutary restraint upon excessive increase of numbers, that the supply of food maintains perpetually a due ratio to the demand. The result is, that the surface of the land and depths of the waters are ever crowded with myriads of animated beings, the pleasures of whose life are coextensive with its duration; and which throughout the little day of existence that is allotted to them, fulfill with joy the functions for which they were created.

We may find a certain amusing charm in Buckland's vision today, but such arguments did begin to address "the problem of evil" for many of Buckland's contemporaries—how could a benevolent God create such a world of carnage and bloodshed? Yet this argument could not abolish the problem of evil entirely, for nature includes many phenomena far more horrible in our eyes than simple predation. I suspect that nothing evokes greater disgust in most of us than slow destruction of a host by an internal parasite—gradual ingestion, bit by bit, from the inside. In no other way can I explain why *Alien*, an uninspired, grade-C, formula horror film, should have won such a following. That single scene of Mr. Alien, popping forth as a baby parasite from the body of a human host, was both sickening and stunning. Our nineteenth-century forebears maintained similar feelings. The greatest challenge to their concept of a benevolent deity was not simple predation—but slow death by parasitic ingestion. The classic case, treated at length by all great naturalists, invoked the so-called ichneumon fly. Buckland had sidestepped the major issue.

The "ichneumon fly," which provoked such concern among natural theologians, was actually a composite creature representing the habits of an enormous tribe. The Ichneumonoidea are a group of wasps, not flies, that include more species than all the vertebrates combined (wasps, with ants and bees, constitute the order Hymenoptera; flies, with their two wings—wasps have four—form the order Diptera). In addition, many non-ichneumonid wasps of similar habits were often cited for the same grisly details. Thus, the famous story did not merely implicate a single aberrant species (perhaps a perverse leakage from Satan's realm), but hundreds of thousands—a large chunk of what could only be God's creation.

The ichneumons, like most wasps, generally live freely as adults but pass their larval life as parasites feeding on the bodies of other animals, almost invariably members of their own phylum, the Arthropoda. The most common victims are caterpillars (butterfly and moth larvae), but some ichneumons prefer aphids and others attack spiders. Most hosts are parasitized as larvae, but some adults are attacked, and many tiny ichneumons inject their brood directly into the egg of their host.

The free-flying females locate an appropriate host and then convert it to a food factory for their own young. Parasitologists speak of ectoparasitism when the uninvited guest lives on the surface of its host, and endoparasitism when the parasite dwells within. Among endoparasitic ichneumons, adult females pierce the host with their ovipositor and deposit eggs within. (The ovipositor, a thin tube extending backward from the wasp's rear end, may be many times as long as the body itself.) Usually, the host is not otherwise inconvenienced for the moment, at least until the eggs hatch and the ichneumon larvae begin their grim work of interior excavation.

Among ectoparasites, however, many females lay their eggs directly upon the host's body. Since an active host would easily dislodge the egg, the ichneumon mother often simultaneously injects a toxin that paralyzes the caterpillar or other victim. The paralysis may be permanent, and the caterpillar lies, alive but immobile, with the agent of its future destruction secure on its belly. The egg hatches, the helpless caterpillar twitches, the wasp larva pierces and begins its grisly feast.

Since a dead and decaying caterpillar will do the wasp larva no good, it eats a pattern that cannot help but recall, in our inappropriate, anthropocentric interpretation, the ancient English penalty of treason—drawing and quartering, with its explicit object of extracting as much torment as possible by keeping the victim alive and sentient. As the king's executioner drew out and burned his client's entrails, so does the ichneumon larva eat fat bodies and digestive organs first, keeping the caterpillar alive by preserving intact the essential heart and central nervous system. Finally, the larva completes its work and kills its victim, leaving behind the caterpillar's empty shell. Is it any wonder that ichneumons, not snakes or lions, stood as the paramount challenge to God's benevolence during the heyday of natural theology?

As I read through the nineteenth- and twentieth-century literature on ichneumons, nothing amused me more than the tension between an intellectual knowledge that wasps should not be described in human

terms and a literary or emotional inability to avoid the familiar categories
of epic and narrative, pain and destruction, victim and vanquisher. We
seem to be caught in the mythic structures of our own cultural sagas,
quite unable, even in our basic descriptions, to use any other language
than the metaphors of battle and conquest. We cannot render this corner
of natural history as anything but story, combining the themes of grim
horror and fascination and usually ending not so much with pity for the
caterpillars as with admiration for the efficiency of the ichneumon.

I detect two basic themes in most epic descriptions: the struggles of
prey and the ruthless efficiency of parasites. Although we acknowledge
that we may be witnessing little more than automatic instinct or physiological reaction, still we describe the defenses of hosts as though they
represented conscious struggles. Thus, aphids kick and caterpillars may
wriggle violently as wasps attempt to insert their ovipositors. The pupa
of the tortoiseshell butterfly (usually considered an inert creature silently
awaiting its conversion from duckling to swan) may contort its abdominal
region so sharply that attacking wasps are thrown into the air. The
caterpillars of *Hapalia*, when attacked by the wasp *Apanteles machaeralis*,
drop suddenly from their leaves and suspend themselves in air by a silken
thread. But the wasp may run down the thread and insert its eggs
nonetheless. Some hosts can encapsulate the injected egg with blood cells
that aggregate and harden, thus suffocating the parasite.

J. H. Fabre, the great nineteenth-century French entomologist, who
remains to this day the preeminently literate natural historian of insects,
made a special study of parasitic wasps and wrote with an unabashed
anthropocentrism about the struggles of paralyzed victims (see his books
Insect Life and *The Wonders of Instinct*). He describes some imperfectly
paralyzed caterpillars that struggle so violently every time a parasite
approaches that the wasp larvae must feed with unusual caution. They
attach themselves to a silken strand from the roof of their burrow and
descend upon a safe and exposed part of the caterpillar:

> The grub is at dinner: head downwards, it is digging into the limp belly of one
> of the caterpillars. . . . At the least sign of danger in the heap of caterpillars,
> the larva retreats . . . and climbs back to the ceiling, where the swarming
> rabble cannot reach it. When peace is restored, it slides down [its silken cord]
> and returns to table, with its head over the viands and its rear upturned and
> ready to withdraw in case of need.

In another chapter, he describes the fate of a paralyzed cricket:

> One may see the cricket, bitten to the quick, vainly move its antennae and
> abdominal styles, open and close its empty jaws, and even move a foot, but the
> larva is safe and searches its vitals with impunity. What an awful nightmare
> for the paralyzed cricket!

Fabre even learned to feed paralyzed victims by placing a syrup of sugar and water on their mouthparts—thus showing that they remained alive, sentient, and (by implication) grateful for any palliation of their inevitable fate. If Jesus, immobile and thirsting on the cross, received only vinegar from his tormentors, Fabre at least could make an ending bittersweet.

The second theme, ruthless efficiency of the parasites, leads to the opposite conclusion—grudging admiration for the victors. We learn of their skill in capturing dangerous hosts often many times larger then themselves. Caterpillars may be easy game, but psammocharid wasps prefer spiders. They must insert their ovipositors in a safe and precise spot. Some leave a paralyzed spider in its own burrow. *Planiceps hirsutus*, for example, parasitizes a California trapdoor spider. It searches for spider tubes on sand dunes, then digs into nearby sand to disturb the spider's home and drives it out. When the spider emerges, the wasp attacks, paralyzes its victim, drags it back into its own tube, shuts and fastens the trapdoor, and deposits a single egg upon the spider's abdomen. Other psammocharids will drag a heavy spider back to a previously prepared cluster of clay or mud cells. Some amputate a spider's legs to make the passage easier. Others fly back over water, skimming a buoyant spider along the surface.

Some wasps must battle with other parasites over a host's body. *Rhyssella curvipes* can detect the larvae of wood wasps deep within alder wood and drill down to a potential victim with its sharply ridged ovipositor. *Pseudorhyssa alpestris*, a related parasite, cannot drill directly into wood since its slender ovipositor bears only rudimentary cutting ridges. It locates the holes made by *Rhyssella*, inserts its ovipositor, and lays an egg on the host (already conveniently paralyzed by *Rhyssella*), right next to the egg deposited by its relative. The two eggs hatch at about the same time, but the larva of *Pseudorhyssa* has a bigger head bearing much larger mandibles. *Pseudorhyssa* seizes the smaller *Rhyssella* larva, destroys it, and proceeds to feast upon a banquet already well prepared.

Other praises for the efficiency of mothers invoke the themes of early, quick, and often. Many ichneumons don't even wait for their hosts to develop into larvae, but parasitize the egg directly (larval wasps may then either drain the egg itself or enter the developing host larva). Others simply move fast. *Apanteles militaris* can deposit up to seventy-two eggs in a single second. Still others are doggedly persistent. *Aphidius gomezi* females produce up to 1,500 eggs and can parasitize as many as 600 aphids in a single working day. In a bizarre twist upon "often," some wasps indulge in polyembryony, a kind of iterated supertwining. A single egg divides into cells that aggregate into as many as 500 individuals. Since some polyembryonic wasps parasitize caterpillars much larger than themselves and may lay up to six eggs in each, as many as 3,000 larvae may develop within, and feed upon a single host. These wasps are endoparasites and do not paralyze their victims. The caterpillars writhe back and forth, not (one suspects) from pain, but merely in response to the commotion induced by thousands of wasp larvae feeding within.

Maternal efficiency is often matched by larval aptitude. I have already mentioned the pattern of eating less essential parts first, thus keeping the host alive and fresh to its final and merciful dispatch. After the larva digests every edible morsel of its victim (if only to prevent later fouling of its abode by decaying tissue), it may still use the outer shell of its host. One aphid parasite cuts a hole in the bottom of its victim's shell, glues the skeleton to a leaf by sticky secretions from its salivary gland, and then spins a cocoon to pupate within the aphid's shell.

In using inappropriate anthropocentric language for this romp through the natural history of ichneumons, I have tried to emphasize just why these wasps became a preeminent challenge to natural theology—the antiquated doctrine that attempted to infer God's essence from the products of his creation. I have used twentieth-century examples for the most part, but all themes were known and stressed by the great nineteenth-century natural theologians. How then did they square the habits of these wasps with the goodness of God? How did they extract themselves from this dilemma of their own making?

The strategies were as varied as the practitioners; they shared only the theme of special pleading for an a priori doctrine—our naturalists knew that God's benevolence was lurking somewhere behind all these tales of apparent horror. Charles Lyell, for example, in the first edition of his epochal *Principles of Geology* (1830–1833), decided that caterpillars posed such a threat to vegetation that any natural checks upon them could only reflect well upon a creating deity, for caterpillars would destroy human agriculture "did not Providence put causes in operation to keep them in due bounds."

The Reverend William Kirby, rector of Barham, and Britain's foremost entomologist, chose to ignore the plight of caterpillars and focused instead upon the virtue of mother love displayed by wasps in provisioning their young with such care.

> The great object of the female is to discover a proper nidus for her eggs. In search of this she is in constant motion. Is the caterpillar of a butterfly or moth the appropriate food for her young? You see her alight upon the plants where they are most usually to be met with, run quickly over them, carefully examining every leaf, and, having found the unfortunate object of her search, insert her sting into its flesh, and there deposit an egg. ... The active Ichneumon braves every danger, and does not desist until her courage and address have insured subsistence for one of her future progeny.

Kirby found this solicitude all the more remarkable because the female wasp will never see her child and enjoy the pleasures of parenthood. Yet love compels her to danger nonetheless:

> A very large proportion of them are doomed to die before their young come into existence. But in these the passion is not extinguished. . . . When you witness the solicitude with which they provide for the security and sustenance of their future young, you can scarcely deny to them love for a progeny they are never destined to behold.

Kirby also put in a good word for the marauding larvae, praising them for their forbearance in eating selectively to keep their caterpillar alive. Would we all husband our resources with such care!

> In this strange and apparently cruel operation one circumstance is truly remarkable. The larva of the Ichneumon, though every day, perhaps for months, it gnaws the inside of the caterpillar, and though at last it has devoured almost every part of it except the skin and intestines, carefully all this time it avoids injuring the vital organs, as if aware that its own existence depends on that of the insect upon which it preys! . . . What would be the impression which a similar instance amongst the race of quadrupeds would make upon us? If, for example, an animal . . . should be found to feed upon the inside of a dog, devouring only those parts not essential to life, while it cautiously left uninjured the heart, arteries, lungs, and intestines—should we not regard such an instance as a perfect prodigy, as an example of instinctive forbearance almost miraculous? [The last three quotes come from the 1856, and last pre-Darwinian, edition of Kirby and Spence's *Introduction to Entomology.*]

This tradition of attempting to read moral meaning from nature did not cease with the triumph of evolutionary theory in 1859—for evolution could be read as God's chosen method of peopling our planet, and ethical messages might still populate nature. Thus, St. George Mivart, one of Darwin's most effective evolutionary critics and a devout Catholic, argued that "many amiable and excellent people" had been misled by the apparent suffering of animals for two reasons. First, whatever the pain, "physical suffering and moral evil are simply incommensurable." Since beasts are not moral agents, their feelings cannot bear any ethical message. But secondly, lest our visceral sensitivities still be aroused, Mivart assures us that animals must feel little, if any, pain. Using a favorite racist argument of the time—that "primitive" people suffer far less than advanced and cultured folk—Mivart extrapolated further down the ladder of life into a realm of very limited pain indeed: Physical suffering, he argued,

> depends greatly upon the mental condition of the sufferer. Only during consciousness does it exist, and only in the most highly organized men does it reach its acme. The author has been assured that lower races of men appear less keenly sensitive to physical suffering than do more cultivated and refined

human beings. Thus only in man can there really be any intense degree of suffering, because only in him is there that intellectual recollection of past moments and that anticipation of future ones, which constitute in great part the bitterness of suffering. The momentary pang, the present pain, which beasts endure, though real enough, is yet, doubtless, not to be compared as to its intensity with the suffering which is produced in man through his high prerogative of self-consciousness (from *Genesis of Species*, 1871).

It took Darwin himself to derail this ancient tradition—and he proceeded in the gentle way so characteristic of his radical intellectual approach to nearly everything. The ichneumons also troubled Darwin greatly and he wrote of them to Asa Gray in 1860:

I own that I cannot see as plainly as others do, and as I should wish to do, evidence of design and beneficence on all sides of us. There seems to me too much misery in the world. I cannot persuade myself that a beneficent and omnipotent God would have designedly created the Ichneumonidae with the express intention of their feeding within the living bodies of Caterpillars, or that a cat should play with mice.

Indeed, he had written with more passion to Joseph Hooker in 1856: "What a book a devil's chaplain might write on the clumsy, wasteful, blundering, low, and horribly cruel works of nature!"

This honest admission—that nature is often (by our standards) cruel and that all previous attempts to find a lurking goodness behind everything represent just so much special pleading—can lead in two directions. One might retain the principle that nature holds moral messages, but reverse the usual perspective and claim that morality consists in understanding the ways of nature and doing the opposite. Thomas Henry Huxley advanced this argument in his famous essay on *Evolution and Ethics* (1893):

The practice of that which is ethically best—what we call goodness or virtue —involves a course of conduct which, in all respects, is opposed to that which leads to success in the cosmic struggle for existence. In place of ruthless self-assertion it demands self-restraint; in place of thrusting aside, or treading down, all competitors, it requires that the individual shall not merely respect, but shall help his fellows. . . . It repudiates the gladiatorial theory of existence. . . . Laws and moral precepts are directed to the end of curbing the cosmic process.

The other argument, radical in Darwin's day but more familiar now, holds that nature simply is as we find it. Our failure to discern a universal good does not record any lack of insight or ingenuity, but merely demonstrates that nature contains no moral messages framed in human terms. Morality is a subject for philosophers, theologians, students of the humanities, indeed for all thinking people. The answers will not be read passively from nature; they do not, and cannot, arise from the data of science. The factual state of the world does not teach us how we, with our powers for good and evil, should alter or preserve it in the most ethical manner.

Darwin himself tended toward this view, although he could not, as a man of his time, thoroughly abandon the idea that laws of nature might reflect some higher purpose. He clearly recognized that specific manifestations of those laws—cats playing with mice, and ichneumon larvae eating caterpillars—could not embody ethical messages, but he somehow hoped that unknown higher laws might exist "with the details, whether good or bad, left to the working out of what we may call chance."

Since ichneumons are a detail, and since natural selection is a law regulating details, the answer to the ancient dilemma of why such cruelty (in our terms) exists in nature can only be that there isn't any answer—and that framing the question "in our terms" is thoroughly inappropriate in a natural world neither made for us nor ruled by us. It just plain happens. It is a strategy that works for ichneumons and that natural selection has programmed into their behavioral repertoire. Caterpillars are not suffering to teach us something; they have simply been outmaneuvered, for now, in the evolutionary game. Perhaps they will evolve a set of adequate defenses sometime in the future, thus sealing the fate of ichneumons. And perhaps, indeed probably, they will not.

Another Huxley, Thomas's grandson Julian, spoke for this position, using as an example—yes, you guessed it—the ubiquitous ichneumons:

> Natural selection, in fact, though like the mills of God in grinding slowly and grinding small, has few other attributes that a civilized religion would call divine. ... Its products are just as likely to be aesthetically, morally, or intellectually repulsive to us as they are to be attractive. We need only think of the ugliness of *Sacculina* or a bladder-worm, the stupidity of a rhinoceros or a stegosaur, the horror of a female mantis devouring its mate or a brood of ichneumon flies slowly eating out a caterpillar.

If nature is nonmoral, then evolution cannot teach any ethical theory at all. The assumption that it can has abetted a panoply of social evils that ideologues falsely read into nature from their beliefs—eugenics and (misnamed) social Darwinism prominently among them. Not only did Darwin eschew any attempt to discover an antireligious ethic in nature, he also expressly stated his personal bewilderment about such deep issues as the problem of evil. Just a few sentences after invoking the ichneumons, and in words that express both the modesty of this splendid man and the compatibility, through lack of contact, between science and true religion, Darwin wrote to Asa Gray,

> I feel most deeply that the whole subject is too profound for the human intellect. A dog might as well speculate on the mind of Newton. Let each man hope and believe what he can.

1983

THE READER

1. Gould identifies two possible arguments on the morality or nonmorality of nature (p. 1156). Does he prefer one to the other? Lorenz, in "The Taming of the Shrew," says, "Man should abstain from judging his innocently-cruel fellow creatures" (p. 888). Does that statement follow from the second argument?.

2. In "The Superorganism" (p. 856), Wilson speaks as a scientist and as one who is concerned about what we should or should not do. Has he eliminated the distinction Gould makes between science and morality?

3. Cohen, in "The Case for the Use of Animals in Biomedical Research" (p. 633), and Regan, in "The Case for Animal Rights" (p. 621), are two philosophers debating animal rights, especially in scientific experiments. Are they arguing science or morality?

THE WRITER

1. At the beginning of his essay, Gould provides a sample of William Buckland's rhetoric, which he says has an "amusing charm," and then launches into his own no less rhetorical discussion. What is his justification for his own rhetoric?

2. Can you describe what the ichneumon does without anthropocentric rhetoric? Write a descriptive paragraph to support your answer.

E. M. Forster

WHAT I BELIEVE

I do not believe in Belief. But this is an age of faith, and there are so many militant creeds that, in self-defence, one has to formulate a creed of one's own. Tolerance, good temper and sympathy are no longer enough in a world which is rent by religious and racial persecution, in a world where ignorance rules, and science, who ought to have ruled, plays the subservient pimp. Tolerance, good temper and sympathy—they are what matter really, and if the human race is not to collapse they must come to the front before long. But for the moment they are not enough, their action is no stronger than a flower, battered beneath a military jackboot. They want stiffening, even if the process coarsens them. Faith, to my mind, is a stiffening process, a sort of mental starch, which ought to be applied as sparingly as possible. I dislike the stuff. I do not believe in it, for its own sake, at all. Herein I probably differ from most people, who believe in Belief, and are only sorry they cannot swallow even more than they do. My law-givers are Erasmus and Montaigne, not Moses and St. Paul. My temple stands not upon Mount Moriah[1] but in that Elysian Field[2] where even the immoral are admitted. My motto is: "Lord, I disbelieve—help thou my unbelief."

I have, however, to live in an Age of Faith—the sort of epoch I used to hear praised when I was a boy. It is extremely unpleasant really. It is bloody in every sense of the word. And I have to keep my end up in it. Where do I start?

With personal relationships. Here is something comparatively solid in a world full of violence and cruelty. Not absolutely solid, for Psychology has split and shattered the idea of a "Person," and has shown that there is something incalculable in each of us, which may at any moment rise to the surface and destroy our normal balance. We don't know what we are like. We can't know what other people are like. How, then, can we put any trust in personal relationships, or cling to them in the gathering political storm? In theory we cannot. But in practice we can and do. Though A is not unchangeably A or B unchangeably B, there can still be love and loyalty between the two. For the purpose of living one has to assume that the personality is solid, and the "self" is an entity, and to ignore all contrary evidence. And since to ignore evidence is one of the characteristics of faith, I certainly can proclaim that I believe in personal relationships.

Starting from them, I get a little order into the contemporary chaos. One must be fond of people and trust them if one is not to make a mess of life, and it is therefore essential that they should not let one down. They often do. The moral of which is that I must, myself, be as reliable as possible, and this I try to be. But reliability is not a matter of contract— that is the main difference between the world of personal relationships and the world of business relationships. It is a matter for the heart, which signs no documents. In other words, reliability is impossible unless there is a natural warmth. Most men possess this warmth, though they often have bad luck and get chilled. Most of them, even when they are politicians, *want* to keep faith. And one can, at all events, show one's own little light here, one's own poor little trembling flame, with the knowledge that it is not the only light that is shining in the darkness, and not the only one which the darkness does not comprehend. Personal relations are despised today. They are regarded as bourgeois luxuries, as products of a time of fair weather which is now past, and we are urged to get rid of them, and to dedicate ourselves to some movement or cause instead. I hate the idea of causes, and if I had to choose between betraying my country and betraying my friend, I hope I should have the guts to betray my country. Such a choice may scandalise the modern reader, and he may stretch out

1. Biblical name for a hill in East Jerusalem, the site of Solomon's Temple.   2. In Greek religion, a happy otherworld for heroes favored by the gods.

his patriotic hand to the telephone at once and ring up the police. It would not have shocked Dante, though. Dante places Brutus and Cassius in the lowest circle of Hell because they had chosen to betray their friend Julius Caesar rather than their country Rome. Probably one will not be asked to make such an agonising choice. Still, there lies at the back of every creed something terrible and hard for which the worshipper may one day be required to suffer, and there is even a terror and a hardness in this creed of personal relationships, urbane and mild though it sounds. Love and loyalty to an individual can run counter to the claims of the State. When they do—down with the State, say I, which means that the State would down me.

This brings me along to Democracy, "even Love, the Beloved Republic, which feeds upon Freedom and lives." Democracy is not a Beloved Republic really, and never will be. But it is less hateful than other contemporary forms of government, and to that extent it deserves our support. It does start from the assumption that the individual is important, and that all types are needed to make a civilisation. It does not divide its citizens into the bossers and the bossed—as an efficiency-regime tends to do. The people I admire most are those who are sensitive and want to create something or discover something, and do not see life in terms of power, and such people get more of a chance under a democracy than elsewhere. They found religions, great or small, or they produce literature and art, or they do disinterested scientific research, or they may be what is called "ordinary people," who are creative in their private lives, bring up their children decently, for instance, or help their neighbours. All these people need to express themselves; they cannot do so unless society allows them liberty to do so, and the society which allows them most liberty is a democracy.

Democracy has another merit. It allows criticism, and if there is not public criticism there are bound to be hushed-up scandals. That is why I believe in the Press, despite all its lies and vulgarity, and why I believe in Parliament. Parliament is often sneered at because it is a Talking Shop. I believe in it *because* it is a talking shop. I believe in the Private Member who makes himself a nuisance. He gets snubbed and is told that he is cranky or ill-informed, but he does expose abuses which would otherwise never have been mentioned, and very often an abuse gets put right just by being mentioned. Occasionally, too, a well-meaning public official starts losing his head in the cause of efficiency, and thinks himself God Almighty. Such officials are particularly frequent in the Home Office.[3] Well, there will be questions about them in Parliament sooner or later, and then they will have to mind their steps. Whether Parliament is either a representative body or an efficient one is questionable, but I

3. A department of government in Great Britain corresponding to the Department of the Interior in the United States.

value it because it criticises and talks, and because its chatter gets widely reported.

So Two Cheers for Democracy: one because it admits variety and two because it permits criticism. Two cheers are quite enough: there is no occasion to give three. Only Love the Beloved Republic deserves that.

What about Force, though? While we are trying to be sensitive and advanced and affectionate and tolerant, an unpleasant question pops up: does not all society rest upon force? If a government cannot count upon the police and the army, how can it hope to rule? And if an individual gets knocked on the head or sent to a labour camp, of what significance are his opinions?

This dilemma does not worry me as much as it does some. I realise that all society rests upon force. But all the great creative actions, all the decent human relations, occur during the intervals when force has not managed to come to the front. These intervals are what matter. I want them to be as frequent and as lengthy as possible, and I call them "civilisation." Some people idealise force and pull it into the foreground and worship it, instead of keeping it in the background as long as possible. I think they make a mistake, and I think that their opposites, the mystics, err even more when they declare that force does not exist. I believe that it exists, and that one of our jobs is to prevent it from getting out of its box. It gets out sooner or later, and then it destroys us and all the lovely things which we have made. But it is not out all the time, for the fortunate reason that the strong are so stupid. Consider their conduct for a moment in the Niebelung's Ring.[4] The giants there have the guns, or in other words the gold; but they do nothing with it, they do not realise that they are all-powerful, with the result that the catastrophe is delayed and the castle of Walhalla, insecure but glorious, fronts the storms. Fafnir, coiled round his hoard, grumbles and grunts; we can hear him under Europe today; the leaves of the wood already tremble, and the Bird calls its warnings uselessly. Fafnir will destroy us, but by a blessed dispensation he is stupid and slow, and creation goes on just outside the poisonous blast of his breath. The Nietzschean would hurry the monster up, the mystic would say he did not exist, but Wotan, wiser than either, hastens to create warriors before doom declares itself. The Valkyries are symbols not only of courage but of intelligence; they represent the human spirit snatching its opportunity while the going is good, and one of them even finds time to love. Brünnhilde's last song hymns the recurrence of love, and since it is the privilege of art to exaggerate, she goes even further, and proclaims the love which is eternally triumphant and feeds upon freedom, and lives.

So that is what I feel about force and violence. It is, alas! the ultimate

4. Four operas by Richard Wagner, based on a Middle High German legend of the thirteenth century.

reality on this earth, but it does not always get to the front. Some people call its absences "decadence"; I call them "civilisation" and find in such interludes the chief justification for the human experiment. I look the other way until fate strikes me. Whether this is due to courage or to cowardice in my own case I cannot be sure. But I know that if men had not looked the other way in the past, nothing of any value would survive. The people I respect most behave as if they were immortal and as if society was eternal. Both assumptions are false: both of them must be accepted as true if we are to go on eating and working and loving, and are to keep open a few breathing holes for the human spirit. No millennium seems likely to descend upon humanity; no better and stronger League of Nations will be instituted; no form of Christianity and no alternative to Christianity will bring peace to the world or integrity to the individual; no "change of heart" will occur. And yet we need not despair, indeed, we cannot despair; the evidence of history shows us that men have always insisted on behaving creatively under the shadow of the sword; that they have done their artistic and scientific and domestic stuff for the sake of doing it, and that we had better follow their example under the shadow of the aeroplanes. Others, with more vision or courage than myself, see the salvation of humanity ahead, and will dismiss my conception of civilisation as paltry, a sort of tip-and-run[5] game. Certainly it is presumptuous to say that we *cannot* improve, and that Man, who has only been in power for a few thousand years, will never learn to make use of his power. All I mean is that, if people continue to kill one another as they do, the world cannot get better than it is, and that since there are more people than formerly, and their means for destroying one another superior, the world may well get worse. What is good in people—and consequently in the world—is their insistence on creation, their belief in friendship and loyalty for their own sakes; and though Violence remains and is, indeed, the major partner in this muddled establishment, I believe that creativeness remains too, and will always assume direction when violence sleeps. So, though I am not an optimist, I cannot agree with Sophocles that it were better never to have been born. And although, like Horace, I see no evidence that each batch of births is superior to the last, I leave the field open for the more complacent view. This is such a difficult moment to live in, one cannot help getting gloomy and also a bit rattled, and perhaps short-sighted.

In search of a refuge, we may perhaps turn to hero-worship. But here we shall get no help, in my opinion. Hero-worship is a dangerous vice, and one of the minor merits of a democracy is that it does not encourage it, or produce that unmanageable type of citizen known as the Great Man. It produces instead different kinds of small men—a much finer

5. A game similar to cricket in which a batsman is required to run each time he touches a bowled ball with his bat.

achievement. But people who cannot get interested in the variety of life, and cannot make up their own minds, get discontented over this, and they long for a hero to bow down before and to follow blindly. It is significant that a hero is an integral part of the authoritarian stock-in-trade today. An efficiency-regime cannot be run without a few heroes stuck about it to carry off the dullness—much as plums have to be put into a bad pudding to make it palatable. One hero at the top and a smaller one each side of him is a favourite arrangement, and the timid and the bored are comforted by the trinity, and, bowing down, feel exalted and strengthened.

No, I distrust Great Men. They produce a desert of uniformity around them and often a pool of blood too, and I always feel a little man's pleasure when they come a cropper. Every now and then one reads in the newspapers some such statement as: "The coup d'état appears to have failed, and Admiral Toma's whereabouts is at present unknown." Admiral Toma had probably every qualification for being a Great Man—an iron will, personal magnetism, dash, flair, sexlessness—but fate was against him, so he retires to unknown whereabouts instead of parading history with his peers. He fails with a completeness which no artist and no lover can experience, because with them the process of creation is itself an achievement, whereas with him the only possible achievement is success.

I believe in aristocracy, though—if that is the right word, and if a democrat may use it. Not an aristocracy of power, based upon rank and influence, but an aristocracy of the sensitive, the considerate and the plucky. Its members are to be found in all nations and classes, and all through the ages, and there is a secret understanding between them when they meet. They represent the true human tradition, the one permanent victory of our queer race over cruelty and chaos. Thousands of them perish in obscurity, a few are great names. They are sensitive for others as well as for themselves, they are considerate without being fussy, their pluck is not swankiness but the power to endure, and they can take a joke. I give no examples—it is risky to do that—but the reader may as well consider whether this is the type of person he would like to meet and to be, and whether (going farther with me) he would prefer that this type should *not* be an ascetic one. I am against asceticism myself. I am with the old Scotsman who wanted less chastity and more delicacy. I do not feel that my aristocrats are a real aristocracy if they thwart their bodies, since bodies are the instruments through which we register and enjoy the world. Still, I do not insist. This is not a major point. It is clearly possible to be sensitive, considerate and plucky and yet be an ascetic too, if anyone possesses the first three qualities, I will let him in! On they go— an invincible army, yet not a victorious one. The aristocrats, the elect, the chosen, the Best People—all the words that describe them are false, and all attempts to organise them fail. Again and again Authority, seeing their value, has tried to net them and to utilise them as the Egyptian Priesthood or the Christian Church or the Chinese Civil Service or the Group Movement, or some other worthy stunt. But they slip through the net and are gone; when the door is shut, they are no longer in the room; their temple, as one of them remarked, is the Holiness of the Heart's Affection, and their kingdom, though they never possess it, is the wide-open world.

With this type of person knocking about, and constantly crossing one's path if one has eyes to see or hands to feel, the experiment of earthly life cannot be dismissed as a failure. But it may well be hailed as a tragedy, the tragedy being that no device has been found by which these private decencies can be transmitted to public affairs. As soon as people have power they go crooked and sometimes dotty as well, because the possession of power lifts them into a region where normal honesty never pays. For instance, the man who is selling newspapers outside the Houses of Parliament can safely leave his papers to go for a drink and his cap beside them: anyone who takes a paper is sure to drop a copper into the cap. But the men who are inside the Houses of Parliament—they cannot trust one another like that, still less can the Government they compose trust other governments. No caps upon the pavement here, but suspicion, treachery and armaments. The more highly public life is organised the lower does its morality sink; the nations of today behave to each other worse than they ever did in the past, they cheat, rob, bully and bluff, make war without notice, and kill as many women and children as possible; whereas primitive tribes were at all events restrained by taboos. It is a humiliating outlook—though the greater the darkness, the brighter shine the little lights, reassuring one another, signalling: "Well, at all events, I'm still here. I don't like it very much, but how are you?" Unquenchable lights of my aristocracy! Signals of the invincible army! "Come along—anyway, let's have a good time while we can." I think they signal that too.

The Saviour of the future—if ever he comes—will not preach a new Gospel. He will merely utilise my aristocracy, he will make effective the good will and the good temper which are already existing. In other words, he will introduce a new technique. In economics, we are told that if there was a new technique of distribution, there need be no poverty, and people would not starve in one place while crops were being ploughed under in another. A similar change is needed in the sphere of morals and politics. The desire for it is by no means new; it was expressed, for example, in theological terms by Jacopone da Todi over six hundred years ago. "Ordina questo amore, O tu che m'ami," he said; "O thou who lovest me—set this love in order." His prayer was not granted, and I do not myself believe that it ever will be, but here, and not through a change of heart, is our probable route. Not by becoming better, but by ordering and distributing his native goodness, will Man shut up Force into its box, and so gain time to explore the universe and to set his mark upon it worthily. At present he only explores it at odd moments, when Force is looking the other way, and his divine creativeness appears as a trivial byproduct, to be scrapped as soon as the drums beat and the bombers hum.

Such a change, claim the orthodox, can only be made by Christianity, and will be made by it in God's good time: man always has failed and always will fail to organise his own goodness, and it is presumptuous of him to try. This claim—solemn as it is—leaves me cold. I cannot believe that Christianity will ever cope with the present world-wide mess, and I think that such influence as it retains in modern society is due to the money behind it, rather than to its spiritual appeal. It was a spiritual force once, but the indwelling spirit will have to be restated if it is to calm the waters again, and probably restated in a non-Christian form. Naturally a lot of people, and people who are not only good but able and intelligent, will disagree here; they will vehemently deny that Christianity has failed, or they will argue that its failure proceeds from the wickedness of men, and really proves its ultimate success. They have Faith, with a large F. My faith has a very small one, and I only intrude it because these are strenuous and serious days, and one likes to say what one thinks while speech is comparatively free: it may not be free much longer.

The above are the reflections of an individualist and a liberal who has found liberalism crumbling beneath him and at first felt ashamed. Then, looking around, he decided there was no special reason for shame, since other people, whatever they felt, were equally insecure. And as for individualism—there seems no way of getting off this, even if one wanted to. The dictator-hero can grind down his citizens till they are all alike, but he cannot melt them into a single man. That is beyond his power. He can order them to merge, he can incite them to mass-antics, but they are obliged to be born separately, and to die separately, and, owing to these unavoidable termini, will always be running off the totalitarian rails. The memory of birth and the expectation of death always lurk within the human being, making him separate from his fellows and consequently capable of intercourse with them. Naked I came into the world, naked I shall go out of it! And a very good thing too, for it reminds me that I am naked under my shirt, whatever its colour.

1939

Gilbert Highet

THE MYSTERY OF ZEN

The mind need never stop growing. Indeed, one of the few experiences which never pall is the experience of watching one's own mind, and observing how it produces new interests, responds to new stimuli, and develops new thoughts, apparently without effort and almost independently of one's own conscious control. I have seen this happen to myself a hundred times; and every time it happens again, I am equally fascinated and astonished.

Some years ago a publisher sent me a little book for review. I read it, and decided it was too remote from my main interests and too highly specialized. It was a brief account of how a young German philosopher living in Japan had learned how to shoot with a bow and arrow, and how this training had made it possible for him to understand the esoteric doctrines of the Zen sect of Buddhism. Really, what could be more alien to my own life, and to that of everyone I knew, than Zen Buddhism and Japanese archery? So I thought, and put the book away.

Yet I did not forget it. It was well written, and translated into good English. It was delightfully short, and implied much more than it said. Although its theme was extremely odd, it was at least highly individual; I had never read anything like it before or since. It remained in my mind. Its name was *Zen in the Art of Archery*, its author Eugen Herrigel, its publisher Pantheon of New York. One day I took it off the shelf and read it again; this time it seemed even stranger than before and even more unforgettable. Now it began to cohere with other interests of mine. Something I had read of the Japanese art of flower arrangement seemed to connect with it; and then, when I wrote an essay on the peculiar Japanese poems called *haiku*, other links began to grow. Finally I had to read the book once more with care, and to go through some other works which illuminated the same subject. I am still grappling with the theme; I have not got anywhere near understanding it fully; but I have learned a good deal, and I am grateful to the little book which refused to be forgotten.

The author, a German philosopher, got a job teaching philosophy at the University of Tokyo (apparently between the wars), and he did what Germans in foreign countries do not usually do: he determined to adapt himself and to learn from his hosts. In particular, he had always been interested in mysticism—which, for every earnest philosopher, poses a problem that is all the more inescapable because it is virtually insoluble. Zen Buddhism is not the only mystical doctrine to be found in the East, but it is one of the most highly developed and certainly one of the most difficult to approach. Herrigel knew that there were scarcely any books which did more than skirt the edge of the subject, and that the best of all books on Zen (those by the philosopher D. T. Suzuki) constantly emphasize that Zen can never be learned from books, can never be studied as we can study other disciplines such as logic or mathematics. Therefore he began to look for a Japanese thinker who could teach him directly.

At once he met with embarrassed refusals. His Japanese friends explained that he would gain nothing from trying to discuss Zen as a philosopher, that its theories could not be spread out for analysis by a detached mind, and in fact that the normal relationship of teacher and pupil simply did not exist within the sect, because the Zen masters felt it useless to explain things stage by stage and to argue about the various possible interpretations of their doctrine. Herrigel had read enough to be prepared for this. He replied that he did not want to dissect the teachings of the school, because he knew that would be useless. He wanted to become a Zen mystic himself. (This was highly intelligent of him. No one could really penetrate into Christian mysticism without being a devout Christian; no one could appreciate Hindu mystical doctrine without accepting the Hindu view of the universe.) At this, Herrigel's Japanese friends were more forthcoming. They told him that the best way, indeed the only way, for a European to approach Zen mysticism was to learn one of the arts which exemplified it. He was a fairly good rifle shot, so he determined to learn archery; and his wife co-operated with him by taking lessons in painting and flower arrangement. How any philosopher could investigate a mystical doctrine by learning to shoot with a bow and arrow and watching his wife arrange flowers, Herrigel did not ask. He had good sense.

A Zen master who was a teacher of archery agreed to take him as a pupil. The lessons lasted six years, during which he practiced every single day. There are many difficult courses of instruction in the world: the Jesuits, violin virtuosi, Talmudic scholars, all have long and hard training, which in one sense never comes to an end; but Herrigel's training in archery equaled them all in intensity. If I were trying to learn archery, I should expect to begin by looking at a target and shooting arrows at it. He was not even allowed to aim at a target for the first four years. He had to begin by learning how to hold the bow and arrow, and then how to release the arrow; this took ages. The Japanese bow is not like our sporting bow, and the stance of the archer in Japan is different from ours. We hold the bow at shoulder level, stretch our left arm out ahead, pull the string and the nocked arrow to a point either below the chin or sometimes past the right ear, and then shoot. The Japanese hold the bow above the head, and then pull the hands apart to left and right until the left hand comes down to eye level and the right hand comes to rest above the right shoulder; then there is a pause, during which the bow is held at full stretch, with the tip of the three-foot arrow projecting only a few inches beyond the bow; after that, the arrow is loosed. When Herrigel tried this, even without aiming, he found it was almost impossible. His hands trembled. His legs stiffened and grew cramped. His breathing became labored. And of course he could not possibly aim. Week after week he practiced this, with the Master watching him carefully and correcting his strained attitude; week after week he made no progress whatever. Finally he gave up and told his teacher that he could not learn: it was absolutely impossible for him to draw the bow and loose the arrow.

To his astonishment, the Master agreed. He said, "Certainly you cannot. It is because you are not breathing correctly. You must learn to breathe in a steady rhythm, keeping your lungs full most of the time, and drawing in one rapid inspiration with each stage of the process, as you grasp the bow, fit the arrow, raise the bow, draw, pause, and loose the shot. If you do, you will both grow stronger and be able to relax." To prove this, he himself drew his massive bow and told his pupil to feel the muscles of his arms: they were perfectly relaxed, as though he were doing no work whatever.

Herrigel now started breathing exercises; after some time he combined the new rhythm of breathing with the actions of drawing and shooting; and, much to his astonishment, he found that the whole thing, after this complicated process, had become much easier. Or rather, not easier, but different. At times it became quite unconscious. He says himself that he felt he was not breathing, but being breathed; and in time he felt that the occasional shot was not being dispatched by him, but shooting itself. The bow and arrow were in charge; he had become merely a part of them.

All this time, of course, Herrigel did not even attempt to discuss Zen doctrine with his Master. No doubt he knew that he was approaching it, but he concentrated solely on learning how to shoot. Every stage which he surmounted appeared to lead to another stage even more difficult. It took him months to learn how to loosen the bowstring. The problem was this. If he gripped the string and arrowhead tightly, either he froze, so that his hands were slowly pulled together and the shot was wasted, or else he jerked, so that the arrow flew up into the air or down into the ground; and if he was relaxed, then the bowstring and arrow simply *leaked* out of his grasp before he could reach full stretch, and the arrow went nowhere. He explained this problem to the Master. The Master understood perfectly well. He replied, "You must hold the drawn bowstring like a child holding a grownup's finger. You know how firmly a child grips; and yet when it lets go, there is not the slightest jerk— because the child does not think of itself, it is not self-conscious, it does not say, 'I will now let go and do something else,' it merely acts instinctively. That is what you must learn to do. Practice, practice, and practice, and then the string will loose itself at the right moment. The shot will come as effortlessly as snow slipping from a leaf." Day after day, week after week, month after month, Herrigel practiced this; and then, after one shot, the Master suddenly bowed and broke off the lesson. He said "Just then it shot. Not you, but *it*." And gradually thereafter more and more right shots achieved themselves; the young philosopher forgot himself, forgot that he was learning archery for some other purpose, forgot even that he was practicing archery, and became part of that unconsciously active complex, the bow, the string, the arrow, and the man.

Next came the target. After four years, Herrigel was allowed to shoot at the target. But he was strictly forbidden to aim at it. The Master explained that even he himself did not aim; and indeed, when he shot, he was so absorbed in the act, so selfless and unanxious, that his eyes were almost closed. It was difficult, almost impossible, for Herrigel to believe that such shooting could ever be effective; and he risked insulting the Master by suggesting that he ought to be able to hit the target blind-folded. But the Master accepted the challenge. That night, after a cup of tea and long meditation, he went into the archery hall, put on the lights at one end and left the target perfectly dark, with only a thin taper burning in front of it. Then, with habitual grace and precision, and with that strange, almost sleepwalking, selfless confidence that is the heart of Zen, he shot two arrows into the darkness. Herrigel went out to collect them. He found that the first had gone to the heart of the bull's eye, and that the second had actually hit the first arrow and splintered it. The Master showed no pride. He said, "Perhaps, with unconscious memory of the position of the target, *I* shot the first arrow; but the second arrow? *It* shot the second arrow, and *it* brought it to the center of the target."

At last Herrigel began to understand. His progress became faster and faster; easier, too. Perfect shots (perfect because perfectly unconscious) occurred at almost every lesson; and finally, after six years of incessant training, in a public display he was awarded the diploma. He needed no further instruction: he had himself become a Master. His wife meanwhile had become expert both in painting and in the arrangement of flowers— two of the finest of Japanese arts. (I wish she could be persuaded to write a companion volume, called *Zen in the Art of Flower Arrangement*; it would have a wider general appeal than her husband's work.) I gather also from a hint or two in his book that she had taken part in the archery lessons. During one of the most difficult periods in Herrigel's training, when his Master had practically refused to continue teaching him—because Herrigel had tried to cheat by *consciously* opening his hand at the moment of loosing the arrow—his wife had advised him against that solution, and sympathized with him when it was rejected. She in her own way had learned more quickly than he, and reached the final point together with him. All their effort had not been in vain: Herrigel and his wife had really acquired a new and valuable kind of wisdom. Only at this point, when he was about to abandon his lessons forever, did his Master treat him almost as an equal and hint at the innermost doctrines of Zen Buddhism. Only hints he gave; and yet, for the young philosopher who had now become a mystic, they were enough. Herrigel understood the doctrine, not with his logical mind, but with his entire being. He at any rate had solved the mystery of Zen.

Without going through a course of training as absorbing and as complete as Herrigel's, we can probably never penetrate the mystery. The doctrine of Zen cannot be analyzed from without: it must be lived.

But although it cannot be analyzed, it can be hinted at. All the hints that the adherents of this creed give us are interesting. Many are fantastic; some are practically incomprehensible, and yet unforgettable. Put together, they take us toward a way of life which is utterly impossible for westerners living in a western world, and nevertheless has a deep fascination and contains some values which we must respect.

The word Zen means "meditation." (It is the Japanese word, corresponding to the Chinese Ch'an and the Hindu Dhyana.) It is the central idea of a special sect of Buddhism which flourished in China during the Sung period (between a.d. 1000 and 1300) and entered Japan in the twelfth century. Without knowing much about it, we might be certain that the Zen sect was a worthy and noble one, because it produced a quantity of highly distinguished art, specifically painting. And if we knew anything about Buddhism itself, we might say that Zen goes closer than other sects to the heart of Buddha's teaching: because Buddha was trying to found, not a religion with temples and rituals, but a way of life based on meditation. However, there is something eccentric about the Zen life which is hard to trace in Buddha's teaching; there is an active energy which he did not admire, there is a rough grasp on reality which he himself eschewed, there is something like a sense of humor, which he rarely displayed. The gravity and serenity of the Indian preacher are transformed, in Zen, to the earthy liveliness of Chinese and Japanese sages. The lotus brooding calmly on the water has turned into a knotted tree covered with spring blossoms.

In this sense, "meditation" does not mean what we usually think of when we say a philosopher meditates: analysis of reality, a longsustained effort to solve problems of religion and ethics, the logical dissection of the universe. It means something not divisive, but whole; not schematic, but organic; not long-drawn-out, but immediate. It means something more like our words "intuition" and "realization." It means a way of life in which there is no division between thought and action; none of the painful gulf, so well known to all of us, between the unconscious and the conscious mind; and no absolute distinction between the self and the external world, even between the various parts of the external world and the whole.

When the German philosopher took six years of lessons in archery in order to approach the mystical significance of Zen, he was not given direct philosophical instruction. He was merely shown how to breathe, how to hold and loose the bowstring, and finally how to shoot in such a way that the bow and arrow used him as an instrument. There are many such stories about Zen teachers. The strangest I know is one about a fencing master who undertook to train a young man in the art of the sword. The relationship of teacher and pupil is very important, almost sacred, in the Far East; and the pupil hardly ever thinks of leaving a master or objecting to his methods, however extraordinary they may seem. Therefore this young fellow did not at first object when he was made to act as a servant, drawing water, sweeping floors, gathering wood for the fire, and cooking. But after some time he asked for more direct instruction. The master agreed to give it, but produced no swords. The routine went on just as before, except that every now and then the master would strike the young man with a stick. No matter what he was doing, sweeping the floor or weeding in the garden, a blow would descend on him apparently out of nowhere; he had always to be on the alert, and yet he was constantly receiving unexpected cracks on the head or shoulders. After some months of this, he saw his master stooping over a boiling pot full of vegetables; and he thought he would have his revenge. Silently he lifted a stick and brought it down; but without any effort, without even a glance in his direction, his master parried the blow with the lid of the cooking pot. At last, the pupil began to understand the instinctive alert-ness, the effortless perception and avoidance of danger, in which his master had been training him. As soon as he had achieved it, it was child's play for him to learn the management of the sword: he could parry every cut and turn every slash without anxiety, until his opponent, exhausted, left an opening for his counterattack. (The same principle was used by the elderly samurai for selecting his comrades in the Japanese motion picture *The Magnificent Seven*.)

These stories show that Zen meditation does not mean sitting and thinking. On the contrary, it means acting with as little thought as possible. The fencing master trained his pupil to guard against every attack with the same immediate, instinctive rapidity with which our eyelid closes over our eye when something threatens it. His work was aimed at breaking down the wall between thought and act, at completely fusing body and senses and mind so that they might all work together rapidly and effortlessly. When a Zen artist draws a picture, he does it in a rhythm almost the exact reverse of that which is followed by a Western artist. We begin by blocking out the design and then filling in the details, usually working more and more slowly as we approach the completion of the picture. The Zen artist sits down very calmly; examines his brush carefully; prepares his own ink; smooths out the paper on which he will work; falls into a profound silent ecstasy of contemplation—during which he does not think anxiously of various details, composition, brushwork, shades of tone, but rather attempts to become the vehicle through which the subject can express itself in painting; and then, very quickly and almost unconsciously, with sure effortless strokes, draws a picture containing the fewest and most effective lines. Most of the paper is left blank; only the essential is depicted, and that not completely. One long curving line will be enough to show a mountainside; seven streaks will become a group of bamboos bending in the wind; and yet, though technically incomplete, such pictures are unforgettably clear. They show the heart of reality.

All this we can sympathize with, because we can see the results. The young swordsman learns how to fence. The intuitional painter produces a fine picture. But the hardest thing for us to appreciate is that the Zen masters refuse to teach philosophy or religion directly, and deny logic. In fact, they despise logic as an artificial distortion of reality. Many philosophical teachers are difficult to understand because they analyze profound problems with subtle intricacy: such is Aristotle in his *Metaphysics*. Many mystical writers are difficult to understand because, as they themselves admit, they are attempting to use words to describe experiences which are too abstruse for words, so that they have to fall back on imagery and analogy, which they themselves recognize to be poor media, far coarser than the realities with which they have been in contact. But the Zen teachers seem to deny the power of language and thought altogether. For example, if you ask a Zen master what is the ultimate reality, he will answer, without the slightest hesitation, "The bamboo grove at the foot of the hill" or "A branch of plum blossom." Apparently he means that these things, which we can see instantly without effort, or imagine in the flash of a second, are real with the ultimate reality; that nothing is more real than these; and that we ought to grasp ultimates as we grasp simple immediates. A Chinese master was once asked the central question, "What is the Buddha?" He said nothing whatever, but held out his index finger. What did he mean? It is hard to explain; but apparently he meant "Here. Now. Look and realize with the effortlessness of seeing. Do not try to use words. Do not think. Make no efforts toward withdrawal from the world. Expect no sublime ecstasies. Live. All *that* is the ultimate reality, and it can be understood from the motion of a finger as well as from the execution of any complex ritual, from any subtle argument, or from the circling of the starry universe."

In making that gesture, the master was copying the Buddha himself, who once delivered a sermon which is famous, but was hardly understood by his pupils at the time. Without saying a word, he held up a flower and showed it to the gathering. One man, one alone, knew what he meant. The gesture became renowned as the Flower Sermon.

In the annals of Zen there are many cryptic answers to the final question, "What is the Buddha?"—which in our terms means "What is the meaning of life? What is truly real?" For example, one master, when asked "What is the Buddha?" replied, "Your name is Yecho." Another said, "Even the finest artist cannot paint him." Another said, "No nonsense here." And another answered, "The mouth is the gate of woe." My favorite story is about the monk who said to a Master, "Has a dog Buddha-nature too?" The Master replied, "Wu"—which is what the dog himself would have said.

Now, some critics might attack Zen by saying that this is the creed of a savage or an animal. The adherents of Zen would deny that—or more probably they would ignore the criticism, or make some cryptic remark which meant that it was pointless. Their position—if they could ever be persuaded to put in into words—would be this. An animal is instinctively in touch with reality, and so far is living rightly, but it has never had a mind and so cannot perceive the Whole, only that part with which it is in touch. The philosopher sees both the Whole and the parts, and enjoys them all. As for the savage, he exists only through the group; he feels himself as part of a war party or a ceremonial dance team or a ploughing-and-sowing group or the Snake clan; he is not truly an individual at all, and therefore is less than fully human. Zen has at its heart an inner solitude; its aim is to teach us to live, as in the last resort we do all have to live, alone.

A more dangerous criticism of Zen would be that it is nihilism, that its purpose is to abolish thought altogether. (This criticism is handled, but not fully met, by the great Zen authority Suzuki in his *Introduction to Zen Buddhism*.) It can hardly be completely confuted, for after all the central doctrine of Buddhism is—Nothingness. And many of the sayings of Zen masters are truly nihilistic. The first patriarch of the sect in China was asked by the emperor what was the ultimate and holiest principle of Buddhism. He replied, "Vast emptiness, and nothing holy in it." Another who was asked the searching question "Where is the abiding-place for the mind?" answered, "Not in this dualism of good and evil, being and non-being, thought and matter." In fact, thought is an activity which divides. It analyzes, it makes distinctions, it criticizes, it judges, it breaks reality into groups and classes and individuals. The aim of Zen is to abolish that kind of thinking, and to substitute—not unconsciousness, which would be death, but a consciousness that does not analyze but experiences life directly. Although it has no prescribed prayers, no sacred scriptures, no ceremonial rites, no personal god, and no interest in the soul's future destination, Zen is a religion rather than a philosophy. Jung points out that its aim is to produce a religious conversion, a "transformation": and he adds, "The transformation process is incommensurable with intellect." Thought is always interesting, but often painful; Zen is calm and painless. Thought is incomplete; Zen enlightenment brings a sense of completeness. Thought is a process; Zen illumination is a state. But it is a state which cannot be defined. In the Buddhist scriptures there is a dialogue between a master and a pupil in which the pupil tries to discover the exact meaning of such a state. The master says to him, 'If a fire were blazing in front of you, would you know that it was blazing?'

"Yes, master."

"And would you know the reason for its blazing?"

"Yes, because it had a supply of grass and sticks."

"And would you know if it were to go out?"

"Yes, master."

"And on its going out, would you know where the fire had gone? To the east, to the west, to the north, or to the south?"

"The question does not apply, master. For the fire blazed because it had a supply of grass and sticks. When it had consumed this and had no other fuel, then it went out."

"In the same way," replies the master, "no question will apply to the meaning of Nirvana, and no statement will explain it."

Such, then, neither happy nor unhappy but beyond all divisive description, is the condition which students of Zen strive to attain. Small wonder that they can scarcely explain it to us, the unilluminated.

1957

THE READER

1. On p. 1177, Highet says that "Zen is a religion rather than a philosophy." How has he led up to this conclusion? What definitions of "religion" and "philosophy" does he imply?
2. To what extent is Zen "the creed of a savage or an animal"? How does Highet go about refuting this charge?

THE WRITER

1. What difficulties does Highet face in discussing Zen? How does he manage to give a definition in spite of his statement that Zen "cannot be analyzed"?
2. Why does Highet describe the training in archery in such detail?
3. By what means does Highet define "meditation"? Would other means have worked as well? Explain. Write a brief definition of a similar term (perhaps intuition or realization), using an approach similar to Highet's.

Virginia Woolf

THE DEATH OF THE MOTH

Moths that fly by day are not properly to be called moths; they do not excite that pleasant sense of dark autumn nights and ivy-blossom which the commonest yellow-underwing asleep in the shadow of the curtain never fails to rouse in us. They are hybrid creatures, neither gay like butterflies nor sombre like their own species. Nevertheless the present specimen, with his narrow hay-coloured wings, fringed with a tassel of the same colour, seemed to be content with life. It was a pleasant morning, mid-September, mild, benignant, yet with a keener breath than that of the summer months. The plough was already scoring the field opposite the window, and where the share had been, the earth was pressed flat and gleamed with moisture. Such vigour came rolling in from the fields and the down beyond that it was difficult to keep the eyes strictly turned upon the book. The rooks too were keeping one of their annual festivities; soaring round the tree tops until it looked as if a vast net with thousands of black knots in it had been cast up into the air; which, after a few moments sank slowly down upon the trees until every twig seemed to have a knot at the end of it. Then, suddenly, the net would be thrown into the air again in a wider circle this time, with the utmost clamour and vociferation, as though to be thrown into the air and settle slowly down upon the tree tops were a tremendously exciting experience.

The same energy which inspired the rooks, the ploughmen, the horses, and even, it seemed, the lean bare-backed downs, sent the moth fluttering from side to side of his square of the window-pane. One could not help watching him. One was, indeed, conscious of a queer feeling of pity for him. The possibilities of pleasure seemed that morning so enormous and so various that to have only a moth's part in life, and a day moth's at that, appeared a hard fate, and his zest in enjoying his meagre opportunities to the full, pathetic. He flew vigorously to one corner of his compartment, and, after waiting there a second, flew across to the other. What remained for him but to fly to a third corner and then to a fourth? That was all he could do, in spite of the size of the downs, the width of the sky, the far-off smoke of houses, and the romantic voice, now and then, of a steamer out at sea. What he could do he did. Watching him, it seemed as if a fibre, very thin but pure, of the enormous energy of the world had been thrust into his frail and diminutive body. As often as he crossed the pane, I could fancy that a thread of vital light became visible. He was little or nothing but life.

Yet, because he was so small, and so simple a form of the energy that was rolling in at the open window and driving its way through so many narrow and intricate corridors in my own brain and in those of other human beings, there was something marvellous as well as pathetic about him. It was as if someone had taken a tiny bead of pure life and decking it as lightly as possible with down and feathers, had set it dancing and zig-zagging to show us the true nature of life. Thus displayed one could not get over the strangeness of it. One is apt to forget all about life, seeing it humped and bossed and garnished and cumbered so that it has to move with the greatest circumspection and dignity. Again, the thought of all that life might have been had he been born in any other shape caused one to view his simple activities with a kind of pity.

After a time, tired by his dancing apparently, he settled on the window ledge in the sun, and, the queer spectacle being at an end, I forgot about him. Then, looking up, my eye was caught by him. He was trying to resume his dancing, but seemed either so stiff or so awkward that he could only flutter to the bottom of the window-pane; and when he tried to fly across it he failed. Being intent on other matters I watched these futile attempts for a time without thinking, unconsciously waiting for him to resume his flight, as one waits for a machine, that has stopped momenta-rily, to start again without considering the reason of its failure. After perhaps a seventh attempt he slipped from the wooden ledge and fell, fluttering his wings, on to his back on the window sill. The helplessness of his attitude roused me. It flashed upon me that he was in difficulties; he could no longer raise himself; his legs struggled vainly. But, as I stretched out a pencil, meaning to help him to right himself, it came over me that the failure and awkwardness were the approach of death. I laid the pencil down again.

The legs agitated themselves once more. I looked as if for the enemy against which he struggled. I looked out of doors. What had happened there? Presumably it was midday, and work in the fields had stopped. Stillness and quiet had replaced the previous animation. The birds had taken themselves off to feed in the brooks. The horses stood still. Yet the power was there all the same, massed outside indifferent, impersonal, not attending to anything in particular. Somehow it was opposed to the little hay-coloured moth. It was useless to try to do anything. One could only watch the extraordinary efforts made by those tiny legs against an oncom-ing doom which could, had it chosen, have submerged an entire city, not merely a city, but masses of human beings; nothing, I knew, had any chance against death. Nevertheless after a pause of exhaustion the legs fluttered again. It was superb this last protest, and so frantic that he succeeded at last in righting himself. One's sympathies, of course, were all on the side of life. Also, when there was nobody to care or to know, this gigantic effort on the part of an insignificant little moth, against a power of such magnitude, to retain what no one else valued or desired to keep, moved one strangely. Again, somehow, one saw life, a pure bead. I lifted the pencil again, useless though I knew it to be. But even as I did so, the unmistakable tokens of death showed themselves. The body relaxed, and instantly grew stiff. The struggle was over. The insignificant little creature now knew death. As I looked at the dead moth, this minute wayside triumph of so great a force over so mean an antagonist filled me with wonder. Just as life had been strange a few minutes before, so death was now as strange. The moth having righted himself now lay most decently and uncomplainingly composed. O yes, he seemed to say, death is stronger than I am.

1947

THE READER

1. Why does Woolf describe the rooks in some detail, but not the ploughmen?
2. Does Woolf see any resemblances between the moth and human beings? How do you know?
3. In "The New Biography" (p. 738), Woolf speaks of the kind of biography written by Harold Nicolson, in which the biographer uses devices of fiction. Are there any devices of fiction in "The Death of the Moth"? Has she written a biography of the moth? She represents Nicolson as laughing at eminent men; she is very respectful of the insect. What does this suggest about her?

THE WRITER

1. Observe an insect, and describe it from two points of view—one objective and one subjective, or as a scientist might describe it and as a poet or a novelist might describe it.
2. Read Frost's poem "To a Moth Seen in Winter," printed below. Does Frost feel the same way about his moth that Woolf does about hers? Does one author identify with the moth more than the other? Woolf's piece takes place in the fall, Frost's in winter. What is the significance of the difference in seasons? Embody some of your conclusions in a brief essay of comparison.

TO A MOTH SEEN IN WINTER

Here's first a gloveless hand warm from my pocket,
A perch and resting place 'twixt wood and wood,
Bright-black-eyed silvery creature, brushed with brown,
The wings not folded in repose, but spread.
(Who would you be, I wonder, by those marks
If I had moths to friend as I have flowers?)
And now pray tell what lured you with false hope
To make the venture of eternity

And seek the love of kind in wintertime?
But stay and hear me out. I surely think
You make a labor of flight for one so airy
Spending yourself too much in self-support.
Nor will you find love either nor love you.
And what I pity in you is something human,
The old incurable untimeliness,
Only begetter of all ills that are.
But go. You are right. My pity cannot help.
Go till you wet your pinions and are quenched.
You must be made more simply wise than I
To know the hand I stretch impulsively
Across the gulf of well nigh everything
May reach to you, but cannot touch your fate.
I cannot touch your life, much less can save,
Who am tasked to save my own a little while.

3. *Explain whether you think another person looking over Woolf's shoulder would have described the moth differently. How might Petrunkevitch (see "The Spider and the Wasp," p. 905) or Thoreau (see
"The Battle of the Ants," p. 690) have described it?*

Annie Dillard

SIGHT INTO INSIGHT

When I was six or seven years old, growing up in Pittsburgh, I used to
take a penny of my own and hide it for someone else to find. It was a
curious compulsion; sadly, I've never been seized by it since. For some
reason I always "hid" the penny along the same stretch of sidewalk up the
street. I'd cradle it at the roots of a maple, say, or in a hole left by a
chipped-off piece of sidewalk. Then I'd take a piece of chalk and, starting
at either end of the block, draw huge arrows leading up to the penny from
both directions. After I learned to write I labeled the arrows "SURPRISE
AHEAD" or "MONEY THIS WAY." I was greatly excited, during all this
arrowdrawing, at the thought of the first lucky passerby who would
receive in this way, regardless of merit, a free gift from the universe. But I
never lurked about. I'd go straight home and not give the matter another
thought, until, some months later, I would be gripped by the impulse to
hide another penny.

There are lots of things to see, unwrapped gifts and free surprises. The
world is fairly studded and strewn with pennies cast broadside from a

generous hand. But—and this is the point—who gets excited by a mere penny? If you follow one arrow, if you crouch motionless on a bank to watch a tremulous ripple thrill on the water, and are rewarded by the sight of a muskrat kit paddling from its den, will you count that sight a chip of copper only, and go your rueful way? It is very dire poverty indeed for a man to be so malnourished and fatigued that he won't stoop to pick up a penny. But if you cultivate a healthy poverty and simplicity, so that finding a penny will make your day, then, since the world is in fact planted in pennies, you have with your poverty bought a lifetime of days. What you see is what you get.

Unfortunately, nature is very much a now-you-see-it, now-you-don't affair. A fish flashes, then dissolves in the water before my eyes like so much salt. Deer apparently ascend bodily into heaven; the brightest oriole fades into leaves. These disappearances stun me into stillness and concentration; they say of nature that it conceals with a grand nonchalance, and they say of vision that it is a deliberate gift, the revelation of a dancer who for my eyes only flings away her seven veils.

For nature does reveal as well as conceal: now-you-don't-see-it, now-you-do. For a week this September migrating red-winged blackbirds were feeding heavily down by Tinker Creek at the back of the house. One day I went out to investigate the racket; I walked up to a tree, an Osage orange, and a hundred birds flew away. They simply materialized out of the tree. I saw a tree, then a whisk of color, then a tree again. I walked closer and another hundred blackbirds took flight. Not a branch, not a twig budged: the birds were apparently weightless as well as invisible. Or, it was as if the leaves of the Osage orange had been freed from a spell in the form of redwinged blackbirds; they flew from the tree, caught my eye in the sky, and vanished. When I looked again at the tree, the leaves had reassembled as if nothing had happened. Finally I walked directly to the trunk of the tree and a final hundred, the real diehards, appeared, spread, and vanished. How could so many hide in the tree without my seeing them? The Osage orange, unruffled, looked just as it had looked from the house, when three hundred red-winged blackbirds cried from its crown. I looked upstream where they flew, and they were gone. Searching, I couldn't spot one. I wandered upstream to force them to play their hand, but they'd crossed the creek and scattered. One show to a customer. These appearances catch at my throat; they are the free gifts, the bright coppers at the roots of trees.

It's all a matter of keeping my eyes open. Nature is like one of those line drawings that are puzzles for children: Can you find hidden in the tree a duck, a house, a boy, a bucket, a giraffe, and a boot? Specialists can find the most incredibly hidden things. A book I read when I was young recommended an easy way to find caterpillars: you simply find some fresh caterpillar droppings, look up, and there's your caterpillar. More recently an author advised me to set my mind at ease about those piles of cut stems on the ground in grassy fields. Field mice make them; they cut the grass down by degrees to reach the seeds at the head. It seems that when the grass is tightly packed, as in a field of ripe grain, the blade won't topple at a single cut through the stem; instead, the cut stem simply drops vertically, held in the crush of grain. The mouse severs the bottom again and again, the stem keeps dropping an inch at a time, and finally the head is low enough for the mouse to reach the seeds. Meanwhile the mouse is positively littering the field with its little piles of cut stems into which, presumably, the author is constantly stumbling.

If I can't see these minutiae, I still try to keep my eyes open. I'm always on the lookout for ant lion traps in sandy soil, monarch pupae near milkweed, skipper larvae in locust leaves. These things are utterly common, and I've not seen one. I bang on hollow trees near water, but so far no flying squirrels have appeared. In flat country I watch every sunset in hopes of seeing the green ray. The green ray is a seldom-seen streak of light that rises from the sun like a spurting fountain at the moment of sunset; it throbs into the sky for two seconds and disappears. One more reason to keep my eyes open. A photography professor at the University of Florida just happened to see a bird die in midflight; it jerked, died, dropped, and smashed on the ground.

I squint at the wind because I read Stewart Edward White: "I have always maintained that if you looked closely enough you could see the wind—the dim, hardly-made-out, fine débris fleeing high in the air." White was an excellent observer, and devoted an entire chapter of *The Mountains* to the subject of seeing deer: "As soon as you can forget the naturally obvious and construct an artificial obvious, then you too will see deer."

But the artificial obvious is hard to see. My eyes account for less than 1 percent of the weight of my head; I'm bony and dense; I see what I expect. I just don't know what the lover knows; I can't see the artificial obvious that those in the know construct. The herpetologist asks the native, "Are there snakes in that ravine?" "No, sir." And the herpetologist comes home with, yessir, three bags full. Are there butterflies on that mountain? Are the bluets in bloom? Are there arrowheads here, or fossil ferns in the shale?

Peeping through my keyhole I see within the range of only about 30 percent of the light that comes from the sun; the rest is infrared and some little ultraviolet, perfectly apparent to many animals, but invisible to me. A nightmare network of ganglia, charged and firing without my knowledge, cuts and splices what I do see, editing it for my brain. Donald E. Carr points out that the sense impressions of one-celled animals are *not* edited for the brain: "This is philosophically interesting in a rather mournful way, since it means that only the simplest animals perceive the universe as it is."

A fog that won't burn away drifts and flows across my field of vision. When you see fog move against a backdrop of deep pines, you don't see the fog itself, but streaks of clearness floating across the air in dark shreds. So I see only tatters of clearness through a pervading obscurity. I can't distinguish the fog from the overcast sky; I can't be sure if the light is direct or reflected. Everywhere darkness and the presence of the unseen appalls. We estimate now that only one atom dances alone in every cubic meter of intergalactic space. I blink and squint. What planet or power yanks Halley's Comet out of orbit? We haven't seen it yet; it's a question of distance, density, and the pallor of reflected light. We rock, cradled in the swaddling band of darkness. Even the simple darkness of night whispers suggestions to the mind. This summer, in August, I stayed at the creek too late.

Where Tinker Creek flows under the sycamore log bridge to the tear-shaped island, it is slow and shallow, fringed thinly in cattail marsh. At this spot an astonishing bloom of life supports vast breeding populations of insects, fish, reptiles, birds, and mammals. On windless summer evenings I stalk along the creek bank or straddle the sycamore log in absolute stillness, watching for muskrats. The night I stayed too late I was hunched on the log staring spellbound at spreading, reflected stains of lilac on the water. A cloud in the sky suddenly lighted as if turned on by a switch; its reflection just as suddenly materialized on the water upstream, flat and floating, so that I couldn't see the creek bottom, or life in the water under the cloud. Downstream, away from the cloud on the water, water turtles smooth as beans were gliding down with the current in a series of easy, weightless push-offs, as men bound on the moon. I didn't know whether to trace the progress of one turtle I was sure of, risking sticking my face in one of the bridge's spider webs made invisible by the gathering dark, or take a chance on seeing the carp, or scan the mudbank in hope of seeing a muskrat, or follow the last of the swallows who caught at my heart and trailed it after them like streamers as they appeared from directly below, under the log, flying upstream with their tails forked, so fast.

But shadows spread and deepened and stayed. After thousands of years we're still strangers to darkness, fearful aliens in an enemy camp with our arms crossed over our chests. I stirred. A land turtle on the bank, startled, hissed the air from its lungs and withdrew to its shell. An uneasy pink here, an unfathomable blue there, gave great suggestion of lurking beings. Things were going on. I couldn't see whether that rustle I heard was a distant rattle-snake, slit-eyed, or a nearby sparrow kicking in the dry flood debris slung at the foot of a willow. Tremendous action roiled the water everywhere I looked, big action, inexplicable. A tremor welled up beside a gaping muskrat burrow in the bank and I caught my breath, but no muskrat appeared. The ripples continued to fan upstream with a steady, powerful thrust. Night was knitting an eyeless mask over my face, and I still sat transfixed. A distant airplane, a delta wing out of nightmare, made a gliding shadow on the creek's bottom that looked like a stingray cruising upstream. At once a black fin slit the pink cloud on the water, shearing it in two. The two halves merged together and seemed to dissolve before my eyes. Darkness pooled in the cleft of the creek and rose, as water collects in a well. Untamed, dreaming lights flickered over the sky. I saw hints of hulking underwater shadows, two pale splashes out of the water, and round ripples rolling close together from a blackened center.

At last I stared upstream where only the deepest violet remained of the cloud, a cloud so high its underbelly still glowed, its feeble color reflected from a hidden sky lighted in turn by a sun halfway to China. And out of that violet, a sudden enormous black body arced over the water. Head and tail, if there was a head and tail, were both submerged in cloud. I saw only one ebony fling, a headlong dive to darkness; then the waters closed, and the lights went out.

I walked home in a shivering daze, up hill and down. Later I lay openmouthed in bed, my arms flung wide at my sides to steady the whirling darkness. At this latitude I'm spinning 836 miles an hour round the earth's axis; I feel my sweeping fall as a breakneck arc like the dive of dolphins, and the hollow rushing of wind raises the hairs on my neck and the side of my face. In orbit around the sun I'm moving 64,800 miles an hour. The solar system as a whole, like a merry-go-round unhinged, spins, bobs, and blinks at the speed of 43,200 miles an hour along a course set east of Hercules. Someone has piped, and we are dancing a tarantella until the sweat pours. I open my eyes and I see dark, muscled forms curl out of water, with flapping gills and flattened eyes. I close my eyes and I see stars, deep stars giving way to deeper stars, deeper stars bowing to deepest stars at the crown of an infinite cone.

"Still," wrote Van Gogh in a letter, "a great deal of light falls on everything." If we are blinded by darkness, we are also blinded by light. Sometimes here in Virginia at sunset low clouds on the southern or northern horizon are completely invisible in the lighted sky. I only know one is there because I can see its reflection in still water. The first time I discovered this mystery I looked from cloud to no-cloud in bewilderment, checking my bearings over and over, thinking maybe the ark of the covenant was just passing by south of Dead Man Mountain. Only much later did I learn the explanation: polarized light from the sky is very much weakened by reflection, but the light in clouds isn't polarized. So invisible clouds pass among visible clouds, till all slide over the mountains; so a greater light extinguishes a lesser as though it didn't exist.

In the great meteor shower of August, the Perseid, I wail all day for the shooting stars I miss. They're out there showering down committing hara-kiri in a flame of fatal attraction, and hissing perhaps at last into the ocean. But at dawn what looks like a blue dome clamps down over me like a lid'on a pot. The stars and planets could smash and I'd never know. Only a piece of ashen moon occasionally climbs up or down the inside of the dome, and our local star without surcease explodes on our heads. We have really only that one light, one source for all power, and yet we must turn away from it by universal decree. Nobody here on the planet seems aware of this strange, powerful taboo, that we all walk about carefully averting our faces, this way and that, lest our eyes be blasted forever.

Darkness appalls and light dazzles; the scrap of visible light that doesn't hurt my eyes hurts my brain. What I see sets me swaying. Size and distance and the sudden swelling of meanings confuse me, bowl me over. I straddle the sycamore log bridge over Tinker Creek in the summer. I look at the lighted creek bottom: snail tracks tunnel the mud in quavering curves. A crayfish jerks, but by the time I absorb what has happened, he's gone in a billowing smoke screen of silt. I look at the water; minnows and shiners. If I'm thinking minnows, a carp will fill my brain till I scream. I look at the water's surface: skaters, bubbles, and leaves sliding down. Suddenly, my own face, reflected, startles me witless. Those snails have been tracking my face! Finally, with a shuddering wrench of the will, I see clouds, cirrus clouds. I'm dizzy, I fall in.

This looking business is risky. Once I stood on a humped rock on nearby Purgatory Mountain, watching through binoculars the great autumn hawk migration below, until I discovered that I was in danger of joining the hawks on a vertical migration of my own. I was used to binoculars, but not, apparently, to balancing on humped rocks while looking through them. I reeled. Everything advanced and receded by turns; the world was full of unexplained foreshortenings and depths. A distant huge object, a hawk the size of an elephant, turned out to be the browned bough of a nearby loblolly pine. I followed a sharp-shinned hawk against a featureless sky, rotating my head unawares as it flew, and when I lowered the glass a glimpse of my own looming shoulder sent me staggering. What prevents the men at Palomar[1] from falling, voiceless and blinded, from their tiny, vaulted chairs?

I reel in confusion: I don't understand what I see. With the naked eye I can see two million light-years to the Andromeda galaxy. Often I slop some creek water in a jar, and when I get home I dump it in a white china bowl. After the silt settles I return and see tracings of minute snails on the

---

1. An astronomical observatory in California.

bottom, a planarian or two winding round the rim of water, roundworms shimmying, frantically, and finally, when my eyes have adjusted to these dimensions, amoebae. At first the amoebae look like *muscae volitantes*, those curled moving spots you seem to see in your eyes when you stare at a distant wall. Then I see the amoebae as drops of water congealed, bluish, translucent, like chips of sky in the bowl. At length I choose one individual and give myself over to its idea of an evening. I see it dribble a grainy foot before it on its wet, unfathomable way. Do its unedited sense impressions include the fierce focus of my eyes? Shall I take it outside and show it Andromeda, and blow its little endoplasm? I stir the water with a finger, in case it's running out of oxygen. Maybe I should get a tropical aquarium with motorized bubblers and lights, and keep this one for a pet. Yes, it would tell its fissioned descendants, the universe is two feet by five, and if you listen closely you can hear the buzzing music of the spheres.

Oh, it's mysterious, lamplit evenings here in the galaxy, one after the other. It's one of those nights when I wander from window to window, looking for a sign. But I can't see. Terror and a beauty insoluble are a riband of blue woven into the fringe of garments of things both great and small. No culture explains, no bivouac offers real haven or rest. But it could be that we are not seeing something. Galileo thought comets were an optical illusion. This is fertile ground: since we are certain that they're not, we can look at what our scientists have been saying with fresh hope. What if there are *really* gleaming, castellated cities hung up-side-down over the desert sand? What limpid lakes and cool date palms have our caravans always passed untried? Until, one by one, by the blindest of leaps, we light on the road to these places, we must stumble in darkness and hunger. I turn from the window. I'm blind as a bat, sensing only from every direction the echo of my own thin cries.

I chanced on a wonderful book called *Space and Sight*, by Marius Von Senden. When Western surgeons discovered how to perform safe cataract operations, they ranged across Europe and America operating on dozens of men and women of all ages who had been blinded by cataracts since birth. Von Senden collected accounts of such cases; the histories are fascinating. Many doctors had tested their patients' sense perceptions and ideas of space both before and after the operations. The vast majority of patients, of both sexes and all ages, had, in Von Senden's opinion, no idea of space whatsoever. Form, distance, and size were so many meaningless syllables. A patient "had no idea of depth, confusing it with roundness." Before the operation a doctor would give a blind patient a cube and a sphere; the patient would tongue it or feel it with his hands, and name it correctly. After the operation the doctor would show the same objects to the patient without letting him touch them; now he had no clue whatsoever to what he was seeing. One patient called lemonade "square" because it pricked on his tongue as a square shape pricked on the touch of his hands. Of another post-operative patient the doctor writes, "I have found in her no notion of size, for example, not even within the narrow limits which she might have encompassed with the aid of touch. Thus when I asked her to show me how big her mother was, she did not stretch out her hands, but set her two index fingers a few inches apart."

For the newly sighted, vision is pure sensation unencumbered by meaning. When a newly sighted girl saw photographs and paintings, she asked, "'Why do they put those dark marks all over them?' 'Those aren't dark marks,' her mother explained, 'those are shadows. That is one of the ways the eye knows that things have shape. If it were not for shadows, many things would look flat.' 'Well, that's how things do look,' Joan answered. 'Everything looks flat with dark patches.'"

In general the newly sighted see the world as a dazzle of "colorpatches." They are pleased by the sensation of color, and learn quickly to name the colors, but the rest of seeing is tormentingly difficult. Soon after his operation a patient "generally bumps into one of these colour-patches and observes them to be substantial, since they resist him as tactual objects do. In walking about it also strikes him—or can if he pays attention—that he is continually passing in between the colours he sees, that he can go past a visual object, that a part of it then steadily disappears from view; and that in spite of this, however he twists and turns—whether entering the room from the door, for example, or re-turning back to it—he always has a visual space in front of him. Thus he gradually comes to realize that there is also a space behind him, which he does not see."

The mental effort involved in these reasonings proves overwhelming for many patients. It oppresses them to realize that they have been visible to people all along, perhaps unattractively so, without their knowledge or consent. A disheartening number of them refuse to use their new vision, continuing to go over objects with their tongues, and lapsing into apathy and despair.

On the other hand, many newly sighted people speak well of the world, and teach us how dull our own vision is. To one patient, a human hand, unrecognized, is "something bright and then holes." Shown a bunch of grapes, a boy calls out, "It is dark, blue and shiny. . . . It isn't smooth, it has bumps and hollows." A little girl visits a garden. "She is greatly aston-ished, and can scarcely be persuaded to answer, stands speechless in front of the tree, which she only names on taking hold of it, and then as 'the tree with the lights in it.'" Another patient, a twenty-two-year-old girl, was dazzled by the world's brightness and kept her eyes shut for two weeks. When at the end of that time she opened her eyes again, she did not recognize any objects, but "the more she now directed her gaze upon everything about her, the more it could be seen how an expression of gratification and astonishment overspread her features; she repeatedly exclaimed: 'Oh God! How beautiful!'"

I saw color-patches for weeks after I read this wonderful book. It was summer; the peaches were ripe in the valley orchards. When I woke in the morning, color-patches wrapped round my eyes, intricately, leaving not one unfilled spot. All day long I walked among shifting color-patches that parted before me like the Red Sea and closed again in silence, transfigured, wherever I looked back. Some patches swelled and loomed, while others vanished utterly, and dark marks flitted at random over the whole dazzling sweep. But I couldn't sustain the illusion of flatness. I've been around for too long. Form is condemned to an eternal danse macabre with meaning: I couldn't unpeach the peaches. Nor can I remember ever having seen without understanding; the color-patches of infancy are lost. My brain then must have been smooth as any balloon. I'm told I reached for the moon; many babies do. But the color-patches of infancy swelled as meaning filled them; they arrayed themselves in solemn ranks down distance which unrolled and stretched before me like a plain. The moon rocketed away. I live now in a world of shadows that shape and distance color, a world where space makes a kind of terrible sense. What Gnosticism[2] is this, and what physics? The fluttering patch I saw in my nursery window—silver and green and shape-shifting blue—is gone; a row of Lombardy poplars takes its place, mute, across the distant lawn. That humming oblong creature pale as light that stole along the walls of my room at night, stretching exhilaratingly around the corners, is gone, too, gone the night I ate of the bittersweet fruit, put two and two together and puckered forever my brain. Martin Buber tells this tale: "Rabbi Mendel once boasted to his teacher Rabbi Elimelekh that evenings he saw the angel who rolls away the light before the darkness, and mornings the angel who rolls away the darkness before the light. 'Yes,' said Rabbi Elimelekh, 'in my youth I saw that too. Later on you don't see these things anymore.'"

Why didn't someone hand those newly sighted people paints and brushes from the start, when they still didn't know what anything was? Then maybe we all could see color-patches too, the world unraveled from reason, Eden before Adam gave names. The scales would drop from my eyes; I'd see trees like men walking; I'd run down the road against all orders, hallooing and leaping.

Seeing is of course very much a matter of verbalization. Unless I call my attention to what passes before my eyes, I simply won't see it. If

2. Pretension to esoteric spiritual knowledge.

Tinker Mountain erupted, I'd be likely to notice. But if I want to notice the lesser cataclysms of valley life, I have to maintain in my head a running description of the present. It's not that I'm observant; it's just that I talk too much. Otherwise, especially in a strange place, I'll never know what's happening. Like a blind man at the ball game, I need a radio.

When I see this way I analyze and pry. I hurl over logs and roll away stones; I study the bank a square foot at a time, probing and tilting my head. Some days when a mist covers the mountains, when the muskrats won't show and the microscope's mirror shatters, I want to climb up the blank blue dome as a man would storm the inside of a circus tent, wildly, dangling, and with a steel knife claw a rent in the top, peep, and, if I must, fall.

But there is another kind of seeing that involves a letting go. When I see this way I sway transfixed and emptied. The difference between the two ways of seeing is the difference between walking with and without a camera. When I walk with a camera I walk from shot to shot, reading the light on a calibrated meter. When I walk without a camera, my own shutter opens, and the moment's light prints on my own silver gut. When I see this second way I am above all an unscrupulous observer.

It was sunny one evening last summer at Tinker Creek; the sun was low in the sky, upstream. I was sitting on the sycamore log bridge with the sunset at my back, watching the shiners the size of minnows who were feeding over the muddy sand in skittery schools. Again and again, one fish, then another, turned for a split second across the current and flash! the sun shot out from its silver side. I couldn't watch for it. It was always just happening somewhere else, and it drew my vision just as it disappeared: flash! like a sudden dazzle of the thinnest blade, a sparking over a dun and olive ground at chance intervals from every direction. Then I noticed white specks, some sort of pale petals, small, floating from under my feet on the creek's surface, very slow and steady. So I blurred my eyes and gazed toward the brim of my hat and saw a new world. I saw the pale white circles roll up, roll up, like the world's turning, mute and perfect, and I saw the linear flashes, gleaming silver, like stars being born at random down a rolling scroll of time. Something broke and something opened. I filled up like a new wineskin. I breathed an air like light; I saw a light like water. I was the lip of a fountain the creek filled forever; I was ether, the leaf in the zephyr; I was flesh-flake, feather, bone.

When I see this way I see truly. As Thoreau says, I return to my senses. I am the man who watches the baseball game in silence in an empty stadium. I see the game purely; I'm abstracted and dazed. When it's all over and the white-suited players lope off the green field to their shadowed dugouts, I leap to my feet, I cheer and cheer.

But I can't go out and try to see this way. I'll fail, I'll go mad. All I can do is try to gag the commentator, to hush the noise of useless interior babble that keeps me from seeing just as surely as a newspaper dangled before my eyes. The effort is really a discipline requiring a lifetime of dedicated struggle; it marks the literature of saints and monks of every order east and west, under every rule and no rule, discalced and shod. The world's spiritual geniuses seem to discover universally that the mind's muddy river, this ceaseless flow of trivia and trash, cannot be dammed, and that trying to dam it is a waste of effort that might lead to madness. Instead you must allow the muddy river to flow unheeded in the dim channels of consciousness; you raise your sights; you look along it, mildly, acknowledging its presence without interest and gazing beyond it into the realm of the real where subjects and objects act and rest purely, without utterance. "Launch into the deep," says Jacques Ellul, "and you shall see."

The secret of seeing, then, is the pearl of great price. If I thought he could teach me to find it and keep it forever I would stagger barefoot across a hundred deserts after any lunatic at all. But although the pearl may be found, it may not be sought. The literature of illumination reveals this above all: although it comes to those who wait for it, it is always, even to the most practiced and adept, a gift and a total surprise. I return from one walk knowing where the killdeer nests in the field by the creek and the hour the laurel blooms. I return from the same walk a day later scarcely knowing my own name. Litanies hum in my ears; my tongue flaps in my mouth, *Alim non,* alleluia! I cannot cause light; the most I can do is try to put myself in the path of its beam. It is possible, in deep space, to sail on solar wind. Light, be it particle or wave, has force: you rig a giant sail and go. The secret of seeing is to sail on solar wind. Hone and spread your spirit till you yourself are a sail, whetted, translucent, broadside to the merest puff.

When her doctor took her bandages off and led her into the garden, the girl who was no longer blind saw "the tree with the lights in it." It was for this tree I searched through the peach orchards of summer, in the forests of fall and down winter and spring for years. Then one day I was walking along Tinker Creek thinking of nothing at all and I saw the tree with the lights in it. I saw the backyard cedar where the mourning doves roost charged and transfigured, each cell buzzing with flame. I stood on the grass with the lights in it, grass that was wholly fire, utterly focused and utterly dreamed. It was less like seeing than like being for the first time seen, knocked breathless by a powerful glance. The flood of fire abated, but I'm still spending the power. Gradually the lights went out in the cedar, the colors died, the cells unflamed and disappeared. I was still ringing. I had been my whole life a bell, and never knew it until at that moment I was lifted and struck. I have since only very rarely seen the tree with the lights in it. The vision comes and goes, mostly goes, but I live for

it, for the moment when the mountains open and a new light roars in
spate through the crack, and the mountains slam.

1974

THE READER

1. Is the kind of seeing Dillard talks about at the end of her essay the same
   as the one she talks about at the beginning?
2. Why is verbalization so important to seeing (p. 1190)?

THE WRITER

1. What accounts for the intensity of Dillard's description of staying at
   the creek too late (p. 1185)?
2. How does Dillard establish her authority during the course of her
   argument?
3. Dillard says, "I see what I expect." Look at an object or a scene briefly,
   and jot down what you see. Then look at it longer and more intensely,
   and jot down the additional things you see. Write a brief comparison of
   your first view and your later view of the object or scene.

Jean-Paul Sartre

EXISTENTIALISM

Man is nothing else but what he makes of himself. Such is the first
principle of existentialism. It is also what is called subjectivity, the name
we are labeled with when charges are brought against us. But what do we
mean by this, if not that man has a greater dignity than a stone or table?
For we mean that man first exists, that is, that man first of all is the being
who hurls himself toward a future and who is conscious of imagining
himself as being in the future. Man is at the start a plan which is aware of
itself, rather than a patch of moss, a piece of garbage, or a cauliflower;
nothing exists prior to this plan; there is nothing in heaven; man will be
what he will have planned to be. Not what he will want to be. Because by
the word "will" we generally mean a conscious decision, which is subsequent to what we have already made of ourselves. I may want to belong to
a political party, write a book, get married; but all that is only a manifestation of an earlier, more spontaneous choice that is called "will." But if
existence really does precede essence, man is responsible for what he is.
Thus, existentialism's first move is to make every man aware of what he
is and to make the full responsibility of his existence rest on him. And
when we say that a man is responsible for himself, we do not only mean
that he is responsible for his own individuality, but that he is responsible

for all men.

The word "subjectivism" has two meanings, and our opponents play on the two. Subjectivism means, on the one hand, that an individual chooses and makes himself; and, on the other, that it is impossible for man to transcend human subjectivity. The second of these is the essential meaning of existentialism. When we say that man chooses his own self, we mean that every one of us does likewise; but we also mean by that that in making this choice he also chooses all men. In fact, in creating the man that we want to be, there is not a single one of our acts which does not at the same time create an image of man as we think he ought to be. To choose to be this or that is to affirm at the same time the value of what we choose, because we can never choose evil. We always choose the good, and nothing can be good for us without being good for all.

If, on the other hand, existence precedes essence, and if we grant that we exist and fashion our image at one and the same time, the image is valid for everybody and for our whole age. Thus, our responsibility is much greater than we might have supposed, because it involves all mankind. If I am a workingman and choose to join a Christian trade union rather than be a Communist, and if by being a member, I want to show that the best thing for man is resignation, that the kingdom of man is not of this world, I am not only involving my own case—I want to be resigned for everyone. As a result, my action has involved all humanity. To take a more individual matter, if I want to marry, to have children, even if this marriage depends solely on my own circumstances or passion or wish, I am involving all humanity in monogamy and not merely myself. Therefore, I am responsible for myself and for everyone else. I am creating a certain image of man of my own choosing. In choosing myself, I choose man.

This helps us understand what the actual content is of such rather grandiloquent words as anguish, forlornness, despair. As you will see, it's all quite simple.

First, what is meant by anguish? The existentialists say at once that man is anguish. What that means is this: the man who involves himself and who realizes that he is not only the person he chooses to be, but also a lawmaker who is, at the same time, choosing all mankind as well as himself, cannot help escape the feeling of his total and deep responsibility. Of course, there are many people who are not anxious; but we claim that they are hiding their anxiety, that they are fleeing from it. Certainly, many people believe that when they do something, they themselves are the only ones involved, and when someone says to them, "What if everyone acted that way?" they shrug their shoulders and answer, "Everyone doesn't act that way." But really, one should always ask himself, "What would happen if everybody looked at things that way?" There is no escaping this disturbing thought except by a kind of double-dealing. A man who lies and makes excuses for himself by saying "not everybody does that," is someone with an uneasy conscience, because the act of lying implies that a universal value is conferred upon the lie.

Anguish is evident even when it conceals itself. This is the anguish that Kierkegaard called the anguish of Abraham. You know the story: an angel has ordered Abraham to sacrifice his son; if it really were an angel who has come and said, "You are Abraham, you shall sacrifice your son," everything would be all right. But everyone might first wonder, "Is it really an angel, and am I really Abraham? What proof do I have?"

There was a madwoman who had hallucinations; someone used to speak to her on the telephone and give her orders. Her doctor asked her, "Who is it who talks to you?" She answered, "He says it's God." What proof did she really have that it was God? If an angel comes to me, what proof is there that it's an angel? And if I hear voices, what proof is there that they come from heaven and not from hell, or from the subconscious, or a pathological condition? What proves that they are addressed to me? What proof is there that I have been appointed to impose my choice and my conception of man on humanity? I'll never find any proof or sign to convince me of that. If a voice addresses me, it is always for me to decide that this is the angel's voice; if I consider that such an act is a good one, it is I who will choose to say that it is good rather than bad.

Now, I'm not being singled out as an Abraham, and yet at every moment I'm obliged to perform exemplary acts. For every man, everything happens as if all mankind had its eyes fixed on him and were guiding itself by what he does. And every man ought to say to himself, "Am I really the kind of man who has the right to act in such a way that humanity might guide itself by my actions?" And if he does not say that to himself, he is masking his anguish.

There is no question here of the kind of anguish which would lead to quietism, to inaction. It is a matter of a simple sort of anguish that anybody who has had responsibilities is familiar with. For example, when a military officer takes the responsibility for an attack and sends a certain number of men to death, he chooses to do so, and in the main he alone makes the choice. Doubtless, orders come from above, but they are too broad; he interprets them, and on this interpretation depend the lives of ten or fourteen or twenty men. In making a decision he cannot help having a certain anguish. All leaders know this anguish. That doesn't keep them from acting; on the contrary, it is the very condition of their action. For it implies that they envisage a number of possibilities, and when they choose one, they realize that it has value only because it is chosen. We shall see that this kind of anguish, which is the kind that existentialism describes, is explained, in addition, by a direct responsibility to the other men whom it involves. It is not a curtain separating us from action, but is part of action itself.

When we speak of forlornness, a term Heidegger was fond of, we mean only that God does not exist and that we have to face all the consequences of this. This existentialist is strongly opposed to a certain kind of secular ethics which would like to abolish God with the least possible expense. About 1880, some French teachers tried to set up a secular ethics which went something like this: God is a useless and costly hypothesis; we are discarding it; but, meanwhile, in order for there to be an ethics, a society, a civilization, it is essential that certain values be taken seriously and that they be considered as having an a priori existence. It must be obligatory, a priori, to be honest, not to lie, not to beat your wife, to have children, etc., etc. So we're going to try a little device which will make it possible to show that values exist all the same, inscribed in a heaven of ideas, though otherwise God does not exist. In other words—and this, I believe, is the tendency of everything called reformism in France—nothing will be changed if God does not exist. We shall find ourselves with the same norms of honesty, progress, and humanism, and we shall have made of God an outdated hypothesis which will peacefully die off by itself.

The existentialist, on the contrary, thinks it very distressing that God does not exist, because all possibility of finding values in a heaven of ideas disappears along with Him; there can no longer be an a priori Good, since there is no infinite and perfect consciousness to think it. Nowhere is it written that the Good exists, that we must be honest, that we must not lie; because the fact is we are on a plane where there are only men. Dostoievsky said, "If God didn't exist, everything would be possible." That is the very starting point of existentialism. Indeed, everything is permissible if God does not exist, and as a result man is forlorn, because neither within him nor without does he find anything to cling to. He can't start making excuses for himself.

If existence really does precede essence, there is no explaining things away by reference to a fixed and given human nature. In other words, there is no determinism, man is free, man is freedom. On the other hand, if God does not exist, we find no values or commands to turn to which legitimize our conduct. So, in the bright realm of values, we have no excuse behind us, nor justification before us. We are alone, with no excuses.

That is the idea I shall try to convey when I say that man is condemned to be free. Condemned, because he did not create himself, yet, in other respects is free; because, once thrown into the world, he is responsible for everything he does. The existentialist does not believe in the power of passion. He will never agree that a sweeping passion is a ravaging torrent which fatally leads a man to certain acts and is therefore an excuse. He thinks that man is responsible for his passion.

The existentialist does not think that man is going to help himself by finding in the world some omen by which to orient himself. Because he thinks that man will interpret the omen to suit himself. Therefore, he thinks that man, with no support and no aid, is condemned every moment to invent man. Ponge, in a very fine article, has said, "Man is the future of man." That's exactly it. But if it is taken to mean that this future is recorded in heaven, that God sees it, then it is false, because it would really no longer be a future. If it is taken to mean that, whatever a man may be, there is a future to be forged, a virgin future before him, then this remark is sound. But then we are forlorn.

To give you an example which will enable you to understand forlornness better, I shall cite the case of one of my students who came to see me under the following circumstances: his father was on bad terms with his mother, and, moreover, was inclined to be a collaborationist,[1] his older brother had been killed in the German offensive of 1940, and the young man, with somewhat immature but generous feelings, wanted to avenge him. His mother lived alone with him, very much upset by the half-treason of her husband and the death of her older son; the boy was her only consolation.

The boy was faced with the choice of leaving for England and joining the Free French forces—that is, leaving his mother behind—or remaining with his mother and helping her to carry on. He was fully aware that the woman lived only for him and that his going off—and perhaps his death—would plunge her into despair. He was also aware that every act that he did for his mother's sake was a sure thing, in the sense that it was helping her to carry on, whereas every effort he made toward going off and fighting was an uncertain move which might run aground and prove completely useless; for example, on his way to England he might, while passing through Spain, be detained indefinitely in a Spanish camp; he might reach England or Algiers and be stuck in an office at a desk job. As a result, he was faced with two very different kinds of action: one, concrete, immediate, but concerning only one individual; the other concerned an incomparably vaster group, a national collectivity, but for that very reason was dubious, and might be interrupted en route. And, at the same time, he was wavering between two kinds of ethics. On the one hand, an ethics of sympathy, of personal devotion; on the other, a broader ethics, but one whose efficacy was more dubious. He had to choose between the two.

Who could help him choose? Christian doctrine? No. Christian doctrine says, "Be charitable, love your neighbor, take the more rugged path, etc., etc." But which is the more rugged path? Whom should he love as a brother? The fighting man or his mother? Which does the greater good, the vague act of fighting in a group, or the concrete one of helping a

---

1. With the occupying German army, or its puppet government in Vichy.

particular human being to go on living? Who can decide *a priori*? Nobody. No book of ethics can tell him. The Kantian ethics says, "Never treat any person as a means, but as an end." Very well, if I stay with my mother, I'll treat her as an end and not as a means; but by virtue of this very fact, I'm running the risk of treating the people around me who are fighting, as means; and, conversely, if I go to join those who are fighting, I'll be treating them as an end, and, by doing that, I run the risk of treating my mother as a means.

If values are vague, and if they are always too broad for the concrete and specific case that we are considering, the only thing left for us is to trust our instincts. That's what this young man tried to do; and when I saw him, he said, "In the end, feeling is what counts. I ought to choose whichever pushes me in one direction. If I feel that I love my mother enough to sacrifice everything else for her—my desire for vengeance, for action, for adventure—then I'll stay with her. If, on the contrary, I feel that my love for my mother isn't enough, I'll leave."

But how is the value of a feeling determined? What gives his feeling for his mother value? Precisely the fact that he remained with her. I may say that I like so-and-so well enough to sacrifice a certain amount of money for him, but I may say so only if I've done it. I may say "I love my mother well enough to remain with her" if I have remained with her. The only way to determine the value of this affection is, precisely, to perform an act which confirms and defines it. But, since I require this affection to justify my act, I find myself caught in a vicious circle.

On the other hand, Gide has well said that a mock feeling and a true feeling are almost indistinguishable; to decide that I love my mother and will remain with her, or to remain with her by putting on an act, amount somewhat to the same thing. In other words, the feeling is formed by the acts one performs; so, I cannot refer to it in order to act upon it. Which means that I can neither seek within myself the true condition which will impel me to act, nor apply to a system of ethics for concepts which will permit me to act. You will say, "At least, he did go to a teacher for advice." But if you seek advice from a priest, for example, you have chosen this priest; you already knew, more or less, just about what advice he was going to give you. In other words, choosing your adviser is involving yourself. The proof of this is that if you are a Christian, you will say, "Consult a priest." But some priests are collaborating, some are just marking time, some are resisting. Which to choose? If the young man chooses a priest who is resisting or collaborating, he has already decided on the kind of advice he's going to get. Therefore, in coming to see me he knew the answer I was going to give him, and I had only one answer to give: "You're free, choose, that is, invent." No general ethics can show you what is to be done; there are no omens in the world. The Catholics will reply, "But there are." Granted—but, in any case, I myself choose the meaning they have.

When I was a prisoner, I knew a rather remarkable young man who was a Jesuit. He had entered the Jesuit order in the following way: he had had a number of very bad breaks; in childhood, his father died, leaving him in poverty, and he was a scholarship student at a religious institution where he was constantly made to feel that he was being kept out of charity; then, he failed to get any of the honors and distinctions that children like; later on, at about eighteen, he bungled a love affair; finally, at twenty-two, he failed in military training, a childish enough matter, but it was the last straw.

This young fellow might well have felt that he had botched everything. It was a sign of something, but of what? He might have taken refuge in bitterness or despair. But he very wisely looked upon all this as a sign that he was not made for secular triumphs, and that only the triumphs of religion, holiness, and faith were open to him. He saw the hand of God in all this, and so he entered the order. Who can help seeing that he alone decided what the sign meant?

Some other interpretation might have been drawn from this series of setbacks; for example, that he might have done better to turn carpenter or revolutionist. Therefore, he is fully responsible for the interpretation. Forlornness implies that we ourselves choose our being. Forlornness and anguish go together.

As for despair, the term has a very simple meaning. It means that we shall confine ourselves to reckoning only with what depends upon our will, or on the ensemble of probabilities which make our action possible. When we want something, we always have to reckon with probabilities. I may be counting on the arrival of a friend. The friend is coming by rail or streetcar; this supposes that the train will arrive on schedule, or that the streetcar will not jump the track. I am left in the realm of possibility; but possibilities are to be reckoned with only to the point where my action comports with the ensemble of these possibilities, and no further. The moment the possibilities I am considering are not rigorously involved by my action, I ought to disengage myself from them, because no God, no scheme, can adapt the world and its possibilities to my will. When Descartes said, "Conquer yourself rather than the world," he meant essentially the same thing.

The Marxists to whom I have spoken reply, "You can rely on the support of others in your action, which obviously has certain limits because you're not going to live forever. That means: rely on both what others are doing elsewhere to help you, in China, in Russia, and what they will do later on, after your death, to carry on the action and lead it to its fulfillment, which will be the revolution. You even *have* to rely upon that, otherwise you're immoral." I reply at once that I will always rely on fellow-fighters insofar as these comrades are involved with me in a common struggle, in the unity of a party or a group in which I can more or less make my weight felt; that is, one whose ranks I am in as a fighter and whose movements I am aware of at every moment. In such a situation, relying on the unity and will of the party is exactly like counting on the fact that the train will arrive on time or that the car won't jump the track. But, given that man is free and that there is no human nature for me to depend on, I cannot count on men whom I do not know by relying on human goodness or man's concern for the good of society. I don't know what will become of the Russian revolution; I may make an example of it to the extent that at the present time it is apparent that the proletariat plays a part in Russia that it plays in no other nation. But I can't swear that this will inevitably lead to a triumph of the proletariat. I've got to limit myself to what I see.

Given that men are free and that tomorrow they will freely decide what man will be, I cannot be sure that, after my death, fellow-fighters will carry on my work to bring it to its maximum perfection. Tomorrow, after my death, some men may decide to set up Fascism, and the others may be cowardly and muddled enough to let them do it. Fascism will then be the human reality, so much the worse for us.

Actually, things will be as man will have decided they are to be. Does that mean that I should abandon myself to quietism? No. First, I should involve myself; then, act on the old saw, "Nothing ventured, nothing gained." Nor does it mean that I shouldn't belong to a party, but rather that I shall have no illusions and shall do what I can. For example, suppose I ask myself, "Will socialization, as such, ever come about?" I know nothing about it. All I know is that I'm going to do everything in my power to bring it about. Beyond that, I can't count on anything. Quietism is the attitude of people who say, "Let others do what I can't do." The doctrine I am presenting is the very opposite of quietism, since it declares, "There is no reality except in action." Moreover, it goes further, since it adds, "Man is nothing else than his plan; he exists only to the extent that he fulfills himself; he is therefore nothing else than the ensemble of his acts, nothing else than his life."

According to this, we can understand why our doctrine horrifies certain people. Because often the only way they can bear their wretchedness is to think, "Circumstances have been against me. What I've been and done doesn't show my true worth. To be sure, I've had no great love, no great friendship, but that's because I haven't met a man or woman who was worthy. The books I've written haven't been very good because I haven't had the proper leisure. I haven't had children to devote myself to because I didn't find a man with whom I could have spent my life. So there remains within me, unused and quite viable, a host of propensities, inclinations, possibilities, that one wouldn't guess from the mere series of things I've done."

Now, for the existentialist there is really no love other than one which manifests itself in a person's being in love. There is no genius other than one which is expressed in works of art; the genius of Proust is the sum of Proust's works; the genius of Racine is his series of tragedies. Outside of that, there is nothing. Why say that Racine could have written another tragedy, when he didn't write it? A man is involved in life, leaves his impress on it, and outside of that there is nothing. To be sure, this may seem a harsh thought to someone whose life hasn't been a success. But, on the other hand, it prompts people to understand that reality alone is what counts, that dreams, expectations, and hopes warrant no more than to define a man as a disappointed dream, as miscarried hopes, as vain expectations. In other words, to define him negatively and not positively. However, when we say, "You are nothing else than your life," that does not imply that the artist will be judged solely on the basis of his works of art; a thousand other things will contribute toward summing him up. What we mean is that a man is nothing else than a series of undertakings, that he is the sum, the organization, the ensemble of the relationships which make up these undertakings.

When all is said and done, what we are accused of, at bottom, is not our pessimism, but an optimistic toughness. If people throw up to us our works of fiction in which we write about people who are soft, weak, cowardly, and sometimes even downright bad, it's not because these people are soft, weak, cowardly, or bad; because if we were to say, as Zola did, that they are that way because of heredity, the workings of environment, society, because of biological or psychological determinism, people would be reassured. They would say, "Well, that's what we're like, no one can do anything about it." But when the existentialist writes about a coward, he says that this coward is responsible for his cowardice. He's not like that because he has a cowardly heart or lung or brain; he's not like that on account of his physiological make-up; but he's like that because he has made himself a coward by his acts. There's no such thing as a cowardly constitution; there are nervous constitutions; there is poor blood, as the common people say, or strong constitutions. But the man whose blood is poor is not a coward on that account, for what makes cowardice is the act of renouncing or yielding. A constitution is not an act; the coward is defined on the basis of the acts he performs. People feel, in a vague sort of way, that this coward we're talking about is guilty of being a coward, and the thought frightens them. What people would like is that a coward or a hero be born that way. . . .

From these few reflections it is evident that nothing is more unjust than the objections that have been raised against us. Existentialism is nothing else than an attempt to draw all the consequences of a coherent atheistic position. It isn't trying to plunge man into despair at all. But if one calls every attitude of unbelief despair, like the Christians, then the word is not being used in its original sense. Existentialism isn't so atheistic that it wears itself out showing that God doesn't exist. Rather, it declares that even if God did exist, that would change nothing. There you've got our point of view. Not that we believe that God exists, but we think that the problem of His existence is not the issue. In this sense existentialism is optimistic, a doctrine of action, and it is plain dishonesty for Christians to make no distinction between their own despair and ours and then to call us despairing.

1947

THE READER

1. What is the significance of the words "if existence really does precede essence"? What does this mean? What is the force of "if"? Why does Sartre repeat the words later in the essay?
2. Why does Sartre use three separate terms—"anguish," "forlornness," "despair"? What, if any, are the differences among them?
3. Sartre makes a distinction between treating "any person as a means . . . [and] as an end" (p. 1198). What are the implications of this distinction?

THE WRITER

1. What are some of the methods or devices Sartre uses to define existentialism? Why does he use more than one method or device? Compare the techniques that Sartre uses with those that Highet uses in defining Zen (p. 1170).
2. Sartre says that "when we say that a man is responsible for himself, we do not only mean that he is responsible for his own individuality, but that he is responsible for all men." Write a brief essay explaining how, in the existentialist view, this is possible.

Authors

Robert M. Adams (1915–)
American literary critic, editor, and teacher. Educated at Columbia, Adams has taught at Columbia, the University of Wisconsin, Rutgers, Cornell, and the University of California, Los Angeles. He has edited works by Stendhal, Voltaire, Machiavelli, and More, and has written *James Joyce: Common Sense and Beyond* (1966) and *After Joyce: Studies in Fiction after Ulysses* (1977). Since 1962, he has served as an editor of *The Norton Anthology of English Literature.* "Soft Soap and the Nitty-Gritty" originally appeared in *Fair of Speech: The Uses of Euphemism,* a collection of essays on language edited by D. J. Enright (1985).

Aesop (sixth century B.C.)
Legendary Greek storyteller. A collection of Greek fables, orally composed and transmitted, was ascribed to Aesop sometime in the third century A.D. Preserved and copied during the Middle Ages, the fables probably made their way into English through the work of the Dutch scholar Erasmus, who translated them into Latin; Erasmus's Latin text was later rendered into English. The fable has proved to be an enduring literary form, practised in this century by writers as different as Orwell, Golding, and Nabokov.

Woody Allen (1935–)
Popular name of Heywood Allen, born Allen Stewart Konigsberg, American comedian, writer, actor, and film director. Allen began his career as a television comedy writer in the late 1950s. Eventually he became a comedian himself, then a screenwriter, playwright (*Don't Drink the Water,* 1966; *Play It Again, Sam,* 1969), and film director. His films include *Annie Hall* (1977), which won Allen the Academy Award for best director; *Manhattan* (1979);

The Purple Rose of Cairo (1985); and *Hannah and Her Sisters* (1986). Allen's books include *Getting Even* (1971), *Without Feathers* (1975), and *Side Effects* (1980). "Selections from the Allen Notebooks" first appeared in *Without Feathers* (1975).

Maya Angelou (1928–)
American author, playwright, actress, poet, and singer. Born in St. Louis, Angelou attended public schools in Arkansas and California before studying music and dance. In a richly varied career, she has been a cook, streetcar conductor, singer, actress, dancer, and teacher. Author of several volumes of poetry and ten plays (stage, screen, and television), Angelou may be best known for her autobiography, a work-in-progress of which five volumes have been published so far. "Graduation" originally appeared in *I Know Why the Caged Bird Sings* (1970), the first volume of that autobiography.

Hannah Arendt (1906–1975)
German-American political scientist and philosopher. Born in Hanover, Germany, and educated at the University of Heidelberg, Arendt began her academic career in Germany but was forced to flee when Hitler came to power. Arriving in the United States in 1940, she became chief editor for a major publisher and a frequent lecturer on college campuses. Arendt taught at a number of American colleges and universities, finishing her career at the New School for Social Research in New York City. Of the dozen or so major books she wrote, three received greatest attention: *Eichmann in Jerusalem: A Report on the Banality of Evil* (1963); *On Revolution* (1963); and *The Origins of Totalitarianism* (1968). "Denmark and the Jews" comes from *Eichmann in Jerusalem;* in slightly different form, it first appeared in *The New Yorker.*

Michael Arlen (1930–)
American journalist and writer. After receiving his undergraduate degree from Harvard in 1952, Arlen became a reporter for *Life* magazine. Since 1957, he has been a staff writer and television critic for *The New Yorker*. Many of his critical essays have been collected and published in book form: *Living-Room War* (1969); *The View from Highway 1* (1976); *Thirty Seconds* (1980); and *The Camera Age: Essays on Television* (1981). "Griefspeak" first appeared in *Living-Room War*.

Matthew Arnold (1822–1888)
English poet, literary critic, and social critic. Son of distinguished educator Thomas Arnold, Matthew Arnold studied at Balliol College, Oxford, before beginning work as an inspector of schools, a position he held for thirty-five years. Arnold wrote poetry early in his literary career, establishing his reputation with poems like "Stanzas from the Grand Chartreuse" (1855) and "Dover Beach" (1867). The publication of his *Essays in Criticism, First Series* (1867) marked a shift to writing prose. The recurrent topic in Arnold's writing is the problem of living a full and an enjoyable life in a modern industrial society. "Culture" comes from *Culture and Anarchy* (1869), a collection of critical essays considered central to Arnold's thought.

Lord Ashby (1904–)
Eric Ashby, English botanist, writer, and educator. Educated at the University of London and the University of Chicago, Ashby has held teaching appointments in science in England, Australia, and the United States. President and vice-chancellor of the Queen's University, Belfast, from 1950 until 1959, he served as chancellor there from 1970 until 1984. He has written articles and books on education (*Universities: British, Indian, and African*, 1966; *Masters and Scholars*, 1970) and on environmental matters (*Reconciling Man with the Environment*, 1978; *The Politics of Clean Air*, 1981). Made a Life Peer in 1973, Lord Ashby is a Life Fellow of Clare College, Cambridge.

Isaac Asimov (1920–)
American biochemist and science writer. Born in Russia, Asimov was educated in the United States and received a Ph.D. in biochemistry from Columbia. He became a member of the faculty at the School of Medicine, Boston University, in 1949 and he is currently professor of biochemistry there. An extraordinarily prolific author, Asimov has published over 250 books on topics as diverse as mathematics, astronomy, physics, chemistry, biology, mythology, Shakespeare, the Bible, and geography; he also writes science fiction. Among his works: *The Stars, Like the Dust* (1951); *Science, Numbers and I* (1968); *ABC's of the Earth* (1971); *The Road to Infinity* (1979); and *The Exploding Suns: The Secrets of Supernovas* (1985). "The Eureka Phenomenon" comes from *The Left Hand of the Electron* (1972).

Margaret Atwood (1939–)
Canadian poet, novelist, and critic. After study at Victoria College, University of Toronto, and Radcliffe, Atwood became a film-script writer and worked for a marketing-research firm. Though her first book of poems, *Double Persephone*, was published in 1961, it was not until the second, *The Circle Game* (1966), that she began to be recognized. In all, she has published ten volumes of poetry. In the late 1960s, Atwood began writing novels; among them, *Surfacing* (1972; 1973), *Bodily Harm* (1981), and *The Handmaid's Tale* (1985) stand out. She has also written short stories, criticism, and works for children. "Writing the Male Character" comes from *Second Words* (1982), a collection of Atwood's critical essays.

W. H. Auden (1907–1973)
Wystan Hugh Auden, English poet, playwright, librettist, and essayist. Called "the foremost poet of his generation," Auden was born in York, England, and educated at Christ Church College, Oxford. After Oxford, Auden supported himself as a schoolmaster (1928–1933). In 1930, he made his literary debut with the publication of *Poems*. During the 1930s, he and Christopher Isherwood collaborated on three plays: *The Dog beneath the Skin* (1935); *The Ascent of F6* (1936); and *On the Frontier* (1938). In 1939, he settled in the United States and, with the exception of 1956 to 1961, when he was professor of poetry at Oxford, made his home here until 1972. Among the more important collections of his poems are *Another Time* (1940) and *The Shield of Achilles* (1955). He also wrote opera libretti as well as scores of reviews and introductions for books of poetry. Some of these were collected in *The Dyer's Hand* (1962), from

which "Apothegms" comes.

Francis Bacon (1561–1626)
English politician, statesman, and philosopher. Trained as a lawyer, Bacon served as a member of Parliament during the reign of Queen Elizabeth I. After her death, he found favor with King James I and advanced in government service. His career was cut short in 1621 when he was convicted of accepting bribes. Retired, he married and devoted the rest of his life to study and writing texts, among them *The Advancement of Learning* (1605), *Novum Organum* (1620), which contains "Of Simulation and Dissimulation," and *Essays* (various editions, 1597–1625), from which "Of Revenge" comes.

James Baldwin (1924–1987)
American essayist, novelist, and social activist. Baldwin was born in Harlem, the son of a preacher, and grew to maturity in an America disfigured by racism and prejudice. Only after moving to Paris in 1948 did he begin to write. Both his first novel, *Go Tell It on the Mountain* (1953), and his first play, *The Amen Corner* (1955), are autobiographical explorations. Though he would write other plays—for example, *Blues for Mister Charlie* (1964)— Baldwin concentrated his energies on novels like *Giovanni's Room* (1956), *Another Country* (1962), and *If Beale Street Could Talk* (1974) as well as on essays. Collections like *Notes of a Native Son* (1955), from which "Stranger in the Village" comes, *Nobody Knows My Name* (1961), *The Fire Next Time* (1963), and *No Name in the Street* (1972) demonstrate Baldwin's skills as a social critic of insight and passion. A number of his most important essays and reviews have been gathered in *The Price of the Ticket* (1985).

Carl Becker (1873–1945)
American historian and teacher. Educated at the University of Wisconsin, Becker held several teaching appointments (Dartmouth, University of Kansas, University of Minnesota) before joining the faculty of Cornell University, where he taught from 1917 until 1941. The author of fifteen books, Becker wrote "Democracy" for his text *Modern Democracy* (1941).

Wendell Berry (1934–   )
American poet, novelist, and essayist. Born in Kentucky, educated at the University of Kentucky, Berry has been a member of the faculty at the university since 1964. Although he has written novels, his literary reputation rests on his poetry and essays. The world of nature, its precarious balance and our responsibility to sustain it, as well as the people and places of the South form the fabric of his work. Of particular note are *The Hidden Wound* (1970), a prose work on racism; *The Country of Marriage*, poems (1973); *Recollected Essays 1965–1980* (1981); and *The Gift of Good Land, Further Essays Cultural and Agricultural* (1981), from which "Home of the Free" comes.

Tom Bethell (1940–   )
American journalist and writer. Born in London, Bethell attended the Royal Naval College and Trinity College, Oxford. He came to the United States in 1962 and taught mathematics at a private preparatory school in Virginia until 1965. He then became managing editor of *New Orleans* magazine and did free-lance writing and research. Bethell served as editor of the *New Orleans Courier* (1972–1974) and of the *Washington Monthly* (1975–1976) before joining the staff of *Harper's*, where he is now a contributing editor. "Agnostic Evolutionists" originally appeared in *Harper's* (February 1985).

Bruno Bettelheim (1903–   )
American child psychologist, educator, and writer. Born and educated in Vienna, Bettelheim came to the United States in 1939 and joined the faculty of the University of Chicago in 1944, beginning a long and distinguished teaching career there (1944–1973). He has written several dozen books, including *Love Is Not Enough: The Treatment of Emotionally Disturbed Children* (1950); *The Informed Heart: Autonomy in a Mass Age* (1960); *The Children of the Dream* (1969); *The Uses of Enchantment: The Meaning and Importance of Fairy Tales* (1976); and *A Good Enough Parent* (1987). "A Victim" originally appeared in *The Informed Heart*.

Ambrose Bierce (1842–1914?)
American journalist, poet, and writer. After serving in the Civil War and working as a journalist in San Francisco, Bierce went to England, where he wrote comic and satiric sketches for several publications. In 1876, he returned to San Francisco as a reporter for William Randolph Hearst's *Examiner*. Bierce's twelve-volume *Collected Works* (1909–1912) include a generous sampling of his tales, essays, verses, and fables. Today, Bierce may be

best known for *The Devil's Dictionary* (1906), a collection of ironic definitions compiled while he was a Hearst correspondent in Washington, D.C. Selections included in "Prose Forms: Apothegms" come from *The Devil's Dictionary*.

Caroline Bird (1915–)

American journalist, public-relations specialist, and writer. Bird attended Vassar College, graduated from the University of Toledo, and received her master's from the University of Wisconsin (1939). She worked at *Newsweek* and *Fortune* in the 1940s, then moved into public relations, which she left after twenty years to pursue writing full time. Bird is the author of nine books, a number focused on feminist concerns: *Everything a Woman Needs to Know to Get Paid What She's Worth* (1973; revised edition, 1982); *The Two-Paycheck Marriage* (1979); and *The Good Years: Your Life in the Twenty-first Century* (1983). "College Is a Waste of Time and Money" comes from *The Case Against College* (1975).

William Blake (1757–1827)

English poet, artist, and writer. An engraver and illustrator by trade, Blake established a printing shop in London, where he engraved and printed his second volume of poems, *Songs of Innocence* (1789). Blake's poems and illuminations, reflecting an independent spirit seeking freedom from repression, take their inspiration from nature and religion, both being transformed into a deeply personal and unorthodox vision. His *Songs of Experience* (1794) is a masterful lyric series that includes the well-known "Tyger! Tyger! burning bright." "Proverbs of Hell" comes from *The Marriage of Heaven and Hell* (1793), Blake's principal prose work.

Wayne C. Booth (1921–)

American writer, literary critic, and teacher. After receiving a Ph.D. from the University of Chicago in 1950, Booth began a teaching career that has taken him to Haverford College, Earlham College, and back to the University of Chicago, where he is now professor of English. Among Booth's books are *The Rhetoric of Fiction* (1961; revised edition, 1983); *A Rhetoric of Irony* (1974); *Modern Dogma and the Rhetoric of Assent* (1974); and *Critical Understanding: The Powers and Limits of Pluralism* (1979). "Is There Any Knowledge That a Man Must Have?" originally appeared in *The Knowledge Most Worth Having* (1967); "Boring from Within: The Art of the Freshman Essay" was an address given to the Illinois Council of College Teachers (1963).

Jacob Bronowski (1908–1974)

English mathematician, scientist, and writer. Born in Poland, educated in England, where he received a Ph.D. in mathematics from Cambridge in 1933, Bronowski served as a university lecturer before entering government service during World War II. From 1950 until 1963, he was head of research for Britain's National Coal Board; from 1964 until his death, he was a resident fellow at the Salk Institute, La Jolla, California. The author of many books, among them *Science and Human Values* (1956; 1965), *Nature and Knowledge* (1969), *Magic, Science, and Civilization* (published posthumously, 1978), Bronowski achieved fame with the thirteen-part television series, "The Ascent of Man" (1973–1974). "The Nature of Scientific Reasoning" comes from *Science and Human Values*. "The Reach of Imagination" from *Proceedings of the American Academy of Arts and Letters and National Institute of Arts and Letters*, Second Series, No. 17 (1976).

Jerome S. Bruner (1915–)

American psychologist and teacher. Educated at Duke and Harvard, Bruner has made major contributions to understanding how human beings process information. At Harvard from 1945 to 1981, he founded the Center for Cognitive Studies, an interdisciplinary research center devoted to analyzing learning. Bruner has concentrated his research on the development of learning capacities in children. In 1981, he accepted an appointment at the New School for Social Research. Among Bruner's most important books are *A Study of Thinking* (1956); *The Process of Education* (1960); *The Relevance of Education* (1971); *In Search of Mind*, an autobiography (1983); and *Actual Minds, Possible Worlds* (1986). "Freud and the Image of Man" originally appeared in the *Partisan Review* (Summer 1956).

Robert Burchfield (1923–)

British lexicographer and authority on language. Born in New Zealand, Burchfield was educated at Magdalen College, Oxford. After serving as a lecturer in English at Oxford, he became one of the editors for *A Supplement to the Oxford English Dictionary* in 1957; he continues to hold that position. In addition, Burchfield was chief editor of *The Oxford English Dictionaries* from 1971 until 1984. The author of several books (*The Spoken Word*, 1981; *The Spoken Language as an Art Form*, 1981; *The English Language*, 1985), Burchfield is senior research fellow at St. Peter's College, Oxford. "Dictionaries and Ethnic Sensibilities" is a revised version of a talk given on BBC Radio 3 in April, 1978, the text of which was printed in *The Listener* (April 13, 1978) and in *The State of the Language*, edited by Leonard Michaels and Christopher Ricks.

Anthony Burgess (1917–)
[John] Anthony Burgess [Wilson], English novelist, playwright, editor, and writer. Born in Manchester, England, and a graduate of Manchester University, Burgess was a lecturer and teacher of English until 1954. He then became an education officer in the Colonial Service, stationed in Malaya. His writing career began there. In 1959, when he was told that he had a year to live, Burgess returned to England and wrote five novels in one year. Since then he has written several dozen more, including *A Clockwork Orange* (1962), *Enderby Outside* (1968), and *Earthly Powers* (1980). In addition, Burgess has written critical studies, giving special attention to James Joyce and D. H. Lawrence. "Is America Falling Apart?" originally appeared in *The New York Times* in 1971.

Herbert Butterfield (1900–)
British educator and writer. He was educated at Cambridge and has spent his career there, serving in a variety of capacities including professor of modern history (1944–1963), vice-chancellor (1959–1961), and Regius Professor (1963–). A specialist in eighteenth-century English and French history, Butterfield has written a classic study, *The Whig Interpretation of History* (1931) as well as *Lord North and the People* (1949) and *George III and the Historians* (1957). "The Originality of the Old Testament" originally appeared in *Writings on Christianity and History*, a collection of Butterfield's essays edited by C. T. McIntire.

Nigel Calder (1931–)
English research physicist and writer. After earning two degrees at Cambridge, Calder was a research physicist for two years before he joined the staff of the *New Scientist*. In 1966, he left his position as editor to become a free-lance writer. He has published over two dozen books and has adapted a number of them for television. His in-depth knowledge of complex subject matter coupled with his ability to communicate with a broad audience have made his books popular, including *Restless Earth* (1972), *Einstein's Universe* (1979), *Time-Scale* (1983), and *The Green Machines* (1986). "Heads and Tails" is Chapter 4 from *The Comet Is Coming!* (1980).

June Callwood (1924–)
Birth name of June Frayne, Canadian writer and social activist. Callwood began her professional writing career as a journalist (1941–1945). Since 1945, she has been a free-lance writer. From 1975 until 1978, she was hostess for "In Touch," a Canadian Broadcasting Company television program. Callwood has co-written a number of books, including *How to Talk to Practically Anybody about Practically Anything* (with Barbara Walters, 1973), and *Otto Preminger Remembers* (with Otto Preminger, 1977). A resident of Toronto, she is active in social, political, and feminist causes in Canada. "Portrait of Canada" is the Introduction to Callwood's book of the same title (1981).

Edward Hallett Carr (1892–1982)
English historian, journalist, and statesman. After studying classics at Trinity College, Cambridge, Carr spent twenty years in the diplomatic service. In 1936, he became professor of international relations at University College in Wales and began to write about diplomatic history. In 1941, he became assistant editor of *The Times* (London). In 1946, he left teaching and journalism to begin work on his major opus: a fourteen-volume study, *A History of Russia*, completed in 1978. "The Historian and His Facts" comes from Carr's *What Is History?* (1961).

Joyce Cary (1888–1957)
Arthur Joyce Lunel Cary, Anglo-Irish novelist, poet, and political philosopher. Cary studied art in Paris and was educated at Oxford before seeing military service in the Balkan War (1912–1913) and in Africa (1915–1916). Cary was a prolific writer, particularly noted as a novelist; of his twelve novels, *A House of Children* (1941) and *The Horse's Mouth* (1944) stand out. In addition, he wrote poetry, short stories, and a text on esthetics. "Art and Education" comes from "On the Function of the Novelist," which originally appeared in *The New York Times* in 1949.

Lord Chesterfield (1694–1773)

Philip Dormer Stanhope, fourth earl of Chesterfield, English statesman, diplomat, and writer. Though attracted to the literary world as a youth, Chesterfield entered diplomatic service and held important posts in Holland and Ireland. His literary reputation rests on his *Letters*. Addressed to his son Philip and written with near-daily frequency beginning in 1737, they became a handbook of gentlemanly conduct when they were published in 1774. In a now-famous episode, Samuel Johnson sent the *Plan* for his *Dictionary* to Chesterfield but received no response. Even though Chesterfield published two favorable reviews when the *Dictionary* was printed, Johnson, always sensitive to slights, wrote his "Letter to Lord Chesterfield," scorning the nobleman's praise.

Lord Clark (1903–1983)

Kenneth Clark, lord of Saltwood, English art historian and critic. Born into wealth, Clark was educated at Trinity College, Oxford, and studied with art historian Bernard Berenson in Florence. In a distinguished career, Clark held many major appointments, including Keeper of Fine Art at the Ashmolean Museum and director of the National Gallery, London. He published over a dozen books, two of which are considered definitive studies: *Leonardo da Vinci* (1939) and *The Nude* (1955). Lord Clark may be best known for a thirteen-part television series, *Civilisation*, broadcast here in 1970. "The Blot and the Diagram" comes from *Moments of Vision and Other Essays* (1982).

Samuel L. Clemens (1835–1910)

American novelist, journalist, humorist, and writer. First apprenticed as a printer, Clemens was by turns a river-boat pilot, gold prospector, and journalist. Under his nom de plume of Mark Twain, he became famous when his short story "The Celebrated Jumping Frog of Calaveras County" was published in 1867. Clemens wrote a good deal and lectured widely after that. At least two of his novels, *The Adventures of Tom Sawyer* (1876) and *Adventures of Huckleberry Finn* (1885), rank as American classics. "Advice to Youth" is the text of a lecture delivered by Clemens. He dictated "The War Prayer" in 1904 or 1905, but it was not published until 1923 in *Europe and Elsewhere*.

Carl Cohen (1931–)

American philosopher and teacher. After earning a Ph.D. in philosophy at the University of California, Los Angeles (1955), Cohen became a member of the Department of Philosophy at the University of Michigan, Ann Arbor, where he has been professor of philosophy since 1960. With special interests in political philosophy and the philosophy of law, Cohen has published widely in a number of journals. "The Case for the Use of Animals in Biomedical Research" originally appeared in *The New England Journal of Medicine* (October 2, 1986).

Ralph W. Conant (1926–)

American political scientist and writer. Educated at the University of Vermont and the University of Chicago, Conant has pursued interests in public planning, social violence, and politics. He has taught at a number of American schools, including the University of Denver, MIT, Harvard, and Rice. Conant is now president of Public Research, Inc. He has written and edited many books, among them *Problems in Research on Community Violence* (1969) and *The Conant Report: A Study of the Education of Librarians* (1980). While Conant was associate director of the Lemberg Center for the Study of Violence at Brandeis University, he wrote "The Justification of Civil Protest, Nonviolent and Violent"; it originally appeared as "Rioting, Insurrection and Civil Disobedience" in *The American Scholar* 37, no. 3 (Summer, 1968).

Aaron Copland (1900–)

American composer and writer. Copland studied music theory and practice in Paris (1921–1924), then returned to New York. After some experimentation with adapting jazz to classical composition, Copland developed a distinctly American style, incorporating American folk songs and legends into three ballet scores: *Billy the Kid* (1938), *Rodeo* (1942), and *Appalachian Spring* (1944); poetry into *Twelve Poems of Emily Dickinson*, songs for voice and piano (1950); and historical material into *Lincoln Portrait* (1942), for narrator and orchestra. Copland has also written about music. "How We Listen" comes from a collection of his essays, *What to Listen for in Music* (1939).

Malcolm Cowley (1898–)

American critic, poet, editor, and literary historian. Though Cowley has written poetry (*Blue Juniata*, 1929; *The Dry Season*, 1941; *Blue Juniata: Collected Poems*, 1968), he has earned a more important place for himself as a literary historian and memoirist. In *Exile's Return* (1934), *The Literary Situation* (1954), *Think Back on Us: A Contemporary Chronicle of the 1930s* (1967), *A Many-windowed House* (1970), and *A Second Flowering* (1973), Cowley has recorded vital chapters in American literary life. His memoirs, *And I Worked at the Writer's Trade* (1978) and *The Dream of the Golden Mountains* (1980), have amplified and further personalized those chronicles. "The View from 80" comes from a collection of essays with the same title, published in 1980.

Robertson Davies (1913–   )
Canadian novelist, playwright, and critic. Educated in Canada and at Balliol College, Oxford, Davies joined the Old Vic Company, one of England's most prestigious acting troupes, for two seasons. From 1940 to 1962, he worked as a journalist and then became involved in writing and directing for the theater. On his return to Canada, he joined the faculty of the University of Toronto; from 1962 until 1981, he was master of Massey College there. Davies's fiction is generally deemed more important than his journalism and drama. He has written two trilogies—*The Salterton Trilogy* (1951–1958) and *The Deptford Trilogy* (1970–1975)—and four major novels, the most recent of which is *What's Bred in the Bone* (1985). "Ham and Tongue" comes from *One Half of Robertson Davies* (1978), a collection of essays. It is an abridged version of a speech given on April 6, 1977, for The Cosmos Club of Washington, D.C.

Joan Didion (1934–   )
American novelist, essayist, and screenwriter. A native Californian, Didion studied at the University of California, Berkeley. After winning *Vogue* magazine's Prix de Paris contest for excellence in writing, she went to work for the magazine. Didion rose from promotional copywriter to associate feature editor before leaving *Vogue* in 1963, the year her first novel, *Run River*, was published. Since then, she has written three more novels (*Play It As It Lays*, 1971; *A Book of Common Prayer*, 1977; *Democracy*, 1984). A frequent contributor to magazines like *Vogue* and *Harper's Bazaar*, Didion has published two collections of essays (*Slouching towards Bethlehem*, 1969; *The White Album*, 1979). *Salvador*, a work of fiction based on her visit to El Salvador in

1983, marked Didion's growing concern with politics. She is currently working on a novel, *Angel Visits*, and a collection of childhood reminiscences, *Fairytales*. "On Going Home" and "On Keeping a Notebook" originally appeared in *Slouching towards Bethlehem*; "Salvador" comes from *Salvador*; "Georgia O'Keeffe" was written for *The Saturday Evening Post* in 1976, then reprinted in *The White Album*.

Annie Dillard (1945–   )
American poet, critic, and editor. Dillard received a B.A. and an M.A. from Hollins College. A keen observer of the natural world, Dillard published her first collection of poems, *Tickets for a Prayer Wheel*, and a Pulitzer Prize–winning volume of essays, *Pilgrim at Tinker Creek*, in 1974. Since then, she has written four books, including *Living by Fiction* (1982), from which "About Symbol" comes, and *Encounters with Chinese Writers* (1984), a collection of nonfiction pieces. Dillard is a contributing editor for *Harper's* magazine, where "Sight into Insight" originally appeared (February 1974).

Kildare Dobbs (1923–   )
Canadian writer. Born in India and educated at Cambridge, Dobbs spent time in the British foreign service before becoming a journalist and an editor; he is now a free-lance writer. He has written autobiographical sketches (*Running to Paradise*, 1962), short stories (*Pride and Fall*, 1981), and essays, some of which were collected in *Reading the Time* (1968). "The Shatterer of Worlds" originally appeared in that collection.

John Donne (1572–1631)
English poet, essayist, and cleric. Born into an old Roman Catholic family, Donne attended Oxford and Cambridge, but could not receive a degree because of his religion. He studied, though never practiced, law and, after quietly abandoning Catholicism some time during the 1590s, entered government service. In 1615, he was received into the Anglican Church. One of the greatest religious orators of his age, Donne became dean of St. Paul's Cathedral in 1621. Donne's literary reputation rests on his poetry as well as on his sermons (e.g., "Let Me Wither") and devotions (e.g., "Men Are Sleeping Prisoners").

Barbara Ehrenreich (1941–   )
American writer. Educated at Reed Col-

lege and Rockefeller University, where she earned a Ph.D. in biology, Ehrenreich taught at New York University and the State University of New York before becoming a full-time writer and lecturer on women's issues and social policy. A regular contributor to Ms., Vogue, and The New York Times, she has written several important feminist studies: For Her Own Good: 150 Years of the Experts' Advice to Women (co-author, 1978); The Hearts of Men: American Dreams and the Flight from Commitment (1984); and Re-making Love: The Feminization of Sex (co-author, 1986). Her most recent work appears in Mean Season: The Attack on the Welfare State, by Fred Block and others (1987). "College Today: Tune In, Drop Out, and Take the Cash" originally appeared as a "Hers" column in The New York Times (March 7, 1985).

Loren Eiseley (1907–1977)
American anthropologist, historian of science, and poet. Educated at the University of Nebraska and the University of Pennsylvania, Eiseley taught at the University of Kansas, Oberlin, and finally back at the University of Pennsylvania, where he remained for thirty years. A humanist deeply concerned with major ethical issues, he established a national reputation with his writings: The Immense Journey (1957); Darwin's Century (1958); The Firmament of Time (revised edition, 1960); The Night Country (1971), in which "The Brown Wasps" originally appeared; and The Unexpected Universe (1972). A collection of Eiseley's poems, Another Kind of Autumn, was published posthumously in 1977.

Ralph Waldo Emerson (1803–1882)
American poet, philosopher, and essayist. One of the most influential writers of the American tradition, Emerson entered Harvard at the age of fourteen. After graduation in 1821, he taught school for several years before beginning theological studies in 1825. In 1829, he was ordained a Unitarian minister. In 1832, he resigned his pastorate, retiring to Concord, Massachusetts, to a life of study and reflection. With the publication of his first book, Nature in 1836, Emerson became an important force in the development of American Transcendentalism. Emerson's occasional lectures at Harvard and the publication of his Essays (1841) enhanced his reputation. The selections included under "Journals" are from The Journals

and Miscellaneous Notebooks of Ralph Waldo Emerson, edited by George Clark and others (1960–1978).

Daniel Mark Epstein (1948–   )
American poet and playwright. Educated at Kenyon College, Epstein is the author of four books of poetry (No Vacancies in Hell, 1973; The Follies, 1977; Young Men's Gold, 1978; The Book of Fortune, 1982), two plays (Jenny and the Phoenix, 1977; The Gayety Burlesque, 1978), and a collection of essays (Star of Wonder, 1986). He is much concerned with myth and ritual, both political and religious, and with the American character. Epstein is a frequent contributor to The Atlantic, The New Yorker, and The New Criterion, where "The Case of Houdini" originally appeared (October 1986).

William Faulkner (1897–1962)
American novelist. A native of Mississippi, Faulkner lived his whole life there. He attended the University of Mississippi in the town of Oxford. With the help of Sherwood Anderson, he published his first novel, Soldier's Pay, in 1926. His work, which won him a Nobel Prize in 1949, often depicts life in fictional Yoknapatawpha County, an imaginative reconstruction of the area adjacent to Oxford. Faulkner's major novels include The Sound and the Fury (1929), As I Lay Dying (1930), Sanctuary (1931), Light in August (1932), and Absalom! Absalom! (1936). His short stories are included in the collections These Thirteen (1931), Go Down, Moses and Other Stories (1942), and The Collected Stories of William Faulkner (1950).

Robert Finch (1943–   )
American writer. Finch combines a keen interest in the world of the naturalist with a concern for the craft of writing. He has published three books: Common Ground: A Naturalist's Cape Cod (1981); The Primal Place (1983); and Outlands: Journeys to the Outer Edges of Cape Cod (1986). Publicity director for the Cape Cod Museum of Natural History, he also serves on the staff of the Bread Loaf Writers' Conference at Middlebury College. "Very Like a Whale" comes from Common Ground, a collection of essays on the natural environment.

Frances FitzGerald (1940–   )
American journalist and writer. A freelance journalist since her graduation from Radcliffe in 1962, FitzGerald achieved

critical success with her first book, *Fire in the Lake: The Vietnamese and Americans in Vietnam* (1972); it won four major awards, including a Pulitzer Prize and a National Book Award. Since then, she has written two other books: *America Revised: History Schoolbooks in the Twentieth Century* (1979) and *Cities on a Hill: Journeys through American Cultures* (1986). Although FitzGerald regularly contributes to several American periodicals, she is most closely associated with *The New Yorker*, where "Rewriting American History" appeared before being published in *America Revised*.

E. M. Forster (1879–1970)

British novelist, critic, and essayist. Educated at King's College, Cambridge, Forster was closely associated with the Bloomsbury set, a group of literary and artistic figures that included Virginia Woolf. Forster's literary reputation rests on four novels: *Where Angels Fear to Tread* (1905); *A Room with a View* (1908); *Howard's End* (1910); and *A Passage to India* (1924). Some of his essays on life and literature were gathered in *Aspects of the Novel* (1927) and *Two Cheers for Democracy* (1951), where "What I Believe" originally appeared.

Benjamin Franklin (1706–1790)

American statesman, inventor, writer, and diplomat. Apprenticed at the age of twelve to his brother, a Philadelphia printer, Franklin learned all aspects of the trade, from setting type to writing editorials. At the age of twenty-four, he was editor and publisher of the *Pennsylvania Gazette*. In 1733, he began writing *Poor Richard's Almanack*, a collection of aphorisms and advice. He retired from business at the age of forty-two to devote himself to study and research but soon found himself involved in colonial politics. From 1757 until 1763, he was diplomatic representative for the colonies in England. He served as a member of the committee appointed to draft the Declaration of Independence and later as minister to France and delegate to the Paris peace conference that officially concluded the Revolutionary War. "The Convenience of Being 'Reasonable'" comes from Franklin's *Autobiography*, written between 1771 and 1788; the selections from *Poor Richard's Almanack* are from the editions noted in the text.

Ian Frazier (1951–   )

American writer and satirist. A graduate of Harvard, where he wrote for the *Harvard Lampoon*, Frazier has been on the staff of *The New Yorker* since 1975. He contributes humorous sketches as well as factual essays and profiles. He has published two books, both substantially taken from material previously published in *The New Yorker*: *Dating Your Mom* (1986), a collection of humorous pieces, and *Nobody Better, Better Than Nobody* (1987), a volume of five character portraits. "Just a Country Boy" comes from *Dating Your Mom*.

Erich Fromm (1900–1980)

German-American psychoanalyst and social philosopher. Born in Frankfurt, he received a Ph.D. in philosophy from the University of Heidelberg, then trained at the Psychoanalytic Institute in Berlin. He immigrated to the United States in 1934, where he held a succession of academic appointments at Columbia University, Bennington College, Yale University, Michigan State University, and New York University. In establishing a reputation as a gifted and innovative psychoanalyst, Fromm wrote twenty books, among them *Escape from Freedom* (1941), *The Forgotten Language* (1951), *The Sane Society* (1955), and *The Art of Loving* (1956). "The Nature of Symbolic Language" comes from *The Forgotten Language*.

Robert Frost (1874–1963)

American poet, teacher, and lecturer. This quintessential "New England" poet was born in California and spent his childhood there. He studied briefly at Dartmouth and Harvard, married, and tried farming for a while. In 1912, he moved to England, where his first book of poems, *A Boy's Will*, was published. In 1914, his second collection, *North of Boston*, received favorable reviews, and the poet returned to the United States. For the next fifty years, Frost was a respected and successful poet, writing about the people and landscape of New England in a voice sometimes lyric, sometimes humorous, sometimes desolate. During the last part of his life, Frost held a number of teaching appointments and lectured widely on poetry and the role of the poet. "Education by Poetry: A Meditative Monologue," an address delivered at Amherst College in 1930, comes from *Selected Prose of Robert Frost*, edited by Hyde Cox and Edward Connery Latham (1966).

Christopher Fry (1907–)

English playwright, translator, and essayist. A schoolmaster, an actor, and a theatrical director before becoming a successful playwright, Fry has written both plays with spiritual concerns (*Thor, with Angels*, 1949; *A Sleep of Prisoners*, 1951) and popular comedies (*A Phoenix Too Frequent*, 1946; *The Lady's Not for Burning*, 1949). In addition, he has written screenplays, translated works by Anouilh and Giraudoux for the stage, and written essays, including "Laughter," which originally appeared in *Vogue* (January 1951) with the title "Comedy."

Northrop Frye (1912–)

Canadian literary critic and teacher. Educated at the University of Toronto and at Merton College, Oxford, he has been a member of the faculty at Victoria College, University of Toronto, since 1939. Although Frye specializes in Renaissance and Romantic literature, he has also written on Milton, the Bible, and Canadian literature. He has published more than forty books, including *Fearful Symmetry: A Study of William Blake* (1947); *Anatomy of Criticism* (1957); *The Educated Imagination* (1964), from which "The Motive for Metaphor" comes; *The Secular Scripture: A Study of the Structure of Romance* (1976); and *The Great Code: The Bible and Literature* (1982).

Paul Fussell (1924–)

American writer and teacher. After distinguished military service in World War II, Fussell earned a Ph.D. at Harvard and became an instructor of English at Connecticut College. In 1955, he was hired by Rutgers, where he is professor of English today. Fussell's early books deal with poetic theory (*Poetic Meter and Poetic Form*, 1965) and eighteenth-century literature (*Samuel Johnson and the Life of Writing*, 1971). With the publication of *The Great War and Modern Memory* (1975) and *Abroad: British Literary Traveling between the Wars* (1980), his attention has shifted to the twentieth century. In 1983, he published *Class: A Guide through the American Status System*. "My War" comes from *The Boy Scout Handbook and Other Observations* (1982), a collection of Fussell's occasional essays.

John Gardner (1933–1982)

American poet, novelist, critic, and teacher. Educated at Washington University and the State University of Iowa, Gardner wrote poetry and nearly all kinds of prose (novels, short stories, children's books, fairy tales, critical essays) in a distinguished career cut short by his death at age forty-nine in a motorcycle accident. Gardner came to popular attention with his novel *Grendel* (1971), a retelling of the *Beowulf* legend from the monster's point of view. Another novel, *October Light*, won the National Book Critics' Award in 1976. His critical powers were at their sharpest in *On Moral Fiction* (1978), an indictment of much modern writing. "What Writers Do" originally appeared in *Antaeus*, no. 40/41 (Winter/Spring 1981).

Barbara Garson (1941–)

American playwright, social critic, and writer. Garson achieved prominence with *MacBird!*, a two-act play produced in 1967, a parody of *Macbeth* based on the administration of President Lyndon B. Johnson. She has written two other plays: *The Co-op* (co-authored with Fred Gardner, 1972) and *The Dinosaur Door* (1976). "Whistle While You Work" comes from *All the Livelong Day: The Meaning and Demeaning of Routine* (1975).

Willard Gaylin (1925–)

American psychiatrist and psychoanalyst. After receiving an M.D. degree from Case Western Reserve University, Gaylin did advanced work in psychoanalytic medicine at Columbia and opened a private practice in psychiatry. In 1970, he co-founded the Hastings Center, Institute of Society, Ethics and the Life Sciences at Hastings-on-Hudson, New York. His writings reflect a broad range of interests: *In the Service of Their Country: War Resisters in Prison* (1970); *Partial Justice: A Study of Bias in Sentencing* (1974); and *Feelings: Our Vital Signs* (1979). Gaylin's study of the use of the insanity defense, *The Killing of Bonnie Garland: A Question of Justice* (1982), received considerable attention. "What You See Is the Real You" originally appeared in *The New York Times* (October 7, 1977).

Carol Gilligan (1936–)

American educational psychologist. Gilligan did her undergraduate work at Swarthmore, where she studied literature and Gestalt psychology before pursuing graduate work at Harvard. Her doctoral dissertation concerned the moral power of children's stories. Gilligan's postdoctoral work has concentrated on moral development in women. She has written and lectured widely on the results of her research. Particularly provocative are her article "Are Women More Moral Than Men?" (*Ms.*, December 1981) and her book *In a Different Voice* (1982), from which "Images of Relationship" comes.

William Golding (1911–)
English novelist. Educated at Oxford, Golding was a schoolmaster at Bishop Wordsworth's School, Salisbury, before becoming a novelist at the age of forty-three. Golding's novels are strikingly original, characterized by their darkly poetic tone and dense symbolism. His most famous work is *Lord of the Flies* (1954), a story of schoolboys marooned on an island who revert to savagery. Other novels include *Pincher Martin* (1956), *The Spire* (1964), *The Pyramid* (1967), *Rites of Passage* (1980), and *Close Quarters* (1987). In 1983, Golding received the Nobel Prize for literature. "Thinking as a Hobby" originally appeared in *Holiday Magazine* (August 1961).

Stephen Jay Gould (1941–)
American paleontologist, writer, and teacher. Gould grew up in New York City, graduated from Antioch College, and received his Ph.D. from Columbia in 1967, joining Harvard the same year. Now professor of geology and zoology at Harvard, Gould teaches paleontology, biology, and history of science. Witty and fluent, Gould demystifies science for lay readers in essays written for a regular column in *Natural History* magazine and collected in *Ever since Darwin* (1977); *The Panda's Thumb* (1980); *Hen's Teeth and Horse's Toes* (1983); and *The Flamingo's Smile* (1985). His books include *Ontogeny and Phylogeny* (1977) and, most recently, *Time's Arrow, Time's Cycle: Myth and Metaphor in the Discovery of Geological Time* (1987). "Our Allotted Lifetimes" originally appeared in *Natural History*, no. 7 (1977); "Darwin's Middle Road" comes from *The Panda's Thumb*; "Nonmoral Nature" is a chapter from *Hen's Teeth and Horse's Toes*; "The Terrifying Normalcy of AIDS" first appeared in *The New York Times Magazine* (April 19, 1987).

Robert Graves (1895–1985)
British poet, novelist, and classical scholar. After private education, distinguished service in World War I, and study at St. John's College, Oxford, Graves held a brief appointment at the University of Cairo before becoming a professional writer. In a long and prolific career, he published 130 volumes, ranging from poetry and novels to essays, lectures, and criticism. He is perhaps best known for his classic memoir, *Goodbye to All That* (1929); his historical novels, *I, Claudius* (1934) and *King Jesus* (1946); his work on writing, *The Reader over Your Shoulder* (1943); and his study of poetic myth, *The White Goddess* (1948). Graves's classical scholarship provided much of the material for his fiction and poetry. "Mythology" originally appeared as the Introduction to the *Larousse Encyclopedia of Mythology* (1959).

Nathaniel Hawthorne (1804–1864)
American novelist, short-story writer, and essayist. Educated at Bowdoin College, Hawthorne returned to his home in Salem, Massachusetts, and devoted himself to writing tales. In 1837, *Twice-told Tales* appeared, and Hawthorne became a public literary figure. After his marriage in 1842, he and his wife moved to Concord, where they lived for three years. In 1846, Hawthorne was appointed surveyor of the Port of Salem, the first of a number of political positions that would culminate in his appointment as American consul in Liverpool, England (1853). Although he may be best known for his short stories or novels —*The Scarlet Letter* (1850) and *The House of the Seven Gables* (1851) in particular— Hawthorne also wrote a series of valuable sketches for the *Atlantic Monthly*. "Abraham Lincoln" (1862) is one of these.

S. I. Hayakawa (1906–)
Samuel Ichiye Hayakawa, Japanese-American writer, educator, and politician. Before becoming president of San Francisco State College, Hayakawa established himself as a scholar and pioneer in language and semantics with books like *Language in Action* (1941; revised as *Language in Thought and Action*, 1949), *Our Language and Our World* (1959), and *Symbol, Status and Personality* (1963). His tenure as college president (1969–1973) was marked by student demonstrations and protests against authority. Throughout, Hayakawa asserted a firm belief in authority, traditional values, and the rule of law and order. With the same ideas as a campaign platform, he was elected to the United States Senate, where he served from 1977 until 1982. "Sex Is Not a Spectator Sport" comes from a collection of Hayakawa's es-

says, *Through the Communication Barrier* (1979).

Vicki Hearne (1952–)

American animal trainer and writer. A graduate of the University of California, Riverside, Hearne did graduate work in writing at Stanford University before returning to the Riverside campus as a lecturer in writing (1980–1984). Since 1984, she has taught at Yale. Hearne, also a professional animal trainer, works most often with dogs and horses. Her writing, whether it be poetry (*Nervous Horses*, 1980; *In the Absence of Horses*, 1984) or prose (*Adam's Task: Calling Animals by Name*, 1986), reflects her interest in animals. "Horses in Partnership with Time" comes from *Adam's Task*.

Ernest Hemingway (1899–1961)

American novelist and short-story writer. Hemingway began his professional writing career as a journalist, reporting for newspapers in Kansas City and Toronto. In the 1920s, he lived in Paris, a part of the American expatriate community that included Gertrude Stein and Ezra Pound. Hemingway's literary reputation rests on his short stories, collected in volumes like *In Our Time* (1925) and *Men without Women* (1927), and his novels, including *The Sun Also Rises* (1926), *A Farewell to Arms* (1929), and *For Whom the Bell Tolls* (1940). *The Old Man and the Sea* (1952) was the last work published during his lifetime. Hemingway received the Nobel Prize for literature in 1954.

Michael Herr (1940–)

American writer and historian of popular culture. In 1977, Herr published *Dispatches*, a nonfiction account of American involvement in the war in Vietnam; ten years before he had gone there to cover the story for *Esquire*. Herr earned substantial praise for the book and for the narration he wrote for Francis Ford Coppola's film about the war, *Apocalypse Now*. "'How Bad Do You Want to Get to Danang?'" comes from *Dispatches*. A regular contributor to *Esquire*, *The New American Review*, and *Rolling Stone*, Herr recently collaborated on *The Big Room* (1986), a popular history of celebrities in twentieth-century American art.

Gilbert Highet (1906–1978)

American scholar of classical literature, poet, writer, and teacher. Born in Glasgow, Scotland, Highet was educated at the University of Glasgow and Oxford University. From 1932 until 1936, he taught at St. John's College, Oxford, then accepted an appointment at Columbia University, where he taught Greek and Latin literature for thirty years. Considered a master teacher, Highet communicated his enthusiasm for classical literature not only in the classroom, but also in a number of books. Of the fourteen books he wrote, perhaps the most famous are *The Classical Tradition* (1949), *The Art of Teaching* (1950), and *The Anatomy of Satire* (1962). "The Mystery of Zen" comes from *Talents and Geniuses* (1957), a collection of essays by Highet.

John Houseman (1902–)

American actor, director, and teacher. Born in Bucharest, Romania, Houseman came to the United States in 1925 and worked as a grain broker. When the depression ruined his business, he worked in the theater, where writing eventually led to producing and directing. In 1937, Houseman and Orson Welles founded the Mercury Theatre. They also wrote the screenplay for *Citizen Kane* (1941), considered a landmark in American motion-picture history. After World War II, Houseman continued his career as a film producer in Hollywood. He has taught drama at Julliard and has acted in films, including *The Paper Chase* (1974), and television commercials. Houseman has written three volumes of an autobiography: *Run-Through: A Memoir* (1972), from which "The War of the Worlds" comes; *Front and Center* (1979); and *Final Dress* (1983).

Jane Howard (1935–)

American writer. After receiving her undergraduate degree from the University of Michigan, Howard joined *Life* magazine, serving as associate editor and staff writer. Combining the skills of a reporter with the curiosity of a social scientist, Howard has written four books: *Please Touch: A Guided Tour of the Human Potential Movement* (1970); *A Different Woman* (1973; revised edition, 1982); *Families* (1978); and *Margaret Mead: A Life* (1984). "Pomp and Circumstance in Groundhog Hollow" comes from *A Different Woman*.

Langston Hughes (1902–1967)

American poet, playwright, and writer. An extraordinarily prolific writer, Hughes published seventeen volumes of poetry, two novels, seven collections of short stories, and twenty-six plays. Hughes emerged as a key figure in the Harlem Renaissance of the 1920s and 1930s, an awakening of black artists centered in New York City. Encouraged by his fellow artists, Hughes published his first collection of poems, *The Weary Blues* (1926). Although critical response was mixed, the degree of public acceptance achieved by Hughes with this and subsequent works enabled him to become the first black American writer to support himself from his writing and lecturing. "Salvation" is a chapter from Hughes's autobiography *The Big Sea* (1940).

Richard Hugo (1923–1982)

American poet and teacher. Hugo was educated at the University of Washington, and then worked for Boeing (1951–1963), writing poetry in his spare time. In 1964, he joined the Department of English at the University of Montana, eventually becoming professor of English there. From 1977 until his death, Hugo served as judge of the Yale Younger Poets Series. He published nine volumes of poetry, including *The Lady in Kicking Horse Reservoir* (1973) and *White Center* (1980), the novel *Death and the Good Life* (1981), a collection of essays entitled *The Triggering Town* (1979), and the memoir *The Real West Marginal Way: A Poet's Autobiography* (published posthumously, 1986). "How I Never Met Eudora Welty" is a chapter in Hugo's autobiography.

Zora Neale Hurston (1903–1960)

American writer and folklorist. A central figure in the Harlem Renaissance of the 1920s and 1930s, Hurston was born in Eatonville, Florida, daughter of a Baptist preacher and a seamstress. She attended Howard University and received a B.A. from Barnard in 1928, where she studied anthropology and developed an interest in black folk traditions and in oral history. Hurston's writing, pulled from her knowledge of folklore, reveals a vigorous, rhythmical, direct prose style that has influenced later writers. Rediscovered by the women's movement, Hurston's works include plays (e.g., *Mule Bone: A Comedy of Negro Life in Three Acts*, 1931, with Langston Hughes) as well as novels (*Their Eyes Were Watching God*, 1937; *Moses, Man of the Mountain*, 1939; *Seraph on the Suwanee*, 1948). "How It Feels to Be Colored Me" was originally published in *The World Tomorrow*, 11 (May 1928), and was reprinted in *I Love Myself When I'm Laughing* (1975), a collection of Hurston's writings edited by Alice Walker.

Thomas Jefferson (1743–1826)

Third president of the United States, lawyer, architect, and writer. An educated man of significant accomplishments in many fields, Jefferson entered politics in his native state of Virginia, serving in the House of Burgesses and eventually becoming governor (1779–1781). He founded the University of Virginia (1809) and designed both the buildings and curriculum. Jefferson served as secretary of state to Washington (1789–1793), vice-president to John Adams (1797–1801), and president (1801–1809). A fluent stylist, Jefferson wrote books on science, religion, architecture, even Anglo-Saxon grammar, but is probably best known for writing the final draft of the Declaration of Independence. Preliminary drafts were done by committee, but it was to Jefferson that the members turned for the last revision. "George Washington" is taken from a letter written in 1814 to a Dr. Jones.

Jesus (c. 6 B.C.–c. A.D. 30)

Jesus of Nazareth, first-century Jewish religious teacher and preacher. Acknowledged by Christians as the Son of God, Jesus spent his short public career in Palestine, preaching a message of conversion and repentance. One of his favorite teaching devices was the parable, a literary form with a long history and used extensively in rabbinic tradition.

Samuel Johnson (1709–1784)

English lexicographer, critic, moralist, and journalist. In spite of childhood poverty, poor eyesight, and scant advanced education, Johnson achieved renown in his day as wit, conversationalist, and astute observer of the human experience. In 1737, having failed as a schoolmaster, he sought his fortune in London, where he soon found work contributing essays and poems to *The Gentleman's Magazine*. Johnson's literary career prospered as he wrote and published poems, plays, and essays. In 1750, he founded *The Rambler*, a popular periodical containing essays, fables, and criticism: "On Self-Love and Indolence" appeared in *The Rambler* (1751). One of the greatest prose stylists of the English language, Johnson prepared the monumental *Dictionary* (1755) that bears his name, wrote *Rasselas* (1759), a novel from which "The Pyramids" comes, and *Lives of the Poets* (1779–1781).

Carl Gustav Jung (1875–1961)
Swiss psychiatrist and founder of analytic psychology. Jung was educated at the University of Basel and began practice in 1900 at a mental hospital in Zürich. From 1907 to 1913, he and Sigmund Freud collaborated in research on psychiatry and psychoanalysis. In 1914, after the two had severed connections, Jung devoted himself to private practice and writing. A prolific writer, whose *Collected Works* consist of eighteen volumes, Jung did pioneering work on schizophrenia and related personality disorders, and, in the process of classifying personality types, introduced terms like "extrovert," "complex," and "introvert" into the vocabulary of psychiatry. Jung's interest in human creativity led him to posit the existence of a "collective unconscious," a part of the human mind to which human beings relegate unpleasant experiences and from which creativity springs. Among Jung's major books are *The Psychology of Dementia* (1906), *The Psychology of the Unconscious* (1912), and *Psychological Types* (1921). "The Poet" comes from his *Modern Man in Search of a Soul* (1933).

Franz Kafka (1883–1924)
Austrian novelist and short-story writer. A German-speaking Jewish novelist born in Prague, Kafka wrote about isolation and alienation before they became subjects central to twentieth-century art and literature. His literary reputation rests on three novels (*The Trial*, 1925; *The Castle*, 1926; *Amerika*, 1927) and a number of short stories, including "The Metamorphosis" (1915) and "A Hunger Artist" (1924). "Parable of the Law" comes from *The Trial*.

Michael J. Katz (1950–)
American physician and teacher. Katz received his M.D. and Ph.D. degrees from Case Western School. He is a philosopher at Case Western Medical School. "On the Wings of an Angel: An Exploration of the Limits of Biological Enterprise" first appeared in *Harvard Magazine* (September–October 1985).

Garrison Keillor (1942–)
American humorist, writer, and broadcaster. While still an undergraduate at the University of Minnesota, Keillor became a staff announcer at a Minneapolis radio station. He continued to work for KUOM-Radio until 1968. In 1971, he went to work for Minnestota Public Radio in St. Paul,

producing and announcing shows. In 1974, as host and principal writer, Keillor started a weekly program, "A Prairie Home Companion." This two-hour mix of music, monologue, and conversation attained a cult following in its thirteen-year run; Keillor broadcast his last show on June 13, 1987. He now lives in Denmark. "The Tower Project" comes from *Happy to Be Here: Stories and Comic Pieces* (1982). A number of these pieces first appeared in *The New Yorker* and the *Atlantic Monthly*. Keillor has also written *Lake Wobegon Days* (1985), a collection of stories set in the mythical town of Lake Wobegon, Minnesota.

Martin Luther King, Jr. (1929–1968)
American clergyman and civil-rights leader. By the age of twenty-six, King had completed his undergraduate education, finished divinity school, and received a Ph.D. in religion from Boston University. The Montgomery bus boycott (1956) marked King's entry into public politics; blacks in Montgomery, Alabama, boycotted segregated buses, and King took a public stand in their support. Drawing upon the New Testament teachings of Jesus and the principles of passive resistance of Mahatma Gandhi, King advocated nonviolent protest to effect significant social change. In the years following the boycott, he became a major figure in the civil-rights movement, uniting small groups of blacks in their struggle. In 1963, Birmingham, Alabama, the most segregated city in the South, became the focal point for violent confrontations between blacks and whites; 2,400 civil-rights workers, King among them, went to jail. It was then that he wrote his now-famous "Letter from Birmingham Jail." In 1964, at the age of thirty-five, Martin Luther King, Jr. became the youngest person to receive the Nobel Peace Prize. He was assassinated on April 14, 1968, in Memphis, Tennessee.

Arthur Koestler (1905–1983)
British writer. Born in Hungary and educated at the University of Vienna, Koestler worked as an editor of a Cairo newspaper, then as foreign correspondent for several other papers before settling in England in 1941, when his novel, *Darkness at Noon*, appeared. That novel, an indictment of the Communist party, mapped the territory for Koestler's next ten years of work. In the 1950s, however, he turned to writing about a wide range of topics:

psychology, religion, philosophy, evolution, among others. Koestler wrote over forty books, among them *The God That Failed* (1950), *The Ghost in the Machine* (1967), and *The Lion and the Ostrich* (1973). "Gravity and the Holy Ghost" originally appeared in *The Act of Creation* (1964).

Elisabeth Kübler-Ross (1926–)

Swiss-American psychologist. Born and educated in Switzerland, Kübler-Ross has come to prominence in the United States, where she has lived since 1958. Her work is largely a response to what she calls "the horrifying experience of the [postwar European] concentration camps." She has given seminars and written about death and dying not only in order to understand the process better, but also to learn how to care for the terminally ill. "On the Fear of Death" comes from Kübler-Ross's best-selling book *On Death and Dying* (1969). Other books on the subject have followed, including most recently *AIDS: The Ultimate Challenge* (1987).

Thomas S. Kuhn (1922–)

American philosopher. Educated at Harvard, where he earned a Ph.D. in physics, Kuhn is a specialist in the history and philosophy of science. The author of *The Copernican Revolution* (1957) and *The Essential Tension: Selected Studies in Scientific Tradition and Change* (1977), he is perhaps best known for *The Structure of Scientific Revolutions* (1962, 1970), from which "The Route to Normal Science" is taken. Kuhn is currently Laurance S. Rockefeller Professor of Philosophy at MIT.

Dan Lacy (1914–)

American historian, publisher, and writer. After receiving a bachelor's and a master's in history from the University of North Carolina, Lacy taught history there. From 1947 to 1950, he worked in the Library of Congress. He then became assistant administrator of the International Information Administration for the State Department. He spent the next thirty-two years in the publishing business, retiring from McGraw-Hill in 1985. With special interests in history, libraries, and literacy, Lacy has written a dozen books, including five historical books for children. "Reading in an Audiovisual and Electronic Era" originally appeared in *Daedalus* (Winter 1983), the journal of the American Academy of Arts and Sciences.

Susanne K. Langer (1895–1985)

American philosopher and teacher. After studying at Radcliffe, and the University of Vienna, Langer became a tutor in philosophy at Radcliffe, beginning a teaching career that would last more than fifty years. She was particularly interested in esthetics, that branch of philosophy concerned with beauty; her book *Feeling and Form* (1953) is a classic in the field. She also wrote *Problems of Art* (1957), from which "Expressiveness" comes, and a three-volume study, *Mind: An Essay on Human Feeling* (1967–1982).

Margaret Laurence (1926–1987)

Canadian novelist, short-story writer, and essayist. Although Laurence began her professional writing career as a translator, she soon established a reputation as a novelist with *The Stone Angel* (1964) and *A Jest of God* (1966). Between 1964 and 1975, Laurence tried her hand at writing essays and articles, mostly for Canadian periodicals. Laurence, whose life took her across Canada and to Africa, displays a strong sense of geography in her prose. Her work often deals with the search for personal identity in the midst of the conflict between tradition and modernization. "Where the World Began" first appeared in *Maclean's*, a Canadian magazine (December 1972); it was reprinted in *Heart of a Stranger* (1976), a collection of occasional and autobiographical essays by Laurence.

John Leo (1935–)

American journalist and writer. Leo has been a staff writer for the *Village Voice* and *The New York Times*, and associate editor for *Commonweal*, a biweekly journal of public affairs, literature, and the arts. Until recently a senior writer for *Time*, Leo is now a contributor to that magazine, where "Journalese for the Lay Reader" originally appeared (March 18, 1985).

Doris Lessing (1919–)

British novelist and political activist. Lessing was born in Persia but grew up in Southern Rhodesia, where she was largely responsible for her own education. She married and divorced twice before leaving Africa for London in 1949. There, her career as a professional writer of more than thirty books began with the publication of her first novel, *The Grass Is Singing* (1950). The central theme of Lessing's work has been women's quest for identity in a world fragmented by prejudice, ideology, and violence (the *Children of Violence* Series, 1952-1969; *The Golden Notebook*, 1962). In the *Canopus in Argos: Archives* Series (1979-1983), she has turned to science fiction. Her latest work includes two novels about the stages of women's lives (*The Diary of a Good Neighbor*, 1983; *If the Old Could . . .*, 1984) and three political novels (*The Good Terrorist*, 1985; *African Tale*, 1987; *The Wind Blows Away Our Words*, 1987). "My Father" first appeared in the London *Sunday Telegraph* (September 1, 1963); it was reprinted in the collection of essays, review, and interviews entitled *A Small Personal Voice* (1975).

Michael Levin (1943–   )

American philosopher. Educated at Michigan State University and Columbia, Levin was a member of the Department of Philosophy at Columbia from 1968 until 1980. He is currently professor of philosophy at City College of the City University of New York. His research interests include ethics, philosophy, and the mind. The author of a number of scholarly articles, Levin has published *Metaphysics and the Mind-Body Problem* (1979). "The Case for Torture" originally appeared in *Newsweek* (June 7, 1982).

C. S. Lewis (1898–1963)

Clive Staples Lewis, English novelist, literary scholar, and critic. Born in Belfast, Ireland, educated at Oxford, Lewis taught at Oxford from 1925 until 1954. In addition to scholarly writing (*The Allegory of Love*, 1936; *English Literature in the Sixteenth Century*, 1954), Lewis wrote popular books on Christianity (*The Problem of Pain*, 1940; *The Screwtape Letters*, 1942; *The Four Loves*, 1960), science fiction (*Out of the Silent Planet*, 1938), and children's novels (*The Chronicles of Narnia*, 1950-1956). "Three Screwtape Letters" comes from *The Screwtape Letters*.

Abraham Lincoln (1809–1865)

Lawyer, orator, and sixteenth president of the United States (1861-1865). Born in Kentucky, Lincoln was a self-made and self-taught man. His family moved to Illinois in 1830, where Lincoln prepared himself for a career in law. In 1834, he was elected to the first of four terms in the Illinois state legislature and in 1847, to the U.S. Congress. Elected president in 1860, Lincoln sought to preserve the Union amid the strife of the Civil War while he worked for the passage of the Thirteenth Amendment, which would outlaw slavery

everywhere and forever in the United States. Lincoln was assassinated by actor John Wilkes Booth on April 15, 1865. During his first term, Lincoln delivered the Gettysburg Address (1863). Reelected in 1864, he gave his Second Inaugural Address, an eloquent appeal for reconciliation and peace.

Walter Lippmann (1889–1974)

American journalist and political commentator. Esteemed as the dean of American political columnists, Lippmann published twenty books and over 4,000 columns in a career that extended from the presidency of Woodrow Wilson to that of Richard Nixon. Noted for his ability to bring reason to bear in political matters and distinguished by his crisp style, Lippmann was a powerful voice in the American political forum. He began his famous column "Today and Tomorrow" in the *New York Herald Tribune* in 1931. He also wrote for *The New Republic*, *Newsweek*, and the *Atlantic Monthly*, where "The Indispensable Opposition" originally appeared (August 1939).

Konrad Z. Lorenz (1903–   )

Austrian-German scientist. Although he studied medicine at the University of Vienna, Lorenz's early interests lay in the field of animal behavior. *King Solomon's Ring* (1952), from which "The Taming of the Shrew" comes, deals with the behavior of jackdaws, geese, and other animals. *On Aggression* (1963) and *Civilized Man's Eight Deadly Sins* (1974) detail Lorenz's beliefs about humankind's behavior and civilization's harmful effects on people and the environment. With Niko Tinbergen and Karl von Frisch, Lorenz won the Nobel Prize for Physiology or Medicine in 1973.

Niccolò Machiavelli (1469–1527)

Florentine statesman and political philosopher. An aristocrat who held office while Florence was a republic, Machiavelli fell from favor when the Medicis returned to power in 1512. Briefly imprisoned, he was restored to an office of some influence, but he never regained his former importance. Machiavelli's most famous work, *The Prince* (1513), from which "The Morals of the Prince" comes, has exerted considerable literary and political influence.

John McMurtry (1939–   )

Canadian athlete, writer, and teacher. Educated at the University of Toronto, Mc-

Murtry became a professional football player before earning his Ph.D. in philosophy at the University of London. A member of the Department of Philosophy at the University of Guelph since 1970, he has written two books: *The Dimensions of English: A Concise Compendium* (1970) and *The Structure of Marx's World View* (1978). "Kill 'Em! Crush 'Em! Eat 'Em Raw!" originally appeared in the October 1971 issue of the Canadian news magazine *Maclean's.*

John McPhee (1931–)
American writer. After undergraduate work at Princeton and graduate work at Cambridge, McPhee wrote scripts for television dramas before becoming an editor at *Time* magazine (1957–1964). Since 1965, he has been a staff writer for *The New Yorker.* McPhee has written nearly twenty books, among them *Oranges* (1967), *The Curve of Binding Energy* (1974), *Giving Good Weight* (1979), *Coming into the Country* (1977), and *Rising from the Plains* (1986). "The Grizzly" originally appeared in *Coming into the Country.*

Judith Martin (1938–)
American journalist and novelist. After receiving a B.A. from Wellesley, Martin became a reporter for the *Washington Post.* In 1978, she began to write her column, "Dear Miss Manners," in which she dispenses, with wit and zest, advice about etiquette. She has gathered a number of the columns in *Miss Manners' Guide to Excruciatingly Correct Behavior* (1981) and some of her essays and lectures in *Common Courtesy* (1985). She has also written two novels: *Gilbert: A Comedy of Manners* (1982) and *Style and Substance: A Comedy of Manners* (1986). "Some Thoughts on the Mannerly Way of Life" comes from *Miss Manners' Guide to Excruciatingly Correct Behavior.*

H. L. Mencken (1880–1956)
Henry Louis Mencken, American journalist, editor, writer, and social critic. Until the Great Depression, Mencken was a successful writer, popular for his scathing attacks on pretense and organized activities of all kinds, from religion to politics. Most of his material was published either in *The Smart Set,* a magazine of which he was literary editor and then co-editor (1908–1923), or in the *American Mercury,* which he founded in 1924 and edited until 1933. When reading tastes shifted,

Mencken turned his talents to revising his *American Language,* first published in 1919, and to adding two supplements to it, as well as to writing a three-volume autobiography (*Happy Days,* 1940; *Newspaper Days,* 1941; *Heathen Days,* 1943). "Gamalielese" originally appeared in the *Baltimore Sun* (March 7, 1921).

Stanley Milgram (1933–1984)
American social psychologist and film producer. Educated at Queens College and Harvard University, Milgram taught at Yale, Harvard, and the City University of New York, where he was Distinguished Professor of Psychology at the time of his death. He made a series of six films, one of which, *The City and the Self,* won wide acclaim. His research experiments in human behavior attracted considerable attention. His most important book, *Obedience to Authority* (1974), offered some startling conclusions about the power of authority. In unabridged form, "The Perils of Obedience" originally appeared in *Obedience to Authority.*

Jessica Mitford (1917–)
Anglo-American writer and social critic. Born into one of England's most famous aristocratic families, Mitford left for the United States shortly after completing her education (1936). A naturalized American citizen (1944), she has established herself as an investigative reporter with a talent for pungent social criticism. Her study of the American funeral industry, *The American Way of Death* (1963), was followed by *The Trial of Dr. Spock* (1969) and *Kind and Unusual Punishment: The Prison Business* (1973). She has completed two volumes of an autobiography and a book of reminiscences, *Faces of Philip* (1984). "Behind the Formaldehyde Curtain" comes from *The American Way of Death.*

N. Scott Momaday (1934–)
Native American poet, writer, and artist. Momaday grew up on reservations in the Southwest, deeply influenced by the example and traditions of the Kiowa people. He studied at the University of New Mexico and Stanford University before beginning a teaching career. Currently, Momaday teaches at Stanford University. He has published two volumes of poetry, *Angle of Geese and Other Poems* (1973) and *The Gourd Dancer* (1976); a Pulitzer Prize–winning novel, *House Made of Dawn* (1968); an autobiography, *The Names: A Memoir* (1976); and a collection

of Kiowa folktales, *The Way to Rainy Mountain* (1969), from which "The Way to Rainy Mountain" comes.

Charles R. Morris
American investment banker and writer. A graduate of the University of Pennsylvania and its law school, Morris has worked in the public and private sectors, serving as assistant budget director for New York City, secretary of social and health services for the state of Washington, and a vice-president of Chase Manhattan Bank. He has written two books: *The Cost of Good Intentions: New York City and the Liberal Experiment— 1960–1975* (1980) and *A Time of Passion: America 1960–1980* (1984), from which "Civil Disobedience" comes.

Desmond Morris (1928–   )
British zoologist and writer. After receiving a Ph.D. in zoology from Oxford, Morris remained there to do research. In 1959, he became curator of mammals at the London Zoo. During the next eight years, he wrote five books on animals. In 1968, he returned to research at Oxford and began writing books on human and animal behavior: *The Naked Ape* (1967); *The Human Zoo* (1969); *Intimate Behavior* (1971); *Manwatching* (1977); and *Bodywatching* (1985). "Territorial Behavior" comes from *Manwatching*.

Thomas H. Murray (1946–   )
American social psychologist. Educated at Temple University, Murray did graduate work in psychology at Princeton. Although he was trained as an empirical scientist, he is most interested in ethical issues. Until recently, Murray was professor of ethics and public policy at the Institute for Medical Humanities, University of Texas Medical Branch, Galveston, Texas. While he was there, he founded and edited the *Medical Humanities Review*. He is now director of and professor at Case Western Reserve Medical School. "The Growing Danger" originally appeared in *Discovery* (February 1987).

Vladimir Nabokov (1899–1977)
American writer and teacher. Born in Russia, educated at Trinity College, Cambridge, Nabokov came to the United States in 1940 to lecture at Stanford University and stayed for twenty years. While teaching at Wellesley and Cornell, he contributed essays, stories, and poems to several American magazines. Although he was well known in literary circles, Nabokov did not achieve fame until 1958, when his controversial and explicit novel *Lolita* was published. *Lolita* earned Nabokov enough money so that he could retire to Switzerland and write fiction full time. "Good Readers and Good Writers" comes from *Lectures on Literature* (1980), a collection of Nabokov's essays and classroom presentations.

Gloria Naylor (1950–   )
American writer. Naylor received her B.A. from Brooklyn College, and an M.A. in Afro-American studies from Yale. She has been a writer-in-residence at George Washington University. Naylor has written two novels, *The Women of Brewster Place* (1982) and *Linden Hills* (1985). "'Mommy, What Does "Nigger" Mean?'" originally appeared as a "Hers" column in *The New York Times* (February 20, 1986).

John Henry Newman (1801–1890)
English Roman Catholic prelate, poet, novelist, and writer. Educated at Trinity College, Oxford, Newman became a priest in the Anglican Church. He was a major force in the Oxford movement, an effort to reestablish the authority and traditions of the Church of England. In 1845, Newman became Roman Catholic; in 1846, he was ordained in Rome and then returned to England. From 1852 on, he delivered not only sermons, but lectures on education. The latter culminated in one of Newman's finest works, *The Idea of a University Defined and Illustrated* (1852), which ranks with his treatise *An Essay in Aid of a Grammar of Assent* (1870) as a classic statement of belief. Newman wrote two novels (*Loss and Gain* 1848; *Callista*, 1856), an explanation of his conversion (*Apologia Pro Vita Sua*, 1864), and a visionary poem (*The Dream of Gerontius*, 1865). In 1879, he became a cardinal in the Roman Catholic Church. "Knowledge and Virtue" comes from *The Idea of a University*.

Ngũgĩ wa Thiong'o (1936–   )
Formerly known as James T. Ngugi, African novelist and essayist. Educated in Africa and at Leeds University in England, Ngũgĩ wrote his first novel, *The River between Us*, in 1963–1964, but it was not published until 1965, after his *Weep Not Child* (1964). He continues to write novels (*Devil on the Cross*, 1982), but his memoir,

Detained: A Prisoner Writer's Diary (1981), an account of his arrest and detention for teaching his native Gĩkũyũ language, has attracted most attention. "Decolonizing the Mind" is part of the Introduction to Ngũgĩ's Decolonizing the Mind: The Politics of Language in African Literature (1986), the last book he wrote in English.

George Orwell (1903–1950)
Pen name of Eric Blair, English journalist, essayist, novelist, and critic. Born in India and educated in England, Orwell became an officer in the Indian Imperial Police in Burma (1922–1927), a part of his life that he later recounted in a novel, Burmese Days (1934). In 1927, he went to Europe to develop his writing talents. His first book, Down and Out in Paris and London (1933), depicts his years of poverty and struggle while working as a dishwasher and day laborer. Orwell's experiences fighting in the Spanish Civil War are the subject of his memoir, Homage to Catalonia (1938). Of his seven novels, Animal Farm (1945) and Nineteen Eighty-Four (1949), satires directed at totalitarian government, have become twentieth-century classics. Orwell published five collections of essays, including Shooting an Elephant (1950), from which both "Politics and the English Language" and "Shooting an Elephant" come.

Walter Pater (1839–1894)
English novelist and essayist. Educated at King's School, Canterbury, and Queen's College, Oxford, Pater devoted his life to study, reflection, and writing. As a prose stylist, he has few equals in the English language. Pater's first book, Studies in the History of the Renaissance, appeared in 1873. Marius the Epicurean (1885), a novel set in Rome, Imaginary Portraits (1887), a collection of fictional sketches, and Appreciations: With an Essay on Style (1889) followed. "The Mona Lisa" comes from Pater's essay on Leonardo da Vinci in Studies in the History of the Renaissance.

S. J. Perelman (1904–1979)
American humorist, playwright, screenwriter, and journalist. After graduating from Brown University in 1925, Perelman took a job as a cartoonist. Soon afterward, he wrote the screenplays for Monkey Business and Horse Feathers, two of the Marx Brothers' most successful films. Although he wrote a number of stage plays as well, Perelman was most closely associated with

The New Yorker, writing stories, articles, and even cartoon captions from 1931 until 1979. A prolific writer, Perelman is the author of over 450 essays, 10 screenplays, 8 stage plays, and more than a dozen books. "The Machismo Mystique" comes from Vinegar Puss (1975), a collection of Perelman's short stories and essays.

William G. Perry, Jr. (1913–)
American educator. Born in Paris and educated at Harvard, Perry taught at Williams College from 1941 to 1945 before moving to Harvard, where he has been director of the Bureau of Study Counsel since 1948 and professor of education since 1964. With C. P. Whitelock, he wrote the Harvard Reading Course (1948). His Forms of Intellectual and Ethical Development was published in 1968. "Examsmanship and the Liberal Arts: A Study in Educational Epistemology" originally appeared in Examining in Harvard College: A Collection of Essays, by members of the Harvard faculty (1964).

Alexander Petrunkevitch (1875–1964)
Russian-born zoologist and teacher. Petrunkevitch was educated in Russia and Germany before coming to the United States as a lecturer at Harvard in 1904. In 1910, he joined the Department of Zoology at Yale, where he became professor in 1917, and served until 1944. Petrunkevitch was an expert on the behavior of American spiders; his Index Catalogue of Spiders of North, Central, and South America (1911) and An Inquiry into the Natural Classification of Spiders (1933) are classic studies. Petrunkevitch's essay "The Spider and the Wasp" originally appeared in Scientific American (August 1952).

Robert Pirsig (1928–)
American writer and teacher. After receiving a bachelor's and a master's from the University of Minnesota, Pirsig became a college teacher of composition and rhetoric (1959–1962). He then worked as a technical writer (1963–1973). With the publication of Zen and the Art of Motorcycle Maintenance (1974), from which "Concrete, Brick, and Neon" comes, Pirsig became a full-time professional writer.

Plato (c. 428–c. 348 B.C.)
Greek philosopher and teacher. When Socrates died in 339 B.C., Plato went into exile. He returned in the 380s and founded a school, the Academy. He adopted the

Socratic method of teaching, a technique of asking, rather than answering, questions. Although many of Plato's writings take the form of dialogues, he does occasionally, as in the case of "The Allegory of the Cave," use the parable.

Norman Podhoretz (1930–   )
American writer and editor. Educated at Columbia and Cambridge, trained as a literary critic, Podhoretz has long been a powerful voice in American political debate. Associated with *Commentary* since 1955, he has been editor-in-chief of that journal since 1960. Podhoretz has contributed essays to a number of volumes and journals, and has written six books of his own, including *The Bloody Crossroads: Where Literature and Politics Meet* (1986). "My Negro Problem—and Ours" originally appeared in Podhoretz's first book, *Doings and Undoings* (1964).

Neil Postman
American writer and critic, with major interests in linguistics and teaching. Postman's first book, *Television and the Teaching of English* (1961), began a career that has produced nearly two dozen books and many articles, particularly for *Atlantic* and *The Nation*. With the appearance of his *Teaching as a Subversive Activity* (1969), written with Charles Weingartner, Postman emerged as a spokesman for radical educational reform. In 1979, he wrote *Teaching as a Conserving Activity*, in which he asserted that schools must act as conserving agents during times of accelerated social change. Postman is currently professor of media ecology at New York University. "Confusing Levels of Abstraction" originally appeared in *Crazy Talk, Stupid Talk: How We Defeat Ourselves by the Way We Talk and What to Do about It* (1976).

Tom Regan (1938–   )
American philosopher and teacher. After receiving a Ph.D. in philosophy from the University of Virginia, Regan taught at Sweet Briar College before joining the Department of Philosophy at North Carolina State University. He does research in theoretical and applied ethics. "The Case for Animal Rights" originally appeared in *In Defense of Animals* (1985), edited by Peter Singer.

Adrienne Rich (1929–   )
American poet and writer. While she was an undergraduate at Radcliffe, Rich's first book of poetry, *A Change of World*, was chosen by W. H. Auden for the Yale Younger Poet's Prize (1951). Since then, in a career spanning nearly forty years, Rich has published many books of poetry and several collections of provocative essays. An articulate feminist, she has recently published *Your Native Land, Your Life* (1986), a collection of autobiographical poems, and *Bread, Blood, and Poetry* (1986), a volume of prose pieces. "When We Dead Awaken: Writing as Re-Vision," written in 1971, was first published in 1972; it later appeared in Rich's collection of essays and lectures *On Lies, Secrets, and Silence* (1979).

La Rochefoucauld (1613–1680)
François, duc de La Rochefoucauld, French nobleman, soldier, and writer. La Rochefoucauld's literary fame rests on his *Réflexions ou sentences et maximes morales* (1665), better known as *Maxims*. This collection of witty observations about human behavior established him as a moralist of decidedly pragmatic persuasion.

Richard Rodriguez (1944–   )
American writer and teacher. The son of Mexican-American immigrants, Rodriguez learned to speak English in a Catholic grammar school. A proficient student, he received a B.A. from Stanford and an M.A. from Columbia. Enrolled in the doctoral program in English literature at the University of California, Berkeley, Rodriguez won a Fulbright and attended the Warburg Institute in London (1972–1973). Although he returned to Berkeley for a year, he left without earning a Ph.D. In *Hunger of Memory* (1982), from which "Aria" comes, Rodriguez recounts his assimilation into mainstream American society.

Betty Rollin (1936–   )
American writer, journalist, and television reporter. Rollin spent several years as a stage and television actress before beginning a career in journalism, first at *Vogue* (1964), then at *Look* (1965–1971). Since 1971, she has worked as a network correspondent, chiefly for NBC. Rollin is the author of five books, including *First, You Cry* (1976); *Am I Getting Paid for This?: A Romance about Work* (1982); and *Last Wish* (1985). "Motherhood: Who Needs It?" originally appeared in *Look* (September 22, 1970).

Phyllis Rose (1942–   )
American writer and teacher. Educated at Radcliffe, Yale, and Harvard, Rose has been a member of the Department of English at Wesleyan University since 1969. Her major publications include *Woman of Letters: A Life of Virginia Woolf* (1978), *Parallel Lives: Five Victorian Marriages* (1983), and *Writing of Women* (1985). She is a regular contributor to *Vogue*, *The Nation*, *The Atlantic*, and *The New York Times*. "Shopping and Other Spiritual Adventures" originally appeared in a "Hers' column in *The New York Times* (April 12, 1984).

Gilbert Ryle (1900–1976)
English philosopher and essayist. Educated at Oxford, Ryle spent his entire teaching career there, assuming a prominent place in the intellectual life of the university. His first book, *The Concept of Mind* (1949), set forth his "philosophy of the mind." *Dilemmas* (1954) and *Plato's Progress* (1966) further enhanced his reputation as a critical thinker and essayist. From 1945 until 1968, he was Wayneflete Professor of Metaphysical Philosophy at Oxford. "On Forgetting the Difference between Right and Wrong" originally appeared in *Essays in Moral Philosophy* (1958), edited by A. I. Melden.

Oliver Sacks (1933–   )
Anglo-American physician and writer. Son of parents who were medical doctors, Sacks and his three older brothers all became physicians. Educated at Queen's College, Oxford, Sacks earned his M.D. from Middlesex Hospital, London (1960), and then came to the United States for five years' advanced study at UCLA. A practicing neurologist, he has wirtten four books: *Migraine: The Evolution of a Common Disorder* (1970; revised edition, 1985), an exploration of the mind-body connection in illness; *Awakenings* (1973), a study of Sacks's controversial treatment of patients afflicted with sleeping sickness; *A Leg to Stand On* (1984), the story of his own serious injury and recovery; and *The Man Who Mistook His Wife for a Hat and Other Clinical Tales* (1985), a collection of short works from which "The Disembodied Lady" comes.

Carl Sagan (1934–   )
American astronomer and writer. Sagan received a Ph.D. in astronomy and astrophysics from the University of Chicago in 1960. He taught at the University of California, Berkeley, and at Harvard before joining the faculty of Cornell, where he is currently professor of astronomy and director of the Laboratory for Planetary Studies. While Sagan's early writing concerns his work as an astronomer, *The Dragons of Eden* (1977) delves into the subject of human intelligence. Like *Broca's Brain* (1979) and his television series "Cosmos," it extended Sagan's audience considerably. His novel *Contact* (1985) became a best seller. "The Abstractions of Beasts" originally appeared in Sagan's Pulitzer Prize–winning book *The Dragons of Eden*.

Scott Sanders (1945–   )
American writer and teacher. Educated at Brown and Cambridge, Sanders has spent his entire teaching career in the Department of English at Indiana University, where he is now professor of English. He has written scholarly works on literature (*D. H. Lawrence: The World of the Major Novels*, 1974), science fiction (*Fetching the Dead: Stories*, 1984), and studies of American places and people (*Wilderness Plots: Tales about the Settlement of the American Land*, 1983; *Audubon's Early Years*, 1984). His latest work is *The Paradise of Bombs* (1987), a collection of essays on violence in the United States. "Listening to Owls" originally appeared in the *North American Review* (March 1982).

May Sarton (1912–   )
American novelist, poet, and essayist. Born in Belgium, Sarton came to the United States as a child. The daughter of a Harvard professor, she did not attend college. Instead, she pursued a career in the theater, which she left to become a scriptwriter, then an instructor in writing. She now lives on the coast of Maine. Sarton is the author of seventeen novels, among them *The Bridge of Years* (1946), *Kinds of Love* (1970), and *A Reckoning* (1978), as well as fourteen books of poetry, including *Encounter in April* (1937), *The Land of Silence* (1953), and *A Durable Fire* (1972). She has also published several nonfiction works. The selection here comes from *Journal of a Solitude* (1973).

Jean-Paul Sartre (1905–1980)
French playwright, novelist, critic, philosopher, and left-wing activist. After earning an advanced degree in philosophy, Sartre became a provincial schoolmaster, then a playwright and writer of philosophical essays. Described by *The New York*

Times as "a rebel of a thousand causes, a modern Don Quixote," Sartre was a major force in the intellectual life of post-World War II France. His philosophy of existentialism influenced generations of artists and thinkers. Steadfastly independent, Sartre refused both the Nobel Prize for Literature (1964) and the Legion of Honor. He died having completed only three volumes of a four-volume study of Gustave Flaubert. A sampling of his major works includes *The Flies* (1943), *Being and Nothingness* (1943), *No Exit* (1944), and *Life Situations* (1977). "Existentialism" is taken from *Existentialism* (1947).

Jonathan Schell (1943–)
American writer and editor. While he was a graduate student in Far Eastern history at Harvard, Schell, returning from study in Japan, accompanied American forces on their evacuation of the South Vietnamese village of Ben Suc (January 1967) and wrote a series of articles on the operation for *The New Yorker*. A contributing editor to that magazine since 1967, Schell has written four books, the contents of which first appeared in *The New Yorker*: two books on the American war in Vietnam— *The Village of Ben Suc* (1967) and *The Military Half: An Account of Destruction in Quang Ngai and Quang Tin* (1968)—a chronicle of Richard Nixon's presidency —*The Time of Illusion* (1975); and a detailed consideration of the consequences of nuclear war—*The Fate of the Earth* (1982). "The Destructive Power of a One-Megaton Bomb on New York City" and "The Roots of Nuclear Peril" come from *The Fate of the Earth*.

Hans A. Schmitt (1921–)
American historian with special interests in French intellectual history and German constitutional history. Born in Frankfurt, Germany, he and his family fled to the United States to escape Hitler. After receiving a Ph.D. from the University of Chicago, Schmitt began a college teaching career that culminated in his appointment as professor of history at the University of Virginia. He has written a number of books, including *The Path to European Union* (1962), *Charles Peguy* (1967), and *Historians of Modern Europe* (ed., 1971). "January 30, 1933: A Memoir" originally appeared in the *Virginia Quarterly Review* (Winter 1983).

E. F. Schumacher (1911–1977)
British economist and writer. Born in Bonn, Schumacher studied abroad in the 1930s and returned to Germany under Hitler only to flee to England in 1937. Schumacher worked for the British government during World War II, drafting theories for a welfare state. After the war, he became economic adviser to Britain's National Coal Board (1950–1970). His *Small Is Beautiful* (1973), an economic study that advocates small-scale use of technology, became an international best seller. "Levels of Being" is the second chapter in Schumacher's last book, *A Guide for the Perplexed* (1977).

Chief Seattle (c. 1786–1866)
Native American leader. A fierce young warrior, Seattle (also Seathl or Sealth) was chief of the Suquamish, Duwamish, and allied Salish-speaking tribes of the Northwest. In the 1830s, he was converted to Christianity and became an advocate of peace. Local settlers honored him and his work by naming their town Seattle. When the Port Ellicott Treaty of 1855 established reservations for Native Americans, Seattle signed it and lived the rest of his life at the Port Madison Reservation. Because of his example, his people did not become involved in the bloody warfare that marked the history of the territory from 1855 until 1870. Chief Seattle died on June 7, 1866 and was buried at the Suquamish cemetery near Seattle.

George Bernard Shaw (1856–1950)
Irish playwright and essayist. Shaw began his career by writing five unsuccessful novels. When he switched to writing criticism for a number of London publications, he became successful and popular, particularly as a music critic. A committed socialist, he wrote and lectured extensively for the cause. In 1893, Shaw's play *Widowers' Houses* was produced. It was the first of over fifty plays that included *Man and Superman* (1903), *Major Barbara* (1905), *Pygmalion* (1913), *Heartbreak House* (1919), and *Saint Joan* (1924). This man of devastating wit and intense convictions received the Nobel Prize for Literature in 1925. Selections included in "Prose Forms: Apothegms" come from "The Revolutionist's Handbook" in *Man and Superman*.

Nancy Sommers (1951–)
American teacher and writer. A specialist in the theory and practice of composition, Sommers has taught writing at Boston University, the Harvard Graduate School

of Business Administration, New York University, and the University of Oklahoma, where she served as director of composition. At the Rutgers Graduate School of Education, she did her research on the role of revision in the writing process. She is currently associate director of expository writing at Harvard. "Revision Strategies of Student Writers and Experienced Adult Writers" originally appeared in *College Composition and Communication* 31 (December 1980).

Francis E. Sparshott (1926–)
Canadian philosopher and writer. Educated at Oxford, he became a lecturer in philosophy at Victoria College, University of Toronto, in 1950, where he is currently professor of philosophy. Sparshott's particular interests are ethics and esthetics. He has lectured and published in both areas. His most recent book is *The Theory of the Arts* (1982). "Nothing to Say" is the text of the convocation address delivered on June 20, 1984, by Sparshott to the graduates of Victoria College.

Brent Staples (1951–)
American journalist and writer. Born in Chester, Pennsylvania, Staples holds a Ph.D. in psychology from the University of Chicago. He is Assistant Metropolitan Editor of *The New York Times*. His essay "Just Walk On By" appeared in *Ms.* magazine in September 1986. An excerpt, entitled "Black Men and Public Space," was published in *Harper's* (December 1986).

Wallace Stegner (1909–)
American essayist, novelist, and teacher. Influenced by Twain, Cather, and Conrad, Stegner writes of the development of individuals within particular landscapes. Stegner's landscapes are often those of the American West, for he is a serious naturalist with special interest in that area. In a long career, he has written and edited more than forty books, among them the novels *Remembering Laughter* (1937), *The Big Rock Candy Mountain* (1943), and *Recapitulation* (1979), as well as historical narratives like *Mormon Country* (1941) and *The Gathering of Zion: The Story of the Mormon Trail* (1964). Stegner is a member of the Department of English at Stanford University. "The Town Dump" originally appeared in *Wolf Willow: A History, a Story, and a Memory of the Last Plains Frontier* (1963, 1980).

Gloria Steinem (1934–)
American writer and editor. After receiving a B.A. from Smith College, Steinem spent two years studying in India. On her return, she held several positions in publishing and worked as a writer for television, film, and political campaigns until 1968, when she and others founded *New York Magazine*. Founding editor of *Ms.* magazine (1971), Steinem is an influential spokesperson for the women's movement. "The Good News Is: These Are Not the Best Years of Your Life" first appeared in *Ms.* with the title "Why Young Women Are More Conservative." It was reprinted in *Outrageous Acts and Everyday Rebellions* (1983), a collection of Steinem's essays and articles.

Laurence Sterne (1713–1768)
English cleric and novelist. Educated at Jesus College, Cambridge, and ordained in the Anglican Church, Sterne became pastor of a quiet country parish in 1738. In 1759, he gave up some of his duties and started writing *Tristram Shandy*; volumes I and II were published that year. This innovative and witty novel was not completed until 1767, when volume IX was published. In late 1767, shortly before his death, Sterne published another novel, *A Sentimental Journey through France and Italy*. "Of Door Hinges and Life in General" comes from *Tristram Shandy*.

Michael Stone (1948–)
American journalist. "Should Testing for the AIDS Virus Be Mandatory?" is Part III of "Q. and A. on AIDS," which appeared in *New York Magazine* (March 23, 1987).

Jonathan Swift (1667–1745)
Anglo-Irish poet, satirist, and cleric. Born to English parents who resided in Ireland, Swift studied at Trinity College, Dublin, then departed for London (1689). There he became part of the literary and political worlds, beginning his career by writing political pamphlets in support of the Tory cause. Ordained in the Church of Ireland (1695), Swift was appointed dean of St. Patrick's Cathedral, Dublin, in 1713 and held the post until his death. One of the master satirists of the English language, he wrote several scathing attacks on extremism, including *The Tale of a Tub* (1704), *The Battle of the Books* (1704), and *A Modest Proposal* (1729), as well as poetry, but he is probably best known for his novel *Gulliver's Travels* (1726). "The Spider and the Bee" comes from *The Tale of a Tub*.

Dylan Thomas (1914–1953)

Welsh poet and writer. Born and raised in the coal-mining district of Wales, Thomas lived a turbulent life marked by chronic alcoholism that helped bring about his early death. His writing, though, particularly his recollections of childhood, reveals an awareness of the sweetness of living that is expressed in bold, inventive, often playful language. Although he is perhaps best known for his poetry, particularly the verse drama *Under Milk Wood* (1954), Thomas also wrote short stories, plays, and film scripts. *Quite Early One Morning* (1954), a collection of his reminiscences of a Welsh childhood, and especially *A Child's Christmas in Wales* (1954) have become classics. "Memories of Christmas" first appeared in *The Listener* (December 20, 1945). It was later reprinted in *Quite Early One Morning*.

Lewis Thomas (1913–)

American physician, teacher, writer, and humanist. Educated at Princeton and Harvard Medical School, Thomas has specialized in pediatrics, public health, and cancer research. From 1973 until 1980, he served as president of Memorial Sloan-Kettering Cancer Center in New York City; he is currently Emeritus President there. In 1970, Thomas began writing occasional essays for the *New England Journal of Medicine*. A number of these, gathered in *The Lives of a Cell* (1974), established Thomas's reputation as a writer. Since then, three more collections have been published: *The Medusa and the Snail* (1979), *The Youngest Science* (1983), and *Late Night Thoughts on Listening to Mahler's Ninth Symphony* (1983). His most recent work, *The Lasker Awards: Four Decades of Scientific Medical Progress* (1986), traces developments in cancer research. "Humanities and Science" was first published in *Late Night Thoughts*; "Notes on Punctuation" and "On Magic in Medicine" originally appeared in the *New England Journal of Medicine* before publication in *The Medusa and the Snail*; "The Long Habit" appeared in *The Lives of a Cell* after having been published in the *New England Journal of Medicine*.

Henry David Thoreau (1817–1862)

American philosopher, essayist, naturalist, and poet. A graduate of Harvard, Thoreau worked at a number of jobs—schoolmaster, house painter, employee in his father's pencil factory—before becoming a writer and political activist. He became a friend of Emerson's and a member of the Transcendental Club, contributing frequently to its journal *The Dial*. Deeply drawn to the world of nature, he wrote his first book, *A Week on the Concord and Merrimac Rivers* (1849), about his impressions. Thoreau's strong stance against slavery led to his arrest for refusing to pay the Massachusetts poll tax (an act of protest against government sanction of the Mexican War, which he viewed as serving the interests of slaveholders). His eloquent essay defending this act, "Civil Disobedience" (1849), his probing meditation on the solitary life, *Walden* (1854), and his speech, "A Plea for Captain John Brown" (1859), are classic literary documents in the history of American life and thought. "The Battle of the Ants" comes from *Walden*; "Observation" and selections printed here in "Prose Forms: Journals" come from Thoreau's *Journal*.

James Thurber (1894–1961)

American humorist, cartoonist, and writer. Born in Columbus, Ohio, Thurber attended Ohio State University. He started his career as a professional writer working for the *Columbus Dispatch* (1920–1924), then moved on to the *Chicago Tribune* and the *New York Evening Post*. In 1927, encouraged by E. B. White, he became managing editor of and staff writer for *The New Yorker*. Throughout his career he contributed stories, essays, and cartoons to the magazine. Thurber wrote more than thirty books, including *The Owl in the Attic and Other Perplexities* (1931), *The Beast in Me and Other Animals* (1948), and *The Secret Life of Walter Mitty* (1939). "University Days" comes from Thurber's *My Life and Hard Times* (1933); "A Dog's Eye View of Man" comes from his *Thurber's Dogs* (1955); "The Bear Who Let It Alone," "The Rabbits Who Caused All the Trouble," and "The Owl Who Was God" all come from Thurber's *Fables for Our Time* (1940).

Paul Tillich (1886–1965)

German-American philosopher and theologian. Born into a German Lutheran family and educated at several German universities, Tillich served as an army chaplain in World War I. Afterward, he joined the theology faculty of the University of Berlin. When Hitler came to power, Tillich was dismissed from the Chair of Philosophy at Frankfurt University. He fled to the United States, where he spent over twenty years on the faculty of the Union Theological Seminary in New York City. Upon retirement, he became University Professor at Harvard. Tillich's most important work, the three-volume *Systematic Theology*, was published in 1963. Among other important works are *The Eternal Now* (1963) and *A History of Christian Thought* (revised edition 1968). "The Riddle of Inequality" comes from *The Eternal Now*, a collection of Tillich's sermons.

Niko Tinbergen (1907–   )
British zoologist. Born in the Netherlands, Tinbergen studied at the State University of Leyden, receiving his Ph.D. in zoology in 1932. Fascinated since childhood by animals, he spent fourteen months in Greenland observing arctic life. He then joined the faculty at Leyden, conducting research on the homing habits of sand wasps, the mating rituals of butterflies, and the behavior of falcons. In 1949, he became a lecturer at Oxford. His research there on communication systems among gulls led him to the study of autistic children. In 1973, he was one of three scientists to share the Nobel Prize for Physiology or Medicine. Tinbergen's work *The Animal in Its World: Explorations of an Ethologist, 1932–1972* is widely respected. "The Bee-Hunters of Hulshorst," an essay drawn from his experiences at his parents' vacation cottage in the Netherlands, comes from a collection of Tinbergen's essays, *Curious Naturalists* (1958).

John Updike (1932–   )
American poet, fiction writer, and critic. After attending Harvard and Oxford, Updike joined the staff of *The New Yorker*, beginning an association that continues today. He has written over thirty books, including collections of poetry (*The Carpentered Hen and Other Tame Creatures*, 1958; *Seventy Poems*, 1972), short stories (some collected in *The Music School*, 1966; *Trust Me*, 1987), and novels (*The Centaur*, 1963; *The Witches of Eastwick*, 1984; *Roger's Version*, 1986). Today, Updike writes occasional essays, short stories, and poems for *The New Yorker*, while serving as a regular book reviewer for that magazine. "Beer Can" originally appeared in the "Talk of the Town" section of *The New Yorker* (January 18, 1964).

Judith Viorst (1931–   )
American poet, writer, and editor. Viorst began writing poetry as a child and pub-

lished her first book of poems, *The Village Square*, in 1965. But it was not until her second book, *It's Hard to Be Hip over Thirty and Other Tragedies of Married Life* (1968), that she became well known as a writer of humorous verse. Two more volumes, *How Did I Get to Be Forty and Other Atrocities* (1976) and *When Did I Stop Being Twenty and Other Injustices* (1987), followed. A writer of fiction and nonfiction for children, Viorst has also contributed a regular column to *Redbook* magazine since 1972. "Good as Guilt" is taken from *Necessary Losses* (1986), her study of confronting loss and separation as part of emotional and psychological growth.

Alice Walker (1944–   )
American writer. Born in Georgia, the eighth child of sharecroppers, Walker graduated from Sarah Lawrence in 1966. She then lectured and taught at a number of schools. Speaking for and about women of color, she has written four volumes of poetry, three novels, and two collections of short stories. She has also published a biography of Langston Hughes and edited the work of Zora Neale Hurston. Her latest novel, *The Color Purple*, has brought her fame. "Beauty: When the Other Dancer Is the Self" comes from Walker's recent book, *In Search of Our Mother's Gardens: A Collection of Womanist Prose* (1983).

Eudora Welty (1909–   )
American writer, critic, amateur painter, and photographer. Born and brought up in Jackson, Mississippi, Welty has retained her deep attachment to the people and places of the South. After graduating from the University of Wisconsin in 1929 and a year's study at Columbia University's School of Business, she returned to Jackson and eventually found work as a publicity agent for the Works Progress Administration, a New Deal social agency. With the help of Robert Penn Warren and Cleanth Brooks, she had several short stories published, and her literary career was launched. Welty has published four collections of short stories, three novellas, two novels (*The Optimist's Daughter* [1972] won a Pulitzer Prize), two volumes of photographs, and an acclaimed collection of critical essays, *The Eye of the Story* (1978). "Clamorous to Learn" and "One Writer's Beginnings" are taken from her memoir, *One Writer's Beginnings* (1985).

Paul West (1930–)

American critic, poet, and novelist. Born in England and educated at Oxford and Columbia, West taught at Memorial University of Newfoundland from 1957 to 1960 before joining the faculty of the Department of English and Comparative Literature at Pennsylvania State University. A prolific writer, he has published poetry and criticism, but he is best known for his novels, particularly *Words for a Deaf Daughter* (1970) and *The Very Rich Hours of Count Von Stauffenberg* (1980). He is a regular contributor to *The New York Times Book Review*. "A Passion to Learn" originally appeared in the *New American Review* (June 1968).

Richard S. Westfall (1924–)

American professor of history and philosophy of science. Educated at Yale, Westfall has taught at the State University of Iowa, Grinnell, and Indiana State University, where, since 1976, he has been Distinguished Professor of History. A specialist in the work of Isaac Newton, Westfall has published three books on the subject: *Development of Newton's Philosophy of Color* (1962), *Force in Newton's Physics* (1971), and *Never at Rest: A Biography of Isaac Newton* (1980). "The Career of Isaac Newton: A Scientific Life in the Seventeenth Century" originally appeared in *The American Scholar* (Summer 1981).

E. B. White (1899–1985)

American poet, journalist, editor, and essayist. After graduating from Cornell in 1921, White became a reporter, then an advertising copywriter before beginning a sixty-year career on the staff of *The New Yorker*. With Harold Ross, the magazine's founding editor, and Katharine Angell, its literary editor, White made *The New Yorker* the most important publication of its kind in the United States. He wrote poems and articles for the magazine and served as a discreet and helpful editor. Among his many books, three written for children earned him lasting fame: *Stuart Little* (1945), *Charlotte's Web* (1952), and *The Trumpet of the Swan* (1970). White revised and edited William Strunk's text *The Elements of Style*, a classic guide. "Once More to the Lake" originally appeared in "One Man's Meat," White's column for *Harper's Magazine* (October 1941); it was reprinted in *The Essays of E. B. White* (1977). "Progress and Change" also appeared in "One Man's Meat" (December 1938); it was reprinted

in a collection of the same title (1942). "Democracy" first appeared in *The New Yorker* (July 3, 1944); it was reprinted in *The Wild Flag* (1946). "Four Letters on Freedom of Expression" originally appeared as indicated in the text; these and other letters were gathered in a volume, *Letters of E. B. White*, edited by Dorothy Lobrano Guth (1976). "Some Remarks on Humor" is adapted from the Preface to *Subtreasury of American Humor*, edited by Katharine S. White and E. B. White (1941).

Walt Whitman (1819–1892)

American poet and writer. Born on Long Island and raised in Brooklyn, New York, Whitman received scant formal education before going to work at age eleven in a newspaper office. Even though he taught school from 1835 to 1840 and worked at several government posts during his lifetime, Whitman considered himself a writer, publishing poetry, stories, and newspaper articles from the age of nineteen. In 1855, he published *Leaves of Grass*, a series of twelve poems that most scholars consider his finest work. As it evolved through a number of editions, *Leaves of Grass* came to include well over 100 poems, including "Calamus," "Crossing Brooklyn Ferry," and "Out of the Cradle Endlessly Rocking." In his poetry and prose, Whitman celebrates the landscape and people of the United States. Although he was an ardent Democrat, he supported Lincoln; indeed, Lincoln was one of the subjects of Whitman's moving elegy "When Lilacs Last in the Dooryard Bloom'd" (1865). Both "Abraham Lincoln" and "Death of Abraham Lincoln" come from Whitman's *Specimen Days* (1882), which partly consists of diary entries and newspaper articles written during the previous two decades.

Edward O. Wilson (1929–)

American biologist, writer, and teacher. After receiving a Ph.D. in biology from Harvard, Wilson remained there and is now Frank B. Baird, Jr. Professor of Science. Early in his career, Wilson became an expert on ants and social insects. In 1975, his focus shifted to sociobiology. His book *Sociobiology: The New Synthesis* (1975) sets forth the principles of this new science, which interprets behavior in biological terms. Wilson's central thesis, that all human behavior is determined by genetic structures, ignited controversy. Subsequent books—*On Human Nature* (1978);

Genes, Mind and Culture (with Charles Lumsden, 1981); *Promethean Fire* (1983) —present Wilson's further explorations of the subject. His most recent book, *Biophilia: The Human Bond to Other Species* (1984), from which "The Superorganism" comes, is an ethical appeal for the conservation of all life.

Tom Wolfe (1931–   )

American journalist, essayist, and social commentator. After receiving a Ph.D. from Yale, Wolfe began a career in journalism that has taken him from newspapers like the *Washington Post* and *New York Herald Tribune* to magazines like *New York, Esquire,* and *Vanity Fair.* Several of Wolfe's books have established his reputation as a witty social critic and historian of popular culture: *The Kandy-kolored Tangerine-Flake Streamline Baby* (1965), *Radical Chic and Mau-Mauing the Flak Catchers* (1970), and *From Bauhaus to Our House* (1981). Wolfe's chronicle of the American space program, *The Right Stuff* (1979), became a successful film. "The Legend of Junior Johnson" is excerpted from "The Last American Hero" in *The Kandy-kolored Tangerine-Flake Streamline Baby.*

Virginia Woolf (1882–1941)

English novelist, critic, and essayist. The daughter of respected philosopher and writer Sir Leslie Stephen, Woolf educated herself by unrestricted reading in her father's library. She lived at the center of the "Bloomsbury Group," a celebrated gathering of artists, scholars, and writers. Woolf, together with her husband socialist writer Leonard Woolf, founded the Hogarth Press. Her work, whether it be nonfiction or fiction, is marked by a resonant autobiographical voice. *A Room of One's Own* (1929), an historical investigation of women and creativity; *Mrs. Dalloway* (1925), *To the Lighthouse* (1927), and *The Waves* (1931), novels about artistic consciousness and the development of personality; *The Common Reader* (1925, 1932), collections of essays on topics as diverse as literature and automobiles, reveal penetrating intelligence as well as innovations in narrative technique. "My Father: Leslie Stephen," originally entitled "Leslie Stephen, the Philosopher at Home: A Daughter's Memories," was first published in the London *Times* (Nov-

ember 28, 1932), the centenary of his birth; it was later reprinted in *Atlantic Monthly* (March 1950) and in a collection of Woolf's essays, *The Captain's Death Bed* (1950). "The Death of the Moth" first appeared in a collection of essays bearing that title (1942). "Great Men's Houses" originally appeared in *Good Housekeeping* (March 1932). "What the Novelist Gives Us" comes from the essay "How Should One Read a Book?" in *The Second Common Reader* (1932). "In Search of a Room of One's Own" comes from *A Room of One's Own.* "The New Biography" comes from *Granite and Rainbow,* © 1958 by Leonard Woolf.

Al Young (1939–   )

American poet, novelist, and essayist. Born in Mississippi, Young attended the University of Michigan and the University of California, Berkeley. His first book of poems, *Dancing,* appeared in 1969, and his first novel, *Snakes,* in 1970. Since then, he has published more than a dozen books of poetry, fiction, and essays, among them *The Blues Don't Change: New and Selected Poems* (1982); *Bodies and Soul: Musical Memoirs* (volume 1, 1981), *Kinds of Blue* (volume 2, 1984), *Things Ain't What They Used to Be* (volume 3, 1987); and a novel, *Seduction by Night* (1987). Music, particularly jazz and blues, and its great artists and composers are the recurrent themes of Young's fiction, poetry, and popular articles. "'Java Jive,' by the Ink Spots" originally appeared in *Kinds of Blue: Musical Memoirs,* and was reprinted in *Harper's* (February 1985).

William Zinsser (1922–   )

American journalist, writer, and teacher. After graduating from Princeton in 1944 and serving in the army for two years, Zinsser joined the staff of the *New York Herald Tribune* (1946–1959), first as a features editor, then as a drama editor and film critic, and finally as an editorial writer. In 1959, he became a free-lance writer, joining the English faculty at Yale University from 1971 until 1979. Zinsser is the author of more than a dozen books, among them the well-known *On Writing Well: An Informal Guide to Writing Non-Fiction* (1976; revised edition, 1980). "College Pressures" originally appeared in *Blair and Ketchum's Country Journal* (April 1979).

Index

About Symbol, 1006
Abraham Lincoln, 92, 108
Abstractions of Beasts, The, 180
Adams, Robert M., 288
Address, 693
Advice to Youth, 599
Aesop, 1105
Agnostic Evolutionists, 952
Allegory of the Cave, The, 1105
Allen, Woody, 101
Angelou, Maya, 22
Anonymous, 372
Apothegms, 670
Arendt, Hannah, 714
Aria, 315
Arlen, Michael, 719
Arnold, Matthew, 370
Art and Education, 376
Ashby, Lord, 261
Asimov, Isaac, 201
Atwood, Margaret, 1042
Auden, W. H., 670

Bacon, Francis, 365, 592
Baldwin, James, 547
Battle of the Ants, The, 690
Bear Who Let It Alone, The, 587
Beauty: When the Other Dancer Is the
    Self, 52
Becker, Carl, 832
Bee-Hunters of Hulshorst, The, 892
Beer Can, 379
Behind the Formaldehyde Curtain, 443
Berry, Wendell, 391
Bethell, Tom, 952
Bettelheim, Bruno, 41
Bierce, Ambrose, 671
Bird, Caroline, 217
Black Men and Public Space, 440
Blake, William, 674
Blot and the Diagram, The, 1083
Booth, Wayne C., 268, 332
Boring from Within: The Art of the Fresh-
    man Essay, 332

Bronowski, Jacob, 194, 927
Brown Wasps, The, 72
Bruner, Jerome S., 481
Burchfield, Robert, 308
Burgess, Anthony, 384
Butterfield, Herbert, 685

Calder, Nigel, 914
Callwood, June, 112
Career of Isaac Newton: A Scientific Life in
    the Seventeenth Century, The, 931
Carr, Edward Hallett, 751
Cary, Joyce, 376
Case for Animal Rights, The, 621
Case for Torture, The, 619
Case for the Use of Animals in Biomedical
    Research, The, 633
Case of Harry Houdini, The, 159
Chesterfield, Lord, 596
Civil Disobedience, 785
Clamorous to Learn, 212
Clark, Lord, 1083
Clemens, Samuel L., 599, 1115
Cohen, Carl, 633
College Is a Waste of Time and Money,
    217
College Pressures, 234
College Today: Tune In, Drop Out, and
    Take the Cash, 226
Conant, Ralph W., 788
Concrete, Brick, and Neon, 380
Confusing Levels of Abstraction, 187
Convenience of Being "Reasonable," The,
    172
Copland, Aaron, 1078
Cowley, Malcolm, 569
Culture, 370

Darwin's Middle Road, 945
Davies, Robertson, 1035
Death of Abraham Lincoln, 696
Death of the Moth, The, 1179
Declaration of Independence, The, 828

Decolonizing the Mind, 775
Democracy (**Becker**), 832
Democracy (**White**), 833
Denmark and the Jews, 714
Destructive Power of a One-Megaton
     Bomb on New York City, The, 472
Devil's Dictionary, The, 671
Dictionaries and Ethnic Sensibilities, 308
Didion, Joan, 69, 464, 731, 1098
Dillard, Annie, 1006, 1182
Disembodied Lady, The, 538
Dobbs, Kildare, 725
Dog's Eye View of Man, A, 378
Donne, John, 366, 1137

Education by Poetry: A Meditative Mono-
     logue, 1026
Ehrenreich, Barbara, 226
Eiseley, Loren, 72
Emerson, Ralph Waldo, 88
Epstein, Daniel Mark, 159
Eureka Phenomenon, The, 201
Examsmanship and the Liberal Arts: A
     Study in Educational Epistemology, 242
Existentialism, 1193
Expressiveness, 1013

Farewell to Arms, A, 373
Faulkner, William, 376
Finch, Robert, 521
FitzGerald, Frances, 744
Forster, E. M., 1162
Four Letters on Freedom of Expression,
     834
Franklin, Benjamin, 172, 676
Frazier, Ian, 397
Freud and the Image of Man, 481
Frogs Desiring a King, The, 1105
Fromm, Erich, 325
Frost, Robert, 1026
Fry, Christopher, 1074
Frye, Northrop, 997
Fussell, Paul, 44

Gamalielese, 301
Gardner, John, 982
Garson, Barbara, 518
Gaylin, Willard, 664
George Washington, 105
Georgia O'Keeffe, 1098
Gettysburg Address, The, 369
Gilligan, Carol, 488
Golding, William, 173
Good News Is: These Are Not the Best
     Years of Your Life, The, 424
Good Readers and Good Writers, 992
Good as Guilt, 501
Gould, Stephen Jay, 643, 910, 945, 1153

Graduation, 22
Graves, Robert, 1124
Gravity and the Holy Ghost, 920
Great Men's Houses, 142
Griefspeak, 719
Grizzly, The, 381
Growing Danger, The, 650

Ham and Tongue, 1035
Hawthorne, Nathaniel, 108
Hayakawa, S. I., 1064
Heads and Tails, 914
Hearne, Vicki, 1066
Hemingway, Ernest, 373
Herr, Michael, 722
Highet, Gilbert, 1170
Historian and His Facts, The, 751
Home of the Free, 391
Horses in Partnership with Time, 1066
Houseman, John, 704
"How Bad Do You Want to Get to
     Danang?", 722
How I Never Met Eudora Welty, 32
How It Feels to Be Colored Me, 19
How We Listen, 1078
Howard, Jane, 134
Hughes, Langston, 1139
Hugo, Richard, 32
Humanities and Science, 253
Hurston, Zora Neale, 19

Images of Relationship, 488
In Search of a Room of One's Own, 1053
Indispensable Opposition, The, 841
Is America Falling Apart?, 384
Is There Any Knowledge That a Man Must
     Have?, 268

January 30, 1933: A Memoir, 36
"Java Jive," by the Ink Spots, 16
Jefferson, Thomas, 105, 824
Jefferson, Thomas, and Others, 828
Jesus, 1109
Johnson, Samuel, 367, 588, 595
Journal (**Emerson**), 88
Journal (**Thoreau**), 91
Journal of a Solitude, 95
Journalese for the Lay Reader, 298
Jung, Carl Gustav, 1021
Just a Country Boy, 397
Justification of Civil Protest, Nonviolent
     and Violent, The, 788

Kafka, Franz, 1117
Katz, Michael J., 866
Keillor, Garrison, 478
Kill 'Em! Crush 'Em! Eat 'Em Raw!, 399
King, Martin Luther, Jr., 792
Knowledge and Virtue, 368
Koestler, Arthur, 920

Kübler-Ross, Elisabeth, 579
Kuhn, Thomas S., 966

Lacy, Dan, 455
Langer, Susanne K., 1013
Laughter, 1074
Laurence, Margaret, 6
Legend of Junior Johnson, The, 379
Leo, John, 298
Lessing, Doris, 151
Let Me Wither, 1137
Letter from Birmingham Jail, 792
Letter to His Son, 596
Letter to Lord Chesterfield, 595
Levels of Being, 1129
Levin, Michael, 619
Lewis, C. S., 1141
Lincoln, Abraham, 369, 822
Lippmann, Walter, 841
Listening to Owls, 59
Long Habit, The, 575
Lorenz, Konrad Z., 879

Machiavelli, Niccolò, 815
Machismo Mystique, The, 406
Martin, Judith, 602
Maxims, 678
McMurtry, John, 399
McPhee, John, 381
Memories of Christmas, 1
Men Are Sleeping Prisoners, 366
Mencken, H. L., 301
Milgram, Stanley, 606
Mitford, Jessica, 443
Modest Proposal, A, 807
Momaday, N. Scott, 129
"Mommy, What Does 'Nigger' Mean?",
    305
Mona Lisa, The, 371
Morals of the Prince, The, 815
Morris, Charles R., 785
Morris, Desmond, 510
Motherhood: Who Needs It?, 430
Motive for Metaphor, The, 997
Muddy Road, A Parable, Learning to Be
    Silent, 1111
Murray, Thomas, 650
My Father, 151
My Father: Leslie Stephen, 146
My Negro Problem—and Ours, 558
My War, 44
Mystery of Zen, The, 1170
Mythology, 1124

Nabokov, Vladimir, 992
Nature of Scientific Reasoning, The, 927
Nature of Symbolic Language, The, 325
Naylor, Gloria, 305
New Biography, The, 738
Newman, John Henry, 368

Ngũgĩ wa Thiong'o, 775
No Dawn to the East, 372
Nobel Prize Award Speech, 376
Nonmoral Nature, 1153
Notes on Punctuation, 322
Nothing to Say, 283

Observation, 193
Of Door Hinges and Life in General, 368
Of Revenge, 365
Of Simulation and Dissimulation, 592
On Forgetting the Difference between
    Right and Wrong, 655
On Going Home, 69
On Keeping a Notebook, 731
On Magic in Medicine, 450
On Self-Love and Indolence, 588
On the Fear of Death, 579
On the Wings of an Angel: An Exploration
    of the Limits of Biological Enterprise, 866
Once More to the Lake, 79
One Writer's Beginnings, 976
Original Draft of the Declaration of Inde-
    pendence, 824
Originality of the Old Testament, The, 685
Orwell, George, 353, 768
Our Allotted Lifetimes, 910
Owl Who Was God, The, 1123

Parable of the Law, 1117
Parables of the Kingdom, 1109
Passion to Learn, A, 527
Pater, Walter, 371
Perelman, S. J., 406
Perils of Obedience, The, 606
Perry, William G., Jr., 242
Petrunkevitch, Alexander, 905
Pirsig, Robert, 380
Plato, 1105
Podhoretz, Norman, 558
Poet, The, 1021
Politics and the English Language, 353
Pomp and Circumstance in Groundhog
    Hollow, 134
Poor Richard's Almanack, 676
Portrait of Canada, 112
Postman, Neil, 187
Progress and Change, 375
Proverbs of Hell, 674
Pyramids, The, 367

Rabbits Who Caused All the Trouble,
    The, 806
Reach of Imagination, The, 194
Reading in an Audiovisual and Electronic
    Era, 455
Regan, Tom, 621
Revision Strategies of Student Writers and
    Experienced Adult Writers, 344
Revolutionist's Handbook, The, 681

Rewriting American History, 744
Rich, Adrienne, 411
Riddle of Inequality, The, 1147
La Rochefoucauld, 678
Rodriguez, Richard, 315
Rollin, Betty, 430
Roots of Nuclear Peril, The, 848
Rose, Phyllis, 394
Route to Normal Science, The, 966
Ryle, Gilbert, 655

Sacks, Oliver, 538
Sagan, Carl, 180
Salvador, 464
Salvation, 1139
Sanders, Scott, 59
Sarton, May, 95
Sartre, Jean-Paul, 1193
Schell, Jonathan, 472, 848
Schmitt, Hans A., 36
Schumacher, E. F., 1129
Seattle, Chief, 693
Second Inaugural Address, 822
Selections from the Allen Notebooks, 101
Sex Is Not a Spectator Sport, 1064
Shatterer of Worlds, The, 725
Shaw, George Bernard, 681
Shooting an Elephant, 768
Shopping and Other Spiritual Adventures, 394
Should Testing for the AIDS Virus Be Mandatory?, 646
Sight into Insight, 1182
Soft Soap and the Nitty-Gritty, 288
Some Remarks on Humor, 1076
Some Thoughts on the Mannerly Way of Life, 602
Sommers, Nancy, 344
Sparshott, Francis E., 283
Spider and the Bee, The, 1112
Spider and the Wasp, The, 905
Staples, Brent, 440
Stegner, Wallace, 10
Steinem, Gloria, 424
Sterne, Laurence, 368
Stone, Michael, 646
Stranger in the Village, 547
Superorganism, The, 856
Swift, Jonathan, 807, 1112

Taming of the Shrew, The, 879

Terrifying Normalcy of AIDS, The, 643
Territorial Behavior, 510
Thinking as a Hobby, 173
Thomas, Dylan, 1
Thomas, Lewis, 253, 322, 450, 575
Thoreau, Henry David, 91, 193, 690
Three Screwtape Letters, 1141
Thurber, James, 229, 378, 587, 806, 1123
Tillich, Paul, 1147
Tinbergen, Niko, 892
Tower Project, The, 478
Town Dump, The, 10

University Days, 229
University Ideal: A View from Britain, The, 261
Updike, John, 379

Very Like a Whale, 521
Victim, A, 41
View from 80, The, 569
Viorst, Judith, 501

Walker, Alice, 52
War Prayer, The, 1115
War of the Worlds, The, 704
Way to Rainy Mountain, The, 129
Welty, Eudora, 212, 976
West, Paul, 527
Westfall, Richard S., 931
What I Believe, 1162
What Writers Do, 982
What You See Is the Real You, 664
What the Novelist Gives Us, 373
When We Dead Awaken: Writing as Re-Vision, 411
Where the World Began, 6
Whistle While You Work, 518
White, E. B., 79, 375, 833, 834, 1076
Whitman, Walt, 92, 696
Wilson, Edward O., 856
Wolfe, Tom, 379
Woolf, Virginia, 142, 146, 373, 738, 1053, 1179
Writing the Male Character, 1042

Young, Al, 16

Zen Parables, 1111
Zinsser, William, 234

ACKNOWLEDGMENTS

Adams: "Soft Soap and the Nitty-Gritty" © Robert M. Adams 1985. Reprinted from *Fair of Speech: The Uses of Euphemism* edited by D. J. Enright (1985) by permission of Oxford University Press.

Aesop: "The Frogs Desiring a King" reprinted by permission of Prestige Books Inc.

Allen: Selection from *Without Feathers*, by Woody Allen. Copyright © 1972, 1973, 1974, 1975, by Woody Allen. Reprinted by permission of Random House, Inc.

Angelou: "Graduation" from *I Know Why the Caged Bird Sings* by Maya Angelou. Reprinted by permission of Random House, Inc.

Anonymous: "No Dawn to the East" reprinted with permission from Sheridan House, New York: *Indian Cavalcade* by Clark Wissler, 1938, © renewed 1966 by Mary V. Wissler.

Arendt: "Denmark and the Jews" from *Eichmann in Jerusalem* by Hannah Arendt. Copyright © 1963, 1964 by Hannah Arendt. This selection originally appeared in *The New Yorker* in slightly different form. Reprinted by permission of Viking Penguin Inc.

Arlen: "Griefspeak" from *The Living Room War*, Viking Press © 1969 Michael J. Arlen. All rights reserved.

Ashby: "The University Ideal: A View from Britain"reprinted with permission from *LSA*, Spring, 1978.

Asimov: "The Eureka Phenomenon" copyright © 1971 by Mercury Press, Inc. from *The Left Hand of the Electron* by Isaac Asimov. Reprinted by permission of Doubleday, a division of Bantam, Doubleday, and Dell Publishing Group, Inc.

Atwood: "Writing the Male Character" from *Second Words* (Toronto: House of Anansi Press). First published in the United States by Beacon Press, 1984. © 1982 by O. W. Toad Ltd. Reprinted by permission of Beacon Press and House of Anansi Press.

Auden: "Apothegms" plus 3 paragraphs from *The Dyer's Hand*, by W. H. Auden. Copyright © 1962 by W. H. Auden. Reprinted by permission of Random House, Inc.

Baldwin: From *Notes of a Native Son* by James Baldwin. Copyright © 1955 by James Baldwin. Reprinted by permission of Beacon Press.

Becker: "Democracy" from *Modern Democracy* by Carl L. Becker. Copyright 1941 by Yale University Press. Reprinted by permission of the Press.

Berry: "Home of the Free" from *The Gift of Good Land, Further Essays Cultural and Agricultural*, © 1981 by Wendell Berry. Published by North Point Press.

Bethell: "Agnostic Evolutionists" Copyright © 1986 by *Harper's Magazine*. All rights reserved. Reprinted from February 1986 issue by special permission.

Bettelheim: "A Victim" reprinted with permission of Macmillan Publishing Company from *The Informed Heart* by Bruno Bettelheim. Copyright © 1960 by The Free Press, a Corporation.

Bird: "College Is a Waste of Time and Money" from *The Case Against College* by Caroline Bird. Reprinted by permission of the author.

Booth: "Is There Any Knowledge that a Man Must Have?" from *The Knowledge Most Worth Having* © by The University of Chicago. Reprinted by permission of the Press. "Boring from Within: The Art of the Freshman Essay," from an address to the Illinois Council of College Teachers in 1963. © Wayne C. Booth. Reprinted by permission of the author.

Bronowski: "The Nature of Scientific Reasoning" from *Science and Human Values*. Copyright © 1956, 1965, by J. Bronowski. Reprinted by permission of Messner Books, a Simon & Schuster Division of Gulf & Western Corporation. "The Reach of Imagination" from *Proceedings of the American Academy of Arts and Letters and National Institute of Arts and Letters*, Second Series, No. 17. Copyright © 1976. Reprinted by permission of the American Academy and Institute of Arts and Letters.

Bruner: "Freud and the Image of Man," from *Partisan Review*, Volume 23, No. 3, 1956. Reprinted by permission of *Partisan Review*.

Burchfield: "Dictionaries and Ethnic Sensibilities" from *The State of Language* (1980). Originally appeared in *The Listener*, April 13, 1978. Adapted from a talk given on BBC Radio, 1978. Reprinted by permission of the author.

Burgess: "Is America Falling Apart?" from *The New York Times*, November 7, 1971. © 1971 by The New York Times Company. Reprinted by permission.